THE
BASEBALL
CHRONOLOGY

THE
BASEBALL
CHRONOLOGY

The
Complete History
of the Most Important
Events in the
Game of Baseball

Edited by
JAMES CHARLTON

Macmillan Publishing Company
New York

Maxwell Macmillan Canada
Toronto

Maxwell Macmillan International
New York • Oxford • Singapore • Sydney

Macmillan Publishing Company
866 Third Avenue
New York, NY 10022

Maxwell Macmillan Canada, Inc.
1200 Eglinton Avenue East
Suite 200
Don Mills, Ontario M3C 3N1

Macmillan Publishing Company is part of the Maxwell Communication Group of Companies.

Library of Congress Cataloging–in–Publication Data

The Baseball Chronology: the complete history of significant
    events in the game of baseball, edited by James Charlton
        p. cm.
    ISBN 0-02-523971-6
    1. Baseball—History—Chronology.   I. Charlton, James, 1939–
    GV862.5.B37   1991
    796.357—dc20   90-23254
                                                            CIP

Macmillan books are available at special discounts for bulk purchases for sales promotions, premiums, fund-raising, or educational use. For details, contact:

Special Sales Director
Macmillan Publishing Company
866 Third Avenue
New York, NY 10022

10 9 8 7 6 5 4 3 2 1

PRINTED IN THE UNITED STATES OF AMERICA

Produced by James Charlton Associates
New York City

*T*he Baseball Chronology was conceived simply and innocently enough as a daily diary of our national pastime—a day-by-day, linear account of the major events, accomplishments, games, record breakers, pennant races, player and franchise shifts that could be read in context. While I knew it was a substantial project, I thought it could be accomplished in a year or eighteen months; it has taken four years and a great deal of help to finally drag the book across home plate.

The Baseball Chronology is a book that includes all the great moments in the major leagues, individual highlights from the majors and the minors, Negro leagues, Japanese leagues, Latin American ball and collegiate baseball. Many of the games and performances chronicled are familiar to a casual fan, but I think that even the most ardent and knowledgeable reader will find the book a delight of new information. We have tried to give the reader a sense of a season or era, the chance to follow a batting or home-run race, or the pennant chases of each season. The low points, oddities, and tragedies are noted, as well as off-field machinations and activities. All trades of importance and, more recently, free-agent switches, are included.

In addition to the more than fifty people who assisted in some way with this book, several hundred publications were used in the research and fact checking. As any reader of baseball literature knows, there are good sources and then there are sources, and many books in the field include information that is inaccurate. Fortunately, they are in the minority. There are a great number of books and writers I came to rely on for accuracy and that I used to double or triple check information. For questions of statistics, we relied on *The Baseball Encyclopedia* the official publication of major league baseball. If a question or discrepancy arose about a fact or statement, we tried to corroborate it with a primary source such as *The Sporting News*, The New York *Times*, or a local newspaper's box score or account. Other sources included the various publications of The Society for American Baseball Research (SABR). Many early accomplishments are difficult to verify from newspaper accounts. For instance, whether the three bases that Honus Wagner stole in a game were all swiped in the same inning, or whether a turn-of-the century player's 2,000th hit occurred off a starter or reliever. Sportswriters of the day just were not preoccupied with records or the minutie of the game, and their write-ups of a contest are more colorful and less fact filled than is the reportage of today's games. And most fans would probably tip their caps to that.

If a question came up about a score, date, player, or event, and we could not verify it from a reliable source, it was omitted. In a few cases, we found that official records are incomplete or incorrect.

With some items, we checked with the actual source, or checked the fact with the team. This made for some interesting telephone calls, such as the one to the White House to verify a radio announcer's claim that two collegians, Lou Gehrig and George Bush, had hit baseballs out of Columbia's stadium. A Bush aide called back and quoted the President as saying that, alas, he had not hit one out of the park and that he'd certainly recall whether he had matched Gehrig, a hero of his. Did the late Sonny Dunlap actually play in a game in the Arkansas-Missouri League? The sports editor of the Fayetteville newspaper verified that she did, and her brother read us the box score from her 1936 game.

There is an extraordinary amount of information in the book, and given the resources and people involved, it is as accurate as we could make it.

An amazing number of "firsts" are noted in *The Baseball Chronology*, from the first game played on ice to the first night game, the first game broadcast, the first steal of first base, the first baseball song to hit the charts, the first unassisted triple play. And there are no lack of "lasts."

From the last fielder to play barehanded to the last park to install lights. High jinks are recalled, such the "potato pickoff of 1987 and Bill Veeck's stunts ranging from his insertion of Eddie Gaedel into a Browns' game to his "Disco Demolition Night" two decades later. Veeck would have been envious of the Braves' promotion of the 1970s billed as "Headlocks and Wedlocks"— championship wrestling followed by a group wedding at home plate.

Flipping through the year-by-year accounts of the various events, a reader can sense how the game has evolved from the rough and loose sport of the 19th century to the corporate enterprise of today's baseball. But with all its changes, whether lengthening the pitching distance, altering the strike zone or number of strikes, installing artificial turf below or domes above, certain verities remain. Baseball a hundred years ago was central to American life. The December 13th, 1856, issue of the *New York Clipper* stated that "the game of Base Ball is generally considered the National game amongst Americans." Even in the complicated world of today, we can hope that statement is still true.

Many people contributed in some way to this book, either with suggestions, initial research, fact checking or in the various editing stages. Each year's entries were compiled by one contributor, whose work was supplemented and added to by a great many individuals. To all these writers, whose patience I wore out with countless queries, postcards with questions, or entreaties for additional information, my heartfelt thanks.

These include:

Bill Loughman, whose work on the 1845–75 era was incredibly extensive and thorough. The estimable Bob Davids worked on 1876, 1889, 1892, 1898 and 1899. Bob Tieman, chairman of the 19th century committee for the Society for American Baseball Research (SABR), was responsible for the years 1877–1881, 1886, 1888 (along with Bill Loughman). Adie Suehsdorf contributed to the1889, 1897–99, and 1916 sections, Martin LaCoste worked on 1885. Fred Ivor-Campbell worked on 1884. A special thanks to Dean Sullivan, who not only wrote the entries for 1893–95, but contributed additional information and fact checked the entire 19th-century section. Fred Sumner contributed the 1896 section. Bill Loughman contributed to the 1888 and 1897 sections. The tireless Norman Macht wrote the 1890 section and all the years from 1900 to 1929, excepting 1916. The peerless Jack Kavanagh wrote the 1930s section, while Dean Coughenour stepped in and wrote the 1940s. Additions to the 1940s were contributed by Eddie Gold. The St. Louis expert, professor Bill Borst, contributed the 1950s section. Morris Eckhouse contributed the 1960s; Bill Deane of the Baseball Hall of Fame wrote the 1970s, while Shep Long wrote all of the 1980s and 1990. Additional work on the 1980s was contributed by Lloyd Johnson.

Entries for special areas of interest were contributed by the following writers: Peter Bjarkman, head of the Latin American committee for SABR, wrote entries on Latin American baseball; Jim Riley contributed the majority of entries on the Negro Leagues; Dick Clark, head of the Negro League Committee for SABR, also wrote and checked material on the Negro Leagues.

A special thanks to Sheila Buff, who not only contributed the majority of entries on Japanese baseball, but whose idea set this whole project in motion. Additional editing of the Japanese entries was done by Ryuchi Suzuki of the Japanese Baseball Hall of Fame. Bob Carroll contributed information on major league players who also played in the NFL. And additional thanks to Dan Okrent and Steve Taylor for their unique contributions.

There are three people who were exceptionally generous with their time, patience, and baseball knowledge. Adie Suehsdorf, Bob Davids, and John Grabowski all read the entries for the entire book, helped with the editing and rewriting, added information of interest that had been overlooked, and patiently noted an occasional contributor's mistake, or an error of omission or commission by me. Each of these gentlemen has a vast knowledge of baseball and was unfailingly supportive throughout the project. It is a much better book for their involvement.

The mammoth job of editing, collating, checking, indexing and copyediting was ably accomplished by Jennifer Atkinson, Elise Passikoff, Cecilia Oh, Fred Chase, Cindy Behrman, Kevin Charlton, Tim Charlton, Jennifer Cooper, and Susanna Schroeder. A special note of thanks to Stephen McErlain and Bill Dye and their staff at LinoGraphics of New York City. Without their computer expertise and support, this book would be still be in the works.

Finally, a word of thanks for their patient support on this Sisyphean project to Macmillan's publisher Bill Rosen and to the book's good-fielding editor, Rick Wolff.

Jim Charlton
New York City
February, 1991

Throughout *The Baseball Chronology,* we have used a number of abbreviations. Most of these should be familiar to any baseball fan, and all are generally spelled out in the text.

Where a minor league is mentioned for the first time within the text for a particular year, the league is spelled out (for example, Pacific Coast League); when it is mentioned again, the abbreviation is used (PCL). Postal abbreviations are generally used for states, and cities (KC for Kansas City) are occasionally abbreviated. A rare entry might use the scorekeeping numbers (1 through 9) for positions to show how a play was made (for example, a 6-4-3-2 triple play means SS to 2B to 1B to C).

Other abbreviations used in the book are as follows:

1B:	first base(man).
2B:	second base(man).
3B:	third base(man).
AA:	American Association (both the 19th-century major league and the 20th-century minor league).
AB:	at bat(s).
AL:	American League.
ALCS:	American League Championship Series.
AS:	All-Star game.
BBWAA:	The Baseball Writers Association of America.
C:	catcher.
CG:	complete games.
DH:	designated hitter.
E:	error or errors (Es).
ERA:	earned run average.
FL:	Federal League.
HBP:	hit by pitched ball(s).
HR:	homer(s) and home run(s).
IF:	infielder.
IP:	innings pitched.
IPHR:	inside-the-park home runs.
LCS:	League Championship Series.
LF, CF, RF:	used for the outfield positions and to show direction.
LH:	left-handed.
LOB:	left on base.
ML:	Major League(s).
MVP:	Most Valuable Player
NL:	National League.
NLCS:	National League Championship Series.
OF:	outfield(er).
P:	pitcher.
PH:	pinch hitter or to pinch hit.
PL:	19th-century Players' League.
RBI:	run(s) batted in.
RH:	right-handed pitcher or hitter.
SA:	Slugging Average.
SB:	stolen base. SBs is the plural.
SS:	shortstop.
TB:	total bases.
TSN:	The Sporting News.
UA:	Union Association.
WS:	World Series.

1845

SEPTEMBER

23rd The Knickerbocker baseball club of New York is organized at the suggestion of Alexander J. Cartwright, who formulates rules to distinguish his brand of baseball from other forms played throughout the country.

OCTOBER

6th The first recorded baseball game using Cartwright's rules is played between members of the Knickerbocker Club. Only 14 players participate as Duncan Curry's team defeats Alex Cartwright's team 11–8 in a shortened game of only 3 innings. The Knickerbocker Club will play at least 14 recorded games during the fall of 1845.

21st The New York *Herald* has an announcement of an upcoming baseball match this afternoon between the New York Club and the Brooklyn Club at the Elysian Fields, Hoboken, NJ. This game is played under different rules than Cartwright's.

22nd The New York *Morning News* reports that in yesterday's "friendly match of the time honored game of Baseball" the New York Club beat Brooklyn 24–4. A box score of the game is included in the account.

25th In a rematch, the New York club again beats Brooklyn, this time 37–19. The New York *Herald* publishes a box score of the game.

1846

JUNE

19th The first officially recorded baseball match, played under Cartwright's rules, takes place on the Elysian Fields with the New York Club defeating the Knickerbockers 23–1.

1849

APRIL

24th The first baseball uniform is adopted at a meeting of the New York Knickerbocker Club. It consists of blue woolen pantaloons, a white flannel shirt, and a straw hat.

AUGUST

10th Cartwright arrives in San Francisco after he travels across the continent, teaching the game of baseball along the way.

1851

JUNE

3rd The Knickerbockers win their first match of the year 21–11 against the Washington Club. According to Cartwright's rules, the first team to score 21 runs wins the game.

1854

JUNE

30th The first extra-inning game is played with the Knicks losing to the Gothams 21–16 in 16 innings. Even though the 21-run rule is still in effect, this is the first match game ever to exceed 9 innings.

1855

AUGUST

14th The Atlantic Club of Brooklyn is organized. The Atlantics would be the preeminent club of the 1860s. Starting in 1859, they would win the whip-pennant, emblematic of the baseball championship, 8 of 11 years.

1856

SEPTEMBER

15th The first reported game of Canadian baseball is played in London, Ontario, with the London Club defeating the Delaware club 34–33.

DECEMBER

13th The New York *Clipper* states that "the game of Base Ball is generally considered the National game amongst Americans."

1857

JANUARY

22nd The first baseball convention is held in New York. It is called by the Knickerbockers and attended by 16 baseball clubs, all located on Manhattan and Long Island.

MARCH

7th The rules committee states that 9 innings shall constitute an official game rather than a team scoring 9 runs. For the first time, the rules specify 9 men to a side, even though the game has been played that way since 1845.

10th The National Association of Base Ball Players is formed. William H. Van Cott is elected President.

MAY

13th A convention is held in Dedham, MA, attended by representatives of 10 New England baseball clubs. Under the name of "Massachusetts Association of Base Ball Players," playing rules are adopted to illustrate the differences between New England baseball and the "New York Game." Rule four: 2 bases shall be wooden stakes, 4 feet high. Rule 14: If a player is hit with a thrown ball while rounding the bases, he shall be considered out. Other rules specify 100 runs will constitute a game and each side shall consist of 10 to 14 players.

OCTOBER

22nd The Atlantic Club defeats the Eckford Club, both of Brooklyn, to take the best-of-3-games match and claim the championship for 1857. The baseball custom now is that the championship can only be won by a team beating the current titleholder 2 out of 3 games.

1858

JULY

20th The first game to attract wide attention in the New York area is an all-star game between players from New York and Brooklyn. The game is played at the Fashion Race Course on Long Island and is the first at which an admission fee (50¢) is charged. This series introduces Henry Chadwick to the newspaper-reading public, starting a baseball reporting career that will last 50 years.

1859

MARCH

14th The Nassau Base Ball Club is organized on the Princeton campus by members of the class of 1862.

15th At the annual meeting of the National Association of Base Ball Players, rule 36 is amended to read: "No party shall be competent to play in a match who receives compensation for his services."

JULY

1st The first intercollegiate baseball match is played between Amherst and Williams colleges at Pittsfield, MA. Amherst wins 73–32. The game is played under the rules of the "Massachusetts Game."

NOVEMBER

28th The first baseball club on the West Coast is formed, the Eagle Club of San Francisco.

1860

MARCH

14th The 4th annual convention of the National Association of Base Ball Players opens with 62 teams represented. The new rules provide for called strikes on a batter who does not swing at good balls repeatedly pitched to him. The umpire must warn the batter before he calls the first strike on him.

JUNE

30th The Excelsiors of Brooklyn leave for Albany, starting the first tour ever taken by a baseball club. They will travel 1,000 miles in 10 days and play games in Albany, Troy, Buffalo, Rochester, and Newburgh.

JULY

22nd One of the first triple plays in baseball is triggered by Jim Creighton, playing LF for the Excelsiors of New York. With Baltimore runners on 2B and 3B, Creighton makes a spectacular catch of a fly ball. The subsequent throws to 3B and then to 2B complete the triple play.

OCTOBER

22nd The Nassau Base Ball Club of Princeton University plays a 42–42 tie game against a team of former Yale and Princeton collegians.

NOVEMBER

8th The first shutout game ever recorded is won by the Excelsiors of Brooklyn against the St. George Cricket Club 25–0.

1861

FEBRUARY

4th With the players wearing skates, the first baseball game played on ice in the New York area is played on Litchfield's Pond in South Brooklyn. The champion Atlantics defeat the Charter Oak Club 36–27.

SEPTEMBER

21st A unique match is played on the St. George Cricket Club Grounds. One team is composed of 9 players, including Jim Creighton and Dickey Pearce. The other team is composed of 18 players, 9 cricketers from St. George and 9 all-stars from the different area clubs. The 18 players are all in the field at once. When they bat, they are allowed 6 outs per inning. Eight innings are played with Creighton's team winning 45–16.

OCTOBER

21st The greatest event of the season, the Grand Match for the Silver Ball, takes place on the Mutuals' Grounds at Hoboken between all-star teams from Brooklyn and New York. The Silver Ball Trophy is the same size as a regular baseball and will be kept by the club whose members score the most runs during the match. Fifteen thousand fans see the Brooklyn team, behind their star Jim Creighton, defeat New York 18–6.

1862

MAY

15th The Union Baseball Grounds at Marcy Avenue and Rutledge Street in Brooklyn is opened, the first enclosed ball field to charge an admission fee.

OCTOBER

14th The Excelsiors defeat the Unions of Morrisania 13–9. Jim Creighton hits 4 doubles and scores 4 runs, but suffers "an internal injury occasioned by strain" hitting a HR. Considered the premier baseball player of the day, he dies of a ruptured bladder four days later at the age of 21.

1864

DECEMBER

14th The 8th annual meeting of the National Association of Base Ball Players is held. The rules committee recommends adoption of the "fly game," making bounced outs in fair territory illegal.

1865

AUGUST

3rd Twenty thousand spectators watch a match in Hoboken between the Mutuals and the Atlantics. The game is a 5-inning, rain-shortened 13–12 Atlantic victory. This particular game would be immortalized in the Currier and Ives print: *The American National Game of Baseball.*

SEPTEMBER

28th Four thousand spectators gather at Hoboken to watch the Mutuals lose to the Eckford Club 23–11. The Mutual Club meets after the game and charges William Wansley of "willful and designed inattention" with the view of causing Eckford to defeat Mutual. A committee formed to investigate the matter later reports that C Wansley, 3B Duffy, and SS Devyr, received the sum of $100 from Kane McLoughlin to allow McLoughlin to win money on the game. The players will be barred from baseball at the next convention, but are reinstated several years later.

1866

JULY

16th   Lipman Pike of the Athletics of Philadelphia hits 6 HRs, 5 in succession, against the Alert Club of Philadelphia. Final score is 67–25.

23rd   The Cincinnati Baseball Club is organized.

26th   The Olympics of Louisville lure Rochester P Ives to join them for a key game. Three years later Ives will join the Kentucky club and will profit from a special "benefit" game honoring him and 2 recent Cincinnati transfers. Baseball is growing rapidly in Louisville.

OCTOBER

11th   The visiting Star Club loses to the Atlantic Club by a 46–18 score. The game is played in one hour, 50 minutes, with not a ball or a strike called.

DECEMBER

12th   The 10th annual convention of the National Association of Base Ball Players is held with a record 202 clubs sending delegates. Rule changes include the introduction of called balls, with 3 called balls allowing the batter to 1B. This session introduces the pitcher's box, an area 6 feet wide and 4 feet deep, from which the pitcher must deliver the ball.

1867

MAY

1st   *The Bat and Ball*, a newspaper devoted exclusively to "base ball," in its first issue of its 2nd year of publication announces that "this season, which is now opening, bids fair to be one of the most exciting that our National Game is likely to ever know." Another article urges umpires to be more diligent in insuring that pitchers throw where the strikers indicate they want the pitches to be.

4th   Princeton wins the first game of their series with Yale 58–52.

JULY

11th   The National Club of Washington departs on the first western trip ever made by a ball club. They will travel a total of 3,000 miles and cover 5 states.

DECEMBER

9th   The National Association of Base Ball Players bans blacks "on political grounds."

1868

APRIL

25th   The New York *Clipper* announces that it will give a Gold Ball of regulation weight and size to the club proclaimed Champions of 1868. In addition, gold medals will be given to the 9 best players.

JULY

9th   The Red Stockings have a field meet at Cincinnati and John Hatfield throws a baseball a record 396 feet, breaking his own record of 349 feet.

25th   The game for the Championship of American Colleges is played at Worcester, MA, with Harvard defeating Yale 25–17.

AUGUST

4th   The quickest game on record is played at the Union Grounds, Brooklyn. Al Martin holds the Uniques to one run against 37 for the Eckfords in the 50-minute game.

NOVEMBER

11th   The New York State Base Ball Convention at Albany expels the Mutual Club from the Association for reinstating Duffy, a player found guilty of throwing a game in 1865.

DECEMBER

9th   The 12th annual convention of the National Association of Base Ball Players is held in Washington, DC. A new rule states that "no game shall be considered as played unless 5 innings on each side have been completed." The National Association decides to divide the players into classes, and for the first time recognizes professionals.

1869

MAY

4th The Cincinnati Red Stockings, baseball's first admittedly all-professional team, play their first game of the year, defeating the Great Westerns 45–9.

JUNE

8th The largest score on record occurs in a 3-hour game between the Niagara and Colombia clubs, both of Buffalo, NY. The final score is Niagaras 209, Colombias 10.

AUGUST

27th The Red Stockings gain their toughest and most controversial victory in their incredible winning streak. Tied with the Troy Haymakers 17–17 after 5 innings, Troy C William Craver claims to catch a foul tip off the bat of Cal McVey on the first bounce for an out, but the umpire disagrees. After a fierce argument, Troy leaves the field, and Cincinnati is awarded the game by forfeit.

NOVEMBER

5th Seven thousand Cincinnati fans brave the cold weather to watch the Red Stockings win their 60th game of the season without a defeat, beating the visiting Mutual Green Stockings of New York 17–8.

1870

APRIL

25th Cincinnati begins a week of play in New Orleans with a 51–1 rout of the local Pelicans team. The Chicago White Stockings will soon arrive in town, marking the first time teams have gone south for spring training.

JUNE

14th After 84 straight wins, the Cincinnati Red Stockings lose 8–7 to the Atlantics of Brooklyn in the greatest game of the year. Twenty thousand spectators watch at the Capitoline Grounds. The Reds had won 24 games this season and 60 last year without a loss. Today's game is tied at the end of the 9th inning 5–5.

Bob Ferguson scores the winning run in the last of the 11th on a hit by George Zettlein.

JULY

3rd As reported in today's New York *Clipper*, the Knickerbocker Baseball Club of New York is formally withdrawing from the National Association of Base Ball Players to protest the evils that seem to be inherent in professionalism. This will be a forerunner of a strictly amateur association. Speculation is that the professionals will form their own association.

23rd Five thousand spectators jam Dexter Park in Chicago to see the White Stockings play the visiting Mutuals of New York. Mutuals P Rynie Wolters holds the White Stockings to 3 singles and no runs, winning 9–0 for the first shutout game in big-time baseball history. The New York *Herald* will use "Chicagoed" from now on to signify a shutout; the term survives until at least the late 1890s.

27th After 104 victories and several road defeats, the Cincinnati Red Stockings lose their first game at home to the visiting Athletics of Philadelphia 11–7.

AUGUST

16th Fred Goldsmith, an 18-year-old pitcher invited by Henry Chadwick to demonstrate his curveball at the Capitoline Grounds in Brooklyn, succeeds before a large crowd. Chadwick observes: "That which had up to this point been considered an optical illusion and against all rules of philosophy was now an established fact." But Chadwick will soon credit Candy Cummings with the discovery of the "crooked pitch." Goldsmith will win 20 or more games each year between 1880 and 1883.

SEPTEMBER

22nd The Mutuals of New York win the Championship for 1870 by defeating the Atlantics 10–4 at the Union Grounds. The game has such national interest that telegraph wires are strung and inning-by-inning results are sent nationwide.

NOVEMBER

10th At the New York State Base Ball Convention in Albany, a motion prevails that no club in New York composed of colored men should be admitted to the National Association.

21st The Executive Committee of the Red Stockings Baseball Club issues a circular to the members announcing their determination not to employ a professional 9 for 1871.

30th The 14th annual convention of the National Association of Base Ball Clubs is held in New York, the attendance of delegates being smaller than any previous convention. Wansley, Duffy, and Devyr are reinstated to professional baseball, and William H. Craver is expelled for dishonorable play. Rule changes include allowing the batter to overrun 1B after touching it.

1871

MARCH

17th The National Association of Professional Baseball Players is formed in New York. Playing rules will be the same as the amateur players' with the exception of player compensation. Each club will play 5 games with the other clubs and the winner of 3 will have won that championship series. The league championship will be awarded to the team winning the most series against the other teams and not on a total wins or percentage basis as would be done in later years. Teams represented at the convention are: Athletics of Philadelphia, Boston Red Stockings (who hired Harry Wright to represent them after the Cincinnati Reds disbanded), Chicago White Stockings, Eckford of Brooklyn, Forest City of Cleveland, Forest Citys of Rockford, IL, Mutuals of New York, Nationals of Washington, DC, Olympics of Washington, and the Union Club of Troy, NY, known as the Haymakers. Teams not present but playing matches in the first season of the National Association are the Atlantics of Brooklyn and the Kekiongas of Fort Wayne, IN.

APRIL

29th The new ball grounds in Chicago, located at Randolph and Michigan on the lakefront, are opened as the White Stockings and a picked 9 play before 1,500 people. The New York *Clipper* says: "They will have accommodations on their grounds to seat 6,500 people. With the single exception of being somewhat narrow, they will have one of the finest ballparks in the country."

MAY

4th The first game played in the National Association is played at Fort Wayne, between the Kekiongas and the Forest Citys of Cleveland. Bobby Mathews shuts out the Cleveland team 2–0, one of only 4 shutouts in 1871. Jim White makes the first hit, a double.

8th The visiting Boston Reds demolish the Brooklyn Atlantics 25–0 in the worst defeat in the history of the Brooklyn club.

16th The first professional game ever played in Boston is played between the Red Stockings and the visiting Haymakers before 5,000. Boston has Harry Wright playing SS in place of his injured brother George. George will miss half the games played by the Reds, severely hampering their pennant chances. Troy wins 29–14.

25th The heavily favored Mutuals are soundly defeated by the Haymakers of Troy, in Brooklyn, 25–10. Lipman Pike, the Troy 2B, collects 6 hits.

JUNE

5th The eagerly awaited series opens between the White Stockings and the Mutuals before 10,000 at the Union Grounds in Brooklyn. Five of the old Eckfords play for Chicago while 5 of last year's Atlantics play for the Mutuals. Fielding decides the game, as Chicago makes 19 errors to 7 for the Mutuals. New York wins 8–5.

19th After 6 innings of play at Troy, NY, the ball becomes ripped. The umpire decides that it is unfit and calls for another. The Kekiongas, winning at the time 6–3, refuse to allow another ball to be used and refuse to continue to the game. The umpire awards the game to the Haymakers, 9–0.

21st The Kekiongas visit Boston and are shut out by Al Spalding and the Reds 23–0. Ft. Wayne makes only one hit.

22nd Forest City of Cleveland travels to Philadelphia, and while playing an exhibition game against the Experts of Philadelphia, their substitute C Elmer White, chasing a poorly thrown ball, runs into the fence and breaks his arm.

25th From the New York *Sunday Mercury*: Answers to Correspondents—"Of course a player can wear gloves if he likes. A half glove covering the palm of the hand and first joints of the fingers is excellent in saving the hand of the catcher and first baseman."

28th The Philadelphia Athletics outlast the Troy Haymakers 49–33 with each team scoring in all 9 innings. For the Athletics, 4 players score 6 runs and P Dick McBride and John Radcliffe each score 7.

JULY

5th The annual contest between Yale and Harvard results in a 22–19 victory for Harvard. Yale scores 4 runs in the top of the 9th to lead 19–17, only to have Harvard score 5 in the last half to win the game.

7th The Olympics of Washington, at home, score 18 runs in the 6th and defeat Ft. Wayne 32–12.

12th The Boston Reds play the Kekiongas at Fort Wayne with the temperature reading 100 in the shade. Losing 8–6 after 5 innings, the Reds win the match 30–9. Al Spalding, Ross Barnes, and Fred Cone get 5 hits each.

AUGUST

9th The Eckfords of Brooklyn journey to Troy and defeat the Haymakers 10–7. Ned Connors, the Troy 1B, makes 20 putouts in the 9-inning game.

28th At the Union Grounds in Brooklyn, the Chicago White Stockings clinch the season's series with a 6–4 victory over the Mutuals behind the speedy pitching of George Zettlein. This game gives the lie to the current rumors about the leading teams throwing games for gate-money purposes as the Whites could have insured a 5th and deciding game of the series played on their own grounds by losing today's game.

30th The White Stockings journey to Philadelphia where they take the 2nd game out of the 3 played in their championship series. The final score, 6–3, marks the lowest score by the Athletics since they started playing professionally. Zettlein holds the Athletics to 4 hits.

SEPTEMBER

5th With the race for the whip-pennant getting closer, Boston defeats the league-leading White Stockings for their first win in the 3 matches played. With the Whites leading 3–0 after 4 innings, Boston scores 6 in the 5th inning, highlighted by a HR over the LF fence by Charley Gould with Dave Birdsall, McVey, and Spalding on the bases. The final score is 6–3.

29th Boston loses to Chicago and loses the season's series 4 games to one.

OCTOBER

7th The Chicago Fire breaks out at 10 o'clock in the evening. As the Rockford club travels toward Chicago the next day, they see the glow of the fire, turn around and return home. Chicago loses its ballpark and all equipment in the fire. The Whites are leading in the pennant race and must defeat the Haymakers in their remaining 3 games to clinch.

9th The Athletics win the 3rd and deciding game of their series with visiting Troy by scoring 3 runs in the 9th inning to win 15–13.

18th The Athletics defeat the Mutuals 21–7 before a large crowd in Philadelphia. This game puts the Athletics in the position of having only to defeat the homeless White Stockings on the 25th to clinch the whip-pennant, provided the Haymakers can win their series with Chicago.

21st In Troy, NY, the Chicago Whites meet the Haymakers for the first time this season. Chicago, playing a match for the first time since the 29th of September, wins the game 11–5. The White Stockings would lose their next game to Troy and the rest of the series would be rained out. Bad weather prevents the completion of the Troy-Chicago series before the November first official end of the season.

30th The final championship match for 1871 takes place on the Union Grounds in Brooklyn between the Athletics and the Chicago White Stockings. The Championship Committee decrees that today's game will decide the winner of the pennant. Chicago, having played all of its games on the road since the fire, appears in an assorted array of uniforms. Theirs were all lost during the fire. The 4–1 victory by the Athletics gives them the championship for 1871. The final putout in the game is made by Nate Berkenstock, a 40-year-old retired amateur who appears in his only professional game. With a birth year of 1831, he is the oldest player to appear in a NA game.

1872

FEBRUARY

12th William Arthur Cummings, who has been accused of signing contracts with 3 different clubs for the 1872 season, will be allowed to play with the Mutual Club of NY.

MARCH

4th The National Association of Professional Baseball Players holds its annual convention in Cleveland. Eight clubs send delegates. Bob Ferguson, Atlantics IF, is elected president. Each team is required to play a series of 5 games with each club. Whoever wins the most games will be declared champion. The rules will now permit the use of the wrist in pitching.

APRIL

13th A gathering of Cincinnatians takes place on the old Union Grounds to witness the auction of the trophies of the famous Cincinnati Red Stockings Baseball Club. Balls from the Reds' victories of 1869 and 1870 sell for an average of $2–$4 each.

18th The first match of the season is played at Washington, and the Lord Baltimores hand the Olympics their first "Chicago," or shutout game, ever, winning 16–0. Other teams in the professional association are the Atlantics, Athletics, Boston, Cleveland, Eckfords, Haymakers, Nationals, Mutuals, and the Mansfields of Middletown, CT.

26th Troy and Middletown begin their season with a well-pitched game by George Zettlein, now with the Haymakers. For the Mansfields, in their first big-league game, a 10–0 loss, are Tim Murnane and future Hall of Famer Jim O'Rourke. O'Rourke, later a prominent Boston Reds player, will close out a noteworthy career by catching a full game for the New York Giants in 1904.

MAY

4th A cold, blustery day in Philadelphia does not deter 5,000 spectators who turn out to see the season's first game between last year's champions, the Athletics, and the number one contender, the Boston Reds. Philadelphia scores 6 in the 7th inning to win the game 10–7.

20th A dispute stops play in the Baltimore-Athletics game. With one out and Mike McGeary on 2B and Adrian "Cap" Anson on 1B, Anson is thrown out at 2B on an attempted steal on a pitch that gives the batter a base on balls. The umpire calls Anson out on the grounds that he attempted to steal before Denny Mack received the pitch, a ball, entitling him to his base. During the argument, McGeary steps off 3B and is tagged out, ending the inning. A great uproar starts and the game is stopped. The game will be replayed.

29th The first game to be played in Chicago since the Great Fire is played on the new grounds of the Chicago Base Ball Association before an enthusiastic crowd of 4,000. Baltimore defeats Cleveland 5–3.

JUNE

15th During the Athletics-Atlantics game, Tom Barlow bunts the ball and reaches first safely. The New York *Clipper* describes the play: "After the first two strikers had been retired, Barlow, amid much laughter and applause, 'blocked' a ball in front of the home plate and reached first base before the ball did." That is one of only 3 hits off Dick McBride, as the Athletics win 11–1.

JULY

6th Cleveland defeats the Eckford club at the Union Grounds in Brooklyn 24–5. Cleveland C Scott Hastings gets 6 hits and scores 5 runs. Cleveland plays the game with only 8 players.

The Boston team under Harry Wright leaves for one of the islands in Boston's Harbor for 10 days of hunting and fishing for a week's vacation. Boston's record is now 22–1.

26th The National Association holds a special meeting, resolving that, because some teams have dropped out of the race for 1872 (Troy, Nationals, and Olympics), 9 games will be played between contending teams this season instead of 5.

AUGUST

8th Twenty-five hundred people watch the Baltimore Canaries rally for 3 runs in the 9th to tie the

Mutuals 8–8 and then win the game in the 12th 12–8 at the Union Grounds in Brooklyn.

15th The Maple Leaf Club of Guelph, Canada, the Canadian champions, plays the Mutuals on the Union Grounds. The Canadians started their American tour in Baltimore on the 12th, losing 25–5. Yesterday they lost in Philadelphia to the Athletics 35–8. Today, in a close game they lose to the Mutuals 9–4.

19th After the defeat of the Forest Citys of Cleveland by Boston 18–7 at Cleveland, the club disbands. There are now only 6 clubs left playing for the pennant.

SEPTEMBER

1st Albert Thake, 22-year-old LF of the Brooklyn Atlantics, drowns off Fort Hamilton, in New York Harbor, while fishing. A benefit game is arranged by Bob Ferguson between the old Brooklyn Atlantics and members of the 1869 Cincinnati Red Stockings.

14th An unusual play highlights the Athletics-Boston match in Philadelphia. With the Athletics leading 4–1 in the 7th inning, and runners on 1B and 2B, Fergy Malone pops up to SS George Wright. Wright catches the ball in his hat and then throws the ball to 3B after which it is thrown to 2B. Wright claims a double play has been completed, as a batter cannot be retired with a "hat catch," and thus runners Cap Anson and Bob Reach are forced out. The umpire finally gives Malone another at-bat, declaring nobody out. Athletics win 6–4.

OCTOBER

5th Baltimore scores 39 runs on 42 hits to the Atlantics' 14 runs on 11 hits. The ball used was so hard and elastic it was dangerous to try and catch it. Scott Hastings, the Baltimore catcher, scores 6 times on 7 base hits.

8th The "Grand Base Ball Tournament" begins, a series of games played on the Union Grounds in Brooklyn between the 3 major professional clubs: Mutuals, Athletics, and the Reds of Boston. First prize will be $1,800. Today's game ends in a tie, Mutuals 7, Boston 7. The tournament will end October 17th with Philadelphia and Boston splitting the prize money.

15th A contest of throwing the baseball is held on the Union Grounds in Brooklyn, first prize being $25. Six contestants make 3 throws each from CF toward home plate. John Hatfield's last throw carries 133 yards, 1 foot, and 7½ inches to capture first prize and break his 1868 record of 132 yards.

22nd The Boston Red Stockings win the championship of the 1872 season, winning their 39th game by defeating the Eckfords 4–3.

1873

MARCH

3rd Delegates from the existing professional clubs of the country assemble in Baltimore to establish a permanent Professional Association. A constitution is adopted along with Henry Chadwick's code of rules. For the first time a uniform ball must be used in all games.

APRIL

23rd At Boston, 2,000 spectators see the first game of the season between the Philadelphias (today called the Quakers, later called the Phillies) and Boston. Philadelphia scores 4 in the 9th to win 8–5.

MAY

5th Two thousand spectators pay 50¢ at the Union Grounds in Brooklyn and watch Baltimore play the Mutuals. Baltimore scores 3 in the first inning without a base hit and wins 6–1.

14th One of the most exciting, best-played, and closely contested games yet recorded takes place before almost 5,000 between the Philadelphias and the Athletics. The Philadelphias win 5–4 in the 13th as Chick Fulmer scores the winning run.

JUNE

3rd The Boston Reds visit the Union Grounds in Brooklyn to play the Mutuals in a game that goes to 12 innings before Boston wins 6–5. George Wright scores for the Reds on a hit by Ross Barnes.

11th The largest crowd of the year, 10,000, jams the grounds at 25th and Jefferson to see the Athletics play the Philadelphias. The Philadelphias score 5 runs in the 7th to win 7–5.

14th In Boston, 2,000 spectators watch the Reds suffer a shutout for the first time in their history. Dick McBride of the Athletics holds the champions to only 2 hits.

27th Michael J. Kelly, former baseball reporter for the New York *Herald* and editor of the DeWitt baseball guide in 1868, dies of pneumonia at the age of 33. A benefit game for the family will be played between the Atlantics and the Mutuals on July 19th, raising $1,000.

JULY

4th The Resolutes of Elizabeth NJ upset the Red Stocking 11–2 in an a.m. game. The afternoon game is close for 6 innings but Boston scores 5 runs in the 7th, 2 in the 8th, and 21 in the 9th to roll to a 32–3 win.

10th In Philadelphia, 3,000 people see the Philadelphias, favorites for this year's pennant, and Boston, last year's champions, play a wild game with the home team winning 18–17. The teams have decided to cut short the number of games they will play in August due to poor attendance during that month.

18th SS George Wright hits 2 HRs in the 3rd off Candy Cummings to stake Boston to an early lead, but Baltimore rallies for 13 runs against Al Spalding in the last 3 innings to overcome a 14–4 deficit. and defeat the Red Stockings 17–4.

21st One thousand people witness an extraordinary game in Philadelphia between the Athletics and the Lord Baltimores. Lipman Pike's 3-base hit and Tom York's groundout tie the game at the end of 9 innings. The Athletics' 3 runs in the top of the 10th and 2 in the top of the 11th are matched by Baltimore, and it is not until the 13th that Everett Mills scores the winning run for the Baltimores on John Radcliffe's hit. winning 12–11.

22nd Tom Barlow's 6 bunt base hits are not enough to give the Atlantics a victory as the Lord Baltimores win 12–9.

24th Brooklyn's Bob Ferguson umpires a close game between the Mutuals and the Baltimores that ends in a 3-run rally by the Mutes in the last of the 9th to win 11–10. A police escort is needed to get the umpire to the clubhouse. Nat Hicks of the Mutuals and Ferguson get into an altercation, the end result of which is the striking of Hicks's left arm with a bat wielded by the umpire. The men are reconciled after the game, but Hicks's arm is broken in 2 places, and he will not play for the next 2 months.

30th The Philadelphia Athletics play their first game in almost 3 weeks after spending a holiday at Cape May, NJ, to rest from the rigors of the season. They are roughly handled at Boston, with the Reds defeating them 24–10.

AUGUST

16th The Athletics make their reappearance at home, shutting out the Washington Nationals 14–0, with Dick McBride allowing but 5 hits.

Seven thousand people in Chicago see the Boston Reds defeat the Philadelphia Phillies (also referred to as "White Stockings," but not in Chicago) 11–8. After the teams leave Chicago it is announced that a number of players have signed contracts to play in Chicago next year.

At Baltimore's Newington Park, Baltimore OF Lipman Pike races against a horse named "Clarence." Pike has a short lead after 75 yards when the trotter breaks into a run. Pike holds on to win in 10 seconds flat.

OCTOBER

10th After scoring 29 runs on 32 hits yesterday, the Lord Baltimores are held to 2 singles by Bob Mathews, as the Mutuals win the game 7–0.

22nd The Boston Red Stockings clinch the pennant for 1873 by defeating the Washington Nationals 11–8 in Washington. George Wright leads the attack with a triple and 2 singles.

NOVEMBER

6th The first game under the proposed new rule of 10 men and 10 innings is played between the Athletics and the Phillies as a benefit for Ned Cuthbert. The majority present thought the 10th man (a right SS) was an unnecessary innovation.

1874

JANUARY

29th A. G. Spalding arrives in England where he will call on sporting editors and athletes pursuing his plan to bring 2 baseball clubs to England this summer and exhibit American baseball and to play some cricket matches.

FEBRUARY

27th The first match of American baseball ever played in England takes place at the Kennington Oval Cricket Field in London. The match is arranged by Mr. C. Alcock, the cricket editor of the London *Sportsman*, and the participants include several well-known cricketers. Mr. Spalding and Mr. Briggs, of the Beacon Club of Boston, choose up sides and play a 6-inning game.

MARCH

2nd The 4th meeting of the Professional Association takes place at the United States Hotel in Boston. Seven clubs send delegates: Athletics, Chicago, Hartford, Philadelphias, Mutuals, and Boston. The Atlantics are not represented but will play this year. Charles H. Porter of the Bostons is elected president. New rules include the adoption of the batter's box and the prohibition of any player betting on his own team (expulsion) or any other team (forfeiture of pay). The 10-man, 10-inning proposition favored by Chadwick is defeated.

14th A. G. Spalding comes home from his visit to England after arranging the tour of the Athletic and Boston teams this summer. Plans call for the teams to depart from the U.S. on July 16, play baseball and cricket matches in England during August, and leave Liverpool for home on August 26th. The full number of championship matches during the regular baseball season will be played.

APRIL

16th The first championship match of the 1874 season is played in Philadelphia, with the Athletics defeating the Philadelphias (now referred to as the Pearls) 14–5.

22nd The first game of the season in Baltimore finds the home team shut out by the Philadelphias and future Hall of Famer Arthur "Candy" Cummings.

MAY

5th Tommy Bond pitches for the Atlantics in their 1874 opener. It is his first appearance in the National Association. Bond would later win 40 or more games in 3 consecutive seasons in the NL. Today he limits Baltimore to 4 hits as the Atlantics win the game, played at the Union Grounds, 24–3.

9th The Mutuals meet the Athletics at the Union Grounds before 1,000 fans. Another 1,000 wait outside the gate for the end of the 3rd inning when they will be admitted for half price. The Mutuals commit 11 errors in the last half of the 6th inning, but still win 8–5.

13th The first professional championship match in Chicago, by a Chicago team, since the Great Fire of 1871 is played before 4,000 spectators. George Zettlein and the White Stockings defeat the Athletics of Philadelphia 4–0. The Athletics have 10 hits and 21 base runners and yet fail to score.

JUNE

15th Candy Cummings strikes out 6 consecutive Chicago White Stocking batters during an 8–6 victory at Philadelphia.

18th One of the poorest games of baseball ever played between 2 professional clubs occurs in New York as the Mutuals defeat the Chicago White Stockings 38–1. Of the 33 hits collected by the Mutes, Tom Carey makes 6 and scores 6 runs. Chicago had two hits and commits 36 errors.

27th The visiting Chicago Whites lose to the Boston Reds 29–6. P Al Spalding collects 6 hits for the winners.

JULY

4th Chicago celebrates its return home after a 4-week eastern trip by defeating the league-leading Boston Red Stockings 17–16 before 10,000 spectators.

10th   Joe Start, the Mutual 1B, misses the train to Hartford, and the Mutes are forced to play with only 8 players. Hartford wins 13–4.

16th   The Boston and Athletic teams sail from Philadelphia for England. Roundtrip tickets for baseball enthusiasts can be obtained for $100.

AUGUST

3rd   The American visitors play their first game of baseball in London at the Lord's Cricket Grounds as Boston defeats the Athletics 24–7. In the morning, a cricket match between the Americans and the Maryleborne Club is started. At the completion of the match on the 4th, the Americans are victorious 107–105. The American ballplayers will play in 7 cricket matches during the tour and will win all 7. However, the Americans field 18 players while their opponents use 12.

24th   The American tourists arrive in Dublin, Ireland, where they play a baseball game, won by Boston 12–7. They then start a cricket game, finishing tomorrow with the U.S. winning 165–88.

SEPTEMBER

9th   The stockholders of the Philadelphias baseball club vote 26–15 to expel player John J. Radcliffe. Umpire William McLean has testified that Radcliffe approached him before the game at Chicago on July 15th and offered him $175 if he would help Chicago win the game. Four other players were in on the plot: Candy Cummings, Nat Hicks, Bill Craver, and Denny Mack.

12th   Boston's return home after the tour is spoiled by a victory for the Athletics 6–5. Boston still leads the pennant race with a 31-9 record followed by the Mutuals with 29 victories and 17 losses.

14th   To the surprise of 1,000 Boston spectators, Chicago bats Spalding all over the lot with 10 runs on 22 hits while George Zettlein limits the Reds to no runs on 4 hits. Boston's George Wright makes 3 errors.

16th   The Globes, Louisville's first black baseball team, play a charity game for yellow fever sufferers, shaming a pair of local white clubs into following suit to avoid, in the words of the Louisville *Courier-*

Journal, being "outdone by the darkly-complected portion of the human race."

OCTOBER

9th   Five thousand people watch the last match game of the season between the Mutuals and the Boston Reds. Spalding allows only 5 hits, but the Reds lose 4–3. The winning runs score on Joe Start's double and a throwing error.

20th   Tommy Bond, whom Henry Chadwick says "bids fair to be a second Creighton," shuts out the Mutual club on 2 hits as the Atlantics win 5–0.

NOVEMBER

1st   The season ends today with the Boston Red Stockings being declared the champions with a record of 43-17. Boston actually had a record of 52-18 but the Committee throws out the Baltimore games because the team did not complete their schedule.

1875

JANUARY

9th The first game of baseball played on ice this winter in the New York area takes place at Prospect Park in Brooklyn between 2 teams managed by Billy Barnie and Crawford. Barnie's team wins 20–7 in a 5-inning match. Only 2 outs per team constitute an inning.

MARCH

17th The National Amateur Baseball Association meets in Boston. Harry Wright represents the Professionals to try and secure the adoption of a single code of playing rules.

APRIL

11th The New York *Sunday Mercury* describes the activities of the New Haven club during their training for the upcoming season: "First, each man runs a quarter of a mile, then gentle exercise upon the horizontal bar is taken, after which a trial at vaulting on the vaulting horse is indulged; then a series of Indian Club swinging, followed by the whole team pulling about one mile on the rowing apparatus. After all this, the club retires to a bowling alley where they pass and strike balls."

22nd The first championship match between the Athletics and the Philadelphias (called the Pearls or the Fillies) is played in Philadelphia before 2,000 people, including the Boston 9, who stopped on their way to Washington. Highlights are the triple by Cap Anson of the Athletics and the unassisted DP by Levi Meyerle of the Philadelphias. The Athletics win 6–3.

MAY

3rd The Hartfords wallop the Philadelphia Centennials 13–4. Captain Hayhurst discovers that some of the Hartford players are using an illegal bat. The rules state that the bat must be round, but the bat in question has been whittled down almost flat on one side and painted black so as to disguise it. The bat is then removed.

6th Before 5,000, the St. Louis Browns defeat the Chicago White Stockings 10–0 at the Grand Avenue Grounds (later known as Sportsman's Park). St. Louis's George Bradley allows but 4 hits.

8th St. Louis holds the White Stockings scoreless for the first 8 innings and hangs on to win 4–3. The Browns have shut out Chicago for 17 consecutive innings, a feat never before accomplished in baseball.

11th Two hundred people sit through a windstorm in St. Louis to see a remarkable game as the visiting Chicago White Stockings defeat the St. Louis Red Stockings 1–0. Each team gets 6 hits in this, the lowest-scoring game in baseball history at the time.

26th The Centennial club of Philadelphia becomes the first professional club of 1875 to disband. The Centennials have the honor of becoming the first team to sell a ballplayer. The rival Athletics wanted Bill Craver and George Bechtel, so the Athletics paid an official of the Centennials to have the 2 players released and transferred to the Athletic club.

29th At Hamilton Park in New Haven, CT, Mann of Princeton College pitches a no-hitter against Yale and their star pitcher Avery, winning 3–0.

JUNE

5th In St. Louis, the Boston Reds suffer their first defeat of the season after 21 victories and one draw. The Browns' George Bradley holds the Reds to 8 hits. After Bradley makes the last putout, the crowd rushes on the field and lifts him to their shoulders.

19th Henry Chadwick has this to say about today's game: "the finest display of baseball playing and the most exciting contest yet recorded in the annals of the national game." The Chicago Whites and the Dark Blues of Hartford battle 10 scoreless innings before Jim Devlin scores on a fly out by Paul Hines in the 11th to win for Chicago 1–0.

28th An organized gang, having bet on the success of the local 9, interrupt the Boston-Athletic game with the score 12–10 in the last of the 10th inning in favor of Boston. The toughs storm the field preventing further play. Harry Wright says he will not play again in Philadelphia.

JULY

5th The largest crowd ever seen in the St. Louis ballpark, estimated at 15,000, sees the Browns soundly defeat the Chicago White Stockings 13–2. Watching the game are members of the Washington club who, when they return to their hotel, are told that there is no money to pay their way back to Washington. With their club disbanded, the players are given fare and expenses by the St. Louis club.

15th   After discovering that urban rival Cincinnati has revived its professional baseball team, Louisville businessmen form the city's first pro team the same day, allowing them to keep pace on the ball field.

20th   The Chicago *Tribune* states that the Bostons will disband at the end of the season, with the Wrights going to Cincinnati to form a club there. The Chicago White Stockings 9 for 1876 will include Al Spalding, James "Deacon" White, Ross Barnes, and Cal McVey of Boston.

21st   The use of a lively ball is reflected in the score as the Mutuals defeat the Philadelphias 16–13 at the Union Grounds in Brooklyn. Joe Start hits 3 HRs and a triple.

28th   Philadelphia's Joseph E. Borden, also known by the name Josephs, pitches the first no-hitter, beating the Chicago White Stockings 4–0. The game takes one hour and 35 minutes to play.

31st   With 3 months to go in the baseball season, the record now shows Boston in first place with a 37–4 record. The Athletics are 2nd and Hartford 3rd.

AUGUST

9th   The underrated Philadelphias and their sensational P Josephs shut out Jim Galvin and the St. Louis Browns 16–0 on 5 hits. It is the first time the Browns have suffered a shutout in their history.

12th   With the score 1–0 and 2 out in the last of the 9th inning, Hartford's Tom York hits a triple. The next batter, Bob Ferguson, after hitting a number of fouls lefthanded, turns around and bats righthanded, getting a double to tie the score. Rain ends the game with the score Hartford 1, Mutuals 1.

20th   Tommy Bond pitches his 2nd one-hit game in 10 days. Bill Boyd of the Atlantics gets the only hit in the 2–0 victory by Hartford.

21st   The St. Louis Browns defeat the Boston Reds, who are minus the services of Al Spalding, suffering from a strained back. With Boston's Jack Manning

pitching, the Browns win 5–3. George Wright pitches the last 3 innings without allowing a run. This is Spalding's first absence from a professional game in 5 years with the Reds and, before that, 4 years with Rockford.

SEPTEMBER

11th   The first baseball game played with women professionals takes place in Springfield, IL. The diamond is half-sized and a 9-foot high canvas surrounds the entire field. The uniforms are similar to the male version except the pants are shorter. Final score: "Blondes" 42, "Brunettes" 38.

25th   Paul Hines, 2B for Chicago, makes 10 errors, helping Philadelphia to a 15–6 victory.

OCTOBER

24th   The Chicago *Tribune* calls for the formation of an organization of major professional teams: Chicago, Cincinnati, Louisville, Philadelphia, New York, Boston, and Hartford. "Unless the present Professional Association leadership adopts rules to limit the number of teams allowed to participate in the Championship season, all clubs will go broke."

1876

FEBRUARY

2nd Chicago President William Hulbert organizes a meeting in New York to establish a new league. To win the support of 4 eastern clubs, Hulbert proposes that Morgan Bulkeley of the Hartford club be president and Nick Young of Washington be secretary. The National League is officially organized.

12th Al Spalding, pitching star of the National Association, moves from his home in Rockford, IL, with his brother J. Walter Spalding, to Chicago to "open a large emporium where they will sell all kinds of baseball goods." This will be the start of the Spalding sporting goods enterprise.

MARCH

19th The Boston *Herald* reports the first practice of the Red Caps under the direction of George Wright. Manager Harry Wright is still in Florida, recuperating from a severe cold. The team has been weakened considerably by the loss to the Chicago White Stockings of Al Spalding, Cal McVey, and Ross Barnes.

APRIL

8th After 4 great seasons with the Philadelphia Athletics, Adrian "Cap" Anson reports to the Chicago club to play 3B.

22nd In the first National League game, Boston defeats Philadelphia at Athletic Park 6–5. Jim O'Rourke makes the first hit and Joseph Borden, pitching under the name of Josephs, is the winning hurler.

24th Chicago manager Al Spalding pitches the NL's first shutout 4–0 at Louisville.

27th In his 2nd outing, Spalding hurls another shutout over the Louisville Grays, winning 10–0.

MAY

2nd Chicago's Ross Barnes, the great batting star of the National Association, hits the first NL HR, an inside-the-park drive off William "Cherokee" Fisher against the Cincinnati Red Stockings in Cincinnati.

Barnes also hits a triple, single, steals 2 bases, and scores 4 runs.

5th The Chicago team loses its first game, as St. Louis's George Washington Bradley outpitches Spalding 1–0.

13th Dick Higham of the Hartford Dark Blues hits into the first NL triple play against New York. It is the only bright spot for the Mutuals, who lose 28–3.

30th Chicago, with 4 former Boston stars in their lineup, play their first 1876 game in Boston. The crowd, estimated at 14,000, is described as "the largest that ever attended a baseball match in the world." The White Stockings beat the Red Caps 5–1.

JUNE

6th Manager Harry Wright, 41, makes his only 1876 appearance for Boston, in the OF, but Jim Devlin of Louisville deals the "Beantowners" their first shutout of the season 3–0.

10th George Bechtel, RF for Louisville, who was suspended for "crookedness in the last Louisville-Mutuals game," gets in deeper trouble when P Jim Devlin shows his manager a telegram from Bechtel saying, "We can win $100 if you lose the game today."

14th George Hall of the Athletics hits 3 triples and a HR in a 20–5 shellacking of Cincinnati. Teammate Ezra Sutton also hits 3 triples, the only time 2 players have done this in the same game.

17th George Hall and Ezra Sutton again gang up on the hapless Reds. Hall hits 2 HRs, a triple, and 2 singles, and Sutton also collects 5 hits in a 23–15 slaughter. Only 39 HRs will be hit in the NL season; Hall will lead with 5.

27th Little Davey Force of the Athletics goes 6-for-6 against Spalding of Chicago, and Philadelphia scores 4 runs in the 9th to pull out a 14–13 victory.

JULY

8th The Boston *Herald* carries the midseason averages showing hits and errors per game (not per at bat or chance). Chicago's Ross Barnes is the top batter with 2.1 hits per game, and Dave Eggler of the Athletics is the leading fielder with .19 errors per game.

10th The New York Mutuals score one run in the 9th to tie the Louisville Grays and then score 4 in the 16th to win 8–5. Bobby Mathews prevails over Jim Devlin in this longest game of the season. In the previous game on July 8th, the 2 hurlers had battled to a 5–5 tie in 15 innings.

15th George Bradley of St. Louis pitches the league's first no-hitter, defeating Hartford and Tommy Bond 2–0. It is his 3rd shutout over Hartford in the 3-game series.

25th For the 2nd consecutive game, Cal McVey of Chicago collects 6 hits in 7 trips. It also gives him a record 15 hits in 3 games, the scores of which are 18–0 and 30–7 over Louisville, and 23–3 over Cincinnati.

AUGUST

4th Louisville, trailing Chicago by a wide margin with rain threatening in the 5th, decides to stall. They make error after error until the umpire forfeits the game to Chicago. The contest would later be ruled "no game."

12th The versatile Cal McVey has the unusual distinction of both pitching and catching in a 5–0 win over Cincinnati.

18th With the season two-thirds over, the lowly Louisville club plays its first errorless game of the season and beats Cincinnati 4–1.

21st The strain of pitching almost every game is taking its toll on Tommy Bond, the 20-year-old, sore-armed hurler of Hartford. Candy Cummings takes his place and beats Boston 10–4. SS George Wright pitches a scoreless 9th for the Red Caps.

SEPTEMBER

9th Curveballer Candy Cummings of Hartford wins 2 games over Cincinnati, 14–4 in the morning and 8–1 in the afternoon. This marks the first time 2 games are played in the same day.

11th President G. W. Thompson of Philadelphia informs Chicago president Hulbert that the Athletics cannot afford to make their final western trip. He suggests that Chicago and St. Louis (the big drawing clubs) play additional games in Philadelphia and take a larger portion of the receipts. Hulbert turns down the offer.

16th After only 200 watch the New York Mutuals lose to Cincinnati, the club announces that they, like the Athletics, will not make their western trip. Their games in the west will be canceled, leaving a thin schedule of league games the rest of the season.

26th Chicago clinches the pennant with a 7–6 win over Hartford. Cal McVey, the regular 1B and Spalding's backup pitcher, hurls the victory.

OCTOBER

6th Louisville closes out its season with an 11–2 loss to Hartford. Jim Devlin, injured severely during yesterday's game, does not pitch for the first time this season. He will still lead the league in games (68), complete games (66), and innings pitched (622).

20th Boston manager Harry Wright shakes up his lineup, shifting brother George to 2B and inserting another brother, Sam, at SS. It is not the "right" combination as Candy Cummings of Hartford blanks the Red Caps 5–0.

21st Candy Cummings defeats Boston in the last game of the season to give Hartford a season record of 47-21. It is not quite good enough for 2nd place, as St. Louis finishes 45-19, with all of the decisions being credited to the Brown Stockings' superb P George Bradley, who hurls a record 16 shutouts.

23rd The Chicago *Tribune* publishes season-ending batting percentages based on the new method of dividing number of at bats into number of hits. Ross Barnes leads with a .429 average.

DECEMBER

10th After a 5-day league meeting in Cleveland, these results are announced: the Philadelphia Athletics and New York Mutuals are expelled by unanimous vote; a uniform and lively baseball is agreed upon; the playing rules for 1877 are modified, and William Hulbert is elected NL president.

1877

JANUARY

6th Joe Battin reportedly will not sign with the St. Louis Brown Stockings because of the new NL policy of charging players $30 for uniforms and, during road trips, deducting 50¢ a day from salaries to help offset the cost of meals.

13th St. Louis announces the signing of Mike Dorgan for $1,600, much to the surprise of the Syracuse Stars, who claim to hold a signed contract with him.

15th Al Spalding proposes a League Alliance in which independent teams would affiliate with the NL and the NL would honor their contracts. Spalding also promises to honor all contracts signed after March 15th.

24th The Centennial club is organized in San Francisco in an attempt to field the first professional team in California.

FEBRUARY

3rd Cherokee Fisher admits he was paid $100 to lose a game last September while pitching for the West Ends in Milwaukee.

20th The International Association is organized at a meeting of representatives of 17 clubs held in Pittsburgh. Although set up as an alternative to the NL, the IA will go down in history as the first minor league.

21st The IA adopts a $10 admission fee, with an additional $10 required to enter the pennant race. Candy Cummings, pitcher-manager of the Live Oaks of Lynn, MA, is elected president.

MARCH

5th The Hartford club completes arrangements to play its 1877 NL home games in Brooklyn. The club will still be called "Hartford."

10th The IA Indianapolis Blues play the first game of their spring training tour in Galveston, TX, beating the Dallas team 50–0. No NL clubs will travel further south than Memphis this spring.

22nd The NL publishes its 1877 game schedule, the first league-wide schedule ever issued. The failure of the Athletics and the Mutuals to finish the 1876 season has convinced the NL of the necessity of agreeing on a schedule.

APRIL

26th The IA opening game is played in Lynn, MA. The Manchester, NH, team beats the Live Oaks 14–3.

30th The Boston Red Stockings and the Hartford Dark Blues open the NL season with a tie game in Brooklyn, 1–1 in 11 innings. Tommy Bond makes his debut with Boston against his old team. Hartford manager Bob Ferguson, who suspended Bond last year after the pitcher had accused him of throwing games, drives in the only run for the Dark Blues.

Jim Galvin of the Pittsburgh Alleghenies hurls the minor league IA's first shutout, defeating Columbus 2–0.

MAY

1st In a preseason game in St. Louis, the Browns and the Syracuse Stars play a 15-inning scoreless tie, the longest scoreless game played by professional clubs.

2nd The Allegheny (IA) club of Pittsburgh upsets the Boston Red Stockings behind the brilliant work of Jim Galvin. Not only does he pitch a one-hit shutout, he hits a HR said to be the first ball to clear the fence at Pittsburgh's Union Park.

8th Batting champ Ross Barnes goes 2-for-4 in Chicago's opener despite the new rule that makes a ball that goes foul before reaching 1B or 3B a foul ball. The old rule enabled Barnes to hit many safe "fair-foul" balls back past 3B.

12th Chicago makes 21 errors, including passed balls and wild pitches, and loses to Boston 18–9. The winners make 11 errors.

17th At a special league meeting, the NL adopts a livelier version of the Spalding ball for all games.

Umpire John Draper walks off the field in the 8th inning of the Cincinnati-Boston game. John Brockway comes out of the stands to finish the game, but the incident underscores the hazards of having amateurs officiate for the NL.

JUNE

1st The Dark Blues play the Athletics in Hartford, CT, for the 2nd day in a row. With a game against amateurs on June 5th, the "Hartford" club plays only 3 games all season in Hartford.

5th Making his last start as a pitcher, Chicago's Al Spalding fails to retire any of the 5 Cincinnati batters he faces. Spalding's old Rockford teammate, Bob Addy, literally knocks Spalding out of the box with a line drive to the chest.

10th The St. Louis Browns and Cincinnati Reds stage a Sunday exhibition game, the only Sunday game between NL teams that would be played until 1892.

Lip Pike resigns as Cincinnati captain and is succeeded by Bob Addy.

18th Lacking the funds to start their scheduled eastern trip, the Cincinnati club disbands.

21st Cincinnati stockholders move to reorganize the club.

25th Hard luck continues to dog the Cincinnati club, as a heavy windstorm nearly destroys the pavilion at the Cincinnati Baseball Park.

30th Cincinnati signs P Candy Cummings, formerly of the Live Oaks of Lynn. Cummings will join the NL club but will still serve as president of the IA.

JULY

3rd The reorganized Cincinnati Red Stockings reappear in action versus the Louisville Grays, losing 6–3. Whether or not their games will count in the NL standings will not be resolved until the NL meeting in December.

11th Having been struck in the eye by a foul tip one month earlier, Pete Hotaling of the IA Syracuse Stars returns behind the plate wearing a wire mask for protection. Hotaling and teammate Al Hall would often use the mask this summer.

13th After pitching in 88 consecutive games since the start of the NL, an all-time record, George Bradley steps aside for Cal McVey, and Chicago beats Hartford 6–3. The revamped lineup shows Bradley at 3B, Spalding at 1B, and Cap Anson catching.

20th Ed Nolan of Indianapolis pitches his 5th straight shutout, all within a span of 8 days, beating Milwaukee 1–0. His previous shutouts were over Louisville, Syracuse, and Manchester twice. Nolan will total 30 shutouts in 1877 against all levels of opponents.

Slumping Paul Hines receives a letter from Chicago club president William Hulbert threatening him with a release for poor play.

21st Jim Galvin of Pittsburgh beats the Champion City 9 of Springfield, OH, 1–0 on one hit. This game would later be claimed as a perfect game, since only 27 Champion City batters faced the pitcher.

31st Louisville supplants St. Louis in first place, beating the Browns 7–0 despite 13 St. Louis runners reaching 1B.

AUGUST

1st Umpire Dan Devinney charges that St. Louis manager George McManus tried to bribe him with $250 to help the Browns beat the Grays in Louisville. But the home team wins 3–1. St. Louis management will vehemently deny the charges.

2nd Charley Bennett signs with Milwaukee for 1878 when the Milwaukee club's offer of $1,700 was supplemented by a private purse of $300 raised by local fans. The terms are among the most lucrative ever offered by an independent club.

6th The NL rule calls for the home team to submit 3 names of approved local men as a possible umpire for each game, with the visiting team choosing one of them at random. Today in Louisville, Chicago's Cal McVey reaches into the hat and picks out a slip with Devinney's name on it. Disgusted, McVey then grabs the hat and finds that all 3 slips have Devinney's name on them. The incensed White Stockings demand a new umpire and then snap the Grays' 6-game winning streak 7–2.

7th Chicago scores 13 runs in the 2nd inning and trounces Cincinnati 21–7. The rally still stands as the NL record for runs in the 2nd inning.

8th After St. Louis C John Clapp has his cheek smashed by a foul tip, replacement Mike Dorgan goes behind the plate wearing a mask. Though used earlier in the IA, this is perhaps the first use of a catcher's mask in an official NL game.

12th Johnny Quigley, catcher for the Clippers of Harlem, dies from head injuries sustained in a home-plate collision with Dan Brouthers on July 7th in a game against the Actives of Wappingers Falls, NY, while trying to catch a throw home. The 19-year-old Brouthers has already been exonerated by the authorities.

16th Louisville loses in Boston 6–1, but retains first place. Bill Craver takes a called 3rd strike with the tying runs on base, and Jim Devlin fans 4 times, raising suspicions of gambling.

20th Louisville director Charles E. Chase receives an anonymous telegram from Hoboken, NJ, saying that "something is wrong with the Louisville players" and that gamblers were betting on Hartford.

SEPTEMBER

4th Boston beats St. Louis 7–1 to take over first place.

5th Louisville's Jim Devlin and George Hall agree to throw tomorrow's game in Cincinnati for $25 apiece. Louisville will lose the game 1–0.

6th Sam "Buck" Weaver of Milwaukee no-hits the Mutuals of Janesville, to win the Wisconsin state championship. The Janesville battery consists of future stars John Montgomery Ward and Albert Bushong.

Bobby Mitchell of Cincinnati, the first southpaw to pitch in the NL, wins a 1–0 victory over Jim Devlin of Louisville. Teammate Lipman Pike, described as the first Jewish player in the NL, provides the margin with a HR.

15th A 3-team tournament in Pittsburgh, featuring the top 3 non-NL pitchers in the game, Galvin of Allegheny, Nolan of Indianapolis, and McCormick of Syracuse, ends in a tie, with each team 2-2. The tournament moves to Chicago.

22nd Hartford plays Chicago in an NL championship game in New Haven before a crowd of 700. Hartford wins 11–9 with 2 runs in the bottom of the 9th.

23rd The Chicago *Times* denounces the Syracuse-Indianapolis-Allegheny tournament as a "swindle" with the outcomes fixed by gamblers, especially the deciding game won yesterday by the Stars.

24th Two Allegheny players confirm that the Chicago games were "sold" by 2 other players. They add that 3 of the Allegheny club's directors bet upon Syracuse.

27th Boston clinches the NL pennant with a 13–2 victory over Hartford. The league's leading hitter, Jim "Deacon" White, leads the Reds' offense with a 4-for-4 performance.

29th Boston completes its league schedule with its 20th victory in its last 21 games, beating Hartford 8–4. The Reds' final record is 31-17, 42-18 counting Cincinnati games.

OCTOBER

2nd In the final game of the IA season, the London, Ontario, Tecumsehs defeat Pittsburgh 5–2 and win the pennant. Their championship record is 14-4.

20th At an exhibition, LH Bobby Mitchell and RH Tommy Bond offer conclusive proof that a ball can curve. Three stakes are set up in a straight line; Bond curves the ball around the center stake on one side, while Mitchell curves it around on the other side.

26th Louisville club vice president Charles Chase confronts George Hall and Jim Devlin with charges that they threw road games in August and September. Both admit to throwing non-league games and implicate teammates Al Nichols and Bill Craver.

27th The Louisville club formally expels Devlin, Hall, and Nichols for selling games and tampering with other players and expels Craver for "disobedience to positive orders." Craver will deny any wrongdoing.

NOVEMBER

12th The champion Boston Red Stockings play a game against the club's stockholders. The players play lefthanded as a handicap but still win 28–18.

17th The Chicago club secures a lease to Lake Front Park, located downtown at Randolph Street and Michigan Avenue. That is the site used before the Great Chicago Fire of 1871. The White Stockings have been playing at 23rd Street since 1874.

30th At Boston's South End Fair, Andy Leonard wins a gold watch valued at $300 for being voted the league's "most popular player."

DECEMBER

4th At the formal meeting in Cleveland, the NL directors meet and confirm the expulsions of the four Louisville players. The directors also vote to throw out all Cincinnati games from the standings on the grounds that Cincinnati never paid its $100 dues.

5th The NL confirms the actions of the directors and accepts the resignation of the St. Louis club. The Cincinnati Reds are readmitted for 1878. The Indianapolis Hoosiers and the Milwaukee Cream Citys are also admitted.

6th William Hulbert is reelected NL president and Nick Young NL secretary. Hartford is stripped of its membership.

9th August Sloari, operator of the Grand Avenue ballpark in St. Louis, announces that he will take down the stands and stack the lumber now that the pro team has folded. Sportsman's Park would eventually be built at the Grand Avenue site.

1878

JANUARY

5th Milwaukee signs SS Johnny Peters. With 4 years of experience, Peters will be the closest thing to a veteran the new Cream Citys have in the coming season.

The annual stockholders meeting of the pennant-winning Boston club shows that the team lost money despite a league-leading attendance of 51,204 in 1877. Salaries totaling $22,000 more than offset revenues.

16th The Grays, a new club that Benjamin Douglas put together in Providence, is finally organized with Henry Root as president, Douglas is hired as manager, and veteran Tom Carey is signed as captain.

25th The Boston club is reported to be backing a Massachusetts bill outlawing gambling on ball games.

FEBRUARY

6th Providence becomes a member of the NL, bringing membership to 7.

9th Official averages compiled by the IA list Rochester's Steve Brady as first-ever minor league batting champion with a .373 average.

19th The 2nd annual meeting of the IA is held in Buffalo, 28 clubs attending.

MARCH

6th "Being unable to secure a team sufficiently strong to cope with the other nines," Louisville submits its resignation from the NL, reducing the circuit for 1878 to 6 clubs: Boston, Providence, Cincinnati, Indianapolis, Chicago, and Milwaukee.

9th The Cincinnati club puts president J. M. Neff "in full charge of the club." There will be no manager, just a captain from among the players.

13th The Pittsburgh Alleghenies mail their $50 entry fee to the International Association to join, beating the deadline by 2 days. Despite the increase in the price from $10 last year, 13 clubs are entered for the championship.

21st Milwaukee hires Jack Chapman as manager. He had run the Louisville NL team for the previous 2 seasons.

27th The National Association of Amateur Base Ball Players disbands. This organization had traced its roots back to the first National Association founded in 1858.

APRIL

1st The NL meets at Buffalo and adopts a schedule. Then the league owners sign an agreement with 6 of the stronger IA clubs agreeing to drop their demand of a $100 guarantee for exhibition games and to split the gate receipts 50/50.

2nd The NL announces the selection of a staff of 18 umpires for the coming season. The individual clubs will arrange which ones will work which games.

10th Ben Douglas is fired as manager of the Providence Grays for incompetence and insubordination.

13th Three NL teams begin practice, the Indianapolis Blues, the Milwaukee Grays, and the Cincinnati Reds. Ed Nolan of the Blues is given a cap with 2 feathers in it to help the fans pick him out.

20th Chicago's new Lake Front Park is opened with a practice game. This field with its very short RF fence will house the White Stockings (NL) for 8 years.

24th John "Bud" Fowler, a young black hurler with the Chelsea team, wins a 2–1 exhibition game from the Boston Nationals, the 1877 NL champs. Fowler will sign with the Lynn Live Oaks of the International Association. There are claims that Fowler played professionally in New Castle, PA, as early as 1872.

MAY

1st A crowd of 5,500 turns out for the Opening Day game at the brand-new Messer Street Park in Providence, but the Boston Reds (NL) spoil the festivities by nipping the Grays 1–0.

4th Providence returns the favor and spoils Boston's home opener by winning 8–6. Dick Higham hits a 3-run HR over the cozy LF wall at the South End Grounds.

6th Chicago makes one error and turns 4 DPs to beat Indianapolis 3–1. The losing Blues make 7 errors.

8th Providence CF Paul Hines pulls off a spectacular and perhaps unassisted triple play. With men on 2B and 3B and none out in the 8th inning, Boston's Jack Burdock lines one over SS as both runners go. Hines, racing in, catches the ball and keeps going until he touches 3B. This retires the runner who started on 3B, but did it retire the runner who started on 2B but had already rounded 3B? To make sure, Hines throws back to Charley Sweasy to touch 2B. This touches off a lively debate over whether the triple play was unassisted or not, a debate that still continues over a century later.

9th Sam Weaver pitches a no-hitter to lead the Milwaukee Cream Citys to their first NL win, beating Indianapolis 2–1, one run scoring after a walk. One scorer gave a hit to John Clapp of the Blues, but Weaver is generally credited with a no-hitter.

10th Indianapolis scores its first NL win, beating Milwaukee 6–1.

11th Indianapolis edges Milwaukee 1–0 when the Reds are able to field Will Foley's long drive beyond the carriages parked in the LF corner in time to nip Foley's bid for a game-tying HR.

14th A crowd of 1,500 attends the first NL game in Milwaukee and sees the Grays end the Cincinnati Reds' 6-game winning streak with an 8–5 decision.

15th Providence beats Boston 24–5, pounding out 25 hits for 34 bases and running up the score with 12 runs in the 8th inning and 7 more in the 9th.

21st Ed "The Only" Nolan of Indianapolis sets Milwaukee down with just 2 hits, but he barely wins a 6–5 game because of 11 errors and passed balls by his team.

28th After starter Fred Corey gives out, Providence is forced to try its catchers as pitchers. Backstops Lew Brown and Doug Allison pitch the final 6 innings in a 12–4 loss to Milwaukee.

JUNE

6th Boston cannot hold a 15–6 lead but is able to push across a run in the bottom of the 9th to edge Milwaukee 16–15.

12th A great throw for a CF and catcher DP by White Stocking OF John Cassidy in the bottom of the 10th inning saves a 1–0 decision over Milwaukee.

17th After he is awarded 3B in a collision with Cal McVey, Johnny Morrill scores the winning run on a double steal. Boston beats Cincinnati in their first meeting of the year 4–2.

JULY

5th Cincinnati wins to move ahead of Boston in the standings with 17 games won. Boston has won 16 but has lost 4 fewer games.

9th Indianapolis begins a transferred "home" series in St. Louis, losing to Boston 6–3 thanks to 4 errors in the 2nd inning by 2B Joe Quest. The 3-game series will total 1,594 in paid attendance.

11th Blues pitcher Jim McCormick suffers a broken bone in his forearm in the 7th inning and gives up 3 runs in the 8th and 4 in the 9th to lose to Boston 8–4. He will be out of action until the end of August.

15th John Montgomery Ward makes his NL debut pitching for Providence in Cincinnati. The first game is a fiasco, the Grays losing 13–9 thanks to 17 battery errors by Monte Ward and Brown. But the 18-year-old rookie will pitch every inning of every league game for the Grays for the rest of the season.

31st Lip Pike, recently released by Cincinnati, goes 4-for-5 with 3 RBI for Providence, as the Grays beat his old team 9–3.

AUGUST

9th Paul Hines and Monte Ward star as Providence wins 2 from Indianapolis 12–6 in the morning and 8–5 in the afternoon. Ward pitches both games, and Hines amasses 7 hits and 7 RBI.

14th The Indianapolis club expels "The Only" Nolan for leaving the team to attend a fictitious funeral.

19th The NL loses 3 out of 4 exhibition games on this date, Boston beating Rochester 4–2 in 14 innings for the only victory.

26th The Manchester IA club plays an exhibition at the state reform school, and during the game their dressing room is robbed of jewelry and $48 in cash.

31st Al Spalding comes out of retirement to play 2B for Chicago. He goes 2-for-4 but makes 4 errors as the Whites lose to Boston 5–2.

SEPTEMBER

2nd A benefit game played in Chicago raises $682 for yellow fever victims in Memphis.

4th Monte Ward shuts Chicago out for the 2nd day in a row, winning 9–0 on 4 hits this time.

5th Catcher Jim "Deacon" White picks 2 runners off and throws out 3 more trying to steal to lead Cincinnati to a 5–2 victory over Boston.

14th The Red Stockings and Blues play an exhibition game in which they experiment with calling every pitch a ball or a strike and allowing only 6 balls for a walk. The reaction is favorable.

23rd The "Chicagos of 1879," including Ned Williamson and Silver Flint of this year's Indianapolis 9, lose an exhibition game to the Blues 9–7.

26th Boston's Tommy Bond posts his 40th win of the season, beating Providence 4–1.

30th The NL season ends with a Providence win over Boston. For the first time ever, a league completes its entire schedule.

OCTOBER

2nd Buffalo beats Boston 9–5 in 12 innings, giving Bison P Jim Galvin at least one win over each NL club. He will finish 10–5 this year versus NL teams.

3rd The Stars of Syracuse beat Lowell 12–1 and claim the IA pennant. They celebrate with a "grand collation."

8th Buffalo beats Utica and also claims the IA pennant.

18th The Indianapolis club unaccountably finds itself short $2,500. The players are given $60 each in lieu of their salaries due, spelling the end of the Indianapolis Blues.

25th The Buffalo club plays its final game in Jamestown, NY, finishing the season with an overall record of 81-32-3, including 10-7 versus NL teams and 24-8 in official IA games. P Jim Galvin racks up a 72-25-3 record.

NOVEMBER

1st Boston beats Providence in an experimental game with 6 balls for a walk and no outs on foul bounds.

9th The official NL averages give Milwaukee's Abner Dalrymple the batting championship with a .356 average. These figures do not include tie games, however, and counting ties, Providence's Paul Hines would have the lead .358 to .354.

10th Nearly 8,000 come out to the San Francisco National Trotting Park to see the deciding game of the Pacific Coast championship season. The Athletics beat the Californias 9–7 in a game marred by terrible field conditions.

DECEMBER

4th The full NL meets and admits the Stars of Syracuse, Buffalo, and Cleveland. Indianapolis resigns, and the Milwaukee club is given 20 days to pay its creditors and resign honorably or be expelled.

New rules include the following:

- Nonplaying managers are barred from the bench (a rule aimed at Harry Wright of Boston).
- The pitcher's box is narrowed from 6 feet wide to 4 feet wide.
- Every pitch is called either a ball, a strike, or a foul and 9 balls are required for a walk, as opposed to the old rule in which every 3rd bad pitch was a called ball and 3 called balls gave the batter his base.
- A system of fines is established against pitchers who hit batsmen with pitches.
- Pitchers are barred from turning their backs completely to the batters during delivery.
- Batting-order rules are altered to make the first batter in a new inning follow the last batter in the previous inning.

5th In its final session, the NL votes to abolish all outs on the first bounce, both on fouls and 3rd strikes.

29th The Professional Baseball League of Cuba is founded in Havana.

31st It is reported that 8,000,000 bats were sold in the United States during 1878.

1879

JANUARY

26th Troy receives notification of its admission into the NL. The Trojans are already committed to salaries totaling $10,240 for 11 players and a manager.

FEBRUARY

14th The Milwaukee NL club's property (Cream Citys) is sold to satisfy a bankruptcy judgment of $125.61.

18th At the International Association meeting, the 1878 pennant is awarded to Buffalo with a 24-8 record; Syracuse was 23-9. With no Canadian clubs in attendance, the league changes its name to the National Association.

MARCH

21st Entry into the NA pennant race is closed with 9 clubs, including 2 in Albany.

24th The NL meets in Buffalo and adopts an 8-team, 84-game schedule.

25th Despite some vocal opposition from some members, the NL votes to retain its 50¢ minimum admission price. It also reinstitutes the rule making outs of fouls on 3rd strikes caught on the first bounce.

APRIL

1st The Northwest League is formed with Davenport, Omaha, Dubuque, and Rockford. This league refuses to affiliate with the NA or NL, setting its sights at limited attendance and salary standards. In this sense, it is the first minor league.

4th The Providence Grays vote to establish a "bull pen" in CF for which 15¢ admissions can be purchased starting in the 5th inning. This would be a very popular ticket, with a daily rush in the 5th.

24th The NA season opens with the Capital Cities losing to their crosstown rivals the Albanys 3–0.

MAY

1st Opening Day in the NL with 4 games, including the first league games ever in Buffalo and Cleveland.

17th Plagued by catching injuries, the Cleveland Blues give Fred Gunkley a trial. He finishes the game with 10 errors (including passed balls) even though he is shifted to the OF midway through the game. The Blue Stockings lose to the Syracuse Stars 11–3.

30th John Ward of Providence beats Buffalo 4–0 and saves his own shutout with the innovative tactic of backing up home plate on a throw from the OF.

JUNE

2nd J. Lee Richmond, Brown University baseball star, makes his pro debut with the Worcester Ruby Legs by no-hitting Chicago in a 7-inning game 11–0.

9th Back with Brown, Richmond pitches his school to the College Championship by beating Yale 3–2.

13th Will White sprains his ankle while horsing around with Mike Kelly before the game, and Cincinnati is forced to use Cal McVey in the pitcher's box. McVey is pounded for 28 hits, as Providence wins 19–6.

14th Chicago's Frank "Silver" Flint hits a ball over the LF fence in the 9th inning in Troy. He takes only 3 bases on the hit because he wants to force the catcher to play close behind the next batter, giving the hitter a better chance. Chicago still loses 10–9.

20th Oscar Walker of Buffalo becomes the first ML player to strike out 5 times in a 9-inning game.

26th Boston edges Providence 3–2, due largely to a triple play started by C Snyder. He drops a 3rd strike with the bases loaded and begins the throws that result in 3 force outs. The rule eliminating the chance for double and triple plays on dropped 3rd strikes would not be adopted until 1887.

JULY

4th A holiday crowd of more than 5,000 turns out in Philadelphia to see a widely advertised game between 2 women's teams, the New York Blue Stockings and the Philadelphia Red Stockings. The teams, connected with variety theaters, are playing for "the championship of the U.S." The Blue Stockings win 36–24 in a loosely played game cut short when the unruly crowd gets out of control.

15th After having pitched complete games in all of Providence's 73 NL games since he joined the club exactly one year ago, Monte Ward is relieved for the first time in the 4th inning in a 9–0 loss to Cincinnati.

26th Syracuse's Harry McCormick hits a HR in the first and then makes it stand up by beating Boston's Tommy Bond 1–0. This will be the only time in ML history that a pitcher wins his own 1–0 game with first-inning HR.

AUGUST

5th After Providence P Bobby Mathews gives up 6 runs in the first 2 innings, he switches positions with 3B Monte Ward, who pitches shutout ball the rest of the way to rally the Grays to a 7–6 win. Captain George Wright would successfully employ this pitching scheme several more times in the season.

7th An unusual base-path occurrence is the feature in Syracuse. The Star runner from 2B, Mike Dorgan, passes the man from 3B, Hick Carpenter, and crosses the plate before Carpenter is tagged out. There is as yet no specific rule about passing preceding runners, but the umpire calls both men out. The Stars beat Boston 6–5.

13th Chicago and Cincinnati try to play a makeup game, but the home team Reds refuse to play after a downpour of rain. The visiting Whites then appoint one of their traveling party as umpire, and he declares the game a 9–0 forfeit victory for Chicago. It will be declared a legal Chicago victory at the NL meeting in December.

15th Providence takes over first place from Chicago in the NL with a 16–7 pasting of Troy.

Cap Anson plays his final game of 1879 for Chicago. He will leave the club to recuperate from a liver ailment. Anson's illness, coupled with P Terry Larkin's lame arm, will doom Chicago to a 4th-place finish.

SEPTEMBER

9th Tommy Bond of Boston shuts out Chicago again, 10–0 this time, for his 11th and final complete-game shutout of the season. This is the 3rd year in a row that he has led the NL in whitewashes.

10th Facing bankruptcy, the Syracuse Stars fold after winning their final game. Having played Troy only 6 times, the official NL standings are adjusted so that only the first 6 games of the total each team played versus Syracuse would count. This adds a game to Providence's lead.

23rd With Bond injured, Boston manager Harry Wright hires Harvard C Joe Tyng to pitch against Providence. Tyng and the Reds win 7–3.

25th Providence jumps on Tyng for 16 hits and wins 15–4 to clinch a tie for first place.

26th Providence squanders a 6-run lead, but George Wright scores a run in the 9th inning to beat Boston 7–6 and clinch the pennant for the Grays. The Providence crowd stages a wild celebration that delays the formal last out of the game.

29th Will White pitches his 74th complete game of the season for Cincinnati, beating Cleveland 13–1. He will finish with 75 complete games and 680 innings pitched, establishing ML season records that will never be broken.

30th From the 2nd day of the NL meeting, word leaks out of a secret agreement among the owners allowing each club to "reserve" 5 players with whom the other clubs agree not to negotiate. This move is to keep their salaries at current levels or below. This represents the beginning of the reserve system that would develop into management's chief hold over the players for the next century.

OCTOBER

1st The financially strapped Cincinnati club releases its players, and will not pay them the final month's salary.

2nd Chicago's announcement of the signing of Troy's Fred Goldsmith leads to protests from Troy that the new reserve system has already been violated.

16th With the Cincinnati Reds folding, Mike Kelly signs with Chicago for 1880 while on tour with the Whites in California.

NOVEMBER

24th   Although the club reportedly cleared $1,500 in winning the pennant, Providence offers player-manager George Wright a contract calling for a cut of about $300 from his 1879 salary of $2,000. Because Wright was reserved by Providence at the NL meeting, he will receive no offers from other clubs.

DECEMBER

3rd   The annual NL meeting convenes in Buffalo. A new Cincinnati club headed by Justus Thorner and O. P. Caylor is admitted to membership.

4th   NL owners again vote to retain the 50¢ minimum admission charge despite opposition from Troy and Buffalo.
   The following rule changes are made:
   • the number of balls for a walk is reduced from 9 to 8.
   • the catcher must catch the 3rd strike on the fly to put the batter out (the first bounce no longer counting).
   • the final outs of the last half inning need no longer be completed if the team batting last is already ahead.

5th   The NL adopts a rule allowing a club to suspend a player for the remainder of one season and the entire following season for drunkenness or insubordination.

6th   The American College Baseball Association is founded in Springfield, MA.

21st   The Hop Bitters of Rochester, the first North American team to play in Cuba, beat a local team 21–7 in Havana before a crowd of 5,000.

1880

FEBRUARY

5th Worcester is voted into the NL.

12th The Boston club cuts the price of season tickets from $14 to $12 after the Red Stockings failed to win their 3rd straight pennant last season.

25th Yale chooses not to join the American Collegiate Baseball Association because of professional players on other teams.

MARCH

31st Worcester offers Providence $1,000 for the right to negotiate with George Wright.

APRIL

14th The new Cincinnati ballpark on Bank Street is opened with an exhibition game between the Reds and the Washington Nationals. The park seats 3,490 and will serve professional teams in three leagues: NL in 1880, AA in 1882–83, and UA in 1884.

21st George Wright turns down Providence's final contract offer. Since the club has turned down Worcester's offer and will not allow any other club to negotiate with Wright, he will sit out the entire season (except for one game), the first player victimized by the reserve system.

28th Boston C Lew Brown shows up drunk at an exhibition game and is suspended for the season.

MAY

1st Opening Day in the NL. In Cincinnati, the Chicagos spoil the official opening of the new park by beating the Reds 4–3 with 2 runs in the bottom of the 9th. This is the first pro game ended in "sudden death," as the old rules required that the full inning be played out even if the team batting last was already ahead.

7th George Gore of Chicago goes 6-for-6 with 5 runs scored as the White Stockings trounce Cincinnati 20–7. Gore will lead the NL in batting with a .360 average.

10th Jim "Pud" Galvin wires the Buffalo club from San Francisco, accepting terms to play for the Bisons despite his contract to play in the California League.

13th Cleveland's Al Hall suffers a season-ending broken leg in an OF collision with teammate Pete Hotaling.

20th Chicago captain Cap Anson begins using hurlers Larry Corcoran and Fred Goldsmith in alternating games, thereby establishing the first "pitching rotation" ever.

21st In Albany's Riverside Park, Lip Pike hits a ball over the wall and into the river. RF Lon Knight begins to go after the ball in a boat but gives up. Few parks have ground rules about giving the batter an automatic HR on a hit over the fence.

22nd Jim Galvin makes his first appearance of the season for Buffalo, beating Cincinnati 2–1. Galvin had difficulty leaving California, where he was forced to walk 36 miles at one point to avoid local detectives who were trying to hold him to his California League contract.

27th Fred Goldsmith and Chicago shut out Buffalo on 2 hits. The 11–0 win extends the Whites' streak to 13 games, a new NL record.

29th With George Wright in its lineup, Boston upsets Chicago 11–10. Wright scores 2 runs and fields flawlessly, but will play no more games because of protests from Providence, which still has him "reserved."

31st Providence captain Mike McGeary, who has played poorly, is given a "30-day vacation" by the club. The team has a disappointing 8-7 record as 20-year-old Monte Ward takes over as captain.

JUNE

2nd Buffalo fines 1B Oscar Walker $50 for breaking his temperance pledge.

4th Larry Corcoran of Chicago and John Ward of Providence battle to a 1–1 tie in 16 innings, called because of darkness. Sixteen innings would remain the longest game in big-league history until August 17, 1882, when Ward would win 1–0 over Detroit in 18 innings.

10th Charley Jones of Boston hits 2 HRs in one inning, becoming the first of 23 big-leaguers to accomplish this feat. Both HRs come off Buffalo's Tom Poorman in the 8th inning of a 19–3 rout.

12th John Lee Richmond pitches the first perfect game in professional history, leading Worcester to a 1–0 victory over Cleveland. RF Lon Knight saves the no-hitter by throwing out a batter at 1B.

17th John Montgomery Ward pitches a perfect game in Providence against Buffalo, winning 5–0. Losing P Pud Galvin makes the last out. This is the 2nd perfect game in the NL in 6 days.

19th Cleveland's Jack Glasscock goes 5-for-5 with 2 doubles to lead a 27-hit attack against Troy in an 18–6 rout.

26th Abner Dalrymple, George Gore, and Larry Corcoran, all normally lefthanded batters, cross over and bat righthanded against southpaw Lee Richmond and get one hit each as Chicago beats Worcester 4–0.

29th Cleveland beats Boston 6–5 with Sid Gardner pitching his first league game for the season. Jim McCormick had pitched complete games in all of Cleveland's 31 previous NL games.

JULY

8th Chicago wins its 21st consecutive decision, beating Providence 5–4. This streak will be surpassed only once in ML history, by the New York Giants in 1916. The victory raises Chicago's won-lost record to 35-3, far ahead of 2nd-place Providence's 21-16 mark.

10th Cleveland snaps Chicago's long winning streak with a thrilling victory. The game is scoreless until the bottom of the 9th inning. Then Jack Glasscock walks, and Fred Dunlap hits a long drive to the deepest part of the park and circles the bases for an apparent HR. A lively debate ensues as to whether Dunlap gets a HR or whether the game ends the instant Glasscock touches the plate under the new sudden death rule.

11th The Chicago *Tribune* publishes statistics for the White Stocking players, including runs batted in. RBI would be dropped after the end of the season.

17th Rookie Harry Stovey hits his first ML HR, connecting off Jim McCormick as Worcester beats Cleveland 7–1. Stovey will be the first ML player to reach 100 career HRs.

23rd Monte Ward pitches a 5–0 one-hitter against Cincinnati. A leadoff single in the first inning by Blondie Purcell keeps Ward from getting his 2nd no-hitter of the season.

AUGUST

12th After 21 consecutive victories at home, Chicago suffers its first defeat at Lake Front this season, losing to Providence 6–4. The White Stockings had not lost an NL game at home since August 25, 1879.

13th Switching OF and pitching positions 5 times, Fred Corey and Lee Richmond combine to hurl Worcester to a 3–1 victory over Cleveland.

16th Worcester becomes the only team all season to win 2 NL games in one day, beating Cleveland 3–1 in the morning and 8–2 in the afternoon.

19th Pitching his 3rd game in 3 days, Larry Corcoran hurls a no-hitter versus Boston, winning 6–0. He walks none, but 4 men reach on errors. Although the ball is described as "mushy and shapeless," that doesn't stop the White Stockings from making 11 hits, including 4 by George Gore.

20th Jim Galvin pitches a no-hitter against Worcester and Buffalo wins 1–0.

28th Cincinnati commits 9 errors in the 4th inning and 16 in the game as the Reds are trounced by Troy 13–2. 2B Charlie Smith makes 4 errors on his way to an NL record 89 errors by a 2B in one season.

SEPTEMBER

1st Boston OF Charley Jones is suspended by the Boston club for demanding his $378 in back pay and then refusing to play when it is not forthcoming. In reaction to Jones's actions, the club suspends, fines, and blacklists him without paying him anything.

2nd The first night baseball is attempted in Nantasket Beach, MA, between teams from 2 Boston department stores, Jordan Marsh and R. H. White. The Boston *Post* reports the next day that "A clear, pure, bright light was produced, very strong and yet very pleasant to the sight" by the 12 carbon-arc electric lamps. The game ends in a 16–16 tie.

3rd The Rochesters fail to appear for a game against the Nationals in Washington because of a dispute over game receipts. With the Albany club already disbanded, this means the end of the National Association after 4 seasons.

8th The Polo Grounds in New York at 110th Street between 5th and 6th Avenues is leased by the new Metropolitan club being assembled by Jim Mutrie with the backing of John B. Day. The grounds, which have been used for polo matches, will be converted into the first commercial baseball park ever to be built on Manhattan Island.

13th NL secretary Nick Young rules that the final score of the July 10th game in which Fred Dunlap hit the apparent HR in the bottom of the 9th inning should be 2–0, not 1–0, as some contend. Young rules that Dunlap's hit should be a HR and it would be a "gross injustice" to deprive him of one.

15th Providence loses to Boston 5–4 as John O'Rourke of Boston keys the Reds' victory with 4 doubles, becoming the first ML player to hit 4 two-baggers in one game. The younger brother of Jim O'Rourke will lead the NL in RBI and slugging averages.

29th The Polo Grounds is opened with a 4–2 Mets victory over the NA champion Nationals. The crowd of around 2,500 is the largest for a ball game in the New York area in several years.

30th Chicago wins its final game to finish the season with a 67-17 record, establishing an NL record for winning percentage (.798), although winning percentage will not be used officially in the league until 1884. Providence is 2nd, 15 games behind.

OCTOBER

4th At a special NL meeting in Rochester, the league prohibits its members from renting their grounds for use on Sundays and from selling alcoholic beverages on the premises. These rules are aimed at the Cincinnati club, which has done both.

5th The NL makes a statement putting its aggregate losses for the season at $20,000. Blame is placed on high salaries, which run over $14,000 for some clubs.

6th The Cincinnati club refuses to accede to the October 4th restrictions and is thrown out of the NL.

The NL also votes to retain the year-old reserve system.

10th The Boston and Providence clubs release their players, thereby saving themselves 20 days' worth of salary.

NOVEMBER

11th Boston signs P Jim Whitney, considered one of the best hurlers in California, at a salary of $150 per month.

DECEMBER

8th At the annual NL meeting, the league rejects the Nationals' bid for admission, electing Detroit instead, although there is no established club there. The Michigan city is chosen for geographic reasons, since its 1880 population (116,340) is smaller than both Washington's (147,293) and Cincinnati's (255,139), the city being replaced.

9th The NL reelects William Hulbert as president, and adopts several new rules, including:

- Moving the pitcher's box back 5 feet so that its front line is 50 feet from the back point of home plate.
- Again reducing the number of called balls for a walk, from 8 to 7.
- Eliminating substitutions (except in the case of illness or injury), the old rule having allowed subs in the first inning but not thereafter.
- Prohibiting all pinch runners (this rule will be ignored many times).
- Reinstituting the old rule that allowed the fielding team to put out a runner on a foul ball if they can return the ball to the pitcher in his box, and then to the runner's original base before the runner can get back.

1881

JANUARY

11th The first of a series of Tuesday games on ice is played in Chicago using professional and amateur players. These games would be a regular winter feature.

FEBRUARY

11th Veteran Charles "Chick" Fulmer is signed to manage a Philadelphia Athletic team being organized by Charley Mason and Billy Sharsig.

22nd George Wright signs a contract with Boston that he claims will only require him to play games in New England and Troy. He feels his business commitments will not allow him to accompany the Reds on their western road trips.

MARCH

8th The NL meets and adopts an 84-game schedule. An enterprising newsman gets the various magnates to predict the winner in the coming pennant race, Chicago the consensus choice with 5 votes.

The owners vote to stop giving refunds or rain checks for postponed games.

APRIL

2nd The new Detroit club begins practice games by beating Princeton University 7–2. Manager Frank Bancroft has lined up a full schedule of preseason games, considered something of an innovation.

11th The Eastern Association is organized to link independent clubs in a loose pennant race. The clubs include the Nationals, the Mets, Atlantics, Athletics, New Yorks, Quicksteps (of NY), and New Bostons.

22nd Horace Phillips loses his litigation against Hop Bitter owner A. S. Soule stemming from last year's disappearance with club funds and is ordered to repay $1,463.

28th With P George Bradley already sidelined by pneumonia, Detroit signs Will White to a 30-day contract, hoping Bradley will be healthy in a month.

30th The NL season opens with games in Worcester and Chicago.

MAY

4th Boston P Jim Whitney shuts out Providence 4–0. The hardworking righthander will wind up leading the NL in both wins and losses (with a 31-33 record), a feat not repeated in the ML until Phil Niekro does it in 1979.

5th Charley Radbourn makes his NL pitching debut leading Providence to a 4–2 victory over Boston.

14th Having won a judgment for his back salary in an Ohio court, Charley Jones has the local sheriff attach Boston's share of the gate receipts in Cleveland.

18th When Detroit base runner Sadie Houck collides with Bob Ferguson of Troy at 2B, Ferguson becomes indignant and slaps Houck in the face. The Detroit club prefers charges against Ferguson with the league office, but nothing will be done.

19th With the Troy franchise experiencing financial difficulties, various rumors have the club moving to New York, Cincinnati, or Pittsburgh.

20th Chicago resorts to trickery to beat Boston 5–4. Mike Kelly scores the go-ahead run from 2B on a groundout by cutting 3B by some 30 feet.

28th James S. Woodruff is apprehended on charges that he tried to bribe Cleveland's John Clapp to throw a game earlier in the season. By going to the police after the incident, Clapp has earned the nickname "Honest John."

JUNE

9th Buffalo wins a 13-inning thriller 1–0 in Boston to move into a tie for first place with Chicago.

16th Buttercup Dickerson goes 6-for-6 as Worcester beats Buffalo 15–4 and knocks the Bisons out of first place.

18th The Washington Nationals disband, blaming lack of interest since the club failed to land a berth in the NL.

20th A new Red Stocking team in Cincinnati takes the field for the first time. This club would be among the founders of the American Association next year and would eventually become the NL Reds.

22nd Two NL teams play the Mets in the same day, Detroit winning the morning game at the Polo Grounds 5–1, Buffalo winning the afternoon contest 9–1.

24th Returning home from a long road trip, the Chicago White Stockings unveil new lavender uniforms, much to the amusement of the press.

25th Chicago's George Gore steals 7 bases as the Whites beat Providence. Gore steals second 5 times and 3rd twice, scoring 5 runs in 5 trips. This record will be tied only once, by Billy Hamilton on August 31, 1894.

30th There are 217 called balls and other interminable delays in Chicago's 4–1 victory over Troy. The lengthy game takes all of 2 hours and 20 minutes.

JULY

2nd Boston loses in Buffalo 7–4, and the Reds fall to last place for the first time in the clubs' proud 10-year history.

21st Cleveland loses at Akron 4–0 in a game that takes just 1:18 to complete, the shortest game any of the reporters can remember.

AUGUST

9th "The delicious uncertainty of baseball" (New York *Mercury*) is demonstrated at the Polo Grounds when the Atlantics score 11 runs in the 9th inning to beat the Mets 14–12.

11th In the most one-sided game of the NL season, Chicago trounces Detroit 17–0. Fred Goldsmith pitched for Chicago

12th The Providence club is reorganized. New capital is pledged. C. L.Gardiner is the new president, and Robert Morrow replaces James Bullock as manager.

14th Statistics published in the Chicago *Tribune* put Dan Brouthers at the top of the batting list with a .390 average. Cap Anson is second with .377. Official figures at the end of the season will declare Anson batting champ with a .399 average, Brouthers finishing 7th at .318

17th Worcester suspends its captain, Mike Dorgan, and Harry Stovey takes over the post. Lee Richmond, who had quit because of conflicts with Dorgan, rejoins the team.

18th The declining fortunes of the Worcesters receive a further blow when Art Irwin suffers a broken leg during a game in which the team blows an 8–0 lead and has to settle for an 8–8 tie with Providence.

21st The Eclipse club refuses to allow black C M. Fleetwood Walker to play for the visiting Cleveland Whites in a game in Louisville, much to the disgust of many fans and sportswriters. Walker later becomes the first African-American to play ML baseball with the Toledo (AA) club in 1884.

23rd When P Fred Goldsmith is injured in the 3rd inning, substitute Larry Corcoran is called in from the turnstile, where he was monitoring the count for the visiting Chicagos. He pitches 9 innings as the White Stockings win a 12-inning game in Detroit 8–6.

SEPTEMBER

3rd CF Lip Pike makes 3 errors in the 9th inning to give Boston 2 runs and a 3–2 victory over Worcester. The losing club immediately accuses Pike of throwing the game and suspends him.

10th In a game in Albany, Troy's Roger Connor hits the first grand slam in NL history. The blow comes off Worcester's Lee Richmond with 2 out in the bottom of the 9th inning and wins the game 8–7.

15th Buffalo 2B Dave Force makes 2 unassisted DPs, participates in 2 other DPs, and starts a triple play in a 12-inning 7–6 loss at Worcester.

16th Chicago clinches the pennant with a 4–0 victory in Boston.

17th Boston informs its players that it will release them on October 1st and not pay them the last month of their salaries.

23rd Boston LF Joe Hornung makes 10 putouts and one assist as the Reds beat Buffalo 4–3. This one-game record of 11 chances accepted by a LF still stands.

25th Although the league has offered membership to the Mets and the Athletics and been turned down, it is announced that all 8 teams from this year will be back in the NL next season, a first for the league.

29th At an NL meeting in Saratoga Springs, NY, the league adopts a blacklist of players who are barred from playing for or against any NL teams until they are removed by unanimous vote of the league clubs. These men are: Sadie Houck, Lip Pike, Lou Dickerson, Mike Dorgan, Bill Crowley, John Fox, Lew Brown, Emil Gross, and Ed Caskins.

30th The NL meeting adopts an "ironclad" contract that gives the club the right to fine a player for any conduct the club deems detrimental to its interest. Furthermore, the player assumes the responsibility for all risks of injury or illness and must pay for his own medical treatment.

OCTOBER

1st The Mets beat the champion Chicagos in New York 7–4. The Mets are the only nonleague team to have won more than one game versus NL opposition.

8th Chris Von der Ahe, president of the corporation that runs Sportsman's Park in St. Louis, signs the members of the previously independent St. Louis Browns semiprofessional club, giving Von der Ahe control over the players for the first time. This is a key step toward the establishment of the club that would eventually become the St. Louis Cardinals.

10th Cincinnati baseball backers meet in Pittsburgh with H. Denny McKnight and issue a call to other independent club operators to meet November 2nd to form a major league independent of the NL.

15th H. D. McKnight organizes a new Allegheny Baseball Club of Pittsburgh in anticipation of the proposed new league.

31st The Metropolitan club plays its final game of the season. The Mets played 151 games altogether, winning 80 of them. They were 18-43 versus NL teams.

NOVEMBER

2nd The American Association of Professionals is founded with the motto "Liberty to All." The members are St. Louis, Cincinnati, Louisville, Allegheny, Athletic, and Atlantic. This AA will be considered a major league.

3rd The AA elects H. D. McKnight as its president. It votes to honor the NL blacklist in the case of drunkenness but not to abide by the NL reserve clause. The new league will rely on home gate receipts, visiting teams getting just a $65 guarantee on the road, as opposed to the NL's policy of giving 15¢ from each admission to the visitors. The AA will allow Sunday games, liquor sales, and 25¢ tickets, all prohibited by the NL.

DECEMBER

8th The NL adopts a few new playing rules: runners can no longer be put out returning to their bases after foul balls not caught, the fine for pitchers hitting batters with pitches is repealed, and the "blockball" rule allows runners to take as many bases as possible on balls going into the crowd, the fielding team being able to put them out only after returning the ball to the pitcher in his box.

1882

JANUARY

7th The NL will continue the practice of using different color patterns on uniforms for the different positions. Third basemen will wear gray and white uniforms, as the blue and white uniforms originally sought were "impossible to obtain."

20th The Kentucky Legislature modifies a recently passed law which inadvertently prohibited the playing of baseball games in the commonwealth.

FEBRUARY

4th NL players are now responsible for carrying their own bats and uniforms on road trips. They are also required to purchase and keep clean 2 complete uniforms, including the white linen ties to be worn on the field at all times.

25th Providence players and their opponents will be expected to parade down the streets of Providence in full uniform, accompanied by a brass band, on game days in order to encourage attendance.

MARCH

11th In retaliation for the "theft" of Sam Wise and Dasher Troy by the NL, the American Association creates a loophole allowing all players either blacklisted or expelled by the NL to join AA clubs after appealing to a special commission.

APRIL

10th NL president William Hulbert dies in Chicago. A. H. Soden, president of the Boston club, is appointed as temporary replacement.

MAY

5th Cap Anson is called out for walking back to his base after a foul ball, instead of running, as the rule specifies. This rule will be amended at the end of the season.

10th Approximately 1,000 people watch the first Chicago home game for free from a nearby viaduct.

Chicago officials will attempt to eliminate this "unfair opportunity to beat the gate."

13th NL players are told that next season they will not be required to wear the uniforms known as "clown costumes," with different color combinations for each position.

16th The scheduled Cincinnati-Allegheny game is switched to Cincinnati because of floods in Pittsburgh.

27th After breaking his finger in a game against the Metropolitans, Philadelphia IF Mike Moynahan has the finger amputated at the first joint. He will play in the AA for Philadelphia for 2 years before retiring.

JUNE

5th Boston defeats Detroit 10–2. According to the Chicago *Tribune*, this is the first time a team scoring in double figures does so entirely with earned runs.

6th William "Blondie" Purcell of Buffalo is fined $10 for slicing open a soggy baseball. He did this to compel the umpire to put a fresh ball in play so his P Pud Galvin might be able to throw a curve.

22nd In a battle between the top 2 teams, Providence scores 13 runs in the 3rd inning to devastate Detroit 15–5 and maintain its edge in the NL pennant race.

24th Dick Higham becomes the first and only ML umpire to be expelled for dishonesty.

29th In the 4th inning of a game against St. Louis, the Eclipse leave the field to protest the continued use of an incompetent umpire. They also refuse to play the next 2 games, thus forfeiting 3 games to St. Louis. After a special AA meeting, the 2 teams agree to replay the last 2 games.

JULY

4th Buffalo's Pud Galvin wins both ends of a doubleheader against Worcester 9–5 and 18–8.

8th Chicago, in the midst of its first 9-game winning streak of the season, moves into first place with a 3–0 victory over Troy.

12th Worcester beats Boston 4–1 to break a 14-game losing streak.

13th During the 4th inning of a Cincinnati-Baltimore game, umpire Mike Walsh is surrounded on the field by angry spectators after a controversial call and is forced to take refuge in the Baltimore clubhouse for 15 minutes. Cincinnati wins the game 1–0.

18th Louisville hurler Tony Mullane pitches both right- and lefthanded in an AA game against Baltimore, the first time the feat is performed in the major leagues. Starting in the 4th inning he pitches lefthanded whenever Baltimore's lefty hitters are at bat. In addition to continuing to pitch righthanded to righthanded hitters. It works until the 9th when, with 2 outs, Charlie Householder hits his only HR of the year to beat Mullane 9–8.

24th Chicago sets a NL record for runs by beating Cleveland 35–4. Seven Chicago players get 4 or more hits. The record will last until June 29, 1897, when Chicago will run up 36 runs against Louisville.

26th Paul Hines carries Providence into first place going 5-for-5 and scoring 4 runs in a 6–5 victory over Worcester.

AUGUST

17th In what is considered one of the greatest games in the 19th century, Providence beats Detroit 1–0 on an 18th-inning HR by RF Charles Radbourn. This game will serve as the longest shutout in ML history until September 1, 1967, when San Francisco blanks Cincinnati 1–0 in 20 innings.

SEPTEMBER

5th Baltimore plays the first 4 innings of its game against Allegheny without its uniforms, which have been delayed at the Baltimore train station. Allegheny wins the game 3–1.

9th After taking a 1–0 lead in the first inning, Troy loses to Chicago 24–1 in a shortened 8-inning battle. Five Chicago players get 4 hits each.

11th Tony Mullane of the Eclipse pitches a no-hitter over Cincinnati 2–0. The next day Mullane does not allow a hit until the 7th inning, and wins 10–4.

14th Chicago pushes past Providence into first place by defeating them 6–2. Chicago will not relinquish the lead for the rest of the season.

19th Guy Hecker becomes the 2nd Eclipse pitcher in 8 days to throw a no-hitter, defeating Allegheny 3–1.

20th Larry Corcoran pitches the 2nd no-hitter of his career by shutting out Worcester 5–0.

22nd In a special NL meeting Troy and Worcester are kicked out of the league, to be replaced by teams from Philadelphia and New York. When the expelled clubs threaten to boycott the rest of the season, Chicago and Providence agree to play a best-of-9 series after the season to determine the league championship.

In its 20–6 victory over Allegheny, the Eclipse score in every inning.

28th Six dedicated Worcester "cranks" (fans), the smallest "crowd" in ML history, show up to watch their club lose to Troy 4–1. The next day the number of spectators is 25. Worcester loses again to their fellow lame-duck team.

OCTOBER

4th After 22 unsuccessful attempts, Cincinnati becomes the first AA team to defeat an NL team, beating Cleveland 5–2.

6th In the first post-season matchup between AA and NL champions, Cincinnati shuts out Chicago 4–0. The next day Chicago returns the favor by blanking Cincinnati 2–0. At this point Cincinnati, under pressure from the AA, reluctantly cancels the series to avoid expulsion from the league.

14th Columbus, which will join the AA in 1883, is officially incorporated with $5,000 in capital stock.

28th The Athletics reveal that in their first AA season they reaped a $22,000 profit, more than any NL team earned. This helps convince the NL that the AA is a viable league.

NOVEMBER

18th The case of the Allegheny Club versus Charles Bennett is won by Bennett. Prior to the 1882 season Allegheny signed Bennett to a $100 agreement which stated that he would sign an 1883 contract with Allegheny after the season. Instead, Bennett re-signed with Detroit. This case will later have bearing on the fight over the reserve rule during the Players' League War of 1889-90.

DECEMBER

6th   At the NL meeting, Troy and Worcester are officially replaced by New York and Philadelphia. A. G. Mills is elected president. Starting in 1883, pitchers will be charged with an error after a walk, balk, wild pitch, or HBP. Catchers will be charged with an error after a passed ball.

9th   James H. Dudley, manager of a top black club in Richmond, VA, initiates discussion concerning the formation of a black league with teams from New York, Philadelphia, Pittsburgh, Cincinnati, Baltimore, Washington, DC, and Richmond. On February 10, 1883, Pittsburgh manager W. C. Lee expresses interest in the plan, but nothing comes of it.

14th   At its first annual convention, the AA establishes the first permanent staff of umpires in ML history. Previously, the NL and AA umpires were local men hired on game day by the home club.

1883

JANUARY

13th Both of the New York ML clubs will play simultaneously at their Polo Grounds. Their fields will be separated by an 8-foot fence.

31st A Baltimore fan loses a suit against Baltimore player Andrew Burns, who, while batting, accidentally let his bat slip from his hands, hitting the spectator. The judge rules fans had been warned to keep a safe distance from the field.

FEBRUARY

17th At a meeting between the AA and the NL, the Tripartite Agreement (or the National Agreement) is drafted. In it the 2 leagues, along with the Northwestern League, agree to respect each other's contracts, ending a brief period of player raids. Also, the reserve rule is amended to allow each team to reserve 11 players, an increase of 6. The National Agreement will usher in a period of peaceful coexistence, lasting until the Players' League war of 1890.

MARCH

14th In a Northwestern League meeting, Peoria moves to ban blacks in order to prevent Toledo from playing star C Moses Fleetwood Walker. After an "exciting discussion" the motion is withdrawn and Walker is allowed to play.

31st The Olympic Town-Ball Club of Philadelphia, the nation's oldest ball club, celebrates its 50th anniversary.

APRIL

3rd The Cleveland club visits the White House, where President Chester A. Arthur greets them by telling them that "Good ball-players make good citizens."

15th The first weekly issue of *Sporting Life*, edited by Francis Richter, is published in Philadelphia. This outstanding magazine will last, with a brief interruption, until July 1926.

24th In a fit of depression, journeyman player Terry Larkin shoots his wife and a policeman and then attempts to commit suicide. Failing, he tries again the next day. Both his wife and the policeman survive. Larkin will play for several teams in 1884 before retiring.

MAY

3rd John Montgomery Ward becomes the first pitcher in history to hit 2 HRs in a game, giving him a 10–9 victory over Boston.

5th In the first game in Chicago's spectacular new ballpark, featuring 41 uniformed attendants, Detroit scores with 2 out in the bottom of the 9th to win 3–2.

15th In St. Louis a meeting is scheduled to plan the taking of "active steps looking towards the foundation of a Colored League."

22nd Future evangelist Billy Sunday, playing for the Chicago White Stockings has a miserable ML debut, going 0-for-4 with 4 strikeouts.

25th Cleveland forges into a 3-way tie for first place in the NL with Detroit and Providence by defeating New York in 14 innings 4–3.

28th Heavyweight boxing champion John L. Sullivan pitches the Mets to a 20–15 victory in an exhibition game. For his efforts Sullivan pockets half of the proceeds—$1,595. On November 4th Sullivan will pitch another game.

The first of 2 games between Fort Wayne and Indianapolis is played under electric lights.

JUNE

2nd Chicago commits 20 errors, while New York records 10, as New York defeats Chicago 22–7 in the sloppiest game of the year. One player on each team plays error-free.

9th After falling behind 5–2 in the 2nd inning, Boston rallies to whip Detroit 30–8. Paul Radford and Jim Whitney each get 5 hits, and Whitney sets a ML record by scoring 6 runs. This record will stand until 1886.

Philadelphia (NL) receives permission to charge 25¢ for admission, instead of 50¢, to allow them to compete with their popular crosstown rivals, the AA-leading Athletics. Philadelphia's attendance quadruples for the rest of the season.

13th With the Allegheny field "half overflown with water" following a series of floods in Pittsburgh, Columbus overcomes the waterlogged home club 25–10, scoring in every inning.

20th Boston mauls Philadelphia 29–4, as Sam Wise goes 6-for-7 with 4 extra-base hits. Wise, Ezra Sutton, and Joe Hornung each score 5 runs. Philadelphia helps by committing 21 errors.

JULY

3rd Chicago beats Buffalo 31–7, as each Chicago player hits safely and scores at least 3 runs. Abner Dalrymple and Cap Anson each get 5 hits (including 4 doubles), and Dalrymple scores 5 runs. Chicago sets a ML record with 14 doubles, getting 16 extra-base hits and 32 hits overall.

4th Tim Keefe of New York wins both ends of a doubleheader against Columbus 9–3 and 1–0, allowing a 2-game total of 3 hits.

6th Cincinnati thrashes Baltimore 23–0, setting a ML record for the most decisive shutout. The record lasts for 46 days.

19th Buffalo defeats Philadelphia 25–5, getting 27 hits in the process. Dan Brouthers goes 6-for-6 with 2 doubles, and Jim O'Rourke gets 5 hits.

25th Charles Radbourn throws a no-hitter as Providence beats top rival Cleveland 8–0.

26th Joe Gephardt of the Eclipse is forced to miss a game against St. Louis because of temporary paralysis. He will return to the lineup within 2 weeks.

28th In the first recorded game in Hawaii, the Honolulu Club wins over the Oceanic Club 14–13.

AUGUST

7th Providence loses the NL lead permanently with a 6–4 defeat by Boston, while Cleveland beats Buffalo 5–2. For the 2nd straight season Providence holds the NL lead for more than twice as many days as any other team but does not win the pennant.

20th After the Eclipse-Allegheny game, Allegheny players Billy Taylor, Mike Mansell, and George Creamer are each fined $100 and suspended indefinitely for drunkenness.

21st In the most decisive shutout in ML history, Philadelphia routs Providence 28–0.

SEPTEMBER

3rd Philadelphia breaks its 14-game losing streak, the longest of the year, by defeating Providence 6–3.

4th Columbus crushes Baltimore 21–4 behind Tom Brown, who goes 6-for-7 with 5 runs and 4 extra-base hits.

6th Chicago concludes an extraordinarily successful series against Detroit with a 26–6 win. Chicago sets a ML record by scoring 18 runs in the 7th inning. In the inning Tom Burns set records by going 3-for-3 with 2 doubles and a HR and scoring 3 runs. Chicago outscores their opponent in the 3-game series by a combined score of 53–8.

The Athletics cling to their lead in the AA by defeating second-place St. Louis for the 3rd consecutive game. Over 45,000 fans attend the series.

10th Chicago loses to Boston 4–2, breaking its 11-game winning streak, the longest of the season.

11th Boston scores 2 runs in the top of the 9th to top Chicago 3–2, taking over the first place. Boston will not relinquish the lead for the remainder of the season.

12th At a meeting in Pittsburgh, the Union Association is formed. The UA states its intention to ignore the reserve rule.

Cincinnati mauls Allegheny 27–5. Warren "Hick" Carpenter and "Long" John Reilly each get 6 hits, while Reilly also scores 6 runs and hits for the cycle.

13th Hugh "One-Arm" Daily of Cleveland pitches a no-hitter, defeating Philadelphia 1–0.

19th Cincinnati 1B Long John Reilly again hits for the cycle against Philadelphia.

25th The Union League, later known as the Eastern League, is officially formed in New York.

27th Boston officially clinches the NL title, beating Cleveland 4–1.

28th After losing 2 straight games to the Eclipse, the Athletics rally in the bottom of the 10th inning, 7–6, to clinch the AA championship.

OCTOBER

10th   Jim Devlin, a former star pitcher for the Louisville Grays (who was expelled from baseball in 1877 for his role in throwing a series of games at the request of gamblers), dies in Philadelphia. Before his death he served as a policeman.

NOVEMBER

22nd   New York owner John B. Day proposes a resolution to prohibit a team from signing a player who has broken the reserve clause in his contract. This resolution, eventually adopted by both the AA and the NL, effectively changes the reserve rule from a device designed to protect owners from their own greediness to a vindictive weapon to be used against uncooperative players.

24th   The AA agree to expand to 12 teams by admitting Brooklyn, Washington, Indianapolis and Toledo.

DECEMBER

13th   The Ohio League is formed.

15th   In Louisville a "first-class colored team" is formed. The team, later known as the Falls Cities, becomes one of the nation's best black teams. It joins the National Colored Base Ball League (NCBBL) in 1887, but apparently disbands shortly after the collapse of the NCBBL in the first week of its season.

1884

JANUARY

4th The newly organized Union League changes its name to Eastern League to avoid confusion with the new Union Association. The EL continues today as the AAA International League.

P Larry Corcoran, who had signed with Chicago of the outlaw UA, breaks his contract to re-sign with his old club, Chicago's NL White Stockings.

FEBRUARY

9th The grounds of Cincinnati's UA club are flooded under 20 feet of water from the Ohio River. It will cost $3,000 to rebuild the fallen pavilions and fences and restore the field.

18th P/IF Terry Larkin, released from prison after serving several months for beating his wife and shooting a policeman, is rearrested for threatening to shoot his father.

MARCH

4th The NL, meeting in Buffalo, reduces the number of balls required for a walk from 7 to 6. Club owners also agree to provide 2 separate team benches to minimize fraternizing among opposing players during games.

6th High winds in New York destroy much of the fence and blow off part of the Polo Grounds grandstand roof, depositing it a block away.

17th The UA admits a Boston club organized by George Wright, bringing the number of teams to 8. The UA decides to stick with the 7-ball walk rule.

The UA also expands its schedule to 112 games and adopts the percentage system for determining the champion.

The UA season opens with 3 games. Bill Sweeney's 7–3 five-hitter for Baltimore over Washington is the first of what will be a UA-high 40 wins—12 more than his closest rival.

28th During an exhibition game between Philadelphia's Phillies (NL) and Athletics (AA), umpire William McLean, reacting to fans' taunts, hurls a bat into the stands hitting but not injuring a spectator. McLean is arrested after the game, but the charges are soon dropped.

APRIL

2nd The AA eliminates the rule allowing batters hit by pitches to go to 1B, instead giving umpires the authority to fine offending pitchers between $5 and $10.

5th Boston UA 1B James Ryan is said to have "a tremendous reach and can catch equally well with his left or right hand," an important skill to have in an era in which many players do not wear gloves or wear thin fingerless models on both hands.

MAY

1st Rookie John Hamill holds Brooklyn (AA) to 5 singles as Washington wins its opener 12–0. But Washington will win only 11 more games (losing 51) before disbanding in early August, and Hamill will record only one more win (against 17 losses) in his only ML season.

Following Cincinnati's Opening Day loss to Columbus (AA) at the new Cincinnati ballpark, a section of bleachers collapses, injuring many exiting fans, one fatally. This location will be used by Cincinnati ML teams until mid-1970, when the Reds move into Riverfront Stadium.

Moses Fleetwood Walker becomes the first black in the ML when he plays for the Toledo club in the American Association. He goes 0-for-3 in his ML debut, allowing 2 passed balls and committing 4 errors, as his team bows to Louisville 5–1. He will do better in 41 subsequent games before injuries force Toledo to release him in late September. Racial bigotry will prevent his return to ML ball. In July he is joined by his brother Welday, an OF. No other black player appears in a ML uniform until Jackie Robinson in 1947.

2nd New York (AA) fails to take advantage of Jack Lynch's 14 strikeouts and 6-hit pitching and loses to Baltimore 8–3. In 166 innings this year Lynch will total only 32 K's for the Metropolitans.

3rd Charlie Sweeney gets off to a good start by throwing a one-hitter to lead Providence (NL) to a 3–0 win over Buffalo.

Buck Ewing gets a triple, a double, and 3 singles as New York (NL) defeats Detroit 11–3.

5th After pitching in St. Louis on May 4, Tony Mullane of Toledo (AA) is enjoined from playing ball in Missouri until defense of his contract jumping from the St. Louis UA club can be heard in court.

6th Rookie P Larry McKeon of Indianapolis (AA), whose 41 losses will top the major leagues in 1884, pitches a 6-inning no-hitter. Rain halts the game with the score 0–0.

Buffalo P Pud Galvin allows only a first-inning double, but must wait until the 9th before his teammates produce the winning run in a 3–2 battle against Boston.

7th Jack Lynch's one-hitter is enough for victory as the Mets whip Allegheny 8–1.

8th Chicago (UA) stuns the Keystones of Philadelphia with an 8-run rally in the 9th to take an 11–10 win.

10th Washington (AA) C Alex Gardner's first ML game is also his last, as he allows 12 passed balls, a ML record that still stands. Washington loses the game to New York's Mets 11–3.

Altoona (UA) wins its first ML game after 11 straight losses 9–4 over Boston. They will win only 5 more times before disbanding at the end of May.

13th C Thomas "Pat" Deasley of the St. Louis Browns (AA) is arrested for drunkenness and for making insulting comments to ladies. He is released but 6 days later he will be seriously injured in a fight, and his wife will be asked to join the team on its trip to keep him in line.

New York (NL) buries Buffalo 20–5. It is the last pitching win of John Montgomery Ward's ML career, as the one-time teenage ace shifts to the IF and OF.

14th P Charles Radbourn gets 5 hits—the same number he allows Detroit—to spur a 25–3 rout, the most decisive victory in the NL this year. Detroit contributes to its own demise by committing 18 errors, including 5 by RF Fred Wood, whose ML career will total only 13 games.

16th When a foul tip from a Detroit (NL) batter sticks in the mask of Boston C Mike Hines, umpire Van Court calls the batter out on a foul catch. NL Secretary Nick Young will later instruct league umpires not to rule an out in such cases.

18th Hugh Daily of Chicago (UA) throws his 2nd consecutive one-hitter against the Nationals of Washington. He adds to the Nationals' embarrassment today by recording 15 strikeouts.

23rd Larry Corcoran limits Cleveland (NL) to one hit in a 5–0 shutout for Chicago.

24th Against Pittsburgh, Philadelphia Athletics (AA) P Al Atkinson hits the leadoff batter, Ed Swartwood, who steals 2B, takes 3B on a putout, and scores on a passed ball. But Atkinson sets down the next 27 Alleghenies for a near-perfect, no-hit 10–1 win.

After 20 consecutive wins St. Louis (UA) finally falls 8–1 to Boston. The Maroons will finish the season with a .832 percentage, the highest in ML history.

29th Taking advantage of a ground rule change which scores balls hit over the close RF Chicago (NL) fence as HRs (instead of doubles), 5 players hit HR's in the White Stockings' home opener against Detroit. Chicago will hit 142 HRs during the 112-game season (more than 90 percent of them at home) to set a record that will be broken by the 1927 New York Yankees.

Ed Morris (Columbia AA) no-hits Pittsburgh 5–0, allowing only one walk.

30th In the afternoon game of Chicago's doubleheader with Detroit (NL), White Stocking Ned Williamson doubles and hits a ML record 3 HRs as Chicago overwhelms the Wolverines 12–2. Williamson's HRs are his first of 27 (25 at home), which will set a ML season record not broken until Babe Ruth hits 29 in 1919.

31st The Altoona club disbands, the first casualty of the UA, and is replaced by a new club formed in Kansas City.

CF Oscar Walker's 6-for-6 spark a 16–1 Brooklyn (AA) romp over the St. Louis Browns.

JUNE

5th Frank Mountain (Columbus AA) no-hits Washington 12–0. In addition, he hits a HR, possibly the first pitcher to do so.

6th Boston remains a game ahead of Providence at the top of the NL after a 16-inning 1–1 pitchers' duel between Red Stocking Jim Whitney and the Grays' Charlie Radbourn. The game will be the season's longest in the NL.

7th Charlie Sweeney of Providence (NL) strikes out 19 Boston Red Stockings to establish a ML record for a 9-inning game. It will be tied one month later but not broken until Roger Clemens fans 20 on April 29, 1986. Providence's 2–1 win moves it into first place, but Boston will take the next 4 from the Grays to regain the lead.

9th Billy Sunday of Chicago (NL) homers for the 3rd time in 3 games. His season total will be 4.

The Mets edge Louisville 7–5 in 11 innings to tie the Eclipse for first place in the AA with a 20-8 record.

13th Baltimore (AA) management surrounds the playing field with a barbed wire fence to restrain the crowd. Baltimore fans had surged onto the field and manhandled the umpire following a 13-inning tie with Louisville the day before.

14th P Charlie Radbourn of Providence and P Jim Whitney of Boston—rivals in the NL's longest game 8 days earlier—face each other in a 15-inning 4–3 Providence win. The victory starts the Grays on a 10-game win streak that will lift them over Boston into first place.

Noah Brooks's *Our Base Ball Club, and How It Won the Championship*, one of the first works of baseball fiction (and Brooks's 2nd) is advertised in the New York *Clipper*.

16th Buffalo LF Jim O'Rourke hits for the cycle against Chicago as the Bisons beat the White Stockings 20–9.

Two days after his 15-inning loss, in which he struck out 18 Providence batters, Boston (NL) hurler Jim Whitney fans 11 New York Maroons for a 2-game total of 29, stopping New York on one hit 6–1.

Chicago's Larry Corcoran pitches both left- and righthanded in an NL game against Buffalo.

Boston's Jim Whitney restricts New York (NL) to one hit in a 6–1 win.

17th Baltimore (AA) Orioles OF Frank "Gid" Gardner is jailed after severely beating lady friend Effie Jones and a woman who had come to her aid. The charges are dropped, but Orioles manager Billy Barnie will fine Gardner and suspend him indefinitely.

Charles Sweeney pitches his 2nd one-hitter of the year, beating New York (NL) 9–0. Tomorrow teammate Charles Radbourn matches Sweeney's performance in a 15–0 win, Buck Ewing getting the only

New York hit in the 9th. In the last 3 games New York has totaled 3 hits.

24th A Chicago court rules that although the NL lakefront ballpark illegally blocks the lake view and breezes from homes to its west, the White Stockings may continue to use it through the end of the season.

Hoss Radbourn continues to stifle NL bats with a 3-hit 1–0 win with 15 strikeouts over Detroit in 15 innings. In his last 3 games Radbourn had allowed only 6 hits.

27th Chicago ace Larry Corcoran ends the Providence Grays' 10-game winning streak with the NL's first no-hitter of the season. The 6–0 win is Corcoran's third ML no-hitter.

28th In the 6th inning of an AA game at Columbus, several Brooklyn and Columbus players are arrested for playing ball on Sunday. Because of the crowd's anger, though, police permit the players to finish the game before taking them into custody.

30th Providence loses 5–4 to Mike "King" Kelly's HR with 2 out in the bottom of the 9th. Chicago's win, coupled with Boston's 11–2 triumph over Detroit, allows Boston to pass the Grays and move into the NL lead by one-half game.

JULY

2nd Bid McPhee smacks 4 hits, including a HR and a double, to support Gus Shallix's one-hit pitching and give Cincinnati (AA) a 16–1 romp over Washington.

4th Louisville (AA) ace Guy Hecker defeats Brooklyn in a morning game (5–4) and again in the afternoon (8–2) en route to a season total of 52 wins. This remains the AA record.

Boston (UA) 2B Tom O'Brien gets 5 hits, including a ball which disappears into a dirt heap and cannot be dug out in time to prevent O'Brien from circling the bases. Thanks in part to the groundskeeper (or lack thereof) Boston whips Kansas City 23–3.

5th After a 17–2 loss at Cincinnati (AA), Philadelphia Athletic pitcher Al Atkinson deserts his club for Chicago (UA)—the first player to break his contract and join the UA.

6th Louisville slips past New York (AA) into first place with a 5–1 win over Baltimore.

10th Hugh "One Arm" Daily of Chicago (UA), having tied Charlie Sweeney's one-game record of 19 strikeouts in his previous outing July 7th, becomes the first ML pitcher to hurl consecutive one-hitters, defeating Boston 2–1. By season's end Daily will have hurled 4 one-hitters, a ML record equaled by Grover Alexander in 1915.

In the AA's longest game of the season, Louisville ace Guy Hecker emerges after 15 innings a 5–4 victor over Baltimore ace Bob Emslie.

11th P William "Bolliky Bill" Taylor, who deserted St. Louis (UA) after compiling a 25–4 won-loss record, wins in his first outing for Philadelphia's Athletics (AA), a 5–2 four hitter vs. Toledo. He will go on to win 17 more games for the A's in 1884.

12th Boston (NL) C Mert Hackett is struck on his mask by a foul tip, and his forehead is gashed by one of the mask's wires. Louisville (AA) C Dan Sullivan is forced to leave a game the same week when a foul ball breaks through his mask.

19th Boston's (UA) Fred "Dupee" Shaw holds pennant-bound St. Louis to one hit while fanning 18 batters, but loses the game 1–0 when batter Bill Gleason gets all the way to 2B on a dropped 3rd strike and scores on a wild pitch. In his outings of July 16th, 19th, and 21st, Shaw will amass 48 strikeouts, a ML record for 3 consecutive games (as is his 2-game total of 34 strikeouts on July 19th and 21st).

20th Cincinnati star Charley Jones slugs 3 triples to propel his club to a 17–5 rout of Indianapolis. The victory puts the 5th-place Reds within 2 games of the lead in the tight AA race.

22nd Providence star Charles Sweeney is suspended without pay after he refuses to move from the mound to RF in the 9th inning with a safe lead over Philadelphia. Sweeney quits the Grays and jumps to St. Louis (UA), for which he wins 24 games for a season's total of 41. As a result, Charles Radbourn is forced to pitch almost every game for the rest of the year. Sweeney's stubbornness has an immediate effect as substitute P Joseph "Cyclone" Miller surrenders 8 runs and gives the Athletics a 10–6 win.

Columbus (AA) slips into first place past Louisville and the Mets with a 5–1 win over Toledo.

24th The New York Mets move past Columbus into the AA lead, rising from 4th place in 5 days.

30th Lon Knight of Philadelphia (AA) goes 6-for-6 to lead the Athletics to a 19–11 win over Washington.

Showing why they lead the AA, the Metropolitans take their 11th straight win 11–5 over Brooklyn.

AUGUST

4th Buffalo's Pud Galvin no-hits Detroit and wins 18–0.

5th Richmond—a midseason replacement for Washington—makes its AA debut with a 14–0 home loss to the Athletics. The Virginias will finish with a .286 record, some 96 percentage points better than Washington.

The ML debut of Chicago (NL) deaf-mute P Thomas Lynch goes well until the 8th, when his arm gives out. When the umpire refuses to allow Lynch to leave the game, Lynch switches positions with Cap Anson, who proceeds to surrender 5 runs and lose the game to Cleveland 8–5. Lynch, the 2nd deaf-mute in ML history, will never play another game.

6th Chicago's Cap Anson hits 3 HRs in a 13–4 win against Cleveland at Lakefront Park. This gives him 5 HRs in 2 games.

7th Philadelphia Keystone (UA) disbands.

Pud Galvin shuts out Detroit 9–0 with a 3-hitter. In the Buffalo star's last 3 games he has allowed only 4 hits. Galvin's scoreless-inning streak will reach 38 innings before Detroit beats him 1–0 in 12 innings.

9th Charles Radbourn wins an 11-inning thriller 1–0 over 2nd-place Boston after Arthur Irwin hits a ball through a hole in the lathing above the RF wall for a HR. Radbourn is in the midst of a 42-inning streak in which he allows only one run, including 29 consecutive scoreless innings.

16th The minor league NWL reorganizes to shorten travel distances between clubs, dropping Evansville, IN, and one of its strongest teams, Saginaw, MI. Saginaw ace John Clarkson (31-8) is thus freed to sign with Chicago (NL), where his pitching (10-3, 2.14 ERA) will give the White Stockings a lift.

18th Harry Stovey's 3 triples and 2 singles contribute to Philadelphia's 20–1 pounding of Baltimore (AA).

21st The UA game at Washington is halted after 8 innings. Charlie Gagus finishes with a no-hit 12–1 win over Wilmington.

23rd After 9 losses, Toledo (AA) defeats Louisville for the first time, as Tony Mullane outduels Ren Deagle for a 1–0 two-hit victory. Deagle allows only 3 hits himself, but one is to engineering student Frank Olin, whose single drives Mullane home from 2B. Following his brief ML career, Olin will go on to found what is today the giant Olin Corporation.

25th Chicago's UA club completes the transfer of its franchise to Pittsburgh and, in its first game as the Pittsburgh Unions, defeats front-running St. Louis 3–2.

26th Kansas City (UA) manages to score one run against Cincinnati but bows 3–1 before Dick Burns's no-hit pitching.

Eclipse star Guy Hecker registers 17 strikeouts and allows only 6 hits, but 2nd-place Columbus (AA) manages to win 4–3. Despite the loss Hecker will lead the AA with 52 wins—the most in the history of the league—and in strikeouts with 385.

28th New York's Mickey Welch opens a game against Philadelphia by striking out the first 9 men he faces for the all-time ML mark.

SEPTEMBER

2nd Boston (NL) star Charlie Buffington beats Cleveland 4–1 with the aid of 17 strikeouts. Buffinton will finish the year with 48 wins, 2nd only to Radbourn's ML record of 60.

5th With his St. Louis Browns (AA) in 5th place, manager Jimmy Williams resigns to become clerk of the Ohio Republican State Committee. 1B-captain Charlie Comiskey will pilot the Browns to a 16-7 record the rest of the way.

11th The Grays, led by the indefatigable Charles Radbourn, win their 20th consecutive game 9–1 over Cleveland, giving them a 7-game cushion over Boston in the NL race.

When no umpire shows up for the Philadelphia Toledo-(AA) game, rookie Toledo P Hank O'Day is pressed into duty. After an undistinguished pitching career O'Day becomes a full-time umpire. In 1908 he will call New York Giant Fred Merkle out in a late-season game, erasing a game-winning, pennant-

clinching run with one of the most famous umpiring decisions in the history of baseball.

15th Wilmington (UA) disbands. Four days later Pittsburgh (UA) disbands as well.

16th Jim McCormick picks off 4 Boston Unions in an 8–4 Cincinnati victory, one of McCormick's 21 UA wins. Earlier in the season he won 19 games for Cleveland (NL). He will lead the UA in winning percentage and in ERA.

19th The UA decides to drop Pittsburgh and Wilmington and replace them with Milwaukee and Omaha. The latter club will only last for 8 days before being replaced by St. Paul.

20th Louisville moves into 2nd place in the AA, just 2 games behind the Mets, with a 2–1 win over Brooklyn. However, the Eclipse will fall back to 3rd within the week and will remain there for the rest of the season.

Baltimore (AA) hits 6 HRs, including 2 each by Oyster Burns and Jimmy Macullar, to topple Columbus 13–6.

22nd Metropolitan ace Tim Keefe strikes out 12 and gives up his only hit in the 9th in a 12–0 rout of Columbus.

28th Ed Cushman (Milwaukee, UA) no-hits Washington 5–0.

OCTOBER

1st Charlie Getzein (Detroit NL) hurls a 6-inning no-hitter against Philadelphia, winning 1–0.

3rd P Henry Porter of Milwaukee (UA) matches Dupee Shaw's distinction of July 19th as he strikes out 18 batters while losing the game 5–4 to Boston.

4th P Ed Cushman (Milwaukee, UA) follows up his no-hitter of September 28th with 8 more hitless innings before Boston's Ed Callahan loops a 9th-inning single. Cushman wins 2–0.

Sam Kimber (Brooklyn, AA) hurls a 10-inning no-hitter against Toledo, called due to darkness with the score tied 0–0.

5th St. Louis (UA) pitchers Charlie Sweeney and Henry Boyle stop St. Paul without a hit or walk, striking out 9 men, before rain halts play after 5 innings. But the Maroons lose the game when 2 St. Louis errors allow the game's only run. The Sweeney-Boyle performance caps what is still the premier ML season for no-hitters: 12 in all, including one of 10 innings and 7 nine-inning games.

6th   The Mets announce that they will allow ladies to attend their home games for free for the remainder of the season—all of 5 games.

9th   Fred Dunlap's 13th HR helps his St. Louis Maroons (UA) bury the Washington Nationals 11–1. The P will add the HR championship to his UA titles in batting, slugging, on base percentage, hits, doubles, and total bases, the most dominant season by any non-pitcher of the 19th century. He also leads all UA second basemen in fielding average, putouts, assists, DPs, and total chances per game.

Jack Manning hits 3 HRs, getting half of Philadelphia's hits in the process, but his club still falls in Chicago (NL) 19–7. Manning totals only 5 HRs in 1884 and 13 over a 9-year career.

10th   Pat Deasley, who will hit .205 for St. Louis (AA) this year, gets all 3 of his team's hits off Tim Keefe, but cannot prevent the 3–1 loss to New York.

22nd   The weekly *Sporting Life* announces—just one day before the start of the event—that the 2 pennant-winners have agreed to meet in a 3-game series October 23–25 at New York's Polo Grounds to decide "the championship of America."

25th   Hoss Radbourn of Providence wins his 3rd straight over the AA New York Mets, concluding the 3-game series.

30th   Financially troubled despite finishing 2nd to New York in the AA, the Columbus club decides to sell its players to Allegheny of Pittsburgh (AA)—for $6,000—and go out of business.

NOVEMBER

4th   Tony Mullane violates an oral agreement to sign with St. Louis (AA) by signing a Cincinnati (AA) contract for $5,000. The AA suspends Mullane for the 1885 season and fines him $1,000, but allows him to remain with Cincinnati. Over the next 8 years Mullane will win 163 games with the Reds on his way to a career total of 285 victories.

19th   NL president Abraham G. Mills resigns and is replaced by former league secretary Nick Young.

20th   The NL agrees to allow overhand pitching, but rules that pitchers must keep both feet on the ground throughout their pitching motion in order to reduce the velocity of their pitches. They still must throw the ball at the height requested by the batter. In addition, teams are now required to supply a separate bench for each club at their park to limit inter-team fraternization.

DECEMBER

11th   The AA votes to keep its ban on overhand pitching and to continue to allow fouls caught on one bounce to count as outs. It does abolish the tradition of team captains flipping for the honor of batting first. Now the home team will automatically bat first.

18th   Only 5 clubs attend the "annual" UA meeting, one by proxy. The UA will die early in 1885.

1885

JANUARY

3rd The recently disbanded Cleveland Spiders (NL) release their players.

6th Millionaire Henry V. Lucas purchases the Cleveland club and plans to fill the vacancy in the NL with his own St. Louis Maroons.

10th At an NL meeting, St. Louis is admitted to the League, Cleveland's registration is formally accepted, and Detroit has its request to remain in the NL granted, leaving only one opening for 1885.

15th At a Union Association meeting held in Milwaukee, only 2 clubs show up, Milwaukee and Kansas City. It is decided to disband the league.

20th The AA is reorganized, with clubs from St. Louis, Cincinnati, Pittsburgh, Brooklyn, Louisville, New York, and Baltimore.

FEBRUARY

12th The Western League is officially formed, with Indianapolis, Kansas City, Cleveland, Milwaukee, Toledo, and Omaha as the original clubs. It will last until June 23rd.

22nd Boston P Charlie Buffinton invents a baseball "roller skate" that gives pitchers greater impetus and swing in their delivery while still allowing them to keep both feet on the ground.

MARCH

15th A lower court in NY decides that playing baseball on Sunday is a crime. This decision will be overturned, but it will be appealed.

25th A new rule is adopted stating that the pitcher must "do all his throwing to bases before he has taken his stride as if to pitch ball."

APRIL

1st The Spalding Sporting Goods store opens in New York.

3rd The Metropolitans release Tim Keefe and Dude Esterbrook; both players later sign with the NY Giants.

17th The 4 NL players (including Hugh Daily, Orator Shaffer, and Fred Dunlap) who violated the reserve rule in 1884 by signing with the UA before the season started are reinstated with fines of $500 each.

18th The AA season opens with all 8 teams playing.

At an NL meeting, the 5 men who jumped the NL to sign with the UA in 1884 (including John Day, Charlie Sweeney, Dupee Shaw, and Jim McCormick) are reinstated with fines of $1,000.

21st Fred Mann hits the longest HR ever seen at Eclipse Park, over the RF fence in the bottom of the 13th inning to help Alleghenies defeat Louisville 4–3. Since a runner scores ahead of him, he does not get credit for the HR, which would have been his first and only one of the season.

24th Pittsburgh and Cincinnati play 16 innings with the Alleghenies winning 7–6. This is the longest ML game of the year.

29th After the 2nd straight shutout by St. Louis over Cincinnati, Reds manager O. P. Caylor fines his players $25 each for failing to make a run.

MAY

2nd In the NY Giants' opener, Mickey Welch throws a one-hitter against Boston for his first of 44 wins. He and Tim Keefe will combine for 76 victories this year, 2nd in history only to Grays P Hoss Radbourn and Charlie Sweeney, who won 77 in 1884.

2B Joe Gerhardt goes 1-for-3 in the Giants-Reds game. He will set the record for lowest BA ever for a 2B with over 350 at bats by hitting .155.

7th St. Louis (AA) trounces the Athletics 13–1 to take the lead in the standings. They will remain there for the rest of the season.

22nd Boston P Charles Buffinton gets 5 hits in 6 tries while pitching a 6-hitter over Detroit.

27th The New York Giants embarrass Buffalo 24–0 for the worst whitewashing of the ML season. Every Giant gets a hit and scores a run. NY P Mickey Welch scores 5 times and allows the Bisons only 5 hits.

Giants SS John Montgomery Ward graduates from Columbia Law School.

28th NY manages its 3rd shutout in a row, this time against Buffalo 11–0. The Giants have outscored their opponents 52–1 in the last 4 games.

JUNE

2nd St. Louis (AA) loses 7–1 to Baltimore, snapping the Browns' 17-game winning streak, an AA record.

4th The St. Louis Maroons beat Buffalo 8–4 in the last game played at the Palace Park of America. Two days later, the Maroons begin playing at Vandeventer Lot.

6th The first game played at Chicago's new West Side Park proves victorious for the White Stockings, as they beat St. Louis 9–2. Hugh "One-Arm" Daily makes his debut as a Maroon before more than 10,000 spectators.

7th The AA wipes out all restrictions on pitchers using an overhand delivery. The foul bounce out is also removed from the rule book.

12th David Orr, star 1B for NY, goes 6-for-6 and hits for the cycle against the St. Louis Browns.

Brooklyn manager Charlie Hackett tenders his resignation after a 15-25 record.

16th Philadelphia's Henry Larkin goes 6-for-6, scores 4 runs, and hits for the cycle.

AA umpire Jack Valentine officially resigns because certain managers had tried to influence him before games to have calls made in their favor.

17th Brooklyn (AA) P "Phenomenal" Smith loses his debut to St. Louis by a score of 18–5. All 18 runs against the brash lefthander are unearned, due to 14 Brooklyn "errors." When he first joined the team, Smith, who gave himself his nickname, said he was so good that he didn't need his teammates to win. The intentional misplays of his teammates cause club president Lynch to fine the guilty players $500 each, but he reluctantly agrees to release Smith to ensure team harmony.

20th John Clarkson allows only one hit in leading Chicago over the Bisons 5–0. He will lead all NL pitchers in wins (53), complete games (68), strikeouts (318), shutouts (10), and HRs (4).

25th Philadelphia beats Chicago 2–0, handing them their first loss at West Side Park, and breaking their 18-game winning streak.

Ten Dodgers make at least 2 hits each tying a ML record, as Brooklyn defeats Philadelphia 21–14. The 35 total runs and 29 hits by Brooklyn are both season highs. Dodger 3B George Pinckney goes 6-for-6. Philadelphia SS George Strief hits a ML-record 4 triples in the game; he also becomes the first player to get 5 long hits in a game (he also hits a double).

JULY

1st Chicago and Boston combine for 34 runs, the NL season high, as Chicago wins 24–10. A HR hit by Chicago SS Tommy Burns is estimated at 500 feet.

3rd Providence P Jim McCormick beats St. Louis 3–2 for his 200th career victory.

4th An exhibition between 2 old-time clubs is played at the Polo Grounds; the Old Mutual Nine (with pitcher Reno Walters) beats the Old Eckford club (with OF Dave Eggler and 1B Andy Allison) 25–17.

9th George Gore gets 5 long hits in a game by hitting 3 doubles and 2 triples off Providence's ace P Hoss Radbourn.

11th Chicago releases injured P Larry Corcoran. After averaging 34 wins the last 5 seasons, Corcoran wins only 7 games in 1885.

12th Buffalo sells a struggling Pud Galvin (13-19) to Pittsburgh for $5,000. This would be the only year from 1879–89 in which "The Little Steam Engine" doesn't win 20 games.

18th The Browns (AA) lose to the Athletics in St. Louis, snapping their 27-game consecutive-win streak at home, still a ML record.

27th John Clarkson pitches no-hitter in defeating Providence 8–0.

AUGUST

1st The largest paying crowd to date gathers at the Polo Grounds; 13,427 fans watch the Giants defeat the Chicago White Stockings 7–6.

2nd Allegheny P Ed "Cannonball" Morris strikes out 15 Colonels, but still loses 4–1. Morris will lead the AA in complete games (63), innings pitched (581), strikeouts (298), and shutouts (6) this year.

7th Detroit defeats Providence, snapping a ML record 26 straight home wins by Providence over Detroit, dating back to June 2, 1882.

8th All games are canceled in New York City today because of General Ulysses S. Grant's funeral.

15th Louis Henke, 1B for Atlanta (Southern League), dies as a result of injuries received the day before during a game against Nashville.

Athletics manager Lon Knight is fired and temporarily replaced by 1B Harry Stovey; former Athletics manager Charlie Mason is eventually hired as his replacement.

18th Providence 2B Jack Farrell is suspended without pay for obscenities directed at spectators at the home grounds.

26th A line drive caught by NY 1B Roger Connor catches runners at 1B and 2B off guard, enabling Connor and 2B Joe Gerhardt to complete triple play in the first inning against Providence. Connor would take part in another first-inning triple play on September 7th.

27th Providence lays off former batting champ Paul Hines and accuses him of intentionally playing poorly to receive his release. His .358 in 1878 led the NL.

29th Philadelphia's Charles Ferguson pitches a no-hitter over Providence, beating them 1–0.

SEPTEMBER

1st Detroit C Charlie Bennett hits a grand slam in the first inning, leading Detroit to an 8–3 victory over the NY Gothams.

4th Player-manager Cap Anson hits HRs in consecutive innings (6th and 7th), to help Chicago down Buffalo 12–4.

7th NY P Mickey Welch loses to the Phillies 3–1, snapping his personal 17-game winning streak. His last loss was on July 16th, versus Boston.

9th The Grays beat the Phillies 3–1, snapping their 13-game losing streak. This is the last ML game ever played in Providence.

11th Providence suspends ace P Hoss Radbourn and 3B Jerry Denny; Radbourn, the NL's highest-paid player ($6,000), is suspended due to NY beating him 9–1.

19th Buffalo's "Big Four" (Dan Brouthers, Hardy Richardson, Jack Rowe, and Deacon White) are to play for Detroit today, but Nick Young orders umpire Bob Ferguson to forfeit the game to New York. Detroit withdraws the players, and they are forced to play out the season with Buffalo.

28th Harry Stovey hits his AA-leading 13th HR off Pittsburgh's John Hofford. This is also Stovey's 51st career HR, which is the current ML record.

29th More than 10,000 fans crowd West Side Park (seating capacity of 6,000); seats are placed in right and left field, and it is declared that if a ball is hit into the crowd, a triple shall be credited. Chicago hits 5 triples in this manner, and beats NY 7–4.

30th Athletics P Bobby Mathews strikes out 4 Alleghenies in the 7th inning.

Canadian Fred Wood catches his only game for Boston, with brother Pete Wood pitching. This is one of the few brother batteries ever in ML history, preceded only by the White brothers, Deacon and Will, of the 1878 Cincinnati team.

OCTOBER

1st Dave Orr goes 6-for-12 in NY's last 3 games, but still falls one point short in the batting race, finishing 2nd to Louisville's Pete Browning.

The first black professional team is organized by Frank P. Thompson. The team is called the Athletics but will shortly become known as the Cuban Giants.

5th The Athletics beat Brooklyn 9–1 in the last game of the AA season. Athletics P Bobby Mathews wins his 30th of the year (he won the same in 1883 and 1884) and 150th of his career.

7th The last NL game ever played in Buffalo's Olympic Park attracts 12 fans as Providence takes 2 from the Bisons 4–0 and 6–1. Grays P Fred Shaw goes the distance in both victories (each 5 innings), throwing a no-hitter in the first game.

10th Another doubleheader is played between Buffalo and Providence and the Grays again win both games, with Fred Shaw pitching. The Bisons end the season on a 16-game losing streak.

Phillies SS Charlie Bastian goes 5-for-10 in the last 2 games to raise his average up to .167, the lowest ever for a SS with over 350 at bats.

14th　The White Stockings (NL) and Browns (AA) engage in a "World's Championship" series. The winner of the 7-game series is to receive a $1,000 prize. Darkness ends game one after 8 innings, at a 5–5 stalemate.

15th　Game 2 of the championship series is forfeited to Chicago. In the top of the 6th inning, Browns manager Charlie Comiskey calls his men off the field to protest a ruling made by umpire Sullivan.

17th　At a joint meeting in New York between both leagues, a salary maximum of $2,000 and a minimum of $1,000 is set for the upcoming season.

22nd　John Ward and several teammates secretly form the Brotherhood of Professional Base Ball Players. The Brotherhood, strengthened by fights against salary restrictions and abuses of the reserve clause, will become a force to be reckoned with by the end of the decade.

23rd　The "World Series" moves from Pittsburgh to Cincinnati, setting a ML record for the series played in the most (4) cities. (also played in NY and St. Louis.). Chicago takes a 3–2 series lead by beating the Browns 9–2.

24th　The St. Louis Browns defeat Chicago 13–4 in the 7th and last game in their series. The Browns claim the game 2 forfeit didn't count and therefore claim the championship. Each club receives $500.

NOVEMBER

19th　At an NL meeting, it is decided that Buffalo's "Big Four" (Brouthers, Richardson, Rowe, and White) can play in Detroit next season.

28th　President Soden buys the Providence franchise and players for $6,000.

DECEMBER

4th　The NL Metropolitans franchise is sold to millionaire Erastus Wiman. The Metropolitan Exhibition Company receives $25,000 for the transaction.

8th　At an AA meeting in Philadelphia, the Metropolitan club is removed from the Association, and the National club of Washington is admitted. By court order, the Metropolitans will be readmitted.

18th　The Washington Nationals are admitted to the NL, in place of Providence. The Washington club was displaced in the AA by the court's decision that the Mets' franchise could not be revoked.

1886

JANUARY

16th Washington is admitted to the NL, bringing the membership up to 7 teams.

FEBRUARY

5th The patent dispute between Thayer & Wright and A. G. Spalding & Brothers goes to court in Chicago. Thayer is the Harvard pitcher who claimed to have invented the catcher's mask, while G. Wright and Spalding are former teammates on the champion Boston Red Stockings. In the eventual settlement, Thayer's claims will be upheld and he will receive a royalty on masks sold from Spalding's company.

9th Kansas City is admitted to the NL on a one-year trial basis.

27th The Cincinnati AA club is sold by Aaron Stern to John Hauck, a wealthy brewer and banker.

MARCH

2nd The American Association suspends Sam Barkley for signing with Pittsburgh before the dispute over his sale is settled.

The AA adopts new rules. The number of balls needed for a walk is reduced from 7 to 6, the pitcher's box is one foot deeper. Stolen bases are adopted as an official statistic.

4th The NL meets and adopts the stolen base and the 4 foot by 7 foot pitcher's box. But the NL retains 7 balls for a walk and rejects the AA rule giving a batter first base on HPB.

13th From Paris, 40-game winner Bob Caruthers agrees to terms with St. Louis Browns owner Von der Ahe via transatlantic telegraph. Caruther's well-publicized holdout will earn him the nickname "Parisian Bob."

17th *The Sporting News,* the weekly that will become "The Baseball Paper of the World," publishes its first issue.

18th The New York State League admits Buffalo, Toronto, and Hamilton. The inclusion of the Canadian teams causes the league to change its name to the International League.

22nd The AA ousts H. D. McKnight from the presidency. Wheeler Wikoff is the new president.

APRIL

2nd Capitol Park is opened in Washington with an exhibition game. The team will be called the Senators or Statesmen. The new park will carry the nickname "Swampdoodle Grounds."

17th The Opening Day game in Cincinnati is protested when the umpire refuses to put a new ball into play despite the new rule making 2 new balls available at all times.

21st Phil Reccius, the last of 3 ball playing brothers still active, suffers a broken leg, virtually ending his season.

22nd The Mets' lavish new park on Staten Island is opened with a loss to the Athletics 7–6.

Later this summer, cranks (fans) will be able to look at N.Y. harbor from the St, George grandstand and see the Statue of Liberty being assembled.

24th Arlie Latham of the Browns goes 6-for-6 and scores 5 runs as the Browns beat Louisville 15–9.

27th Having failed to get a $1,500 salary from the NL to umpire this season, veteran Bob Ferguson signs with the AA and officiates his first game in Baltimore.

29th Opening Day for the NL. The New York *World* carries woodcuts of live action photographs taken by a "detective" camera, perhaps the first "live" pictures of baseball ever taken.

30th The first NL game in Kansas City is played, the home team losing a tight game with Chicago 6–5 in 13 innings. This game is "recreated" for fans in Chicago at the Central Music Hall.

MAY

1st Al Atkinson pitches his 2nd no-hitter for the Athletics, beating the Mets 3–2. His first no-hitter (May 24, 1884) was also not a shutout.

2nd The Athletics and Brooklyn play to a 19–19 tie at Brooklyn's new Sunday park in Ridgewood.

3rd C Patrick Dealy of Boston has 10 passed balls (still the NL record), and P Ed Stemmeyer adds 5 wild pitches as the Red Caps lose to Washington 12–11.

Stemmeyer will finish the season with another ML record of 64 wild pitches.

14th Charles Comiskey of the Browns prevents a double play by running full tilt into Reds 2B Bid McPhee, enabling the Browns to win 2–1. The Cincinnati fans are irate, but the umpire allows the play. The Browns are gradually making "breaking up the double play" an accepted part of the game.

23rd St. Louis SS Bill Gleason makes 6 errors to give Brooklyn a 13–12 game in 10 innings.

29th The Athletics try to slow the Browns down by loading the base paths with sand. St. Louis captain Comiskey refuses to play and helps the grounds crew remove the sand. The Browns win the 2 games with a total of 14 stolen bases.

31st The first ML crowd of over 20,000 pays to see the afternoon game in New York versus Detroit. The Giants had snapped the Wolverines' 15-game winning streak in the A.M. game, but Detroit wins in the P.M. before 20,632.

JUNE

3rd St. Louis teammates Arlie Latham and Doc Bushong stage a fistfight during a game in Baltimore. They are fined $100 each.

4th Mullane pitches 7 shutout innings, then allows 12 runs in the final 2 frames to lose to Brooklyn 12–7, fueling suspicions that he is throwing games.

9th At an AA meeting in Columbus, Browns owner Chris Von der Ahe pays Comiskey's many fines after Comiskey had steadfastly refused to pay them. The AA threatened to bar Comiskey from all games.

12th Detroit sets a new record by hitting 7 HRs in one game. This record is broken by the Yankees on June 28, 1939. St. Louis P Charley Sweeney allows all 7 HRs.

16th On Opening Day in the Southern League of Colored Base Ballists, the Eclipse of Memphis beats the home Unions of New Orleans 3–1. The SLCBB, the first black professional sports league, will collapse in August.

18th The Cincinnati *Enquirer* publishes a letter purporting to show that Tony Mullane sold ball games

in Philadelphia and Brooklyn to gamblers on the last road trip.

22nd Detroit wins the rubber game of the 3-game series with Chicago 5–4, as an irate Captain Anson is fined $110 by umpire John Gaffney, a record for one game. Anson's Whites trail the Sluggers by 3½ games.

24th The Brooklyn Grays rout Matt Kilroy in the 3rd inning and beat Baltimore 25–1.

26th Black lefthander George Stovey makes his pitching debut with Jersey City of the Eastern League after being purchased from the Cuban Giants, the pioneer all-black touring team.

JULY

1st Jim McCormick raises his record for the season to 16-0 pitching Chicago to a 7–3 victory over New York.

3rd Behind the pitching of Amos Alonzo Stagg, who will make his mark as a football coach, Yale beats Harvard in the deciding game of the college championship.

5th Pittsburgh's (AA) Fred Carroll gets a record 9 hits in a doubleheader.

7th Today's issue of *Sporting Life* shows 5 pitchers in the top 7 spots on the AA batting-average list. Dave Foutz, Bob Caruthers, and Guy Becker play enough at other positions to be contenders for the batting title.

11th During the 2nd Sunday game played in Cincinnati after owner Louis Hauck dropped his objections, a riot breaks out. Umpire George Bradley is hit by a beer mug hurled from the rowdy Cincinnati crowd and retreats to the directors' room in the 6th inning. He returns to complete the game. The Reds lose to the Grays 11–7. The incident strengthens the position of many religious and political leaders that Sunday baseball attracts mostly "hoodlums" and "foreigners" and should therefore be banned. While this advice is followed in most ML cities, Sunday baseball in the Queen City continues and proves to be extremely popular with all "classes" of people.

22nd The news leaks out that Chicago owner Spalding has hired detectives to shadow the White Stocking players and report on their drinking habits. Seven players are fined $25 each.

24th Bill "Adonis" Terry no-hits St. Louis as Brooklyn wins 1–0. Terry walks 2 men, and 3 others reach base on errors.

31st Tom Ramsey pitches a 13-inning 17-strikeout one-hitter to beat Baltimore 2–1. It is Ramsey's 2nd consecutive one-hitter, and the 3rd time in 4 games that the Orioles have gotten only one hit.

AUGUST

7th Washington loses its 12th consecutive game, their 4th losing streak of 10 of more games this season. Veteran manager Mike Scanlin announces that he will retire as soon as a replacement can be found.

8th Rumors of the imminent demise of the St. Louis Maroons abound after star 2B Fred Dunlap is sold to Detroit for $4,700.

9th Tom Ramsey ties the AA record by striking out 17 batters in a 9-inning game as he whips the Mets 6–0.

12th Guy Hecker allows 16 hits and 11 runs and goes 4-for-5 as Louisville wins a 27–11 slugfest against Brooklyn.

15th Guy Hecker scores 7 runs in a game, establishing a ML record. In addition, he hits 3 HRs to tie the existing record.

16th Bob Caruthers becomes the first pitcher to make 4 extra-base hits in a game, but he allows 10 runs in the 8th inning and loses 11–9. Having hit a double and 2 HRs earlier, Caruthers ends the game tagged out at home trying for a 3rd. The defeat ends the Browns' 11-game winning streak.

18th St. Louis Maroon owner Henry Lucas quits baseball, announcing that the club has cost him $27,000 in 3 years. The franchise seems to be on the brink of dissolution but will finish the season.

19th NL umpire John Gaffney agrees to take over as manager of Washington.

20th Matt Kilroy of the Orioles and Joe Miller of the Athletics hurl opposing one-hitters. Baltimore wins 1–0 on first-inning errors.

22nd Just as he reaches the ball on a long hit by Chicken Wolf, Reds CF Abner Powell's pants are grabbed by a stray dog. Wolf circles the bases with the HR that wins the game for Louisville 5–3 in 11 innings.

24th Cap Anson scores 6 runs as Chicago trounces Boston 18–6.

In a rematch of the double one-hitter, Miller allows 4 hits and wins 3–0 over Kilroy, who allows only 2 hits. Kilroy fans 16 Athletics, his high in a season in which he will set the all-time record with 513 strikeouts.

28th Phillie C Deacon McGuire returns to action after suffering a broken finger and commits 8 passed balls.

SEPTEMBER

1st Ed "Cannonball" Crane walks 14 and adds 5 wild pitches and an error in a 15–2 loss to Chicago. Formerly an OF, Crane has been pressed into service as a pitcher for the last-place Statesmen.

10th Dan Brouthers hits 3 HRs, a double, and a single to set an NL mark with 15 total bases, but his Detroit team loses to Chicago 14–8.

11th Connie Mack makes his ML debut with Washington, catching flawlessly and contributing a single as the Senators beat the Phillies 4–3.

23rd Pittsburgh's Pud Galvin walks the first 3 batters and then picks them all off.

25th Browns owner Von der Ahe begins negotiations for a World Championship Series by issuing a challenge to White Stockings owner Spalding.

30th Spalding accepts Von der Ahe's challenge for a "World Series" and proposes a best-of-9 series with the winning club getting the total gross gate receipts. St. Louis will accept the winner-take-all provision, but the series will be best-of-7.

OCTOBER

4th After a contract dispute is settled in court, John "Phenomenal" Smith pitches Detroit to a 4–3 victory in Washington.

6th After 3 one-hitters and 4 two-hitters earlier in the season, Matt Kilroy finally gets a no-hitter, beating Pittsburgh 6–0.

7th   Chicago wins while Detroit ties, giving the White Stockings a 2-game lead with 2 to play.

8th   Lady Baldwin of Detroit beats Philadelphia 11–0 in 8 innings for his 42nd win of the season, an all-time record for a lefthanded pitcher. Eight of those wins, including 5 shutouts, have come against the Phillies, who have not been shut out by any other pitcher this season.

Pittsburgh's Ed Morris beats the Mets 9–0 for his 12th shutout of the season, establishing an all-time record for a lefthander. Morris will finish the season with a 41-20 won-lost record.

9th   Chicago clinches the pennant by beating Boston 12–3 on the final day of the season while Detroit is losing 2 games to Charley Ferguson and the Phillies 5–1 and 6–1.

14th   Aaron Stern buys the Cincinnati Reds back from John Hauck.

15th   The AA season ends with 2 games in Philadelphia. Harry Stovey hits a HR to give him at least a share of the Association leadership for the 4th consecutive season.

18th   The World Championship Series opens in Chicago, with the White Stockings beating the Browns 6–0 behind John Clarkson's 5-hitter.

19th   The Browns win the 2nd game in a 12–0 romp, only 8 innings being played. Bob Caruthers pitches a one-hitter, and Tip O'Neill hits 2 HRs.

20th   Chicago being his home town, Caruthers asks to pitch again. He walks 4 men in the first inning and loses 11–4 in an 8-inning game.

21st   The Series shifts to St. Louis, where the Browns even things with an 8–5 victory in 7 innings. Bill Gleason stars with two 2-run singles.

22nd   With Jim McCormick and Jocko Flynn lame and John Clarkson tired, Chicago tries to use a minor league recruit in the pitcher's box, only to be refused by the Browns. SS Ned Williamson and RF Jimmy Ryan pitch for the Whites. The Browns win easily 10–3 to take a 3-to-2 lead in the best-of-7 series.

23rd   The St. Louis Browns win the World Championship by beating Chicago 4–3 in 10 innings. Pitching his 4th game in 6 days, Clarkson holds St. Louis hitless for 6 innings as Chicago builds a 3–0 lead. The Browns tie the game in the 8th, and Curt

Welch scores the "$15,000" run on a wild pitch in the 10th. St. Louis wins the entire gate receipts from the series ($13,920), with each of 12 players getting about $580.

NOVEMBER

11th   The Executive Council of the Brotherhood of Professional Base Ball Players, formed the previous year, meets and chooses officers. John M. Ward is re-elected president, Dan Brouthers vice president, and Tim Keefe secretary-treasurer.

15th   Cincinnati and St. Louis complete the first trade ever of reserved players, the Browns sending Hugh Nicol to the Reds for Jack Boyle and $400.

16th   The AA and NL Joint Rules Committee announces the new rules code, which includes the following changes, among others:

- 4 strikes for an out;
- 5 balls for a walk;
- A standardized strike zone from the knees to the shoulders;
- Restricting the pitcher to just one forward step in making his delivery;
- Restricting the pitcher to start with one foot on the back line of the box;
- Establishing a 55½-foot pitching distance.

18th   The NL meets and admits Pittsburgh, which had been looking to leave the AA since last spring.

22nd   The AA admits Cleveland to membership to fill the vacancy caused by Pittsburgh's defection

DECEMBER

15th   The AA meets and ratifies the new rules. It also approves the new clause that allows a club to reserve a player for as long as it wants, not just for next year's contract.

1887

JANUARY

1st Brooklyn owner-manager Charles Byrne gives a New Year's bonus of $50 to each of his club's reserve players.

18th A new Kansas City club is founded to play in the Western League. It vows to compete with the local NL team.

FEBRUARY

8th Mike "King" Kelly meets with Chicago owner Albert Spalding for contract talks. Kelly, who won the NL batting championship for the pennant-winning White Stockings, wants the bonus of $375 that Spalding promised for good behavior last year. Spalding refuses to give him the bonus or to rescind the additional $225 withheld from Kelly's salary as fines for drinking.

14th James B. Billings, one of the Boston (NL) club owners, agrees to pay Kelly a $2,000 salary and a $3,000 signing bonus if Boston can buy his reserve rights from Chicago.

16th Chicago announces the sale of Kelly to Boston for $10,000, more than twice the amount ever paid for a player before. With the contract and bonus, Kelly is dubbed a "$15,000 Beauty."

MARCH

1st In preparation for the upcoming National Colored Base Ball League (NCBBL) season, the Falls Citys of Louisville sign Al Prater from Detroit and W.S., Purnsley from the Cuban Giants. In addition, they have recently started construction of a 2000-seat park.

8th The NL franchise in St. Louis is sold to a group from Indianapolis for $12,000, including players. The Maroons will now become the Hoosiers.

9th The Kansas City Cowboys (NL) go out of business with the sale of its players to the league for $6,000. The club's spot in the league has already been taken by Pittsburgh.

13th After a week of conditioning in Macon, Georgia, the Detroit team begins a 6-week spring exhibition tour through the South and Midwest.

14th The National Colored League is organized at a meeting in Baltimore. Six clubs are represented: Lord Baltimore, Pythians (Philadelphia), Keystones (Pittsburgh), Gorhams (New York), Falls City (Louisville), and Resolutes (Boston).

APRIL

16th Opening Day in the A.A. Two rookies, Mike Griffin of the Baltimore Orioles and George "White Wings" Tebeau of Cincinnati, hit HRs in their first ML at bats. They are the first of many to accomplish this.

17th St. Louis Browns owner Chris Von der Ahe purchases 19-year-old St. Louisan Charley "Silver" King from the NL. King, with Kansas City at the end of the last season, had not been picked up by any NL clubs this spring. He would post a 34-11 record in 1887.

19th Chicago mascot Willie Hahn, aged 11, is signed to a regular league contract. "You should have seen the little fellow open his eyes," when a club official read him the abstinence clause.

21st Pop Snyder, the only catcher from the National Association still behind the plate, allows Louisville to steal 10 bases in just 3 innings before being replaced by Jim Toy. The Colonels beat the Cleveland "Babies" 14–7.

22nd Tony Mullane pitches a regular-season game in Missouri for the first time since 1883. The Missouri injunction obtained against him by the St. Louis Unions in 1884 having finally been resolved, Tony leads the Reds to a 5–2 victory over the Browns.

26th Denny Lyons of the Athletics goes 6-for-6, all on clean hits. The A's need every one of them to nip the Mets 18–17.

28th Opening Day in the NL. Of the new clubs, Indianapolis loses a thriller to Detroit in its home opener 4–3, while Pittsburgh is rained out.

30th The Browns set a St. Louis scoring record that still stands by trouncing Cleveland 28–11. Bill Gleason goes 7-for-7, but 4 of his "hits" are walks.

The Phillies open their new $30,000 ballpark on Huntington Avenue and Broad Street. They would remain on this site until 1938.

MAY

1st Charlie Comiskey triples and homers to lead the Browns to a 14–13 victory over Cleveland. St. Louis scores 74 runs in a 4-game sweep and is on its way to becoming the first team ever to score over 1,000 runs in a season.

2nd After winning 31 straight exhibition games and 3 regular-season games, Detroit loses its first of the year, to Pittsburgh and Jim Galvin 8–3.

3rd After opening the season with 10 consecutive losses on the road, the Mets win their home opener on Staten Island from Brooklyn 8–2.

6th The National Colored League, patterned after the NL, opens with a game in Pittsburgh, the Gorhams beating the Keystones 11–8 before a crowd of 1,200. Because of rainouts and small crowds the league, which has been recognized by the National Agreement as a legitimate minor league, will fold on May 16th after only 13 games.

7th Tip O'Neill of the Browns hits for the cycle for the 2nd time in 5 games. In each game, Tip had a walk (counted as a hit) as well as a clean single.

Sam Thompson of Detroit becomes the first of only 6 ML players to hit 2 bases-loaded triples in one game.

9th Ed Morris of the Alleghenies refuses to pitch today's game and is suspended for 3 weeks. Morris is having trouble with the new rules limiting the movement of pitchers in the box.

12th The Browns score 12 runs in the 5th inning and beat the Orioles, who score 10 in the 8th, 22–14. The new 4-strike rule and the restricted pitching motion have generated a big jump in scoring.

16th St. Louis wins its 15th straight game, which will be the longest streak of the year in the ML, beating the Athletics 7–2.

Giants rookie Mike Tiernan makes 5 errors, tying the ML record for an OF. But he contributes a HR as New York beats Indianapolis 11–8.

17th Detroit's Dan Brouthers hits a bases-loaded triple and a bases-loaded homer as the Wolverines outslug the Phillies 19–10.

18th White Stocking rookie Marty Sullivan ties the record by making 5 errors in RF as Chicago loses its 3rd straight in Washington 11–4.

20th Nearly 2 weeks after defeating the Falls Citys in their NCBBL opener in Louisville, the Boston Resolutes finally leave for home after earning enough money for train fare by working as waiters. Their departure, and the circumstances surrounding it, sounds the death knell for the 2nd professional baseball league organized by African Americans.

21st Sam Thompson's 3-run HR is the difference as Detroit beats Washington 4–2. Thompson will be credited with 166 RBI for the season, a 19th-century high.

24th Indianapolis 3B Jerry Denny saves a run by holding King Kelly by the belt as Kelly tries to tag up on a fly ball. The umpire misses the play and does not penalize Denny. But the ploy does not save the Hoosiers from an 8–7, 10-inning defeat in Boston.

26th The Louisville Colonels pile up a club record for runs in a 27–9 rout of Brooklyn.

30th Chicago walks to a 12–11 victory in an A.M. holiday game in New York. Giants P Bill George walks 16 batters to establish a ML mark. Mickey Welch relieves in the 9th and walks one more to give Chicago 17 bases on balls for the game.

JUNE

1st The St. Louis Browns offer to buy a partial interest in the rival Athletic club. The Athletics are losing money, and 2 of the 3 partners want out, but this deal will not come to fruition.

5th Today's Chicago *Tribune* publishes NL batting figures through May 31st that show Fred Carroll (.476), Sam Thompson (.454), and Paul Hines (.438) leading the league. Walks are being counted as hits this year.

9th Mets RF Candy Nelson sets a ML record by starting 3 double plays, 2 on throws to home and one to start an infield rundown. Only 2 other ML outfielders have tied this record: Jack McCarthy (4/26/05) and Ira Flagstead (4/19/26).

13th Sportswriter O. P. Caylor takes over as manager of the Mets. Caylor had managed Cincinnati in 1885 and 1886 while writing for the Cincinnati *Enquirer,* now he is with the New York *Tribune* and managing again.

14th Before an overflow crowd of 15,000, the hometown Orioles score 8 times in the 8th inning to beat the Browns 15–12. St. Louis complains that substitute umpire Lew Daniels, an Oriole player, has robbed them of the victory.

15th The Giants annihilate the Phillies 29–1, setting records for runs scored and allowed that still stand for each club.

16th Before a riotous Baltimore club, Curt Welch of the Browns topples Orioles 2B Bill Greenwood to prevent a DP and is promptly arrested for assault by a policeman on duty at the park. He will be fined $4.50 by a local judge.

17th Boston scores 10 runs in the 10th inning to beat New York 19–9, relief P Mike Tiernan taking the beating.

19th During this Sunday battle with St. Louis, Cincinnati draws a crowd of 10,542, its biggest of the season. However, the Cincinnati *Enquirer* notes that 15,086 fans attended the game. Judging from the Reds' official attendance figures from 1886 to 1888, the *Enquirer* overestimated game attendance by an average of 45 percent per game. The official attendance average during this period was 1,970—1,511 on weekdays and 4,075 on Sundays and major holidays.

21st Tom "Toad" Ramsey of Louisville strikes out 17 Cleveland Babies, a singular achievement under this year's 4-strike rule. The Colonels win in a rout 21–1.

23rd Tip O'Neill goes just 1-for-4 (the "hit" being a "phantom," as sportswriters are calling bases on balls) against Cleveland's Bill Crowell, dropping his AA leading batting average to .516.

27th Highly touted California hurler George Van Haltren makes his ML debut with Chicago and ties the all-time record by walking 16 batters while losing to Boston 17–11. Van Haltren would later star as an OF.

JULY

1st The Phillies and Wolverines set an all-time record by scoring in 15 of the 18 half-innings played.

4th Dave Foutz of the Browns has a banner day at the plate, driving in 9 runs with 2 HRs and 5 hits in the afternoon game of a doubleheader against the Mets after having hit a HR in the morning game. St. Louis wins both 15–2 and 20–3.

6th Alex McKinnon leaves the Alleghenies suffering from symptoms of typhoid fever. He has been having his best season, batting .365 (.340 not counting walks), but will die of the disease within 2 weeks.

10th Enforcing a new law barring business on Sundays, St. Louis police stop today's game and arrest owner Chris Von der Ahe. Within a week, however, a judge will rule baseball exempt from the law.

11th Horace Fogel takes charge of the Indianapolis team as manager. Like Ollie Caylor of the Mets, Fogel is a sportswriter by trade.

14th The Alleghenies agree to the Giants' offer of $2,000 for slumping P Ed Morris. But the deal would fall through because of fan indignation in Pittsburgh.

The International League's Board of Directors meets in Buffalo and declares that no new black players will be allowed in the league.

15th John M. Ward quits as captain of the New York Giants, Buck Ewing succeeding him at the post. Ward is busy organizing the new players' Brotherhood.

18th Paced by George Wood's 2 HRs, the Phillies beat the Wolverines 12–2 for a 3-game sweep.

19th Cap Anson refuses to allow his NL champion Chicago White Sox to play against Newark's George Stovey, an outstanding black pitcher.

20th The International League passes a ban on black players. Although not strictly enforced this season, this action spells the end of the IL as a haven for black ballplayers.

22nd Master Chapman, age 14, pitches for Philadelphia against Cleveland in a 9–0 forfeited game. This is his only ML appearance.

AUGUST

6th Charlie Buffinton of the Phillies allows one real hit and 2 "phantoms" (walks) in shutting out Indianapolis.

9th   Buffinton pitches his 2nd straight one-hitter (not counting walks), beating Chicago 17–4. "Buff" is making a successful comeback after being given up on by Boston last winter.

10th   Tip O'Neill gets his 10th consecutive hit (including one walk but not including one HBP) before being retired by Cleveland pitcher John Kirby.

12th   At the Mets' grounds on Staten Island, Athletic batter Gus Weyhing hits an apparent triple that Indian RF Bob Hogan kicks into the stage of the play "The Fall of Babylon." Since the ground rules at park call for a double on hits into the theatrical set, the umpire orders Weyhing back to 2B. After a futile argument, the Athletics leave the field and forfeit the game.

14th   St. Louis P Dave Foutz suffers a broken thumb when hit by a line drive. When he eventually returns to pitching, he will be ineffective.

15th   John Clarkson and Chicago beat Detroit again, 6–4 this time. Since the NL has just thrown out a protested game previously awarded to the Wolverines, this leaves Chicago and Detroit tied for first place.

16th   Detroit bounces back and beats Clarkson and Chicago 5–3 with a 5-run 4th-inning rally to regain sole possession of first place.

17th   Managing from the press table costs Ollie Caylor and the Mets a game. With a Baltimore runner on 3B in the bottom of the 10th inning, manager Caylor yells last-second instructions to C Bill Holbert. Just as Holbert turns around to look at the press stand, P Al Mays begins his delivery. When Mays sees Holbert turned away, however, he stops, committing a balk that sends the winning run across the plate for the Orioles.

27th   Mike Kelly and Ezra Sutton score 6 runs each as the Beaneaters trounce the Alleghenies 28–14. The score is the biggest ever yielded by a Pittsburgh ML team.

29th   Denny Lyons of the Athletics is held hitless for the first time since May 23rd, ending a 52-game hitting streak. In 2 of those games, however, Lyons's only hits were actually bases on balls.

30th   Blondie Purcell succeeds Tom Burns as the Baltimore Orioles' captain. The high-strung Burns overstepped his bounds yesterday when he threw a ball at the opposing pitcher after grounding out in the 9th inning.

31st   The Mets use 5 pitchers while being bombed by Louisville, becoming the first team ever to use that many in one game. For Louisville, the victory is the 6th in a row.

SEPTEMBER

1st   Following a 3-game sweep at the hands of the Detroits, Boston removes King Kelly as captain and gives the job back to manager-1B John Morrill.

3rd   The Browns win a doubleheader on Staten Island to run their latest winning streak to 12 games and extend their lead in the AA race to 19½ games.

5th   Chicago wins the opening game of their final series against league-leading Detroit 11–7. John Clarkson picks up his 9th victory over the Wolverines, the most ever by a pitcher over a pennant-winning team.

7th   Detroit gets sweet revenge against Clarkson and the White Stockings, beating them twice, 8–2 and 8–4, while amassing 34 hits. The defeat pushes the 2nd-place Chicagos 7 games behind.

11th   The Mets successfully stage a Sunday "home" game in Weehawken, NJ, losing to the Colonels 10–6.

The St. Louis Browns players refuse to play an exhibition game versus the all-black Cuban Giants team, stating in a letter to the owner that "we will cheerfully play against white people at any time and think that by refusing to play [blacks] we are only doing what is right." Arlie Latham is singled out as the leader of the recalcitrant players and is fined.

12th   Jimmy Ryan goes 6-for-6 for Chicago with a single, double, HR, and 3 walks. He also pitches the final 3 innngs to get the win as the White Stockings rally to beat the Phillies 16–13.

14th   Adrian "Cap" Anson is 3-for-5, giving him 17 hits in the last 5 games. His hot streak will win him the NL batting title with an official .421 average (without walks, which are counted as hits, Sam Thompson would have won the title with a .372 mark).

22nd   Elmer Smith of Cincinnati shuts out St. Louis 6–0. The Browns will be blanked in only 2 regular season games, both times by Smith.

28th   Abner Dalrymple hits 2 dramatic HRs in front of his old fans in Chicago, one to tie the game for Pittsburgh in the 8th inning and one to win it 3–2 in the 10th. These are Dalrymple's only HRs of the season.

30th   Connie Mack singles, steals 2B, and scores on John Irwin's first NL hit to give Washington a 1–0 victory over New York.

OCTOBER

1st   Matt Kilroy pitches and wins both games of a doubleheader to close the home season at Oriole Park. This duplicates a feat of July 26th. The fastballer would finish the season with a 46-20 record, the ML-season record for a lefthander.

8th   The Metropolitan franchise and player contracts are sold to AA rival Brooklyn for $15,000. Purchaser Charles Byrne has the Mets play today's game in Brooklyn's Washington Park, where the hapless Indians lose to the Orioles 10–0.

The Phillies finish the NL season with their 26th victory in a row, still the club record. The late spurt jumps them to 2nd place behind Detroit.

9th   The St. Louis Browns end their season with a 95-40 record, besting their 1886 record by 2 wins. This will not be topped until the adoption of the 154-game schedule.

10th   The World Series opens in St. Louis with the Browns beating the Detroits 6–1. P Bob Caruthers holds the Wolverines to 5 hits and has 3 safe hits himself.

12th   Game 3 is the most dramatic of the series, Detroit winning at home 2–1 in 13 innings. St. Louis squanders 13 hits against Charlie Getzien, while Caruthers limits Detroit to 6 real hits.

13th   The best-of-15 WS begins its tour of the other cities with a game in Pittsburgh, Detroit winning 8–0 behind the 2-hit pitching of Lady Baldwin.

19th   Detroit runs its lead in the WS to 7 games to 2 with a 4–2 victory at the Athletics' Park. This follows a 3–1 win at the Phillies' Park on the 17th and a 9–2 rout on the 18th at the old Dartmouth Street Grounds in Boston, where Sam Thompson poled two HRs.

21st   Detroit clinches the World Championship with its 8th victory in game 11 this afternoon in Baltimore 13–3.

26th   The World Series winds up with a game back at Sportsman's Park in St. Louis. St. Louis wins the final game but loses the series, 10 games to 5.

27th   The Brotherhood of Professional Base Ball Players holds a meeting and club representatives pledge not to sign standard contracts until negotiations are held concerning the wording of those documents.

29th   Ned Williamson and Silver Flint sign with Chicago for 1888 despite the Brotherhood pledge.

NOVEMBER

2nd   The Athletics are sold to a syndicate headed by Henry C. Pennypacker. The 3 long time partners, Sharsig, Simmons, and Mason, still hold a sizable block of stock.

3rd   The directors of the Omaha club agree to pay $3,000 per month to manager Frank Selee to bring his team from Oshkosh, where they won the Northwestern League pennant in 1887. Two top stars, outfielders Tommy McCarthy and Dummy Hoy, will spend 1888 in the ML, however, and Selee's Omaha team will finish 4th in the WA race.

14th   Cleveland announces a new uniform design featuring dark blue stripes and piping. The new suit will inspire the nickname "Spider" because of the web-like pattern.

16th   The Joint Rules Committee does away with the 4-strike rule and with the scoring of walks as hits. Five balls for a walk remains the rule.

17th   The NL meets and officially recognizes the Brotherhood by meeting with a committee of 3 players, John Ward, Ned Hanlon, and Dan Brouthers.

18th   The NL adopts a new contract that spells out reserve provisions for the first time. The NL refuses to accept the players' demand that the salary be written out on all contracts, however.

21st   The St. Louis Browns announce a trade with the Athletics that ships Bill Gleason and Curt Welch to Philadelphia for Fred Mann, Chippy McGarr, and Jocko Milligan, plus $3,000. This is the first of a number of trades or sales, mostly to Brooklyn.

DECEMBER

2nd The International League disbands. Syracuse, Toronto, Hamilton, and Buffalo split off to form the International Association, while Newark, Jersey City, Wilkes-Barre, and Scranton become the nucleus of the Central League.

7th The Arbitration Committee meets and grants reserve rights to minor league clubs for the first time.

8th In a controversial move the AA doubles its basic admission price to 50 cents. In late August 1888, the league, suffering from decreases in attendance and revenues, reinstitutes the old admission fee.

12th A baseball reporters association is organized. It pledges to work to standardize scoring practices, especially in the gray area of stolen bases.

13th Von der Ahe completes his biggest deal selling Bob Caruthers to Brooklyn for $8,250. The deal was delayed by Caruthers's negotiations with Brooklyn, but he finally agrees to $5,000 for 1888.

1888

JANUARY

2nd   Fred Dunlap signs with Pittsburgh following the sale of his contract by Detroit. He agrees to a $5,000 salary and a $2,000 bonus, making him the highest-paid player to date.

17th   Kansas City is admitted to the American Association to replace the Mets. Even though the Mets were bought out by Brooklyn, their franchise is only considered suspended until suitable playing facilities in Manhattan can be found.

23rd   Harry Spence is hired to manage the Indianapolis (NL) team.

27th   Brooklyn keeps 5 of the recently purchased Mets players and sells the rest of the squad and 4 Brooklyn players to Kansas City for $7,000.

FEBRUARY

2nd   Indianapolis announces that the roof of its new grandstand will hold 42 private boxes, to be sold to season subscribers only.

MARCH

1st   The Washington NL club leaves on its southern tour a day earlier than scheduled, due to a superstition against starting a trip on a Friday.

2nd   The NL meets in New York and abolishes all discounts from the 50-cent minimum admission price.

20th   Albert Spalding announces a baseball tour to Australia next winter with his Chicago team and a squad of NL all-stars.

25th   The St. Louis Browns open the training season with an exhibition game versus the St. Louis Whites, a new Western Association team. The WA will have clubs in 4 cities that also have NL clubs.

APRIL

1st   The Texas League plays its first game, Houston winning at home 3–1 over Galveston before 3,000 fans.

2nd   The Browns beat Detroit 5–3 in New Orleans in the first game of a World Series rematch from last fall. The games are advertised locally as a "World Championship Series."

3rd   Chicago pitching star John Clarkson is sold to Boston for $10,000. With last year's deal for King Kelly, the Beaneaters have acquired a "$20,000 Battery" from the White Stockings.

18th   At Opening Day in the AA, umpire John Gaffney makes news by standing behind the pitcher with men on base.

23rd   The Athletics pile up 28 runs on 23 hits, 5 walks, and 13 Cleveland errors in making the largest score of the season.

27th   Detroit manager Bill Watkins fines captain Ned Hanlon $10 and suspends P Lady Baldwin without pay after Baldwin and the Wolverines are routed in Indianapolis 16–7, dropping the Wolverines' record to 1-5.

29th   Phillie star Charlie Ferguson, 25, a 4-time 20-game winner, dies of typhoid pneumonia.

MAY

1st   After holding out for a $4,000 salary, Tim Keefe wins his 1888 debut for the Giants, beating Boston 6–1.

3rd   In New York, George Gore goes to LF to start the game, but box-seat holders scream for Mike Slattery, and captain Buck Ewing makes the change.

5th   Gid Gardner plays for the Phillies after being traded from Washington for Cupid Childs. But when Childs refuses to play for the Senators, the trade and today's game are nullified.

6th   Long John Reilly hits 2 HRs, giving him 4 in Cincinnati's 4-game series versus Kansas City. Reilly will finish the season with an AA-leading 13 HRs.

9th   Playing in the close quarters of Indianapolis's Athletic Park, Roger Connor hits 3 HRs and the Giants total 7 to tie the existing records. NY wins 18–4.

   With an 18–6 lead after 7 innings, Louisville righthander Elton Chamberlain pitches the final 2 innings lefthanded, holding Kansas City scoreless.

19th   Senator owner Robert C. Hewitt recalls acting manager Burket to Washington after the team loses its 7th straight on the road. Jim Whitney and the owner's son are left in charge.

22nd Future Hall of Fame slugger Ed Delahanty makes his ML debut with the Phillies, going hitless and making 2 errors at 2B. His contract had been purchased from Wheeling in the Tri-State League for $2,000.

25th Boston opens its new Grand Pavilion, an elaborate double-decked structure. Though the Pavilion seats 2,800, 12,000 see the Beaneaters lose their home opener to the Phillies 4–1.

27th Bill "Adonis" Terry hurls his 2nd career no-hitter, beating Kansas City 4–0. Three men walk and 2 more reach on errors. Terry no-hit St. Louis on July 24, 1886.

30th The Brooklyn Bridegrooms, so called because many players married over the winter, move into first place by winning 2 games from previous leader Cincinnati.

JUNE

6th Henry Porter of the Cowboys pitches a no-hitter against Baltimore, walking one and winning 4–0. Meanwhile, Cleveland and Louisville combine for 50 hits as the Spiders outscore the Colonels 23–19.

8th New Louisville owner Mordecai Davidson accepts manager John Kelly's resignation and announces he will manage the club himself.

In the longest game in the NL this year, Detroit beats John Clarkson and Boston 11–5 in 16 innings.

9th The resurgent Wolverines hold off the Beaneaters 10–9 to post their 7th consecutive victory and move to within 2 games of first place.

10th The Athletics play their first official Sunday home game at Gloucester, NJ, or so they think. The AA secretary will later rule the game illegally rescheduled and throw it out of official records.

12th OF Jimmy Ryan, who homered in the first inning, is brought in to pitch with the bases loaded in the 2nd inning. He shuts out the Giants as the Colts rally to win 4–2 to up their NL lead to 4 games.

13th The last-place Senators finally get a legitimate manager when veteran Ted Sullivan arrives.

14th Reds pitching star Tony Mullane suffers a broken nose when hit by a drive in Kansas City. The injury will keep him out of action for 10 days, but his famous good looks will not be permanently damaged.

18th Two AA umpires work the Cleveland-Athletic game. The 2-umpire system had worked well in last fall's WS, but this is believed to be a regular-season first.

20th Future Hall of Famer 1B Jake Beckley makes his ML debut with Pittsburgh, with a double, triple, and stolen base. Beckley started the season with the St. Louis Whites.

21st George Van Haltren pitches a 6-inning no-hitter beating Pittsburgh for Chicago 1–0. He also pitches a hitless 7th, but since the Colts cannot complete their half before the rain, the official score reverts to 6 innings.

22nd Lou Bierbauer of the Athletics establishes the record for second basemen by making 12 putouts in a 9-inning game. This record will not be tied until August 30th, 1966. Oddly, Bierbauer has no assists and 2 errors in today's game.

25th James "Jumbo" Davis of Kansas City makes 5 errors at 3B as the Cowboys fall to the Browns 10–3. He will finish the season with 91 miscues.

30th With permission from the NL, the Phillies reduce admission to 25 cents. Twelve thousand fans turn out to see a one-hit 7–0 victory over Boston by Charlie Buffinton. After averaging 1,123 admissions at the 50-cent rate, attendance will now jump to an average of 4,010.

JULY

5th The AA meets in St. Louis and refuses to allow its clubs to reduce admission prices from 50 cents to 25 cents. It also adopts a system of double substitute umpires in case the assigned umpire fails to show up for a game, one substitute player from each club sharing the duties.

6th The Brooklyn AA team, led by former Browns Bob Caruthers, Dave Foutz, and Doc Bushong, makes its first appearance of the series in St. Louis and is feted with a parade to the ballpark. The 3 pace the Bridegrooms to a 6–2 victory over the Browns to take over first place.

7th   The Southern League collapses under financial strain. The New Orleans club will join a truncated Texas League later this month.

9th   With slugger Sam Thompson already sidelined with a sore arm, Detroit suffers another crippling injury when Hardie Richardson breaks his ankle and is lost for the season.

14th   The AA's substitute umpire system proves a failure after Brooklyn sub Adonis Terry tells his teammates that he heard KC manager Sam Barkley order sub Jim Donahue to call a Bridegroom runner out in the 9th inning of a 5–4 game. The Grooms walk off the field in protest, forfeiting the game 9–0.

17th   Tommy McCarthy's 6 stolen bases pace the Browns to 15 steals and a 10–3 victory over Kansas City. McCarthy also goes 5-for-5 at the plate.

20th   St. Louis regains the AA lead by beating Kansas City 18–5. The Browns will stay in first place the rest of the season.

22nd   The Cleveland club stages its first Sunday game at Beyerle's Park at Geauga Lake, Ohio, 20 miles southeast of town and just across the county line. A total of 4 Sunday games will be played here this summer.

25th   Toad Ramsey misses the Colonels' getaway train in order to avoid a warrant for his arrest at the railroad station. He is arrested later on the complaint of Louisville saloon owners who charge that Ramsey is overdue paying considerable bar tabs.

26th   Ed Seward of the Athletics pitches a 12–2 no-hitter against the Reds. Seward steals 2 bases and scores 3 times himself.

28th   Jimmy Ryan hits 2 triples, 2 singles, and a HR and pitches 7 innings in relief to lead Chicago to a 21–17 decision over Detroit, dropping Detroit into a first-place tie with the Giants. The Colts trail by 2½ games.

31st   Gus Weyhing pitches the Athletics' 2nd no-hitter in 5 games, stopping Kansas City 4–0.

   The New York Giants take over first place by beating Washington 6–1 while Detroit is losing to Indianapolis 7–5 in 11 innings. New York will retain the lead for the remainder of the season.

AUGUST

2nd   Claiming illness, Brooklyn captain Dave Orr misses the practice session. But later in the day he is spotted at Coney Island, and owner Charles Byrne removes him as captain.

3rd   Cowboy rookie Billy Hamilton, recently purchased from Worcester, steals his first base in the ML. Before returning to the minors in 1902, Sliding Billy will amass 937 stolen bases, a record till 1979.

5th   The Athletics hold a Sunday game at Gloucester, NJ, across the river from Philadelphia, beating the Cowboys 6–0. Gloucester will be the site of 30 AA games through the 1890 season.

7th   At a stormy session in Philadelphia, AA owners finally vote to allow 25-cent admission again but drop the percentage system of paying visitors and replace it with a $130-per-game guarantee.

10th   Tim Keefe wins his 19th consecutive game to break Hoss Radbourn's 1884 record. The Giants nip the Alleghenies 2–1 to win their 10th in a row and 18th in 19 games.

12th   St. Louis's Charles "Silver" King posts his 30th win of the season, besting the Athletics with a 2–0 two-hitter. The game is marred by the collapse of an elevated walkway at Sportsman's Park, but there are no serious injuries.

14th   Tim Keefe's winning streak is stopped at 19 games when Gus Krock and the Colts beat the Giants 4–2 before a crowd of 10,240 at the Polo Grounds.

17th   Washington rookie SS Shorty Fuller sets a record by making 4 errors in one inning, allowing Indianapolis to score 6 runs. Fuller is replaced, and the Senators tie the game 7–7 before new SS George Shoch's 2 errors in the 8th open the way for 4 runs and an 11–7 loss.

20th   St. Louis nudges past Brooklyn 1–0 on brilliant baserunning by Arlie Latham. He opens the game with a single, steals 2B, and scores from 2B on an infield out. Silver King wins the pitchers' duel from Mickey Hughes.

21st   After making 6 errors in the final 2 innings to blow a 2–0 lead, Detroit loses to Indianapolis 8–3 for its 16th consecutive loss.

22nd Two one-hitters in the AA today, Jersey Bakely of Cleveland stopping Cincinnati 3–0 and Silver King of St. Louis beating Brooklyn 4–2. King's bid for a no-hitter ends in the 9th inning when Browns outfielders Tip O'Neill and Harry Lyons allow an easy fly to drop between them.

24th Cap Anson goes 5-for-5, and Jimmy Ryan is 4-for-5 with a HR as the Colts rout the Wolverines 14–4. Anson's .344 batting average and Ryan's 16 HRs will be league-leading figures for the season.

25th Tim Keefe wins his 30th game of the season, beating the Phillies 7–0.

29th Australian-born Joe Quinn makes his debut with Boston a memorable one by hitting a game-winning HR in the bottom of the 9th to beat the Giants' Tim Keefe 2–1.

SEPTEMBER

1st St. Louis slugger Tip O'Neill hits a HR over the fence in the 8th inning and lays down a game-winning bunt single in the 10th inning to beat Athletics ace Ed Seward 3–2. O'Neill will win the AA batting title with a .335 average.

3rd Tim Keefe pitches his 8th shutout of the season, the high mark in the ML this year, but he fails to win when Ben Sanders and the Phillies battle the Giants to an 11-inning scoreless tie.

6th Indianapolis tries its 2nd experimental night game (the first was August 22nd) but the natural-gas illumination is inadequate, and the idea is dropped.

12th New York forfeits a game in Chicago when Buck Ewing is injured and cannot continue. With no uniformed substitutes available, the Giants simply leave the field in the 5th inning.

14th Ed Seward wins his 3rd game in 3 days as the Athletics defeat Brooklyn 4–2. Seward has allowed only 13 hits in the 3 games. He will try again tomorrow and allow only 4 hits but will lose to the Grooms 4–2.

15th Ed Morris of Pittsburgh pitches his 4th consecutive shutout, a record that will be unsurpassed in the NL until 1968. Morris's gems include 1–0 and 2–0 victories over the Phillies, a 7-inning 2–0 win over the Senators, and today's 1–0 win over the Giants.

17th Ed Morris's streak is broken when the Giants score in the 2nd inning on doubles by Ewing and Slattery. The run sends Morris to defeat 1–0.

18th Ben Sanders of the Phillies loses his bid for a perfect game when pitching opponent Gus Krock singles with one out in the 9th inning for the Colts. Sanders wins 6–0.

20th In a doubleheader pitching duel, Tony Mullane beats Ed Seward twice 1–0 and 2–1. The Reds total only 9 hits, while the Athletics get 10.

23rd Cincinnati sells starting players Frank Fennelly and John Corkhill. Without them, the Reds will win 13 of their final 16 games.

27th Little-used Ed "Cannonball" Crane pitches a 7-inning no-hitter for the Giants against the Senators, walking 6 and winning 3–0.

30th With the WA season completed and the warring Kansas City clubs having agreed to merge, the Cowboys move their final home game to the Blues' Exposition Park. The game is a 45-hit slugfest with the Cowboys beating the Athletics 26–14. Monk Cline scores 6 runs for KC.

OCTOBER

1st When Indianapolis scores 3 runs in the top of the 8th inning to take a 4–2 lead at Washington, Senator C Connie Mack suddenly complains of a sore finger. The ensuing delay lasts until darkness and forces the game's end, the score reverting to a 7-inning 2–1 Senator victory.

3rd Both the New York Giants (NL) and St. Louis Browns (AA) clinch their respective pennants today.

4th Ed Crane of the Giants strikes out 4 consecutive batters in the 5th inning, one reaching on a missed 3rd strike. Crane finishes with a one-hit 1–0 victory over rookie John Tener of the Colts.

7th Silver King notches his 45th win of the season, 10 more than any other pitcher will get this year. The 20-year-old righthander will also finish leading the ML in games pitched (66), innings (586), complete games (64), and ERA (1.64).

11th New York P Bill George bats leadoff, goes 3-for-6, and pitches a 3-hitter to beat Indianapolis 13–0.

13th The NL season closes on a prosperous note. The Giants finish with a season attendance of 305,000, a league record.

14th The story breaks that Detroit is selling its players and dropping out of the NL. The Cleveland AA club will join the league and get any leftover players.

16th The 10-game World Series opens in New York with the Giants and Tim Keefe edging the Browns and Silver King 2–1. Each hurler allows only 3 hits.

17th The Browns even the series when Icebox Chamberlain blanks the Giants 3–0 on 6 hits.

18th In game 3, Keefe beats King 4–2 thanks to 3 costly errors by St. Louis C Jack Boyle.

19th The series moves to Brooklyn, where the Giants win 6–3 behind the battery of Cannonball Crane and Willard Brown.

20th The largest crowd of the series, 9,124, sees a dramatic 6–4 Giant victory at the Polo Grounds. Trailing 4–1 in the bottom of the 8th, New York scores 5 times, the go-ahead run scoring as 2 St. Louis fielders collide under a pop fly.

22nd With a 12–5 win in Philadelphia, the Giants take a commanding 5-games-to-1 lead in the World Series.

24th In St. Louis, the Browns stay alive in the WS with a 4-run 8th-inning rally that beats the Giants 7–5. Bill White's 2-run single caps the comeback.

25th The Giants clinch New York's first World Championship 6 games to 2 by trouncing the Browns 11–3. Tim Keefe gets his 4th win of the series.

27th The WS ends with St. Louis getting its 2nd "consolation" victory in a row. Tip O'Neill, who was just 5-for-29 in the first 8 games, hits a bases-loaded HR in today's 18–7 romp after having won yesterday's 14–11 contest with a 3-run HR in the 10th inning.

NOVEMBER

4th Al Spalding's Australia-bound baseball tour stages its first tour game in California, the All-Americans beating the Chicagos 14–4 before a crowd of 10,500 in San Francisco.

10th Detroit organizes a club to compete in the International Association next season.

20th The Joint Rules Committee reduces the number of balls for a walk from 5 to 4, establishing the 4 balls/3 strikes count that remains in effect a century later. It also eliminates an out on a foul tip if the catcher catches it within 10 feet of home plate.

21st Cleveland is formally admitted to the NL to replace Detroit, creating a vacancy in the AA.

22nd The NL adopts a salary classification plan that puts all players into 5 categories with a standard salary for each ranging from $1,500 to $2,500. The scheme is vehemently opposed by the players' Brotherhood.

23rd New York announces the sale of John Montgomery Ward to Washington for a record price of $12,000. But Ward, who is on tour, will eventually cancel the deal by refusing to play for the Senators.

DECEMBER

5th Columbus is admitted to the AA to replace Cleveland.

6th The AA votes against adopting the NL's salary classification system, to the surprise of the press and the delight of the Brotherhood.

15th The Tourists play their first game in Australia, drawing a crowd of 5,500 in Sydney.

17th Former Detroit players Deacon White and Jack Rowe purchase a controlling interest in the minor league Buffalo club. Though their reserve rights have been sold to Pittsburgh, both men announce plans to play in Buffalo next year.

1889

JANUARY

1st   The Around-the-World touring squads play a New Year's game in Melbourne, Australia. The Chicagos beat the All-Americas 9–8.

16th   Dallas catcher Charlie Bradley is shot dead by Tom Angus because Bradley had won the favor of Angus's old girlfriend.

22nd   Facing over $30,000 in debts, the Indianapolis team goes bankrupt and surrenders its franchise to the NL.

FEBRUARY

2nd   A new Indianapolis group, headed by John T. Brush, is granted an NL franchise.

8th   In NYC, workers are dismantling fences at the Polo Grounds to cut a street through the property, leaving the Giants without a home for the coming season.

9th   All-America beats Chicago 10–6 in the shadow of the Pyramids outside Cairo.

19th   The tour stages its first game in Europe, playing in Naples, Italy.

22nd   At the Villa Borghesi outside of Rome, the Chicagos edge the All-Americas 3–2 before a crowd that includes King Humbert of Italy.

MARCH

1st   The Philadelphia Phillies head for Jacksonville, FL, for spring training. No other ML clubs will train in the Deep South this season.

3rd   Bobby Mathews goes to court to try and collect $600 that he claims is owed to him by the Athletics for his services as a "coacher" in 1888. If he collects, it will make him the first paid coach in history.

8th   The touring teams play their only game in Paris, the All-Americas winning 6–2 at Parc Aristotique. Chicago SS Ned Williamson suffers a knee injury sliding on the cinder playing field, disabling him until August 14th and effectively ending his days as a top player.

12th   The Tourists play their first game in England at the Surrey County Cricket Club in Kensington Oval, London, in the presence of the Prince of Wales.

22nd   The All America team beats Chicago 7–6 in England's Old Trafford Cricket Stadium. The Manchester *Guardian* said the "general verdict of the more than 1,000 spectators was that the American game was 'slow' and 'wanting in variety.'

24th   The minor league season opens with the California League in San Francisco and Stockton. This year's new rules include the first legal substitution rule and the reduction of balls for a walk from 5 to 4. The substitution rule, which allows a team to designate one man to be put into the game at the captain's discretion at the end of any inning, would soon be modified.

27th   The final game of the tour is played in Dublin. The group sails for America the next day after playing 28 games overseas.

APRIL

9th   Pete Browning signs with Louisville for $1,600. Browning also delivers a signed pledge of abstinence sworn out before a local judge.

15th   Invited to the White House, the Chicago and All-America squads meet with new President Benjamin Harrison. Harrison proves to be quite a baseball fan and would attend many Washington games during his term in office.

24th   Opening Day in the NL. The New York Giants open their season in Jersey City's Oakland Park, losing to Boston 8–7 before a crowd of 3,042. After just one more game in Jersey City, the Giants would relocate at the Mets' old grounds in Staten Island.

29th   The New York Giants play and win their first game 4–2 at St. George Grounds on Staten Island. This picturesque park, home of the AA Mets in 1886 and 1887, houses the Giants and a production of the play *Nero*. The RF is obliged to play out on top of the stage platform, necessitating the use of rubber-soled shoes in wet weather.

MAY

2nd   The St. Louis Browns nearly go on a sitdown strike in support of teammate William "Yank"

Robinson. Robinson had been suspended and fined after a shouting match with owner Chris Von der Ahe, and his indignant teammates had refused to go to Kansas City for their next series. At the last minute, the players board the train, but they would then drop 3 in a row to the Cowboys amid charges that they are losing on purpose.

4th Indianapolis's Jerry Denny goes 6-for-6 with 4 singles, a double, and a HR to lead the Hoosiers over the Pittsburgh Alleghenies 17–12.

5th Brooklyn forfeits a game to the Athletics 9–0 when the unruly crowd at the Bridegrooms' Sunday grounds in Ridgewood, Queens, overruns the field in the 6th inning.

14th Pittsburgh suspends sore-armed pitchers Ed Morris and Pete Conway so the club won't have to pay their salaries while they're disabled. Morris will return to action June 8th, but Conway is through as a ballplayer because of his injury.

19th Fire destroys most of the stand at Brooklyn's Washington Park while the Bridegrooms are on a road trip.

20th The Kansas City Cowboys, after choosing to bat first, score at least one run in every inning against Brooklyn, winning 18–12. The Cowboys become the 2nd team in AA history to score in all 9 innings, Columbus having done so on June 14, 1883.

24th Willie Kuehne sets a new record by accepting 13 chances at 3B. Kuehne makes 3 putouts and 10 assists without an error, a ML record. His brilliant work enables Pittsburgh to best Washington 9–7.

25th Phillie 2B Ed Delahanty suffers a broken collarbone when he slides into Cleveland 2B Cub Stricker in the 5th inning. Delahanty will be out of action until July 30th.

30th Brooklyn draws the largest crowd in AA history, 22,122, for the Bridegrooms' afternoon game against the Browns. An additional 8,462 saw the morning game, as the teams split.

JUNE

7th Louisville slugger Pete Browning hits for the cycle, going 5-for-6, but the Colonels lose to the Athletics 9–7 in 11 innings for their 14th consecutive defeat. The game is staged in Philadelphia as a benefit for the survivors of the Johnstown flood one week before.

8th Playing for Omaha in the small WA ballpark in St. Paul, Jack Crooks goes 5-for-5 with 4 HRs, 5 runs scored, and 13 RBI to lead Omaha to a 19–15 victory. Crooks would hit .344 with 197 runs scored before being sold to Columbus in late September.

9th Darby O'Brien leads the way with 6 steals as the Bridegrooms steal 11 bases and win 12–2 over Louisville. The hapless Colonel battery is Toad Ramsey and Paul Cook.

13th After the Colonels lose for the 19th time, Louisville owner-manager Mordecai Davidson tells the players he will fine them $25 if they lose the next game.

14th The Athletics win their 14th consecutive game, the longest winning streak in the major leagues in 1889.

15th Only 6 Louisville players show up for the game in Baltimore, the others out in protest against owner Davidson, who owes back pay and is now threatening them with fines. Using 3 local recruits, the Colonels lose their 20th in a row 4–2.

17th With the pay and fine situations unresolved, the Louisville regulars return to the lineup and lose a doubleheader 10–6 and 10–0.

19th Washington CF William "Dummy" Hoy throws out 3 Indianapolis runners at home plate, setting a ML record. Hoy also has a single, 2 doubles, and a stolen base, but the Senators still lose 8–3.

22nd Louisville's losing streak reaches 26 in a row, the all-time ML record, when the Colonels lose 2 heartbreakers to St. Louis 7–6, and 3–2 in 10 innings.

23rd The Colonels win, with Farmer Weaver scoring 3 times and Toad Ramsey pitching, Louisville defeats St. Louis 7–3.

24th Louisville owner Mordecai Davidson resigns as team manager, giving doorkeeper Buck McKinney the title. Actual on-the-field authority remains in the hands of captain Chicken Wolf.

30th Jack Stivetts gets the first base hit and first pitching win of his ML career, pitching St. Louis to a 12–7 victory over Louisville. Stivetts would finish his

11-year career with a .297 batting average and 207 pitching victories.

JULY

2nd President Davidson surrenders his financially strapped Louisville franchise to the AA, unable to pay his players' salaries. New local ownership is announced on July 5th.

8th The New York Giants finally open the new Polo Grounds at 155th Street and 8th Avenue with a 7–5 victory over Pittsburgh. In 25 games in exile on Staten Island and in Jersey City, the Giants drew 57,000 fans. In 38 games in their new Manhattan home, they will draw 144,000.

14th A. G. Spalding's plan for classifying minor leagues is printed across the nation. It calls for strict salary and draft-price limits according to the class of the leagues, features that will serve as the basis for a century to come.

24th Joe Dowie of the Orioles goes 5-for-6 in a 17–3 plastering of Louisville. Dowie would wind up with only 17 hits in his big-league career.

25th A fatigued Horace Phillips is given a vacation from managing the Pittsburgh club, captain Fred Dunlap taking over. On August 1st, Phillips would suffer a mental breakdown and eventually be placed in an asylum.

26th Cleveland loses 8–4 despite a fluke HR by Jay Faatz, who hits a ball that ricochets off of Pittsburgh 3B Jim White's foot and goes into the stands, giving Faatz time to circle the bases.

29th Poor baserunning by the pitcher costs Baltimore dearly against St. Louis. In the 2nd game of a doubleheader, Matt Kilroy pitches a 7-inning no-hitter but has to settle for a 0–0 tie because he fails to touch 3B while scoring a run.

AUGUST

7th Cleveland scores 14 runs in the 3rd inning, still the record for that frame, and beats Washington 20–6. Mike Sullivan, making his first start for the Senators after 5 relief appearances, takes the entire pounding.

15th Larry Twitchell has a 6-for-6 day at the plate with a single, double, 3 triples, and a HR. The 5 extra-base hits tie a record set in 1885. Twitchell also pitches to 2 batters in the 3rd inning before returning to the outfield. Cleveland wins 19–8 over Boston, and becomes the first team in NL history to score in all 9 innings in a single game.

SEPTEMBER

1st After having led the AA race all season except for 3 days in April, St. Louis falls to 2nd place behind Brooklyn after losing to Columbus 6–5 on a 10th-inning HR by Dave Orr.

7th In the most controversial game in AA history, the Browns walk off the field in Brooklyn while leading 4–2 in the 9th inning. They claim it is too dark to play, but the lighted candles in front of their bench by owner Chris Von der Ahe make umpire Fred Goldsmith determined to finish the game no matter what. Several St. Louis players are hit with bottles as they leave the grounds.

8th Claiming they cannot count on their personal safety, the Browns fail to show up for the scheduled Sunday game with the Bridegrooms at Ridgewood. The forfeit pushes the Browns 4½ games behind.

10th New York Giants pitcher Mickey Welch strikes out as the first pinch hitter in ML history.

12th Clarkson pitches and wins both games of a doubleheader for Boston over Cleveland, allowing just 10 hits total in the 3–2 and 5–0 victories, which put Boston 2 games ahead of New York in the race.

13th Hoss Radbourn pitches a complete double-header for Boston, too, but fails to win either game. After losing the opener to the Spiders 3–0, he has to hit a HR himself in the 9th inning of the nightcap to salvage a 4–4 tie.

18th Tommy McCarthy steals 2B, 3B, and home in the 7th inning of a 7–2 St. Louis victory in Kansas City.

23rd An emergency meeting of the American Association Board of Directors reverses the St. Louis forfeit of September 7th, the game being ruled as a 4–2 Browns victory, although the forfeit of September 8th still stands.

25th The Brotherhood of Professional Base ball Players' organizational plan for a new Players' League is leaked to the press in New York. It calls for clubs to be owned jointly by players and capitalists.

27th The Philadelphia NL club releases union activists George Wood and Dan Casey. Meanwhile, the Boston club announces the purchase of the entire WA champion Omaha team for 1890. This latter deal would not actually take place.

OCTOBER

2nd King Kelly shows up drunk and is taken by the police when he threatens umpire McQuade. Boston loses 7–1 and falls behind New York, which wins 6–3. Sam Thompson of the Phillies hits his 20th HR of the season. The AA HR leader, Harry Stovey, hits 19 this season, considered a greater achievement because of the bigger parks in the AA.

4th Both contenders win again, setting up the final day with New York in front of Boston by percentage points .656 to .654. Each team has the option of playing one or two games tomorrow, so NY manager Jim Mutrie is in Pittsburgh to watch the Boston game. He is ready to wire to Cleveland if the Beaneaters are going to play an extra game, so that the Giants can also play one.

5th New York wins the pennant on the final day by beating Cleveland 5–3 while Boston loses in Pittsburgh 6–1. This makes doubleheaders unnecessary.

6th Brooklyn wins its last home game 9–0 over the Athletics in 6 innings before a crowd of 2,488, bringing the Bridegrooms' home attendance for the season to 353,690, a ML record.

9th Charlie Reilly hits a record 2 HRs in his ML debut with Columbus to lead the Babies to a 10–6 victory over the Athletics. Only Bob Nieman (9/14/51) and Bert Campaneris (7/23/64) will match this.

10th Charlie Reilly hits another HR, giving 3 in his first 2 games, as Columbus beats the Athletics 5–0.

18th The best-of-11 World Series between Brooklyn and New York opens at the Polo Grounds with the Bridegrooms winning 12–10 in 8 innings.

19th The Giants bounce back at Washington Park with a 6–2 victory behind the 4-hit pitching of Ed "Cannonball" Crane.

22nd After an off day and a rainout, the WS resumes in New York. The Bridegrooms build up a 6–2 lead and then barely hold on to win 8–7. Umpire John Gaffney calls the game because of darkness in the top of 9th inning with the Giants having the bases loaded and one out.

23rd In a 6-inning game delayed by arguments, the Giants tie the score with a 5-run top of the 6th only to see the Grooms win it in the bottom 10–7 on a 3-run HR by Oyster Burns. Brooklyn leads the series 3 games to one.

24th The Giants pound the Bridegrooms' 40-game winner Bob Caruthers for 11 hits and 24 total bases and win easily 11–3. Battery mates Cannonball Crane and Willard Brown and 2B Danny Richardson all homer for the victors.

25th New York evens the series when Hank O'Day beats Adonis Terry in a 2–1 extra-inning pitchers' duel.

28th The Giants pile up 12 runs in the first 4 innings against Terry and trounce the Grooms 16–7. New York P Crane posts his 4th win of the series.

29th The Giants win their 2nd consecutive WS by taking this year's best-of-11 matchup in 9 games. After spotting the Bridegrooms 2 runs in the first, the Giants rally to win 3–2 behind O'Day's pitching.

NOVEMBER

5th The Brotherhood publishes a "Manifesto" in which it claims that "players have been bought, sold and exchanged as though they were sheep instead of American citizens." This bold statement constitutes a declaration of war between the Brotherhood and ML officials which will soon explode.

7th The Brotherhood and its backers meet to begin preliminary work on the organization of the Players' League.

14th Disgusted by the conduct of the Association and especially the perceived dominance of St. Louis president Von der Ahe, Brooklyn president Charles Byrne and Cincinnati owner Aaron Stern withdraw from the AA and join the NL. Indianapolis and Washington refuse to resign from the league, and that organization decides to go as a 10-club circuit.

15th   Kansas City also drops out of the AA.

25th   Jack Glasscock, claiming that his pledge to the Brotherhood does not constitute a binding contract, signs with the Indianapolis NL club, thus becoming the first "double jumper."

30th   Baltimore drops out of the AA and joins the Atlantic Association.

DECEMBER

16th   The PL is formally organized with Colonel E. A. McAlpin of New York as president. The league will not allow player transfers without the player's consent, excess profits will be split between the capitalists and the players, and prize money will be awarded to the teams in the order of their finish.

17th   The PL adopts some new rules, including the 2-umpire system and an increase in pitching distance from 55½ feet to 57 feet. A lively ball is chosen, assuring high scores in the upcoming season.

18th   The Brotherhood meets and expels members who have signed NL contracts, including Jack Glasscock, John Clarkson, Kid Gleason, and George Miller. Among those expelled, Jake Beckley, Joe Mulvey, and Ed Delahanty would eventually jump back to the PL and be reinstated.

1890

JANUARY

9th Brooklyn is selected by the AA as a new franchise. Syracuse, Rochester, and Toledo were selected earlier. However, the Brooklyn team will be transferred to Baltimore before the end of the season.

16th Samuel Gompers, president of the American Federation of Labor, and 3 other labor leaders pledge support for the PL at a league meeting in Philadelphia.

25th M. P. Betts, secretary of the National League of Great Britain, asks for the addresses of American players living in Great Britain who might be interested in playing in the new league. Few respond.

28th In the first of many lawsuits filed against PL players by their former teams, the judge refuses to grant an injunction against John Ward, president of the Brotherhood. His decision, echoed frequently by other judges, states that the "want of fairness and mutuality" in the standard NL contract, specifically the clauses relating to the reserve rule, "[is] apparent."

FEBRUARY

1st The NL Schedule Committee meets in Pittsburgh and decides on a schedule, but for security reasons does not release it. Pittsburgh NL president Nimick comments that "if I had my way, I would duplicate all the home games of the Brotherhood clubs." Hence the reason for security.

17th New York NL officials fail in an effort to woo star player and Brotherhood officer Buck Ewing to rejoin the Giants. Although he has rejected an offer reported at $33,000 for 3 years, Ewing is later accused by some players of spying for the NL.

MARCH

6th The NL releases a schedule with 10 teams, including the Brooklyn and Cincinnati franchises formerly in the AA. Since the NL is expected to trim back down to 8 teams, the release of this schedule is seen as a ruse to throw off the PL.

27th The application of an all-black club made up of ex–Cuban Giants is rejected by the Inter-State League.

APRIL

19th The NL's biggest Opening Day crowd, 6,311 at Chicago, watches 30-year-old righthander Wild Bill Hutchison beat Cincinnati 5–4, the first of his 42 wins and 65 complete games out of 66 starts. He'll work 603 innings and relieve 5 times while sporting a 2.70 ERA.

22nd Philadelphia and Syracuse (AA) combine for a ML record 19 stolen bases in a single game.

27th St. Louis (AA) P Jack Stivetts strikes out the first 7 Columbus batters he faces. He finishes the game with 12 K's.

MAY

1st The 577 consecutive-game streak of 3B George Pinckney of Brooklyn (NL) comes to an end when he is spiked in a game in Boston, which is later rained out. He has played every inning of the 577 games (almost all of them with Brooklyn, AA) since September 21, 1885, including 2 games as SS and one as 3B-P. The every-inning record would last until surpassed by Cal Ripken, Jr. of Baltimore in 1985.

3rd In this issue of the New York *Clipper*, covering the 2nd week of the season, AA game reports and box scores are omitted, indicating the lack of interest in the AA in the wake of the NL-PL war. For the rest of the season AA fans will have to settle for line scores and occasional league summaries.

5th For the first time in this busy litigation season an injunction is granted against a player, John Pickett. The judge rules that Pickett's acceptance of advance money from his Kansas City club bound him to that club.

8th Cleveland's Willie McGill hurls a complete-game 14–5 victory over Buffalo (PL) at age 16, the youngest ever to perform the feat. The Buffalo lineup includes Connie Mack, Dummy Hoy, and Deacon White, at 42 the oldest player in the ML.

12th A scoreless pitching duel between future Hall of Famers Amos Rusie (New York, NL) and Charles "Kid" Nichols is broken up by a tape measure HR by New York OF Mike Tiernan in the 13th inning.

20th Buffalo plays a 4-game series at Brooklyn during which an attendance of 80 is recorded at one game.

23rd Chicago's 10–8, 10-inning win at Philadelphia is thrown out by NL directors when umpire McQuaid admits he made an error in not allowing Philadelphia to send OF Billy Grey in as a sub during the game.

New York and Pittsburgh (NL) combine for an NL-record 17 stolen bases in a single game.

25th After a Louisville-Syracuse game played in Three Rivers, NY, part of the grandstand collapses, throwing 50 or more people to the ground. No deaths are reported, but many are injured.

30th Chicago NL P Bill Hutchison wins a doubleheader against Brooklyn with 2 complete games 5–1 and 7–3.

Philadelphia PL OF Joe Mulvey makes a "simply wonderful" catch with his left (gloved) hand. Even though almost all players wear gloves now, a one-handed grab is still cause for celebration.

31st New York PL players George Gore, Buck Ewing, and Roger Connor hit consecutive HRs in the 8th inning against Cincinnati. This feat will not be matched until May 10, 1894.

PL secretary Frank Brunell sends a letter to PL umpires notifying them about complaints of "the monotony of games in several cities caused by the apparent apathy of the players."

JUNE

1st Professional baseball is born in England as 4 teams—Derby, Preston, Stoke, and Birmingham—form a league. Four Americans are imported to provide instructions for the teams, made up mostly of English pro footballers.

NL pioneer manager Harry Wright, in his 7th year at Philadelphia, is taken ill and temporarily loses his sight. Club owner Al Reach takes over.

2nd Ed Delahanty of Cleveland (PL) goes 6-for-6 with 5 runs as his club crashes Chicago 20–7.

5th Rookie RHP Billy Rhines, 21, pitches Cincinnati to a 9–1 win over Pittsburgh (NL), starting a 13-game winning streak that moves the Reds to a 33-13 record and 4-game lead over Brooklyn.

In the top of the 3rd inning at a Buffalo-Cleveland PL contest, a bolt of lightning hits the metal ball atop a flagstaff, splintering it and severely damaging the grandstand. No injuries are reported, but panic is widespread.

6th Harry Wright, manager of Philadelphia (NL), is now said to be able to see while wearing colored glasses. A serious illness 5 days earlier had blinded him temporarily, making him the only blind manager in ML history.

10th St. Louis AA P Jack Stivetts hits 2 HRs (and strikes out 10) in a game. He later duplicates this batting feat on August 6, 1891, and on June 12, 1896, making him the first pitcher to achieve this. The only 2 pitchers to match this achievement are Wes Farrell (who had 5 such games) and Don Newcombe.

13th Pittsburgh (NL) begins a tailspin, winning just one of 22 games in heading to a record 113 losses and .169 PCT, the lowest since the NL's first year when Cincinnati was .138 in a 65-game schedule.

15th Lefthanded 2B Bill Greenwood plays SS for Rochester versus Syracuse today and becomes the only lefthanded throwing SS to participate in a triple play.

21st Charles "Silver" King of Chicago (PL) pitches an 8-inning no-hitter, but loses to Brooklyn 1–0. Chicago bats first and King does not pitch the last of the 9th.

23rd In field games, New York (PL) C Harry "Farmer" Vaughan makes a throw of 402 feet 2½ inches, beating John Hatfield's 400 foot 7½ inch record of 1872 and winning a $25 purse.

Rochester and Brooklyn (AA) play an exhibition at Elmira; the players are served with warrants for breaking the Sunday laws.

26th Philadelphia (PL) scores 14 runs in the 6th inning against Buffalo on the way to a 30-run performance.

JULY

7th Brooklyn begins a 15-3 run that brings them closer to PL-leading Boston as Gus Weyhing beats Chicago 4–0 for one of his 30 wins. Boston is never caught and finishes 6½ games in front.

11th Brooklyn moves into the NL lead by beating the Reds 9–2 for its 9th win in a row. The team finishes 6 games in front as the Reds fall to 4th.

12th A local boy named Lewis, whose first name is unknown, shows up at the Brooklyn (PL) ball grounds and is given a tryout by Buffalo. He works 3 innings, is battered for 13 hits, walks 7, and leaves trailing 20–5. Buffalo rallies but loses 28–16. Lewis leaves a 60.00 career ERA in the record books.

15th New York (NL) owner John B. Day tells other NL owners he must have $80,000 or sell out to the PL. Spalding, Anson, Brush, and others come to the rescue to prevent New York's withdrawal from the league.

20th After Rochester beats Columbus in a Sunday game 8–3 at Windsor Beach, both teams are arrested.

23rd Harry Stovey, the leading slugger of the Boston Players' League club, hits his 100th career home run. He is the first ML player to attain this milestone.

26th Philadelphia (PL) downs Buffalo 30–12, scoring 14 in the 6th. Charles "Lady" Baldwin absorbs all the punishment, giving up 28 hits.

27th Brooklyn (AA) leads Columbus 13–8 in the 8th at the Long Island Grounds in a Sunday game when they run out of baseballs and are forced to forfeit the game.

AUGUST

6th Long John Reilly, hitting for the cycle for the 3rd time in his career, leads Cincinnati (NL) to a 16–3 romp over Pittsburgh. This cycle record would later be equaled by Bob Meusel and Babe Herman.

25th Brooklyn (AA) disbands.

The Baltimore club of the Atlantic Association finishes the season in first place.

28th Sid Farrar of Philadelphia (PL) hits 3 triples and knocks in 6 runs in a 15–2 stampede of Buffalo.

SEPTEMBER

1st Brooklyn wins 3 games in one day, feasting on Pittsburgh 10–9, 3–2, and 8–4. The 3 losses extend Pittsburgh's losing streak to 22; it will reach 24 before they win again.

6th Toledo plays at Baltimore (AA) and one player from each side is picked to umpire. With the score 2–2 after 7, the Toledo ump calls the game because of darkness, whereupon the Baltimore ump forfeits the game to the Orioles.

14th When Buffalo (PL) captain Jay Faatz and VP Frank disagree, Connie Mack is appointed captain for the rest of the season, unofficially marking the start of his managing career.

15th Lefthander Ledell "Cannonball" Titcomb, 24, pitches a no-hitter for Rochester over Syracuse (AA) 7–0. It's his only shutout of his last ML season.

17th Out of money, the AA Athletics disband, releasing or selling all players. Among players sold are OF Curt Welch, P Sadie McMahon, and C Wilbert Robinson to Baltimore. The so-called reorganized Athletics will finish out the schedule losing all their remaining 22 games.

OCTOBER

2nd Chicago (PL) P Mark Baldwin beats New York 4–0 for his 34th win versus 24 losses. For the 2nd straight year he pitches 54 complete games and over 500 innings.

3rd Chicago's John Luby (NL) wins his 17th consecutive game of the season, a 3–2 victory over Amos Rusie and the Giants.

9th Cincinnati (NL) owner Aaron Stern sells to PL owners for $40,000. Committees from the 3 leagues meet to begin negotiations toward a settlement of the war. PL owners from Cleveland, Brooklyn, and New York seek consolidation with the NL. A truce, during which all contracts will be respected, is agreed upon. It is left to owners in each city to arrange their own deals.

12th Henry Gastright (Columbus, AA) hurls an 8–inning no-hitter against Toledo, winning 6–0.

17th The AA and NL refuse to permit the PL champion to take part in a World Series. Interest in the post-season meeting of league champions is lukewarm as Brooklyn wins a 9–0 opener over Louisville behind Adonis Terry (26-16). After breaking even in 7 games, with one tie, the teams abandon the series.

20th Upset over PL backers seeking deals without consulting them, the Brotherhood meets and votes to add a players' committee to the 3 league committees for the next meeting. John M. Ward, Ned Hanlon, and Arthur Irwin are elected. Ward makes a long, spirited plea for the players' participation. Al Spalding, eager to split the PL backers and players, argues against them. The original 3 league committees vote 2–1 against the players' involvement. Each PL backer is now out to make his own deal and the PL is dead.

NOVEMBER

22nd At the AA annual meeting in Louisville, the Athletics are expelled for violating the constitution. A new team in Philadelphia is admitted, plus entries from Boston, Washington, and Chicago, replacing Syracuse, Toledo, and Rochester.

DECEMBER

29th After the New York and Pittsburgh PL clubs combine with their NL rivals, Spalding buys out Chicago's PL backer Addison for $18,000, some of which goes to pay off unpaid salaries and reimburse players half of their investments. Spalding gets the club's grandstand, equipment, and player contracts.

1891

JANUARY

14th The NL votes to allow the AA to place a team in Boston, despite the vehement opposition of the owners of the Boston NL club.

16th The NL, AA, and Western Association sign a new National Agreement calling for the creation of a 3-man Board of Control to settle disputes between clubs and leagues.

FEBRUARY

6th The New York Giants' salary list is leaked to the press. It shows a total player payroll of $54,600 with Buck Ewing's $5,500 salary topping the scale.

14th The National Board of Control "reluctantly" awards 3 disputed players (Lou Bierbauer, Harry Stovey, and Connie Mack) to the NL clubs that signed them despite the prior claims of the AA.

17th The AA meets and indignantly unseats President Thurman, then withdraws from the National Agreement. This means "war," and the AA's first move is to switch its franchise from Chicago to Cincinnati to compete with the NL in the Queen City.

21st The National Board of Control, with Thurman still acting as chairman, declares all AA players fair game for contract raiding.

MARCH

1st Pittsburgh and Cleveland are the 2 NL clubs making the heaviest raids against AA player contracts. Pittsburgh further earns its new nickname of "Pirates" by signing Pete Browning and Scott Stratton away from Louisville.

25th Albert G. Spalding retires from active participation in the affairs of the Chicago club and the NL. James A. Hart will assume the club presidency.

APRIL

3rd The Cleveland Spiders beat Pittsburgh 6–3 in St. Augustine in the first spring training game between 2 ML teams ever played in Florida.

6th The International League changes its name to the Eastern Association because it no longer has any Canadian clubs.

8th Opening Day in the AA with 4 games. In St. Louis, the Cincinnati Kellys walk off the field in the 9th inning after new umpire Billy Gleason makes several questionable decisions in favor of his old Browns teammates. Gleason will be fired in 2 days, and the game will be replayed.

11th Clark Griffith, 21 years old, makes his ML debut, pitching the St. Louis Browns to a 13–5 victory over Cincinnati. After spending much of 1892 and 1893 in the minors, Griffith will return to remain active in the majors as a pitcher, manager, and club owner until his death in 1955.

13th The Washington Statesmen (AA) open their new National Park before a crowd of 4,365. This site at 7th Street and Georgia Avenue, N.W., will serve ML baseball in the nation's capital through 1961, except for one 4-year period (1900–1903).

20th Washington 2B Fred Dunlap, once considered the greatest in the game, suffers a career-ending broken leg.

22nd Opening Day in the NL. The largest crowd (17,355) is in New York, where the Giants lose to the Boston Beaneaters 4–3 on a 9th-inning muff by CF George Gore.

26th Local Cincinnati authorities allow the Kellys to play their Sunday game, which is won by the Louisville Colonels (AA) 12–6, but then arrest all the players on charges of violating the state's Blue Laws.

27th The Bridegrooms play their home opener at Eastern Park in the East New York section of Brooklyn. The park was used by the PL club in 1890, and the NL club will occupy it for 7 years. It is located near a complex of streetcar and suburban railroad lines, forcing fans to "dodge trolleys" to get to the gates. This spawns the name "Trolley Dodger" or "Dodgers" for the ball club.

MAY

1st Cleveland opens new League Park at 66th and Lexington with Cy Young pitching the Spiders to a 12–3 victory over the Reds before a crowd of about 9,500.

5th Pittsburgh's Pete Browning bunts into a triple play in the top of the 6th inning and makes an error to allow a run in the bottom of the frame, causing Pittsburgh to lose to the Chicago Colts 1–0.

11th After having played 14 home games this season at Oriole Park, the Baltimore club inaugurates its new Union Park on Huntington Avenue and Barclay Street with an 8–4 victory before 10,412 fans. The Orioles' new home will serve through 1899.

The Louisville Courier-Journal announces that yesterday the John Chapman Club—a top Louisville semi-pro team named for the Colonels' manager—defeated the Mafia Ball Club.

19th The Board of Control rescinds the new scoring rule requiring scorers to compile "runs batted in." This rule, which was adopted last winter, will still be used by the AA, however.

30th Jack Stivetts wins both the morning and afternoon games for the Browns, although he leaves both games early when St. Louis gets out to big leads in both games. The Athletics lose 17–2 and 15–3.

JUNE

7th The Boston Reds regain the AA lead by edging the Browns 6–5 before a St. Louis crowd of 17,439, the largest of the AA season.

10th Cleveland Spiders C Chief Zimmer makes 6 errors, and the opposing Brooklyns steal 10 bases. The Bridegrooms win by only 9–8.

11th Herman Long goes 6-for-6 with 4 runs scored as the Boston Beaneaters climb back over .500 with a 14–6 rout of the Chicago Colts.

13th A new ML attendance record is set as 22,289 jam the Polo Grounds to see the Giants nip the Colts 8–7.

19th Playing on a muddy field, NY 3B Lew Whistler sets a record by making 4 errors in one inning as the Giants lose to the Phillies 11–4.

22nd Tom Lovett of Brooklyn no-hits New York 6–0, giving up 3 walks.

25th Tom Brown and Bill Joyce of the Boston Reds become the first pair in ML history to open a game with back-to-back HRs, starting Boston off to a 13–5 defeat of Sadie McMahon and the Baltimore Orioles.

JULY

3rd The Columbus Buckeyes release Jack O'Connor for habitual drunkenness. He will resurface with Cleveland next year and remain an active player through 1907.

7th Baltimore sets a ML record by leaving 18 men on base in an 8–2 loss to the Cincinnati Kellys. This record would not be broken until September 21, 1956.

16th After Louisville falls into last place in the AA, a Louisville *Courier-Journal* headline asks that someone "Give Them a Commercial Name to Advertise Something Outside the City." This headline reflects the relationship between baseball and business in the 19th-century city.

18th After the AA grants Boston the right to lower its admission price from 50 cents to 25 cents, 4,723 pay to see the Reds beat the Colonels 9–0. Only 986 had attended yesterday's game.

23rd The Boston Reds win their 11th game in a row, beating the Washington Statesmen 6–1 in a 5-inning affair featuring two HRs by captain Hugh Duffy. This constitutes the longest winning streak in the AA.

24th The Browns score in all 8 innings in which they bat, as they trounce Cincinnati 20–12. Frank Dwyer pitches the entire game for the losing Kellys.

25th An over-the-fence drive by Cliff Carroll caps a 4-run rally in the bottom of the 9th to give the Chicago Colts a 15–14 victory in Cleveland. Although the ground rules at this park call for a HR on balls hit over all OF fences, the winning run scores from 2B, so Carroll gets credit for only a double.

27th Future Hall of Famer Joe Kelley makes his ML debut with the Boston Beaneaters, singling off of Mickey Welch in his first at bat.

30th Two ML clubs change managers. Bill McGunnigle takes the reins in Pittsburgh, Ned Hanlon being demoted from manager-captain to just captain. And Dan Shannon replaces Charley Snyder in both capacities with Washington.

31st New York Giants P Amos Rusie hurls a no-hitter against Brooklyn, winning 6–0. He walks 8, hits one, and fans 4.

AUGUST

3rd Scott Stratton shuts out the Philadelphia Athletics on one hit 6–0, to snap Louisville's losing streak at 15 games, the longest in the major leagues this year.

6th Jack Stivetts of the St. Louis Browns hits 2 HRs and strikes out 10 in a game.

7th A run-scoring wild pitch by John Clarkson allows Chicago to beat Boston 6–5 in 10 innings. This makes 4 straight that the Colts have beaten the Beaneaters in extra innings.

17th The AA franchise in Cincinnati folds. Milwaukee of the Western Association is elected to take its place, a move that dooms that minor league. The Brewers sign 4 of the Kellys and several players from other WA clubs. "The King of Ballplayers," Mike Kelly, joins the Boston Reds (AA) and is appointed captain.

18th Milwaukee is victorious in its first AA game, beating the Browns in St. Louis 7–2.

21st George Hemming, who fanned Harry Stovey 5 times on June 30th, fans Stovey 4 times today as the Bridegrooms beat the Beaneaters 8–1.

22nd Walt Wilmot of the Colts draws 6 bases on balls from Spider pitchers Lee Viau and Cy Young to set a ML record for walks in a game. Jimmie Foxx (6/16/38) and Andre Thornton (5/2/84) will be the only players to tie this record.

25th The Boston NL club shocks the baseball world by announcing the signing of King Kelly away from the rival Boston AA club, thereby wrecking peace talks between the leagues. Kelly signs through the 1892 season for a total of $25,000, a figure that will not be topped by any player until the Federal League war of 1914 and 1915.

31st In the season's best pitching duel, Chicago's Bill Hutchinson and New York's Amos Rusie battle to an 11-inning scoreless tie.

SEPTEMBER

4th "Old Man" Cap Anson shows up for today's game wearing a wig and a long white beard, much to the delight of the Chicago crowd. Anson wears this costume throughout the game, which his Colts win

over the Beaneaters 5–3, stretching Chicago's lead to 7 games over Boston.

9th Disgusted with owner Von der Ahe's constant criticism, St. Louis stars Tommy McCarthy and Jack Stivetts sign with the Boston Beaneaters (NL) for 1892.

10th In its first AA home game, the Milwaukee team blasts out a 30–3 triumph to the delight of 2,450 fans. The Brewers would log a record of 14-5 home record by the season's end.

12th Mark Baldwin of Pittsburgh pitches 2 complete-game victories in Brooklyn, winning 13–3 and 8–4 while allowing a total of 11 hits. This gives him 4 wins in 6 days.

14th Wild Bill Hutchinson posts his 40th win of the season, beating Boston 7–1.

18th Billy Hamilton steals 4 bases to pace the Phillies to an 11–6 decision over the Cincinnati Reds. Hamilton will finish the season with a league-leading 115 steals, breaking the 100 mark for the 3rd year in a row.

25th The Boston Reds clinch the AA pennant with a 6–2 victory in Baltimore.

The Boston Beaneaters win their 10th in a row, beating the Phillies 6–3, thanks to 3 errors by 3B Ed Mayer.

28th The Giants arrive in Boston without their two best pitchers (Amos Rusie and John Ewing) and their best hitter (Roger Connor) and arrange to play 5 games in 3 days. They lose the first one 11–3 as the Beaneaters move to within one-half game of Chicago.

30th The Beaneaters complete a 5–game sweep of the Giants and vault into first place in the NL race with just 3 days to go. Chicago president James A. Hart protests the extra makeup games played by the Giants in Boston. Several sportswriters are convinced that the eastern clubs have purposely let Boston win the recent games, especially after 4 Giants are retired at home plate in the final game, which Boston wins 5–3.

OCTOBER

1st Boston clinches the NL pennant with its 17th consecutive victory, 6–1, in Philadelphia, while Chicago is losing to Cincinnati by the same score.

2nd   In the first-ever ML game in Minnesota, the Milwaukee Brewers beat the Columbus Buckeyes 5–0 in Minneapolis's Athletic Park.

Boston wins its 18th in a row as Kid Nichols becomes a 30-game winner for the first of 7 times in his career.

4th   Browns rookie Ted Breitenstein gets his first start on the final day of the season and hurls a no-hitter versus Louisville. He wins 8–0 while walking one and facing the minimum 27 batters.

6th   The AA season closes with Baltimore winning 2 games in Washington to capture 3rd place, one-half game ahead of the Athletics. There will be no all-Boston World Series because of the intransigence of the Beaneater owners.

17th   A New York judge rules that the Giants do not have to put a roof on their bleacher seats, despite a recent ordinance passed by the Board of Aldermen.

NOVEMBER

4th   Charlie Comiskey, having had enough of Browns owner Chris Von der Ahe, signs to manage and captain the NL Cincinnati Reds.

11th   The NL meets and dismisses the charges of collusion and game throwing against the eastern clubs brought by Chicago, thereby formally giving Boston the pennant. The league also plans its strategy for conquering the association by consolidating the 4 strongest AA clubs into a 12-team league for next year.

16th   The Louisville Colonels club is sold at auction to satisfy a $6,359.40 mortgage. The new ownership is headed by Dr. T. Hunt Stuckey.

26th   A series for the championship of the Pacific Coast begins between the champions of the California League (San Jose) and the Pacific Northwest League pennant winners (Portland). The series will last until January 10 with San Jose winning 10 games to 9.

DECEMBER

17th   The American Association passes out of existence after ten years as a settlement is finally reached. Four AA clubs (St. Louis, Louisville, Washington, and Baltimore) join with the NL 8 in a 12-club league formally styled "The National League and American Association of Professional Base Ball Clubs." The other 4 AA clubs are bought out for about $130,000. The NL will allow Sunday games for the first time but will retain its 50 cent minimum admission price.

1892

JANUARY

9th "Slide, Kelly, Slide," by George Gaskin, makes the popular music charts, the first baseball song to do so.

Cap Anson is quoted in the New York *Clipper* as saying that "I don't care if they can't field a little bit. In my experience I have found that a man can be taught to almost stop cannon balls, but it is a very difficult task to teach them to line 'em out."

14th Former Chicago star Frank "Silver" Flint dies of consumption.

FEBRUARY

19th Dan Brouthers, batting champion of the AA while with the Boston Reds in 1891, signs a contract to play with the Brooklyn Nationals. It will be his 5th team in 5 years.

MARCH

1st The first meeting of the united NL and AA takes place in New York. Only 4 teams from the collapsed 1891 AA are invited to join the NL, which will expand to 12 teams with a 154-game schedule split into 2 championship series.

12th A bill before the New York State Assembly seeks "To prohibit the employment of females as baseball players."

APRIL

12th Inaugurating the first 12-team NL season, Amos Rusie of the New York Giants outpitches Tim Keefe of the Philadelphia Phillies 5–4.

The famous Boston Beaneaters battery of John Clarkson and King Kelly is too much for the Senators in Washington. Clarkson helps his cause with a HR in a 14–4 victory.

16th Ohio governor William McKinley participates in the WL opening game in Columbus, which defeats Toldeo 8–5. Ironically, McKinley would never attend a ML game as president.

17th The first Sunday game in NL history features the hometown Cincinnati Reds defeating the St. Louis Browns 5–1. Bid McPhee contributes a HR.

19th Cincinnati's Tony Mullane surrenders only a bunt single in a 3–0 win over the Chicago Colts.

22nd The Pittsburgh Pirates score 12 runs in the first inning against Ted Breitenstein and Bob Caruthers of St. Louis. Elmer Smith of the Pirates gets 2 bases on balls, marking the first time a player is walked twice in one inning.

23rd Bill Shindle of the Baltimore Orioles has 5 errors at shortstop in a 19–9 loss to Boston in the 2nd game of a twin bill. He also makes 2 in the opener. He will make 78 errors by the end of the season.

24th Notre Dame defeats Michigan 6–4 in the first intercollegiate varsity game for the Irish. The Notre Dame winner is pitching and batting star "Ringer" Willie McGill, a former student at the elementary school in the college. Though only 18 years of age, McGill is now in his 4th professional season. He will play for the Cincinnati Reds later in the year.

29th Cleveland Spiders SS Ed McKean accidentally shoots himself through the "fleshy portion" of his finger with a revolver. He will recover within a week and go on to drive in 93 runs, albeit with the lowest batting average and HR total of his career to date.

30th Dr. S. B. Talcott, superintendent of the State Lunatic Asylum in New York, declares in the New York *Clipper* that "I believe that baseball is a homeopathic cure for lunacy. It is a kind of craze in itself, and gives the lunatics a new kind of crazing to relieve them of the malady which afflicts their minds."

MAY

4th Cincinnati players Billy Rhines, Jerry Harrington, and Eddie Burke are disciplined after getting involved in a fight the previous evening. Harrington and Burke are each fined $100, but Rhines—who won 45 games for the Reds over the last 2 years—is suspended without pay for the rest of the season. Nevertheless, Rhines will throw 84 ineffective innings this year.

6th John Clarkson and Elton "Icebox" Chamberlain pitch a 14-inning scoreless tie. Clarkson limits the

Reds to 4 hits, one fewer than the Beaneaters can manage off of Chamberlain.

St. Louis southpaw Ted Breitenstein's no-hitter is broken up in the 9th, when 2 singles produce the Bridegrooms' only runs in a 14–2 loss.

7th Bill Hutchinson hurls a one-hitter, permitting only a Jim O'Rourke 9th-inning single, to lead the Chicago Colts to an 8–0 win over the Giants.

11th Baltimore defeats St. Louis 5–3 in a game in which, according to the New York *Clipper*, the only "curious feature was the fact that all of the runs scored were earned." St. Louis OF John Crooks hits a leadoff HR for the 2nd time in a row.

16th A Supreme Court decision permitting the Baltimore and Ohio Railroad to give reduced rates to groups of 10 or more is a boon to ML baseball teams, who can expect to save 25 percent on transportation costs.

17th Bill Hart of Brooklyn becomes the 3rd pitcher in less than 2 weeks to lose a no-hitter in the 9th inning in a 7–0 victory over Boston.

18th John "Sadie" McMahon loses a no-hitter—and the game—when New York's Denny Lyons singles in the only run in Baltimore's 1–0 loss.

21st George "Hub" Collins, 28-year-old Brooklyn OF and leadoff batter, dies of typhoid fever after a brief illness. He had led the AA in doubles in 1888 and the NL in runs in 1890.

Chicago wins its 11th straight game 1–0 over Pud Galvin and the Pirates. Galvin surrenders only 2 hits in the loss, none before the 8th inning.

24th Brooklyn makes good use of its 14 hits in a 24–4 rout of the Washington Senators. Oyster Burns typifies his club's attack by scoring 4 runs without the benefit of a hit.

26th Boston's John Clarkson loses a no-hitter with 2 outs in the 9th inning, as Hughie Jennings of the Louisville Colonels comes through with a hit.

28th Jimmy Ryan helps Chicago defeat Amos Rusie and New York 10–4 by drawing 5 walks—half of Rusie's total for the game.

JUNE

6th President Benjamin Harrison watches Washington go down to a 7–4 defeat to Cincinnati in 11 innings. It marks the first visit to a ML game by a U.S. president.

7th Henry Larkin of the Senators collects 6 hits, including a triple in a 20–2 victory over Cincinnati.

9th The Orioles explode for 25 hits and swamp St. Louis 25–4. Baltimore fails to score after the 6th inning.

10th Wilbert Robinson, Orioles catcher, goes 7-for-7 and bats in 11 runs, as Baltimore defeats the St. Louis Browns 25–7.

13th NL club owners meet in New York to work out league financial problems. The club assessment is increased from 10 percent to 12¼ percent of the receipts of each game. Team rosters are reduced to 13 players, thus allowing the weaker clubs to sign some of those released.

14th Washington, scoring each of its runs with 2 outs, records a 12–7 win over St. Louis with the help of 5 hits from Patrick "Patsy" Donovan. Despite this performance, Donovan will soon be traded to the Pirates, with whom he will enjoy five .300 seasons en route to a career mark of .301.

24th Cleveland and St. Louis aces Cy Young and Ted Breitenstein battle to a 3–3, 16-inning tie.

Philadelphia wins its 15th consecutive game 6–3 over New York and ties Brooklyn for 2nd place in the NL race. Despite extending the winning streak to 16 four days later, the Phillies will fall back to 3rd on that day and will remain there for the rest of the first half of the season.

30th Tony Mullane of Cincinnati and Ad Gumbert of Chicago pitch 20 innings of a 7–7 standoff. It is the longest game in the 19th century.

Baltimore hurler Charles Buffinton refuses to take a salary cut from $100 a week to $75 a week and is released by the club. Only 31, he will never pitch again in professional ball.

JULY

4th Tony Mullane is the only member of the Reds to object to a salary cut and is given a 10-day notice of his release.

7th Pete Browning's 5 hits contribute to the Reds' 21–2 rout of Baltimore.

9th John Clarkson, signed by the Cleveland Spiders after his release from Boston, responds immediately with an 8–2 win over Tim Keefe and the Phillies.

11th Boston, having clinched the first-half championship, plays an unusual game at Chicago with team members, led by King Kelly, dressed in outlandish costumes and wearing beards. The large crowd is delighted, and the game, a 3–2 win for Boston, is surprisingly well played.

15th NL president Nick Young watches the 2nd-half opener in Washington as Cleveland loses 3–1. A major dispute erupts between umpire Charles Mitchell and Cleveland manager Patsy Tebeau, who is fined $10. Tebeau says, "Make it twenty." The fine is increased by installments to $50 "before Tebeau would quiet down."

The St. Louis Browns stun the champions of the first season, the Boston Beaneaters, with a 20–3 bombardment.

19th In losing 1–0 and 13–0 to the Bridegrooms, St. Louis extends its scoreless streak to 35 innings. The Browns, who have totaled only 15 hits in their last 4 games, will finally score after 38 innings against New York.

21st Tim Keefe of the Phillies outpitches veteran Jim Galvin of St. Louis 2–0. It is Keefe's 326th ML win against 211 losses. Galvin's career mark is 360-306.

Harry Stovey smacks 3 triples and drives in 6 runs in the Orioles' 10–3 win over Pittsburgh.

22nd Female baseball players are not exactly accorded respect in the South. A Louisville *Courier-Journal* article about a mass murderer is tellingly titled "Alice Mitchell Played Ball."

26th Ed Delahanty gets 5 of Philadelphia's 29 hits, including 3 doubles and a triple, in a 26–6 massacre of Cincinnati.

27th Baltimore OF George Van Haltren, who collected 4 straight hits the day before, goes 5-for-5 against St. Louis.

28th The Orioles are embarrassed when an Elkton, MD, amateur hurler named Bill Hawke, signed by St. Louis, defeats Baltimore 2–1.

AUGUST

5th Substituting in LF, Jack Stivetts breaks up a scoreless tie with a 2-run HR for Boston in the 11th to beat Brooklyn.

6th Pitching for Boston, Jack Stivetts tosses an 11–0 no-hitter over the Bridegrooms.

Cincinnati manager Charles Comiskey reaches a temporary salary compromise with P Tony Mullane, who returns to the club but pitches poorly in a 6–1 loss to Chicago. He would soon leave the club to pitch in Butte, MT.

8th Boston gets its 3rd straight shutout, 7–0 over Washington, and moves into a first-place tie with Cleveland. Tomorrow Washington will snap the Beaneaters' 33-inning scoreless streak with an 8–3 win.

10th Baltimore rookie P George Cobb walks on all 5 trips to the plate in his 7–2 victory over Washington. In his only ML season Cobb will record a dismal record of 10-37.

12th The Orioles remove OF posts, around which ropes holding back overflow crowds would be wrapped, after a ball hit by Harry Stovey strikes a post and bounces back toward the infield, forcing Stovey to stop at 2B. Another factor in the decision was an incident 3 days ago in which Oriole RF Frank "Piggy" Ward missed a sure catch when he ran upon a post.

15th Jimmy Ryan of Chicago goes hitless after connecting in 29 consecutive games dating back to July 9th. The team makes 10 errors while losing to Baltimore 9–2.

18th In the course of a 13–4 win over Baltimore, Browns LF Cliff Carroll attempts to field a ground ball, but he misjudges it, and the ball becomes lodged in his shirt pocket. Before he can extricate it the Oriole batter makes it to 3B. St. Louis owner Chris Von der Ahe is so outraged that he fines Carroll $50 and suspends him without pay for the rest of the season. Carroll appeals the fine and the suspension at the end of the season but is turned down.

The Bridegrooms overcome 5 hits by Cap Anson, including 2 triples and a double, to defeat Chicago 7–5.

22nd Louisville's Ben Sanders no-hits Baltimore, winning by a 6–2 count. The Orioles runs score on walks and errors.

James "Bug" Holliday hits 2 HRs and drives in all 6 runs in Cincinnati's 12-inning 6–5 win over Washington.

26th The Colonels' Ben Sanders follows up on his August 22nd no-hitter with a 1-hit 4–0 win over Boston.

After Pittsburgh defeats Philadelphia 11–3, the Phillies accuse the Pirates of doctoring the ball with a greasy rag found in the OF. Pittsburgh denies the accusation.

SEPTEMBER

1st Recently released Pirate P Mark "Fido" Baldwin is arrested in his hometown of Homestead, PA, for alleged complicity in the recent strike and ensuing riot. Baldwin posts $2,000 bail and claims that he was merely a spectator. He will soon rejoin the Pirates and finish the season with a 26-27 record.

5th Jack Stivetts, having his best year with Boston, wins 2 complete games over Louisville 2–1 and 5–2. The first game goes 11 innings.

13th Boston shuts out Washington 9–0. Senator OF Patsy Donovan does his best to stave off defeat with 4 hits, but is thrown out at the plate 3 times.

16th Tim O'Rourke hits a bases-loaded, 2-out, bottom-of-the-9th, 2-strike triple to give Baltimore a stunning 6–5 win over the Pirates.

19th P Charles "Kid" Nichols, Boston's premier hurler, hits a grand slam in the 5th and a bases-loaded triple in the 6th to give the Beaneaters a 14–0 lead over Baltimore. In the bottom of the 6th he has to leave the mound when hit by a batted ball. The Orioles quickly score 11 runs, but still lose 14–11.

21st Cleveland gets its only 2 hits in the 9th inning to stun Pittsburgh 3–2 and to avenge a similar loss to the Pirates yesterday.

26th A fire destroys the Louisville Colonels' ballpark and much of the team's equipment, including all bats and many uniforms. Only the bleachers survive, but home games against Chicago on the 28th and 29th are played and are well attended.

28th Bill Hutchinson pitches both games for Chicago against Louisville, winning the first 5–4 and losing the second 5–3.

In Philadelphia's 11–1 victory over Washington, Jack Clements gets a triple on a ball that lands on top of the RF wall and must be retrieved by Senator OF Larry Twitchell.

29th The Beaneaters overcome 14 errors, including 5 by 2B Joe Quinn, to defeat Washington 12–8. Quinn will led the NL's second basemen in fielding percentage with a mark of .951.

30th Willie Keeler makes his ML debut by singling and scoring for New York, but his efforts cannot prevent a 5–4 loss to Philadelphia.

OCTOBER

1st Cincinnati captain Charles Comiskey, interviewed in the New York *Clipper*, states that "the days of the twelve club league are numbered. The double season plan is a failure…as the public will decide that a team that are [sic] champions up to the Fourth of July ought to be champions all season."

4th Amos Rusie of the Giants pitches 2 complete-game victories over Washington at the Polo Grounds 6–4 and 9–5.

5th Cy Young of Cleveland hurls his league-leading 9th shutout, beating Cincinnati 6–0.

12th Browns C Dick Buckley breaks his arm in a home-plate collision with Colonel OF Tom Brown.

14th The scheduled Boston-Washington game is postponed because the Senators' field has already been reserved by the Columbia Athletic Club for a football game against Princeton.

15th Charles "Bumpus" Jones of Cincinnati, making his ML debut, pitches a no-hit game over Pittsburgh, winning 7–1.

Rookie Willie Keeler, a lefthander, plays 3B for the Giants and collects 3 hits in 4 trips.

Boston's Jack Stivetts hurls a 5-inning no-hitter against Washington, winning by a score of 6–0.

17th To settle the championship of baseball's first split season, Boston, the first-half winner, starts a 5-game series with Cleveland, the 2nd-half champ. Jack Stivetts and Cy Young battle to an 11-inning scoreless tie.

18th In Cleveland, 7,000 fans see Boston nip the home team 4–3 with Harry Staley beating John

Clarkson. The latter had pitched for Boston in the first half before joining Cleveland.

19th Boston wins another one-run contest 3–2 as Stivetts bests Young.

21st The winless Cleveland Spiders move to Boston where Kid Nichols shuts them out 4–0 before 6,547.

24th After a Sunday rest, the Boston Beaneaters sweep the series with their 5th victory 8–3. Only 1,812 fans show up on a cold day.

NOVEMBER

1st Averages for the first 154-game season show that Dan Brouthers of Brooklyn was the top hitter at .335, and Cy Young the top pitcher with 36 wins and 11 losses.

17th NL magnates conclude a 4-day meeting in Chicago where they agree to shorten the 1893 schedule to 132 games and drop the double championship concept. They also pledge to continue to reduce player salaries and other team expenses.

1893

JANUARY

12th NL owners, led by Pittsburgh's A. C. Buckenberger, form the National Cycling Association. They hope to build bicycle tracks in at least 8 of the 12 NL parks.

14th The Cuban Giants, perhaps the nation's best black baseball team, announce their desire to join the proposed Middle States League. Their application is rejected.

25th Cincinnati business manager F. C. Bancroft reminisces about "the time when police had to escort the umpire to the depot, and when cannons were fired when a game was won. That's the sort of baseball you want."

28th It is announced that Bancroft is spending the remainder of the off-season serving as the manager of Linda Gardner's Mastodon Minstrels.

The New York *Clipper* states that "an attempt will be made to change the rules so as to compel outfielders to discard gloves."

FEBRUARY

4th The first recorded version of "Casey at the Bat," as sung by Russell Hunting, hits the music charts. DeWolf Hopper's more famous version will not be released until October 1906.

MARCH

1st John Pickett wins $1,285.72 in a lawsuit against Baltimore, his most recent team. Baltimore had claimed that they did not owe him this sum —Pickett's entire 1892 salary—because he "was slow in his movement, and had a sore arm which incapacitated him from being of service to the club."

7th In arguably the most significant rule change in ML history, the NL eliminates the pitching box and adds a pitcher's rubber 5 feet behind the previous back line of the box, establishing the modern pitching distance of 60 feet 6 inches. In addition, bats flattened on one side to facilitate bunting are banned.

25th Louisville is forced to transfer its only three Sunday games because the suburb of Parkland, in which the Colonels' new ballpark is located, does not permit Sunday play.

APRIL

13th Louisville owners refuse an offer from Milwaukee businessmen for their franchise. Nevertheless, many baseball officials believe Louisville is not a good baseball town and hope that the team is transferred to a bigger, more responsive city like Buffalo.

29th On the 2nd day of the season, the Brooklyn Bridegrooms score 5 runs in the bottom of the 9th to tie the host Philadelphia Phillies, then add 2 more in the 10th to win 11–10.

MAY

5th Ed Stein hurls a one-hitter to lead Brooklyn to a 3–1 win over the Philadelphia Phillies.

10th Brooklyn's joy over beating the New York Giants in the bottom of the last inning for the 2nd straight day is partially dashed as youngster Willie Keeler fractures a bone while sliding. Keeler will miss nearly 2 months of action.

11th George Davis goes 5-for-5 with a HR and a triple to lead New York to a 15–9 win over Philadelphia.

12th Philadelphia gains revenge, scoring 11 runs in the 4th inning en route to an 18–6 rout of New York.

15th After tagging out St. Louis Browns OF Steve Brodie in a collision at the plate, Cincinnati Reds C Henry "Farmer" Vaughn throws a bat at Brodie, hitting him on the shoulder. Vaughn is ejected and fined $25 as St. Louis wins 10–6 and moves past the Cleveland Spiders and the Pittsburgh Pirates into first place

19th Held scoreless for the first 8 innings, both Brooklyn and the Boston Beaneaters score 3 runs in the 9th to send the game into extra innings. Boston's Billy Nash hits the ball over the LF fence in the bottom of the 9th, but he stays on 3B "to bother the pitcher." The tactic works, as Nash does score. Both teams score one run in the 10th—Boston scoring on another Nash blow over the LF fence, which he runs out this time. Boston finally claims the game after a 12-inning struggle 5–4.

22nd In the first game at the Louisville Colonels' new Parkland field, "played by mutual agreement with the pitcher under the old rules," Cincinnati wins 3–1.

24th Connie Mack starts a triple play in the 4th inning and drives in the winning run in the bottom of the 8th to lead Pittsburgh to an 8–7 win over St. Louis.

27th Despite losing at home to Cincinnati 4–1, the Pirates back into first place as the Cleveland Spiders fall to St. Louis 3–2.

30th Jake Beckley successfully pulls the "ancient" hidden-ball trick on Baltimore Oriole Joe Kelley, as Pittsburgh wins 9–1.

Brooklyn's William "Brickyard" Kennedy allows a total of 8 hits in a doubleheader as he beats Louisville 3–0 and 6–2.

JUNE

1st Harry Staley hits 2 HRs while pitching Boston to a 15–4 victory over Louisville.

8th Billy Hamilton gets his 8th consecutive hit as Philadelphia beats Louisville 6–2. In defeat, Colonels 1B Willard Brown sets a ML record for assists with 6.

12th Brooklyn outslugs Cincinnati 14–13 to move into first place.

13th Despite losing Connie Mack with a serious injury in the first inning, Pittsburgh beats Boston 9–7. Mack will be out for 10 weeks.

14th In the 2nd inning Boston's Cliff Carroll makes a phenomenal catch to rob a St. Louis player of a HR. In the bottom of the 9th, Carroll knocks in 2 runs and scores the 3rd and decisive run to propel Boston to an 11–10 win.

George Davis becomes the first player in ML history to hit a HR and a triple in the same inning as his Giants overcome the Chicago Colts 11–10. Davis's feat will not be matched until 1926, when the Detroit Tigers' Bob Fothergill turns the trick.

18th Cincinnati starts matters off by scoring 14 runs in the first inning, then cruises to a 30–12 victory over Louisville. Farmer Vaughn and James "Bug" Holliday lead the way with 9 hits, including 5 extra-base hits, between them.

23rd New York's Roger Connor becomes the 2nd man ever to hit 100 HRs in his career with his 3rd of the season in an 11–5 win at Philadelphia.

Boston moves into first place as Philadelphia loses. However, a Philadelphia victory the next day brings them into a first-place tie with Boston.

26th New York and Cincinnati battle 17 innings to a 5–5 tie.

JULY

1st Boston forges into the NL lead by beating St. Louis 12–5. Philadelphia loses to Cleveland 13–6, as the Spiders stage their 2nd 8-run 9th-inning rally in the last month.

4th The Los Angeles and Stockton clubs of the California League play their 2nd game in 3 days under electric lights.

6th Jack Boyle's 6 hits go to waste as Chicago tops Philadelphia 11–10 in 11 innings. Meanwhile, Boston blows its chance to claim first as it allows Pittsburgh to win 10–9 with 5 runs in the 9th.

7th Philadelphia reclaims first place with a 13–10 win at Chicago.

Louisville officials, frustrated by their inability to sell alcohol or play Sunday baseball in their new ballpark, located in the suburb of Parkland, whose laws proscribe such activities, get permission from the Kentucky Legislature to annex the land on which the ballpark is located without the consent of Parkland residents. Alcohol sales and Sunday baseball commence almost immediately.

13th After Baltimore's Joe Kelley hits a HR against Chicago, his bat disappears. The game is delayed at Kelley's next at bat until his bat is found—along with the bats on the Chicago bench.

14th Right-handed P Tony Mullane, losing to Chicago, pitches the 9th inning lefthanded. Chicago adds 3 more runs to their total and whips Baltimore 10–2.

15th Jake Stenzel hits a HR and a triple, both with the bases loaded, along with 3 other hits as Pittsburgh annihilates Louisville 19–0.

19th Pittsburgh uses 19 hits—all singles—to win in Cleveland 10–6. Pittsburgh is further aided by the defense of LF Elmer Smith, whose use of green glasses to fend off the sun "greatly helped him in his fielding."

22nd   Boston's Tommy Tucker ties a ML record by hitting 4 doubles, including 2 in one inning, in a 7–2 win over New York.

27th   Boston takes the NL lead for good by defeating Baltimore 6–2.

31st   The Philadelphia OF records no chances in a 7–4 loss to Boston.

New York's Mark Baldwin surrenders only 3 hits, but is outdueled by Ed Stein, who pitches his 2nd one-hitter of the season to lead Brooklyn to a 3–0 victory.

AUGUST

2nd   Philadelphia snaps Boston's 9-game winning streak with a 7–4 victory.

5th   Brooklyn unveils its new cleanup hitter—5 foot 4 inches Willie Keeler—in a game against Boston. Despite hitting .313 in this role for his new team, Keeler is released to the Binghamton, NY, team of the Eastern League on August 26th.

6th   Chicago's Jimmy Ryan is lost for the season after suffering injuries in a train accident.

7th   Facing a lefthanded Brooklyn pitcher, New York 1B Roger Connor bats righthanded for the first time in his career and slugs 2 HRs and a single in a 10–3 win.

12th   After making 3 errors in a loss in Cleveland, St. Louis LF Jesse Burkett is criticized for forgetting to follow Elmer Smith's example and wear sunglasses.

14th   The Phillies' Billy Hamilton is diagnosed with typhoid fever, and will miss the remainder of the season.

16th   Bill Hawke of Baltimore pitches a 5–0 no-hitter against Washington.

20th   Chicago C Malachi Kittridge allows a Washington player to score as he sweeps off the plate without calling time out.

24th   After incessant rains, the Polo Grounds OF is flooded with nearly 2 feet of water. Officials respond by moving the diamond 45 feet closer to the grandstand. Chicago handles the conditions better and defeats New York 10–4.

SEPTEMBER

11th   George Davis's 33-game hitting streak is broken as his Giants lose at Cleveland 8–6.

13th   Boston star Tommy McCarthy dislocates 2 toes sliding into 3B against Chicago. His loss is felt as the game ends in an 8-inning 8–8 tie.

21st   John "Bid" McPhee, the Reds' star 2B, wears a glove for the first time. However, he ends the experiment before the end of the season.

28th   After moving into the lead with 3 runs in the top of the 9th, Philadelphia players allow themselves to be retired quickly in order to finish the game before it is called on account of darkness. However, Cleveland foils their plans by scoring 4 runs in the bottom of the 9th to win 11–10.

30th   On the last day of the season St. Louis rookie Duff Cooley goes 6-for-6 to spur his team to a 16–4 thrashing of NL champion Boston.

OCTOBER

14th   Baseball legend Harry Wright suggests that umpires keep the ball-strike count a secret until the at bat is concluded. He feels this rule change will increase offense.

NOVEMBER

21st   Ban Johnson is named president, secretary, and treasurer of the recently reorganized Western League. Under Johnson's leadership the Western League will prosper.

1894

JANUARY

9th   Boston's veteran C Charlie Bennett loses both legs in a horrific train accident. In 1900, Detroit, Bennett's first team, will name its ballpark Bennett Park in his honor.

FEBRUARY

26th   In a series of rule changes designed to help pitchers, foul bunts will now be called strikes, and the infield fly rule is instituted.

MARCH

5th   Browns' owner Chris Von der Ahe, unable to hire either Harry Wright of P.J. Powers as manager, announces that he will manage the club himself. Von der Ahe will eventually name starting infielder George "Doggie" Miller as manager.

12th   Pittsburgh issues free season tickets for ladies good for Tuesday and Friday games.

14th   U.S. Immigration Inspector De Barry will ask the Treasury Department if baseball is a "recognized profession" in order to determine if Buffalo has violated the alien contract labor law by signing two Canadians. Before De Barry gets a reply, Buffalo decides to play only Americans.

APRIL

24th   In a game atypical for 1894, Cy Young throws a 2-hit shutout at Cincinnati 1–0, as the Cleveland Spiders score the winning run in the 9th inning.

Losing 3–1 to the Boston Beaneaters in the 9th inning, the Baltimore Orioles rally for 14 runs to top the defending NL champions 15–3.

MAY

5th   In the 5th inning of the St. Louis–Pittsburgh game, Pirate SS Jack Glasscock, thinking opposing Browns P Emerson "Pink" Hawley deliberately threw at him, hurls his bat at the pitcher and then confronts Hawley on the mound. Glasscock remains in the game and helps Pittsburgh to a hard-fought 6–5 victory

6th   Star Boston SS Herman Long accidentally flicks hot ashes from his cigar into his eye, causing him to miss several games.

7th   Baltimore routs the Washington Senators 17–0 for Baltimore's only shutout of the season.

10th   Frank Shugart, George "Doggie" Miller, and Heinie Peitz of St. Louis hit consecutive HRs in the 7th inning. In all, Shugart hits 3 HRs and Peitz 2, giving St. Louis a total of 6. However, their heroics are to no avail as their club falls to Cincinnati 18–9.

11th   In the course of a 12–7 loss to Philadelphia, Baltimore's star SS Hughie Jennings is hit by 3 Wilfred "Kid" Carsey pitches, establishing a ML record.

15th   In the aftermath of a fierce fight between Baltimore's John McGraw and Boston's Tommy Tucker in the 3rd inning, a devastating fire starts in the RF stands. It rapidly spreads to adjacent blocks, and eventually destroys or severely damages 170 buildings.

16th   Losing to Cincinnati 6–4 in the 8th inning, Louisville's William "Farmer" Weaver hits a grand-slam, and Danny Richardson follows with a solo shot—the last HR of his 11-year career—to spur a 9–7 win.

26th   The Pittsburgh Pirates lead at Cleveland 12–3 in the 8th inning when the home spectators start a seat cushion fight that spills onto the diamond. Pittsburgh is awarded a 9–0 forfeit victory.

29th   Washington breaks its 17-game losing streak by whipping Louisville 12–2.

Pittsburgh moves past Cleveland into first place by edging Baltimore 3–2 as the Spiders, held to 3 hits by Jouett Meekin, lose to New York 2–0.

30th   Boston 2B Bobby Lowe hits HRs in 4 consecutive at bats, including 2 in the 3rd inning, to lead his team to a 20–11 conquest of Cincinnati and a sweep of the doubleheader. In the 2 games Lowe's teammate Herman Long sets a ML record by scoring 9 runs, which has since been tied only once.

JUNE

2nd   Ed Stein throws a 7-inning no-hitter, as Brooklyn edges Chicago 1–0. The previous day the Bridegrooms held Chicago to one hit in a 5–0 win.

Sam Thompson of Philadelphia undergoes surgery on the little finger on his left hand and is expected to miss up to a month.

6th Pittsburgh erupts in the 3rd inning against Boston when Jake Stenzel hits 2 HRs and Denny Lyons and Lou Bierbauer hit one each, setting a ML record for HRs in an inning next tied in 1930. Pittsburgh hits 7 HRs in all in its 27–11 win.

7th Jack Taylor pitches a 2-hit shutout to defeat Cleveland 6–0 and to push his Pittsburgh team ahead of Cleveland into 3rd place.

On a rainy day St. Louis Browns southpaw Ted Breitenstein walks 13 men as Boston avenges a humiliating loss the previous day with a 19–8 rout.

12th Brooklyn's 10-game winning streak is ended when Cincinnati triumphs 5–3. Brooklyn is now in 6th place with a 22-16 record.

15th Philadelphia SS Bob Allen is hit in the face with a pitch in a contest against Cincinnati. Allen will require surgery to save his sight, and his career is all but ended.

16th Ed Delahanty goes 6-for-6 with a double, as Philadelphia tops Cincinnati 19–9.

Despite scoring 26 runs in the 3-game series, Louisville is swept by Boston, extending its losing streak to 18 games. The streak will reach 20 games before the Colonels manage to win.

20th Denny Lyons scores the winning run in the 9th inning to lead Pittsburgh to a 7–6 win over Washington. Lyons gets into scoring position by running from 1B to 3B—across the pitcher's mound—on a fielder's choice. The umpire did not see Lyons's transgression, a common one in the 1890s.

22nd Washington scores in every inning to whip Boston 26–12. In the course of the rout, George "White Wings" Tebeau scores 4 runs without the benefit of a hit.

24th The Chicago Colts score 5 runs in the top of the 9th to take the lead over Baltimore, but the NL leaders respond with 3 runs in the bottom of the inning to claim an 11–10 win.

27th For the first time in nearly a month, covering 24 games, Baltimore fails to score at least 7 runs, losing to Chicago 13–4.

28th Louisville P George Hemming throws an 11-inning 25-hitter, as the Colonels edge Boston 11–9.

30th Future Hall of Famer Fred Clarke sets a record by going 5-for-5 in his first ML game, but Louisville squanders his performance in a 13–6 loss to Philadelphia.

JULY

1st Baltimore is shut out for the first time all season, losing a 6–0 decision to Louisville, of all teams.

7th Boston completes a 3-game sweep of Cleveland, outscoring the Spiders by a 57–23 margin. Every Boston starter got a hit in each of the 3 games, totaling 69 hits in all.

9th Every Brooklyn player commits at least one error, for a team total of 10, helping Louisville to a 20–8 laugher.

New York wins its 11th consecutive game, defeating Cincinnati 13–6, as the Giants soar from 7th place into 3rd.

Baltimore OF Steve Brodie goes 6-for-6 with 3 extra-base hits in a 14–10 victory over Pittsburgh.

11th Cleveland catcher Charles "Chief" Zimmer matches Brodie's performance of 2 days ago by recording 6 straight hits in a 15–10, 10-inning win over Washington.

13th Boston claims first place with a 22–7 bombardment in Cincinnati as Baltimore falls to St. Louis 11–10.

14th A Boston loss and a Baltimore win give both teams a winning percentage of .667 and an equal share of first place.

With its 14–7 win over Philadelphia, Cleveland scores in double figures for the 7th consecutive game, and at least 14 runs for the 6th straight time. By winning 6 of these 7 games, Cleveland maintains its 7th-place standing.

15th Baltimore retakes the NL lead with a 9–8, 11-inning victory over St. Louis.

20th Cincinnati benefits from bottom-of-the-10th-inning HRs by Henry "Farmer" Vaughn and George "Germany" Smith, the latter with 2 outs, to squeak past Pittsburgh 7–6. Pirate OF Elmer Smith is prevented from retrieving the game-winning hit in the LF bleachers, as he is allowed to do according to

Cincinnati ground rules, by overzealous Reds fans. One of them draws a revolver on Smith after he hits several other spectators in a desperate attempt to reach the ball.

23rd Once again Boston draws into a first-place tie with Baltimore, again with a .667 percentage, after a 9–5 victory over New York.

30th Boston completes a 3-game sweep of Baltimore to build a 4-game lead in the NL race.

AUGUST

1st Cap Anson and George Decker each go 5-for-7 with a HR, and Jimmy Ryan scores 5 runs, as Chicago massacres St. Louis 26–8.

5th With Anson at bat in the 6th, a fire breaks out in the grandstand of the West Side Grounds. Hundreds are injured as the 10,000 fans stampede, tearing down barbed wire fencing that had been put up to prevent the 25-cent bleacher fans from mobbing the umpire. The game is called with Chicago winning 8–1.

7th Boston's Jimmy "Foxy Grandpa" Bannon becomes the first player to hit grand slams in consecutive games. Bannon's feat will not be matched until September 24, 1901.

Chicago SS Bill Dahlen goes 0-for-6 to break his 42-game hitting streak. However, his teammates cover for him by defeating Cincinnati 13–11. Leading the way is Walt Wilmot, who steals 4 bases for the 2nd straight game and adds 5 hits.

14th Taking advantage of the unusually small University of Pennsylvania field, visiting Louisville tags 6 HRs, including 2 by Tom Brown, to beat Philadelphia 13–7.

17th Philadelphia, still smarting from Louisville's 6-HR assault 3 days ago, mauls the Colonels 29–4. Sam Thompson leads the stampede by getting 6 hits and hitting for the cycle. Three teammates get 5 hits each as Philadelphia chalks up 36 hits, a ML record.

18th Baltimore retakes the NL lead from Boston with a 17–2 rout over Pittsburgh, while Boston is flattened 19–6 by Cincinnati.

19th The Orioles fall back into 2nd place by 4 percentage points with a 7–5 loss to the Pirates.

20th Washington's Bill Joyce smacks 3 HRs in an 8–7 win over Louisville. Joyce finishes the season with 17 HRs to place 2nd in the NL.

22nd With the Giants up by 6 runs in the 8th, Chicago's Bill Lange comes to the plate wielding a 5 foot 10 inch bat that had been given to Jimmy Ryan by a New York theater manager. Neither the umpire, John McQuaid, nor the Giants object, and Lange, who had struck out twice against Jouett Meekin, hits a soft grounder to 1B Jack Doyle, who mishandles it. New York wins 8–5.

24th Chicago C William "Pop" Schriver catches a ball dropped from the top of the Washington Monument. Later in the day the Colts top Washington 10–5.

25th Amos Rusie throws a one-hitter, as New York hands Louisville its 10th straight loss 5–1.

30th Baltimore edges Louisville 9–8 and moves into first place as Boston falls to St. Louis. The Orioles will hold on to the lead for the rest of the season.

31st Billy Hamilton ties George Gore's ML record by stealing 7 bases in a game against Washington. Hamilton's heroics help Philadelphia to win 11–5 and, therefore, to sweep the doubleheader.

SEPTEMBER

3rd Joe Kelley becomes the 2nd man in ML history to get 9 hits in a doubleheader, as Baltimore sweeps Cleveland to strengthen its hold on first place. It will be 32 years until another player matches Kelley's achievement.

The Louisville *Courier-Journal*, in describing Cap Anson as a "wholesome example to the young ballplayers," states approvingly that "he smokes three cigars a day."

4th New York rallies for 3 runs in the bottom of the 9th to slip by Pittsburgh 14–13 and edge closer to 2nd place in the NL race.

6th For the 2nd time in 3 days, New York beats Pittsburgh by scoring in the bottom of the 9th, allowing them to pass Boston—which loses to Louisville in the Colonels' first victory in 19 games—and move into 2nd place.

16th   Cincinnati beats Baltimore 4–3 in the 2nd game of the doubleheader and snaps the Orioles' 18-game winning streak.

George Decker hits 2 HRs, a double, and a triple to lead Chicago to a 13–5 win over Brooklyn.

22nd   After pitching 12 innings the previous day, Pittsburgh P Philip "Red" Ehret throws a 4-hitter to defeat 2nd-place New York 4–1. For his efforts against New York Ehret wins $100 offered by Baltimore's Wilbert Robinson for the win.

25th   Baltimore clinches the NL pennant by beating Cleveland 14–9.

29th   Plans for the establishment of a new ML, to be called the National Association, are revealed in the New York *Clipper*. NL officials counter with a plan to shrink back to 8 clubs and to create a 2nd club of young players for each NL team to play at home when the parent club is on the road.

30th   Losing to Cincinnati 16–1 in the bottom of the 6th, Cleveland stages a furious comeback, including an 11-run outburst in the 7th, to conclude the season with a 16–16 tie.

OCTOBER

8th   New York whips NL regular season champion Baltimore 16–3 to sweep the best-of-7 Temple Cup series.

NOVEMBER

1st   Former Providence P Charles Sweeney is convicted of manslaughter in San Francisco.

8th   Mike "King" Kelly, probably the most popular baseball player of the 19th century, dies of pneumonia in Boston.

16th   Managers Al Buckenberger (Pittsburgh) and William Barnie (Louisville) and Louisville star Fred Pfeffer are expelled from the NL for planning with officials of the proposed American Association (previously called the National Association). The 2 managers are reinstated before the end of the year, but Pfeffer must wait until the end of February 1895 before he is welcomed back into the fold.

DECEMBER

15th   Veteran manager John Chapman expresses his support of a proposed rule change forbidding all but catchers and 1B from wearing gloves. Citing Cincinnati's Bid McPhee as an example of one of the few remaining outstanding gloveless fielders, Chapman remarks that "as it is now, inferior players with big gloves can get into the game and force good men out."

1895

JANUARY

14th Baltimore's grandstand burns to the ground.

25th Cap Anson notes that "nobody likes to see a play made with the aid of gloves." He is of the opinion that only catchers should be permitted the luxury of wearing gloves.

26th Baseball officials discuss the possibility of reinstating the old pitcher's distance. They are dismayed by the explosion of offense, which resulted in "long drawn out and uninteresting contests…. Besides the brainy pitcher of former days would be given another chance to display his ability in the science of the game."

FEBRUARY

2nd The New York *Clipper* and the Cincinnati *Times-Star* both express disapproval of the proposal of putting numbers on uniforms as a means of identifying individual players. The *Times-Star* advocates a return to the use of "distinctive colors in club uniforms," or the practice of assigning to each position a specific color pattern, first enacted in the early 1880s.

9th New York owner Andrew Freedman institutes reserved grandstand seats to attract businessmen.

27th Responding to the complaints of senior citizens like Cap Anson, the NL restricts the size of gloves for all fielders, save catchers and 1B, to 10 ounces, with a maximum circumference of 14 inches around the palm—in other words, less than 4½ inches across. The NL also rescinds the rule forbidding "intentional discoloring" of the ball, thus allowing players to dirty the baseball to their satisfaction.

MARCH

16th John Brush, owner of the Cincinnati Reds and the Indianapolis team of the Western League, transfers 6 Reds to his minor league team. This sort of exchange becomes increasingly common in the 1890s as owners of more than one team shuttle their players between their teams throughout each season in an attempt to stock their most profitable team of the moment. This strategy causes much distrust among fans, who feel that their loyalties are being trampled.

APRIL

12th In a rare matchup between a ML team and a black team, Cincinnati beats the Page Fence Giants for the 2nd consecutive day.

19th Holy Cross defeats Brown University 13–4 in a game between 2 of the top college teams of this period. The Crusaders have 5 future ML players in their lineup, while the losers have 2. Lou Sockalexis bats 7th and plays LF for the victors, and has 6 SBs.

20th The Cincinnati *Times-Star* sees the ML policy of "farming out promising players to minor league teams" as detrimental to the minors.

MAY

3rd Bobby Lowe scores 6 runs and registers 5 hits, leading Boston to a 27–11 rout of Washington.

5th Heinie Peitz goes 5-for-5 with 3 extra-base hits, but somehow fails to score. St. Louis manages to whip Cincinnati 11–4.

6th The Philadelphia-Louisville game is postponed on account of the running of the Kentucky Derby.

10th During the course of a 14–4 win over St. Louis, Philadelphia slugger Sam Thompson becomes the 3rd man in NL history to hit 100 HRs in a career.

19th Toward the end of the Washington-Cincinnati game the "open seats" collapse "mixing up" about 300 spectators but injuring none.

20th Chicago P Clark Griffith goes 5-for-6 as he and his teammates rout Philadelphia 24–6. Rookie 3B Bill Everett contributes with 4 hits and 5 runs.

29th Jake Beckley hits a 3-run HR to give Pittsburgh an 8–6 win over Washington. Under the rules of the era, which do not allow a team batting in the bottom of the last inning to win by more than one run, Beckley should be credited only with a triple. Apparently the rule is not strictly enforced.

30th After an estimated 18,000 spectators squeeze into Philadelphia's ballpark, the enormous overflow crowd shrinks the size of the OF. Taking advantage of the unique circumstances, Cincinnati RF Charles "Dusty" Miller throws out 4 runners at 1B, but Philadelphia wins in 11 innings 9–8. The 2 teams combine for 16 doubles, 9 by Cincinnati, most resulting from balls hit into the overflow crowd.

JUNE

1st St. Louis 1B Roger Connor gets 6 of his team's 30 hits in a 23–2 burial of New York.

3rd Roger Connor becomes the ML's all-time HR leader, passing Harry Stovey with his 4th round-tripper of the season, and the 112th of his career. This historic HR drives in St. Louis's only 2 runs in a 5–2 loss to Brooklyn.

11th Boston whips Louisville 11–0 and takes first place from Pittsburgh, which has held the top position since the beginning of the season.

15th Future novelist Zane Grey makes his minor league debut playing LF for Findlay, OH, against Wheeling (Tri State League). The Pennsylvania University athlete, playing under the name Zane, fails to get a hit, but walks and scores on a grand slam by brother Romer "Reddy" Grey.

Baltimore shuts out St. Louis 5–0 and replaces Pittsburgh in 2nd place.

JULY

2nd Louisville takes advantage of a 7th-inning fight to score 2 runs amidst the confusion, but still loses to Cincinnati 6–5.

St. Louis scores 11 runs in the first inning on its way to a 15–9 victory over Chicago.

3rd Baltimore beats New York 5–4 in 10 innings to move past Boston into first place.

8th Approaching the midpoint of the season, Baltimore leads 8th-place Philadelphia by only 3½ games. The top 4 teams (Baltimore, Boston, Chicago, and Pittsburgh) are within one game of each other.

15th A 6-run 9th inning lifts Boston to a 12–9 win over Cleveland.

17th Cleveland surges into first place on the strength of a sweep of a doubleheader with Baltimore. Just 2 days ago the Spiders were in 6th place.

21st Baltimore's 10–6 win in Cincinnati, coupled with a Cleveland loss, puts the Orioles back into first place.

22nd Not for long. Baltimore splits a doubleheader with Pittsburgh, and Cleveland tops Washington 8–6 to reclaim first place by one percentage point. Nine teams are still within 6 games of the Spiders.

24th Cleveland shows how it got into first place by scoring 6 runs in the bottom of the 8th inning—after which the game was called—to beat Washington 12–8.

AUGUST

1st The Pirates top Cleveland 2–0 to move into a virtual tie with the Spiders, who lead the NL with a percentage of .59770, compared to Pittsburgh's .59756.

3rd Pittsburgh edges Cleveland 5–4 to claim first place outright. Unfortunately, it is also Pittsburgh's last day in first this season, as Cleveland retakes the lead the next day.

The Capital Colored All-Americans set sail for England with a team of players from Western League clubs.

12th Heavyweight boxing champion Jim Corbett, a good ballplayer and a great gate attraction, plays 1B for the Scranton team in an Eastern League victory over Buffalo. Corbett collects 2 singles and knocks in 2 runs. His brother Joe, who will become a ML pitcher, plays SS.

14th Baltimore moves past Pittsburgh into 2nd place as the Orioles top Boston 9–3 and Pittsburgh falls to Cincinnati.

15th Hughie Jennings handles 20 chances flawlessly at SS as Baltimore triumphs over Boston 11–10 in 15 innings.

New York star George Davis gets 6 hits, but cannot generate enough offense to lead the Giants to victory as Philadelphia mauls them 23–9.

20th Cleveland scores 4 runs in the bottom of the 8th inning in near-total darkness to defeat Washington 8–7. Three of those runs come on a HR the Washington CF does not see.

23rd Baltimore sweeps a doubleheader with the Senators to claim first place from Cleveland. The Orioles have now won 13 consecutive games, a streak which will reach 14 before it is broken.

30th New York SS William "Shorty" Fuller sets a ML record with 11 putouts in a 9-inning game.

31st Fred Clarke of Louisville has his 35-game hitting streak broken in an 8–4 victory over Washington.

SEPTEMBER

9th For the 2nd time in 10 days, last-place Louisville breaks an opponent's winning streak this time by beating the Phillies 9–8, snapping their 12-game streak. On August 30th the Colonels halted Brooklyn's 11-game streak with a 6–5 win.

14th In the 8th inning of the Baltimore-Brooklyn game a foul tip shatters the mask of umpire Tim Hurst, driving a wire into his forehead which strikes an artery. Amazingly, Hurst remains in the game despite the blood.

28th Two days before the end of the season Baltimore finally clinches the NL pennant with a 5–2 victory over the New York Giants. Cleveland's 9–8 win in Louisville goes for naught.

OCTOBER

2nd Cleveland wins the first game of the Temple Cup series over Baltimore 5–4 with 2 runs in the bottom of the 9th.

3rd Legendary manager Harry Wright dies suddenly of pneumonia.

8th Cleveland takes the Temple Cup by beating the Baltimore Orioles for the 4th time in 5 games. The lack of respect accorded the Cup is reflected in the "very cold reception" Cleveland receives after returning from Baltimore on October 9.

12th *Sporting Life* notes that "there has never been a negro player in the National League. Though the colored brethren have turned out some excellent players, the color lines have been drawn very closely around the major body, and no colored man ever got into the ranks."

NOVEMBER

15th Cap Anson makes his stage debut in *A Runaway Colt*. Aside from forgetting a few lines Anson does quite well.

30th *Sporting Life* erroneously claims that "'Bid' McPhee will hardly discard the glove next season now that he is accustomed to wearing it."

DECEMBER

28th Star Chicago SS Bill Dahlen breaks his left arm in a fall.

1896

JANUARY

4th A portion of the fence surrounding the Polo Grounds blows down in a fierce storm.

14th A Chicago jury acquits OF Walter Wilmot of charges of violating the Sabbath law by playing Sunday baseball last year. Charges against other players are subsequently dropped, and the way is cleared for future Sunday ball in Chicago.

18th John Ward, who has not played or managed for the last 2 seasons, objects to being reserved by New York. At the NL meeting in February his appeal is upheld, and Ward is a free agent.

FEBRUARY

1st NL umpires oppose the proposed rule giving them the authority to eject "obstreperous players." They claim that the imposition of fines is a more effective form of discipline.

15th The Louisville infield is being rebuilt with base lines of blue clay. In addition, blue semicircles will radiate out from 1B and 3B, joining at 2B to form, along with the bottom half of the diamond, a heart.

16th New York City Parks Commissioner McMillan announces a plan to cut a street through the Polo Grounds leading to the Speedway, a new privately constructed horse track. The street is never built.

24th The NL adopts changes in the National Agreement. The minor leagues are divided into 6 classifications based on population, and new draft fees are instituted.

The NL forbids players from deliberately soiling baseballs, declares that "a ball cutting the corners of the home plate, and being requisite height, must be called a strike," and empowers umpires to eject players.

29th Western League president Ban Johnson asserts that "the Western League has passed the stage where it should be considered a minor league...it is a first-class organization, and should have the consideration that such an organization warrants." Four years later Johnson will act upon this belief, taking the first steps toward moving the WL—renamed the American League in 1900—to ML status.

MARCH

7th A Chicago writer quoted in the New York *Clipper* notes that "[Bill] Dahlen is one of the few now in the League who came blood new from a punky little league and became a good thing at first jump." Indeed, Dahlen eventually accumulates 2,460 hits and a .272 average over a 21-year career.

APRIL

7th Louisville's Pete Cassidy becomes the first baseball player in history to be X-rayed, as a splinter of bone is removed from his wrist.

13th Organized baseball celebrates Harry Wright Day in honor of the baseball pioneer who had died last October. Veterans of the 1860s play an exhibition game in Rockford, IL, using 1860s rules. In Cincinnati, the 1896 Reds defeat the 1892 Reds 7–3. Other games are played in New York, Philadelphia, Louisville, Washington, and Indianapolis.

16th The 12-team NL season opens, with no franchise changes from last year. The largest Opening Day crowd in the 19th century, 24,500, sees the opener in Philadelphia.

Veteran Cincinnati Reds 2B Bid McPhee opens the season wearing a glove for the first time, and survives several weeks of good-natured ribbing by opponents. He is the last to convert.

20th An overflow crowd of 18,033 at Boston necessitates a ground rule of one base on a hit into the standing crowd. The Beaneaters then pound out 28 singles (and a double) in an 8-inning 21–8 win over Baltimore. This outburst equals the ML record for singles in one game set by Philadelphia against Louisville on August 17, 1894.

29th The Cleveland Spiders score 2 runs in the 2nd inning to break a 22-inning scoreless streak by Pittsburgh Pirate pitchers, but fail to score again and lose 9–2.

MAY

3rd The Louisville Colonels lose their 11th straight game to Cincinnati 5–3.

7th Boston scores in all 8 innings in a 17–1 rout of the hapless Colonels, who help to dig their own grave by committing 10 errors.

8th   The St. Louis Browns dismiss manager Harry Diddlebock for intoxication. Player Arlie Latham and owner Chris Von der Ahe manage 2 games apiece before Von der Ahe settles on Roger Connor.

In the top of the 9th inning, Philadelphia's Billy Nash starts to argue with the umpire over a called strike. Clark Griffith throws a pitch in the midst of the argument which nicks Nash's bat, resulting in a DP. Griffith's quick thinking helps the Chicago Colts take a 5–3 victory.

9th   Washington defeats Pittsburgh 14–9 in a bean-ball battle. Senators pitcher Win Mercer hits 3 Pittsburgh batters while Pirate "Pink" Hawley hits 3 consecutive Washington batters in a disastrous 11-run 7th inning, tying the mark he set on July 4, 1894. Hawley retires in 1900 after only 9 seasons with a still-standing NL record of 195 hit batters.

Baltimore's Hughie Jennings knocks down Reds 3B Charlie Irwin before he can catch Bid McPhee's throw. Jennings scores afterward to give the Orioles a controversial 6–5, 10-inning win over Cincinnati. Umpire Bob Emslie is escorted out of the ballpark by Cincinnati police.

13th   Umpire Tim Keefe forfeits the Boston-Chicago game to Boston. The Beaneaters break a 4–4 tie with 6 runs in the top of the 11th. Flagrant stalling by Chicago in the bottom of the inning leads to the forfeit.

14th   Pittsburgh's Jake Stenzel has 6 hits, all singles, and a stolen base in a 20–4 pounding of Boston.

Despite going 5-for-5 with 2 doubles, Cincinnati's Charles "Dusty" Miller fails to score in the 13–2 win over Brooklyn.

20th   The Brooklyn Bridegrooms pile up a franchise record for runs in beating the Pirates 25–6. They will tie the record on September 23, 1901.

21st   Cy Young gets Cleveland's 8th consecutive win with a 4–1 decision over Boston. The streak has helped the Spiders to solidify their hold on first place.

Louisville gets a rare victory, riding Mike McDermott's 2-hitter to a 1–0 win over Baltimore. This is McDermott's only good performance of the year. In the remaining 56 innings he will pitch this year, he will allow 85 hits.

27th   Cleveland takes advantage of Joett Meekin's 13 walks and 3 wild pitches to beat the New York Giants 11–5. However, the Spiders fall to 2nd in the NL race behind Cincinnati, which whips Washington 10–6.

29th   Baltimore leaps past Cincinnati in the NL race with a 4–1 defeat of the Reds.

Washington P Charlie "Silver" King makes his first ML appearance since 1893 a success, as he wins a 6-hitter over Pittsburgh 6–1.

JUNE

3rd   Baltimore wins its 10th in a row over Pittsburgh. The winning run scores in the bottom of the 9th when P Frank Killen hits Hugh Jennings with a pitch with the bases loaded.

4th   The Reds' Red Ehret wins an 11-hit shutout over Brooklyn 6–0.

5th   Cleveland defeats Baltimore 10–4 for its 2nd straight victory over the defending NL champions and replaces the Orioles in first place.

19th   Chicago defeats Cleveland 8–3 in a turbulent game. In the 7th, umpire Tom Lynch changes a close call at first base and enrages Cleveland manager-1B Patsy Tebeau. Lynch ejects Tebeau but Tebeau refuses to leave the field. The two square off and a near riot ensues. Lynch refuses to continue, and players Cy Young of Cleveland and Bill Dahlen of Chicago alternate as umpires.

Baltimore reclaims first place with a 9–4 triumph over Philadelphia plus Cleveland's 8–3 loss to Chicago.

25th   Jake Stenzel's 5 singles are not enough, as Pittsburgh falls to Chicago 17–10.

27th   In an aftermath to the previous day's brawl, several Cleveland players are brought before a Louisville court on a warrant sworn by Louisville owner Hunt Stuckey. Manager Tebeau is fined $100 for disturbing the peace. Ed McKean and Jimmy McAleer are fined $75 each, and Jesse Burkett, $50.

New York rallies with 5 runs in the bottom of the 9th to defeat Brooklyn 9–8. Harry Davis leads the way with a pair of 3-run doubles.

29th   The NL Board of Directors meets and fines Patsy Tebeau $200 for rowdyism. Tebeau refuses to pay and announces he will seek legal redress. In another action, the board denies the appeal of Amos Rusie against fines levied last year by New York president

Andrew Freedman. Rusie is in the process of sitting out the 1896 season.

JULY

1st Cleveland wins 19–7 over Chicago to run its winning streak to 6. The Spiders are 36-18 and tied for first with Baltimore at 38-19.

2nd Kid Nichols wins a battle of 2-hitters with Washington's James "Doc" McJames to give Boston a 4–2 decision.

3rd New York wastes a triple play and 2 DPs and is whitewashed by Baltimore 6–0.

4th Washington and Philadelphia split a wild doubleheader. Washington wins the opener 13–8, while Philadelphia overcomes a 14–5 deficit to win the nightcap 15–14. The 2 teams combine for a ML record 73 hits for the twin bill. The record is tied on July 6, 1929.

6th After the Pittsburgh-Washington contest, umpire Tim Hurst hits Pirate players Jake Stenzel and Emerson "Pink" Hawley in the jaw in response to repeated verbal attacks by the players during the game. According the the New York *Clipper* "neither player resented the attack."

8th St. Louis suffers its 14th straight loss, the longest losing streak of the season. Roger Connor is fired and replaced as player-manager by Tommy Dowd, who becomes the 5th St. Louis manager of the season.

The Pirates hammer out 22 hits in a driving rain to humiliate Washington 19–0.

13th Ed Delahanty of Philadelphia hits 4 inside-the-park HRs against Chicago, 3 in consecutive at bats. He also has a single and drives in 7 runs. Despite this feat the Phillies lose 9–8.

Cleveland falls to 3rd place (behind Cincinnati and Baltimore) after its 5–2 loss to New York. Spider manager Patsy Tebeau, after being suspended by NL president Nick Young for past transgressions, plays anyway after obtaining restraining orders on umpire Tim Hurst, New York manager Arthur Irwin, and Giant captain William "Kid" Gleason.

Deacon McGuire's 5 hits, including 2 doubles, are enough to lead Washington to a 14–1 win over St. Louis.

15th Bones Ely's 5 hits fail to prevent Pittsburgh's 2–1 loss to Boston.

16th Cincinnati beats Baltimore 5–0 for its 11th straight win. The streak has moved the Reds into first place.

17th Pittsburgh defeats Philadelphia 8–7 in a bizarre finish. The Phillies score 3 runs in the top of the 9th inning to take a 7–5 lead only to see Pittsburgh score 3 in the bottom of the inning for the win. Ely scores the tying run from 3B as the Phillies argue with umpire Bette following a disputed call. Philadelphia had neglected to request time out. Kid Carsey then comes in to relieve Jack Taylor and balks in the winning run.

19th A crowd of 24,900 at Cincinnati is disappointed when the Reds lose to Baltimore 14–6. The Orioles score 9 runs in the 7th to tie Cincinnati for first place.

21st Cleveland shuts out Washington in both games of their doubleheader. Five of the 7 NL games today are shutouts.

23rd Cy Young pitches no-hit ball for 8⅔ innings before surrendering a hit to Ed Delahanty in a 2–0 win over Philadelphia. The win is Cleveland's 6th straight and leaves them one game out of first place.

24th Baltimore wins over St. Louis by forfeit. After the Orioles score the first 5 runs in the top of the 13th to break an 8–8 tie, St. Louis flagrantly delays in the bottom of the inning, prompting umpire Bob Emslie to call the forfeit.

25th The 2nd game of the doubleheader between New York and Pittsburgh is stopped after the top of the 8th with the Pirates ahead 7–2 because the flooding Allegheny has inundated the field.

26th In the 8th inning of Cincinnati's 10–1 win over Cleveland, Cincinnati's Eddie Burke steals 2nd and collides with 2B "Cupid" Childs. The subsequent fistfight is joined by other players, and then Cincinnati fans. More than 50 police are needed to clear the field.

28th Cincinnati's 9–8 win over Cleveland is the Reds' 8th straight victory. Upset by the umpiring, Cleveland player-manager Tebeau comes in to pitch in the 9th with runners on 2B and 3B, no outs, and an 8–8 tie. He promptly gives up the game-winning hit to

Germany Smith. This would be Tebeau's only ML pitching appearance.

St. Louis takes advantage of 18 hits, 13 Louisville errors, and 11 walks to stomp the Colonels 20–5.

31st After a disputed call, Pirates P Frank Killen hits umpire Daniel Lally in the face. When Lally responds in kind, hundreds of Pittsburgh fans charge onto the field. Eventually Killen is arrested for disorderly conduct.

AUGUST

2nd Still Bill Hill's 2-hitter helps Louisville edge Chicago 2–1. In the 6th inning Billy Clingman, in a failed attempt to score the game's first run, spikes Chicago C Tim Donahue. Donahue attempts to retaliate by throwing the ball at Clipman but is prevented from doing so.

6th Cincinnati's Frank Dwyer defeats Pittsburgh 4–2 for his 13th consecutive win.

Philadelphia jumps to a 10–0 lead over Brooklyn, but the Bridegrooms charge back, scoring 2 runs with 2 out in the bottom of the 9th to claim a well-earned 11–10 victory.

8th Baltimore defeats Washington 21–16. Each team hits exactly the same number of singles as its run total, with the 37 singles establishing a still-standing ML record for a 9-inning game. Baltimore star John McGraw makes his first appearance of the season when he pinch-hits in the 3rd. McGraw has been sidelined with typhoid fever. The New York *Clipper* box score for the game credits the Orioles with only 20 singles (plus 3 doubles and a HR), not 21. The record claimed for singles in this game may be suspect.

9th New York announces that Manager Arthur Irwin is going on "vacation" for the rest of the season so that the newly acquired Bill Joyce can take over the managerial reins.

10th The Orioles take sole possession of first place for the first time since July 4th, with their 10th straight win, an 11–4 decision over Washington.

11th Cincinnati suffers its first shutout of the season in a 6–0 setback to Chicago.

12th Napoleon Lajoie, who batted .429 in the New England league, makes his ML debut for the

Philadelphia Phillies. He goes 1-for-5 in a 9–0 win over Washington.

13th After losing to Brooklyn the 2 previous games, Baltimore gains revenge by scoring 10 runs in the first inning and continuing the onslaught to beat the Bridegrooms 19–3.

15th In attempting to tag out Brooklyn's rookie Fielder Jones at 2B, Herman Long accidentally spikes him just above the right eye. Jones is safe, but the Bridegrooms lose to Boston 8–3. Jones is not seriously hurt.

17th Baltimore wins a pair of one-run games from Philadelphia 3–2 and 16–15. The Orioles score 8 runs in the bottom of the 9th to win the nightcap.

19th Cincinnati retakes first place with a 9–7 triumph over Boston, while Baltimore loses by the same score to St. Louis.

Philadelphia becomes the 2nd team in 6 days to score 10 runs in the first inning. Not surprisingly, they defeat Louisville 15–0.

21st Baltimore takes over first place for good with a 7–0 win over St. Louis, while Cincinnati loses 10–9 to Boston.

31st Washington's Win Mercer shuts out Chicago 1–0 in 11 innings for the first Senators shutout since September 17, 1893.

SEPTEMBER

3rd Boston hammers St. Louis with 30 hits in a 28–7 win in the first game of a twin bill. Billy Hamilton, Fred Tenney, and Jimmy Collins each have 5 hits, while Hugh Duffy's 4 hits include 2 HRs.

7th On Labor Day, Baltimore wins a rare triple-header from Louisville 4–3, 9–1, and 12–1 in 8 innings.

William "Brickyard" Kennedy allows only one single to lead Brooklyn to a 6–1 win over Cincinnati.

8th Baltimore wins 2 more from Louisville 10–9 and 3–1. The 5 wins in 2 days give Baltimore a record of 82-34 and a 10-game lead over 2nd-place Cincinnati.

12th The Orioles clinch their 3rd straight NL pennant with a 9–5 win over Brooklyn.

15th After umpire Tim Hurst becomes ill in the 3rd inning of the Brooklyn-Washington game, "local man" John Heydler replaces him. Heydler soon joins the NL on a permanent basis and rises quickly in the hierarchy. In 1918 he is elected president of the NL.

16th Cincinnati shuts out home team Pittsburgh in a doubleheader 11–0 and 4–0. Irate Pittsburgh fans throw stones, a board, and a pop bottle at umpire John Sheridan. He is rescued from a crowd of 200 angry spectators by players from both teams.

19th Cy Young throws a 7-hitter and hits a HR, while Jesse Burkett gets 5 hits, in Cleveland's 21–2 win over Cincinnati.

Kid Nichols wins his 30th game for the 6th straight year in Boston's 3–1 victory over Brooklyn.

21st Pittsburgh manager Connie Mack announces that he will manage the Milwaukee club of the Western League in 1897.

26th Jesse Burkett gets 3 hits for Cleveland in the final game of the season to finish at .410, becoming the first major leaguer to hit .400 in consecutive seasons, a feat later duplicated by Ty Cobb and Rogers Hornsby.

OCTOBER

1st Regular-season WL champion Minneapolis defeats Indianapolis 4-games-to-2 to win the WL title and the Detroit *Free Press* Cup.

2nd Following a rainout, Baltimore and Bill Hoffer defeat 2nd-place Cleveland and Cy Young 7–1 in the first game of the Temple Cup.

3rd Baltimore takes the 2nd game 7–2. The losing pitcher is Bobby Wallace, who will be moved to 3B next season, and later to SS where he builds a Hall of Fame career.

4th The Cuban Giants defeat the Chicago Unions 11–9 and claim the title of black champions of America.

5th Baltimore goes ahead 3–0 with a 6–2 win over the Spiders.

8th Following another rainout, the Orioles defeat Cleveland 5–0 to win the Temple Cup in a 4-game sweep. The Cup games are poorly attended, while the rowdy behavior of both teams does nothing to enhance the stature of the troubled series.

11th The annual NL meeting gets underway in Chicago. Brooklyn owner Ferdinand H. Abell proposes to make all players free agents between January 1st and March 1st and allow all teams to bid on them, subject to a salary limit. The plan is studiously ignored.

12th Volatile New York Giants owner Andrew Freedman is found guilty of an April 22nd assault on baseball writer Edward Hurst. He receives a suspended sentence.

13th The NL votes to award Henry Chadwick $50 per month for life in recognition of his past services to the game.

DECEMBER

1st Amos Rusie, a season-long holdout, announces he will settle with New York and play next season.

1897

MARCH

9th Cleveland signs Holy Cross star Louis Sockalexis to a contract. Sockalexis, a full-blooded Penobscot Indian, soon earns the admiration of Spiders fans with his phenomenal all-around skills. Before long, baseball fans start referring to the Cleveland team as the "Indians." Although Sockalexis will only play parts of 3 seasons due to acute alcoholism, the nickname will be revived in 1915 and become the club's official name.

12th Brooklyn president Charles Byrne and treasurer Abell set a ML record by offering $100,000 for the entire Cleveland franchise. The offer is rejected.

27th Cleveland president Frank DeHaas Robison proposes that NL teams chip in to pay the 1896 salary of New York star Amos Rusie, who refused to play due to a contract dispute. Robison and other NL officials want to avoid Rusie's lawsuit, in which he seeks free agency. Although New York president Andrew Freeman vehemently opposes the NL plan, the $3,000 payment is made and Rusie rejoins the Giants.

APRIL

9th A touring team of 13 Australian players arrives in San Francisco, and President Young encourages the 12 NL teams to arrange exhibition games with the visitors.

17th Manager Gus Schmelz and the Washington Senators visit President McKinley at the White House. Because of other pressing business, the president will be unable to attend the Senators' opener.

19th In the season opener at Boston, a 3-run HR by Nap Lajoie in the top of the 9th gives the Phillies a 6-run lead that holds up despite a last-gasp, 5-run Beaneater rally.

22nd Willie Keeler's single and double in the Orioles' first game begins a streak of safe hits in 44 consecutive games.

A loss to Pittsburgh 4–1 starts Red Donahue, St. Louis Browns righthander, on the way to a league-leading 33 losses. A true workhorse, Donahue will also lead in appearances (46), starts (42), complete

games (38), and hits allowed (484). He will win 11 and have an ERA of 6.13.

24th Nap Lajoie has a big day with 2 singles, one double, 3 triples, and 3 errors in the Phillies' 12–4 win over New York.

27th Amos Rusie, the Giants' "Hoosier Thunderbolt," ends a year-long holdout and returns to the mound to beat Washington 8–3 before 10,000 welcoming New York fans.

MAY

3rd With the Giants leading 7–0 after 2 innings, Washington starts delaying the game in hopes that the imminent rainstorm will wash the game out. Umpire Tom Lynch forfeits the game to New York.

4th Cap Anson Day is celebrated in Chicago during the home opener. Anson plays an errorless game behind the plate and adds a single in Chicago's 5–2 victory.

7th Baltimore survives Duff Cooley's 2 doubles and 3 singles to defeat the Athletics 13–11.

10th Jack Doyle hits an unusual home run for Baltimore, but Washington defeats the Orioles 13–5. The HR is noteworthy in that the ball rolls to the fence where a ladder had been placed. It rolls up the ladder and disappears over the fence.

Nap Lajoie slugs 2 HRs and a double to lead Philadelphia to a 13–1 rout of St. Louis.

11th Duke Farrell, Washington catcher, sets a ML record by throwing out 8 Orioles trying to steal 2B, but the Senators lose anyway 6–3.

14th The Orioles fatten their batting averages with 22 hits against the hapless Browns and romp 20–3.

16th Fans assemble for Cleveland's first Sunday baseball game only to have the police arrest the players after the first inning. Players and umpire Tim Hurst are released on bail provided by Cleveland club owner Frank DeHaas Robison. A test case is made of rookie hurler John Powell. On June 10th he will be found guilty of playing ball on Sunday and fined $5.

17th Pirates pitcher Frank Killen allows 2 hits to defeat Rusie and the Giants 3–2. Pittsburgh's Denny Lyons has 2 fingers broken after being hit by a Rusie pitch.

18th Bill "Scrappy" Joyce's 4 triples pace the New York Giants to an 11–5 win over the Pirates at Pittsburgh. This is the last time this feat is accomplished in ML history. George Streif hit 4, June 25, 1885.

20th Washington OF Kip Selbach steals 5 bases against the Chicago Colts.

Fred Clarke gets 5 hits to help Louisville to a 13-inning 13–12 decision over Brooklyn.

23rd A "shoot the chutes" waterslide opens at Sportsman's Park, St. Louis. With the Browns in last place, owner Von der Ahe is trying to draw customers with a variety of amusement park attractions.

25th Cleveland rallies for 4 runs in the bottom of the 9th to topple the Athletics 10–9.

31st At Boston, the home team scores 25 runs on 29 hits to wallop St. Louis 25–5. Fred Tenney goes 6-for-8.

Using mechanical dummies, "an electrical baseball machine" reproduces the Louisville doubleheader on stage at Philadelphia's McCauley Theater, which has been fitted out like a ballpark. Messages transmitted from the field are translated by "skillful manipulation" of the machine's keyboard into a reenactment.

JUNE

3rd In New York, the Giants stop Louisville in the first of 2 games. Because this game was transferred from Louisville without league consent, no league official is present. Two players, Charlie Dexter and Mike Sullivan, umpire the 6–1 Giant victory. This game will later be dropped from the standings.

7th In the midst of the season's longest winning streak, Boston blanks Pittsburgh 4–0 to move past Cincinnati into 2nd place.

15th Pittsburgh loses to Washington 10–8 despite Gene DeMontreville's 5 hits.

16th Louisville president Harry Pulliam fires manager Rogers and replaces him with 24-year-old OF Fred Clarke. In addition to his $2,400 salary, Clarke gets an extra $500 for managing the team.

The Reds explode for 12 runs in the 3rd inning and whip Brooklyn 15–6.

17th Joett Meekin allows 10 hits and his teammates commit 4 errors, but New York still manages to shut out Cleveland 7–0. The next day the Indians are held to 3 hits and lose 5–0.

19th Frank Killen allows 5 Baltimore hits as he pitches Pittsburgh to victory. Willie Keeler fails to get a hit for the first time in 1897 after 44 straight games.

21st Boston moves into first by posting its 17th straight victory, beating Brooklyn 11–6. Winning pitcher Fred Klobedanz has a single, 2 doubles, and a triple.

22nd Boston's winning streak is halted at 17 as Brooklyn pitcher Bill Kennedy defeats the Beaneaters 7–4.

Baltimore takes advantage of Boston's first loss in 18 games and moves back into first place by defeating New York.

23rd The Beaneaters regain the NL lead with a 13–2 rout of Brooklyn.

24th Dick Harley leads the Browns to a 12-inning 7–6 victory over Pittsburgh by going 6-for-6.

26th Pittsburgh CF Steve Brodie's string of consecutive games ends at 574. His arm is so sore the Pirates go on the road without him. The streak is a 19th-century NL record, but falls 3 games short of George Pinckney's 577 ML mark.

Jack Stenzel hits a solo HR with 2 out in the 9th inning to give the Orioles a 1–0 victory over Boston, its first in an important 3-game series with the NL leaders.

29th Chicago scores in every inning to demolish Louisville 36–7 to set the NL record for runs scored. The Colts pile up 32 hits for 51 bases with Barry McCormick hitting 4 singles, a triple, and a HR in 8 at bats.

30th Southpaw Cy Seymour of the Giants allows 11 walks in a loss to Orioles. He will be a 20-game winner this year and lead all pitchers in strikeouts with 157.

JULY

3rd Boston players present a horseshoe of roses to Giants manager Bill Joyce before the game, then defeat him and the Giants 3–2.

5th With the bases loaded, Pittsburgh's Jim Donnelly hits a ball that goes through Jesse Burkett's legs in LF. Burkett refuses to field it and by the time

SS Ed McKean can get the ball, 4 Pirate runners score. Cleveland loses the game 6–1.

Boston's victory, along with its win the next day, give the Beaneaters an incredible record of 28 wins in 30 games. Nevertheless, the Orioles are still close behind.

The Reds defeat Baltimore 8–5 for their 10th win in 11 games and move past the Orioles into 2nd place in the NL race.

6th   Brooklyn tries for a "Boston 9th-inning finish," but fails, losing to New York 7–5.

9th   The Athletics score in 8 of 9 innings and accumulate 26 hits en route to a 19–7 rout of Cincinnati.

13th   Ed Delahanty has 9 hits in 9 at bats during the Philadelphia-Louisville doubleheader. Philadelphia wins both games 4–3 and 9–7.

14th   Delahanty continues his hard-hitting, going 4-for-5 with 2 singles, a double, and a HR in Philadelphia's 10–5 win over Louisville. Delahanty sets a record with 10 consecutive hits.

15th   Washington 1B Tommy Tucker hits five singles and a double in 6 at bats in the Senators' 16–5 win over the Reds.

16th   A game is played under electric lights at the Clyde Park in San Antonio, TX. Dallas wins the exhibition 10–5.

Owner outrage at player ineptitude is vividly expressed by Washington's president J. Earl Wagner. His Senators, en route to a not-so-bad 7th place, are denounced as "dunghills and quitters."

The Louisville Colonels purchase the contract of Honus Wagner, the Atlantic League's star fielder and batter.

After the Louisville Colonels score 5 runs in the bottom of the 9th to gain a 7–7 tie with New York, the Giants complain that the rally was illegally aided by suspicious calls by the umpire. New York refuses to take the field in the 10th inning, and the Colonels are awarded a 9–0 forfeit victory.

17th   Baltimore's Willie Keeler gets 5 hits and scores 5 runs in a 20–2 rout of Chicago.

18th   Cap Anson makes his career 3,000th hit, a 4th-inning single, as Clark Griffith and the Colts defeat Baltimore 6–3. The feat fails, however, to make the Chicago papers.

19th   Honus Wagner makes his first appearance, singling and stealing 2B as Louisville beats Washington 6–2.

22nd   After a base on balls in the Pittsburgh-Baltimore game, umpire Jack Sheridan moves his station behind the pitcher's box. Pirates P "Pink" Hawley says something to Sheridan, whereupon the umpire strikes Hawley in the face. The pitcher retaliates with 2 blows that knock Sheridan out. After 10 minutes, Sheridan continues and Pittsburgh loses the game.

31st   Brooklyn P Bill Kennedy becomes so upset at umpire Hank O'Day that he throws a ball at him. The ball misses O'Day, who has his back turned, allowing George Davis to score the winning run for the Giants.

Louisville ties a ML record by having 6 batters reach base after being hit by pitchers Mike McDermott and John Grimes of St. Louis.

AUGUST

1st   Louisville is winning 5–4, with St. Louis at bat in the last of the 9th. After Tuck Turner fouls a pitch out of play, substitute umpire Red Donahue gives a new ball to pitcher Herb Cunningham, who promptly rolls it in the dirt. Donahue objects and gives him another ball. Five fresh balls are given the same treatment. Umpire Donahue then forfeits the game to St. Louis.

2nd   Baltimore retakes 2nd place from the Reds with their 22nd straight win over Philadelphia 4–2. The Athletics will gain their first win over the Orioles in nearly 2 years tomorrow.

4th   At Cincinnati, umpire Tim Hurst makes a decision in favor of the Louisville Colonels. A fan throws an empty beer glass onto the field, and Hurst promptly picks it up and hurls it back into the stands. An unfortunate fan is hit and cut seriously. Hurst is arrested for assault and battery.

5th   Duff Cooley gets half of the Athletics' 10 hits and 3 of their 5 runs to lead them to a 5–4, 12-inning win over New York.

6th   In Boston, the Beaneaters edge the Orioles 6–5. In the 8th inning, umpire Lynch loses his temper and strikes Baltimore 1B Jack Doyle on the jaw. It takes the Boston police 10 minutes to restore order. LF Hugh Duffy saves the game for the league leaders by throwing out a runner at home in the bottom of the 9th.

7th The Beaneaters defeat Baltimore for the 2nd straight time and drop the Orioles back into 3rd place.

12th Baltimore regains 2nd place with an 11–7 victory over its favorite opponent, Philadelphia.

13th Chicago's Clark Griffith posts his first career shutout, beating Cincinnati 2–0. The win is the 104th of his career.

14th Today is Bid McPhee Day at Cincinnati. The Reds lose the game, but the veteran 2B, playing in his 16th season, receives a check for $1,800.

19th The Orioles lose the first of 2 consecutive shutouts to Cleveland, breaking their 9-game winning streak.

27th Roger Bresnahan, an 18-year-old player who will ultimately become a Hall of Fame catcher, pitches a shutout in his ML debut for Washington, allowing St. Louis 6 hits while winning 3–0. He will win 3 more games before rejecting a contract he feels is unworthy of his talent and going home to Toledo.

Baltimore sweeps a doubleheader from Boston and takes over first place by 4 percentage points, .683 to .679.

At Philadelphia, Nap Lajoie shows up intoxicated for the game with Pittsburgh and is suspended.

SEPTEMBER

3rd For the first time ever, 2 players, Willie Keeler and Jack Doyle, each get 6 hits in 6 at bats in Baltimore's 22–1 win over St. Louis.

8th St. Louis's Rube Waddell loses his ML debut to the Orioles 5–1. Waddell allows 11 hits, walks 4, and strikes out 2. He will eventually register 2,316 strikeouts.

11th Otherwise undistinguished Washington rookie OF Jake Cettman singles in his first at bat in the 2nd game of a doubleheader to tie Delahanty's record of 10 hits in 10 consecutive times at bat. Cettman was 4-for-4 in yesterday's 9–4 win and 5-for-5 in the first game today, a 19–10 loss to Cincinnati.

17th After having their 17-game winning streak broken yesterday, the Boston Beaneaters help "Kid" Nichols to his 30th win of the season, 17–0 over the Giants.

Baltimore wins its 12th straight game, 11–6 over the Athletics.

18th Cy Young shuts out the Reds 6–0 on a no-hitter, the only one in the NL this year and the first in 4 years. Only 4 men reach 1B, all on errors.

20th Former heavyweight champion James J. Corbett plays 1B for Milwaukee (WL) in a 7–6 win at Minneapolis. Batting cleanup, "Gentleman Jim" singles twice, scores once, and is middle man in a 6-3-2 double play. It is his 29th appearance in a scheduled minor league game.

Brooklyn gives Boston a taste of its own medicine by scoring 12 runs in the first inning and crushing them 22–5.

22nd The Beaneaters defeat Brooklyn 12–0 in their last home game for a 52-13 record at South End grounds. They trail the Orioles by .001 point: .707 to .706.

24th The biggest series of the season starts at Baltimore as 13,000 fans see Boston beat the Orioles 6–4 to take over first place. Boston's record is now 90-37 while Baltimore's is 87-37.

25th Baltimore strikes back by beating Boston 6–3 and moving back into first place.

27th Twenty-five thousand people witness the final game of the series between Baltimore and Boston. The Beaneaters overwhelm the Orioles 19–10. Grandstand overflow puts fans within 20 feet of home plate, while 15 ground-rule doubles fall among OF standees. The Beaneaters put the game away with 9 runs on 11 hits in the 7th inning. Kid Nichols goes the distance for Boston.

After 23 straight defeats by Cincinnati, dating from September 25, 1895, St. Louis wins the team's 12th and last game of the season series 5–4.

30th Boston clinches the 1897 NL pennant—Frank Selee's 4th—with a 12–3 victory over Brooklyn, as Baltimore loses 9–3 to Washington. Their winning percentage of .705 is the highest in Boston history.

OCTOBER

1st St. Louis owner Von der Ahe, losing money as the Browns lose games, takes over as the 4th manager this season, 12th since the team rejoined the NL in 1892.

3rd Chicago finishes the 1897 season by splitting a doubleheader with St. Louis. Cap Anson, now 45 years old, hits 2 HRs in the first game. He steals a base in the nightcap, his final game in a career that spans 26 years.

4th   The contest for the Temple Cup starts with a 13–12 home victory for Boston over Baltimore, before 9,600. Charley "Kid" Nichols and Ted Lewis pitch for the winners; Jerry Nops hurls for the Orioles.

5th   The 2nd game of the series sees Baltimore turn back Boston 13–11 behind Joe Corbett.

9th   Twenty-five hundred fans at Baltimore watch the Orioles win their 3rd game 12–11. The Orioles score 11 times in the first 2 innings off Jack Stivetts.

11th   Baltimore wins the Temple Cup, and $310 for each player, by defeating Boston 9–3. The crowd is so small that management refuses to give the exact number.

15th   W. C. Temple of Pittsburgh, whose trophy has been contested for the last 4 baseball seasons, is dissatisfied with this year's contest. He will attend the league meeting and ask that the Cup be returned to him.

NOVEMBER

13th   At the NL meetings, President Young announces that the Temple Cup Series has been discontinued, and that there will be 2 umpires per game next year.

DECEMBER

31st   Charles H. Ebbets, 38, who "has handled every dollar" entering the Brooklyn club's treasury for the past 15 years, gains a controlling 80 percent interest in the team.

1898

JANUARY

8th NL president Nick Young says he will have the more experienced umpires such as Tom Lynch, Bob Emslie, and Hank O'Day stay behind the plate when he institutes the new 2-umpire system. Previously, the single umpire would move behind the pitcher only with men on base.

31st Cap Anson is fired after 19 years as player-manager of Chicago. Strong-minded Cap, with a record of 1,288 victories and 5 pennants, was enormously popular in Chicago. Former infielder Tom Burns takes over for Chicago, who are now called the Orphans.

FEBRUARY

13th President John T. Brush of the Cincinnati club dismisses criticism of his proposed league resolution to punish players who use vulgar and obscene language on the field, saying newspaper criticism is the result of ignorance.

MARCH

12th Former umpire Tim Hurst arrives in St. Louis to take over management of the Browns. The team will have spring practice at West Baden Springs, IN.

APRIL

2nd Famed heavyweight boxer Jim Corbett, whose brother Joe pitches for Baltimore, claims he made $17,000 last year by playing in well-advertised minor league games for a sizable cut of the gate.

16th The league urges official scorers to award hits, rather than automatic errors, on hard-hit balls that handcuff infielders; to be scrupulous in awarding assists to all players handling balls in rundowns; and to cease awarding hits to batters on fielder's-choice plays.

The Sportsman's Park grandstand is destroyed by fire in the 2nd inning with the Browns at bat against Chicago. Forty persons are injured as a crowd of 6,000 stampedes to escape. Browns manager Tim Hurst, and players help workmen remove debris so that the April 17th day game can be played.

20th John McGraw, Baltimore's feisty 3B, who will lead the league in runs (143) and walks (112), gets 3 of each in an 18–3 drubbing of Boston.

21st Phillies P Bill Duggleby hits a bases-full HR in his first ML at bat, an event never duplicated. The Phillies win 13–4.

22nd Two no-hitters: Baltimore's Jim Hughes against Boston in his 2nd ML start; Cincinnati's Ted Breitenstein against Pittsburgh, marking the first time two 9-inning no-hitters are pitched on the same day.

27th All New York players, including P Cy Seymour, score one or more runs in a 20–6 rout of Washington, which is called after 7 innings.

28th The game at Philadelphia is postponed on account of snow.

30th Opening Day at Brooklyn's new Washington Park attracts 15,000 fans to see a 6–4 Brooklyn loss to Philadelphia. Veteran Sam Thompson hits the first HR in the new park, his last in the ML.

MAY

1st The Board of Discipline of the National Baseball League adopts a set of rules to suppress rowdy ball playing. John T. Brush said the resolution, which he proposed, "has worked like a charm."

3rd Brooklyn's Jimmy Sheckard hits a HR, 2 triples, and a single in a 9–6 defeat of Philadelphia. Eleven total bases will be the season's one-game high mark.

4th Nap Lajoie of the Phillies goes 0-for-4 after 22 hits in the first 11 games.

5th Baltimore manager Ned Hanlon sends a nasty letter to the league president, Nick Young, for scheduling a single game in New York. The Orioles arrived for the game, but were rained out, and Hanlon paid for the futile trip "without receiving a penny."

8th Rookie Harry Steinfeldt, the "wonder from Wonderville," replaces injured Bid McPhee at 2B for the Reds, gets 3 hits against Louisville, and handles 9 chances afield.

10th Amos Rusie of the Giants sets down Brooklyn on one hit and wins 5–0.

11th With the bases full and one out, Oriole RF Tommy O'Brien muffs Bobby Lowe's short fly, recovers the ball, runs in, tags Jimmy Collins at 2B, and steps on the bag to force Chick Stahl and complete an unassisted DP.

17th Boston's Ted Lewis shuts out Brooklyn 12–0, giving up only one hit, a 9th-inning single, to opposing hurler Joe Yeager.

19th Jake Beckley, Reds 1B, hits 3 consecutive triples off Kid Nichols in a 5–4 win over Boston.

22nd A 9th-inning scratch single by Brooklyn batter Fielder Jones breaks up a no-hit effort by Chick Fraser of Louisville, who wins 3–0.

24th The highest run total of the season is scored in a 15–13 Oriole defeat of the Orphans in Chicago. The pitcher yields 36 hits, 10 walks, 2 wild pitches, and 3 hit batsmen.

Pitcher Clark Griffith of Chicago, ejected from the Baltimore game, spews obscene language at umpire Tom Lynch, who threatens him with the Board of Discipline. *Sporting Life* notes "the only witness appears to be catcher Bowerman of Baltimore, who is hardly likely to testify against Griffith."

25th Chicago scores 20 runs off rookie Frank Kitson of Baltimore, who pitched a shutout in his debut May 19th.

30th Cincinnati OF Elmer Smith, a former pitcher, is blanked after hitting in 30 consecutive games dating from Opening Day. The Reds defeat Ralph Miller of Brooklyn 7–2.

JUNE

3rd Jack Clements of St. Louis becomes the first lefty to catch 1,000 games. He drives in the winning run in a 5–4 victory over Baltimore.

6th Bill Dahlen, Chicago SS, hits 3 triples in a 15–2 triumph at Brooklyn.

9th Ed Doheny of the Giants fans 12, but 7 walks, 5 wild pitches, and 6 New York errors give Chicago a 10–8 victory.

P-OF Jack Stivetts breaks a 9th-inning 5–5 tie with Cincinnati as he delivers a game-winning pinch HR, the 3rd such wallop of his career.

10th A hard week for managers: Tom Brown is replaced at Washington by "Dirty Jack" Doyle, Billy Barnie is fired by 9th-place Brooklyn. Barnie's successor, CF Mike Griffin, resigns after 4 games; President Charlie Ebbets fills in. "Scrappy" Bill Joyce is dropped by the New York Giants in favor of Cap Anson, who takes over on the 11th.

13th Former pitcher Charles Sweeney, recently released from San Quentin penitentiary where he served time for manslaughter, officiates in the San Francisco–San Jose game as a California League umpire.

18th Philadelphia deposes manager George Stallings. Club secretary Bill Shettsline, a nonprofessional, will be 15 games above .500 managing for the remaining 103 games.

20th Elmer Flick, who swings a 54-ounce bat, hits 3 triples for the Phillies at St. Louis in a 14–2 victory.

22nd Having lost to Cincinnati 2–1 in 14 innings on June 14th, Chicago P Walter Woods loses to Boston 6–5 in 14 innings. Boston's Ted Lewis relieves Vic Willis with 3 runs in, 2 on, and one out in the first inning, and induces the Orphan batter to hit into a double play. Lewis finally triumphs over Chicago in the longest and one of the best relief efforts of the 19th century.

29th The Western Association disbands due to lack of attendance.

30th The Phillies run up the season's record total of 27 hits, whipping Cincinnati 17–3.

JULY

4th While Cleveland's Cy Young is delivering the ball in the 8th inning, Sam Mertes of Chicago steals home to tie the score. Then he drives in the winning run in the 9th.

5th With the agreement of Atlantic League president Ed Barrow, Lizzie (Stroud) Arlington pitches an inning for Reading against Allentown. The lady hurler gives up two hits but no runs in the first appearance of a woman in organized baseball.

6th Arlie Pond pitches Baltimore to a 15–0 win over Philadelphia in his last game before entering the Army Medical Corps.

7th Criticized for being unable "to handle men in the up-to-day style," Cap Anson resigns as Giants manager with a 9-13 record. Bill Joyce is reappointed on the same day.

8th Frank "Red" Donahue, of the Phillies, no-hits the visiting Beaneaters 5–0. It is the 2nd no-hitter pitched against the champs this season.

15th In Baltimore, Chicago 3B Barry McCormick accuses his team's 1B, Bill Everett, of making a rotten throw, sparking a fistfight. A Baltimore spectator, trying to intervene, is hit. McCormick withdraws from the game, and the Orioles win 10–9.

20th Joe Corbett, the Baltimore hurler who has been holding out all season for a higher salary, spars with brother Jim to prepare him for his fight with Kid McCoy.

22nd Amos Rusie edges Pittsburgh's Frank Killen 1–0 in 13 innings at New York.

28th Honus Wagner's first grand-slam HR comes against New York ace Amos Rusie. Louisville wins 6–4.

29th Faced with a labor boycott in Cleveland, the Spiders transfer their series against Baltimore to Philadelphia.

31st In the first 85 games, Cleveland has played 21 errorless games, and 21 others with only one miscue, considered a "remarkable fielding record."

AUGUST

1st Philadelphia's sensational rookie, southpaw Wiley Piatt, blanks Cleveland 1–0 with a 4-hitter for the 2nd time. He will tally 24 wins and a league-leading 6 shutouts.

10th Second-place Boston wins a doubleheader 7–4 and 6–5 from the league-leading Reds.

15th Only 200 fans watch the 11th-place Senators defeat the 12th-place St. Louis Browns in Washington 10–2.

16th Boston moves into first place, as Kid Nichols downs Chicago and the Giants' Rusie shuts out Cincinnati. The Reds held the lead for 98 days.

21st Walter Thornton of Chicago, a part-time OF, pitches a 2–0 no-hitter over Brooklyn and collects 2 hits.

26th Cleveland plays its final home game of the season and only their 4th in Cleveland since July 9th. With 83 of their final 87 games on the road, the team has earned nicknames such as the Nomads, Exiles, Misfits, and Wanderers.

27th Hughie Jennings, the Orioles SS, has 10 assists in a 6–2 victory at St. Louis. The most for the season will be 561 by the Reds' Tommy Corcoran.

28th Umpire Bob Emslie is too ill to continue after the first game between Baltimore and St. Louis. Orioles Manager Ned Hanlon recommends that Browns' manager Tim Hurst, a former NL umpire, officiate in the 2nd game. The Orioles win 6–2, but "Tiny Tim" is cheered by the crowd.

30th The New York *Press*, concerned about scuffles among players, umpires, and managers and the deterioration of baseball, calls for the return of A. G. Spalding. Before his retirement, "he worked so long and well to place it upon a high plane."

Chicago's Clark Griffith, who will top NL hurlers with an 1.88 ERA, throws a three-hit 1–0 shutout at the Giants.

SEPTEMBER

5th Cleveland outlasts Cincinnati 8–6 in a 14-inning slugfest of 38 hits, 9 of them doubles. Cy Young and "Still Bill" Hill, who allows 21 hits, go all the way.

6th Willie Keeler for Baltimore goes 0-for-5 against Red Donahue of Philadelphia, ending his 25-game hitting streak. He had an earlier 25-game string July 2nd to 30th.

10th Chicago reels off 3 double plays against St. Louis en route to a team total of 149. This total will not be surpassed until 1917 when the St. Louis Cardinals do it with 153. Dahlen to Connor to Everett have far better fielding stats than their more famous successors, Tinker, Evers, and Chance.

14th Buck Freeman, who led all minor leagues with 23 HRs while with Toronto in the Eastern League, hits his first ML HR for Washington in an 8–5 loss to Cleveland.

16th   Jimmy Ryan of Chicago opens the game with Philadelphia with a HR, and his club goes on to a 10–5 win. It is his 17th leadoff HR, easily the highest total in the 19th century.

18th   Buck Freeman continues his heavy hitting, belting 2 homers and a double to lead the Senators to an 8–5 win over Chicago.

20th   Boston overwhelms Louisville 24–4, setting the season's record for runs by one team.

The Kansas City Cowboys win the Western League pennant on the last day of the season, beating Indianapolis 6–5.

23rd   The NL western teams are shellacked on their final eastern trip, winning 23, losing 35. Baltimore takes 10 of 11, but gains no ground on the first-place Beaneaters, who win 9 of 10 and hold a 3½ game lead.

24th   Willie Keeler, now known as "Wee Willie," leads an Oriole attack on Washington's Gus Weyhing with 4 hits and becomes the first player to reach 200 this season.

27th   Jake Beckley accepts a record 22 chances—21 putouts, one assist, no errors—in the Reds' 9-inning win over Cleveland.

28th   Louisville righthander Bert Cunningham wins his 11th straight victory, a record streak for the season. Kid Nichols of Boston would have had 16 straight but for a tie game between victories 9 and 10.

29th   Jimmy Collins hits 2 HRs, one a grand slam, giving Boston an 11–10 win. His league-leading HR total is 15 for the season.

OCTOBER

9th   Jack Taylor of Chicago defeats Jack Taylor of St. Louis 5–4 in 10 innings. The winner is a newcomer who won 28 games for Milwaukee in the Western League. The loser is a veteran of 8 seasons.

11th   Boston defeats the Senators 14–5 and clinches the league championship when Baltimore splits with the Giants.

12th   Sam Leever, Pittsburgh rookie, bests Cleveland's great Cy Young 9–1, to score his first ML victory.

14th   Playing manager Fred Clarke of Louisville goes 4-for-5, including a triple, against Cleveland. This is his 7th 4-hit game, tops for the NL season.

15th   Boston wins its 5th pennant in the decade for Frank Selee, equaling its 102 victories of 1892, but one fewer loss increases its percentage to .685 (102-47). Only 3 of the 12 clubs make a profit, as attendance slacks off.

The Spiders' Jesse Burkett, whose .345 is the league's 3rd-highest mark, goes to the plate for his 624th and final at bat without a HR.

16th   In a throwing contest, Hans Wagner hurls a baseball 403 feet 8 inches to beat the record set by the Mutuals' John Hatfield in 1872. Wagner's distance throw will be exceeded by Larry LeJeune, who will throw for 435 feet on October 3, 1908.

In the season just completed, Baltimore batters were hit by pitches 158 times, an all-time record, which would never be approached. Hugh Jennings led with 42, followed by Dan McGann with 38, and John McGraw with 18.

18th   NL attendance totaled 2,313,250, a drop of 572,381 below 1897. Chicago led with 424,352; the Reds were 2nd with 336,378.

DECEMBER

1st   Club president Andrew Freedman renews the Giants' lease on the Polo Grounds for the next 10 years.

7th   Roy Thomas, University of Pennsylvania outfielder, is signed by the Phillies for 1899. *Sporting Life* calls him the "greatest amateur player of this generation."

19th   John B. Day is picked as the Giants' new manager.

1899

JANUARY

10th Tim Hurst, former NL umpire and St. Louis manager, referees the Tom Sharkey knockout of Kid McCoy in 10 rounds at the Lenox Athletic Club in New York.

FEBRUARY

4th Hugh Jennings will not go south with the Brooklyn team but will get in shape as baseball coach for Cornell University.

7th Under a joint ownership arrangement, several Baltimore players are shifted to Brooklyn, and that club transfers several to the Orioles. Manager Ned Hanlon takes Willie Keeler, Joe Kelley, Hughie Jennings, and others with him while John McGraw and Wilbert Robinson remain in Baltimore. The powerful new Brooklyn team is nicknamed the Superbas.

25th The NL Committee on Rules recommends that umpires be given authority to fine unruly players $10 for a first offense.

MARCH

2nd At the league meeting in New York, an attempt to expel the St. Louis Browns, who had a 39-111 record in 1898, fails by a 7-4 margin. It is also decided that no club may hold more than 18 players on its reserve list.

APRIL

3rd The Robison brothers, owners of the Cleveland franchise, gain control of the St. Louis franchise as well, and redistribute players. St. Louis, which finished 12th in 1898, is enhanced with Cy Young, Jesse Burkett, Bobby Wallace, and manager-1B Patsy Tebeau. Cleveland is greatly weakened by the transfers. The new St. Louis owners change the name of Sportsman's Park to League Park. They also change the color of the team socks from brown to red. The team nickname becomes the Perfectos.

14th On Opening Day, Chicago gives P Clark Griffith plenty of batting support and the Orphans defeat Louisville 15-1. At Washington, lefthanded SS Billy Hulen plays his first game with the Senators, but he goes 0-for-5 and makes an error as they lose to the Phillies.

15th A crowd of 21,000 watches Kid Nichols of Boston outlast Brickyard Kennedy 1-0 in 11 innings when Fred Tenney triples in the crucial run.

18th John McGraw makes his managerial debut with Baltimore by leading the Orioles to a 5-3 win over New York. He would later manage the Giants for 3 decades.

25th Louisville 3B Honus Wagner hits 2 HRs, the 2nd winning it in the 9th over Pittsburgh 2-1. The Colonels sell Nick Altrock to Grand Rapids and Rube Waddell to Columbus.

30th A new ML attendance record is set at Chicago as 27,000 fans watch Nixey Callahan shut out St. Louis 4-0. The crowd spills into the field causing any hit into the crowd to count for only one base.

MAY

1st Cleveland wins its home opener over the Louisville Colonels 5-4 in 14 innings before only 500 fans. They lose the 2nd game of the twin bill 2-1.

3rd Pittsburgh's Jack McCarthy gets a game-winning 3-run HR in the bottom of the 9th when his drive into the corner goes through a door that a fan then shuts before the fielder can reach it. The league eventually orders this game replayed.

8th Harry Wolverton's bases-loaded HR in the bottom of the 9th gives the Chicago Orphans an 8-7 victory over Cleveland.

13th Ed Delahanty of the Phillies, who hit 4 HRs in a game in 1896, collects 4 doubles in a 9-0 victory over New York, the only player to achieve these dual records.

15th Willie Keeler, one of the smallest players and best bunters, drives the ball past startled LF Ed Delahanty of the Phillies for an inside-the-park grand slam and an 8-5 victory for Brooklyn.

17th Cleveland OF Louis Sockalexis is fined in police court for public intoxication. The club releases him, and he signs with Hartford of the Eastern League.

Sporting Life indirectly criticizes joint ownership of 2 clubs with this comment: "Syndicate Baseball

Results—May 17, 1898, Cleveland 16 W, 8 L; May 17, 1899, Cleveland 3 W, 20 L."

25th Deacon Phillippe of Louisville tosses a 7–0 no-hitter against the Giants. He walks 3 batters but would become baseball's best control pitcher with a career average of 1.25 bases on balls per game.

31st Boston RF Chick Stahl goes 6-for-6 in a 16–10 romp over Cleveland.

JUNE

2nd Nap Lajoie homers in the last of the 9th, as the Phillies beat Pittsburgh 4–3.

The hapless Cleveland Spiders blow a 10–0 lead and lose to Brooklyn 11–10.

5th Lave Cross (3B) and Willie Sudhoff (P) are transferred from Cleveland, already doing poorly, to St. Louis.

10th Pittsburgh Pirates rookie 3B Jimmy Williams's batting streak stops at 26 games as Louisville's Deacon Phillippe holds him in check.

16th New York forfeits a game to the Brooklyn Superbas when umpire Tom Burns, ridden mercilessly by the Giants after questionable calls, "won't take it any more" and declares Brooklyn a 9–0 winner.

24th Tom O'Brien of the Giants collects one hit and 3 walks and steals 5 bases, including home, in the 7–2 win over Cleveland.

28th Pittsburgh's Jack McCarthy hits his 3rd HR of the season (a 4th was wiped out in a forfeited game on May 3rd). He will have 3,021 more ML at bats through 1907 without another HR.

JULY

1st Cleveland, which has averaged under 200 fans a game at home, splits a twin bill with Boston and decides to spend the rest of the season on the road. The club's record is 12-49. They will play just 7 more home games and finish the year with a total attendance of 6,088, the lowest in ML history,

3rd Arlie Latham, a colorful 3B in his playing days, makes his debut as an umpire at Pittsburgh.

9th Judge Dunn of Chicago orders city officials to stop interfering with Andrew Brennan, who put seats on the roof of his house near the park and sells tickets to people.

14th Kid Nichols pitches a one-hitter against Pittsburgh, winning 2–0. Opposing hurler Jack Chesbro, in his 2nd game, makes the hit.

15th Boston manager Frank Selee is quoted by *Sporting Life* as saying: "I look upon Lajoie as a ballplaying genius with more natural talent than any ballplayer since Charley Ferguson."

Jimmy Collins of Boston, in the bottom of the 11th with Herman Long on base, hits the ball over the fence to win the game 1–0 against Jesse Tannehill of Pittsburgh. Collins gets credit for a double.

22nd Pittsburgh's leadoff batter, Ginger Beaumont, makes 6 infield hits and scores 6 runs in an 18–4 romp over Philadelphia.

24th Nap Lajoie is confined to bed with water on the knee and will miss about 2 months of the season.

26th Pitcher Jim Hughes of Baltimore steals home in the 5th inning against Louisville and wins the game 3–2.

30th The Colonels Honus Wagner hits 2 inside-the-park HRs in the 2nd game of a twin victory over Cleveland at Louisville.

AUGUST

1st P Jack Powell's HR in the 14th inning gives St. Louis an exciting 8–7 win over Boston. The drive off Kid Nichols goes beyond CF Billy Hamilton and Powell beats the relay. The fans carry Powell to the clubhouse.

In a game between the Colonels and the Giants in Louisville, Honus Wagner steals 2B, 3B and home in the 4th inning. He is the first to accomplish this under the rule change of 1898 that differentiates between advanced bases and stolen bases.

7th Vic Willis of Boston pitches a one-hitter, beating Washington 7–1. However, the Associated Press calls it a no-hitter. The controversial hit was by Bill Dinneen, the opposing hurler. Ultimately the record books would carry it as a no-hitter.

10th After a wild game with Baltimore, St. Louis manager Patsy Tebeau swears at an abusive spectator, and the latter has him arrested and fined.

11th Brooklyn beats Louisville 1–0 on a HBP and a steal of home by Bill Dahlen. Brickyard Kennedy triumphs over Bert Cunningham.

12th The grandstand at Louisville's Eclipse Park burns down. The Colonels will try and make do with a temporary stand.

20th Socks Seybold, powerful slugger from the Atlantic League, makes his debut with Cincinnati. He makes 3 errors in the outfield in a 10–1 loss to St. Louis.

22nd Washington OF Buck Freeman, the league's leading HR hitter with 15, pitches the last 3 innings of a 15–5 loss to Baltimore.

24th Cy Young pitches his 3rd consecutive shutout, allowing the hard-hitting Phillies only 3 hits in a 5–0 win.

28th After an absence of nearly 2 months, the Cleveland club returns home for a series with Boston.

31st John McGraw's 23-year-old wife dies following surgery for appendicitis. Her funeral, with Ned Hanlon, Willie Keeler, Joe Kelley, and Hughie Jennings participating as pallbearers, would be one of the largest in Baltimore history.

SEPTEMBER

2nd Louisville defeats Washington 25–4. There are 8 HRs in the game, but attendance is small. Louisville President Barney Dreyfuss would shortly decide to transfer the last 14 home games to the opponents' grounds.

4th The Superbas, already famous for their late rallies, stage "Brooklyn finishes" in 2 different boroughs, winning the morning game in Brooklyn with 2 in the 9th, and then taking the afternoon game in Manhattan with 4 in the 8th.

7th Hometown Brooklyn loses to Boston 2–1 when Tom "Tido" Daly tries to score the tying run in the bottom of the 9th but is called out by umpire Bob Emslie. When the fans attack Emslie, police and players escort him off the field to the railway station.

8th Pittsburgh's Jimmy Williams, who earlier set a rookie record by hitting in 26 consecutive games, runs his new string to 27 games. He is stopped by Deacon

Phillippe of Louisville, who also stopped his earlier streak.

9th Doc McJames of Brooklyn has a no-hitter until Hugh Duffy of Boston singles with 2 out in the 9th. Nevertheless, the league leaders win 4–0.

Jake Beckley of Cincinnati hits a grand slam, inside-the-park HR in a 12–6 loss to St. Louis. In the same game, Bill Phillips quick-pitches a perfect strike to Burkett, who had stepped out of the batter's box. True to his nickname of "The Crab," Jesse shows irritation and is ejected.

10th OF Sam Crawford makes his ML debut by hitting a triple and single in leading Cincinnati to an 8–7 win over Louisville.

15th Vic Willis's drop ball is working effectively, as no Boston OF records a putout in a 9–4 victory over Pittsburgh. Beaneater Chick Stahl chips in one of the longest HRs ever hit at Boston.

17th A preliminary organization meeting is held in Chicago regarding a proposed new American Association. Among the delegates are Adrian Anson of Chicago, Chris Von der Ahe and Al Spink of St. Louis, and representatives from Milwaukee, New York, Philadelphia, and Washington.

18th After losing 24 games in a row, Cleveland defeats Washington 5–4. The Spiders will go on to lose their next 16 games.

20th Brooklyn buys 3B Zeke Wrigley's contract from Syracuse, although Wrigley has been playing for New York for the past 5 days.

26th St. Louis scores in all 8 of its innings in a 15–3 home win over Cleveland.

OCTOBER

2nd Rube Waddell, back up with Louisville, fans 13 in a 3-hit 6–1 victory at Chicago. It is called after 8 innings because of darkness.

6th Frank "Noodles" Hahn of Cincinnati faces only 28 Louisville batters in a one-hit 8–1 victory. Tommy Leach's single drives in manager Fred Clarke, who had reached base on an error.

7th The Brooklyn Superbas clinch the NL pennant with a 13–2 win over the Giants. Jim Hughes is the winning pitcher.

8th The Chicago Orphans win an unusual double-header. Behind Jack Taylor's first season shutout, they beat Cleveland 11–0 in a morning game at West Side Grounds. In an afternoon game called after 5 innings because of darkness, Chicago beats Louisville and Rube Waddell 7–3.

11th The Western League holds its annual meeting in Chicago and changes its name to the American Baseball League. The AL considers putting clubs in Cleveland and Chicago. President Ban Johnson and St. Paul owner-manager Charles Comiskey give little credibility to the proposed "on paper only" American Association.

12th Buck Freeman hits his 25th HR, a 9th-inning grand slam, but the Senators still lose to New York 9–7.

15th Cincinnati closes out the season with 16–1 and 19–3 victories over the hapless Cleveland Spiders. Bid McPhee, considered the best 2B of the 19th century, plays in both games, which ends his long career. Cleveland finishes deep in the cellar with 20 wins and 134 losses, 84 games out.

17th Brooklyn begins a post-season series with Philadelphia for "gate money and satisfaction." The Phillies get most of the satisfaction, batting the Superbas' Jim Hughes for a 7–4 victory. Lajoie collects 4 hits in 4 trips.

22nd The 6th and last game of the post-season series is played at Hoboken, before 700 shivering spectators. The Phillies win 6–4 to even the series at 3 apiece.

NOVEMBER

2nd Henry Chadwick, called the "Father of Baseball," visits President McKinley in Washington to propose that Army regiments be provided with baseball equipment. This is Chadwick's first presidential interview since his visit with President Lincoln in 1861.

4th Representatives of 7 cities meet in New York regarding the proposed new American Association. Attention focuses on what other city might become the 8th franchise.

11th Chicago Orphans star Bill Lange returns to San Francisco and vows he will never appear on the diamond again. He is only 28.

18th Ban Johnson, president of the new AL, contemplates exchanging players of equal ability with the NL and EL with a view to giving the public new attractions.

25th *Sporting Life* reports that President Freedman of the Giants wants to reduce the NL to 8 clubs and purify the game by eliminating "certain parties who have been unduly prominent in the sport for cheap notoriety and the money there is in it."

DECEMBER

4th Buck Ewing, Cincinnati manager for 5 years, is released.

8th Louisville president Barney Dreyfuss is transferring to the Pittsburgh club (of which he is part owner) most of his top stars, including player-manager Fred Clarke, Hans Wagner, Tommy Leach, and Deacon Phillippe. Louisville is a likely candidate in the reduction of NL franchises from 12 to 8.

15th The NL rules Brooklyn's purchase of Zeke Wrigley in September is illegal and nullifies the 16 games he played for Brooklyn. But Brooklyn still wins the pennant.

22nd AL magnates meet to map out a line of action based on results of the NL meeting. They plan to place a team in Chicago with Charles Comiskey the owner-manager.

1900

JANUARY

12th John McGraw threatens that if the NL drops Baltimore, which is controlled by the owners of the Brooklyn Superbas, he will form an AL team. Two weeks later the NL Circuit Committee recommends buying out Baltimore, Washington, Cleveland, and Louisville and going to an 8-team league. McGraw then organizes a Baltimore club in the AL.

19th Marty Bergen, Boston's regular catcher, kills his wife and children, then takes his own life.

24th The NL Reduction Committee has a secret meeting in Cleveland, supposedly to discuss dropping Louisville, Baltimore, Washington, and Cleveland from the league roster.

FEBRUARY

3rd Rival forces fight for control of the Union Park ball grounds in Baltimore. McGraw's men camp around a fire at 3B. Ned Hanlon, his former manager in Baltimore in the 1890s, now manager of Brooklyn and still president of the Baltimore club in the NL, has forces camped around 1B.

A writer for the New York *Clipper*, overcome by the xenophobia rapidly spreading across the United States, asks, "What is baseball coming to? For nearly half a century things ran smoothly enough until they began to rope in a few ringers, such as [Ed] Abbaticchio, [Louis] Sockalexis, [Ossee] Schreckengost and now Accorsini."

7th John B. "Jack" Taylor, 3-time 20-game winner and 20-game loser, including 29 losses in 1898, dies of Bright's disease at 26.

15th Unable to get backers in Philadelphia, McGraw withdraws Baltimore from AL, ending prospects for the league as a rival to the NL. Two weeks later he will sign to manage Baltimore (NL).

16th Washington sells 8 players, with HR king Buck Freeman and P Bill Dinneen going to Boston, then disbands. Baltimore players are to be transferred to Brooklyn and syndicate baseball ended.

17th Mary Hamilton Von Derbeck becomes owner of the Detroit AL franchise and Bennett Park in lieu of unpaid alimony. However, her ex-husband George

Von Derbeck files the required bond with a Michigan court to cover the due alimony, regains ownership of the club, and sells it to Tiger manager George Stallings on March 6th.

MARCH

8th In New York, the NL meets and votes to go with 8 teams. They pay the Baltimore owners $30,000 for their franchise, with Ebbets and Hanlon reserving the right to sell the players. Cleveland, Louisville, and Washington receive $10,000 each, Louisville owner Barney Dreyfuss sending most of his players to his Pittsburgh team. The circuit will remain the same for 53 years, until the Boston Braves move to Milwaukee in 1953.

9th Buck Ewing, a .303 hitter in his 18-year career (and the only 19th-century catcher in the Hall of Fame), is named bench manager of the Giants. He'll last until July 13th.

The NL votes the following rule changes: a single umpire will work a game, reverting back after an experiment with 2; a balk rule allows only a base runner to advance, not the batter; a change in the shape of home plate to 5-sided to eliminate the corners of the old one-foot by one-foot plate. There had been arguments with pitchers who wanted strikes called when balls went over the corners. With no corners to kick about, owners figure there will be no further arguments over strike calls.

16th At an AL meeting in Chicago Ban Johnson announces that an AL team will be placed in the Windy City, ensuring the stability of the league. Other franchises are in Kansas City, Minneapolis, Milwaukee, Indianapolis, Detroit, Cleveland, and Buffalo. In an agreement with Chicago NL officials the AL club will be situated on the south side of the city and will be permitted to use the nickname "White Stockings," formerly used by the NL team. However, the White Stockings will not be able to use the word "Chicago" in their official name.

23rd John McGraw, Wilbert Robinson, and Bill "Wagon Tongue" Keister, an IF, are sold by Brooklyn to St. Louis for $15,000. McGraw and Robby refuse to report.

APRIL

2nd American Federation of Labor president

Samuel Gompers announces that his organization plans to form a baseball players' union. He feels that with the NL's reduction to 8 teams—and the subsequent loss of income by many players on the 4 disbanded teams—players might overcome their fear and join the union.

13th At the request of club owners in Cincinnati and New York, the NL bans umpire Tim Hurst, considered the most colorful, cantankerous ump, from working in cities whose club owners "object to having a man of that type associated with their grounds, where ladies and gentlemen watch the games."

19th In the NL opener at Boston, 10,000 fans watch the Phils win 19–17 in 10 innings.

On Opening Day in the AL Charlie Bennett throws out the first ball in the Detroit park named for him, but his presence fails to rouse the Tigers, who fall to the no-hit pitching of Buffalo's Morris "Doc" Amole 8–0. In his 2-year NL career, which ended in 1898, Amole compiled a record of 4–10.

24th Reds 1B Jake Beckley will lead the NL with 1,389 putouts, but this day he has no fielding chances. Not until April 27, 1930, will another 1B have such an easy day.

26th The American League opener in Cleveland draws 6,500, a higher mark than the NL team drew there for the entire 1899 season.

30th Brothers Joe, Jim, and Tom Delahanty, playing their 3rd year together with Allentown, open the Atlantic League season by banging out a family total of 11 hits for 20 bases.

MAY

6th The Detroit Tigers play their first Sunday home game at a new park just beyond the city limits. They will use this park for Sunday games for 3 years.

8th John McGraw and Wilbert Robinson end their holdout and sign with the Cardinals. Both contracts have the reserve clause crossed out, freeing McGraw to return to Baltimore in the AL in 1901.

20th Fire breaks out at the Pittsburgh park for the 3rd time in 2 weeks. Police speculate the arsonist is a disgruntled stockholder left out of the new Dreyfuss regime.

26th At Chicago, the Colts beat the Superbas 1–0 in 1 hour, 35 minutes.

28th A fire in Cincinnati nearly destroys the grandstand. The new grandstand will not be built until 1902, and the Reds are forced to play on the road for a month.

31st The Phillies' Nap Lajoie suffers a broken hand trying to punch teammate Elmer Flick. Nap is sidelined and suspended without pay for 5 weeks.

JUNE

2nd Boston wins the season's best slugfest, scoring 4 in the 9th and one in the 10th to beat St. Louis 17–16.

5th Pirates 1B Duff Cooley has 2 putouts in a game against the Phils, the lowest number of putouts ever registered by a 1B in an NL game, before or since. The Phils beat Pittsburgh 6–5.

9th A forerunner of today's players' union is organized in New York. Three delegates from each NL team launch the Player's Protective Association and elect Chief Zimmer president. Their goal is to negotiate contracts and rules changes.

19th In the year's best pitching duel, Clark Griffith of the Cubs and Rube Waddell of the Pirates match 13 innings, before Griffith's double in the last of the 14th drives in the only run.

20th One day after Brooklyn moved into the NL lead for the first time all year, Philadelphia regains first place with a 5–4 win over the Superbas.

21st Brooklyn rallies for 5 in the 9th to beat Philadelphia 8–6 and take over first place. They will hold the lead for the rest of the season.

JULY

3rd At Pittsburgh, Jack Chesbro beats the Beaneaters, 2–1; the Boston battery is Lewis and Clarke.

4th At Cincinnati, Jerry Nops of the Superbas pitches a one-hitter, beating the Reds 2–0. The next day his teammate Frank Kitson also pitches a one-hitter, winning 10–0.

7th   Boston hurler Kid Nichols notches his 300th career victory, beating Chicago 11–4. The win comes 2 months before his 31st birthday, making him the youngest to ever reach the magic figure.

12th   Frank "Noodles" Hahn of Cincinnati twirls a 4–0 no-hitter over Philadelphia. The Reds lefty gives up 5 walks to the visiting Quakers who are playing without Nap Lajoie.

13th   Harry Wolverton of the Phillies hits 3 triples and 2 singles in an 8-inning 23–8 victory at Pittsburgh.

15th   At Detroit, Tigers manager Tommy Burns, afraid the crowd would injure umpire Joe Cantillion after the previous day's hostilities, refuses to let him work, and the game is forfeited to Cleveland. But Indians manager Jim McAleer agrees to play using reserve player Sport McAllister as the ump, and Detroit wins 6–1.

17th   At Brooklyn's Washington Park, the Superbas tie the score against the Giants in the 5th. With 2 men on base, New York captain George Davis takes out pitcher Ed Doheny and brings in rookie Christy Mathewson, just brought up from Norfolk. He hits 3 batters, walks 2, and gives up 6 runs in a 13–7 loss. The New York *Times* says, "Matty has lots of speed and gives promise of making his way."

25th   The Boston Beaneaters score 13 runs in the first against the Cardinals on 10 hits, including 2 triples by Buck Freeman, and 4 errors. The game is shortened by rain after 6 innings and Boston wins 18–5.

26th   Gus Weyhing is released by the Cardinals but does not get the 10 days pay he's entitled to. He gets a deputy sheriff to seize the St. Louis share of the gate at Brooklyn, but it comes to less than the $100 he's claiming.

29th   With all the NL teams in the east, and no Sunday games allowed, 100 players gather in NY. Their demands are: release of players who are not going to be used rather than farming them out, and players to share in the purchase price when they are sold. Says veteran Hughie Jennings, "We are not out to fight the owners, but to resolve injustices in the contracts."

AUGUST

2nd   Following a disputed call, New York manager George Davis leads the crowd in an assault on umpire Terry.

17th   Reds pitcher Bill Phillips punches Phillies batter Roy Thomas after Thomas fouls off a dozen pitches in the 8th inning. Phillips is ejected but the Reds win in the 11th.

18th   Veteran manager Pat Tebeau resigns from the Cards. When 3B John McGraw refuses the job, the Robison brothers, the St. Louis owners, pick Louie Heilbroner, the 4' 9" Cardinals business manager, to run the team for the remainder of 1900. Many of the players refuse to take orders from the diminutive Heilbroner, who will return to the front office the following year. In 1910 he would begin publishing the Baseball Blue Book.

20th   Cy Young is knocked out of the box for the 2nd consecutive game. This is a first in his career.

25th   Criticism of administration in the NL continues. *The Sporting News* offers the new AL editorial encouragement: "An organization opposed to the National League will be welcome because it will mean the elevation of the game if it is successful."

31st   Brickyard Kennedy, en route to his 4th 20-win season for the Dodgers, walks 6 Phillies in a row in the 2nd inning of a 9–4 loss.

SEPTEMBER

5th   While riding on the steps of a crowded streetcar in Philadelphia, Phils 3B Harry Wolverton is struck in the head by a pole beside the tracks, suffering a possible skull fracture. He recovers and finishes his ML career as a player–manager for the Yankees in 1912.

11th   The Giants batter P Nixey Callahan for 23 hits in a 14–3 win over the Chicago Cubs.

12th   Sammy Strang, a rookie 3B, breaks in with 7 hits for the Cubs in a doubleheader against the Giants.

In the AL, Milwaukee takes 2 from Detroit by 2–1 scores, each game taking 1 hour, 20 minutes, the fastest time of the year.

The Reds commit 17 errors in a doubleheader at Brooklyn, losing 7–2 and 13–9, the most errors in one day by any team in the 20th century. Iron Man

McGinnity closes both games for Brooklyn; he has worked in every game for a week.

17th Reds SS Tommy Corcoran, coaching at 3B in a game at Philadelphia, uncovers a wire in the coaching box that leads across the OF to the Phils' locker room, where reserve C Morgan Murphy is reading the opposing catcher's signs and relaying them to the Phils' coach by a buzzer hidden in the dirt.

18th The AL season ends with Chicago 4 games in front. Says the *Reach Guide*: "Effective pitching and sharp fielding were the rule as only 17 batters hit over .300. There was less disorder in the field than the other league, owing to the vigilance of Ban Johnson in protecting umpires."

19th St. Louis C Wilbert Robinson objects to the umpire calling a Brooklyn runner safe at home, and throws the ball at the ump. The umpire swings his mask at Robby and throws him out of the game. Cardinals captain John McGraw refuses to put in another catcher, claiming one is injured and the other suspended. The ump forfeits the game to the Superbas. The Brooklyn fans object to the suspension of play and President Ebbets refunds money to those who want it.

OCTOBER

3rd Brooklyn virtually clinches the NL pennant by winning 2 at Boston 6–4 and 3–1. For manager Ned Hanlon, it is his 5th pennant in 7 years.

8th The Cubs and Reds set a record for ragged fielding that still stands. Chicago boots 17 and Cincinnati 8 as the Reds win both ends of a doubleheader 13–4 and 9–1.

11th The AL announces that in 1901 it intends to put a team in Baltimore led by John McGraw, and one in Washington. But they pledge to stay out of Philadelphia and St. Louis unless the NL starts a fight.

Rube Waddell of Pittsburgh strikes out an NL season-high 12 in a 2–1 win over the Cubs. He will lead the league with 130 strikeouts and a 2.37 ERA.

13th Ban Johnson promises to put the following provisions in all player contracts in the AL: no suspensions for more than 10 days; clubs to pay doctor bills for injuries occurring during a game; if a club abandons the league, its players become free agents after 10 days; no farming or selling without the player's written consent; no reserve clause for more than 3 years or for less salary than the current year; and binding arbitration for disputes.

15th The Pittsburgh *Chronicle-Telegraph* World Title series between first-place Brooklyn and 2nd-place Pittsburgh begins with a 5–2 win for Joe McGinnity over Rube Waddell. The Superbas win the series, the Cup given by the newspapers, and half the gate receipts 3 days later. For his efforts, which include a league-leading 29 wins and 347 innings pitched, McGinnity is given permanent possession of the trophy and a $100 bonus.

20th The Cardinals withhold the final month's pay on all but 5 players, including John McGraw and Wilbur Robinson, citing late hours, dissipation, and gambling as reasons for the poor showing of the team, which finished tied for 5th.

31st Ban Johnson writes a letter to NL president Nick Young seeking peace, based on parity as a ML for the AL.

NOVEMBER

14th The NL rejects the AL as an equal, declaring it an outlaw league outside of the National Agreement, thus inaugurating a state of war. Two weeks later the AA makes it a 3-way battle.

DECEMBER

10th At the NL meetings, rumors fly. Ban Johnson says the AL has signed a lease on a park in Detroit. The Players Protective Association says its members will not sign with the NL.

11th A rumor that the PPA leaders have gone to Philadelphia to meet with Ban Johnson causes NL owners to "have something closely resembling a fit," says the New York *Times*. Players later admit the meeting took place.

12th The NL considers going back to 12 teams to counter AL moves into some cities. The league agrees to hear the players in a public meeting, but rejects all their demands.

14th Suffering from a drop in attendance in 1900, NL owners vote to cut costs with a 16-player limit after May 1. The PPA claims the move is aimed at pressuring players into signing by shrinking the number of jobs.

15th   Amos Rusie, a holdout for 2 years, is traded to the Reds by the Giants for Mathewson. Though only 30, Rusie, a future Hall of Fame pitcher, will not add to the 245 wins he collected in 9 seasons. Appearing in just 3 games in 1901, he will finish with an 0–1 record.

The young Christy Mathewson, just 0–3 with the Giants but 20–2 with Norfolk (Virginia League), is much coveted by Cincinnati owner John T. Brush, who is currently negotiating to buy control of the Giants from the unscrupulous Andrew Freedman. Before he takes over, Brush wants Mathewson in place as a Giants' starter, rather than the "pitched out" Amos Rusie.

1901

JANUARY

4th   The Baltimore AL club incorporates, with John McGraw as manager and part owner.

22nd   Connie Mack, Philadelphia A's manager-GM, signs a 10-year lease on grounds at 29th and Columbia to be called Columbia Park. A contract is set for construction of single-deck stands to hold 7,500.

28th   The AL formally organizes: the Baltimore Orioles, Philadelphia Athletics, and Boston Somersets are admitted to join the Washington Nationals, Cleveland Blues, Detroit Tigers, Milwaukee Brewers, and Chicago White Stockings. Three of the original clubs—Indianapolis, Minneapolis, and Buffalo—are dropped. League power aggregates in Ban Johnson as trustee for all ballpark leases and majority stockholdings, and with authority to buy out refractory franchises. Player limit is 14 per team, schedule will be 140 games.

28th   AL contracts give the Players Protective Association what it asked for, with 5-year limits on the rights to player services.

29th   Newly named Rules Committee of Connie Mack, John McGraw, and Charles Comiskey, after rejecting a proposal to ban the bunt, recommends no changes at this time.

FEBRUARY

8th   News leaks out that Napoleon Lajoie, the Phillies star 2B and leading NL hitter, has jumped to the new Philadelphia AL club, along with pitchers Chick Fraser and Bill Bernhard.

26th   NL officials meet with Charles "Chief" Zimmer, Pittsburgh C and the president of the PPA, and agree to contract concessions granted by the AL for NL players who will agree not to sign with AL clubs. Zimmer promises suspensions for PPA jumpers to the AL.

27th   The NL Rules Committee decrees that all fouls are to count as strikes, except after 2 strikes. To cut the cost of balls fouled and unrecovered, the committee urges that "batsmen who foul off good strikes are to be disciplined." The AL will not adopt this rule for several years. Other new rules: catchers must play within 10 feet of the batter; a ball will be called if the pitcher does not throw to a ready and waiting batter within 20 seconds; players using indecent or improper language will be banished by the umpire. A ball will be called when a batter is hit by a pitch.

MARCH

2nd   Jimmy Collins, Connie Mack's choice for the all-time best 3B, leaves the Boston NL club to manage the AL's new Boston Somersets. The Beaneaters also lose OF Hugh Duffy, who will manage Milwaukee (AL), and C Billy Sullivan, who signs with the Chicago White Stockings.

11th   The Cincinnati *Enquirer* reports that Baltimore manager John McGraw has signed a Cherokee Indian named Tokohoma. It is really black 2B Charlie Grant, who McGraw is trying to pass off as an Indian, but the ruse does not work.

28th   Phillies owner John Rogers files for an injunction prohibiting Nap Lajoie, Bill Bernhard, and Chick Fraser from playing for any other team—the most serious legal test of the reserve clause to date.

APRIL

3rd   Connie Mack accuses Christy Mathewson of reneging on a Philadelphia contact signed in January. The young pitcher had accepted advance money from Mack, but jumped back to the Giants in March. Mack considers going to court, but eventually accepts the loss of the pitcher.

18th   Brooklyn's Jimmy Sheckard has 3 triples against the Phils.

24th   Three rain postponements give Chicago the honor of hosting the first game of the new AL. Roy Patterson's 8–2 win over the Cleveland Blues is the first of 20; with manager Clark Griffith's 24, the White Stockings will win the AL's first pennant.

25th   Detroit scores the greatest Opening Day rally in its AL debut with 10 runs in the bottom of the 9th for a 14–13 victory over the Milwaukee Brewers. Tiger 1B Pop Dillon hits 4 doubles.

Cleveland 2B Erve Beck hits the first HR in AL history off Chicago's John Skopec.

Nap Lajoie has 3 hits in the Athletic' first game, and will have 3 in the 2nd game and 4 in the 3rd on the way to an AL-record .422 batting average.

26th Eight days after the Phillies' opener before 4,593, the Athletics, home opener draws 16,000 for a 5–1 loss to the Senators.

After 6 postponements, the New York Giants down the Brooklyn Superbas 5–3 for the season's first win and Mathewson's first victory.

28th Veteran SS Hugh Jennings, teammate and roommate of John McGraw in Baltimore's great days, will play for Mack's Athletics after getting his law degree at Cornell. McGraw persuades him to play for Baltimore instead, touching off a battle royal with Connie Mack and Ban Johnson. The result is ill feelings that never heal. Jennings winds up playing for the Phillies.

Cleveland P Charles Baker gives up an AL record 23 singles in a 13–1 loss to the White Stockings. He will pitch only one other game, also a loss, in the ML.

29th Admiral George Dewey and other prominent guests watch Washington defeat Baltimore 5–2 in the AL opener in the nation's capital.

MAY

1st An AL first: 2 HRs in one game—by Herm McFarland and Dummy Hoy in the White Sox' 19–9 win over Detroit. The Tigers' 12 errors—10 by the infield—set another AL record, which the White Stockings will tie May 6, 1903, against the Tigers.

4th Fire destroys the grandstand at Sportsman's Park and halts St. Louis and Cincinnati with a 4–4 tie in the 10th inning.

8th Amos Rusie, onetime Hoosier Thunderbolt, makes his first start for the Cincinnati Reds after a 2-year layoff and is bombed 14–3. After 2 more appearances, he goes back to digging ditches, having won 245 games, mostly for the Giants, in 9 years.

In their long-delayed AL home opener, Boston defeats Philadelphia 12–4 behind Cy Young, who has jumped from the St. Louis NL team. He will lead the AL with his 1.62 ERA and 33 wins, which are 41.8 percent of his team's 79 victories. A post-1900 record, it will stand until Steve Carlton wins 45.8 percent of the Phils' 59 wins in 1972.

17th The Philadelphia Common Pleas Court rejects the Phillies' suit against Lajoie, Fraser, and Bernhard. The decision is appealed to the State Supreme Court, but the trio remains with the Athletics all season. Lajoie will hit .422, while Fraser wins 22 and Bernhard 17 for the 4th-place Athletics.

21st Giants fractious owner Andrew Freedman accuses umpire Billy Nash of incompetence and bars him from the Polo Grounds. One Pirate and one Giant are forced to officiate.

23rd Philadelphia's Nap Lajoie is intentionally walked with the bases loaded by the White Stockings.

The Blues score a record 9 runs with 2 outs in the 9th inning to defeat the Nationals 14–13. Cleveland will repeat this feat on August 4, 1920 .

27th 3B Jimmy Burke of Milwaukee makes 4 errors in one inning, a record tied by Cleveland's Ray Chapman in 1914 and the Cubs Len Merullo in 1942.

30th An NL record crowd of 28,500 sees St. Louis beat the Giants 6–5 in 10 innings in the afternoon game of a split holiday doubleheader at New York. Christy Mathewson takes the loss in relief.

JUNE

2nd Milwaukee P Bill Reidy surrenders 10 consecutive hits to the Boston Somersets with 2 outs in the 9th inning to set a ML record. Nine runs score as Milwaukee loses 13–2.

9th Overflow crowds ringing the OFs of small parks is a frequent occurrence. At Cincinnati on this Sunday afternoon, the first-place Giants lead 15–4 after 6 innings before 17,000 fans. Ground-rule doubles multiply, and 19 more runs score in the next 2½ innings. When the crowd edges onto the infield, with the Giants leading 25–13, umpire Bob Emslie forfeits the game to New York. The game registers a record 31 hits and 13 doubles. Only one Giant will return to the team in 1902: 5 will go to the AL, and 3 will retire.

11th The Chicago Cubs Bob Wicker pitches a no-hitter through 9 innings against the Giants. With one out in the 10th, Sam Mertes, who broke up a no-hitter in the 10th inning on May 9th, gets the first and only hit for New York. Wicker wins 1–0 in 12 innings.

18th Trailing its AL rival in attendance, the Boston NL club reduces its admission price from 50 cents to the AL's 25 cents. The Somersets will outdraw the Beaneaters by 200,000 this season.

20th Pittsburgh's Honus Wagner becomes the first 20th-century player to steal home twice in a single game, as Jack Chesbro blanks the Giants 7–0.

21st Righthander Doc Parker of the Reds gives up 21 runs and 26 hits to Brooklyn in his first start of the season and ML farewell appearance.

24th The Reds Bill Phillips gives up 19 runs and 22 hits at Philadelphia, losing 19–1.

JULY

1st Cubs 1B Jack Doyle, harassed by a Polo Grounds fan, jumps into the stands and starts a fight, reinjuring his hand, which he had broken several weeks before. The Giants' "Dummy" Taylor bests the Cubs Jack Taylor 6–4.

8th An 8th-inning decision favoring the Brooklyn Superbas infuriates St. Louis fans. When the 7–5 Brooklyn win ends, they rush umpire Hank O'Day, who suffers a split lip before players and police can rescue him.

10th At a secret meeting, the NL Board of directors votes to abrogate the National Agreement that has governed organized baseball, effective September 30.

15th Christy Mathewson (22 years old) of the Giants pitches a no-hitter, blanking St. Louis 5–0 at League Park. Matty saves his own no-hitter in the 6th when an Otto Krueger hit caroms off 1B Chick Ganzel's glove to Mathewson, who throws back to 1B for a 3–1–3 putout.

24th In a baseball rarity, the Pittsburgh Pirates score in every inning, defeating the Reds 11–2.

30th Ban Johnson says the AL will place a team in St. Louis in 1902. The Milwaukee franchise is seen as the most likely to be transferred.

AUGUST

4th Cincinnati and Pittsburgh players are clocked while running from home plate to 1B. The fastest time for the 90-foot sprint is 3 seconds flat, by Pirates OF Ginger Beaumont.

7th Ban Johnson suspends Baltimore 1B Burt Hart for striking umpire John Haskell. In Cleveland,

Milwaukee manager Hugh Duffy hits umpire Al Mannassau when a fly ball nicking the foul line is called fair, scoring the winning runs for the Blues. Duffy is suspended indefinitely.

10th The National's Dale Gear gives up an AL-record 41 total bases in losing 13–0 to the Athletics. The 23 hits include 4 doubles, 4 triples, and 2 HRs. Philadelphia A's P Snake Wiltse has 2 doubles and 2 triples, becoming only the 3rd hurler to collect 4 extra-base hits in a game.

For the 2nd game in a row, Nap Lajoie of the Athletics hits 2 HRs in a victory over Washington. He will lead the AL with 14. Added to 125 RBI and a .422 batting average, he earns the Triple Crown.

20th Umpire Bob Emslie becomes ill before the 2nd game of the Superbas-Phils twin bill. Phils P Al Orth and Superbas C Jim McGuire fill in for him. However, it is a close game, and Orth is needed as a PH in the 9th. Doc White then becomes the 2nd umpire as Orth hits a single and scores a run. Brooklyn holds on for a 3–2 win.

21st Washington's Win Mercer lives up to his name with an 8–0 win over Chicago. White Stockings SS Frank Shugart is so frustrated he attacks umpire Haskel with his fists and then throws a ball at him. He will be expelled from the league.

SEPTEMBER

3rd Baltimore P Joe McGinnity hurls 2 complete games against Milwaukee, winning 10–0 and losing 6–1.

6th The National Association of Professional Baseball Leagues is formed to help the minor leagues protect their interests.

8th The Players Protective Association instructs members to sign one-year contracts only, and not recognize the reserve clause.

12th McGinnity hurls 2 more complete games, winning over Philadelphia 4–3 and losing 5–4.

15th The White Stockings hit a ML record 5 triples in the 8th inning against Milwaukee. A total of 6 in a game is an AL record not duplicated until September 17, 1920.

The Detroit Tigers beat Cleveland behind Ed Siever with the most lopsided score in AL history: 21–0 (equalled on August 13, 1939). The game is called after 7½ innings to allow Cleveland to catch a train.

19th All games are canceled out of respect for the funeral of President William McKinley, who died September 14th from gunshot wounds.

21st Tom Hughes of Chicago and Boston Beaneater Bill Dinneen pitch 16 scoreless innings before the Cubs score in the 17th on an error, hit batter, force-out, and single. Each pitcher gives up 8 hits.

An AL record that still stands is set when Cleveland and Washington make 22 errors in a double-header, 16 by Cleveland. Washington wins both games 18–7 and 11–3.

24th Jimmy Sheckard becomes the first 20th-century player to hit grand slams in 2 consecutive games, as Brooklyn beats Cincinnati 16–2 the day after a 25–6 win.

29th The AL season ends with the White Stockings in first place by 4 games over Boston. Jimmy Williams of the Baltimore Orioles leads the AL in triples, with 21, 2 years after leading the NL with 27. This feat will be topped by Sam Crawford in 1902–1903.

OCTOBER

6th The Pirates hold off a late surge by the Phillies to finish the NL season with a 7½ game lead.

20th Seven Cardinals, including the 3 top hitters—Jesse Burkett, Emmet Heidrick, and Bobby Wallace—and half the pitching staff, jump to the new St. Louis AL team.

NOVEMBER

5th Sportsman's Park in St. Louis is leased for 5 years by Ban Johnson and Charles Comiskey for an AL team; 2 weeks later the Milwaukee franchise is officially transferred.

DECEMBER

3rd At the league meeting, the Milwaukee franchise is officially dropped from the AL and is replaced by the St. Louis Browns.

14th Suffering from too much infighting and no leadership, 4 NL clubs elect A. G. Spalding as president. Two days later, a court voids the election and enjoins him from serving, and he will eventually quit.

1902

JANUARY

4th   Bill Dinneen, winner of 36 games for the Beaneaters (NL) in the past 2 years, signs with the rival Boston Somersets (AL), for whom he will win 20 or more for the next 3 years.

26th   Lulu Ortman, recently jilted by Boston's Chick Stahl, is arrested in Fort Wayne, IN, after attempting (unsuccessfully) to shoot him.

30th   Dashing Tony Mullane, the first player to have jumped the reserve rule by signing with the St. Louis Unions of the Union Association in 1883, signs a contract with Toledo, of the new American Association (AAA).

FEBRUARY

20th   Nick Young remains as NL president when A. G. Spalding bows out of the battle, but the league will have no effective leadership until 1903.

MARCH

12th   Cincinnati OF "Turkey Mike" Donlin is arrested for assaulting actress Minnie Fields and her escort. Donlin will plead guilty and serve a 6-month sentence.

APRIL

3rd   The NL names club owners Arthur Soden, John T. Brush, and James Hart as an interim committee to run the league.

19th   Righthander Bob Ewing, 29, makes his ML debut with the Reds, and ties a NL record by walking 7 batters in the 4th inning. The Chicago Cubs get 5 runs on one hit en route to a 9–5 win.

21st   The Pennsylvania Supreme Court, reversing a lower court's decision, grants a permanent injunction (effective only in Pennsylvania) barring jumpers Nap Lajoie, Chick Fraser, and Bill Bernhard from playing for the A's, or any team but the Phillies. Not mentioned, but covered by the decision, are: Elmer Flick, Monte Cross, and Bill Duggleby of the A's; Ed Delahanty, Al Orth, Harry Wolverton, and Jack

Townsend of Washington; Ed McFarland (White Stockings) and Red Donahue (Browns).

23rd   St. Louis Cardinals owner Frank DeHaas Robison offers to put up $10,000 that the Pirates will not repeat as NL champions. Pittsburgh players accept the challenge with a matching pool, and go on to win the pennant by 27½ games.

26th   In his ML debut, Cleveland's Addie Joss hurls a one-hitter against the Browns to win 3–0. The only hit is a scratch single by Jesse Burkett.

27th   Cubs rookie RH pitcher Jim St. Vrain, sent up to pinch-hit lefthanded, grounds to Pittsburgh SS Honus Wagner. The confused St. Vrain runs toward 3B as the astonished Wagner throws him out. Pittsburgh wins 2–0.

MAY

6th   A circuit court in St. Louis rules the NL reserve clause unfairly restrictive on 3 defectors who jumped to the Browns. Inability to retrieve jumpers gives the NL a strong push to reconcile differences with the AL.

7th   Elmer Flick signs with Cleveland. *Sporting Life* says that A's officials "presumably consented" to the move.

The Cubs Jack Taylor beats Christy Mathewson 4–0 at Chicago. Cubs manager Frank Selee comments that the distance from the pitcher's mound to the plate looks short. Horace Fogel, the Giants manager, measures the distance and finds the lane is 15 inches short. The subsequent New York protest is upheld, and 2 games are ordered replayed.

8th   Bill Duggleby, the first jumper to return to the Phillies, loses 2–1 to St. Louis. Returnee Chick Fraser will win his first start on May 23rd, 5–2 over Chicago. Harry Wolverton will return after 59 games with the Washington Nationals. All others will remain with their new teams. Of all those that the Athletics acquired, only Monte Cross stays.

16th   Two deaf-mutes face each other for the first time when Dummy Hoy leads off for the Reds against Dummy Taylor of the Giants. The Reds win 5–3 with a 5-run rally in the 9th. Hoy goes 2-for-4.

18th   Frank Isbell, White Stockings 1B, fields a record 26 chances—24 putouts and 2 assists. On June

30th, Cleveland's Charles Hickman will tie the record with 25 putouts and one assist.

23rd Cleveland financier Charles Somers, who is also the president of the Boston club, meets with Lajoie in Philadelphia and guarantees him a 4-year contract at $7,000 per year no matter what the legal outcome of his case. Lajoie had played one game, then sat in the stands. In 1903, Cleveland fans will vote to rename the club the Naps in honor of Lajoie.

24th Bill Bradley, Cleveland 3B, is the AL's first to hit a HR in each of 4 consecutive games, a record not matched until Babe Ruth does it June 25, 1918.

JUNE

2nd Baltimore scores 9 runs in the 3rd inning of a 14–1 victory, as Cleveland kicks in 6 errors, the most boots in one inning by any club in the 20th century.

3rd The Cardinals' Mike O'Neill, a pitcher and one of 4 ML brothers, hits the first pinch grand slam ever, against Boston Beaneater Togie Pittinger. It is an inside-the-park HR at Boston and scores his brother C Jack.

10th Bobby Wallace, slick-fielding St. Louis SS, handles an AL record 17 chances in a 9-inning game while losing 5–4 to Boston. Wallace, whose 25-year career will place him in the Hall of Fame, has 11 assists and 6 putouts, but makes 2 errors.

11th Connie Mack signs Rube Waddell, who was pitching in the Pacific Coast League. He will go 24–7 during the remainder of 1902.

15th Corsicana (Texas League) beats Texarkana, 51–3, as Nig Clarke hits 8 HRs. The team's 53 hits include 21 HRs, mostly over a short OF fence.

25th A federal court judge rules that Brooklyn has no claim on C Deacon McGuire, who jumped to Detroit. Two weeks later, another U.S. judge denies jurisdiction to stop Lajoie from playing for Cleveland, thus ending the Phillies' chances of regaining him legally.

30th Jim Jones, Giants LF, throws 3 base runners out at home in an 8–0 loss to Boston.

Cleveland is the first AL team to hit 3 consecutive HRs in one inning as Lajoie, Piano Legs Hickman, and Bill Bradley connect in the first off St. Louis. Two days later, Ed Delahanty, Bill Coughlin, and

Boileryard Clarke will duplicate the feat for Washington against the White Stockings.

JULY

1st Rube Waddell wins his first game for the Athletics, blanking Baltimore on 2 hits 2–0. He fans the side 3 times, once on 9 pitches, and faces only 27 batters, as C Ossee Schreckengost throws out the 2 base runners. In fanning the side in the 3rd, 6th, and 9th, Waddell strikes out the same 3 men each time: Billy Gilbert, Harry Howell, and John Cronin.

6th Corsicana of the Texas League wins its 27th game in a row, topping Charlotte's record of 25 set earlier this year. Corsicana will finish the year with a 57–9 record.

8th John McGraw, accused by Ban Johnson of trying to wreck the Baltimore and Washington clubs, negotiates his release from the Orioles and officially signs to manage the Giants at $11,000 a year, although he'd already secretly signed a contract several days earlier brought to Baltimore by Giants secretary Fred M. Knowles. Conspiring with NL owners Brush and Freedman, McGraw swings the sale of the Orioles their way, enabling them to release Orioles Dan McGann, Roger Bresnahan, Joe McGinnity, and Jack Cronin for signing by the Giants. Joe Kelley and Cy Seymour go to Brush's Cincinnati Reds.

Righthander Doc Adkins gives up 12 hits and 12 runs in the 6th inning of a Philadelphia 22–9 win over the Boston Somersets. The A's new 2B Danny Murphy does not arrive until the 2nd inning. Taking the field with no batting practice, he is 6-for-6, including a HR, in a sensational debut. The 45 hits by the 2 teams set an AL record.

17th Left with only 5 players available to play, the Orioles forfeit a game to St. Louis and their franchise to the league, which borrows players from other teams and operates the club for the balance of the season.

19th The Giants lose their first game under new manager John McGraw 5–3 to the Phillies. They will end the season in last place.

AUGUST

9th John T. Brush sells the Cincinnati Reds to Julius and Max Fleischmann, George B. Cox, and

August "Garry" Herrmann for $150,000. Brush then buys control of the Giants.

13th In the 6th inning of a game with the Tigers, Harry Davis of the A's attempts a double steal with Dave Fultz, who is on 3B. But Davis does not draw a throw as he goes into 2B. On the next pitch he "steals" 1B. The next time he steals 2B he does draw a throw and Fultz scores from 3B. This double steal maneuver will be attempted in later years by Fred Tenney (July 31, 1908), and Germany Schaefer (September 4, 1908).

In the 2nd game of a doubleheader in Boston, Pirate Honus Wagner steals 2B, 3B, and home in the 7th inning. Wagner also did it in 1899.

14th Little Tommy Leach of Pittsburgh, never considered a long-ball threat, hits 2 HRs over the fence at Boston. He will close out the season with only 6, but it is enough to give him sole leadership of the NL, which totals only 99. Leach's leading number is the lowest since Paul Hines hit 4 in a 60-game schedule in 1878.

16th The Athletics move into first place to stay as 18,675 see them beat Chicago 2–1.

18th The first unassisted triple play ever in a professional game is executed by 1B Hal O'Hagan, of the Rochester Broncos (IL) against Jersey City.

25th Ban Johnson announces the AL's intention to have a New York team in 1903, with Clark Griffith as manager. The Baltimore franchise will be moved.

SEPTEMBER

1st Tinker, Evers, and Chance appear together in the Chicago Cubs lineup for the first time, but not in the positions that will earn them immortality. Johnny Evers, a New York State League rookie, starts at SS, with Joe Tinker at 3B, Frank Chance at 1B, and Bobby Lowe at 2B.

4th Dave Fultz steals 2B, 3B, and home in the 2nd inning against Detroit, as the A's romp 13–3.

9th In Philadelphia, 17,291 see the Athletics beat Baltimore twice, while 172 watch the Phils play Pittsburgh. With the A's 1902 attendance almost 4 times that of the Phillies, and the AL planning to oppose the weak Giants in New York, pressure mounts among NL directors for peace talks.

13th Tinker, Evers, and Chance play their first game as a SS-2B-1B combo for the Chicago Cubs. Germany Schaefer is at 3B.

20th OF-P James "Nixey" Callahan of the White Stockings pitches a no-hitter against Detroit 3–0.

28th The AL season ends with the Athletics 5 games in front of St. Louis Browns. Philadelphia's Socks Seybold hits 16 HRs for the highest total to lead the AL until Babe Ruth's 29 in 1919.

OCTOBER

4th When Pirates owner Barney Dreyfuss demands a game be played despite a rain-soaked field, Cincinnati plays most of its team out of their normal positions. P Rube Vickers, catching, sets a modern ML record with 6 passed balls. Pittsburgh wins 11–2, but Dreyfuss refunds fans' money and the Reds return their share of the gate.

DECEMBER

9th The AL announces purchase of grounds for a stadium in NY, and the next day the NL declares its readiness to make peace.

12th Harry Pulliam is elected president of the NL.

1903

JANUARY

9th At Cincinnati peace talks, the NL proposes a consolidated 12-team league, which the AL rejects. An agreement is reached to coexist peacefully if the AL promises to stay out of Pittsburgh. In the awarding of disputed contracts, the most hotly contested case is that of Sam Crawford, Reds OF who batted .333 and led the NL with 23 triples in 1902. The future Hall of Famer, signed for 1903 by both Detroit and the Reds, is awarded to the Tigers, having signed with them first. He will lead the AL in triples this year with 25.

Despite attempts by John Brush and Andrew Freedman to use their political influence to prevent the AL from finding suitable grounds in New York, Ban Johnson, aided by baseball writer Joe Vila, finds backers. He also finds a ballpark site at 165th Street and Broadway. Frank Farrell and Bill Devery pay $18,000 for the Baltimore franchise and will build a wooden grandstand seating 15,000 on the highest point of Manhattan. The team, logically, will be called the Highlanders.

12th Detroit pitcher Win Mercer, winner of 15 games in 1902, commits suicide by inhaling gas in San Francisco's Occidental Hotel. Mercer had recently been named the Tigers manager.

FEBRUARY

5th The Cubs and White Stockings, the first to play an inter-league series, announce a 15-game preseason City Series.

6th Former ML P and umpire Hardie Henderson is run over and killed by a trolley in Philadelphia.

28th A syndicate headed by Pittsburgh owner Barney Dreyfuss and James Potter buys the Philadelphia Phillies from John Rogers and A. J. Reach for $170,000. It will be another 7 years before ownership interest in more than one team is prohibited.

MARCH

7th In the first trade under the peace treaty, the Giants send their 1902 part-time manager Heinie Smith to Detroit for 2B Kid Gleason, who is immedi-

ately moved to the Phils where he will end a 20-year playing career.

20th The 2 MLs agree to blacklist future contract jumpers.

21st *Sporting Life,* the nation's oldest baseball publication, begins its 21st year. It will close during W W I.

APRIL

4th The Philadelphia Athletics threaten to strike unless they share in the receipts of last fall's City Series. They don't get the money, but they don't strike.

14th Ed Delahanty, one of 5 ML brothers, and the greatest natural hitter of his time, rejoins the Washington Nationals in accordance with the peace terms. A 3-year contract with the Giants at $8,000 a year, signed during the winter, is canceled. The Nationals reimburse the Giants for the $3,000 advanced to Big Ed.

20th The New York Highlanders play their first game, with Jack Chesbro losing 3–1 to Al Orth and Washington.

21st Brooklyn P Henry Schmidt and the Giants' Christy Mathewson keep the ball low on opening day, taking a record 98 total chances by 2 clubs. The Superbas have 23 assists, including 8 by Schmidt in his ML debut; the Giants have 21 in Brooklyn's 2–1 home opener. The record will be tied by the Giants and Reds May 15, 1909.

23rd Butte (Pacific Coast League) makes 2 triple plays in one game against Los Angeles.

The New York Highlanders win their first game 7–2 over Washington.

30th The new AL park opens in New York with an estimated crowd of 16,000 watching the home team beat Washington 6–2.

MAY

6th The White Stockings commit 12 errors, and the Tigers commit 6, for a modern ML record by 2 teams in one game. Chicago salvages a 10–9 victory.

The Pirates Deacon Phillippe, en route to 25 wins, lets one get away when the Cubs score 9 in the 9th for an 11–4 triumph.

8th White Stockings P Nixey Callahan gets 5 hits for the 3rd time, but the 11-inning loss to the St. Louis Browns is the final game he will pitch in the major leagues. He will play other positions until 1913.

16th A record 31,500 at the Polo Grounds see the first-place Giants beat Pittsburgh, but the New Yorkers will soon fade, and the Pirates will win their 3rd straight pennant.

17th With Sunday baseball banned in Cleveland, the Blues and Highlanders play at Columbus, OH. Cleveland's Addie Joss defeats Clark Griffith 9–2.

JUNE

8th Detroit SS Kid Elberfeld, suspended for umpire abuse, is traded to New York for veteran infielders Herman Long and Ernie Courtney. "The Tabasco Kid" will be a key ingredient in the Highlanders' rise as contenders in 1904.

9th The Phils score breaking the Pirates' record run of 6 straight shutouts and 56 scoreless innings. The Giants were blanked twice, Boston 3 times, and the Phils once.

23rd The Boston Pilgrims take—and hold—the AL lead. They will finish 14½ games ahead of the Philadelphia Athletics.

25th Boston Beaneater Wiley Piatt becomes the only 20th-century pitcher to lose 2 complete games in one day, falling to Pittsburgh 1–0 and 5–3.

26th Veteran SS George Davis, 1900–1901 Giants manager who played for the White Stockings in 1902 and was awarded to them as part of the peace treaty, gets the approval of NL president Harry Pulliam to play for the Giants. After Davis plays in 4 games for the Giants, Chicago's owner Charles Comiskey gets an injunction preventing Davis from playing. On July 20th the NL directors vote that Davis cannot play for any team except the White Stockings. Davis sits out the rest of the season but rejoins Chicago in 1904 and finishes a 20-year career with them in 1909.

JULY

2nd Seeing that George Davis is playing for the Giants, Ed Delahanty decides to jump to New York too. Leaving the Nationals in Detroit, he boards an eastbound train. He is put off the train for rowdy, and possibly drunken, behavior. When he tries to walk across the railroad bridge over the Niagara River, he falls to his death. He had a 16-year, .346 batting average.

2nd P Jack Doscher, making his debut with the Chicago Cubs, is the first son of a former ML player to also play in the ML. Father Herm was a 3B with Troy, Chicago, and Cleveland before the turn of the century. Jack will end the season with the Brooklyn Superbas.

17th Rube Waddell is arrested for assaulting a fan who had criticized his pitching. Connie Mack bails him out of jail.

Dan McClelland of the Cuban X-Giants spins the first perfect game in black baseball history, blanking the Penn Park Athletic Club of York, PA, 5–0.

AUGUST

1st Rube Waddell no-hits the Highlanders, except for Kid Elberfelk, who has 4 singles. These, plus a lavish 6 walks, down the A's 3–2. Waddell observes afterward, "If I would have walked him 4 times, I would have pitched a no-hitter."

8th Furious when an old black ball is put into play against Cleveland in the last of the 11th and his objections are ignored by umpire Tommy Connolly, Blues 2B Nap Lajoie hurls the ball over the grandstand, suffering the loss of the game to Detroit by forfeit.

The Giants "Iron Man" Joe McGinnity pitches one of 3 doubleheaders he will win this month, beating Brooklyn 6–1 and 4–3; he also steals home in the 2nd game. On August 1st, he won 2 from Boston 4–1 and 5–2. On August 31st he will beat the Phillies twice. He has now done double work 5 times, including 2 losses on each of the 2 occasions at Baltimore in 1901. The combination of his 434 innings pitched and 31 wins, with Mathewson's 366 IP and 30 wins, will make them the century's most productive one-season duo.

An overhanging gallery atop the LF bleachers at Philadelphia's NL park collapses during a doubleheader with Boston, killing 12 and injuring 282. Philadelphia's remaining home games are played at the AL's Columbia Park.

17th Ban Johnson orders betting suppressed at all AL parks, a noble but futile gesture.

20th The Pirates set an NL mark for inept fielding, making 6 errors in the first inning, giving the Giants 7 runs toward a 13–7 win.

21st Ducky Holmes, White Stockings OF, has 4 assists in a game, tying the ML record. But his team still loses 11–3 to Cy Young and the Pilgrims.

28th Cleveland and St. Louis (AL) players escape serious injury when their train derails near Napoleon, OH.

SEPTEMBER

3rd Cleveland P Jesse Stovall hurls an 11-inning shutout in his first ML start, defeating Detroit 1–0. It is the longest shutout ever in a pitching debut.

11th A new National Agreement signed by the National Association of minor league clubs officially organizes professional baseball under one comprehensive set of rules.

14th Pitcher Red Ames begins his 17-year career with a 5-inning no-hitter for the Giants against St. Louis. The game is called in midafternoon due to darkness.

17th The Boston Pilgrims clinch the AL pennant, beating Cleveland 14–3, but their record of scoring in 17 consecutive innings is stopped in the 7th inning.

Chick Fraser no-hits the Cubs 10–0 for the Phils.

18th In the absence of official sanction, the presidents of pennant-winning clubs sign an agreement to meet in a best-of-9 series for the championship. The Pirates clinch the pennant the next day.

20th A bad day for the Poughkeepsie Giants (Class D Hudson River League) as they drop a quadruple header to Hudson by the scores of 2–1, 6–4, 3–1, and 4–2.

24th Bill Bradley of Cleveland hits for the cycle and adds an extra double for 12 total bases.

OCTOBER

1st The first modern World Series game, also called "Championship of the United States," is played at Boston's Huntington Street park before 16,242. Deacon Phillippe pitches Pittsburgh to a 7–3 win over Cy Young. Pittsburgh RF Jimmy Sebring hits the first HR. 3B Tommy Leach hits 2 triples for the Pirates and winds up with 4, a Series record.

2nd The Boston Pilgrims Bill Dinneen blanks Pittsburgh 3–0 on 3 hits to even the Series. His 4 starts will give him 3 victories, making this the only WS to produce two 3-game winners. Boston LF Patsy Dougherty hits 2 HRs; in 14 WS games they are the only HRs he will hit.

3rd Deacon Phillippe comes back on one day's rest to beat Boston 4–2 before 18,801, the biggest crowd of the Series.

6th A travel day and rainout enable Phillippe to pitch and win again 5–4, before 7,600 at Pittsburgh. Honus Wagner has 3 hits, but will manage just .222 for the WS.

7th Cy Young, who will also pitch in 4 games, stops the Pirates 11–2 on 6 hits. The 36-year-old righthander drives in 3 runs. Pittsburgh P Brickyard Kennedy is ahead 4–2 in the 6th when Wagner makes 2 errors, and Boston scores 6 runs.

8th Bill Dinneen evens the Series with a 6–3 win over Pittsburgh's Sam Leever, who was 25–7 during the season.

10th Three days rest are apparently too much for Phillippe, who gives up first-inning triples to Boston's Jimmy Collins and Chick Stahl for a 2–0 lead. Cy Young wins 7–3.

13th Phillippe pitches his 5th complete game of the Series, losing to Dinneen 3–0. Only 7,455, the smallest crowd of the Series, see Boston win the championship. Deacon's 5 decisions and 44 IP are still WS records.

14th Pittsburgh P Ed Doheny is committed to an insane asylum in Massachusetts after assaulting his nurse with a poker. Doheny had compiled a 16–8 mark.

15th With Pirates owner Dreyfuss putting his club's $6,699.56 gate receipts into the players' pool, the 16 Pirates receive $1,316 each, more than the victorious Boston players' $1,182. Deacon Phillippe receives a bonus and 10 shares of stock in the Pirates for his heroic efforts.

NOVEMBER

11th   Jimmy Collins signs a contract to manage the Pilgrims for 3 years. They will be called the Pilgrims, then the Red Sox during his tenure.

17th   Chicago Cubs SS Joe Tinker tells an interviewer that it is "impossible to fix" a ML baseball game.

DECEMBER

12th   During the post-season City Series in Chicago, the Cubs veteran Jack Taylor is chided for losing 3 games to the White Stockings. He is overheard to say, "Why should I win? I get $100 from [Cubs owner] Hart for winning and $500 for losing." He is traded to the St. Louis Cardinals with rookie C Larry McLean for pitcher Mike O'Neill and a righthander who was 9–13 in his first season, Mordecai "Three Finger" Brown.

Continuing efforts to build a winner in New York, John McGraw acquires 34-year-old SS Bill Dahlen from Brooklyn. McGraw says this is the trade that makesthe Giants into winners. In 1904, Dahlen will top the NL with 80 RBI. When he retires in 1911, he will have fielded more chances than any other SS.

18th   Ban Johnson is reelected AL president and given a raise to $10,000.

20th   P Kid Nichols signs to manage the Cardinals. He will win 21 himself, but the team will finish 4th.

1904

JANUARY

4th   The Highlanders announce plans to play on Sundays at Ridgewood Park on Long Island, but the Brooklyn club objects. Sunday games are legal in Detroit, St. Louis, Chicago, and Cincinnati.

22nd   William H. Yawkey, the 28-year-old heir to a lumber and mining fortune, buys the Detroit Tigers from S. F. Angus for $50,000. New money and Frank Navin's shrewd management will bring 3 straight pennants to the franchise within a few years.

FEBRUARY

1st   The Cards purchase veteran first baseman Jack Beckley from the Cincinnati Reds. The future Hall of Famer will have 4 decreasingly productive years in St. Louis before retiring.

APRIL

17th   The Brooklyn Superbas play their first Sunday game at home, beating Boston 9–1. To circumvent Sunday Blue Laws, no admission is charged, but fans must buy scorecards to enter the grandstand and box seats.

26th   Ty Cobb makes his professional debut for Augusta (South Atlantic League), hitting a double and HR in an 8–7 loss to Columbus.

MAY

4th   Justice Gaynor rules in favor of Brooklyn players arrested for playing baseball on Sunday at Washington Park. In an appeal, Sunday baseball will again be ruled illegal on June 18th.

5th   Boston Pilgrim Cy Young pitches the 2nd of 3 no-hitters, a 3–0 perfect game against the Philadelphia Athletics and Rube Waddell. Eventually Young will go on to complete 24 straight hitless innings, still the record, and 45 shutout innings in a row, a record broken by Don Drysdale's 58 in 1968. For Waddell it is one of 18 losses, the most of his career, against 25 wins. He will strike out 349, a record until Sandy Koufax fans 382 in 1965.

14th   Cubs OF Jack McCarthy sprains an ankle by stepping on the umpire's broom at home plate. NL President Pulliam orders arbiters henceforward to use pocket-sized whisk brooms for housekeeping at home. The AL will comply next year.

27th   The Giants Dan McGann steals 5 bases in one game, a feat not duplicated in the NL until August 24, 1974, by Davey Lopes.

30th   Frank Chance of the Cubs is hit 3 times by P Jack Harper of the Reds in the first game of a double-header. On one of the occasions, he loses consciousness when hit in the head. He continues to play when he comes to, however, and in the 2nd game, he is hit twice by Win Kellum, giving him a record 5 hit by pitched balls for the day. The 2 teams split the holiday twin bill.

JUNE

11th   Bob Wicker pitches 9⅓ hitless innings for the Cubs before losing to the Giants in the 12th 1–0.

16th   Christy Mathewson beats the Cardinals to start a 24-game winning streak against them that will not end until 1908. His 33 victories and McGinnity's 35 will be the most victories by 2 teammates since 1900.

JULY

4th   Jack Chesbro, the New York Highlanders spitballer, wins his 14th in a row, an AL record until Walter Johnson wins 16 straight in 1912.

5th   A Giants 18-game winning streak ends when the Phillies prevail 6–5 in 10 innings. The Giants record is now 53–18, effectively ending the NL race. By September 1, they will lead the Cubs by 15 games. John McGraw and John T. Brush say they have no intention of playing a post-season series with the AL champions. "When we clinch the NL pennant, we'll be champions of the only real major league," says McGraw. As the New York Highlanders battle for the AL pennant, local pressure mounts, but Brush, still angry over the inter-league peace treaty, and McGraw, who despises Ban Johnson, are adamant.

AUGUST

6th Lefthander Nick Altrock of the White Sox (their new nickname), en route to the first of three 20-win seasons, handles 13 fielding chances — the modern ML record for pitchers—in an 8–1 victory over the Athletics. He will finish the year with 49 putouts, an AL record for pitchers.

Prompt action by Boston Pilgrims players Bill Dinneen, Norwood Gibson, Freddy Parent, and Hobe Ferris prevents a tragedy in a Cleveland hotel. Returning to their rooms following the game, the 4 are confronted by a fire sweeping through the 5th floor. They extinguish the blaze and are cited as heroes.

10th Jack Chesbro is knocked out by the White Sox after pitching 30 complete games in a row. For the year he will win 41 games, pitching 48 complete games out of 51 starts for the Highlanders. All are post-1900 records. His 455 innings pitched will be topped only by Ed Walsh's 464 in 1908.

17th Jesse Tannehill, a lefthander who will win 20 games or more 6 times, pitches a no-hitter for Boston against the White Sox 6–0.

24th Willie Keeler collects 2 HRs against the St. Louis Browns in a 9–1 win at New York. Both are inside the park.

SEPTEMBER

3rd Syracuse (Eastern League) beats Scranton 3 times in a tripleheader.

15th Giants rookie Hooks Wiltse wins his 12th straight game, setting a ML mark for consecutive games won at the start of a career. It will be tied by relief hurler Clarence Metzger in 1976.

22nd In the final game of his 19-year career as an OF/C, future Hall of Famer Jim O'Rourke, 52, is the Giants backstop in their 7–5 defeat of the Cincinnati Reds. Their 100th win, it clinches the NL pennant. It is O'Rourke's first ML game since 1893; he gets a single and scores a run.

The Giants .262 will lead the NL in team batting, 31 points below the 1900 leaders. Team batting averages have dropped since then, mainly due to: the change from a diamond-shaped, 10-inch home plate to the 5-sided, 17-inch plate after 1901; the foul-strike rule adopted in 1901; and the introduction of the spitball and other doctored pitches in 1903.

27th Bob Rhoads, Cleveland righthander, holds Boston hitless for 8⅔ innings, before Chick Stahl singles.

30th Doc White, White Sox lefthander, pitches his 5th shutout in 18 days, defeating New York. Of his 7 shutouts for the year, 6 come in September. His scoreless streak will end at 45 innings on October 2nd, when the New York Highlanders score in the first; White then pitches another 8 shutout innings to win 7–1.

OCTOBER

3rd Christy Mathewson of the Giants strikes out 16 Cards in a 3–1 Giants victory. Big 6's 16 strikeouts establishes a new record as he finishes the game in one hour and 15 minutes.

4th New York loses to the Cardinals 7–3 despite Giants Sam Mertes contribution of 4 hits for the cycle.

6th Cardinals P Jack Taylor hurls his 39th consecutive complete game of the season—a modern ML record. His streak started on April 15th.

7th Jack Chesbro pitches the Highlanders to a 3–2 win over Boston for his 41st victory. His 41–12 record will top the AL in wins and percentage; in 1902 with Pittsburgh, his 28–6 topped that league, making him the first to lead both leagues. The win gives New York a half-game lead over Boston.

George Stovall of Cleveland hits his first HR, and it comes off his older brother Jesse, pitching for Detroit in his last game. It marks the first time one brother gives up a HR to another, a feat which will be duplicated by the Ferrells in 1933, and the Niekros in 1976.

Pirates 3B Tommy Leach's 3 putouts and 2 assists help the Pirates beat the Cubs, 6–1. He will finish with 643 total chances, the highest of any 3rd sacker in the 20th Century. Only Pirates third sacker Jimmy Williams, whom Leach replaced, had a higher total (671 in 1889).

8th Despite a 154-game schedule, Detroit OF Jimmy Barrett becomes the first to play in 162 games, as the 7th-place Tigers close their home season, splitting with the Cleveland Blues before 400 spectators. The Tigers set a season record with 10 tie games, 8 of which are replayed.

10th The Pilgrim pitchers achieve 148 complete games—an AL record—as George Winter goes the route in a 1–0 loss to the Highlanders on the final day of the season. Both leagues set marks for total complete games: AL 1,098, NL 1,089.

A doubleheader split will give Boston the AL pennant over the Highlanders. With the score 2–2 in the top of the 9th and a man on 3B, Chesbro has a spitball get away from him for a wild pitch, and Boston's winning run scores. New York wins the 2nd game, but Boston triumphs by 1½ games.

Boston P Bill Dinneen hurls his 37th consecutive complete game of the season for an AL mark.

John McGraw issues a statement saying that he, not president John Brush, was responsible for refusing to play the AL winner in a post season series.

28th After a 4th-place finish, the Cleveland Blues release Bill Armour and name Nap Lajoie manager. Armour takes over the Tigers, where Ed Barrow and Bobby Lowe split the season, as Detroit falls to 7th.

NOVEMBER

8th Umpire Silk O'Loughlin runs for a state assembly seat as a Democrat and loses.

DECEMBER

20th The last-place Phillies send minor-league 1B Del Howard to Pittsburgh for Moose McCormick, Otto Kruger and 1B Kitty Bransfield.

1905

JANUARY

14th   Giants owner John T. Brush, who refused to play the AL pennant winners in 1904, proposes rules governing future World Series.

16th   It seems simple enough on paper; the Red Sox buy OF George Stone from the Senators. The Browns reclaim Frank Huelsman from the Senators, where he had been on loan, and send him along with OF Jesse Burkett to Boston for Stone. Boston then sends Huelsman back to Washington in payment for George Stone.

FEBRUARY

2nd   Hugh Jennings, now managing Baltimore in the Eastern League, is admitted to the Maryland bar after completing law studies at Cornell. Two weeks later Yankees OF Dave Fultz, a Columbia graduate, passes the New York bar exam. In 1912 he will organize and lead the Players' Fraternity.

7th   In Lynn, MA, Rube Waddell prevents a fire by carrying a burning stove out of a store and throwing it into a snowbank. Three days later he flees nearby Peabody to escape charges of assaulting and injuring his wife's parents.

15th   Accused of throwing games, Cardinals righthander Jack Taylor is acquitted by the NL Board of Directors in New York, but he is found guilty of bad conduct and fined $300.

25th   While most clubs go south or stay close to home, the Cubs go to Santa Monica, CA, for spring training.

MARCH

29th   A committee of Washington writers votes for "Nationals" as the AL team nickname, but "Senators" continues as the general favorite.

APRIL

10th   A New York magistrate rules Sunday baseball legal, but the battle will continue in the courts.

12th   The Washington owners offer the players a $1,000 bonus if they finish higher than 8th and $500 for each position higher. They finish 7th, 11 games above St. Louis.

14th   Wait Till Next Year: Boston's Kaiser Wilhelm loses to the Giants 10–1 in the opener at the Polo Grounds before 40,000. He will finish the year 4–22, one of 4 Beaneaters who will lose 20 or more this year. The other 3 are Irv Young, Vic Willis, and Chick Fraser. The only other team ever to have a quartet of 20-game losers will be the Beaneaters again in 1906.

The Cleveland-Detroit game is postponed due to snow.

20th   Due to the late Easter this year, games are played on Good Friday for the first time.

22nd   Having failed to give out rain checks the day before when a storm stopped the game, the Highlanders open the gates for free admission, and 30,000 people jam the park for the clash with Washington.

26th   Jack McCarthy becomes the 2nd OF to complete 3 DPs in one game when he throws out 3 Pirates at home, preserving the 2–1 Chicago Cubs victory.

Barney Dreyfuss, claiming the fans want to see more hitting, calls for abolishing the spitball. But it will remain legal until 1920.

30th   Over 30,000 attend a Sunday game between the Giants and Superbas in Brooklyn. To get around the law, fans make "contributions" for admission.

At Shreveport (Southern League), Harold Smith makes a strikeout-HR against Memphis, when the catcher misses the ball and it goes into the grandstand. No ground rules limit the runner's advance.

At Evansville, IN, future ML umpire Cy Rigler begins the practice of raising his right arm to indicate strikes, so that friends in the bleachers can distinguish calls.

MAY

3rd   Washington leads the AL, the highest position it has attained in any race since 1893. In 3 days it will be supplanted by the Cleveland Naps (formerly the Blues).

17th   Waseda University of Tokyo defeats Los Angeles High School 5–3 in the first game of an American tour. It is the first baseball game ever played by Japanese outside Japan. Waseda starts a power-house tradition at Japan's Big Six universities that continues today.

19th Banished yesterday for abusive behavior, John McGraw roams the Polo Grounds before today's game with the Pirates, shouting insults at Barney Dreyfuss. McGraw accuses him of controlling the NL umpires through league president Harry Pulliam and welshing on gambling debts. McGraw is again ejected during the game. Eight days later, Pulliam levies a $150 fine and a 15-day suspension. Dreyfuss demands an NL hearing. McGraw files for an injunction against the fine and suspension, which the judge eventually grants. On June 1st the NL board meets in Boston and clears McGraw of the Dreyfuss charges, then censures Dreyfuss for engaging in a public altercation with McGraw.

30th Both leagues post record attendance figures for the Memorial Day holiday. Thanks to morning-afternoon doubleheaders, 80,963 attend 8 AL games, 67,806 see 7 NL games.

JUNE

8th Red Ames, 22-year-old righthander, loses to Pittsburgh after winning 9 in a row. A surprise winner for the Giants, Ames will have the best season of his 19-year career, 22–8.

9th Rube Waddell loses after 10 wins in a row; the White Sox beat him 3–2 in 14 innings. Waddell will be 26–11 for the Athletics this year; his 1.48 ERA will be the AL's best.

13th For 8 innings, Christy Mathewson and the Cubs' Mordecai "Three Finger" Brown match no-hitters. The Giants get 2 hits in the 9th to win 1–0, and preserve Matty's 2nd no-hitter. His 31–8 record and 1.27 ERA, with 9 shutouts, will mark his 3rd straight 30-win year.

19th The Giants lose to Cincinnati when New York P Hooks Wiltse accidentally swallows a quid of chewing tobacco that upsets his stomach.

20th A young woman sues the Giants for injury suffered when a foul ball hits her. Judge M. Laughlin rules that patrons attend baseball games at their own risk.

24th Chicago Cubs rookie righthander Ed Reulbach wins an 18-inning duel with the Cards' Jack Taylor 2–1 in St. Louis.

30th Nap Lajoie is sidelined by blood poisoning from neglect of a spike wound. He will play in only 65 games, losing a chance to lead the AL in batting for the 5th straight year.

JULY

1st White Sox P Frank Owen narrowly misses becoming the first to pitch a doubleheader shutout as the Browns score one run off him in the 2 games.

4th In the afternoon game of a doubleheader, Philadelphia's Rube Waddell bests Cy Young in a 20-inning marathon, as the Athletics down Boston 4–2. Philadelphia C Ossee Schreckengost works 28 innings in one day, a ML record.

Bugs Raymond of Charleston, SC (South Atlantic), pitches the morning and afternoon games of a doubleheader, throwing a no-hitter in each game.

12th Three Finger Brown scores the first of 9 straight wins over Christy Mathewson 8–1. Of 28 matches over their careers Brown will win 14.

22nd Weldon Henley of the Athletics pitches a no-hitter against the St. Louis Browns 6–0. He will win only 4 games all season.

31st Charles P. Taft, owner of the Cincinnati *Times-Star* and brother of a future president, finances Charles W. Murphy's purchase of the Chicago Cubs for $125,000.

AUGUST

1st The Giants win their 12th in a row, and 11th straight against Cincinnati 10–5. The Pirates will end the streak at 13 on August 3rd, but the Giants will win the pennant easily, 9 games ahead of Pittsburgh.

2nd The Athletics go into first place as Rube Waddell beats the White Sox, fanning 14. He will lead the AL with 287 strikeouts, the 4th of 6 straight seasons when he tops the league.

4th The Highlanders field a unique battery: Doc Newton pitching and Mike "Doc" Powers catching, but only Powers is a physician.

5th   Highlanders 1B Hal Chase has a record 38 putouts in a doubleheader versus the Browns.

At Pittsburgh, umpire Bauswine forfeits a game to the Pirates with the score tied in the 9th when the Giants argue too long over a call at 3B. Two days later, Honus Wagner is fined $40 and suspended 3 days later for throwing a ball at the ump.

8th   Pittsburgh 2B Dave Brain, who hit 3 triples in a game for St. Louis against Pittsburgh on May 29th, repeats the performance for Pittsburgh against Boston. He is the only player to perform the feat twice in one season.

9th   Mistaking her husband for a burglar, Ty Cobb's mother shoots and kills him. The Georgia Peach will make his ML debut with the Tigers later this month.

10th   Catchers are not expected to hit triples, but Boston Beaneater backstop Pat Moran legs out a trio of 3-base hits against the Pirates. He will be the last catcher to do it.

22nd   John Seridan forfeits a game to Washington in the 11th when the Tigers refuse to resume play after a lengthy dispute.

24th   Chicago's Ed Reulbach defeats Tully Sparks in a 20-inning 2–1 Cubs win over the Phils. It ties the ML mark for the most innings played in a game.

30th   Ty Cobb makes his ML debut, doubling off Jack Chesbro, as Detroit defeats New York 5–3. The 2-bagger is the first of his 4,191 hits, a record topped by Pete Rose with 4,256 in 1986.

SEPTEMBER

3rd   Kid Elberfeld ejected in first game of New York's 4–3 win vs. the A's. In the 2nd game, New York baserunner Willie Keeler collides with A's SS Lave Cross trying to field a ground ball. Two runs score but Umpire Silk O'Loughlin sees no interference, a call so hotly disputed by A's captain Harry Davis that after 8 minutes of arguing he pulls his team and forfeits the game to New York.

5th   When Boston beats the Athletics 3–2 in 13 innings, they score the first runs off Rube Waddell in 44 innings. Waddell strikes out 17.

6th   After Detroit has beaten the White Sox 4 times in 2 days, Chicago's Frank "Piano Mover" Smith pitches a 15–0 no-hitter in the 2nd game of a doubleheader.

8th   Pittsburgh scores 2 runs on 15 hits against the Reds, leaving a still-standing NL record 18 men on base.

14th   Joe Tinker and Johnny Evers engage in a fistfight on the field during an exhibition game in Washington, IN, because Evers took a taxi to the park, leaving his teammates in the hotel lobby. The pair will not speak to each other again.

16th   The Highlanders find themselves a little short on infielders so RF Willie Keeler, who is lefthanded, plays 2B in both games of a twin bill.

20th   Cleveland makes 7 errors in one inning, an AL record, giving the White Sox 8 runs and a 9–6 victory.

Chicago President Charles Comiskey orders a houseboat built for the express purpose of transporting and housing the team during spring training.

23rd   Detroit rookie Ty Cobb, 18, hits his first HR, off Cy Falkenberg, an inside-the-park blow, in an 8–5 loss at Washington.

26th   Chicago White Sox P Ed Walsh hurls 2 complete-game victories over Boston, winning by scores of 10–5 and 3–1. When Doc White leaves the first game without retiring a batter in the first inning, Walsh comes in without warming up. He gives up 5 runs in the first, then blanks Boston the rest of the way.

27th   Pilgrim Bill Dinneen pitches the 4th no-hitter of the season. The White Sox have 26 official at bats against him in the 2–0 Boston win.

28th   In a game that helps decide the pennant, The A's beat the White Sox 3–2, as Topsy Hartsell scores from 2nd base with the winning run in the 7th inning. Harry Davis's RBI single to short left hits Hartsell's mitt which the left fielder had left in the outfield when he came off the field. The A's take the series 2 games to 1, and will finish 2 games ahead of Chicago.

30th   The Athletics take 2 of 3 from Chicago at home to all but end the White Sox' pennant hopes. The final margin is 2 games. The series draws 64,620, a ML record, with thousands more turned away each day.

OCTOBER

2nd The Washington OF has no putouts or assists in a 3–2 win over Chicago.

3rd The National Commission establishes the rules for a World Series and names Hank O'Day and John Sheridan (both NL umps) to umpire it.

Brooklyn hurler Doc Scanlon hurls 2 complete-game victories over St Louis, winning by scores of 4–0 and 3–2.

5th Athletics P Chief Bender has 3 hits, including a triple with 3 on, in an 8–0 victory over Washington. He relieves Andy Coakley in the 2nd game and wins 9–7. Overall, he has 2 wins, 6 hits, and 8 RBI for the day.

6th The Athletics clinch the pennant while losing to the Washington Nationals, as St. Louis defeats the White Sox. Elmer Flick of the Cleveland Naps leads the AL in batting with a .306 mark.

7th Beaneaters 1B Fred Tenney has one assist in the season's final game, giving him an NL record of 152. The mark will be topped by Sid Bream of Pittsburgh, with 166 in 1986.

8th A Pacific Coast League game between the Oakland Oaks and Portland Beavers is attended by one fan. According to newspaper reports, the home-plate umpire, whose job it is to announce lineups, addresses the crowd, "Dear sir..."

9th At Philadelphia, the Giants' Christy Mathewson outpitches 26-game-winner Eddie Plank 3–0 in the first game of the all-shutout Series.

10th At New York, Philadelphia's Chief Bender gives up a mere 4 hits for a 3–0 win.

12th With 2 days rest, Mathewson allows his first and only walk in 27 innings, in a 4-hit 9–0 romp.

13th Joe McGinnity surrenders 5 hits, and Plank 4 hits, but 2 errors deal the A's a 1–0 loss.

14th Mathewson pitches his 3rd shutout in 6 days, giving up 6 hits to Bender's 5. The Giants win 2–0. The A's .161 team BA is the lowest ever for a WS; the teams' combined .185 is also the lowest. Each winning share is worth $1,142. The A's receive $382 each, but the club owners donate their share of the gate, raising the players' checks to $832.22.

DECEMBER

15th After losing a record 29 games this year, veteran righthander Vic Willis is traded by 7th-place Boston NL to Pittsburgh for 3 unimportant players.

16th The Cubs trade OF Jack McCarthy and Billy Maloney, 3B Doc Casey, and pitcher Buttons Briggs to Brooklyn for Jimmy Sheckard, who will take over LF for the NL champions of the next 3 years.

23rd Lave Cross, 38-year-old 3B, is sold to Washington by the Athletics.

1906

JANUARY

5th John McGraw and jockey Tod Sloan open a billiard parlor at 34th Street and Broadway, which soon becomes a popular and profitable hangout for New York's sporting life.

12th The owners of the Boston Beaneaters reject a $250,000 offer for the team, which is destined to finish last again.

20th The Giants sign Christy Mathewson's untalented 19-year-old brother Henry.

MARCH

6th Rookie owner Charles W. Murphy puts the last pieces of a Cubs dynasty in place, trading rookie infielder Hans Lobert and lefthander Jake Weimer to the Cincinnati Reds for 3B Harry Steinfeldt. Not a heavy hitter, Steinfeldt completes the Tinker-Evers-Chance infielder.

APRIL

12th Boston (NL) OF Johnny Bates becomes the first modern player to hit a HR in his first ML AB when he connects in the 2nd inning against the Brooklyn Superbas. Boston hurler Irv Young allows only one hit and wins 2–0.

15th Brooklyn plays a Sunday game against Boston, charging no admission. Fans are asked to drop contributions in a box at the gate.

22nd A new rule puts the umpire in sole charge of all game balls. The home team manager previously had some say as to when a new ball was introduced.

28th It's the only time 2 managers steal home on the same day. Cubs pilot Frank Chance steals in the 9th to give Chicago a 1–0 win over the Reds, and Fred Clarke matches it in the Pirates' 10–1 win over the St. Louis Cardinals.

30th Boston C Jack O'Neill, the eldest of the 4 ML O'Neill brothers, suffers through a long day as the Giants rack up 10 stolen bases, beating the Pilgrims 8–2.

MAY

1st John Lush posts a 1–0 no-hitter over Brooklyn for the Phils, striking out 11. The Philadelphia *Inquirer* states, "The trolley dodgers were triumphantly baffled by Lush's drop curve."

OF Jesse Burkett is released by the Boston Pilgrims (AL) to manage the Worcester team, which he owns.

7th Umpire Tim Hurst strikes New York Highlander manager Clark Griffith in the mouth. Hurst is suspended for 5 days.

Detroit Tigers P Bill Donovan steals 2B, 3B, and home in the 5th inning of an 8–3 victory over Cleveland. He also slugs a triple.

8th Shorthanded because of injuries, Connie Mack puts P Chief Bender in LF in the 6th inning in a game against the Boston Pilgrims. Bender hits 2 HRs, both inside the park. His career total for 16 years will be 6.

11th Tom Jones, St. Louis Browns 1B, has 22 putouts—an AL record that will be tied by the Highlanders' Hal Chase on September 21st, and not again until July 20, 1987, by Don Mattingly.

15th Hooks Wiltse of the Giants becomes the first pitcher of the modern era to fan 4 batters in a single inning, fanning the side after the first Cincinnati batter of the 5th inning reaches base on Roger Bresnahan's 3rd-strike error.

17th Detroit's Ty Cobb's bunt single spoils Rube Waddell's no-hit bid. The Philadelphia A's win 5–0.

21st An 11-game win streak by Philadelphia is stopped by Cleveland 2–1 in 13 innings. The Athletics, Cleveland Naps, and New York Highlanders juggle the top spot in AL standings.

23rd Jiggs Donahue of the White Sox has no putouts at 1B in a game against the Highlanders, a record that can't be broken.

25th Jesse Tannehill snaps the Boston Pilgrims' 20-game losing streak (19 at home) with a 3–0 win over the White Sox—both AL records. Both Boston teams will finish last, while both Chicago teams finish first. It's the first time 2 cities have had 2 winners and 2 cellar-dwellers, and it won't happen again until 1921, when New York has the winners, and Philadelphia the last-placers.

JUNE

1st   Women appear at the Polo Grounds ticket windows for the first time. New ticket-selling machines are also introduced.

2nd   Only 3 games separate the Cubs from the 4th-place Phillies, and Cubs owner Murphy again goes to Cincinnati for help. This time he comes back with Orval Overall, a 6 foot 2 inch, 225-pound righthander who is 4–5 for the Reds. The price: P Bob Wicker and $2,000. Overall will go 12–3 for the Cubs and will help pitch them into 4 World Series in 5 years.

4th   Unable to shake the effects of diphtheria contracted in the spring, a frustrated Christy Mathewson throws a rare tantrum after giving up 4 runs to the Phils on 2 hits and 6 walks, and umpire Bill Klem throws him out of the game.

Bill Coughlin is the 2nd Tiger within a month to steal 2B, 3B, and home; he does this in the 7th inning against Washington during a 13–4 romp. Pitcher Bill Donovan did it on May 7th.

7th   The Cubs score 11 runs in the first inning off Mathewson and Joe McGinnity en route to a 19–0 win. Matty gives up 6 walks.

9th   A 19-game losing streak ends for the Boston Beaneaters (NL) with a 6–3 win over the Cardinals.

14th   The Brooklyn Superbas record 27 putouts and 27 assists in beating the Pirates 6–1.

17th   In another test of Sunday baseball in Brooklyn, the police arrest Superbas president Charles Ebbets and manager Ned Hanlon, the visiting Reds' manager Joe Kelley, and starting P Mal Eason. The case is dismissed as no admission was charged, and the law does not apply to "voluntary contributions."

19th   NL directors pass a resolution urging all clubs to provide dressing rooms for visiting teams. Even those that do, however, offer such primitive facilities that most teams on the road continue to dress at their hotels.

JULY

1st   Righthander Jack Taylor, 8–9 with the St. Louis Cardinals, returns to the Cubs in exchange for 2nd-string C Pete Noonan, rookie P Fred Beebe, and cash. Taylor will help the Cubs by going 12–3 the rest of the year.

5th   Jack Coombs, the A's rookie righthander from Colby College, makes his ML debut, blanking Washington 3–0 for the Athletics.

20th   Brooklyn righthander Mal Eason no-hits the Cardinals 2–0 at St. Louis in his last season as an active player. He will become an NL umpire.

30th   A State Supreme Court judge rules that, despite "voluntary contributions" instead of paid admissions, Brooklyn is conducting a business enterprise and thus violating the law prohibiting Sunday baseball in New York.

AUGUST

2nd   While the Athletics, crippled by injuries, falter, Doc White launches the White Sox on a 19-game winning streak (longest in AL history) with a 3–0 win over Boston. The streak, interrupted only by a 0–0 tie with New York, catapults Chicago from 4th place to first in 10 days. Doc White wins 6 of the 19; Ed Walsh, 7.

3rd   Tom Hughes of the Washington Nationals and Tom Glade of the St. Louis Browns enter the 10th inning with a scoreless tie. Hughes decides he will have to do it on his own and hits a HR for a 1–0 victory. He is the first pitcher to win a 1–0 extra-inning game with his own HR.

6th   John McGraw is suspended indefinitely for abusing umpire James Johnstone.

7th   On McGraw's orders, umpire Johnstone is refused admittance to the Polo Grounds, and the game is forfeited to the Cubs. Giants owner John Brush allows Johnstone to officiate the next day, and the Cubs win 3–2 behind Three Finger Brown and Ed Reulbach. At the month's end, the Cubs will have a 15-game lead.

9th   The Giants have just 2 assists at Pittsburgh, both by P Joe McGinnity, for a ML low. They win, however, 6–0.

13th   The Cubs' Jack Taylor is knocked out by Brooklyn in the 3rd inning, ending a string of 187 complete games and 15 relief appearances in which he finished each game. The record run began June 20th, 1901. In 10 years he will fail to finish only 8 of 286 starts.

18th Wee Willie Keeler is struck out for only the 2nd time this season, both times by spitballer Ed Walsh of the White Sox.

24th The Reds' Jake Weimer pitches a 7-inning no-hitter against Brooklyn, winning 1–0.

30th After pitching a shutout in his ML debut, righthander Slow Joe Doyle of the Highlanders becomes the first player to start out with 2 shutouts when he beats the Nationals 5–0. Of his 23 lifetime victories, 7 will be shutouts. He is nicknamed "Slow" because of his time-consuming pace on the mound.

31st Beset by injuries, the Tigers call 46-year-old Sam Thompson out of retirement; he drives in 2 runs in a 5–1 win over the Browns. Thompson last played in the majors in 1898. He appears in 8 games and bats .226.

In the great tradition of his late brother Ed, Frank Delahanty of New York hits 2 HRs, a triple, and single, and knocks in 7 runs in a 20–5 rout of Washington.

SEPTEMBER

1st The AL's longest game on record takes place in Boston. Rookie Jack Coombs and 24-year-old Joe Harris go the route in a 24-inning struggle, ending with a 4–1 Athletics victory after 4 hours and 47 minutes. Philadelphia's Coombs strikes out 18 and gives up 14 hits. The Pilgrims' Harris fans 14 and yields 16 hits.

The Highlanders win their 6th game in 3 days from Washington, sweeping their 3rd straight doubleheader for an AL record. Three days later, they will move into first place, sweeping Boston 7–0 and 1–0 for their 5th straight doubleheader sweep, a ML record.

With the regular umpires sick from food poisoning, Cub P Carl Lundgren and Cardinal C Pete Noonan umpire. The Cubs win 8–1 for the 14th win in a row at the West Side Grounds.

3rd The Philadelphia Giants win the Negro Championship Cup on Labor Day in Philadelphia before 10,000 fans, black baseball's largest crowd ever. Rube Foster pitches them to a 3–2 victory over the Cuban X-Giants, who have John Henry Lloyd in the lineup.

Kid Elberfeld assaults umpire Silk O'Loughlin and is forcibly removed by police in the first game of

New York's 4–3 win over the Athletics. In the 2nd game, New York base runner Willie Keeler collides with SS Lave Cross trying to field a ground ball, and 2 runs score. O'Loughlin sees no interference, a call so hotly disputed by A's captain Harry Davis that, after 8 minutes of arguing, the umpire forfeits the game to New York.

17th Playing as "Sullivan," Columbia University junior Eddie Collins makes his debut at SS with the Athletics. He gets one hit off Ed Walsh and strikes out twice. Collins will play 25 years in the ML, bat .333, and become a member of the Hall of Fame.

21st At Chicago, the White Sox lose a pair to New York before 20,000, their largest Friday afternoon crowd. Hal Chase has 22 putouts at 1B in the first game, tying the record.

24th Cardinals hurler Stoney McGlynn tosses a 7-inning no-hitter against Brooklyn. The game ends in a 1–1 tie.

26th Rookie OF John Cameron of Boston, after one relief appearance, gets a starting assignment against the Cardinals. Leadoff batter Tom O'Hara beats out an infield single. Al Burch's line drive hits Cameron in the head, and caroms back on a fly to C Jack O'Neill, who throws to Fred Tenney at 1B, doubling off O'Hara. Cameron retires with one assist and a headache. This is his last ML game.

Lefty Leifeld of Pittsburgh hurls a 6-inning no-hitter against Philadelphia, winning 8–0.

The Athletics finally score after being shut out for a ML record 48 consecutive innings, dating back to September 22nd. Harry Davis breaks the long drought with a 2-run double against Cleveland, but the A's still lose 5–3.

OCTOBER

1st Hugh Jennings resigns as Baltimore manager to take over at Detroit for 1907. Infusing the Tigers with aggressive Baltimore spirit, he will win pennants the next 3 years, and stay at the helm for 14.

3rd The smallest crowd in Polo Grounds history—300—watches the Phils beat the Giants 3–1. The Giants will attract about 400,000 over the season and be outdrawn by the Highlanders by about 20,000.

The White Sox clinch the AL pennant during a rain-out at St. Louis, as the Athletics beat New York 3–0.

Chicago achieves the lowest team BA ever for a pennant winner with .228. Hence, the "Hitless Wonders."

4th　The Cubs score their record 116th win of the year, beating the Pirates 4–0 in Pittsburgh. The win gives them a 60–15 road record, an .800 percentage mark that has never been equaled.

Boston (NL) hurlers Vive Lindaman and Irv Young lose 3–2 and 2–1 to Brooklyn. The Beaneaters finish last with 102 losses. Four hardworking hurlers bear the brunt: Young and Gus Dorner each lose 25 games; Lindaman, 23; and Frank "Big Jeff" Pfeffer, 22.

5th　The Giants give Christy Mathewson's brother Henry a starting chance against Boston. He establishes a modern NL record by walking 14, and hits one batter, but completes the 7–1 loss for the only ML decision of his career.

6th　Winning on defense, the Cubs are the first team to finish with fewer than 200 errors; their pitching staff has a combined 1.76 ERA.

9th　Snow flies at West Side Park as the first one-city World Series opens with the Cubs heavy favorites over the AL's "Hitless Wonders." Neither ballpark can accommodate the crowds, so the Chicago *Tribune* recreates the games on mechanical boards displayed at theaters. White Sox starter Nick Altrock and Cubs starter Three Finger Brown give up 4 hits each, but Cubs errors produce 2 unearned runs for a 2–1 White Sox victory.

10th　The Cubs jump on Doc White early, and run (5 SBs) to a 7–1 victory. The highlight of the game is Ed Reulbach's no-hit bid broken by Jiggs Donahue's single in the 7th. The next WS one-hitter will come in 1945, by another Cub—Claude Passeau.

11th　Pitching continues to dominate as Ed Walsh stops the Cubs on 2 hits. The Sox manage just 4 off Jack Pfeister, but one is a triple by George Rohe, with 3 on in the 6th, for a 3–0 win. Walsh fans 12, the record until 1929.

12th　It's Brown's turn to throw a 2-hit shutout, besting Altrock 1–0 and evening the Series.

13th　Mound magic disappears as both Walsh and Reulbach are knocked out. Paced by a WS record 4 doubles by Frank Isbell, the White Sox win the slugfest 8–6.

14th　The Sox jump on Three Finger Brown for 7 runs in the first 2 innings, and coast behind Doc White to a 7–1 Series-ending victory. The Cubs' losers' share is $439.50, the lowest ever.

NOVEMBER

1st　P John McCloskey, 3–2 with the Phils, has better luck off the field. An investment in the Cripple Creek, CO, mine pays off with a rich gold strike.

DECEMBER

11th　Harry Pulliam is reelected president of the NL at a salary of $10,000.

12th　The AL gives Ban Johnson a raise to $15,000 for the remaining 4 years of his contract.

13th　The Athletics sell P Andy Coakley to Cincinnati. A 20-game winner in 1905, he had slipped to 7–8. He will be an effective but hard-luck pitcher for the next 2 years before starting a 37-year career as baseball coach at Columbia University.

26th　NL umpire Hank O'Day suggests that the batter's box be outlined with white rubber strips rather than chalk, making it impossible for hitters to obliterate the lines with their spikes.

1907

JANUARY

10th John McGraw stops a runaway team of horses in Los Angeles, saving 2 young women from injury.

28th In an effort to reduce playing-date conflicts between their leagues, presidents Pulliam and Johnson meet to plan schedules. Conflicting dates are reduced to 27.

MARCH

4th A judgment of $52,000 is awarded to the Baltimore club from Brooklyn. When Baltimore left the NL in 1903, Brooklyn agreed to pay $40,000 for the franchise but never did. The award includes interest.

6th The first suit for damages resulting from the Phillies' 1903 ballpark disaster ends with the acquittal of club owners A. J. Reach and John Rogers.

28th Popular Boston Pilgrims OF Chick Stahl, who replaced Jimmy Collins as manager of the now named Red Sox at the end of the 1906 season, commits suicide at spring training in West Baden Springs, IN. After breakfast he returned to his room and drank 4 oz. of carbolic acid. He left a note: "Boys, I just couldn't help it. You drove me to it." Cy Young starts the season as Boston's manager, but there will be 3 others during the year.

29th Boston OF Cozy Dolan, who had played the full schedule of NL games in 1906, dies of typhoid fever in Louisville, and the NL Doves cancel the remainder of spring training.

APRIL

11th On a cold day in New York, the Giants open against the Phillies before 16,000. A late snowstorm has been cleared, but there are large piles of snow surrounding the field. Frank Corridon is in the 8th inning of a shutout for the Giants when fans, who have been pelting the players with snowballs, begin jumping from the stands and running around the outfield. There are no police on duty at the park, so umpire Bill Klem forfeits the game 9–0 to the Phils.

New York C Roger Bresnahan appears wearing shin guards for the first time in a ML game, although the Phils' Red Dooin had worn papier-mâché guards under his stockings in 1906 while catching and at bat. It will be a few years before detachable guards are adopted by all catchers.

15th The Cleveland club takes out a $100,000 policy to insure its players against injury in railroad accidents.

19th Ed Walsh has his sinker working as he fields 11 assists and 2 putouts during a 1–0 win over the Browns. His total of 13 chances ties the mark Nick Altrock set in 1904.

MAY

3rd Dilatory tactics of the Highlanders' Judd Doyle, whose well-earned nickname is "Slow Joe," lengthen a 10-inning game with the Athletics to a record 3 hours, 7 minutes.

8th Frank Pfeffer of the Boston Doves pitches a 6–0 no-hitter against the Reds. He will be known as "Big Jeff" until his younger, and bigger, brother Ed "Jeff" Pfeffer becomes a star hurler for Brooklyn in 1913.

14th The flagpole at the White Sox ballpark breaks during the pennant-raising ceremonies celebrating the 1906 championship.

20th A 17-game winning streak started by the Giants (after their Opening Day forfeit) comes to an end in a 6–4 loss to St. Louis. The Cubs keep pace; at the end of May the clubs are tied 24–5.

21st NL president Pulliam dismisses the protests of Pittsburgh manager Fred Clarke over Bresnahan's shin guards. As yet, Bresnahan is the only catcher using them.

Mobbed at the Polo Grounds after a game with Chicago, umpires O'Day and Emslie require police protection. The crowd is egged on by McGraw, who will be thrown out of games 7 times this year. The next day AL ump Billy Evans needs a police escort after argumentative Hugh Jennings incites a riot. Jennings is suspended.

26th Ed Walsh hurls a 5-inning no-hitter against New York. The White Sox win 8–1.

31st Kid Elberfield of the Highlanders steals home twice against Boston, alone in the 6th and on a double steal with Hal Chase in the 7th.

JUNE

13th The Boston Red Sox play an exhibition game at Providence, raising $3,140.50 for Chick Stahl's widow. The clubs and players also contribute.

18th Roger Bresnahan of the Giants is hit in the head by a pitch from Andy Coakley of the Cincinnati Reds and is hospitalized. During his convalescence, he will develop a primitive headgear for batters.

19th Miller Huggins, diminutive 2B of the Reds, leads off the game against New York with a HR off Christy Mathewson. The rare occurrence (he hits only 9 in his career) astonishes the home town fans and they celebrate by presenting him with a pair of shoes, a gold watch, a 5-pound box of chocolates, a scarf pin, and a Morris chair.

28th The Nationals steal a record 13 bases off C Branch Rickey in a 16–5 win over New York. Rickey spends the rest of the season as OF-1B.

JULY

8th Bombarded by pop bottles in Brooklyn, irate Cubs manager Frank Chance throws one back into the stands where it cuts a boy's leg. Chance is mobbed and leaves the park in an armored car with a police escort after the Cubs' 5–0 victory.

12th After an absence of 24 days, Bresnahan returns to the lineup and collects 2 hits in a 3–2 win for the Giants against Coakley, the same hurler who hit him with a pitch on June 18th. Bresnahan does not wear the headgear he developed.

16th Ed Walsh sets another fielding record for pitchers, handling 12 assists and 3 putouts in a 13-inning game.

22nd Cincinnati righthander Bob Ewing has the Phils popping up all day; the Reds have no assists in a 10–3 win.

23rd The Austin Senators (Texas League) steal 23 bases and beat San Antonio 44–0.

30th Cincinnati manager Ned Hanlon, whose managing days began in 1889 at Pittsburgh, announces this will be his last season. His record includes 5 pennants—4 at Baltimore, one at Brooklyn.

AUGUST

2nd Hugh Jennings, known for his gyrations on the coaching lines and "Eeyah" war cry, is suspended for 10 days for using a tin whistle while coaching at 3B for the Tigers.

Walter Johnson, 19, debuts with Washington and loses 3–2 to Detroit. The first hit off him is a bunt single by Ty Cobb. Sam Crawford hits an inside-the-park HR.

7th Walter Johnson wins the first of his total 416, 7–2 over Cleveland.

11th In the 2nd game of a doubleheader, shortened to 7 innings by prior agreement, St. Louis Card Ed Karger pitches a perfect game 4–0 against the Boston Doves.

15th Chief Bender wins his 11th straight for the Athletics 4–2 over Cleveland, to tighten the race with the Tigers for the pennant.

18th Detroit's first Sunday game at home since 1902, and the first at Bennett Field, is a 16–3 win over New York.

28th Highlander John "Tacks" Neuer, begins baseball's most successful short career by besting the Red Sox 1–0 in his first start. In one month he will pitch 6 complete games, win 4, including 3 shutouts, and disappear from the ML scene.

SEPTEMBER

1st Cubs P Ed Reulbach, who will be 17–4 with a 1.69 ERA, goes into the 9th with a 2–0 lead over the Cardinals at Chicago. He gives up 8 straight hits, 7 runs, and loses the game. Still shell-shocked, the Cubs are shut out twice the next day by the last-place Cards.

4th For his 32nd birthday tomorrow, Cleveland fans give manager Nap Lajoie a wagonload of gifts, including a live black sheep. Addie Joss pitches a one-hitter against Detroit.

11th Chicago's Doc White blanks the Browns 2–0. However, his one base on balls ends his AL record run of 65⅓ IP without issuing a walk. He will win a career high 27 games and walk only 38 in 291 IP.

14th Washington's Lew Lanford, 21, in one of the worst debuts any pitcher ever suffered, walks 2, hits 2 batters, including Frank LaPorte in the head, throws a wild pitch, and balks—all in the first inning. Six runs score, but it is not all Lanford's fault. Two errors and a passed ball add to his woes.

15th At the Browns-Tigers game in St. Louis, a soda bottle thrown by one Hugo Dusenberg fells umpire Billy Evans. The crowd beats up Hugo before the police come to his rescue; he is fined $100. Evans is carried from the field and hospitalized, but is not very seriously injured.

20th Every player but one is hitless in the Pittsburgh-Brooklyn game, won by the Pirates 2–1. Rookie Nick Maddox allows no Superba hits; manager Fred Clarke gets the only 2 given up by Elmer Stricklett.

22nd Phillies rookie George McQuillan pitches a 6-inning 2–0 win over St. Louis in his ML debut, starting a record string of 25 consecutive shutout innings at the beginning of his ML career. The Reds' Bob Spade makes his debut a 1–0 win over the Giants on the same day.

25th. Pittsburgh's Honus Wagner steals 2B, 3B, and home in the 2nd inning against the Giants.

27th After leading the AL most of the month, the Athletics are beset by pitching problems, and Detroit moves into a tie for first. The Tigers come into Philadelphia for 3 games, and win the first 5–4.

30th An overflow crowd lines the OF at Philadelphia's Columbia Park for the showdown doubleheader between the A's and Tigers. In the first game, the home team gets off to a 7–1 lead against 25-game winner Bill Donovan. But Rube Waddell, who relieves in the 2nd, fails to hold the lead. A 2-run HR by Ty Cobb ties it 8–8 in the 9th. Both teams score once in the 11th; an umpire's ruling costs Philadelphia the game in the 14th. Harry Davis hits a long fly into the crowd in left CF, ordinarily a ground-rule double. As Tiger CF Sam Crawford goes to the crowd's edge, a policeman stands up and moves, either to interfere or to get out of the way. Home plate umpire Silk O'Loughlin says there is no interference, then reverses his ruling when base umpire Tom Connolly offers a different opinion. When play resumes, the Athletics' Danny Murphy hits a long single that would have scored Davis. The game is called because of darkness in the 17th, a 9–9 tie. The 2nd game is never played. The Tigers, in first place, leave for Washington where they will win 4. They will finish 1½ games in front.

Cardinals 1B Ed Konetchy steals home twice in St. Louis' 3 game against Boston. St. Louis sets a ML one-game record with 3 steals of home as Joe Delahanty also scores in the 8th.

OCTOBER

2nd Ty Cobb's 200th hit earns him a $500 bonus; he will get 212 for the year.

3rd The Red Sox end their 16-game losing streak by nipping the Browns 1–0. Cy Morgan is the victor over Harry Howell.

5th Athletics hurler Rube Vickers hurls a 5-inning 4–0 perfect game against Washington. He also wins the first game of the twin bill with a spectacular 12-inning relief effort.

8th The Tigers have game one of the World Series against the Cubs in their grasp—or in C Charlie Schmidt's glove—but it gets away from them. Leading 3–2 in the 9th, Bill Donovan faces pinch hitter Del Howard with 2 on and 2 outs. He fans Howard, but the ball gets away from Schmidt, and the tying run scores. Darkness ends the game after 12 innings.

9th The Tigers score once against Jack Pfiester and lose 3–1. They will not score more than once in any of the remaining games in the WS.

10th Ed Reulbach coasts to a 5–1 win, as the Cubs hit 5 doubles.

11th Orval Overall gives up a triple to Cobb, but the Tigers are tamed again 6–1.

12th It's Three Finger Brown's turn to shut down the Tigers 2–0. Each side has 7 hits, but the Cubs steal 4 bases for a total of 18 for the 5-game series.

DECEMBER

13th Friction between his catchers and the need to strengthen the Giants infield prompt John McGraw to trade Frank Bowerman, Bill Dahlen, Dan McGann, George Browne, and Cecil Ferguson to Boston for young SS Al Bridwell, veteran 1B Fred Tenney, and reserve C Tom Needham.

1908

JANUARY

9th Frank Navin is named president of the Detroit club. Bennett Field will be renamed Navin Field.

FEBRUARY

3rd Chris Von der Ahe, flamboyant former owner of the Browns, files for bankruptcy, claiming $27,000 in debts, and $200 in assets.

7th Exasperated Connie Mack sells his talented but eccentric, unreliable hurler Rube Waddell to the St. Louis Browns for $5,000.

27th The sacrifice fly rule is adopted. No time at bat is charged if a run scores after the catch of a fly ball. The rule will be repealed in 1931, then reinstated or changed several times before permanent acceptance in 1954.

MARCH

16th Pittsburgh's Honus Wagner, 34, announces his retirement. An annual rite of spring, it will not keep him from playing in 151 games, more than in any of the past 10 years, and leading the league in hitting (for the 6th time), hits, total bases, doubles, triples, RBI, and stolen bases. He will miss the Triple Crown by hitting 2 fewer HRs than Tim Jordan's 12.

21st Ty Cobb signs for $4,000 and an $800 bonus if he hits over .300. He will collect the bonus with a league-leading .324, one of only 3 AL regulars to top .300 (the NL has 5) in 1908.

APRIL

2nd After a 2-year investigation, the Mills Committee, formed on the recommendation of Al Spalding and headed by the former NL president A. G. Mills, declares that baseball was invented by Abner Doubleday in Cooperstown, N. in 1839. Overwhelming evidence to the contrary is ignored, but the designation makes James Fenimore Cooper's town the most likely site for a Hall of Fame and museum when these establishments are conceived some 30 years later.

7th The St. Louis clubs play a benefit game, raising $5,000 for the beleaguered Chris Von der Ahe.

19th The National Commission reinstates Jake Stahl and Mike Donlin after fining them $100 each for playing with teams outside organized ball in 1907.

20th "The Father of Baseball," Henry Chadwick, the leading reporter, commentator, scorer, and indefatigable promoter of the game, dies in Brooklyn at age 85.

MAY

12th Orval Overall of the Cubs absorbs his first loss since August 11, 1907, as the Phils end his 14-game winning streak 6–2.

21st Washington lefthander Bill Burns—"Sleepy Bill," whose worst years are still to come—loses a no-hitter, and the game, when Germany Schaefer singles with 2 outs in the 9th to give Detroit a 1–0 win.

23rd Giants 3B Art Devlin ties a record by handling 13 total chances as the Cards beat New York 6–2. Two errors cost him a new record.

JUNE

6th The Athletics hold first place for the last time this year. Tomorrow, the Cleveland Naps will replace them, and the next day the White Sox will take the lead for the first time. They jump from 7th to first in 4 days, as a 13-game winning streak puts them into the race, despite being just three games over .500.

7th The Detroit Tigers turn a triple play against the Boston Red Sox for the 2nd day in a row, but Boston wins 9–5.

22nd Honus Wagner gets hit No. 2,000 against Jake Weimer of the Reds, who wins 4–0 over the Pirates.

24th Charging the Highlander owners with refusing to spend money to build the team, manager Clark Griffith resigns; Kid Elberfeld replaces him. New York fades fast and finishes last with 103 losses.

30th Cy Young's 3rd career no-hitter is an 8–0 Boston win over New York. At 41 years and 3 months, he is the oldest pitcher to turn the no-hit trick. Nolan Ryan will beat him in 1990 at the age of 43.

JULY

4th   Lefthander Hooks Wiltse pitches a 10-inning no-hitter for the Giants over the Phillies 1–0. He loses his bid for a perfect 9 innings when, with 2 outs, Phils P George McQuillan is hit by a pitch.

11th   The White Sox play their 2nd 16-inning game in 2 days, beating Philadelphia 5–4.

21st   NY Giant Mike Donlin is baseball's most popular player, according to a Chicago newspaper contest. He tops Honus Wagner by a wide margin and will be awarded a trophy cup.

29th   Rube Waddell continues to haunt Connie Mack, fanning 16 A's in a 5–4 win for the Browns.

31st   With Dummy Taylor the Boston base runner on 3B, Fred Tenney steals 2B against the Cardinals. On the play, pitcher Bugs Raymond throws to 3B hoping to nab Taylor. On the next pitch, Tenney takes off for 1B as Raymond watches. As Raymond delivers again, Tenney again steals 2B. Newspaper accounts will report that, because of the rules, the Cardinals could have tagged Tenney out while he was standing on 2B base the 2nd time.

AUGUST

4th   The Giants take 2 from Cincinnati 4–3 and 4–1. Christy Mathewson wins both; Andy Coakley loses both. New York moves into 2nd place, 5 percentage points behind the Pirates.

At Brooklyn, the Superbas and St. Louis Cardinals play an entire game with one ball. Brooklyn wins 3–0.

5th   The Nationals' Otis Clymer and Jim Delahanty draw indefinite suspensions for abusing umpire Silk O'Loughlin in Cleveland. Delahanty, a Cleveland native, is later fined $50 and barred from the Cleveland ballpark for one year for his unbecoming conduct.

13th   Cy Young Day is celebrated by 20,000 in Boston. He pitches briefly against an All-Star team that includes Jack Chesbro, Hal Chase, Willie Keeler, Hatty Davis, and George Mullin. The game is interrupted several times for presentations to the great hurler.

21st   Nationals C Gabby Street stands at the base of the Washington Monument and catches the 13th ball dropped from the top, 555 feet up, duplicating the feat performed by Pop Schriver of the Chicago Colts on August 24, 1894. Billy Sullivan of the Chicago White Sox repeats the catch on August 24, 1910.

24th   The Giants gain the NL lead by winning 2 at Pittsburgh. The doubleheader is watched in New York on electric diamonds known as "Compton's Baseball Bulletin" at Madison Square Garden and the Gotham Theatre. Bulletins will display all remaining games. The Giants leave town 3½ games ahead of the Pirates.

27th   With electric bulletin boards also showing the action in Chicago, the Cubs come into New York for a 3-game sweep to move within one-half game of the lead.

SEPTEMBER

4th   In a game, the significance of which will not be recognized until 3 weeks later, the Pirates and Cubs are tied 0–0 in the last of the 10th at Pittsburgh. With 2 outs and the bases loaded, Pittsburgh's Owen Wilson singles to CF, scoring Fred Clarke with the winning run. Warren Gill, on 1B, does not get to 2B but stops short, turns, and heads for the dugout, a common practice. The Cubs' Johnny Evers calls for the ball from Jimmy Slagle, touches 2B, and claims the run does not count as Gill has been forced. The lone umpire, Hank O'Day, has left the field. When queried, he rules that Clarke had already scored, so the run counts. The Cubs protest to league president Pulliam, but are denied. This is the first time the Cubs try this tactic, but not the last.

With a runner on 3B, Germany Schaefer attempts to draw a throw by stealing 2B, but the Cleveland catcher, Nig Clarke, holds on to the ball. With runners on 2B and 3B, Schaefer takes off for 1B and is credited with a stolen base. On the next pitch he takes off again for 2B and arrives safely, this time drawing a throw and allowing Davey Jones to score from 3B. Schaefer is credited with one SB. This is the 2nd time in 5 weeks this prank has been run.

5th   Nap Rucker pitches a no-hitter for Brooklyn against the Boston Doves 6–0, striking out 14 and walking none. Three runners reached 1B on errors.

7th   Nationals P Walter Johnson shuts out the New York Highlanders for the 3rd time in 4 days 4–0. He will pitch 130 shutouts during his career, 23 more than runner-up Grover Alexander.

8th The Pirates set a ML fielding record against the Cardinals by making only 2 assists, both by 2B Charlie Starr.

9th In a 7–3 New York win, the Giants steal 9 bases off Brooklyn's Billy Maloney, an OF pressed into service as a catcher. That's enough to make him quit the game.

10th Detroit takes its 2nd straight extra-inning game from the White Sox, 6–5 in 11 innings, and the Indians beat the Browns, 5–2. The AL race leaves Detroit 75-52, Chicago 72-57, St. Louis 71-57.

12th In the dogfight for the AL pennant, the White Sox play their 4th straight extra-inning game at Detroit, a total of 43 innings. The White Sox win their 2nd straight, while the Browns lose their 2nd in a row to Cleveland.

13th Lancaster (Ohio State League) P Walt "Smoke" Justis hurls his 4th no-hitter of the season, defeating Marion 3–0. His other gems came on July 19th, August 2nd, and September 8th. Justis had no record in 2 ML appearances with Detroit in 1905.

14th Former ML OF Ike Van Zandt commits suicide by shooting himself (age 31).

15th Christy Mathewson defeats the St. Louis Browns for a ML record 24th consecutive time. The winning streak dates back to June 16, 1904.

18th Cleveland's Bob Rhoads pitches a no-hitter against the Red Sox 2–1, beating Frank Arellanes, the only Mexican-American pitcher in the ML.

20th Rube Waddell strikes out 17 Washington Nationals in 10 innings.

Frank Smith pitches a no-hitter for the White Sox against the A's, winning 1–0 and giving up just one walk. It is Smith's 2nd no-hitter. The winning run scores in the bottom of the 9th when Freddy Parent, whom Eddie Plank is walking intentionally, pokes a sacrifice to short RF.

21st Cleveland takes the AL lead, beating New York, while Detroit takes two at St. Louis. With 2 weeks to go, 3½ games separate 4 teams.

22nd The Cubs sweep a doubleheader at New York, 4–3 and 2–1, giving them a 90–53 record versus the Giants' 87–50.

23rd Giants P Mathewson and Cubs P Three Finger Brown battle in the most controversial game ever played. The score is 1–1, with 2 outs in the last of the 9th. The Giants' Harry McCormick is on 3B, and Fred Merkle (19, who is subbing for the sore-legged veteran Fred Tenney), on 1B. Al Bridwell singles, scoring McCormick. Halfway to 2B, Merkle turns and heads for the clubhouse in CF. Johnny Evers secures a ball (Joe McGinnity swears he picked up the ball that was in play and threw it into the stands) and touches 2B as the crowd overruns the field. Umpire O'Day at 1B claims he didn't see the play, but that evening he rules the run does not count, and the game ended with a tie score. (Years later, in an interview, Merkle will describe it this way: "When Bridwell shot that long single, I started across the grass for the clubhouse. Matty was near me. When Evers began shouting for the ball, he noticed something was wrong. Matty caught me by the arm and told me to wait a minute. We walked over toward 2B, and Matty spoke to Emslie. 'How about this, Bob, is there any trouble with the score of the play?' 'It's all right,' said Emslie. 'You've got the game. I don't see anything wrong with the play.' Matty then took me by the arm and we walked to the clubhouse confident that we had won the game.")

24th Pulliam upholds O'Day's delayed decision and declares the game a tie, a decision nobody likes. The Cubs demand the game be forfeited to them as the crowd prevented play from continuing, although darkness would have soon ended it. Both teams appeal. Pulliam sees no inconsistency with the September 4th incident and claims he has merely upheld his umpire on a question of fact in each case. Meanwhile, the Cubs beat the Giants 5–4, taking a one-game lead.

25th Detroit's Ed Summers pitches 2 complete-game wins over the A's. The 2nd game is a 10-inning 2-hit shutout.

26th Ed Reulbach becomes the only pitcher to throw 2 shutouts in one day, blanking Brooklyn 5–0 and 3–0 in under 3 hours. He will complete 44 consecutive scoreless innings, an NL record until Carl Hubbell's 46 in 1933.

27th The Reds' Hans Lobert steals 2B, 3B, and home against St. Louis.

28th Phils C Red Dooin is offered—and rejects—a bribe to lose the final series with the Giants. The incident is not made public until 16 years later. Nothing is proved.

OCTOBER

2nd In a great pitching duel, Ed Walsh is almost perfect, giving up 4 hits and striking out 15 in 8 innings, but Cleveland's Addie Joss is perfect, setting down 27 straight White Sox for a 1–0 victory. The only run scores on a passed ball by Ossee Schreckengost. It is the high point of Joss's career. He will finish 24–12 with a 1.16 ERA.

Only 2 points separate New York, Chicago, and Pittsburgh, as each team takes a turn on top during the final week.

3rd The incident of September 23rd would have become just another odd event in baseball if the Giants had been able to handle the 4th-place Phillies. But rookie lefthander Harry Coveleski, just up from the minor leagues, earns the nickname "Giant Killer" by beating them 3–2, for the 3rd time in 5 days.

At a hearing on the September 23rd incident, Pulliam does not call Merkle or any other players as witnesses, saying he was at the game and saw the events himself. He affirms his earlier decision. Two days later, NL directors meet in Cincinnati and order the game replayed on October 8th.

At a field day in Chicago, Larry LeJeune, who will appear in 24 ML games, makes a 435-foot throw, beating the 1907 mark of 399 feet 10¾ inches.

4th The Cubs and Pirates play their last game of the year before 30,247, the largest crowd ever at West Side Park. The Cubs win 5–2. Then they await the results of the 3 Giants games with Boston. In downtown Pittsburgh, 50,000 people watch the progress of the Cub's game on temporary scoreboards. Fans fill New York's Polo Grounds to watch the action in the same way. Men with megaphones announce each pitch.

5th Ed Walsh of the White Sox tops Detroit 6–1 for his 40th victory and forces the AL pennant race to the final day. He also leads the league in games (66), IP (464), K's (269), complete games (42), saves (6), shutouts (11), and winning percentage (.727). His ERA is 1.42.

6th Having been in 13 of the last 16 games, Ed Walsh does not start the White Sox finale against Detroit. Doc White is hit hard in the 7–0 loss that gives the pennant to the Tigers. Bill Donovan pitches a 2-hitter.

Detroit OF Sam Crawford leads the AL with 7 HRs. Having led the NL with 16 in 1901, he becomes the first player to lead both leagues in that department. The Cardinals have scored 372 runs, the lowest season's total ever.

7th The Giants complete a 3-game sweep in Boston, winning the finale 7–2. The season ends with New York and the Cubs each 98–55, and Pittsburgh 98–56.

8th Later admitting he had nothing on the ball, Mathewson loses to the Cubs 4–2 in the playoff replay of the disputed September 23rd game. Three Finger Brown, relieving Jack Pfiester in the first, gets the win. The Giants played to a record 910,000 in attendance for the year, a figure that will be unmatched until 1920.

10th Ed Reulbach, coasting with a 5–1 lead, tires in the 7th. Brown is unable to stop the Tigers from taking a 6–5 lead in the last of the 8th. But the Cubs jump on reliever Ed Summers, a 24-game winner, for 6 straight hits and 5 runs in the 9th, and Brown gets the win 10–6. For umpire Bill Klem, it is the first of 15 WS he will officiate. Detroit's Ira Thomas, batting for Charley O'Leary, hits the first WS pinch hit when he singles in the 9th. There had been 12 previous pinch-hit attempts in WS play, including the batter before Thomas.

11th In Chicago, Orval Overall doles out 4 hits, and the Cubs break a scoreless deadlock with 6 in the 8th off Bill Donovan for a 6–1 win.

12th Tiger bats roar for the last time, as Jack Pfiester proves an easy target 8–3. Ty Cobb is 4-for-5.

13th Three Finger Brown is in command all the way in a 3–0 four-hitter Cub victory.

14th Before the smallest crowd in WS history— 6,210—the Tigers are tamed on 3 hits by Overall, who fans 10 in a 2–0 win. The Cubs win the series in 5 games.

Upset over seating arrangements at the WS, sports reporters form a professional group that will become the Baseball Writers Association of America.

24th Singing sensation Billy Murray hits the charts with "Take Me Out to the Ball Game," the 2nd, and most popular, of 3 versions to be released within a five-week period. Ironically, Murray's 1903 hit, "Tessie," is quickly adopted by Boston's Royal Rooters as their official theme song, much to the chagrin of Red Sox' opponents.

NOVEMBER

3rd An all-star team leaves San Francisco for a tour of Japan, China, Hawaii, and the Philippines. It will play 40 games before returning on February 15.

22nd The Reach All-Americans defeat Waseda University in Tokyo 5–0, in the first game between a Japanese team and American professionals.

DECEMBER

12th The Cardinals are busy. First they get C Admiral Schlei from the Reds for pitchers Ed Karger and Art Fromme. Then they pack off Schlei, along with P Bugs Raymond and OF Red Murray, to the Giants for veteran catcher Roger Bresnahan. Bresnahan, a future Hall of Famer, will be the player/manager of the Cardinals for the next 4 years.

1909

JANUARY

11th The National Commission approves owner Charles Murphy's payment of a $10,000 bonus to his Cubs for their 1908 WS triumph.

15th Minor leaguer Nicholas Mathewson, brother of Christy, commits suicide by shooting himself at age 22.

FEBRUARY

4th John Clarkson, a 326-game winner of the 19th century, dies at Belmont, MA, at age 47.

17th The NL deprives umpires of the power to fine players and decrees that relief pitchers must retire at least one batter before being relieved.

18th NL president Harry Pulliam, in ill health, is granted a leave of absence. The league secretary, John Heydler, assumes his duties. The NL abolishes Ladies Days, and sets a 25-player limit from May 15 to August 20.

The Boston Red Sox trade Cy Young, who won 21 games at age 41 last season, to the Cleveland Naps for pitchers Charlie Chech and Jack Ryan, and $12,500.

27th Joe "Iron Man" McGinnity, released by the Giants, will pitch in the minor leagues for another 13 years, winning 20 or more in 6 of them. He finished his ML career with 247 wins.

MARCH

31st The National Commission rules that players who jump contracts will be suspended for 5 years. Players joining outlaw organizations will be suspended for 3 years as punishment for going outside organized baseball.

APRIL

8th While at spring training, Hal Chase of the Highlanders contracts smallpox. The entire team is vaccinated and quarantined while traveling north.

12th Billy Sullivan, the White Sox catcher in the first AL game, replaces Fielder Jones as manager.

Philadephia's Shibe Park is dedicated as a record crowd of 31,160 sees 18-year-old John "Stuffy" McInnis make his ML debut at SS. Eddie Plank pitches the A's to an 8–1 win over Boston.

15th Before an Opening Day crowd of 30,000 at New York, Red Ames pitches a no-hitter for 9 innings against the Brooklyn Superbas, ruins it with one out in the 10th, then loses the game 3–0 in the 13th. The Giants OF has no putouts.

18th The Tigers announce plans to build a new concrete and steel stadium. The Pirates name their million-dollar ballpark Forbes Field in honor of the English general who founded Pittsburgh.

20th The National Commission learns that an effort to bribe umpires Klem and Emslie was made before the Giants-Cubs playoff game in 1908. The identity of the alleged briber is not disclosed, but all clubs are notified of the results of the investigation.

23rd In the 6th inning of the Reds-Pirates game in Pittsburgh, Honus Wagner steps across the plate to the other batter's box as Reds P Harry Gaspar delivers the ball. Umpire Bill Klem refuses to call him out. The Pirates win 2–1, but Reds manager Clark Griffith protests. Acting NL president Heydler backs Klem. The league will override Heydler and Klem and order the game replayed September 20th. The Pirates will win 4–3.

26th A's popular C Doc Powers dies at age 38. He developed intestinal problems sustained running into a wall during the Shibe Park opener on April 12th.

27th The White Sox win their 3rd 1–0 game from St. Louis in 3 days. Hits by the 2 teams total only 18.

MAY

2nd Honus Wagner steals his away around the bases in the first inning of a game against the Cubs. It is the 4th time he has performed this feat, an NL record.

5th The Pirates move into first place to stay. The Tigers will lead all the way in the AL, except for one week in May and 2 in mid-August.

9th The St. Louis Cardinals take out a $50,000 life insurance policy on manager Roger Bresnahan for reasons having to do more with publicity than concerns about his health.

11th Fred Toney, later to pitch in the only double no-hitter, throws a 17-inning no-hitter for Winchester (Blue Grass League), winning 1–0. He fans 19 opponents and walks only one.

20th In New York, Honus Wagner is given a silver trophy for winning the 1908 NL batting crown.

25th Righthander George Mullin wins his 9th in a row for Detroit 7–4 over Washington, on his way to a league-leading 29–8 record.

30th The Cardinals score 11 runs in the first inning against the Reds.

31st Pitchers Otto Burns of Decatur and Ed Clarke of Bloomington (Three I League) both go the distance in a 26-inning game won by Decatur 2–1.

JUNE

5th St. Louis admirers give Roger Bresnahan a diamond ring and the rest of the team silk umbrellas; then Cardinal errors give the Giants 6 runs and the game.

8th San Francisco (Pacific Coast League) hurler Cack Henley tosses a 24-inning 1–0 shutout over Oakland, surrendering only 9 hits and one walk in the 3-hour and 35-minute contest.

10th George Mullin's winning streak reaches 11 with a 2–1 win over New York. On the 15th, he will finally lose to the Athletics 5–4.

16th Jim Thorpe makes his baseball pitching debut for Rocky Mount (Eastern Carolina League) with a 4–2 win over Raleigh. It is the professional play in this year that will cause him to lose his medals won in the 1912 Olympics.

19th Walter Johnson has a strange day beating the New York Highlanders 7–4. He gives up just 3 hits, but is unusually wild, issuing 7 walks, uncorking 4 wild pitches, and hitting one batter, while fanning 10.

An exhibition night game featuring 2 amateur teams is played in the Reds' park before 3,000 spectators, including the Cincinnati and Philadelphia teams, which had played there earlier.

22nd The Detroit club buys the rest of the vacant Bennett Field grounds as the site for a new park.

30th Ed Reulbach spoils the Pirates' dedication of Forbes Field before 30,338, beating Vic Willis 3–2. A parade of old-time players precedes the game.

JULY

2nd The White Sox steal 12 bases in the course of a 15–3 win over St. Louis. Three are steals of home, including one by P Ed Walsh in the 6th inning, for a modern record.

3rd Seventeen Cardinals commit errors in a doubleheader loss to the Reds 10–2 and 13–7, to tie a modern ML record.

16th Detroit and Washington play the longest scoreless game in AL history—18 innings. Ed Summers pitches the complete game, holding the Nationals to 7 hits. The Nationals' 30-year-old rookie, Bill "Dolly" Gray, allows only one hit before leaving with an injury in the 9th.

18th Harry Krause of the A's loses in 11 innings to the Browns, ending his 10-game winning streak.

19th Cleveland SS Neal Ball executes the 20th century's first unassisted triple play in the top of the 2nd against the Red Sox. With Heinie Wagner on 2B and Jake Stahl on 1B, Amby McConnell hits a line drive to Ball, who steps on 2B and tags Stahl coming down from 1B. In the last of the 2nd, Ball hits his first AL HR. Cleveland wins 6–1.

22nd For the first of 4 times in his career, Ty Cobb steals 2B, 3B, and home doing it in the 7th inning against the Red Sox. The Tigers beat Boston 6–0.

29th NL president Harry Pulliam, despondent over his inability to handle the problems and controversies of the league, dies of a self-inflicted pistol wound.

30th After winning 13 in a row, Christy Mathewson loses to Pittsburgh 3–1, giving up 4 hits in the first inning. Mathewson's 25–6 and 1.14 ERA will top the NL.

31st For the 2nd time in 2 years—the first was on May 21,1908—Bill Burns has a no-hitter broken up with 2 outs in the 9th, when Washington's Otis Clymer singles. Burns and the White Sox win 1–0. Burns is the only pitcher to suffer this fate twice, until Dave Stieb of Toronto does on September 24 and 30, 1988.

AUGUST

4th Umpire Tim Hurst instigates a riot by spitting at Athletics 2B Eddie Collins, who had questioned a call.

This incident eventually leads to Hurst's banishment from baseball 2 weeks later.

11th John McGraw puts 50-year-old coach Arlie Latham at 2B in a 19–3 romp over St. Louis. Latham goes hitless but handles 2 assists.

14th Ed Reulbach's 14-game winning streak is stopped by the Giants 5–2.

17th Nap Lajoie resigns as Cleveland manager with the team in 6th place, but he remains as a player.

18th Giants player-coach Arlie Latham steals 2B in the Giants' 14–1 win over the Phillies. At 50, he is the oldest player to steal a base.

19th Because of a prolonged stretch of bad weather in the East, the Phillies are rained out for the 10th consecutive day.

23rd With lefthander Jim Pastorius pitching, Brooklyn C Bill Bergen throws out 7 base-stealing Cardinals in a 9–1 St. Louis victory.

The Cubs steal home 3 times in a game against Boston. They waste no time, as Johnny Evers and Del Howard do it in the first, and Solly Hofman in the 2nd. The cards do steal 2 bases. In the first game of the doubleheader, it was Brooklyn's turn as the swiped 6 in a 7–0 win.

27th Still pitching doubleheaders, Joe "Iron Man" McGinnity wins a pair for Newark over Buffalo in the Eastern League.

28th William "Dolly" Gray of Washington enters the record book by walking 8 White Sox in the 2nd inning, 7 in a row (both ML records). The 6 runs scored are enough for a 6–4 Chicago win.

31st The A. J. Reach Company is granted a patent for a cork-centered baseball, which will replace the hard rubber-cored one. This change will be particularly apparent in the NL in 1910–11.

SEPTEMBER

2nd Detroit completes a sweep of every series against visiting eastern teams, winning their 14th in a row to regain first place en route to their 3rd straight pennant.

9th Charles "Moon" Gibson of Pittsburgh catches his 112th consecutive game, breaking Chief Zimmer's 1890 record. His streak will end at 140.

Bill Dinneen, winner of 3 games in the first WS, is released by the St. Louis Browns and becomes an AL umpire, a position he will hold through 1937.

13th Ty Cobb clinches the AL HR title with his 9th round-tripper. It is an inside-the-park drive against the Browns. In fact, all his 9 HRs this season are inside the park, including 2 in one game on July 15th. He is the only player in this century to lead in HRs without hitting one out of the park.

14th John Heydler announces that the NL will use 2 umpires per game in 1910.

16th President Taft attends a Cubs-Giants game in Chicago. Players are introduced to him before the game, in which Christy Mathewson beats Three Finger Brown 3–1.

The University of Wisconsin baseball team arrives in Tokyo to begin a series of games against Japanese schools.

18th Before 35,409, the largest paid baseball attendance ever, Chief Bender beats Bill Donovan and the Tigers 2–0 at Philadelphia to keep the A's in the pennant race. Ty Cobb is the Triple Crown winner with a .377 BA, 9 home runs (all inside the park), and 107 RBI. He also leads the AL with 216 hits, 116 runs, and 296 total bases. His 76 stolen bases make him the only player ever to win a quadruple crown.

22nd Jimmy McAleer, one of the AL's original managers, resigns from the Browns after 8 years, switching to Washington.

25th Washington rookie Bob Groom loses his 19th consecutive game, setting a ML single-season mark.

27th The Pirates set an NL record with their 16th victory in a row, before the Giants stop them 8–7 in the 2nd game of a doubleheader.

OCTOBER

2nd Eddie Grant of the Phils is 7-for-7 against the Giants' Rube Marquard and Christy Mathewson.

Walter Johnson's 6–5 loss to Philadelphia seals the last-place finish for Washington with 110 losses—Johnson and Bob Groom suffering 51 of them. Three years later, when Washington rises to 2nd place, Johnson and Groom will combine for 56 wins.

8th The Pirates, winners of 110 games, face Detroit in the WS, which pits the 2 leagues' top offensive stars, Honus Wagner and Ty Cobb. Pittsburgh manager Fred Clarke starts 27-year-old rookie righthander Babe Adams against Tigers P George Mullin. There are only 11 hits in the game, but one is a HR by Clarke, and the Pirates win 4–1.

9th The Tigers win the 2nd game behind Bill Donovan 7–2. Cobb's steal of home highlights a 3-run 3rd. Detroit has been defenseless against SBs in the past 3 WS, giving up 16 in 5 games to the Cubs in 1907, 15 in 5 games to the Cubs in 1908, and 18 in 7 games to the Pirates this year, for a total of 49 in 17 games, and the highest SB totals in all of WS history.

11th Paced by Honus Wagner's 3 hits, 3 RBI, and 3 stolen bases, the Pirates take game 3, 8–6.

12th George Mullin's 5-hitter, 5–0 victory evens the Series again, as Cobb drives in 2 runs with a double.

13th Babe Adams hurls his 2nd complete-game victory 8–4, despite a double and HR by Sam Crawford. Clarke's 3-run HR breaks a tie and gives the Pirates a 3–2 Series lead.

14th George Mullin outlasts 3 Pirates pitchers for a 5–4 win that sends the Series to a 7th game in Detroit. This is the first WS to go the limit.

16th Babe Adams comes through with a 6-hit 8–0 win. It is his 3rd complete-game victory and gives the Pirates their first World Championship.

NOVEMBER

26th The Phils are sold for $350,000 to a group headed by sportswriter Horace Fogel. Because of his dual roles, Fogel will become the only executive barred from a league meeting.

DECEMBER

15th Kid Elberfeld, who helped make the Highlanders a winner, is sold to Washington for $5,000.

1910

FEBRUARY

15th Both MLs adopt resolutions banning syndicate baseball, which allowed owners to have financial interests in more than one team. The NL votes for a 154-game schedule to open on April 12th, which the AL has already adopted. Other rules: umpires must announce all team changes to spectators; batting orders must be delivered to the umpire at home plate before the game; a batter is out if he crosses the plate from one batter's box to the other while the pitcher is in position to pitch; a base runner is out if he passes another runner before the latter has been put out.

MARCH

1st The National Commission bans mementos given to players on winning World Series teams. This will later be reversed, making way for the traditional winners' watches, rings, and stickpins.

25th Chalmers Auto Company of Detroit offers to award a new car to the batting champs of each league. The National Commission accepts.

APRIL

1st Johnny Kling, who played for a Chicago semipro team while holding out for the entire 1909 season, is reinstated, fined $700, and required to play for the Cubs at his 1908 salary of $4,500.

12th The Reds extend the lease on their park for 20 years at an annual rent of $1,500, with an option to buy at $45,000.

14th William Howard Taft becomes the first president to throw out the first ball at a baseball opener in Washington. Walter Johnson catches it, then pitches the first of his 14 Opening Day Senator games. An easy fly hit into the overflow crowd—a ground-rule double—mars his 3–0 pitching gem. The White Sox' Frank Smith also throws a one-hit opener, against the Browns. By season's end the AL will see 13 one-hitters—a league record.

Although every opener is played, a record run of bad weather will force 85 postponements between April 15th and June 10th, causing chaos in the late-season schedule. Combined with an absence of close

pennant races, this will cause a drop in attendance, which will tip 7,000,000 for the year.

19th A split Patriots Day doubleheader at Boston draws 14,721 for the A.M. game with the Senators and 31,007 for the P.M., a record total attendance for one day. The Red Sox win the opener 2–1 and the afternoon game 5–4.

20th Cleveland's Addie Joss pitches his 2nd no-hitter 1–0 over Chicago. Joss's 10 assists help prevent any infield spoilers.

21st League Park opens in Cleveland with a capacity of 21,000; 18,832 watch Detroit and Ed Willett beat the Naps 5–0.

25th Reds president Garry Herrmann bans the sale of beer and liquor at the Cincinnati park.

MAY

2nd Aided by a 13-game winning streak, the Athletics take first place in the AL. New York will wrest it from them for a brief spell in June; otherwise, the A's will hold the top spot all season.

4th President Taft sees the Reds and the Cardinals at Robinson Field in St. Louis. Reds pitchers will walk 16 in the 12–3 loss, but Taft doesn't stick around. He leaves for Sportsman's Park in hopes of seeing some good baseball and is rewarded by a 3–3, 14-inning battle between the Browns' Joe Lake and the Naps' Cy Young that ends in darkness. There will be a record 19 ties in the AL this year.

5th P Cy Morgan and 2B Eddie Collins of the Athletics and P Dixie Walker and C Gabby Street of the Senators handle all the assists in the 10–1 Philadelphia victory.

10th The Cubs' Heinie Zimmerman makes 4 errors and 4 hits in a 9–5 win.

12th The Athletics Chief Bender pitches a 4–0 no-hitter against the Naps, missing a perfect game with one walk. Bender will be 23–5, one of only two 20-game-win seasons the future Hall of Famer will have in 15 years.

19th The Boston Doves beat the Pirates 6–3 for the first time in 26 tries.

23rd The Reds Dode Paskert steals 2B, 3B, and home in the last inning against Boston.

26th The Pirates' Honus Wagner and John Miller narrowly escape death when their car crashes into the safety gates of a railroad crossing in Carnegie, PA.

JUNE

21st Brooklyn rookie Jack Dalton has 5 straight hits off Christy Mathewson. Dalton will finish 1910 hitting .227.

22nd Congressman John K. Tener, former Chicago White Stockings and Pittsburgh Alleghenies pitcher, wins the Republican nomination for governor of Pennsylvania. He will be elected and will serve as president of the NL while governor.

23rd Giants 3B Art Devlin and 2 teammates are jailed for attacking a Washington Park fan who had been verbally abusing them during an 8–2 triumph over the Superbas.

24th In 8 innings at home, Cubs 1B Art Hofman sets an NL record (and ties Jiggs Donahue's ML mark of 1907) with no putouts. His only assist opportunity is fumbled for an error.

28th Joe Tinker steals home twice in the Cubs' 11–1 win over the Reds.

JULY

1st White Sox Park opens with a 2–0 loss to the Browns. The stadium, since called Comiskey Park, is baseball's biggest and costs $750,000 to build. 24,900 attend the game, 1,100 less than capacity. The game is attended by 24,900, 1,100 less than capacity. This stadium would be closed in the fall of 1990, replaced by a new structure, which is still named Comiskey Park.

19th Cy Young, 43, wins his 500th game 5–4, over Washington in 11 innings.

22nd Bugs Raymond, talented but hard-drinking spitball pitcher, walks the winning run home in New York's 4th straight loss to the Pirates. John McGraw suspends him for the rest of the season.

25th Connie Mack trades Joe Jackson to Cleveland for Bris Lord, a former A's OF.

29th White Sox OF Patsy Dougherty breaks up Detroit's Ed Summers's no-hitter. It is the 4th time in his 10-year career the .284 hitter has ruined someone's no-hitter.

30th The "surprise of the year," according to Ed Bang in *Sporting Life,* "came on July 30th when it was announced that the Naps had secured Joe Jackson from the New Orleans Pelicans for $5,000. It is believed that Connie made the Naps the concession [as part of the Lord-Rath trade] to allow them to purchase Jackson from New Orleans." Jackson had been up with the A's briefly in 1908 and 1909.

31st Cubs rookie King Cole pitches a 7-inning no-hitter for a 4–0 win over St. Louis. Cole will top the NL with a 20–4 record, but will have only one more winning season.

AUGUST

3rd St. Louis manager-C Roger Bresnahan pitches 3⅓ innings, giving up 6 hits and no runs against Brooklyn. He last pitched in 1901, and will end his career with a mark of 4–1 as a hurler.

4th Athletics Jack Coombs and Chicago's Ed Walsh duel 16 innings to a 0–0 tie. Coombs gives up just 3 hits in what he calls his best game. (Working with little rest, he wins 18 of 19 starts in July, August, and September, finishing 30–9 with a 1.30 ERA. His 13 shutouts are the AL record; in 12 other games he gives up just one run.)

13th In the most evenly matched game ever, the Pirates and Superbas each have 8 runs, 13 hits, 38 at bats, 5 strikeouts, 3 walks, 1 hit batter, 1 passed ball, 13 assists, 27 putouts, 2 errors, and use 2 pitchers.

22nd Three HRs by one team in one inning are hit by Pirates Howie Camnitz, Vin Campbell, and Honus Wagner against the Phillies, in the first inning. Camnitz's pop is the only one of his career. Old pro Wagner's is 7-for-7 during the doubleheader.

23rd Fred Clarke makes a record 4 OF assists for Pittsburgh against the Phils.

24th Atop of the Washington Monument, Ed Walsh throws 23 balls before C Billy Sullivan snares one, then catches 2 more, 555 feet below. It duplicates Gabby Street's catch of August 21, 1908. The estimated speed of the ball is 161 feet per second. On the field Walsh will be 18–20 despite a league-leading 1.27 ERA, the only time a pitcher with a losing record loses 20 and leads either league in ERA.

27th Using twenty 137,000 candlepower arc lights, 2 amateur teams play a night game at White Sox Park before 20,000. The first AL night game will be played there in 1939.

Washington 2B Red Killefer sets a ML mark by sacrificing 4 times in the first game of a doubleheader against Detroit.

30th New York's Tom Hughes pitches a no-hitter for 9⅓ innings before giving up a hit to Cleveland Harry Niles. Hughes gives up 5 runs in the 11th and loses 5–0.

SEPTEMBER

5th Jack Coombs begins a streak of 53 shutout innings, topping Doc White's 46 of 1904. Three years later Walter Johnson will top Coombs.

17th Detroit pitcher Ed Summers, a notoriously poor hitter, bounces 2 HRs into the stands in a victory over the A's. They will comprise his career total. He wins 10–3.

19th A game between Mobile and Atlanta (Southern Association) takes just 32 minutes to complete. The game is conducted as an experiment with batters swinging at every good pitch and little time taken between pitches. There are no strikeouts and one walk as Mobile wins 2–1.

23rd George Stallings, convinced that 1B Hal Chase tried to throw a game, but unable to make the charge stick, is replaced by his charismatic 1B as manager of the 2nd-place Highlanders for the season's final 11 games. On his own, Prince Hal will lead the New Yorkers downhill to 6th place in 1911.

25th The Chicago White Sox break Jack Coombs's string of shutout innings at 53 with a run in the 7th. Coombs beats Ed Walsh 3–1 in 14 innings.

30th Browns 3B Ray Jansen gets 4 hits in his ML debut, the only game he will play in the ML.

OCTOBER

1st Rookie Lefty Russell blanks the Red Sox 3–0 in his first start, for Philadelphia's 100th win and his sole ML victory in his 3-year career.

The Cubs' Johnny Evers breaks his ankle sliding home in Cincinnati and will not play in the WS.

9th The battle for the AL batting title is decided on the final day, when Detroit's Ty Cobb edges Cleveland's Nap Lajoie .3850687 to .3840947. Neither man covers himself with glory. Lajoie goes 8-for-8 in a doubleheader with the Browns, accepting 6 "gift" hits on bunt singles on which Browns rookie 3B Red Corridon is purposely stationed too deep to field. The prejudiced St. Louis scorer also credits popular Nap with a "hit" on the Brownie SS's wild throw to 1B. Cobb, meanwhile, rather than risk his average, sits out the last 2 games. Ban Johnson investigates and clears everyone concerned, enabling Cobb to win the 3rd of 9 straight batting crowns. The embarrassed Chalmers Auto Company awards cars to both Ty and Nap. In 1981 The *Sporting News* uncovers an error that, if corrected, would give the championship to Lajoie. The commissioner's committee votes unanimously to leave history unchanged.

The Leland Giants begin a 16-game series in Havana, Cuba. The black team will play a series against the AL champion Detroit Tigers.

12th In a field day at Cincinnati, Hans Lobert circles the bases in 13.8 seconds, and Larry LeJeune throws a ball 426 feet 9½ inches, short of his 1908 record of 435 feet.

With the AL season ending a week earlier than the NL, the champion A's tune up with a 5-game series against an AL all-star team, including Ty Cobb, Tris Speaker, Doc White, Ed Walsh, and Walter Johnson.

15th St. Louis manager Jack O'Connor is fired by Browns president Hedges for his role in the Lajoie batting-title travesty.

17th With sore-armed Eddie Plank unavailable, Connie Mack will squeeze 5 complete games out of 2 pitchers in the WS. Chief Bender's 4–1 three-hitter wins game one for the Athletics at Philadelphia. Frank Baker's 3 hits drive in all the runs needed to beat the Cubs' Orvall Overall.

18th Jack Coombs struggles for a 9–3 win, walking 9 and giving up 8 hits, but strands 14 Cubs, while a 6-run 7th off Three Finger Brown blows open the win for the A's. Eddie Collins has 2 doubles and 2 SBs.

The Reds beat the Indians 8–5 in the 7th game of the first Ohio championship series.

20th The A's dispose of Ed Reulbach in 2 innings, and Coombs coasts on one day's rest 12–5. He helps himself with 3 hits.

Cubs manager Frank Chance becomes the first player ejected from a WS game when umpire Tom Connolly chases him for protesting a Danny Murphy HR drive against a sign over the RF bleachers.

23rd Three Finger Brown comes back to face Coombs, who takes a 2–1 lead into the 7th. The A's get to Brown for 5 runs and a 7–2 win. The crowd of 27,374 is the Series's largest. The A's .316 BA is a WS record.

DECEMBER

13th Former New York Giant Dan McGann, who ended his 13-year career in 1908, shoots himself in a Louisville hotel.

1911

JANUARY

3rd The National Commission adopts a rule that bars World Series winners from playing post-season exhibition games. This obscure rule will lead to a direct confrontation between Babe Ruth and Commissioner Kenesaw Mountain Landis in 1921.

14th Bobby Wallace, the era's outstanding AL SS, is named manager of the Browns. St. Louis will finish last, and he will be an infielder again by June 1912.

FEBRUARY

14th At the NL's annual meeting, the Giants and Phils get an okay for new home uniforms: white flannel with a fine stripe, an innovation that predates the famed Yankee pinstripes by 4 years.

MARCH

17th Plumbers at work on the drain pipes at Washington's ballpark start a fire that burns down the grandstand. Since the water has been shut off, firemen can do nothing. Stands will be rebuilt to play the home opener on schedule.

24th Matthew Stanley Robison, president of the Cardinals, dies unexpectedly. He leaves the club and the bulk of his estate to his niece, Mrs. Helene Hathaway Britton, the first female owner of a ML club.

APRIL

1st NL president Tom Lynch reveals he had asked all umpires to produce certificates as to their eyesight; tests showed all had perfect vision.

4th The idea of selecting a Most Valuable Player is introduced. Hugh Chalmers, the automaker, offers a new car to the player in each league chosen MVP by a committee of baseball writers.

12th President Taft throws out the first ball at Washington's opener, and holdout Walter Johnson signs a 3-year contract at $7,000 a year.

13th With Cleveland leading St. Louis 3–1 in the 9th inning at Cleveland's League Park, the game is stopped because of a severe storm. Many fans are bruised by hailstones.

The night after the Phils knock out Christy Mathewson in the Giants' opener, the Polo Grounds grandstand and LF bleachers go up in flames. President Frank Farrell of the Highlanders invites the Giants to use the AL grounds; the offer is accepted, paving the way for the Giants' invitation for the AL team to use the Polo Grounds when the Hilltop Park lease expires after the 1912 season. A $500,000 steel-and-concrete structure will replace the wooden stands of the Polo Grounds.

15th Walter Johnson ties a ML record by striking out 4 batters in the 5th inning of Washington's 1–0 win against Boston.

17th The Giants pick up 4 stolen bases in a 3–1 win over Brooklyn, the start of a post-1900 record 347 steals for the year.

Addie Joss's funeral is held at Toledo with Billy Sunday preaching the sermon. The funeral is the 2nd largest in the city's history. His teammates insist on being there, forcing postponement of the season opener.

A bill to permit Sunday baseball is refused in the lower house of the New Jersey legislature.

24th Battle Creek of the South Michigan League makes 2 triple plays in the first 2 innings against Grand Rapids, a trick never performed in the ML.

NL President Lynch orders his umpires to stop catchers, especially Roger Bresnahan, from verbally attacking batters.

25th In his last full season as a player, 38-year-old Pirate player-manager Fred Clarke is kept busy with 10 putouts in LF.

MAY

10th The Detroit Tigers lose their first home game of the year 6–2, as New York hands George Mullin his first loss. The Tigers have a 21–2 record and will lead the pack until July 4th.

13th Fred Merkle has 6 RBI as the Giants tee off on 3 St. Louis pitchers for 13 runs in the first inning, including a ML record 10 before an out is recorded. The spree ties a first inning enjoyed by the Boston Beaneaters against the St. Louis Cardinals in 1900. John McGraw decides to save starter Mathewson for another day. Rube Marquard works the last 8 innings and strikes out 14, setting a record for strikeouts by a reliever. The Giants win 19–5.

14th More than 15,000 turn out for Cleveland's first Sunday game, and they see a 14–3 win over the New York Highlanders.

20th A New England League game is called in the 7th inning because of dense fog in Lynn, MA. Lynn is leading until Weaver of Fall River hits a fly ball to the OF with a man on. The Lynn OFs are unable to locate the ball, and the 2 runners score to go ahead 6–5. After a dispute, umpire Walsh rules that the game has to revert to the 6th inning with Lynn winning by a 5–4 score.

22nd Boston (NL) hurler Cliff Curtis sets a ML mark by losing his 23rd consecutive game. The streak began on June 13, 1910.

24th An abdominal ailment sidelines Nap Lajoie. He will get into only 90 games for the year and bat .365.

29th Carrying the Cubs from St. Louis, the Pennsylvania Railroad sets a speed record, covering the 191 miles from Columbus, OH, to Pittsburgh in 215 minutes. Arriving in time for the game, the Cubs win 4–1.

30th After one day at the top, the Cubs drop to 3rd, and New York takes the NL lead, winning 2 from Brooklyn while the Pirates down the Cubs twice. Giants C Art Wilson makes the first 9 putouts in the morning game as 4 Superbas fan, 3 foul out, and 2 are thrown out at home trying to score on base hits.

JUNE

3rd Cub Frank "Wildfire" Schulte's grand slam beats the Giants. Schulte will hit 4 this season, a record tied by Babe Ruth in 1919 and topped by Ernie Banks's 5 in 1955. They are Schulte's only grand slams in his 11-year career.

7th After 2 years on the vaudeville circuit with his wife Mabel Hite, and occasional sojourns to jail for drunkenness and assault, "Turkey Mike" Donlin is reinstated by the National Commission. He rejoins the Giants, but John McGraw's willingness to put up with him ceases after 12 games, and the .333 lifetime hitter is traded to the last-place NL Boston Rustlers.

Pirates pitchers have the Giants hitting the ball on the ground all day. Pittsburgh sets a record of 55 total chances on 28 assists and 27 putouts. Seven errors help the Giants to a 9–4 win.

10th The Cubs trade C Johnny Kling, P Orlie Weaver, P Hank Griffin, and OF Al Kaiser to the Braves for C Peaches Graham, P Cliff Curtis, and OF Bill Collins.

18th Down 13–1 after 5½ innings, the Tigers stage the biggest comeback in ML history to defeat Chicago by a score of 16–15.

27th When the A's Stuffy McInnis steps into the batter's box to lead off and hits a warmup pitch for a HR while the Red Sox are still taking their positions, Boston manager Patsy Donovan protests. The protest in not upheld, but Ban Johnson's time-saving rule, which declared that pitchers had to throw as soon as the batter was in the box, is withdrawn.

28th In the Cubs' 11–1 win over the Reds, Joe Tinker becomes the first player to steal home twice in one game.

JULY

1st Cubs player-manager Frank Chance leaves the game suffering from a blood clot in the brain. Except for 11 brief appearances at 1B over the next 3 years, his playing days are over.

4th In the morning game between Chicago and Detroit, Ed Walsh stops Ty Cobb's 40-game hitting streak, as the White Sox win 7–3. Cobb has batted .491 since the streak started on May 15th.

10th Sherry Magee, star OF of the Phillies, knocks out umpire Bill Finneran with one punch after being ejected for disputing a called 3rd strike. He is suspended for the season, but upon appeal he will be reinstated after 5 weeks.

11th The Federal Express of the New York, New Haven, and Hartford Railroad, carrying the St. Louis Cardinals to Boston, plunges down an 18-foot embankment outside Bridgeport, CT, killing 14 passengers. The team's Pullmans were originally just behind the baggage coaches near the front. When noise prevented the players from sleeping, manager Bresnahan requested the car be changed. The day coach that replaced the players' car was crushed and splintered. The players help remove bodies and rescue the injured, then board a special train to Boston, where the day's game is postponed. The railroad pays each player $25 for his rescue work and for lost belongings.

12th In the first inning of a 9–0 win over the Athletics at Detroit, Ty Cobb walks, then on consecutive pitches steals 2B, 3B, and home off lefty Harry Krause. Cobb's 50 steals of home will top all ML players.

Highlanders 3B Roy Hartzell hits a 3-run double, sacrifice fly, and grand slam to drive in 8 runs, an AL record until Jimmie Foxx's 9 RBI in a game in 1933. New York defeats the Browns 12–2.

17th Boston Red Sox infielder Buck Herzog and OF Doc Miller fail to show up for a game and are suspended by the club. After a conference with the club president, they rejoin the team. John McGraw, anxious to retrieve former Giant Herzog to shore up a weak infielder, will swap C Hank Gowdy and SS Al Bridwell to Boston for Herzog on the 21st.

19th While playing CF for Vernon (Pacific Coast League), Walter Carlisle executes an unassisted triple play in the 6th inning against Los Angeles. With men on 1B and 2B, he makes a spectacular diving catch of a short fly by batter Roy Akin, touches 2B, and runs to 1B to retire both runners.

22nd The Pirates pay St. Paul of the American Association $22,500 for righthander Marty O'Toole, the highest purchase to date. In 1912, O'Toole will be 15–17 and lead the NL with 159 walks. He will last only 2 more years.

Brooklyn hurler Nap Rucker loses a no-hitter with 2 outs in the 9th inning when Cincinnati's Bob Bescher comes through with a hit. Rucker wins the game 1–0.

24th An AL all-star team plays the Naps in Cleveland, raising $12,914 for the late Addie Joss's family. The all-stars win 5–3.

Rochester and Newark of the Eastern League play a doubleheader in 2 hours, 32 minutes.

26th The league-leading Phils are dealt a blow when C-manager Red Dooin suffers a broken leg in a collision at home plate with the Cards' Rebel Oakes.

Christy Mathewson wins his 21st straight game from the Reds 5–3. His hit in the 9th scores 2 to win it.

28th Charley "Victory" Faust shows up at the Giants' hotel in St. Louis asking for a tryout. Manager John McGraw observes the "pitcher," who obviously is no player, and carries him on the team as an unofficial "mascot."

29th Red Sox fireballer Joe Wood hurls a 5–0 no-hitter against the Browns. He walks 2 and hits one batter.

In his last appearance for Cleveland, Cy Young pitches just 3 innings and gives up 5 runs in a 7–1 loss to Washington.

AUGUST

4th Lee Tannehill of the White Sox, the only SS to execute 2 unassisted double plays in one season, makes both of them in the same game versus Washington. Walter Johnson still wins 1–0 for the Senators.

5th Cubs manager Frank Chance suspends Joe Tinker and fines him $150 for indifferent play. He is reinstated the next day.

9th The Pirates lead in the NL race for the first time, but it doesn't last, as the Cubs replace them the next day. The lead changes 26 times, as the top 4 bounce in and out until the Giants emerge on August 24th and build a 7½ game lead over the Cubs.

10th The Detroit club announces that a new grandstand, costing $300,000, will be built for the 1912 season.

13th The Pirates' Elmer Steele throws just 72 pitches in subduing the Superbas. Brooklyn so admires the feat they obtain him on September 16th, but he never wins another game in the ML.

Ty Cobb, apparently believing the Tigers can no longer win the pennant race, begins a vacation.

15th Cy Young, 3–4 at Cleveland, is given his release. He returns to Boston and signs with the Rustlers, where he will close out the year 4–5, and his pitching days with a 511–315 record, 750 complete games, 7,356 IP.

19th Thirty-five thousand gather at the not-yet-completed Polo Grounds to watch the Reds finally get to Mathewson after 22 straight losses, beating him for the first time since May 1908. Matty, after saving the

5–4 opener, starts the nightcap, goes 5 innings, and loses 7–4.

27th Chicago's Ed Walsh pitches a 5–0 no-hitter against the Red Sox. A 4th-inning walk produces the only Red Sox runner. After going 18–20 in 1910, Walsh bounces back to win 27 and lead the AL in games (56), IP (369), and strikeouts (255).

SEPTEMBER

1st In game one, Mathewson gives up 10 hits but beats the Phils 3–2. In game 2, Marquard one-hits the Phils 2–0, walks none, fans 10.

7th The Cubs' Frank Schulte hits his 21st HR and brings in RBI No. 121; he will lead the NL in both. He is the first player to have more than 20 doubles, triples, and HRs in one season. In the AL, Frank Baker's 9 HRs will be tops. Ty Cobb hits 8 HRs but leads in BA, RBI, hits, doubles, triples, total bases, and stolen bases.

Grover Alexander (24 years old), winning a rookie record 28 games, pitches the Phils to a 1–0 win over Boston's 44-year-old Cy Young. Alexander's 31 CG, 367 IP, and 7 shutouts lead the NL. The AL has its own rookie sensation, lefty Vean Gregg, who breaks in for Cleveland with a 23–7 record and miserly 1.81 ERA. Gregg will win 20 his first 3 years, then win just 28 in the next 12 years.

12th In a game billed as a pitchers' duel, Boston's Cy Young and the Giants' Christy Mathewson face each other before 10,000, Boston's largest crowd of the year. Young gives up 3 homers and 9 runs in less than 3 innings. With a 9–0 lead, John McGraw lifts Mathewson after 2 innings, preferring to save his ace for the pennant race against Chicago and Philadelphia. This is the only time the 2 pitchers ever face each other.

15th Washington manager Jimmy McAleer and Robert R. McRoy buy a half-interest in the Red Sox for $150,000.

18th The Giants beat Pittsburgh 7–2, as Larry Doyle steals home twice. The team ties a ML mark by stealing home a total of 3 times in the game.

22nd Cy Young shuts out Pittsburgh 1–0 for his final career victory, number 511. It is Young's 2nd shutout against the Pirates, who lost just 3 of 22 games to Boston in 1911.

24th After 41 straight shutout innings, Grover Alexander is scored on by the Cards.

25th Washington's Wid Conroy, in his final season, sets an AL record for total chances by a 3B with 13 in a 3–2 loss to Cleveland.

John C. Bender, brother of Philadelphia great Chief Bender, dies on the mound during a game played in Edmonton, Alberta.

28th A scant few hundred fans see the worst game in AL history as the Highlanders trounce the Browns 18–12. The teams accumulate 29 hits, 20 walks, and 11 errors. New York scores in each of 7 innings, steals 15 bases—7 off C Jim Stephens in 2 innings, 8 off Nig Clarke.

29th Ty Cobb is fined $100 by the National Commission for playing a Sunday game with a semipro club in New York.

30th In a field day at Chicago, Ed Walsh hits a fungo 419 feet and one-half inch, beating a 413 foot eight and one-half inch drive by Cincinnati's Mike Mitchell on September 11, 1907.

OCTOBER

1st The Giants complete a western trip that ices the pennant by beating the Cubs. Chicago's Jimmy Sheckard sets a NL record by drawing his 147th walk, a mark not broken until Dodger Eddie Stanky's 148 in 1945.

5th The National Commission sells motion picture rights to the WS for $3,500. When the players demand a share of it, the Commission cancels the deal.

6th Cy Young's farewell appearance in a ML game is a letdown, as he loses to Brooklyn 13–3 in his 906th game.

9th With the WS not scheduled to start until the 14th, the Athletics tune up in a series against an AL all-star team. The A's clinched on September 26th in an 11–5 win over Detroit.

10th The first game of the Ohio championship between Cleveland and the Reds is won by Cincinnati 4–0. The next day the St. Louis city series begins, and 2 days later the Chicago series. These postseason matches are popular with the fans and put money in the players' pockets.

11th The first MVPs are announced. Using a point system—8 for a first-place vote, 7 for 2nd, and so on—the 8 voting writers give OF Ty Cobb the maximum 64 points. P Ed Walsh is 2nd, and 2B Eddie Collins 3rd. The NL winner is the Cubs OF Frank "Wildfire" Schulte. Christy Mathewson is 2nd. Winners receive Chalmers automobiles.

14th The Athletics go into the WS minus their star rookie 1B Stuffy McInnis. The veteran Harry Davis replaces him and drives in the first run as Chief Bender tries again to outpitch Christy Mathewson. The Giants are dressed in the same black uniforms they wore in their 1905 conquest of the Mackmen, and this Series starts as their last meeting ended: Mathewson wins it 2–1. The largest crowd ever to watch a ballgame—38,281—is at the Polo Grounds. Gate receipts are $77,379.

16th The World Series resumes today, Monday, and the pitchers continue to dominate. Rube Marquard and Eddie Plank are in command of a 1–1 game when Philadelphia's Eddie Collins doubles in the last of the 6th and Frank Baker hits one over the RF fence for a 3–1 victory.

17th After criticizing his teammate Marquard's pitching to Baker in his newspaper column, Christy Mathewson takes the mound for game 3 against 29-game winner Jack Coombs. Matty takes a 1–0 lead into the 9th. With one out, Baker lines another drive over the RF fence to tie it. With that blow, he becomes "Home Run" Baker to future generations. Errors by 3B Buck Herzog and SS Art Fletcher give the A's 2 unearned runs in the top of the 11th. New York scores once, but the A's win 3–2 behind Jack Coombs's 3-hitter.

24th After 6 days of rain, Chief Bender gets another chance against Mathewson. New York takes a 2–0 first-inning lead. But aided by an overflow crowd in the outfield, the A's collect 7 doubles among their 11 hits, pick up 3 in the 3rd and one in the 4th while Bender shuts down the Giants, and the A's take a 3–1 lead in games.

25th Before 33,228 at the Polo Grounds, the Giants put 3 hits together off Coombs in the last of the 9th for 2 runs and a 3–3 tie. The A's Eddie Plank comes on in the 10th and gives up the winning run in the 4–3 contest. Relief specialist Doc Crandall gets the win after working 2 scoreless innings.

26th Chief Bender cruises to his second victory, a 4-hit 13–2 breeze, capped by a 7-run 7th. Overall, the Giants manage just 13 runs and a .175 BA off Bender, Coombs, and Plank. Because of the NL's extended playing season, this is the latest ending ever for a WS, until the "Earthquake Series" of 1989.

27th A's longtime captain and 1B Harry Davis is named manager of Cleveland.

30th Clark Griffith is named manager at Washington, beginning a stand in the Capital as manager, then owner, that will last until his death in 1955.

NOVEMBER

21st Hal Chase resigns as manager of the Highlanders after a 6th-place finish. He will stay as a player until traded during the 1913 season. Harry Wolverton replaces him.

DECEMBER

12th A rift between the leagues develops over widespread charges of ticket speculation during the WS, and accusations that officials of the Giants and A's were involved. The AL passes a resolution refusing to participate in another WS until it has control of ticket sales in its own parks. The National Commission investigates the charge that speculators were given large blocks of tickets, but takes no action and releases no findings. The following spring, the Commission finds that much scalping has occurred, but there is no evidence either team was involved, and peace is declared.

13th The Boston Doves (aka the Rustlers) are bought by New York politician James E. Gaffney and former player, now attorney, John Montgomery Ward. The team will be called the Braves because of Gaffney's Tammany Hall connections.

14th Phillies owner Barney Dreyfuss proposes that each team in the WS be required to turn over one-fourth of its share of the gate to the league, to be divided among the other teams. Until now, 10 percent of the gross went to the National Commission, 60 percent to the players, and the rest to the 2 pennant-winning clubs. The NL will pass the resolution and send it to the AL. It marks the beginning of changes that ultimately give players of the first 4 clubs a percentage of the WS money.

1912

JANUARY

2nd   Brooklyn Dodgers president Charles Ebbets announces he has purchased grounds to build a new concrete-and-steel stadium to seat 30,000. During the year he will ease his pinched financial condition by selling half the team to Ed and Steve McKeever.

15th   Former Brooklyn P Elmer Stricklett, said to be the inventor of the spitball, is reinstated by the National Commission after playing outside organized baseball for 3 years. But he does not make it back to the major leagues.

23rd   The Japanese Army announces it will send a baseball team to the Philippines to play American soldiers; a U.S. team may go to Japan.

FEBRUARY

1st   Jim Doyle, 30, dies after an appendicitis operation. He had only one full season as 3B with the Cubs, in which he hit .282 with 62 RBI.

APRIL

11th   On Opening Day in Brooklyn, fans storm Washington Park hours before the 4:00 P.M. starting time, causing a near riot. An estimated 30,000 people crowd into the OF and along foul lines. The Giants hit a record 13 ground-rule doubles and are leading 19–3 in the 6th when the game is called due to darkness.

In Cincinnati, the Reds open Redland Field with a 10–6 win over the Cubs.

12th   The Tinker-Evers-Chance double play combination plays its final ML game together. Vic Saier will replace Chance at 1B.

The NL has a small box installed in the ground near home plate in each park to supply umpires with baseballs, eliminating the possibility of home team ballboys influencing which balls are used for which team's turn at bat.

19th   Washington wins its home opener 6–0 over the Athletics. Only 10,000 fans show up as shocking news of the *Titanic* sinking keeps people away.

20th   The Boston Red Sox open in the new Fenway Park with a 7–6 11-inning win over the New York Highlanders before 27,000.

After hitting a game-winning HR in the 10th inning, Cubs OF Jimmy Sheckard forgets and heads for the clubhouse after touching 2B. Teammates yell to him to complete the circuit, which he does. The manager of the Reds is Hank O'Day, who was the umpire that day in 1908 when Fred Merkle failed to touch 2B.

Detroit opens remodeled Navin Park and beats Cleveland 6–5 in 11 innings before 24,384.

21st   Reds SS Jimmy Esmond, a .195 hitter, hits the first HR at Redland Park, his only one of the year. It's an inside-the-park blow. Nobody will hit one out of the Cincinnati park until Pat Duncan does it on June 2, 1921.

MAY

1st   George Sisler, a University of Michigan freshman, strikes out 20 in 7 innings.

3rd   Leading 18–5 after 8 innings, A's pitchers give up a record 9th-inning outburst of 10 runs to New York before Eddie Plank stops them at 18–15.

4th   The Giants pilfer 9 bases in a 4–3 win over the Phils. They will run away with 319 SBs and the NL pennant by 10 games.

Phils 3B Hans Lobert, one of the fastest men in the game, chases a foul ball into the stands in New York and breaks his kneecap.

9th   Roy Akin of Houston, who hit the ball that led to Walter Carlisle's remarkable unassisted triple play at Los Angeles the year before, turns the tables. Playing 3B against Waco (Texas League), he catches a hit-and-run bunt, steps on 3B, and then tags the runner coming down from 2B.

15th   After the Reds' Hod Eller and Brooklyn's Al Mamaux match 12 scoreless innings, the Reds pour across 10 in the 13th to win 10–0.

Ty Cobb charges into the stands in New York and attacks heckler Claude Lueker. Other fans and Tigers mix it up before order is restored. Ban Johnson suspends Cobb indefinitely for the incident.

17th   Boston's Fenway Park, built at a cost of $350,000, is formally dedicated, but the White Sox take a 5–2 win before an overflow crowd.

18th The Tiger players protest Cobb's suspension and vote to strike. Faced with a $5,000 fine for failing to field a team, club owner Frank Navin orders manager Hugh Jennings to sign up some local amateurs. Aloysius Travers, Bill Leinhauser, Dan McGarvey, Billy Maharg (whose real name was Graham, "Maharg" reversed), Jim McGarr, Pat Meany, Jack Coffey, Hap Ward, and Ed Irvin put on Tiger uniforms. Two Detroit coaches, Joe Sugden, 41, and Jim McGuire, 48, complete the lineup. The Athletics win 24–2, as Travers goes all the way for Detroit, giving up 26 hits and 24 runs in 8 innings. Irvin hits 2 triples in 3 at bats and closes his ML career with a 2.000 slugging average. Only one ever plays another ML game: Maharg will bat once for the Phils in 1916. He will also be involved as a conspirator in the Black Sox scandal of 1919.

19th President Ban Johnson meets with the Tigers and tells them they will play in Washington the next day or never again. Led by Cobb, they go back to work. Cobb is fined $50, and his suspension will be lifted May 26th. Players who had signed the strike telegram sent to Johnson are fined $100 each. A new players' organization will be formed as a result of the incident.

20th John T. Brush invites the Highlanders to use the larger Polo Grounds for their holiday doubleheader May 30th.

22nd The Giants complete a western trip in first place. They will win 9 straight, before losing to St. Louis 5–1 on May 31st, and will open a 14-game lead.

29th The Red Sox take 2 from Washington 21–8 and 12–11. There are 59 hits for 77 total bases.

30th The Nationals buy 1B Chick Gandil for $10,000 from Montreal of the International League. Washington begins a 17-game winning streak—16 on the road—that will be stopped on June 19th.

Three doubleheader sweeps—Chicago Green Sox over Richmond, Virginia Rebels; Cincinnati over Reading, Pennsylvania, and Pittsburgh Filipinos over Cleveland—end a short, futile season of the would-be ML competitor, the United States League. Poorly organized and financed, the season began May 1st and collapsed largely through the failure of New York franchise to attract fans. The Filipinos, so named because old Pittsburgh favorite Deacon Phillippe was manager, had the best record: 16–8. Players and fields were barely above semipro level, but promoters will be heard from again with the advent of the Federal League.

At New York, the morning game draws 18,000, while 38,000 crowd the afternoon contest. The Giants win both, 8–6 and 5–1, over the Phils.

JUNE

10th The Red Sox take the AL lead and are never dethroned, finishing 14 games ahead of Washington.

13th Christy Mathewson wins his 300th game 3–2 over the Cubs, in his 10th straight 20-win season.

14th "Deerfoot" Clyde Milan steals 5 bases as the Nationals beat Cleveland for their 15th straight win.

20th The Giants take a 14–2 lead into the 9th at Boston, then score 7 more. The Braves rally for 10 in the last of the 9th, but lose 21–12. The 17 runs are the NL post-1900 record scored by 2 teams in the 9th. The Giants P Ernie Shore is making his ML debut in this game. He surrenders 8 hits, 1 walk, and 10 runs (3 earned) in one inning of work in relief, but is credited with a save. It is his only appearance in the NL.

JULY

3rd The Giants Rube Marquard nips Nap Rucker 2–1 to capture his 19th straight game this season. With 2 end-of-year wins in 1911, he has 21 in a row in regular season play. Both marks are records. On the 8th, the Cubs will beat him, but he will ultimately compile a league-leading 26 victories against 11 defeats. Today's game is the Giants' 16th consecutive win. Brooklyn will end the streak tomorrow.

4th Three weeks after the Tigers ask waivers on George Mullin, he pitches himself a birthday present at Detroit, a 7–0 no-hitter over the Browns. In the morning game, a 9–3 Detroit win, Ty Cobb steals 2B, 3B, and home in the 5th inning.

Boston's Smokey Joe Wood suffers his worst loss of the year, a 16–4 shellacking at the hands of the Athletics. Eddie Plank beats Wood, who will finish the year at 34–5. Wood will win his next start on August 8th, the first of 16 in a row.

6th In Brooklyn, the cornerstone is put in place and construction on Ebbets Field begins.

7th To fend off possible future challenges to the legality of the standard contract and its reserve clause, new wording provides for compensation to the player for the right to renew. A player's salary is specified as 75 percent for his services and 25 percent for the privilege of reserving them for the following season.

15th A U.S. team defeats the Swedish Vesteras Club 13–3 in a one-game Olympic exhibition in Stockholm, Sweden.

19th Ty Cobb strokes 7 hits in a doubleheader to give him a ML record of 14 in 2 consecutive twin bills against the Athletics. He also pummeled them for 7 hits on the 17th.

20th Ray Caldwell of the Highlanders, inserted as a pinch runner, steals home for the tying run in an eventual 4–3 win over Cleveland. He then pitches a 4–0 victory in the second game.

23rd Iron Man McGinnity is *still* pitching doubleheaders, winning a pair of games for Newark against Rochester (International League) at age 41.

25th Fleet OF Max Carey goes hitless, but steals 4 bases and scores 5 runs in the Pirates 12–3 win over the Phils. Carey will lead the NL in thefts 10 times, and retire with 738.

29th For the first time, a NL team loses a game because of the rule that holds runners in place when a batted ball hits an umpire. A double by the Giants' Buck Herzog drives in 2 runs, but the ball hits umpire Garner Bush, and the runs do not count.

31st The Braves and Pirates play 19 innings, lefty Otto Hess going all the way for Boston. The Pirates score 3 in the 19th, and the Braves come back with 2, losing 7–6. The day before, the Braves had gone 14 to beat St. Louis.

AUGUST

1st Rube Marquard is fined $25 by the National Commission for pitching an inning in a semipro game in Port Chester, NY, on a day off.

6th Inspired in part by the Cobb suspension and the Tigers' brief strike in May, the formation of a Players' Fraternity is announced, headed by attorney and former player Dave Fultz. Leading players include Cobb, Mathewson, Mickey Doolan, and Jake Daubert. The goals are to oppose contract violations,

rowdyism, and anything that may "impair a player's ability." At one point, a strike will be called for a Brooklyn attempt to send an obscure player, Harry Kraft, down to Newark, but many teams balk at the strike call, and it is rescinded.

7th Browns manager-1B George Stovall makes 7 assists, topping Bill Brown's record of 6 in a game for Louisville in 1893.

11th Cleveland's Joe Jackson becomes the 2nd AL player to steal home twice in a game. He steals home in the first inning, and then in the 7th, he steals 2B, 3B, and home.

12th Cubs owner Charles Murphy hints that the Cards and other clubs go easy against McGraw's Giants. Later Phils' owner Horace Fogel, a former Giants manager whose ownership of the Phils is seen as a front for Murphy and financial backer Charles Raft of Cincinnati, echoes the accusation and charges NL umpires with favoring the Giants. It will lead to Fogel's being expelled from the NL.

15th Little-known Guy Zinn, Highlanders OF, steals home twice in a 5–4 win over Detroit; this will add to last-place New York's record of 18 steals of home for the year.

16th Walter Johnson and Joe Wood are in pursuit of Rube Marquard's 19-game win streak. Johnson picks on the White Sox for his 14th straight, a 2-hitter, tying Jack Chesbro's 1904 mark. A week later Joe Wood wins number 13.

20th Washington hurler Jay Cashion tosses a 6-inning no-hitter against Cleveland, winning 2–0. He will win only 11 other games in his ML career.

21st Thomas C. Noyes, president and part owner of the Senators, dies, opening the way for Clark Griffith to eventually become club owner.

26th Walter Johnson's 16-game winning streak ends under rules that have since been changed. In the 2nd game of a doubleheader against the Browns, he relieves Tom Hughes with one out and 2 on in the 7th inning of a 2–2 game. The 2 runners score and the Nationals lose 4–3. The 2 runs are charged to Johnson, not Hughes.

27th It takes a one-hitter by Art Fromme, but the Reds finally beat New York, and Mathewson 2–0. The Giants' lead shrinks to 3½ games over the Cubs.

In response to demands for an alternative way to rate pitchers besides wins and losses, the NL will officially keep ERA's for the first time; the Giants Jeff Tesreau will lead the league at 1.96. Despite an increase in .300 hitters from 22 to 32 this year, there will be 19 pitchers with ERA's under 3.00. The AL will not make ERA part of their official statistics until 1913.

30th Lefty Earl Hamilton, 22, pitches his only shutout of the year, a no-hitter in the Browns' 5–1 win over Detroit. Ty Cobb scores on an error after a walk.

SEPTEMBER

6th Jeff Tesreau pitches a 3–0 no-hitter over the Phils, the first modern rookie to perform the feat.

In one of the more dramatic matchups in history, Walter Johnson, who had won 16 straight games before losing, takes the mound in a doubleheader nightcap against Joe Wood, who is seeking his 14th straight win. Wood strikes out 9 and beats the visiting Senators 1–0.

7th Arthur "Bugs" Raymond, 30, is found dead at the Hotel Valey in Chicago, 2 days after his skull was fractured in a fight at a ballpark. Raymond last pitched for the Giants in 1911.

Eddie Collins steals 6 bases in the Athletics' 9–7 defeat of Detroit, a post-1900 record that is still unmatched. Remarkably, on the 22nd, he will repeat with 6 against the Browns. With 63 for the season, he will run 2nd to Clyde "Deerfoot" Milan's 88.

14th Former ML player and current president of the Connecticut League "Orator Jim" O'Rourke catches a complete game for New Haven (Connecticut League) at age 60.

15th Boston's Joe Wood wins his 16th straight game as he bests the Browns 2–1 in a game called after 8 innings because of darkness.

16th The Pirates' 2–1 win over Brooklyn is their 12th in a row; they will overtake the Cubs and finish 2nd.

17th CF Casey Stengel breaks in with Brooklyn and has 4 singles, a walk, 2 SB, and 2 RBI in the 7–3 win over Pittsburgh.

20th Joe Wood's bid for a 17th straight victory falls short as Detroit beats Boston 6–4 on 2 unearned runs. Wood gives up 7 hits and, in the 3rd, walks 4 in a row.

22nd Eleven days after stealing 6 bases in a game, Eddie Collins does it again. Included in his 6 swipes are 3B and home, as the A's beat the Browns 6–2.

27th Eddie Plank goes 19 innings for the A's against Bob Groom and Walter Johnson of the Nationals, and takes a 5–4 loss when Eddie Collins's wild throw lets the winning run score.

28th Having recovered from an operation, Frank Chance is released by the Cubs. He will manage the newly named New York Yankees for 2 years.

OCTOBER

2nd In the fight for 2nd place, Cubs C Dick Cotter bats out of turn against Pittsburgh. Pirates manager Fred Clarke doesn't realize it until the game is over, but his protest is later upheld by NL President Lynch.

5th The Red Sox defeat the A's 3–0 for their 105th win of the season, an AL record until the 1927 Yankees' 110.

6th Pirates OF Owen "Chief" Wilson hits his 36th triple, a ML season record that still stands. Trying to stretch it into a HR, he is nipped at the plate.

Cubs 3B Heinie Zimmerman, 0-for-3 in his final game, has just 2 hits in the last week, but he holds on to win the Triple Crown, leading by one in HRs and RBI.

8th The WS opens. Giants manager John McGraw goes with Jeff Tesreau, his most effective late-season pitcher, against the Red Sox. Smokey Joe Wood fans 11 and wins 4–3 before 35,730 at New York.

9th Three errors by Giants SS Art Fletcher help put Christy Mathewson behind 4–2 until the team rallies for 3 in the 8th when Duffy Lewis muffs a fly ball by Fred Snodgrass. Boston ties it in the last of the 8th. The Giants push across a run in the 10th off reliever "Sea Lion" Hall, but Tris Speaker blasts a triple to deep center. Apparently out at home trying to stretch it into a HR, he is safe when C Art Wilson, who has just entered the game, drops the throw for New York's 5th error. Darkness ends the game at 6–6 after 11 innings.

10th In game 3, New York evens the Series behind Rube Marquard, who blanks the Red Sox until the 9th. A spectacular catch in deep LF by Josh Devore with 2 men on saves a 2–1 victory.

11th Joe Wood faces Tesreau again in New York. Despite giving up 9 hits, Wood walks none and works out of several jams for a 3–1 win.

12th In Boston for game 5, the Red Sox scratch only 2 runs off Mathewson on 5 hits, but 18-game winner Hugh Bedient holds the Giants to 3 hits. The 2–1 win gives Boston a 3–1 Series edge.

14th The Giants come out swinging against Bucky O'Brien: 4 singles, 2 doubles, 3 stolen bases, and a balk produce 5 runs. New York's Marquard gives up 2 in the 2nd, and that's all the scoring for the day.

15th In game 7 on a cold day in Boston, the Giants catch up with Joe Wood's smoke, teeing off for 6 runs on 7 hits before the 32,694 fans have settled down. Jeff Tesreau wobbles to an 11–4 win and the Series is tied at 3 all. The only Boston bright spot is Tris Speaker's unassisted double play in the 8th, the only one by an OF in WS play.

16th In the Series finale, Mathewson squares off against Hugh Bedient in quest of his first win of the Series. He takes a 1–0 lead into the 7th, but with one out, Boston manager Jake Stahl hits a pop-up to short LF. The ball drops among Art Fletcher, Josh Devore, and Fred Snodgrass. Honus Wagner walks, and with 2 outs, pinch hitter Olaf Henriksen doubles home the tying run. Smokey Joe Wood relieves Bedient, and the 2 aces match zeroes until "Red" Murray doubles and Merkle singles in the 10th to give New York a 2–1 lead. In the last of the 10th, pinch hitter Clyde Engle lifts a can of corn to CF Snodgrass, who drops the ball. Snodgrass then makes a great catch of a long drive by Harry Hooper. Steve Yerkes walks, bringing up Tris Speaker, who pops a high foul along the 1B line. C Chief Meyers chases it, but it drops a few feet from 1B Merkle, who could have taken it easily. Reprieved, Speaker then singles in the tying run and sends Yerkes to 3B. After Duffy Lewis is walked intentionally, 3B Larry Gardner hits a long fly to Devore that scores Yerkes with the winning run. The Red Sox earn $4,024.68 each; the Giants' share is $2,566.47 each.

17th Phils owner Horace Fogel will be tried by the NL directors for his charges against Cardinals manager Roger Bresnahan and the NL umps. In November he is found guilty on 5 counts and barred from the NL forever. Bresnahan is released by St. Louis with 4 years remaining on his contract.

24th The Cubs name Johnny Evers to manage the team in 1913. Between 1912 and 1916, each member of the Tinker-Evers-Chance infield will manage the team.

NOVEMBER

4th Miller Huggins is named manager of the St. Louis Cardinals, beginning his 17-year career as a skipper.

9th Frank Chance is sold to the Cincinnati Reds; when all NL clubs waive claims to him in December, the Reds free him to manage the Yankees.

16th The Reds buy infielder Red Corriden from Detroit

26th John T. Brush dies while en route to California by train for his health. His son-in-law, Harry Hempstead, will succeed him as president of the Giants.

DECEMBER

11th The Reds trade outfielderss Mike Mitchell and Pete Knisely, infielders Red Corriden and Art Phelan, and P Bert Humphries to the Cubs for C Harry Chapman, P Grover Lowdermilk, and SS Joe Tinker, who will manage the Reds for one year.

1913

JANUARY

8th Frank Chance inherits Hal Chase and the weakest lineup the New York Yankees will ever have when he signs to manage the team.

10th Sent down to Louisville by the Cubs, Three Finger Brown is bought by Cincinnati. He will be 11–12 with a 2.91 ERA for the 7th-place Reds.

11th With the Phils franchise in disarray following the expulsion of President Horace Fogel, William H. Locke and his cousin William F. Baker buy the club.

22nd The Giants give the Yankees permission to use the Polo Grounds for the 1913 season only, as the lease on the Hilltop grounds has expired. The Yankees will remain as tenants through 1922.

FEBRUARY

1st Jim Thorpe signs with the New York Giants, but the Indian Olympic-medal winner will be more of a gate attraction than a threat at the plate.

MARCH

4th The Yankees are the first team to train outside the U.S. when they travel to Bermuda for spring practice.

8th The Federal League is organized as a 6-team "outlaw" circuit and elects John T. Powers president. It will play 120 games at a level equivalent to the lower minor leagues, but will enhance its status considerably in 1914 to challenge the MLs.

28th St. Louis Browns infielder Buzzy Wares is "traded" to the Montgomery, AL, team in exchange for use of the minor league stadium by the Browns for spring training.

APRIL

5th An exhibition game with the newly christened Yankees opens Ebbets Field; 25,000 are on hand to watch Nap Rucker beat the New Yorkers 3–2. The first HR is hit by Brooklyn's Casey Stengel, who legs out an inside-the-parker.

9th With league approval, the Dodgers play their opener—and first regular-season game at Ebbets Field—a day ahead of the rest of the league. Cold weather keeps the crowd down to about 12,000, and the Phils' Tom Seaton beats Nap Rucker 1–0.

10th President Woodrow Wilson, who receives a gold pass from Ban Johnson, throws out the first ball at Washington's home opener. In their first official game as Yankees, New York loses to Walter Johnson 2–1. After giving up an unearned run in the first, Johnson begins a string of shutout innings that will reach a record 56 before the St. Louis Cardinals score in the 4th on May 14th.

23rd Christy Mathewson sets down the Phils 3–1, throwing just 67 pitches.

25th Perennial spring training holdout Ty Cobb signs for the 1913 season.

Giants pinch-hitting specialist Moose McCormick is called upon to get a hit twice in one at bat. With the winning run on base, he singles to win the game. But umpire Bill Klem says his back was turned and he didn't see it, so McCormick has to try again. This time he hits into a double play.

29th After a game in St. Louis, the Reds' trainer forgets to load the uniforms on the train. In Chicago, they borrow White Sox road uniforms and lose to the Cubs 7–2.

Christy Mathewson beats Nap Rucker 6–0 in 13 innings and gives up no walks. He will not walk a batter for 47 innings, then will top his own record later in the year. During his 25–11 season, Matty will walk 21 and hit none.

MAY

4th The U.S. League tries to compete as a ML, with teams in Baltimore, Brooklyn, Philadelphia, Reading, New York, Newark, Washington, and Lynchburg. They will open May 10th and fold May 12th; Baltimore is the pennant winner with a 2–0 record.

6th Better organized and financed than other aspiring circuits, the Federal League opens modestly and quietly, with clubs in Chicago, Cleveland, Pittsburgh, Indianapolis, St. Louis, Kansas City, and Covington, KY. No attempt is made to sign established ML players. Cy Young manages Cleveland, Deacon Phillippe manages Pittsburgh. After a 6-week season, the pennant winner is Indianapolis.

16th Pirates OF Ed Mensor will draw 8 walks all year, but one of them comes in the 3rd inning against New York, ending Mathewson's string of perfect control at 47 innings.

22nd Ruling that a ballplayer on the field is a "public person," a New York judge throws out cases brought by New York and Boston players against a motion picture company that took movies of the 1912 World Series.

30th John McGraw joins Fred Clarke, Cap Anson, Frank Selee, and Connie Mack as managers who have won 1,000 games.

31st Accusing Hal Chase of playing below his capability, Yankees manager Frank Chance sends him to the White Sox for infielder Rollie Zeider and 1B Babe Borton. Despite his uncertain character and questionable honesty, Chase will be on the scene another 6 years.

JUNE

5th Chris Von der Ahe, 65, owner of the champion St. Louis Browns in the 1880s and 1890s, dies of cirrhosis of the liver.

6th The Yankees, on their way to a 7th-place finish, drop their 13th straight 2–1 to Cleveland. After losing their first 18 home games, they will win one over the White Sox the next day.

11th The Browns end an A's 15-game winning streak, but Philadelphia's 5-game lead over Cleveland will be maintained to the end.

Ivy Olson of Cleveland steals home in the top of the 15th for the winning run over the Red Sox. Jack Graney then steals home for an insurance run, marking the only time teammates would steal home in extra innings in the same game.

16th The Cubs hand Grover Cleveland Alexander his first loss of the year after 10 victories 13–3, cutting the Phils' lead to 3.

19th Wilbur Good hits the first pinch-hit HR in Cubs history.

30th The same ball is used for the entire game in the Reds' 9–6 win over the Cubs.

New York's 11–1 win over the Phils puts the Giants on top to stay.

JULY

12th Philadelphia's Boardwalk Brown walks 15 Tigers in 7⅔ innings, but staggers to a 16–9 win.

15th Jake Stahl, hobbled by a foot injury, resigns as Red Sox manager. C Bill Carrigan replaces him.

18th In blanking the Cards 5–0, Mathewson yields a base on balls, ending a record string of 68 walkless innings pitched.

25th A 15-inning 8–8 tie game between St. Louis and the Nationals is called for darkness. Walter Johnson fans 15 in the last 11 innings, but he hits rookie catcher Sam Agnew with a pitch, breaking his jaw. Browns P Carl Weilman becomes the first player in history to strike out 6 consecutive times in a game.

Pirates OF Max Carey scores 5 runs against the Phils without a hit, reaching first on an error and 4 walks. A student at St. Louis Theological Seminary, he will lead the NL in runs this season. He will lead in stolen bases as well, the first of 10 such seasons.

AUGUST

2nd It's Walter Johnson Day in Washington. President Wilson is on hand to help mark the Big Train's 6th anniversary in a Nationals uniform. Johnson is presented with a silver cup filled with 10-dollar bills, and returns the favor with a 3–2 win over Detroit.

The Federal League takes a big step toward another baseball war, voting to expand into the East.

6th C Larry McLean is traded from the last-place Cardinals to the pennant-contending Giants for Doc Crandall. One of the biggest players of this era at 6 feet 5inches and 230 pounds, the veteran catcher will bat .500 in the WS.

13th Petersburg P Harry Hedgpeth (Virginia League) blanks Richmond twice, by scores of 1–0 and 10–0, both in 9 innings. He gives up only one hit in the opener, while hurling a no-hitter in the 2nd game.

14th William H. Locke, who bought the 2nd-place Phils earlier this year, dies. His cousin William Baker will succeed him.

17th The A's break another attendance record in Cleveland, drawing 25,017 to watch the home team's 6–2 win.

18th Doc Crandall is rescued from the basement: McGraw buys him back 12 days after trading him.

Philadelphia's Erskine Mayer sets an NL mark by surrendering 9 consecutive hits to the Cubs in the 9th inning of their game. The Cubs score 6 runs to win 10–4.

19th Grover Cleveland Alexander matches Mayer by giving up 9 consecutive hits and 6 runs to the Cubs in a 9–4 loss.

28th Walter Johnson's 14-game winning streak is ended, although it takes Boston 11 innings to beat him 1–0. Johnson will lose a record 20 games 1–0 in his career.

30th With 2 outs in the top of the 9th, and the Phils leading 8–6 over New York, umpire Bill Brennan suddenly orders Phils captain Mickey Doolan to have spectators removed from the bleachers, where they are waving hats, newspapers, and handkerchiefs to distract the batters. When Doolan refuses, Brennan forfeits the game to the Giants. The Phils protest, and NL president Lynch reverses the umpire and rules the game an 8–6 Phils win. The Giants then appeal. NL directors say both Brennan and Lynch are wrong, and order the game completed from the point at which it was stopped. The game will be completed October 2.

SEPTEMBER

1st Frederick W. Thayer, inventor of the catcher's mask, dies at 65.

4th Cleveland lefty Vean Gregg strikes out Ty Cobb three times in a row, but Cobb doubles in the winning run in the 12th.

6th Athletics 2B Eddie Collins steals home twice in a game against the Red Sox to tie the ML mark.

10th Honus Wagner is given a souvenir bat carved from a piece of wood taken from naval hero Oliver Perry's flagship *Niagara,* which was sunk in Lake Erie 100 years before.

14th Cubs hurler Larry Cheney hurls a 14-hit shutout against the Giants, defeating them 7–0 while setting a ML record for most hits allowed in a white-

washing. Milt Gaston of Washington will duplicate the feat on July 10, 1928.

15th Frank L. Hough, sports editor of the Philadelphia *Inquirer,* and one of 2 writers who owned 25 percent of the Athletics when the team was founded, dies.

22nd Herb Pennock, 19, aided by Eddie Plank, blanks the Tigers 1–0 to clinch the AL pennant for the A's.

27th The Giants lose to Brooklyn, but the pennant is theirs, as the Phils also lose.

29th Walter Johnson wins his 36th game and 12th shutout of the year, defeating the Athletics 1–0 on George McBride Day, a day honoring the Nationals' captain and SS.

OCTOBER

2nd The Giants and Phils wrap up the season with 7 games in 3 days. The August 30th game, called in the 9th, is completed for a Phillie victory. The following doubleheader is split. Tomorrow the Giants will win one and tie one. The day after they will win both.

4th Despite the Dodgers' 6th-place finish, 1B Jake Daubert earns a new Chalmers automobile as the NL MVP. Daubert led the NL at .350 and will repeat his batting title in 1914.

Washington manager Clark Griffith uses an unheard-of 8 pitchers in an end-of-season farce game with Boston. At age 43, he pitches one inning himself, and coach John Ryan, also 43, catches him.

7th Rube Marquard gets the call for the Giants against Philadelphia's Chief Bender in game one of the WS. Bender yields 11 hits, but Frank Baker's HR and 3 RBI pace a 6–4 win over the New Yorkers.

8th Christy Mathewson ties the Series, shutting the Athletics out for 10 innings to beat Eddie Plank 3–0. Mathewson also brings in the winning run with a double in the 10th.

9th In game 3, the A's have no trouble solving Jeff Tesreau. Rookie P Bullet Joe Bush throws a 5-hit 8–2 win before 36,896 at the Polo Grounds, the largest crowd of the Series.

10th　The bottom of the Athletics batting order—Jack Barry, Wally Schang, and Chief Bender—drives in all the runs, as Bender wins his 4th straight WS game 6–5.

11th　John McGraw loses his 3rd straight WS. In game 5, Mathewson is good, but Plank is better; his 2-hitter wins the 3–1 finale. Frank Baker at .450 and Eddie Collins at .421 lead a strong A's offense.

12th　John McGraw hosts a reunion for Hugh Jennings and the old Orioles. After a night of heavy drinking, he blames his longtime friend, business partner, and teammate Wilbert Robinson for too many coaching mistakes in the Series. Robbie replies that McGraw made more mistakes than anybody. McGraw fires him. Eyewitnesses say Robbie douses McGraw with a glass of beer and leaves. They won't speak to each other for 17 years. Six days later Robbie will begin a legendary 18 years as Brooklyn manager. The team will carry the nickname Robins, as well as Dodgers, during his tenure.

19th　The Giants and White Sox, fortified with other players, start their world tour in Cincinnati. After a 31-game tour to Seattle, they will head for the Philippines, Australia, China, and Japan.

NOVEMBER

2nd　St. Louis Browns manager George Stovall is the first ML player to jump to the Federal League, signing to manage Kansas City. With glib salesman Jim Gilmore as its president, and backed by several millionaires, including oil magnate Harry Sinclair and Brooklyn baker Robert Ward, the Feds declare open war 2 weeks later by announcing they will not honor the ML's reserve clause. It will prove a long, costly struggle, similar to the AL's beginnings, but with more losers than winners.

17th　Former star P Rube Waddell is picked up in St. Louis, wandering around the streets and suffering from consumption.

24th　Joe Tinker is out as Reds manager, but is still their property as a player. On December 12th he will be sold to Brooklyn for $25,000, $10,000 of which goes to him. P Earl Yingling and OF Herbie Moran are sent to Cincinnati later as part of the deal. When Charles Ebbets puts off signing Tinker, he jumps to the Feds, signing to manage Chicago for $12,000.

DECEMBER

6th　Exhibition teams made up of White Sox and Giants players make a Tokyo stop as part of their world tour and play each other at Keio University Stadium. The Sox win 9–4. The next day, a combined team defeats Keio University 16–3, then the White Sox beat the Giants 12–3. Nearly a decade will pass before American professionals again play in Japan.

9th　John K. Tener, onetime pitcher and congressman, now governor of Pennsylvania, is elected NL president for four years. John Heydler is elected secretary.

12th　The Reds trade OF Bob Bescher to the Giants for Buck Herzog, who replaces Tinker as manager and SS.

1914

JANUARY

6th The National Commission grants some demands of the Players' Fraternity: players to be notified in writing of their transfer or release and to receive a copy of their contract; players with 10 years in the ML are eligible to become free agents; clubs will pay traveling expenses to spring training and furnish all uniforms; all parks to have a blank green wall behind the pitcher in CF.

FEBRUARY

1st The White Sox and Giants play a 3–3 tie in Cairo. The next day a triple play will be made in the shadow of the Pyramids.

3rd A joint NL-AL rules committee decrees that: a runner touched or held by a coach while rounding 3B is out; coaches may now assist other members of their team, not just base runners; the frequently violated rule requiring pitchers to stand behind the rubber until ready to pitch is rescinded—they may now stand on the rubber; base runners are now not permitted to run on an infield fly. A move to eliminate the intentional walk is defeated.

9th Veteran umpire Hank O'Day, who managed the Reds in 1912, signs to skipper the Cubs.

The world tourists arrive in Rome where they stage a demonstration of the game. After a private audience with the Pope, they travel to Paris. They will be rained out in Paris and end the tour in England on February 26th before King George V.

11th Declining to remain with the Cubs as a player, Johnny Evers goes to the Boston Braves.

21st Charles W. Murphy sells the Cubs to Charles P. Taft of Cincinnati.

APRIL

1st Future Hall of Famer Rube Waddell, weakened by a heroic effort to help contain a winter flood in Kentucky, dies at 37 of tuberculosis in a San Antonio sanitarium.

8th An attempt to legalize Sunday baseball in Massachusetts is defeated.

13th After building 8 new ballparks in 3 months, the Federal League opens with the Baltimore Terrapins beating Buffalo 3–2 before 27,140. Winning P Jack Quinn will win 26 and lose 14. Indianapolis will win the pennant, led by rookie Benny Kauff's league-leading .370 batting average. Ex-Pirate Claude Hendrix will be 29–11.

20th The 25-player limit is suspended in the AL and NL. With uncertainty over who has signed with what teams, it is almost impossible to know how many players may be on the roster at any one time.

22nd At age 19, Babe Ruth's first professional game (as a pitcher) is a 6-hit 6–0 win for Baltimore (International League) over Buffalo. The 2nd batter he faces is Joe McCarthy, the manager he will play for 17 years later with New York. Ruth is 2-for-4.

25th Browns catcher Frank Crossin throws out Detroit's Sam Crawford at 2B, and the return throw from Del Pratt nips Ty Cobb at home, for a rare double play on a double steal. the Tigers win anyway 4–0.

MAY

14th The White Sox' Jim Scott pitches a no-hitter for 9 innings, then loses to Washington 1–0 in the 10th. The first hit is by Chick Gandil, who scores on Howard Shanks's hit. It is the first of a record 3 no-hitters that White Sox rookie C Ray Schalk will catch in his 17 years with the team.

16th Jeff Tesreau's no-hit bid against Pittsburgh is spoiled with 2 outs in the 9th when Joe Kelly gets a hit. Tesreau wins 2–0 against Pittsburgh.

26th Red Sox righthander Rube Foster's string of 42 consecutive scoreless innings is stopped by Cleveland in the 5th inning. The Naps prevail 3–2.

31st Joe Benz, who will be the AL's leading loser with 19, no-hits Cleveland 6–1 at Comiskey Park.

JUNE

3rd P Chief Johnson jumps from Cincinnati to Kansas City (FL); a judge grants a permanent injunction against him playing for KC, but he pitches for the Packers through 1915.

5th Opelika (Georgia-Alabama League) P John Cantley slugs 3 grand slams and a single for 15 RBI in a game against Talladega, winning the contest 19–1.

JULY

5th Big Ed Walsh makes his first start since straining his right arm in 1913 spring training. He lasts 7 innings in a White Sox win over Cleveland 6–3.

7th Suffering heavy losses from Federal League competition in Baltimore, the Orioles' (IL) owner Jack Dunn offers Babe Ruth (plus Ernie Shore and C Ben Egan) for $10,000 to old friend Connie Mack, who refuses, pleading poverty. Cincinnati, which has a working agreement giving them the choice of 2 players, takes OF George Twombley and SS Claud Derrick. Dunn finally peddles his threesome to new owner Joe Lannin of the Red Sox for a reported $25,000.

9th Austin of the Texas League loses its 27th straight.

Ossee Schreckengost, 39, peripatetic catcher (7 teams) best known as battery and roommate of Rube Waddell while with the Athletics, dies of uremia at Philadelphia. Skilled defensively on the field, Schreckengost was an eccentric off. He had it written into his contract that Waddell could not eat crackers in bed.

11th Babe Ruth breaks in with Boston, pitching a 4–3 win over Cleveland. In his first ML time at bat, Ruth strikes out. He will be 2–1 with Boston, spending most of the year at Providence (IL).

Only 26 people see Newark (IL) fade 2–0 at Baltimore.

17th Giants OF Red Murray is knocked unconscious by lightning after catching a fly ball that ends a 21-inning victory over Pittsburgh. Murray is uninjured. Pittsburgh's Babe Adams pitches all 21 innings without yielding a single walk, the longest non-walk game in ML history.

Rube Marquard and Babe Adams go 21 innings before Larry Doyle's HR gives the Giants a 3–1 win over the Pirates. Adams yields no walks and 12 hits; Marquard walks 2 (one intentional) and yields 15 hits. This is the last game Marquard will win in 1914. He will lose 10 straight on his way to a 12–22 record for the Giants this year.

In the 6th, Honus Wagner goes from first to 3B on a hit by Jim Viox. When New York CF Bob Bescher throws to 3B Milt Stock, the ball bounces out of his hands and disappears. Wanger scores before its discovered that the ball had bounced up under his arm and stayed there as he ran home. Wagner is called out for interference. The Pirates protest.

19th The Braves get 3 runs in the 9th to beat the Reds 3–2 and climb out of last place on their way to the pennant. During that journey, they will pass the Reds going the other way, as today's loss starts the Reds' fall from 2nd place to last.

AUGUST

3rd Against Detroit in the 2nd inning, Les Nunamaker, Yankees catcher, becomes the only man in the 20th century to throw out 3 would-be base stealers in an inning.

11th Boston Braves P Lefty Tyler begins a string of 23 shutout innings, but Red Ames of the Reds matches him today in a 13-inning 0–0 tie. Four days later, Tyler will beat Christy Mathewson 2–0 in 10.

After missing 6 weeks, first with broken ribs, then a broken thumb, Ty Cobb signs a new 3-year contract and returns to the lineup. He and Sam Crawford had been offered double their salaries to jump to the Feds. Cobb will get into just 97 games, but he will win another batting crown at .368. Under existing rules his 345 at bats are enough to qualify.

15th Brooklyn 1B Jake Daubert ties a ML record by recording 4 sacrifices in the 2nd game of a doubleheader sweep against Philadelphia 8–4, 13–5.

23rd The Giants lose to Cincinnati 3–2, and the Braves move into a tie for first place. Four days later a 3–2 loss to St. Louis will drop the Braves back to 3rd. The next day a doubleheader sweep will bounce them back to 2nd.

31st Jack Fournier, 1B of the White Sox, hits 2 HRs off Walter Johnson, both inside the park. The 2nd comes in the 10th to give Chicago a 4–3 victory. He will be the only player to hit 2 HRs off the Big Train in one game until August 13, 1926, when Lou Gehrig will connect twice.

Walter Johnson relieves in the 8th inning with his Senators holding a 3–2 lead over the White Sox. On the first pitch, Jack Fournier hits a HR to tie the game.

Fournier next at bat up comes in the 10th and he homers again to give the Sox a 4–3 win. This is the first time Johnson has been reached for 2 HRs in a game by the same batter (Gehrig will match it in 1926). The night before the Sox beat Johnson 2–1 and Fournier was 3-for-3 with 2 triples against the "Big Train."

SEPTEMBER

2nd   The NL lead seesaws. Beaten by Brooklyn 6–2 while the Braves win 2, the Giants drop out of first place for the first time since May 30. The next day they sweep 2 from Brooklyn and retake the top spot.

5th   Pitching for Providence in the IL, 19-year-old Babe Ruth beats Toronto 9–0 with a one-hitter, and hits his only minor league HR.

7th   The Braves and Giants play an A.M.-P.M. twin bill in Boston on Labor Day. To accommodate the crowds, the Braves have moved their home games to Fenway Park. The contenders draw 74,163 on the day.

Floods severely damage the Kansas City Packers' (FL) ballpark, washing away fences and demolishing the clubhouse.

9th   George A. Davis, a Harvard law student, pitches the only shutout of his brief career, a 7–0 no-hitter for the first-place Braves over the Phils. The spitballer walks the bases loaded with no outs in the 5th, but "he rose to the occasion to prove his perfect candidacy to a niche in the hall of stars," writes the Boston *Post*. He will be 3–3 this year and next, then hang up his glove to start a law practice.

12th   Yankee SS Roger Peckinpaugh, 23, replaces Frank Chance and becomes the all-time youngest manager, and the 7th in the club's 12-year existence. He will win 9 of 17 games and will manage next at Cleveland in 1928.

19th   Ed Lafitte pitches a 6–2 no-hitter for the Brooklyn Tip-Tops (FL) over the Kansas City Packers. Wildness costs him the 2 runs. He will lead the FL with 127 walks.

22nd   Boston (AL) P Ray Collins hurls 2 complete-game victories over the Tigers, winning by scores of 5–3 and 5–0.

23rd   After dropping their 19th straight in the first of 2 at Boston, the Reds break the longest losing streak in the club's history (and 3rd longest in the NL) when Charles "King" Lear wins his only game of the year and only shutout ever, 3–0.

Rube Marquard loses his 12th in a row, as the Cards sink the Giants twice, but the Cards fall short of overtaking New York in 2nd place by 2½ games.

27th   The Athletics clinch the AL pennant.

Cleveland 2B Nap Lajoie collects his 3,000th ML hit, as the Indians defeat the Yankees 5–3.

29th   The Boston Braves, who were in last place in mid-July, clinch the pennant with a sensational second-half drive.

OCTOBER

1st   Phillies OF Gavvy Cravath hits HR No. 19 to lead the NL. He also leads NL OF with 34 assists in RF.

6th   The Brooklyn Robins (aka the Dodgers) split with Boston and finish 5th, their highest level since 1907. The Braves lose regular 3B Red Smith, who breaks his right leg sliding into 1B.

In the Federal League, the Chicago Whales lose to Kansas City while the Indianapolis Hoosiers beat St. Louis, giving Indianapolis a 1½ game pennant margin. Five .300 hitters, led by Benny Kauff's .370, pace the winners. For the Whales, Claude Hendrix is the FL's top pitcher, 29–11.

9th   The Boston Braves go into the WS as underdogs, despite their strong finish. Only one regular, LF Joe Connolly, hit .300. Their strengths are pitchers Dick Rudolph, George "Lefty" Tyler, and "Seattle Bill" James, 2B Johnny Evers, who wins Chalmers's final MVP automobile, and SS Rabbit Maranville, their cleanup hitter. The Philadelphia A's Eddie Collins, with a .344 BA, wins the Chalmers AL award with 63 of 64 possible points. The A's have 7 pitchers with 10 or more wins, led by Chief Bender's 17–3. Bender's WS magic is quickly dispelled as the Braves knock him out in the 6th. Rudolph coasts to a 5-hit 7–1 victory. Hank Gowdy has a single, double, and triple. He will hit a WS record .545, and Evers, .438. Only Ruth will top Gowdy with .625 in 1928. Bender makes his last WS appearance, finishing with a record 59 strikeouts.

10th   In game 2, Bill James and Eddie Plank match zeroes for 8. In the 9th, Boston's Charlie Deal doubles, steals 3B, and scores on Les Mann's single. James gives up 2 hits.

12th　Joe Bush, 17–10 for the A's, faces Lefty Tyler in game 3. Tied 2–2 in the 10th, Home Run Baker drives in his only 2 runs of the Series, but a HR by Gowdy starts a game-tying rally. After James comes on and sets the A's down for 2 innings, Gowdy doubles. Bush gives up a walk, then throws a sacrifice bunt past Baker at 3B allowing pinch runner Les Mann to score the winning run.

13th　The first WS sweep in history belongs to the Braves—the only WS the franchise will ever win. Bob Shawkey and Herb Pennock allow just 6 hits, but one is a 2-run single by Evers, as Rudolph wins 3–1.

18th　NL and AL all-star teams, featuring stars such as Grover Alexander, Jeff Tesreau, Joe Bush, and Bill James, start an exhibition tour that will take them to Hawaii after wandering throughout the West. The NL will win 29 of the 50 games played.

20th　Veteran C Pat Moran is named manager of the 6th-place Phils.

NOVEMBER

1st　Connie Mack begins cleaning house, asks waivers on Jack Coombs, Eddie Plank, and Chief Bender. Colby Jack goes to Brooklyn (NL). Plank and Bender escape Mack's maneuvering by jumping to the Federal League. Although all have some life left in their soupbones, they are near their careers' end, and departure is more sentimental than serious. Mack's excuse: retrenchment. Despite the pennant, Philadelphia fans did not support the A's and the club lost $50,000.

5th　The Court of Appeals upholds a ban on Sunday baseball in Washington, DC.

18th　Roger Bresnahan signs to manage the Cubs.

DECEMBER

4th　Walter Johnson accepts an advance from the FL Chicago Whales. Clark Griffith threatens to take Johnson to court, claiming he has paid Johnson for the reserve option in his contract. Ban Johnson says Johnson was on the market and is "damaged goods," worth getting rid of. Griffith travels to Coffeyville, KS, to persuade his franchise player that the option clause is legal and binding. Whales manager Joe Tinker says he has signed Johnson for $16,000 and given him a $6,000 bonus. Two weeks later Griffith signs Johnson for 3 years at $12,500 per year and returns the bonus to the Feds.

6th　Indoor baseball is a winter fad in some cities. In Chicago $2,000 is raised at an indoor game for the benefit of the family of Jimmy Doyle, deceased former Chicago 3B.

7th　Chief Bender signs a 2-year deal with the Federal League; he will be assigned to Baltimore.

8th　After weeks of rumors, the bomb drops: Connie Mack sells Eddie Collins, generally regarded as the game's finest position player, to the White Sox for $50,000. Collins signs a 5-year contract worth $75,000 and gets $15,000 as a signing bonus. The deal breaks up the A's "$100,000 infield" and raises conjecture that Mack, too, will leave to manage the Yankees.

The NL votes to hold the 1915 player limit to 21 per team.

14th　Former Giants pitcher and mascot Charley "Victory" Faust is confined to the Western Hospital for the Insane.

17th　Charles Comiskey pulls a surprise, reaching down to Peoria and naming Clarence "Pants" Rowland, scout and minor league executive, to manage his White Sox.

31st　Ban Johnson's efforts to strengthen the New York Yankees succeed when he arranges the purchase of the team by Colonel Jacob Ruppert and Cap Huston for $460,000. The new owners will name longtime Detroit P Bill Donovan as manager.

1915

JANUARY

2nd   The Cardinals try to prevent OF Lee Magee, 25, from playing for the Brooklyn Tip-Tops. Like most such suits, it will fail. Magee will play and manage in the Federal League.

4th   Hans Lobert, "fastest man" in the NL, is traded by the Phils to the Giants for righthander Al Demaree, infielder Milt Stock, and C Bert Adams.

5th   The FL sues organized baseball, claiming it to be an illegal trust and asking that it be dissolved and all contracts voided. The case is filed in U.S. court in Chicago, before Judge Kenesaw Mountain Landis. He will stall his decision, and peace is declared at the end of the year. The league shifts players to beef up teams in key cities. Benny Kauff, the FL's answer to Ty Cobb, is moved from Indianapolis to Brooklyn.

Thirteen years after a Pennsylvania Supreme Court decision effectively banned him from playing for the Athletics, Nap Lajoie rejoins them. With Lajoie leaving Cleveland, a local newpaper will run a contest to rename the Naps. The winning nickname will be the Indians, after the late Lou Sockalexis, a Penobscot Indian who was a popular Cleveland player in the late 1890's.

9th   The National Commission declares University of Michigan senior George Sisler a free agent after a 2-year fight. The Pirates' owner Barney Dreyfuss claimed rights to Sisler, who had signed a contract as a minor but never played pro ball. After graduating, Sisler will sign with the St. Louis Browns, managed by his former college coach, Branch Rickey.

24th   In a retreat from the FL competition, the Baltimore Orioles of the International League move to Richmond, VA. With the demise of the FL, the Orioles will return to Baltimore.

FEBRUARY

3rd   The AL bans the emery ball, a pitch introduced by Russ Ford in 1910.

11th   The International League tries to put a team in the Bronx, but Giants president Hempstead objects.

16th   Home Run Baker, 28, announces retirement following a contract dispute with Connie Mack. He will sit out the 1915 season.

APRIL

14th   The A's Herb Pennock comes within one out of pitching the first Opening Day no-hitter. A scratch single by Harry Hooper is the Red Sox' only hit in a 5–0 loss.

15th   Rube Marquard, who lost 22 games for the Giants in 1914, pitches a 2–0 no-hitter over Brooklyn in the Giants' 2nd game of the season. The loser is Nap Rucker, who pitched a no-hitter in 1908.

19th   St. Louis Cardinals righthander Lee Meadows makes his NL debut and becomes the first player to wear glasses regularly on the field since P Will White in 1886. Later in the season, Carmen Hill will become the 2nd pitcher to do so.

22nd   A's newly acquired 2B Nap Lajoie makes 5 errors in a 7–6 loss to the Boston Red Sox. He is the last of 7 players to boot that many in one game.

24th   Frank Allen, Pittsburgh (FL) lefty, pitches a 2–0 no-hitter against the St. Louis Terriers. Allen will win 23 for Pittsburgh, who will finish 3rd just a half game back of the first-place Chicago Whales and the 2nd-place Terriers.

29th   FL star Benny Kauff jumps from the Brookfeds to the Giants. When Boston refuses to play if Kauff is in the Giants' lineup, ump Quigley forfeits the game to New York. The 2 teams agree to play an exhibition game. The other ump, Mal Eason, telephones NL president John Tener, who declares Kauff ineligible until reinstated and orders Eason to forfeit the game to Boston. Meanwhile, the Braves win the exhibition game 13–8. The next day Tener rules this the official game, and both forfeits are canceled. Kauff goes back to Brooklyn where he leads the FL at .342, and McGraw has to wait until next year to sign him.

MAY

6th   Red Sox P Babe Ruth hits his first ML HR off the Yankees Jack Warhop in the 3rd inning at New York's Polo Grounds. Ruth has 2 other hits but loses the game in the 13th.

12th White Sox righthander Red Faber throws just 67 pitches in beating Washington 4–1 on 3 hits.

A's C Wally Schang nails an AL-record 6 would-be base stealers in a 3–0 Browns victory.

15th Claude Hendrix pitches a 10–0 no-hitter for Chicago (FL) over Pittsburgh.

29th Connie Mack waives Herb Pennock to the Red Sox.

JUNE

4th Tim Hurst, colorful umpire who was often in the center of controversy, dies at 49.

Ty Cobb steals home in a 3–0 Detroit win. Yankee pitcher Ray Caldwell is so angry at the safe call he throws his mitt in the air and is promptly ejected by umpire Silk O'Laughlin. It is Cobb's 2nd steal of home while Caldwell is on the mound (the first had been on May 12th, 1911).

5th Grover Alexander loses a no-hitter, but wins 3–0 when the Cards' Arthur Butler singles with 2 outs in the 9th. Alexander will pitch 4 one-hitters this season.

9th The Phils move into first place, as Alexander holds the Cubs hitless until the 7th. Alexander will be 31–10 and lead the NL with a 1.55 ERA, 36 CG, 376 IP, 241 strikeouts, and 12 shutouts.

11th Yankees P Ray Caldwell hits a pinch HR for the 2nd day in a row. Nobody else in the AL repeats the feat until Joe Cronin in 1943. The next day Caldwell will hit another, but he is on the mound in that game.

13th Philadelphia Athletics lefty Bruno Haas makes his debut against New York. He walks 16, and throws 3 wild pitches as he goes all the way in the 15–7 loss, his only ML decision.

17th George "Zip" Zabel comes out of the Cubs bullpen with 2 outs in the first and winds up with a 4–3 19-inning win over Brooklyn in the longest relief job ever.

18th Ty Cobb steals home twice in a game against Washington, on the front end of double and triple steals. Both steals come with Joe Boehling on the mound. Bull Henry is the starting catcher, but he leaves in the first with a spike wound from Cobb. The 5th-inning steal is with Buff Williams behind the plate. The steals make the difference in the 5–3 Detroit win.

Charley "Victory" Faust, 34, dies of pulmonary tuberculosis while confined to the Western Hospital for the Insane in Washington State.

23rd For the 5th time this month, Ty Cobb steals home, doing it in a 4–2 Tiger win over the St. Louis Browns.

JULY

2nd The A's sell Jack Barry for $8,000 to Boston. Five days later, they will sell Bob Shawkey to the Yankees for $18,000. Shawkey will win 168 games while wearing the Yankees new pinstripes.

8th The Pirates make just 2 assists, both by 2B Jim Viox, in a 9-inning game to tie a record set by the Giants August 9, 1906. On July 22, 1906, the Cincinnati Reds had no assists in a 7-inning game versus the Phils.

14th White Sox P Red Faber steals 3 bases in the 4th inning against the A's. With the White Sox leading 4–2 in the 4th and rain threatening, the A's try to delay the game. Joe Bush purposely hits Faber with a pitch, and Faber, trying to speed up the game, tries to get thrown out by stealing. Little effort is made to retire him, and he scores Chicago's 5th run. His "steal" of home turns out to be the winning run, as rain never materializes, and Chicago wins 6–4.

17th The Cubs end Alexander's 9-game win streak 4–0. Chicago and Philadelphia are deadlocked for the NL lead. In the AL, the White Sox spend their last day on top. The Tigers will challenge Boston down the stretch.

19th The Nationals come out running, stealing a record 8 bases against the Cleveland Indians in the first inning. Catcher Steve O'Neill is the victim of 3 SBs by Danny Moeller, 2 each by Clyde Milan and Ed Ainsmith, and one by George McBride in the 11–4 Washington win.

23rd Jack Ness of Oakland (Pacific Coast League) has his 49-game hitting streak stopped. He bats .440 in the longest streak thus far in organized baseball.

29th At 41, Honus Wagner becomes the oldest player in this century to hit a grand slam. It is inside the park against Jeff Pfeffer of Brooklyn in an 8–2 win. The record will stand until Tony Perez hits a grand slam on May 13, 1985, one day short of his 43rd birthday.

31st Dave Davenport of St. Louis (FL) splits a pair of 1–0 games in a doubleheader with Buffalo, winning the first and losing the 2nd. He becomes the only pitcher to be involved in two 1–0 decisions in one day.

AUGUST

7th As Brooklyn's rookie pitcher steps to the mound, St. Louis manager Miller Huggins, coaching at 3B, calls for the ball. The rookie obliges, Huggins steps aside, and the Cardinal runner scores. A change in the rules will prevent such trickery in the future.

8th Hank O'Day, who managed the Cubs in 1914, returns to umpiring.

16th Miles Main of Kansas City (FL) pitches a 5–0 no-hitter versus Buffalo.

17th Lefty Rube Benton pitches a 3–2 win for Pittsburgh over Chicago, but both the Cubs and Giants protest, claiming he belongs to New York. A week later, NL directors agree with them, upholding his purchase by the Giants from the Reds.

Fritz Maisel of the Yankees steals 2B, 3B, and home in the 9th inning against Philadelphia.

18th The new Braves Field opens in Boston. An estimated 46,500 jam the park to see the Braves beat the Cards 3–1.

Wilbur Good becomes the first Cub to steal 2B, 3B, and home in an inning. He does it in the 6th of a 9–0 beating of Brooklyn.

Asahi Shimbun, a Japanese newspaper, sponsors the first National High School baseball tournament. It is an instant success and will continue every August (except during W W II) to the present. It will often be called the Koshien Tournament, after the stadium near Osaka where the games will be played starting in 1924.

20th The White Sox obtain Joe Jackson from Cleveland in exchange for OF Robert Roth, OF Larry Chappell, P Ed Klepfer, and $31,500.

22nd In the 2nd inning of game one of a doubleheader versus Detroit, the crowd sees the Nationals score a run with no times at bat. Chick Gandil and Merito Acosta walk; Buff Williams sacrifices, and George McBride hits a sacrifice fly, scoring Gandil.

Acosta is caught off 2B when OF Bobby Veach throws to Ossie Vitt. Washington's Walter Johnson goes on to win 8–1 and snap the Tigers' 9-game win streak.

In the FL, Newark takes 2 from Pittsburgh and leads by one percentage point over Kansas City, with Pittsburgh 3rd and Chicago 4th, only 1½ games separating the teams. The race is so close by season's end Newark will be 5th, six games out. Chicago will win it by one point with 86-66 to St. Louis 87-67 and Pittsburgh's 86-67. There will be nine 20-game winners, led by George McConnell's 25-10 for the Whales, the only year McConnell wins more than 8 games.

29th George Sisler pitches against Walter Johnson and wins 2–1. He will be 4–4 for the Browns and 1–2 next year before moving permanently to 1B.

30th Three-time 20-game winner Larry Cheney is traded by the Cubs to Brooklyn for OF Joe Schultz.

31st Rube Marquard goes to Brooklyn on waivers.

Only 2 runners reach base as the Cubs' Jimmy Lavender pitches a 2–0 no-hitter against the Giants, the only shutout in his 11–16 season.

SEPTEMBER

3rd Cleveland 1B Jay Kirke swings at a wild pitch for strike 3 and reaches 1B. Cleveland beats the White Sox, who protest on the grounds that the rules did not permit Kirke to take 1B. The protest is upheld and the game ordered replayed.

7th The St. Louis Terriers' Dave Davenport, strikeout leader of the FL, pitches a 3–0 no-hitter over the Whales, one of his 10 shutouts and 22 wins. St. Louis will play 2 more games than Chicago and split them, thus trailing the Whales at season's end by one percentage point. Chicago will be 86–66; St. Louis, 87–67, and the Pittsburgh Rebels, 86–67. A percentage difference of .004, it is the closest bunching of the top 3 teams in any ML race.

8th Fred Clarke resigns as Pirates manager having won 4 pennants in 19 years.

10th Sporting goods manufacturer A. G. Spalding, one of the original players, managers, and executives of the NL, dies at 65 in Point Loma, CA.

22nd   Having loaned the Braves the use of their larger park in 1914, the Boston Red Sox request the use of the new, larger NL park for this year's WS.

29th   The Phils clinch their first pennant on Grover Alexander's 4th one-hitter and 12th shutout of the year 5–0 over the defending champion Braves.

30th   The Red Sox clinch the AL pennant by beating Detroit, giving them a 2½-game margin. The Tigers will win 100 games, the first time a runner-up has reached that mark.

OCTOBER

3rd   The Chicago Whales (FL) clinch the pennant by winning the 2nd game of a doubleheader with the Pittsburgh Rebels.

Ty Cobb steals his 96th base of the season against Cleveland's Steve O'Neil for a new ML season record. He also sets a record for caught stealing with 38.

6th   Rookie Elmer Myers, pitching in his first game, strikes out 12 Yankees, an AL record, as he wins 4–0.

8th   Babe Ruth's only appearance in this season's WS comes in the first game as a pinch hitter for Red Sox starter Ernie Shore. Grover Alexander holds a 3–1 lead in the 9th, as Ruth grounds out. He will sit out the rest of the Series.

9th   Playing game 2 in tiny Baker Bowl in Philadelphia, Boston's 19-game winner Rube Foster allows the Phils 3 hits and drives in the winning run to break a 1–1 tie in the 9th against Erskine Mayer. President Wilson is the first president to attend a WS game.

11th   In Boston, an unprecedented 42,300 are on hand for game 3 and see another 1–1 duel, which is decided in the 9th when Duffy Lewis singles home Harry Hooper for a 2–1 hometown win. Dutch Leonard walks none, yields 3 hits, and sets down the last 20 Phils to face him.

12th   In game 4, 41,096 see another 2–1 Boston victory, as Ernie Shore gets the win over surprise starter George Chalmers. Gavvy Cravath triples and scores the Phils' lone run.

13th   Back home, the Phils get 4 runs early off Rube Foster. The Red Sox break a tie in the 9th for the 3rd time, as reliever Eppa Rixey gives up Harry Hooper's 2nd HR of the game, and Boston wins the Series 4–1.

DECEMBER

22nd   Organized baseball and the Federal League sign a peace treaty at Cincinnati, ending their 2-year war. Feds agree to go out of existence, but the ML pay an enormous price: $600,000 for distribution to FL owners; amalgamation of 2 Fed franchises, one each into NL and AL; recognition of Fed players' eligibility, and agreement to bid for them in a Fed-controlled auction. Baltimore gets short shrift and balks, but conferees, eager for settlement, defer its claims—a decision they will repent at leisure.

1916

JANUARY

4th   The St. Louis Browns are the first of 2 ML franchises awarded to Federal League owners. Philip de Catesby Ball, ice-manufacturing tycoon and principal stockholder of the Feds' St. Louis Terriers, pays a reported $525,000 for the Browns and replaces manager Branch Rickey with his own Fielder Jones.

5th   The NL, happy to be rid of fractious Cubs owner Charles W. Murphy, allows Charles H. Weeghman, owner of a restaurant chain and president of the Federal League Chicago Whales, to buy the Cubs for $500,000. Whales manager Joe Tinker succeeds Roger Bresnahan. The Cubs will play in the FL's newly built stadium, soon to become Wrigley Field.

8th   Profiting handsomely on his 1913 investment of $187,000, owner James E. Gaffney sells his Boston Braves for $500,000 to Harvard's famous football coach, Percy Haughton, and a banker associate.

14th   Lee Magee, player-manager of the Brooklyn Tip-Tops, is sold to the Yankees for about $25,000, becoming the first Federal Leaguer welcomed back to organized baseball.

17th   John McGraw's Giants buy the Feds' top star, Benny Kauff, from the Tip-Tops; their best catcher, Bill Rariden, from the Newark Peps; and spitballer Fred Anderson, from the Buffalo Buffeds (aka the Blues), for about $65,000.

19th   A list of 123 Federal League players with free-agent status under the terms of the peace agreement is released by the National Association.

21st   The Yankees buy lefthanded P Nick Cullop from Kansas City (FL), infielder Joe Gedeon from Salt Lake City (PCL), and veteran Germany Schaefer from Newark (FL).

FEBRUARY

7th   The Federal League's year-old suit charging antitrust violations by organized baseball is dismissed by mutual consent in U.S. District Court in Chicago by Judge Kenesaw M. Landis.

8th   The NL votes down a proposal by Charlie Ebbets of Brooklyn to limit the number of 25-cent seats clubs can sell to 2,000. Boston has 10,000 such seats; St. Louis, 9,000, Philadelphia, 6,500, and Cincinnati, 4,000.

9th   The NL votes down a proposal by the Giants, Braves, and Cubs to increase club player limit from 21 to 22. (The Reds want to decrease to 20.)

   The NL celebrates its 40th anniversary with a Waldorf-Astoria banquet. The NL's first president, Morgan G. Bulkeley, is present. The chief speaker is former president William H. Taft.

10th   C Chief Meyers is waived to Brooklyn by the Giants. The Braves also claim him. Owners Ebbets and Haughton toss a coin to determine Meyers's fate, and Ebbets wins the right to claim him.

15th   The Yankees buy Frank "Home Run" Baker from the Athletics for $37,500. He sat out the 1915 season.

16th   Energetic recruiting by Ban Johnson produces a pair of Chicago contractors to take over the Cleveland franchise from Charles W. Somers, a lavish spender at the AL's creation but now in financial difficulties. J. C. Dunn and P. S. McCarthy pay $500,000—$60,000 less than the asking price. E. S. Barnard will stay on as vice president; Lee Fohl, as manager.

MARCH

3rd   Jack Dunn, owner of the IL Orioles, buys the park built by the Baltimore Terrapins (FL).

5th   The NL meeting of February 1916 announced that it had come to the league's attention that "some of the diamonds" didn't measure properly. On this day, John Heydler's office circulates to clubs news of the Chicago Cubs pitching distance, and orders engineer certification. On May 7, 1902, a Chicago Cubs 4–0 victory over the Giants had been thrown out because the mound was too close to the batter's box.

APRIL

8th   Tris Speaker declares he is a holdout when Boston owner Joseph Lannin proposes cutting his salary from $11,000 to $9,000. The Red Sox, in anticipation of resolving the contract dispute by trading Speaker, purchase the hard-throwing OF Tilly Walker from the Browns.

12th On Opening Day, young Babe Ruth goes 8 ⅓ innings for a 2–1 win over the Athletics at Boston. A poor throw by Charlie Pick, A's 3B, is the first of his 42 errors—worst for any 20th-century 3B. This contributes to his overall .899 fielding average, a mark that Butch Hobson would equal in 1978.

Harry Coveleski gives up 3 hits, but gets 4 himself, as the Tigers beat the White Sox in Chicago. Hundreds of fans complain that their clothes are ruined by fresh green paint recently applied to the grandstand seats.

13th Babe Adams, the Pirates bellwether, pitches a one-hit shutout against the Cardinals. He will win only one more game this season.

Cleveland C Steve O'Neill completes a double play (with SS Ray Chapman), the first of 36, a ML season record that still stands.

15th White Sox C Ray Schalk steals twice against Detroit en route to a season total of 30, a record for catchers until 1982 when John Wathan nicks 36.

16th Now with Cleveland, Boston's Tris Speaker doubles against the Tigers Hooks Dauss, the first of 41 that will tie him with teammate Jack Graney for the AL lead, and one of an all-time career high of 792. Indians top Detroit 4–3.

17th Sam Crawford's consecutive-game streak ends at 472. He played in every Tiger game in 1913 through 1915.

Detroit scores a 12-inning 3–1 victory over Stan Coveleski in his first year at Cleveland. Righthander George Cunningham pitches when Tiger ace Harry Coveleski refuses to pitch against his younger brother.

18th "Pete" Alexander (Grover Cleveland) blanks the Braves with 5 hits at the Baker Bowl. It is his first shutout of the year; 15 will follow.

22nd The A's Jack Nabors tops the Red Sox 6–2. His only victory of the season evens his record at 1–1. He will follow with 19 straight losses.

23rd The Giants are saved from a humiliating exhibition loss to the Long Branch Cubans at West Side Park, Jersey City, when rain halts the game in the first inning with the Cubans leading 8–1.

29th Buck Weaver (3B) and Jack Fournier (1B) execute the season's first triple play in the 3–1 White Sox win at St. Louis.

Innovative owner Charles Weeghman allows Cub fans to keep balls hit into stands.

MAY

9th Thirty walks are allowed at Philadelphia as Detroit overwhelms the A's 16–2. Eighteen of the walks are issued by the A's on their way to a season total of 715. Not until 1938 will a team (the St. Louis Browns with 737) top that.

14th The Cardinals rookie Rogers Hornsby hits his first HR. It is inside the park against the Brooklyn Dodgers at spacious Robison Field in St. Louis.

29th Christy Mathewson beats the Braves 3–0 for the Giants' 17th consecutive win on the road.

JUNE

16th Tom Hughes of the Braves pitches a no-hitter over the Pirates, 6 years after pitching a 9-inning no-hitter for the Yanks, before losing 5–0 to Cleveland in 11.

20th Tilly Walker's HR over the LF wall is the only HR the Red Sox will hit at Fenway this season. Boston SS Everett Scott starts a string of 1,307 consecutive games, all played at SS. He will complete the streak as a Yankee. It will be the best until Gehrig's 2,130.

21st Rube Foster of the Red Sox no-hits the Yankees 2–0, for the first no-hitter in Fenway Park, beating Bob Shawkey 2–0.

26th Cleveland players, in a game with the White Sox, wear numbers on their sleeves, marking the first time players are identified by numbers corresponding to those on the scorecard.

28th Rogers Hornsby, playing his first full season for St. Louis, has a 5-hit day, totaling 12 bases.

JULY

1st At age 42 years and 4 months, Honus Wagner is the oldest player to hit an inside-the-park HR. He connects for the Pirates in the 4th inning at Cincinnati.

4th Joe Jackson goes 3-for-5 against the Athletics. In 30 games since May 31st, he has hit 55-for-104, a .524 BA.

18th Umpire Bill "Lord" Byron forfeits a game to Brooklyn in the 10th at Chicago when Hippo Vaughn, protesting alleged sign stealing, refuses to pitch.

20th Christy Mathewson is traded to Cincinnati with Giants CF Edd Roush and 3B Bill McKechnie for Buck Herzog and Red Killefer. A longtime nemesis of the Reds, Mathewson will manage, and a new team nickname will be coined: "Matties."

26th Tigers favorite Harry Heilmann gets an appreciative hand from the crowd for having dived into the Detroit River last night to save a woman from drowning.

AUGUST

8th The Athletics set an AL record with their 19th loss in a row on the road. The streak began on July 25th, making it a record for losses in 2 weeks.

9th The A's end a 20-game losing streak, beating Detroit 7–1.

15th Babe Ruth outduels Walter Johnson 1–0 in 13 innings.

20th Giants 1B Fred Merkle is traded to Brooklyn for C Lew McCarty. Brooklyn needs help because regular 1B Jake Daubert is hurt.

23rd Ty Cobb goes from 1B to 3B on a teammate's single to LF, then steals home when A's 3B Charlie Pick holds the ball. Detroit wins 10–3.

26th After being knocked out of the box in 3 innings yesterday against Cleveland, the A's Joe Bush gets revenge by no-hitting Cleveland 5–0 in Philadelphia. It is Nap Lajoie's last ML game. He goes 1-for-3 with a triple, and hits just .280 for the year; his last at bat is a fly to RF.

30th Following his previous start when he lasted one-third of an inning against St. Louis, Hubert "Dutch" Leonard of the Red Sox no-hits the Browns 4–0.

SEPTEMBER

4th To help draw a crowd, and because of their longtime rivalry, Christy Mathewson and Three Finger Brown close out their careers in the same game. Matty, now the manager of the Reds, wins 10–8 in his only game not pitched in a Giants uniform. Cub Vic Saier

hits a 3-run HR off Matty, the 5th time he has hit a 4-bagger off him, the most Matty has given up to any one hitter. Mathewson and Brown have dueled 25 times since 1903, with Brown, now back with the Cubs, winning 12 and losing 10; Matty was 12–13.

8th Switch-hitter Wally Schang of the A's hits HRs from both sides of the plate against the Yankees. Only a handful of people see the rare feat on a rainy day.

17th St. Louis Browns P George Sisler wins 1–0 over Walter Johnson. It is his last win, as he soon becomes a regular 1B. He will also play 2 games as a lefthanded 3B.

23rd Grover Cleveland Alexander beats Cincinnati twice 7–3 and 4–0 at Philadelphia.

24th Marty Kavanaugh, Indians utility man, hits the AL's first pinch-hit grand slam for Cleveland in a 5–3 win over the Red Sox. The ball rolls through a hole in the fence and cannot be retrieved in time for a play at the plate.

26th Washington manager Griffith excuses several regulars for the remaining games of the season so he can use some new players. Included is Walter Johnson, who has already won 25 games for the 7th-place club. In a league-leading 371 IP, he did not give up a HR, an all-time record.

29th Boston P Babe Ruth closes the season with his 23rd win, topping New York 3–0. It is his 9th shutout and reduces his ERA to 1.75. In 324 IP he gave up no HRs.

30th In his 153rd game, Tiger 3B Ossie Vitt raises his season total chances to 615, a mark that will stand for 21 years.

Red Sox CF Tilly Walker, imitating Tris Speaker, his predecessor, dashes in for a low line drive and beats the runner back to 2B for an unassisted DP. It is an important play, as Dutch Leonard defeats Nick Cullop of the Yankees 1–0 in the 10th on Harry Hooper's sacrifice fly.

OCTOBER

1st Eight stolen bases by the Browns against Detroit raises their team total to 234, an AL mark that will stand until the Oakland Athletics' 341 in 1976.

2nd Grover Cleveland Alexander 3-hits the Braves for a 2–0 win, his 33rd, and his 16th shutout.

5th With the Braves ahead 4–1 in the 8th inning, Phils manager Pat Moran puts pudgy Billy McHarg in as a pinch hitter. McHarg grounds out and then plays LF before returning to his real duties as chauffeur for Phils C Bill Killifer. McHarg also appeared in 2 innings as a replacement Tiger in 1912.

7th Despite a 4-run Brooklyn rally in the 9th, the Red Sox defeat Rube Marquard 6–5 to win game 1 of the WS at Braves Field. Ernie Shore gets the win, Carl Mays a save. The Sox turn 4 double plays.

9th Babe Ruth outpitches Sherry Smith to win game 2 of the WS 2–1 in the 14th. This is the start of 29⅔ scoreless World Series innings pitched. Ruth allows one run in the first.

10th In game 3, Larry Gardner's HR over the RF fence at Brooklyn brings the Sox within a run 4–3, but Jeff Pfeffer, in relief of Jack Coombs, shuts them down. Carl Mays takes the loss. Charlie Ebbets becomes the first owner to raise the price of WS grandstand seats to $5—up from $3.

11th Rube Marquard, Larry Cheney, and Nap Rucker yield 10 hits as the Red Sox win game 4 easily 6–2. The Brooklyn Robins score twice in the first, but Larry Gardner's 2nd HR, an inside-the-park blast, scores 3 in the 2nd and puts Boston ahead to stay. Dutch Leonard holds his foes to 5 hits.

12th Boston's 4–1 win in game 5 ends the Series. The Red Sox had 22 shares of $3,826. The Dodgers, less generous, $2,834.

16th Brooklyn owner Charles Ebbets rewards manager Wilbert Robinson with a $5,000 bonus for a job well done.

NOVEMBER

1st Harry H. Frazee, New York theater owner and producer, buys the Red Sox for $675,000.

DECEMBER

2nd Under pressure from the Players' Fraternity, the National Commission orders that injured players shall get full pay for the duration of their contracts. The injury clause previously let clubs suspend players after 15 days pay.

8th The National Commission fines 51 players $25 to $100 for performing in post-season exhibitions. Among the guilty: Babe Ruth, Jack Barry, Duffy Lewis, 10 other Red Sox players, and Ty Cobb.

1917

FEBRUARY

13th Tim Murnane, 64, 1B on the original Boston NL team of 1876 and later a leading Boston baseball writer, dies in Boston.

24th Smokey Joe Wood, his arm dead at 26, is sold by the Red Sox to Cleveland for $15,000. He will become an OF after one last, losing start on the mound, and will play 5 more years.

APRIL

10th The U.S. entry into W W I and a cold, wet spring combine to put a damper on the start of the season; 48 NL games will be postponed in the first month. Half the ML clubs will show losses this year, and 8 of the 20 minor leagues will fold before the season is over. The AL gets the Army to assign drill sergeants to each team for daily pregame drills. A final contest will be held for a $500 prize. The St. Louis Browns will take the money.

11th Babe Ruth beats the Yankees, pitching a 3-hit 10–3 win for the Red Sox in the opener. By the end of May he will be 10-3 on the way to his best year (24–13) and a league-leading 35 complete games.

14th Chicago's Eddie Cicotte pitches a no-hitter over the Browns, winning easily 11–0. Cicotte's 28 wins and 1.53 ERA will top the AL.

24th The Yankees lefty George Mogridge pitches a no-hitter in Fenway Park for a 2–1 New York win. It is the 2nd of what will be an AL record 5 no-hitters. The Yankees score on 2 walks, an error, and a sacrifice fly.

MAY

2nd The Cubs lefthander Hippo Vaughn and righthander Fred Toney of the Reds toe the mound in Chicago for a one-of-a-kind game. The Reds put up an all righthanded batting order, benching Ed Roush, who will lead the NL with a .341 BA. At the end of 9, both pitchers have no-hitters. With one out in the top of the 10th and men on 2B and 3B, Jim Thorpe hits a swinging bunt near the mound. Vaughn picks it up and throws home, but C Art Wilson freezes; the ball hits his chest protector, and Larry Kopf slides in safe for the only run. Fred Toney sets the Cubs down in order

and has the 4th 10-inning no-hitter to date. The run scored by the Reds is their first in 34 innings.

5th St. Louis Browns P Ernie Koob gets a 1–0 no-hitter over the White Sox' Ed Cicotte. It's the last shutout the 24-year-old pitcher will toss. George Sisler drives in the Browns' run. A first-inning tainted hit by Buck Weaver was changed to an error after much discussion with umpires and players. The following day, the writers' association will take a mail vote on a resolution that a scorer's decision could not be reversed.

6th No-hitters are thrown on consecutive days, as the Browns' Bob Groom no-hits the White Sox 3–0 in the 2nd game of the doubleheader. This year, Groom will be the losingest pitcher in the AL for the 3rd time. He lost a record-setting 19 straight games as a rookie with Washington in 1909. The Browns also win the first game 8–4 in 10 innings, with Groom throwing the last 2 hitless innings. But Chicago will soon win 16 of 17 to overtake the sprinting Red Sox.

20th Cleveland P Jim "Sarge" Bagby steals home in the 7th, and the Indians beat the A's 5–2.

23rd Grover Alexander of the Phils allows the Reds only 2 hits; he collects 3 himself, including a HR, and wins 5–1.

25th Down 5–0 in the 9th, Tris Speaker of the Indians ignites a rally by stealing home against the Yankees. Five more runs follow and they win 6–5.

31st Ty Cobb starts a 35-game hitting streak, going 1-for-4 against Ray Caldwell in Detroit's 2–0 win over New York.

JUNE

1st Hank Gowdy is the first ML player to enlist when he signs up in the Ohio National Guard. He will play until he reports for duty July 15th.

Guy Morton of Cleveland shuts out the Red Sox 3–0, on one hit (a rifle shot over 2B by rival P Ruth). Ray Chapman and Bobby Roth both steal home in the 4th.

8th After a game in Cincinnati, John McGraw takes a swing at umpire Bill "Lord" Byron as they are leaving the field, splitting Byron's lip. NL President John Tener fines McGraw $500 and suspends him for 16 days. McGraw sounds off to writer Sid Mercer about the general shortcomings of Tener and his umpires.

When McGraw's quotes are published, he signs a statement denying he'd said what was printed. The Baseball Writers Association protests, forcing another NL meeting at which Tener finds McGraw guilty and fines him another $1,000. Mercer, a friend of McGraw's, quits the beat and never speaks to McGraw again.

9th The White Sox move into first place in the AL. They will swap the top spot with the Red Sox until August 18th when they will pull away to a final 9-game margin.

17th The Giants and Yankees play the first Sunday game in New York for a war charity; 21,000 fans turn out

21st In a game against Salt Lake City, Red McKee of the San Francisco Seals (PCL), forgets the bases are loaded and attempts to steal 3B. His ploy works as the startled pitcher is called for a balk.

22nd Honus Wagner is given a day in Pittsburgh in honor of his unretirement for one more year.

23rd In Boston, Babe Ruth starts against Washington. He walks leadoff man Eddie Foster, griping to plate umpire Brick Owens after each pitch. On ball 4, Ruth plants a right to the umpire's jaw. He is ejected, and Ernie Shore relieves. Foster is caught stealing, and Shore retires all 26 men he faces in a 4–0 win, getting credit in the books for a perfect game. Ruth is not fined, but draws a 10-day suspension.

JULY

1st Reds Fred Toney pitches a doubleheader, beating the Pirates 4–1 and 5–1. He walks one and allows 3 hits in each game, the fewest hits allowed by any pitcher winning 2 games in one day.

The Robins (Dodgers) play their first Sunday game in Brooklyn, charging regular admission and beating the Phils 3–2. Admission is charged for a pregame band concert and military drill exhibition before the game to benefit wartime charities. When the band concert ends ticket sales stop to conform with the Sunday baseball laws. More than 12,000 attend.

10th The Yankees righthander Ray Caldwell pitches 9⅔ innings of scoreless relief, picking up a 7–5 win over the the Browns in 17 innings.

30th The Tigers Ty Cobb, Bobby Veach, and Ossie Vitt follow each other in the lineup, each going 5-for-5 for a 16–4 win over Washington.

AUGUST

19th Coaching at 3B in a 1–1 game against Washington, Ty Cobb gives base runner "Tioga" George Burns a shove when Burns stops at 3B on a long hit; Burns keeps going and scores the winning run. Clark Griffith protests, and Ban Johnson upholds him, as the rules now ban coaches from touching a runner. The game is replayed, and Washington wins 2–0.

21st Reds rookie righthander Hod Eller fans the side on 9 pitches in the 9th inning, beating the Giants 7–5, and breaking Slim Sallee's 10-game winning streak.

Now with the Philadelphia Phils, Chief Bender, 34, pitches his 3rd straight shutout, winning 6–0 over the Cubs. In his last active season, Bender will turn in 4 shutouts and win 8 with 2 losses and a 1.67 ERA. His mound partner from the glory days of the A's, Eddie Plank, will also close out his career, ending the season 5–6 for the St. Louis Browns with a 1.79 ERA.

22nd Brooklyn and the Pirates play their 3rd straight extra-inning game in Ebbets Field. The Robins win it 6–5 in 22 innings.

SEPTEMBER

3rd Trying to keep the Phils in the race, Grover Alexander does double duty, beating Brooklyn 6–0 and 9–3. He will win 30 for the 3rd straight year, with a league-leading 1.86 ERA.

8th When Browns owner Phil Ball accuses his players of lying down on the job because they dislike manager Fielder Jones, SS Doc Lavan and 2B Del Pratt sue him for $50,000 damages for alleged slanderous statements in St. Louis newspapers.

18th For the 2nd time this month, a pitcher beats Brooklyn twice in one day, as the Cardinals' Bill Doak wins 2–0 and 12–4.

27th The Red Sox play a benefit game against an all-star team and Babe Ruth throws a shut out. More than $14,000 is raised for the family of Tim

Murnane, who died February 13th. Murnane had played and managed in Boston in the 19th century.

30th Detroit's future Hall of Fame OF Sam Crawford retires from ML baseball at 37. In addition to his career-record 312 three-base hits, he has hit 50 inside-the-park HRs. He will play in the PCL for several years.

Cleveland's leadoff man, OF Jack Graney, walks once in a 2–1 win over Washington to lead the AL with 94 walks despite a .241 BA. No other player will lead a league in walks with so low a BA until Gene Tenace with Oakland in 1974 draws 110 walks with a .211 BA. In 1919 Graney will walk 105 times and bat .234.

OCTOBER

4th Braves southpaw Art Nehf's 40-inning scoreless streak is ended by the Robins in the 8th. Brooklyn beats Boston 5–1.

6th Before the WS starts, Charles Comiskey offers one percent of his team's WS share to Clark Griffith's Bat and Ball Fund for American soldiers in France. In Chicago, Happy Felsch's HR is the difference as Ed Cicotte beats the Giants' Slim Sallee 2–1 in the Series opener.

7th In game 2 New York's Ferdie Schupp doesn't get out of the 2nd inning, and reliever Fred Anderson is bombed in a 5-run 4th, as the 14 White Sox hits produce a 7–2 win for Red Faber. Faber's pitching is better than his baserunning; in the 5th inning, he tries to steal 3B, only to find teammate Buck Weaver occupying it.

10th The White Sox are stifled by Rube Benton, who becomes the first lefty to pitch a WS shutout. Dave Robertson, the NL's leading HR hitter with 12, triples and scores the first of two 4th-inning runs for a 2–0 New York win. Robertson will lead all batters in the Series with a .500 average.

11th Ferdie Schupp fares better against Faber in game 4; Benny Kauff hits 2 HRs, which are more than enough for a 5–0 win to even the Series.

13th Game 5 sees White Sox southpaw Reb Russell relieved by Cicotte. Russell gave up 2 hits and a walk to the first 3 batters he faced. In a sloppy game marred by 3 New York and 6 Chicago errors, the White Sox break a 5–5 tie with 3 in the 8th. Red Faber, working the last 2 innings, is the winning pitcher.

15th After Red Faber and Rube Benton match 3 scoreless innings, Eddie Collins leads off the 4th and hits a grounder to Heinie Zimmerman at 3B. Collins takes 2nd when the throw goes past 1B Walter Holke. Joe Jackson's fly to RF is dropped by Dave Robertson, and Collins goes to 3B. When Happy Felsch hits one back to the pitcher, Collins breaks for home. Benton throws to 3B to catch Collins, and C Bill Rariden comes up the line. But Collins keeps running and slides home safely with Zimmerman in pursuit. Zimmerman will be blamed for chasing the runner, but nobody was covering home plate. The Giants come back with 2 on Buck Herzog's triple in the 4th, but Faber wins his 3rd of the Series 4–2. The winners earn $3,669.32 each; the losers $2,442.21. One-fourth of each team's share, about $4,000 each, is divided equally among the clubs in each league.

16th The day after the WS ends, the Giants and White Sox play an exhibition game for 600 soldiers at Garden City, NY. The Sox win 6–4.

26th Miller Huggins, who managed the Cardinals to a 3rd-place finish, is signed to run the Yankees by owner Jake Ruppert. Co-owner Til Huston, who favored Wilbert Robinson for the job, has a falling out with partner Ruppert and will sell his half interest to Ruppert in 1923.

DECEMBER

11th The Phils sell Grover Alexander and "Reindeer" Bill Killefer to the Cubs for righthander "Iron" Mike Prendergast, C Pickles Dillhoefer, and $55,000.

13th Connie Mack and the Phillies need money. He sells P Joe Bush, C Wally Schang, and OF Amos Strunk to the Red Sox for sore–armed P Vean Gregg, OF Merlin Kopp, C Pinch Thomas, and $60,000.

1918

JANUARY

2nd   Brooklyn sends OF Casey Stengel and infielder George Cutshaw to Pittsburgh for P Burleigh Grimes, P Al Mamaux, and infielder Chuck Ward.

10th   Connie Mack alarms Philadelphia by dealing Stuffy McInnis, the last player in his $100,000 infield, to Boston for players to be announced. The furor dies down when Mack announces he has received 3B Larry Gardner, OF Clarence "Tilly" Walker, and C Hick Cady.

22nd   The Yankees trade P Nick Cullop, P Urban Shocker, C Les Nunamaker, 2B Fritz Maisel, and infielder Joe Gedeon to the Browns for P Eddie Plank and 2B Del Pratt. Plank retires, but Pratt gives New York 3 good years at 2B.

FEBRUARY

23rd   Barney Dreyfuss of the Rules Committee launches a campaign to ban the spitter. He will succeed next year.

APRIL

4th   Determined not to be a wartime casualty, the International League reorganizes. The Richmond, Montreal, and Providence franchises are replaced by Binghamton, Jersey City, and Syracuse. Expenses are slashed, causing the resignation of president Ed Barrow, who will go on to greater glory with the Boston Red Sox. The IL will be the only minor league to play its full schedule this year.

7th   In the A.M. game of a doubleheader in Los Angeles, Doc Crandall's no-hit bid against Salt Lake City (Pacific Coast League) is spoiled with 2 outs in the 9th by Crandall's brother Karl, but Los Angeles wins 14–0.

15th   The AL season opens with Babe Ruth pitching a 4-hit 7–1 victory over the A's. Red Sox manager Ed Barrow will start Ruth's conversion to slugger by working him into 72 games as OF-1B.

16th   In their season openers, the Reds' Pete Schneider and the Red Sox' Carl Mays each pitch one-hitters. The Giants play before a record crowd of 30,000 at the Polo Grounds, beating Brooklyn 6–4.

18th   With 2 Tigers on base in the 9th, Cleveland CF Tris Speaker turns an unassisted double play. On April 29th, he will make the same play against Chicago, the 4th unassisted DP of his career. He will share the career record with Cleveland teammate, Elmer Smith.

27th   The Giants' 9–0 winning start and the Dodgers' 0–9 losing streak are stopped as Brooklyn's Larry Cheney wins 5–3.

30th   Grover Alexander, 2–1 in 3 starts for the Cubs, joins the Army after receiving his draft notice on April 18th.

MAY

6th   Brooklyn's Dan Griner has a no-hitter with 2 outs in the 9th, but gives up a hit to Phillie Gavvy Cravath. He nevertheless wins 2–0.

10th   Pittsburgh's lefty Earl Hamilton is 6–0 with an 0.83 ERA after beating the Giants. He then enlists in the Navy.

13th   The Phils' Joe Oeschger pitches 9 no-hit innings, but they come after the Cards put together 2 hits and a walk for 3 runs in the first inning of a 10-inning 3–3 tie.

14th   Sunday baseball is made legal in Washington, DC. District commissioners rescind the ban in view of the large increase in the city's wartime population and the need for recreation and amusement facilities.

15th   Former player-manager Patsy Tebeau commits suicide in St. Louis.

19th   In Washington's first Sunday game, the Senators beat Cleveland 1–0 in 18 innings. More than 15,000 fans are in attendance.

20th   Braves 3B Red Smith makes an out after 10 straight hits over 5 games.

24th   Former P Joe Wood hits a HR in the 19th for a 3–2 Cleveland win over New York. Home Run Baker's 11 assists tie the AL record for 3B in an extra-inning game.

JUNE

1st Losing 5–4 against the Yankees, the Tigers load the bases in the 9th with no outs. Chick Gandil lines a shot to 3B Frank Baker, who turns it into a game-ending triple play.

3rd Boston lefty Hub Leonard pitches his 2nd no-hitter, beating the Tigers' all-right-handed lineup in Detroit 5–0, and allowing just a first-inning walk. Babe Ruth, playing CF, slugs a first-inning HR, his 2nd in 2 days. Ty Cobb, out a week with an injured shoulder, pinch-hits in the 9th and fouls out.

5th The Giants score 3 in the 9th to beat Pittsburgh 4–3 and move into first place.

17th The National Commission rules that P Scott Perry, who has been winning games for the Athletics, belongs to the Boston Braves. Although purchased by the Braves from Atlanta in 1917, the deal was not completed. While on Atlanta's ineligible list, he was sold to Connie Mack. Aroused by Perry's AL success, the Braves enter their proper claim. Mack breaks precedent, goes outside organized baseball to civil court, and gets an injunction against Boston. The NL, having sat still for the loss of George Sisler, is furious; President John K. Tener resigns. John Heydler succeeds him and arranges a compromise solution: Mack pays Boston $2,500 and keeps Perry (henceforth a loser). The clubs' anger at player-allocation decisions will ultimately topple the National Commission, making way for Judge K.M. Landis.

22nd It's a hot day in New York, and umpires George Hildebrand and Billy Evans don't show up, so Giants coach Mike Donlin and Browns trainer Bits Bierhalter take their places. The game takes 15 innings to reach an inconclusive 4–4 tie.

30th In the 10th, Babe Ruth hits his 11th HR to beat Walter Johnson 3–1 and boost the Red Sox back into first place. Ruth is playing CF when not pitching.

JULY

6th The Reds' Pete Schneider takes a 10–0 one-hitter versus the Phils into the 9th, but walks the first 6 batters. Two relievers later, the Phils have 9 runs, but lose 10–9.

7th Rabbit Maranville gets a 10-day leave from the Navy and hits .316 in 11 games for the Braves before going back to sea.

8th Although Babe Ruth's blast over the fence in Fenway scores in Amos Strunk, as the Sox win 1–0 over Cleveland, prevailing rules reduce Babe's HR to a triple. He will tie for the AL title with 11 HRs, even though he plays just 95 games.

17th Chicago's Lefty Tyler goes 21 innings against Milt Watson to beat the Phils 2–1.

19th Washington C Eddie Ainsmith applies for deferment from the draft. Secretary of War Newton D. Baker rules that baseball is not an essential occupation and all players of draft age are subject to the "work-in-essential-industries-or-fight" rule. The ruling sends many players to work in shipyards and other defense industries, where they can play part-time or semipro. Ban Johnson says the AL will close down July 21st, but the next day both leagues vote to continue. A week later, Baker exempts players from the rule until September 1st. Both leagues vote to cut the season short, and end on Labor Day, September 2nd.

25th Walter Johnson gives up one hit (a triple by George Sisler) in the first 11 innings of a 15-inning, 4-hit 1–0 win.

27th Dodger rookie righthander Harry Heitmann, stationed in Brooklyn by the Navy after a 17–6 record at Rochester (IL), surrenders 4 runs on 4 straight Cardinal hits and is removed having retired his initial batter. It's his last ML appearance.

AUGUST

1st Pittsburgh and Boston play a record 20 scoreless innings; the Pirates win 2–0 in 21. Art Nehf goes all the way for Boston.

9th Reds manager Christy Mathewson suspects Hal Chase of taking bribes to fix games, and suspends him "for indifferent play." Chase will be reinstated and play for the Giants in 1919.

19th Walter Johnson beats St. Louis 4–3 in 14 innings. The Big Train will work in 15 extra-inning games, including 2 of 18 innings, one of 16 innings, and another of 15 innings.

24th Secretary Baker grants an extended exemption to players in the WS; 3 days later the National

Commission gets an official approval to play from General Enoch Crowder, providing that 10 percent of the revenues go to war charities.

26th   Ban Johnson casts the deciding vote in a National Commission decision awarding the disputed services of P Jack Quinn to the Yankees for 1919 over the claim of the White Sox, for whom Quinn was 5–1 this year.

27th   Christy Mathewson resigns as Reds manager to accept a commission as a captain in the chemical warfare branch of the Army.

28th   Tris Speaker is suspended for the remainder of the season because of his assault on umpire Tom Connolly following a dispute at home plate in a game in Philadelphia.

30th   Carl Mays of the Red Sox wins 2 games 12–0 and 4–1 over the A's to finish at 21–13.

The Giants beat Brooklyn 1–0 in 57 minutes, scoring their lone run in the 9th. Jack Coombs takes the loss.

31st   The Red Sox clinch the pennant, winning the first of a twin bill from the A's 6–1, as Ruth wins his 9th game in his last 11 starts.

SEPTEMBER

1st   Ty Cobb pitches 2 innings against the Browns while the Browns' George Sisler pitches one scoreless inning. The Browns win 6–2 as Sisler hits a double off of Cobb.

5th   In order to cut down on the use of trains, the first 3 games of the WS are played in Chicago, the next 3 in Boston. The Cubs switch their home games to Comiskey Park with its larger seating capacity. Babe Ruth, having completed 13 scoreless innings in his first WS 2 years ago, adds 9 more in edging Hippo Vaughn 1–0 in the opener. Also when 2B Dave Shean bats for Boston, he becomes the oldest player (40 years, 3 months, 18 days) ever to play in the WS until 1930.

During the 7th-inning stretch, a military band plays "The Star Spangled Banner." From then on, it is played at every WS game, every season opener, and whenever a band is present to play it, though it is not yet adopted as the national anthem. The custom of playing it before every game will begin during WWII,

when the installation of public address systems makes it practical.

6th   In game 2, Lefty Tyler drives in 2 runs in the Cubs' 3-run second. The Red Sox get one in the 9th and that's all the scoring for the day, with Tyler beating Joe Bush.

7th   On one day's rest, Hippo Vaughn gives up only 7 hits, but Carl Mays wins a 2–1 duel. Game 3 ends with the Cubs' Charlie Pick caught in a rundown between 3B and home while trying to score on a passed ball.

9th   In game 4, Ruth bats in 2 runs on a triple in the 4th and pitches 7 scoreless innings before the Cubs tie it in the 8th. Shufflin' Phil Douglas relieves for Chicago in the last of the 8th and throws away the game, first by a wild pitch, then an error. Ruth is the winning pitcher, but Mays relieves with 2 on and no out in the 9th.

Finners Quinlan, OF who last played in 1915, is wounded fighting in a battle at Argonne Wood, France. He loses an eye and his right leg.

10th   Players on both sides threaten to strike unless they are guaranteed $2,500 to the winners and $1,000 each for the losers. They back off, however, when told they will appear greedy while their countrymen are fighting a war. There are no fines, but no WS rings or mementos are given out this year. On the field, Hippo Vaughn comes back with 2 days of rest and blanks the Red Sox 3–0 on 5 hits in game 5.

11th   The Red Sox win the WS in game 6 on Carl Mays's 2nd victory, a 2–1 three-hitter. With 2 on and 2 out in the 3rd, utility OF George Whiteman lines a hard drive to RF. Max Flack drops it, allowing the only runs off Lefty Tyler. Cubs pitchers compile a 1.04 ERA, while Boston's .186 BA is the lowest ever for a WS winner. The Red Sox will realize $1,102 each, the Cubs $671, the smallest winner's share ever earned.

OCTOBER

5th   NL infielder Eddie Grant is killed in action in the Argonne forest in France.

7th   Former Detroit P Bun Troy, born in Germany, is killed in Meuse, France.

NOVEMBER

1st Former OF Alex Burr is killed in France on his 25th birthday.

9th Braves OF Larry Chappell, 27, dies of influenza at an army camp.

DECEMBER

10th NL secretary John Heydler is elected president of the league.

18th Duffy Lewis returns from the military, and is traded by the Red Sox to the Yankees. He goes along with Ernie Shore and Dutch Leonard for Ray Caldwell, Slim Love, Roxy Walters, and Frank Gilhooley.

31st Kid Gleason replaces Pants Rowland as White Sox manager following the team's skid to 5th.

Giants pitcher Fred Toney is sentenced to 4 months in jail after he pleads guilty to violating the Mann Act, which prohibits taking a woman across state lines for immoral purposes.

1919

JANUARY

14th John McGraw, Charles A. Stoneham, and Tammany politician Judge Francis X. McQuade buy controlling interest in the Giants from the John Brush estate. Having drawn just 265,000 fans in 1918, the club is sold at a bargain price. The 3 will spend many days in courtrooms fighting among themselves, and fending off government charges about Stoneham's business practices.

30th The Reds hire Pat Moran as manager when no word is received from manager Christy Mathewson, who is still in France.

FEBRUARY

1st After winning an out-of-court settlement of his suit against the Dodgers for the balance of his salary ($2,150) when the 1918 season ended a month early, former MVP Jake Daubert is traded to the Reds for OF Tommy Griffith.

5th Charges brought in 1918 by Reds owner Garry Herrmann and manager Mathewson against Hal Chase for betting against his team and throwing games in collusion with gamblers are dismissed by NL president John Heydler. Heydler decides Chase's sometimes indifferent play was due to "carelessness." Two weeks later John McGraw trades 1B Walter Holke and C Bull Rariden to the Reds for Chase.

MARCH

1st Connie Mack makes one of his biggest player mistakes, trading 3B Larry Gardner, OF Charlie Jamieson, and P Elmer Myers to Cleveland for OF Braggo Roth. Roth will be shipped on to Boston by midseason. Gardner will put in 6 more .300 years, and Jamieson will be a top leadoff man and .303 hitter for the next 14 years.

4th John McGraw gives up on lefty Slim Sallee, selling him to the Reds. McGraw will buy him back next year.

6th The Giants announce they will fly to Philadelphia for their opener. But they take the train when the time comes.

APRIL

18th Brooklyn's Larry Kopf returns to the Reds in exchange for OF Lee Magee.

19th Pushed through the legislature by future New York City mayor Jimmy Walker, a bill legalizing Sunday baseball in the state is signed by Governor Al Smith.

23rd Anticipating a poor season at the gate, the major leagues open a reduced 140-game season. Despite the lack of close races, attendance remains high all year and every club will show a profit.

The season opens in Washington with General March, Army Chief of Staff, throwing out the first ball. Walter Johnson wins a 1–0, 13-inning duel with the A's Scott Perry.

30th Joe Oeschger goes 20 innings for the Phils in a 9–9 tie against Brooklyn's Burleigh Grimes. Both teams score 3 in the 19th. Oeschger walks 5, gives up 22 hits. Grimes walks 5, gives up 15 hits.

MAY

4th The Giants play their first legal Sunday game at home, before 35,000 fans, losing to the Phils 4–3. More than 25,000 turn out in Brooklyn the same day. By early June, the Giants will outdraw their 1918 attendance.

The A's collect 18 hits, but lose to Washington 12–6, leaving an AL-record-tying 17 on base.

11th After a scoreless 12-inning game the day before, the Yankees and Senators (AKA Nationals) complete 27 innings of action with no decision, going 15 innings in a 4–4 draw.

Cincinnati righthander Hod Eller pitches a 6–0 no-hitter over the Cards.

Walter Johnson retires 28 consecutive batters during a 12-inning scoreless tie against Jack Quinn and the New York Yankees. Future football immortal George Halas, batting leadoff for New York, fans twice and goes 0-for-5.

15th The Reds bomb Al Mamaux for 10 runs in the 13th to beat Brooklyn 10–0. Reds RF Alfred "Greasy" Neale has a record 10 putouts. Hod Eller's scoreless string will end at 22, but he will go on to win 10 in a row.

21st The Giants send Jim Thorpe to Boston for the $1,500 waiver price.

23rd It's Hank Gowdy Day in Boston, the catcher's first game after returning from the Army. He hits the first pitch he sees for a single.

25th Ever-popular Casey Stengel, now a Pirate, is good-naturedly applauded when he comes to bat in the 7th inning, doffs his cap in response, and to everyone's delight releases an "irate but much relieved" sparrow he had hidden there.

30th At the end of the day, the White Sox lead the AL by 4 games. They will be overtaken briefly by Cleveland, then the Yankees, during the next 6 weeks before taking the lead to stay.

JUNE

4th After battling through 20 innings on April 30th, the Phils and Brooklyn go 18, but this time the Phils win it 10–9.

8th The Giants, leading 10–3 in the 9th, ignore the Phils' base runners. Four get to 1B, and each steals 2B and 3B, tying the record for SB in one inning set by Washington July 19, 1915.

9th Rube Marquard breaks a leg running the bases, limiting him to a 3–3 record for the Dodgers.

Browns 1B George Sisler beats Washington 2–1 with 2 hits off Walter Johnson, driving in one run and scoring the other. He also makes an assist and putout when he gets a glove on a ground ball hit wide of 1B. The ball bounds toward 2B, and Sisler gets back to 1B to take the throw in time.

14th White Sox ace Eddie Cicotte beats the A's for the 12th straight time en route to 29 wins versus 7 losses and a 1.82 ERA.

15th A rain check dispute arises. Cincinnati rain checks read "not to be used after 4 and a half innings have been completed." But the game is called with the Reds at bat with one out in the bottom of the 5th and the game tied 1–1. The Reds honor the rain checks, but the Braves demand their share of the gate ($2,600), as a legal game has been played, based on the wording of the rain check. In a compromise, the Braves accept $1,300, and the other 6 clubs agree to share the cost. In future all rain checks will read "not good after five innings."

23rd Red Sox 1B Stuffy McInnis makes his first error of the year after handling 526 chances.

White Sox CF Happy Felsch handles a record-tying 12 chances in a 9-inning game. Only Harry Bay of Cleveland in 1904 has been so busy.

JULY

1st Going 5-for-5 in a 9–4 win over the Phils, Brooklyn's Ed Konetchy gets his 10th straight hit, tying Jake Gettman's record with Washington in 1897. Both will be topped by Walt Dropo in 1952.

6th The Reds take 2 from Pittsburgh to move into first place. The Reds and Giants will seesaw back and forth until August 1st, when the Reds gradually begin to pull away, sprinting at the end to a 9-game lead.

William Veeck, former sportswriter, replaces Fred Mitchell as Cubs president, but Mitchell remains manager for Chicago.

7th In the first game of a doubleheader against the Giants, the Phillies steal 8 bases in the 9th but lose 10–5. Fred Luderus, Eddie Sicking, Hick Cady, and Gavvy Cravath each have 2 thefts.

8th Jack Coombs resigns as manager of the last-place Phils. Slugger Gavvy Cravath replaces him.

10th After PH Joe Harris triples with 3 on base to give Cleveland a 7–3 lead in the last of the 8th, reliever Elmer Myers gives up a run, then loads the bases on walks. In comes little-used lefty Fritz Coumbe. Up steps Babe Ruth who hit his 2nd HR of the day for an 8–7 Red Sox win. Out goes Indians' manager Lee Fohl, fired for the move. In comes CF Tris Speaker to manage the Tribe. He will bring them home in 2nd place and stay as skipper for 7 years.

13th Submarine P Carl Mays quits the mound after 2 innings at Chicago, blaming his teammates for lack of support afield. In defiance of Ban Johnson's order that no action be taken until Mays is returned to good standing, Boston owner Harry Frazee trades Mays to the Yankees for pitchers Bob McGraw Allen Russell and $40,000. Johnson suspends Mays indefinitely and orders umpires not to let him pitch for New York. The Yankees get a court order restraining Johnson from interfering, further eroding Johnson's authority and standing. The AL directors will reinstate Mays. In retaliation, on October 29th the National Commission will refuse to recognize the Yankees' 3rd-place finish and will withhold the players' share of the pool. New York's owners will pay out of their own pockets.

AUGUST

6th   In each of the first 3 innings of Brooklyn's 6–1 victory over the Reds, Jimmy Johnston faces a different Cincinnati pitcher and raps each one for a single.

8th   Casey Stengel is traded to the Phils for Possum Whitted, who will bat .389 for the Pirates in the last 35 games.

10th   More than 28,00 crowd Wrigley Field to watch Grover Cleveland Alexander shut the Giants out, 2–0

11th   Cleveland's Tris Speaker ties an AL record, scoring 5 runs in a 15–9 win at New York.

14th   Babe Ruth hits No. 17, the first of 7 HRs in 12 days, which will include his 4th grand slam, an AL record until 1959. The Yankees overcome Muddy Ruel's hitting into a triple play and beat the Tigers in 15 innings 5–4.

Chicago White Sox CF Happy Felsch ties the ML record with 4 OF assists in one game, but Boston beats the White Sox 15–6.

The Dodgers waste no time in splitting a pair with the Cubs, losing 2–0 in an hour and 10 minutes, then winning 1–0 in one hour and 7 minutes.

16th   The Browns set an AL record with 53 total chances against the A's, but lose 7–4. The Browns have 26 assists and St. Louis 1B George Sisler has 17 putouts. With no putouts, the St. Louis outfielders have the day off.

17th   The Tigers draw a record 31,500 at home, but lose 4–2 to the Senators in 11 innings. Ten ground-rule doubles are hit into the crowd lining the OF.

20th   Wichita OF Joe Wilhoit (Western League) fails to get a hit, ending a 69-game streak in which he collected 155 hits in 299 at bats for a .505 batting average. The previous record was 49 by Oakland's Jack Ness (Pacific Coast League) in 1915.

24th   Cleveland P Ray Caldwell is flattened by a bolt of lightning in his debut with the team. He recovers to get the final out of the game, and defeats Philadelphia 2–1.

26th   Giants 1B Hal Chase handles 35 chances against the Pirates in a doubleheader.

SEPTEMBER

2nd   The National Commission recommends a best-of-9 World Series. The lengthier WS is seen as a sign of greed and is abandoned after 3 years.

8th   Babe Ruth hits HR No. 26 off Jack Quinn in New York, breaking Buck Freeman's 1899 HR mark of 25.

10th   The Indians' Ray "Slim" Caldwell, struck by lightning 2 weeks earlier, no-hits his former teammates the Yankees 3–0 at the Polo Grounds.

16th   Dutch Ruether beats the Giants 4–3 to clinch the Reds' first pennant since American Association days.

20th   Babe Ruth ties Ned Williamson's ML HR mark of 27 with a game-winner off Lefty Williams of the White Sox. Four days later he will hit No. 28 over the roof of the Polo Grounds.

21st   The Cubs beat the Braves 3–0 in 58 minutes. It takes the Dodgers 55 minutes to beat the Reds 3–1. Slim Sallee throws 65 pitches, topping Christy Mathewson's 69-pitch CG. One week later the Giants will close the season beating the Phils 6–1 in a record 51 minutes.

24th   The White Sox' 6–5 win over St. Louis clinches the pennant; the final margin will be 3½ games over the Indians.

The Brooklyn Robins defeat the Phillies twice on Fred Luderus Day in Philadelphia. The 2nd game is the 525th in a row played by the Philadelphia 1B, who is presented with a diamond stickpin and gold watch between games to commemorate his endurance effort. He will end the season with a consecutive-game streak of 553.

Boston's Waite Hoyt pitches 9 perfect innings against the Yankees, but they come in between the 4th and the 13th in which he gives up hits. He loses 2–1 in the 13th.

27th   Babe Ruth's 29th HR is his first of the year in Washington; he is the first to hit one in every park in the league in one season.

OCTOBER

1st   Just before the start of the WS, the highly favored White Sox became the betting underdogs. A year later the White Sox will become the Black Sox, and 8 of them—pitchers Eddie Cicotte and Lefty Williams, outfielders Joe Jackson and Happy Felsch, 1B Chick Gandil, SS Swede Risberg, 3B Buck Weaver, and utility infielder Fred McMullin—will be barred from baseball for taking part in throwing the Series. It will take that long for the story to unfold, as most observers at the time see nothing amiss when the Series opens in Cincinnati.

Eddie Cicotte, a 29-game winner, is driven to cover in a 5-run 4th. Cincinnati's Dutch Ruether pitches a 6-hitter, and has 3 RBI on 2 triples and a single for a 9–1 win. Reds OF Greasy Neale, the only man to play in a WS, coach a football team in the Rose Bowl, and become a pro football Hall of Fame coach, also has 3 hits. He will top the Reds with .357 for the Series.

2nd In game 2 after an easy 3 innings, Lefty Williams walks 3 Reds, gives up a single to Edd Roush and a triple to Larry Kopf, and the Reds lead 3–0. Slim Sallee scatters 10 hits as Risberg and Gandil fail in the clutch. The final score is 4–2. Joe Jackson has 3 hits; his .375 BA will make it appear later that he was trying.

Charles Comiskey tells NL president Heydler that Sox manager Kid Gleason is suspicious of his players. Heydler confers with Ban Johnson, who takes no action, fearing it will look like revenge against Comiskey, with whom he has been feuding. As the games unfold, reporters Ring Lardner and Christy Mathewson do not like what they see. Chicago reporter Hugh Fullerton will raise questions during the winter. Comiskey will offer a reward for information, but the 1920 season will open with the same lineup for Chicago, minus Chick Gandil, who will be in the PCL.

3rd Back in Chicago, 5 foot 7 inch rookie lefty Dickie Kerr pitches a 3-hitter, as Chicago wins 3–0. Joe Jackson is 2-for-3 and Gandil drives in 2 runs. Ray Fisher takes the loss. Cuban Adolfo Luque becomes the first Latin American ML player to appear in a WS game, pitching one inning of relief for the Reds in game 3 at Comiskey Park.

4th Ed Cicotte makes 2 errors in one inning of game 4 to give the Reds the only runs of the game. He walks none and gives up 5 hits, but Jimmie Ring gives up only 3 hits and wins 2–0.

6th After a Sunday rainout, Hod Eller blanks the Sox on 3 hits, fanning 6 in a row — Gandil, Risberg,

Ray Schalk, Williams, Leibold, and Eddie Collins — in the 2nd and 3rd. Once again a big inning gives the Reds a victory. A couple of hits, some slow fielding, and poor throws by Jackson and Happy Felsch result in 4 Reds scoring in the 6th for a 5–0 win, their 4th in 5 games. Lefty Williams is the loser. Sox C Schalk is the 2nd man to be thrown out of a WS game when he disagrees with the call on Heinie Groh's slide at home.

7th Happy Felsch's error and 2 boots by Swede Risberg help put Dickie Kerr in the hole 4–0, but Felsch, Weaver, and Jackson combine for 7 hits as the Sox win 5–4. Dutch Ruether doesn't survive the 6th; Jimmie Ring is the loser, as Kerr wins his 2nd.

8th Ed Cicotte pitches game 7, and the Sox play like they mean it. Joe Jackson and Felsch drive in 2 each for a 4–1 win. The Reds make 4 errors behind Slim Sallee's pitching, before 32,006 Cincinnati fans who pay a record WS game receipt total of $101,768.

9th Lefty Williams gets one man out in the first before departing. The Reds lead 4–0, and go on to give Hod Eller a 10–5 victory and the Reds the world title in 8 games. Joe Jackson hits the only HR of the Series. Eddie Collins's 3 hits give him a total of 42 in WS play, a record broken in 1930 by Frank Frisch, and bettered by Lou Gehrig in 1938. A SB by Collins is his 14th in WS competition, a record tied by Lou Brock in 1968.

NOVEMBER

10th Clark Griffith becomes a club owner and president when he joins Philadelphia grain broker William Richardson in buying controlling interest in the Washington Senators for $175,000. Griffith, unable to get financial help from the AL, mortgages his Montana ranch to raise funds.

DECEMBER

10th The NL votes to ban the spitball's use by all new pitchers. The ban will be formally worked out by the Rules Committee in February.

With the opposition led by New York, Boston, and Chicago, the AL directors pass a resolution accusing Ban Johnson of overstepping his duties. They demand that league files be turned over to them and that an auditor review all financial accounts.

26th Although it will not be officially announced until January, the Yankees buy Babe Ruth from financially pressed Harry Frazee, paying $100,000 (one-fourth cash, plus $25,000 a year at 6 percent) plus guaranteeing a $300,000 loan with Fenway Park as collateral.

1920

JANUARY

5th The Yankees announce the purchase of Babe Ruth; it had been delayed until Ruth agreed to terms believed to be $40,000 total for 2 years.

12th A plan developed by Charles Ebbets many years ago is finally adopted: the annual drafting of players from the minor leagues will be done in inverse order to the teams' final standings.

FEBRUARY

9th The Joint Rules Committee bans all foreign substances or other alterations to the ball by pitchers, including saliva, resin, talcum powder, paraffin, and the shine and emery ball. A pitcher caught cheating will be suspended for 10 days. The AL allows each club to name just 2 pitchers who will be allowed to use the pitch for one more season. The NL allows each club to name all its spitball pitchers. No pitchers other than those designated will be permitted to use it, and none at all after 1920. Other rules changes: the adoption of writer Fred Lieb's proposal that a game-winning HR with men on base be counted as a HR even if its run is not needed to win the game. Also, the intentional walk is banned, and everything that happens in a protested game will go in the records.

10th At a joint meeting, all bleacher prices are raised to 50 cents, pavilion to 75 cents, and grandstand to $1.00. Clubs may set aside bleacher space for kids under 14 at 15 and 25 cents if they wish. The May 15th–August 30th player limits are raised from 21 to 25. The AL prohibits player transfers after July 1st; the NL, after August 20th.

12th "Home Run" Baker's wife, Ottalee, dies at 31, leaving 2 small children. Baker will miss the entire season to stay home and take care of the children, returning in 1921 to hit .294.

Dissatisfaction with the National Commission system comes to a head. The NL votes 6–2 for a one-man commission; the AL votes 6–2 for the status quo. Chairman Garry Herrmann resigns, stating his belief that no club owner should serve on the governing board. When the 2 leagues cannot agree on a chairman, it is left to the league presidents to decide disputes.

13th The Negro National League (chartered as the National Association of Colored Professional Baseball Clubs) is organized at a meeting at the YMCA in Kansas City, MO.

MAY

1st Detroit loses its first 13 games, equaling Washington's lowly start of 1904.

In Boston, Brooklyn's Leon Cadore and the Braves' Joe Oeschger duel 26 innings to a 1–1 tie in the longest game ever played in the ML. Oeschger shuts out the Dodgers for the last 21 innings, topping Art Nehf's 20 scoreless frames in a row on August 1, 1918. He gives up 9 hits, and Cadore allows 12, in the 3-hour, 50-minute game. The Dodgers lose to the Phils at home in 13 innings the next day, then return to Boston for a Monday game where they lose again in 19. For 58 innings work in 3 days, they are 0–2. An unusual double play occurs in the 17th inning when the bases are loaded with one out. A grounder to P Oeschger results in a throw home, forcing the runner. C Hank Gowdy's throw to 1B Walter Holke is fumbled, and when the runner tries to score from 2B, the throw back to Gowdy nips the sliding Ed Konetchy.

Babe Ruth hits his first HR as a Yankee in a 6–0 win over the Red Sox. The HR clears the roof of the Polo Grounds.

11th For the first time in 7 years, a player hits 3 triples in a game. Ross Youngs does the trick for the Giants at Cincinnati, but the Giants lose 9–4.

14th Walter Johnson wins 9–8 over Detroit for his 300th victory.

20th The Phils hit the cellar, having fallen from first in 17 days. With the season all but over, Phils manager Gavvy Cravath will start fast-working P Lee Meadows every Saturday at home, so Cravath can get an early start to his weekend cottage.

Requested by Cubs officials, policemen disguised as soldiers, farmers, and bootblacks raid the bleachers and arrest 24 fans for gambling. Meanwhile, Grover Alexander blanks the Phillies 6–0.

31st P Grover Alexander homers in the bottom of the 10th to win his own game 3–2 against the Reds in Chicago. It is his 11th straight victory.

JUNE

4th Grover Alexander loses his first after 11 wins. He will be 27–14 for the 5th-place Cubs, and his 1.91 ERA will be the only one under 2.00.

5th A's vice president Thomas Shibe denies charges that the baseballs currently being used are livelier. Shibe, a member of the firm that manufactures the balls, cites the abolition of the spitball and other "freak" pitches as the reason for the increase in HRs this season.

8th The Reds' Edd Roush falls asleep in CF during a long argument in the IF. Heinie Groh goes out to wake him, but the ump ejects Roush for delaying the game.

Failing in his efforts to buy Rogers Hornsby from St. Louis, John McGraw picks up the NL's top SS, Dave Bancroft, from the Phils for over-the-hill SS Art Fletcher, P Bill Hubbell, and cash.

9th Former Chicago OF Lee Magee loses his suit against the Cubs. He had charged that he was released without just cause last February. While on the witness stand, Magee admitted to having bet on a ball game between Boston and Cincinnati on July 25, 1918, while a member of the Reds.

26th Lou Gehrig gets his first national mention when, as a high school junior for New York City's School of Commerce, he steals the show in a high school championship game against Lane Tech in Chicago. His grand-slam HR in the 8th gives the NY team a 12–8 victory. Scouts sit with open mouths as the ball sails out of the NL park (later known as Wrigley Field).

JULY

1st Walter Johnson pitches a no-hitter, his first, against the Red Sox at Fenway. An error by Bucky Harris costs him a perfect game, but Harris's hit drives in Washington's only run. The next day Johnson comes up with the first sore arm of his life and is useless for the rest of the year, finishing 8–10.

6th The Yankees score 14 in the 5th and beat Washington 17–0. It's the biggest inning ever until the Red Sox score 17 in a 1953 game.

10th After banging out 11 straight hits, Tris Speaker is stopped by Tom Zachary of Washington.

It's the record until Pinky Higgins of the Red Sox racks up 12 in a row in 1938. Speaker will hit .388 for the season.

13th The fans are flocking to see the mighty Ruth hit home runs (12 in June). A twin bill with the Browns draws a Polo Grounds record of 38,823, the 3rd record-breaker of the year.

15th Babe Ruth ties his 1919 record of 29 HRs with a game-winner in the 13th to beat the Browns 13–10. Two days later, he will break it by hitting 2 off Chicago White Sox P Dickie Kerr.

16th The Pirates' Earl Hamilton runs out of steam after pitching 16 scoreless innings against the Giants, and loses 7–0 in 17.

AUGUST

7th Following an all-night drinking bout and a fight at the Lamb's Club in New York, John McGraw will be indicted for violating the Volstead (Prohibition) Act and charged with assault, but he will be acquitted. He will also be called to testify in Chicago hearings investigating gambling and bribery among players, including Hal Chase and Heinie Zimmerman.

10th Failure to cover 1B in the 7th costs Bill Doak a no-hitter in the Cards' 5–1 win over the Phils. Doak, a good-fielding pitcher, invented a glove with an adjustable pocket. The Rawlings Sporting Goods company began producing a Bill Doak glove in the spring of this year.

16th Cleveland SS Ray Chapman, 29, is beaned by a Carl Mays pitch. A righthanded batter who crowds the plate, Chapman freezes and fails to get out of the way of the submarine delivery. He is carried from the field and dies the next day from a fractured skull. Mays, a surly, unpopular pitcher, is the target of fans' and players' outrage. Chapman, a Cleveland favorite since breaking in in 1912, had been married the previous year. In October his wife will receive a full World Series share, $3,986.34. The incident has no effect on Mays's pitching. One week later he will blank Detroit 10–0, and go on to win 26 and lose 11. Joe Sewell will be called up to take Chapman's place, and for 14 years he will be the hardest man in baseball to strike out.

19th The Indians beat New York 3–2. They leave town with a half-game lead over Chicago and 1½ over the Yankees, in what will be the tightest race since 1908.

SEPTEMBER

14th   The Yankees take 5 of 6 from Cleveland and Detroit and lead the AL. The White Sox then beat them 3 times, and they fall back to 3rd.

17th   The Tigers Bobby Veach and the Giants George Burns hit for the cycle, the only time it has ever happened twice in the same day.

20th   Cincinnati 2B Maurice Rath, who will hit only 2 HRs in 506 ABs, collects both of them against the Giants. They are inside-the-park HRs in the 7th and 8th innings.

22nd   A Chicago grand jury convenes to investigate charges that 8 White Sox players conspired to fix the 1919 World Series.

24th   In the first game of 2, Babe Ruth hits his 50th HR in the first inning, off the Senators Jose Acosta. He hits number 51 in a 4-for-4 second game to give the Yankees a 2–1 sweep.

25th   Lefty Williams beats Cleveland 5–1 to pull the White Sox within a half game of first place.

26th   In his last game of the season, Pittsburgh's Babe Adams walks one in an 8–0 loss to the Reds. He has walked 18 in 263 IP, making him the stingiest pitcher ever for one season.

28th   The grand jury indicts the 8 Chicago players in the 1919 WS scandal. Charles Comiskey immediately suspends them. With the heart of the team sidelined, Chicago falls back and the Indians win by 2. The Yankees finish third, 3 back. Had the grand jury come out with its findings a week later, the White Sox might have won, causing the cancellation of the WS and the voiding of their pennant. For Cleveland it is their first pennant in any league after 39 years of trying. The Indians' victory is due primarily to a .303 team BA (the Browns lead the league at .308) and the pitching of Jim Bagby, 31-12, Stan Coveleski, 24-14, and Ray Caldwell, 20-10. A big boost came from Duster Mails, brought up from the Pacific Coast League in June, who won 7 without a loss on a 1.85 ERA. Despite the heavy hitting in the AL, there are ten 20-game winners; the White Sox have 4 of them—Red Faber, Eddie Cicotte, Dickie Kerr, and Lefty Williams.

Yankees owners Jacob Ruppert and Cap Huston send a telegram to Chicago owner Charles Comiskey offering to place their entire team at his disposal, following the suspension of 8 players in the scandal. Comiskey says he cannot accept the proposal.

29th   Babe Ruth hits HR No. 54 in Philadelphia as the Yankees win 7–2. That is more than any other team total except the Phils. He is responsible for 241 of his team's 838 runs, even though he misses 12 games, with a modern record 158 runs scored, beating Ty Cobb's 147 in 1911.

OCTOBER

1st   In their first game following the indictment, the White Sox lose to St. Louis 8–6, while the Indians split with Detroit. Chicago trails by 2 with 2 to play.

2nd   Dickie Kerr beats the St. Louis Browns 10–7, but Cleveland wins 10–1 to clinch the pennant.

The Pirates and Reds, battling for 3rd place, play a tripleheader in Pittsburgh. The Reds win the first two 13–4 and 7–3, and the Pirates the finale 6–0. It's the only "tribill" played this century.

Shaken by the possible effects of the scandal surrounding baseball, club owners begin a series of meetings to reform the game. Albert D. Lasker, a Chicago advertising man and minority stockholder, of the Cubs, proposes a 3-man board of nonbaseball men, with the chairman to be paid $25,000 year. Among the names mentioned: Judge Kenesaw Mountain Landis, former president William Howard Taft, General George Pershing, Senator Hiram Johnson, General Leonard Wood, and ex–treasury secretary William McAdoo.

3rd   In the Browns' 16–7 win over Chicago, George Sisler gets his 257th hit of the season to set a ML record. He also hurls a scoreless 9th inning in relief.

Cincinnati P Dazzy Swartz makes his big-league debut. He hurls a 12-inning complete game, taking the loss. He never plays another game in the ML.

5th   The tradition of low-scoring WS games continues when the Indians manage to collect only 5 hits off Brooklyn's Rube Marquard (10-7) and 2 relievers. Stan Coveleski's (24-14) 5-hitter gives the Indians a 3–1 opening win.

6th   When Wheeler Johnston pinch-hits for Cleveland in the 9th inning of game 2, his brother Jimmy is playing 3B for Brooklyn. They become the first brothers to take opposite sides in a WS. Spitballer Burleigh Grimes (23-11) strands 10 Indians while the

Robins chip away at Jim Bagby (31-12) for 3 single tallies and a 3–0 Series evener.

7th Two Brooklyn runs in the first lead to a quick exit for Cleveland starter Ray Caldwell (20-10). John "Duster" Mails and George Uhle shut down the Robins, but southpaw Sherry Smith (11-9) gives up 3 hits; the visitors' only run results from an error by Zack Wheat on Tris Speaker's double. It's a 2–1 win, and 2–1 Series lead for Brooklyn.

9th For their first WS game on the lakefront, 25,734 Indians fans watch their home team. score 2 in the first and 2 in the 3rd off Leon Cadore (15-14) and Al Mamaux. Cleveland wins game 4, 5–1.

10th In the bottom of the first of an event-laden game, Grimes gives up hits to Charlie Jamieson, Bill Wambsganss, and Speaker. OF Elmer Smith then hits the first grand slam in WS history. In the 3rd, P Jim Bagby comes up with 2 on and crashes another Grimes delivery for a 3-run HR, the first ever by a pitcher in WS play. Bagby is roughed for 13 hits, but he gets out of jams with the aid of 3 DPs and an unassisted triple play. In the 5th with Pete Kilduff on 2B and Otto Miller on 1B, relief pitcher Clarence Mitchell hits a line drive at SS Wambsganss, who steps on 2B and tags the off-and-running Miller before he can retreat. Cleveland dominates 8–1.

11th In game 6, Brooklyn's P Sherry Smith gives up a 6th-inning single to Tris Speaker and double to George Burns. That's all the scoring for the day, as Duster Mails yields 3 hits for a 1–0 win and 4–2 lead for Cleveland in the best-of-9 series.

12th Stan Coveleski wins his 3rd game of the Series, and the Indians wrap it up, as Dodger bats are silent again. Burleigh Grimes is nicked for single scores in the 4th, 5th, and 7th, for a 3–0 loss. Utility IF Jack Sheehan plays 3B for Brooklyn and gets his 2nd hit of the Series, the same number of hits he had during the season. These 4 are his only ML hits.

13th A WS victory celebration in Wade Park brings out more than 50,000 Clevelanders, whose enthusiasm tears up chairs and stages, dunks some people in the park lake, and blocks downtown streets most of the night.

18th NL directors meet in New York, joined by Jacob Ruppert, Cap Huston, Charles Comiskey, and Harry Frazee of the AL. They name a committee to draw up an agreement along the lines of Albert

Lasker's proposal, and give the 5 AL clubs still backing Ban Johnson an ultimatum: come in by November 1st or the Yankees, White Sox, and Red Sox will pull out of the AL and join a 12-team NL (with a team in Detroit to complete the roster). The AL 5 turns it down, and bluff and counterbluff blow through the autumn air.

23rd The Chicago grand jury indictment adds the names of former featherweight boxing champ Abe Attell, Hal Chase, and Bill Burns as go-betweens in the WS scandal. Confessions, later repudiated, are signed by Ed Cicotte, Joe Jackson, Lefty Williams, and Happy Felsch.

29th The Yankees sign Red Sox manager Ed Barrow as business manager, completing the front office team that will build the game's most successful record. Hugh Duffy replaces Barrow in Boston.

NOVEMBER

8th At a meeting to depose Ban Johnson, a new 12-team National League, made up of the dissenting 11 teams plus one of the 5 teams loyal to Johnson, is agreed to. John Heydler will be its president and Judge Landis the proposed chairman of the new commission. With no stomach for another war, 4 of the 5 AL clubs still backing Johnson agree to a joint meeting November 12th in Chicago.

12th With Ban Johnson barred from the meeting, the 16 ML clubs settle their differences. The 12-team-league idea is discarded, and the 2 leagues will continue with their same identities. The owners unanimously elect Kenesaw Mountain Landis chairman for 7 years. Judge Landis accepts, but only as sole commissioner with final authority over the players and owners, while remaining a federal judge (with his $7,500 federal salary deducted from the baseball salary of $50,000). The agreement will be signed on January 12, 1921, when he is to begin his duties.

DECEMBER

6th A 5-year-old lawsuit that awarded $264,000 damages to the Baltimore Federal League club on April 12, 1919, is reversed by a court of appeals, which upholds the reserve clause and holds that baseball is not interstate commerce nor subject to antitrust laws. The original was initiated because the Baltimore

Feds were not included in the settlement of the Federal League war. They wanted a ML team in Baltimore and did not get it.

15th At NL meetings, Rube Marquard, fined in Cleveland for ticket scalping during the WS, is traded to the Reds for Dutch Ruether. The NL reveals a most telling statistic, pointing out the changes in the game: the use of 27,924 baseballs during the season, an increase of 10,248 over 1919.

The Yankees' Ed Barrow pries future Hall of Fame P Waite Hoyt, C Wally Schang, lefty Harry Harper, and IF Mike McNally from his former Boston team in exchange for 2B Del Pratt, C Muddy Ruel, P Hank Thormahlen, OF Sammy Vick, and cash.

17th The AL votes to allow pitchers who used the spitball in 1920 to continue using it as long as they are in the league. The NL will do the same. There will be 17 in all.

18th On his 34th birthday, Ty Cobb signs to manage the Tigers for $32,500, making him the highest-paid player and 2nd to John McGraw among managers. He replaces Hugh Jennings, who resigns after 14 years to join his old teammate McGraw as assistant manager of the Giants. In other managerial changes at the ML meetings: Lee Fohl replaces Jimmy Burke with the Browns; Clark Griffith, now president of the Senators, gives up the managing job to SS George McBride; George Stallings buys the Rochester club and leaves the Boston Braves, replaced by Fred Mitchell from the Cubs, who is replaced by Johnny Evers; former Yankees skipper Bill Donovan takes over the Phils from Gavvy Cravath.

1921

JANUARY

21st Judge Kenesaw Mountain Landis officially takes over as baseball's commissioner.

22nd The Reds trade P Jimmy Ring and OF Greasy Neale to the Phils for lefty Eppa Rixey, who led the NL with 22 losses in 1920. Rixey will pitch his way into the Hall of Fame over the next 13 years.

FEBRUARY

23rd The Pirates obtain SS Rabbit Maranville from Boston. They give up OF Billy Southworth, OF Fred Nicholson, IF Walter Barbare, and $15,000.

MARCH

4th After 12 years with the Red Sox, OF Harry Hooper goes to the White Sox for OF Nemo Leibold and OF Shano Collins.

21st P Gene Paulette is barred from organized baseball for life for taking part in throwing games. He appeared in one game for the Cardinals in 1918.

APRIL

13th In the season opener for the Yankees, Ruth goes 5-for-5, as New York and Carl Mays beat the A's 11–1.

With former president Woodrow Wilson, new president Warren G. Harding, and VP Calvin Coolidge watching, the Senators lose their home opener 6–3 to the Red Sox. Walter Johnson leaves after 4 innings, the first time he has failed to finish an opening game.

MAY

4th The Giants end Brooklyn's winning streak at 11 games 3–2.

7th Bob Meusel of the Yankees hits for the cycle, and his triple with 2 on beats the Senators 6–5 in the 9th. Former president Wilson witnesses the exciting game in Washington.

13th Giants OF Benny Kauff, FL batting champ in 1914 and 1915, is acquitted of auto theft charges, but Judge Landis bars him from baseball on the basis of undesirable character and reputation. Kauff goes to court for reinstatement, but fails.

28th The league-leading Pirates protest their 4–3, 10-inning loss to the Reds. When hot-tempered Reds P Dolf Luque throws the ball into the Cincinnati dugout, Clyde Barnhart tries to take 3B and is thrown out. The Pirates claim the ball was dead when it went into the dugout. NL president Heydler will sustain the protest and order the game continued with the score 3–3 in the last of the 8th. The Pirates win the replay 4–3 on June 30th.

30th A memorial to Captain Eddie Grant, killed in action in the Argonne Forest October 20, 1918, is unveiled at the Polo Grounds.

Red Sox 1B Stuffy McInnis makes an error, the only one he will make all year. The next day he begins an errorless streak of 163 games and 1,625 chances.

31st The Senators bang out 8 straight hits, including 2 triples, off Waite Hoyt in a 7-run 2nd inning, and beat New York 11–5.

JUNE

1st John McGraw wants Reds 3B Heinie Groh, but Groh, still holding out for $15,000, is put on the ineligible list by the Reds. Groh offers to sign only if he'll be sold to New York. Commissioner Landis vetoes the deal and will reinstate him only if Groh stays with the Reds all season. The decision costs Groh a WS share, but he'll move to New York in 1922.

2nd Reds OF Pat Duncan is the first to hit a fair ball out of Redland Park this season; he will hit just 2 HRs all year.

4th The Pirates' Wilbur Cooper, who with Burleigh Grimes will lead the NL with 22 wins, loses his first after 8 straight victories when the Giants drub him 12–0. The Giants are on top, but only for a few days; the Pirates will regain the lead.

6th Babe Ruth hits a HR off Jim Bagby of Cleveland. The 4-bagger is the 120th of his career, breaking the post-1900 career mark of Gavvy Cravath.

The Detroit Stars' Bill Gatewood pitches the first no-hitter in Negro League history, defeating the Cuban Stars 4–0.

7th The only game canceled because of a murder occurs at Kingsport, TN (Appalachian League), when the body of a slain girl is found at the ballpark. To prevent the trail from becoming confused for bloodhounds, police close the park and cancel the game against Knoxville.

8th Babe Ruth is arrested for speeding in New York, fined $100, and held in jail until 4:00 P.M. Game time is 3:15, so a uniform is taken to him. He changes in jail and follows a police escort to the ballpark where he enters with New York trailing 3–2. They rally for a 4–3 win.

13th The first pitch to Ruth goes 460 feet into the CF bleachers in the Polo Grounds, the first HR ever hit to that spot. He adds HR number 21 in a 13–8 win over Detroit. He also pitches 5 innings for the win, giving up 4 runs, but striking out Ty Cobb. The next day Ruth hits 2 more HRs, his 6th and 7th in 5 games, in a 9–6 win.

Umpires in both leagues begin the practice of rubbing dirt into the balls before each game, using a special clay supplied by A's coach Lena Blackburne from his New Jersey farm.

14th NL P Ray Fisher is placed permanently on the ineligible list by Commissioner Landis for alleged contract jumping. Fisher had left the Reds, thinking he was being placed on the voluntary retired list, in order to become a baseball coach at the University of Michigan. He will serve there for 38 years.

JULY

1st Casey Stengel is traded from the last-place Phils to the 2nd-place Giants, along with IF Johnny Rawlings and P Red Causey for IF Goldie Rapp and outfielders Lance Richbourg and Lee King.

8th In Detroit, RF Harry Heilmann hits a HR that measures 610 feet.

An order is issued that allows fans to keep balls hit into the stands in Pittsburgh.

12th Babe Ruth hits his 137th career HR, passing 19th-century star Roger Connor's record 136.

16th At age 63, Arthur Irwin, pioneer player, manager, and executive who began in the NL in 1880, jumps to his death from a ship in the Atlantic Ocean.

18th The Black Sox trial begins in Chicago.

21st Red Faber wins his 20th game, but it is not easy. He goes 14 innings before edging the A's 2–1. There will be five 20-game winners in the AL, 4 in the NL.

The Indians bang out 9 doubles, and the Yankees 7 for an AL record 16 in Cleveland's 17–8 win. The Indians cling to a 2-game lead.

25th Max Carey flags down 11 flies in CF in the Pirates' 6–3 win over New York, tying 3 others for the NL record.

29th As part of Cleveland's 125th anniversary celebration, Cy Young, 54, makes a 2-inning appearance on the mound in an old-timers' game. Chief Zimmer, 60, is his catcher.

John McGraw buys OF Irish Meusel, who is hitting .353 but has been suspended by the Phillies for lackadaisical play. McGraw gives up 3 bench warmers and $30,000. The Giants take 3 from the Reds and go into the NL lead for the first time. They will fall back by 7 games before coming on with a rush in September.

AUGUST

2nd A Chicago jury brings in a verdict of not guilty against the Black Sox. That night, jurors and defendants celebrate with a party in an Italian restaurant. Ignoring the verdict, Judge Landis bans all 8 defendants from baseball for life.

5th The first radio broadcast of a ML game is heard over KDKA in Pittsburgh. The Pirates-Phils game is announced by Harold Arlin. The Pirates score 3 runs in the 8th inning, beating the Phils 8–5. Arlin, who broadcast the first football game between Pittsburgh and West Virginia, is the grandfather of future San Diego Padre Steve Arlin.

11th The Yankees move one percentage point ahead of the Indians with a 7–3 win over the A's. The 2 teams will run even through September.

13th Boston Braves P John "Mule" Watson hurls 2 complete-game victories over the Phillies, winning by scores of 4–3 and 8–0. It is the 3rd doubleheader he has pitched, the first 2 being with the A's in 1918.

15th A streak of 10 straight hits by the Browns' George Sisler is stopped by Detroit.

19th Ty Cobb gets hit No. 3,000 off Boston P Elmer Myers. At 34, he's the youngest ever to do so.

23rd The Pirates arrive in New York for a 5-game series with a 7½ game lead. They leave town with a 2½ game lead and 5 of the 10 straight losses the Giants will pin on them down the stretch.

28th Babe Ruth starts a record streak in which he gets at least one extra-base hit in 9 straight games. Into the record books go his 119 extra-base hits, 177 runs, and 457 total bases. His .846 slugging average is one point behind that of a year ago.

Jimmy Dykes handles an AL record 17 chances at 2B for the A's, as they beat St. Louis 12–4.

30th The Cubs and Braves each pull a triple play, but they do not help. The Cubs lose to the Giants 5–3, and Boston falls to the Reds 6–4.

31st In the Reds' 7–3 win over the Braves, the 2 infields accept 28 chances, tying the ML record.

SEPTEMBER

5th In the Labor Day afternoon game at Boston, won by the Red Sox 8–2, the Yankees OF makes a record 5 assists, 4 by Bob Meusel. Meusel, with one of the strongest arms in baseball, will lead the AL in assists in 1921 and 1922.

Walter Johnson breaks Cy Young's career strike-out mark by fanning 7 Yankees to run his total to 2,287.

The Browns Urban Shocker takes his first loss after winning 9 in a row. Elmer Smith's 2 HRs pace a 10–5 Indians win in a morning game. In the afternoon game Smith hits another one. Having hit one in Detroit the day before, Smith now has 7 straight hits in 3 games for 22 total bases.

9th An AL record for total runs and hits is made when Chicago beats Detroit 20–15. Each team has 20 hits.

15th Four A's pitchers help the Indians win 17–3, contributing 16 walks. Among them is the starting pitcher Arliss Taylor, appearing in his only ML game. He fans one batter—Joe Sewell, the hardest batter to strike out in ML history.

Babe Ruth hits HR No. 55 in New York's 10–6 win over the Browns.

17th The Giants win their 10th in a row over the Pirates, and their 10th straight, 6–1. They will go on to finish 4 in front of the Pirates.

23rd The Indians come to New York, trailing by 2 points, for a 4-game showdown. Waite Hoyt's arm and Ruth's 3 doubles beat them 4–2.

26th Ruth hits Nos. 57 and 58 to beat the Indians 8–7, and the Yankees take a 2½ game lead. The 4 games draw a record 147,000 people.

OCTOBER

1st White Sox C Ray Schalk makes a putout at 1B. When the Indians' speedy Charlie Jamison singles to RF, Schalk jogs around 1B in case Jamieson takes too wide a turn toward 2B, which he does. Schalk takes a throw from the OF and makes the putout. Schalk is the only catcher to make a putout at every base.

The Yankees clinch their first pennant by sweeping 2 from the A's. Final margin is 4½ games.

2nd The Yankees close the season by beating the Red Sox 7–6. Ruth hits No. 59 off Curt Fullerton; for the team it is No. 134. Stuffy McInnis completes his 119th consecutive errorless game, and Boston SS Everett Scott plays his 832nd consecutive game.

5th In the first one-city WS since 1906, the Polo Grounds will be the site for all 9 games. Carl Mays (27-9) is at his best, needing 86 pitches to set the Giants down with 5 hits—4 of them by Frank Frisch. Ruth drives in the first run of the Series in the opening inning of this 3–0 Yankee win. Mike McNally, subbing for Frank Baker at 3B, steals home in the 5th while Phil Douglas (15-10) is winding up. The game is broadcast on KDKA radio, with Grantland Rice announcing. It is the only game of the season's WS to be aired.

6th In the opener, Johnny Rawlings and Frank Frisch collected the only Giants hits. In game 2 it's the same story. Waite Hoyt (19-13) surrenders 2 singles in another 3–0 Yankee win. Art Nehf (20-10) deserves better, allowing just 3 hits; but 3 errors and 2 mental lapses by the Giants, plus a steal of home by Bob Meusel, put the Giants down 2–0. The 5 hits are the fewest ever in a WS game.

7th The Giants bats wake up against Bob Shawkey (18-12) and 3 other pitchers. A 20-hit barrage and 8-run 8th sink the Yanks 13–5. Jesse Barnes (15-9) gets the win.

9th After a rainout, a Sunday crowd of 36,371 watches Carl Mays and Phil Douglas square off for game 4. Mays works 5 hitless innings, while a run-scoring triple by Wally Schang gives the Yanks a 1–0 lead. The Giants club 7 hits in the last 2 innings for 4 runs. Ruth's first WS homer comes in the 9th, but the Giants win 4–2.

10th In game 5 an unearned run in the first is all the Giants can manage off Waite Hoyt, despite 10 hits and a walk. A 1–1 game is decided in the 4th when Ruth surprises the Giants IF with a perfect bunt, then makes it home on Meusel's double off Art Nehf. Bob Meusel scores on a sacrifice fly, and 3–1 is the result. The 35,758 spectators bring the players' pool to a record $302,522.23.

11th Miller Huggins gambles in Game 6 with lefty Harry Harper (4-3), and the Yankees drive Fred Toney (18-11) to cover with 3 in the first. But the Giants come back with 3 in the 2nd, and continue the attack against Bob Shawkey while Jess Barnes slams the door, striking out 10, including 7 in a row sandwiched around 4 walks. Emil "Irish" Meusel and Frank Snyder homer for the Giants in an 8–5 win. It is Barnes's 2nd WS win in relief.

12th Carl Mays and Phil Douglas meet again, and again Mays has perfect control (he gives up no walks in 26 innings). He yields 6 hits, but a 7th-inning error by Aaron Ward at 2B, followed by Snyder's double, break a 1–1 tie and give Douglas his 2nd win.

13th Waite Hoyt and Art Nehf come back for game 8 with 2 days rest. With 2 on and 2 outs in the first, Giants 1B George Kelly hits a grounder to short that goes through Roger Peckinpaugh, and a run scores. Not another Giant reaches 3B the rest of the day. After Aaron Ward walks in the 9th, Frank "Home Run" Baker hits a drive toward right, but 2B Johnny Rawlings spears it and throws him out while on the ground. Ward heads for 3B and is gunned down by a throw from Kelly to Frisch to end the Series. Hoyt does not allow an earned run in 3 complete games. The Giants are the first to lose the first 2 games and come back to win the Series.

16th In defiance of a Landis ban on WS participants playing post-season exhibitions, Ruth, Bob Meusel, and P Bill Piercy launch a barnstorming tour in Buffalo. Five days later, they cut it short in Scranton. In the meantime Ruth openly challenges Landis to act. The judge does, fining the players their WS shares—$3,362.26—and suspending them until May 20th of the following season.

Judge Landis outlaws gentleman's agreements and cover-ups of players optioned to the minors without proper paperwork. He declares 6 players free agents, including Heinie Manush, who will ride a 17-year .330 BA into the Hall of Fame in 1964.

DECEMBER

6th John McGraw finally gets Heinie Groh from the Reds; it costs him C Mike Gonzalez, OF George Burns, and $250,000.

20th At the ML meetings, the AL votes to return to the best-of-7 WS; the NL votes to keep the 5-of-9. Judge Landis casts the deciding vote, and the 4-of-7 format is reinstated.

The Yankees raid Boston again, and come away with P Bullet Joe Bush, SS Everett Scott, and P Sad Sam Jones in exchange for SS Roger Peckinpaugh (who goes on to Washington), pitchers Jack Quinn, Rip Collins, and Bill Piercy, and $50,000.

22nd Socks Seybold, the holder of the AL season HR record before Ruth, dies at 51 when his car plunges over an embankment.

1922

JANUARY

10th   The following round-robin deal benefits everyone: Roger Peckinpaugh goes from Boston to Washington; Joe Dugan, from the Athletics to Boston; and OF Bing Miller and P Jose Acosta, from Washington to Philadelphia. Acosta will be sold to Chicago on February 4th.

13th   Buck Weaver, one of the 8 Black Sox, applies unsuccessfully for reinstatement.

14th   OF Clyde Milan is named manager of the Washington Senators.

Ben Shibe, half-owner and president of the Athletics since their AL start in 1906, dies at 84. A partner in the A. J. Reach sporting goods company, Shibe invented the machinery that made possible the manufacture of standard baseballs.

18th   The Cubs buy OF Jigger Statz and P Vic Aldridge from Los Angeles for 8 players and cash.

24th   Brooklyn buys SS Sam Crane from Cincinnati. He will play in 3 games and later be convicted of murder. He will be visited in prison by Connie Mack, who works for his parole and gives him a job.

FEBRUARY

4th   Joe Harris, formerly with Cleveland, is reinstated by Judge Landis because of his good war record. Harris had been on the ineligible list for having played with and against ineligible players in independent games. "His service in France, where he was gassed after bitter fighting, caused him to do things he might not have done," says Judge Landis in reinstating him.

9th   Landis cracks down on phony player deals. He fines the Cards and Tigers $150 each, and 3 minor league clubs a total of $1,400 for violating waiver rules. In March, he will assess the Giants $1,764 for the improper transfer of a player.

18th   Judge Landis resigns his federal judgeship, claiming the 2 jobs (judge and commissioner) took up too much time.

The Reds trade P Rube Marquard and SS Larry Kopf to Boston for P Jack Scott.

22nd   Cards C Pickles Dillhoefer, 26, dies from typhoid fever following an operation.

MARCH

6th   Babe Ruth signs for 3 years at $52,000 a year. The next-highest paid New York player is Home Run Baker at $16,000.

30th   Christy Mathewson is elected the first president of the "B" Club of Bucknell.

APRIL

12th   There are no playing managers in the NL for the first time since 1900. Long considered an economic necessity, the dual role is no longer essential. It will be 1930 before the AL has all bench managers.

President Warren Harding throws out the first ball in Washington, as the Senators beat the Yankees 6–5.

Giants SS Dave Bancroft handles 2 assists and 3 putouts in a 4–3 Opening Day loss to Brooklyn. He will handle 1.046 for the year, putting him even with Rabbit Maranville's 1914 record as the most active shortstops of any season.

13th   Dazzy Vance, 31, makes his Brooklyn debut and loses to the Giants' Phil Douglas 4–3. In 1915 when Vance made one start for the Pirates, it was Douglas who beat him. Since then Vance has been in the minors. Despite his late start, the 6 foot 2 inch righthander will win 197 in 14 years and a place in the Hall of Fame in 1955.

15th   The Giants pummel 3 Dodger pitchers for 11 runs in the first inning, winning 17–10.

18th   Willie Kamm makes his debut for the White Sox in a 6–5 loss at Cleveland. He hits a double and handles 2 chances afield. The first $100,000 priced minor league player (bought from the San Francisco Seals), Kamm will be voted by Chicago fans the all-time White Sox 3B.

22nd   The Browns' Ken Williams hits 3 HRs against the White Sox, with George Sisler on base each time. Given a head start by the suspended Ruth, he will take the HR and RBI titles and become the first 30-30 man, with 39 HRs and 37 SBs.

25th   Ken Williams smashes his 6th HR in 4 days, tying Ruth's 1921 feat. On the 29th he'll pole 2 more.

29th The NY Giants hit 4 inside-the-park HRs in one windswept game in spacious Braves Field in Boston. George Kelly hits 2, and Ross Youngs and Dave Bancroft hit the others.

30th Johnny Mostil, fleet-footed White Sox CF, moves over to LF and makes two outstanding catches to save Charlie Robertson's 2–0 perfect game over Detroit. It's the only game Mostil ever plays in LF. Play is stopped twice after Ty Cobb and Harry Heilmann complain that Robertson is doctoring the ball.

MAY

5th The Giants evict their AL tenants as of the end of the year, so the Yankees sign a contract to build their own $750,000 stadium on a site they had held an option on since 1920.

7th Giants righthander Jesse Barnes walks Cy Williams in the 5th to spoil a 6–0 perfect no-hitter over the Phils.

Pirates rookie Walter Mueller hits a HR on the first ML pitch he sees, and it comes from Grover Alexander. The box score credits the HR to teammate Ray Rohwer. In 4 years Mueller will hit one more HR.

8th Sam Breadon buys controlling interest in the Cardinals. He and Branch Rickey will combine to create one of baseball's most successful operations.

15th In a game at New York, Ty Cobb beats out a grounder to SS Everett Scott. Veteran writer Fred Lieb scores it a hit in the box score he files with the Associated Press. But official scorer John Kieran of the *Times* gives an error to Scott. At the season's end, the AL official records, based on AP box scores, list Cobb at .401. New York writers complain unsuccessfully, claiming it should be .399, based on the official scorer's stats.

20th Babe Ruth and Bob Meusel, suspended on October 16, 1921, by Judge Landis, return to the New York lineup and go hitless. Two days later Ruth will hit his first HR of the year. The Browns, down 2–0 after 7, score one in the 8th and 7 in the 9th, 6 of them coming after the game-ending out has apparently been called by ump Ollie Chill at first base.

25th Babe Ruth is suspended one day and fined $200 for throwing dirt on an ump after being called

out on a play at 2B, then going into the stands after a heckler. He is also stripped of his title as team captain.

29th The U.S. Supreme Court rules baseball is not interstate commerce, and the Baltimore Feds lose their case. The request for a rehearing will be denied.

30th Between games of the holiday doubleheader, the Cubs swap OF Max Flack to the Cards for OF Cliff Heathcote. The players, who both played in the morning game, trade uniforms and play for their new teams in the afternoon. Heathcote goes 0-for-3 as a Card, 2-for-4 as a Cub. Flack goes 0-for-4 in the first game, 1–for-4 in the 2nd, as the Cubs win both. Cubs SS Charlie Hollocher strikes out for the first time this year, on a Bill Doak spitter. A .304 career hitter, he will whiff 5 times in 1922. In 3 years he will fan 33 times in 372 games.

With the score at 8–8 in the bottom of the 10th inning in game 2 of a Giants-Phils twin bill at Baker Bowl, C Butch Henline bats with Cy Williams on 1B and Curt Walker on 3B. Henline lines an apparent 3-run HR into the LF stands, and Walker scores the winning run. Henline reaches 2B before heading for the CF clubhouse, but as Williams had not scored at that point, Henline is credited with just a double, making the final score 9–8. The Philadelphia *Evening Bulletin* noted that, "it would have been a home run if Williams had completed the circuit, but they were serving ice cream and frankfurters in the clubhouse and when he reached second base his feet naturally strayed through center field."

George Burns, now a member of the Reds, steals home against the Pirates in the 3rd. A double steal with Greasy Neale, it is his 28th career steal of home and gives him a new NL record formerly held by Honus Wagner.

JUNE

3rd Indians 1B Stuffy McInnis makes an error, his first in 163 games.

9th James C. Dunn, who brought Cleveland its first pennant as Indians president in 1920, dies. He is succeeded by former newspaperman Ernest S. Barnard, who will later become AL president.

10th The Giants raise their WS pennant on George Burns Day; it's the first appearance at the Polo Grounds for the popular OF now with the Reds after 10 years in a Giants uniform.

12th   The Cards get 10 straight hits in the 6th to beat the Phils 14–8, tying their own record of September 17, 1920. One of the hits is a HR by SS Specs Toporcer, the first nonpitcher to wear glasses. But Toporcer's first ML HR is negated when he passes base runner Doc Lavan.

19th   Babe Ruth explodes at umpire Bill Dinneen and gets his 4th suspension of the year.

28th   Walter Johnson wins another 1–0 battle, this one over the Yankees, for his 3rd straight shutout and 97th in all.

Christy Mathewson, in a sanitarium for treatment of tuberculosis, throws out the first pitch for a game at Saranac Lake, NY.

JULY

2nd   A's OF Tilly Walker hits 2 HRs, giving him 4 in 2 days, as the A's lose to New York 9–3. He will finish with 37 for the year, 2 ahead of Ruth. The Athletics, with the AL's winningest pitcher in Eddie Rommel (27-13) and losingest in Slim Harriss (9-20) will lead the AL with 114 HRs and climb out of the cellar.

5th   The Cards' Rogers Hornsby hits his 20th HR, tying Ken Williams of the AL for HR leadership.

The first game ever played in Hungary takes place in Budapest.

7th   Pirates OF Max Carey is the busiest man on the field in an 18-inning 9–8 loss to the Giants. He gets 6 hits, draws 3 walks, has 3 SBs, including one of home, and catches 7 flies. His 51 SBs in 53 attempts is the highest success rate ever achieved by a SB leader. His record of 31 straight steals without being caught will be broken by Davey Lopes's 38 in 1975.

Commissioner Landis bars ML teams from playing in Montreal.

8th   Reds righthander Pete Donohue beats the Phils 7–1. A 3-time 20-game winner in 9 years with the Reds, Donohue will beat the Phils 20 straight times.

17th   Ty Cobb gets 5 hits in a game for the 4th time this year, setting an AL mark. His previous 5-hit contests were on May 7th, July 7th, and July 12th.

22nd   When the Cards go into first place by beating Boston while the Reds are downing the Giants, it is the first time both St. Louis teams are ever on top together.

23rd   When umpires Brick Owens and Tom Connolly miss a train, the Detroit and St. Louis trainers, Bits Bierhalter and Howley, are pressed into service.

The Yankees pick up 3B Joe Dugan and one-time Cleveland WS hero Elmer Smith from Boston, giving up OF Elmer Miller, SS Chick Fewster, SS John Mitchell, and P Lefty O'Doul. This deal leads to a rule barring nonwaiver trades after June 15th.

Ed Roush ends his holdout and signs with the Reds.

Cubs 1B Ray Grimes homers in Chicago's 4–1 win over Brooklyn, giving him at least one RBI per game for 17 in a row, a ML record.

28th   The Yanks move back into first when Sad Sam Jones beats Ray Kolp. Browns lefty Dave Danforth gets a 10-day suspension for using a foreign substance on the ball.

The AL announces plans to erect a $100,000 monument to baseball in East Potomac Park, Washington. It never gets built.

New York will lead for 85 days, the Browns for 65. The Browns hold a 3-game lead when owner Phil Ball gives the team a $5,000 bonus. At the end of the season he will distribute another $20,000, from $1,000 to top stars to $200 for each sub. They will also get $662 each from the AL for 2nd place.

30th   The Giants send pitchers Fred Toney and Larry Benton to the Braves with $100,000 and bring back righthander Hugh McMillan. Toney refuses to report and stays in New York. When Benton develops into a consistent pitcher, the Giants will buy him back.

AUGUST

4th   The Cards pass New York and move into first again, as the Cubs score a 3–2 win over the Giants.

5th   Tommy McCarthy, a top OF of the 1890s, dies at 58. He will enter the Hall of Fame in 1946. On the 14th, an all-star team will beat the Red Sox in a benefit game that raises more than $5,000 for his family.

In the midst of a 13-game winning streak that carries them into 3rd place, the Pirates set a unique record. Beginning with a 9–3 win over the Braves, every man in the lineup gets at least one hit — including pitchers and subs—for 5 games in a row. On August 7th and 8th, they set an NL mark with 49 hits in 2 games, 17–10 and 19–8 wins over the Phils.

7th   Ken Williams hits 2 HRs in the 6th inning as the Browns score 9 times against Washington in a 16–6 win. Williams is the first to do so since the 1890s.

8th   The Giants Shufflin' Phil Douglas is suspended and fined $100 by John McGraw. (Douglas, an alcoholic, and McGraw did not enjoy the best of relationships after McGraw forced Douglas to undergo a terrible treatment for alcoholism.) Douglas writes a letter to St. Louis Cardinals OF Les Mann, his former roommate at Chicago, offering to disappear if they make it worth his while, lest he help McGraw win the pennant. Mann turns the letter over to Branch Rickey, who relays it to Commissioner Landis. In Pittsburgh on the 16th, Douglas admits he wrote the letter, and Landis bars him from baseball. Douglas was 11-4 at the time, with the lowest ERA on the club (2.63).

Pittsburgh makes a ML record 46 hits in a doubleheader against Philadelphia.

13th   The New York Yankees Everett Scott nears 1,000 consecutive games played, but it takes an extra effort to keep the streak alive. He spends $40 to hire a car to get to Chicago in time for the game after a train he is on is wrecked.

14th   Lizzie Murphy plays 1B for an AL all-star team in an exhibition game against the Boston Red Sox, making her the first female to play for a ML team. The all-stars win 3–2.

15th   In a game between Chicago and Boston, 35 singles are hit—21 by the White Sox, 14 by the Red Sox—an AL record. Chicago wins 19–11.

25th   One of the most poorly pitched ML games ever played takes place in Chicago. The Cubs edge the Phils 26–23. There are 51 hits, 23 walks, and 10 errors. The Phils have the bases loaded in the 9th when the game ends, making a total of 16 left on base; the Cubs leave 9. When the Cubs score 14 in the 4th to take a 25–6 lead, OF Marty Callaghan bats 3 times, getting 2 hits and striking out. Time of game: 3:01. Modern records are set for total runs and hits. The 14-run inning ties the Yankees' mark of July 6, 1920. Cliff Heathcote of the Cubs sets a modern NL record by reaching base 7 times in the 9-inning game.

30th   After hitting HR No. 28 in the first inning, Babe Ruth argues too strongly over a called strike on his next AB, and he is thrown out of the game.

Suspended for the 5th time of the year, he is out for 3 days.

SEPTEMBER

5th   At the start of the day, both New York teams are on top, and both Boston teams are on the bottom. But today, the Red Sox will take 2 and knock the leaders off their perch. Babe Ruth hits his last regular season HR in the Polo Grounds. He gets it off Herb Pennock, who also gave up Ruth's first Polo Grounds homer.

8th   The Yankees go back on top, this time to stay, beating the Senators while the Browns lose to Detroit.

9th   Danville's Otto Pahlman (III League) has his 50-game hitting streak stopped.

11th   The Yankees play their farewell home game in the Polo Grounds. An estimated 40,000 overflow the stadium with another 25,000 turned away. Joe Bush beats the Philadelphia A's 10–3 in the opener, and Waite Hoyt takes the second 2–1. Plans are in the works to expand the park to 56,000 capacity. This is the last regular season AL game at the Polo Grounds. The Yanks will play their next 18 games on the road, and then open in Yankee Stadium next spring.

13th   The Browns announce that George Sisler has severely strained ligaments and cannot lift his right arm over his head. He might be out for the remainder of the season, jeopardizing the Browns' pennant chances and Sisler's 39-game hitting streak. Ironically, the injury occured when Sisler tried to catch a throw on a hit by Ty Cobb, whose streak he is trying to break.

Baltimore wins its 4th straight International League pennant.

15th   C Butch Henline is the first NL player to hit 3 homers in a game since 1897, as the Phils beat the Cards 10–9.

16th   Pennant fever rages in St. Louis, as the Yankees come to town with a half-game lead. Bob Shawkey outpitches Urban Shocker 2–1, as Sisler ties Cobb's 1911 record by hitting in his 40th straight game. While chasing a fly ball in the 9th, New York OF Whitey Witt is hit in the head and knocked cold by a soda bottle thrown from the bleachers. Ban Johnson will initially offer a $1,000 reward for the name of the bottle-thrower. Then, to calm the crowds, the AL offers the theory that Witt stepped on the bottle and it flew up and hit him. The incident leads to a ban on the sale of bottled drinks in ballparks.

17th Browns southpaw Hub Pruett, who has fanned Ruth 9 of 10 times over the season, is reached for a HR by the Bambino, but he still beats the Yankees 5–1. George Sisler extends his streak to 41 games.

18th Whitey Witt, his head bandaged from being hit by the bottle, drives in 2 in the 9th for a 3–2 New York win, and they leave town 1½ in front. They will finish one game on top, clinching the pennant on the 30th with a 3–1 win in Boston. Sisler is stopped by New York's Joe Bush, the same pitcher he had started the streak against on July 27th.

20th Rogers Hornsby is stopped by Burleigh Grimes of Brooklyn after hitting in 33 straight games.

21st The AL reinstates the MVP award, last given in 1914, appointing a committee of one writer from each city, headed by I. E. Sanborn of the Chicago *Tribune*. As a player-manager, Ty Cobb is not eligible. The trophy goes to George Sisler. The NL will pick up the idea 2 years later.

24th Rogers Hornsby hits his 41st and 42nd HRs of the year, connecting off brothers Jesse and Virgil Barnes of the Giants.

25th The Giants beat St. Louis to clinch John McGraw's 8th pennant and the Giants' 10th in 41 years in the NL.

OCTOBER

1st Rogers Hornsby's 3-for-5 on the last day puts him at .401, the first .400-hitter in the NL since Ed Delahanty in 1899. His NL-record 250 hits top Willie Keeler's 243 in 1897. Hornsby wins the Triple Crown with 152 RBI and 42 HRs. His 102 extra-base hits will be the NL's tops until Chuck Klein's 107 in 1930.

4th For the first time, the entire WS will be broadcast over the radio. Writer Grantland Rice does the announcing for station WJZ, Newark; it is relayed to WYG in Schenectady.

For the first time since 1908, 2 repeaters meet in the WS. The Yankees get there with an all righthanded starting pitching staff; the Giants on a .305 BA. In a return to the 7-game format, the Giants will win 4 games while scoring in only 5 innings. The Yankees'

Joe Bush (26-7) leads Art Nehf (19-13) 2–0 when Irish Meusel's 2-run single and Pep Young's sacrifice fly score 3 runs in the 8th for a 3–2 win in game 1. Rosy Ryan (17-12) gets the win in relief.

5th Bob Shawkey (20-12) goes the route, with the Giants scoring 3 in the first and the Yanks getting single tallies in the first, 4th, and 8th. A near-riot erupts among the 36,514 fans when umpire George Hildebrand, acting on umpire Bill Klem's advice, calls the game, a 3–3 tie, due to darkness after 10 innings. The fans think there's light enough to continue. It takes a police escort to get Judge Landis out of the park and away from the unruly mob. That night he bends over backwards to negate the public's opinion that the game might have been called to provide an extra day's gate by donating the $120,554 receipts to charities. Half will go to New York charities, and half to disabled soldiers.

6th The Giants Jack Scott (8-2 with the Giants) fires a 4-hitter as a surprise starter in game 3, after Hugh McQuillan (6-5 with NY) warms up to face Waite Hoyt (19-12). Scott gets the Yanks to hit 18 grounders. Frank Frisch's 2 RBI are more than enough in the 3–0 win. With 2 hits in each game so far, Frisch will bat .471. Heinie Groh, hitting safely in every game, will be at .474.

7th Judge Landis insists game 4 be played despite a heavy rain. Again one big inning—a 4-run fourth off Carl Mays (13-4)—is enough for McQuillan to squeeze out a 4–3 win. Aaron Ward's 2nd HR of the Series is all the long-ball clout the Yankees will display.

8th The Yanks score first, but the Giants score 2 in the 3rd and 3 in the 8th to win the finale 5–3, as Art Nehf hands Joe Bush his 2nd loss.

18th The Tigers trade pitchers Carl Holling and Howard Ehmke, along with infielder Danny Clark, outfielder Babe Herman, and $25,000 to Boston for 2B Del Pratt and P Rip Collins. Pratt has 2 more .300 seasons left; Collins and Ehmke provide long-term benefits to their clubs. Herman, 19, won't make it to the big leagues until 1926, and then it will be with Brooklyn.

30th The Giants pay $65,000 and 3 players to Baltimore for Jack Bentley, "another Babe Ruth." Bentley hit .349 and was 13-1 as a pitcher in 1922 (41-5 since 1920). The 3 players are to be delivered by

March 20, 1923, and if not satisfactory to Baltimore, the Giants will pay $2,500 per man instead.

NOVEMBER

1st Former A's C Ira Thomas buys the Shreveport club in the Texas League for $75,000. Other former players who own pieces of minor league clubs include Ty Cobb (Augusta), Eddie Collins (Baltimore), and George Stallings (Rochester).

7th The Phils fire manager Kaiser Wilhelm. Art Fletcher succeeds him.

Morgan G. Bulkeley, first president of the NL and later governor of Connecticut and U.S. senator, dies. As president of the Hartford club, he presided over the NL's first meeting and headed the league for one year.

15th Former Providence OF Paul Hines is arrested on charges of pickpocketing. The 69-year-old Hines made a famous play in a game on May 8, 1878—the disputed first unassisted triple play.

27th Cards OF Austin McHenry, 27, dies from a brain tumor. After hitting .350 with 17 HRs in 1921, he became ill during the 1922 season and was hitting .303 when forced to quit.

DECEMBER

5th Connie Mack spends money to begin building another winner. He sends $40,000 and several players to Portland (Pacific Coast League) for 3B Sammy Hale.

12th Jake Ruppert agrees to buy out his partner Colonel Huston and gains full control of the Yankees.

13th The Phils buy IF Heinie Sand from Salt Lake City (PCL) for 4 players and cash. A competent SS, Sand will be the object of an alleged bribery scheme that causes another scandal.

Alarmed at the increase in HR hitting (1,054 in the major leagues, up from 936), some AL owners back a zoning system setting a minimum of 300 feet for a ball to be called a HR. The motion dies. In another action, the league requires each club to furnish 2 home uniforms per player, plus extra caps and stockings on the road, to improve the players' appearance. In NL meetings, Charles Ebbets proposes putting numbers on players' sleeves or caps. It's left to each club to do as it wishes.

14th In a joint meeting, the ban on nonwaiver trades after June 15th is approved. The NL favors a 50-player limit until June 15th, the AL votes for 40. Judge Landis breaks the deadlock in favor of 40. Compensation of WS umpires is changed from a percentage of the players' pool to a flat $2,000.

Still smarting over the rejection of the official scorer's decision in the Ty Cobb case, the national baseball writers' group meets and votes to back the New York group's protest. Fred Lieb, who had filled in the AP box score giving Cobb the disputed hit, asks Ban Johnson to revise the records to .399 for Cobb. Johnson complains of not receiving box scores from some writers, who are appointed by the clubs as official scorers.

16th The Eastern Colored League (chartered as the Mutual Association of Eastern Colored Baseball Clubs) is formally organized. The league will complete 5 seasons before folding in midsummer of 1928.

1923

JANUARY

3rd   The Yankees pluck 2 rookies from the Red Sox, P George Pipgras and OF Harvey Hendrick, in exchange for 2nd-string C Al DeVormer.

30th   The Red Sox send P Herb Pennock to New York in exchange for IF Norm McMillan, P George Murray, OF Camp Skinner, and $50,000.

FEBRUARY

10th   C Muddy Ruel and P Allen Russell go from the Red Sox to Washington for C Val Picinich and outfielder Howard Shanks and Ed Goebel.

11th   Jack Fournier comes to the Brooklyn Robins in a trade that sends C Hy Myers to St. Louis. Fournier, a Cardinal 1B for years, says he'll quit if he has to move, but gives in and plays another 5 years.

20th   Christy Mathewson becomes president of the Boston Braves after buying the club for $300,000 with New York attorney Judge Emil Fuchs and Bostonian James McDonough. The deal does not include Braves Field, which still belongs to James Gaffney. There are also 85 minority stockholders.

MARCH

6th   The Cardinals announce that their players will wear numerals on their uniforms, and number them according to the batting order.

7th   After sitting out most of last season, 35-year-old Fred Toney signs for one more year with the Cards.

The New England American Legion appeals to Commissioner Landis to discontinue morning games on Memorial Day. The request is turned down.

8th   Judge Landis allows former Giants lefthanded P Rube Benton to return to the NL. Benton had admitted prior knowledge of the 1919 WS fix, but he remained in baseball, winning 22 for St. Paul (American Association). NL President Heydler disagrees with Landis, calling Benton "undesirable," but does not stop the Reds from signing him. Benton, 35, will be 14-10 for the 2nd-place Reds.

APRIL

3rd   Two "Black Sox" sue the White Sox. Swede Risberg and Happy Felsch seek $400,000 damages and $6,750 back salary for conspiracy and injury to reputation, but their suit will be unsuccessful.

17th   Record Opening Day crowds turn out in Chicago—more than 33,000—for the Cubs' dedication of their greatly enlarged and remodeled park, and in Cincinnati, where 30,338 watch the Reds win an 11-inning 3-2 contest over the Cards.

In the longest NL opener to date, Brooklyn and Philadelphia battle to a 14-inning 5–5 tie. Dutch Ruether, who beat the Phils 7 straight in 1922, goes the distance.

18th   The debut of Yankee Stadium is a huge success with an announced attendance of 74,217. Bob Shawkey, aided by Babe Ruth's 3-run HR, beats Howard Ehmke and the Red Sox 4–1.

20th   The Cubs win 12–11 over the Pirates on Gabby Hartnett's 9th-inning HR. There are 8 HRs in the game, 6 by the Cubs, who had hit 4 the day before. The Cubs will hit 90 for the year, more than double their team total of 42 last year.

22nd   The first Sunday game at Yankee Stadium draws an estimated 60,000, but the Yankees suffer their first loss of the year, 4–3 to Washington.

24th   President Warren G. Harding attends the game at Yankee Stadium and sees Babe Ruth hit a HR in a 4–0 win over the Senators.

26th   The Giants receive their 1922 WS rings, then beat the Braves 7–3 in their home opener, despite a record-tying 5 double plays by Boston. Giants 1B George "Highpockets" Kelly ties a record, handling 22 chances in the field.

30th   Phils OF Fred "Cy" Williams starts an unprecedented slugging spree, going 2-for-4 in a 12–3 loss to the Braves. In 15 games in the Baker Bowl, he will accumulate 65 total bases on 11 singles, 5 doubles, 11 home runs, and 29 RBI. He will lead the NL with 41 HRs, equal to Ruth's AL top total, but his BA will drop to .293, his only sub-.300 mark during a 7-year stretch.

MAY

2nd Walter Johnson gets his 100th shutout, and New York SS Everett Scott gets a gold medal from the AL for playing in his 1,000th consecutive game, as Washington defeats the Yankees 3–0.

3rd Pirates 1B Charlie Grimm starts a 25-game hitting streak that is stopped by Dick Rudolph, the 1914 Braves hero, who comes off the coaching lines to make 4 starts for Boston.

7th Tigers 3B Bob Jones ties an AL record with 9 assists; Willie Kamm will match it for the White Sox on September 30th.

11th The Phils and Cards bash a record 10 HRs out of Baker Bowl; Cy Williams has 3 of them in the Phils' 20–14 win.

OF Pete Schneider strokes 5 HRs, including 2 grand slams, in a game for Vernon (Pacific Coast League). The former ML pitcher drives in 14 runs in a 35–11 victory over Salt Lake City.

12th P Hollis "Sloppy" Thurston goes from the Browns to the White Sox.

13th Washington rookie Wally Warmoth strikes out Cleveland SS Joe Sewell twice. It is the first of only 2 times in his 14-year career that Sewell will fan twice in the same contest.

17th When the Giants return big southpaw Rube Walberg to Portland (PCL) after a 2-game trial, the A's buy him. He'll be 4-8 in the first of his 15 ML seasons.

Grover Alexander issues a walk after starting the season with 52 IP without a pass for the Cubs. He walks 3 in a 7–4 win over the Phils.

21st Formal transfer of T. L. Huston's interest in the Yankees to Jake Ruppert is completed for $1.5 million. Ten days later Ruppert buys 2 more sets of uniforms so his players can wear a clean outfit every day, an unprecedented move.

25th Ty Cobb scores his 1,741st run, passing Honus Wagner's record.

30th After playing before the NL's biggest crowd (41,000) in the P.M. game of the holiday twin bill against Brooklyn, the Giants head west with a 4-game lead over the Pirates. Five regulars will bat over .300, and three will top 100 RBI, led by NL leader Irish Meusel's 125. At 3B, rookie Travis Jackson takes over for gimpy Heinie Groh. With 5 future Hall of Famers in the lineup and 8 on the roster during the season, the Giants will be the first team to hold first place from opening to closing day and the only NL team to have done it. With average pitching, they win just 95 games, but it's enough for a 4½ game margin over the Reds.

JUNE

1st The Giants score in every inning, beating the Phils 22–8. It's been done only once since, by the Cardinals on September 13, 1964.

7th John McGraw ships P Jesse Barnes and C Earl Smith to the Braves for P Mule Watson and C Hank Gowdy.

8th After Browns C Pat Collins leaves the game after pinch-running in the 2nd inning, A's manager Connie Mack gives the okay for him to come back as a pinch hitter for P Ray Kolp in the 9th. He walks.

13th Rogers Hornsby, out since May 24th, comes back with 3 hits. He'll "slump" to .384 but still capture his 4th straight title.

17th Reds IF Sammy Bohne spoils Brooklyn's Dazzy Vance's no-hitter with a 9th inning 2-out single.

JULY

7th Cleveland scores in every inning against the Red Sox, but playing at home, the team does not bat in the 9th. In the 8 innings, they run up an AL-record 27 runs, including 13 in the 6th, for a 27–3 win. In 3 innings, Lefty O'Doul gives up 16 runs on 11 hits and 8 walks. This is his last season as a ML pitcher, but he will return to the ML in 1928 as an OF. The Indians keep it up, scoring 3 in the first inning of the 2nd game en route to a 8–5 win.

10th Cardinals rookie P Johnny Stuart hurls 2 complete-game victories over Boston, winning by scores of 11–1 and 6–3.

11th Harry Frazee, owner of the Red Sox since 1916, sells out for over $1 million to a group of Ohio businessmen, who bring in veteran front office man Bob Quinn from St. Louis to run the club. Frazee's departure is welcomed by Boston fans who are fed up with the sale of Frazee's best players over the years.

22nd　Walter Johnson notches his 3,000th strikeout on the way to 3,508. He fans 5 in beating Cleveland 3–1.

AUGUST

1st　Stepping in against the Indians Sherrod Smith in the 9th inning, Babe Ruth starts off batting righthanded. After taking a strike, he switches to LH and hits his 25th HR of the season. The Indians still win 5–3. The Babe will bat righty 4 days later.

3rd　No games are played following the death of President Harding in San Francisco on August 2nd. The schedule will also be canceled a week later on the day of his funeral.

5th　Against the Browns, Ruth again bats righthanded. After the Babe hits his 26th and 27th HRs off of Ray Kolp, relief P Elam Vangilder takes no chances with Ruth and walks him intentionally in the 11th and again in the 13th inning. Ruth bats righty against Vangilder. Bob Meusel's single wins the game 9–8.

13th　Pirates OF Max Carey steals 2B, 3B, and home versus Brooklyn. He will again lead the NL with 51. Equally fleet in the field, he will garner 450 putouts and 28 assists. He is the only OF to top 400 putouts 6 times. Richie Ashburn will later do it 9 times.

15th　Senators southpaw George Mogridge becomes the only hurler to steal home in extra innings when he scores an insurance run in the 12th in a 5–1 win over the White Sox.

17th　The Cardinals stop Dazzy Vance after 10 straight wins 8–5.

After 111 games, Babe Ruth is hitting .401 with 31 HRs. He'll wind up with his highest BA, .393. With 205 hits, a ML record 170 walks, and 4 times hit by pitches, Ruth will reach base a record 379 times.

20th　A 4-piece bat used by Ruth is banned by AL president Ban Johnson because of the glue used on it. A protest is made against the Browns' Ken Williams for using a bat with a wooden plug in it. Johnson rules that all bats must be one piece with nothing added except tape extending to 18 inches up the handle.

23rd　Reds 2B Sammy Bohne and OF Pat Duncan deny under oath that they have been approached to throw games with the Giants.

31st　Giants owner Charles Stoneham is indicted by a federal grand jury for perjury. He will also be indicted for mail fraud. He had denied any ownership in 2 bucket-shop operations that had been found guilty of stock frauds; creditors of the 2 firms claimed he retained financial interests in both. Other NL owners are rumored to be forming a pool to buy him out, but Stoneham stays out of jail and in the NL.

SEPTEMBER

4th　Yankee Sam Jones no-hits the Athletics 2–0. Babe Ruth makes the only strikeout of the game as he slips a point behind Detroit's Harry Heilmann in the batting race.

In a twilight charity game, Ruth plays 1B for Philadelphia's Ascension Catholic Club. Ruth scores the only run in a 2–1 loss to the Lit Brothers.

7th　Boston's Howard Ehmke strikes out one while pitching a no-hitter against the A's. "Ehmke's zippy crossfire came out of the shortstop's chest like bad news from a gatling gun" (Philadelphia *Public Ledger*). Preserving the no-hitter is A's P Slim Harriss, who hits the ball to the wall in the 7th and winds up on 2B, but he is called out for failing to touch 1B.

13th　The White Sox buy OF Maurice Archdeacon from Rochester (International League) for $50,000. After batting .402 in 22 games, the little speed merchant will drop to .319, then to .111, then out of sight.

14th　George Burns, 1B for the Boston Red Sox, makes an unassisted triple play on a line drive hit by Cleveland's Frank Brower. He tags out Rube Lutzke and rushes to 2B for the 3rd out before Riggs Stephenson returns.

15th　The Cubs lose 10–6 to the Giants in Chicago. After he makes an out call at 2B, umpire Charlie Moran is pelted by pop bottles. Judge Landis shakes his cane at the angry mob, and play is held up for 15 minutes. John McGraw and the umpires need a police escort at the end of the game.

Paul Strand, RF for Salt Lake City (PCL), makes his 290th hit, a pro baseball record. He will play in 194 games, make 325 hits, including 66 doubles, 13 triples, and 43 HRs, for a .394 BA, with 180 runs and 187 RBI. He also has 612 total chances in the OF. Strand, 30, had come up to the Braves as a pitcher in 1913 and was 6-2 for the 1914 pennant winners, mostly in relief. The Athletics will pay a reported $100,000 (which Mack later says was really $40,000) for him, but he will hit just .167.

17th The Giants' George Kelly homers in the 3rd, 4th, and 5th against the Cubs. New York wins 13–6.

20th The Yanks clinch their 3rd straight pennant, beating St. Louis 4–3 to lead by 18 games. Their final margin is 16.

21st Babe Ruth is the unanimous choice of the AL committee of baseball writers for the MVP award.

24th Bill Terry takes his first swings in a Giants uniform as a pinch hitter. On September 30th he will play his first game at 1B and get his first hit in a 4–3 win over Boston.

27th Signed in June for a $1,500 bonus, and recently brought up from Hartford (Eastern League), Lou Gehrig hits the first of his 493 HRs. It comes off Bill Piercy at Fenway Park in an 8–3 New York win.

Rogers Hornsby is fined $500 and suspended indefinitely by the Cardinals when, feeling ill, he refuses to take the field for a game against the Dodgers, despite the team doctor's opinion that he is in condition to play.

28th The Yankees beat the Red Sox 24–4 with 30 hits in 55 at bats, both AL records.

The Giants beat Brooklyn 3–0 to clinch the NL flag.

Three weeks after both pitchers have thrown no-hitters versus the A's, Sam Jones of the Yankees and Howard Ehmke of the Red Sox clash. It is not Ehmke's day; he is routed after facing 16 batters in an 11-run 6th inning. Babe Ruth hits HR number 38.

OCTOBER

4th Cleveland's Tris Speaker connects against the Browns for his 57th double. His final total of 59 is a record that will be beaten in 1931 by Earl Webb (67), but his career-high 793 are still tops.

Tigers P Herman Pillette loses 9–6 to Chicago for his AL-high 19th loss of the season. His son Duane will lead the AL with 14 losses in 1951.

Allen "Rubber-Arm" Russell pitches in his 52nd game for Washington. A record 47 are in relief. He also works 145 innings as a "fireman," another new mark. He finishes the season with a 9-4 record, 9 saves, and a 2.55 ERA in relief.

6th Braves rookie IF Ernie Padgett pulls an unassisted triple play against the Phils. Padgett's is the first in the NL since 1878. Walter Holke lines out, Cotton Tierney is forced, an Cliff Lee is tagged out.

At season's end, Cincinnati Reds hurler Adolfo "Dolf" Luque of Cuba has a ML-leading won-loss record of 27-8, still the best single-season mark ever posted by a Latin American pitcher in ML play.

7th New York Yankees SS Everett Scott runs his consecutive-game streak to 1,138.

10th It's an all–New York WS for the 3rd time. In the first WS game at Yankee Stadium, the home team takes a quick 3–0 lead, but Heinie Groh triples in 2 runs in a 4-run 3rd that drives Waite Hoyt (17-9) to cover. A 4–4 tie is broken in the top of the 9th by the Giants when Casey Stengel's blast rolls to the OF wall. The sore-legged veteran hobbles around the bases to score the winning run against reliever Joe Bush (19-15) before 55,307 spectators. This is also the first WS to be broadcast on a nationwide radio network. Graham McNamee, aided by baseball writers taking turns, is at the mike. Grantland Rice had broadcast an earlier WS, but not nationally.

11th Babe Ruth hits 2 HRs, and Aaron Ward one, as Herb Pennock (19-6) scatters 9 hits for a 4–2 Yankee win at the Polo Grounds.

12th Yankee Stadium fills with 62,430 fans to see an old-fashioned pitching duel. Once again a Stengel home run is the difference, as Art Nehf (13-10) bests Sam Jones (21-8) 1–0 in game 3.

13th The Yankees score 6 runs in the 2nd off 3 Giants hurlers to help a shaky Bob Shawkey (16-11) to an 8–4 win. Whitey Witt has 3 hits and 2 RBI; for the losers Frank Frisch has 2 hits for the 3rd time, and Ross Youngs has 4.

14th In game 5, the Yankees score 3 in the first and 4 in the 2nd off Jack Bentley (13-8), and Joe Bush spins a 3-hitter for an 8–1 win. Joe Dugan has 4 hits, including a homer.

15th After Babe Ruth's first-inning HR, the Giants peck away at Herb Pennock for 4 runs and take a 4–1 lead into the 8th. With one out, Art Nehf loads the bases on 2 singles and a walk, then walks in a run. Reliever Rosy Ryan forces in another run with a walk to Joe Dugan. Ruth strikes out, but Bob Meusel raps a single that scores the go-ahead runs. Sam Jones holds off the Giants, and the Yankees have their first World Championship.

16th Soon after Babe Ruth receives his WS winner's share of $6,160.46, insurance agent Harry Heilmann, who beat Ruth for the batting title by 10 points, sells him a $50,000 life insurance policy. Beneficiaries are Mrs. Ruth and adopted daughter Dorothy.

19th Citing the unsavory characters associated with the sport, AL president Ban Johnson persuades AL owners to prohibit boxing matches in their parks. The NL declines to go along with it.

23rd Babe Ruth makes a post-season appearance in a Giants uniform, as the Giants defeat the Baltimore Orioles 9–0. Ruth hits a HR over the RF roof at the Polo Grounds. The game is a benefit for destitute former Giants owner John Day.

26th Frank Chance signs to manage the White Sox replacing Kid Gleason, but he will resign February 17, 1924, because of illness. Coach Johnny Evers, named acting manager, will fill the job the entire season.

NOVEMBER

12th John McGraw sends OF Casey Stengel, SS Dave Bancroft, and OF Bill Cunningham to the Braves for P Joe Oeschger and OF Billy Southworth. Bancroft will manage the Braves.

DECEMBER

6th While in Paris, John McGraw announces plans for a tour of Europe by the Giants and White Sox in 1924, as world interest in baseball grows. In Romania, Queen Marie will throw out the first ball to mark the game's debut in July.

10th Traveling to Chicago for the ML meetings, Wild Bill Donovan, New Haven manager, is killed in a train wreck. Donovan was a pitcher for Detroit and ML manager for the Yankees and Phils. New Haven president George Weiss had swapped berths with Donovan and escapes with a minor injury. Phils owner William F. Baker is also on the train, but he is unhurt.

15th Al Szymanski, 21, signed with his hometown Milwaukee club in the spring and was farmed out to Shreveport. Connie Mack secures the rights to his contract while he's still there; at the end of the season he reports to Milwaukee and hits .398 in 24 games. Scorekeepers change his name to Simmons. The A's send IF Heinie Scheer and outfielders Wid Mathews and Frank "Beauty" McGowan to Milwaukee.

1924

JANUARY

7th   The Indians trade veteran C Steve O'Neill, 2B Bill Wambsganss, OF Joe Connolly, and P Danny Boone to Boston for 1B George Burns, 2B Chick Fewster and C Al Walters. Burns gives the Indians a 6th .300 hitter in the lineup.

12th   OF Bobby Veach is sold by the Tigers to Boston.

FEBRUARY

10th   Clark Griffith picks 27-year-old 2B Bucky Harris to manage the Senators.

12th   The NL decides to go along with the AL in offering a $1,000 prize to the player named MVP by a committee of writers.

16th   Boston Braves SS Tony Boeckel dies of injuries received the day before in an automobile accident. He is the first ML player killed in a motor accident.

MARCH

7th   Reds manager Pat Moran, 48, dies at spring training of Bright's disease.

APRIL

15th   The Giants open before the NL's biggest Opening Day crowd, more than 45,000 fans, but lose to Brooklyn 3–2.

The Reds beat the Pirates 6–5 before a home-record crowd of 35,747.

Walter Johnson shuts out the A's 4–0 on Opening Day, his 99th shutout. One of the 4 hits off him is a single by rookie Al Simmons, the first of the 2,927 he will make.

George Sisler returns after missing a full year due to impaired vision caused by severe sinusitis. He is 2-for-4 in the Browns' 7–3 win over the White Sox.

The Cards' Rogers Hornsby is the only batter who ever goes 2-for-5 (against Vic Aldridge of the Cubs) on Opening Day and improves on his BA for the rest of the year. His .424 will be the highest ML BA in the 20th century. The Cardinals open the season with the

players wearing small numbers on their sleeves. The experiment will continue in 1925, then be dropped.

MAY

1st   Yankee rookie Earle Combs breaks his leg and will be out most of the year.

White Sox SS Bill Barrett steals home twice, in the first and the 9th, in a game against Cleveland. He ties the ML mark.

12th   Cincinnati edges past New York into first place in the NL. They'll swap places until June 13th, when a 5–1 win over the Braves boosts the Cubs into the top spot.

23rd   Walter Johnson strikes out 14, including 6 in a row, in a 4–0 one-hitter over the White Sox for his 103rd shutout. Johnson will have his best season in 5 years, going 23-7.

25th   The Red Sox' 6–5 win over the Yankees deadlocks the 2 at the AL top. They'll run neck and neck until June 14th when the Sox begin to unravel.

JUNE

13th   The first-place Yankees come to Detroit with the Tigers close on their heels. New York leads 10–6 in the top of the 9th. Bob Meusel takes a pitch in his back, hurls his bat at P Bert Cole, and charges the mound. Players from both teams start swinging. Fans rush out of the stands, eager to mix it up with players, police, and each other. The fight goes on for nearly 30 minutes while umpire Billy Evans, unable to clear the field, forfeits the game to New York. Cole and Meusel are suspended for 10 days; Meusel is fined $100, and Cole and Ruth $50 each.

14th   Giants 1B George Kelly hits 3 HRs to drive in all 8 New York runs in an 8–6 win over the Reds. Kelly's one-man offensive will be matched by Bob Johnson on June 1, 1938.

The Yankees regain first place with a 6–2 win over the Tigers, but 10 days later the Senators will pass both of them.

25th   Pittsburgh relief hurler Emil Yde doubles in the 9th inning against Chicago to tie the game, then triples in the 14th to win it.

30th   2B Max Bishop and 3B Sammy Hale, the first 2 men in the A's batting order, draw 8 of the 9 walks issued by New York pitchers in the A's 10–3 win. A .271 hitter for 12 years, "Camera Eye" Bishop will draw 1,153 bases on balls, giving him a walk percentage of .204, which is higher than Ruth's and just behind Ted Williams's .207.

JULY

4th   Phils SS Heinie Sand handles 18 chances against the Giants, falling one short of Danny Richardson's record set on June 20, 1892.

11th   Cubs 1B Lee Cotter equals a ML record when he makes 21 putouts and one assist in a game against Brooklyn.

16th   Giants 1B George Kelly hits his 7th HR and becomes the first to hit HRs in 6 consecutive games. He will finish with 21.

17th   On Tuberculosis Day at Sportsman's Park, the Cards' Jesse Haines hurls his only shutout in 2 years, a 5–0 no-hitter over the Braves. "While the majestic northpaw was realizing his lifelong pitching ambitions, the Cardinals were making merry with the right-hand shoots of McNamara" (St. Louis *Globe-Democrat*). It is the first no-hitter by a St. Louis hurler since 1876, and the first-ever NL no-hitter in St. Louis.

19th   Cards rookie righthander Herman Bell holds the Braves hitless until one out in the 8th of the first of 2. Then he does the same until one out in the 5th of game 2, winning both 6–1 and 2–1. He allows only 6 hits in the twin-bill wins.

30th   Bill Sherdel is called out of the Cardinals bullpen to pitch to PH Johnny Mokan of the Phillies. There are no outs in the 8th with runner's on 1B and 2B. Sherdel throws one ball, and Mokan bunts it in the air to Jim Bottomley coming in from 1B. He throws to SS Jimmy Cooney, who doubles the runner at 2B and throws to Hornsby who goes covering 1B. A triple play on one pitch.

AUGUST

1st   Dazzy Vance strikes out 7 Cubs in a row in a 4–0 win for the Dodgers. Vance will lead NL pitchers with 28 wins, a 2.16 ERA, 30 complete games, and 262 strikeouts, as rare a triple crown for a pitcher as the batting version. With Burleigh Grimes's 22-13, Zack Wheat's .375, and Jack Fournier's league-lead-ing 27 HR, the Dodgers will nip at the Giants' heels all season and finish just 1½ games back.

2nd   A's 1B Joe Hauser sets an AL record when he hits 3 HRs and a double for 14 total bases. It'll be broken by Ty Cobb's 16 total bases on May 5, 1925.

8th   The Washington Potomacs of the Eastern Colored League connect for 14 consecutive hits in one inning against South Philadelphia of the Penn-Jersey League.

10th   Ty Cobb steals 2B once, 3B twice, and home once in the Tigers' 13–7 win over Boston that puts them on top in the AL, as the Indians beat the Yankees 7–1.

13th   The Yankees regain the AL lead with 1–0 and 2–1 wins over the Browns.

Red Sox righthander Howard Ehmke has the White Sox popping up all day in his 6–0 win. Only one assist is made by Boston.

25th   Walter Johnson hurls a 7-inning rain-short-ened no-hitter against the Browns, winning by a score of 2–0.

28th   Despite Babe Ruth's 2 HRs, the Senators beat the Yankees 11–6 and move into first place. The Yankees will tie them for 2 days in September, but otherwise the Senators stay on top till the end.

SEPTEMBER

4th   Dazzy Vance chalks up his 12th straight win, and 24th on the year; it's also the Dodgers' 12th straight win.

6th   Spitball hurler Bill Doak pitches the Dodgers into first place with a 1–0 win over Boston. It is Brooklyn's 15th win in a row. The streak ends in a 5–4 Braves win in the 2nd game, and Brooklyn falls back to 3rd place behind the Giants and Pirates.

Urban Shocker of the Browns hurls 2 complete-game victories over the White Sox, winning each contest by a score of 6–2. He fans only one batter in the 2 games.

7th   The Giants bring a half-game lead into Ebbets Field. With the park already packed, some 7,000 fans tear the gates off the hinges and break into the field. The Giants win 8–7.

14th Walter Johnson is elected AL MVP with 55 points. White Sox 2B Eddie Collins is 2nd. He was runner-up to Ruth last year.

16th Cards 1B Jim Bottomley's 3 singles, a double, and 2 HRs produce a ML record 12 RBI in the St. Louis 17–3 win over Brooklyn.

20th Carl Mays wins his 20th for the Reds 9–6 over the Phils, becoming the first pitcher to win 20 for 3 different teams in his career. Grover Alexander's 21 wins for the Cards in 1927 makes him the 2nd; Gaylord Perry will be 3rd in 1978.

22nd The Senators open a 2-game lead as Walter Johnson wins his 14th in a row 8–3 over Chicago.

27th The Giants clinch their 4th straight pennant, beating the Phils 5–1, while Brooklyn is losing 3–2 to Boston.

29th The Senators clinch the pennant in Boston, finishing 2 games in front of the Yankees.

In the next-to-last game of the Western League season, Lyman Lamb of Tulsa hits his 100th 2B hit of the year. It is 25 doubles higher than any other season total in organized baseball.

OCTOBER

1st Another bribery scandal clouds the WS atmosphere. Judge Landis bans Giants OF Jimmy O'Connell and coach Cozy Dolan from the WS after they admit an attempt to bribe Phils SS Heinie Sand to "go easy" in their season-ending series against the Giants. O'Connell implicates Frank Frisch, George Kelly, and Ross Youngs, who deny everything and are cleared by Landis. O'Connell is out of baseball at 23.

4th For the 4th straight year, the Giants are in the series. At 3B is Fred Lindstrom, at 18 years, 10 months, the youngest ever to play in a WS. President Calvin Coolidge is among 35,760 who jam the DC stands in game 1. George Kelly drops a HR into the bleachers in the 2nd, and Terry does the same in the 4th for a 2–0 New York lead. Art Nehf (14-4) gives up one in the 6th. In the last of the 9th, the Senators score to send the game into extra innings. The Giants net 2 runs in the 12th. In the last of the 12th, Washington scores one, but the rally falls a run short, and Walter Johnson (23-7) loses his WS debut. Nehf becomes the 5th pitcher to get 3 hits in a WS game, a feat that will not be repeated until Orel Hershiser does it in 1988.

5th A 2-run HR in the first by Goose Goslin and a solo blast by manager Bucky Harris in the 5th give Tom Zachary (15-9) a 3–0 lead. The Giants tie it in the 9th, but a double by Roger Peckinpaugh scores Joe Judge with the winning run in the bottom of the 9th.

6th Washington's Firpo Marberry (11-12) and the Giants starter Hugh McQuillan (14-8) will be gone by the 4th. The Giants lead 3–0 after 3 and are never caught, for a 6–4 victory. The only HR is hit by Giants reliever Rosy Ryan; it is the only HR he hits in 6 years at New York.

7th The preceding day's record attendance is topped when 49,243 show up in New York to see what turns into Goose Goslin day. The Senators' top batter has 3 singles and a HR for 4 RBI in a 7–4 victory.

8th Walter Johnson tries for a WS win again, but he's far from invincible. Fred Lindstrom is 4-for-5 with 2 RBI, and Johnson's pitching opponent Jack Bentley (16-5) clouts a 2-run homer for a 6–2 New York win.

9th Tom Zachary is touched for a run on 2 hits in the first, but scatters only 5 more hits and issues no passes the rest of the way. The Senators win 2–1.

Reds 1B Jake Daubert dies at 40 from complications during an operation for gallstones and appendicitis.

10th President and Mrs. Coolidge and 31,665 others thrill to the 2nd 3-hour battle of the Series. Bucky Harris starts 23-year-old righthander Curly Ogden (9-8) against Virgil Barnes (16-10), then pulls him after he fans Fred Lindstrom and walks Frisch. In comes lefty George Mogridge (16-11). Bucky Harris lifts one into the temporary seats in LF for a 1–0 lead. In the 6th a single ties it at 1–1, and Harris brings in Firpo Marberry for his 4th appearance. A base hit and 2 costly errors give the Giants a 3–1 lead. In the 8th, PH Nemo Liebold doubles and C Muddy Ruel singles. A walk loads the bases and up comes Harris, who hits a hard bounder to 3B that strikes a pebble and skips over Lindstrom's head and down the LF line as the tying runs score. With one out in the last of the 12th, Giants reliever Jack Bentley gets Muddy Ruel to pop up near home plate, but veteran C Hank Gowdy trips on his discarded mask, and the ball falls to the ground. Ruel then gets his 2nd hit, a double. Walter Johnson reaches 1B on SS Travis Jackson's error. Earl McNeely hits a grounder at Lindstrom, and again the ball takes a bounce over his head. Ruel tears home with Washington's first WS championship.

20th   Kansas City Monarchs manager Jose Mendez takes the mound to spin a 3-hit, 5–0 shutout over the Hilldales to win the final game of the first Negro League World Series. Nip Winters had pitched the first 3 Hilldale wins.

27th   The Cubs trade P Vic Aldridge, 1B George Granthan, and 1B Al Niehaus to Pittsburgh for 1B Charlie Grimm, SS Rabbit Maranville, and P Wilbur Cooper.

DECEMBER

10th   The 2 leagues agree on a permanent rotation for WS play proposed by Charles Ebbets: first 2 games at one league's park, next 3 at the other leagues park, last 2 if needed back at the first league's park, with openers to alternate between leagues. Next year's WS will commence at the NL city.

11th   Eddie Collins signs as player-manager of the White Sox.

17th   The Yankees get 4-time 20-game winner Urban Shocker from the Browns for pitchers Milt Gaston, Joe Giard, and Joe Bush. Shocker will be a mainstay on 2 pennant-winning staffs for New York.

The AL adopts a resolution censuring Ban Johnson for his activities and misconduct in dealing with the commissioner's office, threatening his immediate removal and limiting future activities to internal workings of the AL.

1925

JANUARY

5th   During the White Sox' and Giants' tour of Europe, the French Baseball Federation awards silver medals to John McGraw, Charlie Comiskey, and Hugh Jennings for their efforts to advance the game in France.

FEBRUARY

2nd   The NL inaugurates its Golden Jubilee Year by holding its spring meeting in the same room in New York's Broadway Central Hotel where the league was organized on February 2, 1876.

10th   At the AL meeting, a plan is adopted to alternate the site of future WS openers by league rather than deciding it by a coin toss, with games 1, 2, 6, and 7 in one park and 3, 4, 5 in the other, unless a ban on Sunday baseball interferes in one city. The clubs finishing 4th in the AL will henceforth share in the WS pool. WS umps get a raise to $2,500, while umps in city series will earn $700. The plan was proposed in 1924, but formally adopted at this meeting.

25th   John McGraw arrives in Florida and is installed as president of a real estate development near Bradenton called Pennant Park. With streets named for early Giants heroes, and lots offered for $2,500 to $5,000, McGraw hires a fleet of salesmen and heads north. A year later, the boom will go bust, washed away by 2 hurricanes. McGraw will incur a loss of $100,000 after paying off close friends, players, and other investors.

MARCH

15th   Cubs SS Rabbit Maranville breaks his leg sliding home in a game in Los Angeles. At 33, the injury threatens to end his career, but the Rabbit will be back in the lineup by midseason.

APRIL

5th   Babe Ruth collapses in the railroad station in Asheville, NC, and winds up in a New York hospital. He'll undergo an operation for an ulcer on April 17th and will be in bed till May 26th.

7th   A's long-ball-hitting 1B Joe Hauser is standing still near 1B, minding his own business, when his knee gives way suddenly and the kneecap shatters all by itself. He is out for the season. His other knee will give out in a few years with the same amount of provocation.

13th   Stuffy McInnis is released by the Braves. He'll sign with the Pirates, bat .368 in 59 games, and get into his 5th WS.

14th   In the first regular-season Cubs game to be broadcast on the radio, Quin Ryan announces the contest from the grandstand roof for WGN. Grover Alexander wins for the Cubs 8–2 over the Pirates and adds a single, double, and HR.

Cleveland defeats St. Louis 21–14, with the Indians winning it with 12 in the 8th. Browns manager George Sisler makes 4 errors at 1B.

Two future Hall of Famers make their ML debuts for the A's in the same game. Lefty Grove starts against Boston and leaves in the 4th after walking 4 and striking out nobody. He gives up 5 runs on 6 hits. In the 8th, Mickey Cochrane pinch-hits for C Cy Perkins, singles and stays in behind the plate while the A's go on to score 9 runs in the last 4 innings to win 9–8 in 10 innings. Grove, known as Groves in Baltimore, is also listed that way in the New York *Times* box score. Grove will become the first pitcher to lead the AL in strikeouts and walks in the same year.

18th   Charles Ebbets, Dodgers president, dies on the morning of the opener at Ebbets Field, won by New York 7–1. No NL games will be played on the 21st, the day of his funeral. Ed McKeever, the new club president, will catch a cold that turns into pneumonia and die on May 27th.

22nd   The Cardinals open at home and treat their fans to a post-1900, NL-record, first-inning barrage of 12 hits, scoring 11 runs to beat the Reds 12–3.

26th   With the Indians leading 7–2 at Chicago, the umps forfeit the game to Cleveland when the crowd storms onto the field and refuses to get off.

MAY

1st   The A's introduce another future Hall of Famer, 17-year-old C Jimmie Foxx, who pinch-hits and singles against Washington.

5th Ty Cobb is 6-for-6, including 3 HRs, in Detroit's 14–8 win over the Browns. Cobb's 16 total bases tops Joe Hauser's 14 of August 2, 1924. The next day Cobb hits 2 more HRs, giving him 5 in 2 days, tying Cap Anson's 1884 feat.

Everett Scott is benched by New York manager Miller Huggins, ending his 1,307-game playing streak. Pee Wee Wanninger replaces him at SS. Scott will soon go to Washington on waivers.

7th Pirates SS Glenn Wright pulls a solo triple play at 2B in the 9th, grabbing Jim Bottomley's liner, stepping on the bag before Johnny Cooney can get back, and tagging Hornsby coming down from 1B. The Cards win 10–9.

8th Every NL city will have a Golden Jubilee Day. The first, at Boston, sees former Boston players from 1876 on hand. The Braves beat the Cubs 5–2.

11th Walter Johnson blanks the White Sox 9–0 for his 108th shutout, and he runs his strikeout total to 3,232.

Chicago C Ray Schalk holds on to a ball dropped 460 feet from the top of the Tribune Tower in Chicago.

In a Mississippi Valley League game, 55-year-old former Giants star Joe McGinnity hurls Dubuque to a 7–3 victory over 18-year-old John Welch of Ottumwa.

12th A record 20 HRs are hit in the ML this day.

17th A 9-game winning streak propels the A's past Washington into first place. The A's will hold the top spot through June with the Senators always at their heels.

Washington's lefty Tom Zachary throws the pitch that Tris Speaker socks for his 3,000th hit.

20th George Sisler's 34-game hitting streak is stopped by the A's Lefty Grove and Slim Harriss.

Casey Stengel buys the Worcester club in the Eastern League and arranges for the Braves to send 7 players down to his club.

The Indians score 6 runs in the last of the 9th to beat the Yankees 10–9. Tris Speaker scores the winning run from 1B on a single.

21st The Tigers and Senators combine for 9 double plays, tying the record for a 9-inning game.

24th Reds C Astyanax Douglass breaks in on an argument between Philadelphia's Jimmy Ring and Reds C Ivy Wingo and lands a punch to Ring's jaw. After the game they fight round 2 in the clubhouse.

Ring then follows Douglass to the railroad station where they tangle again.

26th In the Tigers' 8–1 win over the White Sox, Ty Cobb becomes the first to collect 1,000 career extra-base hits. He will finish with 1,139.

27th The Browns have 26 assists in a 10-inning game with the Indians. They have 24 in the first 9 innings for an AL mark.

30th Rogers Hornsby is named manager of the Cardinals, replacing Branch Rickey, who remains as general manager. Hornsby will be the only player-manager to win the triple crown, which he does by topping .400 for the 3rd time in 4 years, hitting .403 with 39 HRs and 143 RBI. His .756 slugging average is still the NL's best. Branch Rickey sells his stock in the club to Hornsby for $50,000, a transaction that will later cause headlines.

Pittsburgh sets a modern NL record by stroking 8 triples in the 2nd game of a doubleheader against the Cardinals.

JUNE

1st Lou Gehrig begins a consecutive-game streak that will surpass Everett Scott's mark by pinch-hitting for Pee Wee Wanninger, the SS who replaced Scott in the Yankees lineup. The next day, 1B Wally Pipp shows up with a headache, and Gehrig takes over. Babe Ruth plays his first game of the season following his illness.

3rd White Sox manager Eddie Collins makes hit No. 3,000 versus Detroit.

4th Veteran hurler Joe Bush, playing RF for the Browns, is called in to pitch to Cleveland pinch hitter Harvey Hendrick with the bases filled and 2 out in the 9th. Hendrick hits the first pitch for a triple, and the Indians win 11–10.

6th Fred Clarke and Honus Wagner are in the line-up of a 1901 Pirates team that plays a brief game as part of Golden Jubilee Day in Pittsburgh. A week later Clarke joins the Pirates as assistant to the president, a move that will lead to a player revolt in which heads roll and pennants are lost.

7th The Reds and Braves turn 5 double plays each in a 12-inning game for a ML record.

12th Against the Pirates, the Giants make a triple play that goes from SS Travis Jackson to C Hank Gowdy to 3B Heinie Groh to RF Ross Youngs to 2B George Kelly to 1B Terry. In the first inning, with Max Carey on 3B and Johnny Rawlings on 2B, Kiki Cuyler taps a slow roller to SS that gets away from Jackson for a few seconds. Carey starts home and is caught, Jackson to Gowdy to 3B Groh. Rawlings, on his way to 3B, heads back to 2B and is run down. Cuyler tries for 2B and gets caught in a rundown.

15th In Shibe Park with the Indians leading 15–4 after 7 innings, many fans leave and miss one of the greatest rallies of the century. The A's score 13 in the 8th for a 17–15 win. The outburst gives P Tom Glass his lone ML victory.

17th The Tigers score 13 runs in the 6th and beat the Yankees 19–1 at Yankee Stadium. It takes 49 minutes to play the top of the 6th, in which there are 7 walks and 6 hits. Eleven runs score before the first out is made.

20th The Reds IF makes 6 double plays against the Giants, winning 4–2 for Eppa Rixey's 7th straight win.

22nd Pittsburgh defeats St. Louis 24–6. Max Carey collects 2 hits in an inning twice, in both the first and 8th frames.

28th A's OF "Broadway" Bill Lamar hits in his 28th straight game; he'll be stopped the next day, but will hit .356.

29th The Senators beat the A's 4–2 to move within a halfgame of the top. The next day Walter Johnson blanks the A's 7–0 to knock them out of the lead.

JULY

1st The Giants move back on top of the NL, taking 2 from the Phils. In the 2nd game, Hack Wilson hits 2 HRs in the 3rd inning of the 16–7 nightcap. The next day the Pirates edge back on top with a 2–1 win over the Reds while New York is rained out.

3rd Brooklyn 2B Milt Stock sets a modern NL record by getting 4 hits in his 4th consecutive game.

4th The Athletics' Lefty Grove battles the Yankees' Herb Pennock 15 innings before taking a 1–0 loss. Pennock is a model of control, issuing no walks and giving up 4 hits.

7th The 7th-place Cubs install Rabbit Maranville as manager, replacing Bill Killefer.

10th Giants OF Hack Wilson is the 7th player to hit 2 HRs in one inning; he does it against the Pirates.

11th George Sisler drives in 7 runs in 2 innings, tripling with the bases full in the 3rd and hitting a grand slam in the 4th, in a Browns 10–5 win over Washington.

15th The A's go back into the lead with a sweep over the White Sox 9–7 and 11–5.

20th Washington veteran Stan Coveleski wins his 12th straight to keep the Senators near the top. He will have his finest year at 20-5 and the AL's best ERA, 2.84.

Dazzy Vance fans 17 in a 10-inning 4–3 Dodger win over the Cubs.

22nd The Yankees buy SS Leo Durocher from Hartford (Eastern League).

23rd The A's move back into first with a 5–4 win over the Red Sox and an assist from Lou Gehrig, who hits the first of his ML-record 23 grand slams to beat Firpo Marberry and the Senators 11–7. A Pittsburgh win and Giants split with the Phils lifts the Pirates back on top.

30th The White Sox stop Coveleski's streak at 13, beating Washington 11–1.

AUGUST

1st The Yankees buy Tony Lazzeri from the Pacific Coast League for spring delivery. Lazzeri will hit 60 HRs with 222 RBI at Salt Lake City and earn the nickname "Poosh-em-up" from his legion of Italian admirers.

4th Every player in each team's lineup has at least one putout in the Indians-Yankees game.

5th Cards RF Jack Smith charges in for a short fly ball and keeps on running, tagging 1B to double up the base runner before he can get back, for a rare unassisted double play.

Lefty Dickie Kerr, on the injured list since 1921, is reinstated and tries a comeback with the White Sox. He'll start twice, lose once, and after 10 relief chores, quit for good.

8th The Giants buy righthander Fred Fitzsimmons from Indianapolis.

15th Little Dickie Kerr, the southpaw who won 2 games for the White Sox in the 1919 WS, makes his first ML appearance since 1921. He has been playing semipro ball rather than accept Charles Comiskey's salary offer. When he relieves Red Faber in the 3rd inning against the Tigers, play is stopped while admirers present him with a floral horseshoe. In 2 innings, he gives up 3 hits and walks 2. The White Sox go on to win 12–5.

19th The Phils finally solve Reds righthander Pete Donohue 5–4, after losing to him 20 straight times.

22nd After a disastrous western trip, the Giants trail the Pirates by 3 as the leaders come to the Polo Grounds for a 5-game series. Before crowds of more than 50,000 at 2 weekend doubleheaders, the Pirates take 3 out of 4. On Monday they beat Wayland Dean 9–2, and the NL race is over. When the Giants go west again, McGraw will stay home. The Pirates boast a team BA of .307 and a deep pitching staff of 5 pitchers winning 15 to 19 games.

28th Although Baker Bowl is considered a bandbox by some, the aggressive Kiki Cuyler of the Pirates hits 2 inside-the-park HRs there in a victory over the Phils.

29th After a night on the town, Babe Ruth shows up late for batting practice. Miller Huggins suspends Ruth and slaps a $5,000 fine on him for disobeying orders on the field and team rules off the field. In the showdown between the Bambino and the tiny manager, Jake Ruppert backs up his manager. Ruth is forced to apologize before he's reinstated 9 days later. The day after his return to the lineup, Ruth hits HR number 300.

The city of Detroit gives a dinner for Ty Cobb honoring his 20 years in a Tiger uniform. He's given a trophy by the city and $10,000 by the club.

SEPTEMBER

10th Bob Meusel, Babe Ruth, and Lou Gehrig hit successive homers in the 4th inning of game one versus the A's; Ruth and OF Ben Paschal hit back-to-back homers in the 4th of game 2, both won by New York.

13th Brooklyn's Dazzy Vance narrowly misses back-to-back no-hitters over Philadelphia, pitching a 10–1 no-hitter 5 days after a 1–0 one-hitter. The Phils' lone run is scored by Chicken Hawks, who reaches 2B on an error. Five days earlier it was Hawks's 2nd-inning single that ruined Vance's no-hitter. On June 17, 1923, Vance lost a no-hitter with 2 out in the 9th.

19th The White Sox take a 15–0 lead against Washington after 5 innings, but Chicago P Ted Lyons will have to pitch to 18 different batters as Senators manager Bucky Harris juggles his lineup and sends in pinch hitters. With a no-hitter going, Lyons continues to bear down. Finally, with 2 out in the 9th, Washington's Bobby Veach gets a base hit. The final is 17-0. Washington outfielder Sam Rice's streak of 9 hits in a row is stopped.

20th Chicago Cubs and Cleveland old-timers play a 6–6, 8-inning tie.

21st Pittsburgh OF Kiki Cuyler ties the NL record by getting his 10th consecutive hit, before he is stopped by the Phils' Art Decatur.

Phils utility player Barney Friberg catches the 8th inning in a 14–4 loss at Pittsburgh, thus playing every position during the year; he will be featured in a Ripley's Believe it or Not cartoon.

The Reds' Sam Crawford hits his 12th and last inside-the-park HR in the 6th in the New York–Cincinnati match. The final score is 12–0.

22nd Brooklyn P Burleigh Grimes hits into 2 double plays and one triple play in an 11–2, 11-inning loss to the Cubs.

The Yankees' Ben Paschal hits 2 inside-the-park HRs in one game, an 11–6 win over the White Sox at Yankee Stadium.

Ramon Herrera, a Cuban IF, makes his debut with the Boston Red Sox. He will bat .385 in 10 games, but will hit only .257 in 74 games in 1926. Herrera is probably the first player of this era to play in both the major leagues and the Negro leagues.

P Burleigh Grimes of Brooklyn has only himself to blame for losing 3–2 to the Cubs in the 12th. While he masterfully scatters 16 hits, he not only goes hitless at the plate but hits into 2 double plays and one triple play.

23rd The Pirates clinch the NL pennant, making 6 double plays in beating the Phils 2–1.

Washington SS Roger Peckinpaugh, a .294 hitter, is named the AL MVP with 45 points; A's OF Al Simmons is 2nd with 41.

Rogers Hornsby will win the MVP honor in the NL, rewriting the offensive record book while bringing the Cards home 4th. Other strong contenders ar Kiki Cuyler, the Pirates top hitter at .357; the Giants' George Kelly; Pirates' SS Glenn Wright; Brooklyn's Dazzy Vance; and Dave Bancroft, who hit .319 and topped NL shortstops in fielding average while managing the 5th-place Braves.

24th Washington takes 2 from Cleveland 4–3 and 6–2 while the A's lose to St. Louis 6–4, and the Senators clinch their 2nd pennant.

26th Philadelphia fans chip in to buy a new automobile for the A's player chosen by the press as MVP. The winner: Al Simmons with 30 points. Mickey Cochrane, a .331 hitter in his first year, is 2nd.

OCTOBER

4th Harry Heilmann gets 6 hits in Detroit's doubleheader win over the Browns to edge out teammate Cobb for the batting crown, .393 to .389. Ty Cobb bats over .300 for the 20th time.

Managers George Sisler of the Browns and Ty Cobb of the Tigers both pitch in relief in the final game of the season for the 2 clubs.

Washington's Firpo Marberry finishes the season with 55 mound appearances, all in relief. He becomes the first exclusive relief hurler appearing in more than 40 games and launches a growing trend that will extend to the present day.

7th Christy Mathewson dies of tuberculosis at Saranac Lake, NY, at the age of 45. At the time of his death he was part owner and president of the Boston Braves.

Walter Johnson (20-7) opens the WS in Pittsburgh. A 5th-inning HR by Pie Traynor is the only damaging blow, as Johnson fans 10 of the heavy-hitting Bucs for a 4–1 win over Lee Meadows (19-10). Sam Rice, Joe Harris, and Ossie Bluege, with 2 hits each, drive in the Senators' runs.

In a cold opener of the annual City Series between the Cubs and the White Sox, the Cubs Grover Alexander and the Southsiders Ted Blankenship each labor 19 innings before darkness stops the game with the score 2–2. The Cubs then win 4 of the next 5 to win the series.

8th Kiki Cuyler's 2-run HR in the 8th breaks a 1–1 tie and gives the Pirates' Vic Aldridge (15-7) a 3–2 win over Stan Coveleski (20-5).

10th For game 3 it's clear but bitterly cold in Washington following a rainstorm that caused the game to be rescheduled. President Coolidge throws out the first ball. The Pirates hold a slim 3–2 lead after 6. A walk and 2 singles score 2 in the 8th for Washington, and Firpo Marberry (8-6) closes it. Joe Harris has 2 hits for the 3rd time; he'll lead the Senators with .440. Sam Rice makes a controversial game-saving play in the 8th, tumbling into the stands in the right corner to spear a long drive by Earl Smith. About 15 seconds later he emerges with the ball. Despite the Pirates' arguments that a fan might have given it to him, ump Cy Rigler calls Smith out. Questioned about it for the rest of his life, Rice leaves a letter, to be opened after his death (in 1974), in which he states: "At no time did I lose possession of the ball."

11th Walter Johnson wins his 3rd straight WS contest over 2 years. He blanks the Bucs on 6 hits but fans just 2. A 3-run HR by Goose Goslin in the 4th followed by Joe Harris's round-tripper give the Senators a 4–0 win and 3–1 Series advantage.

12th Louisville manager Joe McCarthy (American Association) is named to manage the Chicago Cubs.

Stan Coveleski goes out to finish off the Pirates, but a lapse of control costs him 2 in the 3rd. Joe Harris's 3rd HR ties it in the 4th. In the 7th, a walk and 3 hits net 2 runs and drive Coveleski off the mound. The Pirates' 13-hit attack produces a 6–3 win.

13th Back home for game 6 before 43,810, the largest crowd of the Series, Pittsburgh's Ray Kremer (17-8) gives up a first-inning HR to Goose Goslin and a run in the 2nd on Roger Peckinpaugh's RBI double. Joe Ferguson is touched for 2 in 3rd. The tie is broken by 2B Eddie Moore's HR, the 11th in the Series, and Pittsburgh wins 3–2.

The Pirates buy SS Hal Rhyne and OF Paul Waner from San Francisco (PCL).

15th A steady downpour the day before has left the field a muddy mess. It's a short day for Vic Aldridge: 3 walks and 2 hits, and he's out of there with one out in the first. Walter Johnson takes a 4–0 lead to the mound. The Bucs clobber him for 15 hits, good for 24 total bases. Max Carey's 4-for-5 gives him a Series-high .458. The Senators make the most of 7 hits, scoring 7 runs, including Roger Peckinpaugh's HR, the 12th of the Series, a WS record. Johnson would have fared better but for 2 more errors by SS Peckinpaugh, the MVP's 7th and 8th, still the WS record for any position. Ray Kremer picks up his 2nd win with a 4-inning relief effort, as the Senators lose 9–7. The Series breaks all financial records, grossing almost $1.2 million. Winning shares are $5,332.72; losers' $3,734.60.

18th Salt Lake City (PCL) 2B Tony Lazzeri hits his 60th HR of the season in a 12–10 victory over Sacramento in the final game of the year. It is an inside-the-park drive in the 7th off Frank Shellenback.

22nd Marv Goodwin, 34, former righthander for the Cards who joined the Reds at the end of the season, is the first active player to die from injuries sustained in an airplane crash.

NOVEMBER

9th Rabbit Maranville is waived to the Dodgers from the Cubs.

DECEMBER

9th The AL extends Ban Johnson's contract to 1935 and gives him a raise to $40,000.

Nap Lajoie is named commissioner of the Ohio-Pennsylvania League.

10th The A's pick up veteran SS Bill Wambsganss from the Red Sox.

The AL goes on record as opposing the use of resin by pitchers. In a joint meeting, future WS games are set to start at 1:30 P.M.; 2nd-place money withheld from the 8 Black Sox in 1920 is distributed to the other 1920 White Sox; and players signed by August 31st are declared eligible for WS play.

1926

JANUARY

2nd The NY newspapers begin a week-long series of full-page ads featuring a picture of John McGraw with the bold caption "You've followed me in baseball, now follow me in real estate." The ad is for Pennant Park in Sarasota, Florida, and offers lots for $2,000 to $2,500. With a drop-off in land speculation, the development will go belly-up by April, and a distracted McGraw will be hounded by creditors and lot purchasers for a year.

30th The ML Rules Committee agrees that pitchers may have access to a resin bag. On February 8th the AL will refuse to permit its use. On April 28th the league will give in and allow a resin bag on the field, but discourage its use by players.

FEBRUARY

1st Wally Pipp, 33, has lost his Yankee 1B job to Lou Gehrig after 10½ years; the Reds buy him for $7,500.

  The Browns trade P Joe Bush and outfielder Jack Tobin to Washington for P Tom Zachary and win Ballou. Zachary will be back with the Senators next year in time to serve up Ruth's 60th HR.

2nd The NL holds its Golden Jubilee Banquet in New York. Among nearly 1,000 invited guests are 10 players from the 1876 season and 2 umpires, including Billy McLean, who was the umpire for the first NL game.

24th Southpaw Eddie Plank, winner of 327 games in 17 years, dies at 51 in his native Gettysburg, PA.

APRIL

2nd Hugh Jennings, slated to be the Giants assistant manager, is unable to join the team due to illness. Roger Bresnahan replaces him.

13th More than 45,000 at the Polo Grounds watch Brooklyn's Jess Petty post an Opening Day, 3–0 one-hitter over the Giants. The Giants will win 7 in a row after the opener, only to be beaten again by Petty 2–1 on April 24th.

  Walter Johnson takes on A's knuckleballer Eddie Rommel in baseball's greatest opening-day pitchers'

duel, a 15-inning battle won by the Senators 1–0. Johnson gives up 6 walks and fans 12.

20th The Yankees batter Washington 18–5. Among their 22 hits are a HR, 2 doubles, and 2 singles by Ruth, who scores 5 and drives in 8.

22nd The Browns' 5 double plays against the White Sox tie the AL record.

30th Jess Petty wins his first 5 games, and the Dodgers go into first place.

MAY

1st Satchel Paige, 19 years old, makes his debut in the Negro Southern League, pitching Chattanooga to a 5–4 win over Birmingham.

8th Fenway Park bleachers are partially destroyed by a fire.

  The Yankees score 7 in the 2nd but lose to Detroit 14–10, knocking themselves out of the lead; Washington moves into first.

12th Walter Johnson wins the 400th game of his career by defeating the St. Louis Browns 7–4.

15th Led by the NL's 2 top hitters—C Bubbles Hargrave at .353 and OF Cuckoo Christensen at .350—and the pitching of Pete Donohue, Carl Mays, and Eppa Rixey, the Reds move into first place where they'll stay until mid-July.

21st White Sox 1B Earl Sheely hits 3 doubles and a HR at Boston, following 3 doubles in his last 3 at bats the day before. His 7 straight extra-base hits tie the ML record.

22nd At Rogers Hornsby Day in St. Louis, the Cards manager is presented $1,000 in gold and a medal as the NL MVP for 1925.

28th A Boston–New York old-timers' game is played for a Christy Mathewson Memorial at Bucknell before the regular Giants-Braves game in Boston.

  The A's take 2 from the Yankees 2–1 and 6–5, ending New York's 16-game win streak.

JUNE

6th Player-manager Tris Speaker, 38, of the Indians, sporting a lifetime .350 BA, startles players and fans alike when he directs P George Uhle to pinch-hit for him in a close contest with the Yankees. Uhle is a good-hitting hurler, but he flies out.

14th The Giants trade OF Billy Southworth to the Cards for OF Heinie Mueller.

15th After sending OF Bing Miller to St. Louis for OF Baby Doll Jacobson, the A's trade P Slim Harriss, P Freddie Heimach, and Jacobson to the Red Sox for OF Tom Jenkins and P Howard Ehmke, 32. Ehmke, 3-10 at Boston, will be 12-4 for the rest of the year at Philadelphia.

20th A delegation of Coffeyville, KS, fans comes to St. Louis to see their hometown hero, Walter Johnson, pitch against the Browns. Unfortunately, the Big Train cannot hold a 4–0 lead and loses his 7th game in a row 5–4.

22nd The Cardinals pick up 39-year-old Grover Alexander on waivers from the Cubs to help in the pennant chase. He'll be 9-7 down the stretch.

24th Bullet Joe Bush, 1-8 with the Senators, is handed his release. The Pirates will sign him.

26th The Cardinals move into 2nd with a win over the Cubs. The next day Alexander will earn a split with a 4-hitter over his former teammates.

JULY

1st The Pirates break an 8-game losing streak by beating St. Louis. They move into 2nd, dropping the Cards to 3rd.

22nd The Reds score 11 in the 2nd and beat the Braves 13–3. Two days later, the Pirates move past them into the NL lead.

23rd Detroit and Washington take the unheard of time of 2 hours and 40 minutes to play 9 innings. Detroit's 19 hits give them a 9–6 win, but much of the time is consumed by manager Ty Cobb's arguing over a balk call, then trying to have a heckling fan removed from the stands.

24th Lou Gehrig and Babe Ruth demonstrate that power hitting is not the only thing they can do when Lou scores on a double steal with the Babe in a victory over the White Sox. They had pulled the same double steal against the Red Sox on April 13th.

25th Braves coach Art Devlin is riding Reds 3B Babe Pinelli. Coming off the field in the 3rd, Pinelli brushes against him. Devlin swings, starting one of the great baseball fights of the century. Police restore order, but not before Boston OF Frank Wilson is arrested and taken to jail for hitting a police inspector. In the 4th, Boston OF Jimmy Welsh crashes into C Val Picinich in a play at the plate. Picinich takes a poke at him, starting round 2, and is ejected.

AUGUST

4th Stanford star fullback Ernie Nevers pitches his first complete game for the Browns, beating the A's 3-1. Nevers will be 6-12 in his brief baseball life, but he will win a place in the Pro Football Hall of Fame playing with the Duluth Eskimos and Chicago Cardinals (1926–31).

11th Dodgers rookie Babe Herman collects his 9th hit in a row, but flies out to Kiki Cuyler in the 6th to fall short of the record of 10 straight, held by Cuyler and Ed Konetchy.

Tris Speaker hits the 700th double of his career, as the Indians lose to the White Sox 7–2.

13th Pittsburgh players ask that Fred Clarke, assistant to owner Barney Dreyfuss, not be permitted to sit on the bench. Dreyfuss squelches the revolt by releasing Carson Bigbee and Babe Adams, and suspending Max Carey, who has slumped to .222. Carey is waived to the Dodgers.

15th The Braves are at Ebbets Field with Brooklyn's Hank DeBerry on 3B, Dazzy Vance on 2B, and Chick Fewster on 1B. Babe Herman drives the ball against the RF wall, and DeBerry scores. Vance holds up, then rounds 3B headed for home. Fewster stops at 3B. The RF throws home and traps Vance, who heads back to 3B. Herman slides into 3B as Fewster steps off. Herman is out for passing a base runner. Fewster, thinking he's out, too, walks off with Babe, and gets tagged out. Vance, still on 3B, later admits it was his fault, but Herman, who doubles into a double play, gets the blame.

20th The Giants lose their 5th in 6 games 6–2 in St. Louis. Frankie Frisch misses a sign that costs a run. After the game, berated by John McGraw in front of the team, Frisch buys a ticket to New York and leaves the team. Fined $500, McGraw's favorite, and heir apparent, is through with the Giants.

21st It takes Ted Lyons just 67 minutes to no-hit the Red Sox 6–0 for Chicago.

Rabbit Maranville, hitting .235, is released by the Dodgers.

22nd After 3 games with the Tigers are rained out at home, Connie Mack and Tom Shibe decide that Sunday baseball is entitled to be played. Armed with a court injunction preventing police from interfering, they play the first Sunday game ever seen in Philadelphia. A light rain holds the crowd to 10,000, but Lefty Grove sets down the White Sox 3–2 without incident. A court later rules Sunday baseball still illegal; it will be 1934 before that law changes in Philadelphia.

25th The Cardinals regain first place in the NL, but the next day the Pirates retake the high ground.

26th Pittsburgh RF Paul Waner goes 6-for-6, including 2 doubles and a triple, in a game against St. Louis.

27th Veteran P Dutch Ruether is picked up from Washington by the Yankees.

28th The Indians use the same lineup in 2 victories over the Red Sox, including Emil Levsen, who pitches the 6–1 and 5–1 sweep. He strikes out none.

31st Bill Sherdel and Al Sothoron pitch the Cards back into first place with 6–1 and 2–1 wins over the Pirates.

White Sox IF Ray Morehart gets 9 hits in 10 at bats in a doubleheader, a record that has been matched but never broken.

SEPTEMBER

1st Washington and Boston combine for a ML-record 11 sacrifices in a game won by the Senators 7–4.

4th The Reds take first place by beating the Cards. The next day they will reverse positions again.

7th The Red Sox lose their 17th in a row, a 4–2 Yankees win.

9th Five Brooklyn pinch hitters all deliver, including Dick Cox, who gets 2 hits, scores twice, and has 2 RBI in a 9-run 9th inning that sinks the Phils 12–6.

14th The Reds take the NL lead with a 5–1 win over the Dodgers.

17th The Cardinals regain the lead in a 10–1 win over the Phils. The Reds nosedive, losing 7 of their last 9.

24th The Cards beat the Giants 6–4 to clinch their first NL pennant.

25th The Yankees take 2 from the Browns to nail down the AL flag.

26th The Browns beat the Yankees 6–1 and 6–2 in a total time of 2 hours, 7 minutes. The 2nd game is the fastest in AL history: 55 minutes. Ruth hits HR No. 47, more than double the total of anybody in either league. He also leads the AL with 139 runs, 155 RBI, and 144 bases on balls while batting .372, 2nd to Detroit's Heinie Manush.

Browns coach Jimmie Austin, 46 years old, participates in the last game of the season against the Yankees. He contributes to the win by knocking in a run with a double and then stealing home. He is not the oldest to steal a base (Arlie Latham, 50, in 1909), but he is the oldest to steal home.

27th Cleveland 1B George Burns hits his 64th double of the year, as the Indians down Philadelphia 5–4. Indians righthander George Uhle gives up 9 hits in winning his 27th against 11 losses. He leads the AL, despite giving up a league-high 300 hits and 118 walks, and posts a 2.83 ERA. It is his best record in a 17-year, 700-win career.

OCTOBER

2nd Game 1 of the WS before 61,658 at New York belongs to southpaws Herb Pennock (25-11) and Bill Sherdel (16-12). Two hits give the Cards a quick first-inning run. Sherdel issues 3 walks for a New York run without a hit. In the 6th, Babe Ruth slaps a single to left, moves to 2B on a sacrifice, and scores on a Lou Gehrig single for a 2–1 win. It is the first of a record 8 game-winning RBI in WS play.

3rd Grover Alexander (9-7) faces Urban Shocker (19-11) as a record 63,600 look on. The Yankees score twice in the 2nd, but Old Pete sets down the last 21 batters, striking out 10. Billy Southworth and SS Tommy Thevenow collect 3 hits each for a 6–2 St. Louis win. Thevenow, batting .256 for the season, will lead all batters with .417.

In Baltimore, the Bacharach Giants' Red Grier tosses a 10–0 no-hitter against the Chicago American

Giants in the 3rd game of the Negro League World Series. Grier wins just more one game before an unexplained ailment ends his career.

5th Jesse Haines (13-4) stifles the Yanks on 5 hits while the Cards kayo Dutch Ruether (14-9 on the year, 2-5 for the Yanks) in the 5th. Haines helps his own side with a 2-run HR in the 4th. The 4–0 St. Louis win gives them the Series lead.

6th In game 4, the Yankees tee off on Flint Rhem (20-7) and 4 other Cardinal hurlers for 10 runs and 14 hits, while Waite Hoyt (16-12) strands 10 Cardinal runners for a 10–5 win. Babe Ruth hits 3 HRs. Ruth's 3rd clout, in the 6th, is the longest blast ever seen in St. Louis. It clears the park and goes through the window of an auto dealer across the street. In the 4th, Taylor Douthit and Chick Hafey collide in the OF as the ball drops; Douthit is sidelined for the rest of the Series.

7th With the Series tied at 2–2, 39,552 pack Sportsman's Park to watch Herb Pennock and Bill Sherdel duel again. The Cards score first on a double by Jim Bottomley and single by Les Bell. Ragged play costs the Cards a run in the 6th. Tied 2–2 in the 10th, Mark Koenig singles, takes 2B on a wild pitch, and after a sacrifice, comes home on Tony Lazzeri's long fly for a 3–2 Yankees win.

9th Grover Alexander scatters 8 hits in game 6 while the Cards tee off on Bob Shawkey (8-6), Urban Shocker, and Myles Thomas for 10 runs and 13 hits in a 10–2 romp.

10th Only 38,093 show up at the Stadium for the deciding WS contest. Grover Alexander, possibly sleeping off a hangover in the bullpen, barely notices when Jess Haines take a 3–2 lead over Waite Hoyt into the 7th. Haines weakens in the last of the 7th; 3 walks put Earle Combs, Bob Meusel, and Lou Gehrig on base with 2 out and Tony Lazzeri at the plate. Hornsby waves in Alexander. On a 1-1 count Lazzeri hits a line drive into the left-field seats, a few feet to the foul side of the pole, then swings and misses for strike 3. Alexander sets the Yanks down in order until Babe Ruth draws his 11th walk with 2 out in the 9th, and is thrown out trying to steal 2B. The Cards have their first World Championship. Each winner collects $5,584.51, the losers, $3,417.75.

11th The Browns announce that George Sisler will be back as a player but not as manager.

13th Cleveland 1B George Burns is voted AL MVP. Hitting .358, Burns makes 64 doubles, topping Tris Speaker's 59. It'll be the record until Earl Webb's 67 in 1931.

20th Stuffy McInnis is named manager of the Phils.

22nd Manager Lee Fohl resigns after 2 last-place finishes with the Red Sox.

NOVEMBER

3rd Ty Cobb resigns as Tigers manager and announces his retirement from the game. AL umpire and former Tigers IF George Moriarty replaces him. Moriarty is the only man to hold baseball's 4 principal jobs: player, umpire, scout, and manager.

Dan Howley is named St. Louis Browns manager.

11th Eddie Collins is released as White Sox manager; he'll rejoin the A's as a player-coach. C Ray Schalk takes his place.

29th Tris Speaker resigns as Indians manager. Stories of a thrown game and betting on games by Ty Cobb and Speaker gain momentum when Judge Landis holds a secret hearing with the 2 stars and former pitcher-OF Joe Wood. The story and testimony will not be released until December 21st. Former Tiger P Dutch Leonard wrote to Harry Heilmann that he had turned over letters written to him by Joe Wood and Ty Cobb to AL president Ban Johnson, implicating Wood and Cobb in betting on a Tiger-Cleveland game played in Detroit, September 25, 1919. He charged that Cobb and Speaker conspired to let Detroit win to help them gain 3rd-place money. At a secret meeting of AL directors, it was decided to let Cobb and Speaker resign with no publicity. But, as rumors spread, Judge Landis takes charge of the matter and holds the hearings, at which Leonard refuses to appear. Cobb and Wood admit to the letters and say Leonard is angry for having been released to the Pacific Coast League by Cobb. Speaker, not named in the letters, denies everything. Public sympathy is with the stars, but the matter will remain unresolved until January of next year.

30th Bill Carrigan, popular Red Sox manager who won pennants in 1915 and 1916, is drafted out of retirement to resurrect the cellar-dwellers.

DECEMBER

5th   Cardinals C Bob O'Farrell is named NL MVP. O'Farrell caught 146 games and batted .293. He polls 79 points. Reds 2B Hughie Critz is runner-up with 60. Critz set a ML record handling 588 assists, which will be topped by Frank Frisch with 643 in 1927.

11th   Cleveland coach Jack McAllister is named to replace Speaker as Indians manager.

16th   Judge Landis is given a new 7-year term as commissioner with a raise to $65,000.

20th   Rogers Hornsby is traded from the Cardinals to the New York Giants for Frankie Frisch and P Jimmy Ring. Hornsby, after 12 years in St. Louis, will play for 3 teams in the next 3 years.

28th   Bob O'Farrell is named to replace Hornsby as Cards manager.

30th   The Chicago *Tribune* breaks a story that the Tigers had thrown a 4-game series to the White Sox in 1917 to help Chicago win the pennant. Judge Landis will begin a hearing in a week.

1927

JANUARY

1st Charles Ebbets announces the purchase of ground for a new 30,000-seat stadium in Brooklyn. He also announces the release of OF Zack Wheat, a future Hall of Famer.

5th Judge Landis begins a 3-day public hearing on the charges that 4 games played between Chicago and Detroit on September 2 and 3, 1917, had been thrown to the White Sox. The White Sox, Swede Risberg contends, returned the favor for 2 games in 1919. Near the end of the 1917 season, some Chicago players contributed about $45 each to reward Detroit pitchers for winning the last series against Boston, helping Chicago clinch the pennant. No witnesses confirm any part of the story, although Tigers P Bill James denies ever receiving any money, and the others named deny all charges. A week after the hearing opens, Judge Landis clears all the accused, ruling lack of evidence of anything except the practice of players paying another team for winning.

9th In a 3-way deal, P Burleigh Grimes goes from Brooklyn to the Giants, C Butch Henline goes from Philadelphia to Brooklyn, and Giants 2B Fresco Thompson and P Jack Scott wind up with the Phils.

15th Washington veteran SS Roger Peckinpaugh is traded to the White Sox for P Sloppy Thurston and Leo Mangum.

23rd Ban Johnson is given an indefinite leave of absence, due to ill health. Detroit's President Frank Navin is named acting AL president.

27th Citing accuser Dutch Leonard's refusal to appear at the hearings of January 5th, Judge Landis issues a lengthy decision clearing Ty Cobb and Tris Speaker of any wrongdoing and ordering them reinstated by their teams. Both are then made free agents. Connie Mack will sign Cobb on February 8th. Speaker will sign with Washington on January 31st.

31st NL President John Heydler rules that Rogers Hornsby cannot continue to hold stock in the Cardinals and play for the Giants.

FEBRUARY

8th Sad Sam Jones departs the Yankees for St. Louis, traded for P Joe Giard and OF Cedric Durst.

9th The Giants send versatile George Kelly, along with cash, to the Reds for truculent holdout OF Edd Roush.

MARCH

3rd Babe Ruth signs for a reported $70,000 a year for 3 years.

10th In a practice game in spring training, Joe Judge hits a line drive that hits Walter Johnson in the foot, breaking a small bone in the ankle and sidelining him for over two months.

APRIL

1st Giants SS Travis Jackson has an appendicitis operation that puts him out of action for 6 weeks.

8th Four days before the season opens, recently traded Rogers Hornsby breaks the impasse by selling his stock in the Cardinals for $112,000. He receives $86,000 from Sam Breadon, $2,000 from each of the other 7 NL clubs, and an extra $12,000 from the Giants.

12th President Calvin Coolidge throws out the first ball in Washington as the Red Sox win 6–2. Walter Johnson, sidelined with an injury sustained March 10th, misses his last chance to pitch an opener, after winning 9 of 14, including 7 shutouts.

Mark Koenig is 5-for-5 as the Yankees batter Philadelphia's Lefty Grove 8–3 before 65,000, the biggest Opening Day crowd ever. The Yankees will share or hold first place from the first day of the race to the last; a feat unmatched in the AL until the 1984 Tigers.

26th Forty-year-old Ty Cobb has 3 hits, drives in the winning run, and steals home in the 7th inning. He tops that off with a 9th-inning shoestring catch in shallow RF and then traps the runner off first for an unassisted DP to end the game. The A's win a 9–8 squeaker over Boston. Cobb also stole home on April 19th in a 3–1 win over Washington.

28th   The Giants take first place in the NL when the Cubs rake Pirates pitching for 17 hits and 8 walks in a 16–4 win.

MAY

1st   One-year wonder Hod Lisenbee, 28, blanks the Red Sox 6–0 for the Senators in his first ML start. He will be 18-9 with 4 shutouts for the 3rd-place Senators and never have another winning season.

8th   The Yankees draw a record 52,000 to Comiskey Park; Waite Hoyt wins one of his league-leading 22 games 9–0.

17th   Charlie Grimm singles in the winning run in the 22nd inning to give the Cubs a 4–3 win over the Braves at Boston against Bob Smith, who goes the distance. Bob Osborn hurls 14 runless relief innings to win for Chicago.

18th   White Sox players give their former manager Eddie Collins a wristwatch and diamond stickpin on his return to Chicago with the A's.

21st   The Cubs move into first place in the NL when a 9-run 9th inning gives them an 11–6 win and double-header sweep at Brooklyn while the Pirates are beating New York.

30th   Walter Johnson's first appearance of the season is the occasion of the last shutout of his career, No. 113, 3–0 over Boston.

Reading, PA managed by Fred Merkle, defeats Baltimore in the International League to break its 32-game losing streak.

Unassisted triple plays are a rarity, but SS Jimmy Cooney makes one for the Cubs against Pittsburgh as he catches Paul Waner's line drive, steps on 2B to retire Lloyd Waner, and tags Clyde Barnhart going back to 1B.

31st   Detroit 1B Johnny Neun pulls the 2nd unassisted triple play in 2 days. It happens in the 9th against Cleveland to end the game when Neun catches Homer Summa's line drive, touches Charlie Jamieson in the baseline and runs to 2B where he tags the base Glenn Myatt has vacated. Detroit wins 1–0.

JUNE

10th   George Stallings, Rochester (IL) club owner, fires himself as manager.

11th   Fred Werber of the Augusta Tigers (South Atlantic) sets a minor league record by stealing 7 bases. The record will be equaled by Lee Mazzilli and Rickey Henderson.

12th   The Giants trade righthander Hugh McQuillan back to Boston with P Kent Greenfield and IF Doc Farrell for C Zack Taylor, IF Herb Thomas, and P Larry Benton.

16th   The Pirates Lee Meadows wins his 9th of the season to beat Boston 6–0 as Paul Waner hits in his 19th straight game. Waner also has an RBI, the 12th straight game he has done this.

17th   A 12-game winning streak that has lifted the Cubs into 2nd behind the Pirates comes to an end with a loss to the Phils.

18th   It's Charles Lindbergh Day in St. Louis as the transatlantic flyer helps raise the Cardinals NL pennant before a 6–4 win over the Giants.

Continuing a feud that dates back to Smith's days with the Braves, Pirates C Earl Smith decks Braves manager Dave Bancroft with a right to the jaw after they exchange words in the 7th inning. Bancroft is carried off the field. Smith draws a $500 fine and 30-day suspension.

19th   Phils P Jack Scott is the last to pitch 2 complete games in one day, beating the Reds 3–1 and losing 3–0.

21st   Pirates OF Paul Waner's 23-game hitting streak is stopped. Waner, in his 2nd season, will lead the NL with a .380 BA, 237 hits, and 131 RBI. His brother Lloyd will gather 223 hits for a .355 BA in this, rookie year. They pace the 1927 Pirates to a team BA of .305.

JULY

2nd   The Senators complete a sweep of 4 games over the A's and climb into 2nd place on a 9-game winning streak.

7th   Cubs righthander Charlie Root's one-hitter drops the Pirates into 2nd place, with the Cubs on top. In the 2nd of his 16 years with the Cubs, Root will lead the NL with 26 wins and 309 IP.

The Senators trade righthander General Crowder to the Browns for southpaw Tom Zachary.

11th The White Sox tie a ML record with 8 sacrifice bunts against Detroit.

13th Chicago admirers present Eddie Collins, now with the A's, with a new automobile.

18th The Philadelphia A's Ty Cobb makes his 4,000th hit, a double off Sam Gibson of Detroit. Detroit wins 5–3 over Lefty Grove.

19th It's John McGraw Day at the Polo Grounds, in honor of his 25 years as Giants manager. The Cubs spoil the day with an 8–5 win.

Joe Bush is released by the Giants.

22nd Red Lucas of the Reds pitches a 3–0 one-hitter against Dazzy Vance and the Dodgers. The "hit" is a 6th-inning grounder by Hank DeBerry which goes between the legs of Cincinnati 2B Hughie Critz.

26th Max Carey, who played 17 years with the Pirates before he was dismissed, returns to Pittsburgh in a Dodgers uniform and makes a clean steal of home in the 6th inning. It is his 33rd and last steal of home, an NL record.

27th Mel Ott, 18 years old, hits his first ML HR, an inside-the-park round-tripper. It is the only inside-the-park HR he will hit of his 511 career homers.

AUGUST

2nd Washington celebrates Walter Johnson Day on the 20th anniversary of his joining the team. He receives $14,764.05, a silver service, and a Distinguished Service Cross made of gold with 20 diamonds. But the Tigers kayo him in a 3-run 9th to win 7–6.

22nd The Yankees lose their 4th straight for the first time 9–4 to the Indians, despite Babe Ruth's 40th HR. Detroit wins its 13th straight, moving up to 2nd, 12½ games back.

Braves OF Eddie Brown passes Fred Luderus's modern NL mark of 533 consecutive games played (1916–19). Steve Brodie had 574 in 1893–97.

29th In St. Louis, the Yankees win their 18th game against the Browns without a loss 8–3.

31st The Yankees open a home stand by beating the Red Sox 10–3. Ruth hits No. 43 and leads Gehrig by 2. With an 89-37 record, they now lead the 2nd-place A's by 17.

SEPTEMBER

2nd The Cardinals bring Rabbit Maranville back from the minors, buying him from Rochester (IL).

3rd Lefty Grove pitches his only shutout of the year, beating the Yankees 1–0.

Doc Gautreau of the Boston Braves steals home twice in a game against Brooklyn to tie the ML record. This feat will not be repeated until Vic Power does it in 1958.

4th The Pirates beat the Reds and open a 2-game lead in the NL.

7th After blasting 3 HRs in a doubleheader split with the Red Sox the day before, Ruth hits 2 more in a 12–10 win, giving him a record-tying 5 in 3 games. He leads Gehrig 49 HRs to 45.

11th After losing 21 in a row to New York, the Browns win their last meeting 6–2, behind Milt Gaston's 5-hitter. No team has ever swept a 22-game season series. One NL team, the 1909 Cubs, went 21-1 against the Braves.

13th Babe Ruth hits two (52), and the Yankees win a pair from Cleveland to clinch the AL pennant with a 98-41 record and 17-game lead. It is Miller Huggins's 5th pennant, tying him with Connie Mack.

24th The Yankees win their 106th, 6–0 over Detroit, for a new AL high. They will win 110, a record until the 1954 Indians win 111.

25th The Cardinals win 2 to move into 2nd, while the Pirates take 2 from Chicago.

26th The Cubs play their last home date and report a season's attendance of 1,190,000, the first time the Cubs go over a million.

27th Babe Ruth connects for a grand slam off Lefty Grove while Lou Gehrig hits No. 46 in a 7–4 win over the A's. Ruth has 57 with 3 games to play. One of the HRs is a grand slam, the Babe's 2nd in 3 days.

29th Babe Ruth hits 2 HRs to tie his 59 of 1921 in a 15–4 win over Washington.

30th With the score 2–2 in the 8th, Mark Koenig triples and Ruth hits No. 60 off Tom Zachary for a 4–2 win. In the 9th Walter Johnson makes his final appearance as a player. He pinch-hits for Zachary and flies out to Ruth. Ruth hits 17 HRs in September, the highest month's HR output till Rudy York's 18 in August 1937.

OCTOBER

1st The Pirates clinch the NL flag, beating the Reds 9–6. They will finish 1½ games ahead of the Cards and 2 in front of New York.

2nd In the first of 2 games, Detroit's Harry Heilmann hits 2 doubles, a bunt single, and a HR. With the batting title in his pocket, he chooses to play the 2nd game, and collects a single, double, and HR. His 7-for-9 put him at .398 to Philadelphia's Al Simmons's .392. It is the 4th time he will win an alternate-year championship.

The Phils beat the A's 1–0 for the benefit of the Eddie Plank Memorial Fund.

5th With 158 HRs, a .307 team BA, and 6 winning pitchers, the Yanks are the Series favorite. But the Pirates are no slouches with a team BA of .305. OF Kiki Cuyler, a .309 hitter, will see no action in the Series, being passed over for a lighter-hitting OF, as he and manager Donie Bush feud.

Pittsburgh's Ray Kremer (19-8) opens against Waite Hoyt (22-7). In the 3rd, 2 walks and 2 Pirates errors help the Yankees to 3 runs and a 4–1 lead. With 9 hits, the Pirates come close, but the final is 5–4 New York.

6th Two 3-run outbursts by the Yankees off Vic Aldridge (15-10) and a steady 7-hitter by surprise New York starter George Pipgras (10-3) give the Yankees a 6–2 win. Mark Koenig has 3 hits.

7th The 60,695 on hand for game 3 see the Yankees' Herb Pennock (19-8) take an 8–0 lead and a perfect game into the 8th. He retires Glenn Wright, but Pie Traynor breaks the spell with a single, and Clyde Barnhart doubles him home. Pennock settles for a 3-hit 8–1 victory.

8th Down 3-0, the Pirates give the ball to their biggest winner, Carmen Hill (22-11). In the 5th, Ruth's 2nd HR of the Series scores Earle Combs ahead of him for a 3–1 lead. The Pirates tie it in the 7th. In the last of the 9th, Combs walks, Mark Koenig beats out a bunt, and Ruth walks to fill the bases. Reliever Johnny Miljus strikes out Lou Gehrig and Bob Meusel. With 2 strikes on Tony Lazzeri, a wild pitch rolls far enough away for Combs to score the winning run. The Bronx

Bombers are World Champions in 4 straight. Ruth's .400 is good for 7 RBI; Lloyd Waner's .400 tops the Bucs.

11th Lou Gehrig, who established a new ML record with 175 RBI, is named AL MVP. With 56 points, Gehrig wins over Harry Heilmann's 35 and Ted Lyons's 34. Ruth is not considered because former winners are not eligible.

12th In the opening game of the Negro League WS, the Bacharach Giants' Luther Farrell pitches a 3–2 no-hit win over the Chicago American Giants. The game is played in a drizzle and shortened to 7 innings because of darkness.

13th Dave Bancroft resigns as Braves manager; he will play for Brooklyn.

14th Walter Johnson retires as a player. He will sign a 2-year contract to manage Newark (IL) and will later return to the majors as a manager.

17th Ban Johnson, in failing health, retires as AL president after heading the league he started for its first 28 years. Detroit's President Frank Navin is named acting president.

22nd Future Hall of Famer Ross Youngs, one of John McGraw's favorite players, dies of Bright's disease at age 30, cutting short a 10-year career in which he batted .322. Youngs had been accompanied by a specialist as early as 1924, and after the illness had been identified, the Giants hired a nurse to travel with Youngs. He was bedridden in 1927, after appearing in just 95 games in 1926.

23rd Bill Purdy, who hit .355 in his 2nd year with the Reds, scores a touchdown for the Green Bay Packers against the New York Yankees. Purdy's score comes on a 5-yard run.

24th August "Garry" Herrmann, former chairman of the National Commission and 25-year Reds president, resigns.

25th Heinie Groh retires after being released by the Pirates; he signs to manage in the minors.

NOVEMBER

2nd Jack Slattery, Boston College baseball coach, agrees to manage the Braves for a year.

7th Bill McKechnie replaces Bob O'Farrell as St. Louis Cardinals manager, and Burt Shotton moves up from Syracuse (IL) to manage the Phils.

28th AL umpire Billy Evans becomes business manager of the Indians following the purchase of the club by a group headed by Alva Bradley.

The Pirates trade OF Kiki Cuyler to the Cubs for 2B Sparky Adams and OF Pete Scott.

The Yanks release P Bob Shawkey and P Dutch Ruether.

DECEMBER

4th Pirates OF Paul Waner noses out Frank Frisch for NL MVP honors with 72 points to 66. Rogers Hornsby, Cubs P Charlie Root, and Giants SS Travis Jackson also score high.

5th The National Board of Arbitration rules the Texas League cannot place teams in Tulsa and Oklahoma City without permission of the Western League, which now operates in those cities. This landmark decision establishes league property rights in the cities of each circuit.

In an attempt to combat "chain store" baseball, the American Association votes to bar further ownership of its clubs by the ML clubs.

10th Roger Peckinpaugh begins a 6-year term as Indians manager.

11th The Browns sell George Sisler to Washington for $25,000.

12th The NL reports more than 5 million attendance for the league in 1927, a new high. Veteran umpire Hank O'Day is named "player and umpire scout" for the league.

13th Senators president Clark Griffith gains approval to have Washington open the AL season one day before the rest of the league, to celebrate a "National Day" with the U.S. president throwing out the first ball. The AL also installs Ernest S. Barnard as its president.

The Tigers trade OF Heinie Manush and 1B Lu Blue to the Browns for P Elam Vangilder and OF Harry Rice.

The Cards trade P Jimmy Ring to the Phils with C Johnny Schulte for C Bubber Jonnard, SS Jimmy Cooney, and OF Johnny Mokan.

15th The Browns sell HR-hitting Ken Williams to the Red Sox. At 38, Williams is still a .300 hitter, but his HR production will drop to 8.

In a joint meeting, the major leagues turn over $5,000 to the Association of Professional Ball Players to aid ill or disabled former players.

1928

JANUARY

4th   The Yankees buy SS Lyn Lary and IF Jimmy Reese from the Pacific Coast League.

10th   Charles Stoneham announces he has traded Rogers Hornsby to the Braves for C Shanty Hogan and OF Jimmy Welsh.

14th   Alfred J. Reach, founder of the A. J. Reach sporting goods firm, dies at 87. Before 1860, he became the first ballplayer to receive a regular salary when he signed as a catcher with the Philadelphia Athletics for $25 a week.

25th   Tris Speaker, released by Washington, will sign up with the A's.

FEBRUARY

3rd   The NL appoints 2 former players as umpires: OF Sherry Magee and SS Albert "Dolly" Stark. It is a type of vindication for Magee, who was suspended for hitting an umpire in 1911.

SS Jimmy Cooney gets to spend his last ML season with his brother Johnny when the Cards sell him to the Boston Braves.

11th   The Giants and Pirates swap pitchers: Burleigh Grimes for Vic Aldridge.

14th   The ML Advisory Council allots $50,000 to develop a national championship program run by the American Legion.

APRIL

10th   The Senators open a day ahead of the other teams as President Calvin Coolidge throws out the first ball. The Red Sox win 7–5.

12th   The Cards Grover Alexander opens his 18th season by shutting out the Pirates 5–0.

16th   For the first time, a pitcher is deprived of his glove when the Brooklyn captain complains and the ump removes Boston's Charlie Robertson's glove. The New York *Times* reports, "The Robins detected Robertson doing odd stunts with the ball with the aid of his glove. They reported it to umpire Moran who

made Robertson change his glove." Robertson still wins 3–2.

18th   The Cubs set an Opening Day attendance record as a reported 46,000 jam Wrigley Field to see Cincinnati top the Cubs 9–6. The two teams combine for 28 hits.

19th   The Yankees are out of first place for the first time since May 1926, as they lose the morning Patriots Day game in Boston.

The Browns and Tigers pitchers issue 18 walks. Detroit wins 9–8.

20th   Detroit OF Paul Easterling hits his 3rd HR in 3 days, and that's the last he hits for the year.

MAY

1st   Indians outfielders tie the record with 5 assists in a game against the Browns. Rookie Elton Langford has 4 of them, also equaling the record.

3rd   Ty Cobb hits the 700th double of his career while the Athletics lose to the Red Sox 3–1.

10th   The Giants send OF George Harper to the Cards for C Bob O'Farrell.

13th   The Reds move into first place in the NL with a win over the Phils.

14th   Outside the park after a game in Chicago, John McGraw is knocked down by a taxicab and suffers a broken leg that will keep him out of the dugout 6 weeks. Roger Bresnahan takes over.

15th   The Giants make 6 double plays against the Cubs, but lose 10–7.

19th   A 13-game win streak boosts the Cubs into first place. But 3 days later, the Reds will regain the lead with a win over Pittsburgh.

22nd   White Sox CF Johnny Mostil handles 12 chances against the Indians, equaling Happy Felsch's record, also made against Cleveland.

23rd   Jack Slattery quits as Braves manager, and Rogers Hornsby takes over.

Cleveland OF Charlie Jamieson starts a triple play against the White Sox in a 4–3 loss.

28th   The A's buy P George Earnshaw from Baltimore for $50,000 and 2 players.

JUNE

2nd   St. Mary's College football star Larry Bettencourt breaks in at 3B with the Browns. A future member of the College Football Hall of Fame, Bettencourt was an All-American center who will later play for the Green Bay Packers. The $6,000 bonus he receives is a record for a rookie just out of school.

The Phillies defeat the Cardinals 2–1, with all the runs scoring as the result of a record 3 pinch-hit HRs.

6th   Fred Williams hits his 2nd pinch HR in 2 games for the Phils.

8th   Braves OF Eddie Brown is benched, breaking his 618-game playing streak.

The Pirates trade OF Joe Harris and C Johnny Gooch to Brooklyn for C Charlie Hargreaves.

12th   Brooklyn beats the Cubs 13–1, as 3B Harvey Hendrick steals 2B, 3B, and home against Chicago in the 8th.

Chick Hafey's HR beats the Braves for St. Louis, moving them into first place for 2 months as the Cubs, Giants, and Reds stay on their heels.

15th   Ty Cobb, 41 years old, steals home for the 50th and final time in his 24-year career to extend his ML record. It comes in the 8th against the Indians. In a 12–5 Tiger win, Veach, Crawford and Cobb team up for a triple steal.

22nd   Journeyman hurler Hank Johnson of the Yankees blanks the star-studded Athletics 4–0. In the game for Connie Mack's team are Ty Cobb, Mickey Cochrane, Al Simmons, Jimmie Foxx, Eddie Collins, Tris Speaker, and Lefty Grove.

24th   Grover Alexander beats the Reds for the third time in 8 days.

25th   The Giants' Fred Lindstrom strokes 9 hits in a doubleheader against Philadelphia to tie the ML mark.

28th   Babe Ruth slugs 2 HRs to lead the Yankees to a 10–4 victory over the Athletics, and Ty Cobb appears in his 3,000th career game.

30th   The Yankees win 2 from Boston and close out the month 11½ games in front of the A's. Attendance lags, as the race appears over.

JULY

4th   Ray Schalk resigns as White Sox manager; Lena Blackburne replaces him. Blackburne will last one year and in 1930 will start selling his Rubbing Mud from the Delaware River to the AL to use to take the shine off of baseballs. The NL will adopt it in the 1950s.

6th   Urban Shocker, in poor health, is released by the Yankees after one appearance on the mound.

10th   Washington P Milt Gaston surrenders 14 hits in a 9–0 shutout over Cleveland, setting an AL mark and tying the ML standard.

12th   Baseball's biggest battery is recorded, appropriately, with the New York Giants, as Garland "Gob" Buckeye, a 260 pound pro football lineman in the off-season, makes his NL pitching debut with 250 pound Shanty Hogan behind the plate. The Giants lose to the Cardinals.

21st   Jimmie Foxx hits the longest drive ever seen out of Shibe Park as the A's take 2 from St. Louis, increasing their lead over the 3rd-place Browns to 10 games.

22nd   P Red Faber of the White Sox comes up to bat in the 8th with 2 runners on base and the game with the Yankees tied 4–4. He swings twice righthanded against righty Wilcy Moore and misses. He then switches to the left side and knocks in the winning runs with a single to center.

26th   Detroit rookie righthander Vic Sorrell and the Yankees' Waite Hoyt are 1–1 after 11. Twelve hits and 2 walks in the 12th score 11 New York runs in the biggest extra-inning storm ever.

The Phils buy lefthand hitting OF Chuck Klein from Fort Wayne.

29th   The Indians score 8 in the first and 9 in the 2nd in a 24–6 win over the Yankees at home. Johnny Hodapp of the Indians becomes the first AL player to get 2 hits in an inning twice in a game. He strokes 2 singles in both the 2nd and 6th innings of the game. The Yankees' lead shrinks from 11½ games to 6 in one week.

AUGUST

1st   Babe Ruth hits HR No. 42 and is 4 weeks ahead of his 1927 pace.

11th Carl Hubbell's first ML victory is a 4–0 shutout of the Phils. He'll be 10-6 down the stretch and will pitch 16 years with the Giants.

20th Art Shires of the White Sox strokes 4 hits, including a triple, in his ML debut.

23rd The Yankees pick up lefty Tom Zachary on waivers from Washington.

SEPTEMBER

3rd Ty Cobb makes the last of his 4,191 hits, the 724th double of his career, as a pinch hitter in the 9th inning of the first game at Washington. The hit is off Bump Hadley.

Pirates RF Adam Comorosky handles 9 putouts, tying the record for that position.

4th The Braves play a record 9 consecutive double-headers between now and the 15th. They lose 5 of them in a row, including 4 to the Giants.

7th The A's take 2 from Boston and move into a first-place tie with the Yankees, who lose a pair to the Senators.

9th A total of 85,265 jam Yankee Stadium to watch George Pipgras and Waite Hoyt turn back the Athletics 3–0 and 7–3. The A's will take the last game of the series and leave town 1½ back.

At age 38, Yankee P Urban Shocker dies of pneumonia in Denver, where he had gone for his health. Only now does it become known that he had suffered from an enlarged heart and was unable to sleep lying down for 2 years. Shocker, who never had a losing season, was 18-6 in 1927 but appeared in only one game in 1928.

10th The Giants gain 1½ games on the Cards and Cubs by winning 2 from Boston while the leaders lose. New York moves into 2nd the next day with another sweep of the Braves.

11th Ty Cobb makes his last appearance as a batter, popping out against Yankee Hank Johnson to SS Mark Koenig as a pinch hitter in the 9th.

17th Wilcy Moore, the Yankee pitching hero of 1927, goes home with an ailing arm after working just 60 innings.

20th The White Sox beat New York 4–3, and the Yankee lead is cut to one game.

A crowd of 50,000 at the Polo Grounds sees the Giants and Cardinals split a doubleheader. The Cards take the first game 8–5 behind George Harper's 3 HRs. The Giants take the nightcap 7–4 to remain 2 games behind the NL-leading Cardinals.

26th The Cardinals lose to Brooklyn and hold a half-game lead over New York.

28th George Pipgras survives an 11-6 win over the Tigers to clinch the AL pennant for the Yankees. The A's finish 2½ games out.

Browns P Alvin Crowder beats his former teammates the Senators 4–3 to finish with the AL best record, 21-5. He will later win 50 in 2 years for the Senators.

29th The Cardinals win the NL pennant with a 3–1 win at Boston while the Cubs are beating New York. The final margin is 2 games over the Giants, 4 over the Cubs.

30th Washington OF Goose Goslin gets 2 hits for the 3rd day in a row to edge Browns OF Heinie Manush .379 to .378 for his only batting title in his 18-year career.

OCTOBER

4th The Cardinals lack the Yankees' power, but have a .325 hitter in Jim Bottomley, who tied with Hack Wilson for NL HR honors with 31 and led in RBI with 136. St. Louis has a solid IF defense with Frankie Frisch, the venerable Rabbit Maranville, and their fleet OF, led by Taylor Douthit, whose 547 putouts and 566 total chances in CF have set post-1900 records.

The first game is a swift execution before 61,425 at New York. Babe Ruth has a single and double and scores twice, once on Bob Meusel's 4th-inning HR, and Lou Gehrig is 2-for-4 with 2 RBI off Bill Sherdel (21-10). Waite Hoyt (23-7) sets the Cards down with 3 hits, one a solo HR by Bottomley in the 7th, for a 4–1 win.

5th Grover Alexander (16-9) faces George Pipgras (24-13) in game 2. Gehrig unloads a 3-run HR in the first. The Cards tie in the 2nd, but Pipgras shuts them out on 2 hits the rest of the way. Alexander is nicked for one in the 2nd and is driven to cover by a 4-run outburst in the 3rd and it's 9–3 New York. Ruth is 2-for-3, and Gehrig has 3 more RBI.

7th Veteran Tom Zachary (3-3 with New York) gets a start against the Cards' Jesse Haines (20-8). Two infield hits followed by a triple give the Cards 2 runs. Lou Gehrig leads off the 2nd with a booming HR, and in the 4th the sharp-fielding Taylor Douthit misplays a single before a 2-run HR by Gehrig. Three runs in the 8th give New York a 6–3 lead that stands up when Zachary goes all the way for a 7–3 win. Ruth and Gehrig have 2 hits each, and Gehrig another 3 RBI.

9th After a rainout, Waite Hoyt and Bill Sherdel are back on the mound for game 4. After 6 innings, the Cards hold a 2–1 lead. With one out in the 7th, Ruth hits a HR, his 2nd of the game, and Gehrig follows suit. When Meusel singles, in comes Alexander to face Tony Lazzeri. Lazzeri doubles and later scores the 4th run of the inning. In the 8th, Cedric Durst, subbing for Earle Combs, hits one out of the park, and Ruth follows with his 3rd HR of the game. Final score is 7–3 and the Yanks sweep their 2nd straight WS. Ruth's World Series BA of .625 is still unmatched; with Gehrig's .545 and a record 9 RBI, they also set individual and team offensive records for hits, HRs, total bases, and at bats in a game.

15th Walter Johnson signs a 3-year contract to manage the Senators.

16th Gordon "Mickey" Cochrane wins AL MVP honors, edging Heinie Manush by 2 points. Neither Ruth nor Gehrig is eligible, having won before.

17th George Moriarty resigns as Tigers manager and is replaced by ousted Washington skipper Bucky Harris. Moriarty will return to the ranks of the AL umpires.

29th The Giants send OF Lefty O'Doul and cash to the Phils for OF Freddy Leach.

NOVEMBER

3rd The Cubs get Rogers Hornsby from the Braves in exchange for $200,000, IF Fred Maguire, P Percy Jones, C Lou Legett, former A's P Harry Seibold, and P Bruce Cunningham. Braves owner-president Judge Emil Fuchs also decides to be his own manager.

Voters in Massachusetts approve Sunday baseball in Boston, provided that the ballpark is more than 1,000 feet from a church. This leaves Pennsylvania as the only state with no Sunday baseball in the major leagues.

Voters in Cleveland approve a bond issue to build a giant municipal stadium near the lakefront to attract events for the 1932 Olympics.

19th The Indians send $50,000 and 2 players to San Francisco (PCL) for OF Earl Averill.

21st The Cardinals sign Billy Southworth as manager; Bill McKechnie goes down to Rochester (IL).

28th The NL buys George Magerkurth from the PCL for $2,000. This is the highest price paid for a new ump.

DECEMBER

2nd Cardinals 1B Jim Bottomley is voted NL MVP with 76 points to 70 for Giants 3B Fred Lindstrom, whose .358 BA was 3rd behind Hornsby and Paul Waner.

11th At the NL meeting, President John Heydler proposes the designated hitter for pitchers to improve and speed up the game. He contends fans are tired of seeing weak-hitting pitchers come to bat.

12th The Pirates buy lefthander Larry French from Portland (PCL).

15th The Red Sox trade Buddy Myer to Washington for P Hod Lisenbee, P Milt Gaston, IF Bobby Reeves, IF Grant Gillis, and OF Elliot Bigelow. Myer will become a top player in the 1930s.

17th At a joint meeting, a rule is changed that ends the practice of minor league teams selling star prospects to friendly ML clubs for high prices, then getting the players back, forcing another ML club to pay the reputed price for the player. Other changes ban the signing of players under the age of 17 and set a $7,500 price tag on any first-year player.

NL President John Heydler's designated hitter idea gets the backing of John McGraw, but the AL is against it.

1929

JANUARY

1st   OF Jim Bell of Cienfuegos becomes the first to connect for 3 HRs in one game during professional league play in Cuba. Bell's feat occurs at Alda Park in a 15–11 victory over Club Havana.

22nd   The Yankees announce they will put numbers on the backs of their uniforms, becoming the first baseball team to start continuous use of the numbers. The first numbers are based on positions in the batting order; thus, Ruth will wear number 3 and Gehrig 4. By 1931 all AL teams will use them; it will be 1933 before all NL players are numbered.

FEBRUARY

20th   The Red Sox announce they will play Sunday games, allowed for the first time in Boston, at Braves Field because Fenway Park is located too close to a church.

APRIL

16th   The Cubs open at Wrigley Field before an estimated 50,000, the biggest Opening Day turnout they've ever had, and beat the Pirates 3–1.

Cleveland OF Earl Averill becomes the first AL player to hit a HR on his first ML time at bat when he blasts an 0-and-2 pitch off Detroit's Earl Whitehill in the Indians' 5–4, 11-inning victory.

17th   President Herbert Hoover throws out the first ball in Washington and then watches the Athletics win 13–4. The previous day's game, marking the opening of season, was rained out.

Babe Ruth and actress Claire Hodgson are married at 5 A.M. to avoid crowds. The Yankee opener with the Red Sox is rained out. The next day, in his first at bat against Red Ruffing, the Babe will hit a HR. Rounding 2nd base, he doffs his cap to Claire in the stands. Gehrig adds a HR in the 6th, and New York wins 7–3.

27th   Brooklyn relief P Clise Dudley becomes the first man to hit a HR at Baker Bowl on the first ML pitch he sees, thrown by Claude Willoughby. Dudley will hit two more in his 4 ML years.

MAY

6th   The AL announces that it will discontinue the MVP award. The NL will abandon it after this year; in 1931 the Baseball Writers Association will pick it up and conduct the balloting from then on.

7th   Yankee southpaw Tom Zachary wins a 6–5 game in relief at St. Louis, the first of his 12 wins without a loss for the year.

8th   The Giants Carl Hubbell pitches an 11–0 no-hitter against the Pirates, allowing just one walk. It's the first by a lefthander since Hub Leonard in 1918. Chick Fullis starts the scoring with a HR in the 2nd, his 3rd in three days. Mel Ott adds 2 HRs to take the NL lead.

11th   After 25 consecutive complete games, White Sox righthander Tommy Thomas comes out in the 5th inning of a 9–2 loss to Washington.

The Indians defeat the Yankees 4–3 in the first game played between 2 teams wearing numbered uniforms.

14th   After a slow start, the Athletics beat Detroit and move past the Yankees into first place, where they will stay for the rest of the year.

18th   Brooklyn and Philadelphia score a ML-record 50 runs in a doubleheader at the Baker Bowl. The Robins (Dodgers) win the opener 20–16, and the Phils take the 2nd game 8–6.

19th   A cloudburst at Yankee Stadium sends a standing-room-only crowd rushing for the exits. A stampede in the RF bleachers leaves 2 dead, 62 injured. Jake Ruppert vows never again to sell more tickets than seats.

Fleet White Sox OF Johnny Mostil, 2-time AL SB leader, breaks his ankle, ending his ML playing days at the age of 33.

24th   Chicago's Ted Lyons and Detroit's George Uhle go 21 innings before the Tigers get a run to win 6–5 in the longest game—3 hours and 31 minutes—ever seen at Comiskey Park. Uhle is the winner, though Vic Sorrell pitches the bottom of the 21st. Lyons, the loser, goes the distance and gives up 24 hits.

26th   Two pinch hitters—Les Bell for the Braves and Pat Crawford for the Giants—hit grand slams in New York's 15–9 victory.

JUNE

3rd HR-hitting 1B Joe "Unser Choe" Hauser is sold by the A's to Cleveland.

16th The Reds beat Burleigh Grimes, ending the Pirate spitballer's 10-game win streak. He'll finish 17-7, the top Pittsburgh hurler.

18th Bill Terry of the Giants gets 9 hits and 6 RBI in a doubleheader against the Dodgers, but the Giants lose both games 8–7 and 7–6.

19th In their 2nd straight doubleheader, The Giants sweep the Phillies, winning 15–14, in 11 innings, and 12–6. Mel Ott has 2 HRs and 4 doubles for the day, while Edd Roush goes 8-for-12. In tomorrow's 11-6 win over the Phils, Ott will have 3 RBI, giving him 11 straight games with at least one ribbie. The 20 year old will have 27 RBI in the 11 games, and will finish the season with 151, 2nd in the NL.

JULY

3rd The Cubs and Reds turn 9 double plays, tying the Detroit-Washington 1925 mark. The 7–5 Chicago win is their 7th in a row, giving them a half-game lead over the Pirates.

The Cubs Hack Wilson jumps into the Reds dugout to fight pitcher Ray Kolp, who has been needling him. Wilson is stopped and ejected before reaching Kolp. The Cubs win 10–5, and that evening, when both teams are at Chicago's Union Station awaiting trains, Wilson floors Reds pitcher Pete Donahue.

5th Cards 1B Jim Bottomley hits the first of 7 HRs he will knock in 5 games.

The Giants use the first public address system in a big-league park for a game against the Pirates.

6th After losing 11 in a row, including a 10–6 loss in the opener, the Cardinals break out in the 2nd game. They score 10 in the first and 10 more in the 5th to wallop the Phils 28–6 on 28 hits. The run and hit totals are NL records. The Cardinals (43) and Phillies (30) combine for a ML-tying 73 hits in the doubleheader at cozy Baker Bowl.

After watching the Tigers belt 8 HRs on the 2nd, 3rd, and 4th, the Browns use the off day to erect a screen in front of the RF pavilion. The screen stretches 156 feet from the foul pole toward CF, 310 feet down the line from home. In the next day's game, Heinie Manush will hit 3 balls off the screen against the Yankees' Waite Hoyt, while Ruth will hit 2 off it in the series. This screen will remain in place into the 1940s, the only stadium with extended OF seating where it is impossible to catch a HR ball.

9th Cardinals OF Chick Hafey, with 8 straight hits in his 2 previous games, gets 2 more before the Phils' "Fidgety Phil" Collins stops him. His 10-for-10 ties the NL record. The Cards win 7–4.

10th The Pirates outslug the Phillies 15–9 at the Baker Bowl. Pittsburgh hits 5 HRs; the Phils, 4, with one HR coming in each inning, a virtually insurmountable record.

18th Trying to curb the hitters, NL president Heydler orders umpires to rub up new balls before each game to remove the gloss.

23rd The Cardinals decide they made a mistake when they sent manager Bill McKechnie to Rochester and brought up Billy Southworth; they swap them back again.

24th The Cubs regain the NL lead; a 9-game winning streak gives them a 4½ game lead.

31st Babe Ruth hits a fungo 447 feet in an unofficial test, beating all trial competition records.

AUGUST

3rd The Cubs complain about the ragged shirt sleeve on Dodger Dazzy Vance's pitching arm, an age-old trick to distract a batter. A rule will be passed enforcing neater dressing habits by pitchers.

4th The Yankees take the opening game of 2 from Cleveland, winning 12–0. In the 2nd game, after trailing 6–5 with 2 out in the top of the 9th, Cleveland scores 9 runs.

10th Grover Alexander beats the Phils 7–1 for his 373rd and last NL victory. He pitches 4 scoreless relief innings to win 11–9 in the 11th.

11th Babe Ruth hits HR No. 500 off Willis Hudlin of Cleveland.

12th OF George Quellich of the Reading Keys (IL) hits a grand slam against Montreal for his 15th consecutive hit over a 4-day period.

14th   It is Charlie Gehringer Day in Detroit, and the popular 2B handles 10 chances in the field, hits 3 singles and a HR, and steals home in a 17–13 win over the Yankees.

17th   The Yankees buy P Lefty Gomez from San Francisco (PCL) for delivery in September 1930.

21st   Cubs 1B Charlie Grimm is sidelined for the rest of the regular season with a hand injury, but he'll be okay for the WS.

23rd   The Cubs buy Lon Warneke, 20, from Alexandria (Cotton State League) for $100.

25th   The largest crowd ever to pack the Reds' ball-park—35,432—watches their team split a pair with the Cubs.

26th   In the 8th inning of a 5–5 game at Wrigley Field, Cubs 3B Norm McMillan hits a line drive down the LF line with the bases loaded. Reds LF Evar Swanson, shaded toward center, can't find the ball, which he sees bounce off a gutter in foul territory. McMillan circles the bases and 4 runs score. Later, Cubs relief P Ken Penner picks up his jacket in the bullpen and discovers the ball in his right sleeve.

Albert G. Mills, NL president 1883–84, author of the National Agreement and original reserve rule that governed baseball's early years, dies at 84.

28th   Donie Bush resigns as Pirates manager; coach Jewel Ens replaces him.

SEPTEMBER

2nd   The Cubs beat the Cards twice 11–7 and 12–10, before 81,000 fans at Wrigley Field. A crowd of 38,000 fans sees the morning game and 43,000 watch the afternoon game. Rogers Hornsby has 2 HRs and Hack Wilson has one.

14th   The A's clinch the AL pennant with a 5–0 win over the White Sox.

15th   In a field day trial, former college track star Reds LF Evar Swanson circles the bases in 13.3 seconds. Two years later, with more sophisticated equipment timing him, he will do it in 13.2 while with Columbus (American Association).

18th   A Pirates loss to the Braves clinches the NL pennant for the Cubs.

24th   The Yankees' Tom Zachary wins his 12th without a loss 5–3 over Boston. His 12-0 season record will not be equaled.

Brooklyn OF Johnny Frederick connects for his 52nd double in the Dodgers' 8–6 loss to the Phils.

The Giants sweep the Braves, 5–4 and 6–5, as Mel Ott hits a homer in each game, his 41st and 42nd HRs of the year. This ties Rogers Hornsby's NL mark.

25th   Three days after turning the team over to coach Art Fletcher, Yankee manager Miller Huggins dies from blood poisoning at New York's St. Vincent Hospital. He was 49. On the day of his funeral in Cincinnati, the AL will cancel all games.

27th   Phils OF Chuck Klein hits HR No. 42, tying Mel Ott and equaling Hornsby's NL record. He'll hit one more to top the NL with 43.

OCTOBER

5th   Mel Ott and Chuck Klein go into today's Giant-Phils doubleheader tied at 42 home runs apiece. In the opener, Ott manages a single, but Klein homers off Carl Hubbell in his first at bat to take the HR lead. In game 2, Ott singles in his first at bat. After that, Phillies pitchers, rather than give Ott a chance to tie Klein, intentionally walk him 5 times. The last walk comes with the bases loaded. Phillie Frank O'Doul gets 6 hits in the 2 games for an NL record of 254 hits for the season.

Reds righthander Rube Ehrhardt, making his only start of the year, becomes one of only 5 men to pitch a shutout in their final ML game. He blanks the Cubs 9–0 on 5 hits for his only win of the year.

6th   While the 3rd-place Indians lose 2 to the 4th-place Browns, Cleveland's Joe Sewell finishes a 152-game schedule with just 4 strikeouts.

Bill Killefer signs to manage the Browns.

Bill McKechnie signs a 4-year contract to manage the Braves.

Former hurler Nick Altrock, 53, now a coach-comedian for the Senators, plays one inning in RF and collects a single in his one AB against the Red Sox. Other graybeards to make season-ending token appearances include Browns coach Jimmie Austin, 49; Braves coach Johnny Evers, 48; and White Sox manager Lena Blackburne, 42, who pitches one-third of an inning.

9th Howard Ehmke (7-2), who has been scouting the Cubs for a week, is the Athletics' surprise starter in game 1 of the WS at Chicago. A crowd of 50,740 Cubs fans watches Ehmke strike out a WS-record 13 that will stand until Brooklyn's Carl Erskine fans 16 Yankees in 1953. He holds the Cards scoreless until the 9th for a 3–1 win. Charlie Root (19-6) yields just 3 hits, but one is a HR by Jimmie Foxx in the 7th.

A 3-run HR by Foxx and a 2-run blast by Al Simmons are enough for a 9–3 A's win over Pat Malone (22-10). George Earnshaw (24-8) is kayoed in a 3-run Cubs 3rd; Lefty Grove comes in and shuts down the Cubs.

11th In Philadelphia, Guy Bush (18-7) is tagged freely but the A's strand 10; Earnshaw comes back with a 6-hitter, striking out 10, but 2 hits, a walk, and an error in the 6th produce 3 tallies for a 3–1 Cubs win.

12th At 45, John Quinn (11-9) gets a start against Root. After giving up a HR to Charlie Grimm with a man on in the 3rd, Quinn serves up 4 straight singles to open the 6th, and in comes Rube Walberg (18-11). The inning ends with the score 7–0. Trailing 8–0 in the 7th, the Athletics, in the greatest rally in World Series history, shake Chicago by scoring 10 runs for a 10–8 victory. The most damaging play is Hack Wilson's misjudgment of a fly from Mule Haas's bat, which goes for a 3-run, inside-the-park HR.

14th After a Sunday off, a special train from Washington brings President and Mrs. Hoover to Shibe Park to see if Howard Ehmke can wind up the Series against Pat Malone. They match zeroes for 3, but with 2 outs in the 4th, a walk and 3 hits give the Cubs a 2–0 lead. Malone stifles the A's with 2 hits and the 2–0 lead holds up into the 9th. The Athletics rally and come up with 3 runs, the winning run scoring on a Bing Miller double, and take the series four games to one.

17th The Yankees sign former P Bob Shawkey as manager.

22nd Phils C Walt Lerian, 26, is killed when a truck hits him.

30th Former C Gabby Street is named manager of the Cardinals.

NOVEMBER

14th The Braves send OF George Harper, P Art Delaney, and cash to Los Angeles (PCL) for OF Wally Berger.

DECEMBER

11th The Cards trade Grover Alexander back to the Phillies with C Harry McCurdy for OF Homer Peel and P Bob McGraw.

The Browns trade C Wally Schang back to the Athletics for 3B Sammy Hale.

20th Bill Carrigan has had enough of managing the Red Sox. He quits, and Heinie Wagner signs on for a year.

1930

JANUARY

8th   Art Nehf, who pitched in 5 World Series, announces his retirement. He won 184 games in his career, last pitching for the Cubs in the 1929 Series.

20th   Commissioner Landis bans boxing for all players in baseball following the brief boxing career of Art Shires. "Whataman" Shires fought football players as well as baseball players, and his challenge to Hack Wilson purportedly prompts the ban.

26th   Carl Mays, whose underhand pitch killed Ray Chapman 10 years earlier, ends his ML career with 208 victories and signs with Portland (Pacific Coast League).

29th   Ken Williams, former AL HR champion and a lifetime .319 batter, goes from the Red Sox to the Yankees for the waiver price. He will be released before the season begins.

FEBRUARY

2nd   The Yankees waive Leo Durocher out of the AL and he is signed by the Reds.

12th   Connie Mack is awarded the prestigious Edward W. Bok Prize given to the Philadelphian who has done the most for the city in the past year. Mack, the first sports figure to be so honored, led the Athletics to a World Championship in 1929.

16th   Judge Landis rules that the Cards cannot farm out C Gus Mancuso. Forced to keep him, the commissioner's edict pays off when Cardinals regular C Jimmie Wilson is injured and Mancuso bats .366 in 76 games.

MARCH

8th   Babe Ruth signs a 2-year contract for $160,000 with New York. At $80,000 per year, he is the highest paid player of all time. When it is pointed out he is earning more money than the President of the United States, Ruth observes: "I had a better year than he did." Ed Barrow, Yankee GM, assures posterity, "No one will ever be paid more than Ruth."

APRIL

9th   Burleigh Grimes, veteran spitballer in a contract dispute with the Pirates, is sold to the Boston Braves. Boston later trades Grimes to the Cardinals, the eventual pennant winner.

14th   President Herbert Hoover continues the tradition of throwing out the first ball on Opening Day in Washington, a day before the rest of the ML teams begin. The Red Sox win 4–3.

15th   Weather curtails the AL Opening Day schedule. Al Simmons ends his holdout, signs a contract, and homers in his first at bat as the A's and Lefty Grove defeat the Yankees 6–2. Ruth's clout in the 3rd inning strikes a loudspeaker in deep right center and bounds back onto the field for a double.

27th   Bud Clancy, White Sox 1B, enters record books without doing a thing. He has no chances in a 9-inning game against St. Louis. The last player to have a game with no plays at 1B was Al McCauley of Washington (American Association) in 1891.

28th   The first night game in organized baseball—played with temporary lights—is played in the Class C Western Association with 1,000 fans on hand. Home team Independence loses to Muskogee 13–3.

29th   Suspicions that the 1930 ball is the liveliest ever increase as 123 runs are scored in 7 ML games.

MAY

2nd   Des Moines (Western League) defeats Wichita 13–6 to open the first ballpark with permanently installed lights. The field is a predecessor of Sec Taylor Stadium.

6th   The Yankees get Red Ruffing from the Red Sox for $50,000 and Cedric Durst.

7th   Chick Hafey has 5 RBI in the 5th inning as the Cards beat the Phils 16–11 to move out of the cellar and begin the climb to an eventual pennant.

8th   Fred Lindstrom has his 2nd 5-hit game of the season, hitting for the cycle as the Giants defeat the Pirates 13–10.

9th   The Yankees and the Tigers OF make only 2 putouts for an AL record which has never been equaled. The NL record for OF idleness is one chance (Pittsburgh versus Brooklyn, August 26, 1910).

12th Umpire Brick Owens calls 5 balks against Cleveland's Milt Shoffner and 3 against Philadelphia's George Earnshaw. Philadelphia wins 13–7.

Giants P Larry Benton sets a modern ML record (since tied several times) by surrendering 6 HRs in a single game. The New Yorkers manage to hold on to win the game against the Cubs 14–12, with the victory going to Benton.

16th Washington wins a doubleheader from Philadelphia and moves into first place.

21st Babe Ruth hits 3 HRs in the first game of a doubleheader against the A's. Max Bishop draws 5 walks for the 2nd time in his career (he is the only player to do this twice). Ruth homers in the 2nd game, and Bishop has 3 more walks.

22nd The Yankees and the Athletics continue the HR barrage as the Yankees take both games of a doubleheader. The 2nd-game score is 20–13. Babe Ruth hits a pair of HRs in each game, as the teams combine to hit 14.

24th Ruth homers in both games of a doubleheader, giving him 9 in one week.

26th Joe Sewell strikes out twice facing lefthander Pat Caraway of the White Sox. It is the last time the Indians 3B will fan this season, striking out only 3 times in 353 at bats.

28th Cubs P Hal Carlson, 38, dies suddenly of stomach ulcers. He is 4-2 at the time, and had won 114 games over a 14-year career.

Philadelphia's Grover Cleveland Alexander makes his last ML appearance, giving up 2 hits and 2 runs in relief as the Braves win 5–1.

30th Del Bissonette, Brooklyn 1B, hits the ball over the RF screen at Ebbets Field. Baserunner Babe Herman, "the Headless Horseman of Ebbets Field," stops to watch and is passed by Bissonette, reducing the HR to a single. Despite this, the Robins, so called for their manager Wilbert Robinson, win a pair of games from the Phillies and take first place.

The Yankees trade 2 stars of the 1927 team, Waite Hoyt and Mark Koenig, to the Tigers for Ownie Carroll and Harry Rice.

The Cubs Rogers Hornsby, already limping after off-season surgery on his heel, breaks an ankle sliding into 3B in a game in St. Louis.

JUNE

1st Danny MacFayden beats the Yankees 7–4 to end a 14-game losing streak for the Red Sox.

The Giants score 12 runs in the 3rd inning of a game with the Braves, winning the nightcap of the doubleheader 16–3.

3rd Grover Cleveland Alexander is released by the Phillies after posting a 0–3 record. He ends his career thinking he has the NL record for most wins at 373, one more than Christy Mathewson. In 1946, a win disallowed in 1902 is restored to Mathewson's record, to leave the 2 pitchers at a tie.

4th Brooklyn makes 8 errors, losing to Pittsburgh at Ebbets Field 12–6.

6th Denny Sothern, Phillies OF, has 4 doubles in a 5-for-5 game.

8th The increased hitting in the NL is reflected in these batting averages: Riggs Stephenson .420; Babe Herman .414; Chuck Klein .401; Harry Heilmann .400; and Bill Terry .399.

9th Chick Hafey, the Cardinals' bespectacled OF, withdraws from the game because of eye trouble. He soon returns to the lineup, but this signals a constant problem with vision and sinus conditions that will hamper his career.

10th Lefty Grove loses his first game of the season, 7–6, in 11 innings to the White Sox. His record is now 7–1.

13th Cleveland beats Philadelphia and takes over first place. Washington trades Goose Goslin to St. Louis for Heinie Manush and Al Crowder. The Senators will regain the popular OF in 1932, and with Manush and Crowder, he will help them win a pennant the following year.

16th The Cardinals acquire spitball veteran Burleigh Grimes from the Braves for another spitballer, Wee Willie Sherdel, and Fred Frankhouse.

18th The Athletics beat Wes Ferrell of the Indians 7–2 with 3 consecutive HRs in the 5th (Al Simmons, Jimmie Foxx, and Bing Miller).

23rd With 2 outs in the 6th inning, Brooklyn makes 10 hits in succession against Pittsburgh to equal the ML record. They begin the 7th inning with 2 more after the 6th inning ends with a runner tagged out at the plate.

Hack Wilson hits for the cycle with 2 singles, a double, triple, and HR and drives in 6 as the Cubs whip the Phils 21–8 at Wrigley.

27th John Quinn, 46-year-old Athletics pitcher, becomes the oldest player to hit a HR when he connects against the Browns and picks up the victory. Fellow sluggers Foxx and Simmons also hit HRs.

A Ladies Day crowd swells the Wrigley Field attendance to a park record 51,556 to watch the Cubs 7–5 win over Brooklyn. Kiki Cuyler's 10th- inning HR is the clincher.

30th Brooklyn, in need of an OF, buys Ike Boone from the San Francisco Missions (PCL) where he was hitting .448 through 83 games. In 1929 Boone compiled an all-time record of 553 total bases while hitting 55 homers and batting .407. Boone wasn't even Brooklyn's first choice; the Robins preferred another PCL batting star, Buzz Arlett, who had his eye injured in a postgame fight with umpire Chet Chadbourne, who slugged the Oakland OF with his mask.

The Cubs move into first place ahead of Brooklyn by defeating the Giants.

JULY

2nd Carl Reynolds of the White Sox hits 3 consecutive HRs in the 2nd game of a doubleheader at Yankee Stadium. Two of them are hit inside the park. The feat is second-billed, as headlines tell of Ruth tearing a nail off his finger on the OF screen.

5th Frankie Frisch, Cardinals 2B, ties the league record with 16 chances in a game in which St. Louis defeats Cincinnati 6–4.

The Phillies lose a doubleheader to the Braves to drop into the cellar for the rest of the season, despite a team batting average of .315.

Marking the first time 2 Negro-League teams play at Yankee Stadium, 20,000 watch the New York Lincoln Giants and the Baltimore Black Sox split a pair. Baltimore's Rap Dixon has 3 HRs and the Giants, Chino Smith has 2 HRs and a triple.

9th Alex Gaston of the Red Sox beats the Senators to stop a 10-game winning streak by the league-leading Senators. In 1929 he halted an 11-game string by the A's, the eventual winners.

The Phillies come from behind in the last of the 9th to defeat the Giants 5–4. Chuck Klein's double off Carl Hubbell drives in Lefty O'Doul from 2nd.

10th Fred Lindstrom of the Giants has 5 hits in a game against the Phillies. This is the 3rd time he has accomplished this feat.

13th The defending champs, the Philadelphia A's, move into first place by beating the Browns, 12–1, and will remain in the lead the rest of the season.

18th Chuck Klein's consecutive-game hitting streak ends at 26. The Phillie outfielder is stopped by journeymen hurlers Al Grabowski and Jim Lindsey of the Cardinals.

21st Four pinch-hit HRs are hit in a doubleheader between Brooklyn and St. Louis. Hal Lee and Harvey Hendrick connect for Brooklyn, and George Puccinelli and Jim Bottomley, for the Cards. The HRs are the first ML hits for both Lee and Puccinelli.

22nd Phillies P Phil Collins hits home runs in the 4th and 5th innings of an 11–5 win over the Pirates. He will hit just 2 more HRs in his 8-year career.

23rd Pie Traynor of the Pirates is responsible for 2 victories over the Phillies. His HR in the 9th seals the first game 2–1, and he comes through with a 3-run HR in the 13th of the nightcap to win 16–15.

24th The Phillies Chuck Klein objects sharply to an 8th-inning strike call by umpire Lou Jorda and is banished for the first time in his career. Also ejected are manager Burt Shotton, captain Fresco Thompson, and 1B Don Hurst. It is necessary to use 42-year-old Cy Williams in RF in the 9th, the only inning of play Klein will miss in 1930.

25th The Athletics pull off triple steals twice in one game against the Indians. Al Simmons, Bing Miller, and Dib Williams are the base thieves in the first inning, and Cochrane, Simmons, and Foxx steal together in the 4th.

26th Phils pitchers continue their consistency, giving up 5 HRs to the Cubs in a 16–2 pasting. Hack Wilson has 3 of the homers, while Gabby Hartnett and winning pitcher Pat Malone add the other two.

27th Cincinnati hurler Ken Ash throws one pitch in relief against the Chicago Cubs and then is lifted for a pinch hitter. Ash's pitch to Charlie Grimm results in a triple play, and Ash receives credit for the 6–5 victory, his last in the ML.

30th Cincinnati loses an exhibition night game at Indianapolis. In 1935 the Reds will inaugurate night baseball in the majors.

AUGUST

2nd Playing under Kansas City's portable light system, the Homestead Grays, 54-year-old hurler Smokey Joe Williams (27 strikeouts) spins a one-hitter to defeat the Monarchs' Chet Brewer (19 strikeouts) 1–0 in a fiercely contested 12-inning matchup. Oscar Charleston scores the only run.

3rd Chuck Klein hits safely in his 26th consecutive game, the 2nd time this season he has run a streak to this length. He will hit safely in 135 of his team's 156 games in 1930.

6th Eugene Mercantelli, under the name Gene Rye, hits 3 HRs in the 8th inning as Waco (Texas) racks up 18 runs in the inning against Beaumont. Waco wins 22–4. Rye will have 39 ML at bats and get 7 hits, all singles. Rye sets 4 organized baseball records for one inning with 12 total bases, 9 extra bases, 3 HRs, and 8 RBI (since tied).

9th John Stone, Detroit OF, hits in his 34th consecutive game as the Tigers beat the White Sox at Comiskey Park.

10th The Phillies win 18–0 as Claude Willoughby defeats the Reds in the first game of a twin bill.

11th The Cubs displace Brooklyn for the league lead, sweeping a 4-game series with the Braves. Cubs P Bud Teachout wins the final game 4–2.

14th Wes Ferrell of Cleveland breezes to a 15–0 win over the league-leading A's for his 20th win.

16th Lefty Grove wins his 20th game of the season, beating the Browns in Philadelphia 4–2.

18th Woody English scores 5 runs and Hack Wilson hits his 42nd HR, as the Cubs crush the Phillies 17–3. Pat Malone hits a HR and goes the distance for the win.

19th Goose Goslin hits 3 consecutive HRs for St. Louis in a game against the Philadelphia A's.

21st Chick Hafey hits for the cycle, as the Cards beat the Phillies at St. Louis 16–6.

23rd The Yankees buy Frank Crosetti from the San Francisco Seals but allow him to play another season in the PCL before reporting. The Yankees will make a similar arrangement for Joe DiMaggio, buying him from the Seals but waiting a year before acquiring him in 1936.

The Giants' Fred Lindstrom has his 24–game hitting streak ended, as the Cubs shock the Giants 3–2. The game is tied 2-all in the bottom of the 9th, when the Cubs load the bases with 2 out. With the count 0-and-2, Tommy Bridges, the runner on 3rd, races safely home, as surprised Giant reliever Joe Heving watches and then completes his deliberate windup with a wide pitch.

25th Tommy Bridges walks 12 Brownies, but Detroit still beats St. Louis 7–5.

26th Hack Wilson hits his 44th HR, breaking Chuck Klein's one-year-old NL record, as the Cubs defeat the Pirates 7–5.

28th The Cards outlast the Cubs 8–7 in a 20-inning game at Wrigley Field.

29th In the Cubs' 2nd successive extra-inning game, Pat Malone beats Burleigh Grimes 9–8 in 13 innings to halt the Cardinals' 9-game win streak. With captain Charlie Grimm out of the lineup with a spike wound, the Cubs sign George Kelly, released a month earlier by Reds.

A little comedy is injected into an 11-inning, 9–8 Braves victory over the Phillies. The Braves Rabbit Maranville makes the 3rd out of the 4th inning in a steal attempt at 2B. He argues vigorously and at length. Fresco Thompson of the Phils finally tires of it, picks up the scrappy little guy and carries him to his position at SS.

31st Bill Hallahan, on the way to becoming the NL strikeout leader, fans 12 as the Cards beat the Cubs 8–3.

At the Polo Grounds, Mel Ott hits 3 consecutive HRs against Boston, but the Giants lose 14–10.

SEPTEMBER

1st The Cardinals take a pair from the Pirates and go into first place. Brooklyn, New York, and Chicago are all bunched at the top of the standings with St. Louis.

4th Rogers Hornsby returns to the Chicago lineup as the Cubs beat the Pirates. Hornsby had been absent since Memorial Day because of a broken ankle.

6th In the first game of a doubleheader, Ted Lyons of Chicago beats Wes Ferrell of Cleveland, ending Ferrell's winning streak at 13. Only 2 bases on balls are issued in the doubleheader.

12th Brooklyn C Al Lopez drives one over the head of Cincinnati LF Bob Meusel, and the ball bounces into the bleachers at Ebbets Field. It will be the ML's last recorded bounce HR, as the NL rules after the season that such a hit will henceforth be a double. The AL had made the change after the 1929 season.

14th Brooklyn becomes the 3rd team in 3 days to lead the NL, beating Cincinnati 8–3 while the Cards split a doubleheader.

15th The Dodgers win their 11th straight, although Babe Herman once again stops to watch a HR disappear for a record 2nd time in one season. This time, Glenn Wright lopes past the awestruck Herman to reduce a HR to a single.

Newspapers carry the story of the disappearance of Cardinals P Flint Rhem on the eve of a crucial series in Brooklyn.

The Cubs split a pair in Philadelphia when Lefty O'Doul pinch-hits a HR to beat the Cubs 12–11 in the first game. It is the 2nd consecutive game that O'Doul has produced pinch-hit HRs. In the 2nd game of the day's doubleheader, Hack Wilson hits his 50th HR to pace the Cubs to a 6–4 win.

16th Brooklyn's collapse begins. The Cardinals tie for first place when Bill Hallahan outduels Dazzy Vance 1–0 in 10 innings.

Flint Rhem returns to the Cardinals with an improbable story that he was kidnapped by gamblers and forced to drink bootleg whiskey.

17th Earl Averill, Cleveland OF, hits 3 HRs in succession and narrowly misses a 4th when the umpire rules a long drive foul. He hits another HR the first time up in the 2nd game of the doubleheader.

The Braves Wally Berger adds 3 HRs in a doubleheader against the Reds en route to a rookie record.

18th The Philadelphia Athletics win the AL championship for the 2nd year in a row, defeating the White Sox 14–10.

The Cards finish a 3-game sweep of Brooklyn at Ebbets Field.

20th Joe Hauser of the Baltimore Orioles (International League) sets a new minor league record by hitting his 63rd HR.

Hack Wilson hits no HRs but gets his 176th RBI, passing Lou Gehrig's 1927 ML record.

23rd There are 42 hits in the Phillies, 19–16 loss to the pennant-bound Cardinals. RF Chuck Klein makes his 44th assist, well above the record of 39 set by Mike Mitchell with the Reds in 1907.

25th Joe McCarthy, not receiving the support of Cubs owner William Wrigley, resigns as manager. Rogers Hornsby is named to finish the season.

Harry Hooper, former Red Sox and White Sox star OF, is named baseball coach at Princeton University.

26th Jesse Haines pitches the St. Louis Cards to a 10–5 pennant-clinching win over the Pittsburgh Pirates.

27th Hack Wilson clubs 2 HRs to finish with a still-standing NL record of 56. The Cubs win 13–8 over the Reds at Wrigley as Pat Malone wins his 20th of the year.

Almost overlooked is Wally Berger's 38th HR for the Braves, at Ebbets Field, as Boston tops Brooklyn 7–1. It is a record for rookies and still stands as an NL record.

Gehrig plays the last of 885 consecutive games at 1B. In the next game, the season's finale, he will take Ruth's LF position.

28th Babe Ruth returns to the scene of his youthful fame, the pitcher's mound at Fenway Park, and hurls a 9–3 complete game win over the Red Sox.

The Cubs bring down the season's curtain as Wilson has his 189th and 190th RBI in a 12–11 victory over the Reds. Wilson's major league RBI record will remain untouched.

Bill Terry goes hitless as the Giants edge the Dodgers for 3rd place with a 10-inning win over the Phillies at the Polo Grounds. He finishes at .401, and is the last NL player to hit over .400. The Giants set a 20th-century single season batting average record of .319 (the Philadelphia Phillies hit .349 in 1894).

Dizzy Dean scatters 3 hits for a 3–1 victory in his ML debut. The 19-year-old rookie, fresh from the Texas League, pitches the final game of the season for the pennant-winning Cardinals.

OCTOBER

1st The World Series opens with a Wednesday game at Philadelphia's Shibe Park. The defending World Champion Athletics are held to 5 hits by Burleigh Grimes. Lefty Grove limits the Cards to a pair of runs, as the A's capitalize on their power. Their 5 hits include HRs by Mickey Cochrane and Al Simmons, 2 triples and a double, providing Philadelphia with single runs in 5 different innings and a 5–2 victory.

2nd Flint Rhem is a surprise starter for the Cardinals but he fails to astonish the Athletics batters. He gives up 6 earned runs in less than 4 innings, all the Athletics need to win 6–1 behind George Earnshaw's 6-hit pitching.

4th Bill Hallahan blanks the A's 5–0, giving up 5 walks and 7 hits. Philadelphia A's hurler Jack Quinn, at age 46, pitches 2 innings of relief against the St. Louis Cardinals, thereby becoming the oldest player to appear in a WS game.

5th Jesse Haines pitches a brilliant 4-hitter to beat Lefty Grove and the A's 3–1, thereby evening up the Series.

6th The A's take the lead in the Series, 3 games to 2, when George Earnshaw and Lefty Grove combine to shut out the Cardinals, 2–0, on 3 hits. Philadelphia's runs come in the top of the 9th when Burleigh Grimes is tagged for a long 2-run HR by Jimmie Foxx.

8th George Earnshaw finishes off the Cardinals 7–1, pitching shutout ball until the 9th inning. He is clearly the pitching star of the WS with 2 wins and 7 shutout innings of a game in which reliever Lefty Grove got the decision. Despite the "lively" 1930 ball and the many outstanding hitters on both sides, it is a pitching-dominated Series. The Cards bat only .200 as a team and the A's .197. The A's staff has a combined ERA of 1.73.

10th The New York Yankees announce they have signed Joe McCarthy to manage the team for 4 years. The Cubs made him available one year after he had led them to a pennant, and the Yankees lost no time in signing him. McCarthy will lead New York to 8 pennants and 7 World Championships before resigning in 1946.

With no MVP award for the second year in a row, the Associated Press polls its members and names Joe Cronin unofficial AL MVP for 1930. The Baseball Writers Association names Hack Wilson the MVP of the NL. The Cubs give Wilson a bonus of $1,000, the monetary reward which the MVP title had carried as an official league honor.

14th Brooklyn sends a bundle of cash to the last-place Phillies, together with some 2nd-line players, to obtain Lefty O'Doul and Fresco Thompson.

NOVEMBER

2nd E. S. Barnard completes his 3-year contract as president of the AL. Among Barnard's innovations have been the establishment of an umpire's school and the recodifying of the rule book. He also led the effort to eliminate the sacrifice fly scoring rule (with inflated averages resulting from the livelier baseball, the batter no longer needed the benefit of not being charged a time at bat when his fly ball advanced a runner).

6th The Pirates trade SS Dick Bartell, a .320 hitter, to the Phillies for defensive star SS Tommy Thevenow, and P Claude Willoughby.

10th Veteran Jim Vaughn is reinstated by Judge Landis after 8 years of ineligibility. Vaughn, who had lost a double no-hitter to Fred Toney in 1917, had jumped the Cubs in 1922. He chose to pitch for a semipro team following a salary dispute with Chicago. He will go to spring training with the Cubs in 1931 but will fail to make the team at age 43.

23rd At the Polo grounds, Browns outfielder Red Badgro, playing for the NFL New York Giants, catches a TD pass against the Green Bay Packers. It is Badgro's 3rd TD catch of the season, all from Benny Friedman. In 1981, Badgro will be elected to the Hall of Fame—for football.

25th *The Sporting News,* also acting to fill the MVP void, announces its selection of Bill Terry as the Most Valuable Player in the NL, and Joe Cronin in the AL.

DECEMBER

1st   Shano Collins, a native New Englander, is appointed manager of the perennial last-place Boston Red Sox.

9th   At its annual meeting, the AL reelects E. S. Barnard to a 5-year term.

Rube Foster, one of the most prominent figures in black baseball history, dies. The founder of the Negro National League, he excelled as a player, manager, and executive.

11th   The BBWAA votes to continue the custom of selecting an MVP for each league. Beginning in 1931 the annual vote of the BBWAA will designate a player for this honor in each league. Previous MVP winners will be able to repeat under the new rules, something that was prohibited by the AL in the 1920s.

12th   The Rules Committee of baseball issues a greatly revised code, reducing the number of rules by combining many. Not only is the sacrifice rule abolished but also the rule awarding HRs when the ball bounces into the stands. This had already been in effect in the AL but not the NL.

13th   The 15-year career of George Sisler ends as the Boston Braves release him. A lifetime .340 hitter who twice led the AL with averages above .400, Sisler would be among the first to be elected to the Baseball Hall of Fame, enshrined in 1939.

15th   Chief Bender is signed by the New York Giants as a pitching coach. He had coached baseball at the Naval Academy in 1930.

1931

JANUARY

5th Mrs. Lucille Thomas becomes the first woman to buy a professional baseball team, purchasing the Topeka franchise in the Western League.

19th Acting under a new draft agreement with the Pacific Coast League, Brooklyn purchases the contract of Ernie Lombardi from Oakland.

20th Joe Sewell, released by the Cleveland Indians, signs with the New York Yankees.

26th Another Oakland star, Buzz Arlett, long coveted by ML teams and long withheld by Oakland, is sold to the Phillies.

The Boston Braves release veteran pitcher Johnny Cooney. He had held out in 1930, insisting he could bat well enough to stay in baseball. After several years in the minors, he will return to the NL as a Braves OF and be runner-up to NL batting champ Pete Reiser in 1940.

The International League accepts the open draft imposed by the major leagues. Until this time the top minor leagues could control their players and refuse to sell them.

FEBRUARY

5th Hack Wilson, who set still-standing NL HR and ML RBI records for the Cubs in 1930, signs with them for $35,000.

15th The New York Yankees' training site in St. Petersburg is renamed Miller Huggins Field in honor of the team's late manager.

21st The Chicago White Sox and the New York Giants become the first ML teams to meet in a night game. They collect 23 hits in a 10-inning exhibition game played in Houston, at Buffs Stadium.

Brooklyn arrives in Cuba to play 5 intersquad games.

27th Finally cut loose by the New York Giants, for whom he refused to play in 1930 in a seasonlong holdout over salary terms, 2-time batting champ Edd Roush returns to the Cincinnati Reds.

E. S. Barnard, recently reappointed AL president, dies at 57. He had succeeded Ban Johnson in 1927.

28th Ban Johnson dies after a long illness. He had created the AL and been its dynamic, dictatorial leader until subdued by the advent of Judge Landis, who took office as the first commissioner in January 1921.

APRIL

2nd Miss Jackie Mitchell, a 17-year-old gate attraction for Joe Engel's Chattanooga Lookouts (Southern Association), pitches against the New York Yankees in an exhibition game in Chattanooga. Babe Ruth waves wildly at 2 pitches and watches a 3rd strike go by. Lou Gehrig gallantly times his 3 swings to miss the ball, but unsmiling Tony Lazzeri, after first trying to bunt, walks and Miss Mitchell leaves the game. The final score is 14–4 Yankees. In 1933 Mitchell will pitch for the House of David team.

14th President Herbert Hoover throws out the first ball at Washington. Lefty Grove, in relief, gets the first win of what will be his greatest season.

22nd Babe Ruth collides with Charlie Berry, Red Sox catcher and former pro football player, while trying to score on a sacrifice fly. Ruth is carried off the field at Fenway Park and taken to a hospital.

24th Rogers Hornsby, player/manager of the Chicago Cubs, hits 3 consecutive HRs to beat the Pirates at Forbes Field 10–6.

26th Dusty Cooke, Yankee RF, is hurt diving for a fly ball off the bat of Ossie Bluege of Washington. 1B Gehrig winds up playing the ball, which becomes an inside-the-park HR. With Babe Ruth still sidelined, the shorthanded Yankees send P Red Ruffing to the outfield. The game's most significant play comes with Lyn Lary on base when Lou Gehrig's drive into the CF stands at Washington bounces back and is caught by CF Harry Rice. According to the rules, this is a home run, but when Lary sees Rice catching the ball, he thinks it's the final out of the inning. Unnoticed by Joe McCarthy, coaching at 3B, Lary heads for the dugout after crossing 3B. Gehrig circles the bases. He is called out and gets credit for a triple instead of a HR and loses 2 RBI. As a result Gehrig will end the season tied for the HR title with Babe Ruth and will have "only" 184 RBI.

27th Wally Berger, Boston Braves CF, ties the modern mark for the outfield by recording 4 assists, helping Socks Seibold shut out the Phillies 2–0.

29th Wes Ferrell pitches a 9–0 no-hit game for Cleveland against the St. Louis Browns. His brother, Rick, almost gets a hit for the Browns when he beats out a grounder that is ruled an error. Ferrell strikes out 8 and bats in 4 runs with a HR and a double.

MAY

2nd Hack Wilson hits his first HR of 1931 as the Cards beat the Cubs 6–3 at St. Louis. After hitting 56 homers last year, Wilson will hit only 13 in a disaster-ridden season.

4th Lou Gehrig and Babe Ruth, back in the lineup, switch positions to spare Ruth's lame leg. The Red Sox beat the Yankees as Gehrig makes an error. It is the last game in which Gehrig plays OF.

11th The Philadelphia A's gain first place, never to relinquish it. Al Simmons, who will repeat as batting champion, drives in a run for the 11th consecutive game, and Lefty Grove, on his way to 31 wins, beats Chicago 5–2.

17th Willie Kamm, star White Sox 3B, is traded to Cleveland for Lew Fonseca, who will manage Chicago next season.

21st Dazzy Vance is knocked cold by a line drive while leading the Phillies 3–2 with 2 outs in the 9th inning. John Quinn gets the last out for Brooklyn.

25th The A's win their 17th in a row, 2 behind the White Sox' AL record, beating the Yankees 4–2 at Philadelphia. The streak ends the next day when Lefty Gomez stops the A's 6–2.

27th AL Secretary Will Harridge is elected to succeed E. S. Barnard as president of the league.

The Giants surge past the Cards to move into first place, beating Boston 7–4.

30th The Cards retake first place and hold it the rest of the season, as they win a Memorial Day double-header and the Giants lose a pair to Brooklyn. In the 2nd game at the Polo Grounds, Robins 3B Wally Gilbert has 6 consecutive hits but falls one short of the ML record held by his manager, Wilbert Robinson.

Despite the Baker Bowl's reputation as a HR haven, no one had hit a ball over the stadium wall since 1922. But Wally Berger, Boston Braves slugger, clears it in a 10–9 loss to the Phillies.

31st After hitting in 27 consecutive games Al Simmons is stopped in a darkness-shortened game between the A's and the Red Sox at Fenway Park.

Yankee Earle Combs' hitting streak ends at 29, although the Yankees beat Washington in a rain-shortened 7-inning game.

JUNE

4th After hitting safely in his last 8 times at bat, Oscar Melillo, the slick-fielding but light-hitting 2B of the Browns, is stopped by Red Ruffing of the Yankees. St. Louis wins 8–6.

7th With Sunday baseball still prohibited in Philadelphia, the A's make a one-day trip to Detroit. They win 12–2, and leave 18 men on base.

13th Adam Comorosky, the Pittsburgh OF who made an unassisted DP on May 31, makes another as the Giants win 6–4.

15th Cut-down day for ML rosters brings the retirement of Eddie Collins and Harry Heilmann. Collins becomes a coach for the A's. Heilmann will return briefly to the Reds in 1932.

17th Tommy Connolly, who had umpired the first AL game in 1901, retires as an active arbiter to become supervisor of AL umpires.

21st George Earnshaw notches the 12th consecutive victory for the A's 6–5 at Chicago.

24th Bill Sweeney, Red Sox 1B, makes 21 putouts, one fewer than Hal Chase's 1906 record. Boston outfielders have no putouts as the Red Sox lose 7–3 in Cleveland.

28th Records for catching fly balls are set in a doubleheader as the A's beat the Tigers 9–1 and 5–1. The Detroit OF make 24 putouts, and Philadelphia adds 19 for a 2-team total of 43 in the 2 games.

30th The New York Giants' Ethan Allen pinch-hits a grand slam off the Cubs' Pat Malone to tie the game, but Chicago scores again to win at the Polo Grounds 11–10. Sparky Adams also homers in the game, his first since 1925. He had been to bat 3,104 times without a HR.

The Athletics buy veteran Waite Hoyt from Detroit.

JULY

2nd Babe Ruth homers to drive in a run for the 11th consecutive game as the Yankees drub Detroit 12–1. Ruth has 18 RBI in the string.

7th The Browns and the White Sox play a 12-inning game in which not a single strikeout is recorded. It is the longest whiffless game in ML history. Chicago wins 10–9.

9th Fred Lindstrom breaks his ankle sliding into 3B. He will be out of the lineup until early August, leaving the Giants with only 3 outfielders.

12th The largest crowd in the history of Sportsman's Park in St. Louis, 45,715 (in a ballpark with 35,000 seats), creates a travesty and permanently distorts the record for doubles hit in a game. Easy fly balls drop for ground-rule doubles among the fans encroaching on the field. There are 32 doubles hit in 2 games, 11 in the first and 21 in the 2nd, for records both for the most doubles in one game and for a doubleheader.

18th John McGraw is ejected from a game in St. Louis after he rages over an out call on the Giants Chick Fullis. A telegram McGraw receives before the next game causes another tantrum, as NL president Heydler fines him $150 and suspends him for 3 days.

24th Babe Herman hits for the cycle for the 2nd time this season, but the Robins lose at Pittsburgh 8–7.

25th Pittsburgh's Larry French pitches a 14-inning game, the longest NL contest of the season, to beat Brooklyn 3–2.

26th The Yankees split a doubleheader with the White Sox, taking the 2nd game 22–5 with 9 batters scoring 2 or more runs each.

27th Riggs Stephenson, Cubs OF, breaks an ankle in a game with the Phillies, as Chicago loses 6–5 at Wrigley Field.

28th The White Sox record an AL-record 12 hits in the 8th inning against the Yankees. They score 11 runs as Bob Fothergill homers and triples to win 14–12.

29th Cleveland's Wes Ferrell shuts out Washington 6–0, scattering 10 hits, as the Senators leave 15 runners on base.

AUGUST

2nd The Red Sox and the Yankees split a Sunday doubleheader before a record 40,000, played at Braves Field because of religious restrictions involving Fenway. Former Boston P Red Ruffing wins the first game 4–1, and ex-New Yorker Wilcy Moore blanks his former mates 1–0 in the nightcap. It will be the last time the Yankees are shut out in 308 games.

5th For the 2nd time in his career, Jim Bottomley has 6 hits in 6 at bats, as the Cards defeat Pittsburgh 16–2.

The Cubs edge the Reds 3–2 at Wrigley Field when Leo Durocher boots a ground ball hit by Kiki Cuyler. It ends a string of 251 errorless chances in 53 games for Durocher.

8th Washington's Bobby Burke, a little-known left-hander, throws a 5–0 no-hitter against Boston. Burke will finish the year 8 and 3, the best mark of his 10-year career. "Burke didn't throw more than a half dozen curves all afternoon," said plate umpire George Moriarty.

13th Tony Cuccinello wakes up the last-place Reds by going 6-for-6 in the first game of a doubleheader against Boston.

18th Lou Gehrig is hitless in Detroit, as he plays his 1,000th consecutive game. He is 307 short of Everett Scott's record streak.

19th Lefty Grove wins his 16th consecutive game, tying the AL record set by Walter Johnson and Joe Wood in 1912.

20th Tony Frietas, who will win 342 minor league games, is let out of jail to pitch for Sacramento (PCL) against the Missions. He wins, and then returns to finish a 5-day sentence for speeding.

21st Babe Ruth hits his 600th HR, off George Blaeholder of the Browns, as the Yankees win 11–7. Lou Gehrig homers immediately after the Babe's historic blow. In their 10 years as teammates, they will homer in the same inning 19 times and in the same game 72 times.

23rd Lefty Grove is frustrated in his effort to win a record-breaking 17th game in a row, as Johnny Moore misjudges a routine fly ball to allow the game's lone run. The volatile Grove is outraged that Al Simmons, the regular OF, misses the game, which is won by Dick Coffman of the Browns 1–0.

29th Gehrig knocks Lefty Grove out of the box with a 6th-inning grand slam, but the A's still win 7–4.

31st Wes Ferrell of Cleveland hits 2 HRs, as he beats the White Sox 13–5 at Chicago. He will end his career with a record 37 HRs as a hurler, plus one as a pinch hitter.

The A's win their 22nd game in a row, beating the Red Sox at home. This mark will stand until the Boston Red Sox win 23 straight in July of 1988.

SEPTEMBER

1st Gehrig hits his 3rd grand slam in 4 days and his 6th HR in consecutive games when he connects in a 5–1 win over the Red Sox.

6th Homestead Grays ace Smokey Joe Williams fashions a 2-hit, 6–2 win over the St. Louis Stars in the Negro NL Championship Series. The Grays will win in 6 games.

7th Van Lingle Mungo, Uncle Robby's last find as a pitcher, reports to Brooklyn from Hartford and shuts out Boston 2–0. In his first start he fans 7 and hits a HR and a single.

In the morning game of a doubleheader in Philadelphia, the Yankees begin with 8 walks and score 8 times in the first inning.

9th To raise funds to help the unemployed in the Depression, the Yankees, Giants, and Robins agree to a series of benefit games. Sixty thousand fans, paying regular prices, raise $59,000 in the first matchup, as Babe Ruth homers and the Yankees beat the Giants 7–2.

13th Yankee Tony Lazzeri steals 2B and home in the 12th to give Lefty Gomez a 2–1 win over Detroit.

Guy Bush of the Cubs pitches his 2nd one-hitter of the season, against the Braves. His first was against the Cards on August 9th.

15th The Philadelphia Athletics clinch the pennant, beating Cleveland at home. Eddie Rommel, veteran knuckleball pitcher for the A's, is the winning hurler, as Connie Mack wins his 3rd successive pennant. It is Mack's 9th, and last, AL championship.

16th World Series tickets can now be printed as the St. Louis Cardinals repeat as NL champions. They beat the Phillies 6–3 and prepare for a rematch of the 1930 WS.

17th On his 32nd birthday, OF Earl Webb of the Red Sox sets the still-standing ML record for 2-base hits at 65. He will finish the season with 67. He would have had 68, but on August 4th the league corrected a May 1st box score, turning what had been credited as a double into a single.

18th Burleigh Grimes hits Mel Ott in the head with a pitch in a game at St. Louis. The Giants OF is hospitalized with a concussion and is out for the season.

19th Lefty Grove wins his 30th game, beating the White Sox 2–1. He is the first to win 30 since Jim Bagby of Cleveland in 1920 and will be the last AL hurler to do so until Denny McLain in 1968.

20th Lou Gehrig drives in 4 runs to break his old RBI mark of 175, set in 1927. By the season's end he will have a total of 184.

Before a game with Brooklyn, Sparky Adams, Cards 3B, injures his ankle. He can see only limited action in the WS, leaving a chance for Andy High to shine as his substitute. Gabby Street, 48-year-old Cardinal manager, catches the last 3 innings of the game against the Robins.

22nd In a 13-inning game at Forbes Field, Hal Finney, Pirates C, has no putouts in a 3–2 win over Philadelphia. Paul Waner draws 5 walks, and 20 runners are left on base, as Heine Meine wins his 19th game to tie for the lead in the NL.

24th The round-robin playoff among New York City's 3 ML teams, to raise money for the unemployed, concludes with Brooklyn losing to both the Giants and the Yankees at the Polo Grounds. Again, a near capacity crowd turns out and adds $48,000 to bring the fund to $108,000. In field events held between games, Babe Ruth, normally a lefthanded hitter, bats right and wins the fungo hitting contest. He breaks the old distance record held by Big Ed Walsh. Ruth's drive lands in deep center field, 421 feet away. The old record, set 20 years earlier, was 419½ feet.

27th Lou Gehrig hits a HR to tie Babe Ruth at 46 while the Yankees beat Lefty Grove and deny him his 32nd victory.

The most desperately contested battle for individual honors takes place in the race for the NL batting title. Chick Hafey, who reported late due to a contract dispute, goes into the final doubleheader with the Reds batting .353, 4 points over Bill Terry, last year's champ. Hafey gets only one hit in 8 times at bat to drop to .349. Bill Terry's Giants are playing archenemy Brooklyn at Ebbets Field. Brooklyn, in their last game as the Robins, wins 12–3, and Terry gets only one hit in 4 times at bat. The title goes to Hafey, who batted .3488 to Terry's .3486. Jim Bottomley, Hafey's Cardinal teammate, finishes at .3481.

OCTOBER

1st   Pepper Martin, an unheralded rookie, gets 3 hits, but the A's Lefty Grove coasts to an easy 6–2 victory in the WS opener in St. Louis.

2nd   The Cards even the WS as Wild Bill Hallahan shuts out the A's 2–0 despite 7 walks and a wild pitch. Pepper Martin continues to steal the Series, scoring from 2B on a base hit in the 2nd inning and sliding in a cloud of dust on a squeeze play in the 8th. He has 2 stolen bases, but the game almost gets away on a bonehead play by the usually savvy Cardinal C Jimmy Wilson. With 2 on base in the 9th, and 2 outs, PH Johnny Moore swings at a ball in the dirt and misses. Wilson needs only to throw the ball to 1B. Instead, he throws it to 3B, and everyone is safe. Fortunately for Wilson's reputation, Jim Bottomley makes a sensational catch, leaning into the box seats to get the final out on a pop foul by Max Bishop.

5th   Because of a Pennsylvania law banning baseball on Sunday, an extra day is added as the Series moves to Philadelphia. Lefty Grove pitches the 3rd game with 3 days rest. However, Burleigh Grimes, who had lost twice to Grove in 1930, has a no-hitter until the 8th inning, winning 5–2. Pepper Martin continues to excite the crowds with 2 more hits, scoring twice.

6th   The A's George Earnshaw evens the WS with a 3–0 shutout, giving up 2 hits to the red-hot Pepper Martin. Jimmie Foxx hits a ball over the LF stands, judged one of the longest drives ever at Shibe Park.

7th   Connie Mack, who surprised everyone in 1929 by starting veteran Howard Ehmke in the WS opener, tries the ploy with Waite Hoyt. Pitching in his 7th WS, Hoyt falls victim to Pepper Martin, who homers and drives in 4 runs with 3 hits. Hallahan wins for the Cards 5–1.

9th   With the Series back in St. Louis, Lefty Grove evens matters by containing Pepper Martin and winning easily 8–1.

10th   Connie Mack sends George Earnshaw out to win the final game as he had in 1930. However, Burleigh Grimes carries a 4–0 lead into the 9th before he weakens. The A's score twice and have 2 runners on base with 2 outs when Bill Hallahan rescues Grimes. Max Bishop flies to Pepper Martin for the final out as the Cardinals take the Series 4 games to 3. As in the 1929 and 1930 WS, the A's finish the 1931 WS with no stolen bases.

15th   Sportswriter Fred Lieb leads an all-star squad on a barnstorming trip to Hawaii and Japan. Among those aboard ship are Lou Gehrig, Frank Frisch, Rabbit Maranville, Willie Kamm, Al Simmons, Lefty O'Doul, Mickey Cochrane, and Lefty Grove.

20th   Frankie Frisch, the Cardinals' fiery field leader, is named MVP of the NL. He led in stolen bases with 28, hit .313, and was chosen for his all-around excellence.

23rd   Brooklyn announces Wilbert Robinson is through as manager and the club will be called the Robins only in the past tense. Max Carey, a no-nonsense sort, will take over next year.

26th   Charles Comiskey dies at age 72. The White Sox owner and a pioneer player, he never recovered from the betrayal of the 1919 WS.

29th   Lefty Grove, the A's P who won 31 games, is named the AL's MVP. He led the league in strikeouts for the 7th straight season and topped all pitchers in winning percentage, ERA, and complete games.

NOVEMBER

2nd   The team of ML stars arrives in Japan for its tour. The team will win all 17 games it plays.

13th   Jacob Ruppert, Yankee owner, buys the Newark franchise in the International League. During the decade the Bears will dominate the league and send a steady stream of players to New York.

30th   George Gibson comes out of retirement to manage Pittsburgh. Ten years earlier he had led the Pirates to 3 first-division finishes.

DECEMBER

2nd   Toronto sells Ken Strong to Detroit. A former All-American football player at NYU, Strong hit .340. However, a botched operation on his wrist during the winter leaves him unable to throw effectively, and he settles for a pro football career with the New York Giants that eventually takes him to that sport's Hall of Fame.

4th   Bump Hadley, Jackie Hayes, and Sad Sam Jones are traded from Washington to the White Sox for Carl Reynolds and John Kerr.

9th   Baseball owners, fearful of the effects of the Depression, vote to cut squads from 25 players to 23. Both leagues will stop awarding MVP trophies. The NL continues to prohibit uniform numbers.

11th   Despite 2 wins in the WS, spitball veteran Burleigh Grimes is traded by the Cards to the Cubs for the fallen Hack Wilson.

1932

JANUARY

4th   The Depression deepens, and AL costs are cut by dropping an umpire from the AL staff of 11.

Casey Stengel returns from exile in the minor leagues to become coach for the Dodgers.

11th   Bill Terry sends his contract back to the Giants, telling writers he is "thoroughly disgusted." Terry, who just missed the NL batting title, was offered a $9,000 cut from his 1931 contract of $22,500.

14th   Babe Ruth rejects a Yankee offer of $70,000, as the major leagues vow to cut salaries by $1 million.

23rd   The Dodgers acquire Hack Wilson from the Cardinals. The 1930 HR king of the NL costs only $45,000 and a minor league pitcher.

26th   William K. Wrigley, owner of the Cubs since 1919, dies and is buried on Catalina Island. His only son, Philip K. Wrigley, inherits the Cubs and the minor league Los Angeles Angels.

FEBRUARY

8th   Waite Hoyt is released by the Philadelphia Athletics and will sign with Brooklyn.

12th   George Weiss, GM of the Baltimore Orioles (International League), joins the Yankee front office. He will eventually run the club during its years under Casey Stengel's managing.

MARCH

3rd   Boston (AL) P Ed Morris dies of knife wounds inflicted in a fight at a party given in his honor.

14th   Babe Herman is traded to Cincinnati by the Dodgers. Catching prospect Ernie Lombardi goes with him. The Dodgers acquire Tony Cuccinello, Joe Stripp, and Clyde Sukeforth.

16th   Babe Ruth signs for $75,000.

APRIL

6th   The Albuquerque Dons (Class D Arizona-Texas League) open the season with a 43–15 win over the El Paso Longhorns.

8th   The Dodgers buy George Kelly, former Giants, star, from Minneapolis.

11th   President Herbert Hoover continues the tradition of throwing out the first ball at Washington to start the season. The Senators win in the 10th on Heinie Manush's double off Boston's Danny MacFayden, giving Al Crowder a 1–0 victory.

Holdout Chick Hafey, last year's batting champ, is traded by the Cardinals to the Reds.

17th   Bill Terry, Giants 1B, ties the NL record with 21 putouts. The Giants shut out Boston 5–0 on Hal Schumacher's 2-hitter.

20th   The Yankees draw the largest paid attendance, 55,452, for any home opener. Babe Ruth homers, as Lefty Gomez beats Lefty Grove, and the Yankees defeat the Athletics 8–3.

21st   Lefty O'Doul, injured in spring training, plays his first game for Brooklyn and has 2 hits.

Terry hits his 6th HR in 4 games, as the Giants outslug the Phillies 13–8.

Mark Koenig is released by Detroit to the San Francisco Missions (PCL). He will make a dramatic return with the Cubs late in the season.

24th   The Cubs' Kiki Cuyler breaks a bone in his left foot, as Chicago beats Pittsburgh 12–3.

27th   Cardinals manager Gabby Street is fined by the NL for breaking the rule prohibiting talking with spectators.

MAY

1st   The New York Yankees reacquire relief ace Wilcy Moore from the Red Sox.

11th   Cardinal Wild Bill Hallahan lives up to his name with 3 wild pitches in the 12th inning in a game that Brooklyn wins at St. Louis 6–3. He ties the record set by Jake Weimer of the Cubs on May 10, 1903.

16th   The Yankees score their 4th straight shutout to equal the record set by Cleveland and Boston in 1903 and 1906. Johnny Allen, George Pipgras, Red Ruffing, and Lefty Gomez are the hurlers.

19th   The NL rescinds its unpopular rule prohibiting players from talking to fans.

20th Paul Waner equals the ML record with 4 doubles in a game. He will break Chuck Klein's NL season record with 62.

30th A plaque in memory of Miller Huggins, former Yankee manager, is dedicated at Yankee Stadium. It is the first of an array of monuments erected in the ballpark.

Umpire George Moriarty fights with White Sox players under the stands after Cleveland wins a doubleheader. Chicago claims the umpire deliberately made wrong calls. Moriarty breaks his fist knocking down Milt Gaston, but he is pummeled by manager Lew Fonseca and catchers Charlie Berry and Frank Grube.

JUNE

2nd Buzz Arlett hits 4 consecutive HRs for Baltimore, as they edge Reading 14–13 in an IL game.

3rd John McGraw, who came to New York in 1902, resigns as manager of the Giants and is replaced by Bill Terry, the team's star 1B.

Lou Gehrig hits 4 consecutive HRs and narrowly misses a 5th in the Yankees-Athletics slugfest won by New York 20–13. Tony Lazzeri hits for the cycle, and the teams set a still-standing record for extra bases on long hits in a single game (41).

4th The Phillies get Cardinals problem P Flint Rhem.

5th The Red Sox sell star P Danny MacFayden to the Yankees for $50,000 and players.

7th P John Quinn, at 47, becomes the oldest player to have an extra-base hit (a double) and bat in a run, as the Dodgers beat the Cubs 9–2.

Waite Hoyt is unconditionally released by the Dodgers.

13th Dale Alexander and Roy Johnson are traded by Detroit to Boston for Earl Webb. Alexander, batting only .250, will hit .372 with Boston and will edge out Jimmie Foxx for the batting title by 3 points.

20th Roger Cramer of the A's has 6 hits in consecutive times at bat in a 9-inning game. Cramer will do this again in 1935, the only AL player to repeat the feat.

22nd The NL, at a meeting of club presidents, finally approves players wearing numbers. The AL had started in 1929.

23rd Lou Gehrig plays his 1,103rd successive game in a New York uniform, equaling Joe Sewell's record with one team (Cleveland).

Goose Goslin of the St. Louis Browns hits 3 HRs in a game for the 3rd time.

Waite Hoyt signs with the Giants.

JULY

4th Baltimore's (IL) Buzz Arlett again hits 4 HRs in a game, one grand slam from the right side of the plate, and the other 3 HRs from the left side, with Reading again the victim. It is the 2nd time Arlett has accomplished the feat in 5 weeks.

Yankees C Bill Dickey breaks Carl Reynolds' jaw with a punch, sidelining the Senators OF indefinitely. Dickey is suspended for 30 days and assessed a $1,000 fine.

6th Cubs SS Bill Jurges is shot twice in his Chicago hotel room by a spurned girlfriend, Violet Popovich Valli. In a scuffle for the gun, Jurges is hit in the shoulder and hand. Jurges fails to prosecute, and Valli will be signed to a 22-week contract to sing in local nightclubs and theaters. She is billed as "Violet (What I Did for Love) Valli—the Most Talked About Girl in Chicago."

9th Yankees OF Ben Chapman has 3 HRs in the 2nd game of a doubleheader with Detroit at Yankee Stadium. Two are inside the park, as the Yankees win 14–9.

10th An extraordinary 18-inning game is won by the Athletics at Cleveland, 18–17. A's winning P Eddie Rommel pitches 17 innings in relief, giving up a record 33 hits. To save train fare for a single-date appearance, Connie Mack brought only 2 pitchers. The starting pitcher is knocked out after one inning and only Rommel is left. Johnny Burnett of Cleveland has 9 hits in 11 at bats.

18th Washington 3B Ossie Bluege equals the AL record with 5 walks in the first game of a doubleheader won by Detroit 8–6 and 2–1.

22nd Billy Jurges, shot on July 6, returns to the Cubs lineup.

23rd Cleveland P Wes Ferrell makes 10 assists in a 12-inning game, but loses to the White Sox 6–5. The record in both leagues is 12.

31st Cleveland plays its first game in new Municipal Stadium before a crowd in excess of 80,000 (paid attendance of 76,979), but Mel Harder loses to the A's Lefty Grove 1–0 on Cochrane's RBI single.

AUGUST

1st The Indians drop another 1–0 game to the A's at Municipal Stadium, as Rube Walberg beats Wes Ferrell.

2nd Rogers Hornsby is fired as manager of the Chicago Cubs, and 1B Charlie Grimm is put in charge.

4th Bill Dickey returns to the Yankees lineup after his month's suspension with a grand slam and 3 singles, as New York beats Chicago 15–3.

5th Detroit P Tommy Bridges has a brush with baseball immortality when he retires the first 26 Washington Senators to face him, before surrendering a hit to pinch hitter Dave Harris. The Tigers win the game 13–0.

11th Rookie SS Arky Vaughan makes a crucial error in the 10th inning, and the Cubs top the Pirates 3–2 to take first place.

12th AL president Will Harridge upholds Detroit's protest of its August 1st game against NY and orders it replayed on September 8. Detroit had protested because Tony Lazzeri's and Ben Chapman's batting order was orally reversed after the lineup cards were handed in before the game.

13th Bill Terry, Mel Ott, and Fred Lindstrom hit HRs on consecutive pitches in the 4th inning, but the Giants lose 18–9 to Brooklyn. In game 2 the Dodgers' Joe Stripp, Lefty O'Doul, and Tony Cuccinello hit first-inning HRs off Waite Hoyt. Brooklyn wins 5–4.

It looks like the Yankees scoring streak might be broken, but P Red Ruffing hits a HR in the 10th to beat Al Thomas of the Senators 1–0. Tom Hughes, in 1906, was the last ML pitcher to hit an extra-inning, game-winning HR.

Commissioner Landis clears Rogers Hornsby of charges of fraudulently "borrowing" money from Cubs players. The Chicago papers said Hornsby had obtained money from players, either loaned to him to bet on horse races, or to share in joint ventures. When Hornsby is fined, the players want refunds. Hornsby wants a lump payoff by the Cubs, who refuse. Landis holds several hearings, and as he doesn't punish anyone, it is taken as exoneration.

14th John Quinn, at 49, becomes the oldest P to win a ML game. He relieves Van Mungo in the 9th with the game between Brooklyn and New York tied at 1–1. The Dodgers win in the 10th after Johnny Frederick hits a pinch-hit HR off Carl Hubbell in the 9th to tie. It is Frederick's 4th pinch-hit HR of the year, for a new ML record. He will have 6 by the season's end.

Cardinals rookie Dizzy Dean fans 6 Cubs in a row, one less than the record, and wins 2–1 in the 10th.

17th The Cubs and the Braves play 19 innings, the longest game of the season, with Chicago winning 3–2. Guy Bush wins in relief. The following day he will again beat the Braves with a brief extra-inning outing.

21st Wes Ferrell becomes the first 20th-century pitcher to win 20 or more games in each of his first 4 seasons, beating Washington 11–5.

23rd The Cubs have only one assist in a 5–1 win, sweeping the Phillies in 4 straight. The fielding mark equals the ML record.

28th The Red Sox "eclipse" the Indians in the 2nd game of a doubleheader 4–3 in 11 innings. The game was previously scheduled for August 31, but a solar eclipse was due and blackened the ballpark for 20 minutes, so the game is played today instead.

29th Detroit C Ray Hayworth makes his first error of the season after handling 439 chances without a miscue dating back to September 2, 1931.

30th Wes Ferrell is suspended 10 days by the Indians for insubordination.

31st Detroit P Chief Hogsett hits 2 HRs, as the Tigers end Tony Freitas' winning streak at 10 with a 5–4 victory over the A's.

SEPTEMBER

3rd Dizzy Dean stops the Cubs' winning streak in the 2nd game of a doubleheader after Chicago wins its 14th straight in the opener.

Jimmie Foxx of the A's poles his 50th and 51st HRs to become the 3rd player to reach 50 in a season, joining Babe Ruth and Hack Wilson.

7th Earl Grace, Pirates C, makes a wild throw to end a streak of 110 consecutive errorless games. It is Grace's only error of the season for a still-standing NL record.

8th The Yankees and Tigers replay protested August 1st game as the nightcap of a doubleheader, but end in a 7–7 tie. Official records get confused and have never been completely corrected. After the game, Babe Ruth experiences abdominal pains he believes are an appendicitis attack. He will be out of the lineup indefinitely. Sam Byrd, subbing for Ruth in the opener, collects 5 hits for the Yankees, including 2 HRs in a 5–4 win.

9th The Tigers beat the Yankees 14–13 in a 14-inning game in which Lou Gehrig drives in 8 runs. He has performed the feat twice before.

10th Dodger OF Johnny Frederick hits his record 6th pinch-hit HR of the season. It is a dramatic 9th-inning, 2-run shot that beats Burleigh Grimes and the Cubs 4–3. Frederick's 6 pinch-hit HRs doubles the previous record of 3 held by Ham Hyatt in 1913, Cy Williams in 1928, and Pat Crawford in 1929.

11th Joe Schultz, Jr., 14-year-old son of Houston (Texas League) manager Joe Schultz, is inserted into a game against Galveston as a pinch hitter. He hits a single, steals 2B and 3B, and scores a run. Fritz, the black batboy, also bats, but is fanned by Thormahlen after trying to sacrifice.

The New York Yankees clinch the AL pennant with their 100th victory, as George Pipgras defeats the Indians 9–3 at Cleveland.

The Cardinals sign Branch Rickey to a 5-year contract as GM and director of the farm system.

John Quinn earns his 247th ML victory at age 49. It is the final win of his career.

20th The Chicago Cubs clinch the NL pennant when Kiki Cuyler hits a triple with the bases loaded for a 5–2 win over Pittsburgh.

Babe Ruth returns to the Yankees lineup.

22nd The Cubs announce WS shares and snub former manager Rogers Hornsby. Late-season arrival Mark Koenig gets just a half share.

25th Paul Waner sets a new NL record with his 62nd double, as the Pirates defeat the Cardinals 7–1.

Jimmie Foxx hits his 58th HR in the last game of the season to finish 2 short of Ruth's 1927 record of 60.

Alvin Crowder of the Senators wins his 15th straight game, one short of the AL record held by Walter Johnson, Smokey Joe Wood, and Lefty Grove.

26th Chuck Klein closes the season with 38 HRs and 20 SBs and becomes the only player of the lively-ball era (1920 and after) to lead his league in these 2 departments.

28th Connie Mack begins dismantling the Athletics by selling Al Simmons, Jimmie Dykes, and Mule Haas to the White Sox for $100,000.

In the opening game of the WS, Lou Gehrig's HR leads the Yankees to a 12–6 win over the Cubs.

29th Lefty Gomez breezes to a 5–2 win over the Cubs, and Gehrig gets 3 hits for the Yankees' 2nd victory.

OCTOBER

1st The WS moves to Chicago, and the Yankees continue to torment the Cubs. In the fifth inning, Babe Ruth waits until he has 2 strikes and then gestures to P Charlie Root. He belts the next pitch into the CF bleachers. It is Ruth's 2nd HR of the game. Gehrig also hammers out 2 round-trippers.

On the West Coast, a 17-year-old San Francisco player appears in his first game with the Seals (PCL). SS Joe DiMaggio has one hit against the Missions.

2nd The demoralized Cubs lose 13–6, as the Yankees sweep the Series. Tony Lazzeri hits 2 HRs, and Earle Combs, one. Wilcy Moore gets the win in relief. Combs ties a WS record with 4 runs scored, and Bill Dickey ties another with 6 at bats.

4th Clark Griffith announces that Walter Johnson will not be the manager of the Senators in 1933.

8th Washington names 27-year-old SS Joe Cronin manager.

10th The Giants get C Gus Mancuso from the Cards for 4 players, including veteran Bob O'Farrell.

12th NY Yankees manager Joe McCarthy signs a 3-year contract.

14th Judge Landis rejects Rogers Hornsby's appeal for a share of the Cubs' WS money.

19th The BBWAA MVP awards are announced, with Jimmie Foxx winning in the AL and Chuck Klein in the NL.

24th Rogers Hornsby signs to play with the St. Louis Cardinals, whom he had managed to the World Championship in 1926.

NOVEMBER

10th Donie Bush, pennant-winning manager of Minneapolis (American Association), is named manager of the Cincinnati Reds.

22nd Cardinals SS Charley Gelbert has his leg shattered in a hunting accident in Chambersburg, PA. He will return as a part-time infielder in 1935 and will play until 1940.

29th The New York Giants release pitchers Waite Hoyt and Clarence Mitchell.

30th The Chicago Cubs get Babe Herman from the Cincinnati Reds for Rollie Hemsley and 3 others.

DECEMBER

14th William A. Heydler is elected to another 4-year term as president of the NL.

The Senators swap Sam West, Carl Reynolds, and Lloyd Brown, along with $20,000, for former Senator Goose Goslin, lefthander Walter Stewart, and OF Fred Schulte. They also get Earl Whitehill from Detroit for Firpo Marberry and Carl Fischer.

15th A joint meeting of AL and NL owners approves the concept of "chain store" baseball, developed as the St. Louis Cardinal farm system, despite strenuous objections by Judge Landis.

17th Jim Bottomley is traded by the Cardinals to the Reds for Owen Carroll and Estel Crabtree.

29th The Boston Braves buy Giants C Shanty Hogan for $25,000.

1933

JANUARY

7th Baseball Commissioner Landis voluntarily cuts his salary by 40 percent as a signal that all salaries are to be trimmed because of the Depression.

The Washington Senators get veteran C Luke Sewell from Cleveland.

21st Pittsburgh signs veteran Waite Hoyt.

27th Veteran 1B Joe Judge of the Senators is released. He will sign with the Dodgers.

FEBRUARY

2nd Honus Wagner rejoins the Pirates as a coach and goodwill ambassador.

9th Dodger pitching ace Dazzy Vance is traded to the Cardinals with infielder Gordon Slade for Owen Carroll and Jake Flowers.

25th Multimillionaire sportsman Tom Yawkey and former star player Eddie Collins buy the Boston Red Sox from Robert Quinn.

MARCH

11th Rogers Hornsby, out of baseball since being fired as Cubs manager in August 1932, joins the Cardinals in spring training as a player. He will return to 2B after a 6-year absence from St. Louis.

During an exhibition game in Los Angeles between the Cubs and the Giants, a substantial earthquake occurs. Players from both teams huddle around 2B until the tremors stop.

24th Babe Ruth signs for $52,000, down from last year's $75,000. The large cut is significant of the Depression era.

29th Chicago Cubs OF Kiki Cuyler, who missed the first half of 1932 with a broken left leg, breaks his other leg in another spring training accident. He will be out until June 22.

APRIL

11th The Cardinals trade Chick Hafey to the Reds for Harvey Hendrick, Benny Frey, and cash.

12th Joe Cronin debuts as Washington manager, and the Senators Alvin Crowder wins his 16th successive game over 2 seasons, 4–1 from Philadelphia.

13th Browns OF Sammy West goes 6-for-6 in an 11-inning victory over the White Sox. He has 5 singles and a double, all off Ted Lyons.

15th Schoolboy Rowe of Detroit makes his first ML start and shuts out the White Sox 3–0.

20th White Sox OF Al Simmons makes an unassisted double play against the Browns.

Umpire Charlie Pfirman officiates in his 1,700th consecutive NL game, as Carl Hubbell pitches the Giants to a 1–0 victory over the Braves.

23rd Lou Gehrig's consecutive-game streak is threatened when he is knocked unconscious by an Earl Whitehill pitch in the New York-Washington game. He recovers and finishes the game.

24th Giants player/manager Bill Terry is hit by a pitch in a game with the Dodgers, breaking his wrist. He will be out 3 weeks, ending his consecutive-game streak at 468.

Governor Pinchot of Pennsylvania signs a bill legalizing Sunday baseball under local option. A statewide referendum will be on the ballot in November.

25th Russ Van Atta makes a spectacular debut for the Yankees, winning 16–0 over the Senators while getting 4 hits in a game marred by a wild free-for-all. Ben Chapman, Buddy Myer, and Earl Whitehill are suspended 5 days and fined $100 each.

Phillies SS Dick Bartell equals the ML record with 4 doubles in 4 at bats in a game with Boston.

29th Washington C Luke Sewell makes a rare double play, tagging out first Lou Gehrig and then Dixie Walker attempting to score, as the Senators beat the Yankees 6–3.

MAY

5th Pepper Martin of the Cardinals hits for the cycle against the Phillies.

6th The Reds sign Jack Quinn 2 months short of his 50th birthday.

Senators 2B Buddy Myer is carried off the field unconscious after being hit by a Whit Wyatt pitch, as Washington beats Detroit 6–2.

7th Reds SS Leo Durocher and Cardinals P Paul Derringer are the principals in a trade that gives St. Louis a player to replace Charley Gelbert, the victim of a hunting accident in November.

9th The Red Sox get Rick Ferrell and Lloyd Brown from the St. Louis Browns for cash and a player. They sell Earl Webb to the White Sox.

12th The Red Sox pay the Yankees $100,000 for P George Pipgras, rookie SS Bill Werber, and Dusty Cooke.

15th The major leagues advance the cut-down date a month, limiting rosters to 23 players on May 15 instead of June 15.

16th Washington and Cleveland break a ML record by using 11 pitchers in a 12-inning game won by the Senators 11–10. Cecil Travis plays his first ML game and gets 5 hits.

18th The first ML All-Star Game is announced for July 6 at Comiskey Park. It will be played as part of the Chicago World's Fair celebration and is sponsored by the Chicago *Tribune*. Fans will pick the players.

22nd Joe Sewell of the Yankees fans for the first time this season. He will strike out only 3 more times in 524 at bats.

26th Phillies OF Chuck Klein hits for the cycle for the 2nd time in his career, as the Cards win 5–4 in 14 innings.

27th The White Sox tally 3 in their half of the 8th inning to take an 11–3 lead against New York. The Yankees storm back with 12 runs in the bottom half 8th inning with Bill Dickey's grand slam the big blow. The combined total of 15 runs is a new AL record for one inning. The final reads 15–11.

JUNE

3rd Walter "Jumbo" Brown, the biggest player in the major leagues (260-295 lbs), fans a dozen A's batters in 6⅓ innings of strong relief to gain a victory for the Yanks.

Connie Mack suspends overweight P George Earnshaw and fines him $500 for failure to get into shape.

4th The Giants, with Terry back in the lineup, gain first place with a doubleheader win over the Dodgers, 3–0 and 6–4.

8th Jimmie Foxx homers in his first 3 at bats, as the A's outscore the Yankees 14–10. He had homered his last time up the previous day to give him 4 consecutive HRs.

9th Walter Johnson takes over as Cleveland manager.

Foxx ties a ML record with another HR, his 5th in 3 games, but the A's bow to the Yankees 7–6.

Luke Appling hits a HR in the 14th inning to give the White Sox a 10–9 win over the Tigers.

10th The Giants never lose the league lead after Freddie Fitzsimmons beats Philadelphia 5–2.

12th On a day off, the Giants team accompanies P Hal Schumacher to St. Lawrence University where he receives his diploma. After graduation, Schumacher pitches the first 2 innings in a game against his old college teammates. He gives up one hit, as the Giants win 12–4.

14th Lou Gehrig's consecutive-game streak survives, even though he and manger McCarthy are thrown out of a game. Joe McCarthy is suspended 3 games but Gehrig's streak, now at 1,249, continues.

15th The Dodgers send Lefty O'Doul, last year's batting champ, and 20-game winner Watson Clark to the Giants for Sam Leslie. The two Brooklyn stars have struggled during the year.

23rd The Senators take over first place, winning their 3rd in a row over the White Sox while the Yankees break even in St. Louis.

24th Arky Vaughan hits for the cycle, as the Pirates beat the Dodgers 15–3.

28th Spitballer Jack Quinn, one week short of his 50th birthday, loses his final career decision as the Dodgers edge the Reds 6–5.

2B Billy Herman sets fielding records with 11 putouts in the first game and 16 for the twin bill, as the Cubs take a pair from the Phillies, 9–5 and 8–3.

29th Ethan Allen of the Cards races around the bases for an inside-the-park HR at the Polo Grounds, but is out for batting out of turn.

JULY

2nd Carl Hubbell pitches an entire 18-inning shutout for the Giants over the Cardinals to tie a record for the longest 1–0 game. He strikes out 12 and walks none, allowing only 6 hits in a duel with Tex Carleton, who goes the first 16 innings. In game 2, played in semidarkness, Roy Parmelee wins 1–0 on a Johnny Vergez HR. The notoriously wild Giants' pitcher does not issue a walk and strikes out 13.

4th   The Washington Senators widen their lead over the 2nd-place Yankees to 2½ games with a double-bill win before 77,365 holiday fans at Yankee Stadium, 6–5 in 10 innings and 3–2.

The New York Giants have their NL lead cut to 5 games when the Braves take a pair in Boston, 3–0 and 8–3.

6th   The first ML All-Star Game is played at Comiskey Park, and Babe Ruth is the star. His 2-run HR is the margin of victory in the AL's 4–2 win. John McGraw comes out of retirement to manage the NL.

7th   Phillies 2B Mickey Finn dies following an abdominal operation.

16th   Red Lucas of the Reds pitches a 15-inning 1–0 win over Roy Parmelee and the Giants in the opener of a doubleheader.

18th   The Yankees win their 9th straight and take the lead from the Senators, beating the White Sox 5–4.

19th   For the first time, brothers on opposite teams homer in the same game. Red Sox C Rick Ferrell hits his HR off brother Wes of Cleveland. Wes hits his off Hank Johnson in the 3rd inning. He will wind up his career with 38 HRs in 548 games. Rick will hit only 28 in 1,884 games.

24th   Frank Frisch is appointed manager of the St. Louis Cardinals, replacing Gabby Street.

26th   Rogers Hornsby swaps St. Louis uniforms, leaving the Cards to manage the Browns.

The 61-game batting streak of San Francisco's (PCL) 18-year-old rookie, Joe DiMaggio, is stopped by Ed Walsh, Jr. of Oakland.

Lou Gehrig is thrown out of the second game in a doubleheader against Boston. Had it been the first game, his consecutive-game streak would have ended.

30th   The Cards Dizzy Dean sets a 20th-century ML record with 17 strikeouts in the first game of a doubleheader with the Cubs. His teammate, C Jimmie Wilson, totals 18 putouts, also a new record.

Burleigh Grimes, 9 days short of his 40th birthday, is released by the Cubs and signs with the Cardinals.

AUGUST

1st   Carl Hubbell breaks Ed Ruelbach's 1908 NL record for consecutive scoreless innings, with 45⅓, although the Giants lose to Boston 3–1.

2nd   The A's Mickey Cochrane hits for the cycle for the 2nd time in his career, against the Yankees in a 16–3 drubbing.

3rd   The Yankees are shut out by the A's and Lefty Grove, 7–0, for their first scoreless game since August 2, 1931. They had tallied in 308 games in a row, during which they scored 1,986 runs (6.5 per game) to 1,434 for the opposition, which New York hurlers blanked 22 times.

5th   Browns OF Sammy West equals the ML record with 4 extra-base hits in a 12-inning, 10–9 win over the White Sox. He hits one double, 2 triples, and a HR.

6th   A's 3B Pinky Higgins hits for the cycle in a 12–8 win over the Senators.

11th   The Senators score 6 times in the final inning to top the Red Sox as both teams use a record-tying 11 pitchers in the game.

12th   Brooklyn's longtime manager, Wilbert Robinson, is appointed president of the Atlanta Crackers (SA) and will also manage the club. He is 69.

14th   Jimmie Foxx hits for the cycle and drives in 9 runs to break the AL record, as the A's beat the Indians 11–5. A record 8 players will hit for the cycle this year.

17th   Lou Gehrig plays his 1,308th consecutive game to break Everett Scott's mark, as the Browns edge the Yankees 7–6 in 10 innings.

Earl Averill hits for the cycle, as the Indians beat the A's 15–4.

20th   Powered by Turkey Stearnes' 41st HR, the Chicago American Giants (Negro League) defeat the Nashville Elite Giants in a twin bill for their 28th consecutive victory.

21st   The Yankees and White Sox play an 18-inning game which ends in a 3–3 tie.

22nd   The front-running Senators are stopped after 13 straight wins when Detroit rookie Hank Greenberg homers in the 9th.

William Veeck, president of the Chicago Cubs, urges a midsummer series of inter-league games. He also proposes a split season.

26th   Cleveland's Wes Ferrell stops Heinie Manush's hitting streak at 33, as Washington loses 5–4 in 11 innings.

31st   The Giants lose 3B Johnny Vergez for the season due to an appendectomy. Travis Jackson, who has been filling in at SS, shifts to 3B.

SEPTEMBER

4th   In a Labor Day twin bill, Joe Hauser, Minneapolis (AA), hits 3 HRs to reach 65, a new professional record.

7th   Rookie Johnny Marcum of the Philadelphia A's wins his first start with a shutout over Cleveland, 6–0.

9th   Joe Hauser, Minneapolis (AA), hits 2 HRs to set all-time record of 69. Hauser also set the International League record mark at 63, with Baltimore in 1930.

10th   The first Negro League East-West All-Star Game is played at Comiskey Park. Willie Foster goes the distance in the West's 11–7 victory.

11th   Johnny Marcum pitches his 2nd shutout in his 2nd start, as the A's beat the White Sox 8–0.

17th   The Giants spoil Dizzy Dean Day at Sportsman's Park 4–3, but the popular pitcher drives home in a new Buick, given to him by St. Louis fans.

19th   Although they lose to St. Louis 12–3, the Giants clinch the pennant when runner-up Pittsburgh splits a pair in Philadelphia.

21st   Lefty Walter Stewart pitches the pennant-clinching victory over the Browns, as Washington wins 2–1.

23rd   Paul Derringer loses his 27th game for the last-place Reds, the most losses since George Bell (Brooklyn) in 1910.

24th   Detroit's Tommy Bridges reaches the 9th inning with a no-hitter for the 3rd time this season and the 4th time in 2 years. He yields a pair of hits, as

Detroit beats the Browns 7–0. Bucky Harris resigns as manager of the Tigers.

Lefty Grove wins his 24th game, replacing starter Emmett McKeithan after 4 innings and the A's leading 8–3. The final score is 11–4, but Grove's win is tainted. The Athletics "contrived" to give Grove the sure win, so that he could finish the season with more wins than NL star Carl Hubbell, who will finish with 23. AL President Harridge reverses the official scorer's decision and gives the win to McKeithan, but the league eventually returns the win to Grove.

30th   Babe Herman of the Chicago Cubs hits for the cycle in a 12–2 win over the Cardinals. It is the 3rd time he has performed the feat in his career.

OCTOBER

1st   Nick Altrock, clowning coach of the Senators, pinch-hits at age 57 in a 3–0 loss to the A's.

Babe Ruth, in a season-ending stunt, pitches the final game of his career, defeating the Red Sox 6–5 with a complete game. Ruth hits a HR to help his effort.

3rd   The Giants take the opener of the WS at the Polo Grounds, as Carl Hubbell holds the Senators to 5 hits and 3 unearned runs. Washington unravels when Buddy Myer makes a record-tying 3 errors. Mel Ott is the hitting star, tying a WS record with 4-for-4.

4th   Scoring 6 runs in the 6th inning, the Giants make it 2 in a row over Washington. The Senators are again held to 5 hits.

5th   The WS moves to Washington, and Earl Whitehill blanks the Giants 4–0. President Roosevelt throws out the first ball and stays the whole game despite a steady rainfall.

6th   Carl Hubbell wins for the 2nd time, going 11 innings for the 2–1 victory in a pitching duel with Monte Weaver. Heinie Manush is thrown out of the game for brushing umpire Charlie Moran in the 6th inning. Travis Jackson beats out a surprise bunt to open the 11th inning, is sacrificed to 2B on a close play, and scores on a single by Blondy Ryan.

7th   Flags are at half staff to honor William L. Veeck, Chicago Cubs president who died suddenly.

The WS comes to a close when Mel Ott homers in the 10th inning for a 4–3 Giants, victory. Dolf Luque gets the win in relief.

10th Joe Cronin is rewarded with a 3-year contract as player-manager of the Senators.

12th Jimmie Foxx (AL) and Carl Hubbell (NL) are named MVPs by the baseball writers.

22nd Phil Ball, millionaire owner of the St. Louis Browns, dies. Manager Rogers Hornsby will run the team.

31st The St. Louis Cardinals release spitballer Burleigh Grimes.

NOVEMBER

6th Sidney Weil quits as Cincinnati Reds president. Larry MacPhail acquires an interest in the team and is elected director.

15th Cards C Jimmie Wilson is swapped to the Phillies to become manager. St. Louis gets hard-hitting Virgil Davis in exchange.

17th Pittsburgh sends Alan Comorosky and Tony Piet to Cincinnati in exchange for P Red Lucas. As a pitcher, Lucas will feast on the Reds over the rest of his career, going 14–0 against them.

21st Chuck Klein, who won the Triple Crown with the Phillies, is sold to the Chicago Cubs for $125,000 and 3 players.

DECEMBER

3rd Connie Mack sells C Mickey Cochrane to Detroit for $100,000. Cochrane is named manager.

12th At the major leagues' annual meeting, the owners vote Judge Landis another 7-year contract as commissioner. Will Harridge gets a new 5-year pact as AL president.

Connie Mack sells Lefty Grove, Max Bishop, and George Walberg to the Boston Red Sox for $125,000. George Earnshaw goes to the White Sox for $20,000 and another player.

14th Washington's Goose Goslin is traded for Johnny Stone of the Tigers.

15th The major leagues agree on a uniform ball to be livelier than the NL ball of recent seasons, to match the AL balls. Owners also agree to ban Sunday doubleheaders until after June 15th.

29th Yankees owner Jake Ruppert refuses to release Babe Ruth so he can become manager of the Cincinnati Reds.

1934

JANUARY

5th Fire destroys the new CF bleachers under construction at Fenway Park.

10th William Walker is elected president of the Cubs, filling the vacancy created by William Veeck's death during the WS.

15th Babe Ruth accepts a cut of $17,000 and signs a 1934 contract for $35,000.

17th Carl Hubbell, the NL MVP winner, is rewarded with a $18,000 contract by the New York Giants.

19th Judge Landis denies Shoeless Joe Jackson's appeal for reinstatement.

25th Bill Terry, Giants manager, in an interview with New York newspapermen, asks, "Is Brooklyn still in the league?" The jest boomerangs as the Dodgers will rise in wrath at the season's end.

FEBRUARY

3rd The St. Louis Cardinals and Browns discontinue broadcasts from Sportsman's Park. Games had been aired since 1926 but on weekdays for only the last 2 years. The cutback is a response to declining attendance, and the radio broadcasts are thought to keep fans at home.

Powel Crosley, local millionaire, heads a syndicate that buys just over half the stock in the Cincinnati Reds from Sidney Weil. No price is announced. The Reds' home park is renamed Crosley Field.

4th The National Recovery Administration says athletes advertising athletic goods must actually use them or advertisers will lose the NRA Blue Eagle and be fined.

6th Ford Frick, New York newspaperman and sports broadcaster, is named PR director for the NL.

14th Sam Rice is signed by the Cleveland Indians. He will fall 13 short of 3,000 career hits.

15th Boston, Chicago, Detroit, and Cincinnati grant radio broadcast rights.

16th Eppa Rixey of the Cincinnati Reds announces his retirement after 21 seasons and a career 266-251 mark. The next day Urban "Red" Faber retires, leaving a 20-year career mark of 254-212, all with the Chicago White Sox.

23rd Casey Stengel, who had been a Dodger coach, signs a 2-year contract to manage Brooklyn. He replaces Max Carey.

25th John McGraw, in ill health since his retirement as Giants manager early in the 1932 season, dies at his home in New Rochelle, NY, at age 60. His last public appearance had been the 1933 All-Star Game as the NL manager.

MARCH

10th Jimmie Foxx ends his holdout from the A's. The 1933 Triple Crown winner and AL MVP accepts a reported $18,000.

12th Dizzy Dean's younger brother, Paul, ends his holdout. Diz predicts they will win between 40 and 45 games between them. They do even better, winning 49, with Dizzy contributing 30.

20th All-around female athlete Babe Didrickson pitches the first inning for the Philadelphia Athletics in a spring training exhibition game against the Brooklyn Dodgers. She gives up one walk but no hits. Two days later she pitches again, this time one inning for the St. Louis Cardinals against the Red Sox. She is less successful this time, giving up 4 hits and 3 runs in the first inning. Bill Hallahan relieves her. Didrickson does not have an at bat in either game. She will also play several games for the House of David this season. Didrickson is the 2nd of only 2 females to play exhibitions with a ML team (1B Lizzie Murphy played for an AL all-star team on August 14, 1922).

28th Forty-two-year-old Rabbit Maranville breaks his leg sliding home in an exhibition game against the Yankees. The Braves veteran is out for the season. He had broken his leg earlier in spring training of 1926.

APRIL

4th The Red Sox discover that veteran Lefty Grove, bought from the A's, has a sore arm. He will win only 8 games in 1934 but will return to good form in 1935.

5th Three Cincinnati radio stations will broadcast 85 Reds games. Red Barber is hired by Crosley-owned WSAI.

Babe Ruth is to be sponsored by Quaker Oats to do three 15-minute broadcasts a week over NBC. The total of $39,000 for 13 weeks is $4,000 more than Ruth's baseball salary.

8th The Phillies and A's meet in a City Series game before 15,000 fans at Shibe Park for the first legal Sunday baseball game ever played in Philadelphia.

16th Rain in Washington prevents President Franklin D. Roosevelt from throwing out the first ball of the season.

17th Both leagues open with full schedules and draw 180,000 in attendance. The Cubs Lon Warneke gives up a 9th-inning single to Adam Comorosky, winning 6–0 over the Reds. He strikes out 13 in the one-hitter.

21st Moe Berg, little-used Senators catcher, plays his 117th consecutive errorless game, dating back to 1931. It is an AL record.

22nd Lon Warneke pitches his 2nd straight one-hitter, beating Dizzy Dean, as the Cubs romp over the Cards 15–2.

24th President Roosevelt throws out the first ball for the Washington opener, but a rainstorm sends him back to the White House in the 4th inning.

27th Wes Ferrell is suspended by Cleveland for failing to report 10 days after the season has started.

28th Goose Goslin, Detroit OF, hits into 4 DPs, but the Tigers beat Cleveland 4–1.

29th With Pennsylvania's Blue Law repealed, Pittsburgh becomes the last ML city to play a home game on a Sunday, beating the Reds 9–5.

30th Red Ruffing hits a HR in the 9th to defeat Washington and put the Yankees in first place.

MAY

6th The Red Sox score 12 runs in the 4th inning, helped along by a record 4 consecutive triples hit by Carl Reynolds, Moose Solters, Rick Ferrell, and Bucky Walters, to beat Detroit 14–4. The record is 5 set in 1901.

8th The Chicago White Sox name Jimmie Dykes as their new manager, replacing Lew Fonseca, who later will become the motion picture specialist for the ML.

Cardinal P Bill Walker has his arm broken by a batting practice smash by Joe Medwick.

10th Lou Gehrig hits 2 HRs (one a grand slam) and a pair of doubles, tying the record with four long hits, and drives in 7 runs, but leaves the game after 5 innings with a severe cold. During the game Ben Chapman shouts racial remarks at a Jewish fan. In 1947 he will lead the dugout bigots in protest of Jackie Robinson.

15th Buffalo (IL) hits 5 HRs in one inning against Albany. A rookie, Jake Plummer, is beaned by the Albany pitcher after the 5th HR in a row, and a promising career is ruined.

25th The Red Sox buy Wes Ferrell, who was suspended by the Indians, for players and $25,000.

26th Fans will vote for players in the 2nd All-Star Game, to be played on July 10 at the Polo Grounds. The managers will pick the lineups from 20 players chosen.

27th Buck Newsom walks 11 batters but knocks the Yankees out of first place with a 16–7 Browns win. Cleveland moves into the league lead.

30th Minor leaguer Lou Frierson strokes 5 successive HRs for Paris (West Dixie League) in a 17–12 loss.

Cleveland 1B Hal Trosky hits 3 successive HRs in the 2nd game of a Memorial Day doubleheader against the White Sox.

Giants SS Travis Jackson has only one chance in 18 innings at Ebbets Field in a doubleheader against the Dodgers.

Washington's Earl Whitehill pitches a one-hitter, allowing a 9th-inning single by Ben Chapman, to defeat Lefty Gomez of the Yankees 1–0.

JUNE

1st The Dean brothers claim to have "sore arms" that only pay raises can heal. Diz is getting $7,500 and Paul, a rookie, $3,000. The brothers will back down.

3rd The St. Louis Browns tie the AL record with 9 consecutive hits in the 6th inning, beating Cleveland 12–8.

6th Myril Hoag, Yankees OF, ties the AL record with 6 singles in 6 at bats in the first game of a doubleheader with the Red Sox.

The Cubs get 6 runs in the 13th inning to beat the Cards 12–6. In a row with umpire Cy Rigler, Frank Frisch is hit in the jaw by the ump's mask. Both are fined $100.

8th With the Midwest sweltering in a heat wave, Larry MacPhail flies the Reds from St. Louis to Chicago to spare players a Pullman ride. Six players opt for the train, but the rest make the first air flight by a ML team.

9th Sore-armed Lefty Grove gives up 6 doubles, 5 consecutive, in the 8th inning as the Senators beat the Red Sox 8–1.

10th Doc Cramer hits for the cycle, but the Yankees still beat the A's 7–3 on Gehrig's grand slam.

11th The Cubs send Dolph Camilli and cash to the Phillies for Don Hurst. Camilli will later win the 1941 MVP with the Dodgers, while Hurst hits .199 for the Cubs and disappears.

13th Billy Urbanski, Braves SS, has 4 walks and 2 sacrifices for no at bats in 6 plate appearances against the Cardinals. Rival SS, slick-fielding Leo Durocher, makes 4 errors in the 9–0 Boston rout.

14th The Red Sox sell a star player unknowingly. They peddle infielder Bucky Walters to the Phillies where he will convert to pitcher and subsequently win the 1939 MVP with the Reds.

16th A's OF Bob Johnson ties the AL record going 6-for-6 with 2 HRs, a double, and 3 singles.

18th After 8 straight wins, rookie Paul Dean, in relief, loses the first game of his ML career.

19th Pie Traynor (3B) replaces George Gibson as Pirates manager.

22nd Bill Terry and Joe Cronin, managers of the 1933 pennant winners, are named to head the All-Star teams, establishing a precedent that is still followed.

Detroit takes over first place, beating Washington 11–3, dislodging the Yankees who lose 4–1 to Cleveland.

23rd The Cards beat the Dodgers 5–4 with the win credited to Bill Hallahan, who relieved in the 6th inning and gave up a run. In the bottom half, the Cards scored 5 runs, and Dizzy Dean comes in and shut out Brooklyn the last 3 innings. The official scorer refers the decision on the winning pitcher to NL president

Heydler, who gives it to Dean, eventually making his 30-win season possible.

24th Babe Ruth hits a grand slam in a 5–0 win over the White Sox after being hitless in his last 21 at bats.

25th Johnny Broaca, Yankee P, fans 5 times in a row while beating the White Sox 13–2. Gehrig hits for the cycle, and the Yankees regain first place from the Tigers, who lose 13–11 in Philadelphia.

26th Paul Dean wins his 10th game against one loss, defeating the Giants 13–7. Dizzy's record is 10–3.

27th The temperature reaches 115 degrees at Sportsman's Park in St. Louis. Dizzy Dean leaves the game with 2 out, the score tied 7–7 in the top of the 9th, relieved by Jim Mooney. When Bill Delancey homers in the bottom of the inning to win the game, Dean is given credit for the win.

28th Cincinnati P Red Lucas makes his 100th consecutive start without a relief appearance in a game where umpire Beans Reardon is overcome by heat at Crosley Field. Umps at the time wore heavy blue coats despite the weather.

29th Lou Gehrig is beaned in an exhibition game played in Norfolk, VA.

30th Gehrig plays and has 3 triples at Washington. However, the game is rained out after 4½ innings, depriving Gehrig of a record.

Tiger Gee Walker is picked off base twice in a game against the Browns. His team will suspend him for 10 days for his ineptitude.

JULY

1st The Cardinals outlast the Reds 8–6 in an 18-inning first game of a double bill in Cincinnati. Dizzy Dean and Tony Frietas duel for 17 innings.

Bill Terry is the top vote-getter in the All-Star balloting. Babe Ruth leads all AL outfielders.

2nd The Cardinals protest a game with the Cubs in a dispute over a delayed call on an infield fly by veteran umpire Bill Klem.

4th When Dodgers manager Casey Stengel comes out to the mound to remove P Boom Boom Beck from the game in Philadelphia's Baker Bowl, the frustrated Beck turns and fires the ball at the tin wall in RF.

Dodgers OF Hack Wilson, not paying attention to the happenings, hears the ball, hurries to retrieve it, and fires a strike to 2B to prevent the imaginary runner from advancing.

After the finish of the holiday doubleheaders by all the teams, the Giants, by winning 2 from the Braves at the Polo Grounds, have a clear lead. They are 3½ games ahead of the Cubs and 4½ in front of the Cardinals.

The AL race has seesawed between the Yankees and Detroit with New York only one game ahead. The improved Red Sox are 6½ behind, and Washington, last year's winner, 7 back and dropping fast.

Satchel Paige pitches a 4–0 no-hitter against the Negro League Homestead Grays in Pittsburgh, with only a walk and an error spoiling a perfect game. After this performance, Paige drives to Chicago to shut out the Chicago American Giants 1–0 in 12 innings, giving him 2 shutouts in 2 different cities in the same day.

5th Lou Gehrig hits an inside-the-park grand slam, as the Yankees beat the Senators 8–3. It is his 4th of the season and 17th overall, passing Babe Ruth's career total. Gehrig will eventually set a career record of 23 grand slams. Gehrig now has 321 career HRS to Ruth's 698.

8th Max Bishop has 8 walks in a doubleheader, tying his own ML record.

10th The 2nd annual All-Star Game produces Carl Hubbell's amazing feat of striking out 5 future Hall of Famers in a row. Off to a shaky start with 2 on base in the first inning, Hubbell uses his screwball to fan Ruth, Gehrig, and Foxx. He adds Al Simmons and Joe Cronin to start the 2nd. After 3 scoreless innings he leaves with the NL ahead 4–0. The AL rallies, scoring 9 runs off Warneke, Mungo, and Dean, while Mel Harder pitches 5 shutout innings in relief of Red Ruffing to hold the lead. Frisch and Medwick hit HRs. Earl Averill's 3 RBI are decisive for the AL 9–7 victory.

12th Schoolboy Rowe fans 11 Yankees in a 4–2 win that puts the Tigers back in first place.

Chuck Klein is out of the Cubs lineup because of injuries as they beat the Braves 7–4. He is batting .331 with 19 HRs and 65 RBI, but will miss much of the 2nd half and never again will return to the high level of performance previously shown.

13th Babe Ruth hits his 700th HR to win the game at Detroit's Navin Field and put the Yankees back in first place. Lou Gehrig has a lumbago seizure and is helped off the field.

14th Gehrig's consecutive-game string is extended by having him lead off, listed in the lineup as SS. He singles and leaves the game.

15th Gehrig returns to 1B and goes 4-for-4, including 3 doubles, off Schoolboy Rowe, but the Yankees lose to Detroit 8–3.

Waite Hoyt, now with the Pirates, has a one-hitter against the Braves, winning 5–0.

17th Babe Ruth draws his 2,000th base on balls at Cleveland. He will retire with a still untopped walk record of 2,056.

Although Bob Johnson, Jimmie Foxx, and Pinky Higgins hit successive HRs in the 4th inning, St. Louis Browns P Jack Knott perseveres to beat the A's 7–4.

Lon Warneke, Cubs mound ace, intentionally walks a batter in the 7th to load the bases and bring up the Giants P Roy Parmelee. He hits a grand slam for a 5–3 win.

NL President William Heydler upholds the Cards protest of a loss to the Cubs on July 2. The game will be resumed from the point at which umpire Klem waited too long to call an infield fly and be played prior to a scheduled July 31st game.

18th Twenty-two players hit safely in the Cleveland 15–14 win over New York. Babe Ruth is hit in the leg by the ball and will be out for 10 days. It is the 2nd time an injury has sidelined him this season.

22nd Dazzy Vance's last hurrah? He wins the last complete game he will ever pitch and notches his 2,000th strikeout to beat the Braves 4–2 for the Cardinals.

24th Yankee CF Earle Combs crashes into the wall at Sportsman's Park in St. Louis and suffers a fractured skull. New York calls up George Selkirk but learns he broke his arm the same day playing for Newark.

28th The veteran Waite Hoyt stops Dizzy Dean's win streak at 10 with a 5–4 win in Pittsburgh.

Chuck Dressen, who will win pennants in Brooklyn and manage 16 seasons in the ML, begins by replacing Bob O'Farrell at the helm for the Cincinnati Reds.

Pittsburgh's Red Lucas, whose hitting keeps him in the lineup in close games, is relieved after 250 consecutive innings as a starting pitcher.

29th Flint Rhem comes within a lazily fielded bunted ball to 3B of pitching a no-hitter for Boston against the Dodgers. He wins 1–0.

31st When the Cards and the Cubs resume playing the protested game of July 2 at Wrigley Field, Chicago still wins. The final score this time is 7–1 instead of 7–4.

AUGUST

2nd Walter Johnson is hospitalized with pleurisy, and Willie Kamm takes over as interim Cleveland manager.

4th Phillies P Reggie Grabowski surrenders 11 hits in the 9th inning of the 2nd game against the Giants for a modern NL record. Eleven runs score in the inning, as New York wins 21–4.

5th While 3 teammates stand watching, a fly ball by Foxx drops for a double, the only hit given up by Lefty Gomez in the 3–1 win by the Yankees over the A's.

7th Dizzy Dean becomes the first pitcher to reach 20 wins this season with a 2–0 shutout over the Reds.

8th Wilbert Robinson dies in Atlanta. Beloved as "Uncle Robbie," the jovial and bemused manager of the Dodgers for 18 seasons, his 7-for-7 day with Baltimore still stands as a ML record.

10th Babe Ruth announces 1934 is definitely his final season as a regular player. He says he will seek a managerial role and will pinch-hit.

12th Making a farewell appearance in Boston, Babe Ruth draws a record 46,766 fans, with an estimated 20,000 turned away at Fenway Park where he began his career as a pitcher 20 years ago. Ruth singles and doubles in the first game, but the Yankees lose to Wes Ferrell 6–4. Walks hold him to one official at bat in the 2nd game, which the Yankees win, and he leaves the field to standing cheers in the 8th inning.

13th In a preview of the WS, the Cardinals play the Tigers in an exhibition game in Detroit. The Deans refuse to make the trip, having both pitched the day before. Dizzy is fined $100 and Paul $50.

14th The Deans are suspended by the Cards and Dizzy is charged for 2 uniforms he tore up—the 2nd for the benefit of the photographers.

The largest weekday crowd in history watches as the Tigers sweep a pair at Yankee Stadium. It is the Tigers' 14th straight; Schoolboy Rowe has won 13 in succession. The next day the Yankees will end the Tiger streak.

16th Dizzy Dean takes his appeal to Judge Landis in Chicago, who schedules a hearing in St. Louis.

17th Ed Coleman of the A's hits 3 consecutive HRs in the first game of a doubleheader, a 9–8 win in 10 innings over the White Sox.

Paul Dean accepts the fine and is reinstated.

19th The Harvard University varsity team tours Japan, winning only 5 of 11 games against collegiate and club teams.

20th Judge Landis rules against Dizzy Dean. The Cards end his suspension, and Dean returns to the team to avoid further loss in salary.

22nd P Wes Ferrell hits 2 HRs in a 10-inning, 3–2 win for the Red Sox over the White Sox. It is the 2nd time this season he has a pair of HRs, and the 3rd in his career. He will hit 2 HRs in a game 6 times before he finishes.

25th Schoolboy Rowe, Detroit's sensational rookie P, defeats the Senators 4–2 for his 16th win in a row, tying the AL record held by Walter Johnson, Joe Wood, and Lefty Grove.

29th A capacity crowd at Shibe Park sees Detroit's Schoolboy Rowe fail to win his 17th straight. He is knocked from the box in the 7th inning of the 2nd-game, 13–5 loss to Philadelphia.

SEPTEMBER

3rd Labor Day doubleheaders define the standings for the final pennant surge. Detroit, rained out in Chicago, holds a 5-game lead over the Yankees, who split a pair with the A's. Gomez wins his 24th and 10th straight in the opener, and Foxx hits his 40th HR in the 2nd.

Washington's player-manager Joe Cronin collides with Boston's Wes Ferrell in a play at 1B. Cronin fractures a bone in his arm and is out for the season. The Senators, last year's champs, will finish 7th.

In the NL, the Giants are rained out but move 6 games ahead of the Cardinals, as the Deans have a double disaster in Pittsburgh. Paul loses the first game

12–2, and Dizzy fails to hold the lead in the 2nd game and is the losing pitcher with a final score of 6–5. The Cards drop to a tie with the Cubs, who split a pair with the Reds.

7th Lou Gehrig and Jimmie Foxx, heirs to Babe Ruth's HR championship role, are in battle for the title. Gehrig hits his 44th in Chicago, and Foxx, his 41st in Detroit.

9th In one of the most memorable games in the Negro League history, Pittsburgh Crawfords' Satchel Paige duals the Philadelphia Stars' Slim Jones to a 1–1 stalemate, called after 9 innings due to darkness. Paige strikes out 12, and Jones, 9, before 30,000 at Yankee Stadium.

10th Dizzy Dean wins his 25th game, beating the Phillies 4–1. It is the 5th straight for the Cards, now 4 games behind.

13th Lefty Gomez pitches a 3-hitter against the Indians for his 25th win.

Judge Landis sells the WS broadcast rights to the Ford Motor Company for $100,000. Previously no fee had been charged.

With his fianceé, Edna Mae Skinner of Oklahoma, watching, Schoolboy Rowe halts the Tiger skid with a 2–0 win over Washington. He asks in a radio interview: "How'm I doing, Edna?"

14th Buck Newsom walks the first 4 batters and departs the first game of the doubleheader, which the Browns will lose to the A's 9–7. He starts the 2nd game with 4 straight strikeouts and wins 5–2.

16th The largest turnout in Polo Grounds history, 62,573, suffers as the Deans take 2 from the Giants. Diz needs relief from Tex Carleton for a 5–3 opener, but Paul goes 11 innings for a 3–1 win.

17th The Yankees reach Detroit for a last-chance series and lose the opener, as veteran Al Crowder beats Lefty Gomez with a 3–0 shutout.

18th Buck Newsom of the Browns continues the unusual, losing a no-hitter with 2 out in the 10th inning. Two walks and a single produce the game's only run as Boston's Wes Ferrell hurls a 10-hit shutout 1–0.

19th Tom Yawkey decides to eliminate advertising on fences at Fenway Park.

21st The Deans shut out the Dodgers. After Dizzy gives up just 3 hits in a 13–0 victory, allowing no hits

until the 8th, Paul wins a no-hitter 3–0. Diz says: "If'n Paul had told me he was gonna pitch a no-hitter, I'd of throwed one, too."

24th Idle Detroit wins the pennant, as the Red Sox beat the Yankees 5–0 in the season's finale at Yankee Stadium. Ruth walks in the first inning, limps to 1B, and leaves for a pinch runner in his last home game.

The Cardinals beat the Cubs 3–1 and move 2 games behind the Giants.

25th Lou Gehrig plays his 1,500th consecutive game. His 48th HR is a personal high.

Diz wins his 28th, beating the Pirates 3–2. The Giants lead is cut to one game when the Phillies rally in the 9th for a 5–4 win.

27th The Cards close to one-half game of the idle Giants, beating the Reds 13–7. Cincinnati SS Gordon Slade makes 3 errors in the first inning.

28th The Cardinals gain a tie for first. The Giants are idle, as Dizzy Dean, on 2 days rest, shuts out the Reds 4–0 for his 29th win.

29th Brooklyn's Van Mungo knocks the Giants out of the lead at the Polo Grounds 5–1 while Paul Dean is beating the Reds in St. Louis 6–1.

Babe Ruth hits his last HR as a Yankee, as New York splits a doubleheader in Washington.

30th Coach Charley O'Leary scores a run as a pinch hitter for the Browns at age 52—the oldest ML player ever to do so.

Dizzy Dean clinches the pennant with his 30th win, 9–0 over the Reds, as the Dodgers again beat the Giants 8–5.

Babe Ruth is hitless in his last game in a Yankee uniform.

OCTOBER

3rd Dizzy Dean wins the opening game of the WS 8–3, as Detroit manager Mickey Cochrane holds back his ace, Schoolboy Rowe. Veteran Al Crowder is ineffective as the Cardinals romp. Joe Medwick homers in a 4-for-4 day while the Tigers make 5 errors.

4th Schoolboy Rowe evens the Series with a 12-inning, 3–2 win, shutting out the Cardinals over the final 9. The Tigers tie the game in the 9th inning and win on Goose Goslin's single.

5th With no need for a travel delay, the teams move to St. Louis, and Paul Dean puts the Cardinals ahead with a 4–1 win. He pitches shutout ball until the 9th.

6th It is the Cardinals turn to play poorly, and they make 5 errors to lose 10–4. Dizzy Dean, used as a pinch runner, is carried off the field after being hit in the head by Billy Rogell's throw. Hank Greenberg ties the WS record with 4 hits.

7th Tommy Bridges beats Dizzy Dean 3–1 to put the Tigers within a game of the World Championship. The Series heads back to Detroit.

8th Paul Dean holds off the Tigers in a pitching duel with Schoolboy Rowe, winning 4–3. Weak-hitting Leo Durocher has 3 hits, as does Tigers manager Mickey Cochrane.

9th Dizzy Dean makes good his boast that "me and Paul will win all 4 games." He humbles Detroit 11–0, as the Tigers go to pieces. When Joe Medwick slides roughly into 3B in the 6th inning, he tangles with Marv Owen. Irate Tigers fans in the temporary LF stands then launch a barrage of fruit at Medwick, halting the game. With the score at 9–0, Commissioner Landis removes Medwick from the game "for his own safety."

While the Cardinals celebrate their WS victory in St. Louis, their top farm team, Columbus, wins the final game of a 9-game Junior WS. The American Association representatives beat Toronto of the International League in the 2nd game of a playoff doubleheader.

11th Burleigh Grimes is released by the Pirates. He is the last official spitball pitcher.

14th Underpaid by the Cardinals, the Deans reap profits on a barnstorming tour. Each makes $5,000 in a game against Chicago semipros.

21st An all-star team led by Babe Ruth and Connie Mack sails on tour to Hawaii and Japan. Players with wives include Lou Gehrig, Jimmie Foxx, Charlie Gehringer, Lefty Gomez, Earl Averill, and Lefty O'Doul.

23rd P. K. Wrigley buys more shares in the Cubs and replaces William Walker as president. He gives player/manager Charlie Grimm complete control.

26th Washington player-manager Joe Cronin is sold to the Boston Red Sox for $225,000 and Lyn Lary. Recently married to Mildred Robertson, Clark Griffith's niece and adopted daughter, Cronin is signed to a 5-year contract.

NOVEMBER

1st The Giants obtain Dick Bartell from the Phillies for 4 players and cash.

2nd William Heydler resigns as NL president due to poor health.

3rd Although Lou Gehrig wins the Triple Crown with 49 HRs, 165 RBI, and a .363 BA, Mickey Cochrane, with 2 HRs, 76 RBI, and a .320 BA, is named AL MVP. Dizzy Dean, with a 30-7 record, is chosen as NL MVP.

8th Ford Frick, NL publicity director, is named league president. He will eventually become commissioner.

13th Bucky Harris, who had been "Boy Manager" of the 1924 and 1925 AL champion Senators, is hired back by Washington to replace youthful Joe Cronin, who has been sold to Boston.

18th Al Schacht leaves Washington to join Boston as a coach, breaking up the clown act he had performed with Nick Altrock.

20th Seventeen-year-old Eiji Sawamura gives up one hit, a HR to Gehrig, as the touring American all-stars win in Japan 1–0. At one point Sawamura strikes out 4 in a row—Gehringer, Ruth, Foxx, and Gehrig. The all-stars easily win the other 15 games against high school and post-college players. College players in Japan are prohibited from playing against foreigners.

22nd The Pirates and Cubs make a trade which brings Chicago a needed lefty in Larry French, as well as Fred Lindstrom. They send Guy Bush, Jim Weaver, and Babe Herman to Pittsburgh.

DECEMBER

11th The 1935 All-Star Game is assigned to Cleveland. Frank Frisch and Mickey Cochrane, rival managers in the St. Louis–Detroit WS, will manage their league's teams.

The NL votes to permit night baseball, authorizing a maximum of 7 games by any team installing lights.

The AL does not grant permission for night games until 1937.

13th The Cardinals sell minor league prospect Johnny Mize to Cincinnati. He is later returned because of a suspect knee and does not make his debut until 1936.

19th The Yankees send 5 players to San Francisco as part of the payment for Joe DiMaggio. He will play another season in the Pacific Coast League and will report at the end of 1935.

26th Matsutaro Shoriki, head of Yomiuri Newspapers, announces the official formation of Japan's first professional team, the Tokyo-based Yomiuri Giants. The team is made up of players signed to compete against the American all-star team. Professional league play, with 6 teams, does not begin until 1936.

Judge Landis plays Scrooge to the Dodgers and denies their claim to the services of teenager Johnny Vander Meer.

1935

JANUARY

14th Fading A's star Bing Miller is sold to the Red Sox.

22nd The Senators get Bump Hadley from the St. Louis Browns in a trade for Luke Sewell, who is passed on to the Chicago White Sox.

FEBRUARY

6th Dizzy Dean declares himself a holdout, demanding $25,000. He signs the next day for $19,500.

13th French-Canadian OF Gus Dugas, obtained by Montreal (IL) from Washington, signs a contract written in French.

19th Lou Gehrig signs for $30,000.

26th Babe Ruth is released by the Yankees to sign with the Boston Braves for $20,000 and a share in the team's profits.

MARCH

26th The Yankees buy Pat Malone from the Cards.

29th The Cardinals release Dazzy Vance, who returns to Brooklyn for his final season.

APRIL

14th Cincinnati returns Johnny Mize to St. Louis, getting a $55,000 refund on the provisional purchase.

16th Babe Ruth's NL debut draws the largest Opening Day crowd, 25,000, in Braves' history. The Babe's 2-hit debut includes a 430-foot HR off Carl Hubbell, as Boston beats New York 4–2.

17th President Roosevelt throws out the first ball at the delayed Washington opener. Jimmie Foxx homers, but the Senators beat the A's 4–3.

18th Detroit's Jo Jo White ties an AL record with 5 walks.

21st Cleveland sets a new AL record, playing a total of 41 innings in their 3rd consecutive overtime game: 14 innings against St. Louis (win 2–1), 24 innings against Detroit (win 2–1), and 13 innings against Detroit (lose 3–2).

Philadelphia's Blondy Ryan ties a ML record by turning 5 DPs against the Giants. The Phillies make 6 DPs in all to equal the NL record.

28th Trade unions direct their attention at the Cardinals, voting to boycott their games because team captain Leo Durocher made an antiunion statement in behalf of his wife's dress business. The ballpark is eventually picketed to protest nonunion ushers, gate men, and vendors.

MAY

4th Jimmie Foxx scores 5 runs, as the A's beat the Indians 12–1.

8th Reds backstop Ernie Lombardi equals the ML record with 4 doubles in consecutive innings, each off a different pitcher. The slow-footed Lombardi also has a "long single" in the 23-hit, 15–4 win over the Phillies.

9th The Braves Rabbit Maranville sets a new record for NL service by appearing in his 23rd season. It is his first appearance since breaking his ankle in last year's spring training.

Charley Gelbert of the Cardinals plays his first game since a 1932 hunting accident almost severed his leg.

15th Lou Gehrig steals home in a 4–0 Yankee win over the Tigers. It is his 15th and last steal of home, all of which were double steals.

The Giants make Dolf Luque a coach, the Browns buy Russ Van Atta from the Yankees, and the Dodgers obtain George Earnshaw on waivers from the White Sox.

19th Pittsburgh 1B Gus Suhr injures his hand and leaves the game with the Dodgers. He plays in the OF one inning the next day to continue his consecutive-game streak, which eventually reaches a NL record 822.

21st Buck Newsom is sold by the Browns to the Senators for $40,000.

22nd The Albany Senators (IL) sign Alabama Pitts, legendary athletic star and parolee from Sing Sing prison.

23rd Cleveland has an internal problem between manager Walter Johnson and veteran 3B Willie

Kamm. Judge Landis refuses to intervene, and Kamm is eventually made a scout while Johnson continues his shaky tenure, which will not last the season.

24th   The Cincinnati Reds host the Philadelphia Phillies in the first ML night game, winning 2–1. On the initiative of Larry MacPhail, FDR throws the switch at the White House to turn on the lights. The Reds will play 7 night games, one each against the other NL teams.

25th   Babe Ruth has a last hurrah, hitting 3 HRs at Pittsburgh. The final one, the last of his 714 career HRs, is the first to clear the RF grandstand at Forbes Field and is measured at 600 feet.

27th   The Red Sox get Oscar Melillo, star 2B, from the Browns, for Moose Solters and cash.

28th   Washington's Buck Newsom (later to be called Bobo) is hit on the knee by a line drive by Cleveland's Earl Averill in the 3rd inning. After he finishes the game, it is discovered that his kneecap is broken. Washington loses 5–4.

30th   The Memorial Day twin bill at the Polo Grounds breaks all NL attendance records when 63,943 see the Giants take a pair from the Dodgers.

Babe Ruth plays only the first inning of the opener of a doubleheader between Boston and Philadelphia at Baker Bowl. It is his final ML appearance.

Joe Medwick has 3 doubles and a triple in the first game, a 12–5 Cards win over the Reds. The Cards take game 2, as Medwick contributes another 3 hits.

The Yankees move into first place in the AL with a double win over the Senators.

JUNE

2nd   Babe Ruth announces his retirement as a player at age 40.

P George Pipgras is released by the Red Sox and later becomes an AL umpire.

5th   Rookie White Sox P John Whitehead, who had won his first 8 starts, loses to the Browns 2–0.

6th   Alabama Pitts, signed May 22nd, is released from prison on parole, but Albany (IL) withdraws its offer when controversy rages over his right to play.

8th   Lou Gehrig collides with Carl Reynolds on a play at 1B and leaves the game with arm and shoulder injuries. His consecutive streak is preserved, in part, by a rainout of the next day's game and an open date.

9th   The Cardinals become the 10th team in history to score in every inning, beating the Cubs 13–2 at St. Louis.

10th   Paul Waner, Arky Vaughan, and Pep Young hit successive HRs in the 8th inning for the Pirates against the Reds.

14th   Playing for Kansas City (AA), 1932 AL batting champ Dale Alexander hits 4 successive HRs off future ML hurler Steve Sundra at Minneapolis.

16th   Senators OF John Stone adds 8 hits to 4 made yesterday with 2 triples, 2 doubles, and 4 singles in a doubleheader split with the Browns. Stone scores 5 runs in the opener.

17th   Recently released P Fred Marberry joins the AL umpiring staff.

Judge Landis rules Alabama Pitts may play for the Albany Senators (IL) but only in regular season games—no exhibitions.

18th   All 7 scheduled ML games are rained out.

21st   Babe Herman, on waivers from Pittsburgh, returns to Cincinnati.

23rd   Alabama Pitts plays his first game for Albany (IL), going 2-for-5.

26th   Lloyd Waner has a still-standing ML record 18 putouts in CF in a doubleheader as the Pirates take a pair from the Braves at Boston.

28th   Earl Averill's consecutive-game streak ends at 673 when he is injured in a pre-4th fireworks accident.

29th   Despite Joe Medwick's hitting for the cycle, Paul Dean and the Cardinals are beaten 8–6 by the Reds.

JULY

1st   Yankees OF George Selkirk suggests a cinder path, 6 feet wide, be installed in the outfield so a player knows when he is nearing the wall.

3rd   The Cubs drop Kiki Cuyler to cut their payroll. He will sign with the Reds 2 days later.

Giants SS Dick Bartell plays a 10-inning game with no fielding chances.

4th   The Cardinals move into 2nd place with a twin win over the Cubs, but the Giants hold a 9-game lead at the season's midpoint.

5th   Tony Cuccinello, with Brooklyn, and brother Al, with New York, both homer in a game at the Polo Grounds. The next time brothers homer in a game against each other will be on June 30, 1950, when Joe and Dom DiMaggio do it.

7th   Phillies 2B Lou Chiozza ties a NL record with 11 assists in a 9–1 win over Boston.

At a special meeting, the AL owners raise the waiver price to $7,500.

8th   The AL continues its All-Star Game reign, winning the 3rd event, at Cleveland's Municipal Stadium 4–1. Jimmie Foxx is the hitting star with a homer and 3 RBI.

10th   Hal Schumacher wins his 11th consecutive game as the Giants beat the Pirates 10–3.

The Tigers' win streak ends, despite a record-tying 10 doubles in a 12–11 loss in Washington.

11th   Pete Fox's hitting streak is stopped after 29 games.

13th   The A's Doc Cramer has a 6-for-6 game, tying the AL mark for the 2nd time. He had also done it in 1932.

17th   Bill Werber of the Red Sox ties the ML record with 4 doubles in the opening game of a doubleheader with Cleveland. The Sox win the pair 13–5 and 3–1.

23rd   Paul Dean puts the Cards in first place with a win in the opener of a doubleheader with the Giants. The Giants regain the lead in the nightcap with an 8–2 win.

24th   The Tigers shut out the Yankees 4–2 to go ahead by one-half game, but are a fraction of a percentage point behind.

26th   Jesse Hill's line drive bounces off the head of P Ed Linke back to C Jack Redmond on the fly, who throws to 2B to double off Ben Chapman, as the Senators knock the Yankees out of first. Linke will be hospitalized for 2 days.

28th   Ted Lyons ties a ML record with 2 doubles in the same inning while beating the Browns 14–6.

31st   The Reds oversell their night game, and 30,000 jam in for the match against the Cards. Kitty

Burke, a female fan, slips under the ropes around the infield and grabs a bat. Paul Dean lobs a pitch and she grounds out. Manager Frisch demands it count as an at bat.

Judge Emil Fuchs, president of the Boston Braves since 1925, forfeits his majority stock and retires.

Two AL pitchers each hit 2 HRs in a game. Wes Ferrell clouts a couple against Buck Newsom of the Browns and knocks in 4 runs in a 6–4 win for Boston. Mel Harder hits 2 for Cleveland but loses 6–4 to the White Sox. No other hurlers will hit 2 HRs this season.

AUGUST

2nd   Phillies 1B Dolph Camilli makes 3 errors in the first inning, a ML record. He will lead the NL in fielding, however, in 1937.

4th   Walter Johnson resigns as Cleveland manager and is replaced by Steve O'Neill.

5th   In a rain-soaked game between the Yankees and the Red Sox, Lou Gehrig leaves in the 4th inning with another lumbago attack. The teams engage in stalling and hurry-up tactics, and AL President Heydler fines managers Cronin and McCarthy $100 each.

10th   George Selkirk drives in 8 runs, one short of Jimmie Foxx's AL record, with 2 HRs and a single.

11th   Wally Berger hits a HR, 2 doubles, and a triple, to tie the modern record for extra-base hits in a game.

14th   The largest midweek crowd in NL history, 50,868, sees the Giants and Cards split at the Polo Grounds.

Schoolboy Rowe beats the Senators 18–2 and also goes 5-for-5 at the plate. His hits include a double and a triple, and he scores 3 and knocks in 3.

15th   Phillies 3B Johnny Vergez starts 4 DPs to equal the ML record set by Pie Traynor.

23rd   NL President Ford Frick announces an undisclosed punishment of umpires Reardon and Sears for arguing with Cincinnati fans on July 11.

24th   Giants OF Hank Leiber ties the ML record with 2 HRs during an 8-run, 2nd-inning assault on the Cubs.

25th   Earle Combs of the Yankees collides with teammate Red Rolfe on a fly ball and suffers a severe shoulder injury. It will contribute to his decision to retire at the end of the season.

26th Lumbering 1B Zeke Bonura of the White Sox steals home with 2 outs in the 15th inning to beat the Yankees 9–8.

27th The Yankees outslug the White Sox 13–10 in the first game of 2. In the 2nd game, Lou Gehrig ties an AL record with 5 walks as the Yanks lose 4–3.

31st Vern Kennedy pitches the first AL no-hitter since 1931, and the first ever in Comiskey Park, blanking Cleveland 5–0. He also is the batting star with a bases-loaded triple.

SEPTEMBER

3rd Judge Landis rules against a $1,500 fine the Reds imposed on injured Chick Hafey, who had left the team for his home in California after asking to be placed on the voluntary disabled list. Hafey had chronic sinus and sight problems in addition to an injured shoulder. Landis grants Hafey's request and places him on the list.

5th Terry Moore of the Cardinals goes 6-for-6 against the Braves.

7th Boston's Joe Cronin lines a drive off the head of Cleveland 3B Odell Hale. The ball caroms to SS Bill Knickerbocker, who starts a triple play that ends the game.

14th The Cubs defeat the Dodgers for their 11th straight win and go into first place.

17th Dodger OF Len Koenecke, dropped by the team, hires a private plane. During the flight he gets into a fight with the pilot and dies when he is hit over the head with a fire extinguisher.

19th The Cubs complete a 4-game sweep of the Giants, beating Carl Hubbell for their 16th straight win, the most in the NL since the 1924 Dodgers won 15.

20th The Pittsburgh Crawfords beat the New York Cubans to win the Negro NL Championship 3–0 behind the pitching of Leroy Matlock and the extra-base hits of Josh Gibson, Cool Papa Bell and Oscar Charleston.

21st The Detroit Tigers clinch the pennant with a double win over the St. Louis Browns.

22nd The Boston Braves lose their 110th game for a new NL record. They will lose 115, which remains the record until the 1962 expansion New York Mets lose 120 in a 162-game schedule.

27th The Cubs clinch the NL pennant in the first game of a doubleheader with the Cardinals, as Bill Lee wins his 20th. By winning the 2nd game, the Cubs extend their win streak to 21 games.

29th Washington's Buddy Myer goes 4-for-5 to edge out Cleveland's Joe Vosmik for the AL batting title, .349 to .348.

After winning the first game 3–2 against Detroit, the White Sox tie the AL record with 10 singles in the 2nd inning of game 2 off Eldon Auker. The Sox win 14–2, as Auker loses his 7th against 18 wins, still the best percentage in the AL.

OCTOBER

2nd The WS opens in Detroit and Lon Warneke, the Cubs ace, shuts out the Tigers and Schoolboy Rowe 3–0.

3rd The Tigers even the Series behind Tommy Bridges 8–3, but lose Hank Greenberg who injures his wrist trying to score from first on a single.

4th AL umpire George Moriarty chases Chicago manager Charlie Grimm and SS Billy Jurges in the 3rd inning. After Chicago ties the game in the bottom of the 9th, Detroit scores an unearned run to win in 11.

5th Detroit's Al Crowder outduels Tex Carleton 2–1 when the Cubs allow an unearned run in the 6th.

6th Lon Warneke keeps the Cubs alive with 6 innings of shutout ball for his 2nd win. Bill Lee relieves in the 2–1 victory.

7th The Tigers end the Series in 6 games behind Tommy Bridges' second complete game 4–3. Goose Goslin's single, with 2 out in the bottom of the 9th, wins the game.

20th Hank Greenberg is named AL MVP by the BBWAA; Wes Ferrell is runner-up.

23rd Gabby Hartnett is selected by the BBWAA as the NL MVP, with Dizzy Dean the runner-up.

24th Judge Landis levies $200 fines on umpire George Moriarty, Cubs manager Charlie Grimm, and

Chicago players Woody English, Billy Jurges, and Billy Herman for their conduct in the WS.

NOVEMBER

4th   Cal Hubbard, pro football tackle with the Green Bay Packers, 1929-35, joins the AL umpiring staff.

6th   P Sad Sam Jones, after 21 successive but not always successful AL seasons, is released by the Chicago White Sox.

26th   The NL takes over the bankrupt, last-place Boston Braves franchise after several failed attempts to buy the club. The league takes over only temporarily, until matters can be straightened out.

DECEMBER

9th   The Giants get Burgess Whitehead from the Cardinals for Roy Parmelee, Phil Weintraub, and cash.

10th   Jimmie Foxx, with Johnny Marcum, is sold by the A's to the Red Sox for $150,000; Al Simmons is sold by the White Sox to the Tigers for $75,000.

The NL accepts Bob Quinn, who had been GM of the Brooklyn Dodgers, as president of the new ownership of the Braves.

Ford Frick is reelected NL president for 2 years and given a raise. The AL votes down night ball and awards a $500 cash prize for batting leaders retroactive to include Buddy Myer in 1935.

The Hanshin Tigers of Osaka are officially formed to become Japan's 2nd professional team.

11th   The Yankees trade Johnny Allen to Cleveland for Monte Pearson and Steve Sundra.

14th   Fred Marberry resigns as AL umpire to sign with the Giants as a pitcher.

17th   Heinie Manush is traded from Washington to the Boston Red Sox for Roy Johnson and Carl Reynolds.

21st   The Dodgers trade Ray Benge, Tony Cuccinello, Al Lopez, and Bobby Reis to the Braves for P Ed Brandt and OF Randy Moore.

1936

JANUARY

4th As the 2nd part of the December 10th deal for Jimmie Foxx, the Boston Red Sox get Doc Cramer and Eric "Boob" McNair from the A's for Henry Johnson, Al Niemiec, and $75,000.

15th IRS figures for 1934 show Branch Rickey as the highest paid man in baseball at $49,470. Commissioner Landis had voluntarily taken a cut in 1933 from $65,000 to $40,000 because of the Depression.

Horace Stoneham is elected president of the New York Giants, succeeding his late father.

The Chunichi Dragons of Nagoya, Japan, are officially formed. Eight days later the Hankyu Braves of Nishinomiya are formed.

17th The Yankees trade Jimmy DeShong and Jesse Hill to Washington for Bump Hadley and Roy Johnson.

30th The new owners of the Boston Braves ask newspapermen to pick a new nickname for the team from suggestions made by fans. They choose the Bees, but the name will not catch on. It will be scrapped after the 1940 season.

FEBRUARY

2nd The baseball writers vote for the first players to be named to the new Baseball Hall of Fame. Ty Cobb, Babe Ruth, Honus Wagner, Christy Mathewson, and Walter Johnson each receive the requisite 75 percent of ballots cast. Active players also are eligible in this first election, with Hornsby finishing 9th, Cochrane 10th, Gehrig 15th, and Foxx 19th. Tainted former star Hal Chase receives 11 votes for 25th place, and Joe Jackson has 2 votes to tie for 36th place.

20th The Giants buy back 1B Sam Leslie from the Dodgers.

MARCH

1st After spring training with Lefty O'Doul's San Francisco Seals (PCL), the Yomiuri Giants of Japan beat the Seals 5–0. On March 5th they will win again 11–7.

5th The St. Louis Cardinals, without the Dean brothers, who are once again holdouts, visit Cuba and are beaten by the Cuban all-stars. Luis Tiant, Sr., whose son will win 229 ML games, is the starting pitcher for the Cubans.

17th Much-heralded rookie Joe DiMaggio makes his debut with the Yankees, getting 4 hits, including a triple. The day is marred when the Cardinals win 8–7.

21st The Cincinnati Reds trade Jim Bottomley to the St. Louis Browns for Johnny Burnett.

Joe DiMaggio runs his spring training record to 12-for-20, in an 11–2 Yankee victory over the newly named Boston Bees. Before the next game is played, the prize rookie is left unattended with his foot in a diathermy machine. The resulting burn ends his spring training and delays his ML debut until May.

23rd After an acrimonious holdout, Dizzy Dean signs for a reported $24,000 and an understanding that the only fines levied will be major ones.

24th Paul Dean follows his brother into the fold and signs for $10,000.

26th Hank Greenberg signs a Tiger's contract for $20,000, and Red Ruffing accepts $12,000 from the Yankees.

APRIL

14th In a 12-7 loss to Cubs, Cardinals rookie Eddie Morgan pinch-hits and drives the first ML pitch he sees for a HR, the only one he'll hit in a 39-game career.

16th Red Sox player-manager Joe Cronin breaks his thumb on a force play. He will miss almost half the season.

23rd Dodgers OF Randy Moore breaks his leg sliding into 2B and will miss most of the season.

26th Brooklyn SS Ben Geraghty reaches base twice on interference by Philadelphia C Earl Grace for a ML record.

29th Roy Parmelee, former Giants P, beats Carl Hubbell 2–1 in a 17-inning duel.

Tiger Hank Greenberg breaks his wrist in a base-line collision with Washington's Jake Powell. He is finished for the season.

The first professional baseball game in Japan is played. Nagoya defeats Daitokyo; the score is 8–5.

30th Tigers player/manager Mickey Cochrane breaks a finger and is lost to the World Champions for most of the season.

MAY

3rd Joe DiMaggio makes his regular-season debut with the Yankees and has 3 hits, one a triple, as New York routs St. Louis 14–5.

10th Joe Sullivan, Detroit P, weakens after 12 innings of scoreless relief and Cleveland edges Detroit 9–7.

The Yankees move into first place and remain there the rest of the season.

12th After the Dodgers beat Dizzy Dean at Ebbets Field, Cardinal SS Leo Durocher and Casey Stengel agree to meet under the stands and the Dodger manager gets a cut lip in a brief fight.

16th Pittsburgh P Waite Hoyt has an emergency appendectomy.

20th The Giants take first place from the Cardinals, defeating them at the Polo Grounds 10–7. The next day, Paul Dean will pitch the Cards back on top, as the NL lead seesaws.

21st The Phillies reacquire Chuck Klein from the Cubs, along with P Fabian Kowalik and a reported $50,000, for P Curt Davis and OF Ethan Allen.

23rd Pepper Martin scores in his 13th consecutive game.

24th Yankees 2B Tony Lazzeri sets several slugging marks with 2 grand slams, a 3rd HR, and a triple for 15 total bases in a 25–2 slaughter of the Athletics at Shibe Park. He has hit 7 HRs in 4 games and 6 in three games. He also sets a new AL mark of 11 RBI in one game.

27th Carl Hubbell beats the Dodgers 5–4 in 12 innings for his 6th win, as the Giants tie the Cardinals for first place.

Cleveland OF Bruce Campbell is released from the hospital after a 3rd attack of spinal meningitis.

31st P Chief Hogsett, making his first appearance with the last-place Browns, hits 4 Detroit batters to tie the ML record.

JUNE

5th Lou Gehrig plays in his 1,700th consecutive game, as the Yankees beat Cleveland 4–3.

6th Stu Martin, Cardinals 2B, ties the ML mark with 11 assists in the first game of a St. Louis-New York doubleheader.

7th George Selkirk's HR in the 16th gives Red Ruffing a 5–4 win over Oral Hildebrand of the Indians. Ruffing has 3 hits, including a HR. There are no strikeouts in the long game.

10th Brooklyn's Van Mungo jumps the team in Pittsburgh, complaining of poor support and demanding to be traded.

13th Van Mungo rejoins the Dodgers and pitches the final 3 innings of the 2nd game of a doubleheader.

14th The Yankees trade Ben Chapman to the Senators for Jake Powell.

Pirates 1B Gus Suhr completes a string of 70 consecutive errorless games for a NL record.

19th Joe McCarthy is named to manage the AL All-Stars, rather than the high-strung Mickey Cochrane, who is very close to a nervous breakdown.

21st Van Mungo stops the Cubs' win streak at 15, leaving them a half game behind the Cards, who lose to the Giants.

Mickey Cochrane checks out of the hospital and goes to a Wyoming ranch to recover his health.

24th Joe DiMaggio ties 3 ML records in New York's 10-run 5th inning against the White Sox, hitting 2 HRs for 8 total bases. With 2 doubles, he equals the modern record of 4 long hits in a game.

25th Brooklyn's Van Mungo ties the ML record with 7 consecutive strikeouts, but loses to the Reds 5–4.

28th Larry French and Bill Lee pitch the Cubs to twin shutouts 3-0 and 6-0 over the Giants and replace the Cardinals in the league lead.

JULY

1st Powel Crosley, Jr. exercises his 2-year option and buys controlling interest in the Cincinnati Reds.

2nd Cleveland OF Bruce Campbell, recently returned from a bout with spinal meningitis, goes 6-

for-6 in the first game of a doubleheader. He singles in his first AB in the nightcap.

7th   The NL, having lost the first 3 All-Star Games, wins 4–3 at Fenway Park. After Dizzy Dean and Carl Hubbell each pitch scoreless 3-inning stints, Curt Davis is hammered by the AL, including Lou Gehrig's HR, but Lon Warneke shuts the door. Meanwhile, the NL is helped by Joe DiMaggio's loose fielding and error and Augie Galan's HR. NL plays its starting line-up except for 2 late-inning pinch hitters.

9th   Philadelphia's Chuck Klein hits 4 HRs in 5 at bats in a 10-inning game at Forbes Field. His final HR beats the Pirates 9–6.

11th   Dizzy Dean is knocked unconscious by a line drive off the bat of Burgess Whitehead and is carried off the field.

13th   Bill Lee wins a 1–0 duel from Carl Hubbell, as the Cubs move into first place. It is the last game the Giant will lose in 1936; he will win his next 16 decisions.

15th   Cincinnati plays the first Ladies Night game, beating Brooklyn 5–3.

Mickey Cochrane rejoins the Tigers in New York, as they split a doubleheader with the Yankees.

17th   Carl Hubbell starts his winning streak, beating Pittsburgh 6–0. The Giants hit 4 triples in the first inning. Joe Moore, Mel Ott, and Hank Leiber hit them in succession, and Eddie Mayo adds one later in the inning to equal the NL record.

Red Rolfe, Lou Gehrig, and Bill Dickey hit 3rd-inning HRs against Detroit to tie the AL record.

18th   The Chicago White Sox and Philadelphia A's set an AL record for most runs scored by 2 teams, as the White Sox win 21–14. Chicago OF Rip Radcliff ties an AL record with 6 hits in 7 at bats in the 9-inning game.

19th   Bob Feller makes his ML debut in relief. He pitches the 8th inning at Washington, giving up no hits and fanning one.

21st   Cardinals slugger Joe Medwick has 10 hits in succession to equal the NL record. He had 7 hits in his last 7 times at bat in a doubleheader on the 19th, and he hit safely in his first 3 today before being stopped by the Giants Carl Hubbell.

Mickey Cochrane has a relapse, and Del Baker again takes charge of the Tigers.

25th   Philadelphia A's C Frankie Hayes equals a ML record with 4 doubles in a game against Cleveland.

26th   Umpire Bill Summers is knocked unconscious by a pop bottle thrown from an unruly crowd at Comiskey Park. Judge Landis, on hand to watch the game, offers a $5,000 reward over the PA system for the culprit, but only draws more boos.

27th   Cleveland's Roy Weatherly sets an AL rookie record by hitting in his 20th consecutive game.

28th   Joe DiMaggio and Myril Hoag collide while chasing Tiger Goose Goslin's long fly ball. Both are knocked unconscious and Hoag is hospitalized with a severe concussion. Goslin gets an inside-the-park HR.

30th   Kiki Cuyler of the Reds has 8 straight hits during a doubleheader with the Phils.

The Boston Red Sox, led by owner Tom Yawkey and accompanied by AL President Will Harridge, fly from St. Louis to Chicago aboard one plane. In 1934, the Reds flew from Cincinnati to Chicago, but divided the players among 3 planes.

AUGUST

4th   The Cardinals regain first place, beating the Cubs 6–1, and dropping them to 2nd place.

9th   The Cubs move back into first place by taking 2 from Pittsburgh while the Cards lose a pair to Cincinnati.

10th   The Cards are back in first place, beating the Cubs in a game interrupted by a fight between former teammates Dizzy Dean and Tex Carleton.

Buddy Myer, last year's AL batting champ, is sent home by Washington to recover from a season/long stomach ailment.

12th   The largest crowd ever to watch a baseball game, between 90,000 and 125,000, sees a "demonstration game" as an event of the 1936 Olympics in Berlin. The world amateurs beat the U.S. amateurs 6–5. Carson Thompson pitches 4 hitless innings in relief.

21st   Wes Ferrell, in a tantrum for what he considers shabby support, walks off the mound during a Yankee rally and is suspended and fined $1,000 by Boston manager Joe Cronin. It is the second time in 5 days he has walked off the mound, having done it in Boston last Sunday in a game against the Senators. Ferrell, furious when he hears about the fine, says he will not pay it. "They can suspend me or trade me, but they're not getting any dough from me." The Red Sox lift the suspension in 4 days and will trade Ferrell after the season.

Babe Herman, who quit the Reds in a dispute over a bonus, rejoins the team on orders from Commissioner Landis.

22nd Washington ties an AL record when Red Kress, Joe Kuhel, and Carl Reynolds hit HRs in the 4th inning.

23rd Seventeen-year-old Bob Feller makes his first start and strikes out 15, one less than the AL record, as Cleveland beats St. Louis 4–1.

25th The Giants win their 13th straight and take over first place.

28th The Giants win their 15th in a row, beating Pittsburgh 7–4 in 14 innings. First base coach Bill Terry inserted himself as a pinch hitter and delivered a bases-loaded single to break the 1–1 tie in the 14th. The streak will be stopped the next day by Red Lucas.

31st Yankees manager Joe McCarthy consents to Dixie Walker as a temporary substitute while the White Sox patch up Mike Kreevich, who is spiked on a play. Walker runs for Kreevich but does not replace him in the outfield.

SEPTEMBER

7th Sonny Dunlap, an All-American girls A.A.U. basketball player for the Tulsa Stenos, is in RF for the Fayetteville Bears in a 5–1 win over Cassville (Class D Arkansas-Missouri League). She goes hitless in 3 trips but hits the ball hard. She is the first woman to play an entire game, and represents the 2nd and last time a woman plays in the minors.

9th The Yankees sweep the Indians 11–3 and 12–9 to clinch the pennant on the earliest date ever.

11th Hod Lisenbee of the Philadelphia A's ties a ML record for hits allowed, giving up 26 in a 17–2 rout by the White Sox.

12th Kid Elberfeld pinch-hits at age 61 for his Fulton (Kitty League) team and grounds out to 3B.

13th Bob Feller, still only 17, breaks the AL record and ties the ML mark with 17 strikeouts, defeating the A's 5–2.

The Cardinals and Giants split a doubleheader at the Polo Grounds before 64,417, the largest crowd in the 60-year history of the NL.

14th Pittsburgh's Paul Waner ties Rogers Hornsby's modern NL record, reaching 200 hits for the 7th time.

15th Johnny Allen wins his 20th for Cleveland, though he is forced to leave the game with a back injury, after hurling 5 innings of no-hit ball.

18th Larry MacPhail abruptly quits as the Reds GM. He will be replaced by Warren Giles.

23rd Pitching in the 10th straight Giants game, Carl Hubbell notches his 16th consecutive victory, his 26th of the year. He resumes the streak next year to reach a record 24 wins in a row.

24th The Giants clinch the pennant, winning 2–1 in the 10th of the opening game of a doubleheader with the Boston Bees. P Hal Schumacher singles in the winning run.

The AL batting crown is decided when Luke Appling of the White Sox goes 4-for-4 in the 2nd game of a doubleheader with Cleveland. Runner-up Earl Averill is held hitless. Appling will coast to a 10-point margin at .388.

25th Joe Medwick sets a still-standing NL record with his 64th double.

27th When Johnny Mize is thrown out in the 7th inning for arguing, rookie 1B Walt Alston subs. In his only ML game, the future Hall of Fame manager makes one error in 2 chances and is fanned by Lon Warneke in his only at bat.

28th The Boston Red Sox release Heinie Manush, and make Bing Miller a coach to replace Al Schacht, who will begin to barnstorm as the "Clown Prince of Baseball."

30th In the WS opener, Carl Hubbell scatters 7 hits and limits the Yankees to a solo HR by George Selkirk. The Giants take a decisive 6–1 win.

OCTOBER

1st Rain postpones the 2nd WS game.

2nd The Yankees score a still-standing record 18 runs, as they demolish the Giants 18–4. Lefty Gomez coasts to a 6-hit win, while every member of the Yankees lineup makes a hit and scores at least one run. Lazzeri hits a grand slam, the first in WS play since 1920.

3rd Game 3 shifts to Yankee Stadium and a new attendance record of 64,842. Lou Gehrig's solo HR is matched by the Giants' Jimmy Ripple, with the deciding run of the Yankees 2–1 squeaker coming on an infield hit.

4th Another attendance record is set at Yankee Stadium, with 66,669 people watching Lou Gehrig lead the way to a 5–2 win behind Monte Pearson's pitching.

5th The Giants stave off a final Yankee victory with a 5–4 win for Hal Schumacher in 10 innings.

6th The Yankees roll to a 13–5 Series-ending victory. Lefty Gomez is the winning pitcher. In the 6 games the Yankees score 43 runs to the Giants' 23.

7th The 7th-place Brooklyn Dodgers fire manager Casey Stengel with a year remaining on his contract.

8th The Cardinals trade 1B Ripper Collins and P Roy Parmelee to the Cubs for Chicago's star P Lon Warneke.

15th Cincinnati rewards Chuck Dressen with a new managerial contract.

16th Lou Gehrig, who hit 49 HRs, scored 167 runs, knocked in 152, and batted .354, is voted AL MVP by the BBWAA.

20th Carl Hubbell, 26-6, edges out Dizzy Dean, 24-13, for MVP honors in the NL.

NOVEMBER

5th Burleigh Grimes is named manager of the Brooklyn Dodgers.

12th Following the death of Phil Ball, wealthy owner of the St. Louis Browns, his estate sells the team to a syndicate headed by Donald L. Barnes and William O. DeWitt. As the new owners of Sportsman's Park, they announce their intention to install lights and bring night baseball to the AL.

29th Judge Landis declares Lee Handley and Johnny Peacock of the Cincinnati Reds free agents. They had been covered up on minor league teams by the Reds.

DECEMBER

2nd The Cards sell Virgil Davis and Charley Gelbert to the Reds, and the Browns buy Ethan Allen from the Cubs.

3rd The Dodgers "sell" Frenchy Bordagaray, Dutch Leonard, and Jimmy Jordan to the Cardinals, but the exchange is understood to be a continuation of the September 7th transaction, which brought the Dodgers Tom Winsett and Eddie Morgan from the Cards' AA farm team.

4th The Dodgers trade Lonny Frey to the Cubs for Woody English and Roy Henshaw. The Boston Bees buy Vince DiMaggio from San Diego (PCL). The Dodgers get Cookie Lavagetto and Ralph Birkofer from Pittsburgh in exchange for Ed Brandt.

8th In a 3-way deal, the Indians send Thornton Lee to the White Sox, who ship Jack Salveson to the Senators, who transfer Earl Whitehill to Cleveland.

9th The Red Sox trade Bill Werber to Philadelphia for Pinky Higgins.

The AL okays night baseball for St. Louis. The NL adopts a new design for home plate. It will have beveled edges, the first change in 50 years. The AL adopts a rule stating that no batter can be batting champion unless he has 400 or more at bats.

10th Commissioner Landis announces his ruling on the Bob Feller case. Feller joined Cleveland in July and Des Moines (Western League) protested, claiming the pitcher for themselves. Landis let Feller stay with Cleveland, pending his final ruling, which is announced today in favor of the Indians.

1937

JANUARY

6th   The Giants buy SS Tommy Thevenow from Cincinnati.

17th   Cleveland gets Moose Solters, Ivy Andrews, and Lyn Lary from the St. Louis Browns for Joe Vosmik, Bill Knickerbocker, and Oral Hildebrand.

19th   Nap Lajoie, Tris Speaker, and Cy Young are voted into the Baseball Hall of Fame by the BBWAA.

FEBRUARY

11th   Connie Mack is interviewed on a television demonstration by Philco.

17th   The Yankees buy Babe Dahlgren from the Red Sox.

27th   The Negro American League announces the schedule for their inaugural season.

MARCH

13th   Lou Gehrig agrees to $38,000, plus a $750 bonus for signing.

20th   Josh Gibson and Judy Johnson, 2 future Hall of Famers, are traded to the Homestead Grays for 2 journeyman players and $2,500. The transaction is called the biggest deal in Negro baseball history.

APRIL

1st   Babe Herman is sold by Cincinnati to Detroit.

2nd   Dizzy Dean, Paul Dean, and Joe Medwick have a scuffle in a Tampa hotel lobby with New York *News* reporter Jack Miley and Chicago *Times* writer Irv Kupcinet.

4th   In an Indians-Giants exhibition game, Hank Leiber is beaned by a Bob Feller fastball and will miss most of the upcoming season.

9th   The 1936 batting champ, Paul Waner, ends his holdout and signs a contract with Pittsburgh.

14th   Judge Landis declares Tommy Henrich a free agent, voiding his Cleveland contract. This is another of the cover-up situations Landis hated, and the bal-ance of the scale for letting Cleveland keep Bob Feller. Henrich will sign with the Yankees 4 days later.

19th   The Phillies open in Boston with a double-header win against the Bees 2–1 and 1–0.

20th   Gee Walker of the Tigers becomes the only player to hit for the cycle on Opening Day when he performs the feat against the Cleveland Indians, hitting in reverse order for a HR, triple, double, and single. Detroit wins 4–3.

22nd   Satchel Paige and Josh Gibson are among 18 black players who jump to the Dominican Republic league. Negro League owners regard this as desertion and plan to ban the players from the league. In May, Paige will be banned for life.

23rd   Carl Hubbell's first start of the season is a 3-hitter against the Boston Bees. For the Giants ace, it is his 17th straight win, dating back to July 17 of last year.

Jersey City, now a Giants farm team, returns to the International League with the largest crowd, 31,294, in minor league history.

25th   Giants rookie P Cliff Melton strikes out 13 in his first ML game but loses to the Boston Bees 3–1.

28th   In a game against the Reds, Cubs P Larry French gets a bone broken in his right hand when he is hit by Ernie Lombardi's line drive.

30th   Duke All-American football star Ace Parker pinch-hits a HR in his first ML at bat for the Athletics. Parker will have just one more HR on his way to a .117 average this year, but will do better on the gridiron. He will score 2 TDs for the Brooklyn Dodgers at Pittsburgh on November 21st and will eventually be elected to the Football Hall of Fame. He, thereby joins Hoyt Wilhelm and Earl Averill as one of just 3 Hall of Famers to hit a HR in their first at-bat.

After a long holdout, Dolph Camilli signs with the Phillies.

MAY

3rd   The Giants equal a ML record, playing a 9-inning game against the Bees with no chances for their outfielders.

4th   Ripper Collins, Joe Marty, and John Bottarini homer for the Cubs in the 8th inning against the Phils, as visiting Chicago wins 14–7.

9th   Reds C Ernie Lombardi ties the modern ML record with 6 hits in 6 consecutive times at bat, as Cincinnati routs Philadelphia 21–10.

12th   Joe Medwick ties a ML record with 4 extra-base hits: 2 HRs and a pair of doubles.

Chick Hafey is restored to active duty with the Reds after a 2-year retirement.

13th   Washington's Joe Kuhel ties the modern ML record with 3 triples in a game at Chicago.

16th   Browns 3B Harlond Clift equals the AL record with 9 assists. By the end of the season, Clift will set a new record for total chances and the still-standing mark of 405 assists.

19th   Dizzy Dean instigates another donnybrook following a number of knockdown pitches in a game with the Giants. Losing 4–1 to Carl Hubbell in the 9th, Dean knocks down Jimmy Ripple with a pitch. Ripple follows with a bunt on the first base side in a effort to make Dean field the ball. The bunt, however, bounces to 2B Jimmy Brown, who prepares to throw to Johnny Mize at 1B. Dean, who had started toward the ball, keeps running and barrels into Ripple. The two benches empty, and when the field is cleared by the umpires and policemen, the batter Ripple, who was never put out at first base, is credited with a single. The only player who doesn't leave the bench is Hubbell, who wins his 6th straight game of the year and 22nd regular-season decision in a row.

23rd   Van Mungo is fined $1,000 by the Dodgers, suspended for 3 days, and given a bill for $1,500 worth of damage done to a hotel room following a ruckus with teammates trying to get him to bed at 4 A.M..

25th   After hitting a HR against the Yankees in his prior at bat, Mickey Cochrane suffers a skull fracture from a Bump Hadley pitch. Coach Del Baker will run the team for the hospitalized Detroit leader, who will never return to active play.

26th   Joe McCarthy of the Yankees and Bill Terry of the Giants are named to manage the All-Star teams. Judge Landis announces that the managers, not the fans, will pick the teams, and increases the squads from 21 to 23 players.

27th   Hubbell pitches 2 innings in relief and wins his 24th straight game when Mel Ott hits a 9th-inning HR for a 3–2 victory over the Reds.

31st   A Memorial Day crowd of 61,756, the 2nd-largest crowd in Polo Grounds history, sees the Dodgers end Carl Hubbell's consecutive-game winning streak at 24 over 2 seasons. Brooklyn routs King Carl in the 4th inning and wins 10–3.

JUNE

1st   White Sox P Bill Dietrich pitches an 8–0 no-hitter against the Browns. It is the 3rd no-hitter Luke Sewell has caught, having previously been behind the plate for Wes Ferrell in 1931 and Vern Kennedy in 1935.

2nd   NL President Ford Frick suspends Dizzy Dean for refusing to retract statements made after a balk call in the May 19th game, which led to an on-field brawl. Dean forces a meeting with the press at which he denies the statements, and his suspension is lifted a few days later.

3rd   Josh Gibson is credited with a drive that hits just 2 feet below the rim of Yankee Stadium, about 580 feet from home plate. It is estimated that the ball would have traveled nearly 700 feet.

5th   Gus Suhr's NL record of 822 consecutive games, started on September 11, 1931, ends when he attends his mother's funeral in San Francisco.

6th   Umpires declare the Cardinals winners of the 2nd game with the Phils when the Phils stall and delay until a Sunday curfew of 7 P.M. is reached.

One of baseball's rarest feats takes place when Woody English of the Dodgers wins a suit by hitting the sign of clothier Abe Stark at the base of the Ebbets Field scoreboard.

8th   The White Sox take first place from the Yankees, beating New York 5–4 for their 10th straight win.

9th   Mickey Cochrane is taken off Detroit's active-player roster. 3B Marv Owen is sidelined with a broken bone in his hand, and Rudy York is recalled from Toledo to replace him.

10th   Bobo Newsom and Ben Chapman are traded by Washington to Boston for Wes and Rick Ferrell, and Mel Almada.

11th   In one of the Giants' worst trades, popular Fred Fitzsimmons is sent to Brooklyn for rookie prospect Tom Baker.

It is Zeke Bonura Day at Comiskey Park. Zeke paces the White Sox to a 14–8 win over the Senators, as he knocks in 5 runs with a HR, 2 doubles, and a single, after receiving a car in pregame ceremonies.

15th   The Boston Bees sell star OF Wally Berger to the New York Giants for $35,000 and P Frank Gabler.

21st   Johnny Allen, off to a 4–0 start for Cleveland, has an appendectomy in Boston and will miss 8 weeks of the season.

25th   Cubs switch-hitter Augie Galan becomes the first NL player to hit HRs from both sides of the plate in the same game as Chicago beats Brooklyn 11–2.

JULY

2nd   Rollie Hemsley is suspended by the Browns for violation of training rules.

4th   After the July 4th games are played, the Yankees have opened a 3½ game lead over the White Sox. The NL league lead is a narrow one-game margin held by Chicago over New York.

7th   Lou Gehrig leads the AL All-Stars over the NL 8–3 with a HR, double, and 4 RBI. FDR attends the game in Washington. Dizzy Dean's toe is fractured by a drive off the bat of Earl Averill. After the injury Dean is unable to pitch with the same delivery. He uses an unnatural motion, causing an arm injury from which he never recovers.

12th   The Phillies score 6 runs in the 7th inning to beat Hal Schumacher and the Giants 6–3. With the bases loaded in the first, Giants OF Mel Ott starts an unusual 9–2–5 triple play. But the highlight of the game comes when umpire Bill Klem ejects Giants manager Bill Terry for the first time in Terry's 15-year career.

13th   The Cardinals' Pepper Martin is fined $200 for violation of training rules.

14th   Boston's Fabian Gaffke ties the AL record by scoring 5 runs against the St. Louis Browns.

15th   The Athletics snap a 15-game losing streak, beating the White Sox 3–1.

19th   P Johnny Broaca is fined $250 and suspended indefinitely by the Yankees for jumping the club.

21st   Rogers Hornsby is fired as manager of the St. Louis Browns for playing the horses; Jim Bottomley takes over.

25th   Washington's Mel Almada ties the ML record by scoring 5 runs in the first game of a doubleheader. When he adds 4 in the 2nd game, he sets an 18-inning record.

26th   Mickey Cochrane resumes command of the Detroit Tigers as a bench manager.

AUGUST

1st   Lou Gehrig hits for the cycle against the Browns, as the Yankees win 14–5. It is the 2nd time he has performed this feat in his career.

Hank Leiber pinch-hits for the Giants, his first appearance since early May, following his hospitalization as a result of the Feller beaning in spring training.

3rd   A Tuesday crowd of 66,767 watches at Yankee Stadium as Lou Gehrig plays his 1,900th consecutive game.

Cardinals C Mickey Owen becomes the 3rd NL backstop ever to make an unassisted DP, as the Cards beat the Bees 5–2.

4th   Joe Medwick again ties the ML record with 4 extra base hits in a game. It is the 3rd time he has performed the feat.

6th   For the first time in the 20th century, the first 2 batters in a game—Roy Johnson and Rabbit Warstler of the Boston Bees—lead off with HRs. They do it off Cubs P Tex Carleton.

In a 10-inning game Cleveland outfielders have no chances against the Yankees. In the 10th inning Joe DiMaggio hits a drive which 3B Odell Hale deflects into foul territory. One umpire calls it foul, so the Indians LF fails to chase after the ball. But the other umpire overrules the first, allowing the winning run to score because of the OF's idleness. Cleveland protest of the game will be upheld.

10th   Washington 3B Buddy Lewis makes 4 errors in a game with the A's, tying the record set in 1901.

Cubs 1B Ripper Collins fractures his right ankle sliding into home plate in a game with Pittsburgh.

13th   The Hellenic Societies of Chicago hold a day for Alex Kampouris of the visiting Reds. He gets a car, and the Cubs get a 22–6 win, as Kampouris makes 3 errors and fans twice.

14th Tigers P Eldon Auker hits 2 HRs while beating the Browns. Detroit wins 16–1 and 20–7 and scores an AL record 36 runs in the doubleheader to move into 2nd place, 10 games behind the Yankees.

17th The first ML night game to start one day and end the next ends at 12:02 AM in Cincinnati, as the Cards beat the Reds 8–6.

21st Brooklyn OF Johnny Cooney ties the ML record with 4 extra-base hits: 3 doubles and a triple.

25th Cleveland's Bob Feller strikes out 16 Red Sox, one less than his own AL record, in an 8–1 victory.

27th Fred Frankhouse of the Dodgers loses his chance to pitch a full no-hitter when rain stops the game with 2 out in the 8th; the hitless Reds lose 5–0.

28th Van Mungo is suspended indefinitely for insubordination after rejecting the Dodger trainer's program to cure his sore arm.

29th The A's set a new AL record in the opener of a doubleheader with the White Sox by scoring 12 runs in the first inning, 6 of which are driven in by Bob Johnson.

31st Detroit's rookie Rudy York sets a new record for HRs in a month, hitting his 17th and 18th to eclipse Babe Ruth's mark set in September 1927. He knocks in 7 runs against Pete Appleton, as Detroit beats Washington 12–3.

SEPTEMBER

1st The Giants sign Bill Terry to a 5-year contract as manager and farm director at $40,000 a year.

2nd For the second time this season, the first 2 batters in a game—the White Sox Boze Berger and Mike Kreevich—hit HRs.

4th Mike Kreevich of the White Sox ties a ML record with 4 doubles.

6th The Giants take a Labor Day pair from the Phillies and move 3 games ahead of the Cubs, who split with the Reds.

13th Manager Charlie Dressen presses Reds GM Warren Giles for a contract renewal and is fired. Chief scout Bobby Wallace takes over the last-place team.

15th AL President Will Harridge upholds Cleveland's protest of the August 6 Yankee win, and the entire game is replayed as the 2nd game of a doubleheader. The protested game is called a tie with all stats retained except those following the disputed call.

16th Future Hall of Famer Martin Dihigo pitches the first professional no-hit, no-run game on Mexican soil, a 4–0 victory against Nogales at Veracruz. In 1938, Dihigo will lead the Mexican league in 4 categories: ERA (0.90), wins (18-2), strikeouts (184), and batting (.387).

17th Cleveland's Johnny Allen wins his 12th straight without a loss, equaling Tom Zachary's 1929 record of 12-0.

18th Pittsburgh OF Paul Waner establishes a 20th-century NL record with his 8th year of 200 or more hits.

19th Hank Greenberg's HR in Detroit's 8–1 win over New York is the first ever hit into the CF stands at Yankee Stadium.

23rd The Yankees lose 9–5 but clinch the pennant when the Red Sox beat Detroit.

29th New York rookie Cliff Melton wins his 20th game in the opening game of a doubleheader, but the Phillies beat the Giants in the 2nd game, preventing New York from clinching the flag. They will do this the following day when Carl Hubbell wins his 22nd game.

OCTOBER

2nd Thirty-four-year-old rookie Jim Turner of the Boston Bees wins his 20th game. The next day, fellow first-year pitcher Lou Fette will also win his 20th.

Rudy York of Detroit hits his 35th HR, tying the 1934 AL record of Hal Trosky for rookies.

3rd Johnny Allen's effort to tie the AL record of 16 straight wins is frustrated when Detroit's Jake Wade beats him with a one-hit shutout 1–0 on the final day of the season.

The Pirates take a closing day doubleheader from the Reds, extending their win streak to 10, and the Reds' losing run to 14. The Pirates beat the Reds 21 of 22 games, tying the ML record set by the Cubs over the Braves in 1909.

4th Cincinnati releases 38-year-old Kiki Cuyler. He will sign with Brooklyn.

5th Leo Durocher is traded to the Dodgers by the Cardinals for Johnny Cooney, Joe Stripp, Jim Bucher, and Roy Henshaw.

6th Carl Hubbell and Lefty Gomez duel in the opening game of the WS, a rematch of last year's teams. The Yankees score 7 runs in the 6th inning on 5 singles, 3 walks, and 2 errors. Tony Lazzeri homers in the bottom of the 8th to make the final score 8–1.

7th The Yankees win the 2nd game, again by an 8–1 score, with Red Ruffing beating Cliff Melton. Ruffing fans 8 and drives in 3 runs with 2 hits.

8th The Yankees continue their mastery over the Giants, who unravel with 4 errors. Monte Pearson and Johnny Murphy combine to pitch a 5-hitter, winning 5–1.

9th Carl Hubbell staves off a Yankee sweep with a 6-hit, 7–3 victory. The Giants score 6 runs in the 2nd inning.

10th Lefty Gomez wins again, and the Yankees wrap up the Series. Gomez himself knocks in the winning run in the 4–2 clincher. It is a record 5th WS win, without a loss, for Gomez. Another record comes when the Yankees complete the Series without an error.

15th Boston Bees manager Bill McKechnie signs a contract to lead Cincinnati.

The Yankees release Tony Lazzeri who later signs as a player-coach with the Chicago Cubs.

20th Ossie Vitt, the highly successful manager of the Newark Bears (IL), becomes the new manager of the Cleveland Indians, replacing Steve O'Neil.

25th Casey Stengel is signed to manage the Boston Bees.

NOVEMBER

2nd AL batting champ Charlie Gehringer is named MVP by the BBWAA.

9th St. Louis Cardinals Triple Crown winner Joe Medwick is named NL MVP by the BBWAA.

DECEMBER

2nd Gerald Walker, Marv Owen, and Mike Tresh are traded by Detroit to the White Sox for Vern Kennedy, Tony Piet, and Dixie Walker.

6th It is announced that Ford Frick has been reelected president of the NL for 3 years.

7th Five of baseball's pioneers are added to the Hall of Fame: Connie Mack, John McGraw, Morgan Bulkeley, Ban Johnson, and George Wright.

The NL extends permission for night baseball but the AL refuses to permit arc light games.

The Red Sox acquire the contract of 19-year-old Ted Williams from San Diego (PCL). He will not report to Boston until 1939.

1938

JANUARY

18th Grover Cleveland Alexander is elected to the Baseball Hall of Fame, the only player to get the required 75 percent of the BBWAA votes.

19th Larry MacPhail is announced as the new general manager of the Brooklyn Dodgers.

FEBRUARY

22nd The Cardinals sign Texas Christian University All-American football star and Washington Redskins quarterback Sammy Baugh as an infielder. He will be assigned first to Columbus and then Rochester.

MARCH

6th Brooklyn's Larry MacPhail buys Dolph Camilli, slugging Phillie 1B, for $45,000.

23rd Judge Landis frees 74 Cardinal minor leaguers, among them Pete Reiser, in yet another attempt to halt the cover-up he perceived the farm system caused. MacPhail makes a pact with Branch Rickey to take the unknown player and swap him back in the future, but Reiser's ability is too great to hide.

27th White Sox SS Luke Appling, sliding into 2nd in an exhibition game against the Cubs, breaks his leg and will miss almost half the season.

APRIL

3rd Goose Goslin, released by Detroit, returns for his 3rd stint with the Senators.

15th The Dodgers buy OF Ernie Koy from the Yankees.

16th Dizzy Dean is sold by the Cardinals to the Chicago Cubs. The Cubs pay $200,000 and send P Curt Davis and Clyde Shoun to St. Louis. The Cardinals also buy Tuck Stainback from the Cubs for $15,000.

19th In the top of the first inning at Philadelphia, Dodger Ernie Koy homers in his first ML at bat. In the bottom of the inning, leadoff man Emmett Mueller also hits a HR in his first time up in the ML.

20th Bob Feller pitches the first of 12 career one-hitters, beating the Browns 9–0.

21st The Dodgers Tot Pressnell shuts out the Phillies 9–0 in his first ML start.

24th Goose Goslin's pinch-hit HR is the 5th of his career, for a new AL record, but the Yankees beat the Senators 4–3.

30th Aided by grand slams by Gene Moore and Harl Maggert, the Bees beat the Phillies 16–11.

Pittsburgh 3B Bill Brubaker sets a modern ML record with 4 errors in a game with Cincinnati.

MAY

2nd Pinky Higgins equals the 2-day-old ML mark for errors by a 3B, making 4 for Boston against Philadelphia.

University of California All-American football star Sam Chapman signs with the Athletics for a $8,500 bonus.

The Giants announce that 2B Burgess Whitehead is out for the season following a nervous breakdown.

3rd Lefty Grove defeats the Tigers 4–3 in 10 innings for the first of a record 20 consecutive victories at his home field, Fenway Park in Boston. He will not lose there until May 12, 1941.

5th Harold Kelleher of the Phillies faces 16 batters in the 6th inning, as the Cubs score 12 runs. Both marks are NL records off one hurler in a single inning. The Cubs win 21–2 with Joe Marty tallying 4 runs, 4 RBI, and 4 hits.

6th OF Bob Seeds of the Newark Bears (IL) hits 4 HRs in succession and drives in 12 runs against Buffalo. Tomorrow he will slam 3 more. His 7 HRs in the 2–day barrage account for 17 RBI and 30 total bases.

18th After Bobo Newsom equals the AL record with 6 consecutive strikeouts, Joe DiMaggio hits his 2nd HR of the game, and Newsom and the Browns lose to New York 11–7.

21st The power-laden Yankees give little support to P Spud Chandler, but he hits a HR in the 8th to gain a 1–0 victory over Thornton Lee and the White Sox.

22nd The Dodgers announce contracts to install lights at Ebbets Field. The first night game will be played there on June 15th.

30th The largest crowd in Yankee Stadium history, 83,533, sees Red Ruffing end Lefty Grove's 8-game winning streak in a 10–0 victory over the Red Sox. Six thousand fans are turned away, and 511 are given refunds because there is no place to sit.

Rudy York hits his 3rd grand slam of the month, as the Tigers beat the Browns 10–9 in the first game of a holiday pair.

31st Lou Gehrig plays his 2,000th consecutive game.

JUNE

3rd NL President Ford Frick orders the May 14th game at Sportsman's Park replayed, upholding the Reds protest of the Cardinals' 7–6, 10-inning win. Dusty Cooke's disputed triple is ruled a HR for the Reds OF. One umpire had signaled Cooke's hit a HR, and Cooke slowed down, only to be tagged out.

Bill Lee of the Cubs blanks the Bees for his 3rd straight shutout, and Chicago moves to within 1½ games of the Giants, who lose their 4th straight to the Pirates.

5th The Cubs take first place, beating the Phillies while the Reds top the Giants.

6th The Reds get Wally Berger from the Giants for Alex Kampouris.

7th Umpire Bill McGowan orders Cleveland P Johnny Allen to cut off part of a shirt sleeve which dangles as he pitches, distracting the batter. Allen refuses and walks off the mound. He is fined $250, and the shirt later makes its way to the Hall of Fame museum in Cooperstown, NY.

8th New York regains the lead with a double win at Wrigley Field.

10th Red Sox rookie P Bill Lefebvre homers in his first ML at bat, and only plate appearance for the season, off Monty Stratton of the White Sox, but Lefebvre is hammered by the White Sox for a 15–2 loss. He is the first AL player to homer in his only at bat, and it will be his only ML HR.

11th Cincinnati lefthander Johnny Vander Meer pitches a no-hitter against Boston, winning 3–0.

Vander Meer, in his first full season, strikes out 4 to increase his league-leading total to 56.

Cardinals OF Terry Moore sustains a concussion after crashing into a wall at Sportsman's Park.

12th The A's beat the Browns 8–3, as Bob Johnson bats in all the runs with 3 HRs and a single.

13th Philadelphia's Bucky Walters is sold to the Reds for $55,000 plus players Virgil Davis and Al Hollingsworth.

15th Johnny Vander Meer stuns baseball by pitching his 2nd successive no-hitter, defeating the Dodgers 6–0, as Brooklyn plays the first night game ever at Ebbets Field. In front of 38,748 fans, including spectator Babe Ruth, Vandy strikes out 7 and walks 8, including 3 walks in the 9th. A force at home and a fly ball end the game. In a pregame event, Ernie Koy, with a 10-yard start, beats Olympic champion Jesse Owens in the 100-yard dash.

16th Jimmie Foxx is walked a record 6 consecutive times by Browns pitchers, as the Red Sox win 12–8.

18th Babe Ruth is signed as a Dodgers coach for the rest of the season. He is in uniform for batting demonstrations the following day.

19th The Reds Johnny Vander Meer extends his string of hitless innings to 21⅔ before Debs Garms singles for Boston in the 4th.

21st Red Sox 3B Pinky Higgins extends his consecutive-hit string to 12, with 8 hits in a doubleheader with Detroit. He will strike out against Vern Kennedy in his first at bat the following day.

22nd Chicago's Hank Steinbacher gets 6 hits in 6 at bats as the White Sox pound Washington 16–3.

26th Carl Hubbell wins his 200th game, as the Giants beat the Cubs and stretch their lead over the 2nd-place Reds to 2 games.

30th The Phillies play their final game in the Baker Bowl, losing 14–1 to the Giants. They will play future games in A's-owned Shibe Park.

JULY

1st Dodgers C Babe Phelps fractures the thumb on his throwing hand for the 2nd time this year.

6th The NL wins the 6th All-Star Game 4–1, with the aid of fine pitching and 4 AL errors. Starter Johnny Vander Meer gets the win.

9th Carl Hubbell is routed when Boston's Tony Cuccinello, Max West, and Elbie Fletcher hit successive 4th-inning HRs.

11th The Dodgers buy former ML hurler Whitlow Wyatt from Milwaukee (American Association).

12th The Pirates take the NL lead for the first time, beating the Cubs for their 12th straight win.

15th Terry Moore returns to the Cardinal lineup following his June 11th concussion. He gets 3 hits to help St. Louis snap an 8-game losing streak.

20th Johnny Mize of the Cardinals has 3 HRs in a game for the 2nd time this season, in a game against the Giants.

C Gabby Hartnett replaces Charlie Grimm as manager of the 3rd-place Cubs.

25th Cleveland's Johnny Allen has his 12-game win streak snapped by the Red Sox.

27th Hank Greenberg of the Tigers, who had hit HRs his last 2 at bats the day before, homers his first 2 times up to tie the ML record of 4 in a row.

29th In a postgame radio interview with Bob Elson, Jake Powell of the Yankees will make headlines with remarks about "beating up niggers and then throwing them in jail" as part of his off-season duties as a policeman. For the statements, Judge Landis suspends Powell for 10 days.

New York's Spud Chandler pitches 15 innings as the Yankees beat the White Sox 7–3.

AUGUST

1st Al Munro Elias, founder of the Elias Sports Bureau and for many years the official statistician of the NL and IL, dies in New York City at age 67.

2nd Larry MacPhail has official baseballs dyed dandelion yellow, and they are used in the first game of a doubleheader between the Dodgers and Cardinals at Ebbets Field. The Dodgers win 6–2, but Johnny Mize hits one of Freddie Fitzsimmons's knuckleballs for the first "yellow" HR.

5th Forty-year-old Browns P Fred "Cactus" Johnson wins his first ML game since 1923. He won 252 minor leagues games in his career.

6th Mickey Cochrane is fired as Detroit manager.

Former AL P George Pipgras joins the league's umpiring staff.

Cincinnati has only one assist in a game with the Dodgers, tying the ML record held by 4 clubs.

18th When Detroit's Billy Rogell walks his first time up, it is his 7th consecutive base on balls, a new AL record.

Carl Hubbell is forced to leave the mound in a 5–3 loss to the Dodgers when he experiences sharp elbow pains in his pitching arm.

20th Lou Gehrig hits a first-inning grand slam, the 23rd and last of his career for a still-standing record. It comes off Buck Ross in an 11–3 victory over the A's.

Indians C Frank Pytlak and C Hank Helf break the all-time altitude mark by catching baseballs dropped from the 706-foot Cleveland Terminal Tower.

22nd Carl Hubbell has an arm operation for bone chips in his elbow and is finished for the season.

24th Virgil Trucks strikes out his 418th batter—the highest season total in organized ball—for Andalusia in an Alabama-Florida League game.

25th St. Louis Browns' George McQuinn's 34-game hitting string is stopped 7 short of George Sisler's AL record.

27th Joe DiMaggio has 3 triples in the first game of a doubleheader with Cleveland, an 8–7 win in New York. Monte Pearson has a no-hitter in the 2nd game, winning his 10th straight game, 13–0. The Yankees, playing their 6th successive doubleheader, increase their AL lead to 12 games.

28th On Connie Mack Day at Shibe Park, the A's win a doubleheader from the White Sox, setting a league record by playing their 7th successive twin bill in 8 days.

SEPTEMBER

3rd Rudy York of the Tigers hits his 4th grand slam, tying the ML season record.

5th C Babe Phelps of the Dodgers breaks a bone in his throwing hand for the 3rd time this season.

9th Lou Gehrig plays his 2,100th consecutive game and has 4 hits to bring his average over .300.

10th Jimmie Foxx of the Red Sox hits 2 HRs in a game for the 9th time this season, breaking a record held by Babe Ruth and Hack Wilson.

11th Frank Frisch is fired as Cardinals manager, and Cuban-born coach Mike Gonzalez takes charge.

13th A special committee names Alexander Cartwright to Baseball's Hall of Fame for originating the sport's basic concepts. Henry Chadwick, inventor of the box score and the first baseball writer, is also honored.

15th Pirates P Jim Tobin puts Mel Ott in the record book, hitting him with a pitch 3 times. Tobin wins 7–2.

Brothers Lloyd and Paul Waner of the Pirates hit consecutive HRs off Cliff Melton in the 5th inning at the Polo Grounds.

18th Although they drop a doubleheader to the Browns, the Yankees clinch the pennant.

22nd Bill Lee of the Cubs pitches his 4th consecutive shutout, matching the feat of Ed Reulbach (1908) and Grover Alexander (1911).

The Pirates take 2 from the Dodgers and remain in first place by 3½ games.

23rd The Cubs take 2 from the Phillies while the Reds trim the Pirates in 12 innings, cutting Pittsburgh's lead to 2 games.

27th Hank Greenberg again hits 2 HRs, extending his record to 11 times in the same season. They are the last he will hit this season, as he falls 2 short of Ruth's 1927 record of 60.

With the Pirates 1½ game up on the Cubs, Dizzy Dean shuts out the Bucs for 8 innings. In the 9th Bill Lee relieves Dean, and the Cubs win 2–1.

28th Cubs manager Gabby Hartnett hits the "homer in the gloaming" against Mace Brown in the bottom of the 9th to break a 5–5 tie and put the Cubs in first place ahead of the Pirates. With 2 outs and none on base, the umpires intended to call the game because of darkness after Hartnett's turn at bat.

30th Jimmie Wilson resigns as manager of the Phillies. He will be replaced by Doc Prothro.

OCTOBER

1st The Cubs clinch the pennant, beating the Cards in the 2nd game of a twin bill while the Reds beat the Pirates.

2nd Bob Feller sets a ML strikeout record by fanning 18 Tigers. At one point Feller has 6 straight strikeouts yet loses 4–1 to Harry Eisenstat's 4-hitter.

Bobo Newsom wins his 20th game for the 7th-place Browns.

5th Bill Dickey ties a WS record with 4 hits, as Red Ruffing pitches the Yankees to a 3–1 win in the Series opener at Wrigley Field.

6th Lefty Gomez sets a record with his 6th WS victory without a loss, defeating the Cubs 6–3.

8th The Series moves to Yankee Stadium, and New York rolls to its 3rd straight win, with Monte Pearson beating Clay Bryant 5–2. Bill Dickey and Joe Gordon homer.

9th The Yankees become the first team to win 3 successive World Championships, defeating the Cubs by a score of 8–3, as Red Ruffing wins his 2nd game and the Yankees sweep.

10th Burleigh Grimes is dismissed as Dodgers manager. Leo Durocher will be named as his replacement 2 days later.

NOVEMBER

1st NL batting champ Ernie Lombardi is named MVP by the BBWAA. Chicago P Bill Lee is runner-up.

2nd Jimmie Foxx is voted MVP of the AL for the 3rd time, with Yankees C Bill Dickey 2nd in the voting.

6th The 3 DiMaggio brothers play together for the first time, making up an outfield for an all-star team in a West Coast charity game.

The St. Louis Cardinals hire Ray Blades to manage the team in 1939.

7th Fred Haney is signed to manage the St. Louis Browns.

28th The White Sox 25-year-old pitching star Monty Stratton has his leg amputated following a hunting accident.

DECEMBER

6th The Giants trade Dick Bartell, Hank Leiber, and Gus Mancuso to the Cubs for Bill Jurges, Frank Demaree, and Ken O'Dea.

Larry MacPhail ends an agreement with the Yankees and Giants to ban broadcasts in the New York area and sells the radio rights of the Dodgers games to Wheaties.

11th The Giants get slugger Zeke Bonura from Washington for $20,000 and 2 minor league players.

13th Fred Frankhouse returns to the Boston Bees, and Joe Stripp goes to Brooklyn in a player swap. In a separate transaction, the Dodgers send Buddy Hassett and Jimmy Outlaw to the Bees for Gene Moore and Ira Hutchinson.

14th The major leagues agree on a standard ball but disagree on increasing rosters from 23 to 25 players. Judge Landis will decide on 25. The NL grants Cincinnati its season opener a day before the rest of the league in recognition of baseball's 100th anniversary and the 1869 Red Stockings being the first professional team. The AL permits Cleveland and Philadelphia to play night games. Will Harridge is elected to a 10-year-term as AL president.

1939

JANUARY

13th   Yankee owner Colonel Jacob Ruppert dies.

17th   Ed Barrow is elected president to succeed Colonel Ruppert.

24th   George Sisler, Eddie Collins, and Willie Keeler are elected to the Baseball Hall of Fame by the BBWAA.

MARCH

22nd   Pete Reiser, 0-for-3 yesterday against the Yankees, starts his 2nd spring training game for the Dodgers. He homers in his first at bat against the Cardinals, and follows with a walk and 2 singles. He will have 10 straight hits before striking out 3 times against the Yankees Orel Hildebrand on the 28th. When Jack Haley relieves Hildebrand, Reiser hits a HR off him. Reiser will go north with Brooklyn and play in an April 15th exhibition against the Yankees in Ebbets Field before being farmed out to Elmira.

APRIL

20th   A minor league attendance record is set at Jersey City as 45,112 see the Giants farm team play Newark (International League).

The Red Sox show off rookie Ted Williams in the opener in New York. He collects a double off Red Ruffing, who wins 2–0. Gehrig goes hitless in the only game featuring the 2 great sluggers. Other notables in what will become a historic box score include Joe DiMaggio, Bill Dickey, Jimmie Foxx, Joe Cronin, Bobby Doerr, and Lefty Grove.

23rd   Chicago's Marv Owen equals a ML record with 4 doubles, as the White Sox trounce the Browns 17–4.

29th   In the 7th game of the season, Joe DiMaggio makes a sharp turn while fielding a liner against the Senators, and tears muscles in his right foot. The Yankees lose the game and DiMaggio will miss the next 35 games.

MAY

1st   The White Sox and Cubs play a benefit game for Monty Stratton at Comiskey Park and raise a purse of almost $30,000.

2nd   Lou Gehrig voluntarily benches himself "for the good of the team." His consecutive-game string stops at 2,130. Babe Dahlgren, his replacement, has a HR and double, as the Yankees rout Detroit 22–2.

3rd   Washington 1B Jimmy Wasdell makes 4 errors to equal the ML mark.

4th   Executive vice president Larry MacPhail is elected president of the Brooklyn Dodgers.

5th   The A's Sam Chapman hits for the cycle. Tomorrow he will homer in his first 2 at bats.

8th   Phil Cavarretta of the Cubs breaks his leg sliding.

Chuck Klein hits a pinch triple with the bases loaded off the Reds Johnny Vander Meer, and the Phils win 8–7.

10th   Bill Klem, behind the plate at the Reds game in Philadelphia, celebrates his 35th anniversary as a NL umpire.

Phillies rookie C Dave Coble catches a ball dropped from the 521-foot-high Philadelphia City Hall.

11th   The Yankees take over first place, and remain there the rest of the season.

13th   In a 10-player deal, Bobo Newsom goes from the St. Louis Browns, with Beau Bell, Red Kress, and Jim Walkup, to Detroit for Vern Kennedy, Bob Harris, George Gill, Roxie Lawson, Chet Laabs, and Mark Christman. It is one of the biggest trades of the 1930s.

16th   The first AL night game is played at Shibe Park, with Cleveland beating the A's 8–3 in 10 innings.

17th   The first baseball game ever televised, Princeton against Columbia at Baker Field, Columbia's home field, is seen by a handful of viewers via W2XBS in New York City. Bill Stern announces, as Princeton wins 2–1 in 10 innings. The 2nd game of the doubleheader is not televised.

Brooklyn and Chicago play a 19-inning 9–9 tie game at Wrigley Field.

Boston Bees P Fred Frankhouse beans Harry Craft of the Reds and is accused of throwing spitballs.

23rd P Boots Poffenberger is suspended by the Dodgers and fined $400 for breaking training rules.

26th Cincinnati takes over first place and holds the lead for the rest of the season.

27th Charlie Gehringer hits for the cycle against the Browns.

28th Robert Joyce, who gave up 2 HRs to George Selkirk yesterday, relieves for the A's. Selkirk hits 2 more HRs off Joyce, giving him 4 HRs in 4 at bats against the same pitcher in 2 successive games.

29th The Cubs get Claude Passeau from the Phillies for Kirby Higbe, Joe Marty, and Ray Harrell.

30th In an attempt to spruce up their appearance, NL umpires wear white gabardine trousers with blue jackets.

JUNE

5th The Philadelphia A's sign Duke University All-American running back Eric Tipton.

7th In his first at bat since April 29th, Joe DiMaggio triples to pace the Yankees to a 5–2 win over the White Sox at Comiskey Park.

12th The greatest gathering of members and future inductees of the Baseball Hall of Fame assembles in Cooperstown, NY, for the dedication of the museum. A 6-inning game at Doubleday Field presents lineups studded with players who will be elected in the future, as Babe Ruth, Ty Cobb, Honus Wagner, Walter Johnson, Grover Alexander, Nap Lajoie, George Sisler, Eddie Collins, Tris Speaker, Cy Young, and Connie Mack accept their plaques.

14th Veteran OF Earl Averill is swapped by Cleveland to Detroit for Harry Eisenstat and cash.

18th Dizzy Dean of the Cubs, trying to regain his old form, beats Brooklyn 1–0 on Gabby Hartnett's HR.

21st The New York Yankees announce Lou Gehrig's retirement, based on the report that he has amyotrophic lateral sclerosis. The 36-year-old star will remain with the team as captain.

25th Cleveland batters Ben Chapman, Hal Trosky, and Jeff Heath homer in the 7th inning to tie a ML record, while beating Philadelphia 8–4.

27th The Dodgers and Bees play a 23-inning, 2–2 game at Boston, called on account of darkness after 5 hours and 15 minutes. Whit Wyatt pitches 16 innings for the Dodgers.

28th The Yankees hit 8 HRs in the first game of a doubleheader with the A's, and 5 more in the nightcap. Both are ML records, as is the 53 total bases in a doubleheader. Joe DiMaggio, Babe Dahlgren, and Joe Gordon each hit 3 HRs. The Yankees win the opener 23–2 and take the nightcap 10–0.

JULY

2nd In a doubleheader with the Dodgers before 51,435 at the Polo Grounds, the fireworks start 2 days early. The Dodgers take a uneventful opener 3–2, but in the 4th inning of the nitecap, Dodger player-manager Leo Durocher ends the inning by grounding into a DP and spikes 1B Zeke Bonura as he crosses the bag. Bonura takes off after Durocher, chases him down the RF line, and throws his mitt at him. He finally wrestles him to the ground. Both players are ejected, and the Giants go on to win 6–4. To Bonura's charge of intentional spiking, the Lip retorts, "If that big clown hadn't got his foot in my way, I wouldn't have been close to him."

3rd Cleveland's Ben Chapman ties the modern ML record with 3 triples, as Bob Feller notches his 13th victory 4–2.

Johnny Mize equals a NL record with 4 extra-base hits—double, triple, and 2 HRs—in the Cards' 5–3 win over the Cubs.

4th A tearful Lou Gehrig tells 61,808 fans at Yankee Stadium, "I consider myself the luckiest man on the face of the earth," Gehrig's uniform number 4 is retired, the first ML player so honored.

The Red Sox's Jim Tabor hits 4 HRs as Boston sweeps Philadelphia 17–7 and 18–12. Three of his HRs, including a record-tying 2 grand slams, come in the nightcap. He totals 19 bases and 11 RBI in the 2 slugfests.

5th Yankees rookie P Atley Donald wins his 10th game without a loss.

7th   Sacramento (PCL) beats San Francisco 5–4 in an exhibition game played inside Folsom Prison.

9th   The Red Sox win 4–3 and 5–3 to sweep a 5-game series in Yankee Stadium. The Yankee lead is now 6½ games. Joe Cronin drives in runs in both games, giving him 12 games in a row with RBI.

11th   With another Yankee-dominated lineup, the AL defeats the NL 3–1 in the 7th All-Star Game, at Yankee Stadium. Cincinnati OF Ival Goodman fractures his shoulder diving for a ball.

14th   The Yankees tie the AL record with only one assist, as Ruffing wins 8–3 over the Tigers.

15th   A disputed call on a fly ball down the LF foul line at the Polo Grounds touches off a melee in which the Giants Billy Jurges and umpire George Magerkurth spit at each other. Both will be fined $150 and suspended for 10 days. NL President Ford Frick announces that 2-foot screens are to be installed inside all foul poles to prevent future arguments. The Al eventually also adopts the rule. The Giants lose 8–4 to the Reds and will add another 8 in a row to take them out of contention.

16th   Bees All-Star SS Eddie Miller collides with teammate OF Al Simmons and fractures a bone in his ankle. He will be out for the season.

22nd   A Boston Bees fan, outraged when Al Lopez drops a pop foul, his 2nd and the team's 7th of the game, jumps from the stands to punch the Boston catcher.

23rd   The Dodgers use the new yellow-colored baseball again, but the Cardinals see it better in a 12–0 win.

24th   The Detroit Tigers release oft-injured Dixie Walker. He signs with Brooklyn, with whom he will have his most productive year.

25th   Unbeaten rookie Atley Donald wins his 12th in a row for the Yankees, beating the Browns 5–1.

With the score tied 3–3, Cleveland scores 9 runs and Philadelphia 5 in a record-setting 9th inning.

Salisbury's (Eastern Shore League) Count Henri S. "Hank" Bertrand de la Vigne, known as the only titled pitcher in baseball, wins his 11th of the year, beating Milford 8–0 and striking out 11. The Count will be 14–9 for the year, but he will never make it to the majors.

31st   The Cardinals, partial to MacPhail's yellow-dyed baseballs, use them at Sportsman's Park to beat the Dodgers 5–2.

The Pirates buy baseball's tallest player, 6'9" P Johnny Gee from Syracuse (IL).

AUGUST

3rd   Veteran C Joe Sprinz of the San Francisco Seals (PCL) tries to break the altitude record for a catch as a stunt at the Treasure Island Exhibition. A ball is dropped 800 feet from a blimp and hits him in the face. He suffers a compound fracture of the jaw and loses several teeth.

4th   Mike Kreevich of the Chicago White Sox equals the ML record by grounding into 4 successive DPs against the Washington Senators.

13th   The Giants hit 3 successive HRs in the 4th inning, with Joe Moore, Alex Kampouris, and P Bill Lohrman connecting. The Giants add 4 more HRs in the game to beat the Phils 11–2.

The Yankees beat the A's 21–0 to equal the ML record for lopsided shutouts. Joe DiMaggio and Babe Dahlgren each have 2 HRs, one each inside the park. Red Ruffing collects 4 hits along with the victory.

16th   The Giants suspend 2B Burgess Whitehead, who will show up the next day in full uniform at Yankee Stadium and ask to work out. Yankee manager Joe McCarthy refuses. Whitehead rejoins the Giants a few days later, but he will be suspended again in mid-September after leaving the team.

25th   Red Rolfe scores for the Yankees in his 18th consecutive game, giving him a total of 30 runs.

26th   The first ML baseball game is telecast from Ebbets Field as the Reds play the Dodgers in a double-header. Red Barber broadcasts the game over W2XBS. The Dodgers take the first game 6–2, and the Reds take the 2nd 5–1.

28th   Cleveland OF Jeff Heath punches a taunting fan leaning over the railing, but the umpires miss the incident and he goes unpunished.

SEPTEMBER

2nd   Nine players hit homers, as the Giants beat the Dodgers 10–6 in the opener of a doubleheader at the

Polo Grounds, falling one short of the record for two teams in one game set in 1923.

3rd With the Sunday curfew impending, the Yankees stall to avoid a loss in Boston. Irate Fenway fans litter the field with cushions and debris. Umpire Cal Hubbard forfeits the game to the Yankees, but AL President Will Harridge subsequently overrules him and fines the Yankees for their tactics.

4th After Labor Day games, the Reds lead the Cards by 4 games. In the AL, the Yankees are 14½ ahead.

8th Twenty-year-old Bob Feller becomes the youngest 20th-century pitcher to win 20 games, as Cleveland beats St. Louis 12–1.

9th Jimmie Foxx is operated on for appendicitis, and will be out for the season. His 35 HRs will still win the title.

16th The New York Yankees clinch their 4th successive pennant with a win over Detroit.

17th The Dodgers pull within one game of the 3rd-place Cubs, taking 2 at Wrigley Field. The yellow-dyed ball is used in the first game.

19th Ted Williams hits a HR off Thornton Lee, one of 31 HRs he will hit in his rookie season. Williams will homer off Thornton's son, Ron Lee, 21 years later.

21st The NL announces that for the first time in the 20th century, games will be transferred from one city to another. The Dodgers' doubleheader in Philadelphia will be moved to Brooklyn in an effort to top one million paid attendance.

23rd Brooklyn 3B Cookie Lavagetto goes 6-for-6. Brooklyn beats Philadelphia 22–4.

24th OF Johnny Cooney of the Boston Bees, playing at the Polo Grounds, hits his first HR after 15 years as P/OF in the ML. Tomorrow he will repeat the feat, hitting his last HR in what will be a 20-year career.

27th The hometown White Sox play the first "day-night" doubleheader against Cleveland, but lose both games 5–2 and 7–5. Fans are charged separate admissions for each game.

28th Cincinnati clinches the pennant with Paul Derringer defeating 2nd-place St. Louis 5–3.

30th White Sox reliever Clint Brown sets a ML record with his 61st relief appearance.

OCTOBER

3rd Frank Frisch abandons the broadcasting booth to return to managing, signing for 2 years with the Pirates.

4th The WS, with the Yankees as heavy favorites, begins in New York. The pitching of Red Ruffing for New York and Paul Derringer for Cincinnati produces a tense, low-scoring duel that is tied 1–1 until the last of the 9th, when Yankees C Bill Dickey singles home the winning run.

5th The Yankees P Monte Pearson does not allow a base hit until one out in the 8th. The Reds are shut out 4–0. Babe Dahlgren hits a HR and double.

7th The Series resumes at Crosley Field, and Yankee power proves too much for the Reds. Bump Hadley pitches well enough in relief of Lefty Gomez to wrap up a 7–3 victory. Yankees OF Charlie Keller hits 2 HRs.

8th In the 10th inning of game 4, the Reds make 3 errors and watch in shock as the Yankees run wild. The inning is climaxed by Joe DiMaggio's slide across the plate left unguarded by Ernie Lombardi, who was stunned by a kick in the groin by the preceding runner, Charlie Keller. The Yankees sweep the Reds and win their 4th straight World Championship.

11th Bucky Harris signs to manage Washington again.

17th Bucky Walters is voted NL MVP by the BBWAA, with Johnny Mize 2nd.

24th The AL MVP is Joe DiMaggio, with Jimmie Foxx the runner-up, in the BBWAA poll.

NOVEMBER

12th The youngest of the 3 DiMaggio brothers, Dom, is bought by the Boston Red Sox from San Francisco (PCL).

P Victor Starfin wins his 42nd game in a 96-game season, leading the Yomiuri Giants to the pennant, setting a post-1900 world record for season victories that will be equaled (by Kazuhisa Inao in 1961) but never broken. Starfin, the 6'4" son of Russian immigrants, was exempt from the military call-up of able-bodied Japanese, and from 1936-55 he won 303 games, the first in Japanese baseball to top the 300 mark. He is the only non-Japanese player in the Japanese baseball Hall of Fame.

29th Judge Landis fines Brooklyn, Detroit, and the St. Louis farm club, Columbus, for manipulating player contracts. He frees 7 farm hands.

DECEMBER

6th In a trade of veteran shortstops–or "worn-out shortstops," as one newspaper described it–the Cubs acquire Billy Rogell from the Detroit Tigers for Dick Bartell. Rogell, who injured his arm playing handball the previous year, will hit just .136 before hanging up his spikes. The Tigers will release "Rowdy Richard" 5 games into the 1941 season, but he will stick with the Giants until 1946.

The Braves are busy clearing their pitching staff. JimTurner goes to the Reds for 1B Les Scarsella and cash, while Johnny Lanning is sent to Pittsburgh for P Jim Tobin and cash. On December 8th, P Danny MacFaydan joins Tobin in a trade for P Bill Swift.

7th Lou Gehrig, age 36, is elected to Baseball's Hall of Fame.

8th The White Sox trade Gee Walker to the Senators for Pete Appleton and Taffy Wright. The Dodgers get Gus Mancuso and Newt Kimball from the Cubs for Al Todd.

9th Wally Moses is traded by the Philadelphia A's to Detroit for Benny McCoy and George Coffman. The deal is later voided by Judge Landis, who declares McCoy a free agent because of a Tigers cover-up. He gets a $10,000 bonus to sign with the A's.

11th The Yomiuri Giants beat the Hanshin Tigers 4–2 to clinch the Japanese league pennant. The Giants will win the pennant for the next 4 years.

1940

JANUARY

14th   Commissioner Kenesaw Landis gives free agency to 91 Detroit players and farm hands. Citing cover-ups of the movement of players within its organization, Landis hands freedom to Roy Cullenbine, Benny McCoy, Lloyd Dietz, and Steve Rachunok from the parent roster and orders $47,250 paid as compensation to 14 players. Johnny Sain is one of 23 players who will later make it to the ML. Landis's edict nullifies a deal which would have brought Wally Moses to the Tigers for Benny McCoy and George Coffman. McCoy is the plum of the emancipation, and several clubs bid for the 2B. Connie Mack keeps Moses and signs McCoy for a $45,000 bonus and 2-season contract at $10,000 a year.

FEBRUARY

15th   The Tiger roster lists Hank Greenberg as an OF. The willingness of the team's leading power hitter to switch, at a contract boost, from 1B allows manager Del Baker to find a position for Rudy York. Also on the list are Dick Bartell, traded from the Cubs for Bill Rogell, and Pinky Higgins, who has been shopped around. The 4, along with Barney McCosky and Charlie Gehringer, produce the stuff which will move the Tigers from 5th to first, although its .588 mark will be as low as that of any pennant-winner yet.

29th   The First National Bank of Chicago tries to force a sale of the White Sox by the heirs of the late Louis Comiskey. A local judge denies the effort of the club's principal lender, saying that Mrs. Grace Comiskey can keep the club for their 14-year-old son, Charles II, until he is 35.

MARCH

17th   An inter-league all-star game is played in Florida for the benefit of Finland, which has been attacked by the Soviet Union. Over $20,000 is raised, but the Finlanders give up their battle within a few days of the benefit.

APRIL

16th   Working in 47-degree weather, Bob Feller of the Cleveland Indians throws an Opening Day no-hitter against the Chicago White Sox, winning 1–0 at Comiskey Park. Rollie Hemsley has the only RBI. Edgar Smith is the losing pitcher. It is the first Opening Day no-hitter since 1909.

23rd   A flood at Crosley Field washes out a game against the St. Louis Cardinals, the first time a flood has caused the postponement of an NL game. The teams will later decide to replay the game on May 13th when both teams will be heading east from St. Louis, but they neglect to inform the NL office.

26th   Yankee Red Rolfe has 9 assists at 3B against Boston, but the Red Sox win 8–1.

27th   Rookie SS Lou Boudreau's first ML HR leads off the game against Detroit's Hal Newhouser. He adds another against Prince Hal, as Cleveland wins 4–2.

30th   Tex Carleton of the Brooklyn Dodgers, who dropped to the minors after successful hurling with the Cards and Cubs, tosses a no-hitter, blanking the Cincinnati Reds 3–0. The win is the 9th straight for Brooklyn since Opening Day, which ties a ML record. Carleton had been released by the Minneapolis Millers after the 1939 season, and Brooklyn had signed him as a free agent.

MAY

3rd   The Pirates purchase infielder Debs Garms from the Braves. His .355 will win the 1940 batting championship, although he will have only 358 at bats. Garms will drop to .264 in 1941.

7th   The Dodgers are drubbed by the Cardinals 18–2 when St. Louis totals 49 bases on 20 hits. The Cards have 13 extra base hits, 7 of them HRs. Brooklyn then becomes the first NL team to fly, going from St. Louis to Chicago on 2 planes. The Red Sox flew the same route July 30, 1936, but for reasons of cost and risk, no other teams try the airlines.

8th   The Waner brothers, Lloyd and Paul, lose their places in the Pittsburgh OF when new manager Frank Frisch acquires Vince DiMaggio for Johnny Rizzo in a trade with Cincinnati. Vince takes over CF, flanked by

Maurice Van Robays and Bob Elliott, each playing their first full season.

9th The press reports the impending sale of the Yankees by the Ruppert estate to political bigwigs Jim Farley and Jesse Jones. *The Sporting News* declares the sale will be for $4 million. The imminent sale will resurface on the front page several times during the next year, but it never happens.

10th The minor leagues start with 44 different circuits in operation. Forty-three will finish, the most ever. In 1910, 46 started and 42 completed the season.

13th In a replay of their washed-out game of April 23rd, Johnny Mize of the St. Louis Cardinals hits 3 HRs, and Bill Werber hits 4 doubles in a 14-inning, 8–8 tie with the Reds. The teams had neglected to inform the league office of the game, and no umpires were assigned to Crosley Field. Coach Jim Wilson and P Lon Warneke are pressed into service as umpires before umpire Larry Goetz, at home in Cincinnati on a day off, arrives to officiate. Warneke will later become a full-time umpire.

14th Boston's Jimmie Foxx blasts a HR off White Sox P Johnny Rigney. The ball goes over the LF roof, the longest poke in Comiskey Park history.

15th 1B Art Mahan and 2B Herman Schulte establish themselves as regulars at their positions with the Phillies. Fewer than a dozen players have been 120-or-more-game regulars in their only season in the ML, and the Phillies, again locked in last place, have 2 of them in one season. Neither Phillie will hit .250, but Schulte will top 2B in fielding.

20th Pinky Higgins of the Detroit Tigers hits 3 successive HRs in a 10–7 win over Boston at Briggs Stadium.

21st Jimmie Foxx hits a grand-slam HR for the 2nd day in a row against Detroit in an 11–8 Red Sox win.

24th The New York Giants rip the Boston Bees 8–1 in the first night game at the Polo Grounds before 22,460. Harry Gumbert is the winner.

The Cleveland Indians edge the St. Louis Browns 3–2 in the first night game at Sportsman's Park before 25,562.

JUNE

1st Dizzy Dean is sent by the Cubs to Tulsa to see if the Texas League sun can restore his arm. He will pitch moderately well and is a great ticket seller.

4th The Pirates rout the Boston Braves 14–2 in the first night game at Pittsburgh's Forbes Field.

7th With the Cardinals starting badly (14-24), owner Sam Breadon fires Ray Blades as manager. Bill Southworth is brought back from Rochester to replace him.

8th The Washington Senators tip the Chicago White Sox 1–0 in 18 innings in the first game of a doubleheader at Comiskey Park.

Carl Doyle of the Dodgers gives up 16 hits and 14 runs in 4 innings of relief, as the Reds pound out 27 hits in a 23–2 win. Doyle also manages to hit 4 Cincinnati batters in the game. He will end with 10 Reds hit-batsmen for the season, setting a bitter tone to the Cincinnati-Dodgers rivalry, which will continue through the decade.

12th Brooklyn GM Larry MacPhail perfects his OF and gets one pitcher: Joe Medwick and Curt Davis are acquired from the Cardinals for Ernie Koy, 3 minor leaguers, and $125,000.

13th Bill "Swish" Nicholson of the Cubs is the first player to homer at Cooperstown's Doubleday Field. Ted Williams of the Red Sox is the second as the two teams tie in an exhibition game.

14th Boston Bees 1B Buddy Hassett is stopped after hitting safely in 10 straight at bats. He has one walk during the 3 games in which he hits safely.

15th Harry Danning hits for the cycle, as the Giants beat visiting Pittsburgh. Danning's HR is an inside-the-park hit that lands 460 feet on the fly in front of the Giants' clubhouse. It lodges behind the Eddie Grant memorial, and CF Vince DiMaggio cannot extricate the ball in time.

16th The Cleveland players petition owner Alva Bradley to remove Oscar Vitt as manager. Bradley declines. Nevertheless, the Indians have their best month of the year, settling into first place, which they will hold until the final 2 weeks of the season.

17th Not a single assist will be recorded by any of the Boston Bee infielders in the first game of a doubleheader versus Pittsburgh.

18th Joe Medwick, in the Dodger lineup for 6 days after his trade from the Cardinals, is beaned by St. Louis P Bob Bowman at Ebbets Field in the 2nd game of a doubleheader. The Cards win in 11 innings 7–5, as Bowman is escorted from the park by policemen. Hospitalized, Medwick will return to the lineup after several days, but he is never again a major power hitter. Larry MacPhail wants Bowman banned for life. The night before, Bowman allegedly had a verbal confrontation with Medwick and Leo Durocher in a hotel elevator.

19th In a night game following the Medwick beaning, the Cards make 7 errors in an 8–3 loss to Brooklyn. Slick-fielding Cardinal SS Marty Marion makes 3 errors in the 7th inning.

23rd Billy Jurges of the Giants is hit on the head by a pitched ball thrown by Bucky Walters of the Reds. In 2nd place at the time, the Giants will go 39-61 after the loss of the SS and drop to 6th place.

JULY

4th Ab Wright of Minneapolis (AA) follows one HR in a morning game of a holiday doubleheader with 5 HRs and a triple—19 total bases—against St. Paul.

5th The Brooklyn Dodgers beat Boston 6–2 in 20 innings lasting 5 hours and 19 minutes. The 2 teams' epic marathon ties record-setters of 1920 and 1939.

10th Boston Bees OF Max West, a late replacement for Mel Ott, hits a 3-run HR in the first inning to lead the NL to a 4–0 victory over the AL in the All-Star Game at Sportsman's Park. It is the first shutout in All-Star history. Joe Cronin directs the AL when Joe McCarthy steps aside, stating he has "had the honor often enough."

14th In the aftermath of the beanball wars, Spalding advertises a batting helmet with ear flaps in *The Sporting News*. Players express no interest, but next year Brooklyn will introduce a cap liner, which some batters start to use.

Freddie Fitzsimmons of the Dodgers wins his 200th career game, a 4-hitter over Pittsburgh. Fat Freddy will win 6 games each from the Pirates and Philadelphia on the way to a 16–2 won-loss mark.

19th Buddy Rosar of the Yanks hits for the cycle; Joe Cronin will do it August 2, and Joe Gordon, September 8th.

26th New York P Spud Chandler beats the White Sox with his bat, knocking in 6 runs with a single and 2 HRs, one a grand slam off Pete Appleton. The 6 RBI ties the AL record held by Appleton, George Uhle and Wes Ferrell.

28th King Kong Keller clouts 3 HRs for the New York Yankees in a 10–9 Yanks win over Chicago in the first game of a doubleheader split.

30th Veteran Lou Finney hits so well for the Red Sox early in the season that manager Joe Cronin must make a place for him in the lineup. With rookie Dom DiMaggio joining Ted Williams and Doc Cramer in the OF, Cronin puts Finney at 1B when Jimmie Foxx volunteers to catch. The experiment lasts but a few games.

AUGUST

3rd With Ernie Lombardi hurt, Reds C Willard Hershberger is hitting .309 after taking over. However, depressed in recent weeks, Hershberger commits suicide by slashing his throat in Boston's Copley Plaza Hotel. Hershberger blamed himself for calling wrong pitches in the July 31st 5–4 loss to New York. Leading 4–1, Bucky Walters retired the first two batters in the 9th and had two strikes on each of the next four batters. But Harry Danning and Burgess Whitehead each homered with a man on. Hershberger's father had also committed suicide, in 1928.

4th Jimmie Foxx, who started as a catcher in 1925, goes behind the plate for the Red Sox to catch a 7–3 win for long-time teammate Lefty Grove. Foxx also cracks his 24th HR.

6th Rookie Sid Hudson one-hits the A's on his way to a 17-win season for the hapless Senators. Hudson pitched in Class D the year before.

7th A crowd of 53,997, an NL record for a night game, watches the Dodgers beat the Giants 8–4 under the lights at the Polo Grounds. Only Chicago and Boston are without lights in the NL.

9th The Yankees, at 51-51, seem certain to be out of the running for their 5th straight championship. However, they will go 37-15 the rest of the way and actually make the top for a few hours on September 11th. The Yanks will ultimately finish 3rd, losing 3 straight to the Browns September 15-16.

24th LF Ted Williams of the Boston Red Sox pitches the last 2 innings in a 12–1 loss to the Detroit Tigers. Williams strikes out Tiger slugger Rudy York on 3 pitches. Joe Glenn, who caught Babe Ruth's last pitching appearance in 1933, is Williams's catcher.

25th Lefty Tom George, who started in pro ball in 1907, returns to the mound for York (Interstate League) at age 54, and wins 3–2. He had been inactive for 5 years.

28th Homestead Grays (Negro League) P Ray Brown earns his 27th consecutive victory over a 2-year span when he shuts out the Baltimore Elite Giants 5–0 on a 3-hitter. The win raises his record to 12-0 for the season.

SEPTEMBER

8th In the opener of a doubleheader, Johnny Mize of the St. Louis Cardinals rips 3 consecutive HRs, his second 3-homer game of the season. For "Big John," it is number 38 through 40 HR of the year. Pittsburgh still sweeps the 2 games.

10th Former ML infielder Sam Crane, serving time for the 1930 murder of his former sweetheart and her boyfriend, starts parole proceedings.

11th In a doubleheader, the Yankees' first-game win at Cleveland puts them in first place, the only time they reach that spot. A 2nd game loss drops them out of first.

14th The United States, Hawaii, Cuba, Mexico, Nicaragua, Venezuela, and Puerto Rico meet in the 3rd annual World Amateur Baseball Championship tourney, the first championship series to feature more than 3 participants. Cuba, the host country, is the victor for the 2nd consecutive year. The initial tourney had been held in England in 1939 and was also won by the host country, Great Britain.

16th Rookie Johnny Lucadello of the St. Louis Browns hits HRs from each side of the plate versus the New York Yankees in a 16–4 Browns win. Only Wally Schang, in 1916, had accomplished the same in the AL. Mickey Mantle in 1955 will be the next AL player to do it. These are the only HRs Lucadello will hit all year.

A rhubarb at Ebbets Field results in a suspension and fine for Leo Durocher for "inciting a riot." Perhaps better known from the game is the photo showing an obese Brooklyn fan astride George Magerkurth, pummeling the veteran umpire.

Called up from the Eastern League in August, Phillies rookie Danny Litwhiler singles in both games of 7–1 and 3–2 losses to St. Louis, extending his hitting streak to 21 straight games. He will be stopped tomorrow by Whitey Moore at Cincinnati. He will hit .345 in 36 games.

18th The A's are mired deep in the cellar, but Connie Mack hits all the right buttons today. He sends 4 PHs to the plate in the 9th inning versus Detroit, and all 4 deliver hits.

The Reds clinch the NL flag, outdistancing the Dodgers and the late-rushing Cardinals. Bill McKechnie's Cincinnati team makes only 117 errors during the season, 18 less than any previous team. The .981 fielding mark is the best up to this time. The defense, plus the pitching of Bucky Walters, Paul Derringer, and reliever Joe Beggs, brings the 2nd straight NL flag to the Reds, despite multiple injuries to Ernie Lombardi. The big catcher went down again September 15th, and with Hershberger's suicide, the club turns to 39-year-old coach Jimmy Wilson for some of the backstopping. Wilson will end up as a WS hero.

21st With the Tigers, Indians, and Yankees neck-and-neck, the Tigers boost their lead to 2 games, as Schoolboy Rowe shuts out Cleveland 5–0. Rowe, seemingly washed up after anchoring the staff through Tiger championships in the mid-1930s, will finish at 16-3.

24th George Caster of the Philadelphia Athletics allows 6 HRs in one game against the Boston Red Sox. Ted Williams, Jimmie Foxx, Joe Cronin, and Jim Tabor connect in the 6th inning. Foxx's HR is his 500th.

25th Walker Cooper, recently called up from Columbus (AA), and Mort Cooper, pitching in relief, make up a brother battery in the Cards, 4–3 win over the Reds.

Bobo Newsom wins a clutch doubleheader for the Tigers, pitching 2 innings of relief in the opener against the White Sox, and going the distance in the nightcap for his 21st win.

27th Besides Bobo Newsom (21-5), Schoolboy Rowe (16-3), and Tommy Bridges (12-9), the Tigers pitching staff combines for a losing record. Needing one victory to gain the title, manager Del Baker decides to withhold Newsom and Rowe and picks Floyd Giebell, an obscure rookie just called in from Buffalo. Giebell shuts out the Indians 2–0 to beat Bob Feller, who gives up just 3 hits. Not eligible for the WS, Giebell never wins another game in the ML. During the game, unruly Cleveland fans shower the field with fruit and vegetables. At one point, a basket of green tomatoes is dropped onto Tigers C Birdie Tebbetts' head while he sits in the bullpen.

29th Johnny Rucker, a *Life* magazine cover boy at the start of the season, based on his .346 average with Atlanta and his speed afoot, never quite lives up to the ballyhoo. But this day he drives in 7 runs in 2 consecutive innings, as the Giants whip Boston 14–0.

OCTOBER

2nd The Series opens in Cincinnati, and the Reds lose 7–2, the 10th straight WS loss for a NL team. The Tigers bunch 5 singles, a walk, and an error in the 2nd off Paul Derringer to score 5 runs. Bruce Campbell adds a 2-run HR, and Bobo Newsom rations 8 hits and only one walk. Bobo's father, visiting from South Carolina, dies in a Cincinnati hotel the next morning.

3rd Bucky Walters gives the NL its first Series game victory since Carl Hubbell beat the Yankees in 1937. Jimmy Ripple's 2-run HR in the 3rd provides the margin. Walters gives up only 3 hits, but is lucky to escape a jittery first inning.

4th Detroit bombs 9 hits for 19 bases in the 7th and 8th innings off Jim Turner and successors to win 7–4 in the first game at Briggs Stadium. Tommy Bridges gives up 10 hits but goes the distance.

5th Paul Derringer, who had lost 4 WS starts going back to 1931, finally breaks his jinx. His 5-hitter and Jim Ripple's 3rd-inning double, which knocks Dizzy Trout from the mound, provide a 5–2 win.

6th Detroit regains the advantage with Bobo Newsom pitching even better than he had in the first game. Newsom's 8–0 whitewash is the first Detroit shutout in the WS since 1909.

7th Back in Cincinnati, Bucky Walters evens the Series for the Reds with a 4–0 shutout, scattering 5 hits. Walters also becomes the first pitcher in 14 years to hit a HR in the Series.

8th With only one day's rest, Bobo Newsom comes back for the Tigers and nearly has enough to win. Detroit gets an unearned run off Paul Derringer in the 3rd, and Newsom holds the Reds scoreless through 6 innings. In the 7th, however, Frank McCormick and Jimmy Ripple hit consecutive doubles, and Ripple later ambles in from 3B on Billy Myers's sac fly. Derringer gives up 7 hits in the first 6 innings but sets the Tigers down in order in the final 3 frames. Old Jimmy Wilson catches 6 of the 7 games, hits .353, and has the only SB of the Series. The Reds' share is $5,803 and the Tigers get $3,532.

NOVEMBER

5th Former Washington hurler Walter Johnson, who won 416 games for the Senators, goes down in defeat as a Republican candidate for the U.S. House of Representatives from Maryland.

11th Brooklyn's Larry MacPhail still needs a starting pitcher to make his Dodgers a threat to the Reds. He gets Kirby Higbe from the Phils for $100,000, P Vito Tamulis, and Bill Crouch.

12th Alva Bradley wouldn't fire Oscar Vitt on his players' demand during the season, but he does now. Today he hires Roger Peckinpaugh to become Cleveland boss, the 2nd hitch for Peck.

17th Jimmy Wilson gets his reward for managing the woeful Phillies in the 1930s and for his late-season role with the Reds. He becomes manager of the Cubs.

DECEMBER

4th MacPhail continues his dealing and gets his catcher. The Dodgers trade for Mickey Owen, giving Gus Mancuso and $85,000 to the Cardinals.

The Cubs swap SS Bobby Mattick and OF Jim Cleason to the Reds for SS Billy Myers.

6th The major and minor leagues agree that players taken into the military will not count against roster limits.

10th A curious rule that was designed to "break up the Yankees" is continued by the AL, a rule which prohibits the team winning the championship from trading with any other club.

12th Washington sends Gee Walker to the Red Sox for Doc Cramer. Walker is then packed off to

Cleveland with P Jim Bagby, OF and C Gene Desautels for C Frank Pytlak, Odell Hale and P Joe Dobson.

20th Connie Mack acquires controlling interest in the Athletics from the Shibe family at the price of $42,000.

24th Merry Christmas to Ben Chapman from the Senators who ship him to Cleveland for P Joe Krakauskas.

1941

JANUARY

21st Bob Feller signs with the Indians for a reported $30,000.

31st Paul Waner, released by Pittsburgh in December 1940, signs with Brooklyn.

FEBRUARY

8th The Tigers release OF Earl Averill and sign OF Hoot Evers, out of the University of Illinois.

25th The Yankees sell Babe Dahlgren, the man who took over 1B from Lou Gehrig in 1939, to the Braves.

MARCH

8th Phils P Hugh Mulcahy is the first ML player drafted into military service in W W II.

19th The Giants sign Paul Dean, recently released by the Cardinals. He will go 4-4, and the Giants will give him his release.

APRIL

14th The season opens in Washington, with writers for *The Sporting News* selecting Cincinnati to repeat in the NL and Cleveland to win the AL.

15th Cubs SS Lou Stringer makes 4 errors in his debut, but the Chicago beat the Pittsburgh Pirates 7–4 behind Claude Passeau and a clutch HR by Bill Nicholson.

20th The Dodgers start to wear liners in their caps as a cautious response to the numerous beanball wars of 1940 that hospitalized Joe Medwick, Billy Jurges, and others. The liners are thin enough to be hardly noticeable, but most ML players disdain the protection.

A syndicate of 12 Bostonians buys 73 percent of the Braves, formerly the Bees, for $350,000 from the Charles F. Adams estate.

26th The Chicago Cubs are the first team to install an organ. With Roy Nelson at the keyboard, the Cubs hit sour notes, losing 6–2 to the St. Louis Cardinals.

MAY

3rd Hank Gornicki of the St. Louis Cardinals pitches a one-hitter in his big-league debut, beating the Philadelphia Phillies 6–0. Stan Benjamin's single is the lone hit.

5th Bobo Newsom and the Tigers trounce the Yankees 10–1 in Detroit. Joe DiMaggio is held hitless and has gone 7-for-43 in his last 12 games.

6th The Dodgers snag veteran 2B Billy Herman from the Cubs for OF Charlie Gilbert, IF Johnny Hudson, and cash.

7th The AL MVP of 1940, Hank Greenberg of the Tigers, plays his last game before entering the army. A few days later OF Joe Gallagher of the Dodgers is drafted. No other regular ML player will be drafted during the season, but several others on training rosters will, as contemporary writers phrase it, "join the colors."

14th Browns hurlers walk 19 Athletics. Starter Bob Harris issues 8 of the passes, but the Browns win anyway 10–5.

The Cubs finally give up on Dizzy Dean. Diz gets his release the same day that brother Paul is sent to the minors by the Giants.

15th Joe DiMaggio gets a single in 4 at bats against Ed Smith of the Chicago White Sox to start his 56-game hitting streak.

Rip Radcliff, one of the top AL batters in 1940 for the Browns, is waived to the Tigers as a result of a sudden batting decline.

17th The city of Philadelphia and the state of Pennsylvania declare a legal holiday to honor the A's manager on Connie Mack Day at Shibe Park.

20th OF Taft Wright of the Chicago White Sox doubles to drive in a run and sets an AL record by driving in at least one run in 13 consecutive games. Wright has 22 RBI in the streak, although in 6 of the games he knocked in a run without a hit.

25th Ted Williams raises his batting average over .400 for the first time during the season. His run to be the first since Bill Terry in 1930 to exceed the magic number will be marked in newspapers throughout the season, although it will often give way to the batting streak by Joe DiMaggio.

Pete Reiser hits his only career grand slam to pace the Dodgers to an 8–4 win over the Phils. Reiser's HR comes off Ike Pearson, who had beaned Pete a month earlier.

27th   With the score 1–1 and Hal Schumacher on the mound, umpire Jocko Conlan calls time. The crowd then listens for 45 minutes while President Roosevelt's radio message about the war in Europe is heard on the Polo Grounds' loudspeakers.

28th   The New York Yankees nip the Washington Senators 6–5 in the first night game at Griffith Stadium.

JUNE

1st   After losing 6 straight games in mid-May, the Dodgers begin to show the results of the trades by Larry MacPhail and Leo Durocher. They win their 9th-straight game and are well entrenched in first place.

Mel Ott's 2-run homer, the 400th of his career and his 1,500th RBI, gives the Giants a 3–2 win over the Reds.

2nd   New York Yankees 1B Lou Gehrig dies of amyotrophic lateral sclerosis at age 37 in New York. From that time on, the illness is known primarily as Lou Gehrig's Disease.

6th   The Giants use plastic batting helmets for the first time against the Pirates but lose a doubleheader to the Bucs 5–4 and 4–3.

17th   Joe DiMaggio is credited with a hit in his 30th consecutive game when an easy grounder to short bounces up and hits Luke Appling on the shoulder. Chicago beats the Yankees 8–7.

18th   The Giants play an 11-inning tie in Pittsburgh because of a regulation that states that no inning can be started after 11:50 P.M. The game is held up in the 4th inning so that the fans can listen to a broadcast of the title fight between local favorite Billy Conn and Joe Louis.

28th   White Sox rookie Don Kolloway does it all. He steals 4 bases, including 2nd, 3rd, and home in the 9th, and hits 2 HRs and a single in a 6–4 win over the Indians.

29th   Joe DiMaggio singles against Washington knuckleballer Dutch Leonard in the 6th inning in the first game of a doubleheader to tie George Sisler's AL

consecutive-game hit record of 41. In game 2 he collects a 7th-inning single off Walt Masterson to set the record at 42 games.

JULY

1st   Before 52,832 at Yankee Stadium, Joe DiMaggio leads a sweep of the Red Sox 7–2 and 9–2. The 2nd game is called after 5 innings. DiMaggio has 2 hits in the first game and one in the 2nd to tie Willie Keeler's ML batting streak of 44 games. The Yankees have 25 hits in the 2 games but fail to hit a HR in the first game, ending their AL streak of 25 consecutive games with at least one HR. The previous record, set by the Tigers in 1940, was 17 games.

2nd   Joe DiMaggio extends his consecutive-game hitting streak to 45 by hitting a HR off Boston's Dick Newsome, surpassing Willie Keeler's all-time record.

8th   At the All-Star Game at Briggs Stadium, Ted Williams, hitting .405 at the break, homers off Chicago Cubs P Claude Passeau with two out and 2 on in the 9th inning to give the AL a dramatic 7–5 victory. Williams's 4 RBI are matched by NL SS Arky Vaughan, who hits HRs in the 7th and 8th.

13th   Former ML player Eddie Mayo, playing for Los Angeles (Pacific Coast League), spits in the face of umpire Ray Snyder. PCL President W. C. Tuttle suspends Mayo for one year.

17th   In front of more than 60,000 fans at Cleveland, Joe DiMaggio's hitting streak is ended at 56 games. Indian P AL Smith and Jim Bagby, plus sensational plays by 3B Ken Keltner, stop the Yankee Clipper, but New York edges the Indians 6–5.

25th   Forty-one-year-old Lefty Grove wins his 300th game as the Boston Red Sox defeat the Cleveland Indians 10–6 before a Fenway Ladies Day crowd of 16,000. Though he will make 6 more starts, this will be Grove's last career win.

AUGUST

1st   Lefty Gomez of the New York Yankees pitches a 9–0 shutout over the St. Louis Browns despite walking 11 batters, the most ever issued in a shutout. Fifteen base runners are left stranded by the Browns.

6th   Detroit P Al Benton collects 2 sacrifices in one inning, a ML record.

15th Because of rain, the game between the Red Sox and the Senators is stopped in the 8th inning, with Washington winning 6–3. After a 40-minute wait the game is called. But because of Washington's failure to cover the field in case play is resumed, Boston manager Joe Cronin protests the game. The protest is upheld by league president Will Harridge and the forfeit goes to Boston.

19th Pittsburgh Pirates manager Frankie Frisch is ejected by umpire Jocko Conlan from the 2nd game of a doubleheader when he appears on the field with an umbrella to protest the playing conditions at Brooklyn's Ebbets Field. The rainy argument is later portrayed in a famous oil painting by artist Norman Rockwell.

20th Larry MacPhail stages a fashion show before a Ladies Day crowd at Ebbets Field. Such promotions, as well as the Dodgers pennant race, will push the home gate to over one million fans.

27th Charlie Root uses his arm and then his bat with a clutch single in the 9th inning to win his 200th game. Trailing the Cincinnati Reds 4–3, the Cubs win 6–4 with the 42-year-old Root going the route.

30th The Cardinals Lon Warneke no-hits the Cincinnati Reds 2–0 with only 3 balls hit to the outfield. It is Warneke's 15th victory of the season and, with the Dodgers' doubleheader loss to the Giants, puts St. Louis in first place by 2 percentage points.

SEPTEMBER

1st Rudy York wallops 3 HRs for the Detroit Tigers.

Dolph Camilli hits the 200th HR of his career against the Braves to put the game into extra innings. Camilli gives the Dodgers a 6–5 victory in the 15th inning with his 5th hit of the game. He will end the season with 34 HRs and be selected as the NL MVP.

4th The New York Yankees beat the Boston Red Sox 6–3 to clinch the AL pennant, the earliest date in ML history. The Yankees need only 136 games, giving them a 91-45 record.

10th Johnny Schmitz makes his ML debut and notches a victory by throwing only one pitch in the 9th inning of the Cubs 5–4 victory over the Brooklyn Dodgers.

13th The Dodgers Whit Wyatt beats the Cards Mort Cooper 1–0 in St. Louis. Dixie Walker's double in the 8th is the first Dodger hit. Walker then relays a stolen sign to Billy Herman, who singles him home.

15th After 16 scoreless innings, the Dodgers score 5 in the top of the 17th and beat the Reds 5–1. Johnny Allen pitches 15 innings for Brooklyn, and Hugh Casey wins in relief.

17th Stan Musial makes his ML debut, going 2-for-4 as the St. Louis Cardinals beat the Boston Braves. Musial, who started the season in the Western Association (Class C), will hit .426 in 12 games.

27th Ted Williams starts the day with a .401 batting average and refuses Boston manager Joe Cronin's suggestion that he sit out the season to preserve his average. Against the A's he hits one single in 4 at bats to drop his average to .3995.

You won't find the name of George Pfister in the NL records, though he appears as C for the Dodgers. The NL rules Pfister, who never signed a Brooklyn contract, is the property of Montreal (IL), and his name is removed from the box score.

28th Ted Williams collects 4 hits in 5 at bats in the 12-11 first-game victory in Philadelphia to bring his average to .404. He goes 2-for-3 in game 2 against rookie Fred Caligiuri, who beats Lefty Grove 7–1. Williams will finish the season with a .406 batting average.

A jubilant crowd at Ebbets Field watches as the Dodgers beat the Phillies 6–1 to clinch the pennant. The crowd sets a new attendance record at 1,215,253.

29th Overshadowed by the .406 mark of Ted Williams and the hitting streak of Joe DiMaggio, Jeff Heath of the Indians hits over 20 doubles, triples, and HRs during the season. The Canadian muscleman will finish with 32 doubles, 20 triples, and 24 HRs. It will be 38 years before George Brett will duplicate the feat in the AL.

A crowd estimated at one million jams downtown Brooklyn to cheer the Dodgers in a parade.

OCTOBER

1st Red Ruffing pitches the Yankees to a 3–2 win over the Dodgers at Yankee Stadium in the opening game of the WS. Joe Gordon chips in with a HR and RBI single.

2nd   Dodgers ace Whit Wyatt trims the Yankees in a 3–2 Brooklyn win.

4th   In the 7th inning of a scoreless tie, Yankees pitcher Marius Russo breaks P Fred Fitzsimmons's knee with a line drive. The Yankees score 2 in the 8th off Hugh Casey to win 2–1.

5th   With 2 out in the 9th inning, Dodger C Mickey Owen drops a 3rd strike on Tommy Henrich, which would have given Brooklyn a 4–3 victory over New York. The Yankees then rally for a 7–4 win in the 4th game of the WS.

6th   The New York Yankees top the Brooklyn Dodgers 3–1 to take the WS in 5 games. P Ernie Bonham of the Yankees retires the side on 3 pitches in the 7th inning.

NOVEMBER

25th   Lou Boudreau is named player-manager of the Cleveland Indians. Boudreau, at 24 years, 4 months, and 8 days, is the youngest manager appointed.

27th   Joe DiMaggio is named AL MVP. His 56-game hitting streak edges out Ted Williams and his .406 batting average for the award (291 votes for DiMaggio and 254 for Williams).

DECEMBER

11th   The Giants acquire Johnny Mize from the Cardinals for 3 players and $50,000.

1942

JANUARY

4th Rogers Hornsby becomes the 14th player selected to the Hall of Fame, getting 78 percent of the vote. But Frank Chance with 58 percent and Rube Waddell with 54 percent miss out.

6th Bob Feller, winner of 76 games for the Indians in 3 previous seasons, follows Hank Greenberg into the military. Feller, saying "I've always wanted to be on the winning side," enlists in the Navy and reports to Norfolk, VA, for duty.

15th President Roosevelt gives baseball the go-ahead to play despite W W II. In his famous "green light" letter FDR says, "I honestly think it would be best for the country to keep baseball going." He encourages more night baseball so that war workers may attend.

The Cubs, who had signed contracts to install lights at Wrigley Field, drop their plans because of the military needs for the material.

FEBRUARY

3rd At a special meeting of owners to discuss wartime regulations, they decide to allow 14 night games for each club, with Washington allowed 21. Two All-Star Games will be played, one with a military All-Star team. Curfews are set for night games with no inning to start after 12:50 war time.

5th In one of their best trades ever, The Braves get Tommie Holmes from the Yankees for Buddy Hassett and Gene Moore. Hassett will hit .284, then join the Navy and will not make it back to the ML. The much-travelled Moore will never play for the Yanks. Holmes, with three .300+ seasons in the IL, could not break into New York's all star outfield. In 10 seasons with the Braves he will hit over .300 and win the MVP in 1948.

7th Cincinnati sells C Ernie Lombardi to the Braves.

12th Gordon Houston, an OF with Texarkana in 1940, is the first player in organized baseball to lose his life in W W II.

19th Hal Trosky, suffering from migraine headaches that cannot be treated, retires as 1B of the Indians.

MARCH

1st Can players in the military play for the clubs if on furlough or based near a game site? Owners decide against it.

18th Two black players, Jackie Robinson and Nate Moreland, request a tryout with the Chicago White Sox during spring training at Pasadena. Manager Jimmie Dykes allows them to work out but dismisses the two.

APRIL

1st *The Sporting News* raises its price to 15 cents a copy, $7 per year.

5th The season will start with Lou Boudreau of Cleveland, Mel Ott of the Giants, and Hans Lobert of the Phillies as new managers.

14th Ted Williams opens the season with a 3-run first-inning homer at Fenway Park. He adds 2 other hits and 5 RBI, as the Red Sox beat the A's 8–3.

15th For the first time in nearly 70 years there will be no Spalding or Reach guides. *The Sporting News* takes over the role. Its first edition has some improvements but also some flaws: Additional AL pitching records are missing, and so is Lou Boudreau's entire batting record.

18th Military leaders on the Pacific Coast ask that the PCL limit crowds to 3,000.

21st Only 4 games are played in the ML, but all end in shutouts: Pirate Rip Sewell blanks the Cubs 6–0; Reds P Johnny Vander Meer beat the Cards 1–0 in 11 innings; Cleveland's Jim Bagby nips the Tigers 1–0, and the Browns Al Hollingsworth beats the White Sox 3–0.

26th Alvin Montgomery, C on the Braves training roster, is killed in an auto wreck.

30th A month after selling veteran P Bobo Newsom, who had slipped to 12-20 record after three 20-win seasons, to Washington, the Tigers sell Schoolboy Rowe to the Dodgers. The vet will win just

2 in Brooklyn before making a comeback in Philadelphia.

MAY

2nd Cleveland beats the Senators 12–3 in Washington. The win gives the Indians 13 straight victories.

13th P Jim Tobin of the Boston Braves slams 3 successive HRs to beat the Chicago Cubs at Braves Field. He had a pinch-hit homer the day before. Tobin is the only ML pitcher to accomplish this.

19th Paul Waner, now with the Boston Braves, collects his 3,000th hit off Rip Sewell of the Pittsburgh Pirates, but Bob Elliott of the Pirates hits 2 HRs to help the Pirates win 7–6 in 11 innings. Two days earlier, Waner's grounder bounced off an infielder's glove and had been ruled a hit. Waner, who did not want his 3000th hit to be a tainted one, signalled to the scorekeeper that it was an error, and the ruling was changed.

25th A pulled muscle ends a 652-game playing streak for Cincinnati 1B Frank McCormick.

28th New York's Lefty Gomez, self-described as the worst-hitting pitcher in baseball, bangs out 4 hits in pitching a 4-hit, 16–1 victory over Washington. They are his last ML hits.

31st Against the Pirates, the Reds Clyde Vollmer hits a home run on his first ML pitch, the 4th major leaguer to do so. The Reds go on to win 3–0 in this 2nd game of a doubleheader.

Before 22,000 at Griffith Stadium, Satchel Paige pitches 5 innings to defeat the Dizzy Dean All-Stars 8–1. Dean pitches just the first inning. The game a week earlier, in which Paige won 3–1 at Wrigley Field, drew 29,000. Judge Landis will prohibit a scheduled July 4th matchup because the first 2 games outdrew ML games.

JUNE

1st Jimmie Foxx crosses leagues, waived by the Red Sox to the Cubs.

Army-Navy relief games by each team are publicized war efforts by organized baseball. The game at Ebbets Field contributes $60,000 from a crowd of 43,000, but the Phillies' game at Shibe Park draws only 2,000 fans and $3,000.

2nd Red Sox star Ted Williams enlists as a Navy aviator. He will finish the season with his team as will many other players who enlist or await draft, which moves slowly despite the early discouragements of the war. Among AL regulars of 1941 who are now in the service: Johnny Rigney, Joe Grace, John Berardino, Cecil Travis, Bob Feller, Pat Mullin, Buddy Lewis, Sam Chapman, Johnny Sturm.

Ted Williams hits 5 HRs in a week, but players are bemoaning a low-voltage ball. HRs will be down for the season by more than 25 percent, and the NL will average less than 4 runs a game per team for the first time since 1920.

4th Muskogee (Western Association) OF Allen McElreath is declared permanently ineligible by minor league head George Trautman for attempting to induce a teammate to throw a game.

6th Gene Stack of the White Sox, the first player drafted from a ML roster, dies of a heart attack following an army ball game.

18th Another brawl between the Cards and the Dodgers at Ebbets Field leads to ejection and fines for Joe Medwick and Frank Crespi. The Dodgers' NL lead is 7½ games.

19th Paul Waner, now with the Braves, joins Cap Anson and Honus Wagner as NL players with 3,000 hits. He hits a single off Pittsburgh's Rip Sewell at Boston.

21st Ted Lyons wins his 250th career game, 6–5 over the Red Sox. A week later he will beat New York's Red Ruffing to match the Yankee hurler's 251 career wins. The White Sox veteran will finish the season with 20 complete games in 20 starts, lead the AL with a 2.10 ERA, then enter the Marine Corps at age 42.

JULY

4th In the 8th inning of an 8–4 Negro League victory over the Newark Eagles at Yankee Stadium, Baltimore Elite Giants spitball ace Bill Byrd beans Eagles manager Willie Wells. Wells is carried from the field, and the incident causes him to design a batting helmet. When he steps into the batter's box Thursday he will be wearing a modified construction worker's hardhat.

5th Peanuts "Nyassas" Davis pitches and bats the Cincinnati Clowns to a 7–4 victory over the Baltimore Grays in the new Negro Major League. Davis's receiver Pepper Bassett catches the last inning in a rocking chair.

6th First-inning HRs by Lou Boudreau and Rudy York off Mort Cooper lead the AL to a 3–1 triumph over the NL in the All-Star Game at the Polo Grounds. Mickey Owen also homers for the 3rd run. He does not hit a single HR during the regular schedule.

7th A military all-star team that includes Bob Feller, Cecil Travis, Sam Chapman, Benny McCoy, Johnny Sturm, and Frank Pytlak loses 5–0 to AL stars in a game at Cleveland in front of more than 60,000 fans. Jim Bagby wins against his Indian teammate Feller. Military relief receives $160,000.

15th "There is no rule, formal or informal, against the hiring of Negro players," says Judge Landis in response to an editorial in the New York *Daily Worker* newspaper.

17th The Browns, under Luke Sewell, achieve an 8-game win streak with doubleheader victories 4–2 and 11–1 over the A's. Chet Laabs blasts HRs in both games. During the 8 game streak, Laabs hits 8 HRs. He will finish 2nd to Ted Williams in the AL with 27 HRs.

19th The Brooklyn lead of 8 games is cut as the Cards win 3 of 4. The larger blow, however, is a concussion suffered by Pete Reiser after crashing into an OF wall at Sportsman's Park chasing an Enos Slaughter 11th-inning fly. Reiser drops the ball upon impact, and Slaughter scores an inside-the-park HR for a 7–6 Cards' win. Hitting .379 at the time, Reiser will see his average fall to .310 after the injury. His 20 stolen bases will still lead the NL.

P Mike Ryba of the Red Sox catches both games of a doubleheader against the Indians at Fenway Park.

21st At Forbes Field, the Monarchs (Negro League) Satchel Paige performs one of his legendary feats. Years earlier, Paige told Josh Gibson that one day he would strike him out with the bases loaded. With a man on, 2 outs, and Gibson 3rd up, Paige walks the next 2 Grays to bring Gibson up. Satchel tells the crowd what is going to happen. "Three fastballs, Josh," Paige tells him, then proceeds to strike him out.

23rd After giving up a lead-off bloop single, Newark Eagles Leon Day strikes out 18 Baltimore Elite Giants to set a Negro League record.

26th Clyde McCullough hits 3 consecutive HRs, but the Chicago Cubs lose 4–3 to Philadelphia Phillies.

27th The New York *Daily Worker* announces that Pittsburgh Pirates owner Benny Benswanger will arrange a tryout for Roy Campanella, Sammy T. Hughes, and David Barnhill. In August, Campanella and Hughes will jump their team during a tight pennant race to "showcase" for the ML.

AUGUST

3rd A military relief game at the Polo Grounds with the Dodgers attracts a Polo Grounds record crowd of 57,303. The Giants, losing 7–4, have 2 on and no out in the 9th when the game is called. A government order mandates that lights must be turned out at 9:10. Giants President Horace Stoneham states that twilight games would be terminated since "playing against the clock was too tough."

4th The Giants-Dodgers game ends in a 1–1 tie as Pee Wee Reese's grand slam in the top of the 9th is wiped out. As was the case the day before, the game is called because of the government's 9:10 curfew on lights. It is the last twilight game played at the Polo Grounds.

The Dodgers have held the NL lead for 144 days. The margin over the Cardinals is down to 10 games. Until the season's end, Brooklyn will win 17, lose 18.

6th An editorial in *The Sporting News* argues for segregation on the diamond. The column states that members of each race "prefer to draw their talents from their own ranks and both groups know their crowd psychology and do not care to run the risk of damaging their own game."

Lou Novikoff, who led 4 minor leagues in hitting in consecutive years but was a bust with the Cubs in 1941, moves into the top 5 among NL hitters at .316. In his last at bat of the year, Novikoff will get a "gift hit" when the opposing pitcher lets a light grounder come to a stop so he can maintain a .300 batting average for the season.

9th The Chicago Cubs beat the Cincinnati Reds 10–8 in 18 innings at Cincinnati. The Reds tie the score in the 9th, 10th, and 12th innings before the Cubs hang on. Stan Hack collects 5 hits and 3 runs.

As a warmup to the upcoming series at St. Louis with Brooklyn, the Cardinals win their 7th straight, a 7–2 win over Pittsburgh behind rookie Johnny Beazley.

11th At Cleveland, in the first game of a twi-nighter, Indian P Al Milner has a no-hitter until Doc Cramer singles with 2 out in the 9th. But the game with Detroit ends in a 14-inning scoreless tie because the rules state the game cannot be continued under the lights. Indians C Gene Desautels catches the entire game without a putout (no strikeouts) or assist.

14th The Yankees turn 7 DPs in an 11–2 win over the Athletics.

23rd Seven of 8 scheduled games are shutouts. The one that isn't is by White Sox veteran Ted Lyons. Taking a regular Sunday start, he wins his 256th career game, a 3-hitter 3–1 victory over Cleveland.

Walter Johnson pitching to Babe Ruth is the pregame attraction that draws 69,000 for the New York-Washington game at Yankee Stadium that provides $80,000 for Army-Navy relief. Ruth hits the fifth pitch into the right-field stands, and then adds one more shot before circling the bases. Sixteen relief games contribute $523,000 during the season.

24th C Clyde McCullough, SS Lennie Merullo, and 1B Phil Cavarretta combine on a triple play in the top of the 11th, and Bill Nicholson HRs in the bottom half of the inning, as the Chicago Cubs stun the Cincinnati Reds 5–4.

25th Brooklyn's Whit Wyatt and the Cards Mont Cooper duel for 13 scoreless innings. St. Louis wins 2–1 in the 14th.

26th Johnny Beazley wins his 16th game of the year, 2–1 over the Dodgers in 10 innings. The win caps a sweep of Brooklyn, with Max Lanier having edged Larry French in the opener 2 days before.

28th Dodger Pete Reiser, hitless in his last 13 trips and with his batting average down 35 points in 6 weeks, enters the hospital with a torn thigh ligament.

30th The Giants' Mel Ott collects his 2,500th hit in a 5–5 tie in Chicago.

31st Larry MacPhail seeks insurance for the Dodger pennant run by buying Bobo Newsom from

the Senators. The veteran responds by shutting out Cincinnati 2–0 three days later. Blanking the Reds is not difficult. Bill McKechnie's team will hit .231 for the season, the lowest in the ML since the Highlanders hit .229 in 1914 and Brooklyn .229 in 1910.

SEPTEMBER

1st After going 24-9 in July and 25-8 in August, the Cardinals are still 3⅔ games behind Brooklyn.

11th Eddie Freed of the Philadelphia Phillies collects one single, 2 doubles, and a triple in his ML debut, but the Reds win 8–5 in 11 innings. The 5'6" Freed will total only 10 hits during his brief ML career.

12th Mort Cooper wins his 20th game and 8th shutout, stopping Brooklyn 3–0. St. Louis finally catches the Dodgers when Max Lanier wins the second game 2–1.

13th Chicago Cub SS Lennie Merullo makes a ML record 4 errors in the 2nd inning of the nightcap against the Boston Braves. Merullo's son is born today and is named Boots. The Cubs win 12–8 after losing the first game 10–6.

Following their showdown the day before at Ebbets Field, both the Dodgers and Cardinals have doubleheaders this day. The Cards salvage a split with the Phillies, but Brooklyn loses both games to Cincinnati. The Dodgers recover sufficiently to win their final 8 games and finish with 104 wins, 4 more than their pennant level of 1941, but the Cards win 106, winning 43 of their final 52 games.

14th With all the NL hubbub, the Yankees go about their lofty business, clinching the flag against Cleveland 8–3. Ernie Bonham wins his 20th game, and DiMaggio strokes 4 hits.

In the Negro League WS, Leon Day, pitching for the Homestead Grays, fans 12 in beating Satchel Paige and the Kansas City Monarchs 4–1 in Game 4. The Monarchs protest, contending that Day and 3 other players were picked up from other teams. Day's win is disallowed, and the Monarchs sweep the 4 games.

23rd Larry French of the Brooklyn Dodgers pitches a brilliant one-hitter, beating the Philadelphia Phillies 6–0 for his 197th career win. After a brief relief stint on the 26th, he will join the U.S. Navy, rise through the ranks and retire in 1969 with the rank of captain. Larry MacPhail, the 52-year-old Dodger president, also announces today that he is quitting at the end of the season to reenter the army.

25th With the Giants' 3rd-place finish secure, OF Hank Lieber pitches a complete-game 9–1 loss against the Phillies at the Polo Grounds. He yields 9 hits and strikes out 5 in his only ML pitching appearance. The Phils score 5 of their runs without a hit.

26th Youngsters, admitted free for bringing scrap metal to aid the war effort, get restless and invade the field at the Polo Grounds in the 8th inning of the 2nd game with the Giants leading 5–2. Umpire Ziggy Sears forfeits the game 9–0 to the Braves. Boston P Warren Spahn is not charged with a loss, although he was losing at the time of the forfeit. But he is given credit for a complete game, his only one in 4 appearances for the year.

27th The Red Sox Tex Hughson wins his 22nd to tie Mort Cooper for the ML lead, as the Red Sox edge the Yankees. A Fenway Park crowd of 26,166— including 4,293 youngsters who gained free admission by bringing 29,000 pounds of scrap metal—watches Hughson scatter 11 hits. Ted Williams, in his final appearance before entering the war, has a single to finish the season at .356 and wins his second straight batting title. Teammate Johnny Pesky is 2nd at .331. Williams also leads the ML in HRs (36), RBI (137), runs (141), and walks (145).

The Cardinals clinch the NL pennant by winning the first game of a doubleheader from the Cubs. The final score is 9–2.

Phils outfielder Dan Litwhiler completes his 151st errorless game of the season in a game against the Dodgers. Litwhiler becomes the first OF to avoid an error the entire season. He has 308 putouts and 9 assists on the year.

30th Down 7–0 to Red Ruffing in the Series opener, the Cardinals storm back for four 9th-inning runs, not enough to win but enough to portend the result of the WS.

OCTOBER

1st Behind 3–0, the Yankees tie it up in the top of the 8th, but rookie Stan Musial singles in Enos Slaughter in the bottom of the inning to forge a 4–3 Cardinal victory.

3rd Ernie White shuts out New York on 6 hits, winning 2–0. Arguments during the game result in $200 fines for Joe Gordon and Frank Crosetti; the latter is also suspended for the first 30 days of the 1943 season for shoving umpire Bill Summers.

4th The Cards get 6 runs in the 4th, but the Yankees tie the game with 5 in the 6th. St. Louis scores 3 more runs to win 9–6 in a 22-hit game.

5th Whitey Kurowski's 2-run HR in the 9th inning gives St. Louis a 4–2 WS triumph and enables the Cardinals to upset the New York Yankees in 5 games.

NOVEMBER

1st Larry MacPhail enters the army. The Dodgers look to St. Louis for leadership. After 2 decades in St. Louis, Branch Rickey splits with owner Sam Breadon. He will sign to become GM at Brooklyn.

3rd Ted Williams is the ML Triple Crown winner, but the writers select 2B Joe Gordon by 21 votes as AL MVP. Gordon of the New York Yankees leads the AL with 95 strikeouts, the most ground balls hit into double plays (22), and the most errors at his position (28). P Mort Cooper gets the MVP honor in the NL.

DECEMBER

1st At ML meetings in Chicago, the owners decide to restrict travel to a 3-trip schedule, rather than the customary 4. Spring training in 1943 will be limited to locations north of the Potomac or Ohio rivers and east of the Mississippi.

11th Cardinals GM Branch Rickey, possibly motivated by a clause in his contract that gives him 20% of the team's profits, trades slugger John Mize to the Giants for 3 players and $50,000. Yesterday he sold C/OF Don Padgett to Brooklyn for $30,000. Padgett will enter the Navy without playing a game for the Dodgers, and Brooklyn will try unsuccessfully to get their money back from Rickey.

1943

JANUARY

1st Negro League star Josh Gibson suffers a nervous breakdown and is admitted to St. Francis hospital for rest and treatment. He will be released in time to go to Hot Springs, AR, to get in shape for the baseball season.

4th A wartime tone for the season is set when Red Ruffing, just months short of his 38th birthday, and minus 4 toes, is drafted into the army.

5th Teams agree to start the season later than usual and prepare to train in northern areas. Resorts, armories, and university facilities are chosen for training sites. The Dodgers will train at Bear Mountain, NY; Cards, at Cape Girardeau, MO; the Yankees, in Atlantic City.

25th The Yankees send Lefty Gomez to the Boston Braves for cash. He will be released without playing a game and will sign with Washington on May 24th.

27th The Cubs pay cash to the Reds to get P Paul Derringer.

FEBRUARY

2nd After experimenting with a vest worn over knit jerseys, the Cubs return to conventional baggy flannels for 1943. The outfitting change saves the organization $2,000 on the cost for uniforms.

9th The NL is looking for a buyer for the Phillies, whose owner, Gerry Nugent, has fallen in arrears on rent and bank loans. The league pays $10 a share for 4,685 out of 5,000 outstanding shares in club.

17th Joe DiMaggio, drawing $43,500 from the Yankees, trades in his salary for the $50 a month as an army enlisted man. DiMag, in his customary quiet style, gives no notice to the club.

18th The NL finds a buyer for the Philadelphia club. He is William D. Cox, a New York lumberman.

20th Phil Wrigley and Branch Rickey charter the All-American Girls Softball League. The league will operate around the Chicago area and is formed as a sports backup in case the government shuts down ML baseball. The league will later change its name and

switch to hardball with a pitching distance of 40 feet and bases 68 feet apart.

24th The Texas League announces it will quit for the duration of the war. The Cardinals, with 260 farm players in the service, will reduce farm clubs from 22 to 6. Only 9 minor leagues will start the 1943 season. Advertisements for players appear in the *The Sporting News*.

26th The Phils sign Bucky Harris as manager. It is the 4th ML club Harris has led, not counting 2 stints— later 3—at Washington. Clark Griffith, Rogers Hornsby, Donie Bush, and Bill McKechnie have also managed 4 clubs.

MARCH

13th The major leagues approve an official ball, which will be made from reclaimed cork and balata in the interior, materials not needed in the war effort. Officials insist the ball will have the resiliency of the 1939 ball, but the players will express dismay that they cannot drive the new ball and point out the dearth of runs and homers in 1942 even with the old ball.

20th LF Bob Johnson, a star for the Athletics since 1933, is traded to the Senators for 3B Bob Estalella and Jimmy Pofahl.

APRIL

20th The season starts, 2 weeks later than customary. Stalwarts such as Joe DiMaggio, Ted Williams, Enos Slaughter and Johnny Mize are gone, among some 60 players who could have been classified as regulars in the 1942 season.

Braves manager Casey Stengel is struck by a taxi, fractures a leg, and will miss much of the season. The cabdriver is nominated Sportsman of the Year in Boston by a local newspaper, weary of Stengel's humor in the face of the Braves' pitiful record.

21st Travel restrictions limit the crowd to 4,000 in St. Louis as the Browns Al Hollingsworth blanks the White Sox 3–0, the Browns' 7th consecutive Opening Day win.

22nd Despite going 4-for-4 in a 5–2 win at Ebbets Field, the Giants' Mel Ott declares the new baseballs hit like overripe grapefruits. Reds slugger Frank

McCormick adds, "It was like hitting a piece of cement."

24th A spokesman for A. G. Spalding defends the ball, saying the 11 shutouts in the first 29 games are the result of it being "too wet and too cold. In time the new ball will prove to be just as lively as the old one." A few days later the company admits that the balls contain an inferior grade of rubber cement, which has hardened. The teams agree to use up their stock of balls left over from the 1942 season while a new supply of higher-quality balls is made.

25th Rufe Gentry of Buffalo (International League) wins an 11-inning no-hitter against Newark 1–0. The last IL no-hitter of this length was thrown by Toronto's Urban Shocker on July 22, 1916.

MAY

4th Baseball Commissioner Ford Frick demonstrates the revised "balata ball" to reporters by bouncing it on his office carpet. This ball will prove to be 50 percent livelier than the 1942 one. When introduced in games on May 9th, 6 HRs will be hit in 4 doubleheaders compared with 9 HRs hit with the previous ball in the first 72 games.

14th The Detroit Tigers play their 4th straight extra-inning game.

The only Class E league in minor league history—the Twin Ports League—qualifies for play. It is a semi-industrial league located in the northern Minnesota mining area.

21st The Chicago White Sox top the Washington Senators 1–0 in 1 hour, 29 minutes, the shortest night game in AL history.

24th After his release from the Braves, Lefty Gomez signs with the Senators. He will pitch in only one game, which he loses.

27th Johnny Allen, incensed over a balk call, attacks umpire George Barr and is suspended for 30 days and fined $200.

30th The Cubs play 32 games before hitting a home run. Bill Nicholson hits the first Cubs blast of the year against the Braves in the club's 1,120th at bat of the season.

31st Mort Cooper gives up a 7th inning hit to Billy Jurges in stopping the Dodgers on a one-hitter 7–0. Jurges' fly ball loops down the foul line.

JUNE

1st Rip Sewell of the Pirates throws his dew-drop ball in a game. Sewell loops the ball 18 to 20 feet high on its way to the strike zone. Later it is called a blooper or eephus ball. The pitch is more than a gag, and Sewell is on his way to a 20-win season.

2nd The Red Sox and the Browns play 4 consecutive extra-inning games, working 45 innings in games May 31 and June 2. Both leagues will set records for extra-inning activity, 91 in the AL, 80 in the NL.

4th Mort Cooper of the St. Louis Cardinals pitches back-to-back one-hitters, beating the Brooklyn Dodgers on May 31 and the Philadelphia Phillies on June 4. Hits by Billy Herman on May 31 and by Jimmy Wasdell of the Phils deprive him of no-hitters. Cooper has 6 wins and 3 shutouts on the way to his 2nd 20-win year.

12th Roy Weatherly of the Yankees, who caught 10 fly balls in a game April 28, does it again. He is the first OF to have 10 putouts in a game twice in one season.

17th Player-manager Joe Cronin of the Red Sox hits two 3-run pinch HRs, one in each game of a doubleheader, as Boston beats the St. Louis Browns 5–4 and loses 8–7. He had hit a 3-run pinch HR 2 nights before against the A's, 3 HRs in his last 4 ABs. He will pinch-hit 42 times this year with 18 hits, including an AL record 5 pinch-hit HRs.

Player-manager Mel Ott of the Giants walks 5 times in a game versus Brooklyn. Ott also received 5 free passes in games in 1929 and 1933. With a base on balls in his last trip to the plate on the previous day and again on his first at bat the next day, Ott garners 7 consecutive walks.

18th Not a single putout will come the way of Detroit 1B Rudy York.

JULY

1st *The Sporting News* switches to a tabloid format from a standard metro layout as a means of saving newsprint.

10th Brooklyn scores 10 runs in the first and 4th innings as they whip the visiting Pirates 23–6. This follows a pregame attempted strike by the players following Leo Durocher's 3-game suspension of P Bobo Newsom for insubordination. Minutes before the game SS Arky Vaughan handed his uniform to Durocher and refused to play. Durocher called for volunteers to play, but by game time he had just a battery of Curt Davis and Bobby Bragan. Branch Rickey intervened, and Vaughan and the others agreed to play. Newsom, 9-4, will be traded to the Browns on July 15th.

Homestead Grays owner Rufus "Sonnyman" Jackson is jailed after a confrontation with Mexicans trying to sign his players. Jackson will retain his players and win the Negro League World Championship.

12th In Boston, a team of Armed Forces all-stars managed by Babe Ruth and featuring Joe DiMaggio and Ted Williams plays the Braves in a fund-raising effort. Ruth pinch-hits in the 8th and flies out to right. The all-stars win 9–8 on a Williams HR.

13th The AL edges the NL 5–3 at Shibe Park in the first All-Star Game played under the lights. Bobby Doerr of the Red Sox is the hitting hero with a 3-run HR off Mort Cooper in the 2nd inning. Vince DiMaggio of the Pirates has a single, triple and HR in 3 trips. Doerr also handled 6 fielding chances. At the All-Star break he had handled 307 errorless chances, dating back to May 20th. His AL streak will end at 349 chances, a record he will break in 1948.

23rd Outfielders Luis Olmo, Augie Galan, and Stan Bordagaray of the Dodgers account for 18 putouts in a game against Cincinnati.

30th Phil Cavarretta of the Chicago Cubs HRs off the RF foul pole against Johnny Allen of the Brooklyn Dodgers. The ball is retrieved, and Bill Nicholson hits the next pitch out of Wrigley Field. The result: one ball, one pitcher, 2 pitches, 2 HRs. The Cubs go on to beat the Dodgers 13–2.

31st Dodger Dolf Camilli, the league's MVP in 1941, is traded with Johnny Allen to the Giants for Bill Sayles, Bill Lohrman, and Joe Orengo. Camilli declines to report his new team and retires to a California ranch for the season. The next year he will manage in the PCL and in 1945 will return briefly to the Red Sox.

AUGUST

1st Players losses to the military have taken some of the competition out of Cards-Brooklyn confrontations, but the brawling doesn't stop. A duster aimed at Stan Musial by Dodger P Les Webber clears both benches.

6th Rip Sewell, now throwing his blooper pitch some 25 feet high, loses to the Cardinals after 11 straight wins. He has won 18 already but will get only 3 more victories the rest of the season.

7th The Giants strand 18 runners in a 9–6 loss to the Phillies. Mel Ott's team leaves 2 runners on in every inning to symbolize their dreary season that will result in 98 losses and the first Giant tailend finish since 1915.

17th Nick Etten of the Yankees singles twice off White Sox hurler Bill Dietrich, breaking a 17-game stretch in which Etten didn't single. Six of the games were hitless, but Etten either doubled or homered in the other games. The Yankee lead is now 9½ games with the Bombers winning their 9th straight series, most of which are now 4 games as a result of wartime travel. The streak of winning each series will stretch to 13 before being broken by the Senators.

18th In a trade that will benefit Wasington, the Senators send Ellis Clary, Ox Miller and cash to the Browns for Johnny Niggeling and Harlond Clift. Niggeling will split 48 decisions as a Senator, while Miller will win just 3 in St. Louis.

24th The Philadelphia Athletics drop their 20th game in a row, losing to Chicago 6–5. This ties the AL record. They dodge the bullet in game 2 by scoring 8 runs in the 2nd inning to win 8–1.

31st Detroit's Rudy York hits 2 HRs to bring his August home run total to 17, one less than his 1937 record for home runs in a single month, which he also set in August.

SEPTEMBER

6th Woody Williams of the Cincinnati Reds collects his 10th straight hit in 2 games. He is stopped by the Cubs Eddie Hanyzewski. Prior to the run, Williams had only 39 ML hits.

P Carl Scheib of the Philadelphia Athletics becomes the youngest player to appear in an AL game at age 16 years, 248 days. He gives up 2 hits in ⅔ of an inning but retires the side.

18th The Cardinals clinch the NL pennant. Howie Pollet, Max Lanier, and Mort Cooper will rank 1-2-3 in NL ERA, and Al Brazle at 1.53 and Harry Brecheen at 2.27 are near the same level. For hitting, Redbirds prime with George Kurowski, Walker Cooper, and Stan Musial, who in his 2nd season hits .357 and has 220 hits, 347 total bases, 48 doubles, 20 triples.

20th The hottest club at the end of the season is the Senators, who win 10 straight and 15 in a row at home, including a doubleheader win today over the Yankees. The Bombers, however, will clinch the flag on Sept. 25 with a 2–1 win over the Tigers in 14 innings.

24th A crowd of 314, the smallest in Wrigley Field history, see Andy Pafko make his Cubs debut. Pafko drives in 4 runs with a double and a single in 3 at bats, as the Cubs top the Phillies 7–4 in a 5-inning downpour.

OCTOBER

2nd The Yankees take 2 from the Browns 5–1 and 7–6 for their 14th sweep of a doubleheader, an AL mark. Bud Metheny hits a HR in the opener for the Yankees 100th roundtripper of the season.

The season finishes with attendance off some 13 percent from the year before. The Dodgers and Tigers, both good for a million in contending years, each drop below 700,000. Only the Phils, under new ownership, have a significant increases, from 230,000 to 467,000. NL attendance falls from 8.9 million to 7.7 million.

5th Many ML players have gone into the war, including several key Yankees and Cardinals players. Nevertheless, both these clubs are back in the Series. New York wins the opener at Yankee Stadium 4–2 behind Spud Chandler, who will later be named 1943 AL MVP.

6th Robert Cooper, father of P Mort Cooper and C Walker Cooper, dies at his home in Independence, MO, but both players decide to play in the WS. Mort goes on to beat the New York Yankees 4–3, resurrecting memories of 1942 when the Yankees lost 4 straight after winning the opener. Marty Marion and Ray Sanders homer.

7th The attendance is nearly 70,000 as the Yankees take the lead on a 6–2 win helped by 4 Cardinal errors.

10th Marius Russo, of little use during the season, pitches and bats the Yankees to a 2–1 win.

11th Bill Dickey's 2-run HR off Mort Cooper in the 6th gives the Yanks the championship. Spud Chandler gives up 10 hits but strands 11 in the 2–0 victory. Chandler won 2 games and compiled an 0.50 ERA. A full share is worth $6,139 to the New York players; the Cards get $4,321 each. The Series grosses $1.1 million at the gate, receives $100,000 for broadcast rights, and donates $308,000 to War Funds.

25th Dodger manager Leo Durocher signs his 1944 contract, which calls for a base salary of $20,000 plus $5,000 for every 100,000 fans over 600,000.

NOVEMBER

1st League statistics show the White Sox Luke Appling leading the AL hitters with .328, the lowest since Cobb hit .324 to lead in 1908. Conversely, of course, the pitchers' marks were topped by Spud Chandler's 1.64 ERA, the best since 1919. Spud also has the best percentage at .833, on a 20-4 won-lost mark. The White Sox aging OF Wally Moses stole 56 bases after stealing only 3 two years before. The veteran Mel Ott hits only .234 for his Giants, but he still has 18 homers—all in the Polo Grounds.

11th The MVPs for both leagues are named. Spud Chandler wins it in the AL; Stan Musial, in the NL.

23rd Commissioner Landis rules that Phils owner William D. Cox is permanently ineligible to hold office or be employed in baseball for having bet on his own team. The Carpenter family of Delaware will buy the Philadelphia club and Bob Carpenter, age 28, will become president. The Phils, in an effort to change their image, will conduct a contest for a new name. The winning entry, the Blue Jays, submitted by a Mrs. John Crooks, will be the unofficial team name for 1944-45 until abandoned in 1946.

DECEMBER

2nd With only 9 minor leagues operating during the season, the minor league convention in New York has an incipient revolt to oust longtime head William G. Bramham in favor of Frank Shaughnessy, president of the International League, who had 5 pledges. But Bramham rules that 15 nonoperating circuits which had paid dues are eligible to vote. Five of the leagues had given proxies. A later appeal to Commissioner Landis fails.

30th Happy New Year to a couple of Babes. The Phillies send 1B Babe Dahlgren to Pittsburgh for catcher Babe Phelps and cash.

1944

JANUARY

5th Longtime AL 3B Joe Dugan, hit by a car while crossing a Boston street, escapes with a slight concussion and a lacerated scalp.

8th Bill Terry announces he is through with baseball and plans to enter the cotton business.

27th Lou Pirini, Guido Rugo, and Joseph Maney buy control of the Braves and oust Casey Stengel as manager.

FEBRUARY

2nd The leagues meet at New York to discuss postwar action. They decide players with war service will be guaranteed 30 days of trial at pay and restrictions of their release or assignment. Military service will count as playing time.

12th Bob Coleman, after 23 years of managing in the minors, is named to pilot the Boston Braves.

18th Fifteen-year-old Joe Nuxhall signs a contract with the Cincinnati Reds just one day after playing in a high school basketball game.

29th Brooklyn Dodger 1B Howie Schultz is rejected for military service a 2nd time. At 6 foot 6 inches Schultz is deemed too tall.

MARCH

1st The Browns send veteran C Rick Ferrell to Washington for Gene Moore and cash.

8th The Detroit Tigers invite 6 foot 11 inch Ralph Siewert to spring training.

15th The Senators start training with 5 knuckleballers likely to make the staff: Dutch Leonard, Roger Wolff, Mickey Haefner, John Niggeling, and Bill Lefebvre. Pity C Rick Ferrell, who will have to corral the flutterballs.

29th Oakland loans Los Angeles 3 players for a PCL exhibition game after 5 Los Angeles players suffer various injuries in an automobile accident. Los Angeles beats Oakland 6–2.

30th Branch Rickey suggests pooling of surplus players if ML 4F players are drafted for military service. Nothing comes of the suggestion.

APRIL

1st Gerald Juzek pitches 3 innings for Los Angeles in a PCL exhibition game less than 2 years after suffering a severe leg wound while fighting in Guadalcanal. Juzek was told he would never walk again.

16th Jack Hand of the Associated Press names the Yankees, White Sox, and Senators as favorites to win the AL pennant. Like most observers, he picks the Browns to finish last.

18th All 16 ML teams see action on Opening Day. But Bobby Doerr, Tex Hughson, and Mort Cooper are the only established stars still on the wartime rosters. A potential star among the new crop of rookies is George Kell, now Connie Mack's 3B, who last year with Lancaster (Inter-State League) led all minor league hitters with a .396 average.

Hank Borowy of the Yankees shuts out the Red Sox 3–0, as Johnny Lindell hits the first HR of 1944.

19th The Giants defeat the Braves 2–1, as Mel Ott hits the first NL HR of the year and the 464th of his career.

20th The major league career of Mike Kosman ends after a 30-yard dash. Sent in to pinch-run for Steve Mesner at 3rd base for the Cubs, Kosman is thrown out at the plate and never appears in another box score.

21st Mike Kreevich hits 2 HRs, as the Browns beat the White Sox 5–3. In the preceding 3 years, a period involving 297 games, Kreevich tallied just one homer.

22nd The Yankees hand out 1943 WS rings before beating the Senators 6–3.

23rd Jim Tobin tosses a one-hitter in the Braves' home opener as Philadelphia 2B Ford Mullen gets the only hit in the 6th inning. In his previous start Tobin lost a 3-hitter to the Giants.

26th Frank McCormick homers in the bottom of the 13th inning as Bucky Walters and the Reds beat the Cardinals 1–0.

27th Boston knuckleballer Jim Tobin hits a HR and no-hits the Brooklyn Dodgers 2–0 before a midweek crowd of 1,984 at Braves Field. Tobin walks Paul Waner to lead off the game, then retires 26 consecutive batters before again walking Waner with 2 outs in the 9th inning.

29th The White Sox beat the Browns 4–3 to hand St. Louis their first loss after 9 wins.

30th Before 58,000 at the Polo Grounds, the Giants pummel the Dodgers 26–8. Player/manager Mel Ott reaches base 7 times, scoring 6 runs for the 2nd time in his career, and Phil Weintraub drives in 11 runs with a homer, triple, and 2 doubles. Dodger pitchers gives up 17 walks, including 6 in a row. But the Dodgers earn a split as Hal Gregg wins the nitecap 5–4.

Elmer Gedeon, who played briefly for the Senators in the outfield in 1939, is killed in air action over France.

MAY

1st George Myatt of the Washington Senators collects 6 hits in 6 at bats, as the Nats pound out 20 hits to beat Boston 11–4.

Jimmie Wilson resigns as manager of the Cubs.

2nd Phillies P Charley Schanz takes a 1–0 no-hitter into the 7th inning before giving up a 2-run HR to Joe Medwick of the Giants. Schanz wins his own game by clearing the bases with a triple in the 9th.

3rd Joe Cronin, making his 1944 debut at 1B, makes putouts at both ends of a doubleplay, one out at 1B and the other at 3B.

4th Joe Cicero, actor Clark Gable's cousin, hits 3 HRs, 2 of which are grand slams, for 10 RBI, as Newark beats Montreal 17–8 in the International League.

5th The Senators beat the Athletics 11–8, as both teams combine for 33 hits.

Charlie Grimm resigns as manager of the Milwaukee Brewers in the American Association to take over the Cubs. Casey Stengel is named manager in Milwaukee.

7th The Cubs lose to the Pirates 6–5 and ruin Grimm's 2nd debut as Cubs manager.

9th Joe McCarthy returns as Yankees manager after missing much of spring training and the early season due to illness.

10th Mel Harder wins his 200th career game as Cleveland defeats the Red Sox 5–4. He is the 50th to reach this mark.

Cardinal ace Mort Cooper picks up his first win of the season as the Cards beat the Dodgers 4–2.

11th The Cubs beat the Phillies 5–3 to snap a 13-game losing streak after Charlie Grimm gave a 4-leaf clover to starting P Eddie Hanyzewski, who wore it under his cap.   The Cubs are now 1-13 on the year.

Hal Trosky, making a comeback with the White Sox after having retired for 2 years because of migraine headaches, steals home in the 16th to break a 2–2 tie in a 4–2 win over the A's. By inning, it is the latest steal of home, a feat Willie Davis will duplicate in 1964.

12th The Giants purchase 6 foot 9 inches Johnny Gee from the Pirates. Gee has a ML record of 5-8, but his chief attraction is that he is too tall for the draft. He will compile a 2-4 record for the Giants.

13th Joe Page, just called up from Newark, throws a 5-hitter, as the Yankees defeat the Indians 5–1.

14th Connie Ryan singles with 2 outs in the 8th inning, as Reds P Bucky Walters fires a one-hitter against the Braves.

15th Reds reliever Clyde Shoun, making his first start of the season, throws a no-hitter to nip the Boston Braves 1–0. Only 1,014 see the 32-year-old lefty top Jim Tobin, who had thrown one in April. Reds reserve 3B Chuck Aleno accounts for the sole run with his only 1944 HR.

Frankie Hayes hits a grand slam in the 9th inning off the Tigers Rufe Gentry, as the Athletics win 6–2.

16th The White Sox beat the Yankees 10–4 to stop Hank Borowy's 2-year winning streak at 11.

17th Bobby Doerr hits for the cycle, but Red Sox hurlers walk 14 batters, as Boston loses to the Browns 12–8.

18th Rufe Gentry wins his own game with an RBI single in the 8th inning. The Tigers defeat the Athletics 1–0.

20th Mel Harder of the Indians and Paul Derringer of the Cubs both win their 201st career games.

22nd The Cincinnati Clowns of the Negro American League defeat the Great Lakes Naval Center Negro team 7–5.

23rd Wartime restrictions are eased, and the Polo Grounds is the scene of the first night game in metro New York since 1941. The Giants Bill Voiselle loses a 2–1, 9th-inning lead because an apparent last-out fly ball is dropped by CF Johnny Rucker when Charles Mead runs into him. Two runners score and the Dodgers win 3–2.

Milwaukee defeats Toledo 28–0 in an American Association game.

24th Frankie Hayes of the Athletics hits his 2nd grand slam in 10 days. This one comes against the Tigers.

25th On Mel Harder appreciation night in Cleveland, the Indians and Harder drop a 4–2 decision to the Senators. Harder scores both of the Indian runs.

26th The Red Sox defeat the Browns 4–2 in 11 innings, although Browns P Nels Potter retires the first 23 batters he faces.

The 1943 Negro League World Champions, the Homestead Grays, defeat the Fore River Shipyard team of the New England Industrial League 1–0 in a game played at Fenway Park.

30th Dizzy Trout leads off the bottom of the 9th with a HR to win his own game as the Tigers beat the Yankees 2–1. Hal Newhouser finishes off the nightcap with a complete-game, 4–1 win.

Mel Ott hits 3 HRs, as the Giants sweep 2 from the Cubs 6–5 and 5–4.

31st Al Unser hits his only 1944 HR, a pinch-hit grand slam with 2 outs in the bottom of the 9th, to help the Tigers beat the Yankees 6–2.

Nap Reyes goes 3-for-4 with 2 HRs and 6 RBI, as the Giants beat the Cubs by a score of 8–5.

Cal McLish, 18 years old, picks up his first ML victory in a Dodgers' 8–4 win over the Pirates.

John McKelvey, last surviving member of the National Association (1871-75), dies at Rochester, NY. At age 96, he was the oldest former ML player.

JUNE

1st Stan Spence goes 6-for-6 with a HR and 5 singles in the Senators' 11–5 win over the Browns.

Hal Newhouser picks up a victory in relief as the Tigers beat the Yankees 4–3 on Don Ross's 16th-inning RBI.

Dick Barrett, the winning pitcher in the Phillies 8–7 win over the Reds, has a double, triple, 4 RBI, plus 3 wild pitches.

2nd Mel Ott hits 2 HRs in the Giants' 6–4 win over the Pirates. These are Ott's 7th and 8th HRs in his last 10 games.

The Tigers beat the Red Sox 4–1 for their 7th straight win, as Red Sox SS Eddie Lake tosses 2 hit-less innings in relief.

4th In Hawaii, Joe DiMaggio hits a 435-foot HR, but the 7th Army Force team loses 6–2 to a Navy team, as former ML P Bob Harris throw a 4-hitter for the Navy.

6th All ML games are canceled as the country's focus is turned toward Europe while allied forces invade occupied France.

7th Detroit's Hal Newhouser is wild and issues 9 passes in 6 innings as the White Sox defeat the Tigers by the score of 3–1.

8th Bucky Walters of the Reds outduels Max Lanier of the Cardinals 2–1. The Cardinal run, scored in the 9th, is the first they have scored off the Reds righty in 45 innings.

Three runs score for the Cubs on one wild pitch by Pirates rookie Art Cuccurullo.

The Cubs trade reserve infielder Eddie Stanky to the Dodgers for P Bob Chipman.

10th P Joe Nuxhall of the Cincinnati Reds is the youngest player in ML history. Nuxhall, only 15 years, 10 months old, pitches ⅔ of an inning in an 18–0 loss to the St. Louis Cardinals. He manages to give up 5 walks and 2 hits before Bill McKechnie takes him out.

11th Gene Moore hits a pinch-hit grand slam in the bottom of the 7th off Joe Heving of Cleveland to give the Browns a 4–2 win in a doubleheader split with St. Louis. The Cardinals win the other game 13–1.

The Giants takes a doubleheader from the Phillies by identical scores of 6–5. In the first game the Giants use 22 players, including 5 pitchers, 3 catchers, 3 second basemen, 3 pinch hitters, and 2 pinch runners.

12th The Giants defeat the Dodgers 15–9, as Mel Ott and Phil Weintraub each homer twice.

13th Al Simmons, 42, comes to bat for the first time in 1944 in the 9th inning of the Athletics' 7–2 loss to the Red Sox. He hits into a double play.

14th Bucky Walters beats the Pirates 3–2 in 11 innings to become the season's first 10-game winner.

15th Tex Hughson runs his record to 9-2 with a 5–1 victory over the Athletics, as the Red Sox win their 9th in a row. Less than 800 fans are in attendance in Boston.

16th Milo Candini shuts out the Red Sox 4–0 to end the Boston win streak at 9.

Whit Wyatt wins his first game of the year as the Dodgers beat the Phillies 4–3. Phils P Bill Lee takes a one-hitter into the 9th inning but loses the game on 2 errors.

18th The White Sox take a pair from the Indians in Cleveland by the scores of 3–2 and 7–6. The White Sox win the first game on a 10th-inning HR by Wally Moses, who, in the twin bill, has 2 triples, a double, and a single.

Cal McLish is knocked from the mound by a 5-run outburst by the Phillies in the first inning of a Philadelphia 6–2 victory over the Dodgers. The 18-year-old McLish is followed to the mound by Dodgers hurlers Ralph Branca, also 18, and Charley Osgood, 17, in his only major league appearance.

22nd Ron Northey homers in the top of the 15th for a 1–0 Phillies win over the Braves.

Jim Tobin throws his 2nd no-hitter, winning 7–0 in the 2nd game of a doubleheader against Philadelphia. The game is called in the 5th inning because of darkness.

23rd The Dodgers Ed Head tosses a 2-hitter against the Phillies as Philadelphia infielder Charley Letchas accounts for both Phillies hits.

24th The Cardinals beat the Pirates 16–0 as Cards hurler Mort Cooper tosses a 3-hitter while his teammates pound out 22 hits.

JULY

4th Baltimore's Oriole Park, erected in 1914 for the Federal League, burns down. The team moves to the city's unroofed Municipal Stadium. It will be used this way until a second tier is added when the St. Louis Browns move in for the 1954 season.

11th Phil Cavarretta of the Cubs sets an All-Star Game record by reaching base 5 successive times on a triple, single, and 3 walks, as the NL romps 7–1.

13th A .300 hitter as a rookie for the Tigers in 1943, Dick Wakefield finishes Navy air training and then is released from the service pending assignment. He rejoins the Tigers and will hit .355 the rest of the season, pushing Detroit near the flag despite the loss of 12 of its first 13 home games. In the first week after the All-Star Game, Wakefield homers twice, and goes 9-for-24.

16th The Dodgers score 8 unearned runs against the Braves to win 8–5 and break their 16-game losing streak. They will lose another 5 in a row.

20th The Browns Nelson Potter becomes the first pitcher suspended for throwing spitballs. He is banished for 10 days for allegedly "putting an illegal substance on the ball." Potter will return and win 19 games for St. Louis.

23rd After hitting 4 consecutive HRs in 2 games, Bill Nicholson of the Chicago Cubs is walked intentionally with the bases loaded in the 7th inning of the 2nd game against the New York Giants. The Cubs rally to tie, but the Giants win 12–10. Nicholson has hit 6 HRs within 48 hours (one on Friday night, one on Saturday, and the 4 today).

30th The 4th straight bad start by Bucky Walters of Cincinnati will deprive him of the ERA title. Bucky gives up 27 runs in 24 innings after a brilliant start of the season. He will recover to win 23 games and finish with an ERA of 2.40, but teammate Ed Heusser will be the ERA champ with 2.38.

AUGUST

3rd Tommy Brown, just 16 years and 8 months old, plays SS for Brooklyn in both games of a twin bill loss, 6–2 and 7–1, to the Cubs. He hits a double and scores a run.

9th The Browns win their 9th straight game for the 2nd time this season in a 3–2 win over the Yankees in New York. They lead by 6½ games. St Louis's other team, the Cardinals, after winning 26 in July, now leads the NL by 16½ games.

10th Red Barrett of the Boston Braves throws only 58 pitches and shuts out the Cincinnati Reds 2–0. This is the ML record for fewest pitches in a 9-inning game. The game takes one hour, 15 minutes, the shortest night game ever.

17th Yankee OF Johnny Lindell, converted from a pitcher the year before, hits 4 straight doubles to share a ML mark.

29th The Cardinals beat the Reds 3–0 as Ted Wilks (14-1) wins his 11th in a row. He will lose his next start, September 2nd in Pittsburgh, 5–4.

Braves 3B Damon Phillips has 11 assists versus the Giants, equaling an 1884 mark.

SEPTEMBER

1st The Giants lose to Brooklyn 8–1, as Giant Joe Medwick is hit on the elbow and leaves the game for treatment. With both teams out of the race, Dodgers manager Leo Durocher agrees to allow Medwick to reenter the game if Durocher can pick the pinch runner for him. He selects slow-footed Gus Mancuso, who is promptly erased on a DP ground ball.

3rd After losing 13 of 17 games and dropping from first place, the Browns turn back their principal rival, the Tigers, behind Jack Kramer. Two days later, neither St. Louis nor Detroit is at the AL top. It's the Yankees, who have come from nowhere.

15th Radio announcer Bill Stern reports on a scandal involving the Browns. A Chicago newspaper attributes the Browns' recent slump to the fact that the team wants a larger park for the WS. Four days later, Stern repudiates the story.

16th Jack Kramer's one-hitter against the White Sox puts the Browns back into first place.

21st The Cardinals finally clinch the NL flag with a 5–4 win over Boston. Twenty games ahead on September 1, the Cards then blew 15 of the next 20 games. They will finish with 105 victories and their 3rd title under Billy Southworth, whose clubs won 316 games in 3 years. Pittsburgh finishes 14½ games behind.

Reds OF Dain Clay has no chances in a 21-inning doubleheader.

25th Going into the final Monday of the season, the Tigers hold a one-game lead over the Browns with the Yankees now out of the running. Russ Christopher of the A's beats the Tigers 2–1 to produce a tie for the lead.

27th The Browns give the lead back by insisting on playing the Red Sox in the rain under the arcs and then losing 4–1. The Red Sox had just lost 10 straight.

29th The final series of the year begins. Trailing Detroit by one game, the Browns have 4 games with the Yankees, who are three games out of first place. With rainouts the night before, all contenders play doubleheaders.

The Browns are last in the AL in attendance, and only 6,172 fans watch St. Louis sweep the doubleheader. Jack Kramer wins the opener 4–1, and Nels Potter wins a 1–0 shutout over the Yankees Hank Borowy, even though St. Louis batters get but 2 hits. In Detroit, the Tigers split with 2 of the Washington knuckleballers, beating Johnny Niggeling 5–2 in the opener but losing to Mickey Haefner 9–2 in the nightcap.

30th Hal Newhouser wins his 29th as Detroit whips Washington 7–3.

The Browns remain tied with Detroit as Dennis Galehouse goes all the way, winning 2–0 for his 9th victory of the year. Paid attendance is 12,982.

OCTOBER

1st In Detroit 45,565 watch 27-game winner Dizzy Trout, pitching on one day's rest, lose to Washington knuckleballer Dutch Leonard 4–1. Prior to that, Leonard had lost 7 straight to Detroit in 1943-44. Years later, Leonard reports he had received a phone call offering him $20,000 to throw the game.

The Browns have their first sellout in 20 years as 37,815 pack Sportsman's Park. St. Louis clinches the flag on the final day of the season by sweeping the Yankees and winning 5–2 on a pair of 2-run HRs by Chet Laabs. Sig Jakucki is the winning pitcher.

4th The first all-St. Louis WS opens with the Browns beating the Cardinals 2–1 on George McQuinn's HR. Denny Galehouse is the winning P. It is the first Series in which all the games are played west of the Mississippi River. The Series is dubbed the Streetcar Series and is played with no days off.

5th Ken O'Dea's pinch single in the 11th drives in Ray Sanders for a Cardinals' 3–2 win. Two errors by Potter and one by Mark Christman give the Cards 2, early-inning, unearned runs.

6th   The Browns take a 2–1 game lead with a 6–2 victory for Jack Kramer, who fans 10. Five singles and a wild pitch by Fred Schmidt give the Browns 4 runs in the 3rd.

7th   The Cards even the Series with a 5–1 win by Harry Brecheen, who strands 10 runners.

8th   Mort Cooper strikes out 12; Denny Galehouse, 10. But the Cards get the runs to win 3–0.

9th   Emil Verban drives in 3 runs as the Cardinals top the Browns 3–1 and win the Series in 6 games. Ted Wilks allows no one to reach base in 3⅔ innings of relief, fanning 4 pinch hitters. George McQuinn hits .438 for the Series. The winners get $4,626 each; the Browns take $2,743, the lowest player shares since 1933.

NOVEMBER

1st   Total attendance in the 2 leagues is 8.9 million. No team draws over a million, as Detroit leads with 923,000.

23rd   Five groups totaling 23 players, managers, umpires, and writers visit war theaters as part of the USO program. Included are Mel Ott, Dutch Leonard, Frankie Frisch, Bucky Walters, Harry Heilmann, Carl Hubbell, Freddie Fitzsimmons, Bill Summers, Beans Reardon, Johnny Lindell, Tuck Stainback, Steve O'Neill, Leo Durocher, Joe Medwick, Nick Etten, Dixie Walker, Paul Waner, and Rip Sewell.

25th   Kenesaw Mountain Landis, baseball's first commissioner, dies of a heart attack at age 78 in Chicago. The Commissioner had ruled over baseball since November 1920 in the wake of the Black Sox scandal, and wielded authority perhaps unparalleled in any other industry. Landis had entered the hospital on October 2nd. He will be named to the Hall of Fame on December 9th by a special committee which he formed on August 4th.

28th   Hal Newhouser is named MVP in the AL gathering 4 more votes than teammate Dizzy Trout. Newhouser's 29 wins contrasts with 9-9-8-8 win totals in previous years. His 2.22 ERA is bettered by Trout (2.12), who also has 27 wins.

DECEMBER

21st   NL averages show Brooklyn's Dixie Walker at the top of the hitters with a .357 mark, ahead of Stan Musial at .347. In an even closer vote than occurred in the AL, the NL MVP award goes to fielding wizard Marty Marion, who tallies one more vote than Cubs slugger Bill Nicholson. The Cardinals erred only 112 times and averaged .982, both better than previous records held by the 1940 Reds.

28th   Former Washington 3B Buddy Lewis wins the Distinguished Flying Cross for precision flying over the Burma War Theater.

1945

JANUARY

7th In the most violent incident in Cuban baseball history, OF Roberto Ortiz of Almendares attacks umpire Bernardino Rodriguez in a dispute at home plate and knocks the umpire unconscious.

10th Baseball writers again fail to elect a new Hall of Famer. Frank Chance, Rube Waddell, and Ed Walsh come closest, but none get the required three-fourths of the vote.

25th Training rosters list 260 players who are classified 4F for military service, and quality of big-league play will decline even more from 1944 and 1943. But the flow of players will begin to turn around. Rosters will include Al Benton, Tigers; Jim Wallace and Tom Earley, Braves; and Van Mungo of the Giants as players returning from the military.

The Yankees are sold by the Ruppert estate to Larry MacPhail, Dan Topping, and Del Webb for $2.8 million. For that price the trio obtains 400 players, 266 of them in military service, Yankee Stadium, parks in Newark and Kansas City, and leases on other minor league ballparks. Jake Ruppert, who died in 1939, paid more than the new purchase price for the ground on which Yankee Stadium was built in 1923.

FEBRUARY

14th Bob Quinn, president of the Boston Braves since 1936, relinquishes his job as general manager, and his son John takes over the post. The elder Quinn has been in organized baseball since 1900.

MARCH

15th Bert Shepard, a one-legged veteran of the war, tries out as a pitcher for the Senators. The symbol of wartime baseball, outfielder Pete Gray of the Browns, will field and bat with only one arm.

25th A group of blacks appears at the Dodger offices to ask for tryouts for P Terris McDuffie and 1B Dave Thomas. The two will work out for Branch Rickey in Brooklyn on April 7.

APRIL

16th The Boston Red Sox allow 3 blacks—Marvin Williams, Sam Jethroe, and Jackie Robinson—to work out at Fenway Park. None is signed.

17th The season opens. Two rookies released from the military will be the best newcomers in each league: Red Schoendienst, a shortstop in the minors but a leftfielder in his fledgling campaign, and David "Boo" Ferriss, a handsome Mississippian who will win 8 straight games for the Red Sox.

18th Pete Gray, the one-armed OF, plays his ML debut game with the St. Louis Browns. He singles once in four at bats, and has no chances in the outfield.

20th Mickey Grasso, future ML catcher, escapes from a German prisoner-of-war camp. He was captured in February 1942.

24th At a meeting of owners in Cleveland a list of possible successors to Judge Landis is cut to 6: Ford Frick, president of the NL, and 5 politicians, Jim Farley, Carl Vinson, Robert Patterson, Bob Hannegan, and Frank Lausche. Larry MacPhail suggests adding the name of Albert "Happy" Chandler, a Kentucky senator. The list then narrows to Chandler and Hannegan. On the first ballot Chandler leads 11-5, short of the required three-fourths. One vote switches over, and the owners unanimously approve the selection.

25th Baseball writers cannot seem to get any Hall of Fame candidates past the 75 percent requirement, but a committee selected to bring in some old-timers succeeds with a group of turn-of-the-century names: Jimmy Collins, Roger Bresnahan, Fred Clarke, Dan Brouthers, Ed Delahanty, Hugh Jennings, Mike Kelley, Jim O'Rourke, Wilbert Robinson, and Hugh Duffy.

29th In his first ML appearance, Boo Ferriss of the Red Sox survives a first inning, in which he throws 17 balls and loads the bases, to blank the A's 2–0. At bat he is 3-for-3.

30th P Dixie Howell, briefly with Cleveland in 1940, is liberated from a prison camp in Germany.

MAY

6th Boston's Boo Ferriss pitches his 2nd straight shutout, blanking the Yankees 5–0.

13th Boo Ferriss reaches 22 shutout innings before allowing a run versus the Tigers in a 6–2 Red Sox win. This sets an AL record for scoreless innings at the start of a ML career.

18th A wet record. The Detroit Tigers and the Philadelphia Athletics both have 7 straight games postponed because of rain in the past 4 days.

In a 15–12 Dodgers' victory over the Cubs, Brooklyn's Luis Olmo hits a triple and HR, each with the bases loaded. No ML player has done that since. Olmo adds a 2B for good measure. Former OF Ben Chapman is the winning P.

Jimmie Foxx hits the 2nd pinch grand slam of his career, off Ken Burkhart, to give the Phils an 8–7 lead. St. Louis rallies in the 9th to win 11–8.

20th In St. Louis, Pete Gray stars, as the Browns sweep the Yankees 10–1 and 5–2. Gray has 2 RBI on 3 hits in the opener, and in the nightcap he scores the winning run and hauls in 7 fly balls, 3 on spectacular catches.

23rd A 20-game winner for 3 previous seasons, Mort Cooper is traded by the Cardinals to the Braves. Cooper has twice jumped the club in a salary hassle. Threatening to run out again unless his contract is increased from $12,000 to $15,000, Cooper is traded by owner Sam Breadon to the newly affluent Braves for Red Barrett and $60,000 cash.

24th The visiting Giants beat the Reds 7–6 on a pinch homer by colorful Danny Gardella. Gardella had started the day by leaving a suicide note in his hotel room for his roommate 1B Nat Reyes. When Reyes returned to the room a few minutes later, he noticed the open window and read the note. Horrified, he rushed to window to see the grinning face of Gardella, who had been hanging from the window ledge several stories over the street.

27th The White Sox get only 3 hits total in a doubleheader loss to the Red Sox.

JUNE

2nd The Phils Vince DiMaggio hits a pinch grand slam against his old teammates, but the Pirates win 7–6.

9th Brooklyn manager Leo Durocher is arrested on a complaint by a fan that Durocher slugged him while an Ebbets Field cop pinned back his arms. The case will be settled in 1946.

16th Boo Ferriss loses to the Yankees 3–2 after starting his career with 8 victories—4 of them shutouts—for the Red Sox.

19th Allied Commander Dwight Eisenhower, just back from Europe, is given a tremendous round of applause from fans at the Polo Grounds. The Braves beat New York 9–2.

29th Ben Chapman replaces Fred Fitzsimmons as manager of the Philadelphia Blue Jays.

JULY

1st The first of the superstars returns from the war. Hank Greenberg, gone for 4 years, homers in his first game following his release from the army. Charlie Gassaway of the Athletics gives up the blow before 47,700 in a Sunday game at Briggs Stadium. The Tigers lead the Yankees by 3½ games with Chicago and Boston following.

6th The Braves sweep the Pirates 13–5 and 14–8, as Butch Nieman hits a pinch grand slam in the opener. In the 2nd game, Tommy Holmes hits in his 34th consecutive game to pass RogersHornsby's record of 33 in 1922.

P Phil Marchildon rejoins the Athletics. In the Canadian Air Force, he was shot down and in a German prison camp for 9 months.

8th Filling wartime rosters requires going deeper into the bag. The Dodgers bring back Babe Herman from California. He pinch-hits twice against the Cardinals, tripping over 1B on a hit. Guy Bush, Clay Touchstone, and Hod Lisenbee, contemporaries of Babe Herman in the 1920s, will get their chances on the mound. The Babe will go 9-for-34, mostly as a pinch-hitter, sock one HR, and be a popular gate attraction in Brooklyn.

The Cubs take the NL lead by winning 2 from the Phillies, 12–6 and 9–2. They never relinquish first place, despite losing 16 of 22 games to the Cards.

10th The All-Star Game at Fenway Park is canceled because of travel restrictions. During the schedule break, 7 inter-league games are played for war charity. Plans for a USO-sponsored all-star game in Europe do not materialize, although the war in

Germany is over and fighting in the Pacific will be over in 6 weeks.

11th Aaron Robinson, Yankees C, returns from the military. Red Ruffing is back too, and so are Hugh Mulcahy and Buddy Lewis. Charlie Keller will follow, and a couple of dozen former ML players will be in uniform before the season is over.

12th The Chicago Cubs stop Tommy Holmes's modern-day NL hitting streak at 37 games, beating the Boston Braves 6–1 behind Hank Wyse for their 11th victory in a row. The Braves take game two 3–1, as Claude Passeau loses his first after 9 straight wins. . Holmes hits .433 during the streak and will finish at .352, 2nd in the NL. His 9 strikeouts coupled with 28 HRs and 47 doubles is unparalleled for making contact and hitting for average and power.

21st The Detroit Tigers and the Philadelphia Athletics battle to a 1–1 tie in 24 innings. Les Mueller hurls 19⅔ innings for the Tigers. No hurler has matched this endurance feat.

27th The Cubs purchase P Hank Borowy from the New York Yankees in an unexpected waiver deal. Borowy, 10-5 with the Yankees, was put on waivers, apparently to solve a roster problem, and was passed over by 15 teams. The Cubs snatch him for $97,500, and he will help the Cubs win the pennant with an 11-2 record, including 3 wins over the Cardinals down the stretch.

AUGUST

1st Mel Ott hits the 500th HR of his career, a total exceeded only by Babe Ruth and Jimmie Foxx. He will hit 10 more this season and one on Opening Day of 1946 to finish with 511. Of Ott's total, 324 will be hit in the Polo Grounds. When he retires in 1947, he will have failed to hit a HR in Philadelphia after the Baker Bowl was abandoned in 1938.

4th Tom McBride of the Boston Red Sox drives in 6 runs in the 4th inning of the 2nd game of a double-header against the Senators. He doubles and triples off Santiago Ullrich and Joe Cleary, each time with the bases loaded.

8th The Senators Joe Cleary pitches to 9 men and gets one K, his only out, in his only ML appearance.

10th Richard Muckerman buys out Don Barnes's interest in the Browns and now controls 50 percent of the club.

12th The Reds Bill McKechnie, desperate for hitting, selects P Joe Bowman to pinch-hit for Vern Kennedy. Bowman is 0-for-42. He will hit .088 for the season.

13th Branch Rickey becomes the principal stockholder of the Dodgers. He and associates Walter O'Malley and John Smith acquire the 50 percent interest of the Ebbets estate for a reported price of $750,000.

15th Commissioner Happy Chandler sells WS radio rights for $150,000 to Gillette. Ford had been the WS sponsor since 1934, paying $100,000 annually.

Umpire Ernie Stewart is canned by AL President Will Harridge for "disloyalty." Stewart had complained about the pay and taken his case to Chandler. Bill McGowan is the top-paid umpire in the league at $9,000.

18th Scheduled demonstrations at the Polo Grounds and Ebbets Field to end segregation in organized baseball are called off.

19th In game 2 of a doubleheader against the Reds, 37-year-old slugger Jimmie Foxx pitches the first 7 innings for the Philadelphia Blue Jays. He leaves with a 4–1 lead, and Andy Karl saves Foxx's only ML decision. His ERA in 10 ML appearances is 1.52.

20th At the age of 17, SS Tommy Brown of the Brooklyn Dodgers is the youngest player to hit a ML HR. Brown homers off Pirates southpaw Preacher Roe at Ebbets Field.

24th Cleveland ace Bob Feller returns from the Navy and attracts a crowd of 46,477, who watch him strike out 12 and yield only 4 hits in a 4–2 win over Detroit's Hal Newhouser. He will get 9 starts during the remainder of the year, and his 5 wins will include a one-hitter and two 4-hitters. With the war now over, fans are clamoring for entertainment and it is clear Feller is still baseball's number one ticket seller.

28th Against the Phillies, Brooklyn's Tommy Brown hits a triple and then steals home. At 17 he is the youngest to pull off a home steal.

30th Stan Hack of the Cubs becomes No. 82 in the 2,000-hit club. Earlier in the season the Senators' Joe Kuhel and Red Sox OF Bob Johnson made the list.

SEPTEMBER

1st The Phils beat the Braves 8–3 in Boston, as Vince DiMaggio hits his 4th grand slam of the year, tying an ML mark. An injury will shortly end the season for the senior DiMaggio.

4th Long-time Yankee batting practice pitcher Paul Schreiber, who last pitched in the ML in 1923 and the minors in 1931, relieves for the Yankees against Detroit in a Tiger rout. Schreiber gives up no hits in 3⅓ innings, but the Tigers Dizzy Trout wins 10–0.

6th Punching umpire Joe Rue earns an indefinite suspension for the A's C Greek George.

7th Joe Kuhel hits an inside-the-park HR, the only HR hit by a Senator all season at Washington's Griffith Stadium.

9th Dick Fowler of the Philadelphia Athletics returns from 3 years with the Canadian Army and pitches a no-hitter, walking 4 and beating the St. Louis Browns 1–0 in the 2nd game of a doubleheader. A triple by Hal Peck leads to the winning run in the 9th. It is Fowler's first start since his return and his first ML shutout. The no-hitter is the first by an Athletic since 1916.

28th Four bases on balls give Eddie Stanky of the Dodgers 147 walks for the season, tying the mark held by Jimmy Sheckard of the Cubs in 1911.

29th The Cubs clinch the NL flag on Hank Borowy's 4–3 win over Pittsburgh in the first game of a doubleheader. The final margin for Chicago is 3 games over the Cardinals. During the season, the Cubs win 20 doubleheaders.

30th Hank Greenberg's grand-slam HR in the 9th inning on the final day of the season beats the St. Louis Browns 6–3 and clinches the AL pennant for the Detroit Tigers. The Tigers had been assured of a tie on September 26 when Newhouser won his 24th game, an 11–0 shutout of the Indians. There were 3 off days before the season finale today. The 2nd-place Senators had finished the season a week before, on the 23rd, to make Griffith Stadium available for pro football.

George Stirnweiss of the Yankees gets 3 hits on the final day to raise his average to .309. The White Sox games are washed out, depriving the veteran Tony Cuccinello of a shot at the title. The only other .300 hitter playing full time is Johnny Dickshot. Neither Cuccinello or Dickshot ever play another game in the ML. Only Elmer Flick in 1905 and Carl Yastrzemski in 1968 ever lead the AL with a lower average than Stirnweiss, but the latter also leads the AL with 195 hits, 107 runs, 22 triples, 301 SB, 33 TB, and a .476 SA.

Eddie Stanky draws a walk his first time at bat, his 148th walk of the year, from Hugh Mulcahy to break Jimmy Sheckard's mark. The Dodgers beat the Phils 4–1.

OCTOBER

3rd The Tigers and Cubs meet in the WS for the 4th time. Hank Borowy pitches a 6-hitter and Hal Newhouser is roughed up for 8 runs in 3 innings, as the Cubs win 9–0.

4th Returning war vets Virgil Trucks and Hank Greenberg produce a 4–1 Detroit win. Trucks, who pitched in only 5 innings of one game at the end of the season, pitches a complete game, giving up 7 hits. Greenberg's 3-run HR in the 5th wins the game.

5th Claude Passeau of the Chicago Cubs pitches a one-hitter, beating the Detroit Tigers 3–0 in the 3rd game of the WS. Rudy York's 2nd-inning single spoils Passeau's no-hit bid. Bill Nicholson drives in the first run.

6th Tavern owner "Billy Goat" Sianis buys a box seat for his goat for the 4th game of the WS and is escorted out of Wrigley Field. In retaliation Sianis casts a "goat curse" over the Cubs. The Tigers tie the series on Dizzy Trout's 5-hit 4–1 win. Detroit scores all its runs in the 4th, with Hank Greenberg, Roy Cullenbine, Paul Richards, and a force-out scoring the runners.

7th Hal Newhouser beats Hank Borowy 8–4. A 4-run 6th, including Hank Greenberg's double, provides the margin.

8th Stan Hack's double takes a tricky bounce over LF Hank Greenberg's shoulder with 2 outs in the 12th inning to give the Chicago Cubs an 8–7 win in the 6th game of the WS. Borowy pitches 4 scoreless innings in relief.

10th The Tigers tally 5 runs in the first inning and rout the Chicago Cubs 9–3 behind Hal Newhouser, who strikes out 10, enabling Detroit to win baseball's most sloppy WS 4 games to 3. The winners get $6,433 a share, 2nd to the 1937 Yankees share. Each Cub gets $3,930. Total receipts of $1.6 million is a WS record.

15th Attendance in the ML was 10.28 million, breaking the 1940 record. The Tigers led with 1.28 million. The Dodgers, Giants, and Cubs also drew a million.

23rd Branch Rickey announces the signing of Jackie Robinson by the Dodger organization.

29th Happy Chandler, who had continued to serve in the U.S. Senate after becoming commissioner, resigns his political office. He will presently move the commissioner's quarters to Cincinnati.

30th Branch Rickey signs Jackie Robinson to a Montreal (IL) contract for 1946. Black P John Wright also signs.

NOVEMBER

6th Billy Southworth leaves the Cardinals to sign a 3-year contract with the Braves, who are making aggressive moves under Lou Perini and other new owners. Eddie Dyer will become the new Cardinal pilot.

15th The rules are revised for election of modern players to the Hall of Fame. A runoff election is formulated as a way to qualify more players for selection, but it fails to meet its objective as no one reaches the 75 percent requirement in the runoff. Frank Chance, Johnny Evers, Miller Huggins, and Ed Walsh come closest.

DECEMBER

10th At the annual meeting the major leagues head off the quest of the PCL for major status and more territorial protection for upper minors by a new AAA classification for the PCL, American Association, and International Leagues. Returning servicemen are given increased protection for one year and the limiting of rosters to 25 players will be delayed until June 15.

11th The Giants obtain a genuine "pheenom," pitcher/outfielder Clint Hartung, from Minneapolis for $20,000 and 3 players. Much ballyhooed, Hartung hit .358 in 66 games in 1942 for Eau Claire (Northern) while winning 3 games. He was in the military for the next 3 years, and will be for the 1946 season. The New York *World Telegram*'s Tom Meany writes, "Hartung's a sucker if he reports to the Giants. All he has to do is sit at home, wait till he's eligible, and he's a cinch to make the Hall of Fame."

1946

JANUARY

1st George Trautman, head of the American Association, becomes general manager of Detroit, succeeding Jack Zeller, who retires after 25 years with the Tigers.

2nd The White Sox buy P Alex Carrasquel and SS Fred Vaughan from the Senators. Carrasquel will make only 3 appearances for Chicago before being farmed out. When the Sox acquire his nephew Chico in 1949, the Sox will swap Alex for reliever Luis Aloma, who will act as an interpreter for the young Venezualan shortstop.

3rd The Red Sox get Rudy York from Detroit in a trade for Eddie Lake.

5th Walker Cooper goes to the Giants. The sale by the Cardinals for $175,000 is the highest cash deal ever. The Joe Cronin transaction in 1934 and the Dizzy Dean sale in 1938 were larger deals but also involved other players. Cooper was considered the best catcher in the game before his 1945 induction into the Navy.

12th The first professional league game is played in Venezuela, launching the newly constituted 4-team Liga de Beisbol Profesional de Venezuela. The game is won by Magallanes 5–2.

FEBRUARY

9th Pirate southpaw Preacher Roe suffers a brain concussion in an altercation with a referee in an Arkansas basketball game.

15th Detroit's Hank Greenberg signs for $60,000 and then marries New York department store heiress Coral Gimbel 3 days later.

19th Giants OF Danny Gardella becomes the first major leaguer to announce he is jumping to the "outlaw" Mexican League, the first shot in the series of events that will dominate baseball even more than the return of all the war veterans. His attempt to return to the ML a few years later will initiate a major court battle.

28th Alex Carrasquel, White Sox P, signs a 3-year contract with the Mexican League.

MARCH

30th A holdout from the Browns, SS Vern Stephens signs a 5-year deal with the Pasquel brothers to play in Mexico. The Giants dismiss Roy Zimmerman, George Hausmann, and P Sal Maglie for dickering with the Pasquels, and the trio departs for Mexico. One day later Mickey Owen of the Dodgers signs to manage the Mexican club in Torreón. Stephens will play a couple of games in Mexico, then jump back. Owen announces he will return and then changes his mind again.

APRIL

13th Eddie Klepp, a white pitcher signed by the defending Negro League champion Cleveland Buckeyes, is barred from the field in Birmingham, AL.

15th Manager Mel Ott of the Giants hits his 511th and final HR on Opening Day, an 8–4 home victory over the Phils (now back to their original nickname). The next day Ott will injure his knee diving for a ball and will play only occasionally.

The Tigers, Cubs, Reds, Athletics, and Phillies retain their 1945 ticket prices. Other clubs increase admission costs. Typical: $2 to $2.50 for boxes, general admission $1.25, bleachers 60 cents.

18th Robert Murphy, Boston labor relations counsel, announces the formation of the American Baseball Guild.

Jackie Robinson debuts as 2B for the Montreal Royals (International League) and is the first recognized black in organized ball in this century. A HR and 3 singles versus Jersey City start off the season in which he will win the IL batting championship at .349.

20th Bucky Walters, in a tight pitching duel with the Pirates Rip Sewell, steals home in the 6th, but Sewell wins the squeaker 2–1 before 28,000 in Pittsburgh.

21st Cleveland C Frank Hayes catches the last of 1,312 consecutive games as a backstop, a streak begun on October 12, 1943, when he was with the Browns. Virgil Trucks wins 3–2 for the Tigers.

22nd Boston's Eddie Pellagrini homers in his first at bat in the ML, in a 5–4 Red Sox win over Washington.

23rd Ed Head of the Brooklyn Dodgers tosses a no-hitter at the Braves, beating Boston 5–0 before 30,287 at Ebbets Field. It is Head's first ML start since his return from the military.

24th Eleven former players—Joe Tinker, Johnny Evers, Frank Chance, Jess Burkett, Tom McCarthy, Rube Waddell, Eddie Plank, Ed Walsh, Jack Chesbro, Clark Griffith, and Joe McGinnity—are named to the Hall of Fame.

25th Leo Durocher is acquitted of assaulting a baseball fan, John Christian, under the grandstands at Ebbets Field on June 8, 1945. Christian will admit that he received $6,750 from the Dodgers for his injuries.

26th Giants pitchers Ace Adams and Harry Feldman jump to the Mexican League.

28th Two days after buying Goody Rosen and Jack Graham from the Dodgers, the Giants sweep a double-header from Brooklyn 7–3 and 10–4. Rosen is the hitting star and, when the Dodgers end the season in a tie with the Cardinals, fans speculate that the Dodgers traded Rosen 2 days too soon.

30th Dispelling the rumors that he had lost his fast-ball after nearly 4 years in the Navy, Bob Feller of the Cleveland Indians hurls his 2nd no-hitter, beating the New York Yankees 1–0 on Frankie Hayes's HR in the 9th inning.

MAY

2nd In St. Louis, Giants manager Mel Ott informs C Clyde Kluttz at breakfast that he has been traded from New York to the Phillies. Cards manager Eddie Dyer calls Kluttz at lunch to tell him not to pack; St. Louis has just made a trade for him.

4th Washington's Cecil Travis gets 6 straight hits before being stopped by Cleveland's Steve Gromek. A prewar hitting star, Travis has few other starring moments as a player after suffering frozen feet in combat in Europe.

5th P Hank Borowy hits 2 doubles and drives in 4 runs during the Cubs 11-run 7th inning for a 13–1 victory over the Phillies.

Cincinnati fans boo the substitution of Ray Mueller for C Ray Lamanno, who had 3 hits in 4 trips to the plate. Sent in for the final inning to preserve a NL record consecutive-game catching streak of 233 contests, Mueller sits out the next day. Mueller missed only 81 innings during the streak, which began July 31, 1943, and included Army service through 1945.

6th Pinch runner Joffre Cross steals home in the 10th inning, giving the St. Louis Cardinals a 9–8 victory over the Boston Braves.

8th Red Sox SS Johnny Pesky becomes the first player in AL history to score 6 runs in one game, as Boston beats the White Sox 14–10. During the week Pesky also had 11 straight hits before grounding out against Al Milnar of the Browns.

2B Lonnie Frey of the Reds throws out 6 straight runners as part of an 11-assist game against Brooklyn.

11th The New York Giants top the Boston Braves 5–1 in the first night game at Braves Field.

The Red Sox lose the first game after 15 straight wins, as Tiny Bonham beats them 2–0 before 52,011 at Yankee Stadium. The Red Sox are 21-4, 4½ ahead of the Yanks. The 15-game streak is still a Red Sox record.

19th The oldest star to go into the military was the White Sox P Ted Lyons, who finished each of the 20 games he started in 1942. Lyons continues to pitch on the first 5 Sundays of the 1946 season. Although the 46-year-old former Marine has an ERA of 2.32, he loses 3 of his 4 starts.

20th Claude Passeau of the Chicago Cubs makes his first error since September 21, 1941, ending his streak with an all-time pitcher's fielding record of 273 consecutive errorless chances.

A state Supreme Court justice has armed the Yankees with an injunction against the raiding Mexican Leaguers, and the Dodgers and the Cardinals have also turned to the courts for protection and damages. Before any of the relief becomes permanent, however, Max Lanier, Fred Martin, and Lou Klein jump back to the Redbirds.

23rd Police sit along the dugouts of both clubs at Ebbets Field after 2 brawls in 2 days, including a pregame fight between the Dodgers Dixie Walker and the Cubs Lenny Merullo.

24th Ted Lyons, 45 years old, gives up the mound to replace Jimmie Dykes as Chicago White Sox skipper. He is 1-4 but has an ERA of 2.32. The last 28 games he pitched, dating back to 1941, were complete.

Joe McCarthy quits as Yankee manager, and Bill Dickey replaces him.

26th Two-for-42 and hitting .048 for the season, Mel Ott stops playing and only manages the Giants.

27th The outlaw Mexican League scuttles its competition, Mexico's only league entry in organized baseball. There are now 43 minor leagues for 1946.

28th The Washington Senators edge the New York Yankees 2–1 before 49,917 fans in the first night game at Yankee Stadium.

30th In a play that anticipates a scene in *The Natural* by Brooklyn-native Bernard Malamud, the Braves Bama Rowell smashes a HR in the 2nd inning of the second game of a doubleheader at Ebbets Field. The ball shatters the Bulova clock high atop the right-field scoreboard at 4:25 P.M., showering glass down on the Doder's RF Dixie Walker. An hour later the clock stops.

JUNE

3rd The A's release Bobo Newsom at his own request. He becomes a Senator for the fourth time 2 days later.

7th One hour before game time, Pirates players vote 20-16 in favor of a walkout rather than play against the Giants, in order to gain recognition of the American Baseball Guild. To strike, however, requires a two-thirds majority and so the walkout does not occur. Aims of organizer Robert Murphy are not exactly stated, but goals are sometimes identified as a minimum salary of $7,500, arbitration of salary disputes, and players sharing in 50 percent of any sale price.

8th After acquiring Vince DiMaggio from the Phils in May, the Giants sell him to the San Francisco Seals (PCL).

9th In a doubleheader loss in Pittsburgh 2–1 and 5–1, Giants manager Mel Ott is thrown out of each game for protesting calls.

12th The Red Sox 2nd long win streak early in the year—this one 12 games—is broken by Bob Feller's 7–2 win at Boston.

15th Commissioner Happy Chandler bans Mexican jumpers Max Lanier, Fred Martin, and Lou Klein. Chandler mentions a lifetime suspension for the players, but his penalty is later reduced to 5 years.

20th A *Fortune* magazine story gives some rare details of baseball finances, showing the 1945 Yankees revenue of $1.6 million and profit of $306,000, cut to $201,000 after minor league losses. Of the gross income, $896,000 is from home ticket sales.

21st A federal judge rules that the Seattle club does not have to play returning serviceman AL Niemiec but it does have to pay him his $720 a month contract through the season. At midseason 143 players who had ML contracts when they went to war had been released or sent to the minors. Former ML players Van Mungo, Lou Finney, Chubby Dean, Nate Andrews, and Max Butcher are all playing in Class D leagues.

22nd Bill Veeck heads a syndicate which purchases the Cleveland Indians. This launches Veeck on a long career as a lively promoter.

23rd Eddie Waitkus and Marv Rickert of the Chicago Cubs hit back-to-back, inside-the-park HRs in the 4th inning, but the team loses 15–10 to the New York Giants at the Polo Grounds.

24th A bus careens off a Cascade Mountain pass road, killing 9 members of the Spokane (Western International League) club. Jack Lohrke, a young infielder, had gotten off the bus at its last stop before the accident, on orders to report to San Diego. The future Giant and Phil will be known ever after as Lucky.

JULY

2nd The Yankees nip the Red Sox 2–1 before a Stadium crowd of 69,107. Spud Chandler walks 9 in the first 4 innings but takes a no-hitter into the 9th before Bobby Doerr hits a one-out single.

8th A special meeting of clubs deals with Mexican League defections and attempts by players to gain new rights. Some results: $5,000 minimum salary, $25-per-week training-camp expenses, a fixed period for spring training, 25 days for post-season barnstorming, maximum pay cut of 25 percent. A pension fund aimed at providing $100 a month for retired 10-year players will be funded by WS broadcast rights and net proceeds from All-Star Games. Each league will have a player rep to baseball councils. The first player reps named are Yankees P Johnny Murphy and Dodgers OF Dixie Walker.

9th With 7 Red Sox teammates on the AL squad, Ted Williams stages a power show with 2 HRs, 2 singles, a walk, 4 runs scored, and 4 RBI to lead the AL to a 12–0 laugher over the NL at Fenway Park. The highlight of the All-Star Game is Williams's HR off a Rip Sewell blooper pitch.

12th Johnny Sain just misses a perfect no-hitter when Grady Hatton's pop fly drops among three Braves behind 3B. No one else gets on as the Braves win 1–0 in Cincinnati.

13th Al Zarilla of the St. Louis Browns gets 2 triples in the 4th inning against the A's. The Browns win 11–4 at Shibe Park.

14th Player-manager Lou Boudreau of Cleveland hits 4 doubles and one HR, but Ted Williams wallops 3 HRs and drives in 8 runs, as the Boston Red Sox top the Indians 11–10. In the Sox 2nd-game win, the famous Boudreau Shift is born. Boudreau shifts all his players, except the 3B and LF, to the right side of the diamond in an effort to stop Williams. Ted grounds out and walks twice while ignoring the shift.

19th In a Boston-Chicago game, 14 White Sox are banished for jeering umpire Red Jones.

21st Lew Flick of Little Rock (Southern Association) gets 9 straight hits in a 19-inning game. Flick gets 3 more hits in the 2nd game of the double-header.

26th Monty Stratton, who lost a leg in a hunting accident in 1938, wins his 14th game for Sherman (East Texas League). He will finish with 18 victories for the second-division team.

27th Rudy York of Boston hits grand-slam HRs in the 2nd and 5th innings off Tex Shirley of the St. Louis Browns, as the Red Sox win 13–6. Only Tony Lazzeri and Jim Tabor have accomplished this feat before York. York also has a 2-run double to knock in 10 runs. He had 5 RBI against the Browns the day before.

AUGUST

5th Mickey Owen quits his Mexican League team. He and Luis Olmo ask Commissioner Chandler for reinstatement 3 days later.

8th The Dreyfuss family, owners of the Pittsburgh Pirates since 1900, sell the club to a group headed by Frank McKinney and John Galbreath. Singer Bing Crosby is among investors in the team. The Pirates are purchased for a reported $2.5 million.

A single by Frank Hayes deprives Bob Feller of a no-hitter against the White Sox. Hayes was traded by Cleveland in June, just weeks after catching Feller's April 30th no-hitter. It it the 8th one-hitter of Feller's career. His 10 games of less than 2 hits better Addie Joss's old mark of 9.

9th All games are played at night for the first time in ML history, 4 in the AL and 4 in the NL.

11th Stan Musial gets 8 hits in 9 at bats, as the St. Louis Cardinals sweep the Cincinnati Reds 15–4, 7–3.

The Phillies sweep Brooklyn 7–6 and 6–4 to end the string of 18 consecutive Brooklyn wins in Philadelphia, a ML mark. The last Phillie victory at home against the Bums was May 5, 1945.

20th The Pirates vote on whether to accept the Guild as their bargaining agent. The vote is 15-3 against, with 10 abstentions.

22nd Clubs approve a change to a 168-game schedule, but they will rescind the decision at another meeting Sept 16. Television is first recognized, with clubs given rights to their own games. Players jumping to outlaw leagues will not be allowed to apply for reinstatement for 5 years.

31st Luke Sewell quits as manager of the Browns; Zack Taylor will finish the season.

SEPTEMBER

8th With the Red Sox running away with the AL race, attention closes in on Bob Feller's strikeout pace. He reaches 300 today, a number reached by Walter Johnson and Rube Waddell twice each. Can Feller beat Waddell's 347 of 1904? Boudreau finds plenty of innings for Feller to work as the season comes to an end and statisticians discover an error in the Aug 24th box score that shorted the fireballer one strikeout against the A's. Counting that one, Feller ends with 348. Alas! Waddell's old record of 347 was apparently based on the compilations of George Moreland, an early baseball historian, and listed in *Little Red Book*. *TSN* researchers later revise Waddell's total to 349.

Dodger Pete Reiser, even though still as injury-prone as he was before the war, steals 3 bases, including home, in an 11–3 Dodger victory over the Giants. It is his 7th steal of home this year. He will lead the ML with 34 steals despite missing more than 30 games due to injuries.

In the minor leagues Bill Kennedy of Rocky Mount (Coastal Plain League) will be credited with 456 strikeouts, breaking the former mark of 418 set by Virgil Trucks in the Alabama-Florida League in 1938.

11th The Reds and Dodgers play the longest scoreless tie game, 19 innings, at Ebbets Field. The Reds' Johnny Vander Meer pitches the first 15 innings, striking out 14.

13th The Boston Red Sox clinch the AL pennant, edging the Cleveland Indians 1–0 on Ted Williams's inside-the-park HR, the only one of his career. Williams punches the ball over the shift when LF Pat Seerey pulls in behind the SS position. The Boston margin at the season's end will be 12 games.

14th Roy Hamey, president of the American Association, is named general manager of the Pirates by its new owners.

15th After dropping the opener, the Brooklyn Dodgers are stinging the Chicago Cubs 2–0 in the 5th inning when a swarm of gnats descends upon Ebbets Field and causes the game to be postponed.

Ernie Lombardi of the Giants slams the ball 483 feet under the stairway in right-center of the Polo Grounds, but barely makes 3B. It is the 3rd triple in 7 years for Schnozz and the last of his career.

19th Washington's Sherry Robertson leads off with a home run against Cleveland. It is his 2nd consecutive leadoff HR, having connected yesterday in Detroit.

24th Disappointing on the field, the Yankees nevertheless finish their home season with a 2,309,029 attendance. The best previous draw was the 1929 Cubs at 1,485,166. Total ML attendance was 18.5 million, 80 percent more than 1945.

25th Handling 13 chances without an error against the Braves in an 8–0 loss, Giants SS Buddy Kerr runs his errorless streak to 254 chances, breaking Eddie Miller's 1940 record.

The Phils score 5 in the 9th to beat the Dodgers 11–9, a loss that will haunt the Dodgers at the season's end. Phils 1B Frank McCormick makes his first error of the season after a ML record 131 straight errorless games.

29th The Cardinals and the Dodgers end the season tied for the NL lead. Both are 96-58. The first-ever best-of-three championship playoff series will start in 2 days.

OCTOBER

1st Before 26,012 at Ebbets Field the Dodgers manage just 3 hits off Howie Pollet to lose 4–2. Joe Garagiola's 3 hits pace the Cardinals.

3rd The St. Louis Cardinals wallop the Brooklyn Dodgers 8–4 at Ebbets Field to win the NL playoffs 2–0 and advance to the WS. Erv Dusak and Enos Slaughter lead the attack.

6th The WS opens with a Red Sox 3–2 win as Rudy York hits a 10th-inning HR off Howie Pollet. The Sox tie the game in the 9th when an easy grounder to Marty Marion takes a freak bounce and goes through his legs.

7th Harry Brecheen gives up only 4 singles in shutting out the Red Sox 3–0. He also drives in the first run of the game.

9th Boo Ferriss records the 50th shutout in WS history. He holds the opposition to only 6 hits, as the Boston Red Sox blank the St. Louis Cardinals 4–0. Rudy York's 3-run HR in the first is the big blow.

10th Enos Slaughter, Whitney Kurowski, and Joe Garagiola each have 4 hits, and Al Brazle pitches a 12–3 complete game win. The Cards tie a WS record by racking up 20 hits.

11th The Red Sox take the Series lead with a 6–3 win, as Joe Dobson fans 8 in a complete game win. All 3 runs off of Dobson are unearned.

13th Back in St. Louis, Harry Brecheen ties the Series again with a 4–1 win, stopping the Red Sox on 7 hits.

15th Enos Slaughter sprints all the way from 1B and slides into home with the winning run in the 8th inning on Harry Walker's double, as the Cardinals edge the Boston Red Sox 4–3, giving St. Louis the WS 4 games to 3. Harry Brecheen wins 3 games for the Cardinals. Billed as the duel between the 2 best hitters in baseball, the Series sees Stan Musial go 6-for-27 and Ted Williams 5-for-25. With the Series held in 2 small ballparks and the broadcast fees now aimed at a player pension fund, the Cardinal share of $3,748 and the Red Sox portion of $2,140 is the smallest Series payoff since 1918.

NOVEMBER

1st   The right foot of Cleveland owner Bill Veeck is amputated, a result of a war injury in the South Pacific 2 years before. Veeck has had a tremendous impact on promotion in a half season of ownership. A minor but typical change is the regular posting of NL scores on the Cleveland scoreboard, a departure from the long-standing practice of both leagues.

15th   Ted Williams is picked as the AL MVP. A week later the NL names Stan Musial for the honor.

DECEMBER

4th   W. G. Bramham retires as head of the minors. George Trautman will replace him.

6th   The major leagues finally accept the contention that invasion of minor league territory will result in compensation for the entire league. The major league clubs agree to return the selection of the All-Star teams, except for pitchers, to a fan ballot.

20th   The Indians send young OF Gene Woodling to Pittsburgh for veteran receiver Al Lopez. Lopez will play just 61 games in 1947, before taking over as manager of Indianapolis for 3 reasons. He will return to skipper the Indians in 1951.

1947

JANUARY

18th   The Pirates buy 1B Hank Greenberg from the Tigers for a reported $25,000 to $35,000. Greenberg led the AL in HRs with 44 in 1946.

20th   Famed Negro League slugger Josh Gibson dies of a brain tumor at age 35.

21st   Bob Feller signs for "more than $80,000," according to Cleveland owner Bill Veeck.

Dodger manager Leo Durocher marries actress Laraine Day, after she obtains a Mexican divorce.

A rule change that allows voting only for players after 1921 produces 4 new Hall of Famers: Carl Hubbell, Frank Frisch, Mickey Cochrane, and Lefty Grove. Pie Traynor misses selection by 2 votes.

25th   Five Evangeline League (Class D) players are made ineligible for allegedly betting on 1946 playoff games. The group includes P Bill Thomas (35-7 for Houma, LA, in 47 appearances), who is still the all-time win leader in the minors (with 383), 2 Houma teammates, and the Houma manager. Thomas protested, pointing out that he was 5-0 in the playoffs. He and Len Pecou will be reinstated in 1949.

MARCH

1st   New managers in training camps are Billy Herman with Pittsburgh, Muddy Ruel with the Browns, Bucky Harris with the Yankees, and Johnny Neun at Cincinnati. Neun had ended 1946 as manager of the Yankees after both Joe McCarthy and Bill Dickey had quit.

In anticipation of the signing of the first black players, Bill Veeck, a resident of Phoenix, had set up a spring training camp there for the Cleveland Indians. Arizona was chosen because of its relatively tolerant racial climate. During the season, Veeck will sign the first AL black player, Larry Doby, who will train at the Arizona camp. The Giants also set up camp in Arizona, while the Dodgers moved their training camp from Florida to Havana.

8th   In Havana's new Stadium del Cerro, the Dodgers, behind 3 pitchers, beat the Yankees in 10 innings 1–0. Carl Furillo scores on Pete Reiser's double, and Snuffy Stirnweiss's 10th-inning single is the only Yankee hit.

APRIL

1st   Branch Rickey deflects pressure on Jackie Robinson by keeping him in Montreal, although it is clear the contending Dodgers can use the 1946 International League batting king.

4th   The adoption of a ML pension plan is effective immediately.

8th   Giants OF Whitey Lockman, in his 2nd year, breaks his leg sliding into 2B in an exhibition game against the Indians in Sheffield, AL. Lockman will miss all but 2 games of the season.

9th   Commissioner Happy Chandler suspends manager Leo Durocher of the Brooklyn Dodgers for the entire season for incidents detrimental to baseball. Larry MacPhail and the Dodger organization are fined $2,000 each, and Yankee coach Charley Dressen is set down for 30 days. A feud involving Durocher, MacPhail, and Dodger officials rocked the training season. The Yankees' signing of Dressen and Red Corriden, longtime Brooklyn coaches, charges of consorting with Cuban gamblers against MacPhail, and charges and countercharges that Durocher had sought—or been offered—the Yankee managerial post were included in the hearing before Chandler.

10th   Jackie Robinson becomes the first black in the modern ML when the Dodgers purchase his contract from Montreal.

15th   Robinson goes hitless in 3 trips in his debut but handles 11 chances at 1B, a new position for him, in a 5–3 Brooklyn win over the Braves. Coach Clyde Sukeforth, interim manager and the man credited with first scouting Robinson, guides the team to 2 wins before stepping down.

In his NL debut, Hank Greenberg singles home the only run as the Pirates Rip Sewell wins the opener in Chicago 1–0.

16th   The Cubs buy veteran Lonnie Frey from the Reds, but keep him just 9 weeks before selling him to the Yankees.

17th   The Dodgers win 12–6 over the Braves at home, as Robinson gets his first ML hit, off Glenn Elliot.

18th   Scout Burt Shotton is the surprise choice to replace Leo Durocher on the 3rd day of the season. Taken to the stadium in a taxi, Shotton manages the club from the dugout in street clothes, à la Connie Mack.

24th Johnny Mize of the New York Giants hits 3 successive HRs in a 14–5 loss in Boston. It is the 5th time in his career that Mize has hit 3 HRs in one game; he will do it a 6th time with the Yankees in 1950.

27th Today is Babe Ruth Day at all ML parks. A crowd of 58,339 at Yankee Stadium honors the ailing slugger, but the Yankees lose to Sid Hudson and the Washington Senators 1–0.

MAY

1st For the first time Cleveland will play all its games at Municipal Stadium, abandoning League Park, where most weekday games have been played. New owner Bill Veeck installs an inner fence to cut power alleys from 435 to 365 feet. A more celebrated attempt to fuel HRs is at Pittsburgh where the 30-foot reduction of the LF wall is dubbed Greenberg Gardens, for the Pirates' famous acquisition. Hank will hit only 25 HRs for the season, however, but sophomore Ralph Kiner will find the shortened distance more advantageous.

3rd The Cards trade Harry Walker to the Phillies for OF Ron Northey. Although batting only .200 with the Cards, Walker will hit .371 for the Phils in 130 games to finish the season with a league-leading .363 batting average.

8th A movement among Cardinal players to protest its first meeting with Jackie Robinson and the Dodgers is aborted by a clubhouse talk from owner Sam Breadon, according to a story by league president Ford Frick. Breadon denies the story.

9th Heralded rookie Clint Hartung makes his first pitching appearance and throws 6 shutout innings against the Braves. He will start 20 games and compile his best season at 9-7. He will also play 7 games in the OF and bat .309 for the year.

13th Ted Williams hits 2 HRs to LF, the first to that pasture in his career at Fenway Park, as the Red Sox wallop the White Sox 19–6.

16th Johnny Mize of the Giants scores a run in his 16th straight game, helping his team beat the Cubs 5–3. Mize's run eclipses the NL mark of Max Carey

and Fred Lindstrom. Ted Kluszewski will better the league mark 7 years later.

17th A seagull flies over Fenway Park and pelts St. Louis Browns P Ellis Kinder with a smelt.

19th After 22 hitless at bats, Stan Musial sees his average drop to .140. Treated for appendicitis but avoiding surgery, Musial will not reach the .200 level until mid-June, just after the champion Cardinals get out of last place.

20th Athletics C Buddy Rosar drops a pop-up off Walt Judnich's bat for his first error in 147 games and 756 chances. Yogi Berra will extend the record to 148 and 950 in 1957-59, but Rosar's 1946 single-season record of 115 games and 605 errorless chances is still unsurpassed.

22nd The Pirates beat the Braves as both teams combine for 22 hits—all singles. The Pirates have 12.

25th Joe Medwick returns to the Cardinals after a 7-year absence. Ducky has lost his power from his St. Louis heyday, but he will hit .307 as PH and OF against lefthanders.

Giant Buddy Kerr bungles a hard grounder from Bob Elliott for his first error in 384 chances and 69 games, the NL record for SS.

26th The largest single-game crowd to this date, 74,747, sees the Yankees win their 5th straight, defeating the Red Sox 9–3 at Yankee Stadium.

30th Earl Torgeson of the Braves will not record a single putout at 1B, a record of idleness shared in the NL by Rip Collins (twice) and Dolf Camilli of the Phillies in 1937. Later Gary Thomasson and Len Matuszek will have zero putouts in a full game at 1B.

JUNE

8th The Washington Senators edge the Chicago White Sox 1–0 in 18 innings on Al Evan's triple and Sherry Robertson's long fly. It is the 4th 1–0, 18-inning game in history.

13th The Boston Red Sox beat the Chicago White Sox 5–3 before 34,510 "first nighters" in the first night game at Fenway Park.

14th The Reds swipe pitcher Ken Raffensberger and C Hugh Poland from the Phillies for C Al Lakeman. Lakeman won't hit his weight (195 pounds) in 2 seasons in Philadelphia while Raffensberger will win 89 games in a Reds uniform.

18th Ewell Blackwell of the Cincinnati Reds no-hits the Boston Braves at Crosley Field 6–0. Rookie Frankie Baumholtz, who played in the NBA the previous winter, collects with 4 hits.

20th Yale bests Clemson 7–3 in the first game of the NCAA East Regional. Eli 1B George Bush has a single in 4 at bats and steals a base. Winning pitcher Frank Quinn will sign a $50,000 bonus with the Red Sox but never win a ML game.

22nd Ewell Blackwell just misses pitching back-to-back no-hitters when Eddie Stanky of the Brooklyn Dodgers singles with one out in the 9th inning. Blackwell then gets Al Gionfriddo before Jackie Robinson bangs out a 2nd single. Blackwell wins 4–0, his 9th straight win to improve to 11-2. Stanky's hit ends Blackwell's hitless-inning skein at 19.

24th The Dodgers win 4–2 over the Pirates, as Jackie Robinson swipes home for the first of 19 times in his career.

28th Walker Cooper of the Giants hits a HR in his 6th consecutive game to tie a record set by George Kelly in 1924. Cooper had 2 HRs in the first game of the streak, and his shot today helps his brother Mort win 14–6 over the Phils.

JULY

5th Larry Doby of the Cleveland Indians becomes the first black to play in the AL. He strikes out as a pinch hitter, as the Chicago White Sox edge the Indians 6–5. Tomorrow he will go 1-for-5 in his first full game at 1B.

8th Clutch pinch hits by Luke Appling and Stan Spence lead the AL to a 2–1 win over the NL in the All-Star Game at Wrigley Field. Schoolboy Rowe pinch-hits for Johnny Sain, becoming the first player to appear for each side. Rowe pitched 3 innings for the AL in 1936.

10th In a rain-interrupted game before 47,871, Don Black of the Cleveland Indians pitches a no-hitter, beating the Philadelphia Athletics 3–0 in the first game of a doubleheader. It is the first no-hitter at Municipal Stadium.

James "Stormy" Davis, 20-year-old OF of Ballinger (Longhorn League), dies as a result of being hit in the head by a pitched ball. He was hitting .333 with 19 HR in 48 games.

13th Making his 14th ML uniform switch, Bobo Newsom joins the Yanks. His 7-5 record the rest of the way will help the Yankees to the title. The next season Newsom will join the Giants.

17th The Yankees sweep a doubleheader against Cleveland 3–1 and 7–2 to extend their winning streak to an AL record 19 games. The streak matches that of the 1906 White Sox.

Hank Thompson plays 2B for the Browns, the first black in the franchise's history.

18th Freddie Hutchinson of the Tigers shuts out the Yankees 8–0, stopping their winning streak at 19.

Willard Marshall of the New York Giants hits 3 consecutive HRs, as Larry Jansen beats the visiting Reds.

The first 5-for-5 game of his career moves Ted Williams among the top hitters in the AL.

20th The choice rhubarb of the year occurs when umpire Beans Reardon signals that Ron Northey's long fly has gone into the stands. Northey jogs around the bases only to discover C Bruce Edwards awaiting him with the ball. The Cardinals protest is upheld, but the Dodgers will win the replay.

Hank Thompson plays 2B and Willard Brown CF for the St. Louis Browns against the Red Sox. It marks the first time that 2 black players appear in the same ML lineup.

23rd Ralph Kiner hits HRs 24 and 25, breaking the Pirate record of 23 by Johnny Rizzo in 1938 and tied by rookie Kiner last year. Behind HR king Johnny Mize 14 to 3 at the end of May, Kiner will have 25 to Mize's 31 by the end of July.

27th Jake Jones of the Red Sox hits a foul ball along the 3B line in the 6th. Browns P Fred Sanford throws his glove at the ball to prevent it from rolling into fair territory. Umpire Cal Hubbard awards Jones a triple on the basis of the rule about intentionally thrown gloves. In 1954 the rule is changed so that it only applies to fair balls.

30th The New York Giants edge the Cincinnati Reds 6–5 in 10 innings, ending Ewell Blackwell's winning streak at 16 games. All games are complete games and 5 are shutouts.

31st   The Giants lose 8–7 but hit their 55th HR of the month, an NL record. Walker Cooper connects against the Reds.

AUGUST

6th   Can a pinch runner drive in a run? Skeeter Webb of the Tigers takes the paths for Freddie Hutchinson against the Indians and scores. Detroit bats around, and Webb lifts a fly ball that scores a run.

10th   Stan Musial finally lifts his average over .300, and the Cardinals make a run at the Dodgers. Musial will finish at .312, and the Cards, 5 games back of Brooklyn.

13th   Willard Brown of the Browns is the first black to homer in the AL when he hits a pinch inside-the-park blow in a 6–5 win over the Tigers.

16th   Ralph Kiner hits 3 successive HRs for the Pittsburgh Pirates, for a 12–7 win over the Cardinals in a game in which the 2 clubs bang out 10 homers. Kiner matches the ML mark of seven HRs in 4 games, six in 3 games, five in 2 games, and 4 in consecutive at bats. By the end of the month, Kiner will still trail Mize 39 to 43 in a head-to-head HR competition that will only be matched by Roger Maris and Mickey Mantle in 1961.

20th   The Boston Braves hit a million attendance for the first time.

21st   The first Little League World Series tournament is held in Williamsport, PA. The Maynard Midgets of Williamsport, with a tourney batting average of .625, win the WS, 16–7.

24th   The Giants break the Cubs NL record for homers in a season with their 172nd in a 4–0 win by Larry Jansen.

26th   Recently signed by the Dodgers, former Memphis Red Sox (Negro League) P Dan Bankhead becomes the first black ML hurler. The Pirates rock Bankhead for 10 hits in 3⅓ relief innings, but Bankhead joins a small list of players who homer in their first ML at bat.

SEPTEMBER

1st   Jack Lohrke hits a homer off the Braves, number 183 for the season for the Giants, breaking the 1936 team record held by the Yankees. Mel Ott's club had hit 5 HRs in a doubleheader against the Cubs August 24 to break Chicago's 1929 NL record. The Giants will finish with 221 HRs, led by Johnny Mize, Walker Cooper, Willard Marshall, and rookie Bobby Thomson.

3rd   Rookie Bill McCahan of the Philadelphia Athletics no-hits the Washington Senators 3–0. 1B Ferris Fain allows the only runs when his toss to McCahan on an easy grounder in the 2nd inning goes wide. McCahan, the former Duke University star, was the losing pitcher when Don Black threw his no-hitter July 10th. The Senators have not suffered a no-hitter since Ernie Shore pitched his 26-out perfect game in 1917.

8th   Starting P Johnny "Ox" Miller of the Cubs hits a game-winning grand-slam HR in a 4–3 win over the Pittsburgh Pirates, but does not go the required 5 innings to gain the win.

11th   Ralph Kiner hits 3 successive HRs for the Pittsburgh Pirates. He hit 2 on the 9th against the Giants Larry Jansen, as the Pirates lost.

12th   Ralph Kiner hits his record 8th HR in 4 games to pass Johnny Mize in the HR race as Pittsburgh tops the Boston Braves 4–3. The rain of HRs exceeds the 7 in 4 games hit by Tony Lazzeri in 1936. On the 18th Kiner will again pass Mize in the homer derby by belting his 50th of the season. Mize will get his 50th two days later. Kiner will get number 51 on September 23 against Jim Hearn of the Cards, and Mize will tie it up 2 days later off Johnny Sain of Boston. Both players have until the season finales on September 28 to break the tie, but neither will succeed.

17th   Jackie Robinson is named Rookie of the Year by *The Sporting News* 2 weeks before the season is over. At the year's end he has hit .297, led the league in stolen bases and sacrifices. He has 14 bunt hits, and in a game against the Cubs in June he scored from 1B on a sacrifice.

21st   The Braves' Warren Spahn delays the Dodgers' clinching the pennant by shutting them out 4–0 for his 20th win.

22nd Stan Musial collects his 5th hit in a game for the 5th time in one season, tying Ty Cobb's all-time record. Musial hits a HR, a double, and 3 singles against the Boston Braves.

The Dodgers win the pennant while idle. The Cards lose to the Cubs to clinch the Dodgers first title since 1941, this time with a 5-game margin.

25th Giants rookie Larry Jansen wins his 21st game of the season, beating the Braves Red Barrett 2–1. It is Jansen's 10th win in a row, all complete games.

28th On the season's last day, the Browns, desperate for a ticket seller, bring announcer Dizzy Dean in to pitch against the White Sox. Diz gives up only 3 hits in 4 innings and laces a clean single in his only at bat, but a pulled leg muscle forces his retirement. The White Sox score all their runs in the 9th to win 5–2. Even with Diz, the game draws less than 16,000, and the Browns finish the year with only 320,000 attendance, less than half that of 1946. Three days before the finale a Browns' game drew only 350.

29th Joe McCarthy, who led the Yankees to 9 pennants, is coaxed out of retirement and signs to manage the Red Sox. Joe Cronin will become general manager of Tom Yawkey's team.

Hitless the first 4 innings against Brooklyn's Ralph Branca, the Yankees score 5 runs in the 5th inning and win the World Series opener 5–3. A record WS crowd of 73,365 at the Stadium pays $325,828.

OCTOBER

1st New York's Allie Reynolds spaces 9 hits and coasts to a 10–3 victory. Tom Henrich's solo HR in the 5th puts the game away for the Yankees.

2nd The Dodgers squeak to a 9–8 win, jumping on Bobo Newsom and Vic Raschi in the 2nd for 6 runs. Yogi Berra becomes the first player to hit a pinch HR in WS history, hitting one off Brooklyn's Ralph Branca in the 7th inning.

Ex-Giant Danny Gardella, suspended for 5 years for jumping to the Mexican League, files suit for $300,000 in damages. He charges that the reserve clause is "monopolistic and restrains trade." It will be dismissed.

3rd Brooklyn pinch hitter Cookie Lavagetto doubles home 2 runs with 2 out in the bottom of the 9th to break up Floyd Bevens, dramatic no-hit bid and give the Dodgers a 3–2 victory over the Yankees in game 4 at Ebbets Field.

4th Frank Shea throws a 4-hitter and helps his own cause with 2 singles, as the Yankees win 2–1 in Game 5. A Joe DiMaggio HR in the 5th is the margin.

In the Negro League WS, Luis Tiant, Sr., and Pat Scantlebury pitch the New York Cubans to a 6–5 win over the Cleveland Buckeyes in the final game.

5th CF Al Gionfriddo's magnificent catch takes a HR away from Joe DiMaggio, which would have tied the 6th game of the WS at Yankee Stadium. The Brooklyn Dodgers go on to win 8–6. There is another WS attendance record, with a crowd of 74,065 on hand to watch the game.

6th The New York Yankees beat the Brooklyn Dodgers 5–2 to win the WS in 7 games. Relief P Hugh Casey of the Dodgers appears in 6 games, winning 2 while notching an 0.87 ERA. Series heroes Bevens, Gionfriddo, and Lavagetto will not play another ML game.

7th Larry MacPhail resigns as Yankees general manager moments after the final game of the series. Co-owners Dan Topping and Del Webb then buy out MacPhail's one-third interest in the club for $2 million. George Weiss will become GM.

20th Radio rights for the WS sell for $475,000 for 3 years. Every franchise but Pittsburgh has sold 1948 TV rights. The Giants get $400,000 for radio-TV rights from Chesterfield.

NOVEMBER

17th In a major deal that helps the Red Sox, Boston ships Roy Partee, Jim Wilson, Al Widmar, Eddie Pellagrini, Pete Layden and Joe Owstrowski and $310,000 to the Browns for Jack Kramer and Vern Stephens. Stephens will lead the AL in RBI in 2 of the next 3 seasons while averaging 33 HRs each year.

18th The Red Sox acquire All-Star SS Vern Stephens and pitchers Jack Kramer and Ellis Kinder from the Browns in exchange for 10 players and $375,000.

25th Sam Breadon sells the Cardinal empire to Postmaster General Robert Hannegan and Fred Saigh. The price is in excess of $4 million with the new owners getting the Cardinal players, physical assets, 16 minor league franchises, $2.1 million in reserve funds and payment on a new ballpark site, 4 minor league parks, and the lease on Sportsman's Park. Breadon had first acquired an interest in the Cardinals in 1917 and bought control in 1920 for an investment of $350,000.

27th Setting off a storm of controversy, Joe DiMaggio is named American League MVP by a single point over Ted Williams. Williams, the Triple Crown winner, receives 201 points, and is completely left off one writer's ballot. A 10th-place vote would have given Williams the needed 2 points. Williams is selected *The Sporting News* Player of the Year.

DECEMBER

9th The Indians pick up John Berardino from the Browns for Catfish Metkovich and $50,000. Because of a broken finger, Metkovich will be returned to Cleveland, and the Indians will add another $15,000 to complete the deal. At the end of 1952, Berardino will drop baseball as well as the 2nd "r" in his name, and start a successful acting career in Hollywood.

1948

JANUARY

29th Commissioner Happy Chandler fines the Yankees, Cubs, and Phillies $500 each for signing high school players.

30th Herb Pennock, general manager of the Phillies and former star southpaw, collapses in a New York hotel lobby and dies a short time later at a local hospital.

FEBRUARY

24th Ed Lopat goes to the Yankees from the White Sox in exchange for Aaron Robinson, Bill Wight, and Fred Bradley.

27th Newly elected to the Hall of Fame are Herb Pennock and Pie Traynor. Needing 91 votes for selection, Pennock, who died a month before, gets 94 votes, Traynor 93. Just missing are Al Simmons, Charlie Gehringer, and Bill Terry.

MARCH

4th Stan Musial ends his holdout and signs with the Cardinals for $31,000. The next day Harry Brecheen agrees to a St. Louis pact for $16,500.

6th The Braves get veteran 2B Eddie Stanky from the Dodgers for Bama Rowell and $60,000.

APRIL

16th The White Sox beat the Cubs 4–1 at Wrigley Field with Jack Brickhouse at the WGN-TV mike. This is the first telecast in Chicago history.

19th Rookie LH Lou Brissie defeats the Red Sox at Fenway 4–2 in the 2nd game of a doubleheader. Wounded in W W II, Brissie, who has a metal plate in one leg and wears a shinguard as protection, is hit on the shin by a Ted Williams line drive.

20th George Vico of the Tigers hits the first pitch thrown to him in the ML for a HR. Chicago's Joe Haynes is the pitcher.

21st Leo Durocher, back at the helm of the Dodgers after a one-year suspension, uses 24 men in one game, a 9–5 loss to the Giants.

White Sox C Mike Tresh hits his first HR in 787 games, 2,568 at bats. He hit his previous HR in 1940.

24th The Cubs hit 4 home runs at home in a 6–2 win over the Phils. Bill Nicholson's HR, to the right of the Wrigley Field scoreboard, lands on Sheffield Avenue. It bounces off a building and allegedly lands on the hood of a southbound car.

29th Cards relief pitcher Ted Wilks bows 5–4 in 14 innings to the Cincinnati Reds on rookie Hank Sauer's single. It is his first loss after 77 mound appearances dating back to 1945. He had won 12 in a row.

30th A 5-hit game by Stan Musial at Cincinnati is the first of 4 such performances by him during the year. He will do it again on May 19, June 22, and September 22. Only Cobb and Keeler have done it before.

MAY

8th An infield single by Johnny Blatnik of the Phillies in the 7th prevents a perfect game by Harry Brecheen of the Cardinals. Brecheen will become the NL ERA leader with 2.24 and the winning percentage leader on a 20-7 record. The Cards win 5–0.

9th In the 2nd game of the Sunday doubleheader between the Pirates and the Dodgers, the umpire continues the game through a 7 P.M. curfew because he believes Pittsburgh to be stalling with a 5–4 lead. The Dodgers pass the Pirates for a 7–5 score, but Ralph Kiner hits a 3-run HR to carry Pittsburgh to a 10–8 victory. The Pirates are fined $100 for violating the curfew.

16th Pete Gray, one-armed OF with the Browns in 1945, starts his comeback at Elmira after a year out of baseball. He will hit .290 in 82 games.

18th An International League game in Jersey City draws less than 1,700 on a night a Giant telecast is being received in 600 bars in Jersey. The minor leagues, especially in the East, are getting testy over the impact of the major leagues open television policy.

20th In a 13–4 Cleveland win, the Indians collect 18 bases on balls in a game with the Red Sox to tie the AL record.

23rd Joe DiMaggio hits 3 consecutive HRs for the New York Yankees in a 6–5, first-game win against the

Indians. The first 2 HRs are off Bob Feller. The Indians take the nightcap 5–1.

27th Recently retired slugger Hank Greenberg buys an interest in the Cleveland club, becoming the Indians 2nd-largest stockholder.

31st A lefthander for Schenectady (Canadian-American League) named Tom Lasorda strikes out 25 in a 15-inning game against Amsterdam.

JUNE

1st Barney DeForge, pitcher-manager in the Carolina League, and Ed Weingarten, an official of clubs in the Tri-State and Blue Grass Leagues, are barred from baseball for life on charges of bribery, gambling, and game-throwing.

2nd The White Sox acquire Fat Pat Seerey and P Al Gettel from Cleveland for 3B Bob Kennedy.

5th Richie Ashburn of the Phillies hits safely in a 6–5 win at Chicago. It is his 23rd consecutive game starting May 9, a 20th-century NL record for a rookie (Jimmy Williams had streaks of 27 and 26 games in 1899). Alvin Dark will tie it this year and Mike Vail will match it in 1975.

6th Erv Dusak, Red Schoendienst, Enos Slaughter, and Nippy Jones homer in the 6th inning as the St. Louis Cardinals beat the Phillies 11–1.

Ted Williams, Stan Spence, and Vern Stephens hit successive HRs for the Red Sox against Freddie Hutchinson of the Tigers. It is the 2nd 3-straight-HR game by the BoSox during the season, with Spence, Stephens, and Bob Doerr having accomplished the feat off Phil Marchildon of the A's on April 19.

7th The Braves Jim Russell hits one HR batting lefty and one HR batting righty in a 9–5 win over the Cubs. He also hits 2 doubles.

13th The Yankees retire Babe Ruth's No. 3 jersey in the Babe's final appearance at Yankee Stadium on the 25th anniversary of Yankee Stadium. After the ceremonies the Yankees beat the Cleveland Indians 5–3.

15th The Detroit Tigers beat the Philadelphia Athletics 4–1 before a crowd of 54,480 in the first night game at Briggs Stadium. The Tigers are the last AL team to install lights.

Behind Johnny Sain, the Braves beat the Cubs 6–3 to take a one-game NL lead. It is the first game to be telecast in the Boston area; the Red Sox will follow a week later after they return from a road trip.

Cleveland picks up Sam Zoldak from the Browns for Bill Kennedy and $100,000. Kennedy will win 7 for the Browns in 1948, while Zoldak will be 9-6 for the Tribe.

20th Cleveland draws 82,781 for a doubleheader, a ML record for a regular season game that will be broken by the same club in 1954. The Indians will attract 2.6 million for the season, surpassing the Yankees, 1947 attendance.

Ralph Kiner hits HRs every Sunday for 8 successive weeks in May and June. For the year he will hit 17 round trippers in 38 Sunday games.

John Mize, Willard Marshall, and Sid Gordon of the Giants hit HRs in the 8th inning in a 6–4 win against Murry Dickson of the Cardinals.

30th In his first full season as a pitcher, Bob Lemon of the Cleveland Indians pitches a no-hitter, beating the Detroit Tigers 2–0 in front of 49,628 at Briggs Stadium. Lemon has only two scares: Dale Mitchell makes a miraculous catch of a George Kell drive in the 4th and Ken Keltner makes a great stop behind 3B in the 5th.

An 18-year-old lefthander from Rochester, NY, Johnny Antonelli, gets a $75,000 contract from the Braves. Shortly afterward, the Tigers will pay a similar sum to another teenager, catcher Frank House.

JULY

3rd Dick Lane, CF of Muskegon (Central League), hits 5 HRs in a game against Fort Wayne. Lane, who will get a trial with the White Sox in 1949, will hit only 7 other HRs during the year.

4th Ted Williams of the Red Sox faces 3 pitchers in the 7th inning, a first in AL history as Boston scores 14 runs and beats the Philadelphia Athletics 20–8. The 14 runs in one inning is a record, but 5 years later they will do even better with 17 in one inning.

5th Ralph Kiner hits 3 HRs for the Pittsburgh Pirates. Fellow Pirates Johnny Hopp and Wally Westlake team up with Kiner in the outfield for a record 19 putouts.

7th The Indians sign Satchel Paige, fabulous veteran Negro League pitcher. Ridiculed as a Bill Veeck publicity stunt, the 42-year-old Paige will finish at 6-1.

13th Vic Raschi of the Yankees drives in the winning runs with a bases-loaded single in the 4th inning and is the winning pitcher as the AL again tops the NL 5–2 in the All-Star Game at Sportsman's Park. Ted Williams, Joe DiMaggio, George Kell, and Hal Newhouser miss places in the lineup due to injuries.

16th The Chicago Cubs beat the Philadelphia Phillies 3–2 when, with 2 outs and the bases loaded in the 9th inning, rookie Robin Roberts hits Phil Cavarretta and Andy Pafko on the back with successive pitches.

There are 3 managerial changes in one day. Ben Chapman is fired by the Phillies, and Eddie Sawyer gets the job. But the big news is from New York. The Giants remove Mel Ott and replace him with Leo Durocher, who obtains his release from Brooklyn. The Dodgers bring back Burt Shotton. At the end of the season, Bucky Harris of the Yankees, Ted Lyons of the White Sox, and Steve O'Neill of the Tigers will be released.

18th Fat Pat Seerey, chunky Sox OF, hits 4 HRs, his last in the 11th inning, to lead the Chicago White Sox to a 12–11 victory over the Athletics in Philadelphia. Seerey is the 5th ML player to accomplish the feat.

The first 17 Dodgers reach base against the Cardinals with 9 hits, 6 walks, a fielder's choice, and an error before P Hank Behrman whiffs to end the 2nd inning. All other outs are on the bases.

20th An unprecedented suspension of an umpire, the veteran Bill McGowan, is announced by AL President Will Harridge. McGowan is set down for 10 days for throwing a ball-and-strike indicator at Washington players.

24th Five members of the Duluth club in the Northern League are killed, and 13 are injured in a bus-truck crash near St. Paul. The injured include Mel McGabe, future NL manager, and Elmer Schoendienst, brother of the Cardinal infielder, Red.

26th Ruth makes his last public appearance, at the New York premiere of the film *The Babe Ruth Story*. He will die 3 weeks later.

27th Hank Arft has a triple and a HR in his ML debut with the Browns. He will hit .253 for his career.

31st The Braves have lengthened their lead over the Pirates and the Dodgers in the NL. The Red Sox push to the AL top, with the A's hanging in close as the Indians falter.

AUGUST

5th Dodger Gene Hermanski hits 3 successive HRs to help Brooklyn beat the Cubs 6–4.

6th The Reds release Johnny Neun as manager and pick Bucky Walters to succeed him.

12th The Indians wallop the Browns 26–3, coming within one run of the AL record for the most runs scored in a game.

13th The promise of Paige on the mound brings 51,013 to Comiskey Park to see "Ole Satch" pitch his first ML shutout as Cleveland wins 5–0.

16th Babe Ruth dies of throat cancer at age 53 in New York.

17th Tom Henrich hits his 4th grand slam of the season, off the Senators Sid Hudson. to join Ruth, Gehrig, and York—and, later, Al Rosen and Ray Boone—for the AL record. Henrich, who broke in with the Yankees in 1937, had never hit a grand slam before this season.

20th The Indians draw 78,382 for the largest crowd to attend a night game. The Indians go on to beat the Chicago White Sox at Memorial Stadium as Satchel Paige blanks the opposition for the 4th consecutive shutout by Cleveland hurlers. Besides Paige, Gene Bearden, Sam Zoldak, and Bob Lemon had shutouts.

21st Aaron Robinson homers in the 9th off Bob Lemon to help the White Sox beat the Indians 3–2. The run breaks the 47-inning scoreless streak by Indians pitchers. The 1903 Cleveland team had had a run of 41 scoreless innings. Baltimore will extend the record in 1974 to 54 innings.

Representatives of Cuba, Panama, Puerto Rico, and Venezuela, meeting in Havana, agree to stage a 4-country round-robin 12-game tournament to be known as the Serie de Caribe (Caribbean Series) and to be launched in Cuba during February 1949. The Dominican Republic and Mexico will also later participate on a regular basis.

22nd The Dodgers steal 8 bases, including a 5th-inning triple steal with Robinson on the front end. But the Braves win 4–3.

27th Hank Majeski of the Athletics hits 6 doubles in a doubleheader against the Browns, pacing the A's to wins of 6–0 and 9–1.

28th The Dodgers sweep a doubleheader 12–7 and 6–4 against the Cardinals to take over first place ahead of the Braves by 3 percentage points. In the first game, Jackie Robinson hits for the cycle, scores 3 runs, and drives in 2.

31st The Dodgers are even with the Braves, with the Cardinals close behind. In the AL only 2 games separate the Red Sox, Indians, and Yankees. The A's stay within striking distance.

SEPTEMBER

2nd Commissioner Happy Chandler fines the Pirates $2,000 for violating the NL bonus rule. Pittsburgh signed M. L. Lynch as a scout while offering his son Danny a $6,000-a-year contract. Chandler interprets this as an attempt to influence the young second baseman's decision. Danny Lynch is declared a free agent and signs with the Cubs.

5th Amarillo (West Texas-New Mexico League) OF Bob Crues hits 2 HRs against Lubbock to give him 69 for the season, tying Joe Hauser's 1933 mark at Minneapolis. He sets an organized baseball record with 254 RBI in 140 games, hits a record 8 grand slams, while hitting .404.

6th The Tigers and the Browns set an AL mark by using 37 players in their game.

9th Hard-throwing Rex Barney of the Brooklyn Dodgers survives a one-hour rain delay plus showers in the 6th, 8th, and 9th innings and hurls a no-hitter, beating the New York Giants 2–0. It is Barney's 10th win in 2 months, and keeps the 3rd-place Dodgers 3½ games behind the NL-leading Braves.

13th Cleveland P Don Black suffers a cerebral hemorrhage while at bat against the Browns. Black's life will hang in the balance for a week. Owner Bill Veeck of the Indians arranges a benefit game for Black on September 22, a contest that attracts 76,000, and $40,000 of the receipts are turned over to the pitcher.

23rd ⟨The Braves clinch the NL flag by defeating the Giants 3–2. They will finish 6½ games ahead of the Dodgers. Two days before the season is over the Braves will lose their best hitter, OF Jeff Heath, who breaks an ankle sliding home against Brooklyn.

OCTOBER

2nd The Yankees are eliminated from the AL race by losing to the Red Sox 7–5. The Indians are sure of at least a tie by whitewashing Detroit 8–0 behind Feller.

3rd Cleveland can clinch the flag with a win over Detroit, but Hal Newhouser gives up only 5 hits in the 7–1 Detroit victory.

The Red Sox tie for the lead by blasting New York 10–5, despite 4 hits by Joe DiMaggio.

Johnny Mize hits his 40th HR of the year to again tie Ralph Kiner for the NL lead, as was the case in 1947. Kiner had hit his final 1948 HR on September 26. In 1946 rookie Kiner led with 23 to the 22 of Mize, who missed 50 games because of injury.

Luke Easter's grand slam highlights the Homestead Grays' 19-hit assault on the Birmingham Black Barons in the 4th game of the Negro World Series. The Grays will win the Championship in 5 games. This will be the final Negro WS, as the Negro National League becomes a casualty of integration and folds during the winter.

Joe Sewell so dominated the low-strikeout records that part of the heroics of Lou Boudreau in this season is often missed. Boudreau finishes the year with only 9 strikeouts, the best record by a RH batter in the AL since Stuffy McInnis fanned just 5 times in 142 games in 1922.

4th In a one-game playoff for the AL pennant at Fenway Park, the Cleveland Indians beat the Boston Red Sox 8–3 behind rookie knuckleballer Gene Bearden, who wins his 20th game. Player-manager Lou Boudreau gets 4 hits, including 2 HRs. Red Sox manager Joe McCarthy ignores his rotation pitchers to go with journeyman Denny Galehouse (8-7). With the score 1–1 in the 4th, Ken Keltner hits a 3-run HR over the LF fence.

6th In the WS opener in Boston, Phil Masi is called safe at 2B on a disputed call by umpire Bill Stewart on a pickoff attempt in the 8th. Masi then scores on a single by Tommy Holmes as Johnny Sain and the Boston Braves top the Cleveland Indians and Bob Feller 1–0.

7th Cleveland ties the Series on Bob Lemon's 4–1 win. Two runs score in the 4th on hits by Lou Boudreau, Joe Gordon, and Larry Doby.

8th Indian Gene Bearden faces only 30 batters as he turns in a 5-hit, 2–0 win before 70,000 at Cleveland.

9th Before a record WS 81,897, the Indians take a 3-1 Series lead, as Steve Gromek outpitches Johnny Sain. The first HR of the Series, by Larry Doby, is decisive.

10th A 6-run 7th kayoes Bob Feller and 2 successors for the Braves' 11–5 victory. Bob Elliott has 2 HRs, one for 3 runs. The WS crowd is even larger than the day before, 86,288, only to be exceeded in the LA Coliseum in 1959.

11th In Boston, the Cleveland Indians nip the Braves 4–3 to take the WS in 6 games. Rookie lefty Gene Bearden is the pitching hero in relief.

12th The Yankees hire Casey Stengel to manage in 1949.

27th Commissioner Chandler orders free agency for 10 Detroit-owned minor leaguers for the club's coverup of their contracts. One of the players who will make the ML is Bill Serena, with a 6-year career.

NOVEMBER

4th Former OF Jake Powell shoots and kills himself in a Washington, D.C., police station.

10th In a move that will give Chicago their mound ace for the 1950s, Detroit sends young Billy Pierce (3-0 in 1948) to the White Sox for Aaron Robinson. The Tigers even sweeten the deal with $10,000.

30th Player-manager Lou Boudreau is selected the AL MVP. Boudreau had almost been traded to the Browns earlier in the year, but protests by fans kept Lou in Cleveland. After the WS win, owner Bill Veeck commented, "Sometimes the best trades are the ones you never make."

DECEMBER

2nd Stan Musial is picked MVP in the NL. Musial led the NL in batting at .365, runs (135), RBI (131), and in doubles and triples. His 39 HRs were one short of Mize and Kiner.

10th The minors started 58 leagues and 438 clubs this year. All the leagues finished schedules, but when the minor leagues ask for curbs on television into their areas, the ML clubs sidestep the issue.

The Yankees send $100,000 plus young catcher Sherm Lollar and 2 players to St. Louis for Fred Sanford and Roy Partee.

14th The Indians send Eddie Klieman, Eddie Robinson, and P Joe Haynes, acquired from the White Sox 3 weeks earlier for C Joe Tipton, to Washington for Early Wynn and Mickey Vernon. Vernon will go back to the Nats in 1950 but Wynn will stay in Cleveland for 9 seasons and 163 wins.

1949

JANUARY

12th The Giants are fined $2,000, and manager Leo Durocher, $500 for signing Fred Fitzsimmons as a coach while he was still under contract to the Braves. Fitz gets a $500 fine and a 30-day spring training suspension.

25th Lou Boudreau is rewarded for the Indians' championship with a 2-year, $65,000 annual contract as player-manager.

27th Fred Saigh buys out the interest of Robert Hannegan and now controls 90 percent of the Cardinals' stock. Saigh and Hannegan had swung the deal in 1947 with only $60,300 in cash in a $4 million deal. Hannegan came out with $866,000 profit in 2 years.

29th The Pirates get Murry Dickson from St. Louis for $125,000.

FEBRUARY

2nd Brothers Bill and Charlie DeWitt gain control of the Browns by acquiring 57 percent of the stock from Dick Muckerman for $1 million.

7th Joe DiMaggio signs with the Yankees for $100,000, the first six-figure contract in the ML.

9th A federal appeals court orders the $300,000 suit against baseball by Mexican League jumper Danny Gardella back to a lower court for trial.

MARCH

1st The Browns, owners of Sportsman's Park, move to evict the Cardinals in order to gain a rental increase.

2nd Joe DiMaggio leaves the Yankee camp to have an ailing right heel examined at Johns Hopkins hospital.

8th Max Lanier and Fred Martin, late of the Mexican League, file a $2.5 million suit against baseball. A federal judge on April 1 will deny their right to be reinstated.

APRIL

8th Dissension rumors surround the NL title-holder Boston Braves after manager Billy Southworth calls a closed meeting of the club in a South Carolina hotel.

19th At pregame ceremonies marking the season opener in Yankee Stadium, a granite monument to Babe Ruth is unveiled in center field. Plaques honoring Lou Gehrig and Miller Huggins are also presented. Mrs. Babe Ruth, Mayor William O'Dwyer, and Governor Thomas E. Dewey are at the game.

In Brooklyn, the Dodgers pay tribute to Jack "Shorty" Laurice, the "number one" fan and leader of the Ebbets Field "Sym-phony" band. Laurice died in 1948.

Before 53,000 at Detroit, Tigers rookie Johnny Groth homers twice in his first 3 trips against the White Sox.

20th Phils 3B Willie Jones hits 4 consecutive doubles, tying a NL mark with Dick Bartell (1933) and Ernie Lombardi (1935).

24th Lloyd Merriman of the Reds gets a HR and a triple in his first ML game.

28th A New York fan charges Leo Durocher with assault after the Giants lose 15–2 to Brooklyn. Commissioner Chandler suspends Durocher but he is absolved on May 3rd. Chandler criticizes teams for lax security that allows fans on the field.

30th Rocky Nelson hits an "inside-the-glove" 2-run HR in short LF to turn a 9th inning 3–1 Cubs' lead into a 4–3 Cardinals' victory. Cubs CF Andy Pafko's catch is ruled a trap by umpire Al Barlick, as Pafko races in, holding the ball high as runners circle the bases.

MAY

1st Elmer Valo is the first AL player to hit 2 bases-loaded triples when he leads the A's to a 15–9 win in the first of two. Valo has a 3rd bases-loaded triple during the season, to tie the league mark of Shano Collins in 1918.

5th Charlie Gehringer, star 2B of the Tigers between 1925-41, is picked for the Hall of Fame. Two days later, the Old-Timers committee will select Kid Nichols and Three-Finger Brown.

The White Sox abandon their trick LF fence. A 5-foot chicken wire fence erected to cut the distance by 20 feet results in 11 HRs in 8 games, the opponents getting 7 of them. Floyd Baker, an infielder who will play 874 games in the ML, hit his only career HR into "Home Run Lane" on May 4th in an 8–7 loss against Washington. "Home Run Lane" is named after GM Frank Lane.

6th Nine hitless innings in relief are thrown by A's rookie Bobby Shantz in a 13-inning, 5–4, Athletics' win over the Tigers. Shantz gives up a run in the 13th, but old-timer Wally Moses saves him with a 2-run HR.

10th Longtime Cardinal owner Sam Breadon dies. Robert Hannegan, the man to whom he sold the club, will die October 6.

11th The White Sox score in every inning of their 12–8 victory over the Red Sox.

24th Striking out the last 6 St. Paul batters, Maurice McDermott of Louisville (American Association) fans a total of 20 for a new league record.

27th The Indians start so badly, 12-17, that owner Bill Veeck arranges a "2nd Opening Day." The Indians do rise to 2nd place, within 2½ games of the top, but they will finish 3rd, 8 games back.

29th After 44 games and 285 errorless chances, 2B Red Schoendienst of the Cardinals errs against the Pirates.

JUNE

2nd The Philadelphia Phillies hit 5 HRs in the 8th inning, tying the mark set by the 1939 Giants. The Phillie 5 includes Del Ennis, Andy Seminick (2), Pudding Head Jones, and Schoolboy Rowe. Jones adds a triple, and Gran Hamner's 2B jumps the extra base total to 18, still a record. Seminick has 3 HRs in all.

5th Commissioner Happy Chandler lifts the ban on all players who jumped to Mexico, starting in 1946. Only Sal Maglie will make a significant mark after the exile. Lou Klein will be the first jumper to make a ML box score, successfully pinch-hitting on June 16.

9th The Phillies tip the Pirates 4–3 in 18 innings in Philadelphia.
Athletics P Dick Fowler records 9 putouts in a 12-inning 1–0 win over the White Sox.

10th Frank Frisch, who began the season as coach of the Giants, replaces Charlie Grimm as manager of the last-place Cubs.

13th The Giants trade C Walker Cooper to Cincinnati for Ray Mueller.

15th Eddie Waitkus of the Phillies is shot by 19-year-old Ruth Steinhagen at Chicago's Edgewater Beach Hotel. She will later be placed in a mental hospital. Waitkus battles for his life and will come back to play the following season.
Rookie OF Dino Restelli joins the Pirates from San Francisco (PCL) and hits 7 HRs in his first 39 at bats. He will finish with 12, hitting .250 in 72 games, and is out of the league the next year.

16th The Braves bring up 19-year-old Del Crandall from Evansville (IN) and make him their regular catcher.

26th Pat Mullin hits 3 HRs for the Detroit Tigers.

28th After missing the first 69 games of the season because of an ailing heel, Joe DiMaggio wakes to find the pain has disappeared. He returns to the Yankee lineup with a single and a HR that help the Bombers beat the Red Sox 6–4 in a night game at Fenway. He will hit 4 HRs in a 3-game sweep.

29th Mickey Owen and Luis Olmo rejoin the Dodgers from Mexican League exile.

JULY

3rd Giants P Monte Kennedy hits a grand slam and shuts out the Dodgers 16–0.

4th The Dodgers increase their lead to 2 games over the Cardinals by winning the twin bill from the Phillies while the Redbirds, with Max Lanier dropping his first start since reinstatement, divide with the Cubs.

6th The Reds Walker Cooper, acquired on June 13th from the Giants, collects 6 hits in 7 at bats, including 3 HRs, and scores 5 times.

7th Dave Koslo hits the first 2 HRs of his career while beating the Phils 11–3 at the Polo Grounds.

8th Monte Irvin and Hank Thompson, brought up from Jersey City 3 days earlier, are the first blacks to play for the Giants. Thompson, who was also the first black to play for the St. Louis Browns in 1947, starts at 2B, and Irvin pinch-hits in the 8th for Hartung.

12th The NL commits 5 errors, allowing the AL to record an 11–7 triumph in the All-Star Game at Ebbets Field. The contest marks the first appearance of black players—Jackie Robinson, Roy Campanella, and Don Newcombe in the NL lineup and Larry Doby among the AL stars.

24th The Cards trounce the Dodgers 14–1. This win gives St. Louis 3 straight victories at Ebbets Field, as they take over the lead Brooklyn has held through most of the season.

26th Wally Moses gets his 2,000th hit, off Joe Ostrowski of the Browns.

28th A 12-for-25 run raises Jackie Robinson's NL-leading average to .364. Jackie will tail off from that mark but will win the batting title at .342.

Detroit pitcher Dizzy Trout hits a 9th inning grand slam against the Senators to help the Tigers to a victory.

31st Sid Gordon of the New York Giants blasts 2 HRs in the 2nd inning of game 2, as the Giants sweep the Reds 10–0 and 9–0 behind Larry Jansen and Adrian Zabala.

AUGUST

6th Luke Appling appears as SS in his 2,154th game, surpassing Rabbit Maranville's ML mark. Appling will finish with 2,218.

7th Lineup juggling is a Casey Stengel forte as his Yankees suffer injury after injury. Against the Browns, 13 different Yankees score a run in the first game of a doubleheader.

8th Carl Furillo returns to the Dodgers' lineup after an injury and hits .431 in the final 8 weeks of the season. He finishes at .322, fourth best in the league.

9th Dom DiMaggio's 34-game hitting streak is on the line against Vic Raschi and the Yankees. Hitless in his first 4 at bats, Dom hits a sinking line drive in the 8th that his brother Joe catches at his shoetops. The Red Sox win 6–3 to move 5½ games behind the Yankees. Dom had started his streak after going hitless against Raschi.

15th Reports of clubhouse troubles trail the Braves all season. Owner Lou Perini prevails on manager Billy Southworth to take a leave of absence. The team spurts briefly under Johnny Cooney but finishes under

.500 in 4th place. Braves players vote Southworth only a half-share of last year's Series earnings but Happy Chandler restores the full share.

21st A barrage of bottles from the Philadelphia stands as protest of a decision by umpire George Barr over a trapped fly ball results in the first forfeiture in the ML in 7 years. The Giants, who receive this forfeit, gave one away in 1942 when hordes of youngsters invaded the field.

22nd The Giants sell veteran Johnny Mize to the Yankees for $40,000.

26th For choking an umpire in the Florida International League, Miami manager Pepper Martin is fined $100 and suspended for the remaining 2 weeks in the season.

27th Former Mexican Leaguers Max Lanier and Fred Martin drop their $2.5 million suit against baseball.

SEPTEMBER

9th Despite terrorizing the NL with bat and baserunning during the season, Jackie Robinson is picked off base by Dave Koslo, the 4th time this year Giants pitchers have nabbed him.

13th For the 2nd time in his career, Ralph Kiner hits HRs in 4 consecutive at bats, over 2 games. He performed the same feat in 1947. The 2 HRs today are numbers 33 and 34. Kiner's 1949 total will include 25 on the road, 29 at Forbes Field, 14 of them in the bullpen enclosure still known as Greenberg Gardens.

15th Pirates P Ernie Bonham dies following an appendectomy and stomach surgery, just 18 days after his last pitching performance, an 8–2 win over the Phillies. Mrs. Bonham will receive the first benefits under the players pension plan, $90 a month for 10 years.

20th Jackie Robinson steals home in a 5–0 Dodger win against the Cubs. It is his 5th steal of home this year and the 13th in his 3 years in the NL. That is the most in the ML since Ben Chapman stole his 15th and last in 1940, his 11th season.

24th Bob Elliott hits 3 successive HRs for Boston, as the Braves down the Giants 6–4.

Ellis Kinder (15-1 at Fenway Park) pitches a 6-hitter, and Williams lines his 42nd HR to beat the

Yankees 2–0 and pull the Red Sox 1 game behind the Yankees.

25th The Cardinals, in first place for 2 months, win their final home game, and the Dodgers lose to Philadelphia, maintaining the Cards 11½ game lead.

Despite 71 injuries that kept players out of games, Casey Stengel and his Yankees have been in first place all season. But today the Red Sox move into a tie for first place with a 4–1 victory over Allie Reynolds. Ted Williams hits his 43rd HR, and Mel Parnell wins his 25th game of the season. The lefty is 16-3 at Fenway this year. Joe DiMaggio listens to the game from a hospital, bedridden with pneumonia. The Yankees return to New York and are greeted at Grand Central Station by a huge crowd of fans, including Mrs. Babe Ruth, who predicts, "Whoever wins tomorrow should go all the way."

26th Before 67,434 at Yankee Stadium, the Red Sox survive a rhubarb-filled, 7–6 win when Johnny Pesky scores on a disputed squeeze play. Leading by one game, the Sox move on to Washington for a 3-game series before the last 2 games of the year with the Yankees.

27th The Red Sox, winners of 16 out of the last 19 with the Senators, win the opener in Washington 6–4.

28th Facing Ray Scarborough, the Nats' top pitcher, the Red Sox take a 1–0 lead into the 9th only to have Washington tie it up. Mel Parnell, in relief, bounces a curve past C Birdie Tebbetts, and the winning run scores from 3rd.

The Yankees, taking 2 out of 3 games from the Athletics, stay one game behind the Red Sox with 2 games left.

Called up from Toronto in mid-September, Eddie Sanicki of the Phils gets his 3rd hit of the season. All 3 are homers. On September 14 Sanicki had homered with 2 men on his first big-league at bat, against Rip Sewell of the Pirates.

29th The Cardinals lose to former Redbird Murry Dickson, now with the Pirates, 7–2, following a George Munger loss. The Dodgers take 2 from the Braves and a half-game lead.

In the 5th inning against the Dodgers, the Braves Connie Ryan protests against playing in the rain by kneeling on the on-deck circle with his raincoat on. Umpire George Barr ejects Ryan from the game.

30th Boston outlasts Washington 11–9 to move into New York for the showdown for the AL pennant.

Kiner hits his 54th homer and 16th in September, as the Pirates beat Herm Wehmeier and the Reds 3–2. The monthly total eclipses Cy Williams's 1923 NL mark.

OCTOBER

1st The Cards lose to the Cubs, and the Dodgers lose to Philadelphia, preserving the one-game Brooklyn margin.

The Red Sox need to win just one of the final 2 games against New York to clinch the title. Before a crowd of 69,551 at Yankee Stadium, New York overcomes a 4–0 deficit, as Joe Page is nearly untouchable in 5 innings of relief. Johnny Lindell's HR wins it 5–4.

Alex Kellner wins his 20th to finish the season as the A's first 20-game winner since Lefty Grove in 1933. A future pitching trend is foretold by the record of Yankee ace Allie Reynolds (17-6), who finishes only 4 of 31 starts. Dave Koslo of the Giants is the surprise ERA leader in the NL, but his 2.50 mark contains not a single shutout.

2nd The New York Yankees and the Boston Red Sox enter the final day of the season tied for first place. Nearly 70,000 pack Yankee Stadium to see the finale. Vic Raschi nurses a 1–0 lead into the 8th against Ellis Kinder before the Yankees score 4 against a tired Mel Parnell and an unlucky Tex Hughson. A Sox rally falls short, and the Yankees win the game and the pennant 5–3.

George Kell of the Tigers goes 2-for-3 and Ted Williams is hitless in 2 official trips. Kell's final mark is .3429 and Williams's is .3427.

One game back on the final day, the Cards finally win 13–5 over the Cubs and await the progress of the Dodgers against the Phils. The Phillies shell Don Newcombe and tie the game 7–7 in the 6th. The game goes overtime before the Dodgers get 2 in the 10th for the win and the pennant.

In a promotional stunt, the Browns use a different pitcher in each of 9 innings against the Tigers. Detroit wins 4–3.

5th In the Series opener at the stadium, the New York Yankees and Allie Reynolds beat the Brooklyn Dodgers 1–0 on Tommy Henrich's 9th-inning HR off Don Newcombe. Newcombe had struck out 11 and walked none before Henrich's blast. Allie Reynolds gives up only 2 hits and fans 9.

6th Another 1–0 game, and Preacher Roe wins this one for Brooklyn to knot the Series. Gil Hodges' single drives in Jackie Robinson in the 2nd for the winner.

7th The 9th inning decides the 3rd game also. At Ebbetts Field, with the game tied 1–1, the Yanks score 3, the Dodgers 2 in the final stanza. Johnny Mize's 2-run pinch single is the big factor followed by Jerry Coleman's run-scoring hit. Roy Campanella and Luis Olmo hit bases-empty HRs in the bottom of the 9th.

Danny Gardella drops his suit against baseball, settling out of court for a reported $80,000. All other suits by players who had jumped to Mexico have been dropped.

8th Allie Reynolds relieves Lopat with 2 on and 2 out in the 6th, strikes out Johnny Jorgensen on 3 pitches, and then retires the next 9 batters. The Yankees win 6–4.

9th The Yankees pound the Dodgers 10–6 to win the WS in 5 games. Pinch hitter and 3B Bobby Brown is the hitting hero, batting .500 and driving in 5 runs.

26th The San Francisco Seals (PCL), managed by Lefty O'Doul, finish a tour of the Orient that includes 5 games in Japan, one of which draws 100,000.

29th Arguably their best trade ever, the White Sox send C Joe Tipton, who hit .204 in his one season in Chicago, to the Athletics for young Nellie Fox.

NOVEMBER

1st Gillette buys the WS television rights for $1.37 million, the money to be dedicated to the players pension fund.

18th NL batting leader (.342) Jackie Robinson is picked for the NL MVP award.

21st Bill Veeck sells the Indians for $2.2 million to a local syndicate headed by Ellis Ryan. Hank Greenberg will be general manager.

25th Ted Williams, who lost the Triple Crown when his batting average was .0002 below that of George Kell, wins the MVP vote in a landslide. Phil Rizzuto and Joe Page finish 2nd and 3rd in the voting.

26th The Japanese Central League is joined by the Pacific League.

DECEMBER

1st Attendance in the ML is 20.2 million, down from 20.9 in 1948. The Yankees and the Indians each finish with over 2.2 million, but the Browns fall to 270,000. The Browns will try to cover their light attendance with $200,000 obtained in cash in December sales of Bob Dillinger, Gerry Priddy, and Paul Lehner. The Browns get 5 players in the transactions.

12th The AL rejects by a 7-1 vote a proposal to return the spitball to legality. The rules committee also alters the strike zone to the space between the armpits and the top of the knees. The new rule eliminates the batter's shoulders being within the strike zone.

14th In a major trade, the Giants get Alvin Dark and Eddie Stanky from the Braves in a swap for Willard Marshall, Sid Gordon, Buddy Kerr, and Sam Webb.

31st The 1940s is the only decade in ML baseball history in which no new stadiums are built. After Cleveland opened Municipal Stadium in 1932, no new ballpark will be opened until County Stadium in Milwaukee is unveiled in 1953.

The 1940s will end with 8 blacks on ML rosters: 3 each on the Dodgers and Indians, and 2 with the Giants. Although it will be another decade before all ML teams would be integrated, most teams will be playing blacks in the next 2 years. All but the Browns, Cubs, and Reds set attendance records in the 1940s. There were 81 scheduled night games in 1940 and 384 in 1949. The change to playing under the lights is underscored by the release of the 1950 schedule. The Cardinals have permission to open the season with the Pirates in a night game.

1950

JANUARY

6th   Charlie "Jolly Cholly" Grimm resigns as vice president of the Cubs to sign a 3-year contract, for a record $90,000, to manage Dallas (Texas League).

10th   The Cleveland Indians fire coach George C. "Good Kid" Susce when his son, George D., signs with the Red Sox.

18th   The Indians Bob Feller, whose 1949 record was a lackluster 15-14, takes a $20,000 salary cut to $45,000. The pay cut was Feller's own suggestion.

23rd   The AP picks the "Miracle Braves" of 1914 as the greatest sports upset in the 20th century.

31st   The Pirates sign high school P Paul Pettit for a record $100,000 after buying his contract from film producer Fred Stephani, who had signed him to an exclusive contract as an athlete/actor (scouts are barred from doing so prior to graduation under major league baseball's "high-school rule"). Unfortunately, with an eventual 1-2 career mark, he will prove not to be worth the trouble.

FEBRUARY

7th   Red Sox slugger Ted Williams becomes the highest paid player in history, by signing for $125,000.

9th   The White Sox purchase C Phil Masi from the Pirates. He will finish his career with 3 strong years in Chicago.

10th   The Reds sell Johnny "double-no-hit" Vander Meer to the Cubs for an undisclosed amount of cash.

16th   Writers fail to name anyone to the Hall of Fame at Cooperstown. Mel Ott and Bill Terry top the list for enshrinement.

27th   The National Baseball Congress criticizes the bonus rule that keeps young players on a ML bench for 2 seasons.

APRIL

1st   The Hollywood Stars (PCL) open their season clad in shorts and rayon shirts.

10th   Based on his 22 wins for Baltimore (IL) in 1949, St. Louis Browns P Al Widmar quits the team. He threatens a suit against baseball unless the team grants him a pay raise. He will sign within the week.

17th   The first Opening Day night game is played in St. Louis with the Cardinals defeating the Pirates 4–2.

18th   President Harry Truman throws out 2 balls at the Washington opener—one left-handed and the other right-handed—as the Senators beat the A's 8–7. When rain starts falling in the 6th, he puts on a raincoat and remains to the end.

Sam Jethroe becomes the first black to play for the Boston Braves. In his ML debut, he goes 2-for-4, including a HR. Jethroe will go on to become NL Rookie of the Year.

The Indians release veteran Ken Keltner. He signs with the Red Sox the same day but is released on June 6th.

Yankees 2B Billy Martin becomes the first player in history to get 2 base hits in one inning in his first ML game. He doubles on his first at bat in the 8th inning, then singles later in the same frame as the Yanks chalk up a 15–10 win over the Red Sox.

19th   Sid Gordon of the Braves hits the first NL grand slam of the season, as Boston beats the Giants 10-6 at the Polo Grounds. There will be 35 in the league this year, a NL single-season record.

21st   Boston's Vern Stephens slugs a 9th-inning grand slam off the A's Lou Brissie to lead the Red Sox to an 8–2 romp. It was the first of 33 AL grandslams in 1950. The ML season total of 68 is a record.

28th   The Yankees sell OF Dick Wakefield to the White Sox for OF John Ostrowski and cash. Wakefield, a hot hitter in 1943 who has since lost his sparkle, refuses to report unless the Sox restore a $5,500 salary cut inflicted by the Yankees. The deal later falls through.

30th   The A's are pummeled by the Red Sox in a doubleheader, 19–0 and 6–5. First-game highlights are an 11-run 4th inning and a 17-hit barrage, which includes HRs by Ted Williams (2), Vern Stephens, and Bobby Doerr. Bobby Shantz ends the slaughter with 4-plus innings of relief.

MAY

1st The Red Sox bring up slugger Walt Dropo from their Louisville farm club to replace the injured Billy Goodman at 1B.

3rd Yankee Vic Raschi, troubled by the new rule that requires a one-second rest before delivery with men on base, balks 4 times in one game, 2 fewer than the single-season record. Nevertheless, he wins 4–3 over the White Sox.

4th The White Sox, helped by Bob "Sugar" Cain's 5-hitter, embarrass the Yankees 15–0 at the Stadium. The score ties the Yank's team record, set in 1907, for the most runs in a shutout loss. One bright spot for the Yankees in the humiliating defeat is Phil Rizzuto's 3 hits.

6th The Boston Braves hit 5 HRs in a 15–11 trouncing of the Reds. This gives them a record 13 HRs in 3 consecutive games.

7th The Cards humble the Braves 15–0 behind Howie Pollet's 4-hitter.

9th Ralph Kiner of the Pirates hits his 2nd grand slam in 3 days—and the 8th of his career—and drives in 7 runs as the Pirates beat Brooklyn 10–5.

10th The Reds trade veteran C Walker Cooper to the Braves for 2B Connie Ryan.

11th Commissioner Happy Chandler voids the Dick Wakefield deal between the Yankees and the White Sox. The Yanks immediately suspend the OF.

Connecticut House member Abraham Ribicoff introduces legislation for observance of National Baseball Day.

Airplane travel is still a baseball rarity, but a railroad strike forces 5 clubs—the Red Sox, Yankees, Dodgers, Giants, and Reds—to fly home or away to play their next scheduled games. The Senators, with short hops in the prospect, will take the bus.

12th Red Sox star Ted Williams apologizes to the hometown fans for "insulting gestures" he made in response to catcalls prompted by his 2 errors in a doubleheader loss (13–4 and 5–3) to Detroit. Williams' 2nd bobble allowed the Tigers eventual winning run to score.

14th The Pirates Johnny Hopp goes 6-for-6, including 2 HRs, in a 16–9, 2nd-game victory as the Pirates sweep the Cubs. The Pirates won the opener 6–5.

15th The Yankees sell veteran OF Johnny Lindell to the Cardinals and P Clarence "Cuddles" Marshall to the Browns.

17th After 11 straight losses to Max Lanier, the Dodgers finally top the Cardinal lefty 6–2 for the first time since 1943. Don Newcombe is the winning P.

The Yankees reinstate Dick Wakefield, but he is not asked to rejoin the team.

18th Tom Glaviano makes 4 errors at 3B in a 9–8 Cardinal loss to Brooklyn. Three errors come in the 9th—2 wild throws and a boot that lets in the winning score. He ties a ML record set most recently by Dodgers Billy Cox the previous year.

19th Tigers ace Virgil Trucks, a 19-game winner in 1949, hurts his arm and is lost for the season.

20th Three Dodger relief hurlers, Ralph Branca, Jack Banta, and Dan Bankhead, combine to pitch 9⅔ innings of no-hit ball, as Brooklyn beats Pittsburgh 4–3 in 11 innings.

25th The Oakland Oaks of the PCL buy recalcitrant OF Dick Wakefield from the Yanks. New York will not allow him to buy out his own contract.

26th The Athletics make some changes. Connie Mack's son, Earl, who had been assistant manager, assumes the duties of chief scout. Earl, who had hoped to succeed his father as manager, is replaced by Jimmie Dykes. Mickey Cochrane is named general manager.

After a miserable 8–22 start, the last-place White Sox fire Jack Onslow, replacing him with interim manager Red Corriden.

27th Former Tiger great Mickey Cochrane becomes the general manager of the Athletics.

29th Pueblo (Western League) announces that its players will don shorts during the summer.

Team psychologist Dr. David Tracy resigns from the St. Louis Browns after the players fail to cooperate with him.

30th The Dodgers Duke Snider hits 3 HRs in the 2nd-game, 6–4 win of a doubleheader sweep of the Phils at Ebbets Field.

JUNE

1st Marty Marion, Sid Gordon, and Hank Thompson hit grand slams for the Cards (5–2 over Brooklyn), the Braves (14–2 over the Pirates), and the Giants (8–7 in the first of 2 at Cincinnati) respectively.

2nd The Tiger's George Kell hits for the cycle in the 16–5 second-game sweep of a Detroit doubleheader with the A's.

Browns P Harry Dorish steals home in the 5th inning against the Senators, as teammate Hank "Bow Wow" Arft goes 5-for-5 in a 9–3 St. Louis win.

3rd In direct challenge to a new league rule, the St. Louis Cardinals book a Sunday night game with Brooklyn, the first in ML history.

The Braves Sid Gordon slugs his 3rd grand slam of the season, plus a 2nd HR, to account for 7 Braves runs in a 10–6 whipping of Pittsburgh.

7th Junior Stephens and Clyde Vollmer each have 2 HRs and 5 RBI for the Red Sox, as they trounce the lowly Browns 20–4 at Fenway.

8th In the most lopsided score in history, the Boston Red Sox annihilate the St. Louis Browns at Fenway Park 29–4. Bobby Doerr has 3 HRs and 8 RBI; Walt Dropo, 2 HRs and 7 RBI, and Ted Williams, 2 HRs and 5 RBI. Al Zarilla adds 4 doubles. The Red Sox have 28 hits to total 51 for 2 days against the Browns. But Ned Garver, the Browns best hurler, will turn the tables the next day, 12–7.

9th Commissioner Happy Chandler orders the Cardinals to cancel their Sunday night game with the Dodgers. On the advice of NL President Ford Frick, the Cards comply and reschedule it as a July 17th day/night doubleheader.

12th ML baseball names Connie Mack as the Honorary Manager of the All-Star Game.

16th The Detroit Tigers regain the lead and do not relinquish it until August 30th.

The Yankees recall Johnny Mize from Kansas City. He proceeds to wallop 25 HRs and drive in 72 runs in 90 games.

18th In the first inning of the 2nd game of a doubleheader, the Indians score 14 runs on their way to a 21–2 trouncing of the Athletics.

In a blockbuster deal, the Yankees send Jim Delsing, Don Johnson, Snuffy Stirnweiss, Duane Pillette, and $50,000 to the Browns for P Tom Ferrick, Joe Ostrowski, and 2 minor leaguers.

21st Joe DiMaggio gets his 2,000th hit, a 7th-inning single off the Indians Chick Pieretti, as the Yanks win 8–2. DiMaggio joins Luke Appling and Wally Moses as the only active players with 2,000 or more hits.

Renegade ball player Danny Gardella admits accepting a pay-off to drop his suit against baseball. After a monthlong tryout with the Cardinals, Gardella had been sent to their Houston farm club where, shortly afterward, he was released. Gardella argues that he should be paid for the entire year, and he blames his release on his suit against the ML.

22nd Larry Jansen of the Giants wins the first game of a doubleheader with a 3–0 shutout of the Cards, and Dave Koslo follows suit with a 5–0 two-hitter in the 2nd game, giving NY a sweep of the twin bill.

23rd Eleven home runs—a ML record—drive in all the runs scored in a 10–9 Tiger win over the Yankees. Detroit has 4 HRs in one inning as Dizzy Trout, Gerry Priddy, Vic Wertz, and Hoot Evers connect. Pitcher Dizzy Trout's HR is his 2nd lifetime grand slam, off Tommy Byrne. Hoot Evers hits another HR, an inside-the-park game winner in the 9th.

Coach Bibb Falk of the University of Texas leads his team to their 2nd consecutive NCAA baseball title.

24th C Wes Westrum has 3 HRs and a triple, as the Giants beat Cincinnati 12–2. The Giants belt 7 HRs in the game.

25th Ralph Kiner leads the Pirates to a 16–11 win at Brooklyn by hitting for the cycle, adding a 2nd HR, and driving in 8 runs.

The A's Paul Lehner ties an AL record with 11 putouts in LF in a 13–5 win against the White Sox.

28th Roy Smalley of the Cubs hits for the cycle in a 13–5 win over the Cards at Wrigley.

29th In an effort to thwart the ML's signing of black players, Dr. J. B. Martin, the president of the Chicago Giants of the Negro American League, signs two white players, teenagers Lou Chirban and Lou Clarizio.

In what looks like a football score, the Red Sox overpower the A's 22–14 in Philadelphia. The 36 runs establishes an AL mark for runs scored by 2 teams.

Overall, pitchers gave up 21 walks in the debacle. Despite the high score, only one HR was hit—by Ted Williams. The previous record of 35 runs was set by the same 2 clubs in 1901: Boston 23, A's 12. The ML mark is 49 by the Cubs and Phillies on August 25, 1922.

Whitey Ford is called up by the Yankees from Kansas City (AA).

30th Joe and Dom DiMaggio both HR in the same game, a 10–2 Red Sox victory in the nightcap of a doubleheader.

Brownie stalwart P Ned Garver loses the game because of his mental error against the White Sox. In what would have been the winning run in regulation, Garver is called out for his failure to touch 3B when rounding the bases. He loses 3–2 in 13 innings.

JULY

2nd Indian great, Bob Feller, wins his 200th ML game, 5–3 over Detroit in the 2nd game of a double-header split.

3rd With rookie Joe Collins not hitting and Tommy Henrich injured, Casey Stengel asks Joe DiMaggio to play 1B in an experiment. In the 7–2 loss he handles 13 cleanly.

4th Braves slugger Sid Gordon ties the ML season grand slam record with 4 when he hits one against the Phillies. Boston's 12–9 win in game 2 means totals of 40 runs, 55 hits, and 90 total bases for the day.

5th Tommy Byrne hits 4 batters with pitches but survives to get the win in a sloppy 12–8 Yankee victory over the A's. The game also featured 18 walks.

8th Red Schoendienst of the Cards goes 5-for-5 against Pittsburgh, but the Cards lose 7–6. The Bucs win in the 9th when they load the bases and Jack Phillips' long fly ball is seemingly snagged by Stan Musial, but then drops into the bullpen for a grand slam.

10th The Giants pick up P Jim Hearn on waivers from St. Louis.

11th Making a leaping, off-the-wall catch of a Ralph Kiner drive, Ted Williams fractures his left elbow in the All-Star game at Chicago. Remaining in the game, he puts the AL ahead, 3–2, with an RBI sin-

gle. Kiner's 9th-inning HR ties the game, and Red Schoendienst's blast in the 14th wins it.

13th Doctors remove 7 bone fragments from Ted Williams' elbow in a 75-minute operation. He will go on to hit .350 for the rest of 1950 and .336 throughout the rest of his career, including .388 and .328 to lead the AL in 1957 and 1958 respectively.

14th The Waterbury (Colonial League) club has a franchise but no players when the 12-man squad is fired after refusing to board the team bus for 2 scheduled games at Kingston, NY. Strike issues are several: The players claim that the team bus is unsafe; the bus is scheduled to bring them home after the first game and return for the second rather than lay over; 6 players claim that the club reneged on the promise of a pay raise if they were still on the roster on June 2.

15th The Colonial League ceases its operation, citing the competition of TV and radio as the cause of their failure.

16th The ML players connect for 37 HRs today for a new record.

19th The Yankees obtain their first black players, OF Elston Howard and P Frank Barnes. They purchase them from the Kansas City Monarchs and assign them to Muskegon (Central League).

Southpaw Ed Lopat of the Yanks wins 16–1 over the Browns, throwing a 2-hitter in the first game of a doubleheader.

Frank E. McKinney resigns as president of the Pirates. He sells interests in the club to John Galbreath and T. Johnson, with Galbreath assuming the presidency. Vice President Bing Crosby retains his minority interest.

The White Sox purchase 3B Bob Dillinger from the Athletics for $35,000.

20th The Giants beat St. Louis 13–3 with an 8-run 3rd inning. Roy "Stormy" Weatherly has a double and triple in the inning.

22nd Red Sox manager "Old Marse" Joe McCarthy leaves the team, citing ill health as the reason. Steve O'Neill replaces him.

23rd Tigers P Saul Rogovin hits a grand slam off Yankees P Eddie Lopat as the Bengals nip New York 6–5.

Sheldon Jones of the NY Giants pitches a one-hitter against the Cubs, winning 3–0 in the 2nd game of a doubleheader. Larry Jansen won the first 5–3.

25th Phillies P Bubba Church and Robin Roberts shut out the Cubs 7–0 and 1–0 in a doubleheader sweep.

After 10 straight losses at Ebbets Field dating back to 1949, the Cards win 9–5.

26th Brooklyn beats the Cardinals 7–5 as the Dodgers' Jim Russell switch-hits HRs, making him the first switch-hitter in history to do it more than once. Stan Musial hits in his 30th straight game, the longest streak of the decade. He is en route to a .346 BA for the season and his 4th batting title. The Cards, currently 1½ games behind Brooklyn, will begin a slow and steady descent to 5th place.

27th Former Dodger great Kirby "Koiby" Higbe hurls a no-hitter for the Minneapolis Millers American Association against the Columbus Clippers.

28th The Indians' Larry Doby, Al Rosen, and Luke Easter connect for consecutive HRs in a 13–1 whipping of the Red Sox.

30th Del Ennis of the Phils hits his 2nd grand slam in 3 days in a 10–0 pasting of Pittsburgh. Phils take the 2nd game 4–2.

AUGUST

1st Acting on the suggestion of Florida International League President Johnny Burroughs, the last-place St. Petersburg Saints players elect their own manager. Their choice, by a near unanimous vote to succeed Jim Pruitt, who resigned, is recently acquired RF Roxie Huberson. He is the team's 4th manager this season.

2nd Andy Pafko of the Cubs hits 3 HRs in the 2nd game of a doubleheader, but the Cubs lose both to the Giants 11–1 and 8–6.

Larry Doby hits 3 HRs in a game as Cleveland beats Washington 11–0. Besides tossing the shutout, Indians hurler Bob Lemon hits a HR.

Elmer Valo hits for the cycle as the A's thrash the White Sox 10–3.

3rd The Pirates sell Hank Borowy to the Tigers, and the Indians waive Gene Bearden to the Senators.

5th Jim Hearn gives up a leadoff single to Bob Dillinger, then throttles the Pirates the rest of the way for a 5–0 win at the Polo Grounds.

6th Boston P Ellis "Old Folks" Kinder hits a grand slam off White Sox ace Billy Pierce.

Sal Maglie and Larry Jansen of the Giants both hurl 3–0 and 5–0 shutouts against the Pirates in a twin bill.

7th Police bar 3 white players— Lou Chirban, Stan Mierko, and Frank Dyle, all of the Chicago American Giants—from playing in the Negro American League against the Birmingham Black Barons, who sweep a doubleheader.

11th Boston P Vern Bickford no-hits the Dodgers in Boston before 29,008 fans. Bickford has lost only once to Brooklyn since joining Boston 1948. The win puts Boston just 5 games behind the first-place Phillies.

Hitting just .279, Yankee great Joe DiMaggio is benched for the first time in his career. He is currently languishing in a 4-for-38 slump.

RF Ken Wood of the Browns nails 2 Tiger runners in the 8th inning of the 2nd game of a DH, tying a ML mark. The Browns prevail 2–1.

12th The Giants Eddie Stanky is banished by umpire Lon Warneke for refusing to stop waving his arms in an attempt to distract Phillies batter Andy Seminick. Giants manager Leo Durocher had agreed to await a league ruling on the tactic, but after Seminick knocks Hank Thompson unconscious in a collision at 3B, Durocher turns Stanky loose. Later, when Seminick puts a linebacker block on Bill Rigney, Stanky's replacement, both dugouts empty for a brawl. The Phils go on to win 5–4, and the Giants protest Stanky's ouster.

14th NL President Ford Frick reproaches Giant Eddie Stanky and bans his tactics, disallowing the Giants' protest. He also fines Andy Seminick and Bill Rigney for the incident.

15th The Red Sox defeat the Athletics 8–3 and 9–4 to begin a streak in which they reel off 27 of 30, propelling themselves back into the pennant race.

16th Branch Rickey of the Brooklyn Dodgers denies news reports that Jackie Robinson will be traded.

Henry Thompson of the Giants hits 2 HRs, both inside the park, against the Dodgers at the Polo Grounds. He is the first to do this since Terry Moore hit two for the Cardinals at Forbes Field on this same date in 1939.

19th The Gillette Safety Razor Co. pays $800,000 for TV rights to the WS. Radio rights will add another $175,000 more.

25th By sweeping a doubleheader from the Cubs, the Phils move into first place for good, replacing St. Louis.

26th Roy Campanella of the Dodgers hits 3 HRs in a 7–5 win over the Reds at Crosley Field.

27th Yankee Allie Reynolds hurls a 2-hitter in a 2–1 win over the White Sox.

The Indians Ray Boone and Clyde Vollmer of the Red Sox hit grand slams today. Boone's comes in the 7-run 3rd to give Bob Feller a 7–0 cushion. Vollmer's pinch slam against Al Benton in the Sox 6-run 7th gives Boston an 11–9 win.

28th Earle and Roy Mack, Connie's sons by his first marriage, purchase 54 percent interest in the Athletics from Connie Mack, Jr., their younger brother from a 2nd marriage. Earl, Roy and Connie Mack now own the club outright.

At Fenway the Red Sox come back from 10–0 and 12–1 to beat the Indians 15–14. Bob Feller is the loser, this time in his only relief appearance of the season.

30th Eddie Stanky of the Giants walks twice in the 6th inning against the Pirates. He walks 7 straight times over 2 games, tying the ML record. The Giants win 4–0 behind Sal Maglie.

31st Gil Hodges of the Brooklyn Dodgers hits 4 HRs and a single, driving in 9 runs in the Dodgers 19–3 rout of the Boston Braves in Ebbets Field.

SEPTEMBER

3rd Havana (Florida International League) wins its 5th straight pennant. Miami, managed by Pepper Martin, finishes 2nd.

4th Giant hurlers Jim Hearn and Sal Maglie hurl twin shutouts over the Phils, winning 2–0 and 9–0.

5th The Yankees acquire 1B Johnny Hopp, who was 2nd in the NL in hitting with a .340 mark, from the Pirates for an undisclosed amount of cash. The Yanks believe Hopp will provide late season pennant insurance.

Phils lefty Curt Simmons is the first player inducted into the Army as a result of the Korean conflict. He will get one more start before reporting.

Purdue Athletic Director Red Mackey criticizes the Yankees for signing his 19-year-old star P Bill Skowron, who was also expected to be the starting right halfback on the Boilermakers' football squad.

6th Don Newcombe tries for a doubleheader victory against Philadelphia. After winning the first game 2–0, he pitches the 2nd game but leaves in the 7th inning trailing 2–0.

7th Tiger OF Hoot Evers hits for the cycle and knocks in 6 runs in a 13–13, ten-inning tie with Cleveland. The game, ended because of darkness, leaves Detroit in first place by a few percentage points ahead of New York.

9th Sal Maglie of the Giants hurls his 4th consecutive shutout, tying a ML record, and beats the Dodgers 2–0. Alvin Dark's 2 HRs provide the runs.

10th Joe DiMaggio becomes the first player to hit 3 HRs in one game at spacious Griffith Stadium, as the Yanks beat Washington 8–1. The Senators lead the 2nd game 6–2 when rain washes it out in the 4th.

The Red Sox win their 22nd in a row at home from the Athletics. This streak dates back to 1949. The Red Sox won all 11 games two years in a row.

12th Ewell Blackwell pitches his 2nd one-hitter of the season, but loses to Brooklyn 3–1.

The Yankees blow a 6-run lead as Cleveland scores 4 in the 9th inning off Allie Reynolds. Luke Easter's 3-run HR is the big blow, as the Yankees skid to 2nd place, a half game behind Detroit and a half game ahead of Boston.

13th Sal Maglie's string of scoreless innings ends at 45, but he beats the Pirates 3–1 in a rain-shortened 7-inning game. Pirate Gus Bell's 257-foot fly ball barely clears the RF wall at the Polo Grounds.

14th Pinch-hitter Ted Tappe homers in his first ML at bat, but the Reds lose 6–2 to Brooklyn. Reds drop the 2nd game 5–2.

15th For the 6th time, Johnny Mize hits 3 HRs in one game, but the Yankees lose 9–7 at Detroit.

His fractured elbow now healed, Ted Williams returns to the Red Sox lineup and raps a HR and 3 singles in a 12–9 defeat of the Browns. The Red Sox will come within 2 games of the first place Yankees this week, but will end up in 3rd place, behind both New York and Detroit.

Eddie Waitkus of the Phils gets 5 hits for the 3rd time this season, as the Phillies beat the Reds 6–5 in 19 innings. Teammate Del Ennis goes 5-for-10.

18th Dodgers Tommy Brown hits 3 HRs in his team's losing effort. The Cubs' Ron Northey hits his 3rd lifetime pinch grand slam to give Chicago a 9–7 win.

19th Stan Musial hits a homer to pace the Cards to an 8–7 win against Boston. Musial will finish the year at .346 to win his 4th batting title.

20th Thrashing the Cubs 9–6 at Philadelphia, The Phils open a 7½ game lead, their biggest so far. Jim Konstanty, appearing for the 68th time, wins his 16th.

21st The Indians open with 14 runs in the first inning against the Athletics.

Warren Spahn of the Braves wins his 21st game, hurling a 2-hit, 5–0 win over the Cards.

23rd The Athletics erupt for 12 runs against the Senators in the 6th inning to win 16–5. Reserve catcher Joe Astroth hits his first homer, a grand slam, and knocks in a record 6 runs in the big inning.

In what amounts to a political and monetary act of leverage, Brooklyn's Branch Rickey offers to sell his 25 percent interest to real estate mogul William Zeckendorf.

24th P Erv Palica of the Dodgers hits a grand slam off Bubba Church of the Phils. He also pitches a 2-hitter, winning in an 11–0 romp.

Mental lapses crush Tiger hopes. Due to heavy smoke from a Canadian forest fire, Detroit puts on the lights in a Sunday afternoon contest with the Indians. With the bases loaded and one out in a 1–1 game, C Aaron Robinson thinks he has a shot at a DP by just stepping on home. Because of the haze, he did not see 1B Don Kolloway remove the force after fielding the ball hit by slugger Luke Easter. Cleveland wins 2–1 in 10 innings.

25th Both Mel Parnell and Harry Taylor of the Red Sox shut out Philadelphia 8–0 and 3–0. Parnell throws a 3-hitter, and Taylor allows only 2 hits in the nightcap.

27th Phils C Andy Seminick hurts his ankle in the first game of a doubleheader, limiting his effectiveness. He will play the next day and all through the WS, later to find out that he has a bone separation.

28th The Phils lose their 2nd doubleheader in as many days, cutting their lead to 3 games over Brooklyn.

29th The idle Yankees clinch their 2nd consecutive pennant under Casey Stengel, as Cleveland's Bob Lemon sets down Detroit 12–2 for his 23rd win.

The Cardinals name Marty "Mr. Shortstop" Marion as their player-manager for 1951.

The Dodgers win a pair from Boston 7–5 and 7–6, shaving the Phils lead to 2, with 2 head-to-head games at Ebbets Field remaining.

30th Brooklyn pulls within one game, as Erv Palica wins 7–3 over the Phillies.

P Gerry Staley and George Munger combine for a doubleheader sweep of the Cubs when the Cards win 4–0 and 2–0.

OCTOBER

1st In Robin Roberts's 3rd start in 5 days, Dick Sisler's dramatic HR off Don Newcombe in the 10th clinches the pennant 4–1 for the Whiz Kids. It is the Phillies' first pennant in 35 years. In the play that sets the stage for Sisler's heroics, CF Richie Ashburn throws out Dodger runner Cal Abrams at the plate in the bottom of the 9th.

Gus Zernial of the Athletics hits 3 HRs in a 4–3 first-game loss. He adds one more in the nightcap, a 10–6 loss to the White Sox, to tie an AL record.

2nd Dom DiMaggio of the Red Sox is the AL leader in steals with 15, the lowest figure ever recorded and a reflection of the emphasis on heavy hitting throughout the season. The younger DiMag made his contribution there as well, batting a career-high .328, tying for the lead with 11 triples, and leading the AL with 131 runs. His brother Joe led with a .585 slugging percentage despite his August slump.

3rd Baseball rules that Phils lefty Curt Simmons cannot play in the WS despite his being on furlough from the Army.

4th Relief ace Jim Konstanty of the Phils starts and loses to Vic Raschi and the Yankees in Philadelphia 1–0 in Game 1 of the WS..

The Columbus Clippers (AA) win the Little World Series 4 games to 1 with a 6–3 victory over the Baltimore Orioles (IL).

5th Allie Reynolds and the Yankees win again over ace Robin Roberts 5–1 in 10 innings in Philadelphia.

6th Tom Ferrick and the Yanks go up 3 games to none, with a 3–2 win over Russ Meyer and the Phils at Yankee Stadium.

7th Whitey Ford wins his first WS game, 5–2 over Bob Miller at the Stadium. The 4-game sweep gives the Yankees their 13th World Championship.

9th Yankees manager Casey Stengel signs a 2-year pact estimated at between $65,000 and $80,000 a year.

10th The Chicago White Sox hire Seattle Raniers (PCL) manager Paul Richards as their manager for 1951.

16th The Brooklyn Dodgers fail to renew Branch Rickey's contract as president.

Manager Eddie Dyer is out after 5 seasons with the St. Louis Cardinals. He will return to off-season oil and real estate businesses in Houston.

18th Connie Mack retires after 50 years as the manager of the Philadelphia Athletics. Jimmy Dykes replaces him. Mack maintains his position as president of the club.

26th The Baseball Writers of America select Yankee SS Phil Rizzuto as the AL MVP.

Branch Rickey resigns as president of the Brooklyn Dodgers and Walter O'Malley succeeds him. Rickey sells his 25 percent interest in the club for a reported $1.05 million.

NOVEMBER

2nd The baseball writers select Phillies relief P Jim Konstanty as the NL's MVP.

6th Branch Rickey signs a 5-year contract as executive vice president/GM with the Pirates.

8th The Baseball Writers Association of America announces that slugging 1B Walt Dropo of the Boston Red Sox is the Rookie of the Year in the AL. Dropo led the league in RBI with 144.

Commissioner Happy Chandler and player reps agree on the split of the TV-radio rights from the WS.

9th The Associated Press chooses Phillie skipper Eddie Sawyer as Manager of the year.

The baseball writers name Sam Jethroe of the Boston Braves as the NL Rookie of the Year.

The White Sox release Luke Appling, who has been with the Sox since 1930, so he can become the manager of the Memphis Chicks (SA).

10th After 9 years at the helm, the Indians fire their manager, Lou Boudreau, amid the howls of fan protest. Although Boudreau's overall winning percentage is a moderate .529, he won 92 games in a 4th-place finish, his best showing since 97 in the championship year of 1948. Al Lopez, who has piloted Minneapolis (AA) since 1948, takes over with a 2-year contract.

16th League presidents Ford Frick and Will Harridge vote to deposit $950,000 received for WS TV-radio rights into the player's pension fund.

20th Pirate GM Roy Hamey resigns to make way for Branch Rickey.

26th The Gillette Safety Razor Co. signs a 6-year deal, worth an estimated 6 million, with ML baseball for the TV-radio rights for the WS.

27th The Red Sox sign former Cleveland SS great Lou Boudreau as a player to a 2-year contract worth an estimated $150,000.

28th Having ousted Branch Rickey, Walter O'Malley now fires Burt Shotton as manager. Oakland (PCL) manager Chuck Dressen is his replacement.

DECEMBER

5th Mel Ott, who has been working in the Giants farm system, hires on for 2 years in the Oakland managerial spot vacated by Dressen.

11th At the winter meeting, held in St. Petersburg, FL, ML owners vote 9-7 against renewing Commissioner Happy Chandler's contract for a new term, starting in 1951. The Cardinals' Fred Saigh led the opposition to Chandler, who had jeopardized the reserve clause and ordered investigations of the alleged gambling activities of several owners.

12th The owners vote to drop the 4-year old bonus and high school rule. This rule, passed to prevent the wealthy clubs from buying up all the talent, required that "bonus" players must stay on the ML roster after just one season in the minors.

14th The baseball owners choose Lou Perini (Braves), Phil Wrigley (Cubs), Del Webb (Yankees), and Ellis Ryan (Indians) to select a new commissioner as rapidly as possible.

18th Yankee great Tommy "Old Reliable" Henrich calls it a career as a player. He accepts a coaching position with the Yankees.

1951

JANUARY

23rd Guido Rujo sells his interest in the Braves to copartners Lou Perini and Treasurer Joe Many.

26th The baseball writers vote Mel Ott and Jimmie Foxx into the Hall of Fame.

29th Baseball signs a 6-year All-Star Game pact for TV-radio rights calling for $6 million. A number of owners criticize lame duck Commissioner Happy Chandler, stating that in a couple of years the broadcast rights would be worth much more than a million per annum.

FEBRUARY

5th California Governor Earl Warren denies he is a candidate for baseball commissioner.

9th The St. Louis Browns sign Satchel Paige, 45. He had been out of ML baseball since last pitching for the Indians in 1949.

21st The South Carolina House introduces a resolution urging that "Shoeless Joe" Jackson, who was banished from baseball because of his part in the Black Sox Scandal of 1919, be reinstated.

MARCH

9th The St. Louis Browns seek a $600,000 loan to help them stay in St. Louis.

10th The Browns reveal plans to move the club to Milwaukee because of poor attendance.

FBI director J. Edgar Hoover reports that he declined the post of baseball commissioner.

12th Happy Chandler loses his fight to stay in office by a 9-7 vote.

19th Detroit player rep Fred Hutchinson asks that players be allowed a say in choosing the new commissioner.

23rd The Brooklyn Dodgers sign a 21-year lease with the city of Vero Beach, FL, for use of their spring training facilities there.

APRIL

1st The Browns trade infielder George "Snuffy" Stirnweiss and SS Merrill Combs to Cleveland for 3B Fred Marsh and $35,000.

2nd Boston slugger Walt Dropo, the 1950 AL Rookie of the Year, breaks his wrist.

12th Cincinnati President Warren Giles proposes Gen. Douglas MacArthur, recently deposed commander of UN forces in Korea, as the new commissioner.

A UPI poll picks the Red Sox and Giants to win the pennant. An AP poll picks Brooklyn and the Red Sox.

17th The Athletics play their first home Opening Day night game, losing to Washington 6–1.

In the pregame ceremonies at Wrigley Field, Sam Snead tees off from home plate and hits a golf ball off the CF scoreboard. The Cubs follow suit in their home opener, beating the Reds 8–3. Rookie 1B Dee Fondy hits a 2nd-inning bases-loaded triple in his first ML at bat.

18th Southpaw Eddie Lopat of the Yankees 2-hits the Red Sox, winning 6–1. Mickey Mantle goes 1-for-4 in his first game.

21st Gil Coan of the Senators gets 2 triples in the 6th inning at Boston.

22nd Gus Bell of the Pirates goes 5-for-5 against the Cubs, as the Bucs win 7–5.

25th Former Braves P 33-year-old Jim Prendergast contests the reserve clause. His lawyer, Frederic Johnson, who was the attorney for Danny Gardella, files a $150,000 suit, alleging that his client's trade from Syracuse to Beaumont in the Texas League constitutes a breach of the nation's antitrust laws.

RF Bob Usher of the Reds throws out 2 runners in the 5th inning in a 4–3 win against the Cubs.

29th El Paso owner Jack Corbett seeks a writ to prevent Commissioner Happy Chandler from removing records pending outcome of his antitrust suit.

30th In a complex 3-way deal, the White Sox get OF/3B Minnie Minoso from the Indians and OF Paul Lehner from the Athletics. Philadelphia sends P Lou Brissie to Cleveland and gets OF Gus Zernial and Dave Philley from Chicago and P Sam Zoldak and C Ray Murray from Cleveland.

MAY

1st The Yankees' new phenom, Mickey Mantle, connects for his first ML HR, off Randy Gumpert of the White Sox. Minnie Minoso becomes the first black to play for the White Sox. He plays 3B and, facing Vic Raschi in his first ML at bat, rips a HR to CF. The Yankees win 8–3.

New Mexico pitchers walk 21 Arizona batters in college baseball.

3rd Rookie Gil McDougald hits a HR and a triple in the 9th, as the Yanks score 11 runs in the inning to rout St. Louis 17–3.

4th NY Representative Emanuel Celler, citing the case of Danny Gardella, plans a probe of ML baseball for antitrust violations.

6th Pirate P Cliff Chambers throws a no-hitter at the Boston Braves in Boston, winning 3–0. He walks 8 and throws one wild pitch but hangs on to record only the second no-hit game in Pirate history. Chambers, hitting .429, drives in Wally Westlake with the 3rd run in the 8th. The loser is George Estock, a Braves reliever making his only ML start. The loss is his only ML decision.

12th Although Boston's Dom DiMaggio begins his 27-game hitting streak, the longest of the season in the AL, with 3 hits against the Senators, Washington wins 5–4.

15th The White Sox trade lefty Bob Cain to the Tigers for hurler Saul Rogovin.

16th Gus Zernial hits his 7th HR in 4 successive games to tie the ML record, as his A's beat the Browns 7–6.

17th The Browns trade C Les Moss to the Red Sox for C Matt Batts, P Jim Suchecki, Jim McDonald, and $100,000.

The Cards trade Erv Dusak and 1B Glenn "Rocky" Nelson to the Pirates for SS Stan Rojek.

18th Catcher Walker Cooper of the Braves goes 5-for-5 against the Pirates.

20th The Phils defeat the Pirates 17–0 and 12–4, as Richie Ashburn gets 4 hits in each game.

23rd Ted Williams walks 5 times in a game.

Rookie P Bill MacDonald of the Pirates blanks the Phils 6–0 in his first ML start.

24th Cleveland whips the Senators 16–0, with Bob Feller pitching a 2-hitter.

25th Giants rookie Willie Mays, who was hitting .477 with Minneapolis, goes 0-for-5 in his ML debut against the Phils.

26th The Dodgers use 12 different hitters in the number 9 slot, 7 of them pitchers, in losing to the Braves 12–10.

28th After going 0-for-12, Willie Mays connects for his first ML hit, a HR off Braves P Warren Spahn. The Giants lose the game 4–1.

Newly acquired White Sox hurler Saul Rogovin 2-hits the Browns in a 4–2 win.

29th The Indians sign high school star Billy Joe Davidson for a reported $150,000, eclipsing the $100,000 the Pirates paid to Paul Pettit in 1949. Several teams sought the services of the tall lefty, alleged to be the best Indians prospect since Bob Feller.

Indians hurler Bob Lemon one-hits the Tigers 2–1.

JUNE

1st The Pirates waive 1B Dale Long to the Browns, who ship him to San Francisco (PCL).

2nd The Red Sox send 1950 AL Rookie of the Year Walt Dropo to San Diego (PCL) to regain his form.

In an Alabama-Florida League (Class D) game, Dothan OF Ottis Johnson is struck in the head by a fastball thrown by Jack Clifton of Headland. Johnson dies 8 days later.

4th Pirates OF Gus Bell hits for the cycle in a 12–4 win over the Phillies.

5th The Pirates get 1B Dale Long from the St. Louis Browns. They farm him out, and he will not return to the ML until 1955.

The Pirates rookie P Paul LaPalme hurls a 8–0 shutout against the Boston Braves in his first ML start.

8th The Indians repeat history when they stop Dom DiMaggio's 27-game hitting streak, just as they ended his brother Joe's record 56-game streak 10 years before.

13th Oklahoma wins the College WS in Omaha, defeating Tennessee in the final game 3–2.

15th Happy Chandler says that his resignation will become effective on July 15th.

The Cubs trade OF Andy Pafko, P Johnny Schmitz, C Rube Walker, and IF Wayne Terwilliger to Brooklyn for C Bruce Edwards, OF Gene Hermanski, IF Eddie Miksis, and P Joe Hatten.

Pittsburgh sends Cliff "no hit" Chambers and OF Wally Westlake to the Cards for C Joe Garagiola, P Howie Pollet, P Ted Wilks, OF Bill Howerton and 2B Dick Cole.

19th Tommy Holmes replaces Billy Southworth as the Boston Braves manager.

Wally Yonamine, an American of Japanese descent (a Nisei) born in Hawaii, plays his first game with the Yomiuri Giants of Tokyo. He will become the first genuine American star in Japanese baseball, winning batting titles in 1954, 1956, and 1957. In 1957 he will also be the Central League MVP. From 1963 to 1986 he will be active with various teams as a coach or manager.

20th Cleveland IF Bobby Avila hits 3 HRs going 5-for-6. His 15 total bases will stand as a team record until surpassed by Rocky Colavito in 1959.

21st Bill Veeck gets an option to buy the St. Louis Browns from the DeWitts.

22nd Willie Mays, 20, hits a 10th-inning HR, the first of his 22 extra-innings HRs, off 42-year-old Dutch Leonard of the Cubs. It is a 3-run shot that gives the Giants a 9–6 win.

27th Former Cubs farmhand Boyd Tepler brings a $450,000 suit against baseball, the Chicago Cubs, and William Wrigley, citing an arm injury he suffered in 1944. His suit contends that "negligent" coaching allowed him to continue with flaws in his pitching motion that resulted in damage to his arm and the end of his promising career.

JULY

1st Veteran Bob Feller pitches the 3rd no-hitter of his career, tying the record of Cy Young and Larry Corcoran, as he beats Detroit's Bob Cain 2–1

Rookie Bob Chakales shuts out the Tigers in the nightcap for Cleveland's 10th straight win over Detroit.

Philadelphia's Russ Meyer and Jim Konstanty hold Brooklyn to one hit but lose anyway 2–0.

In the 2nd game of a doubleheader, the Browns' Ned Garver, en route to a 20-game season, limits the White Sox to 2 hits, winning 3–1.

2nd Bill Veeck gets the necessary 75 percent of outstanding stock on the last day of his option to buy the St. Louis Browns from Bill and Charlie DeWitt.

3rd Former pitcher Hugh Casey, 37, kills himself with a shotgun blast to the neck.

7th OF Hoot Evers of the Tigers goes 5-for-5 and scores 5 runs against the Indians.

8th The feud between Joe DiMaggio and Casey Stengel reaches a head. In the 2nd inning of a game, because of a misplay in the first, Stengel sends reserve Jackie Jensen out to CF to relieve the Yankee Clipper after he had already taken his position.

Red Schoendienst hits a HR from each side of the plate in game 2, as the Cards beat Pittsburgh 9–8 after losing 6–2.

9th At a joint meeting between players and owners, agreement is reached on night curfews and the retention of the reserve clause.

10th Exploding for a record 4 HRs, the NL trounces the AL 8–3 at the annual All-Star Game at Briggs Stadium in Detroit. Pittsburgh slugger Ralph Kiner hits a HR for the 3rd year in a row.

12th Allie Reynolds of the NY Yankees no-hits Cleveland 1–0 for the first of his 2 no-hitters this season. Gene Woodling's HR off loser Bob Feller is the difference in the 1–0 game.

The Red Sox and White Sox draw a record crowd of 52,592 for a twi-night doubleheader at Comiskey. In the 2nd game Saul Rogovin of the White Sox goes the route in a 17-inning contest, only to lose 5–4. Ellis Kinder of Boston pitches 10 scoreless innings in relief.

13th The Red Sox and White Sox play 19 innings under the lights, tying a ML record. Mickey McDermott pitches the first 17 innings for Boston, as Chicago wins 5–4.

Both Wes Westrum and Davey Williams of the Giants hit grand slams, as the Giants beat St. Louis 14–4 at the Polo Grounds. The win moves New York into 2nd place.

15th The Yanks option rookie Mickey Mantle to Kansas City (AA). They will recall him August 20th.

Athletics lefty Sam Zoldak pitches a one-hitter against the White Sox, winning 5–0 in the 2nd game of a doubleheader.

17th After pitching for Bill Veeck in Cleveland in 1948, Satchel Paige rejoins him with the St. Louis Browns.

18th The Pirates Ralph Kiner hits 3 HRs in a 13–12 slugfest win over the Dodgers.

Congressman Emanuel Celler says that President Harry Truman backs his probe of the reserve clause and sports status under the antitrust legislation.

22nd With the Cubs 10 games under .500 at 35-45, Phil Cavarretta replaces Frankie Frisch as manager. They will go 27-47 the rest of the way to finish in last place.

26th Clyde Vollmer knocks in 6 runs on 3 homers to lead the Red Sox to a 13–10 win over the White Sox.

27th The White Sox, just 3½ games behind New York and Boston, open a 4-game series in New York. Trailing 3–1 in the 9th, the Sox make it 3–2 before rain and the Yankees delay the game. Gil McDougald is thrown out for stalling, and Casey Stengel uses 5 pitchers in the inning. Finally the Yanks win as the game is called.

28th Charlie Gehringer succeeds Billy Evans as GM of the Detroit Tigers.

Clyde Vollmer, who started the month on the bench, continues his explosive fireworks against the Indians. He singles in the tying run in the 15th and then in the 16th hits a grand slam off reliever Bob Feller for an 8–4 Red Sox win. The grand slam is the latest hit in a game in ML history.

29th Before a Stadium crowd of 70,972, the Yankees sweep the White Sox, 8–3 and 2–0. The Sox are now 6½ out of first place.

Willie Mays steals the first of 338 bases. Then P Willie Ramsdell of the Reds picks him off 2B.

30th Ty Cobb testifies before the Emanuel Celler committee, denying that the reserve clause makes "peons" of baseball players. National Association President George Trautman testifies, denying that minors hampered independent teams.

31st The Dodgers Carl Furillo hits his 2nd consecutive lead-off HR against the Cubs.

AUGUST

1st Congressman Celler denies the accusation that his committee wants a 3rd ML. He states that some changes with regard to territorial rights will have to be made.

The Cubs' Eddie Miksis lines a ball to Willie Mays in CF, which caroms off his head for a double.

6th Lameduck Commissioner Happy Chandler testifies in front of the Senate committee, urging that baseball expand out of its eastern area. He adds that some owners see sport only as big business.

7th The Phils shut out the Braves 1–0 in 15 innings in the 2nd game of a doubleheader as Ken Heintzelman bests Warren Spahn.

Senator Edwin C. Johnson backs the reserve clause in his testimony, citing his bill to exempt baseball from antitrust legislation.

11th The Braves take the the first game 8–1 and Brooklyn takes the 2nd 8–4 in the first color telecast of ML games.

12th The Giants start the day 13½ games out of first place. Sal Maglie wins the first game against the Phillies 3–2, and rookie Al Corwin takes the 2nd game 2–1. This launches a spurt of 39 wins in 47 games.

15th Giants P Jim Hearn defeats the Dodgers 3–1 as Willie Mays makes a miraculous play in the 8th. With the score 1–1 and Billy Cox on 3rd, Mays makes a running catch of a Carl Furillo drive in deep right CF and whirls counterclockwise to throw out the astonished Cox.

19th In his most interesting promotional stunt, Bill Veeck signs a 3'7" midget, Eddie Gaedel, who goes to bat wearing the number ⅛ in the first inning of the nightcap with the Tigers. Lefty Bob Cain laughingly walks him on 4 pitches. Jim Delsing then pinch runs. Two days later the ML bars Eddie Gaedel from appearing in any more games.

22nd Jackie Robinson of the Dodgers goes 5-for-6 in the 2nd half of a day/night doubleheader with St. Louis.

Eddie Gaedel is arrested in an early morning fracas with a policeman in Cincinnati. The policeman thought he was a juvenile, too young to be out so late at night.

24th In another of Bill Veeck's legendary PR stunts, "Fans Managers' Night," the Browns defeat the Athletics 5–3. The Browns coaches hold up placards for about a thousand fans, who vote on the options given them.

26th Rookie hurler Niles Jordan of the Phillies blanks the Reds 2–0 in his first ML start.

27th Light-hitting reserve C Del Wilber of the Phillies hits 3 HRs in 3 at bats to provide Ken Johnson with all his support. Johnson beats the Reds 3–0 in the nightcap after Jocko Thompson shuts out Cincinnati 2–0 in the first game.

The Giants win 2 from the Cubs, including a 5–4, twelve-inning complete game victory for Larry Jansen. It is his 17th win.

"The two fine Italian arms of Branca and Furillo had a no-hitter running for eight innings" writes columnist Dick Young; Ralph Branca's no-hitter seems broken by a one-hop shot to RF by Mel Queen, but Carl Furillo guns him out at first. Branca finally gives up 2 Pirate hits in the 9th before winning.

28th The Pirates Howie Pollet shuts out the Giants 2–0 to end their 16-game winning streak, best in the NL since 1935.

The Braves sell P Johnny Sain to the Yankees for $50,000 and a young pitcher named Lew Burdette. It is another late-season insurance measure for the New Yorkers.

SEPTEMBER

1st OF Don Mueller hits 3 HRs in an 8–1 Giants' win over the Dodgers. Mueller's 3rd HR comes after he learns he is a new father.

2nd Don Mueller hits 2 more HRs, giving him 5 in 2 days, to tie an ML mark. Jim Hearn beats the Dodgers 11–2, as the Giants move to 5 games behind Brooklyn.

The Cleveland Indians Harry Simpson, Al Rosen and Luke Easter hit consecutive HRs in the first inning, as Cleveland beats the Browns 5–1.

Tony Ponce of the Phoenix Senators (Southwest International League) hurls his 38th consecutive complete game in beating Yuma 4–2 for his 25th win of the season.

3rd Willie Mays makes another rookie error. After an apparent inside-the-park HR, Phils 3B Tommy Brown appeals, and Mays is called out for failing to touch 3B. He is credited with a double.

5th A's Ferris Fain goes 5-for-5 in the 2nd game of a doubleheader with Washington.

7th In an 18-inning game with the Cubs, the Reds Lloyd Merriman records 12 putouts in CF, tying the NL mark.

Bobby Thomson goes 5-for-5 against the Braves, as the Giants win 7–3.

9th The pennant race heats up, as Dodger ace Don Newcombe 2-hits the Giants 9–0.

12th The last Giant game of the season in St. Louis is rained out. The NL reschedules it for the next afternoon.

13th The Cards split a rare doubleheader, with 2 different teams, defeating the Giants 6–4 in the first game in the afternoon and losing to the Braves in the nightcap. The Cards manage just one hit in losing to Warren Spahn 2–0. It is the first time a team in the NL has played 2 different teams in the same day since the early 20th-century.

14th Browns rookie Bob Nieman hits 2 HRs in his first 2 ML at bats, a record unequalled. They come against Mickey McDermott of the Red Sox, but Boston still wins 9–6.

15th The Cardinals take 11 walks, 5 by Solly Hemus, and beat the Braves 10–1. Boston's starter Dave Cole walks the first 3 batters he faces, then hits Enos Slaughter to force in Hemus.

The first game of the first Dominican WS (Los Grandes Finales) is played between Licey and Escogido in Santiago. Behind the hitting of Alonzo Perry (.400 series average) and the pitching of Marion "Sugar" Caine, Licey wins the opener 8–0 and goes on to take the series 4-1 to become the first champion of Dominican Professional Baseball.

18th Browns Tommy Byrne hits a grand slam off the Senators Sid Hudson in the 9th inning to ice the game 8-0.

19th Larry Doby of the Indians walks 5 times in a 15-2 cakewalk over the Red Sox in Boston. Early Wynn picks up his 20th win.

20th The owners elect NL President Ford Frick as the 3rd commissioner of baseball for a 7-year term at

$65,000 per annum. Warren Giles withdraws on a vote deadlock to open the way for Frick.

21st Rookie P Jackie Collum of the Cardinals hurls a 6–0 2-hitter against the Cubs in his first start.

22nd OF Irv Noren of the Senators records 11 putouts in CF in a 9-inning, 9–1 win over the A's, tying the AL record.

27th Future Hall of Fame basketball player Bill Sharman becomes the only man in history to be thrown out of a NL baseball game without ever having played in one. In a game with the Pirates, umpire Frank Dascoli clears the entire Brooklyn bench after a home plate call by him results in a violent protest. Sharman, up from St. Paul (AA) at the end of the season, is one of the players thrown out. Dascoli's safe call at home on Bob Addie's score results in a 4–3 Dodger loss to the Braves.

Gabe Paul replaces the newly elected NL President Warren Giles as GM of the Cincinnati Reds.

28th Allie Reynolds pitches his 2nd no-hitter of the season, defeating the Red Sox in Yankee Stadium 8–0. It is his 7th shutout of the year. With 2 outs in the 9th, Ted Williams hits a foul pop that catcher Yogi Berra drops. Williams then hits another foul fly that Berra grabs for the last out.

In the 2nd game, the Yankees clinch their 3rd straight pennant under Casey Stengel as Vic Raschi wins 11–3 for his 21st victory. The Yankees are 3½ games ahead of Cleveland with 2 to play.

30th Larry Jansen of the Giants holds on to defeat the Braves 3–2 in Boston.

After a great catch of a Eddie Waitkus drive in the 13th, Jackie Robinson hits a HR the 14th inning to give the Dodgers a critical 9–8 win over the Phils, putting them in a first place tie with the NY Giants. Catcher Andy Seminick of the Phils walks 5 times, the first Phillie to do so in a game.

Browns ace Ned Garver wins his 20th game of the season in defeating the White Sox 9–5. He becomes the only player to win 20 for a last-place team that loses 100 games.

OCTOBER

1st In the NL's first best-of-three play-off since 1946, Ralph Branca of the Dodgers loses to Jim Hearn and the Giants 3–1. Branca serves up HRs to Bobby Thomson and Monte Irvin. It is the first game ever to be broadcast live coast-to-coast.

2nd The Dodgers bounce back as rookie Clem Labine evens the playoff with a 10–0 win, besting the Giants' Sheldon Jones. Home runs are smashed by Jackie Robinson, Gil Hodges, Andy Pafko, and Rube Walker. Willie Mays grounds into 3 DP.

3rd The Giants' Bobby Thomson hits the most famous home run in history, off Ralph Branca. His "shot heard round the world" with 2 runners on and trailing 4–3 in the bottom of the 9th defeats Brooklyn 5–4 and sends the jubilant Giants into the WS.

4th In the opening game of the WS, Monte Irvin steals home in the first inning and collects 4 hits. The Giants defeat Allie Reynolds and the Yankees 5–1 with Dave Koslo going all the way at Yankee Stadium.

5th The Yanks and Eddie Lopat even up the WS by winning 3–1 over Larry Jansen.

S. Iijima of the Daiei Stars (later the Lotte Orions) gets 11 RBI in a single game for a Japanese record. The U.S. ML record is 12, set by Jim Bottomley of St. Louis in 1924; Iijima ties Tony Lazzeri of the NY Yankees who knocked in 11 in 1936.

6th Back at the Polo Grounds, the Giants win 6–2, as Whitey Lockman homers with 2 on in the 5th. The Giants score 5 in the inning after Eddie Stanky kicks the ball out of Phil Rizzuto's glove on a tag play at 2B.

8th The Yankees even up the WS with a 6–2 win, with Allie Reynolds going the distance. Hitless in 11 at bats, DiMaggio collects a homer and single.

9th Gil McDougald becomes the first rookie to hit a grand slam in the WS, as the Yankees win in a romp, 13–1. Ed Lopat wins his 2nd game.

10th Hank Bauer's bases-loaded triple propels the Yankees to a 4–3 win and their 3rd straight championship. Just before the game, Leo Durocher turns over a letter he received to Ford Frick that offers the Giants manager a $15,000 bribe "if the Giants manage to lose the next 3 games."

15th Minor league executive Leslie O'Connor testifies before the Celler committee that ML control over the farm system is harmful to players and the minor leagues. He adds that the majors-minors council plans a pact to speed a West Coast bid for higher status.

16th In a letter written to ML officials, the St. Louis Browns P Ned Garver offers a pay plan that would ameliorate the ill effects of the reserve system he supports. He would have the salaries of players on consistent tail-enders be determined by a rating system by the owners. If the club does not match the "average" salary, then that player should be traded to some other club that can afford his services. Garver adds that he "doesn't care where I play, as long as I get a 'fair' salary."

17th The Yomiuri Giants win the Japan Series over the Nankai Hawks. Incredibly, they will win the pennant 19 times in the next 23 years, including 9 in succession (1965-73).

20th Joe DiMaggio accompanies Lefty O'Doul's all-stars on a tour of Japan. They will win 13 of the 15 games.

23rd Branch Rickey contends that the farm system saved baseball during the Depression. He asks Congress for legislation that will protect it from monopoly suits.

The AP picks Giant manager Leo Durocher as Manager of the Year.

24th UPI names Casey Stengel as Manager of the Year.

Larry MacPhail calls for 4 new major leagues, including a Pacific Coast League.

NOVEMBER

1st The NL votes Brooklyn C Roy Campanella the league's MVP for what will be the first of 3 such awards.

2nd The National Labor Relations Board files unfair labor practices charges against the Indians on a claim the club fired a ticket seller at the union's request. This is the first case against baseball under the Taft-Hartley Act.

6th Dodgers President Walter O'Malley denies the farm system constitutes a monopoly. He cites the Dodgers' deficit in 1950.

7th Representative Emanuel Celler's committee issues financial data from 1945-49 that differs with Walter O'Malley's numbers. According to Celler, the Dodgers made a profit of 2.364 million from 1945-49; the Dodgers' "loss" of $129,318 in 1950 included a

$167,000 loss due to the promotion of the Brooklyn Dodgers professional football team. In his continuing investigation into antitrust violations, Celler says that evidence in his committee suggests altering the reserve clause and that it does limit players.

8th C Yogi Berra of the NY Yankees wins the first of his 3 MVP awards.

13th Lefty O'Doul's all-stars, including Joe DiMaggio, Ferris Fain, and Billy Martin, lose 3–1 to a Pacific League all-star team—only the 2nd time since 1922 that an American professional team has lost to Japan, and the first time to professional players.

15th The baseball writers name Gil McDougald as AL Rookie of the Year.

The White Sox object to McDougald's accolade, offering the statistical accomplishments of their superlative rookie, Minnie Minoso.

18th Former Cub 1B and future TV star of *The Rifleman* Chuck Connors is the first player to oppose the ML draft. Currently the 1B of the LA Angels (PCL), Connors wants to stay in California, instead of going to whatever team might draft him for the ML. The PCL views his refusal in a positive manner, allowing them to ask higher prices for players than what the ML usually offers.

28th The Browns trade C Gus Niarhos to Boston for Les Moss and Tom Wright. The team also signs SS Marty Marion, who has just been released as the Cardinal manager.

DECEMBER

8th The AL alters its restrictions on night games, adopting the NL's suspended game rule and lifting its ban on lights for Sunday games.

10th The Cards trade lefty Max Lanier and OF Chuck Diering to the Giants for 2B Eddie Stanky, who becomes the team's player-manager.

11th Joe DiMaggio officially retires as a member of the New York Yankees with 361 HRs and an average of .325 after 13 seasons. His 56-game, consecutive-game hitting streak in 1941 will stand as one of the all-time best diamond achievements.

1952

JANUARY

9th As the Korean War drags on, the marines give notice that they will recall Ted Williams to active duty.

16th The U.S. Standardization Board clears the way for Stan Musial to get a salary increase to $85,000. Prior to this relaxation of the rules, there was a wage freeze in effect due to the Korean War. Under the new rules, a team is free to raise individual salaries, as long as they do not exceed a complicated formula, based on total team salaries for any one year, from 1946-50, plus 10 percent.

17th Detroit owner Walter O. "Spike" Briggs dies at the age of 74. His son will succeed him in the presidency.

18th The Chicago White Sox accept Vice President Charlie A. Comiskey, Jr.'s resignation. Comiskey's request for more money was refused.

26th Because of poor attendance, the Canadian-American League suspends operations for its 1952 season. This is one of 7 minor leagues that will not operate this year, dropping the total from 50 to 43. The Korean War military obligation is the primary reason.

31st Harry Heilmann with 203 votes and Paul Waner with 195 become the newest members of the Hall of Fame.

The Phils settle their damage suit with former P Art Lopatka out of court. He contends that the Phils made him pitch with a fractured index finger, resulting in damage to his arm. He further contends that when he was no longer of use, the Phillies released him as damaged "goods" in 1947.

A U.S. federal jury awards Mexican owner Jorge Pasquel $35,000 for breach of contract by former Dodger star, Mickey Owen.

FEBRUARY

1st The Dodgers report a $24,000 shortfall in 1951 revenue, sparking a New York district attorney probe. There is a possible error in the WS and post-season play-off revenues.

7th North American P Bill Samson achieves an undistinguished winter league record by walking 14 Vargas batters in 6 innings while pitching for Cerveceria Caracas of the Venezuelan League. This negative feat also matches the ML record set in 1906 by Henry Mathewson of the New York Giants, who needed 9 full innings for an equal display of pitching wildness.

16th Hall of Famer Honus Wagner, 77, retires after 40 years as a ML player and coach. He receives a pension from the Pirates, with whom he spent most of those years.

21st Tommy Fine, North American righthander who posted only 4 ML decisions with the Red Sox and Browns, pitches the only no-hit, no-run game in the history of the Caribbean Series. Fine, hurling for Club Havana (Cuba) against Cervecería Caracas (Venezuela), wins 1–0 in the 4th Serie del Caribe at Panama City.

26th The army swears in Dodger P Don Newcombe.

MARCH

5th Norman Bel Geddes, after designing a 5,000 seat complex for the Dodgers in Vero Beach, FL, states that Walter O'Malley has asked for a stadium design for Brooklyn. It is to have a retractable dome, garage, automatic hotdog vending machines, and artificial turf that can be painted in different colors.

APRIL

2nd Giants slugger Monte Irvin breaks his ankle sliding into 3B in an exhibition game against the Indians in Denver. He will play just 46 games in 1952.

13th Babe Ruth's widow unveils the site of his first HR in Fayetteville, NC.

15th In the last home opener in Braves Field in Boston, 4,694 fans watch Warren Spahn lose 3–2 to Brooklyn's Preacher Roe.

16th The Dodgers Duke Snider goes 5-for-6 in a 14–8 win over the Boston Braves.

17th Umpire Bill Summers turns in 7 members of the White Sox and Indians for "fraternizing" before a game, won by the Indians 7–3. The AL fines the unnamed players $5 each for violating the 1951 rule.

19th Eddie Mathews of the Boston Braves hits his first ML HR off Ken Heintzelman of the Phillies in Philadelphia. The Braves win 4–0.

22nd A federal grand jury cites Cardinal owner Fred Saigh with income tax evasion.

23rd Future Hall of Famer Hoyt Wilhelm of the New York Giants wins his first ML game pitching 5 innings in relief in a 9–5 win. He homers in his first at bat against the Braves' Dick Hoover. It is Wilhelm's only ML HR in 1,070 games.

The NL fines and reprimands league umpire Scotty Robb for pushing Cardinal manger Eddie Stanky. Stanky and player Solly Hemus also receive fines.

Bob Cain of the Browns and Bob Feller of the Indians each pitch a one-hitter, with the Browns prevailing 1–0. It ties a ML record for the fewest hits by 2 teams in a game. Bobby Young hits a triple in the first inning and scores the only run, as the Browns move into first place.

24th Leo Durocher charges that the umpires are ignoring the "quick pitch" rule.

26th Detroit's Art Houtteman's no-hit bid is broken up on a 2-out, 9th-inning hit by Harry Simpson, but the Tigers romp over the Indians 13–0.

28th The St. Louis Browns lend 2 black minor league players, 3B John Britton and P Jim Newberry, to the Hankyu Braves of the Japanese Pacific League, making them the first team to send players outside of the U.S. Abe Saperstein, owner and coach of the world-famous Harlem Globetrotters, negotiates this special example in "lend-lease" for both sides.

29th Cleveland OF "Big Jim" Fridley goes 6-for-6 in a 21–9 romp over the Philadelphia A's. Al Rosen chips in with 3 HRs and 7 RBI, as both teams total 43 hits.

30th Before 24,767 at Ted Williams Day at Fenway Park, the Red Sox slugger plays in his final game before going to Korea as a marine fighter pilot. In his last at bat, Williams hits a game-winning 2-run HR against Detroit's Dizzy Trout to give the Red Sox a 5–3 win.

MAY

3rd The Red Sox beat the Browns 5–2 in Fenway. Odd occurrences interrupt the game. In the bottom of the first, 2 fraternity boys dressed in baseball uniforms run onto the field and start throwing a rubber ball around. Two innings later a one-legged man on crutches jumps onto the field to talk to Browns SS Marty Marion and P Earl Harrist. He then shakes hands with Red Sox base runner Don Lenhardt before being hurried off the field.

4th Boston 1B Faye Throneberry hits his 2nd grand slam of the season off Early Wynn of the Indians. The Red Sox have accounted for all 4 of the AL's grand slams thus far, as the infielder is joined by teammates Walt Dropo and Don "Footsie" Lenhardt.

7th Ben Wade of the Dodgers fans 6 Pirates in a row.

10th CF Wally Post of the Reds records 2 assists in the 4th inning tying a NL mark.

Hank Bauer of the Yankees goes 5-for-6 in an 18–3 romp over Boston.

13th P Ron Necciai of Bristol (Appalachian League) no-hits Welch and strikes out 27 batters, including 4 in one inning, en route. In his next start he will strike out 24 while giving up 2 hits. Necciai will later compile a career 1-6 mark with the Pirates.

15th After pitching 4 no-hitters in the minors, 33-year-old Virgil "Fire" Trucks of Detroit pitches his first in the ML, a 1–0 blanking of the Senators. Vic Wertz's 2-out HR in the 9th off Bob Porterfield wins the game at Briggs Stadium.

17th OF Hank Edwards of the Reds goes 5-for-5 in a 7–3 win over the Phillies.

20th In his first start following his no-hitter, Virgil Trucks and Dick Littlefield combine to 2-hit the Athletics 5–1.

21st After Billy Cox grounds out, the Dodgers score 15 runs in the first inning as 19 consecutive batters reach 1B. Captain Pee Wee Reese walks twice in reaching base safely 3 times. Andy Pafko is thrown out trying to steal 3B, and Duke Snider mercifully strikes out to end the barrage against the Reds. The Dodgers coast at home, 19–1.

22nd The Celler committee finds legislation for government control of baseball to be unnecessary. It says that the sport can solve its own problems, and opposes legislation exempting the reserve clause from antitrust laws.

24th Jimmy Piersall and Billy Martin first exchange insults before a game in Boston, then exchange punches under the stands. When the fight is broken up, Piersall goes to the clubhouse and gets into another brawl with teammate Maury McDermott.

26th Bill Bell, only 18, a Bristol teammate of Ron Necciai, hurls his 2nd consecutive no-hitter in the Appalachian League.

29th The Giants Willie Mays enters the army. Although Mays is hitting just .236, the Giants are 2½ games in first place. They will lose 8 of their next 10 games.

31st Charlie Grimm succeeds Tommy Holmes as manager of the Boston Braves.

JUNE

3rd In a blockbuster trade between Detroit and Boston, the Red Sox send Walt Dropo, Don Lenhardt, Johnny Pesky, Fred Hatfield, and Bill Wight to the Tigers for 3B George Kell, Hoot Evers, Dizzy Trout, and Johnny Lipon.

Y. Yamasaki of the Chunichi Dragons steals 6 bases in a single game for a Japanese record. This ties the AL record of 6 set by Eddie Collins of Philadelphia in 1912; it is one behind the NL record set by George Gore in 1881 and Billy Hamilton of Philadelphia in 1894.

4th Billy Goodman of the Red Sox goes 5-for-5 in a 13–11 slugfest with Cleveland. The Indians Larry Doby hits for the cycle.

6th Bucky Walters succeeds Charlie Grimm as manager of the minor league Milwaukee Brewers after the latter had accepted the Braves job.

7th Sam Jethroe hits the last grand slam in the history of the Boston Braves, as the Braves win the 2nd game of a doubleheader 7–6.

10th After an absence of 5 months, Charlie Comiskey, Jr., rejoins the White Sox as vice president after he was reelected to the board.

The St. Louis Browns fire manager Rogers Hornsby in Boston. The players present owner Bill Veeck with a trophy for freeing them from Rajah's tyranny. The stunt was actually the work of Veeck and team traveling secretary Bill Durney. The Browns name Marty Marion as their player-manager.

Sam Mele of the White Sox hits a 3-run HR and a 3-run triple n the 4th inning of a game at Boston, as Chicago romps 15–2.

11th The Cubs Hank Sauer hits 3 HRs off Curt Simmons at Wrigley Field to account for all the scoring. The Cubs beat the Phillies 3–0.

12th The AL suspends Browns manager Marty Marion indefinitely for pushing umpire Bill McGowan in the previous night's 7–5 loss to Boston.

14th Warren Spahn of the Braves ties the NL record of Jim Whitney with 18 strikeouts against the Cubs in a 15-inning, 3–1 loss. Hal Jeffcoat's 2-run triple wins it, while Spahn's HR is the only Boston score. Meanwhile, Braves scout Dewey Griggs signs Henry Aaron to a Braves contract.

15th The Cardinals, down 11–0, rally to defeat the Giants 14–12. All the Redbird scores come in the last 3 innings, as Solly Hemus ties the game with an 8th-inning HR and adds another in the 9th. The Giants win 3–0 in game 2.

17th The Holy Cross Crusaders defeat the University of Missouri 8–4 to win the NCAA College Baseball title.

19th After 4 straight losses to the Cubs, Carl Erskine of the Dodgers no-hits them 5–0. The only base runner is relief P Willard Ramsdell in the 3rd. Erskine is now 6-1 for the first-place Dodgers.

21st As a publicity stunt, Harrisburg of the Inter-State League signs a woman player, Eleanor Engle, but she does not get into a game. Female ball players are officially banned by minor league President George Trautman shortly after.

27th Phils manager Eddie Sawyer is fired. Steve O'Neill will replace him the next day.

28th Stan Musial tops the All-Star balloting for the 2nd year in a row.

29th The NL suspends manager Leo Durocher for 4 days for misconduct.

The Kansas City Blues slam 10 HRs against St. Paul to set an AA record for most HRs by one team and tie the record for most by 2 teams. St. Paul hits none.

30th Satchel Paige is named to the All-Star team.

JULY

1st The Indians Larry Doby walks 5 times in a 19-inning game.

5th The Tigers fire their manager, Red Rolfe, replacing him with the popular pitcher Freddie Hutchinson.

6th Dodgers P Ben Wade homers twice in an 8–2 win over the Braves.

8th The NL defeats the AL 3–2 behind the pitching of Phils Curt Simmons and Cubs Bob Rush in Philadelphia. The game is ended after 5 innings because of rain. Cub Hank Sauer's homer with Stan Musial aboard in the 4th proves to be the deciding run.

13th Before 26,770 fans, Mike Garcia of the Indians blanks Washington 1–0 on 2 hits in the first game of a doubleheader.

Vic Raschi gives up only one hit as the Yankees rout the Tigers 11–1 in the first game of a doubleheader.

14th Tigers slugger Walt Dropo goes 5-for-5 against New York in an 8–2 win. All 5 hits are singles.

15th Walt Dropo continues his streak in game one going 4-for-4 against the Senators' Walt Masterson. In game 2 he gets 3 hits in his first 3 at bats to run his streak to 12 straight hits. He goes 4-for-5 with 5 RBI, but Washington wins both games 8–2 and 9–8.

The Indian power hitters dazzle the Yankees with a triple steal in the first inning as Al Rosen scores, Larry Doby goes to 3rd, and Luke Easter, in his only ML theft, goes to 2nd.

Johnny Vander Meer, 38, of Beaumont (Texas League) pitches a no-hitter. In 1938 he pitched 2 consecutive ML no-hitters, still a record.

16th Walt Dropo gets 2 more hits, giving him 15 in 4 games, which ties the AL record.

19th The visiting Fitzgerald club (Georgia State League) sends up 12-year-old batboy Joe Relford to bat as a pinch hitter in the 8th inning of a game with Statesboro. The black batboy, who broke the league's color barrier, grounds out, but makes a fine catch in the outfield when he stays in the game. Umpire Ed Kubick, who approved the move, will be fired by the league the next day.

20th League Presidents Will Harridge and Warren Giles become directors of the Hall of Fame.

22nd Detroit's Virgil Trucks gives up one hit in beating Washington 1–0.

28th Rogers Hornsby, after being fired by the St. Louis Browns, replaces another former Brownie manager, Luke Sewell, as manager of the Cincinnati Reds.

30th Baseball Commissioner Ford Frick sets a waiver rule to bar inter-league deals until all clubs bid with the club lowest in the league to get the first pick. He sets the price at $10,000. He also bars all other deals after July 31st.

Journeyman hurler Lou Kretlow fashions his 2nd consecutive 2-hitter, as the White Sox down New York 7–0.

AUGUST

5th Bobby Shantz of the Athletics wins his 20th game.

Danny Menendez, the owner of the Toledo Mud Hens, is indicted and charged with cheating 3 fans out of $1,700 worth of tickets after he failed to keep his promise of keeping the team in Ohio until the end of the season. Menendez moved them to Charleston, WV, midway through the season, where they became the Charleston Senators, and kept the proceeds from 38,000 extra seat sales.

6th St. Louis Browns Satchel Paige, 46, beats Vigil "Fire" Trucks 1–0 in 12 innings.

The Dodgers slaughter the Phils 15–0.

7th Umpire Bill McGowan is suspended indefinitely by the AL. In a game in St. Louis, McGowan had thrown out Tiger P Billy Hoeft, who had been heckling him from the dugout. When St. Louis writers, who had had a stormy relationship over the years with the veteran McGowan, ask him to identify the player, the umpire refuses, then adds an obscene gesture. The writers' complaint results in a suspension.

12th Stu Miller of the Cardinals blanks the Cubs 1–0 in his ML debut. In his next start Miller will lead 2–0 with 2 outs in the 9th only to have a Solly Hemus error allow a run. He will win 2–1.

14th The St. Louis Browns send Ned Garver to the Tigers for slugger Vic Wertz in a deal involving 6 other players.

15th   Phil Cavarretta signs his 1953 contract as manager of the Cubs.

Dick Marlowe of the Buffalo Bisons pitches the 2nd perfect game in the history of the International League, against Baltimore.

18th   The NL suspends Leo Durocher for 5 days and fines him $100 for a row with an umpire.

21st   The Bradford Phillies and the Batavia Clippers of the Pony League play the first double no-hit game in league history. The Clippers win on a walk, sacrifice, WP, and SF. Jim Mitchell loses while Frank Etcherger wins.

25th   In a 1–0 win over the Yankees in Yankee Stadium, Virgil Trucks of the Detroit Tigers pitches his 2nd no-hitter of the season. The no-hitter is in doubt for 3 innings when a play made by SS Johnny Pesky in the 3rd inning is under debate. The official scorer, John Drebinger, records it as an error when Pesky has trouble getting a ball hit by Phil Rizzuto out of his glove. Dan Daniel of The New York *World Telegram* convinces Drebinger that it cannot be ruled an error because the ball was stuck in the fielder's glove, and Rizzuto is awarded a hit. In the 6th inning, with Trucks not having given up another hit, Drebinger calls Pesky in the dugout from the press box, and the SS says that he should be given the error rather than Rizzuto the hit. The call is changed again, and Trucks's no-hitter is preserved. Trucks's record is now 5-15.

Although the game only lasts 7 innings, Bill Bell of Bristol (Appalachian League) pitches his 3rd no-hitter of the season.

28th   The Brooklyn Dodgers set the NL mark for DPs in consecutive games with 23.

31st   The Montreal Royals clinch the International League pennant behind the stellar pitching of lefty Tom Lasorda.

SEPTEMBER

2nd   In the 2nd game of a doubleheader, Washington's Mike Fornieles makes his ML debut and pitches a one-hit, 5–0 shutout against the A's.

Yankee hurlers Tom Gorman and Ewell Blackwell shut the Red Sox out 5–0 and 4–0 in a doubleheader.

3rd   Dick Littlefield of the Browns 2-hits the White Sox, but loses 1–0.

Harry Byrd of the Philadelphia Athletics one-hits the Yankees 3–0.

5th   Raul Sanchez of the Senators pitches a 2–0 whitewash against the Red Sox in the first start of his career.

6th   Sid Gordon of the Braves goes 5-for-8 in the first game of a doubleheader that goes 17 innings, as Boston loses 7–6 to Philadelphia.

7th   The Yankees' Johnny Mize's pinch-hit grand slam gives the Yanks a 5–1 win at Washington. He has now homered in each one of the 15 ML parks, including Sportsman's Park in St. Louis while in each league.

OF Don Grate of Chattanooga sets a record for a long toss of a baseball in Chattanooga's Engel Stadium, with a throw of just one inch better than 434 feet, breaking a 42-year-old mark set by Larry LeJeune on October 3, 1908. Grate will improve his own record to 443 feet 3½ inches on August 23, 1953.

8th   An umpire ejects Giants P Larry Jansen for throwing a beanball. Giants manager Leo Durocher is also suspended and fined $100. Jansen is fined just $25 because of his "excellent conduct record." Brooklyn splits the doubleheader, winning the opener 10–2 and losing the nightcap 3–2. The Dodger lead stays at 5 games.

9th   The Cardinals Stan Musial gets his 2,000th hit, off Curt Simmons, as the Cardinals lose 4–2.

13th   OF Frank Carswell of the Buffalo Bisons wins the International League batting title with a .344 average. He also leads the league in HRs with 30 and has 101 RBI.

Warren Spahn strikes out 6 Pirates in a row en route to an 8–0 win in Boston.

14th   Enos Slaughter of the Cardinals walks twice in the 5th inning. Teammate Stan Musial chips in with a HR and a double in the inning, as St. Louis scores 11 runs against Dave Koslo. The Giants pitcher loses the game 14–4, his first loss to St. Louis after 13 straight victories since June 11, 1950.

15th   In a Cold War move, the Russians decry the American game of baseball by citing their own game of "lapka" as being the progenitor of baseball. They call American players "slaves." The State Department links the Soviet claim as the founders of baseball as part of its "Hate America" campaign.

The Braves play their last game in Boston's Braves Field before moving to Milwaukee, losing to Brooklyn's Joe Black 8–2. The Dodgers clinch a tie for the pennant. The crowd of 8,822 is the Braves' 2nd largest of the season.

16th Joe Gordon, former All-Star 2B for the Yankees and Indians and now manager of Sacramento (PCL), inserts himself as a pinch hitter in each game of a twin bill with Los Angeles and homers on both occasions. The first one is a grand slam that wins the game 4–1.

25th Hal Newhouser of the Tigers wins his 200th game. It is his last win for Detroit, who will release him in early 1953.

26th The Yanks clinch their 4th straight pennant, an 11-inning 5–2 win at Philadelphia behind Ed Lopat and Johnny Sain.

27th The Braves Ed Mathews hits 3 HRs as Boston breaks a 10-game loss streak and beats Brooklyn 11–3. Virgil Jester wins, his last in the majors and the last victory for the Boston Braves franchise.

28th The Braves play a 12-inning, 5–5 tie in Brooklyn in their last game as the Boston Braves. The Dodger pitching staff sets a NL record for most strikeouts in a season with 773 when Jim Hughes fans Sid Gordon in the 12th.

29th The Phils Robin Roberts wins his 28th game, the most in the league since 1935, a 7–4 win over New York. It is Roberts's 30th complete game.

Stan Musial makes his only ML pitching appearance. With his 6th batting title wrapped up, he takes the mound against the Cubs Frank Baumholtz, the runner-up in the batting race. Baumholtz, batting righthanded, reaches base on an error, and Harvey Haddix relieves Musial. The Cubs win 3–0 behind Paul Minner.

OCTOBER

1st In Game 1 of the WS, the Dodgers defeat the Yankees 4–2 at Ebbets Field behind relief ace Joe Black, who started only 2 games during the season.

2nd The Yanks tie up the WS behind the masterful 3-hit pitching of Vic Raschi, who defeats Carl Erskine 7–1. Raschi strikes out 9.

3rd Brooklyn's Preacher Roe wins in Yankee Stadium 5–3. Brooklyn scores 2 runs in the 9th on Yogi Berra's passed ball.

4th The Yankees draw even at home 2–0 behind the shutout pitching of Allie Reynolds. Johnny Mize, inserted at 1B, clubs a HR, single, double, and walk in 4 at bats.

In the famed Little World Series, the Rochester Red Wings(IL) defeat the Kansas City Blues (AA) 4–3.

5th At Yankee Stadium, the seesaw WS battle continues as Brooklyn wins 6–5 in 11 innings when Duke Snider doubles home Billy Cox. Carl Erskine goes all the way for the win.

6th At Ebbets Field, the Yankees even it up for the 3rd time, as Raschi and Reynolds combine for a 3–2 win in Brooklyn. RF Carl Furillo robs Johnny Mize of a HR in the 9th.

7th In Game 7 the Yankees take their 4th consecutive WS championship, as Allie Reynolds, one of 3 relievers, defeats Joe Black 4–2. Billy Martin saves the day by snaring a 2-out, bases-loaded IF pop off the bat of Jackie Robinson. Gil Hodges goes hitless again and is 0-for-21 in the Series. Each Yank will receive a winners' share of $6,026, and each Dodger, a losers' share of $4,200.

23rd The PCL announces a 176-game schedule for 1953.

NOVEMBER

12th The baseball writers name Philadelphia P Bobby Shantz as the AL MVP. He was 24-7 for the 79-75 A's.

The White Sox place OF Jim Rivera on a one-year probation after he is cleared of a rape charge.

19th AL President Will Harridge says there will be greater fines for managers who use abusive language while arguing with umpires.

20th The writers name Cubs slugger Hank Sauer as the NL MVP. The Cubs finished in 5th place, despite Sauer's 37 HRs and 121 RBIs.

Baseball Commissioner Ford Frick states that he thinks the PCL will eventually reach ML status.

21st Dodgers P Joe Black, who had a record of 15-4, is voted NL Rookie of the Year.

22nd   The writers vote Harry Byrd of the Athletics as the AL Rookie of the Year.

25th   The St. Louis Cardinals seek payment from the New York Giants for 2 televised games in an effort to determine the TV and radio rights of visiting teams for revenue.

28th   IL President Frank Shaughnessy reveals plans to form 2 new major leagues by merging the top teams in the American Association and the top teams from the International League. He thinks that in 5 to 6 years, ML baseball will elevate these 2 leagues, along with the Pacific Coast League, which nearly has ML status now.

30th   On a local TV program, Brooklyn Dodger Jackie Robinson charges that the New York Yankee management is racist for its failure to bring up a black player. George Weiss of the Yanks denies the allegations.

DECEMBER

2nd   Dodger executive Buzzie Bavasi dismisses the Yankees reaction to Jackie Robinson's charges. Commissioner Ford Frick plans no action against Robinson.

4th   Detroit trades P Virgil Trucks, along with P Hal White and OF Johnny Groth, to the Browns in exchange for 2B Owen Friend, OF Bob Nieman, and OF J.W. Porter.

5th   ML attendance figures show an 11 percent drop.

6th   The AL approves a 2-league waiver rule curbing inter-league trading after June 15th.

11th   Pittsburgh names Fred Haney as its manager for 1953.

12th   Peter J. McGovern becomes president of the Little League, succeeding Charles Durban, who resigns because of ill health. The Little League began in 1939 with 8 teams in 2 leagues and has grown to over 1,800 leagues in 44 states and several foreign countries.

18th   In a shake-up of the Cleveland Indians, Hank Greenberg stays on as GM, while Ellis W. Ryan resigns as president after losing a showdown.

1953

JANUARY

8th The Cleveland Indians bar night games with the Browns due to St. Louis owner Bill Veeck's refusal to share receipts of the telecasts.

17th The Milwaukee Braves sell OF Andy Pafko back to Brooklyn for Roy Hartsfield and $50,000.

Martin Aarjan Jole, a Dutch player, gets a tryout with a Reds farm club in Columbia, SC. The 22-year-old, reputed to be a power hitter, wrote to Rogers Hornsby, the new Reds manager, asking for a try-out.

21st The Hall of Fame passes over Joe DiMaggio in his first year of eligibility and elects P Dizzy Dean and OF Al Simmons to Cooperstown. Dean gathers 209 votes while Simmons's total of 199 is one more than needed.

22nd U.S. Immigration Commissioner Mackey warns that alien players who jump U.S. pro contracts face deportation under the McCarran-Walter Act.

28th Owner Fred Saigh of the Cardinals is found guilty of income tax evasion and is sentenced to a 15-month jail term. He plans to sell the club. Cardinal Vice President W. Walsingham, Jr., is the acting president until Saigh can divest himself of his stock.

30th The Little League names Peter J. McGovern as its first full-time president. Its office is moved to Williamsport, PA.

31st New York, Cleveland, and Boston retaliate at Bill Veeck, forcing the Browns to play afternoon games. Veeck takes his plan to the AL office to make them pay. The plan is rejected.

FEBRUARY

13th The Athletics change the name of Shibe Park to Connie Mack Stadium, in honor of their longtime owner and manager.

19th Ted Williams safely crash-lands his damaged Panther jet after flying a combat mission in Korea.

20th August A. Busch buys the Cardinals for $3.75 million and pledges not to move the team from St. Louis.

The U.S. Court of Appeals rules that organized baseball is a sport and not a business, affirming the 25-year-old Supreme Court ruling. This effectively dismisses the antitrust suits of Jack Corbett and former Dodger farm hand Walter Kowalski. The $300,000 suit of Corbett, the owner of the Texas League El Paso club, is based on his belief that he lost money when ML baseball prohibited him from signing several players suspended for participation in the Mexican League. Kowalski's $150,000 suit is based on the general principles of the antitrust and restraint-of-trade laws. Their lawyer in these cases is Frederic Johnson, who also represents Danny Gardella in his suit against ML baseball.

MARCH

3rd The Boston Braves, who own the Milwaukee minor league franchise, block the Browns' attempt to shift their franchise to Milwaukee. Lou Perini, Braves owner, invokes his territorial privilege, stating he has not been offered enough.

11th Lou Perini, the owner of the Braves, proposes a ban on the move of any ML franchise to that of a minor league city until October 1st.

13th The NL weighs the offer by the Braves to move its franchise to Milwaukee.

Baltimore Mayor Tom D'Alesandro reports that negotiations with Veeck are underway to move the Browns to Maryland.

14th Mayor Joseph Darst of St. Louis vows to fight the move of the Browns to Baltimore.

16th The AL rejects Veeck's request to move the Browns to Baltimore because he is in control of the team. The rejection is designed to force Veeck out of the AL.

17th Veeck says that he will accept an offer of $2.475 million for his 80 percent of the stock. Baltimore Mayor D'Alesandro seeks a syndicate to buy Veeck out. The group will eventually purchase 206,250 shares at $12 per share, a total purchase price of $2,475,000.

The Braves club gets the use of Milwaukee County Stadium at a low rental.

18th The Milwaukee Braves become the first franchise shift in baseball since 1903 when Baltimore moved to New York. The Braves have been in Boston for 77 years. Milwaukee assumes Pittsburgh's place in the Western Division for scheduling purposes and night games. The Brewers move to Toledo.

20th Senator Edwin C. Johnson offers a bill to give clubs the sole right to ban radio-TV broadcasts of ML games in their own territory. The Antitrust Division of the Justice Department outlawed this practice in 1949. Johnson believes that it started the decline of baseball in small towns and cities throughout the country. His bill will restore the equity between large communities and the small areas.

24th Larry Raines, on leave from military service, plays his first game for the Hankyu Braves. He will stay for the 1954 season, return in 1962, and will end his Japanese career with a BA of .302.

APRIL

5th In the 6th inning of a PCL game against Hollywood, San Diego Padres OF Herb Gorman suffers a heart attack and dies on the way to the hospital.

9th August Busch buys Sportsman's Park for $800,000 from Browns owner Bill Veeck. Busch gives a 5-year lease to the Browns, turning the tables in a manner of speaking, since the Cardinals had been tenants of the Browns since 1920. Busch initially renames Sportsman's Park, Budweiser Park, but in response to protests about the commercialization of his ballpark, Busch renames Budweiser Park, Busch Stadium. The following season his company comes out with a new beer, Busch Bavarian Beer.

The Cincinnati club officially changes its name from Reds to Redlegs, in response to McCarthy Era pressure.

13th In Cincinnati, over 30,000 see the Milwaukee Braves win their first game 2–0 behind Max Surkont.

14th In a 3–2 victory, Braves OF Billy Bruton hits the first ML HR in Milwaukee's County Stadium, in the 10th inning off Gerry Staley of the Cards. This is the first game for the home crowd since 1901 when the Milwaukee Brewers were charter members of the AL.

Bob Lemon of the Indians one-hits the White Sox 6–0. Minnie Minoso's single in the first is the only safety for Chicago.

16th Connie Ryan has 6 consecutive hits, but the Phils lose 14–12 to Pittsburgh. The Phillies score 9 runs in the top of the 5th, and the Pirates come back

with 6 in the bottom to tie the NL record for runs in an inning.

Lefty Billy Pierce of the White Sox throws a one-hitter against the Browns. Bobby Young's double in the 7th is the only St. Louis safety in the 1–0 shutout. Harry Brecheen allows the White Sox just 2 hits in losing.

17th Mickey Mantle hits the longest HR in Griffith Stadium history, a 565-feet shot off of Chuck Stobbs of the Washington Senators. The Yanks win 7–3.

24th Jackie Robinson walks twice in the 6th inning, as the Dodgers score 6 runs en route to a 12–4 pasting of the Giants.

26th Feasting again on Pirates pitching, the Phillies Connie Ryan goes 5-for-5 in a 7–5 win in the first game of a doubleheader.

28th A wild fight occurs after Browns Clint "Scrap Iron" Courtney spikes Phil Rizzuto in the 10th inning in St. Louis. In the brawl, umpire John Stevens dislocates his collarbone. Six players are fined for their actions. Courtney retaliated after being knocked over in the top of the 10th when Gil McDougald scored the go-ahead run in an eventual 7–6 Yankee win.

29th Joe Adcock becomes the first ML player to homer into the CF bleacher seats in the Polo Grounds, over 475 feet away. Luke Easter, in a 1948 Negro League game, and Schoolboy Rowe, in batting practice before a 1933 exhibition game, also accomplished the feat. Lou Brock and Hank Aaron will match it is as well in 1962. The Braves win the game 3–2 on a 9th-inning wild pitch by Hoyt Wilhelm.

30th The Little-Bigger League changes its name to the Babe Ruth League.

MAY

1st The U.S. Court of Appeals denies the $450,000 suit of former pitcher Boyd Tepler made in 1951 against organized baseball, the Cubs, and William Wrigley for an arm injury suffered in 1944. He had contended that negligent coaching, in effect, ended his career prematurely.

2nd Pirates OF Carlos Bernier hits 3 triples in a 12–4 win over the Redlegs.

4th Busch Stadium bans bottles from the park during a game due to fans tossing soda bottles during a 7–6 Browns loss to the Yankees on April 28th.

5th P Bob Porterfield of the Senators hits a grand slam off Bill Wight of Detroit.

6th Bobo Holloman of the St. Louis Browns pitches a no-hitter in his first ML start, only the 3rd rookie to do so, in a 6–0 win over the A's. Within 3 months he will be out of the ML for good, the winner of just 3 games.

The NY Giants tie the NL record for the fewest number of assists in one game with just one, by pitcher Sal Maglie, in a 5–3 win over Chicago.

10th Pittsburgh IF Eddie and Johnny O'Brien become the first twins to play for the same team in the same game.

12th Whitey Ford of the New York Yankees allows only rival pitcher Early Wynn's infield single in the 6th in beating the Indians 7–0. New York increases its lead to 2 games over the 2nd-place Indians.

16th White Sox P Tommy Byrne pinch-hits for Vern Stephens and hits a grand slam off Yankees P Ewell Blackwell in the 9th inning to give Chicago the 5–3 win. Stephens has 10 career grand slams.

After the Braves' Billy Bruton's leadoff single in the first, Phillies P Curt Simmons retires the next 27 batters to win 3–0.

17th The Yanks and Browns use 41 players in a game to set a new ML record.

Carl Erskine of the Dodgers allows only one hit—Gus Bell's 6th-inning bunt single—in a 10–0 victory over the Redlegs in the 2nd game of a doubleheader.

18th Redlegs P Bud Podbielan walks 13 batters in 10 innings against Brooklyn, but holds on to win 2–1 on a Ted Kluszewski homer. The Dodgers strand 18, tieing the NL mark.

22nd Yanks OF Irv Noren lines back to P Bob Porterfield, who starts a triple play. The Senators beat the Yankees 12–4, but New York will not lose again for nearly 4 weeks.

24th A year and 3 days after scoring 15 runs in an inning, the Dodgers explode again. Against the Phillies they score 12 runs in the 8th inning before making an out. Their 2 bases-loaded triples set a modern ML record. The final score is 16–2.

25th The Yankees and Red Sox play the longest 9-inning game to date, lasting 3 hours and 52 minutes.

Ralph Kiner becomes the 12th player to hit 300 HRs with a blast at Forbes Field against the Giants. He has played only 7⅓ seasons.

Russ Meyer of the Dodgers is fined $100 and suspended 3 days for obscene gestures and abusive language picked up by TV close-ups. NL President Warren Giles and Commissioner Ford Frick oppose dugout shots by TV cameras.

The U.S. Supreme Court announces that it will review all the antitrust suits under the Sherman Act with regard to baseball, with the focal point being the reserve clause.

Max Surkont of the Braves fans 8 Reds in a row, establishing a new ML mark, as the Braves win 10–3 in game 2 of a doubleheader. Surkont strikes out 7 in a row before rain delays the game and then strikes out Andy Seminick to start the 5th. Surkont fans 13 on the way to his 6th straight win.

29th 3B Bob Elliot lines a double in the Browns, 6-run 11th inning, as they beat the Tigers 11–5. For Elliot, it is his 2,000th ML hit.

JUNE

3rd Congress cites the research of New York City librarian Robert Henderson in proving that Alexander Cartwright "founded" baseball and not Abner Doubleday. His 1947 book *Bat, Ball and Bishop* documents Cartwright's contributions to the origins of the game of baseball.

4th Pittsburgh trades OF Ralph Kiner, along with C Joe Garagiola, P Howie Pollet, and OF Catfish Metkovich to Chicago (NL) for C Toby Atwell, P Bob Schultz, 1B Preston Ward, 3B George Freese, OF Bob Addis, OF Gene Hermanski, and $150,000.

10th RF Jimmy Piersall of the Red Sox goes 6-for-6 in a 11–2 win over the Browns in the first game of a doubleheader. Piersall is hitless in game 2 as the Sox win 3–2.

14th White Sox hurlers Billy Pierce and Sandy Consuegra throw shutouts at the Red Sox in a doubleheader, winning 6–0 and 1–0. Pierce's gem is a 2-hitter. Chicago also picks up 2 players from the Browns, getting veterans 3B Bob Elliott and P Virgil Trucks for P Lou Kretlow, C Darrell Johnson, and $75,000. St.

Louis had obtained Trucks only 6 months ago from Detroit.

The Yankees sweep the Indians 6–2 and 3–0 before 74,708 to extend their winning streak to 18 games.

15th Duane Pillette of the Browns ends the Yankee win streak at 18 and the Browns team record 14-game losing streak with a 3–1 victory over New York in Yankee Stadium. Johnny Mize becomes the 93rd player in baseball history to get 2,000 hits when he singles in the Yankee run in the 5th.

18th Red Sox rookie OF Gene Stephens becomes the only AL player to get 3 hits in the same inning, as Boston scores 17 in the 7th inning in a 23–3 romp over Detroit. The Red Sox send 23 to the plate in the 7th, getting 14 hits and 6 walks before 3B George Kell flies out to end it.

Ed Lopat and Jim McDonald of the Yanks shut out the hapless St. Louis Browns 5–0 and 3–0 in both ends of a doubleheader.

22nd Senators C Ed Fitzgerald pulls off an unassisted DP against Cleveland in a 7–5 win in the first game of a doubleheader.

25th White Sox manager Paul Richards uses 5 firstbasemen in beating the Yankees 4–2. He brings in Harry Dorish to face 2 batters, moving Billy Pierce to 1B. The Sox 3-game sweep still leaves New York 9 games up on the Indians and 9½ on Chicago.

30th Braves slugger Eddie Mathews has 5 straight hits in a 10 inning 6–4 win over the Redlegs.

JULY

6th The Giants Al Worthington shuts out the Pirates 6–0 in his first ML start.

7th The Browns set the ML mark for consecutive home defeats, as they drop their 20th in succession, 6–3 to the Indians. The streak dates back to June 3rd.

The Dodgers set a ML record for most HRs in consecutive games with 24 games.

8th Cardinals 3B Ray Jablonski goes 5-for-5 against the Reds in a 7–2 win.

11th In his 2nd ML start, Al Worthington shuts out Brooklyn 6–0 for his 2nd shutout. This ties a ML record, last accomplished by Boo Ferriss of the Red Sox in 1945. Worthington stops the Dodgers' consecu-

tive-game HR streak. During the streak Brooklyn smacked 39 HRs, another ML record.

12th Braves slugger Eddie Mathews hits the first grand slam in the history of the Milwaukee franchise, as the Braves sweep 2 from the Cardinals 10–1 and 4–3 in St. Louis.

The Yomiuri and Mainichi newspaper chains inaugurate a program of regular visits by American ML clubs to Japan. The program will be sponsored by the Yomiuri chain alone from 1966.

14th The NL wins its 4th All-Star Game in a row, 5–1 in Cincinnati's Crosley Field behind the stellar pitching of Robin Roberts and Warren Spahn. Cardinal OF Enos Slaughter gets 2 hits, scores twice, and robs Harvey Kuenn of an extra-base blow.

16th The Browns tie a record with 3 successive HRs—by Clint Courtney, Dick Kryhoski, and Jim Dyck—in the first inning. Their 5 bases-empty HRs in 3 innings establishes a new mark. It's enough to beat the Yankees 8–6.

18th Dodger backup 1B Wayne Belardi scores 2 runs in the 8th inning, one on a pinch-hit grand slam. His slam in the 8th is the 3rd Dodger grand slam in 3 games (Gil Hodges connected on the 16th, and Billy Cox, on the 17th). The Dodgers' 8–6 win over the Cardinals puts Brooklyn 3 games ahead of Milwaukee.

1B Whitey Lockman, 3B Hank Thompson, and CF Bobby Thomson hit first inning HRs, as the Giants beat the Cubs 12–7 to move into 4th place.

19th The Giants Whitney Lockman leads off the game with a HR for the 2nd day in a row, as the Giants whip the Braves 7–5.

Boston lefty Mickey McDermott and relief P Ellis Kinder combine for a one-hitter against Cleveland. OF Al Smith's 4th-inning single is the only Tribe safety.

21st The Milwaukee Braves suffer their worst shutout loss in the history of the franchise, losing to the Phils 10–0.

24th The Red Sox sweep the Browns as both Boston pitchers, Mickey McDermott and Bill Henry, hurl 6–0 and 8–0 shutouts.

27th Dizzy Dean and Al Simmons are inducted into the Hall of Fame at Cooperstown. Along with them, the veterans committee enshrines Chief Bender, Bobby Wallace, 19th-century manager Harry Wright, executive Ed Barrow, and umpires Bill Klem and Tom Connolly.

30th The Giants Monte Irvin grounds into 3 DPs, tying a NL record, as Milwaukee wins 5–0.

AUGUST

1st Ben Flowers of the Boston Red Sox sets a ML record with 8 consecutive games pitched in relief, a mark that will later be surpassed.

Warren Spahn of the Braves allows just an infield hit to Richie Ashburn in the 4th in beating Philadelphia 5–0. It is Spahn's 31st career shutout.

3rd Chicago White Sox 1B Ferris Fain brawls in a Maryland cafe. The team fines him $600.

4th Yankees hurler Vic Raschi sets the record for RBI by a pitcher with 7, as the Yanks roll over Detroit 15–0. Raschi singles in 2 in the 2nd, doubles home 3 in the 3rd, and singles home the last 2 in the 8th. His teammates fill his locker with bats after the game.

5th Ben Flowers of the Red Sox shuts out the Browns 5–0 in his first ML start.

6th Ted Williams is back in a Red Sox uniform after military duty in Korea. He will finish with 13 HRs and a .407 mark.

8th Yankee southpaws Whitey Ford and Bob Kuzava hurl 1–0 and 3–0 shutouts against the White Sox. Kuzava gives up only Bob Boyd's double in the 9th.

10th Bob Porterfield of the Senators has his 2nd one-hitter of the season, as he masters the Red Sox 2–0.

11th Brooklyn slugger Duke Snider hits his 2nd slam in 3 days, accounting for all the runs in the Dodgers 4–0 win over the Giants. Carl Erskine allows New York just 2 hits.

12th The Yankees explode for 28 hits off Washington pitching.

The Braves and Cards draw 36,241, a record crowd for a twi-night doubleheader in Milwaukee's County Stadium.

15th 3B Ransom Jackson of the Cubs grounds into 3 DPs against the Braves' as the Cubs lose 2–0. Jackson ties a NL record, later eclipsed by Joe Torre.

17th Bob Kuzava of the Yanks shuts out the Athletics 9–0, allowing 11 hits along the way.

21st ML player reps Ralph Kiner (NL) and Allie Reynolds (AL) hire labor leader John Norman Lewis at $15,000 per annum to give legal advice to players in their negotiations with the owners.

22nd Lewis contends that the players have no desire to form a union, and that he is merely giving legal advice.

23rd Phil Paine, a former Boston Braves pitcher on military service with the U.S. Air Force in Japan, becomes the first ex-ML player to play in Japan. He pitches in 9 games for the Nishitetsu Lions: 4 wins, 3 losses, ERA 1.77.

Chattanooga OF Don Grate betters his 1952 record by throwing a baseball 443 feet 3½ inches. Glen Gorbous will beat it in 1957.

26th Giants OF Dusty Rhodes, hitting just .167, connects for 3 HRs in a row at the Polo Grounds in a 13–4 win over the Cardinals. Teammate Al Dark goes 5-for-5 with his own HR.

30th The Dodgers rip St. Louis 20–4 with the help of 2 big innings. Dodger Jackie Robinson fans twice in the 3rd inning, while Gil Hodges walks twice in the 6th. Roy Campanella's 5 RBIs ties the NL season mark of most RBIs by a catcher (122).

Led by OF Jim Pendleton's 3 HRs, the Braves tie the Yankees' 1939 ML record for the most HRs in a game with 8 in their 19–4 win over Pittsburgh in the first game of a doubleheader. Pendleton is only the 2nd rookie in history to hit 3 HRs in one game. In game 2 of the doubleheader, the Braves hit 4 more HRs to win 11–5. The 12 homers in a doubleheader shatters the previous mark of 9. Eddie Mathews's 4 HRs for the day give him an NL-leading 43; he will end the season with 47 HRs, 30 of them on the road to set an ML record.

SEPTEMBER

4th Despite consecutive HRs by Wes Westrum, Al Corwin, and Whitey Lockman in the 3rd, the Giants lose to the Dodgers 8–6 in a game marred by beanballs and disagreements on calls. Following a Clem Labine brushback on Giants IF Bobby Hofman, Larry Jansen throws at Duke Snider and Roy Campanella in the 8th.

6th The feuding continues, as the Dodgers beat the Giants 6–3 but lose Carl Furillo, the NL's leading hitter at .344, for the rest of the regular season. Furillo is hit on the wrist by a Ruben Gomez pitch in the 2nd. With a 3-2 count on the next batter, Furillo races from 1B into the dugout to swing at Leo Durocher. In the melee, a Giants player steps on Furillo's left hand, breaking a finger.

Roy Campanella sets the ML mark for HRs by a catcher. His 38th tops the NL high of 37 hit by Cubs C Gabby Hartnett in 1930.

7th Campanella sets the ML record for RBI by a catcher when he smacks a 3-run HR in a 6–3 Dodgers' win over the Phils. Campy's 125 breaks Yogi Berra's ML record of 124 set in 1950, and he will finish the season with 142.

9th Mantle's 2-run HR off Chicago's Billy Pierce caps a 7-run 5th inning, as New York wins 9–3 at at Yankee Stadium. Returning to CF after the 5th, Mantle is photographed blowing a huge bubble with a wad of gum. Manager Stengel will publicly rebuke the Mick, who will apologize for the indiscretion. However, Mantle does get an endorsement fee from the Bowman Gum company

12th Carl Erskine defeats the Braves 5–2, as the Dodgers clinch the pennant earlier than any other team in history.

13th Red Sox C Sammy White makes an unassisted DP.

P Bob Trice becomes the first black to appear in a ML game for the Philadelphia Athletics.

14th The Yanks clinch their 5th straight pennant with an 8–5 win over the Indians. 2B Billy Martin has 4 RBI.

Johnny Klippstein of the Cubs stops Duke Snider's hitting streak at 27 consecutive games, the longest in the NL in 1953. The Cubs win 3–1 for their 10th win in a row.

17th Ellis Kinder of the Red Sox sets the AL record for most relief appearances with 62.

The Cubs Ernie Banks goes 0-for-3 and makes an error in his first ML game, as the Phillies win 16–4.

With a record of 64-82, the Cincinnati Redlegs fire Rogers Hornsby as their manager with 8 games left in the season. Coach Buster Mills replaces him for the remainder of the year.

Ferris Fain of the White Sox is sued for $50,000 for his part in an August brawl in a Maryland café.

18th The St. Louis Cardinals appeal the U.S. claim for $215,025 in back taxes from 1947-49.

19th Pirates 3B Danny O'Connell hits safely in his 26th game, a 4–1 loss to the Giants.

20th Ernie Banks of the Cubs hits his first ML HR, against Gerry Staley, but the Cards win 11–6.

22nd The Dodgers tie the record for the most wins in a home park, beating Pittsburgh 5–4. They go an incredible 60-17 at Ebbets Field, tying the record of the St. Louis Cardinals in 1942. Only the 61 wins of the San Francisco Giants in an 81-game home season will surpass the mark.

26th Billy Hunter becomes the last St. Louis Browns player to homer in a game. The Browns lose anyway 6–3 to Chicago.

27th Washington's Mickey Vernon goes into the last game of the season still fighting for the batting title with Cleveland's Al Rosen. Near the end of the game Vernon is hitting .337 when word arrives that Rosen's game is over and Vernon is ahead by .0011 points. The possibility of Vernon coming up to bat again and maybe losing a point is scotched when his teammates contrive to make an out to end the game.

The St. Louis Browns play both their last game in Sportsman's Park and the last game in the franchise's 52-year history. Fittingly, they lose 2–1 to Billy Pierce and the Chicago White Sox in 10 innings for their 100th defeat of the season. Reserve 1B Ed Mickelson drives in Johnny Groth in the 4th inning for the last run of the Browns franchise.

29th The AL adopts a constitutional amendment calling for expansion to 10 teams.

A Baltimore syndicate headed by Baltimore Mayor Tom D'Alesandro buys Bill Veeck's interest in the Browns for 2.475 million. The AL approves the shift of the Browns to Baltimore without Bill Veeck.

30th The Yanks defeat Brooklyn 9–5 in the first game of the WS. Carl Erskine is ineffective, walking the first 3 batters who score on a Hank Bauer triple. The Dodgers tie it up 5–5, and Clem Labine gets the loss in relief.

OCTOBER

1st The Yankees go 2 up as Eddie Lopat beats Preacher Roe 4–2, despite the Dodgers' 9–5 edge in hits.

Bill Veeck resigns as Browns president.

2nd The WS moves to Ebbets Field as Carl Erskine establishes a new Series strikeout record by fanning 14 Yanks, including Mickey Mantle and Joe Collins 4 times each. Roy Campanella breaks a 2–2 tie with a game-winning solo HR in the 8th for a 3–2 Brooklyn win

3rd The Dodgers even up the WS at 2 games apiece, as Duke Snider drives in 4 runs in a 7–3 victory.

4th In Game 5, Mickey Mantle hits a grand slam off Russ Meyer, and the Yanks hold on to win 11–7.

5th The Yanks end the WS in 6 as Billy Martin's 12th WS hit, a record-breaking single to CF in the bottom of the 9th, gives the Yankees their 5th championship in a row. Carl Furillo had tied it up in the 9th with a 2-run HR.

7th Bill Veeck tells stockholders that he faces bankruptcy unless they drop their suit to block the move to Baltimore. The Browns stockholders will drop their suit against Veeck.

8th Cuba defeats Venezuela 4–0 before 32,000 partisan fans in Caracas's University Stadium.

The city of Birmingham, AL, bars Jackie Robinson's Negro-White All-Stars from playing there. Robinson gives in and drops the white players from his group.

13th The Yankees buy the contracts of black players Elston Howard and Vic Power from the Kansas City Blues.

14th The Dodgers force Charley Dressen's resignation as manager when he refuses to sign anything less than a one-year contract. The club reportedly offered him a $7,500 raise, but on the insistence of his wife he tried for a 2-year contract and lost. Dressen immediately signs to manage the Oakland Oaks in the PCL.

17th Bill Veeck wastes no time getting a new job. He becomes a special adviser to Phil Wrigley of the Cubs.

18th The Orioles agree to pay the International League $48,749 for its territorial rights in Baltimore.

The Giants leave on a one-month tour of Japan, Korea, and the Philippines.

28th The "Old Redhead," Red Barber, resigns from the Dodger broadcast booth and takes a job with the rival New York Yankees.

31st After touring Japan with the Giants, Commissioner Ford Frick says that Japanese baseball is the equivalent of Class A in the U.S.

NOVEMBER

3rd The rules committee restores the 1939 sacrifice fly rule, which says a sacrifice fly is not charged as a time at bat.

4th A new balk rule gives the batter an option; if he gets a hit after a balk is called, he has the option of accepting the outcome of the pitch, instead of being limited to the advance of the runner(s).

Eddie Joost succeeds Jimmy Dykes as the manager of the Philadelphia Athletics.

9th The U.S. Supreme Court decides 7-2 that baseball is a sport and not a business and therefore not subject to antitrust laws.

10th The Giants end their tour of Japan. It is reported that each player received just $331 of the $3,000 they were promised.

11th Jimmy Dykes, recently released as the manager of the Athletics, succeeds Marty Marion as the manager of the Baltimore Orioles.

17th The St. Louis Browns' name officially becomes the Baltimore Baseball Club Inc. The Baltimore franchise board officially changes its name to the "Orioles."

24th The Dodgers sign the relatively unknown Walter Alston to a one-year pact as their manager for 1954.

27th Indians 3B Al Rosen is unanimously named the AL's MVP with a record 336 votes. In the NL, Dodger C Roy Campanella is named MVP.

30th The player reps reject Commissioner Ford Frick's plan for a conference on their pension after he bars their attorney's presence.

DECEMBER

1st   The Red Sox trade for hard-hitting Jackie Jensen, sending Maury McDermott and Tom Umphlett to Washington.

9th   The leagues meet and adopt a resolution to set up a committee to weigh ending the pension fund in November of 1955. Hank Greenberg and John Galbreath are on the committee. Broadcast revenues from WS and All-Star games are in dispute.

The leagues raise the minimum salary to $6,000.

10th   Dodgers President Walter O'Malley unveils plans for a new stadium in Brooklyn.

14th   Detroit's Harvey Kuenn is voted AL Rookie of the Year. Kuenn hit .308 for the season.

17th   In a tax-avoidance scheme, the NY Yankees sell Yankee Stadium and Kansas City properties for $6.5 million in a deal with Johnson Corp and the Knights of Columbus, who immediately lease the property back to the Yanks.

22nd   Jack Dunn III, whose family successfully owned and operated the Orioles for years in the International League, officially turns the old team name over to the Baltimore Orioles.

23rd   Dodgers 2B Jim "Junior" Gilliam easily wins NL Rookie of the Year honors over Harvey Haddix and Ray Jablonski. Satchel Paige remains unclaimed on the AL waiver list.

1954

JANUARY

13th   The Pirates trade P Murry Dickson to the Phils for P Andy Hansen and IF Jack "Lucky" Lohrke. Dickson led the league in losses the past 2 years and will lead it again in 1954.

14th   Former Yankee great Joe Dimaggio marries actress Marilyn Monroe.

30th   The Braves trade lefties Johnny Antonelli and Don Liddle, and C Ebba St. Clair to the Giants for slugger Bobby Thomson and Sam Calderone. Antonelli will improve his 12-12 record in 1953 to 21-7 as a Giant and lead the NL in ERA.

FEBRUARY

18th   The Washington Senators get Roy Sievers from the Orioles for Gil Coan.

23rd   The Cards purchase Vic Raschi from the Yankees for $85,000.

MARCH

1st   In his first spring practice, Red Sox slugger Ted Williams breaks his collarbone and will be out until May 15th.

13th   Newly acquired Bobby Thomson of the Braves breaks his ankle sliding into 3B in an exhibition game with the Pirates, thus opening the way for Henry Aaron to start in the OF. Thomson will be out of action until July 14th.

14th   Aaron starts his first game with the Braves, getting 3 hits in a spring training game against the Boston Red Sox.

29th   Phil Cavarretta gives Cubs owner Phil Wrigley an honest assessment of the team's chances, and is fired for his "defeatist attitude," the first manager to be given the gate during spring training. Stan Hack replaces him. Cavarretta is right; the Cubs will drop to 7th.

APRIL

11th   To make room for promising rookie OF Wally Moon, the Cardinals trade long-time great Enos Slaughter to the Yankees. In what turns out to be a good deal for both teams, the Cardinals get CF Bill Virdon, P Mel Wright, and OF Emil Tellinger in return. Virdon will become the NL Rookie of the Year in 1955, and Slaughter will help the Yankees to win 103 games.

13th   Henry Aaron of the Braves makes his ML debut, going hitless in 5 trips to the plate in a 9–8 loss to the Redlegs. Reds LF Jim Greengrass bangs 4 doubles, and rookie teammate Spook Jacobs, in his first ML game, also gets 4 hits.

Back in CF after 2 years in the army, Willie Mays of the Giants hits a 2-run shot that beats Brooklyn 4–3.

Hitting against the Cubs Paul Minner, Cardinal rookie Wally Moon homers in his first ML AB. 1B Tom Alston becomes the first black to play for the St. Louis Cardinals. Minner homers to back his own pitching, as the Cubs win 13–4.

Pittsburgh opens at home for the first time in 61 years and defeats the Phils 4–2 before 32,294. Curt Roberts, the Bucs' first black player, hits a triple against Robin Roberts in the first inning.

The new AL Baltimore Orioles open in Detroit and lose 3–0. The Tigers start fast and will win 12 of their first 18 games.

In the opener in Washington, President Dwight D. Eisenhower is thrilled by Mickey Vernon's 10th inning 2-run homer off Allie Reynolds to beat the Yankees 5–3.

In Boston, Braves Field is renamed BU Field by its new owners, Boston University.

15th   The Orioles Clint Courtney hits the first HR in Memorial Stadium. They draw an Opening Day record crowd of 46,354 in a 3–1 afternoon win against the White Sox.

17th   The wind is blowing out at Wrigley, as the Cards lose 23–13 to the Cubs in a record 3 hour and 43 minute game. Bruce Edwards walks twice in the 5th, as the Cubs score 10 runs. Cubs 3B Randy Jackson has 4 hits, including a HR that hits an apartment building on Waveland Avenue.

Joe Coleman of the Orioles loses a 3-hitter to the Tigers 1–0.

Nino Escalera becomes the first black to play for the Cincinnati Redlegs when he hits a pinch single in a 5–1 loss to the Braves.

18th   The White Sox acquire IF Grady Hatton from the Redlegs.

20th Philadelphia's Alex Kellner allows only a Wayne Terwilliger 8th-inning single in defeating Washington 7–0.

23rd At Sportsman's Park, Henry Aaron hits the first of his 755 ML HRs, off Vic Raschi of St. Louis. The Braves win in 14 innings 7–5.

Jackie Robinson steals home on a triple steal with Gil Hodges and Sandy Amoros in the 6th against the Pirates. Dodgers win 6–5.

Cardinal rookie sensation Wally Moon goes 5-for-5 in a 7–5, 14-inning loss to Milwaukee.

24th Mickey McDermott of the Senators breaks former teammate Boston P Mel Parnell's forearm with a pitch.

25th Giants pitchers Sal Maglie and Johnny Antonelli shut out the Phils in a twin bill 3–0 and 5–0.

In a 12-inning, 7–6 loss to the Cardinals, Braves rookie Hank Aaron goes 5-for-6.

MAY

1st Red Sox IF Billy Goodman's single in the 6th spoils Virgil Trucks's bid for another no-hitter. Trucks, now with the White Sox, wins 3–0.

2nd Stan Musial hits 5 HRs in a doubleheader with the Giants in St. Louis. In attendance is 8-year-old Nate Colbert, who will be the only other player in history to accomplish this feat. The Cards win the first game 10–6. In the nightcap of the doubleheader, Don Mueller goes 5-for-5, the Giants winning 9–7.

The Dodgers bench C Roy Campanella, who is hitting only .167. The next day he will undergo surgery for the removal of bone chips from his left hand.

4th The Phils and Cards set a ML record, later broken, by using 42 players in an 11-inning, 14–10 victory for Philadelphia. The Cards use 8 pitchers and the Phillies use 7.

5th The Senators Roy Sievers draws a bases-loaded walk to beat the White Sox 1–0.

9th Athletic C Wilmer (Billy) Shantz, brother of P Bobby Shantz, hits a grand slam, the first homer of his professional career. He will hit just one more ML HR.

12th The Dodgers option LF Sandy Amoros to Montreal because of weak hitting. They will recall him later in the season.

Tom Brewer of the Red Sox loses a 1–0 three-hitter to the White Sox when he walks 4 in the first. Connie Johnson wins with a 2-hitter, the 2nd Sox 2-hitter in 10 days.

Dodger Gil Hodges's HR in the 5th spoils Lew Burdette's bid for a no-hitter in the Braves 5–1 win.

Rookie CF Wally Moon of the Cards has his 2nd 5-hit game and scores 5 runs in a 13–5 rout of Pittsburgh.

13th Bobby Adams of the Redlegs hits a lead-off HR against Phillies P Robin Roberts. Roberts then retires the next 27 batters in a row to win 8–1.

16th The Indians sweep the A's 12–7 and 6–0 to take over first place. This begins a streak of 11 wins in a row.

The Orioles draw a record Mermorial Stadium crowd of 46,796 for a doubleheader with the Yankees.

Ted Williams returns to action after breaking his collarbone in spring training and goes 8-for-9 with 2 HRs and 7 RBI in a doubleheader against the Tigers. Williams has 3 hits in game one, a 7–6 loss. He goes 5-for-5 in the nightcap, including both HRs, but Boston loses 9–8 in 14 innings.

19th The Phils apologize to 2B Granny Hamner for having him followed by Charles Leland, a detective. Phils owner Robert Carpenter, suspecting that some players were not ready physically and mentally, had hired Leland to follow them. Hamner noticed Leland and reported him to the police, who promptly arrested the detective. Carpenter's apology comes with the Phils tied for 2nd place, a game behind St. Louis.

23rd The White Sox send SS Grady Hatton and cash to the Red Sox for 3B George Kell.

24th In a unique Birdie Tebbets' shift against the Cards Stan Musial, the Redlegs enlist a "4th" OF in place of regular SS Roy McMillan. This causes a box score irregularity because left-handed Nino Escalero is officially listed as a left-handed SS. After all that, Art Fowler strikes out Musial as the Reds win 4–2.

26th Robin Roberts of the Phils stops a personal 7-game losing streak to the Dodgers at Ebbets Field with an 8–6 win over Brooklyn.

The Senators defeat Yankee lefty Eddie Lopat for the first time in 3 years 2–1.

Slugger Gus Zernial hits the last grand slam in the history of the Philadelphia Athletics franchise, as the A's down the Red Sox 6–5.

28th   At the Polo Grounds, the Giants whip the Dodgers 17–6 with a 6-HR barrage. Four of the HRs come in the 8th as Davey Williams, Alvin Dark, Monte Irvin, and Billy Gardner connect off Ben Wade.

31st   The Dodgers send Joe Black, their 1952 relief ace and Rookie of the Year, to their Montreal farm club. His ERA is 11.57 in 5 appearances.

JUNE

2nd   After being banished during a rain-splashed victory over the Braves, Dodger star Jackie Robinson accidentally flings a bat into the stands, injuring a spectator.

3rd   Henry Thompson of the Giants hits 3 HRs and knocks in 8 runs in a 13–8 win against the Cardinals. Willie Mays collects the other 5 RBI on 2 HRs.

5th   Ted Williams catches pneumonia, sidelining him for 3 weeks.

6th   C Clint Courtney of the Orioles makes an unassisted DP in a 7–5 win against the Yankees.

7th   Dodger C Roy Campanella, who hit a home run earlier in the game, steals home in the 12th in a 7–5 victory over St. Louis.

9th   Cards P Harvey Haddix defeats the Dodgers 3–0, the first lefty to shut them out since 1950.

10th   Fred Baczewski of the Redlegs gives up 11 hits to the Phils, but shuts them out 6–0

11th   The Tigers hit 6 HRs in a game against the Athletics, winning 16–5, to get them back to the .500 level. Both 3B Ray Boone and teammate RF Al Kaline hit grand slams.

12th   Jim Wilson, 32, no-hits the Phillies 2–0 before 28,218 in Milwaukee. Robin Roberts takes the loss, his first after 9 straight wins over the Braves. It is Wilson's first start after pitching just 8⅔ innings of relief, giving up 7 runs. Ironically, the Braves asked waivers on Wilson 2 weeks earlier, with no takers.

Behind Bob Feller, the Indians beat the Red Sox 4–3 to take undisputed possession of first place. Feller records his 2,500th strikeout in the game. The Tribe proceeds to win their next 9 games.

13th   Cardinals LF Rip Repulski has 2 hits in each game of a doubleheader against Pittsburgh, to start a string of 10 straight games in which he collects 2 or more hits.

15th   The Giants take over undisputed possession of first place for the first and last time, when Hank Thompson hits a 3-run HR with 2 out in the 9th to beat the Redlegs.

With exactly half the season remaining, former Cardinals CF Terry Moore replaces Phillies manager Steve O'Neill.

The University of Missouri defeats tiny Rollins College in the NCAA championship game 4–1.

16th   1B Ferris Fain of the White Sox hits an inside-the-park grand slam in an 11–6 victory over the A's.

20th   Bobby Hofman, Wes Westrum, and Dusty Rhodes hit consecutive HRs in the 6th inning, as the Giants defeat St. Louis to stay ½ game ahead of the Dodgers.

23rd   Harvey Haddix of the Cardinals yields a run to the Pirates after 37 scoreless innings, winning 7–1.

Dodger lefty Johnny Podres undergoes an appendectomy after being knocked out in 3 straight starts.

The Red Sox pull a triple play but still lose to Baltimore in a 17-inning game that sets a new AL record for time consumed (4:58) and ties an ML mark, set 7 weeks earlier, for players used (42).

25th   The Dodgers hold the Cardinals' hottest hitter, Rip Repulski, to a solitary single, snapping his dual hit streak at 10. He will hit in 5 more consecutive games before going hitless. Over the 10 games, Repulski, in 44 ABs, had 22 hits, half for extra bases.

White Sox 1B Ferris Fain injures his knee in a collision at home plate and is lost for the season.

30th   Tom Morgan of the Yankees hits 3 Red Sox in the 3rd inning of a 6–1 loss. Mickey Mantle's HR against Willard Nixon is the only Yankee tally.

JULY

1st   Joe Cunningham of the Cards hits 2 HRs in a game against Milwaukee, giving him 3 for his first 2 days in the ML, a record unequaled since then. Cardinal ace Harvey Haddix stops a Joe Adcock liner with his knee, but wins 9–2. Haddix never fully recovers during the season from this injury.

2nd 3B George Kell of the White Sox wrenches his knee and is out for 5 weeks.

4th Indians Mike Garcia, Ray Narleski, and Early Wynn, in a rare relief role, shut down the White Sox 2–1, only allowing Minnie Minoso's 9th-inning single.

5th Indians reserve 1B Billy Glynn hits 3 HRs in a row and drives in 8 runs in a 13–6 win over Detroit.

RF Stan Musial outpolls all other NL players in the All-Star balloting.

8th The Giants complete a 3-game sweep of the Dodgers in Ebbets Field to up their lead in the NL to 6½ games.

10th Bob Rush of the Cubs stops Cardinal 2B Red Schoendienst's hitting streak at 28 games, the longest batting streak in 1954.

11th Giants OF Don Mueller hits for the cycle, getting his hits off 4 different pitchers in a 13–7 rout of the Pirates. Five other HRs are added, 3 in the 3rd as Monte Irvin, Whitey Lockman, and Alvin Dark connect.

The Red Sox whip the lowly Athletics 18–0 for one of the worst shutouts in AL history. A's slugger Gus Zernial breaks his collarbone diving for a ball and is out of the lineup until late August.

13th In the All-Star Game, the AL breaks the NL's 4-game winning streak with an 11–9 win. Larry Doby's pinch HR in the 8th, followed by Nellie Fox's 2-run single, ends the highest scoring All-Star Game in history. The 2 teams combine for 31 hits, with the AL amassing 17. The Indians Al Rosen has 2 HRs and 5 RBIs.

15th Phillie CF Richie Ashburn walks 5 times in a 2–1 loss to the Redlegs.

18th The NL awards a forfeit victory over the Cards to the Phils for a stall that follows a first-inning brawl featuring Phils manager Terry Moore and 1B Earl Torgeson, and Cards C Sal Yvars. The Cardinals are under the impression that local ordinances prevent lights being turned on to continue a game. Down 8–1 in the 5th inning of game 2, St. Louis begins stalling.

After winning 13 in a row, the Yankees lose the 2nd game of a doubleheader to Detroit 8–6. They now trail Cleveland by ½ game.

22nd Stengel switches players in an effort to get more power in the Yankee lineup. Phil Rizzuto plays 2B and Mickey Mantle plays SS. Mantle wins the game 3–2 against Chicago with a 10th-inning HR.

24th After Casey Stengel pulls Phil Rizzuto in the 8th for a pinch hitter, he brings in Mickey Mantle again at SS. Mantle plays SS with Willie Miranda at 2B against lefthanded hitters. Against righties, Miranda and Mantle switch positions. Cleveland wins 5–4 to go 2½ games up on New York.

25th White Sox P Jack Harshman sets a team record by striking out 16 in a 5–2 win over Boston.

26th Brooklyn defeats Giant stalwart Sal Maglie in Ebbets Field, roughing him up for 6 runs on 11 hits. Since coming into the NL in 1945, the "Barber" had recorded 10 straight victories in the Brooklyn ball park.

28th Giants OF Dusty Rhodes hits 3 consecutive HRs at the Polo Grounds to back Johnny Antonelli's 10–0 whipping of St. Louis. It is Antonelli's 10th consecutive win. Willie Mays smacks his 36th HR, a 447 foot clout to LF.

30th Against Allie Reynolds, 3B Bob Kennedy hits the first grand slam for the new Baltimore Orioles. The Orioles surpass the top season attendance the Browns had in their 52 years, as they draw 27,385 for the game, giving them 7,000 more than the 712,918 St. Louis drew in 1922.

31st Using a borrowed bat, Dodger killer Joe Adcock hits 4 HRs and a double for 18 total bases in the Braves' 15–7 victory at Ebbets Field. The 18 total bases is a ML mark and, combined with the 7 total bases from the day before, gives him a 2-day tally of 25. The 2-game total ties him with Ty Cobb.

AUGUST

1st Dodgers Clem Labine beans Joe Adcock in the 4th. Though he is wearing a batting helmet, Adcock is taken out of the game as a precautionary measure. His helmet apparently saves him from a serious injury. He will appear in the starting line-up the next day. Gene Conley reciprocates by knocking down Jackie Robinson in the 6th. Robinson ends up scrapping with Eddie Mathews. The Braves win 10–5, their 10th win in a row, as Conley runs his record to 10-5.

The 55-game hitting streak of Waco (Big State) OF Roman Mejias ends. He batted .435 during the streak (97 for 223).

3rd The Dodgers bench Roy Campanella again for his ailing left hand. He plays only sparingly for the rest of the season.

8th The Dodgers score an NL record 13 runs in the 8th off Cincinnati in Ebbets Field to win 20–8. Twelve of the runs are unearned. Gil Hodges gets a triple and a HR in the 8th, while P Clem Labine, who has a career .100 BA, walks twice.

12th Eddie Yost of the Senators draws his 100th walk for the 5th year in a row.

14th Dodgers slugger Duke Snider fans twice in the 6th inning of a game against the Giants, as the Dodgers hold on to a 6–5 victory.

16th In a throwing contest between Jimmy Piersall and Willie Mays before a Red Sox-Giants charity game in Boston, Piersall hurts his arm. He starts the game but leaves midway. He wakes up the following morning with a sore arm that stays with him a year, and he will never throw quite as well again.

20th The Cards hit into 6 DPs against the Redlegs to tie the NL record. The Redlegs win 3–2.

OF Gene Woodling of the Yanks crashes into the wall, breaking a thumb. He is lost for the season.

22nd Rookie Spook Jacobs of the A's steals 4 bases in a 3–2 triumph over the Senators.

24th Robin Roberts is lifted in the 7th as the Braves finally knock out the Phillies ace, winning 5–1. Roberts had pitched 13 straight complete games against the Braves over 3 years, with a 12–1 record.

25th The Dodgers hit 9 HRs in a 2-day sweep of the Redlegs, winning 12–4 and 13–2. Gil Hodges of the Dodgers has 2 RBIs today to knock in 100 runs for the 6th consecutive season.

27th In an 11–0 White Sox win, Chicago 3B Cass Michaels has his head fractured by a pitch from A's Marion Fricano. Michaels is sidelined the rest of the year, and the injury will effectively end his 12-year ML career.

In the championship game of the Little League WS, Schenectady, NY, defeats Colton, CA, 7–5. Future NL Rookie of the Year, Cub 2B Ken Hubbs stars for Colton in 1954. This team later becomes the subject of a best-selling book by Martin Ralbovsky, *Destiny's Darlings*.

29th Giants Dusty Rhodes has 6 extra base hits, 2 doubles, 2 triples, and 2 HRs in 2 games, as the Giants split with the Cardinals, winning 5–4 and losing 7–4.

Orioles bespectacled C Clint Courtney goes 5-for-5, as Baltimore defeats the Senators 5–0.

A disappointed crowd of 45,922 at Milwaukee's County Stadium sees the Dodgers take 2 from the Braves, 12–4 and 11–4. In game one, the Dodgers break a tie with a record 8 runs in the 11th. The Braves establish a new NL attendance mark of 1,841,666 on their way to a season total of 2,131,388.

30th In beating St. Louis 4–1 on 4 hits, Johnny Antonelli becomes the first lefty to win 20 games for the Giants since Carl Hubbell and Cliff Melton in 1937.

The Indians complete an 11-home-game sweep of the Red Sox, the first such sweep since the Yankees blanked St. Louis Browns in 1927.

31st The Indians beat the Yanks 6–1 to record their 26th win of the month, tying the 1931 A's.

SEPTEMBER

1st Redlegs Ted Kluszewski hits 2 HRs to break his own club mark of 40 HRs. He will wind up with 49 for the season. Cincinnati loses to Philadelphia 9–3.

2nd Dodger Russ Meyer beats the Cubs for the 16th consecutive time, dating back to 1950.

Mickey Vernon of the Senators gets his 2,000th hit. He also hits his 19th HR (he will add one more before the end of the season) for a team record for left-handers. Teammate Roy Sievers also sets a team record by hitting his 23rd HR. He will hit one more before the end of the season.

3rd The Yankees snap Bob Lemon's 11-game win streak to beat the Indians 3–2 and move to 3½ games from first place. Mantle's gigantic blast into the RF upper deck in the 6th started the Yankee scoring.

Ted Williams of the Red Sox hits his 362nd HR to put him in 5th place on the all-time list.

5th Hank Aaron goes 4-for-4 in a 9–7 triumph over the Cubs, but breaks his ankle in the 2nd game of a doubleheader and is lost for the remainder of the season.

6th After losing 10 straight, the Pirates sweep the Dodgers in Ebbets Field on "Back the Dodgers Day," winning 9–6 in 12 innings and 9–7. It is their first doubleheader sweep of the Dodgers since 1950 and drops Brooklyn to 3rd.

Eddie Mathews leads the Braves in 2 wins, 13–2 and 6–1, over the Cubs. Mathews has 8 straight hits before lining out in his last at bat. The attendance of 43,207 pushes the Braves over 2 million.

Cuban OF Carlos Paula, the first black to play for the Senators, debuts with a 2-for-4 day as the Nats win 8–1.

7th The Senators and Athletics draw just 460 fans to a game, the smallest crowd in Griffith Stadium history. The Senators win 5–4.

9th The Yanks Enos Slaughter spoils a no-hitter for the 3rd time by getting a single off Orioles P Joe Coleman, who finishes with a one-hitter and a 1–0 shutout.

10th Braves 1B Joe Adcock's HR against the Dodgers in Ebbets Field breaks the NL mark of 9 HRs hit on the road against one club. Billy Loes one-hits the Braves 2–1 in a 4½ inning game halted by rain. Adcock's HR is the Braves only hit.

Attempting to handle Hoyt Wilhelm's knuckleball against the Redlegs, C Ray Katt of the Giants sets an ML record with 4 passed balls in the 8th inning. As Wilhelm winds up in the 8th with 2 out and Bobby Adams on 3B, Adams races home, expecting Katt to make his 5th passed ball. Roy MacMillan swings and misses, and Katt holds on and tags out the red-faced Adams. Cincinnati wins 8–1.

11th Whitey Lockman of the Giants gets a pinch-hit grand slam to beat the Redlegs 7–5. Don Mueller hits in his 20th straight game, duplicating Mays's streak, which ended August 20th.

The Yanks lose to the White Sox 6–5, dropping New York 6½ out of first, the largest deficit in Casey Stengel's years.

12th A record crowd of 86,587 jams Cleveland's Memorial Stadium to see the Indians sweep a double-header from the Yanks, 4–1 and 3–2, behind Bob Lemon and Early Wynn.

The White Sox get their 90th victory, the first time this has happened since 1920. They will win 94 for the season. They sweep the Red Sox 5–3 and 7–5.

13th Redlegs slugger Ted Kluszewski scores a run in a 6–5 loss to the Pirates. Big Klu has scored in 17 consecutive games, a modern record.

14th Willie Mays hits a 1st inning double and scores the only run in a 1–0 win over the Cards. It is Johnny Antonelli's 21st win of the year. Mays's hit is his 82nd extra-base hit, breaking Mel Ott's team record.

16th Phillie Robin Roberts beats the Giants 5–4 in 10 innings and becomes the first NL pitcher since Carl Hubbell to win 20 games 5 years in a row. Hubbell did it in 1933-37.

18th The Giants' Don Mueller makes his 200th hit an inside-the-park HR, making him the first Giant to get 200 hits since Joe Moore in 1936. Willie Mays also has an inside-the park-HR, as the Giants beat the Phils 8–1.

The Indians clinch their 3rd pennant in history and the first since 1920 with a 3–2 win over the Tigers.

19th Detroit's Harvey Kuenn, en route to his 2nd year of 200 hits, goes 5-for-5 in a game which the Tigers lose 4–2 to the Indians.

20th The Giants clinch the pennant as Sal Maglie beats the Dodgers 7–1 in the opener of a series with the Dodgers at Ebbets Field.

Warren Spahn of the Braves beats the Cubs 6–2 to notch his 20th win. Spahn has now won 20 games 6 times.

21st Yankees rookie P Bob Grim wins his 20th, 3–1 over Washington. The victory gives the Yanks 101 wins. The win makes Grim only the 2nd Yankee rookie in history to win 20. The Yankees will finish with 103 victories, just one under the ML record for 2nd place, held by the 1909 Cubs and 1942 Dodgers.

22nd Recently called up from Fort Wayne, Karl Spooner of the Dodgers pitches a 3–0 shutout, fanning 15 Giants in his first ML start. Six of the strikeouts are consecutive.

In the top of the 9th, the Redlegs have runners on 1B and 2B when Bob Borkowski strikes out on a WP. Braves C Del Crandall retrieves the ball and throws to 3B to catch the lead runner. Borkowski takes off for 1B illegally, since 1B is already occupied and there are less than 2 outs. He draws a throw, which hits him in the back and rolls into RF, and he and the runner on 2B score. The umpires decide that Borkowski and the 2B runner are both out. Milwaukee wins 3–1 and the Reds protest. Because the standings of 5 teams are affected by the outcome, Warren Giles will uphold the protest, even though he believes the umpires made the correct decision. The protested game will be played in 2 days and the Braves will hang on to win 4–3.

24th Phillie Murry Dickson loses his 20th game of the season 1–0 to New York's Don Liddle. It marks the 3rd consecutive season he leads the NL in losses.

25th Duke Snider joins teammate Gil Hodges in the 40-HR club, giving the Dodgers two 40-HR sluggers in 2 straight seasons. The Dodgers win 10–5.

Early Wynn 2-hits the Tigers 11–1 for his league-leading 23rd win as the Indians notch their 111th victory, a new AL record eclipsing the 110 wins of the 1927 Yankees.

Although they lose 100 games, the same as in the previous season when the club was in St. Louis, the Orioles draw over a million fans.

26th In his 2nd start, rookie Brooklyn lefty Karl Spooner shuts out Pittsburgh 1–0 on a Gil Hodges HR in the 8th. He fans 12 for a total of 27 strikeouts in his first 2 ML games, establishing a new record. Gil Hodges's 8th-inning HR, his 25th at Ebbets Field (a new club record), gives him 42 for the season, tying him with Duke Snider for the most by a Dodger.

Going into the last day of the NL season, Don Mueller leads in hitting with .3426; Duke Snider is 2nd at .3425, followed by Willie Mays at .3422. The Giants win in 11 innings over the Phillies Robin Roberts, as Mays garners a single, double, and triple in 4 ABs. He finishes at .345 while Mueller slips to .341, the same as Snider.

Art Ditmar of the Athletics defeats the Yanks 8–6 in the last game the franchise will play in Philadelphia before moving to Kansas City. Yankee C Yogi Berra plays his only game at 3B in his career. Mickey Mantle plays SS again in Casey Stengel's "power line-up."

28th Two days after firing Bucky Harris, the Senators sign Chuck Dressen to a 2-year deal to manage in 1955.

29th In Game 1 of the WS, Willie Mays of the Giants makes one of the greatest catches in history when he races back to deep CF in the Polo Grounds to make an over-the-head catch of Indian Vic Wertz's 462-foot drive in the 8th with the score tied at 2–2. Wertz drove in the 2 runs in the first with a triple. In the 10th, Dusty Rhodes hits a pinch-hit, 3-run, 260-foot HR off Bob Lemon to give the Giants a 5–2 victory.

30th With lefty Johnny Antonelli going the distance, the Giants defeat Early Wynn and the Indians 3–1 in game 2. Dusty Rhodes drives in all the Giants runs with a pinch-hit single and a solo HR. The Indians' only score is a first-pitch HR by leadoff hitter Al Smith.

OCTOBER

1st Dusty Rhodes gets his 3rd pinch hit of the WS, driving in 2 runs in the 3rd. He is hitting for OF Monte Irvin, who ironically had 11 hits in the 1951 Series. The Giants' Ruben Gomez easily bests Indians P Mike Garcia 6–2.

2nd In game 4 the Giants sweep the AL team with the best record in history, as they score 4 runs in the 5th to take a 7–0 lead. The final is 7–4 as Don Liddle defeats Bob Lemon.

14th The Phils name Mayo Smith to succeed interim manager Terry Moore as their manager for 1955.

20th Shoichi Kaneda of the Tokyo Swallows strikes out his 350th batter, surpassing the American season record of 348, set by Bob Feller in 1948. Kaneda already holds the single-game strikeout record in Japan with 15 in 1952 and 1954 and will go on to hold almost every Japanese pitching record before retiring in 1969.

28th The ML owners vote down the sale of the Athletics to a Philadelphia syndicate. A week later, Arnold Johnson buys a controlling interest in the Athletics from the Mack family for 3.5 million and moves the team to Kansas City.

NOVEMBER

3rd Members of the Yankees' championship team tour Japan and draw a record crowd of 64,000 when they play the first game against the All-Japan Stars in Osaka. Andy Carey slugs 13 HRs, and Elston Howard bats .468 on the 25-game tour.

17th The Cubs trade Ralph Kiner to the Indians for $60,000 plus OF Gale Wade and P Sam Jones. Kiner's HR total fell to 22 in 1954, though he hit .285.

18th The Athletics give manager Eddie Joost his unconditional release and hire Lou Boudreau to replace him.

In an enormous two-part trade begun on November 14, the Yankees and Orioles exchange 17 players. Included are 1B Dick Kryhoski, pitchers Bob

Turley and Don Larsen, and SS Billy Hunter from Baltimore. To the Orioles go OF Gene Woodling, SS Willie Miranda, pitchers Harry Byrd and Jim McDonald, and catchers Gus Triandos and Hal Smith. The trade will help both teams.

DECEMBER

6th   The Tigers trade 1B Walt Dropo with P Ted Gray and OF Bob Nieman to the White Sox for 1B Ferris Fain and Jack Phillips.

8th   The Cardinals send veteran pitcher Gerry Staley, who had won 84 games for St. Louis in the past 6 seasons, along with 3B Ray Jablonski to the Reds for Frank Smith (8–1 in 1954). After a year in St. Louis the Cards will waive goodbye to Smith and Cincinnati will sign him back.

1955

JANUARY

3rd The Orioles purchase OF Hoot Evers from the Tigers.

11th The Cards trade P Ben Wade to Pittsburgh for P Paul LaPalme.

FEBRUARY

12th Willie Mays and Roberto Clemente hit crucial HRs to lead Santurce (Puerto Rico) to a 4–2 win over Venezuela in the Caribbean Series. Mays's HR comes in the 11th.

17th The Orioles get P Erv Palica from the Dodgers for 1B Frank Kellert and cash. This replaces the Preacher Roe deal, which fell through when the Brooklyn lefty announced his retirement.

MARCH

7th Commissioner Ford Frick states that he favors legalization of the spitter, "a great pitch and one of the easiest to throw."

30th The Yanks sell P Ewell Blackwell and Tom Gorman, plus reserve IF Dick Kryhoski, to the Kansas City Athletics, now in the AL, for $50,000.

APRIL

12th In a 4–2 win over the Reds, Milwaukee rookie OF Chuck Tanner hits a 8th-inning pinch-homer in his first ML AB.

After a big civic parade, the Athletics open their first season in Kansas City with a win over the Tigers, 6–2, before 32,844.

13th The Dodgers open what will be their only World Championship season in Brooklyn by beating Pittsburgh 6–1.

A NL record Opening Day crowd of 43,640 watch the Redlegs play the Braves in Milwaukee's County Stadium.

The Yanks rout the Senators 19–1. Whitey Ford gets 3 hits and only allows 2.

14th The Orioles buy P Jim Wilson from the Braves.

Elston Howard becomes the first black to wear the Yankee uniform. He singles in his first at bat, against the Red Sox, as the Yanks win 8–4.

Brooklyn P Don Newcombe hits 2 HRs in a 10–8 win over the Giants at the Polo Grounds.

16th En route to losing their first 5 games, the Redlegs hit 5 HRs and lose to the Braves 9–5. The Braves Johnny Logan goes 5-for-5.

17th Al Kaline of the Tigers hits 3 HRs in Briggs Stadium, including 2 in the 6th inning to drive in 6 runs. The Tigers rout the A's 16–0, behind Steve Gromek's pitching.

The Cards score 10 in the first and go on to rout the Cubs 14–1.

18th In what can be described as a rare "pitcher's cycle," Pirate hurler Al Grunwald allows a single, double, triple, and HR for 4 runs in a single inning and a 12–3 loss in his first ML game.

21st Brooklyn wins its 10th in a row, trouncing Robin Roberts of the Phils 14–2. This sets a new ML record for consecutive wins to start a season, later broken by Oakland.

22nd Though the Dodgers take a 3–0 lead into the 8th, their streak ends as the Braves' Max Surkont beats Johnny Podres 5–4. Don Zimmer is called out at home on a squeeze play by Jackie Robinson that would have tied the game.

In a rundown between home and 3rd, Yankee 2B Jerry Coleman breaks his collarbone. The Yanks beat the Red Sox 3–0, but Coleman is out for the season.

23rd The White Sox erupt for 29 hits in a 29–6 ripping of Kansas City. C Sherm Lollar becomes the only man in the decade to get 2 hits in one inning twice in the same game. Lollar's feat comes in the 2nd and 6th innings. Chico Carrasquel goes 5-for-6 as the White Sox pound out 7 HRs. Bob Nieman's 7 RBIs lead the Sox offensive attack.

In a celebrated fight with the Dodgers, Alvin Dark takes on Jackie Robinson after the latter bowls over pitcher Sheldon Jones, covering first on a bunt. Jones injures his back in the incident. Brooklyn wins 3–1.

26th Bob Turley of the Yanks fires a one-hitter, fanning 10 in beating the White Sox 5–0.

28th The Kansas City Athletics sign P Vic Raschi, who has just been released by the Cardinals. The

Athletics purchase P Lou Sleater from the Yankees for cash.

30th The Phillies trade C Smoky Burgess, P Steve Ridzik, and OF Stan Palys to the Redlegs for OF Jimmy Greengrass, C Andy Seminick, and OF Glen Gorbous. Then the Phillies buy SS Roy Smalley from the Braves.

Harvey Kuenn of the Tigers goes 5-for-5 in an 11–7 win over the Senators.

MAY

1st Bob Feller one-hits the Red Sox 2–0, with Sammy White's single in the 7th spoiling his bid for a no-hitter in the first game of a doubleheader. In the nightcap, Cleveland's Herb Score fans 16 Boston hitters in a 2–1 win, missing Bob Feller's strikeout record by one.

5th In his first ML start, Dodger southpaw Tom Lasorda throws 3 wild pitches in the same inning, to tie a record. He also receives a spike wound from Wally Moon of the Cardinals in a play at the plate. Lasorda later blames his wildness on his catcher, Roy Campanella.

10th Dodger ace Don Newcombe one-hits the Cubs 3–0. Gene Baker, who singles and is caught stealing, is the only base runner.

11th The Cubs click off 5 DPs in a 10–8 win over Brooklyn, snapping the Dodgers' 11-game winning streak.

The Tigers buy OF Charlie Maxwell from the Orioles.

The A's continue to wheel and deal as they purchase OF Harry Simpson from the Indians and P Ray Herbert from the Tigers. They give cash and P John "Sonny" Dixon to the Yankees in exchange for RF Enos Slaughter and P Johnny Sain.

12th Sam "Toothpick" Jones of the Cubs no-hits the Pirates 4–0, fanning the last 3 batters in the 9th after walking the bases loaded. It is the first no-hitter in Wrigley Field since the double no-hitter of 1917. The Cubs lace 15 hits against Nellie King and Vernon Law.

Washington 3B Eddie Yost's streak ends at 838 straight games because of tonsillitis as teammate Maury McDermott 4-hits the Indians for a 3–0 win.

13th Mickey Mantle of the Yankees homers from both sides of the plate for the first time. In all, Mantle has 3 HRs and a single with 5 RBI as New York beats Detroit 5–2.

15th New York's Irv Noren hits an inside-the-park grand slam in an 8–4 victory over the A's.

18th Cleveland scores 11 runs in the 5th to whip the Red Sox 19–0.

Milwaukee slugger Eddie Mathews undergoes an appendectomy and is lost for 2 weeks.

The Yankees' Bob Grim beans Chicago's Minnie Minoso, putting him out for 2 weeks with a hairline fracture of the skull.

22nd The 2nd game of a Giants-Pirates doubleheader is called at the top of the 9th due to rain, 28 minutes short of the Sunday curfew, with the Giants leading 5–3. If the rain had started before the end of the 8th, the game would have gone to the Pirates by a score of 3–2. The umpires almost ruled it a suspended game rather than a called game, because they felt they had to wait at least half an hour before calling a game, which would set the time 2 minutes after the curfew. But a Giants vice president finds the rule that puts weather and similar conditions first when determining whether a game is called or suspended.

24th The Pirates rout the Dodgers 15–1, their highest score in 172 games. The next day they will sink to the cellar.

26th Dodgers P Don Newcombe becomes the only NL pitcher of the decade to steal home when he hits a triple and steals home in the 9th inning in Pittsburgh. He wins 6–2 over Elroy Face, who pitches one of the few complete games of his career.

27th Norm Zauchin hits 3 HRs and drives in 10 RBIs as the Red Sox slaughter the Senators 16–0.

Bobby Hofman of the Giants hits his 3rd pinch-hit HR of the year, and 9th of his career, tying him with Cy Williams for the record. The Giants trip the Dodgers 3–1.

28th Harry "the Hat" Walker replaces Eddie Stanky as manager of the Cardinals with the team in 5th place with a record of 17-19.

After starting the season on the retired list, Ted Williams of the Red Sox becomes "unretired." He joins the team 2 days later.

29th Larry Doby of the Indians hits the first ML HR over the outer wall in Kansas City, an estimated 500-foot clout. The Indians win 4–2.

30th For the 2nd time this season, Dodger ace Don Newcombe homers twice in the same game, beating New York 10–8.

The Senators P Mickey McDermott beats the Yankees 3–2 with a pinch-hit single in the 10th.

JUNE

1st Duke Snider of the Dodgers hits 3 HRs in Ebbets Field. The Dodgers set a club record with six 4-baggers, as they outlast the Braves 11–8.

3rd Stan Musial hits the 300th HR of his career, a 5th-inning, 3-run shot against Brooklyn's Johnny Podres. The Cards use a NL-record 8 pitchers but still lose 12–5.

The Cards trade veteran C Del Rice to the Braves for OF Pete Whisenant and C Charlie White.

6th The White Sox trade veteran P Harry Dorish to the Orioles for C Les Moss.

7th The White Sox reacquire speedster CF Jim Busby from the Senators for C Clint Courtney, OF Johnny Groth, and P Bob Chakales.

9th The Redlegs trade OF Bob Borkowski and cash to the Dodgers for P Joe Black.

11th The Dodgers win their 6th in a row to increase their lead to 10½ games. The lead will not dip below 10 games for the remainder of the season.

12th After winning 10 in a row, Dodger P Don Newcombe suffers his first defeat of the season 10–1 to the Cubs.

The Indians sweep a doubleheader from the Yanks 7–3 and 10–2. The Cleveland crowd of 69,352 is the largest ML crowd of the season. New York is now just 2½ in front of Chicago.

15th The Tigers buy Earl Torgeson from the Phillies to replace Ferris Fain at 1B.

The Orioles trade OF Gene Woodling and IF Billy Cox to the Indians for OFs Wally Westlake and Dave Pope. When Cox announces his retirement, the Indians get more cash.

The Indians pick up Ted Gray who had just been released by the White Sox.

19th The Giants bench Willie Mays for 2 days for a "rest."

23rd The Yanks' Bob Turley shuts out the Athletics 4–0 on 3 hits to end his 5-game losing streak.

The Redlegs purchase OF Sam Mele from the Red Sox.

24th Washington rookie IF Harmon Killebrew hits his first HR in an 18–7 loss to the Detroit Tigers.

25th Miseries plague the Dodger pitching staff. Russ Meyer goes on the disabled list with a broken collarbone, and Carl Erskine has arm trouble.

27th The Orioles trade 2B Bobby Young to the Indians for IF Hank Majeski.

Boston's young star 1B Harry Agganis dies of complications following a bout with pneumonia.

29th Willie Mays hits the first grand slam of his career, off Clem Labine, and accounts for all the RBI in a 6–1 Giant win over Brooklyn. Roy Campanella has a broken spur in his knee and will miss 2 weeks.

JULY

8th Light-hitting Joe DeMaestri of the Athletics goes 6-for-6 in an 11-inning 11–8 loss to the Tigers.

9th Chicago newspaperman Arch Ward, the originator of the All-Star Game, dies at age 58 as he is leaving to cover his 22nd midseason classic.

Mickey Mantle goes 5-for-5, and Bob Turley tosses a 2-hitter in a 4–0 win over Washington.

Giants P Jim Hearn does it all, hitting 2 HRs. and whipping the Dodgers 10–2 at the Polo Grounds.

12th In the All-Star Game in Milwaukee, the AL takes a 5-run lead on a 3-run HR by Mickey Mantle off Robin Roberts, only to see the NL tie it. Braves P Gene Conley strikes out the side in the 12th, and Stan Musial of the Cards homers off Frank Sullivan of the Red Sox to win it.

13th The Orioles deal OF Hoot Evers to the Indians in exchange for P Bill Wight.

14th The Indians sign 2-time batting champ Ferris Fain as a free agent.

17th In what would be their most important move of the season, the Brooklyn Dodgers bring up rookie pitchers Roger Craig and Don Bessent from the minor leagues. They immediately pay dividends as they beat the Reds in both ends of a doubleheader. Craig wins 6–2 and Bessent matches it 8–5.

Earl Torgeson of the Tigers steals home in the 10th to beat the Yanks 6–5.

18th Newly acquired Jim Wilson of Baltimore 2-hits the White Sox 3–0.

19th Playing like Babe Ruth, Detroit relief P Babe Birrer pitches 4 innings and hits two 3-run HRs.

Chattanooga (SA) OF Jim Lemon clouts 4 home runs in the league's all-star contest, as the all-stars defeat the first-place Birmingham club 10–5.

Pirate hurler Vern Law pitches 18 innings in beating Milwaukee 4–3, giving up just 9 hits and fanning 12.

21st The Redlegs Gus Bell hits 3 solo HRs, but the Phils win 5–3.

Warren Spahn, Braves lefty, hits a 3-run HR to beat the Pirates 5–3.

22nd In the first game of a doubleheader, the Phillies beat the Cardinals 5–3. The win completes an 11-game winning streak, setting a team record. All the wins were at home. They drop the nitecap 8–1.

23rd LF Del Ennis of the Phillies hits 3 HRs and drives in all 7 runs as the Phils win 7–2.

29th Redlegs C Smoky Burgess connects for 3 HRs—one a grand slam— and collects 9 RBI in a 16–5 pounding of the Pirates.

30th The Orioles get P Ed Lopat from the Yankees for P Jim McDonald and cash.

31st On the anniversary of his 4-HR game, Braves 1B Joe Adcock has his arm broken by a pitch from Giant Jim Hearn. He will be out for the season.

The Giants sell P Sal Maglie (9-5) to the Cleveland Indians.

The White Sox suffer a great blow as their leading pitcher, Dick Donovan 13-4, undergoes an emergency appendectomy.

Don Larsen wins 5–2, as the Yanks and Athletics collaborate for 9 DPs, with the New Yorkers turning 6. Cloyd Boyer, who had 3 of his first 8 pitches hit for HRs—by Bauer, Mantle, and Berra—takes the loss.

AUGUST

2nd Johnny Klippstein and Joe Nuxhall of the Redlegs shut out the Phils 2–0 and 4–0 in both ends of a doubleheader.

"Mr. Cub" Ernie Banks hits his 4th grand slam of the season, tying the ML record, as Bob Rush bests the Pirates 12–4.

3rd With his record at 18-1, the Dodgers Don Newcombe loses a 1–0 game to the Cubs Sam Jones.

Frank Lary of the Tigers beats Washington 3–0 on a 2-hitter.

4th Ernie Banks hits 3 HRs at Wrigley against 3 Pirate pitchers, as the Cubs win 11–10.

5th After playing 274 straight games at 2B, Nellie Fox is given a day off by White Sox manager Marty Marion. Fox will come back the next day and play in 798 consecutive games.

7th After a 12-17 record in July, the Yankees are in a 4-team race. Tiger Frank Lary beats New York 4–2 in game one, and New York then earns a critical 3–2 10th-inning win on a Mickey Mantle homer off Babe Birrer. The Yanks finish the day in a virtual tie with Chicago, a ½ game ahead of Cleveland, and 1½ games ahead of Boston.

11th Ted Williams gets his 2,000th hit in a 5–3 Red Sox loss to the Yankees.

13th Larry Doby makes his first error in the OF in 167 games, a new AL record.

14th Cardinals manager Harry Walker pulls a shift by moving P Tom Poholsky to LF and bringing in lefty Luis Arroyo to face slugger Ted Kluszewski of the Redlegs. Big Klu foils the manager by homering. Cards rally to win anyway 5–4.

15th Mickey Mantle homers from both sides of the plate in the same game for the 2nd time in his career, tying the ML mark. The Yanks beat the Orioles 12–6 in game 2 and sweep the doubleheader to move back into first.

19th Robin Roberts of the Phils defeats Don Newcombe of the Dodgers 3–2 to become the first 20-game winner in 1955.

26th Vic Wertz of the Indians is diagnosed as having non-paralytic polio and is lost for the season. He will return next year.

27th Dodger bonus baby Sandy Koufax fans 14 Redlegs in a 7–0 win, as the 2-team total of 23 strike-outs ties a record.

31st Lefty Bill Wight of the Orioles gives up 5 runs in the first and then no-hits his former Indian team-mates for 8 innings. He loses 5–1.

SEPTEMBER

2nd After sitting out since August 7th with a broken rib, SS Alvin Dark of the Giants falls and breaks his shoulder in a game against the Phillies.

Whitey Ford and Mickey Mantle celebrate Billy Martin's return from the army; Ford throws 6 innings of no-hit ball against Washington before Carlos Paula spoils it in the 7th with Washington's only hit. The Yanks win 4–2 as Mantle hits his 36th HR, a 3-run shot. Mantle is 10 HRs ahead of rivals Al Kaline and Ted Williams. New York stays a half game behind the White Sox, who beat the 3rd-place Indians. Billy Martin will hit .300 in September, and New York will go on a 17-6 tear to win the pennant by 3 games.

4th Mickey Mantle's first-inning 3-run HR allows Bob Turley to coast to an 8–3 win over Washington. This is Mantle's last HR of the year.

5th P Don Newcombe wins his 20th game of the season 11–4 over the Phillies. Newk hits his 7th HR of the season to set a new NL record for HRs by a pitcher.

7th Whitey Ford continues his mastery with his 2nd consecutive one-hitter, beating the A's 2–1. Jim Finigan hits a 2-out single in the 7th for the Nats' only hit. Ford is the 5th ML pitcher to throw consecutive one-hitters.

8th Brooklyn clinches the pennant by beating the Braves 10–2 for their 8th straight win. They break their own ML record for the earliest clinching, set in 1953.

9th After losing the opener to the Cubs, the Dodgers win the nitecap 16–9 as pitcher Clem Labine gets his 3rd HR of the year. Labine has just 3 hits all year, but all 3 are HRs. The Dodgers lead is now 16½ games.

10th OF Hank Bauer of the Yankees, pressed into emergency service as a catcher, permits a passed ball, setting up the winning run in a 9–8 loss to the White Sox.

11th RF Enos Slaughter of the A's plays in his 2,000th ML game, getting a pinch single in a 4–3 victory over the Orioles.

In a move to shore up their pitching down the stretch, the Yankees buy Gerry Staley from St. Louis for the waiver price.

14th Herb Score of the Indians breaks Grover Cleveland Alexander's rookie record of 235 strike-outs. He finishes the season with 245.

16th Slugger Mickey Mantle pulls a hamstring muscle running out a bunt. He will make just 2 pinch-hit appearances in September, and he will go to bat in the WS just 10 times.

17th Future Hall of Famer Brooks Robinson goes 2-4 in his first game as the O's top the Senators 3–1.

18th In a 7–5 loss to Brooklyn, Willie Mays hits his 9th HR at Ebbets Field to tie Joe Adcock's mark.

19th Cubs slugger Ernie Banks hits his 5th grand slam of the season to set a new ML mark, but the Cubs lose 6-5 in 12 innings, to the Cardinals.

20th Reserve 1B Frank Kellert's HR is the Dodgers' 200th of the season, making them the first team to hit 200 or more in a season more than once. They did it with 208 in 1953. Robin Roberts surrenders 2 HRs to the Dodgers, making it 40 for the season, a ML record.

Giants slugger Willie Mays poles 2 HRs against the Pirates, giving him 50 for the year, making him only the 7th player in history to accomplish this. The Giants sweep the doubleheader, winning 11–1 and 14–8. Mays's HR in the 2nd game was his 7th in 6 consecutive games.

23rd The Yanks clinch the pennant by beating the Red Sox 3–2.

After a running feud with owner Charlie Comiskey, Jr., Frank Lane resigns as GM of the White Sox.

24th The Giants fail to renew manager Leo Durocher's contract. He resigns and is replaced by Bill Rigney.

The Washington Senators lose their 99th and 100th games of the season, the first time the franchise has ever reached the century mark. The Orioles do the damage 1–0 and 8–5.

25th Bobby Hofman underscores the tone of the season for the Giants as he lines into a season-ending triple play against the Phillies in a 3–1 loss. The Giants win the opener 5–2, as Willie Mays belts his 51st HR of the year.

Detroit OF Al Kaline becomes the youngest batting champ in history, as he takes the AL crown at age 20.

26th The Red Sox beat the Yankees 8–1 as Ted Williams goes 1-for-20. Williams finishes the season at .356, well ahead of Kaline's .340, but does not have enough at bats to win the batting title. The same thing happened in 1954. Williams was walked 136 times in 1954 and 71 times (an AL-leading 17 were intentional) this year. A rule change will be made to recognize plate appearances, not times at bat.

28th The Yanks win the first game of the WS, as Whitey Ford beats Don Newcombe, 6–5. In a controversial play with Frank Kellert at bat, Jackie Robinson steals home in the 8th to bring the Dodgers to within a run of a tie. Films later disclose that Robinson is out by a whisker, but Yankee C Yogi Berra actually balked on the play, receiving Whitey Ford's pitch before Kellert could swing at it.

29th In Game 2, lefty Tommy Byrne defeats Dodger Billy Loes 4–2 to go 2 games up. The pitcher's 2-run single caps a 4-run 4th for the Yanks. Byrne becomes the only lefty to hurl a complete game against Brooklyn in 1955.

30th The Dodgers Johnny Podres defeats Bob Turley who fails to last 2 innings against the Bums. C Roy Campanella leads the attack with 3 hits and 3 RBI, as Brooklyn wins 8–3 behind the strong effort of lefty Johnny Podres.

31st The Series evens up with an 8–5 win. Campanella and Gil Hodges give the Dodgers a 4–3 lead, and Snider's 3-run shot in the 5th insures the victory.

OCTOBER

1st Surprise Brooklyn starter rookie Roger Craig pitches 6 innings for the 5–3 win. Two HRs by Duke Snider and one by Sandy Amoros in the first 5 innings prove too much for New York. Snider, who hit 4 HRs in the 1952 WS, becomes the first player in history to do this more than once.

2nd The Yanks kayo lefty Karl Spooner in the first with 5 runs on 2 walks, 2 singles and Moose Skowron's HR. Ford goes all the way for the 5–1 victory.

3rd No more "wait till next year" as Brooklyn, behind the 2-0 pitching of Johnny Podres, brings its first WS championship to Brooklyn in 8 tries. Sixth-inning replacement Sandy Amoros races over to the wall in LF to one-hand an opposite-field bid for extra bases by Yogi Berra with the tying runs on. Amoros turns and fires to SS Pee Wee Reese who throws a bullet to Gil Hodges at 1B for the DP on Yankee base runner Gil McDougald.

6th The Cards name Frank "Trader" Lane as their new GM.

12th The Cardinals hire Fred Hutchinson as their field manager, replacing Harry Walker.

25th Baseball great Branch Rickey steps down as GM of the Pirates and moves into an advisory role with the Pirates. Joe L. Brown, son of the actor, replaces him.

The White Sox trade Chico Carrasquel and Jim Busby to the Indians for Larry Doby.

NOVEMBER

2nd The Pirates name Bobby Bragan as their new field manager, replacing Fred Haney.

8th The Senators trade stalwarts Mickey Vernon, Bob Porterfield, Johnny Schmitz and Tom Umphlett to the Red Sox for 5 young players.

12th The Cardinals give manager Harry Walker his hat and replace him with Fred Hutchinson. With the departure of Walker, who pinch hit for the Cards during the season, the 1956 season will be the first one in NL history without a player-manager. The AL first went to all bench managers in 1930, then repeated in 1951.

21st In an obvious power struggle for control, the principal founding father of Little League, Carl Stotz, sues the organization for breach of contract. The suit will be settled out of court.

28th The Cubs trade P Hal Jeffcoat to the Redlegs for C Hobie Landrith.

DECEMBER

1st The Tigers bring back P Virgil Trucks in a trade with the White Sox for 3B Bubba Phillips

5th The Cardinals buy P Ellis Kinder from the Bosox.

Carl Stotz plans to set up a rival Little League of his own.

6th Brooklyn trades 3B Don Hoak and OF Walt Moryn to the Cubs for 3B Ransom Jackson.

9th The Dodgers send P Russ Meyer to the Cubs for P Don Elston and cash.

The Phils purchase veteran Frankie Baumholtz from the Cubs.

1956

JANUARY

6th A federal court bars former Little League Commissioner Carl Stotz from forming a rival group. He initiated the suit because he felt the league had grown too big, and that increasing team rosters to 15 players was preventing less able players from getting any real playing time.

The Boston Red Sox sell their Louisville farm club to a Cuban cartel led by Havana businessman Edward F. Wheeler.

19th The City of Hoboken dedicates a plaque honoring the achievements of Alexander Cartwright in organizing early baseball at Elysian Field in the New Jersey city.

27th The New York Giants football team of the NFL switches its home games to Yankee Stadium, leading to speculation that the baseball team will soon vacate the Polo Grounds as well.

FEBRUARY

4th The AL says it will test the automatic intentional walk during spring training.

5th New York Mayor Robert Wagner and Brooklyn Borough President Frank Cashmore sponsor a bill to create a Brooklyn Sports Center Authority to build a $30 million sports center in downtown Brooklyn.

The ML owners reject the players' request for an increase in the minimum salary from $6,000 to $7,000.

6th Dodger President Walter O'Malley backs the Wagner-Cashmore plan, vowing to buy $4 million worth of bonds.

8th The legendary Connie Mack dies at age 93. He began his career with Washington in 1886 as a catcher. After managing the NL Pittsburgh club from 1894-96, he became a prominent figure in Ban Johnson's Western League and a founder of the AL and its Philadelphia franchise in 1901. In 50 years as the Athletics pilot he won 9 pennants and 5 World Championships, but also finished last 17 times.

15th The Pirates and the Kansas City A's cancel an exhibition game in Birmingham, AL, because of a local ordinance barring black players from playing against white players.

16th The courts award Dr. Samuel Shenkman $5,000 in his suit against Dodger C Roy Campanella for surgery on Campy's injured hand on October 20, 1954. Campanella says the doctor never informed him that the charge would be $9,500, a price the catcher considered excessive.

ML owners announce that the players' pension fund will receive 60 percent of WS and All-Star Game radio and TV revenues.

27th The Piedmont League disbands after 37 years in operation.

MARCH

3rd In an effort to keep the Giants in New York, Manhattan Borough President Hulan Jack makes plans for a new 110,000-seat stadium over the New York Central railroad tracks, on a 470,000-foot site stretching from 60th to 72nd streets on Manhattan's West Side. The estimated cost of $75 million for the stadium eventually dooms the project and will be a major factor in Horace Stoneham's decision to move to San Francisco.

The Giants and Indians cancel an exhibition game in Meridian, MS, because of racial violence in neighboring Alabama.

7th The player reps accept the owners' decisions on minimum pay and the WS TV pact. They seek workman's compensation coverage. The player reps rehire J. M. Lewis as their representative.

14th Satchel Paige signs with the Birmingham Black Barons (Negro League) at age 50 to play and manage.

24th The Indians sign OF/1B Sam Mele, just released by the Red Sox.

APRIL

9th The Braves trade 1B George Crowe to the Redlegs for OF Bob "Hurricane" Hazle and righthander Corky Valentine.

16th The Athletics purchase OF Johnny Groth from the Senators.

17th The Yanks and Senators each hit 3 HRs, the only time this has happened on Opening Day. Hitting LH, Mickey Mantle has 2 tape measure blasts over 500 feet off Camilo Pascual, as the Yanks win easily

10–4. For the 4th consecutive opener, President Dwight D. Eisenhower throws out the first ball and stays for 9 innings.

Despite 2 HRs by Dale Long, Pittsburgh loses to New York 4–3 when Willie Mays scores from 2B in the 8th inning on Daryl Spencer's groundout to 2B.

19th A record crowd of 12,214 watches the Dodgers nip the Phillies 5–4 at Jersey City. This is the largest daytime crowd the Dodgers will draw in New Jersey for their 15 games there.

21st Art Ditmar of the Athletics limits the White Sox to 1 hit, winning 15–1.

22nd Yankee P Don Larsen slams a HR with the bases loaded off Frank Sullivan of the Red Sox, as New York wins 13–6.

24th AL umpire Frank Umont is the first to wear glasses in a regular season game, between Detroit and Kansas City. The former NFL tackle (New York Giants) still presents an intimidating appearance to most players and fans.

28th Redlegs rookie LF Frank Robinson hits the first HR of his 586 lifetime blasts, off Cub P Paul Minner in Crosley Field. The Cubs lose the opener 9–1. Cincinnati OF Wally Post hits 4 HRs in a doubleheader sweep for the Redlegs.

29th For the 3rd time in his career, Phillies LF Del Ennis spoils a no-hitter, this time singling off the Giants Ray Monzant, who wins the one-hitter 8–1 anyway in the 2nd game of a doubleheader.

MAY

2nd Twenty-five Giants and 23 Cubs appear in a 17-inning marathon won by the Giants 6–5.

LF Lee Walls of the Pirates goes 5-for-5 against St. Louis in a 10-inning 10–9 loss to St. Louis.

4th The National Braille Press presents to manager Pinky Higgins the Red Sox 1956 schedule, printed in braille for the first time.

5th Pittsburgh trades righthander Max Surkont to the Cards for lefty Luis Arroyo.

7th The Future NL president, Bill White of the NY Giants, homers in his first time up in the ML. The Giants lose to St. Louis 6–3.

11th The Cards trade pitchers Harvey Haddix, Stu Miller, and Ben Flowers to Philadelphia for P Herm Wehmeier and Murry Dickson. They also trade 2B Solly Hemus for SS Bobby Morgan.

12th Carl Erskine pitches his 2nd no-hitter for the Dodgers 4 years after his first, a 3–0 wipeout of the Giants. Two walks gave New York their only base runners.

13th The Braves destroy the Redlegs 15–0 and 6–1. In game one, a Warren Spahn homer contributes to the win.

15th The Dodgers buy P Sal Maglie from the Indians.

16th Cards RF Wally Moon hits the first ML HR in Jersey City, but St. Louis loses 5–3 to the Dodgers.

The Pirates trade 1B Preston Ward to the Indians for C Hank Foiles.

17th The Cards trade the 1955 Rookie of the Year OF Bill Virdon to the Pirates for P Dick Littlefield and OF Bobby Del Greco.

18th Mickey Mantle hits HRs from both sides of the plate for the 3rd time in his career, eclipsing the mark of Jim Russell. The visiting New Yorkers nip Chicago 8–7 in 10 innings.

19th Pirate slugger Dale Long hits a 9th-inning HR against the Cubs for the first of a string of 8 HRs in 8 games.

23rd A group of citizens opposes Hulan Jack's plan to build a new stadium in New York, reputed to cost about $40 million.

24th Mickey Mantle goes 5-for-5 with an intentional walk in an 11–4 win against the Tigers. Mantle is hitting .421.

26th Three Redlegs pitchers—Johnny Klippstein, Hersh Freeman and Joe Black—no-hit the Braves for 9⅔ innings. Klippstein walks 8 in 7 hitless innings before giving way to Freeman for one inning. Black finally gives up a double to Jack Dittmer and loses 2–1 in the 11th.

27th Jim Davis of the Cubs fans 4 Cardinals in the 6th inning of the first of two games. The Cubs lose 11–9.

28th Dale Long of the Pirates connects against the Dodgers Carl Erskine at Forbes Field for his 8th HR in

8 games, a record that will stand until the Yankees Don Mattingly equals it in 1987.

The White Sox buy P Gerry Staley from the Yankees.

29th Gus Bell of the Redlegs hits 3 consecutive HRs, going 5-for-5 in a 10–4 win over the Cubs.

Dodgers P Don Newcombe beats the Pirates 10–1 and blanks Dale Long in 4 ABs, stopping his streak.

30th Bobby Thomson of the Milwaukee Braves hits 4 HRs in a doubleheader as Eddie Mathews, Hank Aaron and Thomson hit first-inning HRs against the Cubs Russ Meyer. Meyer then hits the next batter, Billy Bruton, with a pitch. When Bruton charges the mound, both he and Meyer are ejected. The Braves lose the first game 10–9, but hold on to win the 2nd 11–9. Fifteen HRs in the 2 games tie a ML mark.

Mickey Mantle hits one of the most memorable HRs in his career, in the 2nd game of a doubleheader with the Washington Senators. He tags a pitch from Pedro Ramos that comes within 18 inches of leaving Yankee Stadium, something never accomplished by any major leaguer. The ball was still climbing when it caromed off the upper-stand facade, about 396 feet from home plate. Estimates are that the ball could have traveled more than 600 feet. It is Mantle's 20th HR of the season; no one else has ever hit 20 HRs before June.

JUNE

2nd The Indians massacre the Senators 15–0.

3rd CF Richie Ashburn of the Phils goes 5-for-6 in the 2nd game of a doubleheader against the Cards.

4th The Cards pick up relief P Jim Konstanty, who was released by the Yankees.

13th Milwaukee IF Danny O'Connell hits 3 triples in a game.

Vic Power and teammate Tim Thompson of the Athletics go 5-for-6 in a 13–4 win against the Senators.

The Yankees and the White Sox tie a ML mark by using 9 pinch hitters in their game. The Sox prevail 7–5.

14th The University of Minnesota Gophers defeat Arizona 12–1 at the NCAA finals in Nebraska.

The Cards trade future Hall of Famer 2B Red Schoendienst, C Bill Sarni and P Dick Littlefield to the Giants for SS Alvin Dark, OF Whitey Lockman, C Ray Katt and P Don Liddle.

16th NL President Warren Giles states that bigger players, not livelier balls, account for the present-day hitting feats.

17th In Fred Haney's first games managing the Braves, Joe Adcock hits 3 of his record 13 Ebbets Field HRs in a doubleheader win over Brooklyn before 34,394 fans. In the first game, his game-winning 9th-inning HR off Ed Roebuck lands on the roof, making him the only slugger in history to accomplish this. The ball left the field at the 350-foot mark in LF, clearing the 83-foot wall.

20th At Detroit's Briggs Stadium, Mickey Mantle poles 2 Billy Hoeft pitches into the right CF bleachers, something no other player had done since the bleachers were built in the late 1930s. New York wins 7–4.

23rd Hal Jeffcoat of the Cincinnati Reds hits Dodger SS Don Zimmer in the face with a pitch, breaking his cheekbone. This is the 2nd time that Zimmer suffers an injury that nearly ends his career, and he is out for the season. The Dodgers win 7–6.

Kansas City *Star* reporter Dick Wade says that his stopwatch proves that there were only 9:55 minutes of actual "action" in a game the Athletics won from the Senators 15–6 (in just 8½ innings). Wade calculated the time the ball was in play, allowing a second for each pitch that was taken or fouled off.

24th Ed Bailey of the Reds hits 3 HRs in a 10–6 first-game win against the Dodgers. The Reds win the nitecap 2–1.

26th Robin Roberts and the Phillies hand the Braves a 4–2 loss. It was the first loss for the Braves after 11 wins under new manager Fred Haney.

JULY

1st Mickey Mantle switch-hits HRs in the same game for the 4th time in his career. The Yankees win 8–6 over Washington.

2nd NBC pays $16.25 million for the TV-radio rights to the All-Star Game and the WS. The players' pension fund will get 60 percent of the revenues.

6th Jim Busby of the Indians hits his 2nd grand slam in as many days as the Tribe beats the A's 4–2.

Ford Frick inaugurates the Cy Young Award, to honor to outstanding pitcher each year. The BBWAA will do the voting. Only one pitcher will be honored each year until 1967, when a pitcher in each league will be selected.

8th   The Giants connect for a team-record 7 HRs in a 11–1 home win over the Pirates. Willie Mays, Daryl Spencer, and Wes Westrum each connect for 2. Hank Thompson, Westrum, and Spencer hit consecutive HRs in the 4th inning.

Boston's Ted Williams becomes the 12th player to drive in 1,500 runs when he hits a single in the 2nd game of a doubleheader against the Orioles. The Red Sox sweep, winning 9–0 and 8–4.

10th   In the All-Star Game, Ken Boyer of the Cardinals makes 3 sparkling plays at 3B and gets 3 hits as the NL defeats the AL 7–3. Willie Mays, Mickey Mantle, Ted Williams, and Stan Musial all homer. Mays's pinch-hit 2-run HR off of Whitey Ford is his 7th straight hit against the Yankee lefty.

11th   The White Sox purchase Cardinal relief P Ellis Kinder.

14th   Boston lefty Mel Parnell pitches a no-hitter against the White Sox at Fenway Park, winning 4–0. It is only Parnell's 3rd win against 2 losses and is the 6th straight loss for 2nd-place Chicago. The no-hitter is the first for the Red Sox since 1923. Parnell will go 4–4 before a torn muscle in his pitching arm ends his career as the Red Sox' winningest southpaw.

15th   Wally Burnette of Kansas City shuts out Washington 8–0 in his first start.

Hank Aaron of the Braves hits in the second game of a doubleheader sweep of the Pirates, the Braves winning 3–2 and 4–1. This is the start of a 25-game hit streak for Aaron, the longest of the season.

16th   A group headed by Fred Knorr and John Fetzer buys the Detroit Tigers and Briggs Stadium for a record $5.5 million.

17th   Red Sox pitchers Tom Brewer and Bob Porterfield sweep the Athletics 10–0 and 4–0.

21st   Junior Gilliam of the Brooklyn Dodgers makes 12 assists at 2B to set a modern ML record. Dodger captain Pee Wee Reese gets his 2,000th ML hit, one of 5 active major leaguers to reach the mark. But St. Louis wins 13–6.

22nd   The Hall of Fame announces special rules governing elections. Writers should vote every 2 years, alternating with the veterans committee; because of criticism, this will revert back in 1962. To be eligible players must have been retired as a player for 5 years.

23rd   Joe Cronin and Hank Greenberg are officially inducted into the Hall of Fame at Cooperstown, NY.

24th   New York City Mayor Robert Wagner appoints Charles J. Mylod as chairman and R. E. Blum and C. A. Allen as members of the newly created Brooklyn Sports Center Authority. He reveals plans for a 50,000-seat stadium bounded by Warren Street and Fourth, Flatbush and Fifth Avenues. Robert Moses prefers a different Brooklyn site.

25th   Brooklyn's RF Carl Furillo is the first Dodger player to homer in Jersey City, as the Dodgers lose to the Reds 2–1.

27th   3B Hector Lopez and 1B Vic Power of the Athletics each have 5 hits in a 14-inning game 10–9 loss to New York.

Gil Hodges's grand slam clips the Cubs 4–3, as the Dodgers move to 5 games behind the Braves.

29th   Herb Score and Hank Aguirre of the Indians sweep Baltimore 3–0 and 4–0.

AUGUST

2nd   Boston's Jackie Jensen knocks in 9 RBIs as the Red Sox bag the Tigers 18–3.

7th   The Boston Red Sox fine Ted Williams $5,000 for spitting at Boston fans, as the Red Sox edge the Yanks in 11 innings on Williams's bases-loaded walk. It is Williams's 3rd spitting incident in 3 weeks. The spitting started after the crowd of 36,350, a record for night games at Fenway Park, started booing the Splendid Splinter for muffing Mickey Mantle's wind-blown fly in the 11th. Before the game, RF Jackie Jensen had to be restrained by teammates from going into the stands after a heckler. The previous year Jensen had challenged a fan to come out of the stands.

The largest crowd in minor league history (57,000) see Miami's 50-year-old Satchel Paige beat Columbus (IL) in the Orange Bowl.

9th   Longtime Dodger announcer Connie Desmond resigns from the broadcast booth.

The Senators get a license to sell beer at Griffith Stadium.

10th   Cincinnati C Ed Bailey hits a grand slam as the Redlegs win 8–1 over Milwaukee to move into 2nd place, a half game behind the Braves and a half game ahead of the Dodgers.

12th   Shreveport's Ken Guettler sets the Texas League mark with his 56th HR. He will finish the season with 62.

15th   The Dodgers and Giants draw 26,385 for a night-game record at Jersey City. A Willie Mays HR is the only scoring as Johnny Antonelli shuts out the Dodgers 1–0.

18th   Redlegs OF Bob Thurman hits 3 consecutive HRs; Ted Kluszewski and Frank Robinson add 2 each, and Wally Post, one, in a 13–4 win over Milwaukee at Crosley Field. The 8 HRs tie a ML record.

23rd   Led by Nellie Fox's 7 straight hits, the White Sox sweep the Yankees. Mickey Mantle has a bunt single, triple and HR in the 6–4 nightcap loss but trails Fox in season hits, 158 to 155. But the Mick still leads in the Triple Crown race.

25th   To make room for Enos Slaughter, the Yankees give Phil "the Scooter" Rizzuto his unconditional release. Through the instigation of Ballantine Beer, Rizzuto will be in the announcing booth next year, replacing Jim Woods.

26th   The Yankees announce the purchase of OF Enos Slaughter from Kansas City.

27th   Curt Roberts of Columbus (IL) hits 4 HRs in a row in a 7-inning game against the Havana Cubans.

28th   The Giants sign 17-year-old lefty Mike McCormick to a bonus contract.

31st   President Dwight D. Eisenhower is in attendance as Jim Lemon of the Senators slugs 3 consecutive HRs in a night game against the Yankees, but New York still wins 6–4.

SEPTEMBER

3rd   The Braves set a home night-game record by drawing 47,604 to see a doubleheader split with the Redlegs, winning the first 3–2 and losing the second 7–5. Their lead is still 3½ games.

5th   The Red Sox wallop the Senators 16–0 in the 2nd game after taking game one 7–5. In the nightcap, the Sox bang out 20 safeties with every starter getting a hit.

Joe Bauman, of Roswell (Class C Longhorn League) hits 3 HRs in a twin bill win over Artesia, giving him an all-time season record of 72 round trippers.

11th   Yogi Berra ties the ML career record for HRs by a catcher in the Yankees' 9–5 victory over Kansas City. His 236th—and the Yankees' 177th of the season—tie him with Cub great Gabby Hartnett.

Frank Robinson ties the NL record for HRs by a rookie with 38 in an 11–5 Redlegs win over New York.

18th   Mickey Mantle hits his 50th HR, only the 8th to do so, in the 11th off of Chicago's Billy Pierce, as New York wins 3–2 to clinch another pennant.

Cleveland sweeps a doubleheader from Washington behind Herb Score and Mike Garcia, 1–0 and 6–0.

19th   In a rain-shortened 6 inning game, Bob Lemon of the Indians wins 6–0 for his 20th victory of the year.

For the 3rd time in his career, P Don Newcombe hits 2 HRs in one game in a 17–2 laugher. The win puts the Dodgers a half game in front of the Braves.

21st   1B Bill Skowron has 5 hits, but the Yankees strand a record 20 base runners in losing to the Red Sox in Boston, 13–9. Mickey Mantle sends a 480-foot HR into the CF bleachers that lands a foot from the top. His 3 hits raise his average to .352, 4 points behind Ted Williams.

23rd   Pittsburgh and Brooklyn draw the largest crowd, 44,932, in Forbes Field history. Curfew stops the game with 2 outs in the 9th and Brooklyn leading 8–3. The postponement leaves Milwaukee ½ game ahead of the Dodgers.

24th   NL President Warren Giles waives the 12:50 A.M. curfew for games that may affect the outcome of the pennant race. Brooklyn wins the postponed game, but loses the regular game to Pittsburgh 6–5.

25th   At Ebbets Field, Sal Maglie of the Dodgers no-hits the Phils 5–0 for his 12th win against 4 losses. The win keeps Brooklyn ½ game behind the Braves who beat Cincinnati 7–1.

In the wake of the Ted Williams spitting incident, the Massachusetts State Legislature passes a bill to fine fans for profanity during a game. The bill is later killed.

26th Vic Wertz of the Indians hits 4 doubles and a single in an 8–4 win against the Athletics.

Jim Lemon of the Senators sets a ML record for strikeouts by a batter in one season with 138. This surpasses Larry Doby's mark of 121, set in 1953. The Senators lose to the Red Sox 8–4.

Charlie Beamon of the Orioles throws a 1–0 shutout against the Yanks in his first ML start.

29th The Cincinnati Redlegs tie the 1947 Giants record of 221 HRs in a season in beating the Cubs 9–6.

Mickey Mantle has only one hit against Boston pitching, but it is his 52nd HR. In the 2 late-season series against Boston, Mantle has 7 hits in 14 at bats, while Ted Williams has just 3 hits in 20 at bats. Mantle wins the Triple Crown with a .353 batting average, 52 HRs, and 130 RBI. The Yanks and the Red Sox use a record 44 players in the game. The 26 used by New York set a new ML mark.

The Dodgers sweep a pair from the Pirates 6–2 and 3–1, as Milwaukee loses to St. Louis in 12 innings. The Dodgers now lead by one game with just one game to go.

30th Sandy Amoros and Duke Snider each hit 2 HRs, as the Brooklyn Dodgers win 8–6 to cop the pennant on the last day of the season.

Red Schoendienst of the NY Giants gets the 2,000th hit of his ML career, but the Giants lose 4–2 to the Braves.

Al Lopez, manager of the Indians since 1951, resigns and is replaced by Kirby Farrell. Lopez, who won 470 while losing 354 for a .570 percentage, had one pennant and five 2nd-place finishes in his 6 years at the helm.

White Sox hurler Jim Derrington becomes the youngest pitcher in modern history to start a game. He loses to Kansas City 7–6 at the age of 16 years and 10 months.

OCTOBER

2nd The Comiskey Park broadcast booth catches fire, causing damage estimated at $100,000.

3rd Sal Maglie and the Dodgers defeat the Yankees 6–3 in the first game of the WS.

4th Rain delays Game 2 of the WS.

5th The Dodgers come back from a 6–0 deficit in Game 2 to win 13–8 behind the sterling relief pitching of Don Bessent. Yankee C Yogi Berra becomes the only player in WS history to hit a grand slam in a losing cause as he sends one over the RF screen off Don Newcombe in the 2nd.

Owner Clark Griffith of the Senators says the club is considering moving to the West Coast because of the delay in building a new Washington stadium.

6th The Yanks regroup at home and defeat Brooklyn 5–3 in Game 3, with Whitey Ford going the distance and Enos Slaughter hitting a 3-run HR.

7th In Game 4, the Yanks even the WS at 2 apiece with a 6–2 win in Yankee Stadium. Righty Tom Sturdivant holds Brooklyn to 6 hits.

8th Series history is made by Don Larsen of the Yankees, who pitches a perfect game to defeat the Dodgers 2–0 in Game 5. He requires only 97 pitches. Sal Maglie matches him until Mickey Mantle homers in the 4th.

9th The Dodgers bounce back. Clem Labine comes out of the bullpen to pitch a 1–0 victory in 10 innings. Enos Slaughter misjudges Jackie Robinson's fly ball, and Jim Gilliam scores from 2B.

10th The Yankees win their first WS championship in 3 years as Johnny Kucks sets down the Bums 9–0. Yogi Berra hits a pair of 2-run HRs and Bill Skowron hits a grand slam. Don Newcombe takes the loss, his 4th in Series competition.

11th AL President Will Harridge bars the shift of the Senators to the West Coast, unless unanimously approved by the other AL owners.

John Holland is named GM of the Cubs. Charlie Grimm becomes vice president.

The Phillies buy Jim Hearn from the Giants and send Stu Miller to the Giants farm club in Minneapolis.

17th The Senators announce they will study bids from Louisville and San Francisco.

18th The Brooklyn Dodgers begin an exhibition tour of Japan.

19th Playing below par after their 7-game WS loss to the Yankees, the Dodgers lose the first game of an exhibition series in Japan to the Yomiuri Giants 5–4.

Nonetheless, the Dodgers will win 14, lose 4, and tie one in the series.

24th The AP names Cincinnati manager Birdie Tebbetts as its NL Manager of the Year.

25th White Sox manager Marty Marion resigns. AL Lopez is the new manager.

30th The Dodgers sell Ebbets Field to a real estate group. They agree to stay until 1959, with an option to stay until 1961.

NOVEMBER

14th The Pittsburgh Pirates say the franchise may have to move unless a new municipal stadium is built to replace Forbes Field.

20th The Cardinals trade OF Rip Repulski and SS Bobby Morgan to the Phillies for OF Del Ennis.

21st Don Newcombe, who won the 1949 Rookie of the Year Award, wins the NL MVP and the first-ever Cy Young Award.

DECEMBER

1st Cincinnati slugger Frank Robinson is unanimously voted the NL Rookie of the Year. White Sox SS Luis Aparicio is voted AL Rookie of the Year with 22 points, beating out Oriole Tito Francona and Indian Rocky Colavito.

In front of an estimated 100,000 at the Melbourne Cricket Grounds, a U.S. Army team beats an Australian all-star team 11–5 in an Olympic exhibition game. Sergeant Vance Sutton hits a grand slam.

3rd The Tigers send pitchers Ned Garver, Gene Host, and Virgil Trucks, 1B Wayne Belardi and $20,000 to the Athletics for pitchers Bill Harrington, Jack Crimian, 1B Eddie Robinson, and 3B Jim Finigan.

10th The AL club owners vote for a 3-game play-off in case of a tie at the end of the regular season.

The Cubs buy perennial backup C Charlie Silvera from the Yankees. They also trade pitchers "Sad Sam" Jones and Jim Davis, IF Eddie Miksis, and C Hobie Landrith to the Cardinals for pitchers Tom Poholsky and Jackie Collum, C Ray Katt, and a minor league pitcher.

11th A players organization is established with Bob Feller as president.

13th The Dodgers trade Jackie Robinson to the Giants for P Dick Littlefield and $35,000. Robinson retires rather than accept the trade.

18th Former Yankee SS Phil Rizzuto signs as a Yankee radio-TV announcer.

1957

JANUARY

4th The Dodgers buy a 44-passenger twin-engine airplane for $775,000, which they will use to transport the club during the season. They are the first team to own their own plane.

5th Jackie Robinson retires, voiding the December deal with the Giants.

10th Commissioner Ford Frick rules that singer Bing Crosby can keep his "token" stock in the Detroit Tigers, even though he owns part of the Pittsburgh Pirates.

15th The Brooklyn Dodgers extend their 5-year lease on Ebbets Field by signing a new 3-year lease with real estate developer Marvin Kratter, who bought the field in 1953.

26th Joseph F. Cairnes succeeds Lou Perini as president of the Braves.

29th With the advent of coast-to-coast air travel, ML baseball weighs a plan for a player pool to be used in the event of an air disaster.

FEBRUARY

1st Club owners approve a new 5-year player pension plan, effective April 1st. It offers more liberal benefits and includes all players, coaches, and trainers eligible for the 1947 plan. The owners reject the players' request to raise the minimum salary from $6,000 to $7,500.

4th The BBWAA elects manager Joe McCarthy and Detroit's Wahoo Sam Crawford to the Hall of Fame

14th The Georgia Senate unanimously approves Senator Leon Butts's bill barring blacks from playing baseball with whites. Religious gatherings are the only exceptions to this bill.

15th A Boston newspaper claims that Ted Williams never paid his $5,000 fine for spitting at the crowd. It refers to him mockingly as the "Splendid Spitter."

21st In an ominous development for Brooklyn, Walter O'Malley "trades" minor league franchises with Phil Wrigley of the Cubs, giving up the Dodgers' Ft. Worth (Texas) club in return for the Cubs' Los Angeles Angels (PCL).

22nd Walter O'Malley says the Dodgers may play 10 exhibitions in California in 1958.

25th The U.S. Supreme Court decides 6-3 that baseball is the only professional sport exempt from antitrust laws. The issue arises when pro football seeks similar protection from the laws.

MARCH

6th The Dodgers Walter O'Malley confers with Los Angeles Mayor Norris Poulson and other officials of the city.

11th Representative Emanuel Celler, whose committee investigated baseball, calls Ford Frick a "czar" who wishes to "gag" officials; Frick had cautioned ML owners about commenting on the recent Supreme Court decision on pro football coming under antitrust rules.

18th In what is believed to be the largest offer for a player ever made, the Indians reject a million-dollar offer for lefty Herb Score from Red Sox GM Joe Cronin. Cleveland GM Hank Greenberg refuses, saying that the team is interested in building for the future, not in selling its best ballplayers.

21st *Television Age* reports that the major leagues will get $9.3 million for TV-radio rights in 1957.

APRIL

16th The Phillies set an Opening Day record at Connie Mack Stadium as 37,667 fans pay to see the Dodgers Gino Cimoli hit a 12-inning HR to win the game 7–6.

18th About 150 black fans reject seats in the segregated section of Durham Athletic Park in the Carolina League after being denied seats in the non-segregated section.

New York Parks Commissioner Robert Moses proposes a new 78-acre tract in Flushing Meadows as a site for a new NL stadium. The plan, submitted to Mayor Robert Wagner, includes a 50,000-seat stadium with a plastic dome, to be built by the Parks Department.

19th Harvey R. Hansen succeeds Fred Knorr as president of the Detroit Tigers.

21st Reds' baserunner Don Hoak breaks up a DP by fielding a Wally Post ground ball and flipping it to Braves SS Johnny Logan. The umpire calls Hoak out for interference but Post is given a single on the play. The Braves win 3–1. In yesterday's 5–4 loss to the Braves, baserunner Johnny Temple let Gus Bell's ground ball hit him with the same result; Temple out for interfering and Bell awarded a single.

22nd John Kennedy becomes the first black to play for the Philadelphia Phillies, making them the last NL team to integrate. Kennedy pinch runs for Hemus in the 5–1 loss to Brooklyn. He will play only briefly in 5 games, 2 at 3B, and will go hitless.

24th Chicago Cub pitchers walk 9 Reds in the 5th inning, an NL mark, as Cincinnati wins 9–5. Moe Drabowsky starts with 4 walks, Jackie Collum adds 3 and Jim Brosnan has 2 passes.

The NY Board of Estimates fails to act on the Moses plan as outlined by Mayor Wagner.

25th ML baseball hastily adopts a rule which prohibits a base runner from interfering with a batted ball in any way. This is a result of the recent Reds' actions in games against the Braves

26th Walter "Spike" Briggs of the Detroit Tigers resigns as executive vice-president, GM and director after a row with the front office. He is the last member of the Briggs family to hold an official position with the team.

27th The AL finally concedes and suspends a game when the Senators and Orioles are interrupted by a power failure at the end of the 5th inning.

MAY

5th In the 2nd game of a 3–1 and 4–1 doubleheader sweep of the Phils, the Cardinals Wally Moon begins a 24-game hitting streak, the longest of the season in the NL.

7th Gil McDougald of the Yankees hits a wicked line-drive that strikes Cleveland's Herb Score in the right eye. Score, with a broken nose and lacerations, is carried off the field on a stretcher. Lemon relieves and wins the game 2–1. Score will return the following year but his pitching will not be the same.

8th Boston slugger Ted Williams hits 3 HRs and drives in 4 as the Red Sox stop Chicago 4–1.

10th Mayor George Christopher of San Francisco confers with Horace Stoneham on a possible shift of the Giants franchise to the West Coast.

15th When Ted Williams comes up to bat for the Red Sox, manager Paul Richards moves White Sox P Harry Dorish to 3B. After reliever Billy Pierce retires the slugger, Dorish returns to the mound to relieve himself, and go on to finish the game for a 9–7 win in 11 innings.

16th The Yankees celebrate Billy Martin's 29th birthday in a raucous fashion. An ensuing fight at Manhattan's Copacabana Club leads to $5,500 in fines and the eventual trade of Billy to Kansas City. Hank Bauer allegedly starts the fight by hitting a patron, although Bauer denies it. The Yanks fine Ford, Bauer, Berra, Mantle and Martin $1,000 each and Kucks $500.

21st Boston baseball writers reaffirm their decision to bar women from the press box and refuse to allow Doris O'Donnell, a Cleveland feature writer traveling with the Indians, to sit in the Fenway Park press area.

For his part in the Copacabana incident, Yankee OF Hank Bauer is arraigned. He is eventually cleared and threatens to sue the alleged victim, Edward Jones, who suffered a concussion and a broken jaw.

22nd The Red Sox set an AL record by smashing 4 HRs in the 6th inning in an 11–0 win over Cleveland. Gene Mauch, Ted Williams, Dick Gernert, and Frank Malzone do the honors. Williams had set the record with Jimmie Foxx, Joe Cronin, and Jim Tabor in 1940.

24th In his first ML game, Cubs rookie Frank Ernaga hits a solo HR in the 2nd inning and follows with a run-scoring triple in the 4th against Warren Spahn. The Cubs beat the Braves 5–1 at Wrigley Field.

26th Rookie Dick Drott of the Cubs strikes out 15 Braves, including Hank Aaron 4 times, en route to a 7–5 victory.

28th The NL approves the proposed moves of the Dodgers and the Giants to the West Coast, provided both clubs make their request before October 1st and move at the same time.

29th NY Mayor Robert Wagner says he plans to confer with the Giants and Dodgers about the proposed move, but that the city will not be "blackjacked" into anything.

Four PCL teams may seek as much as $6.7 million in indemnities if both the Los Angeles Angels and the San Francisco Seals withdraw from the league.

30th   Walter O'Malley rejects a Queens group's offer to buy the Dodgers.

The Ohio legislature passes a bill to aid the Cincinnati Redlegs in building a new stadium.

JUNE

1st   Braves pitchers Warren Spahn and Gene Conley stop Wally Moon's 24-game streak, but Cards 40-year-old Murry Dickson wins 7–1.

2nd   Moe Drabowsky of the Cubs ties a NL record by hitting 4 batters in the first game of a doubleheader against the Reds. Cubs lose 6–4.

4th   Billy Pierce of the White Sox wins 1–0 in a 10-inning masterpiece before 38,490, against the Red Sox. Chicago maintains its 5-game lead over New York.

5th   In Jersey City, Don Drysdale pitches the first of his 49 ML shutouts, as the Dodgers win 4–0 over the Cubs.

6th   Umpires wait in vain for fog-drenched Ebbets Field to clear. With the Dodgers ahead 1–0, Cubs LF Bob Speake loses sight of a fly ball, and batter Charlie Neal gets a double. After a delay of an hour and 26 minutes the game is called, the first time ever because of fog.

11th   In a 7–2 loss to the Braves, Dodger C Roy Campanella hits his 237th career HR, surpassing career marks of Gabby Hartnett and Yogi Berra. The Braves move ½ game behind the leading Reds.

12th   Mickey Mantle again hits HRs from both sides of the plate, and drives in 4 runs, but the Yankees lose to Chicago 7–6.

The University of California wins the NCAA championship, defeating Penn State 1–0 in the final game.

Cardinal Stan Musial plays in his 823rd game for a new NL consecutive-game streak, beating Gus Suhr's record. Larry Jackson beats the Phils 4–0 to improve his record to 8-2; he has now beaten every NL team this season.

13th   For the 2nd time this year, the Red Sox Ted Williams hits 3 HRs in a game, a 9–2 win over the Indians. Williams is the first to do this in the AL.

15th   In more fallout over the Copacabana incident, the Yankees trade Billy Martin to Kansas City with SS Woodie Held and OF Bob Martyn for P Ryne Duren, 2B Milt Graff and OFs Harry Simpson and Jim Pisoni.

16th   The White Sox rally to defeat the Senators, as relief P Dixie Howell hits 2 HRs.

21st   One month after graduating from high school, Cardinals P Von McDaniel, 18, 2-hits the Dodgers in his first ML start, 2–0. He holds the Dodgers hitless until the 6th inning.

23rd   Prime Minister Kishi of Japan, wearing a Yankees cap, is one of 63,787 fans at Yankee Stadium to see New York split with Chicago, winning the first 9–2 and dropping the 2nd game 4–3. Mickey Mantle goes 6-for-9 as the Yankees maintain their ½ game lead over Chicago. Mantle is leading the AL in hitting, HRs and is one behind the Senators' Roy Sievers in RBIs.

Oriole Skinny Brown blanks the Tigers 6–0 to start a string of 4 shutouts for the O's staff.

28th   By stuffing the ballot box, Cincinnati fans elect 8 Redlegs as starters in the All-Star Game. Over protests from Reds fans, Commissioner Ford Frick names Stan Musial, Willie Mays, and Hank Aaron to replace Reds Gus Bell, George Crowe, and Wally Post in the starting lineup. In the final vote tally, Musial is the only non-Redleg who would have started.

Ray Moore blanks Cleveland 6–0 as the Orioles pitching staff hurls its 4th consecutive shutout, for a new AL mark.

Ponca City and Greenville (Sooner State League) turn triple plays in successive half innings. Greenville turns theirs in the bottom of the first, while Ponca City follows with one in the top half of the 2nd.

29th   NL President Warren Giles proposes that fan All-Star voting be limited to those actually attending a game.

30th   The Braves sweep a doubleheader from Pittsburgh 7–4 and 6–5 to take a ½ lead over the 2nd-place Reds.

JULY

1st P George Zuverink and C Frank Zupo of the Orioles become the first "Z-battery" in history. The end result is a 3–2 loss to the Yanks.

Cincinnati fans threaten to sue Commissioner Ford Frick unless Bell, Crowe, and Post are restored to the All-Star team.

2nd The Women's Christian Temperance Union charges that baseball has become "beerball," since so many broadcasts are sponsored by breweries.

4th George Crowe of the Reds goes 5-for-5 against his old Braves teammates, but Milwaukee wins 10–7.

8th The owners decide to re-elect Commissioner Ford Frick to another 7-year term when his present contract is up in 1958.

9th At Busch Stadium in St. Louis, the AL nips the NL 6–5 in the 24th All-Star Game. Both teams score 3 in the 9th inning, but Minnie Minoso's running catch with the bases loaded chokes off the NL's last-half rally.

11th In Pittsburgh, Braves IF Felix Mantilla and OF Billy Bruton collide while chasing a pop fly. Mantilla will miss 19 games while Bruton will suffer knee damage and be out almost a year.

14th Bill Skowron of the Yanks hits an ML-record 2nd pinch-hit grand slam of the season, off Jim Wilson of the White Sox, in the 2nd game of a doubleheader. Skowron's hit comes in the 9th as the Yanks score 6 runs to win 6–4. The White Sox take the first game 3–1.

P Billy Hoeft of the Tigers hits 2 HRs and a single against the Orioles Skinny Brown, as Detroit wins 10–2.

18th In what will later be revealed as false testimony, Kansas City A's owner Arnold Johnson denies before the Celler committee that he had any ties to the Yankee ownership or has favored them in any trades.

Ernie Banks and Chuck Tanner of the Cubs both hit inside-the-park homers at spacious Forbes Field. The Cubs nip Pittsburgh 6–5.

Horace Stoneham says that the Giants will quit New York after the season. He says he has not heard anything more from San Francisco and that his move is not contingent on that of the Dodgers. He sees a new stadium or joint occupancy with the Yankees as the only reason for the Giants to stay in New York.

Dodger slugger Gil Hodges hits his 12th career grand slam to tie the NL record of Rogers Hornsby and Ralph Kiner, as the Dodgers edge the Cards 10–9. St. Louis remains a game behind the Phils. The slam comes against the Cardinals Wilmer Mizell.

Gene Woodling of the Indians throws out 2 Washington runners from LF in the first inning, tying a ML record. Washington wins 4–0.

19th Testifying before the Celler committee, PCL President Leslie O'Connor holds that 90 percent of all good ballplayers are monopolized through the farm teams. He adds that the major leagues may control as many as 1,098 players.

21st Cubs relief P Jim Brosnan falls on the mound while warming up, injuring his Achilles tendon. He leaves the game without throwing a single pitch to a batter.

23rd Mickey Mantle hits for the cycle, and adds a SB, against Chicago's Bob Keegan. The Yankees win 10–6.

26th Jim Bunning of the Tigers 2-hits New York 3–2, but one of the hits is Mickey Mantle's 9th left-handed HR, the 200th HR of his career.

30th Ron Northey hits his 9th pinch-hit HR, off Buster Freeman, enabling the Phillies to beat the Reds 8–5.

31st The Pirates lose to the Braves and Bob Buhl 4–2. Bucs manager Bobby Bragan is ejected in the bottom of the 5th for making obscene gestures. Before he departs, he strolls onto the field sipping an orange drink through a straw and offers the umpires a drink. Two days later Bragan will be fired by the Pirates.

AUGUST

1st Gil Hodges hits his 13th career grand slam to establish a new NL record. This is the last grand slam in the history of the Brooklyn Dodgers franchise.

Former ML OF Glen Gorbous of Omaha breaks Don Grate's record toss with a heave of 445 feet 10 inches before a home game.

3rd The news that Danny Murtaugh will succeed Bobby Bragan as manager of the Pittsburgh Pirates is leaked to the press, and Bragan hears it on the radio before Joe L. Brown can inform him.

4th Washington defeats Detroit 4–3 as the Senators Roy Sievers hits his 30th HR, his 6th HR in 6 games, to tie an AL record held by Ken Williams and Lou Gehrig.

5th The Brooklyn Sports Authority gets an engineering report on a 50,000-seat stadium in the downtown area. It will cost an estimated $20.7 million, including the land site. Indications are that there will be trouble finding a market for the bond issue.

7th Hank Bauer of the Yanks hits his 2nd consecutive lead-off HR, against Washington, as the first-place Yankees lose 3–2.

11th P Dick Hyde intentionally walks Ted Williams, the 27th time this year the slugger has been handed a free base. Williams will be intentionally walked 33 times this year, the highest AL total since the league started compiling this statistic in 1955.

13th P Lew Burdette of the Braves hits his first 2 HRs and beats the Redlegs 12–4.

Mickey Mantle goes 3-for-3 and drives in 3 runs as the Yankees edge the Red Sox 3–2. Mantle improves his average to .384 while Ted Williams, with 1-for-2, is at .388. A week later Mantle will injure himself when he angrily swings a golf club at a branch and gouges his shinbone. This will effectively take him out of the running for a 2nd-straight triple crown.

17th Richie Ashburn, known for his ability to foul pitches off, hits spectator Alice Roth twice in the same at bat. The first one breaks her nose, and the 2nd one hits her while she is being removed from her seat on a stretcher. Ironically, she is the wife of Earl Roth, the sports editor of the Philadelphia *Bulletin*. The Phils win 3–1 over New York.

19th As Horace Stoneham cites poor attendance as the reason for the Giants' move, the Giants board of directors votes 8-1 to move to California in 1958, as San Francisco promises a new stadium in the Bayview area. The only dissenting vote is by M. Donald Grant.

20th Using a new slow delivery, 35-year-old Bob Keegan of the White Sox pitches a 6–0 no-hitter over Washington, walking just 2. Chuck Stobbs loses his 16th game en route to a league-leading 20 losses. The Sox lose the first game 5–4, but pick up a half game on New York.

Yankee Bob Turley pitches a 2-hitter against Kansas City, but loses 1–0.

23rd Angel Macias, a 12-year-old righthander from Monterrey, Mexico, hurls a perfect 12-inning game over La Mesa, striking out 11 to win the Little League Championship in Williamsport, PA. In the tourney before Williamsport, Macias also pitched left-handed.

24th The Dodgers use 8 pitchers in one game, tying the NL record, in a 13–7 loss to first-place Milwaukee. Johnny Podres leaves after giving up 3 HRs in the 4th. Hank Aaron hits the first grand slam of his career

26th The Red Sox hit 4 HRs and score 10 runs in the 3rd and go on to rip the Athletics 16–0.

Yankee-killer Frank Lary stops New York as Detroit wins 5–2. The New York lead is now down to 3½ games, as they start a crucial series in Chicago. They will win all 3 games with the Sox.

27th Stan Musial, swinging at a 4th-inning pitch, tears a muscle and chips a bone, ending his consecutive- game streak. Four days later he will pinch-run in a game suspended on July 21st, officially giving him 895 consecutive games played.

Hurricane Bob Hazle, hitting .526 since being recalled from Wichita, hits two 2-run HRs, as the Braves beat the Phillies 7–3 for Warren Spahn's 219th career win, moving him to a 6th on the career list. Spahn also hits his 18th career HR, also good for 6th (tie with Schoolboy Rowe) on the career list

31st Steve Dalkowski, legendary minor league fastballer pitching for Kingsport (Appalachian League), strikes out 24, walks 18, hits 4 batters, and throws 6 wild pitches in a row. He loses 9–8.

SEPTEMBER

1st The Yankees purchase Sal "the Barber" Maglie from the Dodgers, but he is ineligible for WS play.

2nd The Braves sweep the Cubs 23–10 and 4–0. The Braves' Bob Hazle has 4 hits in the first game, and teammate Frank Torre scores 6 runs to tie the ML record.

3rd The Dodgers play their last game in Jersey City, as Don Drysdale loses to Philadelphia 3–2 in 12 innings. Brooklyn ends with an 11-4 mark in New Jersey.

Warren Spahn of the Braves hurls his 41st shutout, the most by a NL lefthander, as he beats Chicago 8–0.

16th The Los Angeles City Council approves a 300-acre site in Chavez Ravine for a Dodger stadium if the club will finance a public recreation area.

21st Gail Harris is the last player to hit a HR as a New York Giant, as they beat the Pirates 9–5 in the 2nd game of a doubleheader. Ruben Gomez gains the last New York Giants' victory.

The Cardinals tie a record by using 8 pitchers in one game, but lose 9–8 in 10 innings to the Redlegs and slip 5 games off the pace. Jerry Lynch's 8th-inning HR ties the game; the Redlegs set the NL mark with their 11th pinch-hit HR of the year.

22nd Ted Williams hits his 4th consecutive HR, a grand slam, in 4 official at bats over 4 games, as he is walked 11 times. He ends his HR streak with a single.

Duke Snider's 39th and 40th HRs are the last that will be hit at Ebbets Field. The Duke of Flatbush ties Ralph Kiner's NL mark of hitting at least 40 HRs in 5 consecutive seasons. Phillie Robin Roberts, who has a penchant for throwing HR balls, is the loser, 7–3.

23rd The Milwaukee Braves clinch the pennant by beating the Cardinals 4–2 on Hank Aaron's 11th-inning HR.

24th Hal Griggs of the Senators gets Ted Williams to ground out, breaking the Red Sox slugger's streak of reaching first base 16 consecutive times. Williams later homers to win the game 2–1.

In the last game at Ebbets Field, 6,702 fans watch Dodgers lefty Danny McDevitt prevail over the Pirates 2–0. Gil Hodges has the last RBI.

The Yankees clinch their 23rd pennant and 8th under Casey Stengel, as Kansas City tips the White Sox 6–5.

27th Walter O'Malley says he will waive the oil rights to Chavez Ravine.

In a desperate move, New York City Council President Abe "Hit Sign, Win" Stark says the Dodgers should be urged to enlarge and modernize Ebbets Field.

Owner Paul I. Fagan agrees to rent Seals Stadium to the Giants until Candlestick is ready. Fagan will pay $125,000 in annual taxes, in exchange for the parking concession, against 5 percent of the gross revenue.

Johnny Klippstein of the Reds one-hits the Braves 6–0, with Bob Hazle getting the only safety.

28th Ed Roebuck gets the last Brooklyn victory, an 8–4 win over the hometown Phils.

29th Ernie Banks goes 5-for-5 against the Cardinals.

With 1895 manager Jack Doyle among the 11,606 looking on, the Giants lose their last game at the Polo Grounds 9–1. Pirate P Bob Friend defeats Johnny Antonelli.

The Brooklyn Dodgers lose their final game before moving west, a 2–1 loss to Philadelphia. Roger Craig starts and Koufax relieves as Gilliam scores the only Dodger run.

Bobby Bragan signs with Cleveland to replace manager Kirby Ferrell, released two days earlier.

OCTOBER

2nd Whitey Ford wins 3–1 over Warren Spahn in Game 1 of the Series at Yankee Stadium.

NL President Warren Giles says that the 1958 schedule has no provision in it for a New York team.

3rd In Game 2 Lew Burdette defeats Yankee Bobby Shantz 4–2.

5th The Yankees score 5 in the 7th to cap a 12–3 win, as Don Larsen, in relief of Bob Turley, defeats Bob Buhl. Tony Kubek of the Yankees becomes only the 2nd rookie in WS history to hit 2 HRs in a WS game.

6th With the score tied at 5–5, Eddie Mathews of the Braves evens the WS at 2 games with a 2-run HR in the bottom of the 10th. In the WS first famous "shoeblack incident," pinch hitter Nippy Jones convinces umpire Augie Donatelli that Tommy Byrne's pitch-hit him on the foot.

7th Lew Burdette wins his 2nd against New York—a brilliant 1–0 shutout—to give Milwaukee a 3-2 Series lead.

The Los Angeles City Council approves the Chavez Ravine site for Dodger Stadium by a vote of 10 to 4.

8th The Yankees stay alive as Hank Bauer homers off the foul pole in LF to give the Yankees a 3–2 win behind the 4-hit pitching of Bob Turley. The WS is even at 3 apiece.

9th With Warren Spahn stricken by the flu, Lew Burdette pitches with 2 days rest, achieves his 3rd complete game and 2nd shutout to beat New York 5–0 The Braves win their first WS championship since the

"Miracle Braves" of 1914 beat Connie Mack's Athletics.

15th The Giants trade their Minneapolis franchise to the Red Sox for the San Francisco Seals—franchises only, not the players.

16th Bill Rigney signs a 2-year deal to manage the San Francisco Giants.

21st The Giants purchase the Class A Phoenix team and will convince the PCL to accept the city as a location for the Seals.

The Senators reject the initial overtures of Minneapolis and St. Paul to move the team there.

24th The Cincinnati Redlegs decline to move their franchise to Roosevelt Stadium in Jersey City.

28th Crooner Bing Crosby seeks to sell his stock in the Pirates to his son, while he investigates purchasing additional stock in the Detroit Tigers.

29th The Dodgers sign former manager Charley Dressen as a coach.

31st Yogi Berra says that the Yankees returned the money collected in fines to the players involved in the Copacabana fight.

NOVEMBER

1st The Nishitetsu Lions sweep the Yomiuri Giants in the Japanese WS.

7th The AP poll names Phillies P Jack Sanford its NL Rookie of the Year with 16 votes, beating out teammate 1B Ed Bouchee.

12th Frank Lane resigns as GM of the Cardinals, who replace him with Bing Devine.

14th The AP names Henry Aaron as the 1957 NL MVP with 239 votes. Stan Musial is a close 2nd with 230, and Red Schoendienst is 3rd with 221.

20th Shigeo Nagashima, a star at Rikkyo University, signs with the Yomiuri Giants for a record bonus of $69,000. He will go on to have one of the great careers in Japanese baseball.

22nd Mickey Mantle edges Ted Williams 233 to 209 votes to win the AL MVP. Williams, at 39 years of age, led the league in hitting with a .388 average, hit 38 HRs, and compiled a slugging average of .731. Red Sox owner Tom Yawkey brands the voting "incompe-

tent and unqualified," noting that 2 Chicago writers listed Williams in the 9th and 10th places on their ballots.

NL umpire Larry Goetz is unwillingly "retired" after 36 seasons in the ML.

26th Yoshio (Kaiser) Tanaka, an American citizen of Japanese descent, is named manager of the Hanshin Tigers. He is the first American to manage a Japanese ML team.

28th Warren Spahn of the Braves wins the Cy Young Award as ML Pitcher of the Year almost unanimously. His only competition for the title is the White Sox, Dick Donovan, who received one vote.

29th Mayor Robert Wagner forms a 4-member committee to find a replacement for the Dodgers and Giants in New York City.

DECEMBER

4th ML baseball kills the bonus rule and raises the minimum salary to $7,000.

5th The minor leagues threaten to sue ML baseball if it televises Sunday games in their territory.

The AL purchases a $1.8 million group accident policy to help clubs buy new players in case of a major disaster.

The Cubs send veteran Bob Rush and 2 players to the Braves for C Sammy Taylor and P Taylor Phillips.

In one of their best trades ever, the Cardinals acquire outfielders Curt Flood and Joe Taylor from the Reds for pitchers Marty Kutyna and Ted Wieand. The 19-year-old Flood, who appeared in 8 games for Cincinnati over the past 2 seasons, will anchor the St. Louis OF for the next 12 years.

7th The AP votes Tony Kubek of the Yanks as the Rookie of the Year. Frank Malzone of the Red Sox, the only other candidate, receives one vote.

11th U.S. Congressman Emanuel Celler and Senator Kenneth Keating, both of New York, hint that there might be antitrust action against ML baseball if it televises games as planned, because it jeopardizes the minor leagues.

The Phillies purchase veteran OF Dave Philley from Detroit.

16th The Reds land their 5th pitcher of the month when they acquire Harvey Haddix from the Phillies for OF Wally Post. A week ago they swapped pitchers with the Pirates, picking up veteran Bob Purkey for Don Gross.

17th The Pasadena City Board confers with the Dodgers on the possible temporary use of the Rose Bowl.

19th In a continuing family squabble, Charlie Comiskey, Jr. denies his sister's, Mrs. Dorothy Comiskey Rigney, allegation that he used the "rule or ruin" tactic to gain control of the club.

25th With the backing of Representatives Keating and Celler, the minor league executives urge that ML baseball compensate them for this infringement on their territorial rights.

28th In a swap of first basemen, the Pirates trade Dee Fondy to the Reds for Ted Kluszewski.

CBS states that it will not broadcast baseball into any area at the time a minor league game is scheduled.

1958

JANUARY

6th Willie Mays's $65,000 contract is a record high for the Giants.

11th Representatives Kenneth Keating and Patrick Hillings drop their plan to bring baseball under the nation's antitrust laws.

13th Spokane, Salt Lake City, and Phoenix join the PCL.

Senator Keating of New York proposes a ban within 100-mile radius on telecasts into minor-league territories.

15th In a deal worth over a million dollars, the Yankees announce that they will televise 140 games in the 1958 season. Six days later, the Phillies agree to televise 78 games into the New York City area.

23rd The Washington Senators trade SS Pete Runnels to the Red Sox for 1B Norm Zauchin and OF Albie Pearson.

28th The Tigers trade 3B Jim Finigan and $25,000 to the Giants for IF Ozzie Virgil and 1B Gail Harris.

The Athletics sign P Murry Dickson as a free agent.

29th Dodgers C Roy Campanella suffers a broken neck in an early morning auto accident on Long Island. His spinal column is nearly severed and his legs are permanently paralyzed.

The Indians buy 1B Mickey Vernon from the Red Sox for the waiver price.

Stan Musial signs with the Cardinals for an NL record $100,000.

30th Commissioner Ford Frick announces that players and coaches, rather than the fans, will vote for the All-Star teams this year.

FEBRUARY

4th The Hall of Fame fails to elect any new members for the first time since 1950.

6th Ted Williams signs with the Red Sox for $135,000, making him the highest paid player in ML history.

7th The Dodgers officially become the Los Angeles Dodgers, Inc.

17th Bob Feller signs to announce games for the Mutual Broadcasting System Game of the Week.

20th The Los Angeles Coliseum Commission approves a 2-year pact for use of its facility by the Dodgers.

21st Phillies 1B Ed Bouchee pleads guilty to a series of sex offenses, such as indecent exposure, involving young girls. He will receive a 3-year probationary sentence and enter a rehabilitation program until the end of May.

MARCH

5th Duke Snider, Johnny Podres, and Don Zimmer suffer minor injuries in an auto accident in Vero Beach, FL, as they try to beat a 12:30 A.M. curfew. This is the 3rd accident in 2 months involving Dodger players; Jim Gilliam and his family had an accident shortly after Roy Campanella's.

11th Starting this season, AL batters will be required to wear batting helmets.

18th In a move to change their image, the Dodgers announce that clown Emmett Kelly will not perform in 1958.

20th The Phillies acquire 1B Joe Collins from the Yankees. He decides to retire rather than report, thereby cancelling the deal.

21st The White Sox obtain OF Don Mueller from the Giants for cash.

31st The Indians trade OF Gene Woodling, the versatile Dick Williams, and P Bud Daley to the Orioles for OF Larry Doby and LHP Don Ferrarese.

APRIL

5th Shigeo Nagashima, a rookie phenom, makes his pro debut with the Yomiuri Giants. He is fanned 4 times, but will go on to win the Central League batting title and have one of the distinguished careers in Japanese baseball.

6th The International League votes to open its season in Havana, unless the political and social strife in Cuba worsens.

7th The Dodgers erect a 42-foot screen in LF at the Los Angeles Coliseum to cut down on HRs, since it is only 250 feet down the line.

12th On a recommendation from President Dwight D. Eisenhower, a friend of Branch Rickey's, the Pirates sign Preston Bruce, the son of the doorkeeper at the White House, and send him to Lincoln (Western League).

13th Buffalo refuses to play in Havana despite an IL vote and assurances.

14th The San Francisco Board of Supervisors rejects the plan to move the proposed site for a new stadium from Bayview to downtown.

15th The San Francisco Giants defeat the Los Angeles Dodgers in the first ML game played at Seals Stadium, with Ruben Gomez pitching an 8–0 shutout. Giants SS Daryl Spencer hits the first HR. The Giants set an attendance record for Seals Stadium by drawing 23,192 fans.

OF Bill Tuttle of the Athletics records 2 assists in the 2nd inning, tying a ML record. The A's win 5–0 and beat Herb Score in his first appearance following his injury. Score lasts 3 inning.

17th The Athletics trade P Arnold Portocarrero to Baltimore for P Bud Daley.

18th Following a downtown parade in the morning, the Giants-Dodgers game in Los Angeles sets a NL single-game record with 78,682 fans in attendance, as the Dodgers prevail 6–5. Hank Sauer hits 2 HRs for the Giants, including the first at the Coliseum. After he scores what would have been the tying run in the 9th, Giant Jim Davenport is called out for failing to touch 3B.

21st The A's Frank House scores 2 runs as a pinch hitter in an 8-run 8th inning, as the Athletics trim the Indians 9–4. House's feat is only the 6th occurrence in the ML.

23rd In an ongoing dispute with soap operatic properties, a Chicago Court orders Mrs. Dorothy Comiskey Rigney to distribute stock from her mother's estate, so she can not effectively bar her brother Charles A. Comiskey from sitting on the White Sox Board.

Gil Hodges hits his 300th HR and Pee Wee Reese plays in his 2,000th game, but the Dodgers lose 7–6 to the Cubs. Duke Snider injures his arm before the game

trying to throw a ball out of the Los Angeles Coliseum. Unamused Dodger officials dock him a day's pay.

25th The Dodgers set a record for most fans at a regular season night game as 60,635 attend a game at the Coliseum. Los Angeles beats St. Louis 5–3.

29th Horace Stoneham of the Giants rejects Westinghouse's proposal to televise their games on a non-profit basis.

30th Ted Williams becomes the 10th ML player to get 1,000 extra-base hits. The A's beat Boston 10–4.

MAY

2nd In what nearly turns into a TV war, the Yankees threaten to broadcast their games nationwide if the NL goes ahead with its plans to allow other broadcasts, especially those of the Dodgers and Giants, into New York territory.

4th Light-hitting OF Roman Mejias of the Pirates hits 3 HRs in the opener with San Francisco to lead Pittsburgh to a 6–2 win. The Giants win the nitecap 4–3 in 10 innings.

5th Going into the bottom of the 9th, the Giants trail Pittsburgh 11–1, but rally for 10 runs. Giants rookie 1B Orlando Cepeda's 3rd HR in 3 games ends the scoring, and pinch hitter Don Taussig pops out with the bases loaded to end the game.

6th Giant Mike McCormick, 19, shuts out Pittsburgh 7–0 on 3 infield singles. Orlando Cepeda's first-inning HR helps put the game away.

7th Pirates Bob Skinner, Ted Kluszewski and Frank Thomas hit HRs in the 5th inning at Seals Stadium, but the Giants win 8–6.

8th The Pirates acquire P Bob Porterfield from Boston.

9th The Tigers pick up P Herm Wehmeier from the Cards for cash.

11th Washington P Truman Clevenger gets both the assist and the putout in retiring batter Elston Howard when he is hit by a line drive and the ball bounces off his leg into foul territory near 1B. Clevenger then covers 1B to receive the toss from 1B Norm Zauchin.

12th Willie Mays hits the first grand slam in the history of the San Francisco Giants and adds another HR as Los Angeles loses 12–3.

13th With his pinch double in Wrigley Field off Moe Drabowsky, Stan Musial of the Cardinals becomes the 8th hitter in history to get 3,000 hits. The Cards win 5–3.

Willie Mays goes 5-for-5 against the Dodgers, as the Giants win 16–9. Mays has 2 HRs, 2 triples, and 4 RBI to compete with Daryl Spencer's 2 HRs, triple, double, and 6 RBI.

18th The Indians' Carroll Hardy pinch-hits for Roger Maris and smacks a 3-run HR off Billy Pierce to pace the Tribe's 7–4 win. Hardy will pinch-hit for Ted Williams in 1960.

20th The Cards trade SS Alvin Dark to the Cubs for relief P Jim Brosnan.

30th Cubs Walt Moryn hits 3 HRs in the 2nd game at Wrigley Field as the Cubs sweep the Dodgers 3–2 and 10–8.

31st Braves Hank Aaron, Eddie Mathews, and Wes Covington homer in succession off Ron Kline of the Pirates in an 8–3 win. The same trio hit successive HRs on June 26th last year.

JUNE

2nd Brooks Robinson, in a 2–1 Orioles loss to the Washington Senators, hits into the first triple play of the record 4 of his career.

Yankee P Whitey Ford fans 6 in a row to tie an AL record as he shuts out the White Sox 3–0.

3rd The Dodger referendum passes by a slim margin 24,293 votes. The proposition allows the city to sell 300 acres of Chavez Ravine to the Dodgers for their stadium. The NL president had stated that the Dodgers should vacate Los Angeles if the bill failed.

6th Ozzie Virgil, acquired from the Giants in January, becomes the first black player to appear in a Tiger game. He goes 1-for-5 in the 11–2 win over Washington.

The Little League announces that 4 foreign teams will play in its World Series.

8th Moe Drabowsky of the Cubs beats the Pirates 4–0. Ted Kluszewski's double in the first is the only Pittsburgh hit.

10th The Tigers fire manager Jack Tighe, replacing him with Bill Norman.

13th In a home game between his Columbus (GA) Foxes and the Graceville Oilers (Alabama-Florida League), Tom Kanapky hits HRs in the 6th, 7th, and 8th innings to lead a 22–3 romp. He finishes with 5 hits.

14th P Shoichi Kaneda of the Kokutetsu Swallows wins 7–1 over the Yomiuri Giants, his 28th victory in only 70 days. He wins 20 games or more for his 8th consecutive season.

The Cardinals obtain P Sal Maglie from the Yankees for Joe McClain and $25,000.

15th Yankee killers Jim Bunning and Frank Lary sweep New York 2–0 and 3–0 in a Detroit twin bill.

On the last day of trading, the Yanks send 1954 Rookie of the Year P Bob Grim and OF/1B Harry "Suitcase" Simpson to the Athletics for P Virgil Trucks and RHP Duke Maas. The Tigers trade P Bob Shaw and 1B Ray Boone to the White Sox for OF Tito Francona and P Bill Fischer.

The Indians trade OF Roger Maris, 1B Preston Ward, and LHP Dick Tomanek to the Athletics for 1B Vic Power and SS Woodie Held.

Dick Donovan and Jim Wilson of the White Sox sweep the Orioles 4–0 and 3–0 in a double header. Wilson allows only 2 hits.

16th The Cincinnati Reds acquire Dodger P Don Newcombe.

17th Tigers 3B Ozzie Virgil goes 5-for-5 against Washington as Detroit wins 9–2.

19th The University of Southern California wins the College WS in Omaha, defeating the University of Missouri 8–7 in 12 innings. It is their first of 10 titles under coach Rod Dedeaux.

Early Wynn of the White Sox hurls a 2-hitter in beating Boston 4–0.

21st White Sox lefty Billy Pierce hurls a 2-hitter against the Orioles, winning 2–1.

22nd A game between Olean (New York-Penn League) and Erie is rescheduled from 7:00 P.M. to 4:00 P.M. The Erie Sailors arrive at the Olean ball park 50 minutes after the 4:00 P.M. starting time, and the umpires forfeit the game to Olean.

23rd Carl Willey of the Braves pitches a 7–0 shutout against the Giants in his first ML start. Willey gives up 6 hits, including Willie Mays's 1,000th career hit. Willey is relieved by Don McMahon who becomes the first pitcher to be driven to the mound, when a motor scooter with sidecar delivers him from the bullpen.

26th Hector Lopez of the Kansas City Athletics hits 3 HRs in a 8–6, 12-inning home win against Washington.

Joe Gordon replaces Bobby Bragan as manager of the Cleveland Indians, signing a contract through 1959.

The Braves fall to the Dodgers 4–1 and cut their lead over St. Louis to 1½ games.

27th Billy Pierce of the White Sox retires 26 Washington Senators in a row before pinch-hitter Ed Fitzgerald loops a double for the only base runner. Pierce wins 3–0.

29th Del Ennis of the Cards throws out 2 Phillie runners from LF in the 8th inning, tying a ML mark, but the Phils win in 13 innings 5–4.

JULY

1st The Cubs Tony Taylor hits a ball inside the 3B line that falls into the rain gutter in fair territory at Wrigley Field. San Francisco rookie OF Leon Wagner chases the ball, but is fooled by Cubs relief pitchers staring intently under the bench. Wagner does not look for the ball in the gutter 40 to 50 feet further down. Taylor reaches home on the hit.

2nd The Dodgers split a doubleheader with St Louis, winning 3–2 before dropping the nightcap 6–4. A crowd of 66, 485 see the game at the Coliseum. This puts the Dodgers over the one million mark in just 35 home dates.

ML baseball reinstates 1B Ed Bouchee of the Phils, who was suspended on a morals charge.

6th Cubs pitchers Dick Drott and Don Elston combine on a 1-hit, 6–2 win over the Dodgers. Jim Gilliam's' single in the 7th is the only Los Angeles safety.

With the bases loaded in the 9th inning, Cards reliever Larry Jackson hits Jim Davenport with a pitch to hand the Giants a 5–4 win. In the same situation the

day before, Jackson walked Willie Kirkland to lose 5–4.

7th At the NL meeting, William Shea outlines plans for a $12 million stadium at Flushing Meadows, the eventual site of Shea Stadium.

NL President Warren Giles appoints a committee to study the possible expansion of the league to 10 teams.

8th The AL edges the NL 4–3 in the All-Star Game played at Baltimore's Memorial Stadium. The Yankees Gil McDougald singles to score Boston's Frank Malzone with the deciding run. Billy O'Dell of San Francisco pitches perfect ball for 3 innings and gets the save. This is the first All-Star Game played without an extra-base hit.

Senator Carl Mundt offers legislation to curb franchise shifts.

10th P Lew Burdette of Milwaukee hits 2 HRs and beats the Dodgers 8–4.

12th Orlando Cepeda's 3-run HR off Spahn gives the Giants a 5–3 win and pulls San Francisco to within a half game of the Braves.

13th Orlando Cepeda's 3rd HR in 3 days and Felipe Alou's run-scoring hit in the 9th, give the Giants a 6–5 win over the Braves. San Francisco now leads the Braves by ½ game.

14th Superior Court Judge Praeger voids the Chavez Ravine pact, stating the city cannot sell its land to private concerns. Los Angeles will appeal Judge Praeger's ruling.

16th P Jack Harshman of the Orioles hits 2 HRs in a 6–5 win against the Sox in the nitecap of a doubleheader.

19th The Yanks Norm Siebern has his 2nd 5-hit game of the month, against the Athletics, as New York loses 6–4.

The Red Sox beat the Tigers 7–6 in 12 innings at Fenway Park on a Ted Williams HR.

20th Jim Bunning of the Tigers pitches a 3–0 no-hitter over the Red Sox and fans 12. Only 2 walks and a hit batsman mar Bunning's performance as he wins his 6th game in 7 decisions (8-6). In game 2, Ike Delock wins his 10th straight, 5–2.

22nd   The Phillies replace manager Mayo Smith with Eddie Sawyer, who had managed the club 1948-52.

23rd   Dodger Norm Larker hits a ball just inside the 1B line, which the Pirates believe to be foul. When umpire Vic Delmore signals it fair, P Bob Porterfield picks up the ball from where it had rolled into the bullpen. Though not playing, Porterfield is ejected for intentional interference with a ball in play. Larker is safe on 2B. The Dodgers still lose 11–3 in the double-header opener and are now in last place.

24th   Ted Williams is fined $250 for spitting at the Boston fans again.

28th   For the 6th time in his career, Mickey Mantle hits HRs from both sides of the plate. New York beats the Athletics 14–7.

29th   Ted Williams hits his 17th career grand slam, tying him for 2nd place with Babe Ruth, and behind Lou Gehrig, who had 23. Williams also added a 3-run HR, as Boston beats Detroit 11–8.

AUGUST

10th   In the nightcap of a doubleheader against the Reds, Pirates CF Bill Virdon records 2 assists in the 7th, tying a ML mark. The Reds win 4–3.

14th   Vic Power steals home in the 8th inning and again in the 10th to give the Indians a 10–9 win over Detroit. Power becomes the first AL player since 1927 to steal home twice in the same game. He will have only 3 steals all season.

Manager Birdie Tebbetts of the Reds resigns. Jimmy Dykes takes over as interim manager.

16th   Pirates Frank Thomas clouts 3 consecutive HRs in a 13–4 pasting of the Reds. Pittsburgh is now 7 games behind Milwaukee.

19th   In an oddity, each starting player of the Douglas Copper Kings team hits a HR in a 22–8 rout of the Chihuahua Dorados (Arizona-Mexican League).

22nd   Cleveland Indians Chairman William Daley rejects a $4 million bid for his team

Monterrey, Mexico repeats as Little League WS champions, beating the Kankakee, IL, Yankees 10–1. Hector Torres pitches a 3-hitter for the victory.

23rd   Dodgers P Don Drysdale hits 2 HRs in a 10–1 clipping of the Cards. Veteran Gil Hodges hits the 14th grand slam of his career, a new NL record. It is also the first slam in the history of the Dodgers on the West Coast.

27th   Owner Clark Griffith says that the Senators will probably accept a good offer from Minneapolis/St. Paul, if one is made.

President Dwight D. Eisenhower says that the Senators should improve the team and stay in Washington, DC.

The Braves Bob Trowbridge walks Orlando Cepeda with the bases full in the 12th to give the Giants a 4–3 win. It is the Giants first win in the past 9 games against the Braves.

28th   White Sox 2B Nellie Fox sets a record for consecutive games without striking out (98).

30th   The Orioles Dick Williams plays all 3 OF positions without a single PO or assist in a 7–2 win against Boston.

SEPTEMBER

2nd   Minneapolis announces a $9 million bond issue to improve Metropolitan Stadium.

8th   The Pirates RF Roberto Clemente hits 3 triples in a 4–1 win over Cincinnati.

9th   Athletics 1B Preston Ward hits 3 HRs in a row in an 8–6 win against Baltimore.

11th   Orioles manager Paul Richards lists 3 pitchers in his starting line-up, hoping for a scoring chance in the first inning, at which point he can remove the extra pitchers for a batter of his choice.

12th   The Giants sweep the Phillies 5–2 and 19–2 as Mays has 6 hits to raise his average to .333. Jim Davenport tops him with 7 hits, including a inside-the-park HR in the first inning of game 2, and scores 7 runs.

13th   The Braves Warren Spahn becomes the first lefty to win 20 or more games 9 times, as he beats St. Louis 8–2. Eddie Plank and Lefty Grove each won 20 games 8 times.

14th   The Yankees win their 24th pennant, and 9th under Casey Stengel. This ties Casey for first with Connie Mack for the most AL pennants won.

16th Yankee killer Frank Lary of the Tigers is the 3rd pitcher to beat them 7 times in the same season, as the lefty defeats them 4–2. Ed Walsh (9-1 in 1908) and Ed Cicotte (7-1 in 1916) were the others.

Former AL batting champion George Stirnweiss is killed in a train wreck in Red Bank, NJ.

20th The Orioles P Hoyt Wilhelm, in a rare start, pitches a 1–0 no-hitter against Don Larsen of the Yankees, fanning 8. The Orioles acquired Wilhelm in August for the $20,000 waiver price. The win, Wilhelm's first ML complete game, improves his record to 3-10.

The Giants Ruben Gomez gives up 3 hits, all to Bobby Gene Smith, as the Giants beat St. Louis 5–1. Willie Mays's 3 hits raises his average to .340, and he steals his 30th base.

21st The Cubs 1B Dale Long, a lefty, catches in the 9th inning in a 2–1 loss to the Dodgers.

22nd P Ronnie Kline of the Pirates fans 5 times in a 14-inning game, as his opponents, the Phillies, strike out 21 Bucs. In the 2nd game of the doubleheader, the Phillies Jack Sanford fans 6 Bucs in a row to help his team fan 10 for the game, and a record 31 for the day.

AL President Will Harridge will fine Ted Williams for a bat-throwing incident during Boston's 2–0 win over Washington. After fanning in the 6th, Williams flings his bat into the stands hitting Boston GM's housekeeper, Gladys Heffernan, in the face. She is not badly hurt, and Williams is very apologetic.

23rd For the 2nd time in 1958, P Jack Harshman of the Orioles hits 2 HRs, in a 3–2 win over the Senators.

26th Corpus Christi (Texas League) agrees not to use black players in the Dixie Series with the Southern Association.

28th Ted Williams wins the AL batting title with a .328 mark, edging out teammate Pete Runnels by 6 points. Williams goes 2-for-4 against Washington and Pedro Ramos while Runnels is hitless. Williams hit .403 in his last 55 games.

Two sons of Hall of Famers shine in the White Sox' 11–4 win over Kansas City. Chuck Lindstrom, son of Fred, walks his first time up, then triples in his only ML at bat after being tipped off to the pitch by catcher Frank House. Pitcher Hal Trosky, Jr., making his 2nd ML appearance, relieves in the 6th for the win. It is the last appearance for both players.

29th In a race that goes down to the last game, Richie Ashburn wins the NL batting title with a 3-for-4 day that raises him to .350, 3 percentage points ahead of Mays, despite Willie's 3 hits in the Giant's 7–2 win over St. Louis.

In a 10-inning 6–4 Phillies win in Pittsburgh, the Phils Dave Philley sets a ML record by getting his 8th consecutive pinch hit.

The Cardinals fire manager Fred Hutchinson (69-75 and a 5th-place finish), replacing him with Solly Hemus, who will be a player-manager. Hemus was just acquired from the Phillies for Gene Freese.

Minneapolis (American Association) wins the Little WS, defeating the IL champs, the Montreal Royals, in 4 straight games. This is the 4th time in a row the AA has won the title.

Mayo Smith signs as the new Reds manager, replacing Birdie Tebbetts, who was fired August 14th.

OCTOBER

1st In the WS, the Braves pick up where they left off the previous year, defeating the Yankees behind Warren Spahn 4–3 in 10 innings.

2nd The Braves erupt for 7 runs in the first and go on to defeat the Yankees 13–5. Lew Burdette is shaky but beats New York for the 4th consecutive time. He also chips in with a 3-run HR.

4th Yankee pitchers Don Larsen and Ryne Duren combine for a shutout as New York wins 4–0. Yankee OF Hank Bauer accounts for all 4 runs, including a 2-run homer in the 7th.

A Tokyo schoolboy star named Sadaharu Oh is signed by the Yomiuri Giants for a bonus of ¥13,000,000 (about $55,000). Oh will become one of the most famous players in baseball, setting many world hitting records.

The Sporting News names Washington OF Albie Pearson and Yankee P Ryne Duren as its AL Rookies of the Year; the Giants 1B Orlando Cepeda and P Carl Willey of the Braves as its NL Rookies of the Year.

5th Milwaukee goes up 3 games to one with a 3–0 shutout by Warren Spahn, who allows just 2 hits. The Braves stop Hank Bauer's 17-game WS hitting streak, dating back to 1956.

6th The Yankees finally solve Lew Burdette, scoring 6 runs in the bottom of the 6th and winning 7–0 behind the 5-hit pitching of Bob Turley.

7th The Yanks pull even at 3 games, as Hank Bauer hits his 4th HR of the Series and New York wins 4–3 in 10 innings.

8th The Yankees win the WS handily on Moose Skowron's 3-run HR off Lew Burdette in the 8th that puts the game on ice 6–2. Eddie Mathews strikes out for the 11th time, a record that will stand until 1980 when broken by Willie Wilson of Kansas City. The Braves' 53 strikeouts are also a new WS record. This is Casey Stengel's 7th championship, tying him with Joe McCarthy for the most Series won.

9th Twenty members of the Cardinals embark on an Asian goodwill tour, stopping in Manila and Tokyo.

13th The commissioner fines 22 Milwaukee players $50 each for divulging their WS share.

The ML fines Yankees P Ryne Duren $250 for giving the "choke" sign to an umpire during the WS.

21st P Kazuhisa Inao posts his 4th consecutive win in the Japan Series to bring the Nishitetsu Lions to a dramatic win after losing the first 3 games to the Yomiuri Giants.

NOVEMBER

5th Lee MacPhail becomes GM of the Baltimore Orioles.

11th The AL announces that Kansas City will play 52 night games in 1959, a new league mark.

12th The Yankees Bob Turley wins the Cy Young Award, gathering 5 votes to 4 for last year's winner, Warren Spahn.

13th Mayor Robert Wagner of New York announces preliminary plans for a 3rd ML. Chairman William Shea, of what will become the Continental League, says it is apparent that the NL is going to ignore New York City. He implies that the new league will be free to raid ML rosters.

18th In a power struggle that has been brewing for some time within the Cleveland Indians organization, minority stockholders, led by Hank Greenberg, sell their stock to the majority stockholder, Chairman William Delay, who controls about 34 percent of the stock.

Red Schoendienst of the Braves is diagnosed as having tuberculosis.

20th The Tigers trade Billy Martin and RHP Al Cicotte to Cleveland for relief P Ray Narleski and Don Mossi and SS Ossie Alvarez.

25th The BBWAA names Chicago Cubs slugger Ernie Banks the 1958 MVP. Willie Mays is the runner-up.

26th The AL MVP is Boston slugger Jackie Jensen, winning over New York's Bob Turley and Cleveland's Rocky Colavito.

28th The AL announces that its Opening Day game in 1959 will be the earliest date ever, April 9.

30th Italian baseball commissioner Prince Borghese visits the U.S. to seek aid in organizing Italian teams.

DECEMBER

2nd IL President Frank Shaughnessy reports that club owners are sympathetic to player demands for a pension plan, but says there is no way that $250,000 can be raised to start one.

NL President Warren Giles says he doubts New York City will get a franchise for several years. He says the NL will reject expansion now, even if assured of a stadium and financial backing.

3rd AL President Will Harridge announces his retirement.

The Giants trade P Ruben Gomez and C Valmy Thomas to the Phils for P Jack Sanford. Sanford will win 24 games in 1962 while leading the Giants to a pennant.

The NL reelects Warren Giles to a new 5-year term.

4th The American Association expands to 10 teams by admitting Houston, Dallas, and Fort Worth from the Texas League. This effectively denudes the Texas League, leaving it with 5 teams and a vacancy.

The Dodgers trade OF Gino Cimoli to the Cardinals for OF Wally Moon and RHP Phil Paine.

5th The Phils, under pressure provided by the Yankees' threat to broadcast into their territory, drop any plans for 1959 broadcasts to New York City. The Cards and Pirates follow suit.

10th The University of Pittsburgh agrees to buy Forbes Field from the Pirates and lease it to them for 5 years, or until a new municipal stadium is built.

1959

JANUARY

13th State Senator Joseph W. Cowgill introduces a bill to build a stadium in Camden to induce the nearby Phillies to move to New Jersey. This effort is based on statements by Phillies owner Bob Carpenter that he is thinking of moving the team unless he gets a new stadium.

John Quinn resigns as GM of the Braves and immediately accepts a similar post with the Phillies.

15th The Texas League votes to issue automatic intentional walks instead of throwing 4 wide pitches.

19th The Players Association orders IL members not to sign a pact unless it includes their pension plan.

30th The Cincinnati Reds trade C Smoky Burgess, P Harvey Haddix and 3B Don Hoak to the Pirates for 3B Frank Thomas, RHP Jim Pendleton, OF Johnny Powers, P Whammy Douglas, and cash.

31st Joe Cronin, former Senators and Red Sox SS signs a 7-year pact to become head of the AL.

Caribbean countries agree to use native players in winter ball, no matter how many years they have played in the U.S.

FEBRUARY

1st Zack Wheat, Dodger favorite of the teens and twenties, is unanimously elected to the Hall of Fame by the 11-member veterans committee.

7th White Sox President Mrs. Dorothy Rigney agrees to sell the team to Bill Veeck for a reported $2.7 million. Chicago insurance broker Charles O. Finley allows that he can match the price.

9th Frank D. Lawrence, owner of the Portsmouth, VA, club, files a $250,000 suit against Commissioner Ford Frick and ML baseball for breach of contract, alleging that broadcasts of ML games effectively forced him out of business.

17th The Yankees invite Australian cricket player Norman O'Neill for a tryout at SS. U.S. Davis Cup captain Billy Talbert, while playing tennis in Australia, arranges the deal after hearing of O'Neill's prowess.

MARCH

6th Charlie Comiskey loses his bid to stop the sale of the White Sox to Bill Veeck.

10th Dorothy Comiskey Rigney, granddaughter of the Old Roman, sells her 54 percent ownership in the White Sox to Bill Veeck's syndicate for $2.7 million. Brother Chuck fails in his attempt to match or improve the bid. Comiskey control of the franchise ends after 60 years.

11th The Players Association drops its threat of a strike against the International League.

23rd The Giants send OF/1B Bill White and 3B Ray Jablonski to St. Louis for P Sam Jones.

31st In a trade that helps neither team, Milwaukee trades P Gene Conley, IF Joe Koppe and IF Harry Hanebrink to the Phillies for C Stan Lopata, SS Ted Kazanski and P Johnny O'Brien.

APRIL

7th In an effort to protect its players, Little League moves its pitcher's mound 2 feet back, from 44 to 46.

9th In the 5th against Washington, the Orioles become the first team in history to turn a triple play on Opening Day. Vice President Richard Nixon, a righthander, substitutes for President Dwight D. Eisenhower and watches the Senators win 9–2.

10th Chicago 2B Nellie Fox gets 5 hits in 7 at bats on Opening Day in a 14-inning 9–7 win in Detroit.

11th Don Drysdale hits his 2nd Opening Day HR to become the only pitcher to have 2 career HRs on Opening Day. Unfortunately, his HR is the only Dodger score as he loses to the Cubs 6–1.

Herbert E. Tucker, president of the Boston NAACP, seeks a probe of the Red Sox for alleged discrimination when the team farms out its only black ball player, "Pumpsie" Green. Tucker cites a 12-year history of discrimination toward blacks.

14th The Dodgers set a new night-game record when 61,552 fans pay to see them play in Havana.

Cuban Premier Fidel Castro opens the International League season by tossing out the first ball.

15th William Shea confers with Phillies owner William Carpenter on the possibility of shifting the Phils franchise to New York City.

P Bob Grim of the Athletics hits a grand slam off Barry Latman, as the A's nip the White Sox 10–8.

16th Phillie Dave Philley, who ended 1958 with 8 consecutive pinch hits, starts 1959 with a pinch-hit single in his first AB. Lew Burdette and the Braves win 7–3.

18th Branch Rickey becomes president of the Continental League. He appoints a committee to study problems associated with acquiring players.

Jack Sanford of the Giants allows only a 7th-inning single to Stan Musial in beating St. Louis 8–1.

21st OF Don Demeter of the Dodgers hits 3 HRs, including the game winner in the 11th, in the Los Angeles Coliseum in a 9–7 win against the Giants. One of his HRs is an inside-the-park 4-bagger, as he drives in 6 runs.

Stan Musial breaks up another no-hitter. His 7th-inning double off Glen Hobbie is the Cards' only safety in a 1–0 loss to the Cubs.

22nd Kansas City Athletics relief P George Brunet gives up 5 bases-loaded walks and a bases-loaded HBP, as the White Sox score 11 runs on one hit in the 7th. John Callison has the lone hit and Jim Landis makes 2 outs in the strange inning. There are 3 other bases-loaded walks in the game. Kansas City loses 20–6.

23rd After a conference with Fidel Castro, Havana club president Maduro says the team will stay in Cuba despite the political unrest.

26th The Reds Willard Schmidt is twice hit by pitches in the 3rd inning in an 11–10 win over the Braves. Braves pitchers Bob Rush and Lew Burdette do the plunking.

C Gus Triandos of the Orioles, in attempting to catch Hoyt Wilhelm's knuckleball, allows 4 passed balls for a new AL mark. The O's win the 2nd game of the twin bill 3-2. The game sees 10 pinch hitters, a new ML record.

Los Angeles move into first place ahead of the Braves with a 17–11 win over St. Louis. Charley Neal has 5 hits to lead the Dodgers.

Sadaharu Oh of the Yomiuri Giants hits the first of 868 career HRs.

MAY

1st White Sox, 39, P Early Wynn pitches a one-hitter for a 1–0 victory over Boston. He fans 14 and belts a HR in the 8th for the only run.

The ML executive council approves the Players Association proposal for 2 All-Star Games each year.

The White Sox send OF Lou Skizas and LHP Don Rudolph to the Reds for OF Del Ennis.

The Washington Senators start a baseball lecture series for women.

2nd Frank Robinson of the Reds hits for the cycle, in a 16–4 rout of the Dodgers.

3rd Jimmy Dykes replaces Bill Norman as manager of the Tigers, who are 2-15.

Charley Maxwell, restored to the Tigers lineup although batting only .136, hits 4 consecutive HRs in a doubleheader sweep of the Yankees 4–2 and 8–2.

C Hank Foiles of Pittsburgh makes an unassisted DP in a 2–1 loss to St. Louis.

7th The Los Angeles Coliseum is jammed by 93,103, on "Roy Campanella Night" for an exhibition game between the Dodgers and the New York Yankees. This is the largest crowd in ML history. The Yanks win 6–2.

9th Mrs. Dorothy Rigney, her husband John, and Hank Greenberg all resign their posts with the White Sox.

10th The Giants' Jim Hearn comes on in relief to pitch 1⅓ innings against the Pirates. He allows 2 earned runs when the game is suspended, with the Pirates ahead 6–4. Hearn is released before the game is completed in July and is charged with the loss 2 months after his retirement.

In the first game of a doubleheader, Cubs reliever Elmer Singleton defeats reliever Lindy McDaniel of the Cardinals 10–9. In the nightcap, McDaniel is the winner and Singleton the loser 8–7.

Yogi Berra catches his 148th and last game in his streak of errorless games, which includes 950 chances. The Yanks beat Washington 3–2.

11th At Yankee Stadium, Berra ends his errorless streak by making an error in a 7–6 loss to the Indians

13th Warren Spahn becomes the 3rd NL lefty to win 250 games, beating the Cards 3–2.

15th Massachusetts marks the 100th anniversary of the first college baseball game, between Amherst and Williams. Teams reenact the original contest.

19th Bill Veeck planned a promotion day, giving away prizes between innings of today's game against the Tigers. But due to temperatures in the 30's, the Comiskey Park crowd is sparse. Veeck confers with Chuck Comiskey about cancelling and then goes to umpire Bill Summers, who agrees that the game should not be played. Later, Veeck will say that he did not want the game played because of the risk of injuries to players. But he was glad to have someone else take the heat—meaning Summers.

20th The Yankees sink to last place, the first time since 1940, as Detroit drubs them 13–4.

21st Commissioner Ford Frick announces that he foresees the formation of a 3rd league within 5 years.

22nd Baltimore's Hoyt Wilhelm one-hits the Yankees 5–0, with Jerry Lumpe's single in the 8th the spoiler.

23rd The Athletics' Bud Daley beats the White Sox 16–0, keeping Chicago a ½ game behind Cleveland, a loser to Detroit 6–4.

25th Buffalo seeks membership in the Continental League.

26th In a singular performance, Harvey Haddix of the Pirates pitches a perfect game against Milwaukee for 12 innings, only to lose in the 13th. Felix Mantilla opens the last inning by reaching base on an error. A sacrifice and an intentional walk to Hank Aaron brings up Joe Adcock, who hits one out of the park in right-CF for an apparent 3–0 victory. Aaron pulls a "Merkle," leaving the field, and Adcock passes him on the basepaths. Both are called out as Mantilla scores. Lew Burdette goes all the way for his 8th win, scattering 12 hits.

At Comiskey Park, a helicopter lands behind 2B before a Sox-Indians game, and four midgets dressed as spacemen jump out. Capturing 5'9" Nellie Fox and 5'10" Luis Aparicio, the spacemen, led by Eddie Gaedel, present the 2 with ray guns. Gaedel reportedly says, "I don't want to be taken to your leader; I already know him."

27th League President Warren Giles rules that the final score of the Harvey Haddix perfect game should be amended to 1–0, since both runners Henry Aaron and Joe Adcock were ruled out—Aaron for leaving the field, and Adcock for passing him in the basepath. Adcock is credited with a double and not a HR.

29th President Dwight D. Eisenhower and his White House staff attend a game. He gets slugger Harmon Killebrew's autograph for his grandson David on a HR ball, as Washington defeats the Red Sox 7–6.

31st Seven pitchers record 23 strikeouts in the Cards-Dodgers game tying the NL mark. Koufax is high with 9 as Los Angeles wins 5–3.

JUNE

1st Two-time champ Monterrey, Mexico is barred from 1959 Little League competition for its failure to comply with the rule that specifies using only players from a predetermined geographical area.

9th Joan Payson, a wealthy investor, is identified as the principal backer of a New York franchise in the proposed 3rd league.

10th Rocky Colavito hits 4 consecutive HRs in Baltimore's Memorial Stadium to lead the Indians to an 11–8 win. Colavito joins Lou Gehrig and Bobby Lowe as the only ML players to hit 4 consecutive four-baggers.

12th Giants P Mike McCormick does not yield a single hit in the first 5 innings of a game against the Phillies. In the top of the 6th, he gives up a hit to Richie Ashburn, but the game is called because of rain. The incomplete inning is not included in the records, thereby giving McCormick a 3–0 no-hitter even though he has given up a hit.

18th At a news conference, the Continental League announces that franchises in the 3rd league will be priced at $100 million.

Oklahoma State wins the NCAA college baseball championship, defeating Arizona 5–3 in the deciding game.

14th Ken Boyer of the Cards hits his 3rd weekly inside-the-park HR, this one against the Reds at St. Louis in a 5–4 first-game win. On May 30 he connected at Los Angeles and June 7 at Philadelphia.

21st Milwaukee's Henry Aaron hits three 2-run HRs at Seals Stadium to power the Braves to a 13–3 win over the Giants.

The Indians take two, 4–2 and 5–4, before 68,680 at Yankee Stadium, to increase the Tribe lead to 2 games over Chicago.

22nd Dodger southpaw Sandy Koufax fans 16 Phillies, to set a new record for a night game, and wins 6–2.

23rd The perceived excessive payments of $650,000 to $1,000,000 for Candlestick Park become an issue in Mayor Christopher's bid for reelection in San Francisco.

26th The "Emperor's game," the greatest in Japanese baseball history, is played by the Yomiuri Giants and the Hanshin Tigers, with Emperor Hirohito and his wife attending at Tokyo's Korakuen Stadium. The game is tied 4–4 in the 7th on Giants rookie Sadaharu Oh's 2-run HR, then won 5–4 in the last of the 9th on a HR by the Giant's Shigeo Nagashima. This starts the famed "O-N cannon," the hitting combination of Oh and Nagashima, that will bring the Giants 9 pennants between 1965 and 1973. In all, the O-N cannon hits dual HRs in 106 games.

27th With the players voting, Henry Aaron gets a unanimous vote for the All-Star Game, making him the first player so selected.

28th The Phils Wally Post becomes the only player in baseball history to twice throw out 2 runners from the OF in one inning. The Giants win 6–0.

30th In Chicago, 2 balls are in play at the same time. On a wild pitch from P Bob Anderson, Stan Musial draws a walk. As the pitch gets by C Sammy Taylor, Musial tries for 2B. In what can only be described as a reflex action, umpire Vic Delmore puts another ball in play by mistake. Taylor promptly throws the ball into CF. 3B Al Dark, who chased down the original ball, throws to SS Ernie Banks, who tags out a confused Musial. After a 10-minute conference, the umpires agree that Musial is out. Delmore will be fired because of the boner.

The Giants Sam Jones throws a 2–0 one-hitter against the Dodgers, allowing only Jim Gilliam's controversial single in the 8th, a grounder SS Andre Rodgers has difficulty picking up. Willie Mays's 2-run HR against Don Drysdale accounts for all the scoring.

JULY

2nd Gene Freese hits his 2nd grand slam of the season, off the Reds Jim Brosnan, as the Phils win 7–6. Newcombe wins the nitecap for the Reds 8–4.

3rd Boston fires manager Pinky Higgins, replacing him with Billy Jurges.

4th Yankee Bob Turley turns in another one-hit masterpiece at Washington. A lazy fly in the 9th by PH Julio Becquer drops in front of LF Norm Siebern for the only Senator safety. SS Tony Kubek goes 8-for-10 in the doubleheader, as the Yanks sweep 10–6 and 7–0.

7th The NL defeats the AL 5–4 in the All-Star Game at Forbes Field in Pittsburgh. Willie Mays knocks in Henry Aaron with the deciding run. Don Drysdale pitches perfect ball the first 3 innings.

9th ML baseball announces that the 1960 season will open one week later than this year in hopes of getting better weather.

Ray Herbert and Johnny Kucks of Kansas City sweep the Tigers 5–0 and 4–0 in a doubleheader.

Two 20-year-old Baby Birds—Milt Pappas and Jerry Walker—shut out the Senators 8–0 and 5–0. The Orioles recall young Brooks Robinson from the minors.

11th New Orleans seeks a franchise in the new Continental League.

12th NBC uses outfield TV cameras with 80-inch lenses to show the catchers' signals during a Yankee-Red Sox game. Commissioner Ford Frick requests that they halt its use.

17th In a dispute with the umpires, Cleveland manager Joe Gordon is ejected. Cleveland OF Minnie Minoso refuses to stand in the batter's box until the argument is over. Umpire Frank Umont calls him out on strikes. The enraged Minoso charges Umont and gets the thumb also. The Indians win 8–7 to stay on the heels of Chicago, 2–0 winners over the Yankees.

21st Pumpsie Green pinch runs for the Red Sox, who become the last ML team to play a black player. The next day Green goes 0-for-3 against Early Wynn.

25th Fidel Castro supporters, enjoying a raucous July 26th Celebration in La Gran Stadium in downtown Havana, bring a halt to the IL contest between the Rochester Red Wings and Havana Sugar Kings with random gunshots from the grandstand. Red

Wings 3B coach Frank Verdi and Havana SS Leo Cardenas both suffer minor flesh wounds, which causes manager Cot Deal to pull his players from the field and retreat to their hotel. League officials cancel the remainder of the Havana team's homestand, and eventually relocating the franchise in Newark for the 1960 season.

27th Organizational committee chairman William Shea announces that the Continental League has definite franchises planned for New York City, Houston, Toronto, Denver, and Minneapolis/St. Paul, with interest in 11 other cities. It envisions beginning play in 1961. New York City says it will build a stadium at the Flushing Meadow Park site.

The Dodgers move into first place on Roger Craig's 2–0 win. Joe Pignatano and Don Zimmer hit solo HRs. A year ago on this date the Dodgers were in last place.

30th In his ML debut, Willie McCovey goes 4-for-4 with 2 triples off Robin Roberts to lead the Giants to a 7–2 win over the Phils. McCovey was hitting .372 with 29 HRs at Phoenix when promoted.

The Southern Association suspends Chattanooga 1B Jesse Levan for life because of his involvement as a go-between for gamblers seeking to fix games. His teammate, Waldo Gonzales, receives a one-year suspension.

The PCL's Portland club sues ML baseball for $1.8 million, citing unfair practices through television that could bring the downfall of the minor leagues. They warn the ML not to start a 3rd league or expand.

31st Earl Wilson, the Red Sox' first black pitcher, makes his first start. He gives up no hits against Detroit in 3⅔ innings and leaves with a 4–0 lead after walking 9.

AUGUST

1st P Bob Purkey of the Reds hits a grand slam off Johnny Buzhardt of the Cubs and wins 8–1.

2nd Jim Bunning of the Tigers pitches the only "perfect" inning of the decade striking out 3 Red Sox on 9 pitches. Bunning wins 3–0.

Billy Bruton of the Braves hits 3 triples in an 11–5 win over the Cardinals. Two of the triples are with the bases loaded.

Giants 1B Willie McCovey hits the first of his 521 ML HRs, off Ron Kline, as San Francisco downs the Pirates 5–3. Johnny Antonelli wins his 15th game.

3rd For the first time, there are 2 All-Star Games in the same year. With the managers picking the starting lineup, the AL wins this 2nd contest 5–3, as five HRs are hit at the Los Angeles Coliseum.

5th The Senators lose 7–3, their 18th loss in a row, before Tex Clevenger shuts out the Indians in the nitecap 9–0.

McCovey hits 2 HRs and Mays another as the Giants whip the Braves Bob Buhl 4–1 to move into first place.

10th Ken Boyer of the Cardinals begins a 29-game hitting streak, the longest since Stan Musial's 30-games in 1950. The Giants score 3 in the 9th to win 3–2.

11th Joe Nuxhall fans 4 Braves in the 6th inning, as the Reds win 4–3 to move into 2nd place.

13th The Giants and Cubs set a record for the longest 9-inning game in history, playing 3 hours and 50 minutes. Chicago wins the marathon at Wrigley by a score of 20–9, pounding out 19 hits and 5 HRs.

14th The Red Sox 1B Vic Wertz hits a pinch-hit grand slam off Ryne Duren of the Yanks to pace the 11–6 Boston win. Pete Runnels of the Red Sox walks twice in the same inning of a game.

Reds teammates Vada Pinson and Frank Robinson go 5-for-6 in the first game of a doubleheader. Cincinnati outlast the Phils 15–13.

18th Branch Rickey resigns as chairman of the Pirates to become president of the Continental League.

19th Honolulu seeks a franchise in the Continental League.

20th The A's Bob Cerv hits 3 HRs in an 11–10 loss to Boston.

22nd The Reds Frank Robinson hits 3 HRs in a row against St. Louis, as the Reds win 11–4.

24th New York City Parks Commissioner Robert Moses allocates $150,000 for a preliminary study on building a stadium.

29th Hamtramck, MI, wins the Little League WS at Williamsport, PA.

31st Sandy Koufax breaks Dizzy Dean's NL mark and ties Bob Feller's ML record of 18 strikeouts in a game against the Giants as 82,974 fans watch. He also totals 31 Ks for 2 consecutive games to set a new ML mark. Wally Moon's 3-run, 9th-inning HR wins it 5–2 for the Dodgers.

SEPTEMBER

5th Jim Lemon of Washington knocks in 6 runs in the 3rd inning, on 2 HRs, tying 2 ML records. Washington scores 10 in the inning to triumph over Cleveland 14–2.

6th Sandy Koufax runs his streak to 41 strikeouts in 3 games, for another new ML record, but loses the doubleheader opener 3–0.

The Dodgers set a record for a Coliseum doubleheader when 39,432 fans show up for 2 with the Cubs. The Dodgers split, losing the 2nd game 5–3, to drop 3 games behind the Giants.

10th Mickey Mantle goes 5-for-6, including a HR, in a 12–1 romp over Kansas City's Ray Herbert.

Brothers Jim and Ed Bailey form the battery for the Cincinnati Reds in the 2nd game of a doubleheader against the Cubs. Jim is charged with the 6–3 loss in his ML debut.

11th The Orioles whitewash the White Sox twice 3–0 and 1–0. Jack Fisher and Jerry Walker hurl the shutouts.

The Phillies Robin Roberts beats the Giants 1–0 on a 3-hitter. Roberts also gains revenge on Willie McCovey by ending McCovey's consecutive-game hitting streak at 22 games. Phils CF Richie Ashburn holds the rookie record of 23 games.

Los Angeles defeats Pittsburgh and Elroy Face 5–4. It is Face's first loss after 22 straight wins, 17 of them in 1959. He will end the year at 18-1.

12th Sam Jones's 20th victory of the season, 9–1 over the Phillies, puts the Giants back in first place by a game.

13th Glen Hobbie of the Cubs stops Ken Boyer's hitting streak at 29 games. He was 41-for-117 for a .350 mark over the course of his streak. Hobbie allows just 4 hits in shutting out the Cards 8–0.

The Braves Red Schoendienst returns to the line-up for the first time since being diagnosed as suffering from tuberculosis last November.

15th Carl Yastrzemski plays for Minneapolis (AA), but the game is protested by Omaha because Yaz is not eligible to play until OF Lee Howell leaves for military duty on the 18th.

Dodger SS Maury Wills goes 5-for-5 in a 10-inning, 8–7 win over the Braves. The Dodgers tie the Braves for 2nd, 2 games behind the Giants.

The Giants whip Warren Spahn and the Braves 13–6 behind Jack Sanford. Willie Mays has 4 hits and 5 RBI. The Giants are now 2 games in front with 8 to play.

20th The Giants play their last game in Seals Stadium before moving to Candlestick Park, losing to Los Angeles 8–2. The Dodgers sweep the series and drop the Giants from first to 3rd. The Braves are in 2nd, a half game back.

21st The Braves Warren Spahn notches his 20th win, 8–6, and his 266th NL victory to tie Eppa Rixey of the Phils and Reds for the career high in wins by a lefthander. The Braves and the Dodgers are now tied for the lead in the 3-team pennant race.

22nd The "Go-Go" White Sox clinch their first pennant in 40 years with a 4–2 win over the 2nd-place Indians. Early Wynn gets the win, with Gerry Staley saving the game in the 9th.

23rd The Cubs continue to dash the Giants' pennant hopes as Cal Neeman's 10th-inning HR gives Chicago a 9–8 win. The Cubs won the day before 5–4, on George Altman's 9th-inning, 2-run HR.

24th The Phillies P Humberto Robinson says that gambler Harold Friedman offered him $1,500 to throw a game with the Reds. The pitcher ignores him and hurls a 7–2 win. Friedman is held on bail. Commissioner Ford Frick later commends Robinson for promptly reporting to him.

26th At Milwaukee the Braves beat the Phillies 3–2 behind Warren Spahn's 21st win. He is now ahead of Eppa Rixey as the winningest NL lefty.

The Cubs put the pennant race in a tie by blasting the Dodgers 12–2 at Wrigley. The Cubs tally 18 hits in chasing Johnny Podres.

At St. Louis, Sam Jones pitches a 7-inning no-hitter, but NL President Warren Giles will rule it unofficial after rain wipes out the last 2 innings. But Jones gets credit for his 21st win 4–0 and Willie Mays and Willie McCovey HRs account for the runs.

27th In one of the NL's frequent tight races, the Braves and Dodgers finish in a tie (86-68), with the Giants a close 3rd (83-71). The Dodgers beat Chicago 7–1 while the Braves beat the Phillies 5–2. The Giants drop 2 to the Cardinals, to finish with 7 losses in their final 8 games.

28th In the first game of a best-of-3 playoff, the Dodgers beat the Braves 3–2 in a cold Milwaukee drizzle. Rookie Larry Sherry pitches 7⅔ innings of scoreless relief.

Cubs manager Bob Scheffing resigns and is replaced by Charlie Grimm, who last managed the Cubs from 1932 to 1949.

29th The Dodgers win Game 2 of the playoff 6–5, and take the NL pennant. Los Angeles overcomes a 5–2, 9th-inning deficit to tie the game; they win it in the 12th when Gil Hodges scores from 2nd on Felix Mantilla's off-balance heave past 1B after a difficult chance on Carl Furillo's grounder.

OCTOBER

1st The Go-Go Sox change character at home and hammer the LA Dodgers 11–0 in the first game of the WS, as Ted Kluszewski has 2 HRs and 5 RBI. Early Wynn and Gerry Staley combine for the shutout. Yankee manager Casey Stengel, sitting out only his 2nd Series since 1947, covers the game as a reporter.

Commissioner Ford Frick bars a Chicago auto dealer's plan to give out a free auto for every HR hit by a White Sox player.

2nd In Game 2, the Dodgers score 3 in the 7th to win 4–3 and even up the Series. Charley Neal has 2 HRs for the Dodgers.

4th In Los Angeles The Dodgers win 3–1 behind the pitching of Don Drysdale and Larry Sherry. Carl Furillo's pinch 2-run single in the 7th is the difference. The 92,394 in attendance sets a new WS mark.

The Japanese Baseball Hall of Fame, next to Korakuen Stadium in Tokyo, is dedicated.

5th In Game 4, the Dodgers edge the White Sox 5–4, as Larry Sherry wins in relief of Roger Craig. The Sox tie the game at 4–4 after spotting the Dodgers a 4–0 lead. The previous day's record-crowd is bested by today's attendance of 92,650.

6th White Sox hurler Dick Donovan keeps the Series alive with a splendid 1–0 win over the Dodgers.

Sherm Lollar's DP grounder scores the only run. The attendance mark falls for the 2nd day in a row, as 92,706 fans jam the Coliseum.

8th The Los Angeles Dodgers win 9–3 to take the series in Chicago, again behind Sherry in relief of Johnny Podres. The Dodgers have an 8–0 lead after 4 innings and hold on despite Ted Kluszewski's 3-run HR. The round-tripper gives the slugger a new 6-game RBI record of 10. Chuck Essegian hits his 2nd pinch HR to establish a new record, later equalled by Bernie Carbo of the Red Sox in 1975. Each Dodger receives a record $11,231 winning share. The White Sox get a record $7,275 for losing.

20th Clark Griffith of the Senators says the team will not move the franchise.

21st The Players Association approves 2 All-Star Games in 1960, to be held in Kansas City and New York. The players would like to have them within 4 days of each other.

President Branch Rickey says that a Continental League franchise will be awarded to Buffalo. Montreal, Atlanta, and Dallas/Ft. Worth are still in the running for the remaining 2 slots.

29th The Nankai Hawks of the Pacific League win the Japanese WS by sweeping the Yomiuri Giants 4–0.

Early Wynn of the White Sox wins the Cy Young Award, getting 13 of the 16 votes.

NOVEMBER

4th "Mr. Cub" Ernie Banks wins his 2nd MVP award in a row on the strength of his 45 HRs and 143 RBI. Eddie Mathews finishes 2nd.

12th The White Sox 2B Nellie Fox wins the AL's MVP award. Teammates Luis Aparicio and Early Wynn finish 2nd and 3rd in the voting.

17th William Shea of the Continental League shows sketches of the proposed stadium in New York City with its transparent retractable roof.

Giants slugger Willie McCovey is the NL Rookie of the Year. McCovey gets all 24 votes to make him the 2nd Giant in a row to win the award unanimously.

18th OF Bob Allison of Washington is voted the AL Rookie of the Year. Cleveland's Jim Perry is a distant 2nd.

Kansas City announces that Bob Elliott will be its new manager, replacing the often-ill Harry Craft, who was released at the end of the season.

21st In the first inter-league trade, the Cubs send 1B Jim Marshall and P Dave Hillman to the Red Sox for 1B Dick Gernert.

The Reds trade P Tom Acker to Kansas City for C Frank House.

DECEMBER

5th Representing ML baseball, the Yankees' Yogi Berra visits Italy to present baseball equipment and aid in the sport's development.

7th AL umpires Bill Summers and Ed Rommel retire.

8th AL President Joe Cronin reports that expansion plans are indefinite. Branch Rickey scores him for his indecisiveness.

The Continental League awards a franchise to Atlanta.

11th The Yankees acquire slugger Roger Maris from Kansas City in a 7-player deal that sends P Don Larsen, RF Hank Bauer, 1B Marv Throneberry, and LF Norm Siebern to the Athletics.

The Orioles elect Lee MacPhail as president of the club.

17th In a child-payment hearing related to his divorce, Ted Williams alleges the Red Sox paid him $60,000, not the reported $100,000. He claims his entire yearly income was $83,000.

22nd The Continental League awards its last franchise to Dallas/Ft. Worth.

1960

JANUARY

5th   The Continental League, a proposed 3rd major league, gets an assurance of congressional support from New York Senator Kenneth Keating.

14th   Charles Comiskey, Jr., says Bill Veeck has turned down his offer to buy the White Sox.

16th   Dick Groat scores 14 points, but the football Steelers edge the baseball Pirates 22–20 in overtime in a benefit basketball game.

21st   Stan Musial asks for, and receives, a pay cut from $100,000 to $80,000 a year. Musial says he was overpaid in 1957 and 1958, and his salary should be cut, based on his performance in 1959.

26th   Boston OF Jackie Jensen, 32, announces his retirement from baseball. Jensen will later say, "Looking back, it was foolish to quit. But I thought it would answer my problems [one of which was his great fear of flying]." Jensen will return in 1961 before retiring again for good.

29th   The Illinois Appellate Court says Dorothy Rigney, sister of Charles Comiskey, Jr., was entitled to sell her mother's shares of White Sox stock to Bill Veeck. Her brother brought suit in an effort to gain control of the club.

FEBRUARY

4th   For the 2nd straight year, the BBWAA voters fail to elect a new Hall of Fame member. Edd Roush gets 146 votes, but 202 are necessary for election. Sam Rice (143) and Eppa Rixey (142) are next in line.

The Giants move their offices to Candlestick Park. They will work out of a locker room until the San Francisco facility is completed.

14th   Jim Hearn wins the ML Baseball Players Golf Tournament.

15th   Cienfuegos completes a 6–0 sweep to give Cuba the Caribbean Series championship for the 5th straight year. Camilo Pascual wins 2, including the Series clincher against Puerto Rico.

18th   Walter O'Malley, owner of the Dodgers, completes the purchase of the Chavez Ravine area in Los Angeles by paying $494,000 for property valued at $92,000.

20th   Branch Rickey meets with officials of the proposed Western Carolinas League about pooling talent for Continental League clubs.

23rd   Demolition of Ebbets Field begins. Lucy Monroe sings the National Anthem, and Roy Campanella is given an urn of dirt from behind home plate.

MARCH

9th   Hank Greenberg says efforts to settle the Veeck-Comiskey dispute have failed and that Charles Comiskey refuses to become a minority partner of the Veeck-Greenberg syndicate that controls the White Sox.

13th   The White Sox unveil new road uniforms with the players' names above the number on the back, another innovation by Bill Veeck.

15th   The New Orleans Pelicans cease operation as a member of the Southern Association, and Little Rock replaces them.

24th   Commissioner Ford Frick says he will not allow the Continental League to pool players in the Western Carolinas League as it would violate existing major-minor league agreements.

26th   An Orioles-Reds series scheduled for Havana, Cuba, is moved to Miami by Baltimore chief Lee MacPhail. The Reds, with a farm club in Cuba, want the trip, but the Orioles fear increased political unrest in the area.

APRIL

9th   Black and white fans integrate the stands at City Park Stadium in New Orleans for an Indians-Red Sox exhibition game. Walt Bond hits 2 HRs in Cleveland's 12–8 win.

12th   With 42,269 fans in attendance, the Giants edge the Cardinals 3–1 in the first game at San Francisco's Candlestick Park. Sam Jones pitches a 3-hitter, and Cardinals OF Leon Wagner hits the first HR in the $15 million stadium.

Chuck Essegian's 11th-inning pinch-hit HR beats the Cubs before a record Opening Day crowd (67,550) at Los Angeles. The HR is Essegian's 3rd straight as a pinch hitter, including 2 in the 1959 WS.

In a deal that will haunt the Indians, Frank Lane sends Norm Cash to Detroit for 3B Steve Demeter. Cash will be Detroit's regular 1B for the next 14 years and will hit 373 HRs for them. Demeter will play 4 games for Cleveland.

14th One game into the season, Eddie Sawyer decides he's had it with managing and quits the Phillies. He came to Philadelphia from Toronto (International League) in l948 and has managed no other ML team. Gene Mauch gets the job and begins a 26-year managerial career in the bigs.

16th Sam Jones's no-hit bid is spoiled with 2 out in the 8th by Walt Moryn's pinch HR. The Giants beat the Cubs 6–1.

17th On Easter Sunday, Frank Lane brings AL batting champ Harvey Kuenn to Cleveland and sends co-HR champ Rocky Colavito to Detroit. Colavito, an unparalleled fan favorite in Cleveland, will hit 173 HRs before returning to the Tribe on January 20, 1965. Kuenn will be traded to the Giants after one season.

Eddie Mathews hits his 300th HR, off Robin Roberts, plus a double and triple, as Milwaukee beats Philadelphia 8–4. Only Jimmie Foxx hit his 300th at a younger age.

18th In the AL opener at Washington, a week later than the NL start, President Dwight D. Eisenhower throws out the first ball, then watches Camilo Pascual strike out 15 batters to tie Walter Johnson's record. Boston's only run in a 10–1 loss is a Ted Williams HR.

Cleveland favorite Herb Score, a lefty, is sent to the White Sox for righty Barry Latman.

19th Opening Day in Cleveland takes on added drama as Rocky Colavito makes his debut with the Tigers. He is hitless in 6 ABs and strikes out 4 times. Detroit's Frank Lary and Cleveland's Gary Bell each pitch 10 shutout innings. The Tigers score twice in the 11th, but Jim Piersall's 2-run single off Jim Bunning ties the game. In the 15th, as the ML record for the longest Opening Day game is tied, Al Kaline's 2-run single gives Detroit a 4–2 win.

Before a home crowd of 41,661, Minnie Minoso celebrates his return to the White Sox with a 4th-inning grand slam against Kansas City. Leading off the bottom of the 9th with the score tied 9–9, Minoso hits a solo homer for his 6th RBI.

24th The Yankees score 8 runs against the Orioles before the first out is made, tying an AL record set by Cleveland July 6, 1954, also against Baltimore. The Orioles respond with grand slams by Albie Pearson and Billy Klaus in the 8th and 9th, but New York holds on for a 15–9 triumph.

Lou Berberet's first-inning grand slam off Early Wynn at Detroit is the AL's 3rd of the day, tying the ML record for number of slams on one day in one league. The Tigers beat the White Sox 12–4.

Jimmie Coker's slam for Philadelphia off Ted Wieand of the Reds is the day's 4th. This ties the ML record for most slams in one day, and gives the Phils a 9–5 win.

George Altman of the Cubs earns a "3-ball walk," as umpire Ken Burkhart accidentally counts a balk as a ball in Chicago's game against the Giants.

29th In St. Louis, the Cards crush the Cubs 16–6. Stan Musial plays his 1,000th game at 1B, becoming the first player ever with that many at 2 positions (1,513 in the outfield).

Rio Grande Valley and San Antonio set a new Texas League record by playing 24 innings at San Antonio's Mission Stadium. The Valley Giants score twice in the 24th, ending the 5 hour, 42 minute marathon with a 4–2 win.

30th Pittsburgh has a 10-run 2nd inning in its 8th straight win, 12–7 at Cincinnati.

MAY

1st The Pirates, behind Vern Law's pitching, win their 9th game in a row, 13–2 against the Reds at Cincinnati.

2nd Ron Kline's 7-hitter gives the Cardinals a win and ends Pittsburgh's streak, the club's longest since 1945 for the first-place club. Roy Face issues a bases-loaded walk for his 2nd straight loss.

Playing at a converted football stadium because their own Russwood Park was destroyed by fire, the Memphis Chicks and Birmingham set a Southern League one-game record with 11 HRs, 6 of which clear a RF fence just 204 feet from home plate. Afterward, all drives over the RF fence are declared doubles until home plate can be moved. The Chicks move to Tobey Park in mid-July.

4th When the Cubs pluck Lou Boudreau out of the broadcast booth to replace Charlie Grimm (6-11) as manager, Jolly Cholly takes Lou's chair behind the mike.

The Orioles C Gus Triandos sets ML records with 3 passed balls in one inning (6th) and 4 in one game, but Hoyt Wilhelm, making a rare start, goes 7 innings and gets credit for a 6–4 Baltimore win over the White Sox. Early Wynn records his 2,000th strikeout in a no-decision effort for the Sox.

7th Eddie Bressoud's 3-run HR—a 397-foot, inside-the-park shot off Harvey Haddix—highlights a 6-run rally as the Giants edge Pittsburgh 6–5 at Candlestick Park. San Francisco ties a ML record and sets a NL record by having left just 2 men on base in 2 consecutive games (16 innings), while winning both.

Siblings Larry and Norm Sherry of the Dodgers become the 10th brother battery in ML history. Catcher Norm belts an 11th-inning HR to give his relief-pitching brother Larry a 3–2 win against Philadelphia.

Takehiko Bessho becomes the winningest pitcher in Japan as his Tokyo Giants beat the Hanshin Tigers 6–3. Bessho has 302 wins, one more than Victor Starfin.

10th Joe Ginsberg of the Orioles loses a struggle with Hoyt Wilhelm's knuckler, and ties the record set 6 days earlier by teammate Gus Triandos with 3 passed balls in one inning. Dick Williams of the A's belts a grand slam, as the AL mark of 3 on one day in one league is tied for the 2nd time in 16 days. Williams also doubles in a 9-run 5th inning. Kansas City beats Baltimore 10–0.

Grand slams by Red Sox teammates Vic Wertz and Rip Repulski at Fenway Park give Boston a 9–7 win over Chicago. Repulski's 8th-inning shot off Don Ferrarese is his first AL at bat.

13th Mike McCormick's shutout of the Dodgers is the 3rd straight by San Francisco pitchers, following 2-hitters against Philadelphia by Sam Jones and Jack Sanford. The first-place Giants have 7 straight wins.

Pirate Dick Groat becomes the first NL player since Connie Ryan in 1953 to go 6-for-6. Pittsburgh beats Milwaukee 8–2.

Philadelphia suffers its 3rd straight 1–0 shutout, losing to the Reds in Cincinnati. The Phillies, losers of back-to-back 1–0 games in San Francisco, tie the ML record for straight 1–0 losses. Jim O'Toole's win is Cincinnati's 9th straight.

15th Two days after being traded from the Phillies to the Cubs, Don Cardwell pitches a no-hitter. A brilliant, leaping catch of Carl Sawatski's drive by RF George Altman in the 8th inning saves Cardwell's gem. Ernie Banks's HR paces the 4–0 win, the first no-hitter against the Cards since May 11, 1919.

25th George Crowe's ML-record 11th pinch-hit HR, off Don McMahon, gives the Cardinals a 5–3 win over the Braves. Crowe began the season tied with Smoky Burgess and Gus Zernial in career pinch HRs.

27th Pittsburgh acquires 29-year-old lefty Wilmer "Vinegar Bend" Mizell from the Cardinals, along with LF Dick Gray, for minor leaguers Julian Javier and Ed Bauta.

Since there is no rule limiting the size or shape of the catcher's mitt, Baltimore manager Paul Richards combats the passed-ball problem while catching Hoyt Wilhelm (38 in 1959; 11 so far this year) by devising an oversized mitt to gather in Hoyt's fluttering knuckler. It is half again as large as the standard glove and 40 ounces heavier.

28th Casey Stengel is hospitalized with a virus and high fever. He will miss 13 games. New York goes 7-6 under interim manager Ralph Houk.

JUNE

11th The White Sox set an AL record with just 7 assists in a twi-night doubleheader split against the Red Sox. With 2 assists in the first game and 5 in the 2nd, Chicago also sets an AL record for fewest assists in 2 consecutive games.

12th In a record-tying 3 hour and 52 minute, 9-inning game, Willie McCovey's pinch-hit grand slam, the first slam of his career, and Orlando Cepeda's 3-run double pace the Giants to a 16–7 rout of the Braves.

15th Mexico City and Poza Rica combine to hit 12 HRs in one game, a Mexican League record.

17th A 2-run HR off Wynn Hawkins at Cleveland Municipal Stadium makes Ted Williams the 4th player in ML history to hit 500 HRs. The Red Sox win 3–1.

18th The Giants, a big favorite to win the pennant in a preseason poll of writers taken by *The Sporting News*, change managers, replacing Bill Rigney with Tom Sheehan. Horace Stoneham's team is 33-25 and trails only Pittsburgh. At 66 years, 2 months, and 18 days, Sheehan is the oldest rookie manager in ML history.

24th Willie Mays hits 2 HRs, singles, steals home, and makes 10 putouts to lead the Giants in a 5–3 win at Cincinnati. Mays has 3 RBI and 3 runs scored.

26th Hoping to speed up the election process, the Hall of Fame changes its voting procedures. The new rules allow the Special Veterans Committee to vote annually, rather than every other year, and to induct up to 2 players a year. The BBWAA is authorized to hold a runoff election of the top 30 vote getters if no one is elected in the first ballot.

30th Dick Stuart blasts 3 consecutive HRs, as the Pirates split with the Giants. Stuart drives in 7 runs and joins Ralph Kiner as the 2nd Pirate to hit 3 HRs in a game at Forbes Field. Jack Sanford pitches a 3-hit shutout to give the Giants an 11–0 first-game win. With the 11–6 nitecap victory, Pittsburgh is 3 ahead of the 2nd-place Braves.

JULY

1st A first-refusal option for chief minority stockholder H. Gabriel Murphy to buy the holdings of Washington owner Calvin Griffith expires. Murphy will lose 2 court decisions in efforts to keep Griffith from moving the Senators to Minnesota.

4th Mickey Mantle's 3-run first-inning HR off Hal Woodeshick is the 300th of his career. Mantle becomes the 18th player to join the 300 club, but the Yankees drop a 9–8 decision to Washington.

8th The Cuban revolution led by Fidel Castro brings an end to Havana's International League team. The Sugar Kings relocate in Jersey City, marking that city's return to the IL after a 10-year absence. Poor attendance at Roosevelt Stadium prompts the parent Reds to cease the minor-league operation there following the 1960 season.

11th One-hit shutout pitching by Bob Friend and HRs by Ernie Banks and Del Crandall pace the NL to a 5–4 win over the AL at Kansas City's Municipal Stadium in the first of 2 All-Star Games. Friend has notched 2 of the NL's last 3 All-Star wins.

13th Vern Law becomes the 2nd Pirate to win a 1960 All-Star Game, working 2 scoreless innings.

Stan Musial comes off the NL bench and hits his record 6th and last All-Star Game HR. Willie Mays, Ken Boyer, and Eddie Mathews also homer in the 6–0 NL win, the 3rd shutout in All-Star Game history.

15th San Francisco fog plays havoc with a Giants-Dodgers game. Willie McCovey's invisible triple prompts umpire Frank Dascoli to halt play for 24 minutes. Los Angeles wins 5–3.

17th Batting just .244 and not hitting for power, Willie McCovey, 1959 NL Rookie of the Year, is sent down to Tacoma (Pacific Coast League).

18th The NL votes to expand to 10 clubs if the Continental League does not join organized baseball. The new NL clubs would invade CL territories.

19th In his ML debut, Giant Juan Marichal pitches no-hit ball until Clay Dalrymple pinch-hit singles with 2 out in the 7th. Marichal winds up with 12 strikeouts and a one-hit 2–0 win against the Phillies. Marichal is the first NL P since 1900 to debut with a one-hitter.

Roy Sievers' 21-game hit streak, the longest for any player in 1960, ends, but White Sox teammate Luis Aparicio's inside-the-park HR and Billy Pierce's shutout beat Boston 6–0.

21st Robin Roberts pitches his 3rd career one-hitter, and the 3rd one-hitter of the season in new Candlestick Park. Felipe Alou spoils Roberts's no-hit bid in the 5th inning of a 3–0 Philadelphia win. 3B Joe Morgan fields the hit, but falls down and cannot make a throw.

22nd The Yankees purchase 33-year-old P Luis Arroyo from Jersey City (IL). He will be a key to New York's 1960 pennant and a star in 1961.

23rd Kansas City OF Whitey Herzog hits into the only all-Cuban triple play in ML history. The action goes from Washington P Pedro Ramos, to 1B Julio Becquer, to SS Jose Valdivielso.

24th Chicago's 3rd straight win at Yankee Stadium and 8th straight overall, 6–3 behind Billy Pierce, gives the Sox a 2-game lead atop the AL. Eli Grba beats Herb Score 8–2 in the 2nd game to give New York a twin-bill split.

25th The Bucs return to first place as Bob Friend defeats the Cardinals 4–2 in St. Louis. Pittsburgh will remain atop the NL for the rest of the season.

27th William Shea, chairman of Mayor Robert Wagner's New York baseball committee, announces the formation of the Continental League. The 5 founding cities are New York, Houston, Toronto, Denver, and Minneapolis/St. Paul.

30th Philadelphia P Art Mahaffey, called up from Buffalo, picks off the first 2 batters to get hits against him, but St. Louis still wins 6–3.

31st A game between Memphis and Chattanooga (Southern Association) is postponed because the 94-degree weather is too much for the spectators in Memphis's roofless Tobey Field.

AUGUST

2nd In an agreement with the major leagues, the Continental League abandons plans to join the AL and NL. Walter O'Malley, chairman of the NL Expansion Committee, says, "We immediately will recommend expansion and that we would like to do it in 1961." Braves owner Lou Perini proposes a compromise that 4 of the CL territories be admitted to the current majors in orderly expansion. Branch Rickey's group quickly accepts.

3rd Frank Lane trades managers with Detroit's GM Bill DeWitt. The Indians Joe Gordon (49-46) is dealt to the Tigers for Jimmy Dykes (44-52). For one game, until the pair can change places, Jo-Jo White pilots the Indians and Billy Hitchcock guides the Tigers.

4th Believing that Chicago's Jim Brewer is throwing at him, the Reds 2B Billy Martin throws his bat toward the mound. Then, advancing to retrieve it from Brewer, who has picked it up, Martin launches a hard overhand right that fractures the orbital bone of Brewer's right eye. He requires surgery and will be out of action for a month. The Cubs win 5–3.

9th Phillie Tony Taylor ties a ML record for 2B by going an entire doubleheader (18 innings) without a putout, the first to achieve the feat since Connie Ryan of the Phillies, June 14, 1953.

Indians 1B Vic Power's hit ricochets off the top of the RF fence in Cleveland toward Boston OF Lu Clinton. The ball hits Clinton's foot and is "kicked" over the fence. Umpire Hal Smith rules the hit a HR, since the ball never touched the ground.

14th The Pirates sweep a doubleheader from 2nd-place St. Louis to take a 6-game lead in the NL pennant race. Don Hoak's RBI single in the 11th inning gives Pittsburgh a 3–2 win in the nightcap, following a 9–4 win in the opener.

The Yankees lose a doubleheader to Washington and fall to 3rd place in the AL, a half game behind the Orioles and White Sox. P Camilo Pascual's grand slam is the difference in a 5–4 first-game win. In the 2nd, Mickey Mantle, believing there are 2 outs, jogs to 1B on a grounder to 3B. The Senators turn a DP, with New York OF Roger Maris suffering bruised ribs trying to break it up at 2B. Mantle is heavily booed, and Casey Stengel replaces him with Bob Cerv. The clubs set a ML record by using 17 pinch hitters—9 by the Yankees—in a doubleheader (more than 18 innings), and play a record 24 errorless innings.

15th Mickey Mantle's 2 HRs give New York a 4–3 win and first place in the AL. The 2nd HR comes after C Clint Courtney drops a Mantle foul pop-up. Baltimore's loss is only its 2nd in the last 15 games.

18th Facing just 27 batters, Lew Burdette pitches a 1–0 no-hitter against the Phillies. Tony Gonzalez, the only Phil to reach base, is hit by a Burdette pitch in the 5th inning but erased on a DP. The Milwaukee P also scores the only run of the game.

Bob Sprout sets a Midwest League record with 22 strikeouts, and pitches a 7-inning no-hitter as Decatur defeats Waterloo 3–0. The 18-year-old lefty needs a dropped foul ball for his chance at the record. Sprout will pitch just one game in the ML, with the Angels in 1961.

20th Ted Williams draws the 2,000th walk of his career in the Red Sox' split of a twi-night doubleheader with Baltimore. The Splendid Splinter also clouts HRs 514 and 515 in the twin bill.

25th Boston's Vic Wertz's 2nd career slam as a pinch hitter ties the record set by Bill Skowron in 1957. Ted Williams hits his 516th HR in a 10–7 Boston win.

27th After pitching 32⅔ innings without allowing a run, Braves P Lew Burdette gives up a Felipe Alou HR as San Francisco defeats Milwaukee 3–1.

28th In a battle of New York's chief rivals for the AL pennant, Baltimore's Milt Pappas has Chicago down 3–0 in the 8th. An apparent 3-run HR by Ted Kluszewski is nullified because umpire Ed Hurley calls time just before Pappas delivers. O's prevail 3–1 and take over 2nd place, 2 games behind the Yankees.

30th Boston 2B Pete Runnels goes 6-for-7, as the Red Sox edge the Tigers in the 15-inning opener of a twin bill. His 15th-inning double brings Frank Malzone home with the winning run. Runnels has 3 more hits in the nightcap victory. His 6 hits are the most in an AL game since July 8, 1955. With 9 hits in the doubleheader, Runnels ties the ML record.

SEPTEMBER

2nd In the first game of a doubleheader, Ted Williams homers off Don Lee of the Senators. Williams had homered against Lee's father, Thornton, 20 years earlier. Boston sweeps, winning the first 4–1 and the 2nd game 3–2.

3rd A battle of lefthanders features Sandy Koufax of the LA Dodgers against Mike McCormick of the San Francisco Giants. Felipe Alou's HR gives McCormick a 1–0 win, his 2nd 1–0 win against Los Angeles in 1960.

Al Cicotte of the Toronto Maple Leafs (IL) pitches an 11-inning no-hitter against Montreal.

During a game in Baltimore, plate umpire Larry Napp is struck by foul balls 3 times. Charley Berry finishes the game behind the plate, as Napp is carried off the field.

4th After a ML record 798 consecutive games at 2B, the White Sox' Nellie Fox is hospitalized with a virus. Fox would have gone 1,072 straight games had manager Marty Marion not rested him on August 5, 1955. Billy Goodman replaces Fox.

6th Pittsburgh's All-Star SS Dick Groat suffers a broken wrist when hit by a Lew Burdette pitch. The Pirates captain will be sidelined until the final weekend of the season. Dick Schofield, his replacement, has 3 hits, as the Bucs rally for a 5–3 win. Roy Face finishes a Pittsburgh win for the 30th time in 1960.

12th A crowd of more than 20,000 sees the first-place Pirates dump the Giants 6–1 and sets a new Pittsburgh home attendance record of 1,521,251—4,230 more than the old mark set in 1948.

13th Eighteen-year-old OF Danny Murphy becomes the youngest Cub to hit a HR, but the Reds win 8–6 in Cincinnati. Murphy will play just 49 games for the Cubs from 1960 to 1962. He will come back as a pitcher for the White Sox in 1969 and 1970.

15th Willie Mays ties the modern ML record with 3 triples in a game against the Phillies. His 3-bagger off Turk Farrell gives the Giants an 8–6 win in 11 innings. Mays also strokes a double and single.

16th Warren Spahn, 39 years old, notches his 11th 20-win season with a no-hitter against the Phillies. Spahn also sets a Milwaukee club record with 15 strikeouts in handing the last-place Phils their 90th loss of the year.

18th Don Zimmer, Ron Santo, and George Altman hit 6th-inning HRs as the Cubs beat the Dodgers 5–2 at Wrigley Field. Chicago's biggest HR threat, Ernie Banks, sets a record by drawing his 27th intentional walk of the year.

The surprising 4th-place Senators fall to a game above .500 when Ted Williams's 2-run HR gives Boston a 2–1 win. A late collapse—15 losses in the final 18 games—will drop Washington to 5th place, but that will still be the club's best finish in 7 years. The club will continue its improvement in Minnesota.

Pittsburgh's Vern Law joins the 20-win circle with a complete-game 5–3 win in the first game of a Sunday doubleheader at Cincinnati's Crosley Field.

20th Boston OF Carroll Hardy pinch-hits for Ted Williams, who is forced to leave the game after fouling a ball off his ankle.

25th For the first time since 1927, the Pirates are headed for the WS. While the Bucs play the Braves, the 2nd-place Cardinals are mathematically eliminated by 20-game loser Glen Hobbie's 5–0 win for the Cubs. A gigantic torchlight victory parade in Pittsburgh's Golden Triangle at midnight celebrates the pennant, despite Pittsburgh's 4–2 loss to the Braves.

Ralph Terry clinches the Yankees' 25th pennant with a 4–3 win over the Red Sox. Luis Arroyo saves the win. It is Casey Stengel's 10th pennant in 12 years at New York.

26th In his final ML plate appearance, against Baltimore's Jack Fisher, Ted Williams picks out a 1-1 pitch and drives it 450 feet into the right-CF seats behind the Boston bullpen. It is Williams's 521st and last HR, putting him 3rd on the all-time list. Williams's HR gives the 7th-place Red Sox a 5–4 victory. Williams stays in the dugout, ignoring the crowd's cheers, but when he trots out to LF in the 9th, he is replaced immediately by Carroll Hardy. The Splendid Splinter retires as a standing crowd roars.

27th   Pancho Herrera's 135th strikeout sets an NL record, even though the Phils beat the Braves 5–3.

OCTOBER

2nd   Washington drops a 2–1 decision to Baltimore in the last game ever played by the original-franchise Senators. Pedro Ramos takes the loss for Washington.

3rd   The Yankees head into the WS with a 15-game winning streak after Dale Long's 2-run 9th-inning HR gives them an 8–7 win over the Red Sox. New York's 193 HRs are an AL record, 3 better than the 1956 Yanks. RBI leader Roger Maris drives in 3 runs, but falls one HR short of Mickey Mantle's league-high 40.

Joe Gordon (26-31) resigns as manager of the Tigers, blaming interference by from club president Bill DeWitt.

5th   In a portent of things to come, Bill Mazeroski's 2-run 5th-inning HR off Jim Coates is the difference as Pittsburgh beats New York 6–4 in its first WS win since 1925. Roy Face survives a 2-run 9th-inning Elston Howard HR to preserve Vern Law's victory.

6th   Mickey Mantle's 2 HRs highlight New York's 16–3 victory at Forbes Field, evening the WS. A 7-run 6th inning overwhelms Pittsburgh.

8th   Bombing continues in the Bronx in Game 3. Yankee Bobby Richardson's 6 RBI, including a grand slam off reliever Clem Labine in a 6-run first inning, and Whitey Ford's 4-hitter give the Yanks a 10–0 win and a 2-1 WS lead, spoiling Pittsburgh manager Danny Murtaugh's 43rd birthday.

9th   Vern Law wins again, thanks to his own RBI single and Bill Virdon's 2-run hit. Roy Face retires the final 8 batters in order. Pittsburgh's 3–2 win evens the WS.

10th   Bill Mazeroski stars again. His 2-run double stakes Harvey Haddix to a 3–0 lead. Roy Face is called on once more for another hitless effort to preserve a 5–2 win and 3-2 WS lead for the surprising Pirates.

11th   Radio-television executive John Fetzer buys a controlling interest of the Tigers, giving one man control of the team for the first time since Walter Briggs died in 1952. He offers club president Bill DeWitt a job as his assistant.

12th   Whitey Ford preserves the Yankees hopes with a 7-hit shutout at Pittsburgh. Bob Friend is bombed again as New York coasts 12–0. Bobby Richardson's 2 run-scoring triples give him a WS record of 12 RBI.

14th   In a 9–9 tie, Bill Mazeroski leads off the last of the 9th and hits what is arguably the most dramatic home run in Series history, off Ralph Terry, to give Pittsburgh a 10–9 win and the World Championship. Despite Maz's heroics, Bobby Richardson is the Series MVP.

16th   The NL votes to admit Houston and New York to the league, the first structural change since 1900.

18th   Instituting a mandatory retirement age of 65, New York Yankee co-owners Dan Topping and Del Webb relieve Casey Stengel (1,149-696) as manager. Stengel: "I wasn't retired—they fired me."

20th   Coach Ralph Houk, 41, is named to succeed Stengel. He briefly led the Yankees in 1960 when Stengel was hospitalized.

22nd   The San Francisco Giants lose to their Tokyo counterparts 1–0 in the first of a 16-game exhibition series. They lose again 2–1 to the Japan All-Stars the next day, but finish the series with 11 wins, 4 losses, and one tie.

27th   Trying to jump ahead of the NL, the AL admits Los Angeles and Washington to the league with plans to have the new clubs begin competition in 1961. Calvin Griffith is given permission to move the existing Washington Senators franchise to Minneapolis/St. Paul, MN. League president Joe Cronin says the AL will play a 162-game schedule, with 18 games against each opponent.

31st   The Giants trade IF Andre Rodgers to the Braves for SS Alvin Dark, then sign Dark to a 2-year contract as manager. Dark does not plan to be a playing manager.

NOVEMBER

1st   Balitmore SS Ron Hansen is voted AL Rookie of the Year, getting 22 of 24 votes. The other 2 votes go to teammates Chuck Estrada and Jim Gentile.

2nd   Roger Maris nips Mickey Mantle for the AL's Most Valuable Player award, 225-222, the 2nd-closest vote ever, after the DiMaggio-Williams race in 1947.

Hank Greenberg asks for AL dates at the Los Angeles Coliseum, home of the NL Dodgers. Greenberg and Bill Veeck are expected to run the new LA club in the AL.

George Weiss, recently turned 66, resigns as GM of the Yankees.

3rd Pittsburgh's Vern Law is voted Cy Young Award winner. He outpolls Warren Spahn 8-4.

16th NL batting champion Dick Groat is named league MVP, outpolling Pirate teammate Don Hoak 276-162.

17th The new Washington franchise is awarded to Elwood Quesada, Washington native, W W II hero, and head of the Federal Aviation Agency.

Hank Greenberg drops out of the bidding to run the new AL franchise in Los Angeles.

18th Charlie Finley, 42-year-old insurance tycoon from Gary, IN, makes a formal bid for the new Los Angeles club.

19th Mickey Vernon is hired as the first manager of the new Washington team.

21st Bob Scheffing signs to manage the Tigers after the job is turned down by Casey Stengel.

22nd The AL proposes that both leagues expand to 9 teams in 1961 and begin inter-league play. It will delay entering the Los Angeles market if the NL agrees.

23rd Dodger OF Frank Howard is voted NL Rookie of the Year with 12 of 24 votes.

26th Twins is the appropriate new name chosen for the club transplanted from Washington to the Twin Cities of Minneapolis/St. Paul.

DECEMBER

3rd Cleveland trades OF Harvey Kuenn to San Francisco for OF Willie Kirkland and P Johnny Antonelli.

5th President Joe Cronin suggests that if the NL starts its new New York franchise in 1961, the AL will stay out of Los Angeles until 1962. The NL turned down the suggested compromise of November 22nd because Houston will not be ready in 1961.

6th A group headed by movie star Gene Autry and former football star Bob Reynolds is awarded the new AL Los Angeles Angels. Fred Haney will be GM. Finley withdraws his bid for Los Angeles and offers to purchase control of the Kansas City Athletics.

7th Detroit trades 2B Frank Bolling and a player to be named later (OF Neil Chrisley) to Milwaukee for OF Billy Bruton, 2B Chuck Cottier, C Dick Brown, and P Terry Fox.

14th The Angels and new Senators each select 28 players from a pool of AL talent. Among Los Angeles selections are P Dean Chance, SS Jim Fregosi, 1B Ted Kluszewski, and RF Albie Pearson. Washington selections include P Bobby Shantz, LF Chuck Hinton, OF Gene Woodling, and P Hal Woodeshick.

20th Charlie Finley buys the 52 percent of the A's in the late Arnold Johnson's estate.

21st Cubs owner P. K. Wrigley says Chicago will have no manager, but will use a college of coaches.

23rd Rip Collins is added to Chicago's college of coaches.

1961

JANUARY

1st Briggs Stadium is renamed Tigers Stadium.

3rd Frank Lane quits as GM of the Indians to take the same post with the Athletics.

9th Leo Durocher joins the Dodgers as 3B coach.

The new Minnesota Twins and the American Association finally agree on a $500,000 indemnity payment to the minor league for the Minneapolis/St. Paul territory, ending 2 months of negotiation.

12th Charlie Grimm and Verlon Walker (brother of Rube Walker) are named the 6th and 7th members of the Cubs coaching staff.

24th The A's trade outfielders Whitey Herzog and Russ Snyder to the Orioles for IF Wayne Causey, P Jim Archer, OF Bob Boyd, and OF Al Pilarcik.

28th The International League Board of Directors unanimously votes to move the Montreal franchise to Syracuse, NY.

29th Billy Hamilton and Max Carey are voted into the Baseball Hall of Fame by the Special Veterans Committee.

31st Houston voters approve a bond to finance a luxury domed stadium, the final hurdle standing between the city and ML baseball.

FEBRUARY

7th Jackie Jensen, out of baseball in 1960, signs a $40,000 deal to come back with the Red Sox.

9th Willie Mays signs for $85,000, currently the biggest contract in ML baseball.

16th Charlie Finley purchases the outstanding 48 percent of the Athletics stock to become their sole owner.

MARCH

3rd Frank Robinson is indicted in Cincinnati for carrying a concealed weapon.

14th George Weiss is lured from retirement to become president of the New York Mets.

24th The New York State Senate approves $55 million for a new baseball stadium at Flushing Meadows Park in Queens.

27th In a spring training game Cardinals P Larry Jackson suffers a broken jaw when hit by a fragment of Dodger Duke Snider's broken bat. Jackson will be sidelined 4 weeks.

29th Powel Crosley's will directs the Reds to stay in Cincinnati and be run under nonprofit ownership. The late Crosley's daughter and husband, Stanley Kess, will head the foundation.

31st A Pacific Coast League proposal to use a designated batter for the pitcher is voted down 8-1 by the Professional Baseball Rules Committee. The committee also rules that every club must designate a manager within 30 minutes of game time, a move prompted by the Cubs' college of coaches.

APRIL

3rd Connie Mack Stadium in Philadelphia is sold to J. Schleifer Properties. The park is to be torn down after the 1963 season and replaced by bowling alleys.

6th Vedie Himsl is designated as head coach of the Cubs for the first 2 weeks of the season.

10th The new Washington team loses its first regular-season game 4–3 to the White Sox.

11th Robin Roberts ties Grover Cleveland Alexander's NL record with a 12th-straight Opening Day start, but Philadelphia loses 6–2 to Don Drysdale and the Dodgers.

Ted Kluszewski's 2 HRs highlight the AL Los Angeles Angels first win, as Eli Grba beats Baltimore 7–2.

14th Joe McClain earns the new Senators' first win, defeating Cleveland 3–2.

15th The Dodgers and Pirates tie a ML record by turning 9 DPs (Los Angeles 5, Pittsburgh 4) in a 9-inning 4–1 Buc home win. It is the first time since July 3, 1929, that 9 DPs have been turned in a game.

17th In a 9–5 St. Louis win, Dodger Duke Snider hits his 370th HR, taking 7th place on the all-time list. But the Duke later suffers a broken elbow when hit by Bob Gibson pitch.

23rd Art Mahaffey fans a batter in each inning and 17 in all, a Phillies' record, while beating the Cubs 6–0.

26th Roger Maris hits his first HR of 1961 off Paul Foytack of Detroit, and Mickey Mantle adds HRs from both sides of the plate (for the 8th time), as New York wins 13–10 at Tiger Stadium.

Cincinnati's Jerry Lynch becomes the 6th player in NL history to hit 2 consecutive pinch-hit HRs. This one today is not enough as Chicago wins 3–2.

27th Gabe Paul resigns as GM of the Houston Colt 45s for the same job at Cleveland. He replaces Frank Lane.

28th Five days past his 40th birthday, Warren Spahn becomes the 2nd-oldest ML pitcher (after Cy Young) to hurl a no-hitter, blanking San Francisco 1–0. Hank Aaron drives in the only run off loser Sam Jones. It is Spahn's 290th win and 52nd shutout.

30th Frustrated by a poor start, Jackie Jensen jumps the Red Sox for 8 days.

Using Joey Amalfitano's bat, Willie Mays becomes the 9th player in ML history to enjoy a 4-HR game. His 8 RBI pace the Giants to a 14–4 win at Milwaukee's County Stadium.

Jim Gentile, Gus Triandos, and Ron Hansen hit consecutive HRs in the 2nd inning for the Orioles, as they beat Detroit 4–2 to split a twin bill.

Philadelphia and St. Louis tie a ML record, and set a NL mark, by using 8 pinch hitters in the 8th inning. The Phils finally win in 10 innings 11–7.

MAY

3rd Another brilliant Warren Spahn performance is spoiled when LF Mel Roach's misplay costs the Milwaukee ace a 2nd no-hitter in a row. He settles for a 2-hitter in topping the Dodgers 4–1.

8th The Angels trade P Tex Clevenger and OF Bob Cerv to the Yankees for P Ryne Duren, P Johnny James, and OF Lee Thomas.

9th Jim Gentile becomes the 4th player to hit grand slams in consecutive innings (Tony Lazzeri in 1936, Jim Tabor in 1939, Rudy York in 1946 are the others) when he belts one off Pedro Ramos in the first and adds another off Paul Giel in the 2nd. His 8 RBI in consecutive innings set a ML record. Gentile also

tacks on a sacrifice fly to give him 9 RBI in the 13–5 drubbing of the Twins.

The Indians tie a ML record with just 23 official at bats as Chicago's Herb Score pitches a 2-hit 4–2 win.

10th The Cardinals tie a ML record when 3 pinch hitters strike out in the 9th inning against the Reds. Cincinnati's Bill Henry pitches just the 9th to save the 3–2 win, the Reds' 9th in a row.

12th Bill Monbouquette's 17 strikeouts for the Red Sox are a club record and the most yet by an AL pitcher in a night game. He beats Washington 2–1.

14th Senators pinch hitters tie a ML record by drawing 3 walks in the 9th inning of the 2nd game of a doubleheader against the Red Sox. The Nats edge Boston 2–1.

18th Ray Kendrick ties the California League record with 19 strikeouts in Fresno's 12–3 defeat of Stockton.

Ryne Duren comes in for the Angels and notches 4 strikeouts in the 7th inning against the White Sox. He fans Minnie Minoso, Roy Sievers, J. C. Martin, and Sammy Esposito to tie the ML record. One pitch eludes C Del Rice and results in the winning run. Chicago takes it 6–4.

23rd Norm Cash, Steve Boros, and Dick Brown hit consecutive HRs for the Tigers in a 5–2 win over Minnesota.

28th After losing the first game 14–9 at home to Chicago, the Yankees take the nightcap 5–3 with the help of a Roger Maris HR. Maris's 9th HR of the season is one of 27 hit in today's 7 AL games—a record. Twelve more in 4 NL games make a total of 39, a one-day ML record for 11 games in the 2 leagues.

30th 3B Gene Freese hits 2 HRs, and Joey Jay and the Reds both win their 6th straight game, 8–7. Cincinnati completes a sweep of the Los Angeles, moving into a first-place tie with the Giants. Cincinnati will spend the rest of the season in first place.

Roger Maris, Mickey Mantle, and Moose Skowron each belt 2 HRs, tying the ML record for most players (one club) with multiple HRs in a 9-inning game. New York wins at Fenway Park 12–3.

The Dodgers trade IF Bob Lillis and OF Carl Warwick to St. Louis for IF Daryl Spencer.

JUNE

1st Veteran Vic Wertz hits his first triple in 6 years as he leads the Red Sox to a 7–5 win over Bob Turley and the Yankees. Since June 14, 1955, Wertz has played in 596 games and collected 537 hits, but no 3-baggers.

2nd The Cubs Ernie Banks ties a ML record with 3 run-scoring sacrifice flies in one game. Chicago beats the Reds 7–6.

6th Cleveland's 8th straight win, a 14–3 rout of Washington, moves the Tribe into first place.

Twins manager Cookie Lavagetto is given a week's vacation by owner Calvin Griffith. Coach Sam Mele temporarily replaces Lavagetto.

8th Milwaukee sets a ML record with 4 consecutive HRs in the 7th inning against the Reds. Eddie Mathews and Hank Aaron hit back-to-back HRs off Jim Maloney; Joe Adcock greets reliever Marshall Bridges with another HR, and Frank Thomas sets the record. When these four teammates end their ML careers, they will have hit a combined total of 1,889 homers. For all the bombardment, the Braves lose 10–8.

The Kansas City Athletics hit 3 consecutive triples in a game-deciding, 5-run 3rd inning while trimming the Yankees 9–6 after a first-game loss 6–1.

9th Ryne Duren sets an AL record with 7 straight strikeouts against the Red Sox. He fans 11 batters in a 5–1 win for the Angels.

10th The Braves tie the NL record with 14 HRs in 3 straight games (at least one in each game) as they outscore the Cubs at Wrigley 9–5.

Pitchers Ray Herbert and Don Larsen, 3B Andy Carey, and OF Al Pilarcik of the A's go to the White Sox for pitchers Bob Shaw and Gerry Staley and outfielders Wes Covington and Stan Johnson.

12th An ailing Bill Veeck sells his interest in the White Sox to Arthur Allyn, a minority partner. Allyn also buys Hank Greenberg's stock to acquire a controlling interest. Greenberg remains as GM.

15th Undefeated Ralph Terry's 11-inning 3–2 win at Cleveland moves the Yankees into first place.

16th Detroit's Phil Regan beats New York 4–2 at home, as the Tigers take first place.

Kansas City bonus baby Lew Krausse, Jr., who just graduated from high school, debuts with a 3-hit 4–0 shutout of the Angels before 25,869 fans at Kansas City's Municipal Stadium. His father ended his brief ML career with the Philadelphia A's in 1931 with a shutout.

17th With 2 out and 2 on in the 9th, Mickey Mantle homers into the RF upper deck. Elston Howard follows with a HR, but Detroit hangs on to win 12–10.

18th Pittsburgh takes the first game 5–3 as Don Leppert makes his ML debut with a HR in his first at bat. The Cards salvage a split with a 7–3 nightcap win.

Milwaukee's Hank Aaron, Joe Adcock, and Frank Thomas hit consecutive HRs in a 10–2 triumph at Los Angeles.

Willie Tasby of the Senators and Jim Pagliaroni of the Red Sox swap grand slams in the 9th inning of a lid-lifter at Fenway Park, tying the ML record for slams by 2 teams in one inning. Boston scores 8 runs with 2 out in the 9th for a 13–12 win.

St. Louis Browns midget Eddie Gaedel dies of a heart attack following a mugging in Chicago. He was 36.

19th Charlie Finley makes his first managerial change, booting Joe Gordon (26-33) in favor of Hank Bauer.

23rd Ernie Banks voluntarily takes the bench as a sore knee brings his 717 consecutive-games-played streak to an end.

At home, the Cards win 10–5 over the Giants. With 2 HRs, Stan Musial passes Lou Gehrig on the all-time list for extra-bases hits. Babe Ruth remains first.

Cookie Lavagetto (4-6) is fired as manager of the Twins. Sam Mele again takes control of the club.

Louisville's Howie Bedell's 43-game hit streak ends against Dallas-Fort Worth. Bedell ties the record of Eddie Marshall for the American Association's longest hitting streak.

25th With Vic Power on 1B in the bottom of the 9th, Chuck Essegian pinch-hits a single. Power, thinking it is a HR, waits to shake hands with Essegian, and is forced at 2B.

26th Don DiChiara sets a NYP league record with 4 consecutive HRs in Batavia's 14–9 loss to Jamestown.

27th Gene Green, Willie Tasby, and Dale Long hit consecutive HRs for the Senators, as they trim Cleveland 8–5.

29th With 3 round-trippers at Philadelphia—one a 10th-inning shot to win 8–7—Willie Mays becomes the 4th ML player with 3 or more HRs twice in one season. Manager Gene Mauch's efforts to conceal his starting pitcher and force Al Dark's hand has a Phillie lineup including hurlers Don Ferrarese (batting lead-off, playing CF), Jim Owens (3rd, RF), Chris Short (7th, C), and Ken Lehman (9th, P) against San Francisco. When Dark sends a lefty to the mound, Mauch replaces Ferrarese. Dark then replaces Billy O'Dell with Sam Jones. Mauch replaces Lehman with Dallas Green after 2 batters. All the maneuvering takes 3 hours and 20 minutes.

JULY

6th Solly Hemus (33-41) is fired as manager of the Cardinals and replaced by coach Johnny Keane.

7th Pittsburgh puts Vern Law on the retired list, on doctor's orders, to rest his sore right arm.

9th Sherm Lollar's 9th-inning pinch-hit grand slam for the White Sox crushes Cleveland 7–5. It is the 5th pinch slam in the AL this season and ties the ML record. The Sox also win a 2nd game 9–8. Over the afternoon 8 HRs are hit.

11th Strong winds dominate the first All-Star Game of 1961. A capacity crowd sees P Stu Miller blown off the mound in the 9th inning at Candlestick Park. A balk is called, and it enables the AL to forge a 3–3 tie before losing 5–4 in 10 innings.

13th Mack Jones of the Braves ties the NL record with 4 hits—3 singles and a double—in his ML debut, a 6–5 triumph over St. Louis.

14th Willie Kirkland whacks his 5th HR in 3 games to help the Indians down the Angels 7–5 at Cleveland. His first 4 were in consecutive at bats before and after the All-Star break and tied the ML record. He now has 16 en route to 27 for the year.

17th Following a year-long illness, Ty Cobb succumbs to cancer at age 74 at Emory University Hospital in Atlanta.

Bill White goes 8-for-10 in a doubleheader, as the Cards sweep the Cubs 10–6 and 8–5 at Busch Stadium.

18th Bill White and the Cards continue to beat up on the Cubs, sweeping 8–3 and 7–5. White goes 3-for-4 in each game and ties Ty Cobb's 49-year-old record of 14 hits in consecutive twin bills.

Commissioner Ford Frick rules that Babe Ruth's record of 60 HRs in a 154-game schedule in 1927 "cannot be broken unless some batter hits 61 or more within his club's first 154 games."

Henry Aaron, Joe Adcock, and Joe Torre of the Braves startle the Reds with a triple steal in the 6th inning. For Aaron, it is his first steal of home.

21st With each team stranding 15 base runners, the Angels and Senators tie the ML record for runners left on base by 2 clubs in a 9-inning game. Los Angeles wins 16–5.

Mickey Mantle and Roger Maris slam back-to-back HRs in the first inning for New York, but it takes a 2-out, 9th-inning pinch-hit grand slam by Johnny Blanchard to finally subdue the Red Sox 11–8 at Fenway. The pinch slam is the AL's 6th of the season, a new record.

22nd John Blanchard does it again with a solo pinch-hit HR to start a 3-run 9th-inning Yankee rally to tumble the Red Sox 11–9.

23rd Using 21 pitchers, the Tigers (11) and A's (10) set an AL record for most hurlers used in an 18-inning doubleheader. At 3 hours, 54 minutes, the 2nd game is the longest 9-inning contest in AL history. The entire doubleheader lasts 6 hours, 50 minutes, a ML record. The Tigers sweep 6–4 and 17–14, taking first place by one percentage point.

25th Roger Maris hits 4 HRs, tying the AL record for a twin bill (at least one in each game), as New York beats Chicago 5–1 and 12–0. Mickey Mantle also homers off Frank Baumann in the first game. He ends the day with 38 HRs to 40 for Maris.

26th John Blanchard ties a ML record by hitting his 3rd and 4th HRs in 4 at bats over 3 games. He drives in 4 of the Yankee runs in a 5–2 victory over the White Sox at the Stadium.

29th Duke Snider's pinch HR and Ron Fairly's RBI hit give Los Angeles a 5–4 win at Pittsburgh. The Dodgers take over first place from the Reds.

31st The 2nd All-Star Game of 1961 ends in a 1–1 tie at Fenway Park. Rocky Colavito homers for the AL run. Heavy rains end the exhibition after 9 innings.

AUGUST

3rd A 19–0 rout of St. Louis by Pittsburgh matches the most lopsided shutout in modern NL history. The first had been achieved by the Cubs against the Giants on June 7, 1906.

6th Maury Wills's first HR in 1,167 ML at bats and a double, triple, and HR by Frank Howard give the Dodgers an 11–4 win against Chicago and first place in the NL.

9th Cincinnati wins its 16th straight game against Philadelphia as Joey Jay blanks the Phils 5–0.

11th Warren Spahn's 2–1 victory against the Cubs makes him the 13th 300-game winner.

Vancouver (PCL) steals 9 bases in one inning of a 10–2 win against Salt Lake City.

14th The Phillies lose their 17th straight game 9–2 to the Cubs Dick Ellsworth. It is the 11th straight complete game pitched against Philadelphia.

16th Cincinnati takes the NL lead for good with a shutout sweep 6–0 and 8–0 at Los Angeles before 72,140, a record crowd for a NL doubleheader. Jim O'Toole and Bob Purkey are the winning pitchers.

Chuck Weatherspoon hits his 7th grand slam of the season for Wilson (Carolina League) in a game against Winston-Salem.

Roger Maris ties an AL record with a HR in his 7th straight game, as New York beats Chicago 5–4 in the 9th inning. His 2 blasts off Billy Pierce give him 48, three more than Mickey Mantle.

20th Philadelphia's modern NL-record 23-game losing streak ends when John Buzhardt beats Milwaukee 7–4 in the 2nd of 2 games. The win snaps Milwaukee's 10-game win streak.

The Cubs and Pirates tie an NL record by playing their 3rd straight extra-inning game. The Cubs take this one 1–0. Chicago wins two of the three 11-inning games.

22nd Frank Lane's short tenure as GM of the A's ends when Charlie Finley replaces him with Pat Friday.

Roger Maris becomes the first player to hit his 50th HR in the month of August, as the Yankees lose to the Angels 4–3.

23rd San Francisco pulls within 4 games of first place with a 14–0 rout of the Reds, putting the game away with a record-tying salvo of 5 HRs in the 9th inning. HRs by 6 different Giants tie the ML record for a 9-inning game. San Francisco's 27 total bases in the 9th inning are a modern ML record.

24th Ageless Satchel Paige signs with Portland (PCL). In 25 innings for the Beavers, he will have a 2.88 ERA.

26th Ed Short becomes GM of the White Sox, replacing Hank Greenberg.

27th With first place on the line, Cincinnati rallies from a 5–1 deficit to a 6–5 first-game win over Los Angeles. Ken Johnson is an 8–3 winner in the night-cap, giving the Reds a 3½ game lead in the NL.

Rocky Colavito ties an AL record with 4 HRs in a doubleheader pummeling of the Senators 7–4 and 10–1 at Washington.

SEPTEMBER

1st The AL's biggest crowd, 65,566, sees Whitey Ford and Don Mossi duel at Yankee Stadium as a weekend battle for first place begins. Two-out, 9th-inning hits by Elston Howard, Yogi Berra, and Bill Skowron give New York a 1–0 win over the Tigers.

Paul Richards (38-57) resigns as manager of the Orioles to become GM of the new Houston NL club. Coach Lum Harris takes over.

Cuno Barragan hits his first, and only, HR in his first ML at bat for the Cubs. But the Cubs lose 4–3 in 14 innings to the Giants.

2nd Milwaukee manager Chuck Dressen (71-58) is axed and Executive Vice President Birdie Tebbetts becomes the new skipper.

5th Los Angeles's Lee Thomas ties the ML record with 9 hits in a doubleheader, 5 in the first game and 4, including 3 HRs, in the 2nd. Thomas ties the AL record with 19 total bases in a doubleheader. But Kansas City wins both games 7–3 and 13–12.

14th The Cardinals and Cubs set a NL record by using 72 players in a doubleheader (more than 18 innings). St. Louis leads the way with 37 players and wins twice 8–7 and 6–5.

15th With 10 strikeouts in an 11–2 win against the Braves, Sandy Koufax has 243 strikeouts, most ever for a NL lefty.

20th The Yankees' 155th game of 1961 (including a tie) is Roger Maris's last chance to beat the Babe, in compliance with Commissioner Ford Frick's statement that, for the record to be broken, Maris must do it in the same number of games as Ruth. Maris's 59th HR of the year, off Jack Fisher, is short of the record, but helps New York beat Baltimore 4–2, clinching its 26th AL pennant.

22nd Jim Gentile's 5th grand slam of 1961 ties the ML single-season record in Baltimore's 8–6 win over Chicago. Each of Gentile's slams comes with Chuck Estrada pitching for the Orioles.

23rd An ailing Mickey Mantle's career-high 54th HR, last of the regular season, helps New York beat Boston 8–3.

26th In New York's 159th game, Roger Maris rips a Jack Fisher fastball into the RF seats at Yankee Stadium for his 60th HR. New York beats Baltimore 3–2.

Cincinnati clinches its first NL pennant since 1940. HRs by Frank Robinson and Jerry Lynch give the Reds a 6–3 win at Chicago.

27th Sandy Koufax fans 7 Phils in the course of a 2–1 win to set a NL record for strikeouts in a season: 269. This surpasses Christy Mathewson's 267 in 1903, which was accomplished in 367 innings pitched, as opposed to Koufax's remarkable 255.

OCTOBER

1st Roger Maris's torturous, seasonlong race against Babe Ruth ends in a dramatic at bat against Boston's Tracy Stallard. Maris's classic lefthanded swing sends HR number 61 into the RF stands in "The House That Ruth Built." (Fan Sal Durante grabs the historic HR ball which he sells for $5,000.) New York's 1–0 win gives the Yanks 109 wins, one short of the club's 1927 record.

Setting a ML record, the Cubs and Dodgers use 11 pinch hitters in one 9-inning game, seven of which are used by the Cubs.

2nd Casey Stengel agrees to come out of retirement to manage the NL expansion New York Mets next year.

4th Whitey Ford's 3rd straight WS shutout, with HRs by Elston Howard and Bill Skowron, gives New York a 2–0 win in the opener against Cincinnati at Yankee Stadium.

5th Joey Jay's 4-hitter, Gordy Coleman's 2-run HR, and 2 RBI hits by Johnny Edwards lead Cincinnati to a 6–2 win and even the WS.

The Indians trade CF Jim Piersall to Washington for P Dick Donovan, OF Gene Green, and IF Jim Mahoney.

7th John Blanchard's pinch-hit HR ties the game in the 8th, and Roger Maris's 9th-inning HR off Bob Purkey is the difference in a 3–2 New York win for Luis Arroyo in game 3 of the WS.

8th Five more scoreless innings by Whitey Ford and 4 by Jim Coates silence the Reds. Hector Lopez and Clete Boyer each drive in 2 runs for a 6–0 win. Ford breaks Babe Ruth's WS record of 29⅔ consecutive scoreless innings, running his streak to 32.

9th Super-subs Johnny Blanchard and Hector Lopez spark a 5-run first inning and 13–5 win for New York. Both hit HRs, and Lopez drives in 5 runs. Bud Daley's long relief effort wraps up the Series, as Ralph Houk becomes the 3rd rookie pilot to guide a WS winner.

10th An expansion draft to stock the new NL clubs takes place in Cincinnati. Houston selections include Bobby Shantz, Ken Johnson, Dick Farrell, and Bob Lillis. New York takes Roger Craig, Gil Hodges, Don Zimmer, and Gus Bell among others.

Billy Hitchcock takes Lum Harris's (17-10) place as manager of the Orioles.

11th Kazuhisa "Iron Man" Inao of the Nishitetsu Lions lives up to his nickname and notches his 42nd win of the season, tying the all-time world record since 1893 set by Victor Starfin of the Yomiuri Giants in 1939. He also sets a season strikeout record by fanning 353.

12th Ralph Houk is given a 2-year contract extension to manage the Yankees.

16th   Veteran pitchers Robin Roberts and Billy Loes are purchased by the Yankees and Mets respectively.

18th   The Houston Colt 45s purchase P Hal Woodeshick from the Tigers.

28th   Ground is broken for the Flushing Meadows stadium, the future home of the New York Mets.

31st   A federal judge rules that Birmingham, AL, laws against integrated playing fields are illegal, eliminating the last barrier against integration in the Southern Association.

NOVEMBER

8th   Whitey Ford is voted the Cy Young Award winner over Warren Spahn.

14th   John Fetzer's purchase of the outstanding one-third interest in the Tigers makes him sole owner of the club.

15th   Roger Maris is voted AL MVP with 202 votes to 198 for Mickey Mantle and 157 for Jim Gentile.

16th   Cleveland trades 2B Johnny Temple to Baltimore for 1B Ray Barker, C Harry Chiti, and minor leaguer Art Kay.

22nd   RF Frank Robinson is the first Reds player in 21 years to win the NL MVP, taking 219 of 224 possible votes.

26th   The Professional Baseball Rules Committee votes 8-1 against legalizing the spitball. Only NL supervisor of umpires Cal Hubbard votes in favor.

27th   Chicago trades OF Minnie Minoso to St. Louis for OF/1B Joe Cunningham.

28th   Philadelphia sends P John Buzhardt and IF Charlie Smith to the White Sox for 1B Roy Sievers.

30th   The Giants acquire pitchers Don Larsen and Billy Pierce from the White Sox for pitchers Eddie Fisher, Dom Zanni, and Verle Tiefenthaler and 1B Bob Farley.

Billy Williams of the Cubs is voted NL Rookie of the Year.

DECEMBER

2nd   The ML clubs vote to curb bonuses. All first-year players not on ML rosters, except one minor leaguer, can be drafted by any other club for $8,000. Clubs are expected to be unwilling to pay large bonuses for players who will be subject to a draft for just $8,000.

8th   The Mets purchase OF Richie Ashburn from the Cubs.

13th   Mickey Mantle signs a 1962 contract for $82,000. Only Joe DiMaggio has been paid more by the Yankees.

14th   Roger Maris's request for a $75,000 contract is denied by Yankee GM Roy Hamey.

15th   Charles Comiskey, Jr., sells his 46 percent interest in the White Sox to a group of 11 investors.

18th   Bill DeWitt is elected president of the Reds, and Stanley Kess, chairman of the board.

1962

JANUARY

3rd Ground is broken for the Houston Astrodome.

7th The 61-year-old Three-I League (B) is disbanded by the 6 remaining clubs.

8th Commissioner Ford Frick denies charges that Carl Furillo has been blacklisted by the ML because of a 1959 salary dispute with the Dodgers.

22nd Jackie Jensen again announces his retirement from baseball. This time he means it.

23rd Bob Feller and Jackie Robinson are selected for the Baseball Hall of Fame in their first year of eligibility.

Lawyer Melvin Belli wins a breach-of-warranty suit against the San Francisco Giants on the grounds that his box seat at Candlestick Park is too cold. Belli's suit contends that the seat he bought in 1960, at the cost of $1,597, was supposed to have radiant heating.

24th The Southern Association, which lost New Orleans and Memphis in the last two years and with attendance lagging, suspends operation.

26th Roger Maris and Mickey Mantle sign contracts with Columbia Pictures to star in *Safe at Home!*, a movie that is to be shot during spring training.

28th Edd Roush and Bill McKechnie are added to the Hall of Fame by the Special Veterans Committee.

30th The Milwaukee Braves sign Peter Marchegiano, brother of former heavyweight boxing champ Rocky Marciano, to a minor league contract.

31st Willie Mays signs the biggest contract in baseball, a reported $90,000 for 1962.

FEBRUARY

1st The NL releases its first 162-game schedule.

7th The Red Sox hire former Indianapolis Clowns OF Ed Scott as their first full-time black scout.

Lawyer Melvin Belli obtains a writ laying claim to Willie Mays—among other assets—unless the Giants pay him the judgment awarded by a jury in January. Belli claims the club failed to file a motion for a new trial before the deadline.

8th The Federal Trade Commission accuses Topps Chewing Gum of illegally monopolizing the baseball picture-card industry. In 1980, a court decision will open the door to competition.

27th An architect offers a proposal to encase Candlestick Park in a plastic screen—"saran cloth"—to shield it from the wind.

MARCH

5th Cincinnati 3B Gene Freese suffers a severe ankle fracture in the Reds first intrasquad game. He will not return until August 17th.

6th St. Louis voters approve a bond issue that will fund the improvements necessary to build a new downtown stadium for the Cardinals.

10th Because it does not allow black guests, the Phillies leave Jack Tar Harrison Hotel and move to Rocky Point Motel, 20 miles outside Clearwater, FL.

21st Philadelphia retires P Robin Roberts's number 36.

22nd A former Giant—requesting anonymity—reveals that Bobby Thomson's HR in the 1951 playoffs against the Dodgers was helped by a sign-stealing clubhouse spy. The spying is claimed to have gone on for the last 3 months of the season. Thomson, along with former manager Leo Durocher, vehemently deny that he received help, but a source close to the team confirms the spy operation.

23rd William DeWitt buys the Reds from the Crosley Foundation for $4.625 million.

24th The Phillies trade holdout 3B Andy Carey and IF Lou Vassie to the White Sox for P Cal McLish. Chicago then trades Carey to the Dodgers for IF Ramon Conde and Jim Koranda.

25th Elvin Tappe will be this season's first head coach for the Chicago Cubs, who have operated without a manager since 1960.

APRIL

1st University of Detroit basketball star Dave DeBusschere, also a pitcher, signs with the Chicago White Sox.

2nd The Twins trade P Pedro Ramos to Cleveland for 1B Vic Power and P Dick Stigman.

9th President John F. Kennedy throws out the first ball to open the 1962 baseball season at new District of Columbia Stadium. Despite rain, a record Washington crowd of 42,143 shows up to see Bennie Daniels stop Detroit with a 5-hit, 4–1 win.

10th The Houston Colt 45s begin play before 25,271 fans at Colt Stadium, a temporary facility, adjacent to the land for the Astrodome. Roman Mejias hits two 3-run HRs, and Bobby Shantz pitches Houston to an 11–2 win over the Cubs.

Dodger Stadium, the first ML arena privately financed since Yankee Stadium in 1922-23, opens in Chavez Ravine. With 52,564 fans on hand, the Dodgers inaugurate the $22 million facility with a 6–3 loss to the Reds.

12th Pete Richert of the Dodgers, in his ML debut, fans the first 6 batters he faces against the Reds, tying Karl Spooner's record set on September 22, 1954. This includes 4 strikeouts in the 3rd inning. He wins in relief, giving up no hits or walks and fanning 7 in 3⅓ innings.

13th Just 12,447 Mets' fans welcome the return of NL baseball to New York. Sherman Jones drops a 4–3 decision to the Pirates at the Polo Grounds, which sparkles after a $350,000 face-lift.

Stan Musial scores his 1,869th run—a new NL record. The Cardinals beat the Cubs 8–5 in 15 innings.

17th The Cubs use 5 pitchers in the 8th inning of a 10–6 loss to Pittsburgh, tying an NL mark.

22nd The Pirates win their 10th straight game, matching the ML record to start a season, while the Mets tie a NL record by opening 0-9.

23rd Jay Hook gives the New York Mets their first regular-season victory, a 5-hit 9–1 win at Pittsburgh.

24th Sandy Koufax ties the modern ML record he shares with Bob Feller by fanning 18 Cubs in 9 innings. The Dodgers win 10–2.

Mets manager Casey Stengel is fined $500 by Commissioner Ford Frick for allowing his picture to appear in a beer ad.

26th The Cardinals and Colts play a 17-inning 5–5 tie in a game halted by curfew.

28th Consecutive HRs by Frank Thomas, Charlie Neal, and Gil Hodges in the 6th inning are among a club-record 5 hit by the Mets against Philadelphia. The Mets win 8–6 at Shea

29th The Twins tie a ML record with 6 solo HRs against the Indians in the 2nd game of a Minnesota sweep. The Twins down the Indians 8–4 and 7–3.

In the Mets' 7-run 4th inning, Frank Thomas is twice hit by pitches, from Art Mahaffey and Frank Sullivan of the Phils. Two plunks in an inning are the ML record set in 1959 by the only other player to whom it has happened—Reds P Willard Schmidt. The Mets win 8–0, then lose the 2nd game 10–2.

30th The Phils finally beat Warren Spahn, 6–4, after losing to the Braves lefty 11 games in a row.

MAY

4th The first-place Giants win their 10th straight game, beating the Cubs 11–6.

Arthur Allyn becomes sole owner of the White Sox by purchasing the 46-percent share held by an 11-man Chicago syndicate.

5th Angels rookie Bo Belinsky pitches a no-hitter against the Orioles, the organization from which the cocky lefty was drafted last year. Belinsky has 9 strikeouts and beats Steve Barber 2–0.

6th Mickey Mantle hits HRs right- and lefthanded for the 9th time, in the 2nd game of a doubleheader, as the Yankees win 8–0 over the Senators at the Stadium. In the opener, a 4–2 Nats win, Mantle accounts for both Yankee runs with a lefthanded homer.

7th Former baseball executive Frank Lane signs on as GM of the Chicago Packers of the National Basketball Association.

9th Brooks Robinson becomes the 6th major leaguer to hit grand slams in back-to-back games, as he hits one against Kansas City's Ed Rakow. Baltimore wins 6–3 at home.

The Mets obtain 1B Marv Throneberry from the Baltimore Orioles.

10th Minnesota Lenny Green and Vic Power hit back-to-back HRs off Cleveland's Jim Perry to start the game, tying a ML record. Cleveland comes back to win 9–4.

11th   Minnie Minoso of the Cardinals suffers a fractured skull and broken wrist running into the outfield wall while chasing a Duke Snider triple. The Dodgers win 8–5.

12th   New York Mets relief P Craig Anderson wins both games of a doubleheader against the Braves. He will not win another game in the ML, losing his next 19 decisions, 16 of them this season. Ninth-inning HRs win the games as Hobie Landrith hits one in the opening 3–2 win and Gil Hodges closes a game-two 9–8 victory.

15th   Cubs P Barney Schultz ties Roy Face's ML record by relieving in 9 consecutive games for Chicago.

18th   Mickey Mantle suffers a pulled groin muscle, tears muscles in his right thigh, and injures his left knee trying for an infield hit that becomes the final out of New York's 4–3 loss to Minnesota. He will miss one month.

ML owners approve a Player Development Plan that will ensure the survival of at least 100 minor league clubs for 1963.

The minor leagues are reorganized into 4 classes rather than 7. Classes B, C, and D are grouped as Class A, Classes AA and A become Class AA, and Class AAA remains the same, along with the rookie classification.

19th   Stan Musial gets hit number 3,431, to break Honus Wagner's recognized NL record of 3,430 (since revised to 3,418), as St. Louis downs the Dodgers 8–1. Musial's 9th-inning single comes off Ron Perranoski.

20th   The Indians tie the ML record for most HRs in 6 straight games—21—set by the Giants in July 1954. They win the first game over Detroit 7–6, then lose 8–6 in the nitecap.

21st   The Tribe keeps pounding but lose 10–7 to Baltimore. Three more Cleveland HRs set an AL record for most HRs (26) over 8 straight games.

22nd   Roger Maris, who went all of 1961 without receiving an intentional walk, gets 4 in a 12-inning 2–1 win against the Angels to set an AL record. Maris receives 5 walks in all. Four Yankee pitchers (Whitey Ford, Jim Coates, Bud Daley, and Bob Turley) combine to give up just one hit in 12 innings. Ford leaves after 7 innings because of back spasms, and Coates

gives up the lone hit, a one-out 9th-inning single to Bob Rodgers.

23rd   Yankee rookie Joe Pepitone becomes the 6th player in AL history to hit 2 HRs in one inning. New York's 9-run 8th sinks Kansas City 13–7.

25th   Ernie Banks is beaned by Moe Drabowsky and taken from the field on a stretcher, as Cincinnati beats Chicago 2–1.

26th   Al Kaline suffers a broken right collarbone while making a diving, game-saving catch to seal Detroit's 2–1 win against the Yankees. He will be out until June 23rd.

28th   Former Dodger hurler Don Newcombe signs with the Chunichi Dragons of the Japanese League.

29th   Ernie Banks makes a spectacular return from his May 25th beaning with 3 HRs against the Braves at Wrigley Field. Three teammates hit HRs, as the Cubs outlast the Braves in 10 innings 11–9.

30th   Light-hitting SS Maury Wills becomes the 7th player in ML history to sock HRs from each side of the plate in one game. The Dodgers sweep the Mets 13–6 and 6–5 in New York.

JUNE

1st   The Dodgers sweep Philadelphia 11–4 and 8–5 for a Los Angeles record 13 straight wins. Don Drysdale and Stan Williams pitch the Bums into a first-place tie with the Giants.

6th   Cal McLish and Art Mahaffey pitch Philadelphia to a sweep of the Mets, giving New York 17 straight losses.

12th   The Braves beat the Dodgers 15–2 as the Aaron brothers—Hank and Tommie—hit HRs in the same game for the first time.

14th   The Orioles Charlie Lau ties an AL record with 3 passed balls in the 8th inning, and a total of 4, as Baltimore beats Boston 7–4. No surprise who is pitching: Hoyt Wilhelm.

15th   The Phils score 10 in the 3rd, their biggest one-inning outburst since 1950, and hold on to beat the Reds 13–8.

16th   A limping Mickey Mantle returns after a one-month absence to crack a 3-run pinch-hit HR in the 8th to give New York a 9–7 lead against Cleveland. The Tribe comes back to win it 10–9 in the 9th on Jerry Kindall's 2-run HR. Cleveland now leads the 3rd-place Yankees by a game and will sweep the 4-game series.

17th Lou Brock of the Cubs hits a HR into the right-CF bleachers at the Polo Grounds, 460 feet from home plate, in the first game of a Chicago doubleheader sweep, 8–7 and 4–3. He is the 2nd player to reach those bleacher seats. In the first game loss, Marvelous Marv Throneberry hits an apparent triple, then misses both 1B and 2B, and is called out on an appeal play.

18th Hank Aaron of the Braves reaches the left-CF bleachers at the Polo Grounds, the 2nd player to find the CF bleachers in 2 days and only the 3rd ever. The Braves win 7–1.

22nd Playing 4 hours and 2 minutes, the Braves outscore the Giants 11–9 in the NL's longest 9-inning night game.

Stan Musial becomes the all-time total-base leader, raising his total to 5,864, in the first game against the Phillies. St. Louis wins the opener 7–3 but loses the nightcap 11–3.

23rd Larry Doby, retired from the Cleveland Indians, signs on with the Chunichi Dragons to become, with Don Newcombe, the first former ML players to play for a Japanese team. His season BA will be a mediocre .225.

24th A marathon between the Tigers and Yankees concludes in the 22nd inning when Jack Reed's HR—his only one in the ML—gives New York and Jim Bouton a 9–7 victory. Rocky Colavito has 7 hits for the Tigers. At an even 7 hours, the game is the slowest extra-inning contest in league history.

26th Earl Wilson pitches a no-hitter, his first ML shutout, as Boston beats the Los Angeles Angels 2–0. The righthander also hits a HR off loser Bo Belinsky, who pitched his no-hitter 6 weeks earlier.

28th Roger Maris and Mickey Mantle break a 0–0 tie in the 4th with back-to-back HRs to lead the Yanks to a 4–2 win over the Twins.

30th With the aid of 13 strikeouts and a Frank Howard HR, Sandy Koufax no-hits Bob Miller and the Mets 5–0 in Los Angeles.

JULY

1st Albie Pearson becomes the first player to go hitless in 11 at bats in a doubleheader (both 9-inning games). Los Angeles splits with the Yankees.

The White Sox drop Cleveland to 3rd place while winning a pair 5–4 and 7–6. In the 2nd game they also set a ML record with 3 run-scoring sacrifice flies in one inning.

2nd In the first game of a doubleheader, P Johnny Podres of the Dodgers ties the modern NL record with 8 consecutive strikeouts in a 5–1 win. Stan Williams also wins 4–0, as the Dodgers sweep Philadelphia and move into first place.

4th The Angels win for the 14th time in 20 games and move into first place by sweeping Washington 4–2 and 4–1 in DC.

The San Francisco Giants sign Santa Clara College P Bob Garibaldi for a $150,000 bonus.

6th The Indians regain first place from the Angels, as Ruben Gomez beats Early Wynn and the White Sox 5–3.

8th The Yankees complete a 3-game sweep in Minnesota, winning 7–5, 6–3, and 9–8 to regain first place. They will remain there the rest of the way.

The Dodgers take first place as Don Drysdale saves Sandy Koufax's 13th win 2–0 against San Francisco. Los Angeles will remain in first until the final day of the season.

With HRs in his first 3 at bats, 41-year-old Stan Musial of the Cardinals not only becomes the oldest player to hit 3 in a game but also ties the ML record of 4 straight HRs, as the Cards whip the Mets 15–1. His HR in the 2nd game the day before won the game 3–2.

Cincinnati uses 9 pitchers to win the 13-inning 2nd game against the Houston Colt 45s 12–11. This sets an NL record and ties the ML mark. The Reds also win the first game 12–8.

9th At a meeting held in conjunction with the All-Star Game, the ML players request a reduced schedule for the 1963 season. They also vote unanimously to continue playing 2 All-Star Games each year.

10th Roberto Clemente has 3 hits as the NL wins 3–1 in the first All-Star Game of 1962, at DC Stadium.

13th Orioles C Charley Lau hits 4 doubles in a 10–3 victory over Cleveland.

17th   Sandy Koufax leaves after one inning of a 7–5 loss at Cincinnati. The 14-game winner has a circulatory problem and will be sidelined until late September.

18th   Minnesota is the first AL club to hit 2 grand slams in one inning when Bob Allison and Harmon Killebrew connect in a club-record, 11-run first inning, against Cleveland. The Twins coast home 14–3.

19th   John W. Cox, owner of Yankee Stadium, donates the facility to Rice University.

21st   Houston P Dick Farrell admits to having thrown a spitball to Stan Musial in the previous day's game against the Cardinals.

22nd   Floyd Robinson of the White Sox goes 6-for-6, all singles, as Chicago defeats Boston 7–3 at Fenway Park.

23rd   Bob Feller, Jackie Robinson, Bill McKechnie, and Edd Roush are inducted into the Baseball Hall of Fame in Cooperstown.

25th   Stan Musial becomes the NL's all-time leader in runs batted in with 1,862, driving in both of the Cardinal runs in a 5–2 loss to the Dodgers.

26th   P Gene Conley and IF Pumpsie Green of the Red Sox mysteriously disappear after a game with the Yankees. They leave the team bus in traffic to use a restroom and fail to return. Conley decides he wants to fly to Israel, and goes to the airport, but is refused a ticket because he does not have a visa.

28th   Pumpsie Green returns to the team and is fined.

29th   Gene Conley contacts manager Mike Higgins by telegram, stating that he is "mostly tired," and has "other plans." He will return the next day to the Red Sox and will be fined $2,000.

30th   Homers by Leon Wagner, Pete Runnels, and Rocky Colavito power the AL past the NL 9–4 in the 2nd All-Star Game of 1962.

31st   The NL rejects Commissioner Ford Frick's proposal for inter-league play in 1963.

AUGUST

1st   Nothing less than Bill Monbouquette's no-hitter is necessary to defeat Early Wynn and the White Sox 1–0. The Red Sox pitcher improves his record to 9-10.

Drawing a combined 32 bases on balls in a doubleheader, the Tigers (20) and A's (12) tie an AL record.

3rd   With a pair of HRs for the 3rd straight game, the Mets Frank Thomas becomes the 2nd player in NL history with 6 HRs in 3 consecutive games.

7th   Yankees SS Tony Kubek, in his first at bat after returning from military service, homers in a 14–1 Yankee win over the Twins.

13th   Bert Campaneris of Daytona Beach (Florida State League) pitches ambidextrously in a relief appearance.

15th   Pinch-hit HRs by the Mets Choo Choo Coleman (6th inning) and Jim Hickman (8th) tie the record for pinch HRs by one club in one game, but the Mets still lose to the Phils.

19th   Gino Cimoli, Wayne Causey, and Billy Bryan of the Athletics hit consecutive HRs in the 7th inning, but Elston Howard has 2 HRs and 8 RBI; Bill Skowron, a HR and 4 RBI; Mickey Mantle, a grand slam and 7 RBI, and the Yankees rout the A's 21–7. Mantle adds 2 stolen bases before Jack Reed takes over CF and has 2 at bats.

Cleveland Indians President Mike Wilson dies at age 74.

23rd   Steve Boros matches the AL record for most errors in an inning by a 3B with 4, but Detroit beats Cleveland 8–5, as Al Kaline hits 2 HRs.

24th   Dodger coach Leo Durocher suffers a near-fatal allergic reaction to a penicillin injection while in the clubhouse at the Polo Grounds before a game. An emergency intravenous injection of adrenaline saves his life.

25th   Winning for the 18th time in 21 games—over Houston 7–6—the Reds move within 3 games of first place. Joey Jay wins his 20th game.

Pirates players call off a threatened strike. They had objected to a rained-out game being rescheduled as a night game the day before a doubleheader.

26th   The Twins Jack Kralick no-hits the A's and wins 1–0 on Lenny Green's sacrifice fly off Bill

Fischer. A walk to George Alusik with one out in the 9th puts the only runner on.

Robin Roberts beats Whitey Ford 2–1 on HRs by Brooks Robinson and Jim Gentile to complete a 5-game Oriole sweep of the Yankees. The Twins and Angels are now 3 games behind New York.

The Cubs tie a ML record and set an NL mark with 3 straight sacrifice bunts in one inning.

28th Angels thumpers Lee Thomas, Leon Wagner, and Bob Rodgers hit consecutive HRs in the 4th inning of a 10–5 trouncing of Kansas City.

30th San Francisco's 3–2 win over the Braves is a record-setter, as all 5 runs score on HRs.

SEPTEMBER

2nd Stan Musial's 3,516th hit jumps him over Tris Speaker and into 2nd place behind Ty Cobb, but the Mets beat the Cards 4–3. Although The Man will continue on to 3,630 hits, he cannot overtake Cobb and, in time, Pete Rose and Hank Aaron will surpass him as well.

3rd Jack Sanford of the Giants wins his 20th game and 14th straight at Los Angeles 7–3.

4th Houston finally defeats Philadelphia 4–1 in their final meeting of the season. The Phillies had won all 17 previous contests.

5th Ken Hubbs of the Cubs sets ML records at 2B for consecutive games without an error (78) and consecutive chances accepted (418) without an error. His streak ends with a 4th-inning throwing error as Cincinnati beats Chicago 4–1.

Washington's John Kennedy pinch hits against the Twins and becomes the 9th AL player to debut with a HR in his first at bat.

6th Commissioner Ford Frick announces that any transfer of Bo Belinsky to the Athletics as part of the Dan Osinski deal will be voided due to a technicality in the rules.

The Giants score 4 in the 9th to beat the Dodgers 9–6 and put San Francisco just 1½ games out of first.

7th Four steals bring Maury Wills's season total to 82, one better than Bob Bescher's 1911 mark and a modern NL record. But Pittsburgh beats Los Angeles 10–1, cutting the Dodger lead to one-half game.

12th Washington's Tom Cheney sets a ML mark with 21 strikeouts in a 16-inning game at Baltimore. Bud Zipfel's 16th-inning HR off Dick Hall gives the Senators a 2–1 win.

In the dugout in Cincinnati, Willie Mays collapses from nervous exhaustion. He is taken to the hospital and will miss 4 games. The Giants lose 4–1 and will lose their next 6 to take them apparently out of the race.

13th Washington OF Jim Piersall is arrested for going into the stands after a heckling fan prior to a game against Baltimore. He is charged with disorderly conduct, but later cleared.

14th Jim Piersall is knocked unconscious by a revolving door in his hotel in Baltimore, shortly after the hearing on his arrest.

15th The Pirates beat Jack Sanford 5–1, the first loss by the Giant hurler after 16 straight wins.

18th Bob Aspromonte of the Colt 45s sets an NL record for 3B with his 57th straight errorless game.

Charlie Finley is denied permission to move the Athletics to Dallas-Ft. Worth.

19th Walter Bond and John Romano hit back-to-back HRs twice for the Indians against the Athletics.

23rd A 12–2 Dodger loss at St. Louis is enlivened by Maury Wills, who ties Ty Cobb's long-standing ML single-season record of 96 steals by swiping 2B after singling in the 3rd, and breaks it with a repeat performance in the 7th.

25th Whitey Ford beats Washington 8–3, as the Yankees clinch the AL pennant. Ralph Houk becomes the 5th manager to capture pennants in each of his first 2 seasons.

The Giants keep pace as Billy Pierce beats St. Louis 6–3. Pierce runs his record at Candlestick to 11–0.

29th The Indians and Angels set an AL record with 40 K's in a doubleheader (18 innings). Los Angeles pitchers account for 23 of the strikeouts.

The Giants have a chance to tie for the lead with a makeup doubleheader with Houston. Jack Sanford wins his 24th as the Giants take the opener 12–5. Houston then manages a split behind Bob Bruce's 4–2 victory to leave San Francisco one game back.

30th Willie Mays's 47th HR, an 8th-inning blast off Dick Farrell (10-20), gives the Giants a critical 2–1 win. They then stay in the clubhouse to hear results of the Dodger game.

Gene Oliver's HR off Johnny Podres gives Curt Simmons and St. Louis a 1–0 win against the Dodgers and forces the 4th playoff in NL history.

P Bill Fischer of the Athletics concludes a record string of 84⅓ consecutive innings without allowing a base on balls by walking Detroit OF Bubba Morton on 4 straight pitches. He loses a 6–1 decision to Detroit.

The Cubs turn a triple play and beat New York 5–1, a 20th-century ML record 120th loss for the Mets. C Joe Pignatano of the Mets hits into the triple play in his last at bat in the major leagues.

OCTOBER

1st San Francisco wins the first of the best-of-3 NL playoff as Billy Pierce takes his 12th straight at Candlestick Park, a three-hit, 8–0 victory. Willie Mays hits 2 HRs, giving him 49 in 1962, one more than AL leader Harmon Killebrew.

2nd After 35 straight scoreless innings, the Dodgers break through for 7 runs in the 6th to lead San Francisco by 2. The Giants score twice in the 8th, but a 9th-inning sacrifice fly by Ron Fairly sends Maury Wills home with the winning run 8–7. The Giants tie an NL record by using 8 hurlers in a 9-inning game. At 4 hours and 18 minutes, the game is the longest 9-inning affair in NL history.

3rd A crowd of 45,693, giving the Dodgers a ML-record season attendance of 2,755,184, attends the deciding game of the NL season. In the 7th, Maury Wills collects his 4th single of the day, and his 103rd and 104th steals of the year. But the Giants score 4 in the 9th to win 6–4 and put themselves in the WS.

4th At Candlestick Park, in game one of the WS, Roger Maris stakes Whitey Ford to a 2-run lead with a first-inning, 2-run double. Only RF Felipe Alou's leaping effort keeps Maris's drive in the park. Whitey Ford's record consecutive-shutout-inning streak ends at 33⅔ innings when a surprise bunt by Jose Pagan brings Willie Mays home. Clete Boyer's 7th-inning HR gives the Yankees a 6–2 win, the last of a record 10 WS victories for Ford.

5th Jack Sanford's 3-hitter handcuffs New York and knots the WS. Matty Alou's RBI grounder and

Willie McCovey's HR off Ralph Terry account for San Francisco's 2–0 win.

7th At Yankee Stadium in game 3, Bill Stafford and Billy Pierce match goose eggs for 6 innings. Ed Bailey's 2-run 9th-inning HR ruins Stafford's shutout, but his 4-hitter downs the Giants 3–2.

8th Tom Haller and Chuck Hiller power San Francisco to a WS-tying win 7–3. Haller's 2-run HR puts the Giants in front, and Hiller's surprising grand slam is the margin of victory.

10th Following a rainout, New York overcomes 2 San Francisco leads, and Tom Tresh's 3-run 8th-inning HR off Jack Sanford gives the Yankees and Ralph Terry a 5–3 win.

15th After one day of travel and 3 of rain, Billy Pierce pitches a 3-hitter for a 5–2 Giants win of game 6. Orlando Cepeda breaks his hitless streak with 2 hits and 3 RBI.

16th New York scores the game's only run, as Tony Kubek grounds into a 5th-inning DP. In the 9th, with 2 outs and Matty Alou on 1B, Willie Mays rips a double to right off Ralph Terry, but great fielding by Roger Maris keeps Alou from scoring. Willie McCovey then hits a screaming liner toward right, but 2B Bobby Richardson gloves it, giving the Yankees a 1–0 win and a 2nd straight WS victory. Terry is named WS MVP.

17th Pitchers Larry Jackson and Lindy McDaniel and C Jimmie Schaffer are traded by St. Louis to the Cubs for P Don Cardwell, OF George Altman, and C Moe Thacker.

27th The Detroit Tigers begin a 17-game tour of Japan.

29th Branch Rickey rejoins the Cardinals as a senior consultant for player development.

NOVEMBER

6th Answering rumors that senior consultant Rickey wants Stan Musial to retire, Cardinals owner August Busch says The Man will play until it is time to become a club vice president. Further, Bing Devine is still running the club.

8th Charlie Metro, head coach of the Cubs college of coaches from June 4th to season's end (43-69), is fired.

14th Bob Kennedy joins the Cubs coaching staff as its 8th and final member.

15th Don Drysdale wins the Cy Young Award, outpolling Jack Sanford 14-4.

The White Sox release Early Wynn so that the 299-game winner will be free to deal with other clubs, and earn his 300th.

16th John McHale and 6 former stockholders of the White Sox purchase the Milwaukee Braves from the Perini Corporation for $6,218,480.

19th Pittsburgh trades SS Dick Groat and P Diomedes Olivo to St. Louis for P Don Cardwell and SS Julio Gotay.

20th Sale of the Cleveland Indians is completed as Bill Daley and Gabe Paul take control.

Mickey Mantle is named the AL Most Valuable Player for the 3rd time.

21st Pittsburgh trades 1B Dick Stuart and P Jack Lamabe to Boston for P Don Schwall and C Jim Pagliaroni.

23rd Dodgers SS Maury Wills is named the NL's Most Valuable Player.

25th Boston trades AL batting champ Pete Runnels to Houston for OF Roman Mejias.

29th ML officials and player representatives agree to return to a single All-Star Game in 1963. The players' pension fund will receive 95 percent of the one game's proceeds (rather than 60 percent of the 2 games).

The American Association (AAA) folds, with some of the franchises being absorbed by the International League and the Pacific Coast League.

DECEMBER

3rd Former players Frank Crosetti and John Schulte file suit to halt any increased ML pension benefits that fail to include old-time players.

7th J. G. Taylor Spink, longtime publisher of *The Sporting News,* dies at age 74 in St. Louis.

22nd Harris County voters approve a bond issue to complete the financing of an all-weather stadium to house the Houston Colt 45s.

31st The state of Ohio withdraws a suit against the Reds when owner Bill DeWitt agrees in writing that the club will stay in Cincinnati for 10 years.

1963

JANUARY

5th Hall of Famer Rogers Hornsby dies at age 66 of a heart ailment.

10th The Cubs hire retired Air Force Colonel Robert V. Whitlow as athletic director.

14th The White Sox trade SS Luis Aparicio and OF Al Smith to the Orioles for P Hoyt Wilhelm, OF Dave Nicholson, 3B Pete Ward, and SS Ron Hansen.

26th The ML Rules Committee votes to expand the strike zone, restoring it to pre-1950 standards: from the top of the shoulders to the bottom of the knees.

27th The Hall of Fame Special Veterans Committee votes in Sam Rice, Eppa Rixey, Elmer Flick, and John Clarkson.

29th James M. Johnston, James H. Lemon, and George M. Bunker purchase 80 percent of the Senators, buying out 5 of the original owners, including club president Pete Quesada. Johnston is elected chairman of the board.

FEBRUARY

20th Bob Kennedy is named manager of the Cubs, putting an end to the short-lived college of coaches.

27th Cleveland trades OF Chuck Essegian to the A's for P Jerry Walker.

MARCH

22nd The Mets purchase P Carl Willey from the Braves.

25th Philadelphia purchases P Johnny Klippstein from the Reds.

APRIL

1st The Mets bring the Duke back to New York, purchasing Snider from the Dodgers.

7th A public stock offering of 115,000 shares in the Milwaukee Braves is withdrawn after only 13,000 shares are sold to 1,600 new investors.

8th The Tigers claim young pitcher Denny McLain from the White Sox for the $25,000 waiver price.

11th Warren Spahn's Opening Day, 6–1 victory over the Mets is his first win of the season and the 328th of his career. He thus moves ahead of yesteryear's great Eddie Plank as the all-time winningest lefthander. Except for Duke Snider's HR, no Met gets past 2B.

13th After 11 hitless at bats, Cincinnati 2B Pete Rose records his first ML hit, a triple off Pittsburgh's Bob Friend. Increased enforcement of the balk rule produces a ML record 7 in the Pirates' 12–4 trouncing at Cincinnati. Bob Friend is called for 4 balks.

16th In a 13-inning, 11–10 loss at Minnesota, the Angels use 9 pitchers, tying the ML record for an extra-inning contest.

21st Yakima (Northwest League) C Rico Carty hits 2 HRs in one at bat. The rookie catcher's first blast is nullified because time had been called.

Cincinnati P Jim Owens becomes the first hurler in NL history charged with 3 balks in one inning (the 2nd) in a 7–0 loss at Los Angeles.

27th Pro basketballers Gene Conley of the Celtics and Dave DeBusschere of the Knicks oppose each other as Red Sox and White Sox pitchers. Conley hurls 4+ innings for Boston, while DeBusschere relieves for two-thirds of an inning for Chicago. Boston wins at Fenway 9–5.

MAY

2nd The Twins trade P Jack Kralick to Cleveland for P Jim Perry.

3rd In his first, and only, ML at bat, Orioles pitcher Les "Buster" Narum breaks in with a HR against Detroit's Don Mossi. Six days later Narum is optioned to Rochester.

4th The Braves Bob Shaw shatters the existing balk record when he is called for 5 in a 7–5 loss to the Cubs. Shaw is penalized 3 times in the 3rd inning alone, tying the ML record set the previous week by Jim Owens.

5th The White Sox trade P Dom Zanni to the Reds for P Jim Brosnan.

7th The major leagues approve a $50,000 grant to the National Collegiate Baseball Foundation to operate the new Central Illinois Collegiate League.

8th Pirates LF Willie Stargell's first ML homer and Cubs P Bob Buhl's first ML hit in 88 at bats highlight a 9–5 Chicago win over Pittsburgh.

A Stan Musial HR against the Dodgers gives him 1,357 extra-base hits, surpassing Babe Ruth's ML record. He will get 20 more and permanent possession of 2nd place lifetime. The Cards lose 11–5.

An 8-run 7th inning gives the White Sox an 8–3 win, a sweep of the A's, and the AL lead.

9th Ernie Banks becomes the first NL 1B to register 22 putouts in a game, as the Cubs beat St. Louis 3–1 on Don Cardwell's 2-hitter.

11th Sandy Koufax's comeback from a circulatory ailment in his left index finger continues with a no-hitter against the visiting first place Giants. He walks 2 and fans 4 to run his record to 4–1. Wally Moon homers off loser Juan Marichal in the Dodgers' 8–0 victory.

14th The crackdown on balks by NL pitchers ends with a directive that umpires need not enforce the one-second stop from the stretch position.

17th Don Nottebart pitches the first no-hitter in Houston's ML history with a 4–1 win against the Phils. Carl Warwick goes 4-for-4 with a HR to back Nottebart, now 5–1 for the 9th-place Colt 45s.

19th Billy Bruton ties a ML record for doubles in one game with 4 straight, and Bill Faul pitches a 3-hitter at Washington in his first ML start for Detroit, a 5–1 winner.

21st Jim Maloney ties the modern ML record with 8 consecutive strikeouts against the Braves. Maloney finishes with 16 strikeouts in the 2–0 win, but needs relief help.

22nd The all-time shortest managerial career ends after one game—a loss—when Eddie Yost, who replaced Mickey Vernon (14-26) as the Senators pilot, is replaced by Gil Hodges.

Los Angeles' Don Drysdale beats the Mets 7–3 on two hits—homers by Duke Snider and Tim Harkness.

23rd Pittsburgh trades OF Bob Skinner to the Reds for OF Jerry Lynch.

25th The Indians acquire C Joe Azcue and SS Dick Howser from the A's for C Doc Edwards and $100,000.

26th Cleveland C John Romano suffers a fractured finger as the Indians lose twice to the first-place Orioles 10–6 and 6–1. Reliever Wes Stock wins both games.

28th The first-place Orioles win their 9th straight game, a Robin Roberts 4–2 victory over the A's.

Called out at 1B on a close play for the 2nd time, Roberto Clemente inadvertently strikes umpire Bill Jackowski. Clemente is ejected, fined $250, and suspended for 5 days.

31st Early Wynn signs with the Indians.

JUNE

3rd Chicago's Joe Cunningham is sidelined until Labor Day after fracturing his right collarbone in a collision with Angels 1B Charlie Dees.

5th Mickey Mantle fractures a bone in his left foot and suffers ligament and cartilage damage to the left knee running into the chain link fence at Baltimore. The Mick will be out for 61 games. Whitey Ford beats Milt Pappas 4–3, as the Yankees return to first place.

6th With the bases loaded and one out in the 12th, Cubs reliever Lindy McDaniel picks Willie Mays off 2B and strikes out Ed Bailey. McDaniel then hits a HR in the bottom of the 12th to win 3–2. Chicago moves into a 3-way, first-place tie with St. Louis and San Francisco, its first taste of the lead since May 1958.

8th Baltimore P Chuck Estrada is finished for the season, with bone chips and a spur in his right elbow.

9th The Colt 45s beat the Giants 3–0 in the major leagues' first Sunday night game. The exception is made because of Houston's oppressive daytime heat.

Catcher Tim McCarver of the Cards hits an inside-the-park grand slam against the Mets to give St. Louis an 8–7 win.

12th Rookie OF Vic Davalillo, batting .304, suffers a broken arm when hit by a Hank Aguirre pitch in Cleveland's 12–6 win against the Tigers.

The White Sox Dave Nicholson ties the ML record with 7 strikeouts in a doubleheader split with the Angels. Chicago wins 3–1, then loses 5–0.

14th Cleveland's 19-inning, 3–2 win over the Senators matches the longest game ever played in Cleveland.

15th St. Louis trades C/1B Gene Oliver and minor league P Bob Sadowski to the Braves for P Lew Burdette.

Al Downing's 9–2 win against Detroit puts the Yankees in first place.

Juan Marichal becomes the first Giants P to hurl a no-hitter since Carl Hubbell (5/8/29), and the first Latin American to toss one in the ML. Eighth-inning doubles by Jim Davenport and Chuck Hiller provide the only score in the Giants 1–0 win at Candlestick.

16th Aberdeen (Northern League) 1B Jim Rouse turns an unassisted triple play in a 14–7 loss to Duluth-Superior.

17th Bob Scheffing (24-36) is axed as manager of the Tigers. Dodgers scout Charlie Dressen replaces him.

19th Gates Brown becomes the AL's 11th player to hit a HR in his first at bat. Brown's blow is a pinch-hit blast in the 5th against Boston's Don Heffner at Fenway in a 9–2 Tiger loss.

22nd Philadelphia CF Tony Gonzalez plays his 200th straight errorless game to help rookie Ray Culp beat Roger Craig and the Mets 2–0.

23rd Dropping a 4–0 shutout to Bob Purkey in the first of 2 games at Cincinnati, the Colt 45s tie a ML record with their 4th straight shutout loss. Houston finally breaks a 40-inning scoreless drought in the 2nd inning of the nightcap, but still loses 8–1.

Jimmy Piersall of the New York Mets hits the 100th HR of his ML career and celebrates by running around the bases backwards. Dallas Green of the Phillies, who gave up the HR, is not amused. Neither is Commissioner Ford Frick, who is in the stands.

A ML fielding record is set by Boston's 1B Dick Stuart as "Dr. Strange Glove" handles 3 first-inning grounders and tosses to P Bob Heffner for putouts. Stuart's teammates and Fenway fans give him a standing ovation. The Yankees beat the Sox 8–0.

27th Detroit's Norm Cash achieves a rarity by playing an entire game at 1B without a chance, as the Twins win 10–6.

The Phillie Ray Culp (10-5) beats the Pirates 13–4, but CF Tony Gonzalez's streak of 205 straight errorless games ends with a 7th-inning muff.

A meager crowd of 6,497 fans at Fenway see a great catch. Cleveland OF Al Luplow races full tilt for Dick Williams's drive to right-CF, reaches over the fence, and gloves the ball while flipping over the barrier into the bullpen. Nonetheless, Boston wins 3–2.

JULY

1st The Reds send C Jesse Gonder and cash to the Mets for 3B Charlie Neal and C Sammy Taylor. Cincinnati also sells 2B Don Blasingame to Washington.

2nd At 12:31 A.M. in San Francisco, Willie Mays's round-tripper off Warren Spahn in the bottom of the 16th gives Juan Marichal a 1–0 win, the NL's longest win ended by a HR.

Nipping Curt Simmons and St. Louis 1–0, Don Drysdale puts the Dodgers into first place for good.

5th Minnesota's Zoilo Versalles ties the AL record for SS with 5 errors in a doubleheader (18 innings).

7th 3B Jim Ray Hart debuts with the Giants singling and doubling during a 15-inning, 4–3 squeaker over the Cards at Candlestick. In the 2nd game, Hart suffers a broken collarbone when hit by a Bob Gibson pitch.

8th Reports of Charlie Finley's intention to move the Kansas City A's to Oakland surface during the All-Star break at Cleveland.

9th Willie Mays is held to a single, but dominates a 5–3 NL win in the All-Star Game. He also walks, steals twice, scores twice, bats in a pair, and makes a great catch. It is Stan Musial's 24th All-Star appearance, a record.

13th At Kansas City in the 2nd game of a doubleheader, Cleveland's Early Wynn leaves with a lead after struggling through 5 innings. Four scoreless relief innings by Jerry Walker enable Wynn to score his 300th career victory 7–4.

21st Jerry Lynch's ML record-tying 14th pinch-hit HR, a 3-run shot off the Cubs Lindy McDaniel in the 9th inning, ties the game, and the Bucs win 6–5 in 14 innings. The Cubs take the opener 5–1.

28th The Giants' 8–2 loss at Houston is their 22nd straight away from the Polo Grounds, and matches the ML record by the 1890 Pirates.

31st The Indians become the first AL club to hit 4 straight HRs. Number 8 hitter Woody Held begins with a 2-out blast off Paul Foytack, P Pedro Ramos follows with his 2nd of the game, Tito Francona makes it 3 straight, and rookie SS Larry Brown's first ML 4-bagger finishes the string. The Indians win 9–5 in the opener of 2 with the Angels.

AUGUST

1st Ellis Burton becomes the 8th player to hit HRs left- and righthanded in the same game, helping the Cubs bury the Braves 10–2.

8th Vern Law (4-5) is placed on the retired list with a sore arm. He will come back in 1964.

Frank Howard and Moose Skowron hit back-to-back pinch-hit HRs for the Dodgers, only the 2nd time this has ever occurred, but the Cubs hold on to win 5–4 at Wrigley.

9th Roger Craig's NL record-tying 18-game losing streak ends thanks to Jim Hickman's 9th-inning grand slam off Lindy McDaniel. New York beats the Cubs 7–3.

10th A's pinch-hit star George Alusik suffers a broken wrist when hit by the Indians' Pedro Ramos's pitch.

12th Stan Musial announces he will retire at the end of the year.

16th Jim Ray Hart returns to the hospital when he is beaned by Curt Simmons during an easy 13–0 Cardinal win at San Francisco.

17th Oriole Dick Hall's perfect inning of relief against the Athletics gives him 28 consecutive batters retired since July 24th (5 appearances).

20th The Mets Grover Powell beats the Phils with a 4–0 shutout in his first ML start. It is his only ML victory.

21st Jerry Lynch's ML-record 15th pinch-hit HR gives the Pirates a 7–6 win in Chicago.

Orioles SS Luis Aparicio becomes the first ML player since George Case in 1945 to reach 300 career steals.

23rd 1B Lee Thomas of the Angels ties a ML record by participating in 6 DPs in a 17–0 romp at Washington. 3B Felix Torres starts 4 of them to tie a ML record.

Warren Spahn's 601st start is a modern NL record. Grover Alexander had the previous record of 600.

25th Cleveland batters suffer an AL-record 27 strikeouts in a doubleheader (24 innings) against the Red Sox. The 44 strikeouts for both teams are also a record. The Tribe still manages a split, winning 2–1 after an 8–3 loss.

27th Willie Mays, Orlando Cepeda, and Felipe Alou hit consecutive round-trippers in the 3rd inning of San Francisco's 7–2 win against St. Louis.

29th Minnesota matches the AL record with 8 HRs in a 14–2 opener with Washington, then win the nightcap 10–1.

30th The Twins' power continues in a 5–3 win over the White Sox. Minnesota has 19 HRs in 5 straight games, tying the ML record set by the Giants in 1954.

SEPTEMBER

1st Yankees CF Tom Tresh joins teammate Mickey Mantle among 4 AL and 5 NL players to hit HRs left- and righthanded in one game. The Yanks beat Baltimore 5–4.

P Curt Simmons of the Cardinals drives in a run with a triple in the second and then steals home on a squeeze play. He also knocks in another run and beats the Phils 7–3.

3rd Cubs 3B Ron Santo ties the modern NL record for errors in an inning at 3B with 3 to help the Giants beat Chicago 16–3.

6th Baseball historian Lee Allen says the Indians-Senators game is the 100,000th in ML history. Bennie Daniels celebrates by beating the Tribe 7–2.

7th The Reds Frank Robinson suffers a spike wound requiring 30 stitches when Mets 2B Ron Hunt lands on his left arm.

8th Braves P Warren Spahn ties Christy Mathewson with his 13th 20-win season by notching a 3–2 victory in Philadelphia. At 42, Spahn becomes the oldest 20-game winner.

10th Stan Musial hits a HR in his first at bat as a grandfather, and Bob Gibson (17-8) blanks the Cubs 8–0.

13th The Dodgers split in Philadelphia and lead the Cards by 2½ games.

Jim Bouton's 20th win, 2–0 at Minnesota, clinches the Yankees 28th pennant.

15th The Alou brothers—Felipe, Matty, and Jesus—appear in the San Francisco OF for one inning of a 13–5 win against the Pirates. This necessitates the "benching" of Willie Mays.

16th The Dodgers and Cardinals begin a first-place showdown before 32,442 fans at Busch Stadium. Ron Perranoski saves a 3–1 win for Johnny Podres and the Dodgers.

17th Sandy Koufax gets his 11th shutout, a modern ML season record for a lefty. His 8 strikeouts give him 306, an NL record, as the Dodgers top the Cards 4–0.

18th Rookie Dick Nen crushes St. Louis's pennant hopes with a 9th-inning game-tying HR off reliever Ron Taylor. Ron Perranoski wins 6–5 in 13 innings for a 3-game sweep of the threatening Cards. Nen's HR is his only hit in 8 at bats with the Dodgers.

The last game at the Polo Grounds draws 1,752 fans to see Philadelphia beat New York 5–1. Jim Hickman hits the final New York HR in the historic park.

21st Minnesota's Harmon Killebrew ties an AL record with 4 HRs in a doubleheader, a split with the Red Sox. Minnesota loses 11–2 after winning the opener 13–4.

24th The idle Dodgers clinch their 2nd Los Angeles pennant when Chicago's Lindy McDaniel beats Bob Gibson and the Cards 6–3.

25th Stan Musial is named a vice president of the Cardinals by owner August Busch. His number 6 is retired.

27th Using a lineup of 9 rookies, the Colt 45s lose 10–3 to the Mets. P Jay Dahl loses his only ML game at 17 and will die in an auto accident at 19. Houston 2B Joe Morgan will play 22 years, and 1B Rusty Staub, 23.

29th On Stan Musial Day in St. Louis, The Man has 2 hits, giving him an NL career total of 3,630.

After his 2nd hit, driving in his 1,951st run, Musial retires for a pinch runner as 27,576 roar their approval. The Cards beat the Reds in 14 innings 3–2.

Dave Nicholson suffers his 174th and 175th strikeouts, a ML record, as Washington beats Chicago 9–2.

30th Houston OF John Paciorek goes 3-for-3 in his only ML appearance, driving in 3 runs and scoring 4. Brother Tom will do much better (1970-87).

OCTOBER

1st The season ends, and there are no full-schedule players in the AL for the first time since 1910. Brooks Robinson played in the most games, 161, missing only 1. Ron Santo, Vada Pinson, and Bill White play the full schedule in the NL.

2nd In the WS Opener, Sandy Koufax fans the first 5 batters he faces en route to a WS record 15. John Roseboro's 3-run HR is the difference, as Los Angeles beats the Yankees 5–2 at New York.

3rd In game 2, Johnny Podres scatters 7 hits, Tommy Davis ties a WS record with 2 triples, Willie Davis drives in 2 runs, Moose Skowron homers, and Los Angeles beats Al Downing 4–1 to go 2 up.

5th Fans attending the first WS game at Dodger Stadium see a pitching duel between Don Drysdale and Jim Bouton. A first-inning run is all Los Angeles needs to take a 3-0 WS lead.

6th Sandy Koufax beats the Yanks again 2–1 for a shocking WS sweep for the Dodgers. Whitey Ford gives up only 2 hits, both by Frank Howard, who crashes a long HR in the 5th to start the LA scoring. The Bronx Bombers bat just .171 and score only 4 runs, the 2nd lowest total in WS history.

8th Frank Lane sues Charlie Finley for $144,166 for breach of contract.

10th The Mets take 1B Bill Haas from the Dodgers and P Jack Fisher from the Giants, while Houston grabs P Claude Raymond from the Braves in a supplemental draft for the expansion teams.

12th In the first (and last) Hispanic American major league all-star game, the NL team beats the AL 5–2 at the Polo Grounds. The game features such names as Minnie Minoso, Tony Oliva, Roberto

Clemente, Orlando Cepeda, Julian Javier, Felipe Alou, Luis Aparicio, and Zoilo Versalles. Vic Power receives a pregame award as the number-one Latin player. NL starter Juan Marichal strikes out 6 in 4 innings, though reliever Al McBean is the winner. Pinch hitter Manny Mota drives in 2 against loser Pedro Ramos.

22nd Roy Hamey retires as GM of the Yankees. His surprise replacement is Ralph Houk, who steps up from manager (309-176) after winning 3 pennants in as many seasons.

24th Yogi Berra is appointed manager of the Yankees.

Sandy Koufax is the unanimous winner of the Cy Young Award.

30th Sandy Koufax wins again, outpolling Pittsburgh's Dick Groat 237 to 190 for the NL MVP award.

NOVEMBER

4th The Cards acquire P Roger Craig from the Mets for OF George Altman and P Bill Wakefield.

7th C Elston Howard becomes the first black ever voted AL MVP. New York's Howard tops Detroit's Al Kaline 248 to 148.

18th Detroit sends OF Rocky Colavito, P Bob Anderson, and a reported $50,000 to Kansas City for 2B Jerry Lumpe and pitchers Dave Wickersham and Ed Rakow.

19th Coach Hank Bauer is named to replace Billy Hitchcock (86-76) as manager of the Orioles.

26th Cincinnati 2B Pete Rose is a landslide winner of NL Rookie of the Year honors, taking 17 of 20 votes.

27th Chicago P Gary Peters edges teammate 3B Pete Ward and Minnesota OF Jimmie Hall for AL rookie honors.

The A's acquire 1B Jim Gentile and $25,000 from the Orioles for 1B Norm Siebern.

DECEMBER

1st ML owners agree to allow the expansion clubs 4 protected first-year players who can be optioned to the minors without being subject to a draft.

2nd The Angels trade OF Leon Wagner to Cleveland for P Barry Latman and a player to be named.

The ML Rules Committee bans oversized catcher's mitts, effective in 1965.

3rd OF Felipe Alou, C Ed Bailey, P Billy Hoeft, and a player to be named are sent by the Giants to the Braves for C Del Crandall and pitchers Bob Shaw and Bob Hendley.

4th Cleveland trades OF Willie Kirkland to the Orioles for OF Al Smith and an estimated $25,000.

Detroit P Jim Bunning is traded to the Phillies with C Gus Triandos for OF Don Demeter and P Jack Hamilton.

10th Chicago's 2B Nellie Fox is traded to the Colts for cash, P Jim Golden, and OF Danny Murphy.

12th Minnesota LF Harmon Killebrew undergoes knee surgery.

1964

JANUARY

6th Charlie Finley signs a 2-year pact to move the A's, pending AL approval, from Kansas City to Louisville, KY.

The White Sox introduce powder-blue road uniforms.

15th ML baseball executives vote to hold a free-agent draft in New York City. A new TV pact is also signed.

Willie Mays, the highest-paid player in baseball, signs for $105,000.

16th AL owners vote 9-1 against Charlie Finley's Louisville proposal. Finley is given an ultimatum to sign a lease in Kansas City or lose his franchise.

28th Reds CF Vada Pinson is cleared of assault charges stemming from a September 5, 1963, incident when Cincinnati sportswriter Earl Lawson does not pursue charges further.

29th Pitcher-writer Jim Brosnan is given permission by the White Sox to make his own deal with another team. His in-season writing has been censured by owner Ed Short.

30th The United States Senate Subcommittee on Monopolies begins hearings on baseball.

FEBRUARY

2nd The Hall of Fame Special Veterans Committee tabs Red Faber, Burleigh Grimes, Tim Keefe, Heinie Manush, John Montgomery Ward, and Miller Huggins for induction, the biggest veterans class ever.

15th Cubs 2B Ken Hubbs, 22, dies when his private plane crashes near Provo, UT, while en route to Colton, CA. As a rookie in 1962, Hubbs had played in 78 consecutive games without making an error.

17th Former White Sox SS Luke Appling is voted into the Hall of Fame.

23rd Charlie Finley gives in to AL pressure and signs a 4-year lease with the municipal government to keep the A's in Kansas City. Finley wanted 2 years. His exasperated AL colleagues voted 9-1 that KC's offer was reasonable.

The San Francisco Giants sign P Masanori Murakami, 3B Tatsuhico Tanaka, and C Hiroshi Takahashi—the first Japanese ever to play for American teams. All 3 are assigned to the Magic Valley Cowboys (Pioneer League).

MARCH

5th Atlanta Mayor Ivan Allen, Jr., says he has a verbal commitment from a ML baseball club to move there if a stadium is ready by 1965. A $15 million stadium is approved the next day by the city Board of Aldermen.

9th The ACLU charges the White Sox with violating the rights of P-writer Jim Brosnan.

APRIL

1st Cleveland manager Birdie Tebbetts suffers a heart attack and will be sidelined until July 5th.

2nd Coach George Strickland will manage the Indians in Tebbetts's absence.

3rd P Carl Willey of the Mets suffers a broken jaw when he is hit by a line drive off the bat of Detroit's Gates Brown during a spring training loss. He will be out until June 6th.

8th Houston P Jim Umbricht dies of cancer at age 33. He was 4-3 with a 2.61 ERA in 1963.

9th The Tigers purchase P Larry Sherry from the Dodgers.

14th San Francisco's 5 HRs match the mark for Opening Day round-trippers. Juan Marichal beats Warren Spahn and the Braves 8–4.

Sandy Koufax throws his 9th complete game without allowing a walk as he beats St. Louis 4–0 in his only start as an Opening Day pitcher.

15th Work begins on an $18 million stadium in Atlanta.

17th The Pirates defeat the Mets 4–3 in the first game played at Shea Stadium.

18th Sandy Koufax fans the side on 9 pitches in the 3rd inning, becoming the first pitcher to do it twice, but Cincinnati wins 3–0.

19th Bob Bruce strikes out the Cardinals in order on 9 pitches in the 8th inning of a Houston loss.

21st All runs score on HRs as the Pirates win 8–5 at Wrigley Field, tying a record for the most runs on HRs with no other runs scoring. HRs by 9 different players tie the ML record.

23rd Houston's Ken Johnson becomes the first pitcher ever to hurl a 9-inning no-hitter and lose as Cincinnati wins 1–0. 2B Nellie Fox's error allows the only run.

MAY

1st The visiting Cubs make it look easy, scoring 10 runs in the first inning to shoot down the Colt 45s 11–3. Billy Williams has a grand slam and a single for 5 RBI in the big inning, and adds a run-scoring double in the 8th to lead Chicago.

2nd Minnesota becomes the 3rd club to hit 4 consecutive HRs in one inning. Tony Oliva, Bob Allison, Jimmie Hall, and Harmon Killebrew do the damage in an 11th-inning explosion that gives the Twins a 7–3 win at Kansas City.

3rd Sadaharu Oh of the Yomiuri Giants hits 4 HRs in one 9-inning game against the Hanshin Tigers to set a Japanese record, and tie the American ML record held by 7 players.

5th To foil Oh, the Hiroshima Carp use an exaggerated shift that places all fielders in right and center, leaving LF unguarded. Oh responds by hitting a 400-foot HR to RF.

12th Gary Geiger's recurring ulcer problems force his retirement from the Red Sox for this year.

24th Seven shutouts in both leagues tie the ML record for blankings in one day.

25th Ground is broken for a new stadium in St. Louis.

31st After Juan Marichal's 5–3, first-game win, San Francisco holds a 6–1 lead in the 2nd until New York rallies for 5 to tie in the 7th. Eventually, with 2 out in the 23rd, pinch hitter Del Crandall delivers a run-scoring double off Galen Cisco, and the Giants prevail 8–6 after 7 hours and 22 minutes—a record. Gaylord Perry pitches 10 scoreless innings to get credit for the win. Thirty-two innings and an elapsed time of 9 hours and 50 minutes are doubleheader records, as are 47 strikeouts. New York's 22 K's in the 2nd game are the most by one club in an overtime contest.

JUNE

2nd Dave McNally blanks the A's as the Orioles take first place with a 4–0 win.

The Cards trade P Lew Burdette to the Cubs for P Glen Hobbie.

Giants OF Matty Alou suffers a fractured wrist, as Pittsburgh's Bob Veale beats the Giants 3–1. Alou will miss 5 weeks.

4th Sandy Koufax becomes the 4th pitcher to hurl 3 no-hitters by blanking the NL-leading Phillies 3–0 at Connie Mack Stadium. Koufax strikes out 12 and walks one.

The Angels trade OF Lee Thomas to the Red Sox for OF Lu Clinton.

11th After a 2-week absence, Mickey Mantle returns to the lineup and clouts 2 HRs at Fenway off Bill Monbouquette. The Yankees win easily 8–4.

Charlie Finley fires Ed Lopat (17–35) as manager of the A's, replacing him with Mel McGaha.

13th 2B Bernie Allen of the Twins is hurt in a collision with Don Zimmer. He will be out until August 4th.

14th The Yankees complete a 5-game sweep of the White Sox with two victories 8–3 and 4–3 (in 10) at the Stadium. Chicago falls to 2nd place behind the Orioles.

15th St. Louis acquires OF Lou Brock, with pitchers Jack Spring and Paul Toth, from the Cubs for pitchers Bobby Shantz and Ernie Broglio and OF Doug Clemens.

Cleveland sends P Jim Grant to Minnesota for P Lee Stange and 3B/OF George Banks.

21st On Father's Day at Shea Stadium, Jim Bunning pitches the first perfect game (excluding Don Larsen's 1956 WS effort and Harvey Haddix's 1959 overtime loss) since Charlie Robertson's on April 30, 1922. He also becomes the first pitcher to win no-hitters in both leagues and drives in 2 runs as Philadelphia beats the Mets 6–0.

The Yankees move into first place by 8 percentage points over Baltimore, as they outpitch the White Sox to win 2–0 and 2–1. Mickey Mantle and Elston Howard HRs win it 2–0 for Jim Bouton in the opener against the White Sox, and an error wins the nightcap 2–1 in the 17th. The Yankees sweep 4, giving up just one run in 41 innings, and take 9 games from Chicago in 11 days.

23rd Charlie Lau ties a ML record with 2 pinch hits in the 8th inning of Baltimore's 9–8 win over the Yankees. The O's score 7 runs in the inning after 2 are out.

24th University of Wisconsin star slugger Rick Reichardt signs with the Angels. He receives the biggest bonus ever, an estimated $200,000.

25th Steve Barber's 3-hit 3–1 win gives the Orioles a 3-game sweep of the Yankees and first place in the AL.

27th Cleveland 3B Max Alvis is stricken with spinal meningitis. He will be disabled for 6 weeks but will make the All-Star team in 1965.

JULY

3rd Birdie Tebbetts returns to limited duty as manager of the Indians.

4th Manny Jimenez, who went the entire 1963 season without a HR, hits 3, and goes 4-for-4 for Kansas City against Baltimore. The game ends in a 6–6 tie when halted by a special curfew so a fireworks display can take place in Baltimore.

5th Dennis Bennett beats Juan Marichal 2–1 to give the Phillies a 3-game sweep of the Giants at Candlestick. The Phils hold a 1½ game lead at the All-Star break.

6th The NL and its umpires settle on a contract lasting until December 1969. The league provides increased pension and insurance payments.

7th Johnny Callison's 9th-inning 3-run HR off Dick Radatz caps a 4-run rally and gives the NL a 7–4 win in the All-Star Game at Shea Stadium. This evens the series at 17.

10th Jesus Alou becomes the first Giant with 6 hits in a game in almost 40 years, as San Francisco beats the Cubs 10–3. All 6 hits are against different pitchers.

11th Vic Power of the Angels is fined $250 and suspended 10 days for spitting on ump Jim Honochick after a close play during a doubleheader loss to the White Sox 7–4 and 6–1 the previous day.

14th Jack Sanford of the Giants undergoes arm surgery.

Oriole Bob Johnson's 6th straight hit as a pinch hitter sets an AL mark, but the Yankees win 4–3.

15th Whitey Ford's 2–0 win over the Orioles raises the Yankees to first place.

In the first of 2 with Cleveland, Wes Stock wins his 12th straight game, all in relief, winning 5–3. The A's take the nightcap 3–2 in KC.

16th Steve Barber regains first place for the Orioles with a successful 6–1 outing against the Yankees and Jim Bouton.

17th The first-place O's win again as Robin Roberts shuts out Detroit 5–0, despite giving up 11 hits.

The Phillies regain first place with a 7–5 win against the Pirates. They will hold the lead until September 27th.

18th Ken Boyer, Bill White, and Tim McCarver of the Cards hit consecutive 8th-inning HRs in a 15–7 bombing of the Mets.

Pete Rose hits the only grand slam of his career in the Reds' 14-3 home win against the Phillies.

19th Luis Tiant debuts with a 4-hit 3–0 win for Cleveland at Yankee Stadium.

23rd A's rookie Bert Campaneris sends Minnesota to defeat 4–3 with 2 HRs in his ML debut. The first comes on the first pitch thrown to him by Jim Kaat. The 21-year-old Cuban joins Bob Nieman as the only player since 1900 with 2 HRs in his first ML game.

25th The Twins tie an AL record by using 9 pitchers in a 13-inning game they lose 6–5 to the White Sox. Gerry Fosnow (0-1) is the loser; Don Mossi (2-1)—the 5th Chicago pitcher—is the winner.

26th LF Tony Conigliaro suffers a broken arm in a 6–1 Boston win at Cleveland.

27th Reds manager Fred Hutchinson enters a Cincinnati hospital for further cancer treatment. Dick Sisler takes the helm.

28th The Angels Jim Fregosi hits for the cycle to assure a 3–1 win over the Yankees.

31st Giants P Juan Marichal has back spasms. He will not pitch again until August 25th.

AUGUST

2nd   Detroit P Larry Sherry suffers a fractured left foot when struck by a liner off the bat of Leon Wagner in Cleveland's doubleheader sweep 6–1 and 2–1. Sherry is out for rest of the year.

4th   Fred Hutchinson returns to manage the Reds. They respond by sweeping a pair 5–2 and 4–2 from the Braves.

5th   Ford Frick tells the league presidents and club owners he will not run for another term as commissioner.

7th   Steve Barber and Harvey Haddix beat the Yankees 2–0 to boost the Orioles back into first place.

The Mets trade OF/1B Frank Thomas to Philadelphia for P Gary Kroll, OF Wayne Graham, and cash.

8th   The Angels sign a contract to move to Anaheim in 1966.

12th   Mickey Mantle homers from each side of the plate in the same game for the 10th and final time, a ML record, and New York beats Chicago 7–3 at Yankee Stadium.

13th   CBS buys 80 percent of the Yankees, effective November 2.

Ailing Fred Hutchinson again takes a leave of absence as manager of Reds. Dick Sisler again takes charge.

14th   Bo Belinsky is suspended by the Angels after attacking sportswriter Braven Dyer. Four days later Belinsky is assigned to Hawaii (Pacific Coast League), then suspended for the season when he refuses to report.

16th   Sandy Koufax (19-5) hurts his elbow sliding into 2B in a 3–0 win against St. Louis. He will miss the rest of the season. In the nightcap, Curt Simmons matches Koufax with a 4–0 shutout of the Dodgers. Card CF Curt Flood has 8 straight hits in the doubleheader split.

17th   General manager Bing Devine and business manager Art Routzong of the Cardinals are fired by owner August Busch.

20th   On the New York team bus following a 5–0 White Sox win, Phil Linz begins to play "Mary Had a Little Lamb" on his harmonica. Manager Yogi Berra orders Linz to stop, then slaps the instrument out of his hands when he continues playing. The incident is reported as indicating dissension on the club and Berra's lack of control, as well as the level of Linz's humor.

Orioles LF Boog Powell fractures his right wrist in a collision with the outfield fence in Baltimore's loss at Boston. He will be sidelined until September 5th.

29th   On Elston Howard Night, the Yankees take 2 from Boston 10–2 and 6–1. Joe Pepitone's 3 HRs, including a grand slam, and Roger Maris's 6 singles lead the offense. Mickey Mantle hits HR number 447 in the opener and ties Babe Ruth's career strikeout record (1,330) in the nightcap.

30th   Milwaukee (8) and San Francisco (7) combine to use a ML-record 15 pinch hitters in 2 nine-inning games. The Giants win the opening marathon 15–10, then win 7–4. The Milwaukee refreshment stands, down to $13 in pennies, drop their prices; beer goes from 31 cents to 30 cents, hot dogs from 26 cents to 25 cents, hot sandwiches from 62 cents to 60 cents.

31st   Ground is broken for Anaheim Stadium, future home of next year's California Angels.

SEPTEMBER

1st   Southpaw relief P Masanori Murakami becomes the first ML player from Japan. He debuts in a 4–1 San Francisco loss at New York. His first 11 innings will be scoreless ones.

The Cardinals move past the faltering Giants into 3rd place with a 5–4 win over the Braves. Former Brave, now Cardinals utility C, Bob Uecker hits his first HR of the year in the 9th to win it for the Birds.

2nd   Lee Stange ties the ML record with 4 strikeouts in one inning, as the Indians beat Washington 9–0.

Milt Pappas keeps Baltimore in first place with a one-hit 2–0 win against Minnesota. Zoilo Versalles gets the single.

Boston's Bill Monbouquette pitches a one-hitter, but loses 2–1 to Baltimore. Versalles spoils a no-hitter for the 2nd time in one week with a 6th-inning HR.

7th   Completing a 12-3 home stand, the Cards sweep a Labor Day doubleheader from the Reds 3–2, 3–2, and move into a 2nd-place tie with Cincinnati.

10th The Phils split a 2-game series with the Cards and build a 6-game lead in the NL on Chris Short's 5–1 win.

11th Angels reliever Bob Lee fractures his right hand punching a heckling sailor in Boston.

12th The Orioles' Frank Bertaina and the A's Bob Meyer duel in the ML's 7th double one-hitter. Bertaina prevails 1–0 to earn his only decision of the year.

13th St. Louis becomes the first NL club to score in each inning since the Giants did it on June 1, 1923. They coast 15–2 at Wrigley Field.

16th The White Sox move into a first-place tie (88-61) with Baltimore by besting Detroit 4–1, while the Orioles lose to Minnesota 2–1. The Yanks are one point behind.

17th The Yankees whip the Angels 6–2 to lock on to first place for good with a 2-percentage-point lead over the idle White Sox and Orioles. Roger Maris and Mickey Mantle each have 3 hits. Mantle's include his 2,000th career hit and his 450th HR, his 31st of the year. The Yankees have won 2 in a row and will run their win streak to 11 games.

19th The Colt 45s drop Harry Craft (61-88) as manager. He is replaced by Lum Harris.

Willie Davis steals home in the 16th inning to give the Dodgers a 4–3 win over the Phils.

21st John Tsitouris hurls a 1–0 shutout for the Reds over the first-place Phillies, launching a 10-game Phils' losing streak.

25th Dean Chance beats the Twins' Jim Kaat 1–0 to become the Angels first 20-game winner. Chance's five 1–0 wins in 1964 tie the ML record.

26th The Braves and Phillies set a ML record by using 43 players in a 9-inning game. The Braves' 25 match the 9-inning high mark for NL clubs. Eight of the 25 are pitchers, tying a league mark, but still the stumbling Phils drop their 6th in a row 6–4.

27th Despite 3 HRs by Johnny Callison, the Phils are 14–8 losers to the Braves, who complete a 4-game sweep at Connie Mack Stadium. The Phils' 7th straight loss drops them out of first.

28th Sadaharu Oh hits his 55th HR of Yomiuri's 130-game season. It is his highest total and a Japanese record.

29th The Cards' 4–2 win over the Phils moves them into a first-place tie with the Reds, who lose to the Pirates.

30th The Phillies lose their 10th straight game as Curt Simmons of the Cards beats Jim Bunning 8–5.

A total of 36 strikeouts, 19 by Pittsburgh batters, ties the NL record for whiffs in the Pirates' 1–0 squeaker against the Reds in 16 innings.

In his first ML at bat, pinch hitter Bill Roman debuts with a homer, the only one of his brief ML career. Even so, the Tigers lose to New York 7–6 as a Mickey Mantle HR ignites a 5-run rally. New York takes the nightcap 11–8 for a sweep.

OCTOBER

1st Detroit's Dave Wickersham, in a bid for his 20th win, is ejected by umpire Bill Valentine in the 7th inning of his final start. Wickersham gets the heave-ho for trying to get Valentine's attention by grabbing his shoulder during an argument with Norm Cash. Mickey Lolich enters the 1–1 tie and earns a 4–2 win.

Danny Murtaugh (80-82) resigns as manager of the Pirates for health reasons.

Dave McNally's one-hitter keeps Baltimore in the pennant race, 2½ games behind the Yankees.

2nd The Mets end an 8-game St. Louis win streak when Al Jackson beats Bob Gibson 1–0, but the Cards remain a half game in front of the Reds.

The Orioles score 6 runs in the 2nd to beat Detroit 10–4 in a fog-bound game. Detroit outfielders lose 2 routine fly balls in the O's big inning.

3rd The Yankees clinch their 5th straight pennant, and 29th in the club's history, by defeating Cleveland 8–3.

The Cardinals lose 15–5 to the Mets and fall into a first-place tie with the idle Reds.

Boston fires manager Johnny Pesky (70-90). Billy Herman takes over for the final game of season.

4th Larry Jackson's 9–2 victory over the Giants is his 24th win for the Cubs, the most ever for an 8th-place team. He also sets a ML record for pitchers by fielding 109 chances during the season without an error.

St. Louis wins its first pennant since 1946, cudgeling the Mets 11–5. Bob Gibson wins in relief.

The Phils bomb the Reds 1–0 as both teams finish one game behind St. Louis.

Alvin Dark (90-72) is fired as manager of the Giants and replaced by Herman Franks. The Giants finish in 4th places 3 games off the pace.

7th Ailing Whitey Ford struggles as St. Louis wins the WS opener 9–4 at Busch Stadium. Mike Shannon homers in a 4-run, St. Louis 6th inning. Ray Sadecki and Barney Schultz combine for the win.

8th Rookie Mel Stottlemyre beats Bob Gibson 8–3 to even the WS. The Yanks score 4 in the 9th after Gibson is taken out for a pinch hitter.

9th Charlie Finley says he lost $834,356 in Kansas City this year, a prelude to renewed efforts to move the A's somewhere else.

10th After Jim Bouton and Curt Simmons battle to a 1–1 tie after 8 innings, Mickey Mantle homers on Barney Schultz's first pitch in the 9th, and the Yankees win 2–1.

11th Ken Boyer's grand slam in the 6th inning off Al Downing gives the Cards a 4–3 win in game 4.

12th Tim McCarver's 3-run HR pins a 5–2 loss on Pete Mikkelsen and gives St. Louis a 3-2 WS lead.

14th Roger Maris and Mickey Mantle hit HRs on back-to-back pitches from Curt Simmons, and Joe Pepitone belts Gordie Richardson for a grand slam. New York wins 8–3 at St. Louis and evens the WS.

The Braves say they have a firm lease offer from Atlanta.

15th St. Louis takes an early lead in the deciding WS game 7. Lou Brock's 5th-inning HR triggers a 2nd 3-run frame and a 6–0 lead for Bob Gibson. Mickey Mantle, Clete Boyer, and Phil Linz homer for New York, but it's not enough. The Cards win 7–5 and are the World Champions.

16th The Board of Directors of the Indians votes to keep the club in Cleveland.

17th A WS loss is enough reason for the Yankees to fire manager Yogi Berra (99-63). Johnny Keane (93-69) stuns a St. Louis press conference by resigning as manager of the Cardinals.

19th Fred Hutchinson (60-49) resigns as manager of Reds.

Harry Walker is named manager of the Pirates.

Branch Rickey is fired from his $65,000 per year consulting job with the Cardinals.

20th Johnny Keane pulls another shocker by signing to manage the Yankees.

Red Schoendienst is appointed manager of the Cards.

21st After just 11 years in Milwaukee, the Braves Board of Directors votes to ask the NL for permission to move to Atlanta. Milwaukee County officials sue to block the move.

30th Joe Stanka of the Nankai Hawks wins the Pacific League MVP award. With a season record of 26-7, Stanka pitched his team to 3 straight victories over the Yomiuri Giants to win the Japan Series. In his career with the Hawks (1960-65), and later with the Taiyo Whales (1966), he will win 100 games, the record for an American pitcher.

NOVEMBER

3rd Philadelphia voters approve $25 million to build a new sports stadium.

7th With their home attendance below 800,000 for the past 2 seasons, the NL orders the Braves to stay in Milwaukee in 1965, but permits a move to Atlanta in 1966.

10th The Braves sign a 25-year lease to play in the new Atlanta stadium.

12th Former Cincinnati manager Fred Hutchinson, 45, dies of cancer.

18th Baltimore 3B Brooks Robinson is voted AL MVP, outpolling Mickey Mantle 269 to 171.

23rd The Mets purchase P Warren Spahn from the Braves.

24th 3B Ken Boyer of the Cardinals is voted NL MVP, with 243 votes to 187 for Philadelphia OF Johnny Callison.

29th The Phils trade P Dennis Bennett to the Red Sox for 1B Dick Stuart.

DECEMBER

1st The White Sox trade P Ray Herbert and 1B Jeoff Long to the Phillies for OF Danny Cater and SS Lee Elia.

The Indians obtain OF Chuck Hinton from Washington for 1B Bob Chance and IF/OF Woody Held.

The Houston club officially changes its name from the Colt 45s to the Astros.

4th Baseball approves a free-agent draft. At their winter meetings in Houston, the minor league and major league organizations establish a system, basically like that of professional football, which will take effect in January 1965 and be held every four months thereafter. Choices will be exercised by clubs in inverse order of their previous year's standing. Draftees must be included in their club's 40-man roster or be susceptible to claim at the waiver price the following season.

The majors also restore to the commissioner's office all powers rescinded after Judge Kennesaw Mountain Landis's death in 1944. Principally, they waive their right to take legal action in the event of disagreements with the commissioner and grant him authority to judge whether actions taken by the owners in concert are, automatically "in the best interests of baseball." Voting for the annual All-Star teams is turned back to the fans.

The Dodgers trade OF Frank Howard, P Phil Ortega, P Pete Richert, and 3B Ken McMullen to the Senators for P Claude Osteen, IF John Kennedy, and cash.

The Angels trade P Bo Belinsky to the Phils for P Rudy May and 1B Costen Shockley.

Minnesota acquires versatile Cesar Tovar from the Reds for P Jerry Arrigo.

14th St. Louis trades P Roger Craig and OF Charlie James to the Reds for P Bob Purkey.

15th Tigers owner John Fetzer announces a 2-year television pact between ML baseball and ABC-TV. The network pays $12.2 million to telecast games on 25 Saturdays, Independence Day, and Labor Day.

The Cards purchase OF Tito Francona from the Indians.

26th Bob Lemon is named manager of the Seattle Angels of the Pacific Coast League.

1965

JANUARY

5th   James M. Johnston and James H. Lemon purchase the remaining 40 percent of Senators stock to acquire complete control of the club.

20th   Rocky Colavito returns to Cleveland in a 3-way deal that sends outfielders Jim Landis and Mike Hershberger and P Fred Talbot from the White Sox to Kansas City; C Johnny Romano, OF Tommy Agee, and P Tommy John from Cleveland to Chicago; and C Cam Carreon from the White Sox to the Indians.

31st   Pud Galvin is chosen for Hall of Fame induction by the Special Veterans Committee.

Masanori Murakami, the first Japanese player in the major leagues, says he will not return to the Giants in 1965.

FEBRUARY

1st   The NL clubs adopt an emergency team replacement plan to restock any club struck by disaster.

C Ed Bailey moves from the Braves to the Giants for P Billy O'Dell.

3rd   Braves officials propose a $500,000 payment to county officials if the club's lease to play in Milwaukee can be terminated a year early. The offer is refused.

11th   Braves officials propose to pay 5 cents from each ticket sold to a fund for the purpose of bringing a new ML team to Milwaukee. Teams, Inc., a civic group, accepts the offer, buys out the park for Opening Day, and stages Stand Up for Milwaukee Day.

17th   Commissioner Ford Frick suspends U.S.-Japan baseball relations until the dispute over Masanori Murakami's contract with the Giants is resolved.

MARCH

1st   As Pittsburgh's training camp opens, Roberto Clemente is absent and suffering from malaria. He will report to camp a month late and struggle until mid-May.

7th   Tigers manager Chuck Dressen suffers a mild coronary occlusion. He will be sidelined until May 19th. Coach Bob Swift will be acting manager.

17th   Jackie Robinson is signed as a member of the ABC-TV baseball broadcast team, becoming the first black to receive a network position broadcasting baseball. ABC provides the first-ever nationwide baseball coverage with weekly Saturday broadcasts on a regional basis.

25th   Pittsburgh 2B Bill Mazeroski suffers a broken bone in his right foot. He will not start until May.

APRIL

9th   President Lyndon B. Johnson joins 47,878 fans for the opening of Harris County Domed Stadium (the Astrodome). The Astros win an exhibition with the Yankees 2–1 in 12 innings. Mickey Mantle hits the first HR in the new park.

12th   President Johnson throws out the first ball, as the Red Sox beat the Senators in DC 7–2. Five Boston HRs tie a ML record for an opener and 7 total HRs set a ML record.

17th   In his first full ML game, Orioles LF Curt Blefary hits 2 HRs, as Baltimore loses 12–9 in Boston's home opener.

Don Drysdale ties a ML record by striking out 4 Phils—Wes Covington, Tony Gonzalez, Dick Stuart, and Clay Dalrymple—in order in the 2nd inning, but also gives up 2 HRs to lose 3–2. It is the 8th straight time the Phillies have beaten big Don.

18th   California Angels Rookie Rudy May has a no-hitter ruined in the 8th inning of his ML debut by Jake Wood's double. The Angels lift him after 9 innings of one-hit ball, and Detroit wins in 13 innings.

19th   At a cost of $20,000, the outer Astrodome ceiling is painted because the sun's glare makes fielding fly balls hazardous. This will cause the grass to die and spur the introduction of artificial turf.

28th   Mets announcer Lindsey Nelson broadcasts the Mets-Astros game at the Astrodome from a hanging gondola, 208 feet above 2B.

29th   Masanori Murakami agrees to stay with the Giants in 1965 if he can return to Japan in 1966.

MAY

1st Dodgers LF Tommy Davis suffers a fractured ankle sliding into 2nd base in a 4–2 win over the Giants. Davis will not reappear until October 3rd.

In a 9–8 loss at Detroit, Boston's Chuck Schilling ties a ML record with his 2nd straight pinch-hit HR in back-to-back games. But Boston loses both.

4th Masanori Murakami arrives in San Francisco from Japan to rejoin the Giants as a relief pitcher, ending a bitter contract dispute between the Giants and his home team, the Nankai Hawks. Murakami will have a good season; appearing in 45 games, he wins 4 and loses one, saves 8, gives up 57 hits in 74 innings, fans 85, and walks only 22 while posting an ERA of 3.50.

5th Elston Howard undergoes elbow surgery. The Yankees catcher is out until June 4th.

8th Elmira (Eastern League) beats Springfield 2–1 in 27 innings, a new record for organized baseball's longest game.

A ML-record streak of 438 chances accepted without an error and 89 straight errorless games by Baltimore 2B Jerry Adair ends with his 8th-inning fumble in a 4–3, 15-inning loss to the Tigers.

13th Twenty-five-year-old Angels P Dick Wantz dies following brain surgery for cancer. He appeared in one game last year.

15th Haywood Sullivan replaces Mel McGaha as skipper of the A's.

23rd The Braves trade OF Lee May to the Astros for P Ken Johnson and OF Jim Beauchamp.

25th Nine different Twins (5) and Red Sox (4) hit HRs, tying a ML record. Minnesota wins 17–5.

29th OF Harvey Kuenn, P Bob Hendley and C Ed Bailey are traded from the Giants to the Cubs for C Dick Bertell and 1B/OF Len Gabrielson.

Orioles club president Joe Inglehart sells his 32 percent holding in the club to National Brewing Company President Jerry Hoffberger and club treasurer Zanvyl Krieger.

Mickey Lolich's 10-inning win is Detroit's 2nd straight 2-hit 1–0 win against Cleveland.

31st Chuck Dressen is back managing the Tigers after a preseason heart attack.

JUNE

1st Bob Veale sets a Pittsburgh record with 16 strikeouts and beats Philadelphia 4–0, the 12th straight win for the 7th-place Pirates.

4th The A's receive $100,000, P Jesse Hickman, and 2B Ernie Fazio from Houston for 1B Jim Gentile.

8th Arizona star sophomore Rick Monday, selected by the Athletics, is the first player chosen in the initial ML free-agent draft of high school, college, and sandlot players. Picking 2nd, the Mets take P Les Rohr. On the 10th round they finally take Nolan Ryan. Cincinnati picks Johnny Bench in the 2nd round.

Joe Torre, Eddie Mathews, Hank Aaron, and Gene Oliver hit 10th-inning HRs, as the Braves win 8–2 at Chicago.

11th Lou Klein replaces Bob Kennedy as head coach of the Cubs. Kennedy becomes assistant to GM John Holland.

St. Louis trades pitchers Ron Taylor and Mike Cuellar to the Astros for P Hal Woodeshick.

14th No-hit pitching and 18 strikeouts, tying the NL extra-inning record, net Cincinnati's Jim Maloney a 0–0 tie with the last-place Mets through 10 innings. Johnny Lewis's 11th-inning HR gives New York and reliever Larry Bearnarth a 1–0 win.

15th Tigers P Denny McLain makes a first-inning relief appearance and fans the first 7 batters he faces, setting a ML record. He has 14 strikeouts in 6⅔ innings as Detroit rallies to beat Boston 6–5.

17th Julian Javier suffers a broken finger when hit by a Vern Law pitch. The St. Louis 2B will be out 7 weeks. Pittsburgh's Law wins the game 4–1.

18th The Yankees rout the first-place Twins 10–2 on 4 homers. Mickey Mantle cracks one in the first inning, and his replacement Ross Moschitto hits his first and only ML HR. New York is still 10 back in 7th place.

20th The Atlanta-bound Braves ban sportswriter Lou Chapman from the clubhouse for his "stories of a negative nature" and their "disquieting" effect on players and management. The ban is rescinded a day later upon protest by Milwaukee BBWAA members.

22nd Ray Barker's ML-record-tying 2nd consecutive pinch-hit HR is wasted in a first-game, 6–2 Yankees loss to the A's. Mickey Mantle adds a HR in the opener, but in the 4–2 nightcap win he tries to score from 2nd on a wild pitch and snaps a upper-thigh hamstring. He will be out for 3 weeks. The June 21st *Sports Illustrated* cover features Mantle with the prescient title "New York Yankees: End of an Era?"

29th   Indian Ralph Terry's 8–5 win at Boston gives Cleveland the AL lead.

The Yankees lose Roger Maris for 49 games with bone chips in the heel of his right hand.

JULY

3rd   Horseplay between Phillies teammates Frank Thomas and Richie Allen turns serious when Thomas swings a bat at Allen. Following Philadelphia's 10–8 loss to Cincinnati, Thomas is released and signs with Houston.

5th   Jim Maloney pitches the Reds to a 7–5 win against the Dodgers, as Cincinnati takes the NL lead.

Minnesota takes an AL lead it will not give up, as Dave Boswell and Jim Perry pitch the Twins to a 6–2 and 2–0 sweep of the Red Sox.

6th   Don Demeter of the Phillies plays his record 226th consecutive game without an error in the OF.

8th   Joe Morgan is the first Houston player with 6 hits in a game, but the Braves beat the Astros 9–8 in 12 innings.

9th   Senators LF Frank Howard ties a ML record with 7 strikeouts in Washington's twin-bill split with the Red Sox.

10th   Juan Marichal's 14th win of the year is his 7th shutout, as he 2-hits the Phils 7–0.

13th   Willie Mays's HR, 2 walks, and 2 runs scored pace the NL to a 6–5 All-Star Game victory in Minnesota. Juan Marichal pitches 3 scoreless innings to earn game MVP.

17th   Los Angeles returns to first place, as Claude Osteen beats the Cubs 7–2.

18th   Twins manager Sam Mele is fined $500 and suspended 5 days following an altercation with umpire Bill Valentine in Minnesota's doubleheader split with the Angels.

20th   Mel Stottlemyre of the Yankees becomes the first pitcher to hit an inside-the-park grand slam since Deacon Phillippe did it for the Pirates in 1910.

Stottlemyre's bases-loaded drive assures him a 6–3 victory over the Red Sox.

22nd   Ed Bailey hits a grand slam and drives in 8 runs, as the Cubs beat the Phillies 10–6 at Wrigley Field.

23rd   Dick Stuart homers in a ML-record 23rd different park when he connects at Shea Stadium in Philadelphia's 5–1 win.

27th   The official number of foreigners permitted on each Japanese team is lowered from 3 to 2. The Yomiuri Giants announce they will henceforth have no foreigners—a policy that lasts until 1975, when they sign 2B Davey Johnson.

28th   RF Tony Conigliaro suffers a broken left wrist when hit by a Wes Stock pitch in a 6–0 Boston win. He will miss 24 games.

30th   Milwaukee manager Bobby Bragan says his pitchers threw 75 to 80 spitballs in a 9–2 loss to the Giants. Bragan says he ordered the spitters to prove rules against them are not being enforced.

AUGUST

2nd   Harmon Killebrew suffers a dislocated left elbow in a collision with Baltimore's Russ Snyder. The Twins slugger will miss 48 games.

3rd   Judge Roy Hofheinz purchases 53 percent of Bob Smith's holdings in the Astros, giving Hofheinz a controlling 86 percent of the club's stock.

8th   Recently released by the Mets, Warren Spahn wins his 361st victory and first as a Giant. San Francisco beats the Cards 6–4.

12th   Milwaukee Brewers Baseball Club, Inc. applies for a NL franchise. The nonprofit group has been formed to find a replacement team for the soon-to-be-departing Braves.

15th   Washington 3B Ken McMullen ties an AL record by starting 4 DPs, as the Senators complete a 3-game sweep of Baltimore.

Pinch-hit HRs by Max Alvis in the 9th inning and Leon Wagner in the 11th give Cleveland a 6–4 win against Minnesota. Two pinch-hit HRs in one game tie the ML record.

The Japanese community of San Francisco holds Masanori Murakami Day at Candlestick Park to honor the first Japanese player to have reached the American major leagues. Ordinarily a reliever, Murakami makes his first ML start as the Giants outslug the Phillies 15–9.

18th The Braves take first place when Tony Cloninger beats St. Louis 5–3. Hank Aaron of the Braves hits a HR off Curt Simmons of St. Louis, but has it nullified when umpire Chris Pelekoudas says Aaron stepped out of the batter's box when he made contact.

In a 3–2 Orioles' win over the Red Sox, Brooks Robinson hits into his 3rd triple play against Boston, tying the record of George Sisler in 1921, '22, and '26.

19th Reds P Jim Maloney's 2nd no-hit effort of 1965 is another 0–0 duel through 9 innings, until Reds SS Leo Cardenas homers off the LF foul pole in the 10th at Wrigley Field. Maloney sets a no-hit record by allowing 10 walks, and fans 12 in Cincinnati's 1–0 win.

20th Eddie Mathews hits his 28th HR as the Braves win 4–3 at Pittsburgh. The duo of Mathews and Hank Aaron, 1954–65, becomes the top HR tandem in ML history, passing the Babe Ruth-Lou Gehrig total of 793 HRs while playing together.

Detroit All-Star SS Dick McAuliffe is lost for the season with a broken bone in his left hand suffered diving into 1B, as the 3rd-place Tigers sweep a doubleheader at Boston.

22nd San Francisco's Juan Marichal, batting against LA's Sandy Koufax, complains that C John Roseboro's return throws are too close. He then turns and attacks Roseboro with his bat. A 14-minute brawl ensues before Koufax, Willie Mays, and other peacemakers can restore order. Roseboro suffers a considerable cut on the head. Marichal is suspended 8 playing days and levied a NL-record $1,750 fine.

29th Willie Mays sets a NL record for HRs in one month with his 17th of August, 41st overall, as San Francisco beats the Mets 8–3.

30th Following his doctor's advice, Casey Stengel announces his retirement as manager of the Mets. He will head up Mets scouting in California. Stengel ends a managerial career that included 10 pennants with the Yankees, followed by a dismal 175-404 with the expansion Mets. The 75-year-old Stengel has been in professional baseball since 1910.

31st Boston C Russ Nixon ties a ML record with 3 run-scoring sacrifice flies in the 2nd game at Washington. Boston wins 8–5 after taking the opener 4–0.

SEPTEMBER

1st Sandy Koufax and Don Drysdale lose as the Pirates sweep the Dodgers a doubleheader 3–2 and 2–1 at Pittsburgh.

Cincinnati sweeps the Braves 7–6 and 2–0 to regain first place.

2nd The Cubs beat St. Louis 5–3 at Wrigley Field, as Ernie Banks hits his 400th home run, off Curt Simmons in the 3rd. Banks will end the season with 28 HRs and 106 RBI. Ron Santo and Billy Williams will also knock in over 100 runs, the only team with 3 such sluggers, but the Cubs will finish 8th.

3rd Preparing a move to Anaheim, the Angels change their name from Los Angeles to California.

7th Jim Ray Hart drives in all of San Francisco's runs in a 3–1 win against the Dodgers that gives the Giants a .002 percentage point lead.

8th Bert Campaneris plays all 9 positions against the Angels in a promotion to hype poor attendance at Kansas City. He leaves the game in the 9th after a collision with Angels C Ed Kirkpatrick. The Angels win it in the 13th inning 5–3.

9th A duel between Dodger Sandy Koufax and Bob Hendley of the Cubs is perfect until Dodger LF Lou Johnson walks in the 5th. Following a sacrifice, Johnson steals 3B and scores on C Chris Krug's wild throw. Johnson later gets the game's only hit, a 7th-inning single. Koufax's 4th no-hitter in 4 years is a perfect game. One hit by 2 clubs in a completed 9-inning game is also a record, as is one runner left on base.

11th Tony Cloninger's one-hit, 9–0 win is Milwaukee's 2nd straight one-hitter against the Mets, a ML record. Wade Blasingame, Billy O'Dell, and Phil Niekro combined the day before for a 3–1 win.

12th Washington's Brant Alyea debuts with a pinch-hit HR on the first pitch from Rudy May in his first ML at bat, as the Senators beat the Angels 7–1.

13th Willie Mays's 500th HR (off Don Nottebart) and Juan Marichal's 22nd victory beat Houston 5–1.

The win is the Giants 11th straight and gives them a 2½ game lead.

16th An eventful day in Boston includes the firing of GM Mike Higgins and a no-hitter by Dave Morehead. Boston beats Cleveland 2–0. Morehead lost a no-hitter against Cleveland in 1963 on Fred Whitfield's bad-hop single in the 8th.

Bob Bolin's 5–1 win at Houston gives the Giants 14 straight wins, the longest NL streak since 1951.

18th On Mickey Mantle Day at Yankee Stadium, 50,180 fans see Mantle play his 2,000th game.

20th Just 812 see the soon-to-be Atlanta Braves lose to the Phils in Milwaukee.

Fewer fans (537) see the A's Jim "Catfish" Hunter beat Jim "Mudcat" Grant in Minnesota. Both contests are makeup games.

Pedro Gonzalez of the Indians swings a bat at P Larry Sherry of the Tigers following a Sherry brush-back pitch. Gonzalez is fined $500 by AL President Joe Cronin the following day.

22nd Before 12,577 fans, the Braves end a 13-year stay in Milwaukee against the Dodgers. Despite a Frank Bolling grand slam off Sandy Koufax, the Braves lose 7–6 in 11 innings.

Willie Mays hits his 50th HR, as the first-place Giants beat the Reds 7–5. Mays joins Ralph Kiner as the only players in NL history with multiple 50-HR seasons.

23rd A 20-game winner in 1964, Larry Jackson loses his 20th game of 1965, as the Phillies sweep a twin bill from the Cubs. Jackson is the first pitcher since Murry Dickson of the 1951-52 Pirates to follow a 20-win season with 20 losses.

25th Sandy Koufax blanks the Cardinals 2–0. He fans 12 along the way, raising his record season total to 356. His 2–0 shutout of St. Louis keeps Los Angeles a game behind the Giants.

Another Kansas City publicity stunt makes the great Satchel Paige baseball's oldest performer. At 59, Paige hurls the first 3 innings, garners one strikeout, and allows just one hit, to Carl Yastrzemski in his first ML appearance since 1953. The Red Sox jump on reliever Don Mossi for a 5–2 win.

26th Minnesota gains its first AL pennant by defeating Washington 2–1. Jim Kaat (17-11) wins the clincher.

28th Lou Johnson's 12th-inning HR off Joey Jay gives the Dodgers a 2–1 win over Cincinnati and the NL lead.

The Giants lose to St. Louis 8–6, even though Willie Mays, in his 2,000th career game, hits his 51st HR of the year.

29th Phillies C Pat Corrales sets a ML record by reaching base twice on catcher's interference in one game and 6 times in one season. The Phils beat Chicago 7–6.

30th Don Drysdale (23-12) pitches a 3-hitter and blanks the Braves 4–0. Los Angeles has won 13 straight games, 7 by shutout.

OCTOBER

2nd Sandy Koufax's 2–1 win against the Braves clinches the NL pennant for the Dodgers. With 13 strikeouts, Koufax ups his modern ML single season record to 382. He leads the NL in wins (26), ERA (2.04), complete games (27), and innings pitched (335⅔).

Willie Mays sets a Giants record with his 52nd HR, as Ron Herbel beats the Reds 3–2. Johnny Mize had hit 51 for the Jints in 1947.

Another Mets' marathon twin bill features an 18-inning scoreless tie in which Philadelphia's Chris Short (18-11) fans 18 batters. New York loses the first game 6–0 to Jim Bunning (19-9), setting ML records with 27 scoreless innings and 31 strikeouts in an overtime twin bill.

3rd The Cubs tie a ML record with their 3rd triple play of the season—1B Ernie Banks to SS Don Kessinger—but Pittsburgh wins 6–3 at Forbes Field. Bill Faul is on the mound during each triple play. Submariner Ted Abernathy suffers the loss to Roy Face, but concludes a record season for appearances (84) and consecutive errorless games (84) for a pitcher. He has 31 saves.

Knuckleballer Eddie Fisher of the White Sox sets an AL record with his 82nd appearance, one more than John Wyatt in 1964.

Six Dodgers pitchers, a ML shutout record, combine to blank the Braves 3–0.

"Sudden" Sam McDowell (17-11) loses a 2–1 decision to Baltimore's Steve Barber, but the 22-year-old Tribe southpaw wraps up the AL lead in ERA (2.18) and strikeouts (325). Rocky Colavito plays his

162nd consecutive errorless game (274 chances), a ML season record.

4th Dick Sisler is released as manager of the Reds.

Boston trades P Bill Monbouquette to Detroit for OF George Thomas and IF George Smith.

6th Minnesota's 6-run 3rd inning routs Dodger Don Drysdale and sparks an 8–2 Twins win in the first game of the WS. Jim Grant gets the win.

7th Jim Kaat gives Minnesota a 2-0 WS lead by driving in 2 runs, defeating Sandy Koufax 5–1 at Metropolitan Stadium.

9th Dodgers P Claude Osteen, 5-0 versus Minnesota while with the Senators, remains perfect against the Twins, winning 4–0 in game 3 at Chavez Ravine.

10th In game 4 Don Drysdale evens the WS with a 5-hit 7–2 win. Wes Parker and Lou Johnson hit HRs, as the Dodgers beat Jim Grant.

11th Sandy Koufax's 4-hit, 7–0 win against the Twins puts Los Angeles one win from the championship. Maury Wills ties a WS record with 4 doubles and scores twice.

12th Washington trades OF Woodie Held to Baltimore for C John Orsino.

Milwaukee Brewers Baseball Club, Inc. applies for an AL franchise to replace the Braves.

13th The Twins' Mudcat Grant does it all himself, hitting a 3-run HR and pitching a 5–1 win at Minnesota to knot the WS with the Dodgers.

14th Working on two days rest, Sandy Koufax pitches a 3-hitter and blanks Minnesota 2–0, giving the Dodgers a 2nd World Championship in 3 years. He is named WS MVP.

19th NBC wins a ML television package, including prime-time, All-Star, and WS games.

20th St. Louis trades 3B Ken Boyer to the Mets for P Al Jackson and 3B Charlie Smith.

25th Leo Durocher becomes manager of the Cubs, replacing head coach Lou Klein (48-58).

26th Don Heffner is named manager of the Reds. Dick Sisler (89-73) is out.

27th C Bob Uecker, 1B Bill White, and SS Dick Groat are traded by St. Louis to Philadelphia for P Art Mahaffey, OF Alex Johnson, and C Pat Corrales.

NOVEMBER

3rd Sandy Koufax is named Cy Young Award winner by a unanimous vote.

Athletics P Lew Krausse enjoys one of the finest performances in winter league history, throwing a one-hitter for Caracas against Lara and establishing the following still unsurpassed marks: most strikeouts in a 9-inning game (21), most consecutive strikeouts (10), most strikeouts in 2 consecutive games (33).

4th Al Lopez resigns as manager of the White Sox.

10th Willie Mays is named NL MVP, receiving 224 votes to 177 for Sandy Koufax.

17th Retired Air Force Lieutenant-General William Eckert is unanimously elected commissioner of baseball. Ford Frick leaves office after 14 years.

18th Zoilo Versalles is named AL MVP. The Minnesota SS gets 275 votes to 174 for OF teammate Tony Oliva.

Wes Westrum is named the Mets manager for 1966.

22nd Baltimore OF Curt Blefary edges Angels P Marcelino Lopez for AL Rookie of the Year honors.

26th Dodger 2B Jim Lefebvre is voted NL Rookie of the Year.

28th Haywood Sullivan (54-82) resigns as A's manager to become director of player personnel for the Red Sox. Al Dark replaces him.

DECEMBER

1st Pittsburgh acquires OF Matty Alou from San Francisco for P Joe Gibbon and C Ozzie Virgil.

2nd P Lindy McDaniel and OF Don Landrum are traded by the Cubs to the Giants for C Randy Hundley and P Bill Hands.

Baltimore sends 1B Norm Siebern to the Angels for OF Dick Simpson.

4th Masanori Murakami, 4-1 this year, does not renew his contract with the Giants, signing instead with the Nankai Hawks of Osaka for $40,000.

6th   Baltimore sends OF Jackie Brandt and P Darold Knowles to the Phillies for P Jack Baldschun.

9th   OF Frank Robinson is traded from Cincinnati to the Orioles for pitchers Milt Pappas and Jack Baldschun and OF Dick Simpson. The Reds Bill DeWitt defends the trade by labeling Robinson "an old 30."

While giving a speech in Columbus, MO, Branch Rickey collapses and dies a few days short of his 84th birthday. Player, manager, an extraordinary judge of baseball talent, and a shrewd trader, he became perhaps the game's most influential executive.

12th   Roy Hofheinz fires manager Lum Harris (65-97). Grady Hatton takes over the Astros.

14th   Eddie Stanky is signed to manage the White Sox.

15th   Detroit trades P Phil Regan to the Dodgers for IF Dick Tracewski.

1966

JANUARY

20th The BBWAA voters elect Ted Williams to the Hall of Fame. Williams receives 282 of a possible 302 votes.

25th Tony Kubek announces his retirement owing to a back ailment.

27th Wisconsin State Circuit Court Judge Elmer W. Roller rules that the Braves must stay in Milwaukee, or the NL must promise Wisconsin an expansion team for the 1966 season.

Judge Robert Cannon of Wisconsin is named a full-time administrator of the Players' Association at a $50,000 salary.

FEBRUARY

28th Seeking an unprecedented 3-year, $1.05 million contract to be divided evenly, the Dodgers' Sandy Koufax and Don Drysdale begin a joint holdout.

MARCH

5th Player representatives elect Marvin Miller, assistant to the president of the United Steelworkers, as executive director of the ML Players' Association.

8th The Hall of Fame Special Veterans Committee waives election rules and inducts Casey Stengel, recently retired manager of the Mets.

17th Sandy Koufax and Don Drysdale escalate their threat of retirement by signing movie contracts.

30th Sandy Koufax and Don Drysdale end their 32-day holdout, signing for $130,000 and $105,000 respectively.

APRIL

3rd Tom Seaver, University of Southern California pitcher, signs with the Mets for a reported $50,000 bonus. A selection of the Braves in the January free-agent draft, Seaver was signed by Atlanta's Richmond farm club a month later, after USC had begun its baseball schedule. The violation netted Richmond a $500 fine and forbade Atlanta from signing Seaver for 3 years. However, Seaver was also declared ineligible at the college level, so an unprecedented special draft is held. Three clubs willing to match Richmond's $40,000 contract—the Indians, Phillies, and Mets—participate. New York's name is drawn from a hat as the winner.

5th Don Larsen, last active member of the old St. Louis Browns, is released by the Orioles.

11th A crowd of 44,468, including Vice President Hubert Humphrey, attends a historic opener at Washington. Emmett Ashford becomes the ML's first black umpire in Cleveland's 5–2 win against the Senators.

12th The Braves lose their first game in Atlanta 3–2 to Pittsburgh in 13 innings, with 50,761 fans on hand.

15th Bob Gibson's 9–2 win at Forbes Field is the 18th straight for St. Louis in Pittsburgh. St. Louis ties the ML record set by the Dodgers against the Phillies in 1945-46 for consecutive road wins against one club.

19th In the first regular season game at Anaheim Stadium, California drops a 3–1 decision to the White Sox before 31,660 fans. Rick Reichardt hits the Angels' first regular-season HR in the new facility.

Tommie Sisk finally gives Pittsburgh a home win against the Cardinals 5–3.

21st The Cubs trade pitchers Larry Jackson and Bob Buhl to Philadelphia for young P Ferguson Jenkins, OF Adolfo Phillips, and 1B/OF John Herrnstein. Jenkins was 2–1 for the Phils in 1965 after being brought up from Arkansas (PCL).

24th Pete Richert enters the record books with 7 consecutive strikeouts against the Tigers. Richert still loses a 4–0 decision as the Tigers sweep a pair at Washington.

Atlanta's 5–2 win at Atlanta-Fulton County Stadium in the first game of a doubleheader is an NL-record 18th straight home win against the Mets. "Home" for 17 of those wins was Milwaukee.

28th Cleveland ties the modern ML record with its 10th straight Opening Day win. Sonny Siebert defeats the Angels 2–1.

30th Rick Reichardt hits 2 HRs in the 8th inning, pacing a 16–9 California rout of Boston at Fenway.

MAY

1st   In his 2nd start, Sam McDowell has to settle for a one-hitter. Don Buford's 3rd-inning double is Chicago's only hit in Cleveland's 1–0 win. McDowell becomes the first pitcher since Whitey Ford (September 1955) to pitch back-to-back one-hitters.

3rd   Cleveland regains first place when Luis Tiant (3-0) hurls his 3rd straight shutout and blanks the Yanks 1–0.

4th   Willie Mays hits a NL record 512th HR—topping another Giant, Mel Ott —and the Giants beat the Dodgers 6–1.

Tribe SS Larry Brown and LF Leon Wagner are both hurt in a severe collision at Yankee Stadium. Brown suffers a fractured skull, cheekbone, and nose. Wagner receives a broken nose and slight concussion.

7th   With the Yankees winning only 4 of the first 20 games, GM Ralph Houk fires Johnny Keane (4-16) and installs himself as Yankees manager.

San Francisco sets a modern NL record by scoring 13 runs in the 3rd inning en route to a 15–2 win at St. Louis. The 13 runs are also the most scored in the 3rd inning by two teams.

Dodger Jim Lefebvre hits HRs right- and lefthanded in the same game, as Los Angeles routs Cincinnati 14–2. On June 5th, teammate Wes Parker will match Lefebvre.

8th   Orioles RF Frank Robinson hits the first ball ever hit completely out of Baltimore's Memorial Stadium, a 451-foot shot, ending Luis Tiant's scoreless-innings streak at 27. Baltimore wins 8–3 and ties Cleveland for first place.

In a controversial trade for San Francisco, St. Louis acquires popular 1B Orlando Cepeda from the Giants for P Ray Sadecki. Sadecki will go 3-7 in 1966, and Cepeda will win the MVP in St. Louis in 1967.

In the last game at old Busch Stadium, San Francisco slugs out a 10–5 win over St. Louis.

10th   The Tigers purchase P Johnny Podres from the Los Angeles Dodgers.

12th   The Cardinals open new Busch Memorial Stadium with a 12-inning, 4–3 win over the Braves.

13th   Giant Jim Davenport's 17th-inning HR beats the Mets 5–4 before 56,658 fans, the largest night crowd ever at Shea Stadium. The first-place Giants (22-7) have 12 straight wins.

15th   Rocky Mount (Carolina League) teammates Dick Drago and Darrell Clark each pitch 7-inning no-hitters against Greensboro, Drago winning 5–0 in the opener, Clark 2–0 in the nightcap.

16th   Chuck Dressen suffers his 2nd heart attack in 2 years. Coach Bob Swift again takes the helm of the Tigers.

26th   The Giants Juan Marichal pitches all 14 innings in a 1–0 win over Philadelphia. Jim Bunning matches him for 11 innings before being relieved. Marichal is 9-0.

27th   The White Sox trade 1B/OF Danny Cater to the A's for IF Wayne Causey.

Washington's Phil Ortega becomes the 2nd Senators hurler to fan 7 straight batters, tying the AL record for consecutive strikeouts and winning a 3–2 decision against the Red Sox.

29th   Ron Santo's 10th-inning HR gives the Cubs a 3–2 win over Atlanta. The day before, he beat the Braves with a 3-run, 12th-inning HR in an 8–5 win.

30th   Denny McLain pitches his 2nd one-hitter of the month. Phil Roof's 5th-inning double is Kansas City's only safety in Detroit's 5–2 win.

31st   California's Rick Reichardt ties the ML strike-out record for extra-inning games with 6 K's in a 17-inning, 7–5 loss to the Indians.

Chicago's Ron Santo sets a NL record by appearing in his 364th straight game at 3B, as the Cubs win 2–1 at Pittsburgh.

JUNE

2nd   Boston trades P Dick Radatz to the Indians for pitchers Don McMahon and Lee Stange.

Houston erupts for 8 runs in the 12th inning at Cincinnati to win 11–4. The clubs combine to tie a NL record by scoring 9 runs in the 12th.

3rd   White Sox SS Ron Hansen undergoes surgery for a ruptured spinal disk. He is disabled the rest of the season.

5th   In a 10–5 Bucs win over Houston, Willie Stargell goes 5-for-5, giving him 9 consecutive hits in 2 days.

7th   Bob Gibson (6-5) ties the ML record with 4 strikeouts in one inning (4th), but the St. Louis ace is gone by the end of a 9–1 loss at Pittsburgh.

The New York Mets, picking first in the June free-agent draft, pass up Arizona State OF Reggie Jackson to select C Steve Chilcott. Chilcott will retire after 6 years in the minors and will be the only number-one pick to never play in the major leagues. The A's take Jackson with the 2nd pick.

8th Bob Saverine of the Senators sets an AL record by coming to bat 12 times in a doubleheader (more than 18 innings) without a hit.

9th Minnesota rocks Kansas City with the first 5-HR inning in AL history. Rich Rollins, Zoilo Versalles, Tony Oliva, Don Mincher, and Harmon Killebrew connect in the 7th inning to give the Twins a 9–4 victory.

10th Sonny Siebert pitches a no-hitter against the Senators. Leon Wagner homers off loser Phil Ortega, as first-place Cleveland wins 2–0.

San Francisco sells P Bob Shaw to the Mets.

11th Ernie Banks ties a modern record with 3 triples, as Chicago wins 8–2 in the Astrodome. Chicago OF Adolfo Phillips ties the ML record by striking out 8 times 2 consecutive games (more than 18 innings).

13th The White Sox trade P Eddie Fisher to the Orioles for 2B Jerry Adair and OF John Riddle.

Orioles pitchers Jim Palmer (6-3) and Eddie Watt combine to blank the Yankees 8–0 and give Baltimore an AL lead it will not relinquish.

The Red Sox acquire P John Wyatt, P Rollie Sheldon, and OF Jose Tartabull from the A's for P Ken Sanders, P Guido Grilli, and OF Jim Gosger.

14th Detroit acquires P Earl Wilson and OF Joe Christopher from Boston for OF Don Demeter and P Julio Navarro.

Miami ekes out a 4–3 triumph over St. Petersburg (Florida State League) in 29 innings. It is the longest game not interrupted by a suspension of play in the history of organized ball. Sparky Anderson is the manager for St. Petersburg.

15th Cincinnati trades P Joey Jay to the Braves for P Hank Fischer.

25th Houston 2B Joe Morgan, batting .315, suffers a broken kneecap when hit by a line drive during batting practice. He will miss 40 games.

26th Sandy Koufax (13-2) matches his NL record of 7 consecutive strikeouts in consecutive 9-inning appearances on his way to a 2–1 win in Atlanta.

29th Yankees Bobby Richardson, Mickey Mantle, and Joe Pepitone hit consecutive HRs in the 3rd inning at Fenway Park in New York's 6–5 win.

JULY

2nd Frank Howard, Don Lock, and Ken McMullen hit consecutive HRs with 2 outs in the 6th inning, and Mike McCormick pitches a complete game, as Washington defeats Whitey Ford and the Yankees 10–4.

3rd P Tony Cloninger hits 2 grand slams and drives in 9 runs, as the Braves rout the Giants at Candlestick Park 17–3. Cloninger is the only NL player to hit 2 in a game, and his 9 RBI are a ML record for pitchers.

4th Ron Santo sets a modern-day Cubs' record as he hits in his 28th straight game. The Cubs lose the opener to the Pirates 7–5. The Cubs win the nightcap 6–4, but Santo is held hitless.

6th Despite a doubleheader record 11 RBI by Boog Powell, the Orioles can only split with the A's. They drop the nightcap 9–8 after winning 11–0.

12th St. Louis hosts a hot midsummer All-Star classic. Maury Wills's 10th-inning single scores Tim McCarver, as the NL wins 2–1 in 105-degree heat. Brooks Robinson's stellar game (3 hits, 8 chances) earns him the game MVP.

13th Manager Don Heffner (37-46) is fired by the Reds and replaced by coach Dave Bristol.

14th Interim Detroit skipper Bob Swift is hospitalized, and 3B coach Frank Skaff takes over.

17th Pittsburgh regains the NL lead by sweeping a doubleheader 7–4 and 7–1 from the Giants.

21st Minnesota P Jim Merritt beats the Senators 1–0 and ties an AL mark with 7 straight strikeouts

22nd Gaylord Perry sets a San Francisco record with 15 strikeouts and beats the Phillies 4–1. Clay Dalrymple's one-out 8th-inning single is the first hit against Perry. The Giants (57-39, .594) are two percentage points behind the first-place Pirates (56-38, .596).

23rd Bob Allison of the Twins suffers a broken left hand when hit by a Jim Lonborg pitch during Minnesota's 10–4 win over the Red Sox.

26th Catfish Hunter, Kansas City's top winner, undergoes an appendectomy.

27th The Wisconsin Supreme Court overrules a lower court decision and holds that the state lacks legal jurisdiction to stop the Braves from moving to Atlanta.

28th Rick Reichardt, California's young hitting star, is sidelined with a kidney ailment. He will have a kidney removed in 2 weeks.

AUGUST

1st Houston's Jim Wynn suffers a fractured left wrist, hand, and elbow slamming into the CF fence at Philadelphia. Done for the season, the Toy Cannon will still lead the Astros with 18 HRs. Houston also loses 6–5.

4th Pinch-hit HRs by Mets John Stephenson and Ron Swoboda make the difference in New York's 8–6 defeat of the Giants at Shea Stadium.

7th Lee Bales gets off to a shaky ML start, striking out 4 times, as the Braves beat the Phillies 3–0. Bales equals the NL record of Billy Sunday (May 22, 1883) for most initial-game K's.

9th The Braves fire Bobby Bragan (52-59) and install coach Billy Hitchcock as their new manager.

10th Chuck Dressen dies of a heart attack in Detroit, age 67. He had managed the Tigers earlier in the season.

12th Long-ball lovers enjoy 11 HRs in one game, tying the most in any contest and setting a ML record for an extra-inning contest. Art Shamsky hits 3 for Cincinnati, including 2 in extra innings, but Pittsburgh prevails 13–11 in 13 innings. The Reds' Jerry Lynch smacks his 18th pinch-hit HR for a ML record.

13th Restaurateur Vernon Stouffer buys a controlling interest in the Indians.

14th Art Shamsky hits his 4th consecutive HR, tying the ML record, but the Reds lose again to the Pirates 4–2.

16th Willie Mays hits his 534th HR, matching Jimmie Foxx's record for right-handed batters, as Gaylord Perry beats the Cardinals 3–1.

17th Willie Mays takes 2nd place on the all-time HR list with a 4th-inning blast off Ray Washburn. San Francisco is one-half game out of first place after beating the Cards 4–3.

18th Pittsburgh 3B Jose Pagan ties the modern NL record for errors in an inning with 3, but Pittsburgh coasts to a 9–3 win over the Mets.

20th Gaylord Perry is the first 20-game winner of 1966, pitching the Giants into first place with a 6–1 win against the Braves.

Birdie Tebbetts (66-57) resigns as manager of the Indians. George Strickland is named interim boss.

25th Whitey Ford (2-5) undergoes surgery for a circulatory problem in his left shoulder.

The owners approve a 55 percent raise in contributions to the players' pension fund. It will come from television, WS, and All-Star Game money. Some money will also go to pay the salary of the Players' Association executive director.

26th With Baltimore trailing Boston 2–0 in the 9th inning, Vic Roznovsky and Boog Powell blast back-to-back pinch-hit HRs off Lee Stange to tie the game. Back-to-back pinch HRs occur for only the 3rd time in baseball history. Baltimore wins in the 12th 3–2.

30th Pete Rose becomes the 12th in ML history to hit HRs left- and righthanded in one game, as the Reds win 6–4 over the Cards.

31st Yankees 2B Bobby Richardson, 31, announces his retirement.

SEPTEMBER

8th The Red Sox fire manager Billy Herman (64-82). Pete Runnels is named interim pilot.

11th John Miller becomes the first Yankee to homer in his first ML at bat. He contributes 2 runs in a 4–2 defeat of the Red Sox at Fenway.

Los Angeles regains first place, winning 4–0 and 1–0 behind Sandy Koufax and Larry Miller while Houston suffers its 3rd and 4th consecutive shutouts against the Dodgers.

12th Ron Perranoski of the Dodgers fans the first 6 batters he faces and earns a 3–2 win over the Mets and Tug McGraw.

15th Tom Phoebus of Baltimore begins his ML career with a 2–0 shutout of the Angels.

Seven pitchers are used by the A's in an 11-inning, 1–0 shutout of the Indians. Kansas City wins its 7th straight game.

16th The Mets (5) and Giants (3) tie a ML record by using 8 pinch hitters in the 9th inning as the Mets win 5–4. Willie McCovey hits a 500-ft HR, judged the longest ever at Candlestick Park.

17th Cleveland pitchers set an AL record by fanning 19 batters in the first 9 innings of a 10-inning 6–2 win at Detroit.

18th Kansas City and Washington trade shutouts, the A's winning the first game 3–0 and losing the 2nd in the last of the 9th 1–0. John "Blue Moon" Odom blanks the Senators for 8⅓ innings in the nightcap to run the A's scoreless string to 45⅓ innings. The AL record of 47 was set by Cleveland in 1948.

19th Dan Topping sells his 10 percent stock interest in the Yankees to CBS and resigns as club president. CBS executive Mike Burke succeeds him.

20th Orioles P Tom Phoebus hurls his 2nd straight shutout in his 2nd ML game, blanking the A's 4–0 in Kansas City.

22nd The Orioles beat the A's 6–1 to clinch their first AL pennant. Both Brooks Robinson and Frank Robinson have 2 RBI. Frank Robinson will end the year as the Triple Crown winner, the first to achieve the feat since Mickey Mantle in 1956. He clinches with a batting average of .316, 49 HRs, and 122 RBI.

A crowd of 413, a record low for Yankee Stadium, sees the White Sox beat New York 4–1. Yankee Broadcaster Red Barber insists that TV cameras show the empty seats, a decision that will cost the legendary play-by-play man his job.

28th Larry Jaster (11-5) blanks the Dodgers for the 5th time this season, pitching the Cards to a 2–0 win at St. Louis. Jaster is the first pitcher to accomplish this feat since Grover Cleveland Alexander whitewashed the Reds 5 times in 1916.

The Pirates sweep a doubleheader from the Phillies and move back within 1½ games of the Dodgers.

The Red Sox appoint Dick Williams as manager.

29th Sandy Koufax pitches a 4-hitter, beats the Cards 2–1, and becomes the first ML pitcher to achieve a third 300-strikeout season since Amos Rusie in 1890–92.

30th The White Sox tip the Yankees 6–5 at Comiskey. The Yanks will win their next 2 but finish in 10th place one-half game behind the Red Sox.

OCTOBER

1st The Giants sweep in Pittsburgh 5–4 and 2–0 to move into 2nd place 2 games behind the Dodgers.

2nd Sandy Koufax clinches the 3rd Los Angeles pennant in 4 years, working with just 2 days rest for a 6–3 win at Philadelphia. Koufax sets Los Angeles records with 27 wins and a 1.73 ERA. Philadelphia wins the first game, beating Don Drysdale 4–3.

The Giants beat Pittsburgh 7–4 to finish 1½ behind. A San Francisco rainout will not need to be rescheduled.

St. Louis OF Curt Flood concludes the season with his 159th consecutive errorless game, the most by an NL outfielder in one campaign. Flood handled 396 chances without a miscue.

3rd Mayo Smith signs a 2-year contract to manage the Tigers.

Former Indian Joe Adcock will retire from active play and become manager of the Tribe.

5th With first-inning HRs by Frank Robinson and Brooks Robinson and 11 strikeouts from relief P Moe Drabowsky, the Orioles win game one of the WS 5–2.

6th Los Angeles OF Willie Davis commits 3 errors on two successive 5th-inning plays, as Baltimore scores 3 runs and wins 6–0.

8th In game 3 Paul Blair's HR and Wally Bunker's 6-hit pitching give the Orioles a 1–0 win, as the WS moves to Baltimore.

9th Dave McNally wraps up Baltimore's brilliant pitching display, and a World Championship, with a 4-hit, 1–0 win. Frank Robinson's HR off Don Drysdale gives Baltimore a surprising sweep of the defending champion Dodgers. The 33 consecutive scoreless innings pitched by Baltimore are a WS record.

13th Lee MacPhail is named GM of the Yankees.

17th   Bob Swift, 51, dies at Detroit, losing a bout with cancer. He is the 2nd Tigers manager to pass away this year.

NOVEMBER

1st   Sandy Koufax becomes the first 3-time winner of the Cy Young Award. He is a unanimous winner for the 2nd-straight year. This is the last year that only one award is given for pitchers in both of the MLs.

4th   Maury Wills leaves the Los Angeles club touring Japan, complaining that his injured right knee needs immediate treatment in the U.S. Because treatment apparently consists of visiting Honolulu nightclubs, Wills is later traded to the Pirates.

8th   Frank Robinson of the Orioles is the unanimous choice as AL MVP. He is the first player to win the award in both leagues.

12th   The Dodgers complete an 18-game tour of Japan with a 9-8-1 record, the most losses ever for a ML club touring the Far East.

14th   George Weiss resigns as Mets president and is succeeded by Bing Devine.

16th   Pirate OF Roberto Clemente is named MVP in the NL. He edges Koufax by 10 votes.

18th   Sandy Koufax announces his retirement, due to increasing pain in his arthritic left elbow.

23rd   Chicago OF Tommie Agee is voted AL Rookie of the Year, gathering 16 of the 18 votes. Kansas City P Jim Nash gets the other 2. Agee had been brought up briefly the past 4 seasons before finding a permanent spot this year.

25th   Cincinnati IF Tommy Helms is voted NL Rookie of the Year.

28th   The Pirates purchase P Juan Pizarro from the White Sox, completing a deal that sends P Wilbur Wood to Chicago.

29th   The Mets trade 2B Ron Hunt and OF Jim Hickman to the Dodgers for 2-time batting champ Tommy Davis and OF Derrell Griffith.

The Yankees trade 3B Clete Boyer to the Braves for OF Bill Robinson and a player to be named

A circuit court jury in Chicago awards Jim Brewer $100,000 in damages stemming from his 1960 on-field fight with Billy Martin.

DECEMBER

1st   Dodgers SS Maury Wills is traded to the Pirates for SS Gene Michael and 3B Bob Bailey. A deal has been expected since he bolted the Los Angeles trip to Japan.

2nd   California trades P Dean Chance and a player to be named to the Twins for OF Jimmie Hall, 1B Don Mincher, and P Pete Cimino.

5th   Bill DeWitt sells the Reds to a group of Cincinnati investors for an estimated $7 million.

7th   The Cubs trade P Dick Ellsworth to the Phils for P Ray Culp and cash.

8th   The Yankees trade OF Roger Maris to the Cardinals for 3B Charlie Smith.

12th   By a 4–3 decision, the U.S. Supreme Court refuses to review Wisconsin's suit to prevent the Braves' move to Atlanta, thereby retaining baseball's "umbrella" under antitrust laws.

13th   The Giants trade P Bob Priddy and OF Cap Peterson to the Senators for P Mike McCormick. McCormick will win the Cy Young in 1967.

31st   After 15 seasons with the Braves in 3 different cities, 3B Eddie Mathews is traded to the Astros, with P Arnie Umbach and a player to be named, for P Bob Bruce and OF Dave Nicholson.

1967

JANUARY

6th   Former Yankee's manager Johnny Keane, 55, dies of a heart attack at Houston. It is the 3rd death of a 1966 manager.

23rd   Stan Musial is named GM of the Cards.

29th   Branch Rickey and Lloyd Waner are elected to the Baseball Hall of Fame by a unanimous vote of the Special Veterans Committee.

FEBRUARY

16th   Red Ruffing is selected for the Hall of Fame through a special runoff election, since nobody received the required 75 percent vote in January.

MARCH

3rd   The White Sox are given permission to use a semi-designated hitter in training camp. With home club permission, clubs will be allowed to use a designated pinch hitter twice in the same game.

30th   The Dodgers Willie Davis suffers a broken bone in his ankle that will hamper his performance throughout the season.

APRIL

14th   Red Sox rookie Billy Rohr debuts at Yankee Stadium. He startles everyone by taking a no-hitter to the 9th inning, but Elston Howard lines a 3-2 pitch for a single to right-center with 2 outs. Carl Yastrzemski had kept the no-hitter alive with a spectacular grab of a Tom Tresh drive to deep LF to open the 9th. The Red Sox go on to win 3–0. Rohr will pitch only one more game for Boston before returning to the minors.

25th   Los Angeles 3B Jim Lefebvre commits 3 errors in the 4th inning to help Atlanta win 7–1.

30th   San Francisco concludes its first 3-game sweep at Dodger Stadium, as Bob Bolin beats Don Drysdale 5–1.

Orioles Steve Barber and Stu Miller combine to pitch a no-hitter and lose 2–1 to the first-place Tigers in the first game of a doubleheader, as Barber walks 10 in 8⅔ innings. In his first start of the year, Barber held the Angels hitless for 8⅓ innings. Just 2 hits matches the AL record for fewest safeties by 2 clubs in one game.

MAY

10th   In the 8th inning against Jim Bunning of the Phillies, Hank Aaron drives a ball to deep CF and scores ahead of the relay. It will be the only inside-the-park HR among his 755.

14th   Mickey Mantle becomes the 6th member of the 500-HR club in New York's 6–5 win against Baltimore. Mantle connects batting lefthanded off Stu Miller.

A 62-year-old AL mark is broken when Don Demeter's 8th-inning double in the 2nd game becomes the 28th extra-base hit in the Red Sox's 8–5 and 13–9 victories over Detroit. Fifty hits bombard Fenway, 26 by the Tigers. Each team has 6 homers. The Sox have 9 doubles, the Tigers 6. Boston has one triple. The barrage erases the former record of 27 set by the Red Sox and A's in 1905. The Cards and Cubs established the ML high mark in 1931 with 35.

16th   Philadelphia voters approve a $13 million bond issue to build a new stadium.

On the field, the Phillies tie a NL record with their 11th straight errorless game. But they still lose 4–3 to St. Louis.

17th   The Orioles become the 8th club in AL history with 4 or more HRs in one inning when Andy Etchebarren, Sam Bowens, Boog Powell, and Dave Johnson connect in a 9-run 7th. Those HRs make the difference in a 12–8 Baltimore win over the Red Sox. Boston's Carl Yastrzemski hits 2 homers, one coming in the bottom of the 7th; the total of 5 in one inning equals the ML record.

Philadelphia defenders record just one assist in a 7–1 victory over the Reds. This ties the NL record for fewest assists in a 9-inning game. Jim Bunning is the winning P.

24th   Tommy McCraw belts 3 HRs and drives in 8 runs, as the first-place White Sox bury the Twins 14–1 at Minneapolis.

29th   Orioles 1B Mike Epstein and P Frank Bertaina are traded to the Senators for P Pete Richert.

30th   Yankee Whitey Ford, nearing 41, announces his retirement from baseball. The stylish lefthander closes out with 236 career wins and only 106 losses for a .690 percentage. He played in only 7 games this season.

JUNE

4th   The longest game in modern Orioles history—19 innings —features 21 Washington strikeouts, as the Birds win 7–5. Washington is the 3rd AL club to strike out 21 times in an extra-inning game.

Curt Flood's record string of 568 straight chances without an error ends when he drops a fly ball during a 4–3 win over the Cubs at St. Louis. The Cardinals CF had played a NL-record 227 straight games without an error beginning September 3, 1965.

7th   The last-place Yankees have the first pick in the free-agent draft and use it to take Ron Blomberg. The Cubs tap SS Terry Hughes with the next pick. All 20 first-round picks are high school players, and only 11 will eventually reach the major leagues.

9th   Cal Ermer, who played only one game in the majors, replaces Sam Mele (25-25) as manager of the Twins.

11th   Adolfo Phillips blasts 4 HRs in a doubleheader, 3 in the 2nd game, as the Cubs sweep the Mets at Wrigley Field 5–3 and 18–10. The total of 11, 2nd-game HRs sets a NL record for 2 clubs in 9 innings.

Before the largest AL crowd of 1967, 62,582 at Yankee Stadium, the White Sox regain first place from the Tigers by sweeping a twin bill from New York 2–1 and 3–2.

12th   The Senators and White Sox match up in the longest night game (22 innings, 6 hours, and 38 minutes) in ML history. Washington wins 6–5 when Paul Casanova, who has caught the entire game, singles in the winning run in the bottom of the 22nd.

16th   In a 3–2 Reds' win over the Dodgers, Cincinnati SS Leo Cardenas suffers a broken finger when hit with a pitch by Dodgers P Bill Singer. Cardenas is out until August 15th.

17th   A 9-hour and 5-minute doubleheader between the Tigers and Athletics is the longest ever. The first game includes a rain delay, and the 2nd goes 19 innings before a Dave Duncan HR wins it 6–5 for the A's. Detroit takes the opener 7–6.

18th   The blazing fastball of the Astros Don Wilson overpowers Atlanta with 15 strikeouts in a no-hit 2–0 victory.

A 4–1 St. Louis win at San Francisco gives the Cards a lead in the NL they will not relinquish.

27th   Detroit RF Al Kaline breaks his hand jamming his bat into the bat rack after striking out against Sam McDowell, as the 2nd-place Tigers lose to Cleveland 8–1. Kaline will miss 28 games.

Baltimore RF Frank Robinson is hurt in a 2B collision with Al Weis, as the White Sox beat the Orioles 5–0. Robinson suffers double vision and will miss 28 games.

28th   Relief ace Hoyt Wilhelm of the White Sox extends his ML record for consecutive errorless games to 247. The White Sox win 3–2 at Baltimore.

JULY

2nd   Ferguson Jenkins (11-5) pitches the Cubs into a first-place tie with St. Louis by defeating Cincinnati 4–1.

4th   The Mets end a 19-game losing streak to Juan Marichal with their first win against the Dominican Dandy 8–7. Jack Fisher is the winning pitcher.

Philadelphia C Clay Dalrymple collects 6 walks in a 19-inning doubleheader against the Astros. The Phillies win the first 9–0 and take the nightcap 4–3 in 11 innings.

Atlanta's Phil Niekro gets the best of rookie brother Joe as the Braves beat the Cubs 8–3. It is the first decision between the pair.

12th   Reds 3B Tony Perez ends the longest All-Star Game (15 innings, 3 hours and 41 minutes) with a HR off Catfish Hunter. HRs by NL 3B Richie Allen and AL 3B Brooks Robinson account for the other runs in a 2–1 NL triumph.

14th   Eddie Mathews becomes the 7th member of the 500-HR club, connecting off loser Juan Marichal as the Astros beat the Giants 8–6.

15th   Cardinals P Bob Gibson suffers a fractured right fibula when hit by a Roberto Clemente line drive. Gibson will be sidelined until Labor Day. Pittsburgh wins 6–4.

Kansas City pinch-running specialist Allan Lewis ties the ML record with 2 steals as a pinch runner in one inning. Lewis does his double in the 7th inning of a 3–2 loss at Minnesota.

18th Harry Walker (42-42) is fired as manager of the Pirates. Danny Murtaugh is called back to finish the season.

24th Chicago's 3–1 win at St. Louis puts the Cards and Cubs even atop the NL.

25th Race riots in Detroit force postponement of a Tigers-Orioles game.

26th With a NL-record-tying, 4-run-scoring sacrifice flies in one game, New York wins an 11–5 decision at San Francisco.

29th The Indians trade Rocky Colavito again, this time to the White Sox for OF Jim King and a player to be named.

AUGUST

2nd With homers from both sides of the plate, Pete Rose leads the Reds to a 7–3 win over the Braves. It's a 2nd time for Rose.

3rd Reports of rowdyism on an Athletics flight reach owner Charlie Finley and will result in the release of OF Ken Harrelson and firing of manager Alvin Dark.

The Red Sox acquire C Elston Howard from the Yankees for cash and 2 players to be named.

4th John Fetzer, president of the ML television committee, announces a $50 million, 3-year deal with NBC to televise the WS, All-Star Game, and 28 weekly telecasts.

6th Brooks Robinson of the Orioles hits into the 4th triple play of his career for a ML mark.

9th Minnesota's 20-inning 9–7 loss to the Senators is the longest game in Twins history. Ken McMullen's 20th-inning HR wins it for Washington.

11th In the 2nd inning of the first game of a doubleheader, Al Downing of the Yankees strikes out the side on 9 pitches. The Yanks beat the Indians 5–3.

13th Completing a 3-game sweep of the White Sox, Jim Merritt pitches the Twins into first place with a 3–2 win.

14th Despite a 2–1 loss to the Twins, the Angels are within 1½ games of first place.

18th A baseball tragedy occurs when Tony Conigliaro of the Red Sox is beaned by the Angels Jack Hamilton. Hit on the left cheekbone, just below the eye socket, Conigliaro will miss the rest of 1967 and all of 1968. He was hitting .267 with 20 HRs and 67 RBI in 95 games.

Lew Krausse of the A's is suspended by owner Charlie Finley for rowdyism and conduct unbecoming a ML player.

20th Within 24 hours, Alvin Dark (52-69) is fired, rehired, and fired again as manager of the A's. Luke Appling becomes interim manager.

The Red Sox C Reggie Smith joins the ranks of Mickey Mantle, Pete Rose, and others by hitting HRs left- and righthanded in one game.

21st Charlie Finley releases Ken Harrelson, making him baseball's first free agent. Harrelson is quoted as calling Finley a menace to baseball.

22nd Charlie Finley lifts his suspension of Lew Krausse.

Indian Luis Tiant has 16 strikeouts in a 3–2 win over California.

24th Philadelphia's Richie Allen suffers a severe hand injury while pushing a car. It will sideline him for the remainder of the season.

26th Dean Chance pitches a 2–1 no-hitter, and the Twins sweep Cleveland to take the AL lead. The victory gives Chance a 17-9 record and lowers his ERA to 2.42.

28th Boston signs free-agent OF Ken Harrelson. Harrelson reportedly receives a $75,000 bonus and salary package for 1967 and 1968. Harrelson will homer in his first Boston at bat but will hit just .200 for the Red Sox.

29th The Red Sox tie an AL record it originally set on July 4, 1905, by playing 29 innings in a doubleheader. Boston wins the first against the Yankees 2–1, then drop the nightcap in 20 innings 4–3.

SEPTEMBER

1st Cincinnati's Bob Lee walks Dick Groat with the bases loaded in the 21st inning to give the Giants a 1–0 victory at Candlestick. Twenty scoreless innings tie the ML mark set by the Pirates and the Braves on August 1, 1918, a game Pittsburgh also won in the

21st, 2–0. Gaylord Perry, with 9 one-run losses during the season, pitches the first 16 innings of shutout ball.

2nd Minnesota takes the AL lead on Dave Boswell's 5–0 victory over Denny McLain and Detroit.

6th After the Tigers sweep the A's 8–5 and 6–3, and the White Sox down the Angels 3–2, the top 4 AL teams are separated by a single percentage point. Chicago and Minnesota are 78-61 for .561; Boston and Detroit are 79-62 for .560.

7th The Giants tie their own NL record by using 25 players in a 15-inning 3–2 win over the Astros.

8th The Tigers move into a first-place tie with the Twins, as Eddie Mathews and Jim Northrup hit HRs, and Mickey Lolich beats Tommy John 4–1 at Chicago.

Despite a brilliant relief effort by Dick Kelley, the Braves lose a 4–1 decision at Philadelphia. Kelley ties the NL record for relievers with 6 consecutive strikeouts.

9th A 7-run 9th inning keeps Detroit tied for first place with a 7–3 win at Chicago.

10th Joel Horlen revives Chicago pennant hopes with a 5–0 no-hit win against the Tigers. Detroit hits only two balls to the OF. The Sox win game 2 by a 4–0 score to move a game behind the 2nd-place Red Sox.

Minnesota leads the tight AL race after edging the Orioles 4–2 at Baltimore.

11th A's players agree to drop a grievance filed with the National Labor Relations Board against Charlie Finley. Finley agrees, in writing, that he will not coerce or intimidate his players, or discriminate against them for the threatened action.

Houston ties the NL record by using 8 pitchers in one 9-inning game, defeating Chicago 11–10 at the Astrodome.

14th Walt Bond, who played for the Indians, Astros, and Twins, dies of leukemia at 29.

16th Norm Cash drives in 5 runs and John Hiller goes the distance, enabling Detroit to take the AL lead with a 9–1 win over the Yankees.

18th Bob Gibson pitches St. Louis to a 5–1 win and its 2nd pennant of the decade.

19th Wes Westrum (57-94) resigns as manager of the Mets following a 4–3 loss to the Dodgers. Coach

Salty Parker takes over and will be 4-7 for the rest of the season. Two days later the board of directors announces it will try to obtain Gil Hodges as manager.

20th Steve Carlton of the Cardinals strikes out 16 batters in a 9-inning game but still loses 3–1 to Chris Short and the Phillies.

23rd Three straight sacrifice bunts by the Phillies tie a ML record in a 4–0 win at Los Angeles.

27th Philadelphia's Jim Bunning loses a ML-record-tying 5th 1–0 decision, as Houston's Mike Cuellar outlasts the veteran in 11 innings.

30th Manager Billy Hitchcock (77-82) is fired by the Braves.

Jim Davenport sets an NL record with his 64th straight errorless game—137 chances—at 3B for the Giants.

Boston beats the Twins 6–4 to tie Minnesota for first place. Carl Yastrzemski's 3-run HR, his AL-leading 44th, keys the victory.

OCTOBER

1st Boston clinches the AL pennant with a 5–3 win over Minnesota, Jim Lonborg besting Dean Chance. Carl Yastrzemski goes 4-for-4 and has 10 hits in his final 13 at bats to grab the Triple Crown (.326, 44, 121). Detroit, who could tie for the lead with a sweep, beats California in the opener 6–4. They then drop the 2nd game 8–5.

Joe Adcock (75-87) is fired as manager of the Indians.

Pittsburgh RF Roberto Clemente ends his season with a flourish, winning his 4th batting title with a .357 average by going 2-for-5 with a triple and his 23rd HR, as the Pirates wallop the Astros 10–3.

2nd Ground is broken for a new stadium in Philadelphia.

4th Cardinals LF Lou Brock has 4 hits, 2 stolen bases, and scores twice, as St. Louis edges Boston 2–1 to open the World Series at Fenway Park. Bob Gibson has 10 strikeouts and outduels Jose Santiago, whose HR is Boston's only score.

5th Jim Lonborg pitches the 4th one-hitter in WS history and Yaz (Carl Yastrzemski) hits 2 HRs in Boston's 5–0 win to even the Series.

7th In game 3 St. Louis, Nelson Briles swings the WS toward the Cards with a 7-hit 5–2 win. Lou Brock has 2 more hits, and Mike Shannon homers off loser Gary Bell.

Lum Harris is named manager of the Braves.

8th Bob Gibson is overpowering again in a 5-hit 6–0 win in Game 4. Roger Maris and Tim McCarver each have 2 RBI for St. Louis.

The Braves trade P Denny Lemaster and SS Dennis Menke to the Astros for SS Sonny Jackson and 1B Chuck Harrison.

9th Roger Maris homers for the Cardinals in the 9th, but Jim Lonborg's 3–1 win sends the WS back to Boston.

11th A WS record 3 HRs in one inning—consecutively, by Yaz, Reggie Smith, and Rico Petrocelli—power Boston to an 8–4 win that evens the Series at 3 each.

Gil Hodges leaves Washington to become manager of the Mets. Jim Lemon is named manager of the Senators. New York reportedly pays the Senators $100,000 and later sends P Bill Denehy to Washington as compensation for Hodges.

12th The Cardinals earn their 2nd World Championship of the decade with a 7–2 victory. Bob Gibson notches his 3rd WS win with a 3-hitter, 10 strikeouts, and a 5th-inning HR. Lou Brock has 2 hits and steals 3 bases for a record 7 thefts in a 7-game WS.

13th Larry Sheppard is named manager of the Pirates.

18th The AL approves the Athletics' shift to Oakland, CA. Kansas City is promised a a new team by 1971. When Senator Stuart Symington and Kansas City Mayor Ilus Davis threaten action against the move, AL President Joe Cronin reopens talks, and the expansion deadline is moved to 1969.

19th Senator Stuart Symington blasts A's owner Charlie Finley on the floor of the United States Senate, calling him "one of the most disreputable characters ever to enter the American sports scene."

20th Charlie Finley names Bob Kennedy the first manager of the Oakland A's.

22nd Joe DiMaggio is hired as executive vice president of the A's by Charlie Finley.

30th Arthur Allyn announces that his White Sox will play 9 games in Milwaukee in 1968. Chicago will become the first AL team to play regular season games outside its own city since 1905.

31st San Francisco's Mike McCormick is the NL Cy Young Award winner, as pitchers are honored in each league for the first time.

NOVEMBER

3rd Boston's Jim Lonborg is named AL Cy Young Award winner.

7th Orlando Cepeda of the Cards is the first unanimous selection as NL MVP.

8th The Reds trade OF Art Shamsky to the Mets for IF Bob Johnson.

13th Following a meeting of NL owners, President Warren Giles says the league will not stand in the way of AL expansion to Seattle and Kansas City.

15th Boston's Carl Yastrzemski is the overwhelming selection as AL MVP.

20th Mets P Tom Seaver (16-12) is named NL Rookie of the Year.

21st Cleveland acquires OF Tommy Harper from the Reds for 1B Fred Whitfield and P George Culver.

22nd Minnesota 2B Rod Carew (.292) is the runaway choice for AL Rookie of the Year.

28th The Twins send SS Zoilo Versalles and P Jim Grant to the Dodgers for C John Roseboro and pitchers Bob Miller and Ron Perranoski.

29th The White Sox reacquire SS Luis Aparicio, with OF Russ Snyder and 1B/OF John Matias, from Baltimore for pitchers Bruce Howard and Roger Nelson and IF Don Buford.

The Indians trade OF Chuck Hinton to the Angels for OF Jose Cardenal.

DECEMBER

1st Pacific Northwest Sports, Inc. is awarded one of the 2 AL expansion franchise. The team will play in Seattle.

5th Stan Musial resigns as GM of the Cardinals.

15th Pittsburgh acquires P Jim Bunning from the Phillies for pitchers Woody Fryman, Bill Laxton, and Harold Clem, and IF Don Money.

The Mets trade OF Tommy Davis, P Jack Fisher, P Billy Wynne, and C Dick Booker to the White Sox for OF Tommie Agee and IF Al Weis.

The Red Sox trade C Mike Ryan and cash to the Phillies for P Dick Ellsworth and C/1B Gene Oliver.

1968

JANUARY

11th   Ewing Kauffman becomes owner of the new Kansas City club of the AL.

The Cardinals trade OF Alex Johnson to the Reds for OF Dick Simpson.

23rd   Joe Medwick is voted into the Baseball Hall of Fame.

28th   Goose Goslin and Kiki Cuyler are admitted into the Hall of Fame by unanimous vote of the Special Veterans Committee.

FEBRUARY

6th   Voters in King County (Washington) approve by 62 percent a $40 million bond issue to build a domed, multipurpose stadium.

8th   The Reds trade C Johnny Edwards to the Cardinals for IF Jim Williams and C Pat Corrales.

13th   The White Sox trade SS Ron Hansen and pitchers Dennis Higgins and Steve Jones to Washington for pitchers Bob Priddy and Les Narum and IF Tim Cullen.

The Giants trade C Tom Haller and P Frank Kasheta to the Dodgers for infielders Ron Hunt and Nate Oliver. This is the first trade between the 2 clubs since 1956 when Jackie Robinson was sent to the Giants but retired instead.

21st   The first basic agreement between players and owners is ratified. The agreement runs from January 1, 1968 to December 31, 1969.

The minimum ML player's salary is raised to $10,000. Meal money during the season will be $15 a day (up from $12), and players will get $40 a week for training-camp expenses (up from $25).

MARCH

21st   Royals is chosen as the name of the new Kansas City AL franchise.

23rd   In a spring training game, Cubs P Jim Ellis creates the "Lip Pass" by going to his mouth on a 3-and-1 count to issue an intentional walk.

31st   The name for Seattle's AL club is the Pilots.

APRIL

2nd   Tony Conigliaro returns to Boston with vision trouble. He will miss the 1968 season.

8th   Opening Day is postponed because of the assassination of the Rev. Dr. Martin Luther King, Jr.

14th   New York suffers a 4–3 loss to Minnesota and loses OF Joe Pepitone with a fractured left elbow.

Jim Bunning's first win with Pittsburgh, 3–0 at Los Angeles, is his 40th career shutout and includes his 1,000th NL strikeout, making him the first pitcher since Cy Young with 1,000 in each league.

15th   Three records are smashed when the Astros score an unearned run in the 24th inning to squeeze by the Mets 1–0 after 6 hours and 6 minutes. It is the longest NL game played to completion, the longest ML night game, and the first 23 innings are the longest ML scoreless game. Oddly, the records erased for longest night and scoreless games are less than a year old (June 12 and September 1, 1967). The game ties the AL's longest complete game: A's 4, Red Sox 1, on September 1, 1906.

17th   With a 13–1 rout of the Senators, the Twins are 6-0 and lead the AL.

The A's debut at Oakland-Alameda County Coliseum by losing 4–1 to Baltimore.

19th   The NL owners approve expansion, pending unanimous approval of 2 new teams.

Nolan Ryan of the Mets becomes the 6th pitcher in NL history to strike out the side on 9 pitches. But Los Angeles wins 3–2 at Shea Stadium.

23rd   The Cubs acquire P Phil Regan and OF Jim Hickman from the Dodgers for OF Ted Savage and P Jim Ellis.

27th   Tom Phoebus, the Orioles' top pitcher last year, throws a 6–0 no-hitter against the Red Sox. Brooks Robinson drives in 3 runs and makes a great stab to rob Rico Petrocelli of a hit in the 8th. Converted OF Curt Blefary catches the game.

29th   The Giants Jim Davenport plays his 97th consecutive errorless game at 3B.

MAY

1st   Sudden Sam McDowell of Cleveland strikes out 16 batters and defeats Oakland 3–1.

Phillies P John Boozer is ejected by umpire Ed Vargo at Shea Stadium for throwing spitballs during his warmup pitches. He is only the 2nd ML pitcher to be ejected from a game for throwing spitballs.

6th In a 10–2 loss to Houston, Giants reliever Lindy McDaniel sets a NL record with his 225th consecutive errorless game. The veteran hurler has handled 108 chances consecutively since June 16, 1964.

9th Oakland's Catfish Hunter pitches a perfect game against the Twins, winning 3–0. The 22-year-old righthander hurls the first AL regular season perfecto in 46 years. He strikes out 11 and drives in all 3 A's runs.

10th Denny McLain wins 12–1 at Washington, as the Tigers pass the first-place Orioles. Detroit will remain in the lead for the rest of the season.

13th University of Denver defeats the Air Force Academy 33–29, establishing a record for most runs by a losing team and the most total bases in a game (104).

14th Dodger P Don Drysdale shuts out the Cubs 1–0.

15th The first AL game played in Milwaukee is a 4–2 California win against Chicago before 23,403 fans. This is the first of the 9 games the White Sox will play in Milwaukee in 1968.

16th With his third 2-HR game in 4 games, Senators LF Frank Howard ties the AL record for most HRs (7) in 4 straight games (at least one in each). Washington wins 4–1 at Cleveland.

17th Frank Howard belts a HR for the 5th straight game in Washington's 7–3 loss at Detroit. It is his 8th and the most anyone has hit in a 5-game span.

18th Frank Howard ties the AL record with a HR in his 6th consecutive game. His 10 HRs in the 6 games are the most of all the record holders. Howard's 10 HRs are also the most ever in one week (Sunday through Saturday).

Don Drysdale posts his 2nd consecutive shutout, 1–0 over Houston.

Pirate Bill Mazeroski plays his 392nd straight game, a record for NL 2B, in an 8–3 loss to the Reds.

20th Angels SS Jim Fregosi joins a small group of players by hitting for the cycle a 2nd time, and California beats Boston 5–4 in Anaheim.

21st The Cubs climb above the .500 mark the first time all season with a 6–5 win over the Phillies. Chicago's Billy Williams sets a record for outfielders by playing his 695th straight game.

22nd The Cards fall 2–0, as Don Drysdale's streak reaches 3 consecutive scoreless games.

25th Detroit OF Al Kaline is hit by the A's Lew Krausse's pitch and suffers a broken arm. He will be out until June 30th.

26th Los Angeles downs Houston 5–0 behind Don Drysdale. Now it's 4 straight shutouts.

27th Montreal and San Diego are awarded NL franchises after a 10-hour meeting of league owners.

28th The AL owners agree to the following divisional alignment for 1969: Eastern: Boston, New York, Cleveland, Baltimore, Washington, Detroit; Western: Chicago, Kansas City, Minnesota, Seattle, Oakland, California.

Suffering his 4th straight defeat, Cardinal Bob Gibson (3-5) drops a 3–1 decision to Gaylord Perry and the Giants.

30th Don Drysdale's shutout streak apparently ends when Dick Dietz is hit by a pitch with the bases loaded in the 9th inning, but umpire Harry Wendelstedt rules Dietz did not try to avoid the pitch. Los Angeles wins 3–0, and Drysdale's 5th straight shutout ties the ML record.

JUNE

1st St. Louis reliever Joe Hoerner ties the NL record for relievers with 6 consecutive strikeouts.

2nd Sweeping a doubleheader 6–3 and 3–2 at New York's Shea Stadium, the Cardinals take first place. They will remain atop the NL the rest of the season.

4th With his 6th consecutive shutout, 5–0 over the Pirates at Los Angeles, Don Drysdale establishes two new ML records. He tops Doc White's 64-year-old mark of 5 shutouts, and with 54 scoreless innings he breaks Carl Hubbell's NL string of $4\frac{1}{3}$ in 1933.

At Wrigley, the Mets Jerry Koosman strikes out the leadoff Cub for his 7th straight strikeout, then wins 2–0.

Ewing Kauffman signs a 4-year lease for the Royals to play in Kansas City's Municipal Stadium.

Fresco Thompson succeeds Buzzie Bavasi as general manager of the Dodgers. Bavasi will run the new NL club in San Diego.

6th Tim Foli is the top choice in the regular phase of the free-agent draft. The A's take Pete Broberg with the 2nd pick, but he opts to attend Dartmouth instead. Cecil Cooper lasts until the 27th round. The big winners are the Dodgers, who, in the January draft and the regular and secondary June drafts, select 15 players who end up in the ML. Among them: Davey Lopes, Geoff Zahn, Bill Buckner, Joe Ferguson, Tom Paciorek, Bobby Valentine, Steve Garvey, and Ron Cey.

8th The Mets' game at San Francisco is postponed at the demand of New York players in the aftermath of New York Senator Robert F. Kennedy's assassination. Commissioner William Eckert orders all games delayed until evening. He also orders games at New York and Washington postponed.

Don Drysdale works 4 scoreless innings against Philadelphia before finally allowing a run, after 58⅔ shutout innings, on Howie Bedell's sacrifice fly. Bedell has no other RBI in 1968. Drysdale breaks the ML record of 56 consecutive scoreless innings set by Walter Johnson in 1913. The Dodgers win 5–3.

10th AL games at Baltimore and Chicago are postponed, as mourning for Robert Kennedy continues. Astros Rusty Staub and Bob Aspromonte are fined for not playing. Pittsburgh's Maury Wills also refuses to play and is reportedly punished.

11th The Reds send P Milt Pappas, pitchers Ted Davidson, and IF Bob Johnson to the Braves for pitchers Tony Cloninger and Clay Carroll and IF Woody Woodward.

13th The White Sox trade OF Russ Snyder to the Indians for OF Leon Wagner.

15th Gene Mauch (27-27) is fired as manager of the Phillies. He will be replaced the next day by Bob Skinner.

Chicago's Tommy John becomes the 9th AL pitcher to hit 4 batters in one game, as he nails 4 Tigers in a 7–4 White Sox win.

18th Grady Hatton (23-38) is fired as manager of the Astros. He will be replaced by Harry Walker.

24th Detroit RF Jim Northrup becomes the 6th AL player to hit 2 grand slams in one game, connecting in the 5th inning off Eddie Fisher and in the 6th off Billy Rohr, as the Tigers bomb Cleveland 14–3.

25th San Francisco rookie Bobby Bonds becomes the 2nd player to debut with a grand slam, as Ray Sadecki blanks the Dodgers 9–0. Bonds does it on his 3rd at bat. The only other player to hit a grand slam in his first major league game was William Duggelby of the Philadelphia Nationals, who achieved the feat in 1898.

26th The ML Executive Council decides that both the AL and NL will play 162-game schedules in 1969 and operate two 6-team divisions.

Cardinal Bob Gibson pitches his 5th straight shutout in the first game of a doubleheader with Pittsburgh. Pittsburgh wins the 2nd game 3–1, although the Cardinals stop Maury Wills's 24-game hitting streak.

29th Jim Northrup's 3rd grand slam ties the ML record for slams in a month (Rudy York, May 1938), and sets a ML record for slams in a week. The Tigers win 5–2 over Chicago, as Denny McLain tallies his 14th victory.

JULY

1st A first inning WP allows a run to break Bob Gibson's streak of 47⅔ innings of scoreless pitching. The Cards beat the Dodgers in Los Angeles 8–1. Gibson will pitch 23 innings before giving up another run.

3rd Luis Tiant registers 19 K's in 10 innings, as Cleveland beats Minnesota 1–0. Tiant sets two modern ML records— most strikeouts in a 10-inning game; 32 strikeouts in consecutive games—and ties the modern ML record of 41 strikeouts in 3 successive appearances. He will top the AL in ERA with 1.60.

7th Denny McLain, the major leagues' winningest pitcher with 16, helps Detroit take a 9½ game lead over 2nd-place Cleveland to the All-Star break, as the Tigers sweep the A's 5–4 and 7–6. McLain wins the opener.

Completing a 7-game West Coast winning streak, the Cardinals take a 10-game lead into the All-Star break.

9th Appropriately, pitching dominates the All-Star Game. Willie Mays, playing in place of injured Pete Rose, tallies an unearned run in the first inning against

AL starter Luis Tiant to complete the scoring for the day—the first All-Star effort to end 1–0. Don Drysdale, Juan Marichal, Steve Carlton, Tom Seaver, Ron Reed, and Jerry Koosman hold the AL to 3 hits.

10th   Hank Bauer is fired as manager of the Orioles.

The NL breaks down its 2 divisions for 1969 thus: Eastern: New York, Philadelphia, Pittsburgh, Montreal, Chicago, St. Louis; Western: Los Angeles, San Francisco, Houston, Cincinnati, San Diego, Atlanta.

11th   Groundbreaking takes place for Kansas City's $43 million Jackson County Sports Complex.

Earl Weaver, who never played in the majors, replaces Hank Bauer as manager of the Orioles.

Minnesota rookie Rick Renick is the 16th AL player to hit a HR in his first ML at bat. The Twins beat the Tigers 5–4.

Chicago Cubs P Bill Hands strikes out for the 14th straight time in the 2–0 Cubs win in the nightcap at New York. The 14 straight strikeouts are a ML record.

12th   Eddie Stanky is fired as manager of the White Sox and replaced by Al Lopez.

The Giants trade P Lindy McDaniel to the Yankees for P Bill Monbouquette.

Houston reliever Tom Dukes ties the ML record with his 9th straight relief appearance for the Astros, an 8–1 loss to St. Louis.

14th   Houston's Don Wilson fans 18 batters in a 5–4 win at Cincinnati, tying the ML record set by Bob Feller. He also ties the ML record with 8 strikeouts in a row. For all his efforts, Wilson is not the winner.

16th   Cleveland's Jose Cardenal becomes the 4th OF in ML history with 2 unassisted DPs in one season to help the Tribe to a 2–1 win over the Angels.

23rd   Al Lopez undergoes an emergency appendectomy. Les Moss will serve as White Sox manager during his 36-game absence.

24th   Hoyt Wilhelm's 907th game breaks Cy Young's record for ML pitching appearances, but he loses a 2–1 decision to Oakland.

29th   The Reds George Culver overcomes an upset stomach and an ingrown toenail to pitch a no-hitter against the Phillies, winning 6–1. Two errors give the Phils a run in the 2nd.

30th   Washington SS Ron Hansen turns the 8th unassisted triple play in ML history. Cleveland's Joe Azcue hits a liner to Hansen, who steps on 2B to double Dave Nelson, and tags Russ Snyder sliding into 2B for the 3rd out. Hansen's effort is not enough, as Washington loses 10–1.

31st   Chicago's Billy Williams, Ernie Banks, and Jim Hickman hit 4th-inning HRs as Fergie Jenkins (12-10) beats the Astros 6–1 at Wrigley Field.

AUGUST

2nd   The Senators trade SS Ron Hansen to the White Sox for IF Tim Cullen.

7th   Oakland's Joe Keough makes his ML debut with a first-at bat, HR in the 2nd-game 4–3 win over the Yankees. New York wins the opener 3–0.

8th   Jarry Park is grudgingly approved by Montreal Mayor Jean Drapeau for interim use by the Expos. Montreal officials tell NL President Warren Giles that a new stadium will be ready by 1972.

9th   California pitchers plunk Baltimore batters 3 times in the 7th inning at Memorial Stadium, tying the AL record for hit batsmen in one inning. Baltimore wins 3–0.

11th   Satchel Paige, 62 years or so old, and needing 158 days on a ML payroll to qualify for a pension, is signed by the Braves. He will not pitch a regular-season game for Atlanta and will become a coach on September 30th.

14th   Montreal officially becomes a member of the NL.

16th   Detroit's Denny McLain is 16-0 on the road after blanking the Red Sox 4–0 in Boston. Tigers C Bill Freehan is hit by a pitch in 3 consecutive at bats, painfully tying a ML record.

Philadelphia's Richie Allen ties an NL record by drawing 5 bases on balls in one game, but the Dodgers win 7–5.

18th   Chicago's Phil Regan is ejected by umpire Chris Pelekoudas for throwing a spitball and/or doctored ball in the 2nd game at Wrigley. Pelekoudas does a thorough search on the mound but finds nothing. Cubs executive John Holland protests the game, but the only result is that NL President Warren Giles later orders the umpire to apologize to Regan. Meanwhile, the Reds sweep 2–1 and 6–3.

21st Minnesota's Jim Merritt loses his shutout in the 9th when Mickey Mantle hits a pinch homer, but he wins 3–1. It is Mantle's 534th HR, tying him with Jimmie Foxx for 3rd on the all-time list.

Monte Irvin is named special assistant to Commissioner William Eckert.

23rd After 19 innings, the Tigers-Yankees game is suspended by curfew.

25th Yankees reliever Lindy McDaniel ties the AL record for consecutive batters retired by setting down the first Tiger he faces in the first game, giving him 32 straight batters retired over 4 appearances. New York sweeps 6–5 and 5–4.

27th Sweeping a doubleheader from Oakland 5–3 and 7–2 at Memorial Stadium, the Orioles close within 4 games of first-place Detroit.

31st Steve Blass gets the first out against the Braves, and then moves to LF as Roy Face relieves. Face retires Felix Millan and ties Walter Johnson's ML record of 802 pitching appearances with one club. Blass comes back in and the Pirates go on to win 8–0. Later in the game, the Pirates announce the sale of Face to the Tigers.

It is a tough month for Mets P Jim McAndrews, as he takes his NL-tying 4th shutout loss. Steve Carlton wins for the Cards 2–0.

SEPTEMBER

5th Gene Mauch is named manager of the new Montreal NL club, which is officially named the Expos.

9th Joe Gordon is hired to manage the Royals.

10th Billy Williams hits 3 HRs in a game for the first time in his career. It's all the Cubs' scoring, as they beat the Mets 3–1 behind Bill Hands. Added to two HRs on September 8th, Williams has a ML-record-tying 5 over two straight games.

11th Jim McAndrews of the Mets beats the Cubs 1–0. It is Fergie Jenkins's (17-14) 5th 1–0 loss of the season, which ties a ML record.

14th Denny McLain becomes the first 30-game winner since Dizzy Dean in 1934, as the Tigers beat the A's 5–4.

The Cardinals clinch the NL pennant with a 7–4 win at Houston. Roger Maris hits his 275th, and last, regular-season HR.

16th AL President Joe Cronin fires umpires Al Salerno, an 8-year veteran, and Bill Valentine, with 7 years. They say they have been fired for activities related to starting an umpires union.

17th Gaylord Perry hurls a no-hitter at Candlestick, as the Giants edge the Cards and Bob Gibson 1–0. Ron Hunt's solo HR backs Perry, who evens his record at 14-14.

Detroit clinches the AL pennant with a 2–1 win over the Yankees.

18th Sixteen hours after Perry's feat, Ray Washburn of the Cards makes ML history by hurling a 2nd consecutive no-hitter in one park. Run-scoring hits by Mike Shannon and Curt Flood at Candlestick down the Giants 2–0.

19th Denny McLain's 31st win is overshadowed by Mickey Mantle's 535th HR. McLain says he purposely pipelined a fastball to the aging slugger. The HR gives Mantle undisputed hold of 3rd place on the all-time HR list.

22nd Cesar Tovar becomes the 2nd player to play every position in a game. Minnesota's all-purpose star leads the Twins to a 2–1 win over the Oakland A's. Bert Campaneris of the Kansas City A's was the first to pull off this stunt in 1965.

24th Manager Gil Hodges suffers a heart attack during New York's game with the Braves. He is hospitalized, and Rube Walker takes the helm for the rest of the season.

27th A 1–0 win and 11 strikeouts against the Astros enable Cardinal Bob Gibson to lower his ERA to 1.12, a new NL season mark. His phenomenal campaign includes 28 complete games, 268 strikeouts, and 13 shutouts.

29th Bob Kennedy is fired as Oakland manager.

In a 3–0 loss to the Giants, the Reds Pete Rose goes 1-for-3 to take his first NL batting title with a .335 average.

Carl Yastrzemski maintains a .3005 BA, to win his 2nd straight batting crown with the lowest championship average ever. Yaz is the AL's only .300 hitter: Oakland's Danny Cater is 2nd with .290.

White Sox relief P Wilbur Wood ends his season with a 7–6 win at California and a ML record 88 appearances.

30th AL and NL umpires form a new Association of Major League Umpires. They will strike in the spring of 1969 unless Al Salerno and Bill Valentine are reinstated by the AL.

Cal Ermer is dismissed as manager of the Twins.

OCTOBER

2nd For the first time in history, 2 soon-to-be-named MVPs oppose each other. St. Louis Bob Gibson is nearly untouchable with a WS-record 17 strikeouts and a 4–0 win over Denny McLain. Detroit manager Mayo Smith moves Gold Glove CF Mickey Stanley to SS, improving his offense by opening a spot for Al Kaline.

3rd Detroit's Mickey Lolich evens the Series with a 6-hitter and his first ML HR to defeat St. Louis 8–1.

5th Tim McCarver's 3-run HR off loser Earl Wilson and Orlando Cepeda's 3-run shot off Don McMahon power St. Louis to a 7–3 win and 2–1 WS lead.

6th In Game 4 St. Louis dumps Detroit 10–1. Bob Gibson, fanning 10, earns his 7th straight Series victory. Denny McLain gives up 4 runs, and is relieved in the 3rd after a rain delay. Lou Brock shines with a double, triple, HR, 4 RBI, and a steal that gives him 7 in 4 games.

7th Mickey Lolich saves Detroit, 5–3 with an unlikely assist from Lou Brock. On 2B in the 5th, Brock tries to score standing up on Julian Javier's single and is gunned down by Willie Horton's throw. Al Kaline's bases-loaded single off Joe Hoerner in the 7th scores 2 for the winning margin. Jose Feliciano's modern rendition of the National Anthem before the game stirs controversy.

9th Denny McLain returns to form, scattering 9 singles, as Detroit evens the WS with a 10-run 3rd inning and 13–1 win at St. Louis.

10th Mickey Lolich bests Bob Gibson and brings Detroit its first WS championship since 1945. The hefty lefty hurls a 5-hitter, giving Detroit a 4–1 win.

11th Joe Schultz is named manager of the Seattle Pilots.

Clyde King is named Herman Franks' replacement as manager of the Giants.

Billy Martin is named manager of the Twins.

The Cards trade OF Bobby Tolan and P Wayne Granger to the Reds for OF Vada Pinson.

14th In the NL expansion draft, the Expos choose 30 players, including Maury Wills, Jim Grant, Donn Clendenon, and Manny Mota. San Diego's 30 selections include Dave Giusti, Nate Colbert, Zoilo Versalles, Al McBean, and Clarence Gaston.

15th Roger Nelson is the initial choice of the Royals in the AL expansion draft. Don Mincher is the Pilots' first choice. Other Seattle selections include Tommy Harper, Tommy Davis, Gary Bell, and Lou Piniella. Kansas City chooses Wally Bunker, Moe Drabowsky, Hoyt Wilhelm, and Joe Foy.

21st The Expos purchase 3B Bob Bailey from the Dodgers.

Elston Howard, after 2 seasons withe the Red Sox, announces his retirement.

28th Bob Gibson wins his first Cy Young Award, receiving all 20 votes.

NOVEMBER

1st Denny McLain is the unanimous AL winner of the Cy Young Award.

5th Denny McLain is the unanimous choice as AL MVP.

13th Bob Gibson edges Pete Rose to win the NL MVP award.

19th Yankees P Stan Bahnsen, who was 17-12, is named AL Rookie of the Year.

21st Cincinnati trades SS Leo Cardenas to the Twins for P Jim Merritt.

22nd Cincinnati C Johnny Bench is named NL Rookie of the Year, getting 10½ votes to edge out New York's Jerry Koosman who had 9½. Bench is the 3rd Reds' player in 6 years to be named the top rookie.

DECEMBER

3rd Robert E. Short, Democratic National Committee treasurer, buys the Senators for $10 million. Jim Lemon will retain 15–20 percent.

The Baseball Rules Committee moves to increase offense with new measures to lower the pitching mound, shrink the strike zone, and enforce rules against illegal pitches.

6th William Eckert resigns as commissioner.

12th The Kansas City Royals complete their first trade, sending P Hoyt Wilhelm to the Angels for 2 outfielder/catchers, Ed Kirkpatrick and Dennis Paepke.

17th The owners announce they will increase contributions to the players' pension fund by $1 million to $5.1 million per year. Players vote down the proposal 491–7.

1969

JANUARY

4th   Attorney Jack Reynolds, administrator of the new umpires union, says an economic agreement has been worked out between the AL and umpires that will avert a strike in 1969.

6th   Umpires Al Salerno and Bill Valentine file a grievance against the AL and its president, Joe Cronin. The grievance is filed by the new umpires union with the National Labor Relations Board.

11th   The Cubs obtain veteran reliever Ted Abernathy from the Reds for 3 minor leaguers.

21st   Stan Musial and Roy Campanella are voted into the Hall of Fame by BBWAA members.

22nd   The Expos trade 1B Donn Clendenon and OF Jesus Alou to Houston for OF/1B Rusty Staub.

29th   Washington manager Jim Lemon is fired.

FEBRUARY

2nd   Pitchers Stan Coveleski and Waite Hoyt are voted into the Hall of Fame by the Special Veterans Committee.

3rd   To show strength in their bid for a better pension plan, 125 players meet in New York City.

4th   Attorney Bowie Kuhn is a compromise choice for commissioner of baseball and is elected on a pro-tem basis.

21st   Ted Williams returns to baseball full-time, signing a 5-year contract to manage the Senators.

25th   A pension plan for baseball is agreed on, with players to get $5.45 million per year. They also get a reduction in the years necessary to qualify for a pension from 5 to 4, retroactive to 1959; a percentage of television revenues; lowered minimum age for drawing a pension from 50 to 45; and other benefits.

28th   1B Donn Clendenon announces his retirement.

MARCH

1st   The Yankees' Mickey Mantle retires.

8th   NL President Giles and Commissioner Bowie Kuhn say the Rusty Staub deal stands, that Clendenon belongs to the Expos, and that Montreal and Houston will have to come to agreement on further compensation.

17th   St. Louis trades 1B Orlando Cepeda to Atlanta for C/1B Joe Torre.

26th   An indemnity of $540,000 is paid to the Pacific Coast League for the ML invasion of San Diego and Seattle.

APRIL

3rd   Donn Clendenon ends his retirement and joins the Expos, signing for $50,000 per year.

7th   Bill Singer of the Dodgers is credited with the first official save, as Los Angeles defeats Cincinnati 3–2.

8th   Expansion teams Kansas City Royals, Montreal Expos, San Diego Padres, and Seattle Pilots make things look easy by winning their first regular-season games.

Houston accepts pitchers Jack Billingham and Skip Guinn and an estimated $100,000 from the Expos to complete the Rusty Staub trade.

After a long recovery following a 1967 beaning, Tony Conigliaro starts his first game for Boston. His dramatic 2-run 10th-inning HR gives the Red Sox a brief lead, and his 12th-inning run wins it.

9th   Billy Williams ties the ML record for doubles in a game with 4 straight in Chicago's 11–3 win against the Phillies.

With the Royals Ellie Rodriguez at bat, Bob Oliver tries to steal 2B. Twins C John Roseboro throws the runner out, but has to push Rodriguez's bat out of the way. After several conferences between the umpires, Oliver is sent back to 1B and Rodriguez is called out for interference.

11th   Before 14,993, Seattle successfully inaugurates ML baseball at Sicks' Stadium, as Gary Bell defeats Chicago 7–0. The Pilots will draw just 678,000 for the season.

14th   Montreal nips St. Louis 8–7, as ML baseball comes to Canada. Dan McGinn is the winner at Jarry Park.

16th The Orioles take first place in the AL East with an 11–8 win at Boston, and Baltimore will remain there the rest of the season.

17th Bill Stoneman's first win as a starter is a no-hitter for Montreal at Philadelphia. Rusty Staub's HR, 3 doubles, and 3 RBI pace a 5–0 win.

19th Boston trades last year's 1B Ken Harrelson and pitchers Dick Ellsworth and Juan Pizarro to Cleveland for pitchers Sonny Siebert and Vincente Romo and C Joe Azcue.

25th Giants C Jack Hiatt hits a 2-run first-inning HR and a 13th-inning grand slam to pace a 12–8 victory over Houston. Hiatt has 7 RBI in the game.

26th The Baseball Records Committee says Babe Ruth should be credited with 715 HRs, because one hit recognized as a triple should have been ruled a HR.

27th Harmon Killebrew hits his 400th HR, and the Twins take first place in the AL West by beating Chicago 4–3.

The Giants sweep Houston 8–5 and 4–3 as Willie McCovey hits 3 HRs in each game. McCovey has 8 HRs for the month.

29th San Francisco's hit-by-pitch specialist Ron Hunt ties the ML record when nailed 3 times by Cincinnati pitchers. A Bobby Bonds HR in the 13th seals it for San Francisco 4–3.

30th The Reds Jim Maloney hurls his first 9-inning no-hitter, and 3rd overall. He has 13 strikeouts and Bobby Tolan drives in 4 runs as Cincinnati romps over Houston 10–0.

MAY

1st Houston, no-hit the day before by Cincinnati, answers back, as Don Wilson pitches a 4–0 no-hitter, with 13 strikeouts over the Reds. Houston ties an NL record with just one assist. In Wilson's previous start against Cincinnati, he gave up 6 runs in 5 innings in a 14–0 loss.

2nd Al Lopez (840-650) resigns as White Sox manager for health reasons. Don Gutteridge takes over.

4th The Astros tie a ML record with 7 DPs in a 3–1 win against the Giants. Curt Blefary sets a record for 1B by participating in all 7.

Bob Oliver goes 6-for-6, as the Royals coast over California 15–1.

5th The Baseball Records Committee reverses its earlier decision and decides to stay with the pre-1920 rules on sudden death home runs. This rule stated that a team batting last in the 9th or in extra innings could not win by more than one run. Before 1920 if a player hit an outside-the-park home run with a runner(s) on base, he was not credited with a home run. Babe Ruth (July 8, 1918) and 36 other players "lost" HRs because of the ruling reversal.

12th Cardinal Bob Gibson becomes the 7th NL pitcher to strike out the side on 9 pitches. He does it in the 7th inning of a 6–2 St. Louis win over the Dodgers.

13th Cubs 1B Ernie Banks has 7 RBI, including his 1,500th, in Chicago's 19–0 win against San Diego, matching the biggest shutout margin in modern NL history. Cubs pitcher Dick Selma is the recipient.

14th California and Chicago swap second basemen as Sandy Alomar goes to the Angels and Bobby Knoop to the Sox. P Bob Priddy also goes to California.

15th Willie Horton leaves the Detroit bench during a 2–1 win against Chicago and goes AWOL for 4 days.

16th Seattle scores 6 runs in the 11th inning, then allows 5, but hangs on for a 10–9 win at Boston. Jim Bouton gets the win in the highest-scoring 11th inning ever.

18th Rod Carew steals 2B, 3B, and home in the 3rd inning of Minnesota's 8–2 loss to Detroit. Cesar Tovar also steals 3rd and home that inning to tie a ML record. Detroit's Mickey Lolich and Bill Freehan are the embarrassed battery.

23rd Mickey Lolich sets a Detroit record with 16 strikeouts while defeating Andy Messersmith and the Angels 6–3.

Pittsburgh's rookie 1B Al Oliver ties the ML record with 3 errors in one inning, and the Bucs lose 3–0 at San Francisco.

24th Padres rookie 2B John Sipin debuts with a pair of triples, only the 4th player to do so, in a 7–5 San Diego victory over the Cubs. They are the only triples of his 68-game career.

25th The Cardinals tie a NL record with just one assist in Bob Gibson's 4–0 win at Los Angeles.

26th   Bill Rigney is fired as manager of the Angels, and coach Lefty Phillips is named to succeed him.

28th   In a 7–6 win over Pittsburgh, NL HR leader Lee May of the Reds hits a pair, garnering a ML-record-tying 6 in 3 straight games (at least one in each).

JUNE

7th   The Washington Senators name Jeff Burroughs the number one pick in the June free-agent draft. The Astros choose J. R. Richard as the 2nd pick, and the White Sox follow with 3B Ted Nicholson. Cincinnati picks Ken Griffey on the 29th round, while Kansas City, with a record 90 picks, takes Al Cowens with their 84th choice.

8th   The Expos snap a 20-game losing streak as Jerry Robertson wins 4–3 at Los Angeles.

The White Sox trade P Bob Locker to the Pilots for P Gary Bell.

Mickey Mantle Day in New York. With 60,096 fans on hand, Mantle's number 7 is retired and plaques he exchanges with Joe DiMaggio will hang on the CF wall at Yankee Stadium. DiMaggio's plaque comes as a surprise to the Yankee Clipper. The Yankees then sweep the White Sox 3–1 and 11–2.

9th   Mickey Lolich's 16 strikeouts tie the Detroit record he set May 23rd, but the Tigers drop a 3–2, 10-inning decision to Seattle.

11th   Maury Wills returns to Los Angeles with OF Manny Mota. IF Paul Popovich and OF Ron Fairly are traded to Montreal. The Expos then send Popovich to the Cubs for OF Adolfo Phillips and P Jack Lamabe.

14th   With a 21–7 rout of the Red Sox at Fenway Park, the Oakland A's regain first place in the AL West. Reggie Jackson hits 2 HRs and drives in 10 Oakland runs.

The Yankees trade OF Tom Tresh to the Tigers for OF Ron Woods.

15th   Montreal trades 1B Donn Clendenon to the Mets for IF Kevin Collins and P Steve Renko, Bill Carden, and Dave Colon. The Expos also purchase P Dick Radatz from the Tigers.

Cubs SS Don Kessinger sets a NL record with his 54th-straight errorless game, but Chicago loses 7–6 to start a doubleheader split at Cincinnati.

21st   Minnesota scores a club-record 11 runs in the 10th inning at Oakland. Minnesota's 11 match the New York Yankees' 12th inning of July 26, 1928, for most runs for one club in extra innings. The Twins win 14–4.

22nd   An AL record-tying, 3 straight, 2-out HRs by Ted Kubiak, Reggie Jackson, and Sal Bando power a 7–3 Oakland victory over Minnesota in the first of 2 games.

24th   Richie Allen is suspended indefinitely when he fails to appear for the Phillies game with the Mets.

25th   The Mets (14) and Phillies (13) set a NL record for ineptitude by striking out 27 times in the first 9 innings of a 10-inning game.

28th   San Diego suffers its second 19–0 shutout of the season, as the Dodgers, behind Don Drysdale, match the NL-record shutout margin. The Dodgers score 10 in the first to make it easy.

29th   On Billy Williams Day in Chicago, the Cubs OF passes Stan Musial's NL record for consecutive games played (896). The Cubs sweep the Cardinals 3–1 and 12–1 before 41,060.

JULY

2nd   Reds hurler Jerry Arrigo ties a NL record by hitting 3 Braves in the 2nd inning of a 9–4 Atlanta win. The Braves tie the NL record of 5 hit batters in one game.

4th   The Dodgers take first place in the NL West by sweeping a doubleheader against the Braves in Los Angeles, winning 6–7 and 7–3.

5th   Minnesota regains the AL West lead behind the pitching of Jim Perry and a 13–1 rout of Oakland at Metropolitan Stadium.

AL East leader Baltimore breaks a 3-game losing streak as Dave McNally (12-0) wins his 14th straight game 9–3 at Detroit. Detroit OF Mickey Stanley plays his 220th straight errorless game.

8th   With 3 runs in the 9th inning, the Mets beat the Cubs 4–3, cutting Chicago's lead in the NL East to 4 games.

9th   With one out in the 9th, Chicago's Jimmy Qualls bloops a single to left-CF, the only blemish on

Tom Seaver's 4–0 near-perfect win before a record crowd (59,083) at Shea Stadium.

14th San Diego's Joe Niekro defeats his brother Phil of the Braves 1–0.

16th Rod Carew steals home for the 7th time, as the AL-West leading Twins sweep a twin bill, winning 9–8 and 6–3 from the White Sox. Carew ties Pete Reiser's record for steals of home in a season.

19th Phillie Dick Allen's suspension ends. He incurs a $12,000 fine.

The Twins and Pilots end an 18-inning game after having stranded 44 runners. Minnesota's Jim Perry beats Hohn Gelnar in relief 11–7. The 2 will square off tomorrow with Perry winning again 4–0.

20th Atlanta blanks San Diego 10–0 to grab a one-game lead over Los Angeles and San Francisco in the NL West.

21st A gala All-Star Game banquet in Washington is one of baseball's great events. An all-time team and all-time living team is announced. Babe Ruth is selected Greatest All-Time Player, and Joe DiMaggio, Greatest Living Player.

22nd For the first time, the All-Star Game is postponed due to rain.

23rd Willie McCovey hits 2 HRs as the NL beats the AL 9–3 for its 7th straight All-Star Game win. Mel Stottlemyre starts for the AL when Denny McLain is late arriving from a dental appointment.

25th Tony Conigliaro of the Red Sox suffers a wrenched back while hitting a HR against the Seattle Pilots. The injury forces him to walk slowly around the bases before being replaced. The Red Sox win 7–6.

27th Seattle suffers another heartbreaker, losing 5–3 to Boston in 20 innings at Sicks' Stadium. Tommy Harper hits a HR in the top of the 20th for Boston, and Joe Lahoud hit one in the bottom of the inning for the losers.

30th Houston relief P Fred Gladding singles off Ron Taylor of the New York Mets. It is the only hit of Gladding's career in 63 ML at bats and 450 games.

AUGUST

1st Dick Williams pulls Carl Yastrzemski from the Boston lineup and fines him $500 for "dogging it."

3rd Twin Rich Reese's pinch-hit grand slam off the Orioles' Dave McNally in the 7th ends his 17-game winning streak. McNally, now 15-1 for the year, loses 5–2 to Jim Kaat.

5th Consecutive HRs by Dave Marshall, Ron Hunt, and Bobby Bonds highlight the first of 2 San Francisco wins at Philadelphia. The Giants win game 2 5–3 to regain first place in the NL West by one-half game.

Pirate Willie Stargell hits the first HR completely out of Dodger Stadium. The 512-foot blast comes in an 11–3 Pittsburgh rout of Los Angeles.

6th Jim Merritt pitches the Reds back into first place in the NL East with a 3–2 win against the Mets.

Twins manager Billy Martin punches out his P Dave Boswell after a scuffle between Boswell and teammate Bob Allison. Boswell is hospitalized and requires 20 stitches.

7th Coach George Myatt replaces Bob Skinner as manager of the Phillies.

9th The Giants purchase relief P Don McMahon from the Tigers.

10th Mike Cuellar's (15-9) string of 35 straight batters retired is ended by Cesar Tovar, who also spoils Cuellar's no-hit bid in a 2–0 win against the Twins.

Don Sutton breaks his 13-game losing streak to the Cubs with a 4–2 win at Los Angeles. It was the most losses by any pitcher to one club in ML history.

11th Don Drysdale, the last active member of the Brooklyn Dodgers, retires because of damage to his right shoulder.

12th Citing "personal problems," Yankees 1B Joe Pepitone goes AWOL.

Pirate Jose Pagan's 2nd pinch-hit HR in consecutive appearances ties the ML record, but the Giants win 6–3 at Candlestick.

13th Baltimore's Jim Palmer leaves no doubt about his comeback with a 8–0 no-hitter against Oakland. Reggie Jackson, leading the AL with 42 HRs, walks 3 times, as the A's drop 2 games behind the Twins in the West. Palmer, now 11-2, pushes the O's lead to a comfortable 14½ games.

Commissioner Bowie Kuhn is elected for a 7-year term by unanimous vote of ML owners.

Joe Pepitone returns to the Yankees.

15th Don Sutton (15-11) opens a 9-game eastern swing for Los Angeles with a 9–2 win at Montreal. The Dodgers remain 2 games behind the first-place Reds. Montreal reliever Roy Face makes his final ML appearance, a record 657th consecutive relief effort (excluding his 2 games with the Tigers).

16th In an 8–1 win in Atlanta, St. Louis P Bob Gibson reaches 200 strikeouts (en route to 269) for the 7th season, a NL record.

Seattle's Sicks' Stadium shakes when 250-pound Boog Powell legs out an inside-the-park homer in the 9th. It really isn't that vital, as Baltimore romps 15–3.

19th Cub Ken Holtzman (14-7) pitches the 5th no-hitter of 1969. Ron Santo's 3-run HR off Phil Niekro provides first-place Chicago with a 3–0 win against Atlanta. Holtzman is the first no-hit hurler with no strikeouts since Sam Jones (9/4/23).

John "Swede" Hollison dies in Chicago at age 99. He was the last surviving ML pitcher to throw from a mound 50 feet from home plate. He pitched in one game in 1892.

20th With an 8–5 win at Philadelphia, the Dodgers take first place in the NL West by a half game.

21st Jim Merritt pitches Cincinnati back into the NL West lead with a 5–3 win at St. Louis.

24th Seattle trades P Jim Bouton to Houston for pitchers Dooley Womack and Roric Harrison.

27th New York's 4–1 win at San Diego, its 74th of the year, sets a club record. Chicago loses for the 7th time in the last 8 games and is just 2 games ahead of the Amazing Mets.

28th Detroit OF Jim Northrup goes 6-for-6, the first 6-hit game for Detroit since June 24, 1962, as the Tigers beat the A's 5–3.

At a press conference in New York, Commissioner Bowie Kuhn announces the publication of *The Baseball Encyclopedia* and holds up a copy of the 6½ pound book.

29th Joe Pepitone quits the Yankees after being fined $500 for leaving the bench during a game.

30th Washington 2B Tim Cullen ties a ML record with 3 consecutive errors in the 8th inning, but the Senators beat Oakland 11–3.

31st In their 2nd trade with Seattle within a week, Houston acquires OF Tommy Davis for outfielders Sandy Valdespino and Danny Walton.

SEPTEMBER

1st The Giants move past the Reds into first place with a 12–2 win over Montreal.

2nd Ralph Houk signs a new 3-year contract with the Yankees at $65,000 a season, the highest managerial salary in either league, and Joe Pepitone is reinstated.

4th After hitting in 31 straight games, the 3rd-best streak in NL history, the Dodgers Willie Davis is stopped in a 3–0 loss to San Diego. Al Ferrara drives in all 3 runs.

5th Billy Williams has all 4 of Chicago's hits, as the Cubs lose a 9–2 decision to Steve Blass and the Pirates. Williams sets an NL record for most hits in a game with no other hits, tying the ML record of Norm Elberfeld (August 1, 1903).

9th With a 7–1 win, Tom Seaver hands Chicago its 6th straight loss, giving the Mets a sweep of 2 games. New York now trails the Cubs by one-half game.

Atlanta's Phil Niekro joins the 20-win circle for the first time with a 2–1 defeat of the Dodgers. The victory pulls the Braves into 3rd place, 1½ games from the NL West lead.

10th Ken Boswell's 12th-inning single scores Cleon Jones, as the Mets beat the Expos 3–2 in the first game of a doubleheader. The win puts the Mets in the top spot for the first time in club history. The Cubs' loss drops them out of first after 155 days atop the NL. Chicago will continue to swoon and finish the month with a 9-17 record.

Using a ML record 27 players in one game, the Royals lose 11–4 at California.

12th Juan Marichal (18-10) pitches a one-hitter, as the Giants beat the Reds 1–0, but Atlanta takes the NL West lead by beating Houston 4–3. Tommy Helms's 3rd-inning single is the only hit in what Marichal calls "my best game ever."

Pitchers Jerry Koosman and Don Cardwell hurl 1–0 wins and drive in the winning runs, as the Mets sweep the Pirates.

13th Bobby Bonds becomes the 4th 30-homer, 30-steal player in ML history, but the Reds beat the Giants 6–4. His 32nd steal, on August 13th, erased Willie Mays's SF record of 31.

Baltimore becomes the AL East champs when Tom Phoebus wins the clincher 10–5 over Cleveland.

15th Steve Carlton of the Cardinals fans a ML-record 19 batters and still loses. Ron Swoboda hits a pair of 2-run HRs, and New York beats St. Louis 4–3.

16th Juan Marichal blanks the Braves 2–0, as the Giants regain first place.

17th The great race in the NL West finds San Francisco ahead in the morning, Los Angeles in front in the afternoon, and Atlanta atop the division at the end of the night. Houston nips the Giants 2–1 while Atlanta takes the Dodgers 6–5.

19th Hank Bauer is fired as manager of the Athletics. John McNamara takes over.

20th Bob Moose stops the pennant-bound Mets 4–0 with the NL's record 5th no-hitter of the season. Moose is now 12-3.

22nd Willie Mays joins Babe Ruth in the 600-homer club with a blast off Mike Corkins, while batting for rookie George Foster. Bobby Bonds sets a ML record with his 176th strikeout, as San Francisco beats San Diego 4–2.

The Twins clinch the AL West when Bob Miller beats Kansas City 4–3.

23rd Dick Williams is fired as manager of the Red Sox. Coach Eddie Popowski becomes interim manager.

Umpires Bill Valentine and AL Salerno hit baseball with a $4 million antitrust suit.

John Miller homers for LA in his last ML at bat. In 61 plate appearances over 3 years, Miller's only other HR was on September 11, 1966, for the Yankees—his first ML at bat.

24th Home runs by Donn Clendenon and Ed Charles, and Gary Gentry's 4-hitter, clinch the NL East pennant for the Mets 6–0 against Steve Carlton and the Cards.

25th John Allyn buys 50 percent of the White Sox from brother Arthur, giving him complete control of the club.

26th Larry Shepard is fired as Pittsburgh manager.

28th Cincinnati reliever Wayne Granger sets a ML record with his 89th appearance in a 4–1 win versus Houston.

29th Rico Petrocelli blasts his 40th HR, a season record for SS, as Boston wins 8–5 over Washington. Petrocelli is hitting .301 with only 14 errors in the field.

30th Atlanta's 10th straight win, 3–2 over Cincinnati, clinches the NL West pennant. Hoyt Wilhelm saves Phil Niekro' 23rd win by retiring the last 6 batters.

OCTOBER

2nd A bunt single clinches Pete Rose's (.348) 2nd straight batting title.

The Pilots play what will be their last game in Seattle in a 3–1 loss to Oakland. A crowd of 5,473 fans show up to pay their respects.

Eddie Kasko is named manager of the Red Sox.

4th The first League Championship Series begin in Atlanta and Baltimore. New York survives HRs by Hank Aaron and Tony Gonzalez off Tom Seaver and scores 5 runs off Phil Niekro in the 8th to coast home 9–5. Paul Blair's 12th-inning squeeze bunt gives the Orioles a 4–3 win over Minnesota.

5th New York beats Atlanta 11–6. Tommie Agee, Ken Boswell, and Cleon Jones hit HRs for the Mets; Hank Aaron, for the Braves.

Dave McNally's 3-hitter beats the Twins 1–0.

6th New York rallies twice and wins the first NL Championship Series. Tommie Agee, Ken Boswell, and Wayne Garrett hit HRs and fans swarm the Shea Stadium field after a 7–4 win.

Baltimore wins the first ALCS as Paul Blair delivers 5 hits and Don Buford 4 in an 11–2 win at Minnesota.

7th The Cards trade outfielders Curt Flood and Byron Browne, P Joe Hoerner, and C Tim McCarver to Philadelphia for 1B Richie Allen, 2B Cookie Rojas, and P Jerry Johnson.

8th Dave Bristol is fired as manager of the Reds, and Joe Gordon resigns as manager of the Royals. Charlie Metro replaces Gordon.

9th Sparky Anderson accepts the job as manager of the Reds.

Danny Murtaugh accepts a 3rd term as manager of the Pirates.

10th In his final season, P Masaichi Kaneda of the Yomiuri Giants gets his 400th lifetime win, against 250 losses. During a 20-year career (1950–69), he won 30 games twice and 20 games 14 times. He also holds the Japanese record for strikeouts (4,490), averaging 225 a season, while giving up only 1,809 walks.

Yutaka Enatsu of the Hanshin Tigers strikes out his 401st batter of the season. This puts him 3rd on the all-time list after Matt Kilroy with 513 in 1886 and Old Hoss Radbourn with 441 in 1884.

11th Don Buford's leadoff HR starts a 4–1 Baltimore win at New York to open the WS. Mike Cuellar bests Tom Seaver.

12th New York's Jerry Koosman and Ron Taylor combine on a 2-hitter, as Al Weis's 9th-inning single off loser Dave McNally gives the Mets a 2–1 win to even the WS.

13th Billy Martin (97-65) is fired as manager of the pennant-winning Twins.

14th Tommie Agee and Ed Kranepool hit HRs; Agee makes 2 brilliant catches in CF, and New York wins WS game 3, 5–0 at Baltimore.

15th A memorable WS game pits Tom Seaver against Mike Cuellar. RF Ron Swoboda's questionable dive at Brooks Robinson's sinking liner with runners at 1B and 3B in the 9th inning results in a brilliant catch, even though Frank Robinson tags and scores the tying run. In the 10th, Mets catcher J. C. Martin, running illegally inside the 1B line after a bunt, is hit on the wrist by P Pete Richert's errant throw, enabling pinch runner Rod Gaspar to score from first as the Mets win 2–1.

16th In game 5 Cleon Jones, awarded 1B when shoe polish on the ball proves he was hit by a pitch, scores on Donn Clendenon's HR. Al Weis's HR an inning later ties the game. Ron Swoboda's double and 2 Baltimore errors in the 8th give New York a 5–3 win and the Series. Jerry Koosman completes the Mets amazin' achievement with a 5-hitter.

21st Pittsburgh acquires P Dave Giusti and C Dave Ricketts from St. Louis for 1B/OF Carl Taylor and OF Frank Vanzin.

22nd Bill Rigney is the new manager of the Twins.

24th The New York City Human Rights Division hears arguments on the Bernice Gera case. Gera was rejected by the National Association of Baseball Leagues as the first female umpire. The NABL says she did not meet height, weight, and age standards.

29th Tom Seaver is voted the NL Cy Young Award.

NOVEMBER

6th Denny McLain and Mike Cuellar finish dead even in AL Cy Young Award voting.

12th Minnesota's Harmon Killebrew is voted AL MVP honors.

20th San Francisco's Willie McCovey edges Tom Seaver as NL MVP.

Joe Schultz is fired as manager of the Pilots.

Cleveland trades OF Jose Cardenal to St. Louis for OF Vada Pinson.

24th Dave Bristol is named manager of the Pilots.

25th Kansas City OF Lou Piniella is voted AL Rookie of the Year.

28th Los Angeles 2B Ted Sizemore becomes the 7th Dodger to win NL Rookie of the Year honors.

DECEMBER

3rd In what is rated their best trade ever, the Royals send 3B Joe Foy to the Mets for OF Amos Otis and P Bob Johnson. Foy will not solve the Mets' 3B problems, while Otis will spend 14 years in Kansas City, win 3 gold gloves, and lead the AL in stolen bases once.

4th The Yankees trade 1B Joe Pepitone to the Astros for 1B Curt Blefary.

The Cubs send OF Boots Day to the Cardinals for P Rich Nye.

The Yankees send veteran P Al Downing and C Frank Fernandez to Oakland for 1B Danny Cater and C Ossie Chavarria.

5th Chub Feeney succeeds Warren Giles as president of the NL. He is elected for a 4-year term, beginning January 1, 1970.

11th A Federal Court in New York City rules against the suit of umpires Bill Valentine and Al

Salerno because baseball is exempt from antitrust laws.

12th Cleveland trades pitchers Luis Tiant and Stan Williams to the Twins for 3B Graig Nettles, OF Ted Uhlaender, and pitchers Dean Chance and Bob Miller.

The Mets pick up veteran P Ray Sadecki and OF Dave Marshall from the Giants for OF Jim Gosger and IF Bob Heise.

15th The National Labor Relations Board accepts the case of fired umpires Valentine and Salerno, thereby issuing a challenge to baseball's antitrust status.

18th The White Sox send veteran LH slugger Pete Ward to the Yankees for P Mickey Scott and cash.

29th The New York *Times* reports that Curt Flood will sue baseball and challenge the reserve clause.

1970

JANUARY

1st Chub Feeney takes over as NL president, succeeding Warren Giles, who is retiring.

14th Johnny Murphy, the Mets general manager who had seen his team rise from the NL cellar to the World Championship, dies of a heart attack at age 61. Murphy was a star relief pitcher for the Yankees in the 1930s and early 1940s.

16th Curt Flood, Cardinals Gold Glove outfielder, files a civil lawsuit challenging ML baseball's reserve clause, a suit that will have historic implications. Flood refused to report to the Phillies after he was traded by the Cardinals 3 months ago, contending the baseball rule violates federal antitrust laws.

17th ML teams select a record 357 players in the January phase of the annual free-agent draft, including top pick Chris Chambliss and Chris Speier. Fred Lynn, drafted by the Yankees in the first round, will not sign.

The Sporting News names Willie Mays as Player of the Decade for the 1960s.

20th Lou Boudreau achieves the Hall of Fame, receiving 232 of a possible 300 votes in the BBWAA election. Ralph Kiner finishes 2nd with 167, 58 votes short.

25th Braves ace Phil Niekro undergoes an emergency appendectomy. Niekro's record will dip from 23-13 to 12-18.

FEBRUARY

1st The Hall of Fame Special Committee on Veterans selects former commissioner Ford Frick and former players Earle Combs and Jesse Haines for enshrinement.

13th The NL offices begin their move from Cincinnati to San Francisco, which will be completed February 23rd.

19th Commissioner Bowie Kuhn announces the suspension of Tigers ace Denny McLain, effective April 1st, for McLain's alleged involvement in a bookmaking operation. The suspension will last 3 months.

27th The FBI arrests Lawrence Bankhead in Chicago, charging him with making threatening phone calls to Cubs star Ernie Banks.

28th Pete Rose becomes baseball's first singles hitter to sign a 6-figure contract, coming to terms with Reds general manager Bob Howsam for an estimated $105,000 per year.

MARCH

11th Experimental, lively X-5 baseballs are used in all spring training games played in Arizona and Florida. The results are inconclusive.

19th Indians slugger Ken Harrelson fractures his right leg. He will be sidelined until September.

24th Commissioner Kuhn orders a halt to the use of X-5 balls.

APRIL

1st The Milwaukee Brewers Baseball Club, headed by Bud Selig, purchases the Seattle Pilots for $10,800,000.

7th ML Baseball returns to Wisconsin as the Brewers play their first game in Milwaukee, losing to California 12–0 before a crowd of 37,237.

OF Brant Alyea has 7 RBI to back Jim Perry as the Twins win their opener. Alyea will have 21 RBI in his first 12 games, and in Perry's first 4 starts Alyea will drive in 19 runs.

8th The Phillies acquire minor league 1B Willie Montanez as partial compensation for their loss in the October 7, 1969, deal in which Curt Flood refused to report.

9th Baltimore OF Don Buford hits HRs from both sides of the plate during a 13–1 win over Cleveland.

11th San Francisco beats Cincinnati 2–1, dropping the Reds one-half game out of first place. This will be the only day all season out of first for the Reds, who will set an NL record of 178 days leading the league.

13th Oakland uses gold-colored bases during the club's home opener. The Rules Committee subsequently bans this innovation.

16th Reds ace Jim Maloney suffers a severed Achilles tendon in his left leg while running the bases.

He is replaced by 19-year-old rookie Don Gullett, who earns his first ML victory. Maloney will never win another game in the majors.

18th The Mets Nolan Ryan gives up a leadoff single to Denny Doyle, then shuts out the Phillies without another hit. Ryan fans 15 in the 7–0 triumph.

22nd Tom Seaver strikes out 19 Padres, including the last 10 in succession—both ML records—in winning 2–1 for the Mets. To date, only Steve Carlton has struck out as many in a game in this century, and no one has ever struck out 10 in a row.

25th Tiger P Earl Wilson fans for the 3rd out in the 7th inning against the Twins. On the 3rd strike, Twins C Paul Ratliff traps the ball in the dirt, and must either throw to 1B or tag the batter for the out. Instead he rolls the ball back to the mound. As the Twins head for their dugout, Wilson begins running the bases and is around 3B when OF Brant Alyea retrieves the ball and throws to SS Leo Cardenas, who is standing by home. Wilson turns back to 3B. Cardenas and Alyea run down Wilson for a 7-6-7 out.

26th Don Buford hits a 3-run homer to give Baltimore a 10–9 victory over Kansas City. The Orioles take over first place and will not relinquish that position for the rest of the season.

Willie McCovey and Dick Dietz each hit grand slams as the Giants beat the Expos 11–1 in the first game of a doubleheader.

29th Baltimore's Paul Blair collects 3 homers and 6 RBI in an 18–2 rout of the White Sox.

30th During a 9–2 loss to the Braves, the Cubs Billy Williams becomes the first player in NL history to play in 1,000 consecutive games.

MAY

2nd During a 7–1 loss to the Giants, the Phillies lose both of their catchers, Tim McCarver and Mike Ryan, with broken hands in the same inning. The two will miss a combined total of 197 games.

7th The Yankees Roy White homers from both sides of the plate in a 7–3 win over Oakland.

Wes Parker's 10th inning triple is the game winner in a 7–4 win over the Mets. With the hit, Parker ends the day having hit for the cycle, the first Los Angeles Dodger to turn the trick.

8th A record 30 HRs are hit by NL players in 7 games, including 2 apiece by each of five players.

10th While losing 6–5 to St. Louis, the Braves Hoyt Wilhelm becomes the first pitcher ever to appear in 1,000 games.

11th Ray Culp strikes out the first 6 Angel batters in Anaheim, but Boston loses 2–1 in 16 innings. Culp ties the AL mark.

12th Ernie Banks becomes the 8th member of the 500 HR club, connecting off Pat Jarvis during a 4–3 Cub win over the Braves. It his 1,600th career RBI. Atlanta's Rico Carty, meanwhile, hits safely in his 30th consecutive game.

16th The Reds Jim McGlothlin shuts out the Braves 2–0, stopping Rico Carty's 31-game hitting streak in the process. Carty batted .451 (51-for-113) during the streak, which started April 8th.

17th During a 7–6 Atlanta loss to Cincinnati in the 2nd game of a doubleheader, Hank Aaron collects his 3,000th career hit and his 570th HR. Aaron, the 9th man to amass 3,000 hits, is the first to also have 500 HRs.

22nd Yankee pitcher Mel Stottlemyre walks 11 batters while hurling the first 8⅓ scoreless innings of a 2–0 shutout against Washington. He ties Lefty Gomez's 1941 record for most bases on balls surrendered in a shutout.

Cardinal Steve Carlton strikes out 16 Phillies, but loses 4–3. Two days later, teammate Bob Gibson will also fan 16 Phillies in a 4-hit, 3–1 victory.

23rd Giants manager Clyde King is fired following a 15-inning 17–16 loss to San Diego. Charlie Fox is named as the new skipper.

24th Cleveland's Tony Horton hits 3 HRs versus New York, but the Yankees win anyway 8–7 in 11 innings.

25th Three pitchers on the Nishitetsu Lions are suspended from Japanese baseball for life for participating in a game-fixing scandal in the 1969 season.

29th The Orioles Mike Cuellar strikes out 4 batters in the 4th inning of a 2–0 win over California.

30th All-Star voting is returned to the fans, as computerized punch-card ballots appear in stores and ballparks coast to coast. Since 1958 the All-Star squads had been selected by managers, coaches, and players.

31st Chicago's Luis Aparicio and Walt "No Neck" Williams each collect 5 hits in a slugfest with Boston. The White Sox win 22–13, with Williams scoring 5 times.

Paul Blair is hit by a pitch from California reliever Ken Tatum and carried off the field with a broken nose and fractures. His hitting is never the same following the injury.

JUNE

1st By reprimanding Astro Jim Bouton for writing the controversial book *Ball Four,* Commissioner Kuhn helps put the book on the bestseller list.

4th In the June draft, the Padres select high school catcher Mike Ivie as the number-one pick. Choosing next, the Indians take Stanford P Steve Dunning. The Pirates wait till the 15th round to take Dave Parker.

7th Vic Davalillo of the Cardinals gets 2 pinch hits in the 7th inning of a 10–7 win over the Padres.

8th Players and management end their labor dispute by agreeing to a new standard player contract. Among the players' victories is a raise in the minimum salary from $10,000 to $12,000 per year.

9th Detroit's Willie Horton clubs 3 HRs, including a grand slam, knocking in 7 runs in an 8–3 win over Milwaukee.

12th Pittsburgh's Dock Ellis no-hits San Diego 2–0 in the first game of a doubleheader. Ellis walks 8 and hits one and gets all his support on 2 Willie Stargell HRs.

19th Despite Mike Epstein's 8 RBI, the Senators bow to the Orioles 12–10 in the first game of a doubleheader.

21st Detroit's Cesar Gutierrez goes 7-for-7 to tie a record set in 1892, in a 12-inning 9–8 win over Cleveland. Mickey Stanley's HR wins it for the Tigers. Gutierrez will collect just 128 hits in his entire career.

22nd Rod Carew, batting .376 for the Twins, injures his knee during an attempted double play. The injury will require surgery and sideline him until September.

24th The Reds play their final game at Cincinnati's Crosley Field, beating the Giants 5–4.

Bobby Murcer hits 4 consecutive homers for the Yanks in a doubleheader against Cleveland, including 3 in the 5–4 2nd-game win. Cleveland 1B Tony Horton literally crawls back to the dugout after fanning on 2 of Yankee hurler Steve Hamilton's "Folly floaters."

26th Frank Robinson belts 2 successive grand slams during a 12–2 Oriole romp over the Senators. Dave McNally, Don Buford, and Paul Blair trot home ahead of him on each blow.

28th The Pirates sweep the Cubs in a doubleheader 3–2 and 4–1 in the final games at Pittsburgh's Forbes Field.

30th A sellout crowd of 51,050 is on hand for the dedication of Cincinnati's Riverfront Stadium, but Hank Aaron spoils the show as he hits the park's first home run. The Braves win 8–2.

JULY

1st The return of Denny McLain following his suspension is witnessed by a gathering of 53,863 fans and 71 writers. He is knocked out of the box in the 6th inning, but the Tigers rally to beat the Yankees in the 11th 6–5.

2nd Detroit's Joe Niekro no-hits the Yankees until Horace Clarke singles in the 9th inning. The Tigers win 5–0. This is the 3rd time in the month that Clarke has broken up a no-hitter, having spoiled bids by KC's Jim Rooker (June 4th) and Boston's Sonny Siebert (June 19th).

3rd In pregame ceremonies, Oakland's Clyde Wright is inducted into the National Association of Intercollegiate Athletics (NAIA) Hall of Fame for his pitching while at Carson-Newman College. He then hurls a no-hitter against Oakland, winning 4–0. Reggie Jackson's 400-foot shot to dead center in the 7th is caught.

Mike Lum hits 3 homers as the Braves beat the Padres 8–1 in the first game of a doubleheader.

Indians P Dean Chance is told to remove a tiny flag pin on his cap by umpire Ed Runge in compliance with a rule prohibiting glass buttons and metal objects on uniforms because of their glare.

6th Felix Millan goes 6-for-6 with 4 RBI to help the Braves top the Giants 12–4.

8th Jim Ray Hart ties a modern ML record with 6 RBI in one inning (5th). Hart hits for the cycle as the Giants rout the Braves 13–0.

9th Dalton Jones of the Tigers loses a grand slam against the Red Sox when he passes teammate Don Wert on the basepaths. He is credited with a single.

14th The NL wins its 8th straight All-Star Game, a thrilling 12-inning 5–4 victory in Cincinnati. Pete Rose crashes into Cleveland catcher Ray Fosse to score the winning run.

16th The Reds spoil the Pirates debut in Pittsburgh's Three Rivers Stadium 3–2. Cincinnati's Tony Perez hits the park's first homer, offsetting a later one by hometown Willie Stargell.

18th During a 10–1 win over Montreal, the Giants Willie Mays singles off Mike Wegener. It is career hit number 3,000 for Mays.

20th The Dodgers Bill Singer, who a month earlier lost a no-hitter to Atlanta with 2 outs in the 9th, no-hits the Phillies 5–0, giving up no walks. He strikes out 10 and makes 2 miscues, one a controversial throwing error that pulls 1B Wes Parker off the base. The Phillies' players argue, contending the soft chopper by Don Money should be a hit. Singer had spent 3 weeks in the hospital in June for hepatitis.

21st Clay Kirby has a no-hitter going for 8 innings, but Padres manager Preston Gomez lifts him for a pinch hitter. Reliever Jack Baldschun gives up 3 hits and the Padres lose 3–0. Gomez will repeat the mistake on September 4, 1974.

24th Chicago's Bill Melton ties the ML record by striking out 7 times in a doubleheader split with Detroit.

26th Johnny Bench of the Reds and Orlando Cepeda of the Braves each collect 3 consecutive homers and 7 RBI during respective games with the Cardinals and Cubs.

27th The Expos beat the White Sox 10–6 in the annual Hall of Fame game, following the induction ceremonies for Lou Boudreau, Earle Combs, Ford Frick, and Jesse Haines.

28th A bad day for Angels C Tom Egan: he is charged with 5 passed balls, all with different pitchers, and he drops a throw for an error to permit what would prove to be the winning run in a 6–5 loss to the Yankees.

29th The Cubs purchase 1B/OF Joe Pepitone from the Astros. Pepitone will drive in 31 runs in his first 31 games for his new team.

AUGUST

1st Pittsburgh's Willie Stargell smashes 3 doubles and 2 homers, which ties the ML mark for extra-base hits in a game, and scores 5 runs while driving in 6. Teammate Bob Robertson also collects 5 hits as the Pirates outslug the Braves 20–10.

2nd In their last meeting of the year, Baltimore defeats Kansas City 10–8. It is the Orioles 23rd straight win over the Royals over a 2-year span, a ML mark.

11th Jim Bunning notches his 100th NL victory, a 6–5 Phillies win over the Astros. Bunning and Cy Young are the only pitchers to win 100 games in each league.

12th Curt Flood loses his $4.1 million antitrust suit against baseball, as Federal Judge Irving Ben Cooper upholds the legality of the sport's reserve clause. Cooper does recommend changes in the reserve system, to be achieved through negotiation between players and owners. Less than 6 years later, this recommendation would become a reality.

22nd In a 16-inning game, the Pirates edge the Dodgers 2–1. Roberto Clemente goes 5-for-7 with an RBI and run scored.

23rd Roberto Clemente compiles his 2nd straight 5-hit game during an 11–0 pasting of Los Angeles. He is the first major leaguer this century to collect 10 hits in 2 consecutive games.

28th The Giants Juan Marichal beats the Pirates 5–1 for his 200th ML win.

29th Mickey Mantle returns to the Yankees as first base coach.

SEPTEMBER

1st The Red Sox take an 8–1 lead at Fenway, but Detroit rallies to win 10–9.

2nd Detroit's Gene Lamont homers in his first ML at bat, but the Red Sox this time hold the lead and beat the Tigers 10–1.

3rd After an NL record 1,117 consecutive games, Billy Williams asks to sit one out. Without Williams, the Cubs beat the Phillies 7–2.

7th The White Sox use a ML record 41 players in a doubleheader with Oakland, but lose both games 7–4 and 7–5.

Houston sweeps a doubleheader from San Diego 10–5 and 9–4. In the first game Astro Bob Watson and Padre Ramon Webster each hit grand slams.

9th Bowie Kuhn hands Denny McLain his third suspension of the year, this one is for carrying a gun, plus other unspecified charges, and ends McLain's season with a 3-5 record.

California's Alex Johnson becomes the 3rd player in history to put one into the CF bleachers at Comiskey when he connects in the 6th against Chicago's Billy Wynne.

11th Twenty-one-year-old Vida Blue, recalled from the minors just 8 days earlier, hurls a one-hit shutout as the A's beat the Royals 3–0. Pat Kelly's 8th-inning single is the only hit off the fireballing lefty.

15th The White Sox hire manager Chuck Tanner from the Pacific Coast League. He replaces Don Gutteridge, who had been fired on September 3rd. Coach Bill Adair ran the team in the interim.

19th Syracuse (International League) beats Omaha (American Association) 5–3 in 11 innings, thereby winning the Junior World Series.

Brothers Billy and Tony Conigliaro of the Red Sox hit HRs against the Washington Senators. Billy homers off Jim Hannan in the 4th inning and Tony follows against Joe Grzenda in the 7th.

21st The A's Vida Blue no-hits the Twins 6–0, becoming the youngest pitcher to perform the feat since Paul Dean, 36 years ago to the day. The only base runner against Blue is Harmon Killebrew, who walks in the 4th inning. An Oakland crowd of only 4,284 watches Blue's 2nd ML start.

The Braves trade veteran Hoyt Wilhelm to the Cubs. In December the Cubs will trade him back to Atlanta.

22nd Tommy Harper hits his 30th HR to lead the Brewers to a 4–2 win over the Angels. Harper has 33 stolen bases and becomes the 5th major leaguer to go 30-30 in the same season.

OCTOBER

1st Dal Maxvill of the Cardinals completes the most impotent offensive season (minimum 150 games) in NL history, setting records for fewest at bats (399), hits (80), doubles (5), long hits (7), and lowest batting (.201) and slugging (.223) averages.

The final game at Philadelphia's Connie Mack Stadium is played, the Phillies beating the Expos 2–1. The fans respond by swarming onto and destroying the field and stadium.

The Angels Alex Johnson grounds out and then hits 2 singles in the final game of the season to edge Boston's Carl Yastrzemski for the AL batting title, .3290 to .3286. Johnson leaves the game after his 2nd hit. Yastrzemski goes 12-for-20 over his last 6 games. The Red Sox ended their season September 30th, when New York's Fritz Peterson won his 20th game, 4–3 over Boston.

2nd Billy Martin is announced as the new Tiger manager, replacing Mayo Smith, who was fired a day earlier. The A's Charlie Finley fires manager John McNamara and replaces him with Dick Williams.

3rd Pitcher Mike Cuellar contributes a grand slam as the Orioles explode for 7 runs in the 4th inning to rout the Twins 10–6 in the opening game of the AL Championship Series.

Pete Rose's RBI single in the 10th inning breaks up a scoreless game as the Reds win the NLCS opener 3–0 over Pittsburgh. Gary Nolan gets the shutout victory for Cincinnati, as Dock Ellis takes the loss.

4th ML umpires return after a one-day walkout in quest of higher wages. Minor league umps had been pressed into service for the opening LCS games the day before. There had been rumors of a strike for several days as negotiations between the umpires and ML baseball had reached an impasse.

Bobby Tolan leads the Reds to a 3–1 win as Cincinnati continues to roll over the Pirates in the

NLCS. Tolan tallies 3 hits, including a HR, and scores all 3 of his team's runs.

Dave McNally hurls Baltimore to a 2-0 ALCS lead as the Orioles blast the Twins 11–3. Harmon Killebrew and Tony Oliva hit home runs in a losing cause.

5th Johnny Bench and Tony Perez homer as the Reds beat the Pirates 3–2, while Jim Palmer pitches Baltimore to a 6–1 win over Minnesota. Both teams thus complete sweeps of their respective LCS and advance to the World Series.

St. Louis trades controversial slugger Dick Allen to Los Angeles for 2B Ted Sizemore and C Bob Stinson.

9th The Tigers trade Denny McLain to the Senators in an 8-player deal that also sees OF Elliott Maddox, 3B Aurelio Rodriguez, and P Joe Coleman change teams. This ranks as one of Detroit's best trades ever.

10th Baltimore overcomes a 3–0 deficit to beat the Reds 4–3 in the WS opener at Riverfront Stadium as Boog Powell, Ellie Hendricks, and Brooks Robinson contribute home runs to the winning effort.

11th Boston's Tony Conigliaro (OF) and California's Doug Griffin (2B) switch clubs in a 6-player swap.

The Orioles again overcome a 3–0 deficit to win 6–5, as Powell hits his second WS round-tripper. Baltimore takes a 2-0 advantage in games.

13th The Orioles win their 3rd straight over the Reds 9–3, with winning pitcher Dave McNally slugging a grand slam. Frank Robinson and Don Buford also contribute homers and 3B Brooks Robinson continues his excellence with the glove, as he makes 2 spectacular grabs in the field.

14th Lee May's 8th-inning 3-run homer gives the Reds their first Series win 6–5, and ends the Orioles' 17-game winning streak which started at the end of the regular season.

15th For the 3rd time the Orioles overcome a 3–0 deficit to bury the Reds 9–3 and win the World Championship 4 games to one. Frank Robinson and Merv Rettenmund each homer and drive in 2 runs. Brooks Robinson, the "human vacuum cleaner," easily wins the WS MVP award.

18th Sachio Kinugasa takes his place in the starting lineup of the Hiroshima Carp, playing 3B. Over the next 17 years he will play in 2,215 consecutive games—the durability record of professional baseball, topping Lou Gehrig's 2,130.

NOVEMBER

3rd The Phillies trade Curt Flood to the Senators for 3 minor league players.

Bob Gibson wins the NL Cy Young Award by a 118-51 margin over Giant Gaylord Perry. Gibson posted a 23-7 record for the Cardinals.

6th The Twins Jim Perry wins the AL Cy Young Award in a close race. Perry, who won 24 games during the season, receives 55 points to edge out McNally (47), McDowell (45), and Cuellar (44).

11th Boog Powell, who batted .297 with 35 homers and 114 RBI for Baltimore, is named AL MVP by a 234-157 margin over the Twins Tony Oliva.

18th Johnny Bench wins the NL MVP Award with 326 points, 108 more than the Cubs Billy Williams. Bench had 45 homers, 148 RBI, and a .293 average for the Reds.

21st TSN announces Gold Glove selections. White Sox SS Luis Aparicio wins the 9th and final honor of his career, while Mets OF Tommie Agee becomes the first nonpitcher to win it in each league.

25th Yankee catcher Thurman Munson receives 23 of 24 votes in being named AL Rookie of the Year. Munson batted .302 in 132 games.

27th Carl Morton, who was 18-11 for the last-place Expos, receives the NL Rookie of the Year Award. Morton beats out Reds OF Bernie Carbo, 11 votes to 8.

30th The White Sox trade OF Ken Berry to the Angels for OF Jay Johnstone in a 6-player deal.

DECEMBER

1st Pitchers Tom Phoebus, Al Severinsen, and Fred Beene, and SS Enzo Hernandez, go from the Orioles to the Padres for pitchers Pat Dobson and Tom Dukes. Dobson will win 20 games for the Orioles in 1971.

The Red Sox trade 2B Mike Andrews and SS Luis Alvarado to the White Sox for SS Luis Aparicio.

2nd In a 6-player swap with the Pirates, the Royals acquire SS Fred Patek.

11th The Braves Rico Carty, the leading active ML hitter at .322 lifetime, suffers a fractured knee and ligament damage in a Dominican League game. Carty will miss the entire 1971 season.

14th St. Louis OF Herman Hill drowns in the Caribbean, near Valencia, Venezuela, at age 25. He had been traded from the Twins on October 20th.

21st Jimmy Wynn of the Astros is injured in a stabbing during a domestic quarrel. He will undergo abdominal surgery but will suffer no long-term effects.

1971

JANUARY

7th Reds OF Bobby Tolan suffers a ruptured Achilles tendon while playing basketball. He will miss the entire 1971 season.

11th Tigers P John Hiller, age 27, suffers a heart attack. He will miss the 1971 season before making a remarkable comeback.

21st The BBWAA fails to elect anyone in the annual Hall of Fame election. With 270 votes required, the nearest finishers are Yogi Berra (242) and Early Wynn (240).

29th The Pirates trade OF Matty Alou and P George Brunet to the Cardinals for OF Vic Davalillo and P Nelson Briles.

31st The Hall of Fame Special Veterans Committee selects 7 men for enshrinement: former players Jake Beckley, Joe Kelley, Harry Hooper, Rube Marquard, Chick Hafey, Dave Bancroft, and executive George Weiss.

FEBRUARY

9th Former Negro Leagues P Satchel Paige is nominated for the Hall of Fame. On June 10th the Hall's new Special Committee on the Negro Leagues will formally select Paige for induction.

10th Los Angeles trades OF Andy Kosco to Milwaukee for P Al Downing. Downing will go on to win 20 games for the Dodgers in 1971.

17th Boston's Carl Yastrzemski signs what is believed to be the richest player contract in baseball history: 3 years for a total of $500,000.

20th Ted Kluszewski hits a 500-foot 3-run single to lead the NL team to a 5–3 victory in the annual March of Dimes old-timers' game.

MARCH

1st Willie Mays signs a 2-year contract with the Giants for $165,000 per year.

6th At Mesa, AZ, the A's and Brewers test Charlie Finley's idea of 3-ball walks. The A's win 13–9 in a game featuring 19 free passes.

12th Cubs iron-man C Randy Hundley suffers a severely sprained right knee. He will play only 9 games all season before submitting to surgery.

15th Bernice Gera, a 39-year-old New York housewife, files suit against baseball, claiming violation of her civil rights. Mrs. Gera had completed an umpire school and signed a contract to work in the New York-Pennsylvania League, but her contract had been voided 6 days later with no explanation.

21st The Kansas City Royals new Baseball Academy is officially dedicated. Its stated purpose is "to provide youth with the dual opportunity to pursue an education and at the same time learn the skills of our national pastime."

APRIL

6th Willie Mays, a month shy of his 40th birthday, homers in a 4–0 Opening Day Giants win over the Padres. Mays will go on to hit homers in each of the Giants first 4 games of the season, a ML record.

7th The dismissal of Curt Flood's suit against baseball is upheld by a 3-judge U.S. Circuit Court of Appeals.

9th The A's trade OF/1B Felipe Alou to the Yankees for 2 pitchers.

10th The Phillies debut in new $49.5 million Veterans Stadium, beating Montreal 4–1. Don Money connects for the park's first HR.

17th Willie Horton is 5-for-6 with 2 HRs and 6 RBI, and Detroit needs all of it as they win in 10 innings over Boston 10–9.

19th Longtime Giants announcer Russ Hodges dies at Mill Valley, California.

21st In a 10–2 Pirates win over the Braves, Willie Stargell hits 3 HRs in a game for the 2nd time of the young season. Stargell also turned the trick 11 days earlier.

27th Hank Aaron becomes the 3rd member of the 600-HR club, but one of the other 2 members—the Giants Willie Mays—hits a 10th-inning single to beat Aaron's Braves.

Curt Flood jumps the Senators after 13 games and departs for Denmark, ending his playing career. Flood batted .293 and won 7 Gold Glove Awards during his

15-year tenure in the major leagues. He will continue his antitrust suit which will eventually reach the Supreme Court.

The Pirates lose to the Dodgers 7–5, but Willie Stargell sets a ML record with his 11th HR in the month of April with a shot over the CF wall in Pittsburgh.

30th Oakland dazzles the Indians with a color display as Dick Green, Vida Blue, and Larry Brown score the runs in a 3–1 victory.

MAY

3rd The Toei Flyers set a Japan League record of 5 HRs in one inning, tying the American record held by several teams, most recently the Minnesota Twins in 1966. The record will be tied in 1977 and 1980, and finally broken in 1986.

6th Commissioner Bowie Kuhn signs ML baseball to a $72 million television contract with NBC.

8th The A's trade 1B Don Mincher, P Paul Lindblad, C Frank Fernandez, and cash to the Senators for 1B Mike Epstein and P Darold Knowles.

14th Syracuse blows its 11–1 lead in an International League game as Winnipeg gets 9 HRs to tie the game at 13. Syracuse finally wins 15–13 in the 12th inning.

17th The Red Sox sign P Luis Tiant, who had been released by the Twins and Braves during the preceding 5 weeks, and assign him to Louisville. He will put together three 20-win seasons for the Red Sox in 5 years.

Atlanta's Ralph Garr homers in the 10th and 12th innings of a game against the Mets, tying a ML record for most HRs in extra innings. The Braves win 4–3.

Washington OF Tom McCraw "slugs" a 140-foot HR against the Cleveland Indians. SS Jack Heidemann, CF Vada Pinson, and LF John Lowenstein collide on his short pop fly to left center, and McCraw circles the bases before the ball is retrieved.

23rd Mickey Lolich and Les Cain notch shutouts as the Tigers sweep a doubleheader from the Senators 5–0 and 11–0.

28th The Braves Clete Boyer, involved in a dispute with owner Paul Richards and manager Lum Harris over alleged silly rules and mismanagement, gets his release and retires. Boyer had hit safely in the last 9 games of his career, including 5 HRs and 14 RBI.

29th The Giants trade OF George Foster to the Reds for SS Frank Duffy and P Vern Geishert.

30th Willie Mays hits his 638th career HR for the Giants, adding in the process his NL record 1,950th run scored. Stan Musial had been the record holder with 1,949 runs.

31st The Giants beat the Mets 2–1 in 11 innings to raise their record to 37-14 and open a 10½ game lead over the 2nd-place Dodgers.

JUNE

3rd Cub southpaw Ken Holtzman tosses the 2nd no-hitter of his career, victimizing the Reds 1–0. Holtzman scores the only run, in the 3rd inning.

6th Willie Mays strokes a 12th-inning HR off Joe Hoerner of the Phillies in the 2nd game of a doubleheader, his 22nd—and last—career extra-inning belt, a ML mark.

8th Danny Goodwin is chosen as the first player in the June draft and turns down a reported $50,000 offer from the White Sox to attend Southern University. He will be chosen number one again in 1975. The Padres select P Jay Franklin with the 2nd pick. Future MVP Keith Hernandez lasts until the 42nd round.

9th Expo Steve Renko pitches the first of 2 one-hitters of the season. He beats the Giants 4–0 exactly a month before he will top the Phillies 3–0.

12th Phillies 2B Terry Harmon accepts 18 chances during a 3–0 win over the Padres, setting a modern ML record. Meanwhile, the Phils deal another 2B, veteran Tony Taylor, to the Tigers for 2 minor leaguers.

13th Chico Ruiz allegedly pulls a gun on Angels teammate Alex Johnson in a clubhouse incident. There are no witnesses to the episode, which Ruiz denies, and it is one of a series of problems involving Johnson in 1971.

16th Oakland's 5 solo HRs account for all their scoring in a 5–1 win over Washington. Mike Epstein homers his first 2 times up to give him 4 straight over 2 games.

17th Don Kessinger goes 6-for-6 as the Cubs beat the Cardinals 7–6 in 10 innings.

20th Four grand slams are hit in the ML, by the Braves Earl Williams, the Phillies Deron Johnson, the White Sox Rick Reichardt, and the Pirates Willie Stargell.

21st Indians slugger Ken Harrelson announces his retirement from baseball to join the pro golf tour.

23rd In a singular performance, Phillie Rick Wise no-hits the Reds 4–0 and hits 2 HRs in the game. Wise gets Pete Rose for the last out.

25th Cleon Jones ties an NL record by drawing 6 walks, helping the Mets to a doubleheader sweep of the Expos.

Actor Kurt Russell makes his pro baseball debut for Bend (Northwest League), getting a single, double, and 2 stolen bases. Russell's baseball career would be ended by injury 2 years later.

26th Last year's AL batting king Alex Johnson is suspended by the Angels following a series of incidents (including 5 benchings and 29 fines) resulting from his failure to hustle.

JULY

1st The Mets release 2B Al Weis, a WS hero less than 2 years earlier.

7th Commissioner Kuhn announces that players from the Negro Leagues elected to the Hall of Fame will be given full membership in the museum. It had been previously announced that they would be honored in a separate wing.

9th The A's beat the Angels 1–0 in the longest shutout in AL history—20 innings. Vida Blue strikes out 17 batters in 11 innings for the A's, while the Angels Billy Cowan ties a ML record by fanning 6 times.

Braves SS Leo Foster makes a memorable debut. Against the Pirates, he errs on his first chance, hits into a double play in the 5th, and a triple play in the 7th.

11th Tony Conigliaro, who had gone 0-for-8 with 5 strikeouts for the Angels during their 20-inning loss 2 days earlier, calls a 5 A.M. press conference to announce his retirement. Later tests will show that the sight in his left eye, injured in a 1967 beaning, has deteriorated.

Deron Johnson hits 3 HRs, giving him 4 straight over 2 games, helping the Phils beat the Expos 11–5.

13th In an All-Star Game featuring HRs by Johnny Bench, Hank Aaron, Roberto Clemente, Reggie Jackson, Frank Robinson, and Harmon Killebrew, the AL triumphs at Detroit 6–4. It is the only AL All-Star victory between 1962 and 1983. Jackson's HR goes 520 feet.

15th The Pirates beat the Padres 4–3 in a marathon thriller. Pittsburgh ties the game in the bottom of the 9th, 13th, and 16th innings before winning it on a Roberto Clemente HR in the 17th.

16th Vida Blue boosts his record to 18-3 with a one-hit 4–0 victory over Detroit.

17th Dock Ellis wins his 13th straight as Pittsburgh whips the Padres 9–2.

18th The Pirates sweep a doubleheader from the Dodgers 3–2 and 7–1 to extend their winning streak to 11 games. In the 2nd game, Luke Walker has a no-hitter until Joe Ferguson homers in the 9th inning for Los Angeles.

30th The Indians, with a 42-61 record, fire manager Alvin Dark. Johnny Lipon takes over, but the team goes 18-41 the rest of the season.

31st The Orioles Pat Dobson shuts out the Royals 4–0 for his 8th victory of the month. Since June 16th, Dobson has won 12 straight games.

AUGUST

1st Dave Kingman, in his 2nd ML game, clouts a grand slam for the Giants as the Pirates lose a doubleheader. A day later, Kingman will hit 2 more HRs in a 5–4 loss to the Dodgers.

4th Tommy Walker of Fort Worth (Dixie League) pitches a 15-inning no-hit win over Albuquerque.

7th Vida Blue becomes the first 20-game winner in the major leagues this season with a 1–0 gem over the White Sox.

9th The Indians score 8 runs in the 5th inning to beat the Cubs 13–5 in the annual Hall of Fame game. Earlier, the Hall had inducted Satchel Paige and the 7 others selected in January.

10th Harmon Killebrew becomes the 10th player to amass 500 HRs, and adds his 501st, but the Orioles beat the Twins 5–4.

The Giants Juan Marichal pitches the 50th shutout of his career, a 1–0 squeaker over Montreal. He leads all active hurlers in this category.

Sixteen baseball researchers at Cooperstown form the Society for American Baseball Research (SABR), with founder Robert Davids as president.

14th Before 30,678 Pittsburgh fans, Cardinals ace Bob Gibson, 35, hurls the first no-hitter of his career, an 11–0 shellacking of the Pirates. The Cards make it easy for Gibson by scoring 5 runs in the top of the first inning. Gibson walks 3 and strikes out 10, and paces the offensive with 3 RBIs. Gibson said after the game, "This was the greatest game I've ever pitched anywhere." The win, Gibson's 48th career shutout, improves his record to 11–10 and moves St. Louis to just 5 games behind the first-place Pirates.

15th Vida Blue raises his record to 22-4 as the A's beat the Yankees.

16th Harmon Killebrew, who has a higher percentage of his hits (28.6%) go for home runs than any other player, collects his annual triple in a 11–2 win over the Indians. It marks his 8th season when he will hit exactly one threebagger.

24th Padre Ed Acosta makes his ML pitching debut and shuts out the Phillies 2–0.

Braves OF Rico Carty announces he has suffered permanent damage to his right eye from an altercation with 3 policemen in Atlanta.

27th Detroit's Willie Horton is struck in the eye by a pitch from Chicago's Rich Hinton, sidelining him for 28 games.

28th Phillies hurler Rick Wise hits 2 HRs, including a grand slam, in the 2nd game of a doubleheader. Wise beats the Giants 7–3. Wise also hit 2 HRs in his June no-hitter.

SEPTEMBER

1st The Pirates start what is believed to be the first all-black lineup (including several Latins) in ML history, in a 10–7 win over the Phillies. The lineup: Rennie Stennett, 2B; Gene Clines, CF; Roberto Clemente, RF; Willie Stargell, LF; Manny Sanguillen, C; Dave Cash, 3B; Al Oliver, 1B; Jackie Hernandez, SS; and Dock Ellis, P. Another black, Bob Veale, was one of 3 relievers in the game.

2nd Cesar Cedeno's 200-foot fly ball falls for a grand slam, following a collision of Dodgers 2B and RF. The Astros win 9–3.

Sonny Siebert hits and pitches the Red Sox to a 3–0 win over the Orioles. Siebert hits 2 HRs, the last AL pitcher to do so.

3rd Owner Phil Wrigley takes out newspaper ads criticizing the Cubs players who want to dump manager Leo Durocher. A postscript adds, "If we could only find more team players like Ernie Banks." Banks will play his last game on September 26th.

5th Astros pitcher J. R. Richard makes his ML debut, striking out 15 Giants in a 5–3 win.

The Tigers tie a ML record by using 6 pinch hitters in the 7th inning, but lose 6–5 to the Yankees anyway.

6th Boston uses 2 entirely different 10-man lineups in a doubleheader with New York, but neither succeeds. The Yankees prevail 5–3 and 3–0.

7th Kansas City's Amos Otis collects 4 hits and 5 SBs in a 4–3 win over Milwaukee. Darrell Porter's wild throw on a steal allows Otis to score the winning run.

Jim Northrup goes 5-for-5 with 2 HRs in a 3–2, 11th-inning Tiger win over Washington.

10th Houston's Jack Billingham scores his 2nd straight 1–0 victory, beating Cincinnati 5 days after victimizing San Francisco.

13th Frank Robinson of the Orioles homers in each game of a doubleheader split with Detroit, becoming the 11th member of the 500-HR club.

14th The Dodgers beat the Giants 6–5 to climb within one game of first place in the NL Western Division.

15th Larry Yount is announced as the new pitcher for Houston versus Atlanta. While taking his warmup pitches, Yount injures his arm and must be replaced in what proves to be his only ML appearance. Larry's brother Robin will begin a more successful ML career in 1974.

17th The White Sox defeat the Angels 9–4 with each Chicago player driving in one run.

19th Dodgers Al Downing and Don Sutton hurl shutouts during a 12–0, 4–0 doubleheader triumph over the Braves.

20th The Senators beat the Indians 8–6 in 20 innings, thus completing a suspended game begun 6 days earlier in Cleveland. Meanwhile, Senators owner Bob Short is given permission to move his team to Texas, where they will become the Rangers, a nickname adopted on November 23rd.

21st Dave McNally shuts out the Yankees 5–0 for his 20th win. It is the 4th straight 20-win year for the Oriole ace.

22nd The Phillies leave 14 men on base without scoring in a 2–0 loss to the Expos.

Rochester (International League) beats Denver (American Association) 9–6 to win the Junior WS, 4 games to 3.

24th Wasting a heroic pitching effort by starter Clay Kirby, the Padres lose to the Astros 2–1 in 21 innings. Kirby hurls 15 innings and strikes out 15 men.

The Orioles clinch their division as Mike Cuellar wins his 20th game 9–2 over the Indians. In game 2 of the doubleheader, Pat Dobson cards his 20th win, a 7–0 shutout.

26th Jim Palmer becomes the 4th member of the Orioles 1971 pitching staff to notch his 20th victory. Only one other team in ML history—the 1920 White Sox—boasted four 20-game winners.

Washington P Denny McLain loses his 22nd game of the season, dropping a 6–3 decision to the Red Sox.

Ernie Banks gets his 2,583rd hit, a first-inning single off the Phils Ken Reynolds, but the Cubs lose 5–1. It is the last hit of his 19-year ML career.

28th Arbitrator Lewis Gill rules that Alex Johnson was "emotionally incapacitated" during events leading to his June suspension, and that he should be treated the same as a physically disabled player. Johnson wins nearly $30,000 in back salary from the Angels.

Baltimore achieves 108 wins for the season with doubleheader victories at Boston 10–2 and 5–4. The Orioles become only the 3rd team to win 100 games in 3 straight seasons.

29th In the 6th inning of the Expos 6–5 win over the Cubs, Ron Hunt is hit by a Milt Pappas pitch. It is the 50th HBP for Hunt in 1971, setting a ML record.

30th The Senators, in their final game in Washington, hold a 7–5 lead over the Yankees with 2 outs in the 9th. Fans then swarm onto the field, causing the game to be forfeited to the Yanks.

OCTOBER

2nd The Giants win the first game of the NL Championship Series 5–4 over the Pirates, behind 2-run HRs by Tito Fuentes and Willie McCovey.

3rd Baltimore downs Oakland 5–3 in the ALCS opener, as the Orioles score 4 runs in the 7th inning. OF Paul Blair caps the big inning with a 2-run double.

Bob Robertson crashes 3 HRs and a double, scoring 4 runs and driving home 5, to lead Pittsburgh to a 9–4 triumph.

4th Baltimore wins its 2nd straight game in the ALCS, beating Oakland 5–1 on HRs by Boog Powell (2), Brooks Robinson, and Ellie Hendricks. Four of Baltimore's 7 hits against Catfish Hunter are homers.

5th The Orioles overcome 2 Reggie Jackson HRs to complete a sweep of Oakland in the LCS with a 5–3 victory.

Richie Hebner's homer off Juan Marichal in the 8th inning gives Pittsburgh a 2–1 victory, and a 2–1 lead in the series.

The Angels trade moody OF Alex Johnson and C Gerry Moses to the Indians for outfielders Vada Pinson and Frank Baker, and P Alan Foster.

6th The Pirates outslug the Giants 9–5 to win the LCS 3 games to one, as Richie Hebner's bat takes Pittsburgh into the WS. Hebner has 3 hits and 3 RBI, including a homer.

7th The Angels fire manager Lefty Phillips following a stormy season. Del Rice takes over in 1972.

9th The Orioles win game one of the WS over the Pirates 5–3 behind Dave McNally's 3-hitter and Merv Rettenmund's 3-run homer.

10th Rain washes out game 2 of the WS, the first Series postponement since 1962.

11th Brooks Robinson ties a Series record by reaching base 5 straight times on 3 hits and 2 walks as Baltimore rolls over Pittsburgh 11–3 to take a 2–0 Series advantage.

The Red Sox and the Brewers engineer a 10-player trade that sees P Jim Lonborg, P Ken Brett, and 1B George Scott go to Milwaukee, and P Marty Pattin and OF Tommy Harper head to Boston.

12th As the Series moves to Pittsburgh, Steve Blass 3-hits the Orioles 5–1 to give the Pirates their first win.

13th   Pittsburgh comes back from a 3–0 deficit to beat Baltimore 4–3, as Milt May drives in the winning run in the 8th with a pinch-hit single. It is the first WS game to be played entirely under the lights.

14th   Nelson Briles hurls a 2-hit shutout and Robertson slugs his 6th post-season HR as the Pirates win the 5th game 4–0 and take a 3-2 Series advantage. Roberto Clemente hits safely in his 12th straight WS game.

16th   Brooks Robinson drives in Frank Robinson in the 10th inning to give Baltimore a Series-tying 3–2 win.

17th   Steve Blass hurls a 4-hitter and Clemente homers as the Pirates win game 7 of the WS 2–1, becoming World Champions for the first time since 1960. After the game, 40,000 people riot in downtown Pittsburgh; at least 100 are injured, some seriously.

26th   Vida Blue wins the AL Cy Young Award by a 98-85 margin over the Tigers Mickey Lolich. Blue was 24-8 for the A's, posting 301 strikeouts, 8 shutouts, and a 1.82 ERA. Ferguson Jenkins won the Cy Young Award in the NL.

NOVEMBER

2nd   The Orioles Pat Dobson pitches a no-hitter against the Yomiuri Giants, winning 2–0. It is the first no-hitter in Japanese-American exhibition history. The Orioles compile a record of 12-2-4 on the tour.

10th   Joe Torre, who hit 24 HRs for the Cardinals and led the NL in RBI (137) and batting (.363), wins the MVP Award over Willie Stargell (48, 125, .295). Torre receives 318 points to Stargell's 222.

Vida Blue adds the AL MVP to his list of awards for 1971, easily outpointing teammate Sal Bando 268-182.

20th   TSN announces Gold Glove fielding teams. Among newcomers are OF Amos Otis in the AL and Bobby Bonds in the NL.

22nd   Indians 1B Chris Chambliss outpolls 4 other vote-getters to win the AL Rookie of the Year Award. Chambliss, who batted .275 in 111 games, receives 11 of 24 votes.

23rd   Danny Murtaugh, manager of the World Champion Pirates, announces his retirement for health reasons. Bill Virdon is named to replace him.

24th   C-IF Earl Williams, who belted 33 HRs and knocked in 87 runs for the Braves, wins the NL Rookie of the Year honors. Williams gets 18 of 24 votes, with the others going to Phillie Willie Montanez.

29th   In 3 blockbuster deals, the Cubs trade P Ken Holtzman to the A's for OF Rick Monday; the Giants trade P Gaylord Perry and SS Frank Duffy to the Indians for P Sam McDowell; and the Reds trade 1B Lee May and 2 others to the Astros for 2B Joe Morgan, OF Cesar Geronimo, and P Jack Billingham.

30th   The Twins trade SS Leo Cardenas to the Angels for P Dave LaRoche.

DECEMBER

1st   The Cubs release Ernie Banks and sign him as a coach. Mr. Cub finishes his playing career with 512 HRs and 1,636 RBI.

2nd   Eight trades, involving 30 players, are made in the ML. Among those changing teams are Frank Robinson (to LA), Doyle Alexander (Baltimore), Dick Allen (White Sox), Tommy John (LA), and John Mayberry (KC).

3rd   The Brewers trade OF Jose Cardenal to the Cubs for P Jim Colborn and 2 other players.

10th   The Angels trade SS Jim Fregosi to the Mets for 4 players, including OF Leroy Stanton and P Nolan Ryan.

1972

JANUARY

13th Former umpire, now housewife Bernice Gera wins her suit against baseball, initiated on March 15, 1971. Mrs. Gera is slated to umpire in the New York-Pennsylvania League starting in June.

19th The BBWAA elects Sandy Koufax (344 votes), Yogi Berra (339), and Early Wynn (301) to the Hall of Fame. Koufax makes it in his first try and, at 36, is the youngest honoree in history.

FEBRUARY

2nd The Special Veterans Committee selects former players Lefty Gomez and Ross Youngs, and former AL president William Harridge for the Hall of Fame.

8th Commissioner Bowie Kuhn announces the Hall of Fame selection of Josh Gibson and Buck Leonard by the Special Committee on the Negro Leagues.

9th Angels IF Chico Ruiz dies at age 33 in an auto crash in San Diego.

25th The Cardinals trade P Steve Carlton to the Phillies for P Rick Wise. Carlton will go on to win 241 games and 4 Cy Young awards for the Phils.

MARCH

4th The Texas Rangers (formerly the Washington Senators) trade 2-time Cy Young award winner Denny McLain to the A's for 2 pitchers.

9th Players on the White Sox vote 31-0 in favor of a strike, if necessary, during negotiations between players and owners. The dispute centers around health and pension benefits for players. This is the first of a series of landmark team votes.

22nd The Yankees trade 1B/OF Danny Cater to the Red Sox for relief P Sparky Lyle. In 7 years with the Yanks, Lyle will post a 57-40 record with 141 saves and a 2.41 ERA, win a Cy Young award, and help the team to 3 WS.

Nick Mileti heads a group that purchases the Cleveland Indians from Vernon Stouffer for an estimated $9 million.

30th Marvin Miller, executive director of the Players' Association, completes his canvass of players on the strike issue: 663 vote in favor of a strike, 10 against, and there are 2 abstentions.

APRIL

2nd Mets manager Gil Hodges dies of a heart attack at West Palm Beach, Florida, 2 days shy of his 48th birthday.

5th The Mets trade OF Ken Singleton, 1B-OF Mike Jorgensen, and IF Tim Foli to the Expos for OF Rusty Staub.

6th For the first time in history, the ML season fails to open due to a general player strike. The strike, announced April 1st, will erase 86 games from the ML schedules.

9th President Richard Nixon recommends that both sides of the baseball dispute meet with J. Curtis Counts, director of the Federal Mediation and Conciliation Service.

13th The end of the baseball strike is announced, with an abbreviated schedule to start 2 days later.

15th Reggie Jackson sports a mustache as the A's top the Twins 4–3 in 11 innings. Jackson is reported as the first ML player with facial hair since Wally Schang in 1914.

16th In Chicago, 22-year-old rookie Burt Hooton of the Cubs no-hits the Phillies 4–0. It is Hooton's 4th ML game over 2 seasons and he has allowed just 8 hits in 30 innings. Throwing his knucklecurve, Hooton walks 7 and fans 7.

18th Giants slugger Willie McCovey breaks his right arm in a collision during a win over the Padres. He will be out until June 3rd.

21st The Rangers celebrate their first game in their new home, Arlington Stadium, halfway between Dallas and Fort Worth, by outscoring the Angels 7–6.

27th The Padres fire manager Preston Gomez and replace him with Don Zimmer.

MAY

2nd Oakland's Vida Blue ends a long holdout, signing a contract for $63,000. The young southpaw had received $14,750 in 1971 while winning the AL Cy Young and MVP awards.

11th The Giants trade future Hall of Famer Willie Mays to the Mets for minor league P Charlie Williams and cash.

12th The Brewers edge the Twins 4–3 in a 22-inning marathon. A day later the 2 teams will tangle for another 15 innings, with the Twins coming out on top 4–2.

14th Willie Mays, making a triumphant return to New York with the Mets, hits a game-winning HR against his old teammates. The final score is 5–4.

16th The Cubs Rick Monday hits a single and 3 consecutive HRs, driving in 5 runs in an 8–1 win over the Phillies.

24th California P Don Rose homers in his first ML at bat, and earns a 6–5 victory over the A's and Vida Blue, who is making his first appearance of the season for Oakland. For Rose, it will be his only ML HR, as well as his only win.

28th The Brewers fire manager Dave Bristol, replacing him with Del Crandall.

30th Milwaukee's Skip Lockwood one-hits New York 3–1. Lockwood will be involved in 2 other one-hitters later in the season: June 26th versus Baltimore (with one inning of relief help from Ken Sanders) and August 1st versus Detroit (a 6-inning game).

31st Giants OF Bobby Bonds makes a rare unassisted DP in the 4th inning of a 5–4 loss to the Dodgers.

JUNE

3rd Rusty Staub of the Mets is struck in the right hand by a George Stone pitch during a game with the Braves. Staub will miss 90 contests.

Bobby Murcer and Thurman Munson crack 3-run HRs in the Yankees' 8-run 13th inning to beat the White Sox 18–10. Murcer scores 5 runs on 4 hits.

4th A major league record 8 shutouts are pitched in 16 ML games—5 in the AL, 3 in the NL.

In game 2 of a doubleheader in Chicago, pinch hitter Dick Allen connects with 2 on and 2 out in the 9th inning and drives a Sparky Lyle pitch into the LF upper deck for a dramatic 5–4 White Sox win over the Yankees.

6th Sadaharu Oh of the Yomiuri Giants (Japanese League) hits HRs 499 and 500.

7th The Pirates beat the Padres 1–0 in 18 innings in the 2nd game of a doubleheader.

8th Shortstops are the first 2 picks in the June draft. The Padres make Dave Roberts the number-one selection and the Indians pick Rick Manning number 2.

10th Hank Aaron hits his 14th career grand slam, tying Gil Hodges's NL record, as the Braves defeat the Phillies 15–3. It is career HR 649 for Aaron, enabling him to pass Willie Mays for 2nd place on the all-time list.

18th Larry Bowa's 9th-inning double is the Phillies' only hit as the Astros Jerry Reuss hurls a 10–0 shutout. A day later Houston's Larry Dierker will also spin a one-hitter.

By a 5-3 vote, the U.S. Supreme Court confirms lower court rulings in the Curt Flood case, upholding baseball's exemption from antitrust laws and the legitimacy of its reserve clause. Its decision is narrowly construed, however, and leaves the way open for legislation or collective bargaining to undercut the reserve system. By the year's end the ML owners will destroy it themselves by agreeing to salary arbitration.

24th Culminating a long battle to reach pro baseball, Bernice Gera umpires the first game of a doubleheader between Auburn and Geneva (New York-Pennsylvania League). Several disputes take place and she ejects the Auburn manager. Gera resigns before the 2nd game, leaving in tears.

26th Detroit's Bill Slayback makes his ML debut a good one, allowing no hits for 7 innings against the Yankees. Johnny Callison's single in the 8th is the first hit, but Detroit hangs on to a 4–3 win.

Brewer Billy Conigliaro jumps his club for the comfort of a Massachusetts island retreat.

27th Mickey Lolich is staked to 4–0 lead when the Tigers hit 3 consecutive first-inning HRs against New York's Wade Blasingame, making his AL debut. Aurelio Rodriguez, Al Kaline, and Willie Horton do the damage as Lolich notches his 12th.

29th In a swap of former MVPs, the Braves send 1B Orlando Cepeda to the A's for P Denny McLain.

JULY

2nd Jim Kaat, sporting a 10-2 record and a 2.07 ERA for the White Sox, breaks his pitching hand while sliding. He will miss the remainder of the season.

Reggie Smith homers from both sides of the plate as Boston beats Milwaukee 15–4.

Willie McCovey hits his 14th career grand slam to pace the Giants 9–3 win over the Dodgers. Randy Moffitt wins his first ML game and receives a congratulatory telegram from his sister Billie Jean King, who is playing at Wimbledon.

4th Leron Lee singles in the 9th to break up Tom Seaver's no-hitter, but the Mets shut out the Padres 2–0.

6th The Twins fire manager Bill Rigney, promoting 33-year-old coach Frank Quilici to take his place.

8th The Tigers lose to the White Sox 5–2. Detroit's John Hiller returns to the mound 18 months after suffering a heart attack.

9th The Angels Nolan Ryan strikes out 16 batters, including 8 in a row and three on 9 pitches in the 2nd inning, as he stops the Red Sox on one hit.

10th Phillies GM Paul Owens takes over as field manager after firing Frank Lucchesi.

11th Cub Billy Williams goes 8-for-8 in a doubleheader split with the Astros. The Astros win the opener 6–5, and the Cubs take the nightcap 9–5. Williams is 5-for-5 in the 2nd game.

14th In a ML first, the plate umpire and the catcher in a game are brothers. Bill Haller is the ump and Tom Haller is the Tigers C during a game with the Royals. Kansas City wins 1–0.

18th San Diego's Steve Arlin takes a no-hitter against Philadelphia into the 9th inning before settling for a 2nd straight 2-hitter. During the season, Arlin will notch three 2-hitters, a one-hitter, and a 10-inning one-hit stint, yet compile a 10-21 record.

21st The Dodgers release P Hoyt Wilhelm, ending his Hall of Fame career 2 days before his 49th birthday. Wilhelm appeared in 1,070 games, the most of any ML pitcher.

24th Cubs manager Leo Durocher steps down, turning over the reins to Whitey Lockman.

25th The NL wins the All-Star Game 4–3 at Atlanta behind hometown hero Hank Aaron's 2-run HR and Joe Morgan's 10th-inning RBI single. It is the 7th time the classic has gone into extra innings.

31st Dick Allen becomes the first player since 1950, and the 7th in history, to hit 2 inside-the-park homers in a game. Minnesota's Bert Blyleven is on the mound in the first and the 5th when Allen connects past Danny Darwin in CF. Chicago wins 8–1.

AUGUST

1st Nate Colbert ties one ML record with 5 HRs, and sets another with 13 RBI, as the Padres take a doubleheader from the Braves 9–0 and 11–7. At age 8, on May 2, 1954, Colbert had been at Sportsman's Park in St. Louis to witness Stan Musial hitting 5 HRs in a doubleheader.

Trailing by several runs in a game threatened by rain, Billy Martin has his Detroit Tigers employ stalling tactics while the opposing Milwaukee Brewers try to speed the game up. The game lasts 6 innings, with Del Crandall's Brewers winning 6–0. Umpire Frank Umont recommends a fine of $1,000 for both managers.

2nd The Tigers purchase P Woodie Fryman from the Phillies. Two days later the Bengals will purchase C Duke Sims from the Dodgers. Fryman, just 4-10 for Philadelphia, will go 10-3 for Detroit, while Sims will hit .316 for Detroit in 38 games. The 2 veterans will spark Detroit to the AL Eastern Division title.

5th During a 4–3 win over Cleveland, Detroit SS Ed Brinkman commits an error; this ending his ML-record streak of 72 games and 331 total chances without a miscue.

6th Hank Aaron hits his 660th and 661st HRs for the Braves, the most ever hit by one player for the same franchise.

7th Ron Allen hits 3 HRs as the Yankees beat the Dodgers 8–3 in the annual Hall of Fame game. The contest is preceded by inductions of 8 new members.

Eddie Mathews takes over as Braves manager following the dismissal of Luman Harris.

A horde of grasshoppers invades the field at Midland (Texas League) after the first game of a doubleheader, causing the postponement of the 2nd game.

9th The Cardinals Ted Simmons finally signs his 1972 contract, although he had been playing all season. He is believed to be the first ML player to play without a contract.

11th The A's defeat the White Sox 5–3 on Joe Rudi's 2-run HR in the 19th inning. The game had been renewed after a 3–3 tie in 17 frames the night before.

12th The White Sox top the A's 3–1 in 11 innings. The Sox, who were 8½ games behind Oakland on July 18th, take over first place in the AL West.

13th Bengals manager Billy Martin literally picks his starting lineup out of a hat in an attempt to halt the Tigers' 4-game losing streak. The ploy works as Detroit defeats Cleveland 3–2. Using a regular lineup in the nightcap, the Tigers lose 9–2.

18th Mickey Lolich regains first place for the Tigers as he bests the Angels and Nolan Ryan 2–0. It is Lolich's 19th win.

The Orioles trade C Elrod Hendricks to the Cubs for OF/1B Tommy Davis.

21st Phil Niekro and the Braves beat the Phillies 2–1 in 11 innings to snap Steve Carlton's 15-game winning streak.

23rd Chicago's Dick Allen becomes the 4th ML player (Jimmie Foxx, Hank Greenberg, and Alex Johnson are the others) to hit one into the CF bleachers in Comiskey Park when he connects off New York's Lindy McDaniel. The 2-run homer in the 7th ices the 5–2 win for the Sox. In 1972, all the Chicago Wednesday games are in the afternoon, and Harry Caray announces them while sitting in the CF bleachers. Allen's drive misses Caray by just a few rows.

25th Phillie Ken Reynolds ties a dubious NL record with his 12th straight losing decision from the start of the season after dropping a game 6–1 to the Reds.

26th Leo Durocher, formerly of the Cubs, replaces Harry Walker as manager of the Astros. It is only the 2nd time someone has managed 2 NL teams in the same season. The first was in 1948, when Durocher piloted the Dodgers and the Giants.

27th The Cardinals trade .314 hitter Matty Alou to the A's for 2 players.

The Tigers Willie Horton clouts an 11th-inning 2-run HR to beat Minnesota 5–3 in the opener of 2. In the nightcap, Joe Coleman pitches 11 shutout innings against Minnesota before Aurelio Rodriguez's HR gives him the 1–0 win. This is the 3rd win in a row for the Tigers on 11th-inning homers. Rodriguez hit one to start the streak.

29th During a 3–0 win over St. Louis, San Francisco's Jim Barr retires the first 20 batters to face him. Six days earlier, Barr had gotten out the last 21 men to face him. This gives Barr a ML record of 41 consecutive batsmen retired.

31st Another insurance purchase for the Tigers: they buy slugging 1B/OF Frank Howard from Texas

SEPTEMBER

2nd Milt Pappas of the Cubs hurls a no-hit game in beating the Padres 8–0. Pappas has a perfect game until PH Larry Stahl walks with 2 outs in the 9th inning. Pappas and C Randy Hundley both said of the pitches to Stahl, "They were so close I don't know how Stahl could take them, but they were balls."

6th Behind Mickey Lolich's 20th win, Detroit beats the Orioles in Baltimore 4–3 in the tight pennant race. Lolich had failed in 5 previous outings to win his 20th.

10th A round-robin tournament, replacing the Junior WS, begins, with Hawaii defeating a team of Caribbean all-stars 6–2. The series proves to be a financial and artistic failure.

13th Frank Howard, who is not playing regularly for the Tigers, hits a 3-run homer off Dave McNally of the Orioles for a Detroit victory. It is his 13th career fourbagger off his favorite pitcher. He had hit one with the Rangers on July 18th, and 11 with the Senators 1965-1971.

15th Steve Carlton beats the Expos 5–3, raising his record to 24-9. The rest of the Phillies pitchers have a combined record of 26-80.

16th Expo P Balor Moore extends his scoreless-inning streak to 25 before serving up a 7th-inning 3-run HR to lose to the Phillies 3–1. The homer is the first for Phils rookie Mike Schmidt.

Glenn Beckert sets a dubious ML record by stranding 12 base runners as his Cubs lose to the Mets 18–5.

Joe Coleman wins his 17th game and Dick McAuliffe clouts 2 HRs and drives in 4 to lead Detroit to a 6–2 win in Milwaukee. This is Detroit's 5th win in a row and keeps them a percentage point behind Boston.

19th The A's set a ML record by using 30 players, including a record 10 pinch hitters, in a game against the White Sox. The Sox use 21 players and win 8–7.

20th The Braves score all their runs in the 2nd inning in routing the Astros 13–6. Dusty Baker has 3 at bats in the inning.

Sadaharu Oh of the Yomiuri Giants hits a HR to set a new Japanese record of 7 HRs in 7 consecutive games. Dale Long in 1956 hit in 8 straight, and several players have hit in 6.

21st The Pirates clinch the NL East title with a 6–2 victory over the Mets.

The AL East is a virtual tie as Detroit's Joe Coleman posts his 18th win, a critical 10–3 defeat of first-place Boston. Coleman strikes out 10 and knocks in 3 runs.

27th A's relief star Darold Knowles breaks his thumb, costing him a chance to pitch in the WS. Knowles finishes the season with a 5-1 record, 11 saves, and a 1.36 ERA.

Trailing 5–1, the Tigers score 3 in the 8th and 2 in the 9th to beat the Yankees and Sparky Lyle.

30th During a 5–0 win over the Mets, the Pirates' Roberto Clemente doubles off Jon Matlack in the 4th inning for his 3,000th—and final—career hit in regular-season play.

The Tigers take their 3rd in a row from Milwaukee as John Hiller throws a 5-hitter. Aurelio Rodriguez's 3-run HR is the margin in the 5–1 win. The Tigers now return home to face the Red Sox in a 3-game series that will determine which team wins the East.

OCTOBER

2nd Bill Stoneman of Montreal pitches his 2nd no-hitter, beating the Mets 7–0. The temperature at Jarry Park is 53 degrees as 7,184 watch the doubleheader split.

The Red Sox fall a half game behind Detroit, losing 4–1 to Mickey Lolich before 51,518 at Tiger Stadium. Trailing 1–0 in the 3rd, Carl Yastrzemski hits a triple with 2 on, but Luis Aparicio stumbles twice and scrambles back to 3B, where Yaz is tagged out.

3rd Roric Harrison homers as Baltimore beats Cleveland 4–3 in the 2nd game of a doubleheader. With the DH rule on the horizon, it will be the last HR hit by an AL pitcher.

The Tigers clinch the AL East as Woodie Fryman beats Luis Tiant 3–1 for his 10th win. Chuck Seelbach picks up his 14th save and Al Kaline singles in the winning run for Detroit.

Steve Carlton wins his 27th game for the last-place Phillies, (59-97), as they pound out 6 HRs in an 11–1 win over Chicago. Carlton's total is the highest by a Phillies pitcher in 20 years.

4th Ted Williams manages his final game as the Rangers lose to the Royals 4–0. Williams will be replaced by Whitey Herzog.

5th Yutaka Fukumoto of the Hankyu Braves sets a Japanese single-season record of 113 stolen bases in a 130-game season.

7th Oakland defeats Detroit in the opening game of the AL Championship Series. The Tigers take a 2–1 lead in the 11th inning, but the A's come back with 2 runs in the bottom of the frame. The winning run is scored on Al Kaline's throwing error.

The Pirates score 3 in the first and top the Reds 5–1 in the NLCS opener as Joe Morgan and Al Oliver smash homers.

8th During his club's 5–0 win in the 2nd game of the ALCS, Oakland's Bert Campaneris fires his bat at Detroit P Lerrin LaGrow. Campy, who had been hit by a pitch, is fined and suspended for the rest of the series. LaGrow is also thrown out of the game, but Detroit manages just 3 hits against Blue Moon Odom.

Cincinnati opens the game with 5 straight hits against Bob Moose and wins 5–3 to even the NLCS.

9th The Pirates edge the Reds 3–2 as Manny Sanguillen homers and drives in the winning run in the 8th. Pittsburgh comes within one game of clinching the LCS.

10th Ross Grimsley of the Reds allows but 2 hits—a single and a HR by Roberto Clemente—to even the series with a 7–1 victory.

The Tigers bounce back behind Joe Coleman's 14 strikeouts to beat Oakland 3–0. Bill Freehan's HR supplies the firepower.

11th The Pirates lead the Reds 3–2 in the bottom of the 9th inning of the final game of the NL series. Johnny Bench homers to tie the game, and 2 singles and a Bob Moose wild pitch later, the Reds are NL champs.

The Tigers even the AL series with a 10th-inning 3-run rally to beat the A's 4–3. Jim Northrup bats in the game winner after Dave Hamilton walks home the tying run.

12th Oakland takes the AL flag with a 2–1 win in the 5th game of the LCS. The A's Reggie Jackson steals home, but pulls a hamstring in the process, sidelining him for the WS.

13th Commissioner Kuhn announces that Bert Campaneris will be allowed to play in the WS.

14th Catcher Gene Tenace becomes the first player ever to homer in each of his first 2 WS at bats, leading the A's to a 3–2 opening-game win over the Reds.

15th The A's win 2–1 as Joe Rudi clouts a HR and makes a game-saving catch to back up Catfish Hunter's pitching before a record Cincinnati crowd of 53,224. The A's take a 2-game advantage as the Series moves to Oakland.

17th Rain and hail in Oakland postpone the 3rd game of the Series.

18th With runners at 2B and 3B and a 3-2 count, the A's fake an intentional walk and strike out Johnny Bench looking. Blue Moon Odom strikes out 11, but Cincinnati's Jack Billingham is the winner 1–0.

19th The A's score twice in the bottom of the 9th on 4 straight singles—3 by pinch hitters to win the 4th game 3-2.

20th Pete Rose begins the scoring with a first-pitch HR off Catfish Hunter, and ends it with a 9th-inning RBI single, as the Reds stay alive with a 5–4 triumph.

21st The Reds send the Series to its 7th game with an 8–1 victory, the only game of the Series decided by more than one run. Bench has a HR and Bobby Tolan and Cesar Geronimo each drive in 2 runs.

22nd The A's win their first World Championship in 42 years with a 3–2 victory in game 7. Gene Tenace has 2 RBI in the game. Tenace, who had only 5 HRs in the regular season has 4 in the WS, is named MVP.

24th Hall of Famer Jackie Robinson dies of heart disease at age 53. Robinson had become the first black ML player of this century with the 1947 Dodgers.

Three longtime infielders are released by their respective clubs: Bill Mazeroski (Pirates), Maury Wills (Dodgers), and Julian Javier (Reds).

31st Gaylord Perry wins the AL Cy Young award by a 64-58 margin over Chicago's Wilbur Wood. Perry won 24 games for the 5th-place Indians.

The Phillies trade IF Don Money and 2 others to the Brewers for 4 pitchers, including Jim Lonborg and Ken Brett.

NOVEMBER

2nd Steve Carlton caps off a remarkable season with a unanimous NL Cy Young Award.

The Mets trade pitchers Gary Gentry and Danny Frisella to the Braves for 2B Felix Millan and P George Stone, both of whom will contribute significantly to the Mets 1973 pennant.

15th The White Sox Dick Allen wins the AL MVP Award by an overwhelming margin over Joe Rudi of the A's. Allen led the league in HRs (37), RBI (113), walks (99), and slugging (.603).

21st Boston's Carlton Fisk is the unanimous choice for AL Rookie of the Year, the first time this has happened. The catcher hit 22 HRs and led the AL East with a .293 average. Jon Matlack of the Mets is named the NL Rookie of the Year.

22nd Johnny Bench wins the NL MVP with 263 votes to 211 for runner-up Billy Williams. It is Bench's 2nd award in 3 years.

25th TSN announces Gold Glove Award winners. Pirate Roberto Clemente wins his 12th straight, and Dodger 1B Wes Parker his 6th in a row. Neither will play in 1973.

27th The Indians trade 3B Graig Nettles and C Gerry Moses to the Yankees for C John Ellis, IF Jerry Kenney, and outfielders Charlie Spikes and Rusty Torres.

28th The Dodgers trade OF Frank Robinson, P Bill Singer, and 3 others to the Angels for P Andy Messersmith and 3B Ken McMullen.

30th Twelve transactions, involving 36 players, take place. Among those sent to new clubs are OF

Larry Hisle (to the Twins), 2B Dave Johnson (Braves), and OF Hal McRae (Royals).

DECEMBER

10th The major leagues adopt the Save as an official statistic. A pitcher shall be credited with a save if, when entering a game as a reliever, he finds the tying or winning run on base or at the plate, and he preserves the lead. Or he pitches 3 effective innings and preserves the lead.

The AL votes unanimously to adopt the designated-hitter rule for a 3-year experimental basis. The DH will replace the pitcher in the lineup unless otherwise noted before the start of the game. In the December 1975 meeting the AL will vote to permanently adopt the DH. The NL declines to go along with the AL.

31st A plane carrying Roberto Clemente to Nicaragua on a mercy mission for earthquake victims crashes into the Atlantic Ocean. Clemente, who batted .317 in 18 seasons with the Pirates, is presumed dead at age 38.

1973

JANUARY

3rd A group of investors, headed by shipbuilder George Steinbrenner, purchases the New York Yankees from CBS for $10 million.

18th Orlando Cepeda signs with the Boston Red Sox, making him the first player signed by a team as a designated hitter.

24th Warren Spahn is elected to the Hall of Fame in his first try on the BBWAA ballot, receiving 316 of 380 votes.

28th The Hall of Fame Special Veterans Committee selects players Mickey Welch and George Kelly, plus umpire Billy Evans, for enshrinement.

FEBRUARY

1st Commissioner Bowie Kuhn announces the selection of Monte Irvin for the Hall of Fame by the Special Committee on the Negro Leagues.

8th The ML owners announce that "earlybird" spring training camps are canceled until all bargaining with the Players' Association is concluded.

25th A new 3-year Basic Agreement is reached between players and owners, and spring training is slated to start March 1st. Among the provisions of the agreement are a $15,000 minimum salary, salary arbitration, and the "10 and 5" trade rule, which permits a player with 10 years in the ML, the last 5 of which are with his current team, to veto any trade involving him.

27th White Sox slugger Dick Allen signs a 3-year contract for an estimated $250,000 per year, making him the highest-paid player in ML history.

MARCH

2nd Eddie Bane of Arizona State University pitches a 9–0 perfect game against Cal State Northridge University.

5th Yankee teammates Fritz Peterson and Mike Kekich arrive at spring training and announce that wives and families have been swapped. Even the family dogs were traded.

6th In an exhibition game with the Pirates, the Twins Larry Hisle becomes the first designated hitter in ML history. Hisle makes the new AL rule look good by collecting 2 HRs and 7 RBI.

20th In a special election held by the BBWAA, the late Roberto Clemente receives 393 of 424 votes to earn entry in the Hall of Fame. The Hall's Board of Directors had earlier waived the 5-year-wait rule for Clemente.

24th The Indians trade C Ray Fosse and SS Jack Heidemann to the A's for C Dave Duncan and OF George Hendrick.

27th The Braves release P Denny McLain, ending his stormy big-league career 2 days before his 29th birthday.

29th Orange baseballs, the brainchild of Oakland owner Charlie Finley, are used in the A's 11–5 exhibition loss to the Indians.

APRIL

6th Yankee Ron Blomberg, facing Boston's Luis Tiant, becomes the first official DH in the ML. Blomberg walks with the bases loaded and winds up 1-for-3 in the 15–5 loss to the Red Sox.

7th Cleveland sets day-game and opening-game records as 74,420 fans watch the Indians beat the Tigers 2–1.

10th Kansas City opens its new park, Royals Stadium, with a 12–1 rout of the Rangers. The game is attended by 39,464 fans braving 39-degree weather.

12th Giant Willie McCovey belts 2 HRs in the 4th inning of a 9–3 win over the Astros.

16th Boston's Reggie Smith homers from both sides of the plate during a 9–7 loss to Detroit.

17th Relief hurler Eddie Fisher, trying to become "another Wilbur Wood," beats the Rangers 10–5 in his first complete game in 10 years. It is only the 6th CG of his long career.

19th Al Kaline, 38, steals home on a double steal with Willie Horton as the Tigers defeat Boston 11–7.

27th In 50-degree Detroit weather, Royals rookie Steve Busby no-hits the Tigers 3–0. It is the first Royals no-hitter, and the first in Tiger Stadium since

Virgil Trucks's in 1952. Busby is the first no-hit game pitcher not to bat.

MAY

1st   The Giants score 7 times with 2 outs in the 9th inning to beat the Pirates 8–7. Chris Arnold's pinch grand slam is the big blow.

4th   The Phillies edge the Braves 4–3 in a 20-inning marathon.

7th   Five solo HRs account for all of the Pirates scoring in a 5–4 win over the Dodgers.

8th   Cubs manager Whitey Lockman is ejected during a 12-inning 3–2 win over the Padres. Coach Ernie Banks fills in for the last few innings, technically becoming the ML's first black manager

For the second time in his career, Pirate Willie Stargell poles one out of Dodger Stadium. His blast off Andy Messersmith hits the RF pavilion roof 470 feet away. His first ML HR, a 506-foot shot, came off Alan Foster on August 5, 1969. No other player has hit one out of the stadium.

Former P Ralph Miller dies in Cincinnati at age 100. Miller was the last survivor of 19th-century ball, and the first former ML player to reach the century mark.

In a losing effort against the Giants, Cardinals Bob Gibson makes his 242nd consecutive start. It is a new 20th century record passing that of Red Ruffing, who never pitched in relief the last 10 years of his career.

Cubs Bob Locker pitches in his 500th game, a 3–2 win over the Padres in 12 innings. All have been in relief, a ML record.

9th   The Reds Johnny Bench slugs 3 HRs and knocks in 7 runs in a 9–7 defeat of Steve Carlton and the Phillies. It is the 2nd time Bench has hit 3 HRs in a game against Carlton; the first came on July 26, 1970.

13th   The Yankees tie a ML record by hitting 4 HRs in a shutout game in which no other runs are scored. The mark was originally set by Cleveland on August 2, 1956.

15th   California's Nolan Ryan strikes out 12 and hurls his first career no-hitter in beating Kansas City 3–0. For C Jeff Torborg, it is his 3rd no-hitter.

17th   Angels OF Bobby Valentine breaks a leg trying to scale a wall to prevent a Dick Green HR during a 5–4 loss to the A's.

18th   During a 5–4 win over the Royals, the A's Bill North punches Kansas City P Doug Bird, earning a 3-day league suspension.

19th   Philadelphia's Ken Brett hold Chicago's Glenn Beckert hitless in the first game of a doubleheader, ending his 26-game hitting streak.

20th   In a 5-player deal, Angels 1B Jim Spencer and Rangers 1B Mike Epstein switch teams.

24th   The Dodgers Willie Davis gets 6 hits, the Mets Rusty Staub 5, during a 19-inning game. The Mets win 7–3.

25th   The Giants activate 43-year-old coach Don McMahon as pitcher. McMahon will go 4–0 with 6 saves and a 1.50 ERA the rest of the season, before being released October 9th.

27th   The Padres announce the impending sale of the club to a group that plans to move the team to Washington, DC in 1974.

28th   Chicago's rubber-armed knuckleballer Wilbur Wood wins the completion of a suspended game, then shuts down Cleveland in the regularly scheduled contest. After the White Sox' first 40 games, Wood's record is a remarkable 13-3.

JUNE

2nd   Dodgers 2B Davey Lopes ties the ML record with 3 errors in the first inning of a 6–3 loss to the Expos.

7th   The Rangers make Texas high school P David Clyde the number-one pick in the free-agent draft. He will make his ML debut later this month. Dave Winfield, the number 4 pick, will go straight to the ML. Winfield was also taken in the NBA and NFL drafts. John Stearns is taken 2nd by the Phillies, and the Brewers, picking 3rd, take Robin Yount. Randy Scarbery becomes the first player selected twice in the first round of the regular phase of the draft when the A's take him 23rd. The Astros picked him first in 1970, but he picked college instead.

12th   P Fred Norman, sporting a 1-7 record for the Padres, is traded to the Reds for a minor league pitcher, reserve outfielder, and cash. Norman will go 12-6 the remainder of the season for the Reds.

16th The Orioles Jim Palmer retires the first 25 batters before Ken Suarez singles with one out in the 9th. Palmer holds on for a 2-hit 9–1 win over the Rangers.

17th Darrell Porter and Joe Lahoud each contribute grand slams to Milwaukee's 15–5 rout of Chicago. LaHoud has 6 RBI in the win. It is Milwaukee's 9th straight victory, all on the road.

19th Cleveland's George Hendrick hits a single and 3 consecutive HRs in an 8–7 win over Detroit.

The Reds Pete Rose (single versus the Giants) and the Dodgers Willie Davis (HR versus the Braves) each collects their 2,000th career hit.

20th Chicago's Cy Acosta becomes the first AL pitcher to bat since the DH rule went into effect. Acosta strikes out in the 8th inning, but is credited with an 8–3 victory over California.

Bobby Bonds leads off with a HR, but the Giants lose 7–5 to the Reds. It is Bonds's 22nd leadoff HR, breaking Lou Brock's NL record.

21st Houston's Lee May collects 3 HRs and a single in a 12–2 win over San Diego.

23rd Phillies P Ken Brett beats the Expos 7–2 and hits a HR for a ML-record 4th consecutive game.

27th David Clyde, 18 and fresh out of Houston's Westchester high school, makes his eagerly awaited debut with the Rangers, before 35,698, the largest Rangers' crowd of the year. Clyde, the number one pick in the draft, walks the first 2 Twins he faces, then gets Bob Darwin, George Mitterwald, and Joe Lis on swinging 3rd strikes. Clyde goes 5 innings and gives up only one hit—a 2-run HR—walks 7 and strikes out 8. He is the winner 4–3.

28th During a 2–0 win over the Angels, White Sox star Dick Allen breaks his leg in a collision with Mike Epstein. Allen will come to bat only 5 more times all season.

JULY

1st The Reds, 11 games behind the Dodgers at the beginning of the day, stage two dramatic comebacks to snatch a doubleheader win from LA. Hal King's clutch HR wins the first game 4–3, while Tony Perez's 10th-inning hit wins the 2nd 3–2. This day will be looked upon as the turning point of the National League's Western Division race.

Luis Aparicio of the Red Sox steals the 500th base of his career in a 9–5 loss to Milwaukee. It is the highest total in the AL since Eddie Collins retired in 1930.

3rd Brothers Gaylord (Indians) and Jim (Tigers) Perry pitch against each other for the only time in their careers. Neither finishes the game, but Gaylord is charged with the 5–4 loss. Two Norm Cash HRs help Detroit.

Minnesota's Tony Oliva hits 3 solo HRs during a 7–6 loss to Kansas City.

6th The Expos take 2 in a doubleheader with the Astros 12–8 and 14–6. In the first game John Boccabella hits 2 HRs in the 6th inning for Montreal.

11th Jim Northrup, batting leadoff for Detroit, drives in 8 runs in a 14–2 win over Texas.

13th Montreal's Hal Breeden pinch-hits HRs in each game of a doubleheader split with Atlanta, tying the ML record set by Joe Cronin on June 17, 1943.

Bobby Murcer hits 3 HRs and knocks in all the runs in the Yankees' 5–0 win over the Royals.

15th Before 41,411 in Detroit, Angel Nolan Ryan hurls his 2nd no-hitter of the season in taming the Tigers 6–0. Ryan fans 17 batters, including 8 straight. In the 9th inning, Norm Cash, who had struck out his 3 other times at bat, comes to bat wielding a piano leg. Umpire Ron Luciano points out the illegality and Cash then pops out using a regulation bat.

20th Chicago's Wilbur Wood starts and loses both games of a doubleheader with the Yankees 12–2 and 7–0.

21st Atlanta Brave Hank Aaron hits a Ken Brett fastball into the left-CF stands for a 2-run HR during an 8–4 loss to the Phillies. It is career HR 700 for Aaron, only the 2nd player to reach that milestone.

22nd Reds All-Star SS Dave Concepcion suffers a season-ending broken ankle.

24th The NL wins the All-Star Game at Kansas City 7–1. A record 54 players are used, including Willie Mays, who strikes out in his final All-Star appearance, and Catfish Hunter, who sustains a fractured thumb that will sideline him for 4 weeks. The A's ace has a 15-3 record at the time.

29th Wilbur Wood wins his 20th game of the season as the White Sox beat the Twins 8–6.

30th The Rangers Jim Bibby no-hits first-place Oakland 6–0, while teammate Jeff Burroughs hits the 2nd of 3 grand slams in a 10-day period (July 26th–August 4th). Bobby, who came to Texas in a June 6th trade with the Cardinals, strikes out 13 batters.

31st The Tigers win a pair from the Brewers 6–5 and 9–4 and end Dave May's AL season-best hitting streak at 24 games.

AUGUST

1st Thurman Munson and Carlton Fisk brawl at Fenway. With a 2–2 score in the top of the 9th, Munson, attempting to score from 3rd on a missed bunt, crashes into Fisk and they both come up swinging. Boston wins 3–2 in the bottom of the inning.

4th John Briggs of the Brewers goes 6-for-6 in a 9–4 win over the Indians.

In an outstanding relief performance, Yankee Lindy McDaniel comes to the rescue of Fritz Peterson in the 2nd inning, and allows just one run in 13 innings to earn a 3–2 victory over the Tigers.

5th Braves knuckleballer Phil Niekro no-hits the Padres 9–0 and improves his record to 11-4.

6th Roberto Clemente and Warren Spahn head the list of new inductees at Cooperstown. Clemente is the first Latin-born player to achieve membership at Cooperstown. The Rangers beat the Pirates in the Hall of Fame game 6–4.

7th The Braves purchase Joe Niekro, Phil's pitching brother, from the Tigers.

8th Boston DH Orlando Cepeda ties the ML record with 4 doubles in a 9–4 triumph over Kansas City.

12th The A's, 6 runs behind in the 7th inning, rally to beat the Yankees 13–12 and move to within one game of the first-place Royals in the AL West.

13th Roy White homers from both sides of the plate as the Yankees top the Angels 6–0.

17th Willie Mays hits the 660th—and last—HR of his ML career off Don Gullett of Cincinnati.

21st Cleveland's Walt Williams singles with 2 outs in the 9th, breaking up Stan Bahnsen's no-hitter.

Bahnsen completes the one-hit shutout as the White Sox win 4–0.

26th In a 10–1 win over the Royals, Oriole Paul Blair hits an inside-the-park grand slam off Paul Splittorff. Amos Otis and Steve Hovley collide in midair while chasing Blair's ball to help the O's win their 13th straight.

27th The Orioles beat the Rangers 6–1 for their 14th consecutive victory. It is the longest winning streak in the AL since 1960, and in the major leagues since 1965.

29th Thurman Munson gets a tainted first-inning hit as a pop fly drops between 2 Angels infielders calling for it. It turns out to be the only hit allowed by Nolan Ryan as he beats the Yankees 5–0.

30th The last-place Mets drop to 61-71 after a 10-inning 1–0 loss to Cardinals.

SEPTEMBER

2nd Montreal's Hal Breeden gets 2 triples and 2 HRs in a 12–0 win over Philadelphia.

The Tigers fire Billy Martin due to continuous differences with the front office.

6th The Yankees sell two Alou brothers: Felipe to Montreal and Matty to St. Louis.

The Pirates fire manager Bill Virdon. Danny Murtaugh takes over the club for the 4th and final time.

7th The Rangers fire manager Whitey Herzog. Recently fired Billy Martin takes over the following day.

11th Samuel Ewing sets an unenviable record by striking out 4 times in his first ML game, as the White Sox are throttled by Nolan Ryan and the Angels 3–1.

13th During an 8–6 win over the Padres, the Giants Tito Fuentes ties a ML record by being hit by pitches 3 times.

19th The Angels down the Rangers 6–2 and 9–4 at Arlington Stadium. Frank Robinson homers in the 32nd different park of his ML career—a record.

Chicago's Ron Santo and Billy Williams celebrate their long association together by each hitting their 20th homer of the season in an 8–6 win over Montreal.

It is number 325 for Santo and 376 for Williams in more than 2,000 games together.

20th The Pirates lose 4–3 in 13 innings in New York and their lead over the Mets is cut to one-half game. A Bud Harrelson relay from Cleon Jones nails Richie Zisk at the plate in the bottom of the last inning.

A's speedster Bill North trips over 1B in a 5–4 loss to the Twins, severely spraining his right ankle and costing him both the AL SB crown and a chance to play in the WS.

21st Jim Rice's 3-run HR is the key blow as Pawtucket (International League) defeats Tulsa (American Association) 5–2 to win the Junior WS.

The Mets complete an amazing climb from last place to first, as a 10–2 win over the Pirates raises their record to a modest 77-77. They will finish 82-79, 1½ games ahead of St. Louis, and 2½ ahead of Pittsburgh.

22nd Al Bumbry ties the AL record with 3 triples as the Orioles beat the Brewers 7–1 and clinch the AL East title.

25th The Mets beat the Expos 2–1 on Willie Mays Night at Shea Stadium. "The 'Say Hey' Kid" had announced his retirement 5 days earlier.

26th The Twins Bert Blyleven posts his 2nd one-hitter of the season, beating the A's 4–1.

27th Nolan Ryan fans 16 in 11 innings, beating the Twins 5–4. The final strikeout victim, Rich Reese, is 383 of the season for Ryan, enabling him to surpass the ML record set by Sandy Koufax in 1965.

30th Angel Ron Perranoski announces his retirement after 13 years as one of the premier relief pitchers in the major leagues.

OCTOBER

6th Jim Palmer fans 12 in shutting out the A's 6–0 in the opening game of the AL Championship Series. Meanwhile, Tom Seaver fans 13 and takes a 1–0 lead into the 8th inning of the NL opener, only to be beaten by HRs by Pete Rose and Johnny Bench. The Reds top the Mets 2–1.

7th Jon Matlack gives up 2 hits to Andy Kosco, but none to the rest of the Reds, as the Mets even the series with a 5–0 win.

The A's, led by 2 Sal Bando HRs, even the AL series with a 6–3 triumph over the Orioles.

8th Rusty Staub homers in the first and 2nd innings as the Mets crush the Reds 9–2, in a game featuring a bench-clearing brawl between Rose and Bud Harrelson. Rain postpones the AL game.

9th The Reds beat the Mets 2–1 on a 12th-inning HR by Rose to even the Series 2–2.

Bert Campaneris leads off the 11th with a HR to give Oakland a 2–1 win over Mike Cuellar and the Orioles.

10th Bobby Grich's 8th-inning HR gives Baltimore a come-from-behind 5–4 victory in game 4.

Tom Seaver hurls the Mets into the Series with a 7–2 victory over the Reds. New York has 13 hits in the contest.

11th Catfish Hunter throws a 5-hitter as Oakland wins 3–0 to take the AL flag.

Ralph Houk signs a 3-year contract to manage the Detroit Tigers. He had resigned from the Yankees 11 days earlier.

13th In the WS opener, the Mets hold the A's to 4 hits, but 3 come in the 2-run 2nd inning, allowing the A's to win 2–1.

14th The Mets win game 2, 10–7, scoring 4 runs in an 11th inning featuring the last ML hit by Willie Mays and 2 errors by Oakland 2B Mike Andrews. Andrews is subsequently put on the "disabled list" by Finley, prompting Commissioner Kuhn to intervene. It is the longest WS game (4:13) in history.

16th The A's win game 3 of the WS 3–2 in 11 innings as Bert Campaneris gets the winning RBI. In a private clubhouse meeting, Dick Williams tells A's players he will resign after the Series.

17th The Mets even the Series with a 6–1 win in New York. Rusty Staub goes 4-for-4 with a HR and 5 RBI.

18th The Mets win the 5th game 2–0 behind the 3-hit pitching of Jerry Koosman and Tug McGraw. Cleon Jones doubles in a run in the second and Don Hahn's triple scores the other run.

20th Reggie Jackson hits 2 doubles, scores one run, and knocks in the other 2, as the A's even the Series with a 3–1 win.

21st Oakland wins the World Championship for the 2nd straight year as Campaneris and MVP Jackson homer in the 5–2, 7th-game victory.

22nd The Angels and Brewers engineer a 10-player swap featuring P Clyde Wright and OF Ken Berry going to Milwaukee, and P Skip Lockwood, C Ellie Rodriguez, and OF Ollie Brown heading to California.

23rd Charlie Finley reveals that he will not release Dick Williams from his contract unless he receives adequate compensation from the team that signs him. Williams had resigned following the WS victory 2 days earlier.

The Tigers trade 2B Dick McAuliffe to the Red Sox for OF Ben Oglivie.

25th The Cubs trade 6-time 20-game winner Ferguson Jenkins to the Rangers for 3B Bill Madlock and utility man Vic Harris. Meanwhile, the Giants trade 3-time HR champion Willie McCovey, a Giant since 1959, together with a minor leaguer, to the Padres for P Mike Caldwell.

26th The Red Sox trade P Ken Tatum and OF Reggie Smith to the Cardinals for P Rick Wise and OF Bernie Carbo.

31st The Astros trade P Jerry Reuss to the Pirates for C Milt May.

Tom Seaver wins the NL Cy Young Award, the first time the honor has gone to a player with fewer than 20 wins. Seaver was 19-10 and led the league in ERA (2.08) and strikeouts (251).

NOVEMBER

7th The Cubs trade 2B Glenn Beckert and a minor league player to the Padres for OF Jerry Morales.

14th Reggie Jackson wins the AL MVP Award unanimously. The Oakland star led the league in runs (99), HRs (32), RBI (117), and slugging (.531). Jim Palmer is named the AL Cy Young winner.

21st Pete Rose wins the NL MVP in a controversial vote, edging out Willie Stargell. Rose led the league with 230 hits and won his 3rd batting crown with a .338 mark. Stargell led with 44 HRs, 119 RBI, and a .646 slugging average while batting .299.

24th Bob Gibson wins the last of 9 Gold Gloves on the mound, and Joe Morgan wins the first of 5 at 2B.

27th Gary Matthews outpolls 8 other vote-getters, receiving 11 of 24 nominations for the NL Rookie of the Year Award. The Giants OF batted .300 in 145 games.

28th Oriole Al Bumbry beats out 5 other vote-getters to win AL Rookie of the Year honors. The OF played just 110 games, but tied for the league lead in triples (11) and batted .337.

DECEMBER

4th The Reds trade P Ross Grimsley to the Orioles for OF Merv Rettenmund.

5th Ron Santo becomes the first player to invoke the new 10 and 5 rule. The Cubs want to trade Santo to the Angels for 2 pitchers, but he vetoes the deal.

The Dodgers trade OF Willie Davis to the Expos for relief P Mike Marshall. Marshall will win the Cy Young Award for the Dodgers in 1974.

6th The Astros trade OF Jim Wynn to the Dodgers for P Claude Osteen and Dave Culpepper.

7th A controversial trade for Kansas City: they get veteran P Lindy McDaniel from the Yankees for OF Lou Piniella and P Ken Wright.

In a continuing housecleaning of hometown heroes, the Giants sell future Hall of Famer Juan Marichal to the Red Sox.

11th The Cubs come up with a team Ron Santo will agree to be traded to: Southside rivals the White Sox. P Steve Stone and 3 other players go to the Cubs.

18th The Yankees announce the signing of Dick Williams as manager, precipitating a legal showdown with Charlie Finley. Two days later, AL president Joe Cronin rules that the Yankees cannot sign Williams.

1974

JANUARY

1st Lee MacPhail takes over as AL president, succeeding Joe Cronin, who retires.

3rd Unable to pry Dick Williams away from Finley, the Yankees sign Bill Virdon as manager.

16th The BBWAA elects former Yankee teammates Mickey Mantle and Whitey Ford to the Hall of Fame. Mantle becomes only the 7th player to make it in his first try.

25th Ray Kroc, fast-food entrepreneur (McDonald's), buys the Padres for $12 million.

28th The Hall of Fame Special Veterans Committee selects Sam Thompson, Jim Bottomley, and umpire Jocko Conlan.

FEBRUARY

11th Forty-eight ML players invoke the new arbitration procedure established to settle contract differences. The first is P Dick Woodson (seeking a contract for $29,000) and his team, the Twins (offering $23,000), who present their respective cases to Detroit lawyer and labor arbitrator Harry H. Platt, who must decide on one of the monetary amounts presented. Woodson wins.

13th Speedster James "Cool Papa" Bell is named for Hall of Fame honors by the Special Committee on the Negro Leagues.

MARCH

11th With Hank Aaron needing only one HR to tie Babe Ruth's career record (714), Atlanta plans to save the event for a home audience by benching him on the road. Commissioner Kuhn plans otherwise, ordering the Braves to start Aaron in at least 2 of the team's 3 season-opening games in Cincinnati.

15th Giants 24-game winner Ron Bryant is injured in a swimming pool accident in Yuma, AZ. His record will drop to 3-15 and he will never again be a consistent winner.

19th In a 3-team deal involving the Indians, Tigers, and Yankees, P Jim Perry joins his pitching brother,

Gaylord, in Cleveland. P Ed Farmer and OF No Neck Williams end up on the Yankees, while C Gerry Moses goes to the Motor City.

26th Boston releases future Hall of Famer SS Luis Aparicio, who retires, and DH Orlando Cepeda, who will sign with the Royals.

APRIL

3rd The Dodgers trade P Bruce Ellingsen to the Indians for 17-year-old minor league IF Pedro Guerrero.

4th In his first swing of the season, Hank Aaron hits a 3-run HR off Jack Billingham as the Braves lose to the Reds 7–6. It is HR 714 for Aaron to tie him with the Babe.

5th Streakers and strippers highlight the Opening Day game at Chicago's Comiskey Park. The Angels beat the White Sox 8–2.

8th In the 4th inning, of the Braves home opener against the Dodgers, Henry Aaron parks an Al Downing pitch in the left-CF stands for career HR 715, breaking Ruth's once thought to be unapproachable record. With former teammate Eddie Mathews watching as Braves manager, that makes 1,227 home runs for just 2 players. The Braves win 7-4.

9th New Padres owner Ray Kroc, watching his team losing their 4th straight, 9–2, in their home opener, takes to the public address system in the 8th inning: "Ladies and gentlemen, I suffer with you…. I've never seen such stupid baseball playing in my life." While he is speaking a streaker runs across the field. San Diego scores 3 but loses to Houston 9-5. Hearing of the incident, Commissioner Kuhn will make Kroc apologize to the fans.

12th Robin Yount, 18, collects his first ML hit for the Brewers during a 5–3 loss to the Orioles. The following day, Yount will get his 2nd hit against the O's—a game-winning home run.

14th Yankee Graig Nettles blasts 4 HRs during a doubleheader split with his former team, the Indians. Nettles will go on to tie the ML record with 11 HRs in the month of April.

17th Cubs C George Mitterwald hits a double and 3 HRs, including a grand slam, driving in 8 runs in an 18–9 win over the Pirates.

26th   Colorado defeats Nebraska 2–1 in an NCAA-record 22-inning game. James Smith has 10 at bats.

27th   The Yankees trade 4 pitchers, including Fritz Peterson and Steve Kline, to the Indians for 1B Chris Chambliss and hurlers Dick Tidrow and Cecil Upshaw.

29th   Lee May goes 5-for-5, including 2 homers in the 6th inning, as Houston destroys Chicago 18–2.

MAY

1st   Tom Seaver allows only 3 hits and 2 walks, striking out 16 Dodgers in 12 innings, but the Mets lose in the 14th 2–1.

Dock Ellis of the Pirates hits 3 batters with pitches in the first inning of a 5–3 loss to the Reds.

6th   Oakland P Paul Lindblad makes an errant throw in the first inning of a 6–3 loss to Baltimore. This ends Lindblad's ML-record streak of 385 consecutive errorless games, dating back to August 27, 1966.

27th   The Pirates Ken Brett no-hits the Padres until the 9th inning, settling for a 2-hit 6–0 shutout in the first game of the doubleheader. In the 2nd game, Brett's 2-run pinch triple gives the Bucs an 8–7 win.

30th   Sadaharu Oh becomes the first player in Japanese baseball to hit 600 HRs. Only Babe Ruth, Hank Aaron, and Willie Mays are ahead of Oh—and he will surpass them all.

JUNE

4th   On Ten-Cent Beer Night at Cleveland, unruly fans stumble onto the field and cause the Indians to forfeit the game to the Rangers with the score tied 5–5 in the 9th inning.

5th   Oakland's Reggie Jackson and Bill North engage in a clubhouse fight at Detroit. Jackson injures his shoulder, and Ray Fosse, attempting to separate the combatants, suffers a crushed disk in his neck which virtually ends his season.

7th   The Padres, with their 3rd number-one free-agent pick in 5 years, select Brown University SS Bill Almon. They had selected him 3 years earlier out of high school, but he attended college instead. The Rangers take P Tommy Boggs with the 2nd pick. The

Red Sox, picking 20th, take P Eddie Ford, son of Whitey Ford.

The Giants top Pittsburgh 6–2, dropping the last-place Pirates' record to 18-52, nine games out of first place.

10th   During a 12–0 win over the Astros, Phillie 3B Mike Schmidt hits a ball off the public address speaker hanging from the Astrodome roof, 117 feet up and 300 feet from the plate. Schmidt must settle for a titanic single.

11th   Mel Stottlemyre makes his 272nd consecutive start, with no relief appearances, to set an AL record.

13th   Henry Aaron addresses the House of Representatives in a special Flag Day ceremony. In the chamber is Representative Wilmer Mizell of North Carolina, who, as a southpaw hurler for the Cardinals, served up HR #61 in 1956 and #161 in 1959.

14th   Nolan Ryan strikes out 19 Red Sox in 13 innings, including Cecil Cooper 6 times in a row. The Angels finally win in 15 innings 4–3.

19th   George Scott, who walks to lead off the 2nd inning, is the Brewers' only base runner as the Royals Steve Busby hurls a 2–0 no-hitter. Busby is the first ML pitcher to throw no-hitters in his first 2 seasons.

Runners are passed in 2 different games tonight, depriving Giant Ed Goodson of a HR in a Cardinals-Giants match, and creating confusion in a Pirates 7–3 defeat of the Angels.

21st   The Braves fire manager Eddie Mathews, hiring Clyde King to replace him.

24th   Steve Busby retires the first 9 White Sox to set an AL record with 33 consecutive batsmen retired. The Royals lose, however, 3–1.

27th   The Angels fire manager Bobby Winkles. Whitey Herzog will serve as interim boss for 4 games before Dick Williams assumes the reins.

JULY

3rd   Pitching in his ML-record 13th consecutive game for the Dodgers, Mike Marshall saves Tommy John's 4–1 win over the Reds in the first game of a doubleheader.

4th Mike Marshall picks up a 3–2 win over Reds. Over the past 30 days, Marshall is 9-0 with 3 saves and a 1.82 ERA in 20 appearances.

8th Yankee SS Jim Mason ties the ML record with 4 doubles in a 12–5 win over the Rangers.

11th The Padres release OF Matty Alou. Matty's brother, Felipe, was released by the Brewers on April 29th. Younger brother Jesus keeps the Alou name alive in ML baseball, playing for the A's.

14th The Reds and Pirates split a doubleheader marked by a free-for-all which is later credited with inspiring Pittsburgh and turning its season around.

The Rangers Billy Martin is the first AL manager to be removed by umpires from 2 games in one day.

17th Cardinals pitching great Bob Gibson fans the Reds Cesar Geronimo to become the 2nd hurler to strike out 3,000 batters. Geronimo will become Nolan Ryan's 3,000th K victim 6 years later.

Milwaukee 3B Don Money commits a first-inning error in a 10–5 loss to Minnesota, ending his perfect defensive season after 86 games and 257 chances. Money holds both the NL and AL records for most consecutive chances without an error in a season.

19th Cleveland's Dick Bosman no-hits Oakland 4–0. He has no one but himself to blame for not picking up a rare perfect game. His throwing error in the 4th puts the only A's runner on base.

23rd The NL triumphs in the All-Star Game at Pittsburgh, winning 7–2. Write-in choice Dodger 1B Steve Garvey is the game's MVP.

24th Cubs manager Whitey Lockman steps aside and is replaced by Jim Marshall.

29th Detroit hits 4 consecutive HRs in the first inning in an 8–2 win over the Indians. Al Kaline, Bill Freehan, and Mickey Stanley hit consecutive HRs off Fritz Peterson, and Ed Brinkman connects off Steve Kline.

31st During a 7–4 loss to the Expos, the Cubs Bill Bonham strikes out 4 batters in the 2nd inning, tying the ML record.

Ron Cey drives in 8 runs to lead the Dodgers to a 15–4 victory over the Padres.

AUGUST

1st Detroit's Woodie Fryman stops Milwaukee 2–0, giving up just one hit, a 7th-inning single to Bobby Mitchell.

5th The Pirates win at Montreal, but lose 3B Jose Pagan when his arm is fractured by a pitch. He will return to be a WS hero.

7th As part of a youth movement, the Tigers release 1B Norm Cash and sell OF Jim Northrup to Montreal.

12th Mickey Mantle and Whitey Ford head a group of 6 inductees at Cooperstown.

Nolan Ryan strikes out 19 and walks only 2 as the Angels top the Red Sox 4–2.

17th Cleveland purchases former NL batting champ Rico Carty from Cordoba of the Mexican League. He will hit .363 for the rest of the season.

20th Nolan Ryan strikes out 19 in 11 innings, but loses to the Tigers 1–0 at Anaheim Stadium.

Davey Lopes of the Dodgers hits 3 HRs, a double, and a single in an 18–8 romp over the Cubs. The 15 total bases is the most ever for a leadoff hitter.

22nd Salem (Carolina League) OF Alfredo Edmead is killed in a collision with a teammate during a game with Rocky Mount. The cause of death is given as a massive skull fracture.

24th Davey Lopes steals 5 bases as the Dodgers top the Cardinals 5–0. He is thrown out on his 6th attempt.

27th New York's Benny Ayala homers in his first ML at bat as the Mets top the Astros 4–2.

Hal McRae ties the ML record with 6 extra-base hits—5 doubles and a HR—as the Royals split a doubleheader with the Indians.

28th The Orioles lose to Rangers 4–2, dropping their record to 65-65, 8 games behind the front-running Red Sox.

30th The Rangers Dave Nelson steals 2B, 3B, and home in the same inning, only the 3rd such performance in the major leagues since 1928, but it's not enough as Texas loses to Cleveland 7–3.

31st Portland Mavericks manager Frank Peters rotates his players so that each man plays one inning at each position. It works: Portland beats Tri-Cities (Northwest League) 8–7.

SEPTEMBER

1st   During a 5–3 win over the Tigers, the A's 1B Gene Tenace goes through the entire game without a fielding chance—only the 4th time in ML history that has occurred in that position. In the same game, Detroit's Reggie Sanders homers in his first ML AB.

Lou Brock steals 4 bases in an 8–1 win over the Giants. This gives him 98 steals for the year.

2nd   Boston allows only 2 runs in doubleheader, yet loses both games to Baltimore. Ross Grimsley and Mike Cuellar toss twin 1–0 shutouts.

3rd   The Giants John Montefusco makes his ML debut, homers in his first official time at bat, and pitches 9 innings of relief to earn a 9–5 victory over the Dodgers.

4th   Don Wilson has a no-hitter through 8 innings, but is lifted for a PH by Houston manager Preston Gomez. Reliever Mike Cosgrove gives up a hit, and the Astros lose to the Reds 2–1. Gomez made the same mistake in San Diego on July 21, 1970.

6th   Baltimore sweeps a doubleheader from Cleveland 2–0 and 1–0. Dave McNally and Mike Cuellar notch the 4th and 5th consecutive shutouts for the Orioles, who set an AL record with 54 straight scoreless innings pitched.

7th   During a 3–1 win over Chicago, California's Nolan Ryan has a fastball clocked at 100.8 miles per hour—the fastest pitch ever recorded.

In a game with the Tigers, Graig Nettles loses a single when it is discovered he is using a corked bat. The Yankees win 1–0 on Nettles's earlier HR.

10th   The Cardinals lose to the Phillies 8–2, but Lou Brock breaks Maury Wills's ML record by stealing his 104th and 105th bases of the season. It also gives him 740 career SBs, breaking Max Carey's NL record of 738.

11th   The Mets lose a marathon night game after 7 hours 4 minutes, and 25 innings, the longest game to a decision in ML history. Two Mets errors lead to the Cardinals' winning run. The final is St. Louis 4, New York 3.

13th   The Phillies set an NL record by using 27 players during a 17-inning 7–3 loss to the Cardinals. The Cards had set the record 2 days earlier.

With 16 games remaining, the enigmatic Dick Allen of the White Sox announces he is quitting the team. His 32 HRs, the last of which was hit August 16th, will still be enough to lead the AL.

14th   Graig Nettles homers for the Yankees in the first inning, and brother Jim Nettles homers for the Tigers in the 2nd. Graig's team wins 10–7.

17th   St. Louis beats Pittsburgh 2–1 in 13 innings. It is the 6th straight win for the Cardinals and the 6th straight loss for the Pirates, turning the Bucs' 3½ game lead in the NL East to a 2½ game margin for the Cards.

24th   Al Kaline doubles off Dave McNally for his 3,000th career hit, as the Tigers beat the Orioles 5–4.

Clarence Jones of the Kintetsu Buffaloes hits his 38th HR to become the first American to win a Japanese HR title. He will win again with 36 HRs in 1976.

27th   Baltimore breaks a scoreless tie with the Brewers in the 17th inning to pull out a 1–0 win.

28th   Nolan Ryan pitches his 3rd career no-hitter, victimizing the Twins 4–0. In the process, an Angels hurler strikes out 15 batters for the 6th time this season.

Astro Don Wilson 2-hits the Braves 5–0. It would be Wilson's last ML game, followed barely 3 months later by his suicide.

29th   Lou Brock steals his 118th, and final, base of the season as the Cardinals top the Cubs 7–3.

OCTOBER

1st   The Orioles beat the Tigers 7–6. When the Brewers beat the Yankees 3–2 in 10 innings, the O's become the AL East champions.

2nd   In the Rangers' season finale, Billy Martin allows Ferguson Jenkins to hit for himself rather than use the DH, the first such incident in the AL all season. Jenkins singles to break up the Twins Jim Hughes's no-hitter, scores the Rangers' first run, and goes on to win his 25th game of the season 2–1.

During a 13–0 win over Reds, the Braves Hank Aaron homers off Rawly Eastwick. It is Aaron's 733rd career clout and comes in his last NL at bat.

3rd   Frank Robinson becomes the first black manager in the major leagues, as the Indians name him to replace Ken Aspromonte for the 1975 season.

5th Don Sutton notches a 4-hit shutout to give the Dodgers a 3–0 win over the Pirates in the NL Championship Series opener.

The Orioles beat the A's 6–3 in the AL opener as Paul Blair, Bobby Grich, and Brooks Robinson blast homers.

6th Ron Cey cracks a HR, 2 doubles, and a single, and the Dodgers win the 2nd LCS game 5–2.

The A's even the AL series behind Ken Holtzman's 5–0 shutout and homers by Ray Fosse and Sal Bando.

8th Sal Bando homers again and Vida Blue hurls a 2-hitter to give the A's a 1–0 win and a 2-1 lead in the LCS. Blue fans 7 and walks none.

The Pirates stay alive with a 7–0 win in the NL game as Bruce Kison gets the win. Richie Hebner and Willie Stargell drive in 6 runs between them.

9th Los Angeles advances to the WS with a 12–1 win over the Bucs. Steve Garvey has 2 singles and 2 doubles, and scores 4 runs as Don Sutton wins his 2nd LCS game and 11th in a row.

The A's get just one hit, but draw 11 walks, 9 off loser Mike Cuellar, in beating the Orioles 2–1. Cueller walks Gene Tenace in the 6th to force in a run, and Reggie Jackson doubles in the winning run in the 7th.

10th Former Oakland 2B Mike Andrews files a $2.5 million lawsuit against Charlie Finley over his treatment during the 1973 WS.

11th It is revealed that Oakland ace Hunter has charged owner Charlie Finley with a breach of contract.

12th Oakland slugging star Reggie Jackson connects for a homer off Andy Messersmith to start the scoring, and pitcher Ken Holtzman scores the 2nd run in the 5th on a suicide squeeze. The A's win the WS opener 3–2 as the Dodgers strand 12 base runners.

Sadaharu Oh draws his 166th walk in a 130-game season, setting a Japanese record. At his retirement in 1980, Oh will hold the all-time world record for walks, 2,504, topping Babe Ruth's record of 2,056.

13th Hall of Fame OF Sam Rice dies at Rossmor, Maryland, at age 84, leaving a letter—opened at Cooperstown—confirming his controversial catch in the 1925 WS.

Los Angeles, behind Don Sutton, evens the Series with a 3–2 win. The Dodgers score in the 2nd off Vida Blue, and a 2-run HR by Joe Ferguson in the 6th provides the margin

15th In a Tuesday night game, the surprise starter for the Dodgers is Al Downing. But Catfish Hunter is too much for LA, and Oakland wins another 3–2 game.

16th Ken Holtzman, who hadn't hit all season, belts a 3rd-inning HR and gets the win 5–2 with Rollie Fingers in relief. Oakland scores 4 in the 6th to wrap up the 4th game 5–2.

17th Vida Blue and Don Sutton are tied 2–2 going into the bottom of the 6th when Mike Marshall relieves and retires the side. In the 7th, a shower of debris halts the game for 15 minutes. When play is resumed, Joe Rudi hits Marshall's first pitch for a homer to give the the A's a 3rd 3–2 win, clinching a 3rd straight World Championship for the team.

22nd The Giants and Yankees swap popular star outfielders: Bobby Bonds goes to the Yankees and Bobby Murcer heads to San Francisco.

23rd The Cubs trade sweet-swinging Billy Williams, a fixture at Wrigley for 16 years, to the A's for 2B Manny Trillo and pitchers Darold Knowles and Bob Locker.

Wally Yonamine, an American of Japanese descent, becomes the only non-Japanese manager ever to win the Japan Series when his Chunichi Dragons beat the Lotte Orions.

30th Catfish Hunter is named the AL Cy Young Award winner. He led the league with 25 wins and a 2.49 ERA.

NOVEMBER

2nd The Braves trade Hank Aaron to the Brewers for OF Dave May and a minor league pitcher to be named later. Aaron will finish his ML career in Milwaukee, where he started it in 1954.

Hank Aaron, the HR king of American baseball, and Sadaharu Oh, his Japanese counterpart, square off for a HR contest at Korakuen Stadium. Aaron wins 10–9.

6th The Dodgers Mike Marshall becomes the first relief pitcher to win the Cy Young Award. Ironman Marshall set ML records with 106 appearances and 208 innings in relief.

13th The Dodgers Steve Garvey wins the NL MVP Award with a .312 BA, 21 HRs, and 111 RBI.

20th Jeff Burroughs, the Texas OF who batted .301 with 25 HRs and a league-leading 118 RBI, wins the AL MVP Award.

25th Mike Hargrove of the Rangers takes AL Rookie of the Year honors.

26th Catfish Hunter meets with Charlie Finley in the American Arbitration Association office in New York City for a hearing to determine the validity of Hunter's breach-of-contract claim. Hunter contends that Finley failed to pay $50,000, half of Hunter's salary, to a life insurance fund. The case will go to arbitration.

27th Cardinal OF Bake McBride wins the NL Rookie of the Year Award.

Bowie Kuhn suspend Yankees owner George Steinbrenner for 2 years as a result of Steinbrenner's conviction for illegal campaign contributions to Richard Nixon and others.

DECEMBER

2nd The Red Sox trade OF Tommy Harper to the Angels for IF Bob Heise.

The ML Rules Committee meets in New Orleans. Among the changes is one permitting the use of cowhide, rather than just horsehide, in the manufacture of baseballs.

3rd The Mets trade ace reliever and Shea Stadium favorite Tug McGraw to the Phillies in a 6-player swap, the Astros trade 1B Lee May to the Orioles in a 4-player deal, and the White Sox unload controversial Dick Allen to the Braves. Allen never reports.

4th The Expos trade OF Ken Singleton and P Mike Torrez to the Orioles for P Dave McNally, OF Rich Coggins, and a minor league pitcher.

9th Bobby Tolan traded by Cincinnati for P Clay Kirby on November 9, 1973, finally signs a 1974 contract with the Padres, leading to a withdrawal of the grievance initiated by the Players' Association on his behalf.

13th Catfish Hunter wins his claim against Finley and is declared a free agent by arbitrator Peter Seitz.

19th The race to sign Hunter begins in the law offices of Cherry, Cherry & Flythe in Ahoskie, North Carolina. Yankee and Red Sox representatives are the first arrivals.

31st The Yankees sign Hunter to a 5-year contract worth a reported $3.75 million. This is triple the salary of any other ML player.

1975

JANUARY

5th   Astros P Don Wilson is found dead of monoxide poisoning in his garage in Houston, a suicide victim at age 29.

23rd   Ralph Kiner earns Hall of Fame membership by a single vote.

FEBRUARY

3rd   Billy Herman, Earl Averill, and Bucky Harris are selected for the Hall of Fame by the Special Veterans Committee.

10th   The Special Committee on the Negro Leagues picks William "Judy" Johnson for the Hall of Fame.

25th   The Orioles trade 1B Boog Powell and P Don Hood to the Indians for C Dave Duncan and a minor league OF.

28th   The Mets purchase 1B-OF Dave Kingman from the Giants.

MARCH

5th   Tony Conigliaro signs a contract with Pawtucket (International League) in an attempt to make a comeback.

15th   The Dodgers sign free-agent pitcher Juan Marichal. After two poor outings, Marichal will retire on April 17th, leaving a career record of 243-142, 52 shutouts, and a 2.89 ERA.

21st   Georgia Tech shuts out Earlham 41–0, setting an NCAA record for scoring and for winning margin.

APRIL

5th   The Phillies trade OF Bill Robinson to the Pirates for P Wayne Simpson.

6th   The Astros purchase P Joe Niekro from the Braves.

7th   The Reds open against the Dodgers and go 14 innings before George Foster's infield hit scores the winner 2–1.

8th   Frank Robinson, making his debut as the Indians player-manager, homers in his first at bat (as a DH) during a 5–3 win over the Yankees. It is Robby's 8th Opening Day HR, setting a ML record.

10th   Oakland's Mike Norris shuts out Chicago 9–0 in his ML debut.

17th   During a 14–7 loss to the Mets, the Cardinals Ted Simmons homers from both sides of the plate, while teammate 2B Ted Sizemore ties a ML record with 3 errors in the 6th inning.

23rd   The Yankees Roy White again homers from both sides of the plate, this time in an 11–7 loss to the Red Sox. White last hit switch-hit HRs on August 13, 1973.

25th   The Dodgers Andy Messersmith beats the Giants 6–5 and ties a batting record for pitchers with 3 doubles in one game.

27th   During a 4–3 loss to the Giants, the Reds Johnny Bench suffers a shoulder injury in a home-plate collision with Gary Matthews. Bench will undergo surgery in November.

MAY

1st   Hank Aaron goes 4-for-4, driving in 2 runs in the Brewers 17–3 win over Detroit. This brings his career RBI total to 2,211, breaking Babe Ruth's published record of 2,209. On February 3, 1976, the Records Committee will revise Ruth's total to 2,204; so, in actuality, Aaron set the record on April 18, 1975.

2nd   Cubs P Burt Hooton is traded to the Dodgers for pitchers Geoff Zahn and Eddie Solomon.

3rd   The Reds switch Pete Rose from left field to 3B, opening a lineup spot for utility OF George Foster. Over the next 4 seasons, Foster will average 36 HRs, 117 RBI, and a .302 BA, helping the Reds to two World Championships.

4th   The Giants beat the Astros 8–6 in the first game of a doubleheader at Candlestick. In the 2nd inning, Houston's Bob Watson scores what is calculated as ML baseball's one-millionth run of all time (the Philadelphia Nationals Wes Fisler scored the first run on April 22, 1876).

Met Cleon Jones is arrested in St. Petersburg, Florida, after the police find him naked in a van with a teenage girl who is holding a stash of narcotics. Jones tells the cops that he is "C. Joseph Jones, a laborer."

5th Oakland releases pinch runner Herb Washington. Washington played in 104 ML games without batting, pitching, or fielding, stole 30 bases, and scored 33 runs.

7th The Braves trade C Johnny Oates, along with the contract of Dick Allen, to the Phillies for 2 players and cash. Allen had refused to report to Atlanta following his trade from the White Sox on December 3, 1974.

12th The Royals leave 15 men on base without scoring in a 5–0 loss to the Tigers.

19th San Diego's Randy Jones hurls a 10-inning one-hitter in beating St. Louis 1–0.

20th The Indians trade pitchers Dick Bosman and Jim Perry to the A's for P Blue Moon Odom and cash.

21st The Reds, entering the game with a 20-20 record, 5 games behind the first-place Dodgers, come from behind to beat the Mets 11–4. Cincinnati will go on to win 41 of 50 games and run away with the National League West title.

25th Cleveland's Dennis Eckersley, in his first ML start, hurls a 3-hit shutout in beating Oakland 6–0.

Mickey Lolich's 200th career victory is a rain-shortened, 4–1 win over the White Sox. His catcher is Bill Freehan, who also caught him in his first ML start May 21, 1963.

30th Willie McCovey's grand slam lifts the Padres over the Mets 6–2. It is McCovey's 3rd career pinch slam, tying the ML record held by Ron Northey and Rich Reese. It is Stretch's 16th lifetime bases-loaded homer, tying the NL record held by Aaron.

31st Cesar Tovar gets the only hit for Texas, the 5th time in his career he has had his team's lone hit in a game. The Yankees Catfish Hunter hurls the one-hit 6–0 victory.

Andy Messersmith gets a loss and a save for the Dodgers in Chicago. In a game continued from the previous day, he saves a 3–1 win for Don Sutton, then loses 2–1 to the Cubs on 2 solo HRs.

The Royals beat the Brewers 7–5 in a game bridging the generation gap. Home run leaders Henry Aaron and Harmon Killebrew are in their 22nd ML seasons and winning pitcher Lindy McDaniel is in his 21st. All

three were playing in the majors before Brewers SS Robin Yount was born.

JUNE

1st The Angels Nolan Ryan pitches his 4th career no-hitter, winning 1–0 over the Orioles, to tie the record set by Sandy Koufax. Ryan strikes out 9 and runs his record to 9-3.

4th Danny Goodwin, picked first in the June 1971 free-agent draft, is picked first again, this time by the Angels. The next 4 picks fail to make the major leagues. Montreal finally picks Andre Dawson on the 10th round and the Braves take Glenn Hubbard in the 20th.

Lee Mazzilli of the Visalia Oaks (California) ties the minor league record when he steals 7 bases. He will end the year with 49.

6th Nolan Ryan's bid for a 2nd no-hitter in a row is foiled by Hank Aaron's single in the 6th inning. Ryan gives up one other hit in overpowering the Brewers 6–0.

Cleveland Manager Frank Robinson shows his players how to hit as he connects for two 3-run homers in a 7–5 win over the Rangers.

9th The Dodgers beat the Expos 4–0 and go over the one million mark in home attendance in only their 27th date. This breaks the ML record of 28 days set by the 1948 Indians.

10th The Yankees sponsor Army Day at their temporary home, Shea Stadium (Yankee Stadium is being refurbished). During a ceremonial 21-gun salute, glass is splintered, the park is filled with smoke, part of the fence is blown away, and another part is set afire.

12th Milwaukee defeats Oakland 9–7 to move within 4 games of first. Oakland's Billy Williams's 400th career HR is matched by Hank Aaron's first HR in Milwaukee since 1965.

13th The Indians trade P Gaylord Perry to the Rangers for hurlers Jim Bibby, Jackie Brown, Rick Waits, and an estimated $100,000.

The Yankees Elliott Maddox, hitting .305, is sidelined for the remainder of the season with torn cartilage in his knee. The injury occurs in a fall on the wet Shea Stadium turf during a 2–1 win over the White Sox.

18th Boston rookie Fred Lynn drives in 10 runs with 3 HRs, a triple, and a single during a 15–1 drubbing of Detroit. Lynn's 16 total bases tie an AL record. He is hitting .340 with 14 HRs.

21st The Angels Frank Tanana strikes out 17 Rangers without a walk during a 4–2 win.

30th Baltimore C Dave Duncan ties the ML record with 4 consecutive doubles during an 8–2 win over Boston.

JULY

2nd In a 13–5 win over Detroit, Baltimore C Don Baylor homers his first 3 times up, giving him 4 consecutive HRs over 2 games to tie the ML record.

3rd Fred Lynn's 2nd error of the game allows the Brewers to score in the 10th. The 3–2 win lifts the Brewers into a tie with Boston in the AL East. Milwaukee will fall flat in August and slide to a 5th place finish.

15th The NL rallies for 3 runs in the 9th inning to win the All-Star Game at Milwaukee 6–3. The Cubs Bill Madlock and the Mets Jon Matlack share the game's MVP award.

16th Commissioner Bowie Kuhn is reelected for a 7-year term.

19th Yankee C Thurman Munson's first-inning single and RBI against the Twins are nullified because the tar on his bat handle exceeds the 18-inch limit. Catcher Glenn Borgmann gets the putout.

21st The Mets Felix Millan has 4 straight singles but is wiped out each time when Joe Torre grounds into 4 straight DPs. New York loses 6–2 to the Astros.

Ted Simmons has a 4th-inning HR erased because his grooved bat is illegal. The Cardinals play the game under protest but beat the Padres anyway as rookie Harry Rasmussen wins his ML debut 4–0.

23rd Willie Crawford and Lee Lacy each connect for 9th-inning pinch HRs, but the Dodgers lose anyway 5–4 to the Cardinals.

24th The Royals fire manager Jack McKeon, hiring Whitey Herzog to replace him.

26th Bill Madlock goes 6-for-6 during the Cubs 10-inning 9–8 loss to the Mets.

27th The Mets release OF Cleon Jones, following a suspension for insubordination. He will not be picked up by another team this year, but will play for the White Sox in 1976.

30th P Jose Sosa homers in his first ML at bat as the Astros beat the Padres 8–4. It will be Sosa's only HR in the majors.

AUGUST

2nd Billy Martin becomes the new Yankee manager, replacing Bill Virdon, named by TSN as last year's Manager of the Year. He won't be out of a job for long.

5th The first 8 Phillies hit safely in a game against Bill Bonham and the Cubs, setting a ML record.

6th The Mets fire manager Yogi Berra, promoting coach Roy McMillan as interim skipper.

9th Davey Lopes steals his 32nd consecutive base for the Dodgers without being caught in a 2–0 win over the Mets. This breaks the ML record set by Max Carey in 1922.

13th The A's release P Jim Perry and purchase OF Tommy Harper from the Angels.

15th Frank Tanana pitches an 8–0 shutout as the Angels hand the Tigers their 19th straight loss.

17th During the Reds' 3–1 win over the Pirates, Pete Rose singles off Bruce Kison for career hit number 2,500.

19th The Astros hire Bill Virdon to replace Preston Gomez as manager.

The Cardinals Lynn McGlothen strikes out 3 Reds on 9 pitches in the 2nd inning of a 2–1 victory.

21st Pitching brothers Rick and Paul Reuschel combine to hurl the Cubs to a 7–0 victory over the Dodgers—the first time brothers have collaborated on a shutout.

22nd The Twins Dave McKay homers in his first ML at bat during an 8–4 win over the Tigers.

24th In San Francisco, the Giants Ed Halicki pitches a no-hitter in beating the Mets 6–0 in the 2nd game of a doubleheader.

Lou Brock steals the 800th base of his career as the Cardinals beat the visiting Braves 6–2.

After stealing 2B in the 7th to add to his ML-record of 38 consecutive steals, Davey Lopes is nabbed in the 12th by Montreal C Gary Carter. The Expos score 3 in the 14th off Mike Marshall to beat the Dodgers 5–2.

25th Astro Cliff Johnson hits a HR in the top of the 11th for his 6th in 6 consecutive games, pushing his team to a 4–3 lead. Unfortunately, the game is called due to rain in the bottom half of the inning, and the score reverts to what it was in the 10th, thus erasing Johnson's HR. It deprives Johnson of becoming only the 2nd NL player to hit 6 HRs in 6 consecutive games.

26th The first 8 Pirates hit safely against the Braves, tying the ML record set just 3 weeks earlier by the Phillies.

27th The Twins Craig Kusick ties the ML record by being hit with pitches 3 times in one game, an 11-inning 1–0 win over the Brewers.

29th Chicago's Ken Henderson homers from both sides of the plate during a 4–2 win over Baltimore.

30th The Braves fire Clyde King, naming Connie Ryan as interim manager.

SEPTEMBER

1st Mets ace Tom Seaver shuts out the Pirates 3–0 and reaches 200 strikeouts for a ML-record 8th straight season.

2nd Johnny LeMaster homers in his first ML at bat for the Giants during a 7–3 win over Dodgers. In 12 years and 3,191 at bats, LeMaster will hit only 22 home runs.

3rd After missing 2 games because of the flu, Dodger Steve Garvey returns to the lineup for a 13–2 loss to the Reds, launching a NL record streak of 1,207 consecutive games.

5th Mets C Jerry Grote ties the modern ML record by reaching base on errors 3 times during a 5–2 win over the Cardinals.

7th The Reds clinch the NL West flag with an 8–4 win over the Giants. It is the earliest clinching date in league history.

9th The Cubs Bill Madlock suffers an "incomplete fracture" of his right thumb when hit by a Bruce Kison pitch in a 6–5 win over the Pirates.

14th The Red Sox top the Brewers 8–6 as Robin Yount breaks Mel Ott's 47-year-old record by playing in his 242nd game as a teenager.

15th Late-season call-up Mike Vail extends his hitting streak to a rookie-record 23 straight games as the Mets edge the Expos 3–2.

16th Rennie Stennett ties Wilbert Robinson's ML record, set June 10, 1892, by going 7-for-7 in a 9-inning game. The Pirates 2B collects 2 hits each in the first and 5th innings, and scores 5 of his club's runs in a 22–0 massacre of the Cubs.

20th The A's and Royals set an AL record by using 42 players in a 9-inning game. Oakland wins 16–4.

21st During a 6–5 win over Detroit, Boston rookie star Jim Rice breaks his arm, sidelining him for the rest of the year, including the WS. The Red Sox maintain their 3½ game lead over the Orioles.

26th Burt Hooton wins his 12th straight game, beating J.R. Richard and the Astros 3–2. Happy's 12 in a row is a Dodger record for starting pitchers.

28th In a ML first, 4 pitchers share in a no-hitter, as the A's shut down the Angels 5–0. Vida Blue, Glenn Abbott, Paul Lindblad, and Rollie Fingers are the unique quartet. This is a tune up for the LCS opener against Boston the following Saturday.

Two hours before game time, Milwaukee fires manager Del Crandall. Harvey Kuenn fills in as the Brewers win their finale 7–0. George Scott drives in 2 runs to give him the AL lead with 109.

OCTOBER

1st Montreal fires manager Gene Mauch. Karl Kuehl is named to succeed Mauch.

4th The Reds Don Gullett hurls a complete game, and contributes a HR, a single, and 3 RBI to lead his team to an 8–3 win over Pittsburgh in the opening game of the NL Championship Series. Boston, behind Luis Tiant's 3-hitter, beats Oakland 7–1 in the AL opener.

5th Carl Yastrzemski's 2-run HR is the big blow as the Red Sox win the 2nd LCS game 6–3.

The Reds also win for the 2nd time 6–1, as Tony Perez drives in 3 runs with a HR and single.

7th Pittsburgh's John Candelaria strikes out 14 Reds, but is knocked out of the box by Pete Rose's 8th-inning HR. The Reds complete their sweep of the LCS with a 5–3 win.

The Red Sox match Cincinnati with a 5–3 win and 3-game sweep over Oakland. Yastrzemski makes 2 great plays in the OF and has 2 hits to back Rick Wise's pitching.

Dick Moss, attorney for the Players' Association, files a suit in behalf of Dodgers P Andy Messersmith, contending that Messersmith, having completed his renewal year, now qualifies as a free agent. The All-Star pitcher will finally sign with the Braves after furious bidding.

11th Boston's Luis Tiant shuts down the Big Red Machine and scores the first run as the Red Sox win the opening game of the 1975 WS 6–0.

12th Down 2–1 in the 9th inning, the Reds rally to win the 2nd game 3–2.

14th In a game featuring 6 HRs, 3 by each team, the Reds prevail 6–5 in the 10th inning. The game is marred by a controversial play involving Cincinnati's Ed Armbrister and Boston's Carlton Fisk. Armbrister lays down a sacrifice bunt in the 10th and seemingly hesitates breaking out of the batter's box; Fisk's subsequent throwing error leads to the Reds winning run. The Sox claim interference, to no avail.

15th Luis Tiant throws 163 pitches in winning his 2nd game 5–4, and evening the Series at 2 games apiece.

16th Tony Perez breaks out of an 0-for-15 Series slump with 2 HRs and 4 RBI, as the Reds win the 5th game 6–2. Don Gullett goes 8⅔ innings for the win.

17th The A's fire manager Alvin Dark.

20th For the 3rd consecutive day, rain postpones game 6 of the WS.

21st Fred Lynn's 3-run first-inning HR is matched by teammate Bernie Carbo's pinch 3-run HR in the 8th to tie the game at 6-all. The Sox then fill the bases with no outs in the 9th but fail to bring in a run. But Boston evens the Series again with a dramatic 7–6 victory, won by Fisk's 12th-inning HR off the LF foul pole.

22nd The Sox take a 3–0 lead but the Reds rally to tie it in the 7th. Jim Willoughby is relieved by Jim Burton and Joe Morgan's single wins the deciding game 4–3. Rose is named the WS MVP.

24th Club owners, through the Player Relations Committee, respond to the October 7th Andy Messersmith suit, contending that "claims made by the [Players'] Association are not within the scope of the arbitration panel."

29th Boston's Fred Lynn is the overwhelming choice as AL Rookie of the Year.

30th Giants P John "the Count of" Montefusco outpoints Expos C Gary Carter to win NL Rookie of the Year honors.

NOVEMBER

4th The Orioles Jim Palmer wins his 2nd Cy Young Award, after pacing the AL in wins (23), shutouts (10), and ERA (2.09).

10th The Royals release slugger Harmon Killebrew, ending a 22-year career marked by 573 HRs, good for 5th on the all-time list.

12th The Mets Tom Seaver wins his 3rd Cy Young Award. He led the NL with 22 wins, notched 243 strikeouts, and had a 2.38 ERA.

17th The Dodgers trade outfielders Jim Wynn and Tom Paciorek, and infielders Lee Lacy and Jerry Royster to the Braves for OF Dusty Baker and 1B Ed Goodson.

The Rangers trade 7-time 20-game winner Ferguson Jenkins to the Red Sox for OF Juan Beniquez, 2 pitchers, and cash.

19th By the most overwhelming margin ever, the Reds Joe Morgan is named NL MVP. Morgan batted .327, with 67 SBs, and a league-leading 132 walks.

20th The Giants fire manager Wes Westrum, coaxing Bill Rigney out of retirement to replace him.

22nd The Yankees trade P Pat Dobson to the Indians for OF Oscar Gamble.

24th Gene Mauch signs a 3-year contract to manage the Twins, replacing the fired Frank Quilici.

26th Fred Lynn becomes the first rookie to win MVP honors, taking the AL award. Lynn batted .331

with 21 HRs, 105 RBI, and league-leading figures in runs (103), doubles (47), and slugging (.566).

29th Two Orioles standouts, with a combined total of 24 Gold Glove Awards, are each honored for the last time. Brooks Robinson and Paul Blair are the two making swan songs on TSN fielding team, while outfielders Garry Maddox and Fred Lynn each win the award for the first time.

DECEMBER

4th Ted Turner enters a tentative purchase agreement to buy the Atlanta Braves.

11th In two separate deals, the Yankees acquire pitchers Dock Ellis and Ken Brett, and 2B Willie Randolph from the Pirates for P Doc Medich; and OF Mickey Rivers and P Ed Figueroa from the Angels for OF Bobby Bonds.

12th The Mets trade OF Rusty Staub and P Bill Laxton to the Tigers for P Mickey Lolich and OF Billy Baldwin.

16th The colorful Bill Veeck returns. A group headed by him buys 80 percent of the White Sox from John Allyn.

17th Veeck fires Chuck Tanner and hires old friend Paul Richards to manage the White Sox.

18th Chuck Tanner signs a 3-year contract to manage Oakland.

23rd Arbitrator Peter Seitz announces a landmark decision in favor of the Players' Association, making pitchers Andy Messersmith and Dave McNally free agents. Seitz is immediately fired by John Gaherin, chairman of the owners' Player Relations Committee. McNally, who retired June 8th, will not return to the ML, finishing with a 184-119 career record.

1976

JANUARY

4th Executives of the International Amateur Baseball Association (IABA) meet in Mexico City to end a long-standing feud between delegations, creating in the process a new organization named the Asociacion Internacional de Beisbol Amateur (AINBA). With the United States returning to the IABA fold, after a several-year absence, the first AINBA World Championships are scheduled for Cartagena, Colombia. Manuel Gonzalez Guerra of Cuba is named the first AINBA president.

9th Charles Ruppert, Giants VP and son-in-law of Horace Stoneham, announces the sale of the team to a Toronto group for $13.3 million. The fans' outrage prompts San Francisco mayor George Moscone to get a preliminary injunction preventing the move.

14th Ted Turner completes the purchase of 100 percent of the Atlanta Braves.

22nd Pitchers Robin Roberts and Bob Lemon are voted into the Hall of Fame.

FEBRUARY

1st East Lansing police arrest Dodger reliever Mike Marshall for disobeying the orders set by the Michigan State University police prohibiting him from taking batting practice. MSU feared he would hit balls too far and injure students on an adjacent tennis court. Marshall protests that it is against his rights as an MSU instructor and files a lawsuit against the school.

2nd The Special Veterans Committee selects old-time players Roger Connor and Fred Lindstrom, and umpire Cal Hubbard, for Cooperstown. Hubbard becomes the first man elected to both the Football and Baseball Halls of Fame.

4th Federal Judge John W. Oliver upholds Peter Seitz's decision in the Andy Messersmith free agency case.

9th Oscar Charleston is selected for the Hall of Fame by the Special Committee on the Negro Leagues.

17th Mike Scott of Pepperdine pitches a 3–0 perfect game against California Lutheran University. He will be selected in the 2nd round of the June draft.

23rd ML owners announce that spring training will not open until a new labor contract is agreed upon.

MARCH

1st White Sox owner Bill Veeck opens training camp in Sarasota, Florida, but participation is limited to nonroster players.

2nd The Cubs trade 2B Ted Sizemore to the Dodgers for OF Willie Crawford.

4th In a last-minute deal, the Giants are bought for $8 million by Bob Lurie and Bud Herseth, assuring that team will stay in San Francisco.

17th Commissioner Kuhn orders teams to open spring training camps as soon as possible. All teams will comply within 48 hours.

20th Leo Durocher, hired to manage the Yokohama Taiyo Whales (Japanese League), is sick with hepatitis and asks for a 5-week delay in reporting. The Lip receives a telegram from the Whales stating: Since the championship starts in 20 days, it's better if you stay home and take care of yourself for the remainder of the season."

26th The AL approves the purchase of the new Toronto franchise by the LaBatt's Brewing Company for $7 million.

28th A nearly completed Mets-Dodgers trade, involving ace pitchers Tom Seaver and Don Sutton, is leaked by the New York press. The subsequent public furor causes the Mets to abandon the deal.

APRIL

2nd The A's trade prospective free agents Reggie Jackson and Ken Holtzman, together with a minor league pitcher, to the Orioles for OF Don Baylor and pitchers Mike Torrez and Paul Mitchell.

8th The Brewers open against the Yankees with Hank Aaron driving in 3 runs to back Jim Slaton's 4-hit 5–0 win. Five days later, Slaton will shut out the Tigers.

9th In a classic Opening Day pitchers' duel between the Orioles Jim Palmer and the Red Sox Fergie Jenkins, who would combine for 552 ML wins, Palmer prevails 1–0.

10th The Braves sign free agent Andy Messersmith to a "lifetime contract" worth $1 million.

In the opener in Milwaukee, the Brewers trail 9–6 with the bases loaded in the bottom of the 9th inning at a full County Stadium. Because of crowd noise, Yankee relief P Dave Pagan does not hear the time-out called by 1B Chris Chambliss. Pagan pitches to Don Money, who hits a grand slam. Because of the time-out the HR is nullified. Money bats again, and hits a sacrifice fly. The final score is 9–7 and the Brewers protest the game.

12th The Dodgers-Braves game is rained out in Los Angeles, ending a streak of 724 straight games dating back to the team's first rainout on April 21, 1967. The Braves games of September 11th and 12th will also be rained out.

14th The Mets Dave Kingman hits a HR estimated at 630 feet during a game with the Cubs.

15th Newly remodeled Yankee Stadium is jammed with 52,613 fans for Opening Day ceremonies. The 1923 Yankee team is honored, and Bob Shawkey, winner of the 1923 Stadium opener, throws out the first ball. The Yankees beat the Twins 13–4 on 14 hits, but the only HRs are the 2 hit by Minnesota's Dan Ford.

17th Mike Schmidt leads a Phils' assault with a single, 4 consecutive HRs, and 8 RBI to overcome a 13–2 deficit and beat the Cubs in 10 innings 18–16.

20th Detroit C Milt May, acquired in December 1975, breaks his ankle and is out of action for the 1976 season.

24th Oakland's Bert Campaneris steals 5 bases in an 8–7 win over Cleveland.

25th Cubs OF Rick Monday snatches an American flag from 2 fans who are about to set it on fire in the outfield during a game at Dodger Stadium. The Dodgers win 5–4 in 10 innings. The next day, the Illinois legislature unanimously approves May 4th as Rick Monday Day.

MAY

2nd Jose Cardenal goes 6-for-7, including a double and a HR, driving in 4 runs, as the Cubs edge the Giants 6–5 in the 14-inning first game of a doubleheader.

5th The wind is blowing out at Wrigley as the Dodgers crank out a team-record 7 HRs to outslug the Cubs 14–12.

9th White Sox P Wilbur Wood suffers a fractured kneecap in a 4–2 win over the Tigers. Wood will miss the rest of the season.

13th The Royals beat the White Sox 13–2 as George Brett sets a ML record by collecting 3 hits for the 6th consecutive game. He breaks Rod Carew's record.

15th Mark Fidrych wins his first ML start, a complete-game 2-hit 2–1 victory over the Indians. The Bird holds the Indians hitless for 6 innings, talked to the ball, and tamps down the mound before toeing the rubber each inning.

26th In a scoreless game in Anaheim, Chicago's Ken Brett has a no-hitter with 2 out in the 9th when California's Jerry Remy tops a slow roller down the 3B line. 3B Jorge Orta lets the ball roll and, in a controversial ruling, it is scored a hit, though many thought it ought to be ruled an error. Brett gives up a hit in the 10th to ex-Sox Bill Melton but wins the game 1–0 in 11 innings.

28th Yankees Ed Figueroa and Tippy Martinez beat the Tigers 9–5 and hold Ron LeFlore hitless for the first time since April 17th. LeFlore had hit safely in 30 straight games.

29th The only HR of Joe Niekro's 22-year career comes at the expense of brother Phil as the Astros tie the Braves in the 7th, then win 4–3.

JUNE

1st Detroit reliever John Hiller wins both games 8–7, 7–5 against the Brewers, who blow 6–0 and 2–0 leads. Milwaukee reliever Eddie Rodriguez takes both losses.

The Twins trade P Bert Blyleven and SS Danny Thompson to the Rangers for P Bill Singer, SS Roy Smalley, 3B Mike Cubbage, and $250,000.

4th Dave Kingman hits 3 HRs and knocks in 8 runs during a Mets 11–0 win over the Dodgers at Chavez Ravine.

6th Playing the OF, Expo Gary Carter breaks his thumb in a collision with Pepe Mangual during a 14–8 loss to the Braves, sidelining him for 40 games. The

Expos will decide that Carter might be safer behind the plate.

8th The Houston Astros, picking first in the baseball draft, select Arizona State P Floyd Bannister. Bannister is one of 12 eventual major leaguers from the ASU team, which finished 3rd in the College World Series. The Tigers take P Pat Underwood with the 2nd pick. OF Rickey Henderson lasts until the 4th round.

The Tigers send veteran Joe Coleman, 10–18 in 1975, to the Cubs for cash and a player to be named later.

13th The Braves trade infielders Darrell Evans and Marty Perez to the Giants for 1B Willie Montanez, SS Craig Robinson, and 2 minor league infielders.

15th Rain out! The scheduled game at the Astrodome is canceled when heavy rains make it difficult for the visiting team and umpires to get through flooded streets to the stadium.

18th Commissioner Kuhn voids the A's sales, totaling $3.5 million, of Joe Rudi and Rollie Fingers to the Red Sox, and Vida Blue to the Yankees, saying they are "not in the best interest of baseball." A's owner Charlie Finley files a $10 million damage suit against Kuhn, and will refuse to use any of the 3 players until June 27th.

Henry Aaron hits his 750th career HR in the top of the 9th to give the Brewers a 3–2 win over Oakland. It is Aaron's 3rd HR in 3 games.

22nd Randy Jones pitches the Padres to a 4–2 win over the Giants, and ties Christy Mathewson's 63-year-old NL record by going 68 innings without a base on balls. He receives a standing ovation from the home crowd after striking out Darrell Evans to end the 7th. His streak ends when he walks C Marc Hill leading off the 8th. It is Jones's 13th win of the year.

23rd The Dodgers trade P Mike Marshall to the Braves for P Elias Sosa and IF Lee Lacy.

25th Ranger Toby Harrah becomes the only SS in ML history to go through an entire doubleheader without a fielding chance. At the plate, Harrah makes up for the inactivity, collecting 6 hits, including a grand slam in the opener and another round-tripper in game 2. The Rangers beat the White Sox in the first game 8–4, but lose the nightcap 14–9.

28th With a national television audience looking on, Mark "The Bird" Fidrych beats the Yankees 5–1 in Detroit.

JULY

1st The Indians paste the Toledo Mud Hens 13–1 in an exhibition game in Toledo. Manager Frank Robinson, hitting as the DH, flies out to CF and, while returning to the dugout, exchanges angry words with Hens P Bob Reynolds. Suddenly, Robby flattens Reynolds with a right-left combination and is quickly ejected from the game.

3rd The Tigers rookie sensation Mark Fidrych shuts out the Orioles 4–0 for his 8th straight victory.

4th On the nation's bicentennial anniversary, Philadelphia splits a doubleheader with Pittsburgh 10–5 and 7–1. In the first game, the Phils Tim McCarver loses a grand slam when he passes a teammate on the bases.

8th At Wrigley Field, Randy Jones wins his 16th game of the year for the Padres, an NL record for wins at the All-Star break. He beats the Cubs 6–3. In the 2nd half of the season, the Padres lefty will lose 7 games by one run, 2 of them by 1–0 scores.

9th The Astros Larry Dierker no-hits the Expos 6–0 and evens his record at 8-8. Houston is 4th in the West.

11th Hank Aaron's 10th-inning homer in game 2 gives the Brewers a doubleheader sweep over the Texas Rangers.

In a pre-game promotion at Atlanta-Fulton County Stadium, 34 couples are married at home plate. The nuptials are then followed by Championship Wrestling in an evening billed as "Headlocks and Wedlocks." The Braves then pin a 9–8 loss on the Mets.

12th A tentative agreement between the players and owners on labor contracts is reached. The formal agreement will be announced August 9th.

13th The NL emerges victorious in the annual All-Star Game by a score of 7–1. George Foster, who homers and drives in 3 runs, is named the game's MVP. Rookie Mark Fidrych gives up 2 runs and takes the loss. It is the NL's 13th win in the last 14 games.

19th The Mets Dave Kingman tears ligaments in his thumb diving for a ball in a 4–2 loss to the Braves.

Kingman, who already has 32 HRs for the season, will hit only 5 more after being sidelined for 6 weeks.

20th Hank Aaron hits the 755th, and last, HR of his career, connecting off Dick Drago of the California Angels. Jerry Augustine wins 6–2.

23rd The Angels fire manager Dick Williams. Norm Sherry takes over the reins.

In a game against the Taiyo Whales, Sadaharu Oh of the Yomiuri Giants hits his 700th HR, the only player in Japanese baseball to do so.

28th Blue Moon Odom and Francisco Barrios combine on a no-hitter as the White Sox top the A's 2–1. Odom walks 9 in 5 innings and is lifted after throwing a ball in the 6th. For Odom (2-0), this is his last ML victory.

AUGUST

8th Padres rookie Butch Metzger is credited with a 4–3 victory over the Astros, his 10th win without a defeat.

The White Sox suit up in shorts for the first game of a doubleheader with the Royals—the idea of maverick owner Bill Veeck. The shorts split, the Sox taking the opener 5–2 and losing the nightcap 7–1.

9th Twenty-two-year-old John Candelaria survives a bases-loaded situation in the 3rd inning to hurl a no-hit game to beat the Dodgers 2–0. Candelaria improves his record to 11-4 for the 2nd-place Pirates.

16th With the help of 3 picked-off Oakland runners at 1B, the first such occurrence in the AL since 1910, the Brewers beat Oakland 4–3. Another oddity happens when Oakland's Billy Williams is called out on strikes after refusing to enter the batter's box. He is then thrown out of the game.

17th George Brett steals home in the 10th to give the Royals a 4–3 win over the Indians.

18th The Angels nip the Tigers 5–4 in 11 innings. Nolan Ryan works the first 10, fanning 17.

25th The Yankees edge the Twins 5–4 in a 19-inning marathon.

SEPTEMBER

3rd The Brewers crush the Tigers and Mark Fidrych 11–2 as Mike Hegan hits for the cycle and drives in 6 runs.

Rangers catcher Jim Sundberg records 3 assists in the 5th inning of a 4–1 win over the Royals. He becomes only the 7th perpetrator of this feat in ML history.

10th Nolan Ryan hurls a 3-hit 3–2 victory for California, fanning 18 Chicago batsmen.

11th Minnie Minoso comes to bat for the White Sox after a 12-year hiatus. He goes hitless in his 3 at bats against Frank Tanana, but his appearance makes him one of a handful of ML players to play in 4 decades. His at bat in 1980 will match him with Nick Altrock as a 5-decade player.

12th DH Minnie Minoso singles for the White Sox against the Angels Sid Monge. At 53, Minoso is the oldest ever to collect a hit in the ML.

18th In his last ML appearance as a player, Cleveland manager Frank Robinson pinch-hits in the 8th and singles against the Orioles Rudy May.

22nd Don Sutton wins his 20th game of the year for the Dodgers, beating the Giants 3–1 on a 6-hitter. Sutton will win 324 in his career, but this is the only year he will be a 20-game winner.

26th The Phillies beat the Expos in the first game of a doubleheader to clinch the NL East title. Following the 2nd game, Dick Allen jumps the team in protest of the fact that veteran Tony Taylor is not listed on the post-season roster.

29th John Montefusco walks only Jerry Royster in hurling a no-hitter as the Giants beat the Braves 9–0.

The Dodgers Walter Alston, after 23 years and 2,040 victories, steps down as manager. 3B coach Tommy Lasorda is promoted to the post.

OCTOBER

3rd George Brett edges Royals teammate Hal McRae for the AL batting title, .333 to .332, when his blooper drops in front of Twins OF Steve Brye and skips over his head for an inside-the-park HR. McRae believes the misplay is deliberate, and charges the Twins with racism.

The Cubs Bill Madlock wrests the NL crown from the Reds Ken Griffey by collecting 4 singles in an 11–1 win over the Braves. The hits raise Madlock from .333 to .339, one point ahead of the idle Griffey, who belatedly joins the Reds 8–2 win over the Expos and goes 0-for-2, dipping his average to .336.

Hank Aaron singles in his last ML at bat and drives in his 2,297th run as the 6th–place Brewers lose to the Tigers 5–2.

7th Judge Roy Hofheinz sells the Astros to General Electric and Ford Motor Credit Companies.

9th Pete Rose has 3 hits and George Foster homers as the Reds top the Phillies 6–3 in the first game of the NL Championship Series.

The Yankees beat the Royals 4–1 in the AL opener. George Brett's 2 first-inning errors allow 2 unearned runs, and that is all Catfish Hunter needs as he goes the distance.

Pirates P Bob Moose dies in an auto accident en route to a party celebrating his 29th birthday.

10th Kansas City evens the ALCS with a 7–3 win over New York behind Paul Splittorff's 5⅔ innings of scoreless relief.

The Reds win their 2nd NL game 6–2, as Pedro Borbon saves it with 4 innings of scoreless relief. Pete Rose and Ken Griffey have 2 hits each.

11th In the last of the 8th, leading the Hanshin Tigers 4–1 with 2 out and a full count, Sadaharu Oh socks his 715th HR to pass Babe Ruth's mark. He finishes the season with 716 HRs and takes aim at Hank Aaron's record.

12th The Reds score 7 times in the final 3 innings to secure a 7–6 win and complete a sweep of the LCS. Johnny Bench and George Foster hit successive HRs to start the rally.

In the AL game, Chris Chambliss contributes a HR and 3 RBI to the Yankees come-from-behind 5–3 victory.

13th The Royals even the Series again with a 7–4 win, despite 2 Graig Nettles HRs. Freddie Patek is the big hitter with 3 RBI.

14th In the final LCS game, the Yankees take the early lead only to see the Royals even it up on Brett's 3-run homer in the 8th. Chambliss then connects on a dramatic 9th-inning HR off relief ace Mark Littell to win the game 7–6 and the pennant for the Yankees. By the time Chambliss reaches 2B, he is surrounded by screaming fans who escort him around the bases. After he reaches the dugout he returns with a police escort to make sure he touches 3B and home.

16th Don Gullett and Pedro Borbon combine on a 5-hitter, as the Reds win game 1 of the WS 5–1 over the Yankees. Three hits by Perez, the first WS designated hitter, and a Joe Morgan homer supply the offense.

17th On a cold Sunday night, the Reds gang up on Catfish Hunter for 3 runs, but the Yankees battle back to tie it up. With 2 outs in the 9th inning, Yanks SS Fred Stanley throws Griffey's easy grounder into the dugout. A walk and a Tony Perez single follow and the Yanks lose the second WS game 4–3.

19th At Yankee Stadium, DH Dan Driessen contributes 2 singles and a HR to Cincinnati's 3rd straight WS triumph. The final score is 6–2.

20th Rain cancels game 4 of the WS.

21st The Reds take a 3–0 lead against Ed Figueroa, but the Yankees close it to 3–2. A 4-run splurge in the 9th, topped by Johnny Bench's 2nd HR of the game, ices the Reds 7–2 win, completing a 4-game sweep of the Yankees. WS MVP Johnny Bench has 2 HRs and 5 RBI, and demolishes the Yankees with .533 hitting. Opposing C Thurman Munson had 6 straight singles to tie a WS mark. The 1976 Reds become the first team ever to go through an entire LCS and WS without a defeat.

NOVEMBER

2nd Padre Randy Jones beats out Met Jerry Koosman for the NL Cy Young Award. Jones led the league with 315 innings, and posted a 22-14 record for the 5th-place Padres.

4th The first mass-market free-agent reentry draft is held at New York's Plaza Hotel. Among those available are Reggie Jackson, Joe Rudi, Don Gullett, Gene Tenace, Rollie Fingers, Don Baylor, Bobby Grich, and Willie McCovey.

5th New AL franchises in Seattle and Toronto fill up their rosters by selecting 30 players apiece from unprotected players on other AL rosters. OF Ruppert Jones (Seattle) and IF-OF Bob Bailor (Toronto) are the first choices.

The Pirates trade C Manny Sanguillen and an estimated $100,000 to the A's for manager Chuck Tanner.

Baltimore's Jim Palmer easily outpoints Detroit's sensational rookie Mark Fidrych to win the AL Cy Young Asward.

6th Former Twins relief ace Bill Campbell becomes the first of the free-agent crop to sign with a new team, joining the Red Sox with a contract calling for $1 million over 4 years.

9th Oakland releases Billy Williams, ending his Hall of Fame career with 2,711 hits, 426 HRs, 1,475 RBI, and a .290 average.

17th Minnesota's Rod Carew, who hit .331, wins the AL MVP Award. This is the first year in the past 5 that Carew did not win the batting title.

24th The Reds Joe Morgan outpoints teammate George Foster to win his 2nd straight NL MVP Award. Morgan led with a .576 slugging average, and hit .320, scored 113 runs, knocked in 111, and stole a base.

29th Reggie Jackson signs with the New York Yankees.

DECEMBER

2nd Danny Murtaugh, who had retired 2 months earlier as Pirates manager, dies at Chester, Pennsylvania, of a heart attack at age 59.

4th Aurelio Rodriguez becomes the first AL 3B since 1959 to beat out Brooks Robinson for the Gold Glove Award. Other Newcomers on TSN fielding team include 3B Mike Schmidt, OF Dwight Evans, and C Jim Sundberg, who would combine to win 24 awards.

6th The Red Sox trade 1B Cecil Cooper to the Brewers for 1B George Scott and OF Bernie Carbo.

8th The Indians trade OF George Hendrick to the Padres for 3 players.

10th Rangers SS Danny Thompson, a 7-year veteran, dies of leukemia at Rochester, MN, aged 29.

14th Relief specialist Rollie Fingers signs with the San Diego Padres.

16th Court proceedings in Charlie Finley's $10 million damage suit against Commissioner Kuhn begin in Chicago. At issue is Kuhn's voiding of Finley's attempted player sales in June. The proceedings will take 15 days, and the decision will take 3 months.

1977

JANUARY

1st   Brewers P Danny Frisella, 30, is killed in a dune buggy accident near Phoenix, Arizona.

2nd   Commissioner Kuhn suspends Braves owner Ted Turner for one year as a result of tampering charges in the Gary Matthews free-agency signing, but the Braves are permitted to keep the outfielder.

3rd   The Royals release P Lindy McDaniel, ending his 21-year career. He appeared in 987 games, 2nd only to Hoyt Wilhelm's 1,070.

4th   Mary Shane is hired by the Chicago White Sox as the first woman TV play-by-play announcer.

6th   Angels reserve SS Mike Miley, 23, is killed in an auto crash in Baton Rouge, LA. Miley had been a star football player at LSU and was chosen twice in the first round of the June free-agent draft.

11th   In a 5-player swap, the Cubs send OF Rick Monday to the Dodgers for 1B-OF Bill Buckner and SS Ivan DeJesus.

17th   Kansas City releases Tommy Davis, ending an 18-year career spent with 10 different teams.

19th   The BBWAA elects Ernie Banks to the Hall of Fame in his first year of eligibility.

30th   Edward W. Stack is elected president of the Hall of Fame succeeding the retiring Paul Kerr.

31st   The Special Veterans Committee selects Joe Sewell, Amos Rusie, and Al Lopez for the Hall of Fame.

FEBRUARY

3rd   The Hall of Fame's Special Committee on the Negro Leagues picks Martin Dihigo, the versatile Cuban star, and SS John Lloyd for induction. The committee then dissolves, its functions being taken over by the veterans committee.

11th   The Cubs trade 3B Bill Madlock and 2B Rod Sperring to the Giants for OF Bobby Murcer, IF Steve Ontiveros, and a minor league pitcher.

19th   The A's sell P Paul Lindblad to the Rangers for $400,000, calling into question Bowie Kuhn's policy on player sales. Kuhn had previously voided an Oakland sale of players (6/18/76) as "not being in the best interest of baseball," but had not specified the amount allowable in a player sale.

MARCH

7th   The Braves file suit against Commissioner Kuhn, challenging the severity of the penalty for tampering charges.

15th   The Pirates trade outfielders Tony Armas and Mitchell Page, and 4 pitchers, including Rick Langford, to the A's for 2B Phil Garner, IF Tommy Helms, and P Chris Batton.

17th   Federal Judge Frank McGarr rules in favor of Kuhn, saying that the commissioner acted within his authority in voiding the 1976 player sales engineered by A's owner Charlie Finley.

21st   Mark Fidrych, the 1976 Rookie of the Year, rips the cartilage in his left knee and will undergo surgery 10 days later. The injury will effectively end the fabled career of the Bird.

28th   The Rangers Lenny Randle, angry for having been benched during spring training, attacks 50-year-old manager Frank Lucchesi, sending him to the hospital with a shattered cheekbone. Lucchesi helped precipitate the incident by calling the good-natured Randle "a punk." Randle's days are numbered.

APRIL

5th   The White Sox trade SS Bucky Dent to the Yankees for OF Oscar Gamble, pitchers LaMarr Hoyt and Bob Polinsky, and an estimated $200,000.

6th   The Seattle Mariners make their debut, losing to Frank Tanana and the Angels 7–0.

7th   Al Woods hits a pinch HR in his first ML at bat, as the Toronto Blue Jays make a successful debut versus the White Sox, winning 9–5.

10th   The Indians (13) and Red Sox (6) combine for 19 runs in the 8th inning to set a modern ML record. Cleveland wins 19–9.

12th   The Tigers send popular veteran DH-OF Willie Horton to Texas for P Steve Foucault. Both players will move on after one season.

15th The Expos play their first game in Montreal's Olympic Stadium before a crowd of 57,592. The Phillies win 7–2.

16th Regulations force Oakland P Vida Blue to discard his old, discolored "lucky" cap because it is no longer "identical in color, trim and style" to those of his teammates.

21st Detroit's Dave Rozema shuts down Boston 8–0 for his first ML win.

25th The Reds score 12 runs in the 5th inning, and 23 in the game, in beating the Braves.

26th The Rangers trade Lenny Randle to the Mets for Rick Auerbach and cash.

30th Ron Cey cracks a 7th-inning HR in a 6–4 Dodger win over the Expos. Cey finishes the month with a ML record for April of 29 RBI to lead the Dodgers to a 17-3 start under new manager Tommy Lasorda.

MAY

11th With the Braves mired in a 16-game losing streak, owner Ted Turner takes over as field manager. After the Braves lose again 2–1, Turner is relieved of his new job by NL president Chub Feeney. A league rule prohibits a manager from owning a financial interest in his club.

14th Jim Colborn hurls a no-hit game as Kansas City beats Texas 6–0.

Jim Spencer ties the club mark of 8 RBI as the White Sox scalp the Indians 18–2 at Comiskey Park.

17th The Cubs hit 7 home runs and wallop the Padres 23–6. Three of the HRs are consecutive shots in the 5th by Larry Biittner, Jerry Morales, and Bobby Murcer.

21st Merv Rettenmund hits a 3-run HR in the 21st inning to give the Padres an 11–8 win over the Expos.

22nd The Red Sox split a doubleheader with the Brewers, winning the opener 14–10 and dropping the 2nd 6–0. The 2 teams tie a ML record in game one when they combine for 11 HRs.

26th Rickey Henderson of the Modesto A's (California League) steals 7 bases to tie the minor league record. Henderson will steal 95 in 134 games.

27th OF Lyman Bostock has 12 putouts in the 2nd game of a doubleheader, tying the ML mark, as the Twins sweep the Red Sox.

28th Alvin Dark replaces John McNamara as the Padres manager.

30th Twenty-two-year-old Dennis Eckersley, last year's Rookie of the Year, fires a no-hitter as the Indians top the Angels 1–0. Frank Tanana, with 3 shutouts in his last 4 games, takes the loss.

The Padres sweep a doubleheader from the Giants 12–8 and 9–8. San Diego's Mike Ivie ties an NL record with 5 doubles, while his club ties the ML mark by using 41 players, including 13 pitchers, in the twin bill.

31st The Mets fire manager Joe Frazier, replacing him with 3B Joe Torre.

JUNE

5th The Dodgers retire former manager Walt Alston's uniform, number 24, on Old-Timer's Day. Doug Rau then pitches the current Dodgers to a 4–2 win over the Padres.

7th The White Sox select Harold Baines with the number- one pick in the draft. Bill Veeck had first seen Baines play Little League ball and had followed his career. P Bill Gullickson was taken with the 2nd pick by the Expos, and Milwaukee takes University of Minnesota infielder Paul Molitor with the 3rd pick. Danny Ainge, a potential pro basketball player, is picked in the 15th round.

8th Nolan Ryan notches his 4th career 19-strikeout game, hurling the first 10 innings of a game against Toronto.

10th The A's fire manager Jack McKeon, replacing him with Bobby Winkles.

15th New York fans are in shock as the Mets trade ace P Tom Seaver to the Reds. In return they get P Pat Zachry, IF Doug Flynn, and minor leaguers Steve Henderson and Dan Norman. The Mets also trade slugger Dave Kingman to the Angels for utility player Bobby Valentine and a minor league pitcher.

18th New York's Reggie Jackson loafs after a fly ball during a 10–4 loss to Boston and is taken out by manager Billy Martin. Jackson and Martin nearly come to blows in the dugout as national television cameras watch.

19th The Indians fire manager Frank Robinson, replacing him with Jeff Torborg.

22nd It's not a good year for Texas manager Frank Lucchesi, as Eddie Stanky takes over, leading the club to a 10–8 triumph over the Twins. The next day, the "homesick" Stanky will resign.

26th Carew scores 5 runs and teammate Glenn Adams drives in 8 as the Twins beat the White Sox 19–12.

27th The Giants Willie McCovey smashes 2 HRs in the 6th inning to pace a 14–9 victory over the Reds. McCovey becomes the first player to twice hit 2 HRs in one inning (4/12/73), and also becomes the all-time NL leader with 17 career grand slams.

28th Ken Reitz knocks in 8 runs in a 13–3 St. Louis win over Pittsburgh.

Billy Hunter becomes the Rangers' 4th manager in 6 days. Connie Ryan had filled in after Eddie Stanky's departure.

30th Cliff Johnson hits 3 consecutive home runs, including 2 in the 8th inning, as the Yankees rout the Blue Jays 11–5.

JULY

2nd The White Sox Jim Spencer clubs 2 HRs against the Twins and ties the club record of 8 RBI. Spencer also had 8 RBI on May 14th.

3rd On his 24th birthday, Angel Frank Tanana records his 14th straight complete game in beating the A's 6–4, and raising his record to 12-5. His overworked arm would plague him for the rest of the season, and he would wind up 15-9.

4th The Red Sox wallop 8 HRs, including 7 solo shots, in beating Toronto 9–6. Four HRs come in the 8th inning.

After 8 straight hits, Ron Cey is called out on strikes in the 9th in a 4–0 Dodger win over San Francisco. Cey had 5 hits the day before and 3 straight today.

9th Rafael Garcia of Juarez (Mexican League) hurls his 2nd no-hitter of the season in beating

Durango 3–1. He throttled Nuevo Laredo without a hit on April 16th.

11th The Angels fire manager Norm Sherry. Dave Garcia takes over.

19th At Yankee Stadium, the NL scores 4 times in the opening inning off Jim Palmer, en route to a 7–5 All-Star Game victory. Don Sutton, hurling 3 scoreless innings, is named the game's MVP.

While pursuing Hank Aaron's HR record, Sadaharu Oh breaks one held by Babe Ruth when he draws his 2,057th base on balls.

24th Seattle's John Montague pitches 6⅔ innings of perfect relief against California, giving him 33 consecutive batsmen retired over 2 games to tie the AL record.

25th Pete Rose singles in the 4th inning of the Reds 9–8 loss to the Cardinals. It is Rose's 2,881st career hit, enabling him to surpass Frankie Frisch as the all-time leader among switch-hitters.

26th Padres rookie Gene Richards ties the NL record with 6 hits in an extra-inning contest.

28th The Cubs (6) and Reds (5) combine for 11 HRs to tie the ML record. The Cubs win 16–15 in 13 innings.

29th The Braves Phil Niekro strikes out 4 batters in the 6th inning of a 5–3 win over the Pirates.

AUGUST

1st Willie McCovey hits 2 HRs, including his 18th career grand slam, as the Giants beat Montreal.

3rd Baltimore rookie 1B Eddie Murray homers from both sides of the plate in a 10-inning 8–6 win over Oakland.

7th Mike Torrez snaps a 3-game Yankee losing streak with his 3rd straight victory. The Yankees will win 20 of their next 23 games.

9th The White Sox hit 6 HRs against the Mariners to tie the club mark at Comiskey Park. Eric Soderholm has 2, with Chet Lemon, Oscar Gamble, Jim Essian, and Royle Stillman contributing.

10th Billy Martin installs Reggie Jackson as the Yankees' regular clean-up hitter. The Yanks beat the

A's 6–3, and will win 40 of final 53 games, with Jackson contributing 13 HRs and 49 RBI.

12th For the 2nd straight day, Oakland's Manny Sanguillen foils a no-hit bid. Today's single is off the Orioles Jim Palmer, who settles for a 2-hit 6–0 victory. Yesterday's hit was off the Yankees Mike Torrez, who finished with a 3–0 two-hitter.

The Pirates win twice over the Mets 3–2 and 6–5. In the 2nd game, Mets 2B Felix Millan suffers a broken collarbone in a brawl with catcher Ed Ott, ending Millan's 12-year ML career.

17th Records fall as the Mexican League concludes its season. Ironman hurler Aurelio Lopez of the Mexico City Reds racks up his 30th save to go with a record 19 victories in relief. Veteran Tampico 1B Hector Espino hits only 14 HRs, but raises his career total to 435, a new minor league record. Thirty-eight-year-old Vic Davalillo, the league's top hitter at .384, is purchased by the Dodgers.

21st Pittsburgh's Rennie Stennett, batting .336 for the season, breaks his right leg sliding into 2B during a 5–4 loss to San Francisco.

Graig Nettles's HR and double account for both Yankee runs in a 2–1 win over Texas. The Yankees cut the Red Sox lead to one-half game.

23rd Behind Mickey Rivers's 5-for-5 and Torrez's 7th straight CG contributing to an 8–3 whipping of the White Sox, the Yanks take over first place in the AL East. With the Red Sox losing, the Yankees go ahead by a half game and will stay in first place to the end.

27th Rangers Toby Harrah and Bump Wills hit back-to-back inside-the-park HRs on consecutive pitches, highlighting an 8–2 win over the Yankees, only the 2nd loss for New York in 14 games.

28th Steve Garvey has a career game with 5 extra-base hits, 5 runs, and 5 RBI, as the Dodgers blast the Cardinals 11–0. Garvey's barrage includes 3 doubles and 2 HRs.

29th The Cardinals Lou Brock steals 2B in a 4–3 loss to the Padres. It is career steal 893 for Brock, breaking Ty Cobb's modern record.

31st Hank Aaron's mark of 755 career HRs is tied by Sadaharu Oh.

SEPTEMBER

3rd Sadaharu Oh hits the 756th HR of his career to surpass Hank Aaron's total and make him the most prolific HR hitter in professional baseball history.

8th Cubs reliever Bruce Sutter strikes out the first 6 men he faces, including 3 on 9 pitches in the 9th inning.

10th Toronto's Roy Howell knocks in 9 runs with a single, 2 doubles, and 2 HRs, as the Blue Jays crush the Yankees 19–3. Catfish Hunter takes the loss to finish the season at 9-9.

White Sox knuckleballer Wilbur Wood hits 3 batters in the first inning on the way to a 6–1 loss to the Angels.

13th The Dodgers Dusty Baker drives in a team-record 5 runs in one inning, the 2nd, as Los Angeles whips the Padres 18–4. LA leads the West by 13½ games.

15th The Orioles forfeit to the Blue Jays when manager Earl Weaver pulls his team off the field in the 5th inning citing a hazardous condition—a small tarpaulin held down by bricks on the bullpen mound.

16th Seattle beats Kansas City 4–1 to end the Royals' winning streak at 16 games—the longest in the majors in 24 years.

18th Boston's Ted Cox goes 4-for-4 in his first ML game, a 10–4 win over the Orioles. Cox will get 2 more hits the following day against the Yankees, setting a ML record for straight hits at the start of a career.

19th Former catcher Paddy Livingston dies at age 97, in Cleveland, OH. He was the last surviving player from the AL's first season (1901).

20th The Dodgers clinch the NL Western Division title with a 3–1 win over the Giants.

22nd Bert Blyleven pitches a no-hitter as the Rangers beat the Angels 6–0. Blyleven (14-12) walks one.

24th Jack Brohamer becomes the first White Sox player since Ray Schalk in 1922 to hit for the cycle as Chicago whips the Mariners 8–3. Brohamer also adds a double.

25th Detroit pounds out 18 hits against Boston's Reggie Cleveland, but they still lose 12–5.

OCTOBER

1st The Yankees clinch the AL East title as the Red Sox lose to the Orioles 8–7.

2nd Dusty Baker homers in his final AB of the season during a 6–3 loss to the Astros. It is Baker's 30th HR of the year, enabling him to join teammates Garvey (33), Reggie Smith (32), and Ron Cey (30) in making the Dodgers the first team ever to boast four 30-HR hitters in one season.

4th The Phillies score twice in the 9th inning on singles by Bake McBride, Larry Bowa, and Mike Schmidt, to beat the Dodgers 7–5 in the opening game of the NL Championship Series. Ron Cey blasts a grand slam for Los Angeles in the 7th, and Greg Luzinski homers for the Phils.

5th Dusty Baker's grand slam leads the Dodgers to a 7–1 win over the Phillies as Don Sutton goes the distance for LA.

In the opener of the AL Series, HRs by Hal McRae, John Mayberry, and Al Cowens lead the Royals to a 7–2 triumph over the Yankees.

6th Ron Guidry's 3-hitter gives the Yanks a series-evening 6–2 win over the Royals.

7th Down 5–3 with 2 outs in the 9th inning, the Dodgers catch lightning in a bottle. Pinch hitter Vic Davalillo beats out a 2-strike drag bunt and pinch hitter Manny Mota follows with a long double. Los Angeles pulls out a 6–5 victory.

Kansas City earns a 6–2 win over New York as Hal McRae doubles and scores twice and Dennis Leonard hurls a 4-hitter.

8th Mickey Rivers collects 4 hits as the Yankees even the ALCS 6–4. Sparky Lyle contributes with 5⅔ scoreless relief innings.

The Dodgers clinch the NL flag with a 4–1 win in front of an LCS-record crowd of 64,924 at Philadelphia. Dusty Baker hits a 2-run homer and scores twice as Tommy John allows 7 hits in 9 innings of work.

9th For the 2nd year in succession, the Yanks score in the 9th inning of the 5th game to beat the Royals in the LCS. Mickey Rivers gets the game-winning hit. The final score is New York 5, Kansas City 3.

11th The Yankees win the opening game of the WS 4–3 in 12 innings as Willie Randolph doubles and scores the winning run on a single by Paul Blair.

12th HRs by Ron Cey, Steve Yeager, Reggie Smith, and Steve Garvey lead the Dodgers to a 6–1 win in game 2 of the WS. Burt Hooton goes the distance, allowing just 5 hits.

14th Mike Torrez is the winning pitcher as New York prevails in game 3, 5–3. Mickey Rivers slugs 3 hits, including 2 doubles.

15th The Yankees win 4–2 to take a 3-1 advantage in the WS. Jackson doubles and homers, and Guidry notches a 4-hitter, striking out 7.

16th LA stays alive with a 10–4 victory in game 5. Yeager and Reggie Smith homer as Don Sutton pitches a complete game.

18th Reggie Jackson becomes "Mr. October." Three HRs in 3 swings lead the Yankees to an 8–4, Series-clinching victory.

24th The Brewers fire manager Dave Bristol, replacing him with Bobby Cox.

26th Sparky Lyle becomes the first AL reliever to win the Cy Young Award. Lyle led the league with 72 appearances, posting a 13-5 record with 26 saves and a 2.17 ERA.

NOVEMBER

2nd The Phillies Steve Carlton outpoints the Dodgers Tommy John to win his 2nd Cy Young Award. Carlton led the NL with 23 wins, losing 10, and posting a 2.64 ERA.

4th The 2nd reentry free-agent draft is held at New York's Plaza Hotel. Big names include Lyman Bostock, Goose Gossage, Larry Hisle, Mike Torrez, and Oscar Gamble.

8th Free agent Richie Zisk, formerly of the White Sox, signs a 10-year $2.3 million contract with the Rangers.

9th The Reds George Foster wins the NL MVP Award. Foster batted .320 and led the league in HRs (52), RBI (149), runs (124), total bases (388), and slugging (.631).

16th   Rod Carew wins the AL MVP award. The Twins 1B led the league in runs (128), hits (239), triples (16), and batting (.388).

21st   The Orioles Eddie Murray is named AL Rookie of the Year.

22nd   Montreal's Andre Dawson wins the NL Rookie of the Year Award by one vote over New York's Steve Henderson.

DECEMBER

5th   The White Sox trade C Brian Downing and pitchers Chris Knapp and Dave Frost to the Angels for outfielders Bobby Bonds and Thad Bosley, and minor league P Rich Dotson.

8th   The Rangers engineer a series of deals with the Braves, Mets, and Pirates, unloading a total of 6 players and getting 3 in return. Among those involved are 1B Willie Montanez (to New York), Bert Blyleven (Pittsburgh), and Al Oliver (Texas).

9th   The Brewers trade pitchers Jim Slaton and Rich Folkers to the Tigers for OF Ben Oglivie. The Mariners trade OF Dave Collins to the Reds for P Shane Rawley.

   The A's and Reds announce a deal that will send P Vida Blue to Cincinnati for OF Dave Revering and $1.75 million cash.

14th   The Red Sox trade P Fergie Jenkins to the Rangers for P John Poloni and cash.

1978

JANUARY

19th The BBWAA elects Eddie Mathews to the Hall of Fame. The former 3B is named on 301 of 379 ballots.

25th The Padres trade P Dave Tomlin and an estimated $125,000 in cash to the Rangers for aging P Gaylord Perry. Perry will win the NL Cy Young Award with San Diego in 1978.

30th Commissioner Kuhn voids the Vida Blue deal (12/9/77) between the A's and the Reds, suggesting a restructuring of the trade.

Former P Addie Joss and former executive Larry MacPhail are voted into the Hall of Fame by the Special Veterans Committee.

FEBRUARY

3rd F. J. "Steve" O'Neill becomes the principal owner of the Cleveland Indians under a reorganization of the club's financial structure.

8th The Brewers purchase OF Gorman Thomas from the Rangers.

25th Abandoning the earlier Vida Blue deal, the Reds trade Dave Revering and cash to the A's for P Doug Bair.

28th The Padres trade IF Mike Ivie to the Giants for IF-OF Derrel Thomas.

MARCH

6th The Reds trade P Jack Billingham to the Tigers for 2 minor league players.

15th The A's trade Vida Blue to the Giants for 7 players and an estimated $390,000 in cash.

17th For the St. Patrick's Day exhibition game, the Reds don green uniforms, rather than their traditional red, starting an annual ritual. The Cardinals will follow suit.

21st The Padres fire manager Alvin Dark, replacing him with pitching coach Roger Craig. Dark becomes the only manager besides the Cubs Phil Cavarretta in 1954 to be fired during spring training.

28th The A's release Dick Allen, ending his stormy 15-year career which produced 351 HRs, 1,119 RBI, a .292 batting average, and a .534 slugging mark.

30th The Red Sox trade C Bo Diaz, 3B Ted Cox, and pitchers Rick Wise and Mike Paxton to the Indians for C Fred Kendall and P Dennis Eckersley. Eckersley will win 20 for Boston.

APRIL

1st Starting off with a bang, Sadaharu Oh hits a grand-slam HR on Opening Day. It is his 757th HR.

4th The Royals send slugger John Mayberry to the Blue Jays for an eventual cash settlement.

7th Mark Fidrych scatters 5 hits in beating Toronto 6–2. The Bird, trying to recover from tendinitis that limited him to 11 starts in 1977, will win only 3 more ML games.

The U.S. Court of Appeals upholds an earlier court decision in support of Commissioner Kuhn's voiding of attempted player sales by A's owner Charlie Finley in June 1976. Finley's appeal to the U.S. Supreme Court will be rejected on October 2nd.

9th The Brewers complete a stunning season-opening, 3-game sweep of the Orioles by scores of 11–3, 16–3, and 13–5. Sixto Lezcano, Gorman Thomas, and Cecil Cooper provided the Brewers with a grand slam in each game to set a ML mark.

12th Ranger P Rogelio Moret announces he is going home rather than pitch. In the locker room, the pitcher freezes in a catatonic state, his extended arm holding a bathroom slipper. He is taken to a psychiatric facility and will go on the disabled list for most of the season, appearing in just 6 more games.

13th The Yankees defeat the White Sox 4–2 in their home opener on Reggie Candy Bar Day. Jackson slugs a 3-run HR in the first inning, and the field is showered with candy bars which were given out free to the fans at the game.

14th Darrell Jackson of Orlando (Southern League) makes his pro debut, no-hitting Jacksonville for 9 innings. Orlando wins 1–0 in the 12th.

16th Cardinal Bob Forsch hurls a no-hitter in beating the Phillies 5–0. It is the first no-hitter in St. Louis by a Cardinal since Jesse Haines in 1924.

23rd Reds 2B Joe Morgan commits an error during a 2–1 win over the Giants, ending his ML record streak of 91 consecutive errorless games since July 6, 1977.

24th The Angels Nolan Ryan strikes out 15 Mariners—the 20th time he has had 15 K's in a game—in 9 innings, but leaves without a decision. Seattle prevails 6–5 in the 12th frame.

25th The Cardinals fire manager Vern Rapp. Ken Boyer will take over the reins 4 days later.

Cleveland's Wayne Garland, who signed a lucrative 10-year contract a year earlier, earns his 2nd and final win of the season 6–5 over Toronto. Garland will undergo rotator cuff surgery on May 5th and win only 13 more ML games.

29th Pete Rose crashes 3 HRs and 2 singles in a 14–7 Reds drubbing of the Mets, pushing his career hit total to 2,996.

MAY

5th Pete Rose singles off Montreal's Steve Rogers for career hit 3,000. The Expos beat the Reds 4–3.

14th Dave Kingman drives in 8 runs with a single and 3 HRs, including a 15th-inning 3-run shot that gives the Cubs a 10–7 win over the Dodgers. This is the 2nd time he has enjoyed a 3-HR, 8-RBI day at Dodger Stadium.

16th The White Sox trade OF Bobby Bonds to the Rangers for OF Claudell Washington and OF Rusty Torres.

17th Lee Lacy hits a pinch HR as the Dodgers beat the Pirates 10–1. It is Lacy's 3rd consecutive HR in a pinch-hitting role, setting a ML record. His previous blasts were on May 2nd and 6th.

23rd With Oakland leading the AL Western Division (24-15), manager Bobby Winkles walks off the job. Jack McKeon takes over.

The AL approves the transfer of the Red Sox to a group headed by Jean Yawkey, Buddy LeRoux, and Haywood Sullivan. The purchase price is $15 million. Sullivan had a 7-year catching career for the Red Sox and Royals, while LeRoux was the Boston trainer for 8 years.

24th In a Florida State League game, the Tampa Tarpons push 18 runs across the plate in the 4th inning of a 20–2 win over Daytona Beach. The bizarre frame, which lasts over an hour, features 9 hits, 6 walks, 3 errors, 3 wild pitches, 2 passed balls, and an obstruction call. Fifteen runs score before the inning's first out is recorded.

26th Silvio Martinez, making his last start for Springfield (American Association) before joining the Cardinals, no-hits Omaha 4–0.

30th In his first ML start for the Cardinals, Silvio Martinez hurls a one-hit 8–2 victory over the Mets. Steve Henderson homers in the 7th inning for the lone safety. Martinez will spin 2 one-hitters and two 2–hitters this season.

JUNE

1st The Angels fire manager Dave Garcia. Pirates IF Jim Fregosi is named to replace him.

3rd The Phils Davey Johnson breaks up a 1–1, 9th-inning tie with Los Angeles by hitting his 2nd pinch grand slam of the year. His first came on April 30th when he broke up a 5th-inning tie in San Diego. Johnson is the first ML player to accomplish this feat, but Mike Ivie will duplicate it later this month.

8th Bob Horner, the College Player of the Year, is selected first in the free-agent draft by the Braves. The Blue Jays make Lloyd Moseby the 2nd selection. The Yankees, with 3 first-round selections awarded as compensation in player signings, pick Rex Hudler, Matt Winters, and Brian Ryder. On the 23rd round they take a Clearwater RHP named Howard Johnson, who will make the ML as an infielder. Kent Hrbek lasts until the 17th round.

10th The Orioles score in the 9th inning against the A's to give Jim Palmer his 3rd 1–0 victory in 18 days. The Baltimore ace shut down Detroit on May 24th and New York on June 1st.

12th Jesus Alou, signed by Houston after being out of ML baseball for 2 seasons, goes 4-for-4 to help the Astros to a win over Pittsburgh. Alou is now hitting .343.

13th For the 3rd time in his career, Roy White homers from both sides of the plate in a 5–3 Yankee win over the A's.

The Reds Pete Rose is held hitless during a 1–0 win over Cubs. A 5-for-44 slump has dropped Rose's average to .267. He would not be collared again until August.

14th Bob Horner signs with the Braves for an estimated $175,000 bonus. Two days later he will celebrate his ML debut with a HR off Bert Blyleven of the Pirates.

15th In a swap of pitchers, the Phillies send Gene Garber to the Braves for Dick Ruthven.

16th In the 12th ML season of a career speckled with near-misses, Cincinnati Tom Seaver finally hurls a no-hitter. The Cardinals are the 4–0 victims as Seaver strikes out 3.

17th Ron Guidry strikes out 18 batters in a 4-hit 4–0 shutout of the Angels, setting an AL record for lefthanders. The victory raises the Yankee southpaw's record to 11–0.

20th Toronto is defeated for the 3rd consecutive game by a Canadian-born pitcher. The Blue Jays lose to John Hiller of Detroit, after having previously tasted defeat at the hands of Ferguson Jenkins and Reggie Cleveland of the Texas Rangers.

21st The Angels Dave Machemer homers in his first ML at bat during a 5–2 win over the Twins. Machemer never hits another.

23rd Rubio Malone of Elizabethton (Appalachian League) no-hits Johnson City 8–1. Twenty-six days later, Malone will no-hit Bluefield 6–0.

26th Toronto's Dave McKay and Otto Velez each hit 2 doubles in one inning during a 24–10 rout of Baltimore. The Orioles use C Ellie Hendricks and OF Larry Harlow on the mound during the slugfest.

30th In the first game of a 10–9, 10–5 doubleheader loss to the Braves, Giant Willie McCovey hits his 500th career HR, off Jamie Easterly. McCovey becomes the 12th member of the 500-HR club. Mike Ivie adds his 2nd pinch grand slam of the year in the opener. Jack Clark has 3 HRs in the 2 games.

Larry Doby becomes the 2nd black ML manager, replacing Bob Lemon as skipper of the White Sox. Chicago has a 34-40 record at the time, and would go 37-50 the rest of the way.

31st Pete Rose singles off Phil Niekro to extend his streak to 44 games, as the Reds edge the Braves 3–2. Rose ties Willie Keeler's 81-year-old NL record, achieved when foul balls didn't count as strikes.

JULY

1st The Astros trade C Joe Ferguson to the Dodgers for 2 players to be named later (IF Rafael Landestoy and OF Jeff Leonard).

7th The Brewers Mike Caldwell beats the Yankees Ron Guidry 6–0. For Guidry (13-1), it is his first loss of the season. Caldwell shut out the Yankees 9 days earlier, and will shut them out again on September 19th.

8th Omar Moreno's first-inning single is the Pirates' only hit as the Cardinals Silvio Martinez hurls a 4–0 shutout.

11th At San Diego, the NL wins another All-Star Game 7–3. Steve Garvey singles and triples to earn the game's MVP trophy. Vida Blue starts for the NL, the first pitcher to start for both leagues. Blue also started in 1973 and 1975 for the AL.

14th Umpire Doug Harvey ejects a shocked Dodger P Don Sutton from the game after discovering 3 scuffed balls.

Houston's Ken Forsch defeats the Expos twice in extra innings. He pitches 2 inning in the first game, winning 4–3 in the 13th, and comes back for 2 in the second, winning 5–4 in the 10th.

15th Seattle's Larry Milbourne homers from both sides of the plate in a 7–6 win over Cleveland. These will be Milbourne's only HRs all season, spanning 93 games and 234 at bats.

16th Tulsa's Dave Righetti strikes out 21 Midland batters in 9 innings to set a Texas League record. A Tulsa reliever loses the game 4–2 in extra innings.

17th In the latest incident in his feud with manager Billy Martin, the Yankees Reggie Jackson ignores instructions and attempts to bunt in the 10th inning of a tie game with the Royals. Jackson pops up, the Yanks lose in the 11th, and Martin serves Jackson with a 5-day suspension without pay.

19th The Red Sox beat the Brewers 8–2 to increase their lead in the AL Eastern Division to 9 games over Milwaukee, 12½ over Baltimore, and 14 games over the 4th-place Yankees.

21st The Indians Mike Paxton strikes out 4 batters in the 5th inning of an 11–0 win over the Mariners.

23rd Reggie Jackson returns to the team and the Yankees win their 5th straight 3–1 over the White Sox. The next day, Martin will resign under pressure, giving way to Bob Lemon.

24th Pete Rose singles twice during the Reds' 5–3 win over the Mets, extending his hitting streak to 37 games to tie the modern ML record held by Tommy Holmes. Mets P Pat Zachry kicks the dugout steps in anger, breaking his foot and ending his season.

Ron Guidry raises his record to 23-3 with his 3rd 2-hitter in a row as the Yankees win 4–0 over Cleveland. The two Indian hits are by Duane Kuiper, the 2nd time this year that he has recorded the only hits in a game. The shutout is Guidry's 9th of the year, a team record.

25th The Reds lose to the Mets 9–2, but Rose collects 3 hits to break Tommy Holmes's record.

The Lodi Dodgers (California League) pull off 2 triple plays during an 11–6 win over Fresno. Bob Brenly is a victimized base runner each time. It is the first time a pro team has had 2 triple plays in one game since 1904.

26th Johnny Bench hits his 300th career HR, and Rose hits in his 39th straight game, but the Reds bow to the Mets 12–3.

The Giants Jack Clark has his hitting streak stopped at 26 games during a 2–1 loss to the Cardinals.

27th The Yankees win the first game of a doubleheader 11–0, but the Indians rebound to win the 2nd 17–5. Duane Kuiper ties the ML record with 2 basesloaded triples in the nightcap, only the 3rd player (after Bill Bruton and Elmer Valo) to do so in the 20th century.

29th A surprise announcement at Old-Timers Day in Yankee Stadium: Billy Martin will return to manage the Yanks in 1980. The fans go wild with joy.

30th The Expos crush the Braves 19–0, collecting 28 hits and an NL-record-tying 8 HRs. Andre Dawson, Larry Parrish, Dave Cash, and Dawson again homer in the 4th inning; Parrish has a single and 3 consecutive HRs in the game. The 58 bases break an 85-year-old record held by the Reds.

AUGUST

1st The Braves trounce the Reds 16–4 and stop Pete Rose's hitting streak at 44 games. Larry McWilliams and Gene Garber are the Atlanta pitchers.

7th Eddie Mathews, Addie Joss, and Larry MacPhail are inducted at Cooperstown.

10th A's 2B Mike Edwards ties the ML record with 2 unassisted DPs during a 16–5 loss to the Angels.

12th Peninsula's Marty Bystrom hurls a perfect game over Winston-Salem 3–0 in a Carolina League contest.

13th The Yankees erupt for 5 runs in the 7th inning to take a 5–3 lead over the Orioles before heavy rains force a delay of the game. Baltimore groundskeepers are slow to react, the game is called, the score reverts to the last complete inning. The Orioles win 3–0.

15th The Blue Jays trade DH Rico Carty to the A's for DH Willie Horton and a minor league pitcher.

20th Los Angeles beats New York 5–4. Dodgers Don Sutton and Steve Garvey engage in a clubhouse wrestling match, culminating a long feud.

22nd Ron LeFlore swipes his 27th consecutive base as Detroit beats the Twins 7–3. He began the streak on July 16th.

25th ML umpires stage a one-day strike in defiance of their union contract. Semipro and amateur umps are pressed into service until a restraining order forces the strikers to return.

With 4 amateur umps officiating, Ron Guidry posts his 18th win, beating the A's 7–1. Reggie Jackson's HR drives in his 1,001st career RBI. The win keeps the Yankees 7½ games behind the Red Sox.

30th Sadaharu Oh hits his 34th season HR and the 800th of his career. The ball lands in the shoe of a fan who had removed it to feel more comfortable.

SEPTEMBER

1st Making his ML debut, Oriole Sammy Stewart fans 7 consecutive batters en route to a 9–3 win over the White Sox.

3rd Lee Mazzilli homers from both sides of the plate as the Mets down the Dodgers 8–5.

4th The Pirates Dorian Boyland has a 1-2 count in his first ML AB when the Mets make a pitching change. Rennie Stennett pinch-hits, taking the 3rd strike. The strikeout is charged to Boyland, watching the completion of his historic AB from the bench.

Behind Ron Guidry's 20th win, the Yankees take the first game against Detroit 9–1. New York scores 8 in the 7th. Detroit wins the 2nd 5–4 to keep New York 5 games behind Boston.

5th The Twins Dan Ford costs his team a run during a 4–3 loss to the White Sox. On 3B when a teammate singles, Ford backpedals homeward, signaling Jose Morales to follow him home. Morales arrives there ahead of Ford, who is out for being passed on the bases.

The Expos beat the Cubs 10–8 in a 9-inning game that sees a ML record 45 players participate.

7th The Yankees, 4 games behind the Red Sox in the AL East, arrive in Boston for a crucial 4-game series. The Yanks begin the "Boston Massacre" with a 15–3 rout, which will be followed by 13–2, 7–0, and 7–4 victories. The Yankees outhit the Red Sox 67-21, and outscore them 42-9, in a sweep that leaves the teams in a tie for first place, and caps a remarkable march to the top from 4th place, 14 games out.

14th Jim Bouton, 38, after retiring from pro baseball, earns a 4–1 win for the Braves over the Giants. It is Bouton's first ML victory since 1970, and the last of his career.

The Angels score 13 unearned runs in the 9th inning to cap a 16–1 win over the Rangers.

15th The Dodgers become the first ML team ever to draw 3 million fans. Jay Blood is the historic 3 millionth spectator as the Dodgers shut out the Braves 5–0. The victory is dampened when coach Jim Gilliam suffers a brain hemorrhage.

Phil Garner hits his 2nd grand slam in 2 days as the Pirates beat the Expos 6–1. Garner is the first NL player to have slams in consecutive games since Jimmy Sheckard (9/23, 24/01).

19th During a 12–11 win over the Cubs, the Pirates' 38-year-old, lead-footed Willie Stargell attempts to steal 2B. The Cubs' SS waits with the ball as Stargell slides 10 feet short of the base, signaling "time-out."

21st The Cubs tie an NL record by using 27 players during a 14-inning 3–2 loss to the Pirates.

23rd The Angels 27-year-old OF Lyman Bostock, a .311 lifetime hitter, is killed by a shotgun blast while riding in a car in Gary, IN. The shot was meant for one of the other passengers in the car.

24th Ron Guidry gains his 3rd 2-hit shutout of the month 2–0 over the Indians. The Yankees ace had victimized the Red Sox on September 9th (7–0) and 15th (4–0).

26th New York District Court Judge Constance Baker Motley rules that women sportswriters cannot be banned from locker rooms in the state.

Baltimore's Mike Flanagan has a no-hitter against Cleveland with 2 outs in the 9th inning. Gary Alexander's HR and 2 singles follow, and Don Stanhouse must come in to save the 3–1 Orioles win.

30th Baltimore 2B Rich Dauer makes his only error of the season in the final game, a 5–4 loss to Detroit. Dauer's 86 games and 425 chances without miscue are AL records.

The Phillies overcome a first-inning grand slam by Willie Stargell to beat the Pirates 10–8 and finally clinch the NL East title. Winning P Randy Lerch contributes 2 HRs to his cause.

OCTOBER

1st Rangers manager Billy Hunter is fired following a 9–4 victory over the Mariners. Seattle's Kevin Pasley homers in what will be his last ML at bat.

2nd The Yankees and Red Sox, tied for first at the end of the regular season, play a dramatic one-game playoff at Fenway for the AL East title. New York prevails 5–4 behind Bucky Dent's 3-run HR off Mike Torrez and Guidry's 25th win against just 3 losses. Guidry's .893 percentage is a ML record for a 20-game winner. Goose Gossage saves the game, getting Yaz to pop out with 2 on and 2 out in the 9th.

3rd Reggie Jackson, "Mr. October," hits a 3-run HR, a single, and a double, to lead the Yankees to a 7–1 win over the Royals in the opening game of the AL Championship Series.

4th Steve Garvey smashes 2 HRs and a triple to pace the Dodgers to a 9–5 win over the Phillies in the opener of the NLCS.

Kansas City notches 16 hits off 3 Yankee pitchers to even the AL series with a 10–4 win.

5th   Tommy John notches a 4-hit shutout to beat the Phils 4–0, as Davey Lopes drives in 3 runs. The Dodgers lead 2 games to none.

6th   Despite 3 HRs by George Brett, the Yankees pull out a 6–5 win in the 3rd game of the LCS. Thurman Munson's homer in the 8th gives the Yanks a 2-1 series lead.

The Phillies stay alive with a 9–4 win in the NL game, led by the pitching and hitting (HR, single, 4 RBI) of Steve Carlton.

7th   The Dodgers win the NLCS 4–3 as Bill Russell's 10th-inning single scores Ron Cey. Dusty Baker collects 4 hits for Los Angeles.

Veteran Roy White leads the Yanks to victory, snapping a 1–1 tie with a HR in the 6th inning. New York gains its 3rd straight championship series over Kansas City.

8th   Dodgers coach Jim Gilliam dies at Inglewood, CA, aged 49.

10th   Davey Lopes collects 2 HRs and 5 RBI to lead the Dodgers to an 11–5 victory over the Yankees in game 1 of the WS.

11th   The Dodgers go 2 games up with a 4–3 win in game 2. Ron Cey drives in all the Dodger runs and Reggie Jackson does the same for the Yankees. Bob Welch saves Burt Hooton's win in dramatic fashion by striking out Jackson in the 9th inning.

13th   Graig Nettles's spectacular defense at 3B highlights the Yankees' first WS win 5–1. Ron Guidry goes 9 innings and gets the victory.

14th   Lou Piniella's 10th-inning single scores Roy White with the winning run as New York evens the Series with a 4–3 win.

15th   The Yankees pummel the Dodgers with 18 hits to win the 5th game 12–2. Bucky Dent, Mickey Rivers, and Brian Doyle have 3 hits each.

17th   The Yanks win their 4th straight game 7–2 to clinch their 2nd consecutive WS over the Dodgers as Doyle and Series MVP Dent have 3 hits apiece.

19th   The White Sox fire Larry Doby, naming Don Kessinger as player-manager for the 1979 season.

25th   The Padres Gaylord Perry becomes the first pitcher to win the Cy Young Award in both leagues.

Perry copped the NL honors with a 21-6 record and a 2.72 ERA.

NOVEMBER

1st   Guidry is the unanimous choice for the AL Cy Young Award. The southpaw led the league in wins, percentage, shutouts (9), and ERA (1.74).

4th   The 3rd annual reentry free-agent draft is held at the Plaza Hotel, New York City. Pete Rose, Tommy John, and Darrell Evans are the biggest names among the eligible players.

7th   Boston's Jim Rice outpoints New York's Ron Guidry, 353-291, to win the AL MVP Award. Rice led the league in hits (213), triples (15), HRs (46), RBI (139), and slugging (.600), and became the first AL player to accumulate 400 total bases in a season since Joe DiMaggio in 1937.

13th   Luis Tiant, formerly of the Red Sox, becomes the first to sign with a new club following the reentry draft. The pitching star joins the Yankees.

15th   The Pirates Dave Parker wins the NL MVP Award, 320-194 over the Dodgers Steve Garvey. Parker had 30 HRs, 117 RBI, and league-leading figures in batting (.334), slugging (.585), and total bases (340).

21st   Brave Bob Horner edges Padre Ozzie Smith to win the NL Rookie of the Year Award. Horner batted .266 with 23 HRs in just 323 at bats.

22nd   2B Lou Whitaker, who batted .285 for the Tigers, wins the AL Rookie of the Year, receiving 21 of 28 votes.

The Yankees sign Tommy John, a reentry free agent formerly with the Dodgers.

The Ford Motor Credit Company purchases holdings of the General Electric Credit Company, thereby acquiring 100 percent interest in the Houston Astros.

28th   The Reds fire manager Sparky Anderson after 9 years, during which the club averaged 96 wins per season and won 5 divisional titles, 4 league pennants, and 2 World Championships.

The Orioles sign pitcher Steve Stone, a reentry free agent formerly with the White Sox.

DECEMBER

2nd TSN announces the Gold Glove winners. SS Mark Belanger wins for the 8th and final time, while 1B Keith Hernandez and C Bob Boone are each honored for the first time.

4th The annual ML draft is held at Orlando, FL. Only 7 players are selected.

5th Free agent Pete Rose signs a 4-year, $3.2 million contract with the Phillies, temporarily making him the highest-paid athlete in team sports.

7th The Red Sox trade P Bill Lee to the Expos for IF Stan Papi.

8th The Rangers trade 3B-SS Toby Harrah to the Indians for 3B Buddy Bell.

20th Willard Mullin, 76, the nation's top sports cartoonist and creator of the "Brooklyn Bum," dies at Corpus Christi, TX.

Don Blasingame is named manager of the Hanshin Tigers, the first American not of Japanese descent to lead a Japanese team.

1979

JANUARY

5th   The Twins re-sign reentry free agent P Mike Marshall.

17th   Danny O'Brien signs a contract as president and chief executive officer of the Mariners, 9 days after resigning as the Rangers GM.

23rd   Willie Mays receives 409 of 432 votes in the BBWAA election to earn enshrinement in the Hall of Fame.

FEBRUARY

3rd   The Twins trade 7-time batting champion Rod Carew to the Angels for OF Ken Landreaux, 3B Dave Engle, and 2 pitchers.

7th   Minor league P Jesse Orosco becomes the "player to be named later," going to the Mets in compensation for P Jerry Koosman, who had been sent to the Twins.

11th   Phillies P Larry Christenson falls during a charity bicycle caravan, fracturing his collarbone.

23rd   The Phillies trade 5 players to the Cubs for 2B Manny Trillo, OF Greg Gross, and C Dave Rader.

MARCH

7th   The Special Veterans Committee selects Warren Giles and slugger Hack Wilson for the Hall of Fame.

The exhibition season opens with semipro and amateur umpires in place of ML arbiters, who are staging a collective holdout.

9th   Commissioner Kuhn issues a notice to all clubs urging that reporters, regardless of sex, be treated equally in the matter of access to locker rooms.

26th   The Padres and Giants announce that the 1980 exhibition series between the 2 teams will be played in Tokyo. But Giants owner Bob Lurie leaves the decision up to his players and they reject the agreement.

27th   The Phillies trade 3B Richie Hebner and 2B Jose Moreno to the Mets for P Nino Espinosa.

30th   Fifty of 52 ML umpires meet in Chicago and reject new offers from the AL and NL.

APRIL

4th   More than 20 umpires picket the ML season opener at Cincinnati. The game goes ahead anyway and the Giants beat the Reds 11–5.

5th   Baltimore manager Earl Weaver wins his 1,000th game as a skipper.

6th   The Astros beat the Braves 2–1. Atlanta loses the services of Rookie of the Year 3B Bob Horner for the next 32 games due to an ankle injury.

7th   In the earliest no-hitter in ML history, the Astros Ken Forsch shuts downs the Braves 6–0. Together with Bob Forsch, who hurled a no-hitter in 1978, the brothers become the first to pitch no-hit games.

Clemson defeats North Carolina State 41–9, tying the NCAA record for scoring.

10th   The White Sox lose their season opener 10–2 to the Blue Jays. Their play is so pathetic that Chicago owner Bill Veeck offers every fan at the game free admission to the Sox' next contest.

J. R. Richard throws a ML record 6 wild pitches in the Astrodome against the Dodgers, but strikes out 13 and wins 2–1.

17th   At Oakland, only 653 fans show up to watch the A's beat the Mariners 6–5.

19th   Following a 6–3 loss to the Orioles, Yankees Goose Gossage and Cliff Johnson brawl in the clubhouse. Gossage sustains a sprained ligament in his left thumb, and will be sidelined until July 12th.

20th   After the fight, Reggie Jackson predicts that Cliff Johnson's days as a Yankee are numbered. He is proved correct when Johnson is traded to Cleveland on June 15th for Don Hood.

24th   Substitute umpires consult 28 minutes over a decision, change their minds twice, and finally issue a compromise decision. Both the Mets and the Giants play the game under protest; the Mets win 10–3.

28th   Eddie Murray hits his first career grand slam to give the Orioles a 6–4 win over the White Sox.

30th In a Carolina League game, Alexandria's Gary Pellant homers from both sides of the plate in the same inning, leading a 20–7 assault over Salem.

MAY

1st Phil Niekro earns his 200th career win as the Braves beat the Pirates 5–2. The event is saddened by the collapse of Atlanta's popular GM, Bill Lucas, who will die the next day.

3rd Bobby Bonds hits his 300th HR, against Moose Haas in a 6–1 loss to Milwaukee. He has 413 SBs at the time and becomes the 2nd player, after Willie Mays, to have 300 SBs and 300 HRs.

8th During an 8–7 loss to Texas, Kansas City loses 2 regulars, both as a result of being hit by pitches from Ed Farmer. OF Al Cowens suffers a fractured jaw and will miss 21 games. 2B Frank White sustains a broken hand and will sit out 33 contests. Farmer will be traded 3 times in the next 12 months. On June 20, 1980, Cowens will hit a grounder off Farmer and charge the mound.

9th Four bench-clearing brawls and 2 grand slams (Gary Mathews and John Milner) highlight the Pirates wild 17–9 victory over the Braves. Substitute umpires eject 5 players, 4 managers, and a coach.

13th The Padres Randy Jones steals 2B against the Mets in a 5–4 San Diego victory. He is the first pitcher in the team's 11-year history to do so.

 Willie Wilson hits the first of 5 inside-the-park HRs he will collect in 1979, helping the Royals to a 14–5 triumph over the White Sox.

16th NL owners approve the sale of the Astros from the Ford Motor Credit Company to John J. McMullen for a reported $19 million.

17th The wind is *really* blowing out at Wrigley as the Cubs (6) and the Phillies (5) combine for a ML-record-tying 11 HRs during a wild 10-inning slugfest won 23–22 by the Phils. Dave Kingman has 3 HRs and 6 RBI for the Cubs. Teammate Bill Buckner has a grand slam and 7 RBI. Mike Schmidt's 2 HRs include the game-winner in the 10th.

18th Dale Murphy has 3 HRs in 3 at bats, knocking in 5 runs, to pace the Braves to a 6–4 victory over the Giants.

19th ML umpires return to work, 2 days after a labor agreement is reached in New York.

23rd The Rangers Al Oliver hits 3 HRs in a 7–2 win over the Twins.

24th Billy Martin issues a public apology to Reno sportswriter Ray Hagar, with whom he brawled last November. Hagar had filed suit for assault, leading to an out-of-court settlement.

25th Seven different Dodgers, including P Rick Sutcliffe, hit HRs as Los Angeles buries the visiting Reds 17–6.

 At Candlestick Park, the Braves take a 4–1 lead in the 4th with 2 HRs, and the Giants answer back with 3 HR in same inning. Jack Clark adds one in 8th for a 6–4 win.

30th New York's Cliff Johnson crashes into home plate umpire Lou DiMuro in the 11th inning in a game against Milwaukee. DiMuro, unconscious for 32 minutes, is taken to the hospital.

31st Pat Underwood makes his ML debut for Detroit, pitching 8⅓ innings in shutting out Toronto 1–0. The losing pitcher is Pat's brother, Tom.

 The Expos complete a series sweep over the Phillies, each win by shutout. Scott Sanderson is the 1–0 winner today, following whitewashes by teammates Steve Rogers (9–0) and Bill Lee (2–0).

JUNE

7th Charlotte's Mike Boddicker sets a Southern League record with 18 strikeouts in an 8–2 win over Knoxville.

8th The Mariners make Al Chambers the number-one pick in the free-agent draft. The Mets take UCLA P Tim Leary with the 2nd pick. The Blue Jays, picking 3rd, take high school C Jay Schroeder, who will play football for UCLA and the NFL, but will never catch in the ML. Kansas City picks football players on the 4th (Dan Marino) and the 17th (John Elway) rounds.

9th Nolan Ryan strikes out 16 batters in a 4-hit 9–1 Angels victory over the Tigers.

 Charlie Manuel, playing for the Kintetsu Buffaloes, is critically injured when a brushback pitch fractures his jaw in 7 places. Hitting .371 with 24 HRs and 60 RBI at the time, Manuel will earn the respect of the fans for his determined comeback effort.

11th   The Cardinals Ted Simmons homers from both sides of the plate in a 9–7 win over the Dodgers.

12th   The Tigers fire manager Les Moss, hiring Sparky Anderson.

13th   The Astros trade slugger Bob Watson to the Red Sox for 2 minor league pitchers and cash.

14th   For the 2nd straight day, Willie Aikens hits a grand slam, leading the Royals to a 10–2 win over the Blue Jays.

The Giants lose to the Cubs 8–6, but Willie McCovey hits his 513rd career HR off Dennis Lamp. McCovey becomes the all-time lefthanded HR hitter in NL history.

15th   Willie Wilson homers from both sides of the plate, including a 3-run inside-the-park job in the 9th inning, to lead Kansas City to a 14–11 victory over Milwaukee.

19th   In New York 36,211 fans show up to witness the return of Billy Martin as Yankee manager, but the Yanks lose to the Blue Jays 5–4. Martin had been named to replace Bob Lemon (34-31) the previous day, and begins his 2nd stint as New York's skipper, a season earlier than previously announced.

24th   Rickey Henderson makes his ML debut for Oakland in a 5–1 loss to Texas in the first game of a doubleheader. Henderson has a single and double in 4 at bats, and steals the first base of his ML career.

Redbirds Ted Simmons suffers a broken bone in his left wrist during a 6–2 loss to the Mets. He will miss 28 games.

28th   The Pirates trade pitchers Ed Whitson, Al Holland, and Fred Breining to the Giants for P Dave Roberts and infielders Bill Madlock and Lenny Randle.

30th   The Cubs, led by Mike Vail's grand slam, score 5 runs in the top of the 11th to break a 3–3 tie with the Mets. New York storms back with 6 runs in the bottom of the frame to win the game 9–8.

Less than halfway into its maiden season, the Inter-American League—planned as a new Triple-A circuit—folds. The Miami Amigos, with a 43-17 record, are declared the league champions.

JULY

1st   Boston speedster Jerry Remy, batting .304 on the season, injures a knee sliding home during a 6–5 loss to the Yankees. Remy will appear in only 7 more games all year.

2nd   Indians manager Jeff Torborg announces his resignation effective at the end of the season. Three weeks later he will be fired and replaced by Dave Garcia.

4th   The Phillies Steve Carlton shuts out the Mets 1–0 on a one-hitter, but the Phils manage to lose 3 other hurlers on the same day: Larry Christenson pulls a groin muscle, Dick Ruthven goes on the disabled list, and Randy Lerch fractures his thumb in a brawl.

7th   Mike Schmidt homers in his first 3 times up for the Phillies, to give him a ML-record-tying 4 straight over 2 games. Schmidt flies to the warning track in his next at bat, and the Phils lose 8–6 to the Giants. Schmidt will hit 3 more HRs in the next 3 games to tie the NL record of 7 HRs in 5 games.

8th   Ben Oglivie has 3 HRs in 3 at bats as the Brewers beat the Tigers 5–4 in the first game of a doubleheader. Olgivie drives in the winning run in the 2nd game as the Brewers take it 3–1.

10th   Philadelphia's Del Unser homers in his 3rd consecutive pinch-hit appearance (June 30th, July 5th) to tie the ML record set by Lee Lacy in 1978. The Phillies beat the Padres 6–5.

12th   The Tigers win the first game of a scheduled doubleheader 4–1 on Disco Demolition Night at Comiskey Park. Thousands of fans swarm onto the field, littering and tearing it up, and causing the White Sox to forfeit the 2nd game.

13th   California's Nolan Ryan and Boston's Steve Renko each lose no-hitters in the 9th inning, and each settle for one-hit victories: 6–1 over New York, and 2–0 over Oakland, respectively.

14th   Chicago's Claudell Washington has 3 HRs and 5 RBI in a 12–4 defeat of Detroit.

15th   The Geneva Cubs score 15 runs in the 9th inning to cap a 29–4 romp over the Utica Blue Jays in a New York-Pennsylvania League game. Scott Fletcher paces the attack with 2 singles, 4 doubles, a HR, and 8 RBI.

17th The NL wins its 8th straight All-Star Game 7–6 at Seattle. Lee Mazzilli homers to tie the game in the 8th, and walks in the 9th to bring in the winning run. Dave Parker, with 2 outstanding throws, is named the game's MVP, and Pete Rose plays a record 5th All-Star position.

20th Rusty Staub, a spring holdout who got off to a slow start, is traded by Detroit to former team Montreal for a minor league player to be named later.

22nd The Royals George Brett has 3 HRs and 5 RBI in a 7–6 win over the Rangers.

24th In the first game of a doubleheader, Seattle C Bob Stinson ties a ML record by allowing 2 Baltimore batters to reach base on catcher's interference.

27th The Brewers edge the Yankees 6–5 and Cecil Cooper becomes the 4th AL player this month to hit 3 HRs in a game.

28th The Cubs Dave Kingman has a single and 3 consecutive HRs during a 6–4 loss to the Mets. It is Kingman's 2nd 3-HR game of the season (May 17th), and enables him to tie the ML record with 5 HRs over 2 consecutive games.

AUGUST

1st Following the Yankees-White Sox game, members of the New York club create a minor scandal by autographing the bare behind of a young woman who boards the team bus outside Comiskey Park.

In an 8-player deal, the Rangers send OF Oscar Gamble to the Yankees and acquire OF Mickey Rivers.

2nd Yankees C Thurman Munson, 32, perishes at Canton, Ohio, in a crash of the plane he was piloting. A crowd of 51,151 will attend the memorial tribute at Yankee Stadium the following day.

3rd Tony LaRussa takes over as manager of the White Sox, a day after the resignation of Don Kessinger.

4th During a 6–2 loss to the Astros, Braves knuckleballer Phil Niekro ties modern ML records with 4 wild pitches in one inning (5th) and 6 in one game.

5th The Phillies beat the Pirates 12–8 in the first game of a doubleheader. Philadelphia's Greg Luzinski and Pittsburgh's John Milner each hit a grand slam,

and Rose collects his 2,427th career single to break Honus Wagner's NL record.

The Red Sox demolish the Brewers in a doubleheader 7–2 and 19–5. The Sox amass 27 hits in the 2nd game.

Willie Mays, Warren Giles, and Hack Wilson are inducted into the Hall of Fame.

6th The Rangers blast the Padres 12–5 in the Hall of Fame game featuring a record 9 HRs.

8th Oakland's Matt Keough loses to California 8–1, running his season record to 0-14, and tying a dubious ML record.

9th Longtime Dodgers owner Walter O'Malley dies at age 75.

11th The Pirates Ed Ott hits a grand slam off Phillie reliever Tug McGraw in the 8th inning as the Bucs win 14–11. It is the 4th grand slam that McGraw has yielded this year, setting a new NL mark and tying him for this questionable honor with Detroit's Ray Narleski (1959).

13th Lou Brock collects his 3,000th career hit, a single off Dennis Lamp, as the Cardinals top the Cubs 3–2.

14th The Astros Joaquin Andujar hurls a 4-hitter, and hits a 2-run inside-the-park homer, to defeat the Expos 2–1.

15th Eddie Murray, no gazelle, surprises the White Sox with a 12th-inning steal of home to give the Orioles a 2–1 win.

21st The Mets win a protested game against the Astros 5–0. With 2 outs in the 9th inning, Houston's Jeff Leonard flies to CF to apparently end the game. Umpire Doug Harvey rules that time had been called, and orders Leonard back to the plate. He then singles to left. The Mets were without a 1B, however, so the umps order Leonard to bat once more. He flies to LF to end the game.

23rd Commissioner Kuhn slaps Padres owner Ray Kroc with a $100,000 fine for tampering, following remarks Kroc made about potential free agents Joe Morgan and Graig Nettles.

25th Angel Don Baylor knocks in 8 runs during a 24–2 slaughter of the Blue Jays. California amasses 26 hits.

28th   The Dodgers release P Andy Messersmith, ending his 12-year NL career with a 130-99 record and 2.86 ERA.

29th   Eddie Murray drives in all the Baltimore runs during a 7–4 win in the 2nd game of a doubleheader with the Twins. Murray belts 3 consecutive HRs—2 righthanded, one lefthanded.

Kansas City blasts Milwaukee pitching for an 18–8 victory. Milwaukee finally uses 3B Sal Bando, 2B Jim Gantner and C Buck Martinez in relief.

31st   The Phillies fire Danny Ozark, senior manager (since 1973) in the NL. Farm director Dallas Green takes over.

SEPTEMBER

1st   Carney Lansford hits 3 consecutive HRs as the Angels down the Indians 7–4.

5th   Matt Keough of the A's beats the Brewers 6–1 for his first victory after 14 straight losses. He ended 1978 with 4 defeats and barely avoided tying the AL record of 19 consecutive losses.

6th   The Giants fire manger Joe Altobelli, promoting coach Dave Bristol in his place.

12th   Boston's Carl Yastrzemski singles off New York's Jim Beattie for his 3,000th career hit. The Sox win 9–2 and Yaz becomes the first AL player to collect both 3,000 hits and 400 HRs.

15th   Boston's Bob Watson hits for the cycle in a 10–2 win over the Orioles. Watson becomes the first player to accomplish the feat in the AL and NL.

16th   Willie Wilson hits his 5th inside-the-park homer this season in a 6–3 loss to Seattle at Kansas City. It is the most IPHR hit in a season since Kiki Cuyler hit 8 for the Pirates in 1925.

17th   The Royals George Brett collects his 20th triple of the season in a 16–4 romp over the Angels. Brett becomes the 6th player ever, and the first since Willie Mays in 1957, to collect 20 doubles, 20 triples, and 20 HRs in the same season. He will finish with totals of 42, 20, and 23.

18th   Yanks manager Billy Martin reportedly pays rookie P Bob Kammeyer $100 to hit former Yankee Cliff Johnson with a pitch in a game against Cleveland.

19th   Bruce Sutter saves both games in Chicago's doubleheader victory over the Mets. His 37 saves tie the NL mark.

21st   Royal infielder U. L. Washington homers from both sides of the plate during a 13–4 win over the A's. These are the first homers of Washington's 3-year career.

23rd   St. Louis legend Lou Brock steals the 938th—and final—base of his career in a 7–4 win against the New York Mets. He tops 19th century speedster Billy Hamilton by one.

24th   Pete Rose singles in the Phillies 7–2 loss to the Cardinals, giving him 200 hits in a season for the 10th time. He breaks the ML record of 9 formerly held by Ty Cobb. Rose hits safely in his 18th straight game, and will extend it to 23 by the end of the season.

Herman Franks resigns as Cubs manager, and is replaced by Preston Gomez.

25th   Mickey and Rick Mahler hurl in the same game as the Braves fall to the Astros 8–0. It is the most recent instance of brothers pitching for the same team in the same game.

Frank Tanana pitches a 4–1 victory over the Royals to clinch the AL division title for the Angels.

26th   Atlanta's Phil Niekro notches his 20th win of the season by beating his brother Joe, the NL's only other 20-game winner in 1979, 9–4. The Niekro brothers are the second pair (the other was Jim and Gaylord Perry) to win 20 games in the same year, and Phil Niekro, who finishes at 21-20, is the first pitcher since Wilbur Wood in 1973 to win and lose 20 games the same year, and the first NL pitcher to do so since 1905.

28th   Switch-hitting Cardinal SS Garry Templeton collects 3 hits against the Mets and becomes the first player to get 100 hits from each side of the plate. During the last 9 games, he batted exclusively righthanded to set the record.

Frank Pastore shuts out the Braves 3–0 as the Reds clinch the NL West title.

29th   The Astros J. R. Richard shuts out the Dodgers 3–0 and fans 11 batters to break his own modern NL record for strikeouts by a righthander. Richard finishes with 313 K's, 10 more than in 1978. One of 5 Dodgers hits is a single by Manny Mota, his 146th pinch hit, breaking the mark of 145 formerly held by Smoky Burgess.

30th Minnesota's Jerry Koosman defeats Milwaukee 5–0 on the final day of the season for his 20th win of the year. It is the only time the Brewers are shut out the entire year, as they fail to tie a record set by the Yankees in 1932.

Two ML managers bite the dust. The Padres fire Roger Craig and the Blue Jays do the same to Roy Hartsfield. San Diego will hire broadcaster Jerry Coleman the next day, while Toronto will hire scout Bobby Mattick on October 18th.

OCTOBER

2nd In the opening game of the NL Championship Series, Willie Stargell hits a 3-run HR in the 11th inning to give the Pirates a 5–2 victory over the Reds.

3rd John Lowenstein's 3-run HR in the bottom of the 10th inning gives the Orioles a 6–3 win over the Angels in the first game of the ALCS.

The Pirates win in the 10th inning 3–2 as Omar Moreno and Dave Parker smack singles that snap a 2–2 tie.

4th Baltimore takes a 9–1 lead in the LCS game, but the Angels score 7 runs in the last 4 innings only to fall short 9–8. Eddie Murray drives in 4 runs for the Orioles.

5th The Pirates complete a sweep of the LCS, beating the Reds 7–1. Stargell hits another HR and is named series MVP.

The Angels score 2 in the bottom of the 9th inning of the AL game to avert elimination 4–3. Larry Harlow doubles in the winning run.

6th Scott McGregor's 8–0 shutout gives the Orioles the AL pennant. Pat Kelly notches 3 RBI with a HR and a single.

10th The Orioles score 5 times in the first inning of the WS, hanging on to defeat the Pirates 5–4 in game 1. Dave Parker has 4 hits for the losers.

11th Manny Sanguillen's pinch-hit, 2-out single in the 9th scores Ed Ott and breaks a 2–2 tie as the Pirates win 3–2 and even the Series at one game apiece.

12th Kiko Garcia collects 4 hits and 4 RBI to lead the Orioles to an 8–4 triumph in game 3.

13th Baltimore scores 6 runs in the 8th inning en route to a 9–6 win, taking a 3-games-to-one advantage. Pinch-hit doubles by John Lowenstein and Terry Crowley drive in 4 runs.

14th Bill Madlock has 4 hits and Tim Foli drives in 3 runs as the Pirates stay alive with a 7–1 victory.

16th John Candelaria and Kent Tekulve combine on a 4–0 shutout as the Pirates send the WS to its 7th game. Omar Moreno notches 3 singles.

17th In game 7, Stargell's 3rd WS homer propels Pittsburgh to its 3rd straight win 4–1, and the World Championship. Pops is named Series MVP.

23rd Billy Martin is involved in a barroom altercation with Joseph Cooper, a Minnesota marshmallow salesman. Cooper requires 15 stitches to close a gash in his lip.

26th Commissioner Kuhn notifies Hall of Famer Willie Mays that if he accepts a position with Bally Manufacturing Corporation, owner of several gambling casinos, he must disassociate himself from ML baseball. Mays, a part-time coach and goodwill ambassador for the Mets, will relinquish his duties upon accepting Bally's job offer on October 29th.

28th George Steinbrenner announces that Billy Martin is fired again as a result of his recent barroom fight. Dick Howser is named to replace him.

31st Mike Flanagan, who posted a 23-9 record for the Orioles, is named the winner of the AL Cy Young Award by a comfortable margin over the Yankees Tommy John.

NOVEMBER

1st Edward Bennett Williams buys the Orioles from Jerold Hoffberger for a reported $12.3 million.

In separate deals, the Yankees acquire OF Ruppert Jones from the Mariners and C Rick Cerone from the Blue Jays, giving up 7 players, including 1B Chris Chambliss, SS Damaso Garcia, OF Juan Beniquez, and P Jim Beattie.

2nd Nolan Ryan and Joe Morgan are the top names available in the reentry draft held at New York's Plaza Hotel.

3rd Teams of U.S. all-stars depart on an exhibition tour of Japan. The NL stars will win 4 of 7 games versus the AL, and the combined forces will split a pair of games with the Japanese all-stars.

7th Reliever Bruce Sutter, who had a 2.23 ERA and saved 37 of the Cubs' 80 victories, wins the NL Cy Young Award by a 72-66 margin over the Astros Joe Niekro.

8th The Yankees ink 1B-DH Bob Watson and P Rudy May, the first reentry free agents to sign long-term contracts with new teams.

Mets president Lorinda de Roulet announces the team is for sale, beginning a 2-month bidding war.

13th For the first time in history, 2 players share the MVP Award. The NL co-winners are Willie Stargell, the Pirates spiritual leader, who batted .281 with 32 HRs; and the Cardinals Keith Hernandez, who led the NL in runs (116), doubles (48), and batting (.344).

14th The Dodgers sign reentry free agent P Dave Goltz, formerly of the Twins, to a 6-year, $3 million pact.

California's Don Baylor, who led the AL in runs and RBI, is named the league's MVP.

16th The Red Sox sign 1B Tony Perez, a reentry free agent formerly with the Expos.

17th On a flight to Austin, TX, Daniel Okrent sketches out the first draft of rules for what would become Rotisserie League Baseball. Had the friends he was seeing not ignored these rules, the Rotisserie League would have been called Pit League, after the Austin barbeque joint where Okrent first unveiled them. Two weeks later in New York, he pitches the idea to a more receptive group with whom Okrent lunched monthly at La Rotisserie Francaise.

19th The Astros sign reentry free agent Nolan Ryan, formerly of the Angels, to a 4-year, $4.5 million contract, making him the highest-paid player in the ML.

20th The Braves sign reliever Al Hrabosky, "the Mad Hungarian," a reentry free agent formerly with the Royals, to a 5-year pact worth $2.2 million.

26th 3B John Castino, who batted .285 for the Twins, and SS Alfredo Griffin, who hit .287 for the Blue Jays, tie for the AL Rookie of the Year award, each receiving 7 of the 28 votes. The deadlock precipitates a change in the voting system, effective in 1980.

28th P Rick Sutcliffe, who went 17-10 for the sub-.500 Dodgers, receives 20 of 24 votes to earn the NL Rookie of the Year honors.

29th Commissioner Kuhn lets Martin off with a warning, following the October 23rd incident.

DECEMBER

1st Padres OF Dave Winfield and Texas 3B Buddy Bell are first-time honorees as TSN announces the 1979 Gold Glove teams.

7th The Cardinals trade OF Jerry Mumphrey and P John Denny to the Indians for OF Bobby Bonds. The Tigers swap OF Ron LeFlore to the Expos for P Dan Schatzeder.

12th The Giants sign reentry free agents 2B Rennie Stennett, C Milt May, and OF Jim Wohlford to contracts worth a total of $4.825 million.

31st The Basic Agreement between players and owners expires, precipitating more than 19 months of bitter negotiations, culminating in the 1981 player strike.

1980

JANUARY

9th Al Kaline and Duke Snider are elected to the Hall of Fame by the BBWAA. Kaline is the 10th player to be elected in his first year of eligibility, while Snider is making his 11th appearance on the ballot.

24th Nelson Doubleday and Fred Wilpon head a group of investors which purchases the New York Mets for a reported $21.1 million, the highest price paid to date for a ML baseball franchise. Doubleday, whose publishing company supplied 80 percent of the purchase price, will serve as chairman of the board, while Wilpon, a former teammate of Sandy Koufax's at Brooklyn's Lafayette High School, will be president and chief operating officer.

31st Joe Morgan, a 2-time NL MVP for the Cincinnati Reds, signs as a free agent with the Houston Astros.

FEBRUARY

12th The AL's offer to buy out the remaining 8 years of the Oakland A's lease at the Oakland Coliseum expires, effectively blocking the sale of the club from Charlie Finley to oil man Marvin Davis. Davis had planned to move the club to Denver, but the Oakland Coliseum Board, backed by the city council, refused the league's $4 million offer.

15th The San Diego Padres trade 41-year-old pitcher Gaylord Perry and a pair of minor leaguers to the Texas Rangers for 1B Willie Montanez.

16th Brewers coach Harvey Kuenn has his right leg amputated below the knee after 4 operations to remove a blood clot.

17th While taping separate interviews at KNBC-TV studios in Burbank, CA, Giants coach Jim Lefebvre and Dodgers manager Tommy Lasorda trade punches after a brief argument, leaving Lasorda with a bloody lip. Lefebvre had been a Dodger coach in 1979 until he was fired by Lasorda.

20th Just 4 months after being fired by the Yankees for the 2nd time, Billy Martin signs a 2-year contract to manage the Oakland A's.

MARCH

6th Brewers manager George Bamberger suffers a heart attack at the club's Sun City, AZ, training camp. Coach Buck Rodgers is named interim manager for Bamberger, who will undergo quintuple coronary bypass surgery on March 26th and will not return to the dugout until June 6th.

8th Rangers owner Brad Corbett agrees to sell the club to a group of investors headed by Fort Worth businessman Eddie Chiles.

While waiting for the team bus outside his hotel during the Cleveland Indians 3-game exhibition series against the Mexico City Reds, rookie OF Joe Charboneau is stabbed by a crazed fan wielding a ball-point pen. The pen penetrates one inch and strikes a rib, sidelining Charboneau for 4 days, but he will recover to win the AL Rookie of the Year award.

10th The National Labor Relations Board rules in favor of the umpires' union in its dispute with the National League. The union had demanded that the NL release its umpire evaluations, particularly those of the "scabs" who were retained after filling in for striking umpires in 1979.

12th Slugger Chuck Klein and former Red Sox owner Tom Yawkey are elected to the Hall of Fame by the Special Veterans Committee. Yawkey is the first club owner selected who never served as a player, manager, or general manager.

31st The Expos trade 1B-OF Rusty Staub to the Rangers for IF Chris Smith and OF LaRue Washington.

APRIL

1st After failing to come up with a new collective bargaining agreement with the owners, the Executive Board of the Players' Association votes unanimously to cancel the 92 remaining exhibition games and to strike on May 22nd if a deal has not been reached by then. During spring training, the players had voted 971-1 in favor of a strike. The lone dissenter was Kansas City's Jerry Terrell, who voted no for religious reasons.

9th The Reds Tom Seaver is scratched from his Opening Day start against the Braves because of the flu, and his replacement, Frank Pastore, tosses a 3-hit shutout.

11th   Giants 3B Darrell Evans makes 3 errors in the 7th inning of a 5–3 loss to the Padres. This ties the NL record for errors by a 3B in one inning.

12th   In his first game in the NL since 1971, Astros pitcher Nolan Ryan hits his first career home run, a 3-run shot off the Dodgers Don Sutton. Ryan leaves the game with a 5–4 lead, but Los Angeles wins 6–5 in 17 innings.

The Milwaukee Brewers tie a ML record with 2 grand slams in the 2nd inning of a 16–1 rout of the Red Sox. Cecil Cooper and Don Money connect against starter Mike Torrez and reliever Chuck Rainey, respectively.

13th   In his first ML start, Cincinnati's Charlie Liebrandt shuts out the Braves 5–0.

16th   Oakland's Matt Keough matches last season's victory total with his 2nd win in as many starts 6–1 over Seattle. Keough was 2-17 in 1979.

18th   The winless Braves shut out the undefeated Reds 5–0 behind Rick Matula's 5-hitter. Cincinnati had opened the season with 8 consecutive wins, the best start in club history.

19th   Houston's J. R. Richard fires a one-hitter against the Dodgers, striking out 12 in a 2–0 victory. Reggie Smith's infield roller in the 4th inning is LA's lone hit.

22nd   In a classic Wrigley Field slugfest, the Cubs beat the Cardinals 16–12 on Barry Foote's 2-out grand slam in the bottom of the 9th. Foote drives in 8 runs overall with 4 hits and 2 home runs, and teammate Ivan DeJesus hits for the cycle to help Chicago rally from a 12–5 deficit.

23rd   Angels P Bruce Kison settles for a one-hitter when Minnesota's Ken Landreaux rips a double with one out in the 9th inning of California's 17–0 romp. It is the 2nd time in a year that Kison has lost a no-hitter with one out in the 9th. For Landreaux, the hit marks the beginning of a 31-game hitting streak.

25th   Larry Parrish belts 3 home runs and drives in all 7 of the Expos' runs in an 11-inning 8–7 loss to the Braves.

Making his first appearance in Minnesota since his fight with a marshmallow salesman there last fall, A's manager Billy Martin has to be restrained by umpires from attacking a fan who was pelting him with marshmallows during the Twins' 10–3 victory.

26th   Steve Carlton of the Phillies sets the modern NL record with his 6th career one-hitter, a 7–0 shutout of former team the Cardinals.

27th   The Twins score 10 runs in the first inning on their way to a 20–11 thrashing of the A's. Minnesota starter Geoff Zahn can't hold the 10–0 lead, allowing 8 runs in 4⅓ innings, and Doug Corbett picks up the win in relief.

29th   The Brewers smash 7 home runs in a 14–1 rout of the Indians. Ben Oglivie and Sal Bando lead the way with 2 apiece.

30th   Kansas City's Larry Gura pitches a one-hitter against the Blue Jays for his 3rd shutout in 5 starts, surrendering only a 7th-inning double to Damaso Garcia. Losing pitcher Jesse Jefferson holds the Royals hitless for 6⅔ innings in the 3–0 loss.

MAY

1st   Pittsburgh's Bill "Mad Dog" Madlock is fined $5,000 and suspended 15 games by NL president Chub Feeney for poking umpire Jerry Crawford in the face with his glove after being called out on strikes with the bases loaded. Madlock appeals and remains in uniform, but finally withdraws the appeal and begins serving the suspension on June 6th, after disgruntled NL umpires threaten to eject him from every game he tries to play in.

Pete Falcone ties the modern ML record by striking out the first 6 batters of the game, but his Mets lose to the Phillies 2–1. Falcone finishes with 8 strikeouts in 7 innings.

3rd   Rangers pitcher Ferguson Jenkins defeats the Orioles 3–2 to become only the 4th pitcher to win 100 games in each league. He won 149 games for the Phillies and Cubs before joining the AL in 1974.

Giants 1B Willie McCovey hits his 521st and final career home run off Montreal's Scott Sanderson, tying him with Ted Williams on the all-time list. He will retire on June 6th.

4th   Royals catcher Darrell Porter, returning to the starting lineup after spending 6 weeks in alcohol and drug rehabilitation, drives in 3 runs in Kansas City's 5–3 win over Boston.

Toronto's Otto Velez ties an AL record with 4 home runs in a doubleheader sweep of Cleveland. Velez homers 3 times in the opener, including a grand slam in the first inning and a game winner in the bottom of the 10th, and finishes the day with 10 RBI.

White Sox 1B Mike Squires catches the final inning of an 11–1 loss to the Brewers, becoming the first lefthander to catch in the majors since Dale Long in 1958.

7th Kansas City collects 9 consecutive hits (one shy of the AL record set by Boston in 1901) in an 8-run 4th inning, and goes on to defeat Texas 12–5.

13th Ray Knight breaks out of an 0-for-15 slump by homering twice in the 5th inning of a 15–4 win over the Mets. He is the first Red ever to hit 2 home runs in one inning.

Fred Lynn hits for the cycle as the Red Sox beat the Twins 10–5.

14th The Royals pitching staff issues 14 walks in a 16–3 loss to the Yankees. Reliever Larry Christenson is the main culprit, walking 7 batters in just 1⅔ innings.

23rd Five hours after the midnight deadline passes, the players and owners avert a strike by announcing a new 4-year basic agreement. The new deal raises the minimum salary from $21,000 to $30,000 and increases the clubs' contributions to the players' pension fund, but the major issue of free-agent compensation remains unresolved.

Ferguson Jenkins of the Rangers wins his 250th career game, a 3–1 two-hitter versus Oakland.

29th Dodger Bob Welch faces the minimum 27 batters in a 3–0 one-hitter against the Braves. The lone Atlanta base runner is Larvell Blanks, who singles in the 4th inning and is erased on a double play.

Johnny Bench hits 3 home runs off Randy Jones in Cincinnati's 5–3 win over San Diego. It is the 3rd 3-HR game of his career.

30th John Hiller, 37, who recovered from a 1971 heart attack to become one of baseball's best relievers, retires. His 545 games pitched are the most in Tiger history.

31st Ken Landreaux goes 0-for-4 in Minnesota's 11–1 loss to the Orioles Scott McGregor, ending his hitting streak at 31 consecutive games. It is the longest streak in the AL since Dom DiMaggio's 34-game streak in 1949.

The Boston Red Sox hit 6 home runs—4 in the 4th inning, 3 in succession—but lose to the Brewers 19–8.

JUNE

1st The Cleveland Indians tie a ML record with 4 sacrifice flies (Ron Hassey, Dave Rosello, Gary Alexander, and Del Alston) in an 8–7 loss to the Mariners. Seattle adds one more, tying the 2-team single-game record of 5.

3rd The New York Mets select 18-year-old Darryl Strawberry from Los Angeles's Crenshaw High School with the first pick in the annual June free-agent draft. The Blue Jays then pick SS Garry Harris.

6th Minnesota's Geoff Zahn one-hits the Blue Jays 5–0, allowing only a John Mayberry single with 2 out in the 7th.

Cardinals manager Ken Boyer is fired between games of a doubleheader loss to the Expos; he will be replaced the following day by Whitey Herzog, who led the Kansas City Royals to 3 consecutive AL West titles from 1976-78. St. Louis has the worst record in the major leagues (18-34).

11th Houston's J. R. Richard pitches his 3rd consecutive shutout 3–0 versus the Cubs.

12th Mike Easler hits for the cycle to lead Pittsburgh to a 10–6 win over Cincinnati.

13th Pete Rose goes 4-for-5 to move past Honus Wagner into 5th place on the all-time hit list with 3,431. Philadelphia starts the game with 7 consecutive hits and goes on to beat San Diego 9–6.

15th Cleveland's Jorge Orta goes 6-for-6 (5 singles and a double) in a 14–5 rout of the Twins, tying the AL record for hits in a 9-inning game.

20th Leonard Smith, the man who killed Angels outfielder Lyman Bostock with a shotgun blast on September 23, 1978, but was later acquitted of the crime by reason of insanity, is released from Logansport State Hospital and allowed to return to his home in Gary, IN, because psychiatrists say he is no longer mentally ill.

Five foot 4 inch Fred Patek, one of the smallest players of his era, hits 3 home runs in California's 20–2 rout of the Red Sox at Fenway Park. Patek will end the year with 5.

22nd Claudell Washington hits his first 3 NL home runs to lead the Mets to a 9–6 win at Los Angeles and snap a 7-game losing streak.

25th Five Cleveland pitchers issue 14 walks, including 5 with the bases loaded, in a 13–3 loss to Detroit.

26th Commissioner Bowie Kuhn voids the Yankees' drafting of highly touted high school short-stop Billy Cannon, Jr. Four teams had complained that Billy Cannon, Sr., college football's Heismann Trophy winner in 1959, misled them with telegrams saying that his son would go to college, in the hopes that he would then be drafted by the Yankees. In a special draft, the Indians will pick Cannon but he chooses to attend Texas A & M instead. The young Cannon will be drafted number one by the Dallas Cowboys in 1984.

27th The Dodgers Jerry Reuss pitches an 8–0 no-hitter against the Giants at Candlestick Park. Reuss, who strikes out only 2 but doesn't walk a batter, is deprived of a perfect game when SS Bill Russell throws wildly to 1B on Jack Clark's easy grounder in the first inning.

JULY

2nd Chicago's Ross Baumgarten allows only a 7th-inning single to Rod Carew en route to a one-hit 1–0 shutout of the Angels. Baumgarten will finish the season 2-12.

3rd The ML's largest crowd in 7 years (73,096) watches Wayne Garland 2-hit the Yankees 7–0 at Cleveland Stadium.

Ken Landreaux ties the modern ML record with 3 triples in Minnesota's 10–3 win over Texas.

4th Nolan Ryan fans the Reds Cesar Geronimo to become the 4th pitcher ever to reach 3,000 career strikeouts. Ironically, Geronimo was also Bob Gibson's 3,000th career strikeout victim. Despite the milestone, Ryan allows 6 runs in 4⅓ innings and Houston loses 8–1.

6th Steve Carlton (14-4) becomes the major leagues' lefthanded strikeout king, fanning 7 Cardinals in an 8–3 Phillies win to bring his career total to 2,836. Mickey Lolich had held the record with 2,832.

The NL wins its 9th consecutive All-Star Game 4–2 at Dodger Stadium. Reds outfielder Ken Griffey goes 2-for-3 with a solo HR to win the game's MVP Award.

11th The Dodgers sell knuckleballer Charlie Hough to the Rangers for an undisclosed sum.

16th Despite much speculation that he is simply malingering, the Astros place star pitcher J. R. Richard on the 21-day disabled list with a mystery arm problem. The 6 foot 8 inch righthander is 10-4 with a 1.89 ERA and 119 strikeouts in 114 innings, but has removed himself from 10 games this year complaining of fatigue and a "dead arm." On July 23rd, Richard will check into a hospital for a series of physical and psychological tests to determine the cause of his "erratic" behavior.

The California Supreme Court rules that Ted Giannoulas, better known as the man inside the San Diego Chicken suit, can appear publicly in chicken suits similar to the one that brought him fame, but not bearing the call letters of San Diego's KGB radio station. The station had fired Giannoulas when he began appearing publicly in the suit without permission, and claimed it had all rights to the costume, which was first used as a promotional device in 1975.

22nd Atlanta's Bob Horner belts 2 home runs in a 7–5 win over the Expos, giving him 15 homers in his last 23 games and 13 in the month of July, just 2 short of the ML record shared by Hank Greenberg, Joe DiMaggio, and Joe Adcock. Horner will hit one more home run in July, and finish the season with a career-high 35.

24th Hours after signing a new 5-year contract that will boost his salary to $1 million per year, Kansas City's George Brett goes 2-for-4 in a 12–4 win over Chicago to raise his batting average to .379. The Royals lead 2nd-place Texas by 11 games in the AL West.

25th The Cubs fire manager Preston Gomez and replace him with Joey Amalfitano. Chicago is 38-52, last in the NL East.

In the first game of a doubleheader split with the Braves, Mike Schmidt hits his 25th and 26th home runs of the season to pass Del Ennis as the Phillies' all-time HR leader with 261.

30th Attempting to throw for the first time since being hospitalized for tests last week, J. R. Richard suffers a stroke and is rushed to Houston's Methodist Hospital for emergency surgery to remove a life-threatening blood clot in his neck. He will never pitch in the major leagues again.

31st The Rangers beat the Orioles 7–4, snapping pitcher Steve Stone's 14-game winning streak. Stone was 2 shy of the AL record of 16 consecutive wins.

AUGUST

3rd Al Kaline, Duke Snider, Chuck Klein, and Tom Yawkey are inducted into baseball's Hall of Fame in Cooperstown, NY.

4th The Seattle Mariners fire manager Darrell Johnson and replace him with Maury Wills, who becomes the 3rd black manager in ML history. Seattle had lost 9 games in a row and 20 of 24 since the All-Star break.

5th Expos manager Dick Williams wins his 1,000th career game 11–5 over the Mets at Olympic Stadium. He is 3rd in wins among active managers behind Gene Mauch and Earl Weaver.

10th Steve McCatty becomes the 4th A's starter to pitch a 14-inning complete game this season, losing 2–1 to Seattle despite pitching a 6-hitter. Teammates Matt Keough (on May 17th), Mike Norris (June 11th), and Rick Langford (July 20th) have also pitched 14-inning complete games for manager Billy Martin, who will later be widely criticized for ruining their arms through overwork.

11th Reggie Jackson hits his 400th career home run off Chicago's Britt Burns in the 3rd inning of a 3–1 Yankees victory.

12th Tiger Stadium is packed with 48,361 fans to see Mark Fidrych's return to the big leagues, a 5–4 loss to the Red Sox. The 1976 AL Rookie of the Year will go 2-3 with a 5.73 ERA in what will be his final attempt to come back from injury, and his last ML season.

13th The Yankees trade righty Ken Clay and a player to be named later to the Rangers for 41-year-old pitcher Gaylord Perry.

15th Oakland's Rick Langford (13-9) defeats the Mariners 11–3 for his 17th consecutive complete game, the most in the majors since Robin Roberts's 20 in a row in 1953.

17th George Brett goes 4-for-4 with 5 RBI in Kansas City's 8–3 win over Texas, raising his batting average to .401 and extending his hitting streak to 29 consecutive games.

Al Oliver belts 4 home runs—one in the opener and 3 in the nightcap—as the Rangers sweep a doubleheader from the Tigers. He is the 2nd AL player to hit 4 home runs in a doubleheader this season.

19th Jon Matlack holds George Brett hitless, snapping his hitting streak at 30 consecutive games, but Kansas City rallies for 3 runs in the 9th to beat Texas 4–3. Brett batted .467 during the streak and knocked in 42 runs.

Baltimore's Steve Stone becomes the first 20-game winner in the major leagues this season, holding the Angels hitless for 7⅓ innings on the way to a 5–2 victory.

20th Cleveland's Dan Spillner, who entered the game with a 5.45 ERA, is 2 outs from a no-hitter when White Sox rookie Leo Sutherland singles. Spillner settles for a 3–0 one-hitter.

Pittsburgh's Omar Moreno steals his 70th base of the season, becoming the first player this century with 3 consecutive 70-steal seasons. The fleet outfielder swiped 71 in 1978, 77 in 1979, and will finish 1980 with a career-high 96.

George Brett pushes his average to .406 with a 3-for-3 outing in a 5–3 win over Texas.

Tom Brookens, the Tigers' number-8 hitter, goes 5-for-5 with a triple and a home run and also starts a triple play in an 8–6 win over Milwaukee.

22nd Admitting that he can no longer compete financially in baseball's inflated economy, colorful owner Bill Veeck agrees to sell the Chicago White Sox to Youngstown, Ohio, shopping-mall magnate Eddie DeBartolo, Sr. for a reported $20 million. The sale will fall through, however, when AL owners twice fail to give Veeck the 10 votes needed for approval.

23rd A's owner Charlie Finley sells the club for $12.7 million to the Haas family of San Francisco, owners of the Levi Strauss clothing empire, thus keeping the team in Oakland.

24th Twins manager Gene Mauch resigns following a 3–2 loss to the Tigers. He will be replaced by John Goryl.

25th At Toronto's Exhibition Stadium, Rangers P Ferguson Jenkins is arrested for possession of illegal drugs after customs officials discover an estimated $500 worth of cocaine, marijuana, and hashish in his suitcase. The arrest stuns the entire country, where

Jenkins, a Canadian citizen, is considered a national hero.

27th Phillies Steve Carlton (20-7) becomes the first NL pitcher to win 20 games this season, combining with Tug McGraw to beat the Dodgers 4–3.

29th The Cardinals promote manager Whitey Herzog to general manager, replacing John Claiborne, who was fired on August 18th. Red Schoendienst will serve as interim field manager, but on October 24th the Cardinals announce that Herzog will return as manager in 1981 while retaining his GM duties.

SEPTEMBER

1st Tigers OF Al Cowens and White Sox reliever Ed Farmer publicly end their long-running feud by shaking hands at home plate prior to Chicago's 11–3 win at Tiger Stadium. The feud began in 1979 when Farmer broke Cowens's jaw with a pitch, and flared again this June 20th when Cowens hit a ground ball off Farmer and attacked the pitcher instead of running to 1B. Cowens was suspended for 7 games and a warrant was issued for his arrest in Illinois, forcing him to skip last week's Tigers-White Sox series in Chicago. Farmer agreed to drop the charges in exchange for a handshake, and the 2 players brought out the lineup cards before today's game.

5th Insisting his decision is not health-related, George Bamberger announces that he will step down as the Brewers manager following tomorrow's game against Texas. He will be replaced by Buck Rodgers.

7th The Oakland A's pitch their ML-record 78th complete game of the season as Steve McCatty beats the Orioles 5–2.

8th Commissioner Bowie Kuhn suspends Ferguson Jenkins indefinitely as a result of his August 25th drug arrest in Toronto. On September 22nd, the suspension will be overturned by arbitrator Raymond Goetz, the first time ever a commissioner's decision is overruled by an arbitrator.

10th Expos 21-year-old P Bill Gullickson strikes out 18 Cubs in a 4–2 win at Olympic Stadium, setting a ML record for rookies and falling one short of the all-time record for strikeouts in a 9-inning game. The win keeps Montreal one-half game ahead of Philadelphia in the NL East.

11th In a 6–5 win over the Cubs, Montreal's Ron LeFlore steals his 91st base of the season and Rodney Scott steals his 58th, breaking the ML record for stolen bases by teammates in one season. Lou Brock and Bake McBride set the record with the 1974 Cardinals.

14th Eddie Murray hits 3 HRs, but Baltimore loses to Toronto 4–3 in 13 innings to fall 5 games behind the first-place Yankees in the AL East.

17th After surrendering a 2-run home run to Rusty Staub, Rick Langford is removed with 2 outs in the 9th inning of Oakland's 6–4 win over Texas, ending his consecutive complete-game streak at 22.

The Royals become the first team to clinch a division title, as Dennis Leonard shuts out the Angels 5–0 in the first game of a doubleheader.

18th Willie Wilson steals 2B and 3B in the 2nd inning of Kansas City's 5–2 win over the Angels, giving him an AL-record 28 consecutive stolen bases without being caught. Ron LeFlore had set the previous record in 1978.

20th George Brett goes 0-for-4 in a 9–0 loss to the A's dropping his average below .400 for good. He is now hitting .396 and will finish the season at .390.

24th The Braves, with 24,897 watching, beat the Astros 4–2 at Atlanta-Fulton County Stadium, pushing the Braves over the one million attendance mark for the season. The 11 other NL teams have already reached that milestone, making this the first season ever in which all the teams in one league have done so.

25th San Diego's Jerry Mumphrey steals his 50th base of the season in a 5–3 loss to the Reds, making the Padres the first team in major-league history to have 3 players with 50 steals in the same season—Mumphrey, Ozzie Smith, and Gene Richards.

29th In the race for the NL East title, the Phillies remain one-half game behind Montreal by scoring 3 times in the bottom of the 15th inning to beat the Cubs 6–5. Earlier in the day, the Expos defeated the Cardinals 5–2 on pinch hitter John Tamargo's 3-run home run in the bottom of the 9th.

30th A's OF Rickey Henderson sets the AL single-season stolen base record with his 98th in a 5–1 win over the White Sox, breaking Ty Cobb's record of 96 set in 1915. Henderson will finish the season with 100 stolen bases.

The smallest crowd in Shea Stadium history (1,754) watches the Mets beat the Pirates 3–2.

OCTOBER

1st Batting 9th, Milwaukee's Charlie Moore hits for the cycle to lead the Brewers to a 10–7 win over the Angels.

Don Zimmer is fired as manager of the Boston Red Sox. Johnny Pesky will finish the season as interim manager.

2nd The Phillies move into a first-place tie with the Expos by beating Chicago 4–2. The 2 clubs will close out the season with 3 games in Montreal starting tomorrow.

4th Mike Schmidt's 2-run home run in the top of the 11th inning gives Philadelphia a 6–4 win over Montreal, clinching the NL East title for the Phillies. The home run is Schmidt's 48th of the season, breaking Eddie Mathews's single-season record for 3B set in 1953.

The Yankees clinch their 4th AL East title in 5 seasons, beating Detroit 5–2 in the first game of a doubleheader. Reggie Jackson hits his 41st home run of the season and will share the AL home run crown with Milwaukee's Ben Oglivie.

In a 17–1 rout of the Twins, Kansas City's Willie Wilson becomes the first ML player ever to be credited with 700 at-bats in one season and sets the AL record for singles in a season with 183, eclipsing the mark Sam Rice set in 1925. Wilson also becomes only the 2nd player in history to collect 100 hits from each side of the plate, matching the feat accomplished by Garry Templeton in 1979. The loss ends Minnesota's club-record 12-game winning streak.

5th Capping an improbable comeback, the Dodgers beat the Astros for the 3rd day in a row to force a one-game playoff for the NL West title. Los Angeles trailed Houston by 3 games with 3 games left in the season, and won all 3 by a single run.

On the final day of the regular season, Seattle's Mike Parrott surrenders an RBI double to the Rangers Johnny Grubb in the bottom of the 9th to lose 3–2. The loss is Parrott's 16th in a row since winning on Opening Day.

Jerry Coleman is fired as manager of the last-place San Diego Padres. He will return to the club's broadcasting booth, where he had spent the previous 8 seasons, and will be replaced by former Senators slugger Frank Howard.

6th The Astros whip the Dodgers 7–1 in a one-game playoff at Dodger Stadium. Art Howe drives in 4 runs with a HR and 2 singles and Joe Niekro wins his 20th game of the season to put Houston in the post-season for the first time since entering the major leagues in 1962.

7th Phillies stars shine in the NLCS opener. Steve Carlton and Tug McGraw hold the Astos to one run, and Greg Luzinski cracks a 2-run homer. Final score is 3–1.

8th Knotted in the 10th inning, Houston explodes for 4 runs. Philly gets one back, but it's not enough as they lose 7–4.

Kansas City coasts in the first ALCS game, downing post-season rivals the Yankees 7–2.

9th KC wins again, but this time they have to tag out Yankee Willie Randolph at the plate to end the game 3–2.

10th A scoreless pitchers' duel in Houston ends in the bottom of the 11th inning on Joe Morgan's leadoff triple and Denny Walling's sacrifice fly. Houston is up 2 games to one.

George Brett puts Kansas City into its first World Series by belting a 3-run HR off the Yankees Rich Gossage in the 7th inning, giving the Royals a 4–2 win and a 3-game sweep of the LCS. It's sweet revenge for 3 ALCS losses to the Bombers.

11th In one of the most exciting and controversial games in playoff history, the Phillies tie the NLCS at 2 games apiece with a 10-inning 5–3 win over the Astros. In the 4th inning, Houston is deprived of an apparent triple play when the umpires rule that pitcher Vern Ruhle had trapped Garry Maddox's soft line drive. In the 6th, Houston loses a run when Gary Woods leaves the base early on Luis Pujol's would-be sacrifice fly.

12th The Phillies capture their first NL title since 1950 with a 10-inning 8–7 win over the Astros in the 5th and final game of the NLCS. Each of the last 4 games was decided in extra innings.

14th Philadelphia pitcher Bob Walk becomes the first rookie to start a World Series opener since Joe Black in 1952, and the Phillies rally from a 4–0 deficit to beat the Royals 7–6. Kansas City's Willie Aikens hits a pair of homers, becoming only the 3rd player to do so in his first WS game.

15th George Brett is forced out of game 2 of the World Series in the 6th inning with a severe case of hemorrhoids, and Philadelphia wins 6–4 to take a 2-0 lead. Brett will undergo surgery tomorrow and return for game 3.

17th Back from surgery, George Brett goes 2-for-4 with a home run and double.

18th Willie Aikens slugs 2 more home runs to lead the Royals to a 5–3 win and even the World Series at 2-2.

19th A 9th-inning rally for 2 runs against Dan Quisenberry gives game 5 to the Phils by a 4–3 margin.

21st The Phillies win the first World Championship in their 98-year history by beating the Royals 4–1 in game 6 of the World Series. Philadelphia's Mike Schmidt is named MVP, hitting .381 with 2 home runs and 7 RBI, while KC's Willie Wilson is the goat, striking out a record 12 times (including the final out of the series with the bases loaded) and hitting only .154.

27th In a shocking announcement, Astros owner John McMullen fires president and GM Tal Smith, replacing him with Al Rosen, former GM of the Yankees. Smith will soon be named ML Executive of the Year. The move prompts a rebellion among the Astros 20 limited owners (who together own over 60 percent of the club), and on November 24th McMullen will give up his sole authority to run the club, accepting a position on the club's newly formed executive committee instead.

Ralph Houk, who managed the Yankees and Tigers for 16 years before retiring in 1978, is named manager of the Red Sox.

NOVEMBER

4th Steve Carlton joins Sandy Koufax, Tom Seaver, and Jim Palmer as the only pitchers to win 3 Cy Young Awards, garnering 23 of 24 first-place votes to take NL honors. Carlton was 24-9 with a 2.34 ERA and led the NL with 286 strikeouts.

Forty-year-old Sadaharu Oh, professional baseball's all-time home run king with 868 in 22 seasons in Japan, retires.

6th Mariners GM Lou Gorman, who had been with the club since its inception, resigns to become vice president of the New York Mets.

12th Baltimore's Steve Stone, who led the AL in wins with a 25-7 record, edges Oakland's Mike Norris for the AL Cy Young Award.

Don Zimmer is named manager of the Texas Rangers, becoming the 10th manager in the club's 9-year history.

14th Free-agent OF Claudell Washington signs a 5-year contract with the Atlanta Braves.

18th Despite having missed 45 games with injuries, George Brett is named AL MVP. The 27-year-old 3B's .390 average was the highest in the ML since Ted Williams's .406 in 1941, and he added 24 home runs and 118 RBI to lead Kansas City to its first AL pennant.

21st Ending weeks of speculation that he would be fired despite having led the Yankees to 103 wins last season, manager Dick Howser "resigns" and is immediately replaced by GM Gene Michael.

26th Mike Schmidt is a unanimous choice as NL MVP. The slugging 3B hit .286 with career highs of 48 home runs and 121 RBI.

Outfielder Ron LeFlore, who hit .257 with 97 stolen bases for the Expos last season, signs as a free agent with the Chicago White Sox.

DECEMBER

1st Dodgers pitcher Steve Howe wins the NL Rookie of the Year Award, edging the Expos Bill Gullickson and the Cardinals Lonnie Smith. Howe was 7-9 with a 2.65 ERA and 17 saves.

3rd Don Sutton, 35, the winningest pitcher in Los Angeles Dodgers' history, signs a 4-year contract with the Houston Astros. Sutton was 13-5 in 1980 with a league-leading 2.21 ERA.

Indians outfielder "Super Joe" Charboneau, who hit .289 with 23 HR and 87 RBI, is named AL Rookie of the Year.

8th The Cardinals and Padres complete the first major trade at the annual winter meetings in Dallas, TX. Reliever Rollie Fingers, who won 11 games and saved 23 for San Diego in 1980, and 24-year-old catcher Terry Kennedy, who hit .254 for St. Louis, are the keys in the 11-player swap.

9th Giants manager Dave Bristol is fired.

The Cubs trade reliever Bruce Sutter, the 1979 NL Cy Young Award winner, to the Cardinals for 3B Ken Reitz, OF-1B Leon Durham, and a player to be named.

The Pirates trade P Bert Blyleven and C Manny Sanguillen to the Indians for P Bob Owchinko, P Victor Cruz, C Gary Alexander, and minor league P Rafael Vasquez.

10th The Red Sox trade SS Rick Burleson and 3B Butch Hobson to the Angels for 3B Carney Lansford, CF Rick Miller, and P Mark Clear.

12th The Cardinals make their 3rd major trade, sending the recently acquired Rollie Fingers, C Ted Simmons, and P Pete Vuckovich to the Brewers in exchange for P Lary Sorensen, OF Sixto Lezcano, and minor leaguers OF David Green and P Dave LaPoint. Fingers and Vuckovich will win the AL Cy Young Award for the Brewers in 1981 and 1982, respectively.

15th Outfielder Dave Winfield becomes the highest-paid player in baseball when he signs a 10-year, $15 million contract with the New York Yankees.

18th Ferguson Jenkins is convicted on cocaine possession charges in a Canadian court, but has the verdict immediately erased by Judge Gerald Young because of his years of "exemplary" conduct.

1981

JANUARY

12th Gaylord Perry, 42, signs a one-year contract with the Atlanta Braves.

14th Frank Robinson is named manager of the San Francisco Giants.

15th In his first year of eligibility, former Cardinals P Bob Gibson is the only person elected to the Hall of Fame by the BBWAA. Players falling short of the 301 votes needed for election include Don Drysdale (243), Gil Hodges (241), Harmon Killebrew (239), Hoyt Wilhelm (238), and Juan Marichal (233).

21st The Reds trade 4-time Gold Glove winner Cesar Geronimo to the Royals for minor league IF German Barranca.

23rd Faced with the possibility of losing star OF Fred Lynn to free agency because of a front-office blunder, the Red Sox trade Lynn and P Steve Renko to the Angels for pitchers Frank Tanana and Jim Dorsey and OF Joe Rudi. The Players' Association contends that Lynn and C Carlton Fisk are free agents because the Red Sox failed to mail their new contracts by the deadline provided for in the Basic Agreement. Lynn signs a 4-year deal with the Angels and agrees to drop his case. Fisk's case will go to arbitration.

29th AL owners approve the sales of 2 franchises, the White Sox to Jerry Reinsdorf and Eddie Einhorn for $20 million, and 80 percent of the Mariners to George Argyros for $10.4 million.

FEBRUARY

9th Joe Morgan, 37, signs a one-year contract with the Giants.

12th Arbitrator Raymond Goetz supports the Players' Association and declares Red Sox catcher Carlton Fisk a free agent on the grounds that the club mailed his 1981 contract 2 days after the December 20th deadline.

25th The Executive Board of the Players' Association votes unanimously to strike on May 29th if the issue of free-agent compensation remains unresolved. That deadline will be extended briefly, however, when the Players' Association's unfair labor practices complaint is heard by the National Labor Relations Board.

28th The Mets trade OF Steve Henderson and an estimated $100,000 to the Cubs for slugger Dave Kingman, who led the NL with 48 HRs in 1979.

MARCH

7th The Braves trade OF Jeff Burroughs to the Mariners for P Carlos Diaz.

9th Free agent Carlton Fisk agrees to a contract with the Chicago White Sox.

11th Johnny Mize and Rube Foster are elected to the Hall of Fame by the Special Veterans Committee. Mize hit .312 with 359 HRs in 15 ML seasons for the Cardinals and Giants, while Foster was a star Negro League pitcher, manager, and Negro League organizer in the first quarter of the 20th century.

13th The Angels sign Rick Burleson to a 6-year, $4.2 million contract, making him the highest-paid SS in baseball history. Burleson was entering the last year of a 4-year contract that paid him $125,000 per year.

19th Blue Jays 3B and All-American basketball player Danny Ainge drives the length of the court for a lay-up with 2 seconds to play, giving Brigham Young University a 51–50 upset victory over 7th-ranked Notre Dame in the NCAA East Regional semifinals. Ainge will hit .187 in 86 games for Toronto this season, retire, then sign to play for the NBA Boston Celtics.

22nd Orioles manager Earl Weaver is suspended for 3 days by AL president Lee MacPhail for removing his club from the field and forfeiting a spring training game to the Royals. It is the 4th career suspension for Weaver, who was upset that the umpires did not provide him with an official batting order after Kansas City made numerous substitutions.

25th The Braves trade OF Gary Matthews to the Phillies for P Bob Walk.

30th The Twins trade OF Ken Landreaux to the Dodgers for OF-3B Mickey Hatcher, minor-leaguer Kelly Snider, and P Matt Reeves.

The Phillies sell OF Greg Luzinski to the White Sox, who will use him as a full-time DH.

APRIL

9th   Pressed into service on Opening Day when scheduled starter Jerry Reuss pulls a calf muscle, Dodgers pitcher Fernando Valenzuela shuts out the Astros 2–0 on 5 hits in his first ML start.

10th   In his first game for Chicago, Carlton Fisk belts a 3-run home run in the 8th inning to lead Chicago to a 5–3 win over his former Red Sox teammates at Fenway Park.

11th   After 15 seasons as a Dodger, Don Sutton makes his debut with the Astros and is pounded by his former club for 6 runs in 4 innings. Los Angeles wins 7–4.

17th   After winning their first 8 games of the season on the road, the Oakland A's pound Seattle 16–1 in their home opener before a crowd of 50,256.

18th   Reds Tom Seaver strikes out Keith Hernandez in the 4th inning of a 10–4 loss to the Cardinals, becoming the 5th pitcher in ML history with 3,000 career strikeouts.

The Pawtucket Red Sox and Rochester Red Wings (International League) play 32 innings before suspending play at 4:07 a.m. on April 19th with the score tied 2–2. The game is already the longest in professional baseball history, surpassing a 29-inning Florida State League contest in 1966, and will be resumed on June 23rd.

19th   In the first game of a doubleheader the Oakland A's set the ML record for consecutive wins at the start of the season, running their record to 11-0 with a 6–1 win over Seattle. The Mariners win the nightcap 3–2 on Richie Zisk's solo home run in the 8th inning.

22nd   Dodgers rookie Fernando Valenzuela tosses his 3rd shutout in 4 starts, strikes out 11, and drives in the game's only run with a single in a 1–0 win over Houston.

25th   Mariners manager Maury Wills is suspended for 2 games after ordering Seattle's grounds crew to enlarge the batter's boxes by one foot prior to its game with Oakland. The A's had been complaining that Seattle's Tom Paciorek frequently stepped out of the box while hitting.

26th   Oakland runs its record to 17-1 with a 9–4 win over the Mariners.

27th   "Fernandomania" hits fever pitch at Dodger Stadium as a sellout crowd watches the 20-year-old rookie pitch his 4th shutout in 5 starts 5–0 versus the Giants. Valenzuela is 5-0 with a 0.20 ERA and is batting .438.

28th   Ken Singleton's consecutive-hit streak is snapped at 10 when he grounds into a double play off Chicago's Rich Dotson in the Orioles' 8–6 loss. Singleton singles and homers in his first 2 at bats after going 4-for-4 in each of the previous 2 games.

29th   Philadelphia's Steve Carlton strikes out the side (Tim Raines, Jerry Manuel, and Tim Wallach) in the first inning of a 6–2 win over the Expos to become the first lefthander in ML history (and 6th pitcher overall) to record 3,000 career strikeouts.

The Cubs score 5 times with 2 out in the bottom of the 8th to beat St. Louis 6–1 and snap a 12-game losing streak. The Cardinals had won 8 in a row.

MAY

1st   Frank White's 4th-inning sacrifice fly off Steve Comer ends the Rangers' consecutive-scoreless-inning streak at 39, and Kansas City goes on to a 4–0 win. Texas pitchers had tossed 4 consecutive shutouts, one shy of the AL record.

3rd   The Blue Jays end a 19-game losing streak at Memorial Stadium, beating the Orioles 4–2. It is their first win in Baltimore since July 1978.

4th   Yankee reliever Ron Davis strikes out the last 8 batters of the game in a 4–2 win over the Angels, tying Nolan Ryan's AL record for consecutive strikeouts and setting a new record for consecutive strikeouts by a reliever.

6th   Mariners manager Maury Wills is fired and replaced by Rene Lachemann. Seattle was 6-18, the worst start in the club's 5-year history. In Lachemann's first game, Seattle pounds Milwaukee 12–1 and pitcher Mike Parrott snaps his personal 18-game losing streak, one shy of the AL record.

Cleveland's Bert Blyleven holds Toronto hitless for 8 innings before Lloyd Moseby doubles to lead off the 9th, and Blyleven settles for a 4–1 two-hitter.

9th   Tom Paciorek hits his 2nd game-winning, bottom-of-the-9th HR in as many games, a 3-run blow giving the Mariners a 6–5 win over the Twins. The previous night, Paciorek led off the 9th with a solo homer to give Seattle a 3–2 win over the Yankees.

10th   Montreal's Charlie Lea, a native of France, no-hits the Giants 4–0, walking 4 and striking out 8 in the 2nd game of a doubleheader. It is the first no-hitter at Olympic Stadium, which opened for baseball in 1977.

11th   Boston's Rick Miller goes 5-for-5 with a ML-record-tying 4 doubles in a 7–6 win over Toronto.

14th   The largest Dodger Stadium crowd in 7 years (53,906) watches Fernando Valenzuela run his record to 8-0 with a 3–2 win over the Expos.

15th   The Indians Len Barker pitches the 9th perfect game in 20th century ML history 3–0 over the Blue Jays before just 7,290 fans on a rainy night in Cleveland. Last year's AL strikeout leader, Barker fans 11.

16th   Houston's Craig Reynolds ties the modern ML record with 3 triples in a 6–1 win over the Cubs.

18th   Fernando Valenzuela finally loses 4–0 to the Phillies. His ERA "rises" to 0.90.

19th   Pirates Jim Bibby gives up a leadoff single to the Braves Terry Harper in the first inning, then retires the next 27 batters for a one-hit 5–0 victory.

22nd   Coach Billy Gardner replaces the fired John Goryl as manager of the Twins. Minnesota (11-25) had lost 8 consecutive games, but shuts out Kansas City 7–0 in Gardner's managerial debut.

25th   Texas utilityman Bill Stein drives in the winning run with a pinch single in the bottom of the 9th inning of a 4–3 win over Minnesota. It is Stein's 7th consecutive pinch hit, a new AL record.

Carl Yastrzemski plays in his 3,000th ML game, scoring the winning run in Boston's 8–7 triumph over Cleveland. Yaz joins Ty Cobb, Stan Musial, and Hank Aaron as the only major leaguers to appear in 3,000 games.

27th   Angel 3B Doug DeCinces hits a pair of home runs for the 3rd time in 6 games to lead California to a 6–5 win over the Yankees. DeCinces also homered twice against Detroit on May 23rd and against the Yankees on May 25th. He had no homers this year prior to the streak.

28th   Angels manager Jim Fregosi, who led the club to a 22-25 record, 7½ games off the pace in the AL West, becomes the 3rd AL skipper to be fired this month. He is replaced by Gene Mauch.

29th   A's manager Billy Martin flies into a rage and heaves 2 handfuls of dirt on home plate umpire Terry Cooney's back after being ejected for arguing ball and strike calls. He will be suspended by AL president Lee MacPhail for 7 days.

Montreal trades OF Ellis Valentine to the Mets for P Jeff Reardon, OF Dan Norman, and a player to be named. Valentine will play just 159 games for the Mets, while Reardon will blossom into one of baseball's best relievers.

31st   Playing before their 10th consecutive home sellout, the Dodgers pound the Reds 16–4 and raise their season attendance to 1,026,725 in 22 dates. It is the earliest any team has cracked the one million attendance barrier.

JUNE

3rd   Royals C Jerry Grote hits a grand slam (his first home run since 1976) and goes 3-for-4 with a club-record 7 RBI to lead Kansas City to a 12–9 win over Seattle. Grote had returned from a 2-year retirement to win a spot with the Royals as a free agent during spring training.

5th   Houston's Nolan Ryan passes Early Wynn as baseball's all-time walk leader, walking 2 batters in a 3–0 win over the Mets to raise his total to 1,777. Ryan also fans 10 batters while pitching a 5-hitter.

8th   The Seattle Mariners take Oral Roberts University righthander Mike Moore with the first pick overall in the annual amateur draft. The Cubs take Wichita State's Joe Carter with the 2nd pick. The Yankees use their first round pick to take Stanford QB John Elway.

10th   Phillies 1B Pete Rose singles off Nolan Ryan in the first inning to tie Stan Musial as the NL's all-time hit leader with 3,630, then strikes out in his next 3 at bats. Rose's single is the only hit off Ryan until the 8th inning, when Philadelphia scores 5 times for a 5–4 win over Houston.

11th   The White Sox beat the Yankees 3–2, handing pitcher Doug Bird his first loss since August 16, 1978.

The journeyman righthander had won 12 consecutive decisions.

12th   At 12:30 A.M., after meeting with the owners for most of the previous day, players' union chief Marvin Miller announces, "We have accomplished nothing. The strike is on," thus beginning the longest labor action in American sports history. By the time the season resumes on August 10th, 706 games (38 percent of the ML schedule) will have been canceled.

23rd   Dave Koza scores Marty Barrett with a bases-loaded single in the bottom of the 33rd inning, giving Pawtucket a 3–2 win over Rochester and ending the longest game in professional baseball history. The game had been suspended April 19th after 32 innings and 8 hours, 7 minutes of play, but the continuation took only 18 minutes to complete. Bob Ojeda pitches one inning to earn the win. Future ML stars Wade Boggs and Cal Ripken go a combined 6-for-25.

JULY

31st   Fifty days after the strike began, the players and owners finally hammer out an agreement that features a complicated pooling system for free-agent compensation. Free agents will be classified according to their statistics, with teams losing "Type A" players entitled to select one player from the available compensation pool. Each team will be allowed to withhold 26 players from the pool, while a maximum of 5 clubs can agree not to sign any Type A free agents and therefore not have to contribute to the pool at all.

AUGUST

6th   As a result of the nearly 2-month interruption in play because of the strike the ML owners elect to split the 1981 season into 2 halves, with the first-place teams from each half in each division (or a wild-card team if the same club wins both halves) meeting in a best-of-five divisional playoff series. The A's, Yankees, Phillies, and Dodgers suddenly find themselves guaranteed playoff spots as first-half champions.

9th   Expos C Gary Carter hits a pair of solo home runs and Phillies 3B Mike Schmidt adds a 2-run shot in the 8th off Rollie Fingers to give the NL a 5–4 win in the All-Star Game. It is the NL's 10th win in a row and 17th in the last 18 games.

10th   After a 2-month wait, Pete Rose finally breaks Stan Musial's NL hit record, singling off Mark Littell in the 8th inning of Philadelphia's 7–3 loss to St. Louis. Rose now has 3,631 career hits.

Seattle's Julio Cruz is caught stealing by California's Ed Ott on a pitchout, ending his consecutive stolen base streak at 32. Cruz tied the AL record set by Willie Wilson.

14th   Mike Schmidt hits his 300th career home run off Mike Scott as Philadelphia beats the Mets 8–4.

Mariners OF Jeff Burroughs hits 3 home runs in a 13–3 win over the Twins, giving Seattle a split of a doubleheader.

24th   In his first ML game, Kent Hrbek homers in the 12th inning to give the Twins a 3–2 win over the Yankees at Yankee Stadium. The 21-year-old 1B grew up in Bloomington, MN, less than a mile from Metropolitan Stadium, and jumped directly to his hometown club from Class-A Visalia (California League), where he was hitting .380 with 27 HRs and 112 RBI.

25th   Chicago's Dennis Lamp loses his no-hitter when the Brewers Robin Yount leads off the 9th inning with a bloop double. Lamp settles for a one-hit 5–1 win.

26th   Cards SS Garry Templeton is suspended indefinitely and fined $5,000 by manager-GM Whitey Herzog after making obscene gestures to the crowd following his ejection in the 3rd inning of a 9–4 win over the Giants. He will return to the lineup on September 15th.

28th   Tim Laudner becomes the 2nd Twins player in 4 days to homer in his first ML game, a 6–0 win over the Tigers.

29th   Phillies farmhand Jeff Stone steals his 121st base of the season for Spartanburg (South Atlantic League), breaking the all-time professional record set last season by Alan Wiggins. Stone will finish the season with 122 SBs, a record that will not last through 1982.

31st   Royals manager Jim Frey is fired and replaced by Dick Howser, whose Yankees lost to Frey's Royals in last season's AL Championship Series. Kansas City was 10-10 in the 2nd half of the season, 30-40 overall.

SEPTEMBER

4th   In the conclusion of the longest game in Fenway Park history, the Mariners beat the Red Sox 8–7 in 20 innings on Joe Simpson's run-scoring triple. The game began on September 3rd, but was suspended after 19 innings.

5th   Milwaukee's Jim Slaton pitches a no-hitter for 8 innings, then is knocked out of the box in the 9th without retiring a batter. Two singles and a HR cut the Brewers' lead to 5–3, but Rollie Fingers retires the final 3 batters for his 22nd save.

6th   Despite having won the first-half pennant, Yankee manager Gene Michael is replaced by Bob Lemon, who managed the club in 1978-79. The Yankees are only 2 games above .500 in the 2nd half of the season.

7th   Dave Magadan is named MVP as West Tampa, FL, defeats Richmond, VA, 6–4 to win the American Legion World Series. Magadan was 11-for-24 at the plate and also pitched a complete-game win over Omaha.

8th   Houston's Cesar Cedeno is fined $5,000 but not suspended after attacking a fan during the Astros 3–2 loss to the Braves. Witnesses said that 3 men in the box seats had been loudly berating Cedeno's wife and making remarks about the 1973 incident in which he was convicted of involuntary manslaughter for the accidental shooting death of a young woman in the Dominican Republic.

Citing his "lack of communication" with the players, the Expos fire manager Dick Williams and replace him with Jim Fanning, who has been an executive with the club since it joined the NL in 1969.

12th   Red Sox rookie Bob Ojeda no-hits the Yankees for 8 innings at Yankee Stadium before Rick Cerone and Dave Winfield lead off the 9th with back-to-back doubles. Reliever Mark Clear preserves a 2–1 win.

17th   Fernando Valenzuela sets the NL rookie record with his 8th shutout of the season, a 2–0 three-hitter versus the Braves. He had shared the record with Irv "Cy the Second" Young (1905), Grover Alexander (1911), and Jerry Koosman (1968).

21st   Steve Carlton fans 12 Expos in 10 innings to break Bob Gibson's NL strikeout record (Carlton now has 3,128), but the Phillies lose to the Expos 1–0 in 17 innings. Montreal's Bryn Smith retires just one batter, but picks up his first ML victory.

26th   Nolan Ryan no-hits the Dodgers 5–0 to become the only ML pitcher to toss 5 career no-hitters. Ryan had shared the record of 4 with Dodger great Sandy Koufax, but had not pitched a no-hitter since June 1, 1975. The 34-year-old Ryan strikes out 11 and retires the last 19 batters in a row while lowering his league-leading ERA to 1.74.

27th   In the first game of a doubleheader with Chicago, Oakland ties an AL record with 8 straight singles in the bottom of the first inning, but blows its 5–0 lead and loses 9–5. The White Sox take the nightcap 10–3.

30th   In the last ML game at Minnesota's Metropolitan Stadium, Kansas City clinches at least a tie for the AL West 2nd-half title with a 5–2 win over the Twins. Next season, the Twins will play in the brand-new Hubert H. Humphrey Metrodome in downtown Minneapolis.

OCTOBER

3rd   In Cincinnati, Bob Horner homers twice and scores the winning run on Ron Oester's 8th-inning throwing error to give the Braves a 4–3 win over the Reds and give the Astros the 2nd-half title in the NL West. Cincinnati, which lost the first-half title to the Dodgers by one-half game, will finish with the best overall record (66-42) in the major leagues, but will not make the playoffs.

The Brewers (since 1970) and Expos (1969) clinch their first-ever post-season appearances. Milwaukee beats Detroit 2–1 to wrap up the 2nd-half title in the AL East, while Montreal edges New York 5–4 to win the NL East's 2nd playoff spot.

4th   With one game remaining in the season, the Mets fire manager Joe Torre and his entire coaching staff. The team finishes 41-62.

5th   Kansas City shuts out Cleveland 9–0 in the first game of a scheduled doubleheader to clinch the 2nd-half title in the AL West. The 2nd game is canceled as irrelevant.

6th   In the National League Western Division playoff opener, Nolan Ryan pitches the Astros to a 3–1 win over LA.

Oakland coasts past KC to a 4–0 victory behind the 4-hit complete-game shutout of Mike Norris in the opening game of the American League Western Division playoff.

7th The Expos down Philly 3–1 in game one of the National League Eastern Division playoff.

Ron Davis and Goose Gossage provide a 1-2 relief punch that Milwaukee cannot survive, losing to the Yankees 5–3 in the opening game of the American League Eastern Division playoff.

Houston pitching continues to sparkle as 3 pitchers combine to shut out the Dodgers for 11 innings, resulting in a 1–0 Astro victory, and putting Houston up 2 games to none in the-best-of-5 series.

Another series of excellent pitching: the A's Steve McCatty goes the distance in a 2–1 win over the Royals.

Atlanta fires manager Bobby Cox. Eight days later, Cox will sign a one-year contract to manage the Toronto Blue Jays.

8th Philly loses to the Expos by an identical 3–1 score, putting them in the hole 2 games to none.

Dave Righetti and Davis and Gossage in relief are too much for the Brewers as they are shut out 3–0. All the Yankee scoring comes on HRs by Reggie Jackson and Lou Piniella.

9th The Phillies bats wake up, collecting 13 hits in a 6–2 win over Montreal.

Facing elimination, the Dodgers get the pitching this time and down Houston 6–1.

The Brewers, also facing elimination, beat the Yanks in the 8th inning 5–3 on Paul Molitor's home run.

The A's sweep Kansas City by winning 4–1. In the 3 games, last year's pennant winners score only 2 runs.

10th A pinch homer by George Vukovich in the bottom of the 10th inning gives Tug McGraw and the Phillies a 6–5 win over Montreal and ties up the series 2-2.

Another series is tied up at 2-2 as Fernando Valenzuela wins over the Astros 2–1.

On a cold day in New York, Milwaukee stays alive by winning 2–1. This is the 3rd series knotted at 2-all.

11th Steve Rogers wins the playoff for Montreal over Philadelphia by twirling a 6-hit shutout and knocking in 2 of his team's runs in a 3–0 victory.

After being down 2 games to none, LA shuts out Houston 4–0 behind Jerry Reuss to take the playoff.

Yankee bats are too much for the Brewers. Three HRs, including the 2nd of the series by Jackson, and 13 hits provide a 7–3 win and a trip to the ALCS.

13th Los Angeles takes game one of the NLCS 5–1 over Montreal.

In the ALCS opener against Oakland, Yankee pitching once again asserts itself, as Tommy John, Ron Davis, and Goose Gossage combine to hold up Graig Nettles's first-inning 3-run double 3–1.

The Padres fire manager Frank Howard and his entire coaching staff. San Diego finished last in the NL West in each half of the season.

14th In game 2 of the ALCS, Yankee Graig Nettles singles twice in a 7-run 4th inning to become the first player ever to collect 2 hits in one inning in LCS play. New York sets LCS records for runs and hits (19) in a 13–3 rout of Oakland.

Montreal downs LA 3–0 behind Ray Burris's 5-hitter.

15th The Yankees wrap up their 33rd AL pennant with a 4–0 win over the A's, completing a 3-game sweep of the ALCS.

Less than a year after leading the club to its only World Championship, Phillies manager Dallas Green jumps to the Cubs to become their general manager.

16th Montreal wins 4–1 over Los Angeles behind Steve Rogers.

17th Tied 1–1 going into the 8th, Steve Garvey's 2-run homer puts LA ahead in what will be a 7–1 victory over the Expos. The series is now tied 2–2.

19th In game 5 of the NLCS, Rick Monday hits a solo home run with 2 out in the top of the 9th against Montreal to give Los Angeles a 2–1 victory and a trip to the World Series.

20th In a WS rematch of the 1978 teams, the Yankees take game one over the Dodgers 5–3.

21st Goose Gossage gets his 2nd save in as many days as he preserves Tommy John's win 3–0 in game 2.

22nd Dallas Green hires one of his Phillie coaches, Lee Elia, to manage the Cubs.

23rd Despite an uncharacteristic poor performance (9 hits, 7 walks) Fernando Valenzuela goes the distance in the Dodgers' 5–4 come-from-behind win. The deciding run scores on a double play.

Joe Torre signs a 3-year contract to manage the Braves.

24th Another come-from-behind victory for LA 8–7, helped by poor Yankee fielding in the outfield, ties the Series at 2 games apiece.

25th Back-to-back HRs by Pedro Guerrero and Steve Yeager off Yankee ace Ron Guidry give the Dodgers their 3rd consecutive win 2–1.

After his club loses game 5 of the World Series, Yankee owner George Steinbrenner scuffles with 2 (he says) fans in a hotel elevator and emerges with a fat lip and a broken hand.

28th Pedro Guerrero drives in 5 runs and the Dodgers beat the Yankees 9–2 to win the World Series in 6 games. In a remarkable post season, the Dodgers came from behind to win 3 series (down 2–0 to Houston and 2–0 to Montreal in the best-of-5 series). Guerrero, Ron Cey, and Steve Yeager (2 home runs) are named co-MVPs, while OF Dave Winfield and relief pitcher George Frazier are the goats for New York. Winfield was just 1-for-21, while Frazier tied a WS record by losing 3 games. The record was set by the White Sox Lefty Williams in 1919, but Williams, one of the 8 "Black Sox," probably was losing on purpose.

29th Bill Giles, the Phillies vice president for the past 11 years, heads a group of investors which purchases the club for just over $30 million, the highest price paid to date for a ML club. Giles is the son of longtime NL president Warren C. Giles.

NOVEMBER

3rd Brewers Rollie Fingers (28 saves, 1.04 ERA) wins the AL Cy Young Award, collecting 22 of 28 possible first-place votes. The other 6 go to Oakland's Steve McCatty.

4th The Reds trade OF Ken Griffey to the Yankees for P Fred Toliver and minor-leaguer Brian Ryder.

The Phillies announce that Pat Corrales will manage the club in 1982, replacing Dallas Green, who quit to become Cubs GM.

11th Fernando Valenzuela becomes the first rookie ever to win a Cy Young Award, edging the Reds Tom Seaver 70-67 for NL honors. He was the first rookie

since Herb Score in 1955 to lead his league in strikeouts with 180.

15th Cubs IF Steve Macko dies of cancer at the age of 27. He did not play at all in 1981 because of the illness, but hit .250 in 25 games in 1979-80.

18th Phillies 3B Mike Schmidt wins his 2nd consecutive NL MVP Award, joining Ernie Banks and Joe Morgan as the only NL players to win the award back-to-back. Schmidt hit .316 with 31 HRs and 91 RBI in the abbreviated season and also led the league in runs and walks.

Dick Williams, fired by the Expos on September 7th, is named manager of the Padres. It is the 5th club Williams has managed since taking over the Red Sox in 1967.

25th Rollie Fingers becomes the first relief pitcher ever to win the AL MVP Award, edging Oakland's Rickey Henderson 319-308.

27th The Tigers trade OF Steve Kemp to the White Sox for OF Chet Lemon.

30th Yankees P Dave Righetti (8-4, 2.06 in 1981) wins the AL Rookie of the Year Award.

DECEMBER

2nd Fernando Valenzuela becomes the 3rd consecutive Dodger to win the NL Rookie of the Year Award. Expos OF Tim Raines, who hit .304 with 71 stolen bases, is 2nd.

4th Oakland signs free-agent OF-1B Joe Rudi, who hit just .180 in 49 games for the Red Sox last season, to a 2-year contract.

8th In the first major deal of the winter meetings, the Cubs trade P Mike Krukow to the Phillies for pitchers Dickie Noles and Dan Larson and versatile Keith Moreland.

9th One day after announcing that manager Bob Lemon will return in 1982, the Yankees announce that former manager Gene Michael, whom Lemon replaced on September 6th, will return as manager for the 1983 season. They won't wait that long.

The Dodgers trade 1979 Rookie of the Year Rick Sutcliffe, unhappy with his exile to the Dodger bullpen, and infielder Jack Perconte to the Indians for OF Jorge Orta. Orta will hit just .217 for the Dodgers next season, while Sutcliffe will lead the AL in ERA.

The Giants trade OF Larry Herndon to the Tigers for pitcher Dan Schatzeder and minor leaguer Mike Chris.

10th In what would be a blockbuster swap of outstanding young shortstops, the Cardinals trade Garry Templeton and OF Sixto Lezcano to the Padres for Ozzie Smith and P Steve Mura. The deal is put on hold, however, when Smith is unable to work out an acceptable contract with his new club.

11th Veteran free-agent infielders Joe Morgan and Mark Belanger sign one-year contracts with the Giants and Dodgers, respectively.

Seattle trades OF Tom Paciorek to the White Sox for C Jim Essian, IF Todd Cruz, and Rod Allen.

15th Free-agent P Ron Guidry re-signs with the Yankees for a reported $3.6 million over 4 years.

18th The Reds swap 3B Ray Knight to the Astros for OF Cesar Cedeno.

21st Twenty-two-year-old Royals pitcher Mike Jones, who was 6-3, 3.20 in the 2nd half of 1981 and was projected to be the club's 3rd starter next year, is listed in guarded condition after crashing his car while driving under the influence near Rochester, NY. Jones will not pitch in the majors again until 1984.

23rd The Yankees sign free-agent OF Dave Collins for a reported $750,000 a year for at least 3 years. Collins hit .272 for the Reds in 1981 and stole 79 bases in 1979.

1982

JANUARY

5th Free-agent pitcher Frank Tanana, 4-10 for Boston last season, signs a 2-year contract with Texas.

9th Former Red Sox OF Tony Conigliaro, in Boston to interview for a broadcasting position, suffers a massive heart attack while being driven to the airport by his brother Billy and lapses into a coma. The 37-year-old Tony C. will remain hospitalized until March 2nd.

13th Hank Aaron and Frank Robinson become the 12th and 13th players elected to the Hall of Fame by the BBWAA in their first year of eligibility. Aaron falls 9 votes shy of becoming the first-ever unanimous selection, and his 97.8 election percentage is 2nd only to Ty Cobb's 98.2 percent in the inaugural 1936 election.

22nd Free-agent OF Reggie Jackson ends his tumultuous 5 seasons as a Yankee by signing a reported 4-year contract with the California Angels for nearly $1 million per year.

27th Philadelphia sends veteran SS Larry Bowa and minor league infielder Ryne Sandberg to the Cubs in exchange for SS Ivan DeJesus.

28th The Orioles trade 3B Doug DeCinces and minor league P Jeff Schneider to the Angels for OF Dan Ford.

29th Wayne Garland, baseball's first millionaire free agent, is waived by the Indians with 5 seasons remaining on his 10-year contract. Garland was 3-7 with a 5.79 ERA in 1981.

FEBRUARY

3rd Minor league C Angel Rodriguez, who played for the Pirates' Alexandria club (Carolina League) last season, is suspended from organized baseball for one year for telling opposing Latin American batters what pitches were coming. Rodriguez had been suspended by the Pirates last season after being caught in the act during an August 19th game against Lynchburg.

8th The Dodgers break up the longest-playing infield unit in ML history by trading veteran 2B Davey Lopes to the A's for minor-leaguer Lance Hudson.

Lopes, 1B Steve Garvey, 3B Ron Cey, and SS Bill Russell had been the Dodgers' starting infield since 1974.

10th The Mets agree to a new 5-year contract with slugging OF George Foster, completing a trade that sends pitchers Jim Kern and Greg Harris and C Alex Trevino to the Reds.

11th The Ozzie Smith for Garry Templeton deal finally goes through, more than 2 months after it was first announced. Smith's new salary with the Cardinals will be determined by an outside arbitrator.

16th Bake McBride becomes the 3rd starter from the Phillies' 1980 World Championship squad to be traded or sold since Bill Giles bought the club last October. The Indians get him in exchange for pitcher Sid Monge.

MARCH

5th Needing just 3 wins to reach 300 for his career, Gaylord Perry signs a one-year contract with the Seattle Mariners.

10th Travis Jackson and Happy Chandler are elected to the Hall of Fame by the Special Veterans Committee. Jackson hit .291 in 15 seasons as the New York Giants SS in the 1920s and 30s, while Chandler was baseball's 2nd commissioner and oversaw—and encouraged—the dismantling of the color barrier in 1947.

24th Fernando Valenzuela ends his holdout and reports to the Dodgers' spring training camp in Vero Beach, Florida. After earning just $42,500 while winning the NL Cy Young and Rookie of the Year Awards last season, the 21-year-old lefthander had asked for a raise to $1 million in 1982. The Dodgers unilaterally renewed his contract for a reported $350,000 instead.

30th The Giants trade pitchers Vida Blue and Bob Tufts to the Royals for pitchers Renie Martin, Craig Chamberlain, and Atlee Hammaker.

The Dodgers trade OF Rudy Law to the White Sox for minor leaguers Cecil Espy and Bert Geiger.

31st The Expos trade 3B-OF Larry Parrish and minor league 1B Dave Hostetler to the Rangers for veteran OF-1B Al Oliver.

APRIL

1st The Mets ship popular OF Lee Mazzilli to the Rangers for minor league pitchers Ron Darling and Walt Terrell.

2nd In an exhibition game against the Padres, A's pitcher Steve McCatty steps to the plate wielding a 15-inch toy bat on the instructions of manager Billy Martin, who was upset that his club was not allowed to use a DH in spring training games at NL parks. Home plate umpire Jim Quick refuses to let McCatty use the bat, and McCatty takes 3 called strikes.

5th Forty-three-year-old Jim Kaat pitches one inning for the Cardinals in a season-opening 14–3 rout of the Astros, setting a new ML record for pitchers by playing in his 24th consecutive season.

6th The largest crowd ever to see a baseball game in Minnesota—52,279—turns out for the inaugural game at the brand-new Hubert H. Humphrey Metrodome. Twins rookie 3B Gary Gaetti goes 4-for-4 with a pair of home runs, but Seattle wins 11–7.

9th Former White Sox pitcher Francisco Barrios, 28, dies of heart attack in his native Mexico. Barrios was 14-7 for Chicago in 1977, but had recurring shoulder trouble, as well as drug and alcohol problems.

10th The Yankees trade relief pitcher Ron Davis and minor leaguers Paul Boris and Greg Gagne to the Twins for veteran IF Roy Smalley.

14th In the longest game ever played at Anaheim Stadium, the Angels beat Seattle 4–3 on Bob Boone's RBI single in the bottom of the 20th inning. The game began yesterday, but was suspended after 17 innings. In the scheduled game, California wins again 2–1 in 10 innings.

17th Lured by a cap night promotion, a stadium-record 61,640 fans pack Anaheim Stadium and see Brian Downing homer twice to lead the Angels to a 6–2 win over the Twins. In the 6th inning, SS Rick Burleson tears his rotator cuff making a throw to 1B and will be lost for the season.

20th By defeating Cincinnati 4–2 for its 12th victory in a row, Atlanta breaks the modern ML record for consecutive wins at the start of a season. Steve Bedrosian pitches 4⅓ innings of relief to earn his first ML win.

22nd After opening the season with 13 straight wins the Braves finally lose 2–1 to the Reds.

24th The Cardinals win their 12th game in a row 7–4 over the Phillies. St. Louis will finally lose tomorrow 8–4 to Philadelphia, as Steve Carlton wins his first game of the season after 4 straight defeats.

25th Just 14 games into the season, George Steinbrenner fires manager Bob Lemon and replaces him with Gene Michael, the man Lemon had replaced last September.

27th Todd Cruz, the Mariners' number-9 hitter, hits an 11th-inning home run for the 2nd straight game, helping Seattle to a 7–4 win over Cleveland. On April 25th, Cruz's solo home run in the bottom of the 11th capped a 4-for-4 day and gave the Mariners a 5–4 win over the Twins.

28th The Cubs Dickie Noles pitches his first career complete game, a 6–0 one-hitter over Tom Seaver and the Reds. The only hit off Noles is Eddie Milner's single leading off the 4th inning.

Bob Bailor's sacrifice fly in the top of the 15th inning scores Mookie Wilson with the winning run as the Mets beat the Padres 5–4, ending San Diego's winning streak at 11 games. It is the 3rd winning streak of 10 or more games in the NL this year.

Pete Rose goes 5-for-5 to tie Max Carey for the NL record with 9 career 5-hit games, as Philadelphia scores 6 times in the top of the 9th to beat Los Angeles 9–3.

MAY

4th Twins rookie OF Jim Eisenreich, who suffers from a nervous disorder known as Tourette's Syndrome, is forced to remove himself from a 5–3 loss to the Red Sox when he is taunted mercilessly by bleacher fans and his violent twitching becomes uncontrollable. Eisenreich, who was hitting .310 after making the jump from A ball to the major leagues, will be hospitalized on May 9th and will make several unsuccessful comeback attempts before retiring in 1984. He will ultimately return to the majors with the Royals in 1987.

5th Cincinnati ties the modern ML record with 4 sacrifice flies in an 8–7 loss to Houston.

6th Gaylord Perry becomes the 15th pitcher to win 300 career games, beating the Yankees 7–3 at the

Kingdome. Perry is the first pitcher to reach that plateau since Early Wynn in 1963.

11th The Twins trade ace reliever Doug Corbett and 2B Rob Wilfong to California for minor leaguers Tom Brunansky and Mike Walters and cash.

12th In their 2nd major trade in as many days, the Twins deal C Butch Wynegar and P Roger Erickson to the Yankees for IF Larry Milbourne, minor leaguers John Pacella and Pete Filson, and cash. The Twins' frugal owner, Calvin Griffith, is roundly criticized for the deals, in which he appears to be unloading high-salaried veterans at the expense of a winning ball club.

Brewers Paul Molitor hits 3 solo home runs, but Milwaukee loses 9–7 to Kansas City.

14th Kent Hrbek of the Twins goes 0-for-5 in an 11-inning 4–2 loss to the Tigers, ending his hitting streak at 23. The game is marred by a bench-clearing brawl in which Tigers P Dave Rozema tears knee ligaments, sidelining him for the rest of the season. Rozema is 3-0 with a 1.63 ERA.

18th Tigers Larry Herndon hits 3 home runs in an 11–9 win over Oakland, and in the process becomes the 14th player in ML history to hit home runs in 4 consecutive plate appearances. On May 16th, he homered in his final at bat to give Detroit a 7–6 win over Minnesota.

25th Ferguson Jenkins of the Cubs fans Garry Templeton in the 3rd inning of a 2–1 loss to the Padres to become the 7th pitcher in ML history to record 3,000 career strikeouts.

Jim Palmer wins his 250th career game for Baltimore, 10–3 over the Rangers.

29th The Indians beat the White Sox 5–2, handing pitcher LaMarr Hoyt his first loss of the season. Hoyt had started the season 9-0 and had won 14 consecutive decisions since last August 27th.

JUNE

1st Rickey Henderson steals 2 bases in a 3–2 win over the Red Sox to give him 51 SBs in 51 games, the fastest anyone has ever reached 50 SBs in a season.

2nd San Diego's Juan Eichelberger one-hits the Cubs 3–1, allowing only a questionable 2nd-inning single to Scot Thompson. Thompson's ground ball

skips off the glove of 2B Tim Flannery and is ruled a hit.

Milwaukee fires manager Buck Rodgers and replaces him with batting coach Harvey Kuenn.

4th Brad Havens and Terry Felton combine to shut out Baltimore 6–0, snapping the Twins' club-record 14-game losing streak. The last-place Twins were 3-26 in the month of May.

7th Steve Garvey plays in his 1,000th consecutive game and goes 0-for-4 in a 4–3 loss to the Braves. Garvey's streak is the 5th longest in ML history.

The Cubs select SS Shawon Dunston, who batted .790 this season for Brooklyn's Thomas Jefferson HS, with the first pick in the annual June free-agent draft. The Blue Jays then pick SS Augie Schmidt. Dwight Gooden is the 5th taken. The Yankees select high school SS Bo Jackson in the 2nd round, but he opts for Auburn instead.

8th Dodgers farmhand Sid Fernandez pitches his 2nd no-hitter of the season for Vero Beach (Florida State League), earning a promotion to Triple-A Albuquerque of the Pacific Coast League. Earlier this season Fernandez no-hit Winter Haven on April 24th and fanned 21 Lakeland batters on May 14th.

9th Steve Carlton strikes out 16 while handing the Cubs their 10th consecutive loss 4–2.

11th Jerry Reuss pitches his 2nd one-hitter of the season, allowing a leadoff double to the Reds Eddie Milner in the first inning, then retiring the next 27 batters for an 11–1 victory. It is the 2nd time in his career that Reuss has missed a perfect game by one batter.

12th A's RF Tony Armas sets a pair of ML records for the position with 11 putouts and 12 total chances in an 8–1 win over the Blue Jays. Harry Schafer's record of 11 total chances had stood since 1877.

14th Despite making 6 errors, the Cubs beat the Phillies 12–11 to snap a 13-game losing streak which tied the club record set in 1944.

16th Twins rookie Frank Viola allows one run in 7 innings to record his first ML win 5–2 over the Royals.

18th Cleveland's Toby Harrah goes 4-for-5 in a 10–3 win over the Red Sox to raise his ML-leading average to a sizzling .387. He will finish the season at .304.

Reggie Jackson collects his 2,000th career hit, a solo home run off Dennis Lamp in California's 7–2 win over the White Sox.

20th Phillies Pete Rose plays in his 3,000th ML game (a 3–1 loss to the Pirates), joining Ty Cobb, Stan Musial, Hank Aaron, and Carl Yastrzemski as the only players to reach that plateau.

Milwaukee's Ben Oglivie smacks 3 home runs in a 7–5 win over Detroit. It is the 2nd 3-homer game of his career.

22nd Pete Rose doubles off John Stuper in the 3rd inning of a 3–2 loss to the Cardinals for his 3,772nd career hit, moving him past Hank Aaron into 2nd place on baseball's all-time list.

Rangers Rick Honeycutt shuts out California 4–0, snapping Rod Carew's 25-game hitting streak in the process. The streak was the longest of Carew's career and the longest in Angels history.

Red Sox rookie Wade Boggs hits his first ML home run in the bottom of the 11th inning to give Boston a 5–4 win over Detroit. Boggs will finally crack the starting lineup for good after the next day's game, in which regular 3B Carney Lansford severely sprains his ankle while unsuccessfully trying to stretch a triple into an inside-the-park home run. Boggs hits .390 in Lansford's absence and .349 for the season.

26th Despite managing just one hit in each game, the Appleton Foxes (Midwest League) sweep a doubleheader from the Wisconsin Rapids 2–1 and 1–0.

27th The Braves tie the ML record with 7 double plays in a 2–0 win over Cincinnati.

JULY

2nd Boston's Tony Perez singles off Milwaukee's Bob McClure for his 2,500th career hit.

3rd A County Stadium-record crowd of 55,716 watches the Brewers shut out the Red Sox 7–0 to move into a first-place tie with Boston in the AL East.

7th Harold Baines belts 3 home runs, including a grand slam, to lead the White Sox to a 7–0 win over Detroit.

Houston's Don Sutton wins his 250th career game, a 5–1 four-hitter against the Cubs.

8th Billy Martin records his 1,000th career win as a manager as the A's beat the Yankees 6–3.

10th The Rangers Larry Parrish hits his 3rd grand slam of the week in a 6–5 win over the Tigers, tying the ML record set by Detroit's Jim Northrup in 1968. Parrish also hit grand slams July 4th against Oakland and July 7th against Boston.

13th Reds SS Dave Concepcion hits a 2-run home run in the 2nd inning to spark the NL to its 11th consecutive win in the All-Star Game 4–1. The NL has now won 19 of the last 20 contests.

19th In the first annual Cracker Jack Oldtimers Classic at Washington's Robert F. Kennedy Stadium, 75-year-old Luke Appling hits a 250-foot homer off Warren Spahn to help the AL to a 7–2 win over the NL in a 5-inning battle of retired baseball stars.

21st Mired in last place in the NL West, 24 games below .500, the Reds fire manager John McNamara and replace him with 3B coach Russ Nixon.

25th Steve Carlton pitches his 50th career shutout, a 1–0 five-hitter against the Dodgers and Jerry Reuss.

28th Atlanta's Phil Niekro (10-3) posts his 250th career win 8–6 over the Padres. The 43-year-old knuckleballer will finish the season 17-4, leading the major leagues in winning percentage.

After a 3–2 loss to the Brewers, Rangers manager Don Zimmer is fired and replaced by Darrell Johnson. During the 1976 season, Zimmer had replaced Johnson as manager of the Boston Red Sox.

31st Phillies 2B Manny Trillo misplays Bill Buckner's grounder in the 7th inning of a 2–0 win over the Cubs, ending his errorless string at 89 games and 479 consecutive chances. He falls 2 games short of Joe Morgan's record 91-game streak, and his 479 straight chances set a ML record.

AUGUST

1st Hank Aaron, Frank Robinson, Travis Jackson, and Happy Chandler are inducted into the baseball Hall of Fame at Cooperstown, New York.

2nd Oakland's Rickey Henderson steals his 100th base of the season in a 6–5 win over Seattle, tying the AL record he set last season and leaving him with 56 games to break Lou Brock's single-season record of 118. Henderson is the first player ever to steal 100 bases twice.

3rd The White Sox sweep a doubleheader at Yankee Stadium 1–0 and 14–2, prompting Yankees owner George Steinbrenner to fire manager Gene Michael and replace him with pitching coach Clyde King. King is the Yankees' 3rd manager this season.

Kansas City's Frank White completes the cycle with an RBI triple in the bottom of the 9th to give the Royals a 6–5 win over the Tigers.

4th OF Joel Youngblood becomes the first ML player ever to play for 2 different teams in 2 different cities on the same day, and collects a hit in each game. After going 1-for-2 off Fergie Jenkins in an afternoon game at Wrigley Field, Youngblood is traded from the Mets to the Expos and flies to Philadelphia in time enter the game that night in the 6th inning, going 1-for-1 off Steve Carlton.

6th Jack Clark and Reggie Smith hit back-to-back home runs twice in San Francisco's 7–6 win over Houston. The Giants trail 6–4 in the 9th inning before Clark and Smith homer to send the game into extra innings.

Just 5 days after hitting 3 home runs in a 5–4 loss to the Twins, California's Doug DeCinces hits 3 more home runs in a 9–5 win at Seattle, joining Ted Williams as the only AL players ever to hit 3 home runs in a game twice in the same season.

The Yankees trade Bucky Dent to the Rangers for Lee Mazzilli. Dent was hitting only .169 and had lost his starting SS job to Roy Smalley.

10th Bob Lillis replaces Bill Virdon as manager of the Houston Astros. Virdon was the senior manager in the NL, having managed the Astros since 1975.

11th Houston's Nolan Ryan pitches his 8th career one-hitter 3–0 at San Diego. Terry Kennedy's 5th-inning single is the only Padres hit.

Twins Terry Felton (0-11) is the losing pitcher in 6–3 loss to California, dropping his career record to 0-14, the worst individual start in ML history. Felton will never win a ML game, finishing his career with an 0-16 record.

14th Atlanta snaps an 11-game losing streak with a 6–5 win over the Padres and moves back within 1½ games of first-place Los Angeles in the NL West. Atlanta had held first place since April 27th before the streak.

17th Cincinnati's Mario Soto fans 15 Mets in a 9–2 victory to raise his league-leading total to 209. He will finish the season with 274 strikeouts, 2nd only to Steve Carlton's 286.

18th In the completion of a game suspended the previous day after 17 innings, the Dodgers beat the Cubs 2–1 in 21 innings despite running out of position players and having to use pitchers Fernando Valenzuela and Bob Welch in the outfield. Jerry Reuss pitches the final 4 innings for the win, then starts the regularly scheduled game and wins again 7–4.

20th Padres rookie Alan Wiggins is suspended for one month by Commissioner Bowie Kuhn as a result of his July 21st arrest for cocaine possession.

21st Milwaukee's Rollie Fingers records his 300th career save in a 3–2 win at Seattle, becoming the first player to reach that milestone.

22nd Third-string catcher Glenn Brummer steals home with the bases loaded and 2 out in the bottom of the 12th inning to give the Cardinals a 5–4 win over the Giants. Brummer, who was running on his own, will steal just 4 bases in his ML career.

23rd Seattle pitcher Gaylord Perry is ejected in the 7th inning of a 4–3 loss to the Red Sox for doctoring the baseball. It is the first time in his 20 ML seasons that the self-proclaimed spitball king has been bounced for that offense.

24th Kansas City's John Wathan steals his 31st base of the season in a 5–3 win over the Rangers, breaking the single-season record for catchers set by Ray Schalk in 1916. Wathan will finish the season with a career-high 36 SBs.

27th Rickey Henderson steals 4 bases in Oakland's 5–4 loss to Milwaukee to raise his total to 122 and break Lou Brock's single-season record of 118. The record-breaking 119th steal comes off pitcher Doc Medich and catcher Ted Simmons on a 3rd-inning pitchout.

30th In an effort to bolster its pitching staff for the pennant race, Milwaukee trades minor leaguers Kevin Bass, Frank DiPino, and Mike Madden to the Astros for veteran starter Don Sutton.

31st The Mets lose their 15th in a row 4–0 on Nolan Ryan's 2-hitter. The Mets will finally win the following day, beating the Astros 5–1.

SEPTEMBER

4th Jim Palmer one-hits the Twins 3–0 for Baltimore to get his 11th consecutive victory. The only hit is Gary Gaetti's 2-out single in the 5th inning.

5th Despite managing just one hit—Al Oliver's solo home run in the 2nd inning—the Expos beat the Braves 2–1 on Rafael Ramirez's error in the bottom of the 9th.

6th In an 8–2 win over the Yankees, Benny Ayala belts the Orioles' 11th pinch home run of the season to break the AL record set by the 1961 Yankees. The win is Baltimore's 9th in a row.

Retiring 1B Willie Stargell is saluted by 38,000 fans on his day at Pittsburgh's Three Rivers Stadium. The 41-year-old slugger delivers a pinch single in the Pirates' 6–1 win over the Mets.

7th Pirates Jason Thompson hits his 30th home run of the season in a 9–5 win over the Mets, becoming just the 8th player in history to hit 30 home runs in a season in each league. Thompson hit 31 home runs for the Tigers in 1977.

11th Nine months after re-signing him to a 3-year, $2 million contract, the Indians trade pitcher John Denny to Philadelphia for minor leaguers Jerry Reed, LeRoy Smith, and Wil Culmer.

13th Steve Carlton (20-9) shuts out St. Louis 2–0 on 3 hits and raps a solo home run to become the major league's first 20-game winner this season.

14th Richie Hebner and Bill Madlock hit grand slams to lead the Pirates to a 15–5 rout of the Cubs.

22nd Light-hitting SS Chris Speier goes 3-for-5 with a club-record 8 RBI as Montreal beats Philadelphia 11–4.

24th In the completion of a game suspended on July 9th, the Tigers beat Cleveland 4–3 when reliever Ed Glynn uncorks a wild pitch with the bases loaded and one out in the bottom of the 18th inning.

27th Willie McGee's 3-run inside-the-park home run in the first inning sparks the Cardinals to a 4–2 win over the Expos, clinching their first NL East title since divisional play began in 1969.

Atlanta's Phil Niekro shuts out the Giants on 2 hits 7–0 to push the Braves back into a first-place tie with the Dodgers in the NL West. The Dodgers have lost 6 straight games.

28th In the first game of a doubleheader, Toronto's Jim Clancy is deprived of a no-hitter when the Twins Randy Bush leads off the 9th inning with a broken-bat single. Clancy had retired all 24 batters he faced before Bush singled, and settles for a 3–0 one-hitter.

Detroit's Lance Parrish hits his 31st home run of the season in a 9–6 win over the Orioles, breaking the AL single-season record for catchers that he had shared with Yogi Berra and Gus Triandos.

OCTOBER

1st Trailing the first-place Brewers in the AL East, the Orioles sweep a doubleheader with them 8–3 and 7–1 to cut their deficit to one game.

Mets pitcher Terry Leach tosses a 10-inning one-hitter against the Phillies, finally winning 1–0 on Hubie Brooks's sacrifice fly. Juan Samuel's 5th-inning triple is the Phillies sole hit.

2nd The Angels clinch the AL West title with a 6–4 win over the Rangers.

Baltimore routs Milwaukee 11–3 to set up a winner-take-all showdown for the AL East title season finale.

Houston hands the Reds their 100th loss of the season, 4–2, a first for the franchise.

3rd Robin Yount smacks 2 home runs and a triple as Milwaukee whips Baltimore 10–2 to win the AL East championship. Don Sutton, 4-1 since being acquired by the Brewers in late August, is the winning pitcher. Despite Yount's fine game, he loses the AL batting title .332 to .331 to Kansas City's Willie Wilson, who sat out the Royals' final game.

Atlanta loses 5–1 to San Diego, but clinches the NL West title anyway when San Francisco beats the 2nd-place Dodgers 5–3.

Expos manager Jim Fanning resigns following the club's season-ending 6–1 win over the Pirates and will return to the club's front office. His 102-87 record as manager is the best in club history.

5th Angels Don Baylor collects 5 RBI, tying an LCS record, as California takes game one 8–3 over Milwaukee.

6th California goes 2 up on Milwaukee, helped by Reggie Jackson's HR and Bruce Kison's 5-hitter, winning 4–2.

7th After rain washed out a 1–0 Atlanta lead in the 5th inning of yesterday's NLCS opener, St. Louis crushes the Braves 7–0. Bob Forsch fires a 3-hitter.

8th The pitching of veteran Don Sutton, and a 2-run home run by Paul Molitor, stave off elimination in the Brewers' game against California.

9th The Brewers even the series, beating California 9–5. Reserve OF Mark Brouhard has 3 hits, 3 RBI, and scores 4 runs for the winners.

After losing another game to rain, the Braves Phil Niekro is able to start the 3rd game of the NLCS after only 2 days rest, but St. Louis wins 4–3.

10th St. Louis wins its first NL pennant since 1968 by defeating the Braves 6–2 to complete a 3-game sweep of the NLCS. Catcher Darrell Porter, who hit .556, is named series MVP.

In game 5 of the ALCS, the Brewers complete their comeback from a 2–0 deficit by edging the Angels 4–3 to earn their first-ever trip to the World Series. Angels OF Fred Lynn bats .611 for the series and is named MVP in a losing cause.

12th Paul Molitor goes 5-for-6 to become the first player ever to collect 5 hits in a World Series game, and teammate Robin Yount goes 4-for-6 as the Brewers rout the Cardinals 10–0 in game one.

13th St. Louis rallies to win 5–4 and even the WS.

15th Willie McGee has 2 HRs to drive in 4 runs, and makes a great catch to save another run. Joaquin Andujar wins 6–2 despite having to leave the game after being hit by a line drive.

16th Four Cardinal pitchers are helpless to stop the Brewers from rallying to a 7–5 win after Dave LaPoint's error in the 7th.

17th Robin Yount records his 2nd 4-hit game of the Series to lead the Brewers to a 6–4 win in game 5 and give Milwaukee a 3-2 lead overall. Yount is the first player ever to have two 4-hit games in one World Series.

19th The Cards sit through 2 rain delays to easily win game 6 by a 13–1 score.

Rather than give him the contract extension he requested, A's president Roy Eisenhardt fires manager Billy Martin, who led the club to a 68-94 record this season after winning the AL West in 1981.

20th St. Louis rallies for 3 runs in the 6th and Bruce Sutter saves the 7th game 6–3 win to give the Cards the World Championship.

22nd Despite having led his club to the AL West title, hard-luck Gene Mauch resigns as manager of the Angels. He will be replaced on November 2nd by John McNamara, who was fired in July as manager of the Reds.

26th Steve Carlton wins the NL Cy Young Award for the 4th time, a record unmatched by any pitcher. The Phils 37-year-old lefthander, who led the NL in wins (23), innings (295⅔), strikeouts (286), and shutouts (6), was a previous winner in 1972, 1977, and 1980. He joins Walter Johnson and Willie Mays as the only players to be voted MVP or Cy Young winner 10 or more years apart.

NOVEMBER

1st At a meeting in Chicago, the ML owners vote not to renew Commissioner Bowie Kuhn's contract, which will expire next August. The AL owners voted in favor of Kuhn 11-3, the NL 7-5. But his 18 votes left him 2 shy of the three-fourths majority required for reelection. Kuhn will remain on the job until a successor is found.

Thirty-eight-year-old Doug Rader, who spent the last 3 seasons as manager of the Padres' Triple-A farm club, will pilot the Texas Rangers. The former infielder becomes the club's 12th manager in its 12-year life.

3rd Pete Vuckovich becomes the Brewers' 2nd consecutive AL Cy Young Award winner, edging Jim Palmer. Vuckovich was 18-6 with a 3.34 ERA for the AL champions, and has the highest winning percentage in the majors for the past 2 seasons.

4th Yankees coach Mike Ferraro lands his first ML managing job, signing a 2-year contract to lead the Cleveland Indians. He will be fired before the end of the 1983 season.

9th Robin Yount, who hit .331 for Milwaukee and led the league in hits (210), doubles (46), and slugging percentage (.578), is a unanimous choice as AL MVP.

11th Joe Altobelli succeeds the retired Earl Weaver as Oriole manager. Altobelli is the 2nd Yankee coach to take a managing job this month, and will be Baltimore's first new pilot since 1968.

17th Dale Murphy wins the NL MVP Award, becoming the first Brave to be so honored since Hank Aaron in 1957. The centerfielder hit .281 with 36 HR, 109 RBI, 113 runs, and 23 stolen bases.

22nd 2B Steve Sax is named NL Rookie of the Year, the 4th consecutive Dodger to win the award. Sax hit .282 and stole 49 bases as Davey Lopes's replacement in the Los Angeles infield.

24th Cal Ripken, Jr., who hit .264 with 28 HRs as a SS-3B for the Orioles, is named AL Rookie of the Year.

DECEMBER

1st Free-agent slugger Don Baylor signs a reported 5-year, $5 million contract with the Yankees.

6th The Red Sox trade 3B Carney Lansford, OF Garry Hancock, and minor leaguer Jerry King to Oakland for OF Tony Armas and C Jeff Newman.

Kenneth Moffett, who helped mediate the 1981 baseball strike settlement, is named to succeed Marvin Miller as executive director of the ML Baseball Players' Association.

9th The Phillies trade 2B Manny Trillo, OF George Vukovich, SS Julio Franco, catcher Jerry Willard, and pitcher Jay Baller to the Indians for 24-year-old OF Von Hayes. Hayes hit .250 with 14 HRs and 32 SBs for Cleveland last season and is considered a potential star.

In what will turn out to be a pair of unwise deals, the Yankees sign free-agent OF Steve Kemp to a 5-year contract, and trade OF Dave Collins, pitcher Mike Morgan, and minor leaguer Fred McGriff to the Blue Jays for P Dale Murray and minor leaguer Tom Dodd.

13th Free-agent P Floyd Bannister, who led the AL with 209 strikeouts at Seattle last season, signs a 5-year contract with the White Sox for a reported $4.5 million.

14th The Giants trade veteran 2B Joe Morgan and reliever Al Holland to the Phillies for pitchers Mike Krukow and Mark Davis and minor leaguer Charles Penigar.

16th Tom Seaver agrees to a new contract with the Mets, completing a trade that sends him back to New York from Cincinnati. The Reds receive pitcher Charlie Puleo and minor leaguers Lloyd McClendon and Jason Felice for the 3-time Cy Young Award winner, who was 5-13 with a 5.50 ERA in 1982.

21st Free-agent 1B Steve Garvey signs a 5-year contract with the San Diego Padres.

22nd Versatile Lee Mazzilli is traded for the 3rd time this year. The Yankees send him to the Pirates for 4 minor leaguers, including pitcher Tim Burke.

1983

JANUARY

10th New York Supreme Court Justice Richard Lane issues a preliminary injunction barring the Yankees from playing their season-opening series against the Tigers in Denver. The club had sought to move the games because it feared off-season renovations to Yankee Stadium would not be completed for the April 11th-13th series.

11th For the 3rd time in 8 years, George Steinbrenner hires Billy Martin as Yankee manager. Martin replaces Clyde King, who will move to the front office.

12th Brooks Robinson and Juan Marichal are elected to the Hall of Fame by the BBWAA. Robinson becomes the 14th player elected in his first year of eligibility.

13th The Red Sox trade veteran P Mike Torrez to the Mets for minor leaguer 3B Mike Davis.

17th Bob Horner agrees to a 4-year contract with the Atlanta Braves that will pay him up to $6 million, including $400,000 in bonuses if he keeps his weight below 215 pounds.

19th The Dodgers trade veteran 3B Ron Cey to the Cubs for minor leaguers Vance Lovelace and Dan Cataline.

Ozzie Smith becomes baseball's first $1 million shortstop, signing a 3-year contract with the Cardinals.

26th The White Sox trade pitchers Steve Trout and Warren Brusstar to the Cubs for pitchers Randy Martz and Dick Tidrow and infielders Pat Tabler and Scott Fletcher.

31st The Phillies sign veteran 1B Tony Perez to a one-year contract.

FEBRUARY

7th As compensation for the loss of free-agent pitcher Floyd Bannister to the White Sox, the Mariners select 20-year-old minor league infielder Danny Tartabull from the Reds organization. Tartabull hit .227 for Waterbury (Eastern League) last season.

8th One day after taking a job as director of sports promotions for Claridge Hotel and Casino in Atlantic City, NJ, Mickey Mantle is ordered to sever his ties with ML baseball by Commissioner Kuhn. Mantle joins fellow Hall of Famer Willie Mays as players banned from baseball by Kuhn for involvement with legalized gambling.

19th Fernando Valenzuela wins his salary arbitration case with the Dodgers and becomes the first player to win a $1 million salary through that process. The Dodgers had offered Valenzuela $750,000 for the 1983 season.

MARCH

3rd Steve Carlton agrees to a 4-year, $4.15 million contract with the Phillies that will make him the highest-paid pitcher in baseball history.

10th Walter Alston, who managed the Dodgers to 4 World Championships, and George Kell, who hit .306 over 15 ML seasons, are elected to the Hall of Fame by the Special Veterans Committee.

15th Cy Young Award winner Pete Vuckovich is found to have a torn rotator cuff in his pitching shoulder that will sideline him for almost the entire 1983 season.

24th The Executive Board of the International Olympic Committee agrees to stage a 6-team exhibition baseball tournament as part of the 1984 Summer Olympics to be held in Los Angeles.

APRIL

5th In his first appearance as a Met since 1977, Tom Seaver combines with Doug Sisk to shut out the Phillies 2–0 on 5 hits. It is Seaver's 14th NL Opening Day assignment, tying Walter Johnson's record with Washington.

7th ML Baseball, ABC, and NBC agree to terms of a 6-year television package worth $1.2 billion. The 2 networks will continue to alternate coverage of the playoffs, World Series, and All-Star Game through the 1989 season, with each of the 26 clubs receiving $7 million per year in return. The last package gave each club $1.9 million per year.

15th Detroit P Milt Wilcox is one out away from a perfect game when pinch hitter Jerry Hairston singles, and Wilcox settles for a 6–0 one-hitter over the White

Sox. This is only the 3rd time in ML history a no-hit bid has been stopped with one out to go.

The Astros avoid the worst start in modern ML history by beating the Expos 7–6 in 10 innings for their first win of the season in 10 games.

16th Montreal's Charlie Lea pitches the ML's 2nd one-hitter in as many days, shutting out the Astros 2–0. The only Houston hit is Terry Puhl's pinch single with 2 out in the 8th inning.

Padres 1B Steve Garvey plays in his 1,118th consecutive game, breaking Billy Williams's NL record. Garvey goes 2-for-4 in an 8–5 Padres loss at Los Angeles.

17th Nolan Ryan fans 7 Expos in a 6–3 Houston win to become only the 2nd pitcher to record 3,500 career strikeouts.

20th George Brett belts 3 home runs, the last a 2-run shot in the top of the 9th inning, and drives in 7 runs to lead the Royals to an 8–7 win over Detroit.

27th In a 4–2 win over the Expos, Nolan Ryan strikes out Brad Mills to move a strikeout ahead of Walter Johnson and become baseball's all-time leader at 3,509.

Fred Lynn and Darryl Sconiers hit grand slams to lead California to a 13–3 win over the Tigers. This is a first for the Angels club.

30th El Paso beats Beaumont 35–21 to break the Texas League's 80-year-old record for total runs scored in a game. A 25-mph wind blowing out to right field at El Paso's Dudley Field was a big help to hitters. The only starter on either team without an RBI was the winners' SS Ernest Riles.

MAY

4th Johnny Bench collects his 2,000th career hit, a single off Steve Carlton in a 9–4 Cincinnati loss to the Phillies.

6th Angels Rod Carew goes 3-for-4 in a 4–2 win over the Tigers to raise his batting average to an even .500 (48-for-96). Carew will finish the season at .339.

14th Ben Oglivie slugs 3 home runs as the Brewers come from behind to beat Boston 8–7 in 10 innings. Oglivie's 3rd homer ties the score at 6–6 in the bottom of the 9th.

Toronto's Luis Leal and Roy Lee Jackson combine to one-hit the Indians 8–1, allowing only an 8th-inning single to Chris Bando. Starter Leal pitches 5 innings, and is replaced by Jackson after a 1:42 rain delay.

16th Mets rookie Darryl Strawberry hits his first ML home run in an 11–4 rout of the Padres.

Despite six 9th-inning runs on solo home runs by Dave Engle and Bobby Mitchell and 2-run shots by Gary Gaetti and Mickey Hatcher, the Twins lose 7–6 to Oakland.

18th Chicago's Rich Dotson pitches a one-hitter against the Orioles, and loses 1–0. Baltimore's lone hit is Dan Ford's 8th-inning home run.

20th In a 5–0 loss to the Padres, Steve Carlton strikes out 4 batters to move past Walter Johnson into 2nd place on baseball's all-time strikeout list. Carlton's 3,511 strikeouts leave him 10 behind Nolan Ryan, who broke Johnson's record earlier this season.

22nd The Phillies make a pair of trades, sending P Sid Monge to the Padres for OF Joe Lefebvre and P Dick Ruthven and minor leaguer Bill Johnson to the Cubs for P Willie Hernandez.

25th In a 6–0 loss to the Braves, Pirates Jim Bibby and Jim Winn combine to walk 7 consecutive batters in the 3rd inning, tying the ML record set by the Senators Dolly Gray in 1909.

29th Dodgers pitcher Steve Howe is readmitted to a drug treatment center after suffering a relapse of the cocaine problem for which he had sought treatment after last season. Howe hadn't allowed an earned run in his 14 appearances this season.

31th AL President Lee MacPhail suspends Yankees owner George Steinbrenner for one week, citing "repeated problems" with the outspoken owner's public criticism of umpires. Steinbrenner, who had been fined $50,000 by Commissioner Kuhn during spring training for berating some NL umpires, cannot attend games or be in his Yankee Stadium office during the suspension.

JUNE

3rd George Bamberger resigns as manager of the New York Mets, whose 16-30 record is the big-leagues' worst. He will be replaced by Frank Howard, who managed the Padres in 1981.

6th The Twins select pitcher Tim Belcher with the first pick in the annual June free-agent draft, but Belcher will reject their $125,000 signing bonus offer and pitch for Team USA in the Pan American Games instead. He is the only first-rounder who doesn't sign. Belcher will be the first selected in the January 1984 draft. The Reds take Kurt Stillwell with the 2nd pick. Roger Clemens is taken with the 19th pick.

The Brewers trade OF Gorman Thomas and pitchers Jamie Easterly and Ernie Camacho to the Indians for OF Rick Manning and pitcher Rick Waits.

7th Steve Carlton overtakes Nolan Ryan as baseball's all-time strikeout leader, fanning 6 batters in a 2–1 loss to the Cardinals to bring his career total to 3,526. In Houston, Ryan strikes out 3 Giants while getting no decision in the Astros' 4–2 win, leaving him with 3,525.

11th Cardinals OF Lonnie Smith checks into a drug rehabilitation program, joining the Phillies Dickie Noles and the Dodgers Steve Howe, as the 3rd ML player to leave his team because of a substance-abuse problem this season.

12th In the first complete game of his career in which he does not walk at least one batter, Nolan Ryan strikes out 11 Padres in a 2–0 shutout to move back into a first-place tie with Steve Carlton with 3,535 career strikeouts. The 2 will trade the lead back and forth start by start for much of the summer, but by the end of the season Carlton will have pulled ahead, 3,709 to 3,677.

15th In what will turn out to be a terrible trade for St. Louis, the Cardinals trade 1B Keith Hernandez to the Mets for pitchers Neil Allen and Rick Ownbey.

Darrell Evans hits 3 home runs in a Giants 7–1 win over the Astros to give him a ML-leading 18 for the season. Evans will finish the season with 30 HRs.

17th Bob Welch pitches a 6-hitter and hits his first career homer to lead the Dodgers past the Reds 1–0.

24th Milwaukee's Don Sutton strikes out Alan Bannister in the 8th inning of a 3–2 win over Cleveland to become the 8th pitcher in ML history with 3,000 career strikeouts. County Stadium is packed with 46,037 fans for the game, mostly to welcome back popular OF Gorman Thomas, who was traded to Cleveland earlier this month.

25th After 8 straight losses, Rene Lachemann is fired as manager of the Mariners and replaced by Del Crandall.

26th Mets Rusty Staub delivers his 8th consecutive pinch hit in the 9th inning of an 8–4 loss to the Phillies, tying Dave Philley for the all-time ML record. Staub's streak will be snapped by Cards Bruce Sutter 3 days from now.

Baltimore's Storm Davis holds the Tigers hitless for 8 innings, then needs help from reliever Tippy Martinez to complete a 3–1 victory. Pinch hitter Rick Leach, who had been in a 3-for-35 slump, breaks up the no-hit bid with his first home run of the year leading off the 9th.

29th Mark Fidrych, in the 2nd year of an extended comeback attempt with the Pawtucket Red Sox (International League), retires. The 1976 AL Rookie of the Year was 2–5 with a 9.68 ERA.

JULY

1st Arbitrator Raymond Goetz rules that the 43 players who were on the Disabled List during the 1981 players' strike are not entitled to their salaries for that period. The decision saves the club owners about $2.5 million.

3rd The Rangers explode for 12 runs in the 15th inning of a 16–4 win over the A's, setting a new ML record for runs in a single extra inning.

4th Dave Righetti pitches the Yankees' first no-hitter since Don Larsen's perfect game in the 1956 World Series, handcuffing the Red Sox 4–0 before a holiday crowd of 41,077 at Yankee Stadium.

6th In the 50th anniversary All-Star Game at Chicago's Comiskey Park, the AL routs the NL 13–3 for its first win since 1971. The AL breaks the game open with 7 runs in the 4th inning, highlighted by Fred Lynn's grand slam—the first ever in All-Star competition. It is Lynn's 4th All-Star homer, tying him with Ted Williams for the AL record.

10th It takes Milwaukee 4 hours and 11 minutes to beat Chicago 12–9, the slowest 9-inning game in AL history.

11th With his club in the NL West cellar, 15½ games behind the Braves, Reds president Dick Wagner is fired by the club's general partners.

17th Dodgers 2B Steve Sax commits his 21st throwing error of the season in a 10–0 loss to the Phillies. Sax, who has struggled all year with even the most routine throws to 1B, will lead all ML 2nd basemen with 30 errors this season.

18th Despite being in first place in the NL East, the Phillies fire manager Pat Corrales because the team is "not playing up to its potential." GM Paul Owens will manage the club instead.

20th Two outs away from a no-hitter against the Astros, Phillies P Charles Hudson gives up a bloop single to Craig Reynolds and back-to-back home runs to Denny Walling and Dickie Thon before settling down for a 10–3 victory.

22nd Angels OF Brian Downing misplays Chet Lemon's line drive in the 6th inning of a 13–11 loss to Detroit, ending his AL-record consecutive-errorless-game streak at 244.

24th In the memorable "Pine Tar Game" at Yankee Stadium, George Brett hits an apparent 2-run home run off Rich Gossage to give the Royals a 5–4 lead with 2 outs in the 9th inning, only to have it taken away when Yankees manager Billy Martin points out that the pine tar on Brett's bat handle exceeds the 17 inches allowed in the rules. As a result, Brett is called out for illegally batting the ball, giving New York a 4–3 victory. The Royals immediately protest, and AL President Lee MacPhail overrules his umpires for the first time saying that, while the rules should certainly be rewritten and clarified, the home run will stand and the game will be resumed from that point on August 18th.

27th While picking up his first win as a member of the Royals, Gaylord Perry joins Nolan Ryan and Steve Carlton as the 3rd pitcher this season to reach 3,500 career strikeouts, fanning 4 Indians in a 5–4 victory to raise his total to 3,501.

29th Steve Garvey's consecutive-game streak ends at 1,207 when he dislocates his left thumb in a home-plate collision with Braves pitcher Pascual Perez, and the injury keeps him from playing the 2nd game of the doubleheader.

31st Brooks Robinson, Juan Marichal, George Kell, and Walter Alston are inducted into the Hall of Fame at Cooperstown, New York, bringing the total number of inductees to 184.

In the 2nd game of a doubleheader, Pirates rookie Jose DeLeon holds the Mets hitless for 8⅓ innings before Hubie Brooks singles, but Mets starter Mike Torrez pitches 11 shutout innings himself and New York goes on to win 1–0 in 12 innings. In his previous start, DeLeon had held the Padres hitless for 6⅓ innings.

The Indians fire manager Mike Ferraro and replace him with Pat Corrales, who was fired earlier this month by the Phillies.

AUGUST

3rd Nolan Ryan pitches his 9th career one-hitter, striking out 10 Padres on the way to a 1–0 victory. Tim Flannery's 3rd-inning single is San Diego's only hit.

4th While warming up before the 5th inning of the Yankees 3–1 win over the Blue Jays game at Toronto's Exhibition Stadium, New York OF Dave Winfield accidentally kills a seagull with a thrown ball. After the game, Winfield is brought to the Ontario Provincial Police station on charges of cruelty to animals and is forced to post a $500 bond before being released. The charges will be dropped the following day.

5th AL president Lee MacPhail suspends Yankees manager Billy Martin for the 2nd time this season because of continuing abuse of umpires. Martin is suspended for 2 games for calling umpire Dale Ford "a stone liar" after a July 31st game with the White Sox. He earned a 3-game suspension earlier this year for kicking dirt on umpire Drew Coble.

6th Walt Terrell becomes the first pitcher in 5 years to homer twice in one game, belting a pair of 2-run shots off Ferguson Jenkins to lead New York to a 4–1 win over the Cubs.

10th Al Oliver collects his 2,500th career hit, a 7th-inning single off Carlos Diaz, as the Expos beat the Mets 5–3.

15th Braves Bob Horner, who was hitting .303 with 20 HRs and 68 RBI, breaks his right wrist sliding into 2B during a 4–0 loss to the Padres and will be sidelined for the rest of the season. In Atlanta, the injury is widely attributed to the "Chief Noc-A-Homa Jinx," which seems to strike whenever the Braves remove their mascot's outfield teepee in order to sell more tickets.

18th In the continuation of the "Pine Tar Game," Hal McRae strikes out and Dan Quisenberry retires the Yankees in order in the bottom of the 9th to preserve the Royals' 5–4 victory. The conclusion took just 12 minutes (and 16 pitches) and, as the only game scheduled at the Stadium, was witnessed by a crowd of 1,245.

19th The Dodgers trade pitchers Dave Stewart and Ricky Wright to Texas for star pitcher Rick Honeycutt, who was 14-8 with an AL-best 2.42 ERA for the Rangers. Honeycutt will go 2-3 down the stretch for the Dodgers, but still wins the AL ERA title because his 174⅔ innings pitched were already enough to qualify.

20th Pittsburgh's Jose DeLeon takes a no-hitter into the 7th inning for the 3rd time this season, but Cincinnati's Dan Driessen doubles with 2 out to spoil the gem. DeLeon finishes with 13 strikeouts in a 4–0 two-hitter.

21st Class A outfielders Vince Coleman (Macon, South Atlantic League) and Donnell Nixon (Bakersfield, California League) each break Rickey Henderson's single-season record by stealing their 131st bases of the season. Coleman will finish the season with 145 stolen bases, despite having missed 31 games with a broken hand. Nixon will tally 144.

22nd The Cubs replace Lee Elia with Charlie Fox, a special assistant to GM Dallas Green who managed the Giants to the NL West title in 1971. Chicago is in 5th place in the NL East with a 54-69 record.

23rd Kansas City's Amos Otis notches his 2,000th career hit, a single in a 10–2 win over the White Sox.

24th 1B Pete Rose does not play in the Phillies 5–3 loss to the Giants, ending his consecutive games played streak at 745. Manager Paul Owens had planned to use Rose as a pinch hitter in the 10th inning, but Joel Youngblood ends the game with a 2-run home run off Steve Carlton in the bottom of the 9th.

Cubs Chuck Rainey is one out away from a no-hitter when the Reds Eddie Milner singles to center on the first pitch. Rainey settles for a 3–0 one-hitter, his first complete game of the season.

25th The Louisville Redbirds (American Association) become the first minor league team to draw one million fans in a season, as 31,258 watch them beat Evansville 7–0 to clinch the Eastern Division title. Louisville will finish the season with an attendance of 1,052,438.

28th Greg Luzinski becomes the first player to park 3 home runs onto the roof at Comiskey Park, connecting off Boston's Oil Can Boyd in a 6–2 Chicago victory. Jimmie Foxx and Ted Williams each accomplished the feat twice.

The Indians trade pitcher Len Barker to the Braves for Rick Behenna, cash, and 2 players to be named later who turn out to be OF Brett Butler and 3B Brook Jacoby.

SEPTEMBER

3rd Trailing 5–3, the Indians erupt for 10 runs in the top of the 9th inning and go on to defeat Oakland 13–6. The A's set a ML record by using 6 pitchers in the inning.

8th Yankees OF Steve Kemp will miss the rest of the season with a fractured cheekbone after being struck in the face by an Omar Moreno line drive during batting practice in Milwaukee. Kemp hit just .242 with 12 HR and 49 RBI in the first year of his 5-year, $5.45 million contract.

9th White Sox Britt Burns pitches a one-hit 11–0 win over the Angels. California's sole hit is Mike Brown's single with 2 out in the 7th.

11th LaMarr Hoyt (20-10) becomes the major leagues' first 20-game winner this season by beating California 5–4 in 10 innings.

Los Angeles scores 4 runs in the bottom of the 9th to beat Atlanta 7–6 and widen their NL West lead over the 2nd-place Braves to 3 games.

13th Dan Quisenberry breaks John Hiller's all-time single-season save record, recording the final 2 outs of the Royals' 4–3 win over the Angels for his 39th save of the season.

Oakland's Rickey Henderson steals 3 bases in a 6–5 win over Texas to give him 101 for the season and a ML-record 3 consecutive seasons with 100 or more.

Mets C Mike Fitzgerald becomes the 48th player in ML history to hit a home run in his first at bat, connecting for a solo shot off Tony Ghelfi in the 2nd inning of New York's 5–1 win over Philadelphia.

16th Minnesota's Tim Teufel goes 5-for-5 with a triple and the first 2 home runs of his ML career in an 11–4 win over the Blue Jays.

17th The Chicago White Sox clinch their first-ever AL West championship, beating Seattle 4–3 on Harold Baines's sacrifice fly in the bottom of the 9th.

A record regular-season crowd of 53,790 packs Cincinnati's Riverfront Stadium on Johnny Bench Night, and the retiring superstar responds with a 2–run home run and a single. But the Reds lose to Houston 4–3.

19th Phillies 2B Joe Morgan celebrates his 40th birthday by going 4-for-5 with 2 home runs in a 7–6 win over the Cubs. He will go 4-for-5 again tomorrow in an 8–5 win over the Cubs.

Denver (AA) beats Portland (PCL) 5–4 to give the Tidewater Tides (IL) the championship in the first AAA World Series. Manager Davey Johnson's Tides won 3 of their 4 games in the double round-robin tournament to edge 2nd-place Portland, which finished 2–2.

20th The Tigers rap 10 consecutive hits on the way to an 11-run first inning against Baltimore, tying the AL record set by Boston in 1901. Detroit wins 14–1 in a rain-shortened 5-inning game.

23rd Steve Carlton becomes the 16th pitcher in ML history to win 300 games and the Phillies inch closer to the NL East title with a 6–2 win over the Cardinals.

Troubled Dodger reliever Steve Howe is suspended once again because of his chronic drug problem after missing the club's flight to Atlanta and refusing to take a urinalysis upon his arrival. Howe, who had 18 saves and a 1.44 ERA despite spending part of the season in a drug rehabilitation program, will not be eligible for post-season play.

24th In the 9th inning of Atlanta's 3–2 win over Los Angeles, Braves OF Dale Murphy walks, steals 2B, and scores the winning run on Rafael Ramirez's single. The stolen base makes him only the 6th player in ML history to hit 30 HRs and steal 30 bases in the same season.

25th Baltimore clinches the AL East title with a 5–1 win over Milwaukee, as Storm Davis and Tippy Martinez combine on a 6-hitter.

26th Cardinals Bob Forsch pitches his 2nd career no-hitter 3–0 against the Expos. Forsch allows just 2 base runners while becoming the first Cardinal and 25th pitcher overall to throw more than one no-hitter.

27th Tim Raines becomes the first player since Ty Cobb to steal 70 bases and drive in 70 runs in the same season, going 3-for-4 with a home run, a stolen base, and 4 RBI in Montreal's 10–4 win over St. Louis.

28th Whipping the Cubs 13-6 for their 12th win in their last 13 games, the Phillies clinch the NL East championship. Bo Diaz goes 5-for-5 with a pair of home runs and Joe Morgan records his 3rd 4-hit game of the month.

29th In his 9th ML start, Oakland's Mike Warren pitches a no-hitter against the White Sox 3–0. It is the first no-hitter by a rookie since Jim Bibby's on July 30, 1973.

30th The Dodgers beat the Giants 4–3 and the Padres beat the Braves 3–2, giving Los Angeles the NL West title. Orel Hershiser pitches the final 2 innings in relief of Fernando Valenzuela to record his first ML save.

In a 9-4 win over the Mariners, Chicago's LaMarr Hoyt records his 13th win in a row to raise his record to 24-10, and Greg Luzinski hits his 32nd home run to set a new single-season record for designated hitters.

OCTOBER

2nd In his final ML game, Carl Yastrzemski plays left field and goes 1-for-3 as the Red Sox beat Cleveland 3–1 at Fenway Park.

Rusty Staub's 2-run pinch double with 2 out in the bottom of the 9th gives the Mets a 5–4 win over the Expos in their season finale and gives Staub 25 RBI as a pinch hitter this season, tying the ML record shared by Joe Cronin and Jerry Lynch. After the game the Mets fire manager Frank Howard.

3rd Less than a year after leading the club to its first World Series, Brewers manager Harvey Kuenn is fired and replaced by Rene Lachemann. Milwaukee finished 5th in the AL East this season with an 87-75 record.

4th In the NLCS opener, Mike Schmidt's first-inning homer and Al Holland's clutch relief pitching to get out of an 8th-inning bases-loaded jam are enough for Philadelphia to top Los Angeles 1–0.

Having finished last in the NL West for the 2nd straight year, the Reds drop manager Russ Nixon and replace him with Vern Rapp.

5th Five-hit pitching by LaMarr Hoyt is the margin in the 2–1 White Sox victory over the Orioles in game 1 of the ALCS.

Fernando Valenzuela wins the 2nd game for the Dodgers downing Philly 4–1.

6th Orioles rookie Mike Boddicker ties the LCS record with 14 strikeouts in a 4–0 shutout of the White Sox, evening the series at 1–1.

Jim Frey will manage the Cubs, succeeding interim manager Charlie Fox, who has returned to the front office after the season.

7th The Orioles waltz in game 3, beating the Sox 11–1. In the NL game, rookie Charlie Hudson goes the distance for Philadelphia, winning 7–2, aided by Gary Matthews's 3-for-3 with 4 RBI.

8th The Phillies and Orioles each win game 4 of their respective LCS to advance to the World Series. Philadelphia gets home runs from Gary Matthews and Sixto Lezcano in another 7–2 victory, while Baltimore's Tito Landrum hits a solo home run in the top of the 10th inning to break a scoreless tie and spark the Orioles to a 3–0 win.

10th John E. Fetzer sells the Tigers to Michigan businessman Tom Monaghan, the founder and president of Domino's Pizza.

11th In the WS opener, homers account for all the scoring as the Phillies top Baltimore 2–1.

12th In game 2, Mike Boddicker pitches a 4–1 three-hitter to tie the Series 1–1. He has yet to allow an earned run in 18 post-season innings, and is the first rookie to pitch a 3-hitter in the World Series since Dickie Kerr in 1919.

14th The Orioles rally to win game 3 by a 3–2 margin. Jim Palmer wins and his batterymate Rick Dempsey has 2 doubles.

15th Rich Daner has 3 hits and 3 RBI to lead Baltimore to a 5–4 Series win.

16th Eddie Murray slams a pair of home runs and Scott McGregor pitches a 5-hitter as the Orioles beat the Phillies 5–0 and win the World Series 4–1. Baltimore catcher Rick Dempsey, who hit .385 with 4 doubles and a home run, is the Series MVP.

25th White Sox pitcher LaMarr Hoyt, who led the AL with 24 wins but whose 3.66 ERA was not among the league's 15 best, wins the AL Cy Young Award, beating out the Royals Dan Quisenberry and the Tigers Jack Morris.

NOVEMBER

2nd John Denny wins the NL Cy Young Award, collecting 20 of 24 first-place votes to defeat runner-up Mario Soto. Denny was 19-6 with a 2.37 ERA for the NL champion Phillies.

8th Atlanta's Dale Murphy wins his 2nd consecutive NL MVP Award, joining Ernie Banks, Joe Morgan, and Mike Schmidt, who also accomplished that feat. Murphy hit .302 with 36 HRs, 121 RBI, and 30 SBs this season, and received 21 of a possible 24 first-place votes.

9th University of Alabama 1B Dave Magadan, who led the NCAA with a .535 batting average last season, wins the Golden Spike Award as the United States's outstanding amateur baseball player.

15th Cal Ripken is named MVP of the AL, edging Orioles teammate Eddie Murray. Ripken hit .318 and led the league in hits (211) and runs (111) while playing every inning of every game, and is the first player ever to win the Rookie of the Year and MVP Awards in consecutive seasons.

17th Kansas City Royals teammates Willie Wilson, Willie Aikens, and Jerry Martin, who, along with former teammate Vida Blue, had pleaded guilty to attempting to purchase cocaine, are each sentenced to 3 months in prison.

21st Darryl Strawberry becomes the first non-Dodger since 1978 to win the NL Rookie of the Year Award. Strawberry hit .257 for the Mets with 26 home runs and 74 RBI and also stole 19 bases.

The Mariners trade reliever Bill Caudill and a player to be named later (minor leaguer Darren Akerfelds) to the A's for catcher Bob Kearney and pitcher Dave Beard.

22nd White Sox OF Ron Kittle, who hit .254 with 35 HRs and 100 RBI, but also struck out a league-leading 150 times, wins the AL Rookie of the Year Award. Cleveland's Julio Franco and Baltimore's Mike Boddicker finish 2nd and 3rd.

The Players' Association fires executive director Kenneth Moffett and chooses Donald Fehr as his successor.

DECEMBER

5th   The Phillies trade veteran 1B Tony Perez to Cincinnati for a player to be named later.

6th   The Pirates trade OF Mike Easler to the Red Sox for lefthanded starter John Tudor.

7th   In a complicated 3-team swap, pitcher Scott Sanderson is traded from the Expos to the Cubs. Montreal receives pitcher Gary Lucas from San Diego, and the Padres get P Craig Lefferts, 1B-OF Carmelo Martinez, and 3B Fritz Connally from Chicago.

The Mariners trade 2B Tony Bernazard to the Indians for OF Gorman Thomas and IF Jack Perconte.

The Reds sign their first major free agent: OF Dave Parker, who accepts a 2-year contract.

The Royals trade P Mike Armstrong and minor league catcher Duane Dewey to the Yankees for slugger Steve Balboni and P Roger Erickson.

8th   Dr. Bobby Brown, who played 3B for the Yankees before embarking on a successful medical career, is elected president of the AL by the club owners.

Ill-advisedly, the Dodgers send pitching prospect Sid Fernandez and SS Ross Jones to the Mets in exchange for utility players Carlos Diaz and Bob Bailor.

13th   Forty-year-old Joe Morgan signs a one-year contract with the Oakland A's—his 5th club since 1979.

15th   Commissioner Kuhn suspends convicted Kansas City Royals Willie Wilson, Willie Aikens, and Jerry Martin, and Dodgers pitcher Steve Howe for one season without pay for their use of illegal drugs. The suspensions will be shortened by an arbitrator.

16th   George Steinbrenner fires Billy Martin as manager of the Yankees for the 3rd time, replacing him with Yogi Berra and giving Martin a front-office job.

19th   Cy Young Award winner Vida Blue is sentenced to 90 days in prison, and recently convicted and suspended 1B Willie Aikens is traded by Kansas City to Toronto for DH Jorge Orta.

The Pirates sign free-agent OF Amos Otis, a 5-time AL All-Star, to a one-year contract.

The Tigers sign free-agent slugger Darrell Evans, who hit .277 with 30 home runs for the Giants in 1983.

22nd   Free-agent reliever Kent Tekulve re-signs with the Pirates. In 1983 he had 18 saves and a 1.64 ERA for Pittsburgh.

Pete Rose wins a lawsuit against the Internal Revenue Service and is awarded a $36,083 tax refund for 1978.

28th   Free-agent OF Warren Cromartie signs a reported 3-year, $2.5 million contract to play for Japan's Tokyo Yomiuri Giants. The 30-year-old Cromartie, who hit .278 for the Expos last season, is the best American player to jump to Japan while still in his prime.

1984

JANUARY

5th The Yankees sign veteran free agent Phil Niekro to a 2-year contract, giving the club 6 starting pitchers. Dave Righetti will move to the bullpen to ease the logjam and to fill the void that will be left by the departure of Rich Gossage, who says he will not re-sign with New York.

9th Braves Pascual Perez is arrested for cocaine possession in his native Dominican Republic. Under local law he will remain in jail until his trial, forcing him to miss the beginning of the season. Perez maintains that he was given the packet by a woman he did not know and was unaware of what it contained.

10th Luis Aparicio, Harmon Killebrew, and Don Drysdale are elected to the Hall of Fame by the BBWAA.

12th Rich Gossage signs with the San Diego Padres.

20th In a move that stuns New York fans, the White Sox draft Tom Seaver as compensation for losing Type A free agent Dennis Lamp to the Blue Jays. The Mets left Seaver off their protected list assuming —wrongly—that no team would want to select the aging star, who finished 1983 with a 9-14 record and a 3.55 ERA.

Free agent Pete Rose signs a one-year contract with the Expos.

30th After failing to trade him, the Mets give veteran slugger Dave Kingman his release. Kingman hit .198 with 13 home runs last year, but will find a new home as Oakland's designated hitter.

FEBRUARY

4th The Indians trade 3B Toby Harrah and minor leaguer Rick Brown to the Yankees for P Danny Boitano, C Otis Nixon, and minor leaguer Guy Elston.

8th One day after losing Type A free agent Tom Underwood to the Orioles, the A's "steal" pitcher Tim Belcher from the Yankees as compensation. The number-one selection in last June's draft, Belcher did not sign with the Twins and was available in the January draft. The Yankees signed him on February 2nd, only

to lose him because they had already submitted their list of 26 protected players.

9th The Dodgers waive 2-time NL All-Star Dusty Baker, who had vetoed a trade to Oakland during the winter meetings.

20th Pedro Guerrero becomes the highest-paid Dodger in history, signing a 5-year contract that will reportedly pay him $7 million.

27th The Expos trade Al Oliver to the Giants for pitcher Fred Breining and Max Venable.

MARCH

3rd Peter Ueberroth, the highly successful chairman of the Los Angeles Olympic Organizing Committee for the upcoming Summer Games, is elected to a 5-year term as commissioner of baseball. Ueberroth will take office on October 1st, succeeding Bowie Kuhn.

4th Two outstanding defensive players, SS Pee Wee Reese and catcher Rick Ferrell, are elected to the Hall of Fame by the Special Veterans Committee. Reese hit .269 in 16 seasons with the Dodgers while Ferrell batted .281 with just 28 home runs in 18 seasons for the Browns, Red Sox, and Senators.

16th The Mets sign suspended OF Jerry Martin as a free agent.

17th Ferguson Jenkins is given his unconditional release by the Cubs. He was 6-9 with a 4.30 ERA last season.

18th White Sox coach Charlie Lau, renowned hitting instructor, dies at the age of 50 after a long bout with cancer. Lau, whose ML average was .255, earned his fame as the Royals batting coach from 1971-78, where his star pupil was George Brett.

19th Denny McLain, the last ML pitcher to achieve a 30-win season, is indicted on various charges of racketeering, loan-sharking, extortion, and cocaine possession.

23rd 1B-DH Willie Aikens, now with the Blue Jays, is released from prison.

27th The Phillies trade outfielders Gary Matthews and Bob Dernier and pitcher Porfi Altiamirano to the Cubs for reliever Bill Campbell and catcher Mike

Diaz. Matthews was the MVP of the NLCS last season, while Campbell led the NL with 82 appearances.

J. R. Richard is released by the Astros, ending his professional baseball career. Richard was 0-2 with a 13.68 ERA in 6 starts for Tucson (Pacific Coast League) last season.

30th The Yankees trade new author and veteran 3B Graig Nettles to the Padres for rookie P Dennis Rasmussen and a minor leaguer to be named later. Nettles's controversial book *Balls,* in which he criticizes Steinbrenner, will be not be officially published until April 30th, but the bound books available now make his days in pinstripes numbered.

APRIL

3rd Arbitrator Richard Bloch rules that the Royals Willie Wilson and the Mets Jerry Martin can return to action on May 15th, the day their year-long suspensions are first due to be reviewed.

7th Tigers Jack Morris no-hits the White Sox 4–0 at Comiskey Park, walking 6 and striking out 8.

Dwight Gooden allows one run in 5 innings in his ML debut, earning the win in the Mets' 3–2 victory over Houston. At 19, he is the youngest NL player.

8th Tom Seaver makes an inauspicious AL debut, allowing 5 runs in 4⅓ innings in Chicago's 7–3 loss to Detroit.

In a 3–1 loss to the Mets, Astros SS Dickie Thon is hit in the face by a Mike Torrez pitch and will miss the rest of the season with blurred vision.

Admitting he has a cocaine problem, Pittsburgh's Rod Scurry checks into a 30-day drug rehabilitation program. He will return to action on May 13th.

13th Pete Rose lashes a double off Jerry Koosman in a 5–1 Expos victory over the Phillies to join Ty Cobb as the only player to reach 4,000 career hits.

16th Dave Kingman hits 3 home runs—including his 12th career grand slam—and drives in 8 runs in the A's 9–6 win over the Mariners. It is Kingman's 5th career 3-HR game, one shy of the ML record held by Johnny Mize.

17th Commissioner Bowie Kuhn suspends Braves pitcher Pascual Perez until May 15th as a result of his off-season drug arrest in the Dominican Republic, but an independent arbitrator will overturn the suspension because of lack of evidence.

19th Kansas City's Bret Saberhagen picks up his first ML victory as the Royals beat the Tigers 5–2. It is the first loss of the season for the red-hot Tigers, who began the year 9–0 and will never fall out of first place in the AL East.

21st Montreal's David Palmer, who missed all of the 1983 season following elbow surgery, pitches a rain-shortened 5-inning perfect game 4–0 against the Cardinals to give the Expos a doubleheader sweep. It is the 4th perfect game of less than 9 innings in ML history.

The Tigers beat the White Sox 4–1, ending LaMarr Hoyt's personal 15-game winning streak.

27th Mike Hargrove's bases-loaded double in the top of the 19th inning leads Cleveland to an 8–4 win over Detroit in a game that takes 5 hours and 44 minutes to complete. It is only the 2nd loss of the season for the 16–2 Tigers.

MAY

2nd LaMarr Hoyt faces 27 batters in a 3–0 one-hitter against the Yankees. New York's only hit is Don Mattingly's opposite-field blooper in the 7th inning, which is followed by a double play.

3rd Bobby Ojeda strikes out a career-high 10 batters and outduels Jack Morris as the Red Sox beat the Tigers 1–0, handing Detroit (19-4) a 2nd consecutive loss.

6th Cal Ripken hits for the cycle in Baltimore's 6–1 win over Texas, completing the feat with a solo home run in the 9th inning.

9th The longest—and slowest—game in AL history ends in the 25th inning when Harold Baines homers off Chuck Porter to give the White Sox a 7–6 victory over the Brewers. The game falls one inning shy of the ML record, but takes by far the most time to play: 8 hours and 6 minutes. The contest was suspended yesterday after 17 innings with the score tied 3–3, and each team scores 3 more runs in the 21st. Tom Seaver pitches the final inning to earn the win, then wins the regularly scheduled game as well 5–4.

Umpire Joe West ejects 2 television cameramen from Shea Stadium when they allow the Mets to view replays of a controversial play at the plate in which Hubie Brooks was called out.

11th The Tigers improve their record to 26-4 with an 8–2 win over the Angels and establish a new record for the best 30-game start in ML history, eclipsing the Dodgers 25-5 mark in 1955.

12th Cincinnati's Mario Soto is one out away from a no-hitter when the Cardinals George Hendrick hits a home run to tie the game 1–1. The Reds then rally for a run in the bottom of the 9th to give Soto a one-hit 2–1 victory.

16th Steve Carlton lifts a grand slam off Fernando Valenzuela to lead the Phillies to a 7–2 win over the Dodgers.

Carlton Fisk hits for the cycle in a losing effort as Kansas City tops Chicago 7–6.

The Twins sell 51,863 tickets to their 8–7 loss to the Blue Jays, but only 6,346 fans show up for the game. The skewed numbers are the result of a massive ticket buyout plan organized by Minneapolis businessman Harvey Mackay to keep the Twins in Minnesota; if the club does not sell 2.41 million tickets this season it can break its lease with the Metrodome. Taking advantage of reduced prices on the Family Day promotion, Mackay pays $218,718 for 44,166 tickets.

The Orioles release veteran pitcher Jim Palmer, who was 0–3 with a 9.17 ERA this season. Palmer is asked to retire and accept a job with the organization, but he declines, hoping to find a roster spot on another ML team.

20th Boston's Roger Clemens strikes out 7 batters in 7 innings en route to his first ML victory 5–4 over the Twins.

23rd In a rematch against Steve Carlton, who hit a grand slam off him on May 16th, Fernando Valenzuela strikes out 15 Phillies while pitching the Dodgers to a 3-hit 1–0 victory.

24th Detroit (35-5) beats California 5–1 for its 17th consecutive win on the road, breaking the AL record set by the 1912 Senators, and tying the ML mark set by the 1916 Giants. The Tigers will finally lose tomorrow in Seattle 7–3.

An hour after beating Baltimore 3–2, Oakland fires manager Steve Boros and replaces him with coach Jackie Moore. Boros, who was criticized as being "too nice," had led the A's to a 20-24 start, just 2½ games off the pace in the weak AL West.

25th The Red Sox trade P Dennis Eckersley and minor leaguer Mike Brumley to the Cubs for veteran

Bill Buckner, who had been benched in Chicago in favor of Leon Durham but will immediately become Boston's starting 1B.

29th Braves 3B Bob Horner breaks his wrist diving for a ball against the Cubs and will be sidelined for the rest of the season. Horner broke the same wrist last year and missed the final 43 games.

31st Mario Soto is suspended for 5 days by NL president Chub Feeney for his role in a 32-minute melee that marred the Reds-Cubs game on May 27th. After shoving 3B umpire Steve Ripley, who had signaled that Ron Cey's long fly ball was a 3-run home run (it was later ruled foul), a bat-wielding Soto then tried to attack a park vendor who had thrown a bag of ice at him. Soto will be suspended again for 5 more days later in the season for his June 16th fight with Claudell Washington.

JUNE

1st Phillies 1B Len Matuszek has no putouts in a 12–3 loss to the Cubs. It is the 18th time in ML history a 1B has accomplished that feat.

4th The New York Mets select 17-year-old Shawn Abner with the first pick in the annual June free-agent draft. Thirteen members of the U.S. Olympic team are drafted in the first round.

6th Anthony Perry is killed when he falls from the upper deck of Candlestick Park following a Giants-Braves game. Witnesses say Perry was leaning over the railing and shouting at the Giants, who had lost 5–4 in 11 innings.

9th Greg Luzinski becomes the 10th player in ML history to hit grand slams in consecutive games when he connects off the Twins Mike Walters in the 7th inning of an 8–4 White Sox victory. The previous day, Luzinski sparked the Sox to a 6–1 win with a first-inning grand slam off Frank Viola.

Pete O'Brien's bizarre sacrifice fly gives Texas a 4–3, 12-inning win over Oakland. With the bases loaded and one out in the bottom of the 12th, A's leftfielder Garry Hancock catches O'Brien's deep fly ball, then intentionally drops it when he realizes he is in foul territory. The umpires rule that the catch had been made, however, and Wayne Tolleson trots home from 3B with the winning run.

13th In a deal that will pay off in the short run with an NL East Championship, the Cubs trade outfielders Mel Hall and Joe Carter and minor leaguer Darryl Banks to the Indians for P George Frazier, C Ron Hassey, and P Rick Sutcliffe. Sutcliffe will go 16–1 for the Cubs the rest of the season and win the NL Cy Young Award.

15th The Cardinals trade 3B Ken Oberkfell to the Braves for pitcher Ken Dayley and 1B Mike Jorgensen. Oberkfell was leading St. Louis with a .309 batting average.

20th Dave Kingman hits his 3rd grand slam of the season in the first inning of the A's 8–1 win over Kansas City. Kingman's 14 grand slams are the most among active players.

22nd In a teary home plate ceremony before the Twins-White Sox game at the Metrodome, Calvin Griffith and his sister, Thelma Haynes, sign a letter of intent to sell their 52 percent ownership of the Twins to Minneapolis banker Carl Pohlad for $32 million. Griffith and his sister had been involved with the franchise since 1922, when they were adopted by owner Clark Griffith when the team was the Washington Senators.

Rick Monday, baseball's first-ever first pick in the June free-agent draft (by the Kansas City A's in 1965) is released by the Dodgers, ending a 19-year ML career.

23rd At Wrigley Field, Cubs Ryne Sandberg goes 5-for-6 with game-tying home runs off Cardinals relief ace Bruce Sutter in both the 9th and 10th innings, and drives in 7 runs to lead Chicago to a 12–11 win in 11 innings. Willie McGee hits for the cycle and drives in 6 runs in a losing cause.

24th Oakland's Joe Morgan hits his 265th career home run as a 2B, breaking Rogers Hornsby's ML record for that position. Morgan, who has 267 home runs overall, connects off Frank Tanana in the first inning of the A's 4–2 win over Texas.

26th Pirates Jason Thompson hits a pair of home runs in each game of a doubleheader split with the Cubs.

28th Dwight Evans hits a 3-run home run in the bottom of the 11th inning to complete the cycle and give Boston a 9–6 win over Seattle.

29th Twins rookie Andre David hits a 2-run home run off Jack Morris in his first ML at bat to spark Minnesota to a 5–3 win over Detroit. It is the only home run David will ever hit in the big leagues.

Pete Rose plays in his 3,309th ML game, surpassing Carl Yastrzemski as the all-time leader. Rose goes 0-for-5, but Montreal beats Cincinnati 7–3.

Orel Hershiser scatters 9 hits to lead the Dodgers past the Cubs and Rick Sutcliffe 7–1. Hershiser will not miss another start until he injures his shoulder in 1990, and Sutcliffe will not lose again in the regular season.

JULY

1st Royals Paul Splittorff, whose 166 victories in 13 seasons are the most in club history, retires.

4th Phil Niekro strikes out 5 batters in the Yankees 5–0 win over Texas to become the 9th pitcher in ML history to record 3,000 career strikeouts.

Jim Rice caps a 5-for-6 day with a grand slam in the bottom of the 10th inning to give Boston a 13–9 win over Oakland.

10th On the 50th anniversary of Carl Hubbell's legendary 5 consecutive strikeouts in the 1934 All-Star Game, NL pitchers Fernando Valenzuela and Dwight Gooden combine to fan 6 batters in a row for a new All-Star Game record in the NL's 3–1 triumph. After Valenzuela whiffs Dave Winfield, Reggie Jackson, and George Brett in the 4th inning, Gooden, the youngest All-Star ever at age 19, fans Lance Parrish, Chet Lemon, and Alvin Davis in the 5th.

19th Orel Hershiser pitches his 3rd straight shutout for the Dodgers, striking out 9 in a 10–0 two-hitter at St. Louis.

20th Trailing 3–1 entering the 9th inning, Toronto scores 11 times and hangs on to beat Seattle 12–7.

23rd Angels Mike Witt strikes out 16 Mariners in a 7–1 victory.

26th San Diego's Tony Gwynn goes 3-for-4 in an 8–2 win over Cincinnati to raise his batting average to .362, best in the majors. Gwynn will finish the season at .351 to win his first NL batting title.

Commissioner Bowie Kuhn announces that free-agent pitcher Vida Blue will be suspended for the remainder of the season as a result of his conviction on cocaine possession charges last November.

The Expos trade P Andy McGaffigan and minor leaguer Jim Jefferson to the Reds for 1B Dan Driessen.

27th Pete Rose collects his 3,053rd career single off Steve Carlton in the 7th inning of Montreal's 6–1 win over Philadelphia, passing Ty Cobb as baseball's all-time singles king.

AUGUST

3rd Brewers reliever Rollie Fingers (23 saves, 1.96 ERA) undergoes back surgery to alleviate a herniated disk and will miss the remainder of the season.

5th Toronto's Cliff Johnson hits his 19th career pinch home run, breaking the ML record of 18 he had shared with Jerry Lynch. Johnson's 8th-inning blast gives the Blue Jays a 4–3 win over the Orioles.

Frank Robinson, who had led his club to a 42-64 record, is fired as manager of the Giants and will be replaced Danny Ozark.

7th Bill Buckner and Tony Armas each hit grand slams off Tigers ace Jack Morris to spark the Red Sox to a 12–7 victory in the first game of a doubleheader split.

8th The Cubs tighten their grip on first place in the NL East with a 7–6 win over the Mets at Wrigley Field, completing a 4-game series sweep.

12th Harmon Killebrew, Rick Ferrell, Don Drysdale, Pee Wee Reese, and Luis Aparicio are inducted into the Hall of Fame at Cooperstown, New York.

In one of the ugliest brawl-filled games in ML history, the Braves beat the Padres 5–3 in Atlanta. The trouble begins when Atlanta's Pascual Perez hits Alan Wiggins in the back with the first pitch of the game, and escalates as the Padres pitchers retaliate by throwing at Perez all 4 times he comes to the plate. All in all, the game features 2 bench-clearing brawls, the 2nd of which includes several fans, and 19 ejections, including both managers and both replacement managers. Padres manager Dick Williams will be suspended for 10 days and fined $10,000, while Braves manager Joe Torre and 5 players will each receive 3-game suspensions.

16th After a 5½ year absence, Pete Rose is reunited with his hometown Cincinnati Reds when the Expos trade him for infielder Tom Lawless, and the Reds immediately name him player-manager, replacing Vern Rapp.

20th The Giants trade veteran 1B Al Oliver, whom they acquired from Montreal in February, and pitcher Renie Martin to the Phillies for P George Riley and minor leaguer Kelly Downs.

21st Red Sox rookie Roger Clemens strikes out 15 and walks none as Boston whips Kansas City 11–1.

24th Despite allowing just one hit—an RBI single to Dave Parker in the 7th inning—Pittsburgh's Jose DeLeon loses to the Reds 2–0. DeLeon walks 3 and strikes out 8 but is beaten by Jeff Russell, who tosses a 3-hitter of his own.

30th In a 9–3 win over the Twins, Red Sox slugger Jim Rice grounds into his 33rd double play of the season to break the ML record set by Jackie Jensen in 1954. By season's end, Rice will extend his new record to 36.

Bill Virdon is fired as manager of the Expos and will be replaced by Jim Fanning.

SEPTEMBER

1st Two weeks after being given a vote of confidence by club owner George Argyros, Mariners manager Del Crandall is fired and replaced by 3B coach Chuck Cottier.

3rd Bruce Sutter breaks the NL record for saves in a season with his 38th in the Cardinals' 7–3 win over the Mets.

7th Dwight Gooden pitches a one-hitter and strikes out 11 in a 10–0 rout of the Cubs. The only hit is Keith Moreland's slow roller in the 5th inning, which 3B Ray Knight fields but can't get out of his glove. Gooden's 11 strikeouts give him 236 for the season, breaking the NL rookie record set by Grover Alexander in 1911.

12th Dwight Gooden strikes out 16 Pirates in a 2–0 victory to break Herb Score's ML rookie strikeout record of 245.

14th Rookie Mark Langston (15-9) becomes the first Mariner to win 15 games in a season by beating the Royals 2–1 on a 5-hitter.

17th Reggie Jackson hits his 500th career home run in the 7th inning off Bud Black, but the Royals beat California 10–1 to move into first place in the AL West. Jackson is the 13th player in ML history to hit 500 home runs.

Harold Baines slugs 3 home runs to lead the White Sox to a 7–3 win over the Twins and drop Minnesota into 2nd place in the AL West.

Dwight Gooden strikes out 16 batters for the 2nd straight start to tie the ML record of 32 strikeouts in consecutive games, but balks home the winning run in the 8th inning of a 2–1 loss to the Phillies. It is Gooden's 5th straight outing with 10 or more strike-outs.

18th The Tigers clinch the AL East championship with a 3–0 win over the Brewers as starter Randy O'Neal records his first ML win. Detroit becomes the 4th team this century to be in first place every day of the season, joining the 1923 Giants, the 1927 Yankees, and the 1955 Dodgers.

Tim Raines becomes the first player in ML history with 4 consecutive 70-stolen-base seasons by stealing 4 in Montreal's 7–4 win over St. Louis.

20th The Padres clinch their first NL West title since entering the league in 1969 with a 5–4 win over the Giants. The key blow is winning pitcher Tim Lollar's 3-run home run, his 3rd home run of the season.

The first-place Cubs break 2 million in home attendance for the first time as 33,651 watch them lose to Pittsburgh 7–6.

23rd Sparky Anderson becomes the first manager ever to win 100 games in a season with 2 different clubs as the Tigers beat the Yankees 4–1. Anderson had led the Reds to 100-win seasons in 1970, 1975, and 1976.

24th Rick Sutcliffe pitches a 2-hitter in a 4–1 win over Pittsburgh to clinch the NL East title for the Cubs, who will be making their first post-season appearance since 1945. The win is Sutcliffe's 14th in a row.

25th Red Sox manager Ralph Houk, 65, announces he will retire at the end of the season.

26th Philadelphia's Juan Samuel breaks Tim Raines's record for steals by a rookie with his 72nd in a 7–1 loss to the Mets. Raines had set the record of 71 in the strike-shortened 1981 season.

28th Bruce Sutter ties the ML record with his 45th save of the season in the Cardinals 4–1, 10-inning win over the Cubs. Starter Joaquin Andujar (20-14) allows 2 hits over 9 innings to win his 20th game.

Kansas City clinches the AL West title with a 6–5 win over Oakland.

30th On the final day of the regular season, California's Mike Witt fans 10 and needs just 97 pitches to complete a perfect game 1–0 over Texas. Witt's gem is the first 9-inning perfect game in Angels history and the first in the major leagues since Len Barker's in 1981.

In the dramatic race for the AL batting title, Don Mattingly goes 4-for-5 in the Yankees season-ending 4–2 win over the Tigers to edge teammate Dave Winfield .343 to .340. Winfield goes 1-for-4.

The ML umpires announce that they will go on strike at the 2 LCS scheduled to begin October 2nd in an effort to improve their pay and job security and to change the method by which post-season assignments are determined. ML officials say the games will go on as scheduled using amateur umpires if necessary.

Phillies interim manager Paul Owens resigns following a season-ending doubleheader loss to the Pirates and will move into the club's front office. Coach John Felske will succeed Owens as manager next season.

OCTOBER

1st Peter Ueberroth begins his 5-year term as commissioner of baseball.

Braves manager Joe Torre is fired by owner Ted Turner and replaced by Eddie Haas. Atlanta was 80-82 this season, 12 games behind the first-place Padres.

2nd In the first LCS game played with replacement umpires, the Cubs clobber the Padres 13-0 to take a 1–0 lead in the NL series. Chicago hits 5 home runs at Wrigley Field, including one by starting pitcher Rick Sutcliffe.

The ALCS opens with a convincing 8–1 Tiger trouncing of KC.

3rd Steve "Rainbow" Trout scatters 5 hits and Lee Smith slams the door in the Cubs' 4–2 victory over the Padres.

The Royals rally with RBI pinch hits in the 7th and 8th innings, but John Grubb's 2-run double in the 11th gives the win to the Tigers 5–3.

4th   The Padres take a lead in an NLCS game for the first time, and they go on to down Chicago 7–1.

5th   In game 3, Milt Wilcox and Willie Hernandez combine on a 1–0 three-hitter to give the Tigers a 3-game sweep of the Royals in the ALCS.

6th   Steve Garvey's 2-run home run in the bottom of the 9th inning gives San Diego a 7–5 win over Chicago and evens the NLCS at 2–2.

7th   The striking ML umpires return to work in time for game 5 of the NLCS, and San Diego rallies for 4 runs in the 7th inning to beat Chicago 6–3 and earn its first trip to the World Series.

9th   The Tigers win the WS opener as Jack Morris pitches a complete-game 3-2 victory. Larry Herndon's 2-run HR in the 5th is the margin.

Despite being offered another one-year contract, Angels manager John McNamara resigns. He will be named manager of the Red Sox on the 18th.

10th   Reliever Andy Hawkins allows just one hit in 5⅓ innings to give San Diego a 5–3 win in game 2.

12th   San Diego pitchers tie the WS record by issuing 11 walks in a 5–2 loss to the Tigers in game 3. Detroit leads the Series 2–1.

13th   In game 4, Jack Morris wins again 4–2. A pair of 2-run HRs by Allan Trammell provide all the Motor City scoring.

14th   Series MVP Kirk Gibson blasts 2 upper-deck home runs at Tiger Stadium in game 5, including a 3-run shot off Rich Gossage in the 8th inning, to lead Detroit to an 8–4 win and its first World Championship since 1968.

16th   Gene Mauch, who resigned as the Angels' manager after the 1982 season, is hired again.

23rd   Rick Sutcliffe, who was 16–1 for the Cubs after arriving from Cleveland 2 days before the June 15th trading deadline, is a unanimous choice as NL Cy Young Award winner. Overall, Sutcliffe was 20–6 with a 3.64 ERA.

30th   Tigers reliever Willie Hernandez wins the AL Cy Young Award, edging fellow reliever Dan Quisenberry of the Royals. Hernandez was 9–3 with 32 saves and a 1.92 ERA.

The Giants name Jim Davenport manager for the 1985 season.

NOVEMBER

6th   Willie Hernandez wins the AL MVP Award, joining Rollie Fingers as the only relief pitchers to be named MVP and Cy Young Award winner in the same season.

13th   Ryne Sandberg wins the NL MVP Award, becoming the first Cub to do so since Ernie Banks in 1959. Sandberg hit .314 with 19 home runs and 32 stolen bases and led the NL in runs (114) and triples (19).

20th   Four days after his 20th birthday, Mets pitcher Dwight Gooden becomes the youngest player ever to win the NL Rookie of the Year Award. Gooden was 17-9 with a 2.60 ERA and a ML-leading 276 strike-outs.

22nd   Seattle's Alvin Davis easily wins the AL Rookie of the Year Award over Mark Langston and Kirby Puckett.

27th   The 1984 AL Gold Glove team is announced, and it is made up of the same 9 players as the 1983 team: catcher Lance Parrish, 1B Eddie Murray, 2B Lou Whitaker, 3B Buddy Bell, SS Alan Trammell, outfielders Dwight Evans, Dave Winfield, and Dwayne Murphy, and pitcher Ron Guidry.

DECEMBER

5th   The A's send base-stealing OF Rickey Henderson and P Bert Bradley to the Yankees in exchange for pitchers Jay Howell and Jose Rijo, OF Stan Javier, and minor leaguers Tim Birtsas and Eric Plunk. On the same day, the Yankees trade C Rick Cerone to the Braves for P Brian Fisher.

6th   The White Sox trade 1983 AL Cy Young Award winner LaMarr Hoyt and 2 minor leaguers to the Padres for P Tim Lollar, IF-OF Luis Salazar, and minor leaguers Ozzie Guillen and Bill Long. SS Guillen will win the AL Rookie of the Year Award next season.

10th   Expos catcher Gary Carter becomes the 3rd All-Star caliber player in 5 days to be traded, going to the Mets in exchange for IF-OF Hubie Brooks, C Mike Fitzgerald, OF Herm Winningham, and minor league P Floyd Youmans.

11th   OF Fred Lynn, a free agent, signs a 4-year contract with the Orioles.

27th Free-agent pitcher Ed Whitson, 14–8 for the Padres, begins a nightmarish association with the Yankees by signing a 5-year, $4.4 million contract.

31st Despite 6 weeks of negotiations, the Basic Agreement between the players and owners that was reached after the 1981 strike expires. The players are now seeking increased contributions to their pension plan from the clubs' additional television revenues, while the owners are hoping to slow the rapid growth of player salaries.

1985

JANUARY

7th   Lou Brock, the major leagues' all-time stolen base king, and Hoyt Wilhelm, who rewrote the record book on relief pitching, are elected to the Hall of Fame by the BBWAA.

8th   The Padres sign free-agent reliever Tim Stoddard to a 3-year, $1.5 million contract. Stoddard was 10-6 with 7 saves for the Cubs last season.

18th   In a 4-team trade, the Brewers send catcher Jim Sundberg to Kansas City and receive pitchers Danny Darwin from Texas and Tim Leary from the Mets. The Mets receive pitcher Frank Wills from the Royals, who also send catcher Don Slaught to Texas.

FEBRUARY

1st   In an effort to add some much-needed power to their lineup, St. Louis trades OF-1B David Green, SS Jose Uribe, P Dave LaPoint, and OF-1B Gary Rajsich to the Giants for slugging 1B Jack Clark.

11th   Twins 1B Kent Hrbek signs a new contract that makes him the club's first $1 million player.

21st   Tim Raines is awarded a $1.2 million salary for 1985 by arbitrator John Roberts, the largest award to date through that process. The 25-year-old Raines hit .309 for the Expos last season and stole 75 bases.

27th   The Yankees trade veteran IF Toby Harrah to the Rangers for OF Billy Sample and a player to be named later. The palindromic infielder was a member of the original Rangers in 1972.

MARCH

6th   Enos Slaughter and Arky Vaughan are elected to the Hall of Fame by the Special Veterans Committee.

8th   Dave Stieb, the ace of the Toronto staff for the past 5 seasons, signs an 11-year contract that could be worth up to $25 million with deferred payments and incentives.

16th   Denny McLain, winner of the AL Cy Young Award in 1968, is convicted of racketeering, extortion, and cocaine possession in Tampa, Florida.

18th   Commissioner Ueberroth reinstates Hall of Famers Willie Mays and Mickey Mantle, who had been banned from association with organized baseball by Bowie Kuhn due to their employment by Atlantic City casinos.

25th   An Illinois judge rules that state and city laws which effectively ban night baseball at Chicago's Wrigley Field are constitutional. After being forced to give up a home game during the 1984 NLCS, and threatened with playing future post-season games at another stadium entirely in order to accommodate network television's prime-time schedules, the Cubs had sued to overturn the laws.

28th   The April 1st issue of *Sports Illustrated* contains a fictitious article about a Mets pitching prospect named Sidd Finch, whose fastball has been timed at 168 MPH. Author George Plimpton offers bogus quotes from real-life members of the Mets, as well as several staged photos, and fools readers nationwide.

APRIL

3rd   The Players' Association agrees to the owners' proposal to expand the 1985 League Championship Series from the best-of-5 games to best-of-7.

9th   In his first game as a member of the Mets, catcher Gary Carter hits a solo home run in the bottom of the 10th inning to give New York a 6–5 Opening Day win over the Cardinals at Shea Stadium.

A year and a day after being hit in the face by a Mike Torrez pitch, Astros SS Dickie Thon returns to the Astros lineup and goes 1-for-4 off Fernando Valenzuela in Houston's 2–1 win over the Dodgers. Thon will hit just .207 before going back on the DL with recurring vision problems.

11th   Gorman Thomas, recovering from rotator cuff surgery, smashes 3 home runs in Seattle's 14–6 rout of Oakland. The Mariners set a one-game club record with 7 home runs.

13th   Rollie Fingers records his 217th AL save in Milwaukee's 6–5 win over Texas, breaking Sparky Lyle's record. Fingers already holds the ML record with 325.

20th   The Phillies and Pirates swap relief pitchers, Al Holland going to Pittsburgh, Kent Tekulve to Philadelphia.

24th Pete Vuckovich records his first win for Milwaukee since his Cy Young Award winning season of 1982, pitching 7 innings of the Brewers 3–2 win over Chicago. He had been sidelined most of the past 2 seasons with shoulder problems.

26th The Dodgers Orel Hershiser pitches his 2nd consecutive shutout, a 2–0 one-hitter against the Padres. San Diego's lone hit is Tony Gwynn's 4th-inning single.

28th After the Yankees lose to the White Sox 4–3 on a bases-loaded walk in the bottom of the 9th, manager Yogi Berra is replaced by Billy Martin, who begins his 4th term in the job.

Mickey Hatcher goes 4-for-5 as the Twins post their 8th consecutive win, 10–1 over Oakland. Hatcher was 5-for-5 the day before, giving him a club record 9 consecutive hits.

29th Larry Parrish belts 3 home runs to power the Rangers to a 7–5 win over the Yankees. It is Parrish's 4th career 3-HR game but his first in the AL, making him only the 5th player to accomplish the feat in each league.

30th Dale Murphy drives in his 28th and 29th runs of the season in Atlanta's 8–4 win over the Reds, tying Ron Cey's 1977 record for RBI in the month of April.

MAY

1st Toronto's Jimmy Key beats the Royals 6–3 to become the first lefthanded starter to win for the Blue Jays since Paul Mirabella on October 4, 1980, a span of 614 games.

8th Seattle's Mike Moore no-hits the Rangers for 8 innings, then is driven from the game on 4 hits in the 9th, but the Mariners hang on for a 4–2 victory.

12th Giants pitcher Jim Gott belts 2 home runs as San Francisco beats St. Louis 5–4 in 10 innings.

13th Trailing 8–0 after 2 innings, the Yankees rally to beat Minnesota 9–8 on Don Mattingly's 3-run home run off Ron Davis with 2 out in the bottom of the 9th.

17th The Cardinals trade OF Lonnie Smith to the Royals for minor leaguer John Morris, unloading Smith's $850,000 salary and clearing the way for rookie OF Vince Coleman to play every day.

The Rangers fire manager Doug Rader and replace him with Mets 3B coach Bobby Valentine. Texas was 9-23 under Rader, the worst record in the majors.

20th The Indians-Brewers game at Cleveland Stadium becomes the first one rained out this season, ending a record string of 458 ML games played since Opening Day without a payoff on a rain check. Since 1900, no season had survived without at least one April shower.

30th San Diego's Andy Hawkins runs his record to 10-0 with a 5–4 win over the Expos. He is the major leagues' first 10-game winner this season.

31st Danny Cox retires the first 23 Reds he faces before Dave Concepcion singles with 2 out in the 8th. Cox settles for a 2-hit 5–0 shutout.

JUNE

3rd The Brewers select University of North Carolina catcher B. J. Surhoff with the first pick in what will prove to be an extremely fruitful free-agent draft. Surhoff was the catcher for the U.S. Olympic Team last summer, and fellow Olympians Will Clark (Mississippi State), Bobby Witt (University of Oklahoma), and Barry Larkin (University of Michigan) are drafted 2nd, 3rd, and 4th by the Giants, Rangers, and Reds, respectively.

6th Jimmy Key holds the Tigers hitless for 8 innings before Tom Brookens leads off the 9th with a single, but gets no decision in Toronto's eventual 2–0, 12-inning win. Key and Tigers starter Dan Petry each pitch 10 shutout innings.

11th Von Hayes becomes the first ML player ever to hit 2 home runs in the first inning, leading off with a home run and capping a 9-run outburst with a grand slam, as the Phillies go on to rout the Mets 26–7. The 26 runs in one game are a club record and the most in the NL since 1944.

12th White Sox pitcher Bruce Tanner, son of Pirates manager Chuck Tanner, beats Seattle 6–3 in his ML debut. It is Tanner's first and last ML victory.

14th Cleveland's Bert Blyleven notches his 200th career win, a 5–1 complete game against Oakland.

One day after his successor Joe Altobelli was fired as manager of the Orioles, Earl Weaver comes out of retirement to manage the club. Weaver led Baltimore to 6 AL titles from 1968-82.

15th Seattle's infield records 21 assists in a 2–1 win over Kansas City, tying the ML record last accomplished by the Brooklyn Dodgers in 1935.

19th The Dodgers score 4 runs in the 7th inning to beat the Padres 5–1 and hand Andy Hawkins (11-0) his first loss of the season.

20th Reggie Jackson's 513th home run sparks the Angels to a 4–0 win over the Indians and moves him past Ernie Banks and Eddie Mathews into 10th place on the all-time list.

21st Twins manager Billy Gardner is fired and replaced by Baltimore pitching coach Ray Miller.

22nd In his first ML at bat, Curt Ford delivers a pinch single off Lee Smith to give St. Louis a 2–1 win over the Cubs and sole possession of first place in the NL East. Chicago, which had been clinging to first place, has now lost 11 in a row.

26th Minnesota's Ken Schrom one-hits Kansas City, but needs a 2-run single from Roy Smalley in the bottom of the 9th to secure the 2–1 victory. Willie Wilson's 3rd-inning single is the only Royals hit.

The Cubs beat the Mets 7–3, ending a club-record-tying losing streak at 13 games.

27th San Francisco's Jeffrey Leonard hits for the cycle in a 7–6 loss to the Reds. He is the first Giant to do so since Dave Kingman in 1972.

The Padres trade 2B Alan Wiggins to the Orioles for pitcher Roy Lee Jackson and a player to be named later. Wiggins, who recently completed his 2nd stay at a drug rehabilitation center, was never reactivated by the Padres, who vowed that he would never play for them again.

30th In his final at bat of the month, Pedro Guerrero delivers a 2-run home run off Bruce Sutter to give the Dodgers a 4–3 win over the Braves. It is Guerrero's 15th home run in June (19th overall), tying the ML record.

Cleveland beats Seattle 7–3 to snap the Mariners' club-record 9-game winning streak.

JULY

2nd Houston's Joe Niekro wins his 200th career game 3–2 over the Padres. Joe and Phil Niekro join Jim and Gaylord Perry as the only pitching brother combinations to win at least 200 games per pitcher.

4th In a marathon game that borders on the surreal, the Mets endure 2 rain delays and 6:10 of playing time to beat the Braves 16–13 in 19 innings on Fireworks Night in Atlanta. The Mets had taken a 10–8 lead in the top of the 13th inning, only to watch the Braves tie it up. The Mets score again in the 18th, but relief hurler Rick Camp (a .060 hitter who was batting because Atlanta had no more position players available to pinch-hit) ties the score with his first ML home run on a 2-out 2-strike pitch in the bottom of the inning. No pitcher ever homered that late in a game before. Finally the Mets erupt for 5 runs in the 19th off Camp and Atlanta can respond only with 2. Keith Hernandez hits for the cycle for the Mets, and the game ends at 3:55 A.M. on July 5th, the latest finish in ML history. At 4:01 A.M. the post-game fireworks display begins, causing local residents to think the city is under attack.

9th The Blue Jays trade 1B-OF Len Matuszek to the Dodgers for veteran Al Oliver, who joins his 5th club in the last 3 seasons.

11th Nolan Ryan becomes the first pitcher to record 4,000 strikeouts, fanning Danny Heep in the 6th inning of Houston's 4–3 win over the Mets. Ryan finishes with 11 strikeouts in 7 innings but gets no decision.

16th The NL beats the AL 6–1 at Minnesota's Metrodome for its 13th win in the last 14 All-Star Games. San Diego's LaMarr Hoyt allows one unearned run in 3 innings and is named MVP.

23rd Oddibe McDowell becomes the first Texas Ranger to hit for the cycle, going 5-for-5 in an 8–4 win over Cleveland.

26th Wade Boggs goes 0-for-3 in Boston's 6–2 win over Seattle to halt his hitting streak at 28 games, the longest in the major leagues since 1980.

28th Lou Brock, Enos Slaughter, Arky Vaughan, and Hoyt Wilhelm are inducted into the Hall of Fame in a ceremony in Cooperstown, New York.

Darrell Evans hits his 300th career home run off Ken Schrom to lead Detroit to a 3–2 win over the Twins.

AUGUST

1st Vince Coleman steals 2 bases in the first inning of the Cardinals' 9–8 loss to the Cubs to run his season total to 74, breaking the ML rookie record of 72 set last season by Juan Samuel.

The Indians trade veteran P Bert Blyleven to the Twins for OF Jim Weaver, P Curt Wardle, and SS Jay Bell.

2nd The last-place Pirates unload 3 of their veteran players, trading pitchers John Candelaria and Al Holland and OF George Hendrick to the Angels for OF Mike Brown and pitchers Pat Clements and Bob Kipper.

4th In a day of milestones, Tom Seaver becomes the 17th pitcher to win 300 games and Rod Carew becomes the 16th player ever to collect 3,000 career hits. Seaver pitches the White Sox to a 4–1 six-hit victory on Phil Rizzuto Day at Yankee Stadium as 54,032 New Yorkers cheer him on, while Carew bloops a single to left off Frank Viola in the 3rd inning of the Angels 6–5 win over the Twins.

5th Darryl Strawberry belts 3 home runs to lead the Mets to a 7–2 win over the Cubs and vault the Mets into first place in the NL East.

6th For the 2nd time in 5 years the Players' Association stages a midseason strike. But unlike the 50-day strike that interrupted the 1981 season, this one will be settled by the following day and all 25 canceled games will be made up. The new collective bargaining agreement, which runs through 1989, raises the ML minimum salary to $60,000, extends the time of service required to be eligible for salary arbitration from 2 years to 3, and eliminates the free-agent compensation pool that resulted from the 1981 strike settlement.

8th Cardinals pitcher John Tudor one-hits the Cubs 8–0 for his 6th shutout of the season, allowing only Leon Durham's 5th-inning single. Tudor started the season 1-7 but will win 20 of his last 21 decisions to finish 21-8.

10th Oakland's Dave Kingman becomes the 21st player to hit 400 career home runs, belting a 2-run shot off Matt Young in the first inning of the A's 11–5 win at Seattle.

Willie McGee goes 7-for-10 in the Cardinals' doubleheader sweep of the Phillies to raise his batting average to .351. McGee will lead the NL with a .353 mark this season.

13th Seattle's infield again ties the ML record for assists with 21 against California.

17th Reggie Jackson hits his 522nd career home run off Oakland's Bill Krueger to move past Ted Williams and Willie McCovey into 8th place on the all-time list.

20th Dwight Gooden fans 16 batters on the way to his 13th consecutive victory 5–0 over the Giants, raising his season strikeout total to 208. Gooden (19-3) joins Herb Score as the only pitchers this century to strike out 200 batters in each of their first 2 seasons.

23rd Joaquin Andujar becomes baseball's first 20-game winner this season, beating Atlanta 6–2 for the Cardinals. Andujar is the first NL pitcher to post consecutive 20-win seasons since Joe Niekro in 1979-80.

24th Three outs away from a no-hitter against the White Sox, Toronto's Dave Stieb surrenders consecutive home runs to Vance Law and Bryan Little and is driven from the game. His replacement, Gary Lavelle, gives up a 3rd-straight home run to Harold Baines before Tom Henke comes in to save the 6–3 win.

26th Eddie Murray belts 3 home runs and drives in 9 runs as the Orioles crush the Angels 17–3.

25th Dwight Gooden wins his 14th consecutive game and his 20th of the season 9–3 over the Padres. Gooden will finish the season 24-4.

26th The Braves fire manager Eddie Haas, who led the club to a 50-71 record and 12 losses in its last 13 games. Bobby Wine will serve as interim manager.

29th In the Yankees 4–0 win over the Angels, Don Baylor is hit by a pitch (from Kirk McCaskill) for the 190th time, breaking the AL record of 189 set by Minnie Minoso.

The Rangers trade veteran slugger Cliff Johnson to Toronto for 3 minor leaguers. Johnson had left the Blue Jays after last season to sign with Texas as a free agent.

The Reds trade veteran OF Cesar Cedeno to the Cardinals for minor leaguer Mark Jackson. Cedeno will help St. Louis to the NL East title by batting .434 in 28 games.

31st   The Pirates trade 3-time batting champion Bill Madlock to the Dodgers for prospects R. J. Reynolds, Cecil Espy, and Sid Bream.

San Francisco's Jim Gott and Mark Davis combine to beat the Mets 3–2, ending Dwight Gooden's personal 14-game winning streak.

SEPTEMBER

4th   One day after hitting 3 home runs in an 8–3 win over the Padres, Gary Carter hits 2 more to lead the Mets to a 9–2 win at San Diego, tying the ML record of 5 home runs in 2 games. He is the 13th player to accomplish the feat.

6th   The Royals sweep a doubleheader from Milwaukee 4–3 and 7–1 to move past California into first place in the AL West.

10th   To bolster their pitching staff for the pennant race, the Angels acquire veteran Don Sutton from the A's for 2 players to be named later.

11th   Pete Rose becomes baseball's all-time hit leader, singling to left center off Eric Show in the first inning of the Reds' 2–0 win over San Diego. His 4,192nd career hit breaks Ty Cobb's record before 47,237 fans at Cincinnati's Riverfront Stadium. Rose had tied the record at Wrigley Field on September 8th with a single off the Cubs Reggie Patterson in a game that was later suspended due to darkness, enabling Rose to break the record at home.

John Tudor allows 3 hits in 10 innings for his 3rd consecutive shutout, outdueling Dwight Gooden and the Mets 1–0 to move St. Louis back into a first-place tie with New York in the NL East. Cesar Cedeno's 10th-inning homer provides the game's only run.

Milwaukee beats New York 4–3 to end the Yankees' winning streak at 11 games. New York now trails first-place Toronto by 2½ games in the AL East.

13th   The Rangers trade P Dave Stewart to the Phillies for pitcher Rich Surhoff, whose brother B. J. was the first pick in the amateur draft in June.

15th   The Yankees trade minor league pitcher Jim Deshaies and two other minor leaguers to be named later to the Astros for 40-year-old Joe Niekro, reuniting the Niekro brothers as teammates for the first time since 1974 with the Braves.

18th   Rich Gedman hits for the cycle and drives in 7 runs as the Red Sox rout Toronto 13–1.

19th   Vince Coleman steals his 100th base of the season and teammate Tom Herr drives in his 100th run, but the Cardinals lose to the Phillies 6–3.

20th   A federal jury in Pittsburgh convicts Curtis Strong of 11 counts of cocaine distribution after a trial whose prosecution witnesses revealed how widely the drug problem afflicts major league baseball. Prominent players who were granted immunity from prosecution in exchange for testimony include Dave Parker, Lonnie Smith, Keith Hernandez, Jeffrey Leonard, and Tim Raines.

22nd   One night after scuffling with a patron in the bar of the Yankees' Baltimore hotel, manager Billy Martin has his right arm broken by pitcher Ed Whitson in an early-morning brawl in the same bar.

Ron Guidry becomes the AL's first 20-game winner this season as the Yankees beat Baltimore 5–4.

24th   Expos OF Andre Dawson slugs 3 home runs, including a pair of 3-run shots in a 12-run 5th inning, to lead Montreal to a wild 17–15 win over the Cubs at Wrigley Field. Dawson joins Willie McCovey as the only players to hit 2 home runs in one inning on 2 different occasions, and his 6 RBI in one inning tie the ML record last accomplished by Jim Ray Hart in 1970.

25th   Rickey Henderson steals his 75th base of the season in the Yankees 10–2 win over Detroit, breaking the club record of 74 set by Fritz Maisel in 1914.

Mike Greenwell hits his first ML home run in the top of the 13th inning to give the Red Sox a 4–2 win at Toronto.

26th   John Tudor picks up his 20th win of the season with his ML-leading 10th shutout, a 5–0 four-hitter against the Phillies.

28th   Cincinnati's Tom Browning becomes the first rookie since Bob Grim in 1954 to win 20 games, raising his record to 20–9 with a 5–2 win over Houston. He is the first Reds pitcher to win 20 since Jim Merritt in 1970.

OCTOBER

1st   In the first game of a 3-game showdown between the Mets and Cardinals, Ron Darling and John Tudor each pitch 10 shutout innings before Darryl Strawberry belts a titanic home run off reliever Ken Dayley. The Mets' 1–0, 11-inning win cuts the Cardinals' lead in the NL East to 2 games.

2nd The Dodgers clinch the NL West title with a 9–3 win over the Braves. Orel Hershiser raises his record to 19-3 with his 11th consecutive victory.

Tigers 1B Darrell Evans hits his ML-leading 40th home run of the season and becomes the first player to have a 40 HR season in each league. Evans hit 41 homers for the Braves in 1973.

5th The Cardinals, Royals, and Blue Jays all clinch their division championships. John Tudor pitches a 4-hitter and Cesar Cedeno goes 3-for-3 with a HR, as St. Louis beats the Cubs 7–1. Willie Wilson singles home the winning run as Kansas City beats Oakland 5–4 in 10 innings. Doyle Alexander pitches a 5-hitter, as Toronto beats 2nd-place New York 5–1 to wrap up its first AL East crown.

6th Phil Niekro finally wins his 300th career game 8–0 over the Blue Jays on the final day of the regular season. At 46, he is the oldest hurler ever to pitch a complete-game shutout.

Hubie Brooks drives in his 100th run of the season in Montreal's season-ending 2–1 win over the Mets, becoming the first NL shortstop with 100 RBI since Ernie Banks in 1960.

7th The Giants trade pitcher Dave LaPoint, catcher Matt Nokes, and minor league pitcher Eric King to the Tigers for pitcher Juan Berenguer, catcher Bob Melvin, and a player to be named later.

NL Managers Chuck Tanner and Bob Lillis are fired by the Pirates and Astros, respectively. Lillis is offered a front-office job, while Tanner will be hired to manage the Braves just 3 days later.

8th Orioles manager Earl Weaver signs a one-year contract to manage the club again in 1986.

Dave Stieb allows only 3 hits in 8 innings as Toronto downs KC 6–1 in the ALCS opener, the first in Canada.

9th The Royals come from behind to tie the Blue Jays in the 9th and go ahead in the 10th, but lose 6–5 in the bottom of the inning.

The first game of the NLCS results in a 4–1 Dodger win over St. Louis's John Tudor, only his 2nd loss in his last 22 decisions.

10th Every Dodger starter has a hit, and LA rolls 8–2 over St. Louis.

11th George Brett's bat (4-for-4, 4 runs, 3 RBI, 11 total bases) bails out 20-game winner Bret Saberhagen, and the Royals squeak past Toronto 6–5.

12th In game 4 of the ALCS, Al Oliver's 2-run pinch double in the 9th inning gives Toronto a 3–1 win over Kansas City and a 3-1 lead in the series. Until this year's best-of-7 format was adopted, the 3 wins would have sent the Blue Jays to the World Series.

St. Louis runs the Dodgers out of Busch Stadium 4–2. The Cardinals' first 3 runs are aided by 3 stolen bases and 2 errant pickoff attempts.

13th The Royals stave off elimination behind Danny Jackson's 8-hit shutout 2-0 over the Blue Jays.

The Cardinals rout the Dodgers 12–2 to even the NLCS at 2-2, but also lose rookie sensation Vince Coleman to one of the more bizarre injuries in ML history. Coleman is stretching before the game when his left leg becomes caught in Busch Stadium's automated tarpaulin as it unrolls across the infield, trapping him for about 30 seconds. He is removed from the field on a stretcher and will not play again this year.

14th Ozzie Smith homers off Tom Niedenfuer with one out in the bottom of the 9th to give the Cardinals a 3-2 lead in the NLCS. It is the switch-hitting Smith's first ML home run while batting lefthanded.

15th The Royals once again stave off elimination to the Blue Jays, aided by George Brett's 3rd HR of the series, all off Doyle Alexander. The Royals win 5–3.

16th Baseball gets its first intrastate World Series since 1974, as the Royals and Cardinals win their respective playoff series. Kansas City beats Toronto 6–2 in game 7 to cap a comeback from a 3-games-to-1 deficit. While in Los Angeles, Jack Clark drills a 3-run home run off Tom Niedenfuer with 2 outs in the top of the 9th and 1B open to give the Cardinals a 7–5 victory and a 4-2 series win.

19th St. Louis wins the opener of the "I-70 Series" behind ace John Tudor 3–1.

20th After giving up just 2 hits in 8 innings, Charlie Liebrandt is raked with 3 two-out hits and loses 4–2. St. Louis leads 2-0.

22nd Bret Saberhagen gives Kansas City their first WS win with a 9-inning 6–1 win.

23rd John Tudor wins again as he pitches a 9 inning, 3–0 shutout.

24th The Royals get a 2nd 9-inning effort, this time from Danny Jackson, to win again 6–1. Cards rookie reliever Todd Worrell strikes out all 6 batters he faces.

25th The Angels announce that they will not offer 7-time batting champion Rod Carew a new contract for the 1986 season, effectively ending his 19-year career. Carew finishes with 3,053 hits and a .328 career batting average.

The Blue Jays name 3B coach Jimy Williams manager, replacing Bobby Cox, who resigned to become GM of the Braves.

26th Aided by a blown call, a bungled pop-up, and a passed ball, Kansas City scores 2 runs in the bottom of the 9th to beat St. Louis 2–1 and even the World Series at 3 games apiece. The Cardinals are 3 outs away from the World Championship when Jorge Orta reaches base on a disputed infield single. The next batter, Steve Balboni, lofts a foul pop that Clark loses track of and lets fall untouched, then singles. After Darrell Porter's passed ball puts runners on 2B and 3B and Hal McRae is intentionally walked to load the bases, pinch hitter Dane Iorg singles home 2 runs to end the game.

27th The Royals rout the Cardinals 11–0 in game 7 to become only the 6th team to rally from a 3-1 deficit and win the World Series. Series MVP Bret Saberhagen pitches the shutout while Cardinals ace John Tudor allows 5 runs in 2⅓ innings and fellow 20-game winner Joaquin Andujar is ejected for arguing balls and strikes during Kansas City's 6-run 5th inning. The Cardinals finish the WS with a .185 team batting average, lowest ever for a 7-game Series.

Billy Martin is fired by the Yankees for an unprecedented 4th time and is replaced by former Yankees OF Lou Piniella, who had been the team's hitting instructor since retiring as a player in 1984.

29th Cardinals pitcher Joaquin Andujar is suspended for the first 10 games of the 1986 season as a result of his game 7 tantrum during which he twice bumped home plate umpire Don Denkinger.

NOVEMBER

14th The Brewers release 39-year-old P Rollie Fingers, the major leagues' all-time saves leader with 341.

18th Willie McGee wins the NL MVP Award, capping a season in which he led the league in batting average (.353) and hits (216) and also stole 56 bases for St. Louis.

Dwight Gooden (NL) and Bret Saberhagen (AL) win the Cy Young Award in their respective leagues.

20th Don Mattingly easily wins the AL MVP Award with a .324 average, becoming the first player from a nonchampionship team to do so since 1978.

Jim Leyland is named manager of the Pirates for the 1986 season.

25th White Sox SS Ozzie Guillen, who hit .273 with just 12 errors in 150 games, is named AL Rookie of the Year. Milwaukee lefty Teddy Higuera finishes 2nd.

27th Vince Coleman, who stole 110 bases for the Cardinals, joins Frank Robinson, Orlando Cepeda, and Willie McCovey as the only unanimous winners of the NL Rookie of the Year Award.

DECEMBER

10th In the first major swap of the winter meetings, the A's trade C Mike Heath and P Tim Conroy to the Cardinals for Joaquin Andujar, 21-game winner with a volatile temperament.

11th The Giants send 2B Manny Trillo to the Cubs for SS Dave Owen, and C Alex Trevino to the Dodgers for OF Candy Maldonado; the Phillies trade pitchers John Denny and Jeff Gray to the Reds for OF Gary Redus and P Tom Hume, and the Dodgers trade veteran catcher Steve Yeager to the Mariners for P Ed Vande Berg.

12th The Yankees trade P Joe Cowley and C Ron Hassey to the White Sox for P Britt Burns and minor leaguers Mike Soper and Glen Braxton.

18th The Giants trade strikeout-prone slugger Rob Deer to the Brewers for minor leaguers Eric Pilkington and Dean Freeland.

19th The Expos trade P Bill Gullickson and C Sal Butera to the Reds for pitchers Jay Tibbs, Andy McGaffigan, and John Stuper, and C Dann Bilardello.

1986

JANUARY

8th Willie McCovey is the only player elected this year to the Hall of Fame by the BBWAA, and becomes the 16th player elected in his first year of eligibility. Billy Williams falls 4 votes shy of the 319 needed for election.

16th The Twins trade 2B Tim Teufel and minor leaguer Pat Crosby to the Mets for minor leaguers Billy Beane, Bill Latham, and Joe Klink, and also trade C Dave Engle to the Tigers for IF Chris Pittaro and minor leaguer Alex Sanchez.

28th Free-agent C Darrell Porter signs a one-year contract with Texas.

FEBRUARY

6th Free-agent P Al Holland, who saved just 5 games for 3 teams last season, signs with the Yankees.

13th Two months after being traded from the Yankees to the White Sox, C Ron Hassey is traded back to the Yankees along with 3 minor leaguers in exchange for P Neil Allen, C Scott Bradley, and minor leaguer Glen Braxton.

21st Rollie Fingers loses a chance to continue his career with the Cincinnati Reds when he refuses to shave his trademark handlebar mustache to comply with the club's policy. Says Fingers: "I'm not about to shave it off just to play baseball."

23rd Despite losing his arbitration case, Boston's Wade Boggs receives the largest salary ever awarded through that process, $1.35 million.

24th High-tension Dick Williams resigns as manager of the Padres. He will be replaced by low-key Steve Boros.

27th Nine days after being arrested on drug possession charges for the 2nd time in a month, LaMarr Hoyt checks into a drug rehabilitation program and will miss most of the Padres' spring training. Hoyt was 16-8 with a 3.47 ERA last season.

28th In baseball's sternest disciplinary move since the Black Sox were banished for life, Commissioner Ueberroth gives 7 players who were admitted drug users a choice of a year's suspension without pay or heavy fines and career-long drug testing, along with 100 hours of drug-related community service. Joaquin Andujar, Jeffrey Leonard, Enos Cabell, Keith Hernandez, Dave Parker, Dale Berra, and Lonnie Smith will be fined 10 percent of their annual salaries, while 14 other players will receive lesser penalties for their involvement with illegal drugs.

MARCH

5th The Braves trade C Rick Cerone and a pair of minor leaguers to the Brewers for C Ted Simmons.

10th Ernie Lombardi, the NL MVP in 1938, and Bobby Doerr, a 9-time AL All-Star, are elected to the Hall of Fame by the Special Veterans Committee.

21st Pittsburgh Associates, a coalition of 13 public and private investors, purchases the Pirates from the Galbreath family for $21.8 million.

 The Yankees announce that their most celebrated off-season acquisition, 26-year-old pitcher Britt Burns, will not pitch at all this season because of a chronic deteriorating hip condition.

27th Major league baseball's Rules Committee votes to change the DH rule for the WS, allowing a DH to be used in all games played in the AL club's home park. Since 1976, the DH had been used in all games in alternating years.

28th The Yankees and Red Sox swap designated hitters: Mike Easler goes to New York for Don Baylor.

 Four days before his 47th birthday, the Yankees waive pitcher Phil Niekro. He will be signed by the Indians on April 3rd.

31st Danny Cox, who was 18-9 for the NL champion Cardinals last season, injures his ankle jumping off a seawall while fishing and will be placed on the disabled list.

APRIL

1st In a purge of its pitching staff, Atlanta releases veterans Pascual Perez, Len Barker, Terry Forster, and Rick Camp.

3rd Pedro Guerrero, the Dodgers most productive hitter, ruptures a tendon in his left knee while sliding into 3B in an exhibition game and will be sidelined for at least 3 months.

7th On Opening Day at Tiger Stadium, Boston's Dwight Evans achieves a ML first by hitting a home run off Jack Morris on the first pitch of the entire season, but Detroit's Kirk Gibson later hits 2 home runs of his own to lead the Tigers to a 6–5 victory.

8th After hitting a 2-run home run to tie the score in the bottom of the 9th, Seattle's Jim Presley belts a grand slam with 2 out in the bottom of the 10th to give the Mariners an 8–4 season-opening win over the Angels.

12th Making his first start in nearly 3 years, Kansas City's Dennis Leonard shuts out Toronto 1–0 on 3 hits. Leonard, a 3-time 20-game winner, had undergone 4 knee operations since tearing a tendon during the 1983 season.

19th Oakland's Jose Rijo sets a club record with 16 strikeouts in 8 innings as the A's beat Seattle 7–2. The 2 clubs combine for 30 strikeouts overall, setting the modern ML record for a 9-inning game.

20th San Francisco's Vida Blue wins his 200th career game, combining with Jeff Robinson to shut out the Padres 4–0.

25th One out after Graig Nettles had tied the score with a solo home run in the bottom of the 12th inning, Padres reliever Craig Lefferts belts his first ML home run to beat the Giants 9–8.

26th The game between the Angels and Twins is delayed for 9 minutes when strong winds tear a hole in the Metrodome roof, causing suspended lights and speakers to sag toward the field. The roof is reinflated and California rallies for 6 runs in the 9th to win 7–6.

27th The Mets win their 9th consecutive game 5–3 at St. Louis, and in the process end John Tudor's 18-game winning streak at Busch Stadium. Kevin Mitchell hits his first ML home run for the Mets.

29th Twenty-three-year-old Red Sox pitcher Roger Clemens strikes out 20 batters in a 3–1 win over Seattle, breaking the ML record of 19 shared by Nolan Ryan, Steve Carlton, and Tom Seaver. Clemens doesn't walk a batter, allows just 3 hits, and ties the AL record with 8 consecutive strikeouts in the middle innings.

Reds pitcher Mario Soto ties the ML record by surrendering home runs to Andre Dawson, Hubie Brooks, Tim Wallach, and Mike Fitzgerald in the 4th inning of a 7–4 loss to the Expos.

30th The Mariners strike out 16 more times in a 9–4 loss to the Red Sox, setting a ML record of 36 strikeouts in 2 consecutive games.

MAY

1st Zane Smith strikes out 12 batters as the Braves beat the Mets 7–2, ending New York's club-record-tying 11-game winning streak.

3rd Minnesota's Kirby Puckett hits a home run on the game's first pitch (from Walt Terrell) for the 2nd consecutive night, but the Twins lose to the Tigers 7–4. The night before Puckett hit Jack Morris's first pitch for a home run to spark the Twins to a 10–1 victory.

Cubs 3B Ron Cey hits his 300th and 301st home runs and Chicago scores 4 times in the top of the 9th to beat San Francisco 6–5.

Don Mattingly ties the ML record with 3 sacrifice flies in the Yankees 9–4 win over the Rangers.

7th Thirty-six-year-old Phillies OF Garry Maddox, an 8-time Gold Glove winner, retires. Only Roberto Clemente and Willie Mays have won more Gold Gloves in the outfield.

8th Chuck Cottier is fired as manager of the Mariners. He will be replaced tomorrow by Dick Williams, who resigned as manager of the Padres in February.

12th Texas routs Cleveland 19–2, handing the Indians their 4th straight loss after they had won 10 in a row to move into a first–place tie in the AL East. Tom Paciorek goes 5-for-6 to lead the Rangers' 22-hit attack.

13th Helped by an unusual 3-6-1-2-4 triple play in the first inning, Seattle goes on to defeat Milwaukee 8–5. After Randy Ready and Ernest Riles walk to open the game, Cecil Cooper hits a bouncer to 1B Alvin Davis, who throws to 2B to force Riles. Cooper beats the return throw to 1B, but Ready is thrown out trying to score, and Cooper is thrown out at 2B trying to advance during the play at the plate.

14th Reggie Jackson of the Angels homers off Roger Clemens to move past Mickey Mantle on the all-time list with 537, but Boston scores 3 runs in the top of the 9th to win 8–5.

16th   A's infielder Tony Phillips (5-for-5) hits for the cycle and drives in 4 runs as Oakland beats Baltimore 8–4.

20th   Milwaukee falls behind 8–0 in the top of the first inning, then storms back to defeat Cleveland 12–9.

25th   George Brett collects his 2,000th hit, off Bryan Clark in the 4th inning of Kansas City's 2–1, 17-inning victory over the White Sox. Brett finishes the day 1-for-7, while Scott Bankhead picks up his first ML win.

Roger Clemens no-hits the Rangers for 7⅔ innings before Oddibe McDowell singles and Clemens settles for a 2-hit 7–1 victory that improves his record to 8-0.

26th   Houston's Jim Deshaies records his first ML win, striking out 10 Cardinals in 7 innings in the Astros' 4–1 victory.

28th   In his 2nd start for the White Sox since being recalled from Triple A Buffalo, Joe Cowley sets a ML record by striking out the first 7 Rangers he faces, but still surrenders 6 runs in 4⅓ innings and loses 6–3. He finishes with 8 strikeouts. Cowley's record will be broken by Jim Deshaies before season's end.

30th   Mike Fitzgerald's homer and single are the Expos only hits in their 1–0 victory over Houston. Bryn Smith and Jeff Reardon combine on a 3-hitter for Montreal.

31st   Wade Boggs raises his average to .402 with a 5-for-5 game as Boston beats Minnesota 7–2. Boggs will hit .357 this year to win his 3rd AL batting title.

JUNE

1st   George Brett hits his 200th career home run in the 8th inning off Rangers rookie Mitch Williams as Kansas City defeats Texas 5–3. Ruben Sierra collects his first ML hit for the Rangers, a 3-run homer.

2nd   Oakland draws 7 walks in a 7-run first inning against Detroit and ultimately wins 7–1.

4th   Joe Niekro no-hits the Angels for 7⅔ innings before Gary Pettis doubles, and Niekro combines with Al Holland for an easy 11–0 one-hitter. Dave Winfield homers twice for the Yankees.

Pirates OF Barry Bonds, the son of former ML star Bobby Bonds, goes 4-for-5 with his first ML home run (off Craig McMurtry) as Pittsburgh whips Atlanta 12–3.

7th   University of Arkansas's Jeff King is the first choice in the June draft. The Pirates take the 3B. Gregg Swindell is the next pick. Neither will sign for 6 weeks but Swindell will be in the major leagues after just 3 starts in the minors. Bo Jackson is taken in the 4th round by the Royals and College Pitcher of the Year Mike Loynd is taken by Texas in the 7th Round.

8th   In the longest 9-inning game by time in AL history, Baltimore's Lee Lacy goes 4-for-6 with 3 home runs and 6 RBI as the Orioles club the Yankees 18–9. The game features 9 pitchers, 36 hits, and 16 walks, and takes 4:16 to complete.

Floyd Youmans pitches a one-hitter and hits his first ML home run as the Expos rout the Phillies 12–0. Glenn Wilson's infield single in the 2nd is the only hit off Youmans, who walks 7.

10th   The NL announces that Yale University president A. Bartlett Giamatti will be its next president, after Chub Feeney's retirement in December.

12th   Juan Beniquez joins Lee Lacy as the 2nd unlikely Oriole to hit 3 home runs in a game this month, connecting for 3 solo shots in Baltimore's 7–5 loss to the Yankees. Between them, Beniquez and Lacy will hit 17 home runs this season.

The Cubs (23-33) fire manager Jim Frey and 3B coach Don Zimmer, replacing Frey with Gene Michael.

16th   Rangers knuckleballer Charlie Hough pitches a one-hitter against the Angels but loses 2–1. With 2 outs to go for a no-hitter, George Wright drops Jack Howell's fly ball for an error. A single ties the score, and 2 passed balls by Orlando Mercado bring the 2nd runner around.

The Orioles trade Dennis Martinez, whose ERA had swelled to over 5.00 the last 3 seasons, to the Expos for player to be named later.

18th   California's Don Sutton becomes the 19th pitcher in ML history to win 300 games, beating the Rangers 3–1 on a 3-hitter.

20th   After leading the club to a 26-38 record, Tony LaRussa is fired as manager of the White Sox and replaced by Jim Fregosi. LaRussa will be hired to manage the A's early next month.

21st Bo Jackson, college football's Heisman Trophy winner in 1985 and the first pick (by Tampa Bay) in the NFL draft, stuns observers nationwide by signing with the Kansas City Royals instead.

22nd San Francisco sweeps a doubleheader from Houston 4–2 and 3–2 and leapfrogs past the Astros into first place in the NL West.

23rd The Phillies set a club record with 11 doubles, and Juan Samuel hits a pair of 3-run home runs in a 19–1 drubbing of the Cubs at Veterans Stadium.

Mike LaCoss pitches a 3-hitter and belts his first ML home run as the Giants pound the Padres 18–1.

The Braves tie the NL 9-inning record by leaving 18 runners on base in a 6–5 win over the Dodgers.

25th Kirk McCaskill one-hits the Rangers 7–1, vaulting California past Texas into first place in the AL West. The Rangers' only hit is Steve Buechele's 3rd-inning home run.

Mark Langston sets a Mariners record with 15 strikeouts in a 6–1 three-hitter against the White Sox.

The Phillies give 41-year-old Steve Carlton his unconditional release and call up Bruce Ruffin to take his place in the starting rotation.

26th The A's fire manager Jackie Moore and name Jeff Newman his interim replacement. They will eventually hire recently ousted White Sox manager Tony LaRussa.

27th Give him an A for effort. San Francisco 2B Robby Thompson is caught stealing 4 times in the Giants 7–6, 12-inning win over the Reds, establishing a new ML record. Thompson was thrown out by Bo Diaz in the 4th, 6th, 9th, and 11th innings.

29th Detroit beats Milwaukee 9–5 in the first game of a doubleheader split, making Tigers manager Sparky Anderson the first manager ever to win 600 games in each league.

30th Bo Jackson makes his professional baseball debut with the Memphis Chicks and goes 1-for-4 with 2 strikeouts.

The Yankees trade OF Ken Griffey to the Braves for OF Claudell Washington and SS Paul Zuvella.19

JULY

2nd After 14 wins, Roger Clemens suffer his first loss as Toronto scores 3 times in the 8th inning to down Boston 4–2. Clemens was one game short of the AL record for consecutive wins at the start of a season.

6th Bob Horner becomes the 11th player to hit 4 home runs in a game, but it isn't enough as the Braves fall to the Expos 11–8. Horner is the first to hit his 4 home runs in a losing cause.

9th Atlanta's Dale Murphy does not play in the Braves 7–3 win over the Phillies, ending his consecutive-game streak at 740. Murphy hadn't missed a game since September 1981.

The Padres trade P Tim Stoddard to the Yankees for P Ed Whitson, who had become the target of such fan abuse in New York that manager Lou Piniella would no longer pitch him in Yankee Stadium.

10th Oil Can Boyd (11-6) flies into a rage after learning that he has been left off the AL All-Star team and storms out of Fenway Park prior to Boston's game against the Angels. He will be suspended indefinitely by the Red Sox and eventually scuffle with local police before checking into a hospital for psychiatric testing.

15th At the Houston Astrodome, the AL wins the All-Star Game 3–2 for its 2nd triumph in the last 15 years. AL starter Roger Clemens pitches 3 perfect innings to win the game's MVP Award.

18th The Royals announce that 50-year-old manager Dick Howser, who led the club to a World Championship last season, will miss the rest of the season to undergo treatment for a brain tumor that is later revealed to be malignant. 3B coach Mike Ferraro will manage the club in Howser's absence.

19th Mets players Ron Darling, Tim Teufel, Bob Ojeda, and Rick Aguilera are arrested following an early-morning fight with off-duty police officers working as security guards outside a Houston bar, but are all released in time for their Astros game that evening. On January 26th Darling and Teufel will be fined $200 while charges against Ojeda and Aguilera will be dropped.

22nd Ken Griffey hits 3 solo home runs but Atlanta falls to Philadelphia 5–4 in 11 innings. Griffey is the 2nd Brave this month to hit 3 or more home runs in a losing cause.

30th C Ron Hassey is traded for the 3rd time in 8 months, this time going to Chicago in a deal that brings OF-DH Ron Kittle, SS Wayne Tolleson, and C Joel Skinner to New York.

31st Brian Downing and Bob Boone each hit grand slams off Oakland's Eric Plunk to lead the Angels to an 8–5 victory.

AUGUST

1st Minnesota's Bert Blyleven pitches a 2-hitter and strikes out a club-record 15 batters to become the 10th pitcher with 3,000 career strikeouts. Kirby Puckett hits for the cycle as the Twins romp 10–1 over the A's.

2nd Dodgers Alejandro Pena and Tom Niedenfuer combine to one-hit the Reds 7–1, allowing only Eddie Milner's leadoff home run off Pena in the 6th inning. It is the 5th time Milner has collected the only hit in a one-hitter, tying Cesar Tovar's ML record.

3rd Willie McCovey, Bobby Doerr, and Ernie Lombardi are inducted into baseball's Hall of Fame in Cooperstown, New York.

4th White Sox pitcher Jose DeLeon (2-0) beats Boston's Roger Clemens (17-4) for the 2nd time in 5 days 1–0 at Fenway Park. DeLeon and the White Sox also won 7–2 on July 30th.

5th The Reds pound the Giants' new pitcher Steve Carlton for 7 runs in 3⅓ innings to win 11–6. Carlton records his 4,000th strikeout to join Nolan Ryan as the only pitchers to reach that plateau. The Giants will release Carlton on the 7th and he will join the White Sox.

6th In a wild game that features a ML-record 3 grand slams, Texas scores 7 runs in the final 2 innings to beat Baltimore 13–11. Toby Harrah's grand slam in the 2nd gives the Rangers a 5–0 lead, but Baltimore rallies for 9 runs in the 4th thanks to grand slams by Larry Sheets and Jim Dwyer, the 5th time in ML history a team has hit 2 grand slams in one inning.

The Mets release outfielder George Foster, the last NL player to hit 50 HRs in one season. Foster will play 15 games for the White Sox before retiring for good.

10th Pitcher Bob Forsch hits a grand slam to lead the Cardinals to a 5–4 win over the Pirates, and reliever Todd Worrell records his 24th save to break the ML rookie record set by Doug Corbett in 1980.

17th The Red Sox trade highly touted SS Rey Quinones and P Mike Trujillo to the Mariners for SS Spike Owen and OF Dave Henderson.

20th Tigers Walt Terrell is one out away from a no-hitter when Wally Joyner doubles and Terrell settles for a one-hit 3–0 win over the Angels.

Philadelphia's Don Carman pitches a perfect game until Bob Brenly doubles leading off the 9th, and Carman ends up combining with Steve Bedrosian for a 10-inning 1–0 win over the Giants. Juan Samuel's home run in the top of the 10th provides the game's only run.

21st Newly acquired SS Spike Owen ties the ML record by scoring 6 runs in Boston's 24–5 thrashing of Cleveland.

25th A's 3B Mark McGwire hits his first ML home run—a 450-foot blast to center field off Walt Terrell—as Oakland beats Detroit 8–4 at Tiger Stadium.

27th Nolan Ryan posts his 250th career victory, allowing one hit in 6 innings as the Astros beat the Cubs 7–1.

29th Cleveland's Joe Carter belts 3 home runs and singles twice as the Indians beat the Red Sox 7–3 at Fenway Park.

California scores 8 runs in the bottom of the 9th inning, the final 4 coming on Dick Schofield's 2-out grand slam off Willie Hernandez, to beat Detroit 13–12.

30th Roger Clemens becomes the major leagues' first 20-game winner this season, striking out 11 Indians in a 7–3 victory to raise his record to 20-4.

SEPTEMBER

1st A's rookie Jose Canseco goes 4-for-5 and hits his 28th home run to become the first ML player with 100 RBI this season. Oakland defeats New York 9–8.

7th Floyd Youmans and Tim Burke combine to one-hit the Giants but lose 1–0 as Mike Krukow tosses a 2-hit shutout. Mike Aldrete's first-inning double drives in the game's only run.

12th The Twins fire manager Ray Miller and replace him with coach Tom Kelly.

13th The Rangers set a club record with 7 home runs in a 14–1 rout of Minnesota. Five of the home runs come off Twins starter Bert Blyleven, who will yield a ML-record 50 this season.

14th Giants Bob Brenly, a catcher subbing at 3B, ties a ML record by committing 4 errors in one inning of San Francisco's 7–6 victory over the Braves. Brenly atones for his errors with a homer in the 5th, a game-tying 2-run single in the 7th, and a 2-out game-winning home run in the bottom of the 9th.

Bo Jackson slugs his first ML home run—a 475-foot blast believed to be the longest to date at Royals Stadium—as Kansas City downs Seattle 10–3.

17th The Mets clinch the NL East Championship with a 4–2 win over the Cubs at Shea Stadium as Dwight Gooden tosses a 6-hitter. The Mets will win 108 games this season, most in the NL since the 1975 Reds.

19th White Sox pitcher Joe Cowley, who had been demoted to the minors earlier in the season, pitches an ugly no-hitter against the Angels. Cowley walks 7 batters and allows a sacrifice fly as Chicago wins 7–1.

20th San Diego's Tony Gwynn steals 5 bases in a 10–6 loss to the Astros, tying the modern NL record for steals in one game.

21st In his ML debut, San Diego's Jimmy Jones pitches a one-hitter against the Astros, allowing only a 3rd-inning triple to opposing pitcher Bob Knepper on the way to a 5–0 win.

22nd Dodgers ace Fernando Valenzuela becomes the NL's first 20-game winner this season, beating the Astros 9–2.

23rd Houston's Jim Deshaies strikes out the first 8 batters of the game on the way to a 2-hit 4–0 win over the Dodgers, breaking the ML record of 7 set by Joe Cowley on May 28th. Deshaies finishes with 10 strike-outs.

25th Houston's Mike Scott pitches a 2–0 no-hitter against the Giants at the Astrodome, clinching the NL West title for the Astros. It is the first time a pennant has ever been decided by a no-hitter, and the 3rd consecutive game in which Astros pitchers have allowed 2 hits or less.

In George Bamberger's last game as manager of the Brewers, Teddy Higuera beats Baltimore 9–3 to become the major leagues' 3rd 20-game winner this season. Tom Trebelhorn replaces Bamberger, who is retiring voluntarily.

26th California clinches the AL West title with an 8–3 win over Texas. Brian Downing belts 2 home runs for the Angels.

27th Jack Morris shuts out the Yankees 1–0 in 10 innings, raising his record to 20-8 and snapping Don Mattingly's hitting streak at 24 consecutive games.

28th The Red Sox become the last team to win their division, wrapping up the AL East with a 12–3 rout of the 2nd-place Blue Jays at Fenway Park.

29th Cleveland 2B Jay Bell becomes the 10th player in history to hit a home run on the first ML pitch he sees, but the Indians fall to the Twins 6–5. Bell's home run is the 47th of the season against Bert Blyleven, breaking the ML record of 46 home runs allowed by Robin Roberts in 1956.

OCTOBER

2nd Don Mattingly sets a Yankees record with his 232nd hit of the season in a 6–1 win over the Red Sox, eclipsing the mark set by Earle Combs in 1927. Mattingly will finish the season with 238 hits and a .352 batting average.

Mike Scott strikes out 8 Giants in a 2–1 Astros victory to run his season total to 306, joining Sandy Koufax and J. R. Richard as the only NL pitchers to fan 300 batters in one season. Scott loses his bid for a 2nd consecutive no-hitter when Will Clark doubles in the 7th inning.

3rd Baltimore loses to Detroit 6–3, assuring the Orioles of their first last-place finish since moving from St. Louis in 1954.

4th On the next-to-last day of the season, Dave Righetti saves both ends of the Yankees doubleheader sweep of the Red Sox to give him a ML-record 46 saves. Bruce Sutter and Dan Quisenberry had shared the record with 45.

6th The Orioles announce that 3B coach Cal Ripken, Sr., father of star SS Cal Ripken, Jr., will manage the club in 1987.

7th In the ALCS opener, California behind Mike Witt downs Boston's 20-game winner Roger Clemens 8–1.

8th Houston takes a 1–0 lead over the Mets in the NLCS as Mike Scott ties the NLCS record with 14 strikeouts. Glenn Davis's 2nd-inning solo HR off Dwight Gooden is the game's only run.

Angel errors and a lost fly ball in the late-afternoon sun hand the Red Sox a 9–2 victory in game 2.

9th   The Mets Bob Ojeda goes the distance even though giving up 10 hits, as New York wins 5–1.

10th   The Angels score 5 runs in the 6th, 7th, and 8th innings to down the Red Sox 5–3.

The Royals announce that Dick Howser, who underwent surgery for a brain tumor in July, will return to manage the club next season.

11th   Trailing 3–0 entering the bottom of the 9th inning, California rallies for 3 runs off Roger Clemens and Calvin Schiraldi, and goes on to defeat the Red Sox 4–3 in 11 innings to take a 3-1 lead in the ALCS.

Len Dykstra's 2-run home run off Dave Smith with one out in the bottom of the 9th gives the Mets a 6–5 win over the Astros and a 2-1 lead in the NLCS.

12th   One loss away from elimination and trailing 5–2 entering the 9th, the Red Sox stage one of the most improbable comebacks in post-season history, a 7–6 over the Angels in 11 innings. After Don Baylor's 9th-inning home run reduces the deficit to 5–4, reserve outfielder Dave Henderson slugs a 2-out, 2-run home run off Donnie Moore to give Boston a 6–5 lead. California ties the score with a run in the bottom of the 9th but Henderson, who had appeared to be the goat when he dropped Bobby Grich's long fly ball over the fence for a home run in the 7th inning, delivers a sacrifice fly in the 11th for the winning run.

Mike Scott baffles the Mets for a 2nd time, yielding only 3 hits in a 3–1 Astros victory.

Norm Cash, 1961 AL batting champion, drowns in Lake Michigan, a victim of a boating accident. He was 51.

13th   The International Olympic Committee announces that baseball will become a full medal sport at the 1992 Summer Games.

14th   Boston scores 5 in the 3rd to beat California 10–4. The ALCS series is now tied at 3 apiece.

Breaking out of a 1-for-21 slump, Mets C Gary Carter drives in the winning run of the Mets 2–1 win in the bottom of the 12th, rendering meaningless Nolan Ryan's 9 innings of 2-hit, 12-strikeout pitching.

15th   In the longest game in post-season history, the Mets beat the Astros 7–6 in 16 innings to earn their first trip to the World Series since 1973. New York scores 3 runs in the top of the 9th to force extra innings. The Mets score 3 more runs in the top of the 16th and Houston answers with 2 of its own before Jesse Orosco fans Kevin Bass to end the game.

Boston routs California 8–1 in the 7th game of the ALCS and advances to the World Series. The game caps yet another heartbreaking failure for Angels skipper Gene Mauch, who in game 5 was one strike away from reaching his first World Series in 25 seasons as a ML manager. After the game, veteran 2B Bobby Grich retires.

18th   Boston wins game one of the World Series 1–0 when Tim Teufel botches Rich Gedman's routine grounder in the 7th inning, allowing Jim Rice to score the game's only run. Bruce Hurst and Calvin Schiraldi combine on a 4-hitter for the Red Sox.

19th   Boston has 18 hits against Doc Gooden and 4 relievers to give the Red Sox a 9–3 win.

21st   Len Dykstra's leadoff HR helps Bob Ojeda beat his old team 7–1 to give the Mets their first win.

22nd   Gary Carter hits 2 home runs to lead the Mets to a 6–2 win at Fenway Park and even the Series at 2-2.

23rd   Mets ace Dwight Gooden loses again as Bruce Hurst gives up 10 hits but wins 4–2 for Boston.

24th   Bill Russell, 38, announces his retirement. He was the last member of the Dodgers Garvey-Lopes-Russell-Cey infield and is 2nd on the club's all-time games-played list with 2,183.

25th   Trailing 5–3 with 2 out and no one on base in the bottom of the 10th inning, New York rallies to win game 6 of the World Series 6–5 and force a deciding 7th game. After Gary Carter, Kevin Mitchell, and Ray Knight single, Bob Stanley uncorks a wild pitch that permits the tying run to score, and a hobbled Bill Buckner lets Mookie Wilson's slow bouncer skip through his legs, allowing Knight to score the winning run.

27th   The Mets win game 7 of the World Series 8–5 at Shea Stadium. 3B Ray Knight, whose home run triggers a 3-run rally in the 7th inning, is named MVP.

28th   Former Phillies SS Larry Bowa is named manager of the Padres, replacing Steve Boros.

29th Padres pitcher LaMarr Hoyt is arrested at the U.S.-Mexico border for possession of illegal drugs, the 3rd time he has been arrested on drug charges. He will be sentenced to 45 days in jail on December 16th.

30th San Diego trades C Terry Kennedy and minor leaguer Mark Williamson to the Orioles for P Storm Davis.

NOVEMBER

11th Houston's Mike Scott (18-10) beats Fernando Valenzuela (21-11) for the NL Cy Young Award, garnering 15 first-place votes to Valenzuela's 9.

Forty-five-year-old player-manager Pete Rose is dropped from the Reds' 40-man ML roster to make room for pitcher Pat Pacillo. Rose will continue to manage the club.

12th Roger Clemens wins the AL Cy Young Award unanimously, joining Denny McLain (1968) as the only pitchers to do so.

13th Dave Stewart, who went 9-5 for his hometown A's after being released by the Phillies in May, signs a 2-year contract with Oakland.

14th The Doubleday Publishing Company agrees to sell the World Champion Mets to Nelson Doubleday and Fred Wilpon for $80.75 million. The company had purchased the Mets for a then-record $21.1 million in 1980.

18th Roger Clemens becomes the first starting pitcher to win the AL MVP Award since Vida Blue in 1971, receiving 19 of a possible 28 first-place votes to defeat runner-up Don Mattingly.

19th Phillies 3B Mike Schmidt wins the NL MVP Award, joining Stan Musial and Roy Campanella as the only 3-time winners. Schmidt led the NL with 37 HRs and 119 RBI.

24th Cardinals reliever Todd Worrell, who led the NL with 36 saves, is named NL Rookie of the Year. Worrell had helped St. Louis to the 1985 World Series as a late-season call-up but was still a rookie as defined by the BBWAA.

In yet another unwise trade of prospects for aging veterans, the Yankees deal pitchers Brian Fisher, Doug Drabek, and Logan Easley to the Pirates for pitchers Rick Rhoden, Cecilio Guante, and Pat Clements.

Drabek will win the NL Cy Young Award for Pittsburgh in 1990.

The Twins announce that interim manager Tom Kelly will return on a permanent basis next season.

25th Jose Canseco wins the AL Rookie of the Year Award, becoming the first A's player to do so since Harry Byrd in 1952.

DECEMBER

11th In the first 2 major trades of the winter meetings, the Dodgers send 1B Greg Brock to the Brewers for pitchers Tim Leary and Tim Crews. The Mariners trade OF Danny Tartabull and P Rick Luecken to Kansas City for pitchers Scott Bankhead, Steve Shields, and Mike Kingery.

12th The Mets trade versatile rookie Kevin Mitchell, prospects Stan Jefferson and Shawn Abner, and 2 minor leaguers to the Padres for OF Kevin McReynolds, P Gene Walter, and minor leaguer Adam Ging.

The Yankees trade Mike Easler and minor leaguer Tom Barrett to the Phillies for P Charles Hudson and minor leaguer Jeff Knox, and also re-sign free-agent OF Claudell Washington to fill Easler's DH position.

19th After finding no other clubs interested in signing him, free-agent pitcher and 20-game winner Jack Morris agrees to salary arbitration with the Tigers while at the same time accusing the ML owners of collusion against free agents. Morris had offered to sign a one-year contract, with salary to be determined by an arbitrator, with either the Yankees, Angels, Twins, or Phillies, but was turned down by all 4.

Michael Sergio, a Mets fan who parachuted into Shea Stadium during game 6 of the World Series, is sentenced to 100 hours of community service and fined $500.

24th Free agent OF Gary Ward signs with the New York Yankees.

1987

JANUARY

8th   Ten free agents (Tim Raines, Lance Parrish, Bob Horner, Andre Dawson, Rich Gedman, Ron Guidry, Bob Boone, Doyle Alexander, Toby Harrah, and Gary Roenicke) fail to meet a midnight deadline and thus will not be allowed to re-sign with their former clubs until May1st if they are not offered contracts by new teams. The general lack of interest in the players will become the focus of the Players' Association's first anti-collusion suit against the owners.

14th   Catfish Hunter and Billy Williams are elected to the Hall of Fame by the BBWAA.

21st   Free agent Vida Blue signs with the Oakland A's.

Free agent Gary Roenicke, who spent last season with the Yankees after 8 years with the Orioles, signs with the Atlanta Braves.

29th   Red Sox Wade Boggs avoids going to salary arbitration for the 3rd consecutive year by signing a 3-year contract worth over $5 million.

30th   The Cubs trade veteran 3B Ron Cey to the A's for IF Luis Quinones.

FEBRUARY

2nd   Three-time 20-game winner Dennis Leonard, who returned to the majors last season after a 3-year absence due to a knee injury, announces his retirement. Leonard was 8-13 with a 4.44 ERA for the Royals in 1986.

The Blue Jays trade 2B Damaso Garcia and P Luis Leal to the Braves for P Craig McMurtry.

3rd   The Expos trade ace reliever Jeff Reardon and C Tom Nieto to the Twins for P Neal Heaton, C Jeff Reed, and a pair of minor leaguers.

7th   Dodgers pitcher Orel Hershiser becomes only the 2nd player ever forced to accept a pay cut through salary arbitration when he is awarded $800,000 for the 1987 season, a 20 percent cut (the maximum allowed by the Basic Agreement) from his 1986 salary. Hershiser was 14-14 with a 3.85 ERA in 1986.

11th   Free-agent 3B Ray Knight, who earlier had rejected an $800,000 one-year contract offer from the

Mets, signs with the Orioles for $475,000 plus incentives and an option for a 2nd year.

13th   Tigers Jack Morris is awarded a $1.85 million salary by arbitrator Richard Bloch, the highest amount awarded to date through that process.

17th   Don Mattingly wins a $1.975 million salary in his arbitration case against the Yankees, eclipsing Jack Morris's record amount of just 4 days ago.

19th   Less than one month after signing with the club as a free agent, pitcher Vida Blue stuns the A's by announcing his retirement.

23rd   Just 3 days after training camp opens, an extremely frail Dick Howser abandons his attempt to come back from a brain tumor and gives up his position as Royals manager. Billy Gardner is named his successor.

25th   In the wake of 3 drug-related incidents over the past 12 months, LaMarr Hoyt is banished from baseball for the 1987 season by Commissioner Ueberroth. On June 16th an arbitrator will reduce Hoyt's suspension to 60 days and order the Padres to reinstate him.

MARCH

3rd   Ray Dandridge, a legendary 3B from the Negro Leagues, is the only player elected to the Hall of Fame by the Special Veterans Committee.

6th   Free agent Andre Dawson signs a one-year contract with the Cubs for the bargain-basement price of $650,000. Dawson, who had offered to sign a contract with the dollar amount left blank just so he could play on the natural grass at Wrigley Field and save his fragile knees, will hit 49 home runs and win the NL MVP Award this season.

26th   The Phillies trade OF Gary Redus to the White Sox for pitcher Joe Cowley.

27th   In what will turn out to be an extremely lopsided trade, the Mets send C Ed Hearn and minor leaguers Rick Anderson and Mauro Gozzo to the Royals in exchange for David Cone and minor leaguer Chris Jelic. Cone will blossom into one of the NL's better starters, posting a 20-3 record for the Mets in 1988.

APRIL

1st After testing positive for cocaine during spring training, Mets ace Dwight Gooden avoids suspension by agreeing to enter a drug rehabilitation program.

St. Louis sends highly regarded youngsters OF Andy Van Slyke, C Mike LaValliere, and P Mike Dunne to Pittsburgh in exchange for All-Star catcher Tony Pena.

3rd The Cubs trade veteran pitcher Dennis Eckersley and minor leaguer Dan Roan to the A's for 3 minor leaguers.

7th Atlanta's Rick Mahler ties the NL record with his 3rd Opening Day shutout, a 6–0 three-hitter over the Phillies.

8th Faced with a storm of public criticism, the Dodgers fire vice president Al Campanis for racially insensitive remarks he made on the April 6th telecast of ABC-TV's Nightline news show. Campanis had said that blacks may lack "some of the necessities to be a field manager or general manager."

9th Gary Carter drives in his 1,000th career run with an 8th-inning single that scores Len Dykstra as the Mets defeat Pittsburgh 4–2.

13th San Diego sets a ML record when its first 3 batters of the game—Marvell Wynne, Tony Gwynn, and John Kruk—all homer off the Giants Roger Mason, but the Giants come back to win 13–6.

Free-agent 3B Bob Horner, unable to find a ML club interested in his services, signs a one-year contract with Japan's Yakult Swallows.

15th Twenty-two-year-old Juan Nieves throws the first no-hitter in Brewers history 7–0 at Baltimore, and Milwaukee runs its record to 9-0.

18th Mike Schmidt hits his 500th career home run, a 3-run shot off Pittsburgh's Don Robinson in the top of the 9th inning to give the Phillies an 8–6 win. Schmidt is the 15th ML player to reach the 500-HR plateau.

19th Dale Sveum's 2–run home run off Greg Harris caps a 5-run rally in the bottom of the 9th inning and gives the Brewers a 6–4 win over Texas and a 12-0 record, breaking the 1981 A's record for the best start in AL history.

Cardinals ace John Tudor suffers a broken leg when Mets catcher Barry Lyons crashes into the St. Louis dugout while chasing a foul pop. Tudor, who was not pitching in the 4–2 Cardinals win, will be sidelined until August 1st.

21st The White Sox beat the Brewers 7–1, ending their season-opening winning streak at 13 games. Milwaukee's 13-0 start tied the ML record set by the 1982 Braves.

27th Boston's Don Baylor collects his 2,000th ML hit, a single off Curt Young in a 5–2 loss to the A's.

29th Andre Dawson goes 5-for-5 while hitting for the cycle to lead the Cubs to an 8–4 win over the Giants at Wrigley Field.

MAY

1st Free-agents Ron Guidry (Yankees), Rich Gedman (Red Sox), Bob Boone (Angels), and Tim Raines (Expos) all re-sign with their former clubs on the first day that they are allowed to do so. Doyle Alexander will re-sign with the Braves on May 5th.

2nd After having missed spring training, Montreal's Tim Raines debuts with a 10th-inning grand slam. His 4-for-5 leads the Expos to an 11–7 win over the Mets.

Graig Nettles and Dion James each hit grand slams to lead the Braves to a 12–4 rout of the Astros. It is the first time since July 3, 1966 (when pitcher Tony Cloninger did it by himself), that the Braves have hit 2 grand slams in one game.

3rd Eric Davis belts 3 home runs, including a grand slam, to lead Cincinnati to a 9–6 win at Philadelphia.

4th Candy Maldonado hits for the cycle to lead San Francisco's 21-hit attack in a 10–7 win over St. Louis.

Tim Wallach hits 3 home runs and drives in 6 runs, but Montreal loses to Atlanta 10–7.

9th Eddie Murray homers from each side of the plate for the 2nd consecutive game, a ML first. Murray's 4 home runs in 2 days help the Orioles to 7–6 and 15–6 wins over the White Sox.

After going 15 years without one, Chris Speier hits his 2nd grand slam in a week to lead San Francisco to a 9–4 win over Pittsburgh. Speier also connected for a grand slam against the Cardinals on May 5th.

17th Terry Kennedy hits Baltimore's only home run in a 3–2 win over the Angels, ending the Orioles' streak of 9 consecutive games with at least 2 home runs. The Orioles will go on to hit HRs in 14 consecutive games.

19th Despite getting a club-record 13 strikeouts from pitcher Ted Higuera, Milwaukee loses its 12th straight game 5–1 to the White Sox. The Brewers, who started the season 13-0, are now 20-15 and in 3rd place in the AL East.

Bill Buckner raps his 2,500th career hit, a single off Bret Saberhagen in Boston's 4–1 loss to Kansas City.

27th Greg Gross joins 1987's record-setting HR parade with his first home run since 1978, a 2-run shot in the top of the 8th that sparks the Phillies to a 6–4 win over San Diego. An all-time record 4,458 home runs will be hit in the major leagues this season.

28th Cleveland's Joe Carter hits 3 home runs in a game in Boston's Fenway Park for the 2nd time in his career, but the Indians fall to the Red Sox 12–8.

30th Eric Davis ties a ML record by hitting his 3rd grand slam of the month in a 6–2 win over the Pirates.

JUNE

1st Phil Niekro wins his 314th career game as Cleveland beats Detroit 9–6, moving the Niekro brothers (Phil and Joe) past Gaylord and Jim Perry into first place on the all-time brothers' victory list. The Niekros have now combined for 530 career wins.

Dwight Evans hits his 300th career home run in Boston's 9–5 loss to the Twins, joining teammates Jim Rice and Don Baylor in the 300-HR club.

2nd The Mariners select Cincinnati high schooler Ken Griffey, Jr., the son of Braves OF Ken Griffey, with the first pick overall in the free-agent draft.

3rd The Cubs rout Houston 22–7 at Wrigley Field in a game that features a ML-record-tying 3 grand slams. Keith Moreland and Brian Dayett hit grand slams for Chicago and Billy Hatcher connects for the Astros to equal the record set by the Orioles and Rangers last August 6th.

5th Dwight Gooden returns from drug rehabilitation and allows one run in 6⅔ innings to earn the win as the Mets beat the Pirates 5–1 at Shea Stadium.

6th The Yankees trade knuckleballer Joe Niekro to the Twins for C Mark Salas.

11th Having traded for him last December, the Phillies deal Mike Easler back to the Yankees for a pair of minor leaguers.

12th The first-place Blue Jays set a club record with their 10th straight victory 8–5 over the Orioles. Toronto leads New York by 3 games in the AL East and will win 11 in a row before bowing to Baltimore on June 14th.

14th Mike Schmidt hits 3 home runs in a game for the 3rd time in his career to lead the Phillies to an 11–6 win over the Expos. His 2nd home run is also his 2,000th career hit, and his 3rd gives him 511 career homers, tying him with Mel Ott on the all-time list.

17th Dick Howser dies at St. Luke's Hospital in Kansas City. He led the Royals to their first World Championship in 1985, but was forced to give up managing during the 1986 season because of a brain tumor. His uniform number, 10, will be retired by the club on July 3rd.

18th With his club in 5th place in the NL East, Phillies manager John Felske is fired and replaced by 3B coach Lee Elia.

22nd Tom Seaver abandons his comeback attempt with the injury-riddled Mets and retires with a career W-L record of 311-205, an ERA of 2.86, 3,640 strikeouts (3rd on the all-time list behind Nolan Ryan and Steve Carlton), and 61 shutouts (7th).

26th Wade Boggs has his hitting streak snapped at 25 consecutive games and Roger Clemens fails to hold a 9–0, 2nd-inning lead as Boston loses to New York 12–11 in 10 innings.

27th Tony Gwynn goes 3-for-4 in San Diego's 8–4 win over Atlanta to raise his batting average to .387. Gwynn will finish the season at .370 to win his 2nd NL batting title.

Darrell Evans slugs a 2-run home run in the first inning off Mike Boddicker for his 2,000th career hit, but his Tigers lose to Baltimore 4–2.

28th One day after hitting 3 home runs in Oakland's 13–3 rout of the Indians, A's rookie 1B Mark McGwire hits 2 more in a 10–0 Oakland romp to tie the ML record of 5 homers in 2 games.

Don Baylor moves ahead of Ron Hunt as the major leagues' all-time hit-by-pitch king when the Yankees Rick Rhoden plunks him during a 6–2 loss to the Red Sox. It is the 244th time that Baylor has been hit by the pitch.

Pinch hitter Greg Gross breaks up Ron Darling's no-hitter with a leadoff triple in the 8th inning and 2 Phillies rallies beat the Mets 5–4.

29th In the first game of Philadelphia's double-header sweep of Pittsburgh, Steve Bedrosian records his 12th consecutive save (in 12 appearances) to break the ML record set by Sparky Lyle in 1975.

JULY

2nd Houston's Glenn Davis ends Steve Bedrosian's record-setting streak of 13 consecutive saves by belting a 3-run home run in the top of the 9th inning to give the Astros a 7–6 win over the Phillies.

Jim Eisenreich, making a comeback after being forced out of the major leagues by a nervous disorder in 1984, hits his first ML home run since 1982 to lead the Royals to a 10–3 win over his former club, the Twins.

4th In a 7-player swap, the Padres trade pitchers Dave Dravecky and Craig Lefferts and OF Kevin Mitchell to the Giants for 3B Chris Brown and pitchers Keith Comstock, Mark Davis, and Mark Grant. In 1989, Mitchell will win the MVP Award for the Giants, and Davis will win the Cy Young for the Padres.

8th Floyd Youmans pitches a one-hitter to beat the Astros and Nolan Ryan 1–0. Houston's lone hit is an 8th-inning single by Kevin Bass.

9th Mike Schmidt hits his 513th career home run off Atlanta's Zane Smith to move past Eddie Mathews and Ernie Banks into 10th place on the all-time list, but the Phillies lose to the Braves 11–6.

11th Billy Ripken, 22, joins his brother Cal in the Orioles starting lineup in Baltimore's 2–1 loss to the Twins. Orioles manager Cal Ripken, Sr. is the first to manage 2 sons in the majors.

12th The Yankees trade P Bob Tewksbury and 2 minor league pitchers to the Cubs for Steve Trout, who has just pitched back-to-back shutouts.

14th Tim Raines caps a 3-for-3 performance in the All-Star Game with a 2-run triple in the top of the 13th inning, giving the NL a 2–0 victory.

The BBWAA votes to rename the Rookie of the Year Award in honor of Jackie Robinson, who broke baseball's color barrier on the way to winning the first Rookie of the Year Award in 1947.

15th The Indians fire manager Pat Corrales, replacing him with bullpen coach Doc Edwards. Cleveland is in last place in the AL East, 23 games behind, after finishing 84-78 in 1986.

18th Don Mattingly hits a home run in his 8th consecutive game, tying the ML record set by Dale Long in 1956, but the Yankees lose to Texas 7–2. His streak will end tomorrow when the Rangers romp 20–3.

20th Don Mattingly ties another ML record, this time in the field, as he makes 22 putouts in the Yankees 7–1 win over the Twins. The feat was last accomplished in the AL by Hal Chase in 1906.

23rd The Red Sox waive Bill Buckner, the goat of last season's World Series loss to the Mets, and promote slugger Sam Horn from Pawtucket .

26th Catfish Hunter, Billy Williams, and Ray Dandridge are inducted into the baseball Hall of Fame in Cooperstown, New York.

Paul Molitor ties a ML record with 3 stolen bases in the first inning of Milwaukee's 7–4 win over the A's.

27th The Salt Lake City Trappers lose 7–5 to the Billings Mustangs, ending their professional-record winning streak at 29 consecutive games. The Trappers, who hadn't lost since June 24th, broke the old record of 27 straight wins with a 13–3 rout of the Pocatello Giants on July 25th.

28th Montreal's Jeff Reed makes 3 errors in the 7th inning of an 8–3 loss to the Cubs, tying the ML record for catchers.

29th The Royals trade SS Buddy Biancalana to the Astros for pitching prospect Mel Stottlemyre, Jr.

30th The Pirates trade P Don Robinson to the Giants for minor league catcher Mackey Sasser and cash. The Indians trade fading veteran Steve Carlton to the Twins for a player to be named later.

31st Eddie Murray hits his 299th and 300th career home runs to lead Baltimore to an 8–4 win over Texas.

AUGUST 1987

AUGUST

1st Andre Dawson hits 3 home runs and drives in all 5 Chicago runs as the Cubs beat the Phillies 5–3.

2nd Eric Davis becomes the 7th player in ML history to hit 30 home runs and steal 30 bases in one season by drilling his 30th homer in the bottom of the 11th to give the Reds a 5–4 win over the Giants.

Royals rookie 3B Kevin Seitzer goes 6-for-6 with 2 home runs and 7 RBI in a 13–5 rout of the Red Sox, tying the AL record for hits in a 9-inning game.

Rangers pitcher Bobby Witt ties the ML record by striking out 4 Orioles in the 2nd inning of a 5–2 win. Witt finishes the game with 11 strikeouts.

3rd Twins Joe Niekro is caught with a file on the mound and is ejected during the 4th inning of Minnesota's 11–3 win over California. He will be suspended for 10 games by AL president Bobby Brown, who doesn't buy Niekro's story that he had been filing his nails on the bench and stuck the file in his back pocket when the inning started.

Jack Morris ties the AL record with 5 wild pitches in a 4–2, 10-inning loss to the Royals. Morris will scatter 23 wild pitches this season to set a new ML record.

6th Rich Gossage earns his 287th career save in San Diego's 7–4 win over Atlanta to move past Bruce Sutter into 2nd place on the all-time list.

10th Phillies pitcher Kevin Gross becomes the 2nd pitcher in 8 days to be ejected for scuffing the baseball when umpires discover sandpaper in his glove during the 5th inning of a 4–2 win over the Cubs. Like Joe Niekro, Gross will be suspended for 10 games.

Cardinals 1B Jack Clark sets an NL record by drawing a walk in his 16th consecutive game, a 6–0 win over Pittsburgh.

12th The Braves send veteran pitcher Doyle Alexander to the Tigers in exchange for minor leaguer John Smoltz. Alexander will help lead the Tigers to the AL East title by posting a perfect 9-0.

13th The Cardinals outfield sets a ML record by failing to record a single putout in a 4–2, 13-inning win over the Phillies. The previous mark was held by the 1905 St. Louis Browns, who played an 11-inning game with no outfield putouts.

14th Oakland's Mark McGwire slugs his 39th home run of the season in a 12-inning 7–6 win over California, breaking the ML record for rookies shared by Wally Berger and Frank Robinson. McGwire will finish the season with a whopping 49 homers.

15th At the Pan American games in Indianapolis, the U.S.A. and Cuba are tied with 2 outs in the 9th when Ty Griffin hits a 2-run HR to win it. For Cuba it is their first loss in 20 years of Pan Am competition.

16th Tim Raines goes 5-for-5 and hits for the cycle to lead the Expos to a 10–7 win over Pittsburgh.

The wind is blowing out at Wrigley as the Mets pound the Cubs 23–10 at Wrigley Field, setting a club record for runs scored in a game.

20th Pittsburgh unloads another veteran pitcher, trading Rick Reuschel to the Giants for pitchers Jeff Robinson and Scott Medvin.

21st Dale Murphy hits his 300th career home run as Atlanta beats Pittsburgh 5–4.

Andre Dawson belts his 39th and 40th home runs of the season and Lee Smith picks up his 30th save in Chicago's 7–5 win over the Astros.

26th Paul Molitor goes 0-for-4 in Milwaukee's 1–0, 10-inning win over the Indians, ending his hitting streak at 39 consecutive games. His streak was the 7th longest in ML history and the longest in the AL since Joe DiMaggio's 56-game streak in 1941. Molitor faces rookie John Farrell all 4 times, and is on deck when Rick Manning ends the game with a run-scoring pinch single in the bottom of the 10th.

The Yankees and Reds exchange starting pitchers, with Dennis Rasmussen going to Cincinnati for Bill Gullickson.

27th The Royals fire manager Billy Gardner, who replaced Dick Howser in spring training, and replace him with John Wathan, the former Kansas City catcher who was managing the club's Triple A Omaha affiliate. In Wathan's ML managerial debut, the Royals win 3–2 on George Brett's 10th-inning home run to move within 3 games of first-place Minnesota.

28th Mike Schmidt continues to climb baseball's all-time home run list, passing both Ted Williams and Willie McCovey with the 522nd of his career in an 8–1 win over San Diego.

29th Nolan Ryan passes the 200-strikeout barrier for a ML-record 11th time, fanning 7 Pirates in 6 innings of an 8–2 Astros loss.

633

Two AL West contenders attempt to bolster their rosters for the stretch run. The Angels trade 2 minor leaguers for Pittsburgh 2B Johnny Ray, and the A's send minor leaguer Tim Belcher to the Dodgers for P Rick Honeycutt.

30th Kirby Puckett goes 6-for-6 with 2 home runs in Minnesota's 10–6 win over Milwaukee, tying the AL record for hits in a 9-inning game. Combined with yesterday's 4-for-5, two-HR performance, Puckett has a ML-record-tying 10 hits in 2 games.

With knuckleballer Charlie Hough on the mound, Rangers catcher Geno Petralli ties the ML record by allowing 6 passed balls in a 7–0 loss to Detroit. Eight days earlier Petralli had 5 passed balls in an 8–6 win over Chicago, also with Hough pitching.

The A's get P Storm Davis from the Padres for 2 players to be named later.

31st The Blue Jays trade minor leaguer Oswaldo Peraza and a player to be named later to the Orioles for veteran lefthander Mike Flanagan, then release Phil Niekro to make room for Flanagan on the roster.

SEPTEMBER

1st Williamsport (Eastern League) Bills catcher Dave Bresnahan introduces a new wrinkle to baseball—the hidden potato. With a Reading runner, Rick Rudblad, on 3B, Bresnahan returns from a time out with a shaved potato hidden in his mitt. On the next pitch he throws the potato wildly on a pickoff attempt. When the runner trots home, Bresnahan tags him out with the real ball. The umpire, unamused, rules the runner safe, gives the catcher an error, and fines him $50. Bresnahan replied, "I thought it'd be a do-over."

The Red Sox trade 2 heroes from their 1986 AL Championship team, sending DH Don Baylor to the Twins and OF Dave Henderson to the Giants for players to be named later.

In a 3–2 loss to the Cubs, Houston's Billy Hatcher becomes the first player this season to be ejected for using an illegal bat, and will eventually be suspended for 10 games by NL president Bart Giamatti. Baseball has seen a rash of protests regarding allegedly doctored bats this season, partly in response to the record number of home runs being hit.

2nd The parent Phillies don't find Bresnahan's potato gag funny either, and release him. Bresnahan, hitting .149, explains, " we were 27 games out, what

the hell?" The following night, their last game of the season, the Williamsport Bills admit any fan for a $1 and a potato. On each potato, Bresnahan autographs, "this spuds for you."

Tom Candiotti pitches his 2nd one-hitter of the season, but also walks 7 batters and makes an error as the Indians lose to Detroit 2–1. Matt Nokes's single with 2 out in the 8th is the Tigers' only hit.

5th Carlton Fisk clubs his 300th career home run off Danny Jackson, but the White Sox lose to the Royals 4–2.

6th The Dodgers beat the Mets 3–2 in 16 innings to end their losing streak at 9 games, the club's worst since 1973.

8th With the Cubs in 5th place in the NL East (68-68, 13 games behind), the club fires manager Gene Michael and replaces him with Frank Lucchesi.

9th Nolan Ryan strikes out 16 Giants in 8 innings during Houston's 4–2 victory to take over the ML strikeout lead with 226. Ryan will finish the season with 270 strikeouts, tops in the major leagues.

11th Howard Johnson steals his 30th base of the season in the Mets 6–4, 10-inning loss to the Cardinals, becoming the 8th player ever to hit 30 HRs and steal 30 bases in one season. Mets starter Ron Darling tears ligaments in his thumb while fielding a Vince Coleman bunt during the game and will miss the rest of the season.

13th Chicago's Floyd Bannister faces the minimum 27 batters in a 2–0 one-hitter against Seattle, striking out 10 while walking none. Hard-luck loser Mark Langston pitches a 2-hitter for the Mariners.

14th In an 18–3 rout of the Orioles, the Blue Jays erupt for a ML-record 10 home runs. Ernie Whitt leads the parade with 3 round trippers, Rance Mulliniks and George Bell hit 2, and Lloyd Moseby, Rob Ducey, and Fred McGriff each add one. Mike Hart hits one for Baltimore to tie the 2-team ML record of 11.

15th Mets 1B Keith Hernandez collects his 2,000th ML hit as New York pounds Chicago 12–4. Earlier in the day the 2nd-place Mets obtained pitcher John Candelaria from the Angels for a pair of minor leaguers.

16th In a 6–4 win, California's Bob Boone catches his 1,919th ML game to break the record held by Hall of Famer Al Lopez.

Cleveland's Joe Carter joins the 30-30 club, stealing his 30th base of the season in a 5–3 loss to Seattle.

21st Darryl Strawberry joins Howard Johnson as the first teammates ever to achieve 30 homers and 30 steals in the same season, stealing 2 bases in the Mets 7–1 win at Chicago. Strawberry is only the 10th member of the 30-30 club, but the 4th to accomplish the feat this season.

22nd Wade Boggs goes 2-for-4 in Boston's 8–5 loss to Detroit, reaching the 200-hit plateau for an AL-record tying 5th consecutive year. Al Simmons and Charlie Gehringer are the only other AL players to do so.

23rd Bill Madlock collects his 2,000th career hit as the Tigers beat Boston 4–0 on Doyle Alexander's 2-hitter.

Albert Hall hits for the cycle in Atlanta's 5–4 win over Houston, becoming the first Brave to do so since 1910.

26th Padres catcher Benito Santiago extends his hitting streak to 28 games in a 3–1 loss to the Dodgers, setting a new ML record for rookies. Pittsburgh's Jimmy Williams had held the record with a 27-game streak in 1899.

27th Phil Niekro makes his final ML appearance and is pounded for 5 runs in 3 innings in Atlanta's 15–6 loss to the Giants. Niekro, who had been released earlier in the season by Toronto, agreed to pitch one last game for the Braves, the team he spent his first 19 ML seasons with.

Shea Stadium is packed with 48,588 fans to see the Mets clobber the Pirates 12–3, making the Mets the 2nd franchise in ML history to break the 3 million barrier in season attendance. St. Louis will also draw 3 million fans this season.

28th The Giants and Twins win their divisions, ending 16- and 17-year championship droughts, respectively. San Francisco clinches its first NL West title since 1971 with a 5–4 win at San Diego, while Minnesota clinches its first AL West title since 1970 with a 5–3 win at Texas.

Kevin Seitzer goes 2-for-4 in Kansas City's 5–1 loss to Seattle to become the first rookie since Tony Oliva and Dick Allen in 1964 to collect 200 hits.

29th Don Mattingly hits his ML-record 6th grand slam of the season off Boston's Bruce Hurst in a 6–0 Yankees victory, eclipsing the mark shared by Ernie Banks (1955) and Jim Gentile (1961).

Giants OF Jessie Reid hits a home run off San Diego's Jimmy Jones in his first ML at bat to help the Giants to a 5–3 victory.

30th Oakland's Dave Stewart becomes the major leagues' first 20-game winner this season as the A's beat the Indians 4–3.

OCTOBER

1st Danny Cox pitches a 5-hitter and the Cardinals beat the Expos 8–2 to clinch the NL East championship.

3rd Benito Santiago goes 0-for-3 against Orel Hershiser in San Diego's 1–0 win over Los Angeles, ending his ML-rookie-record hitting streak at 34 consecutive games. Santiago's streak is also the longest ever by a catcher.

4th On the last day of the regular season, Detroit beats 2nd-place Toronto 1–0 at Tiger Stadium to win the AL East title. The Tigers were one game behind the Blue Jays entering their 3-game season-ending showdown, and won each game by a single run (4–3, 3–2, and 1–0). Frank Tanana outduels Jimmy Key in the finale, and Larry Herndon's 2nd-inning home run provides the game's only run.

Roger Clemens closes out his season with a 2-hit, 12-strikeout, 4–0 win over the Brewers, improving his record to 20-9.

6th St. Louis takes the NLCS opener 5–3 over the Giants behind the hitting and pitching of Greg Mathews.

7th San Francisco's Dave Dravecky shuts out St. Louis 5–0 to even the NL series.

In the ALCS opener, Gary Gaetti's 2 HRs are the difference in Minnesota's 8–5 win over Detroit at home.

8th Minnesota wins again as Bert Blyleven beats the Bengals ace Jack Morris 6–3.

9th Trailing 4–0, the Cardinals rally to down the Giants 6–5 at Candlestick.

10th Jeffrey Leonard sets a playoff record with a home run in his 4th consecutive game, sparking the

Giants to a 4–2 win over the Cardinals that evens the NLCS at 2 games apiece. Leonard's 4 home runs tie the record for most home runs in one LCS shared by Bob Robertson and Steve Garvey.

Leading 6–0, the Tigers hold on to beat the Twins 7–6.

11th Minnesota takes a 3-1 edge with a 5–3 win at Detroit.

The Giants take a 3-2 lead in the series, defeating the Cards 6-3.

12th Minnesota beats Detroit 9–5 in game 5 of the ALCS to wrap up its first AL championship since 1965. 3B Gary Gaetti is named MVP.

13th John Tudor and 2 relievers shut down the Giants 1–0 to even the NLCS at 3-3.

14th Danny Cox pitches the Cardinals' 2nd consecutive shutout 6–0 over the Giants in game 7 of the NLCS, to send St. Louis to the World Series for the 3rd time in the 1980s. Giants OF Jeffrey Leonard (.417, 4 HRs) is named series MVP.

17th In the first indoor World Series game ever (at Minnesota's Metrodome), Dan Gladden's grand slam caps a 7-run 4th inning and leads the Twins to a 10–1 win over St. Louis in game one. It is the first World Series grand slam since 1970.

18th The Twins win their 2nd straight WS game 8–4, tallying 7 runs in the 4th inning.

19th Billy Martin is named manager of the Yankees for a bizarre 5th time, replacing Lou Piniella, who replaced Martin, and who is "promoted" to general manager. Piniella led the Yankees to an 89-73 record in 1987, 4th in the AL East.

20th The Cards get all their runs in the 7th to win 3–1 in game 3.

21st With the help of a 3-run HR by Tom Lawless, St. Louis wins 7–2 to even the WS.

22nd Danny Cox gives the Redbirds a 4–2 victory in game 5.

24th Kent Hrbek belts the Twins 2nd grand slam of the World Series to lead a comeback from a 5–2 deficit, and the Twins win game 6, 11–5 to even the series at 3 games apiece. The home team has won all 6 games, with game 7 to be played in Minnesota tomorrow.

25th Series MVP Frank Viola and reliever Jeff Reardon hold the Cardinals to 6 hits as the Twins capture game seven 4–2 to win their first World Championship in Minnesota. The franchise's last World Championship came in 1924 as the Washington Senators.

29th Dallas Green resigns as president and general manager of the Cubs, citing "philosophical differences" with the Tribune Company, which owns the club.

NOVEMBER

3rd Oakland 1B Mark McGwire wins the AL Rookie of the Year Award, joining Carlton Fisk (1972) as the only player to win that league's award unanimously.

4th Padres catcher Benito Santiago is a unanimous selection as the NL Rookie of the Year, while Pirates pitcher Mike Dunne is the second choice on 22 of 24 ballots.

6th The Royals trade pitcher Danny Jackson and SS Angel Salazar to the Reds for pitcher Ted Power and SS Kurt Stillwell.

10th In the closest vote in the award's history, Steve Bedrosian edges Rick Sutcliffe 57-55 to win the NL Cy Young Award. Bedrosian is the 3rd reliever ever to win the award in the NL.

11th Roger Clemens becomes the first pitcher since Jim Palmer in 1975-76 to win consecutive Cy Young Awards, collecting 21 of 28 first-place votes to easily beat runner-up Jimmy Key.

Jim Frey, who managed the Cubs to the 1984 NL East title and spent last season as a broadcaster for the club, is named the club's director of baseball operations. His first major move will be to hire longtime friend Don Zimmer as manager on November 20th.

17th George Bell becomes the first Blue Jay ever to win the AL MVP Award, edging Detroit's Alan Trammell 332-311. Bell hit .308 last season with 47 home runs and a league-leading 134 RBI.

18th Cubs OF Andre Dawson becomes the first player from a last-place club ever to win an MVP Award, taking NL honors for his .287-49-137 season.

DECEMBER

1st Free-agent OF Brett Butler signs a 2-year contract with the Giants. He hit .295 with 33 SBs for Cleveland in 1987.

5th The Tigers swap pitcher Dan Petry to the Angels for centerfielder Gary Pettis.

7th Free-agent OF Bob Dernier, who hit a career-high .317 with 31 stolen bases for the Cubs last season, signs a one-year contract with his original ML club, the Phillies.

8th Cincinnati trades OF Dave Parker to the A's for pitchers Jose Rijo and Tim Birtsas, the Braves trade SS Rafael Ramirez to the Astros for a pair of minor leaguers, and in the day's biggest (and most lopsided) deal, the Cubs send dominating reliever Lee Smith to the Red Sox for pitchers Al Nipper and Calvin Schiraldi.

10th The White Sox trade ace lefthander Floyd Bannister (16-11 last season) and Dave Cochrane to the Royals for John Davis, Melido Perez, Greg Hibbard, and Chuck Mount.

11th In a 3-team trade, the Dodgers acquire relief pitcher Jesse Orosco from the Mets and relief pitcher Jay Howell and SS Alfredo Griffin from the A's, and send pitchers Bob Welch and Matt Young to Oakland and minor leaguer Jack Savage to New York. The Mets receive two A's minor leaguers to complete the deal, pitchers Kevin Tapani and Wally Whitehurst.

In the first trade ever between the Yankees and Mets that involves a ML player, the Mets send SS Rafael Santana and a minor leaguer to the Bronx for C Phil Lombardi and minor leaguers Darren Reed, and Steve Fry.

22nd The Yankees send P Steve Trout and OF Henry Cotto to Seattle for pitchers Lee Guetterman and Clay Parker and minor leaguer Wade Taylor.

1988

JANUARY

6th   Free-agent slugger Jack Clark signs with the New York Yankees, while free agent Paul Molitor re-signs with the Brewers.

8th   Faced with a midnight deadline to re-sign with the Yankees, pitcher Bill Gullickson agrees to a 2-year contract with Japan's Tokyo Giants instead.

12th   Former Pirates slugger Willie Stargell is the only player elected this year to the Hall of Fame by the BBWAA, and becomes the 17th player to be elected in his first year of eligibility. Jim Bunning falls 4 votes shy of the 321 needed for election in his 13th year on the ballot.

13th   Steve Garvey retires. He hit just .211 last season and was not offered a new contract by the Padres.

14th   After playing last season with Japan's Yakult Swallows, Bob Horner signs a one-year contract with the Cardinals, who need a power-hitting 1B to replace Jack Clark.

22nd   As a result of the Players' Association's 1985 collusion suit against the owners, arbitrator Thomas Roberts declares 7 players no-risk free agents until March 1st, giving them a chance to sign with other clubs despite already having contracts. The 7 are Kirk Gibson, Carlton Fisk, Donnie Moore, Joe Niekro, Butch Wynegar, Tom Brookens, and Juan Beniquez.

29th   Detroit's Kirk Gibson signs a 3-year contract with the Dodgers. Gibson will be the only one of the 7 no-risk free agents to change clubs.

FEBRUARY

9th   Don Baylor signs a one-year contract with the A's.

12th   The Padres trade reliever Rich Gossage to the Cubs for IF Keith Moreland in a deal that also includes a pair of minor leaguers.

23rd   A committee of Chicago aldermen vote 7-2 to allow the Cubs to install lights and play up to 18 night games a year at Wrigley Field. The Cubs had feared losing the 1990 All-Star Game, as well as future play-off and World Series games, if lights were not installed.

27th   3B Ray Knight is traded from Baltimore to Detroit for P Mark Thurmond.

MARCH

1st   For the first time since 1956 the Special Veterans Committee does not elect anyone to the Hall of Fame. Phil Rizzuto, Leo Durocher, Joe Gordon, and Gil Hodges are among the candidates passed over.

11th   Angels manager Gene Mauch, 62, takes a leave of absence for health reasons and is replaced by Cookie Rojas. Mauch will announce his retirement on March 27th.

17th   Newly acquired Yankee Jack Clark tears a tendon in his calf while hitting a home run in a spring training game against the Orioles and will miss the start of the regular season.

21st   The Phillies trade 3B Rick Schu and outfielders Jeff Stone and Keith Hughes to the Orioles for OF Mike Young.

30th   Reds OF Eddie Milner is suspended for the 1988 season by Commissioner Ueberroth after suffering a relapse of his cocaine problem.

APRIL

4th   Toronto's George Bell, the defending AL MVP, hits home runs as the Blue Jays beat Kansas City 5–3 on Opening Day. Bell will go 5-for-5 in Toronto's 2nd game of the season.

The Mets set an Opening Day record with 6 home runs in a 10–6 win over the Expos. Darryl Strawberry and Kevin McReynolds each connect twice for New York, with Strawberry's 2nd blast believed to be the longest ever hit at Olympic Stadium (estimated at 525 feet).

7th   Reds rookie Chris Sabo ties a ML record with 11 assists at 3B in Cincinnati's 8–1 win over St. Louis.

12th   After leading his club to an 0-6 start, Orioles manager Cal Ripken, Sr. is fired and replaced by Frank Robinson. Ripken was 68-101 since taking over for Earl Weaver last season.

Rangers pitcher Bobby Witt ties the AL record by committing 4 balks in a 4–1 loss to the Tigers.

13th   Oakland's Rick Honeycutt becomes the 2nd pitcher in as many days to tie the AL's 28-year-old balk record by committing 4 balks in 4 innings while saving a 12–7 win over Seattle. A ML-record 924 balks will be called this season after umpires are instructed to interpret the "complete stop" rule more strictly.

17th After 10 consecutive losses the Braves win their first game of the season 3–1 over the Dodgers. Atlanta's 0-10 start is the worst in NL history but not the worst in the major leagues this year.

20th The Orioles set a ML record for consecutive losses at the start of a season, falling to 0-14 with an 8–6 loss to the Brewers. The 1904 Senators and 1920 Tigers each lost their first 13 games of the season. It's not over yet for the O's.

Claudell Washington hits the 10,000th home run in Yankees history and Jack Clark hits his first AL home run in the top of the 10th inning to give New York a 7–6 win over Minnesota. The Yankees are the first ML club to hit 10,000 homers.

22nd The Cardinals trade veteran 2B Tom Herr to the Twins for OF Tom Brunansky.

26th Keith Hernandez hits 2 home runs (one is a grand slam) and drives in 7 runs to reach the 1,000 career RBI mark as the Mets pound the Braves 13–4.

27th Nolan Ryan no-hits the Phillies for 8⅓ innings before Mike Schmidt singles and Ryan ends up getting no decision in Houston's eventual 3–2, 10-inning win.

28th The Orioles set an AL record with their 21st consecutive loss 4–2 to the Twins, breaking the record shared by the 1906 Red Sox and the 1916 and 1943 A's.

29th Baltimore pounds Chicago 9–0 for its first win of the season, ending its losing streak. Mark Williamson and Dave Schmidt combine on the shutout.

30th Dave Winfield drives in his 28th and 29th runs of the season in New York's 15–3 rout of Texas, tying the ML record for RBI in April.

MAY

2nd Reds manager Pete Rose is suspended for 30 days by NL president Bart Giamatti, the stiffest suspension ever levied against a manager for an on-field incident. On April 30th Rose shoved umpire Dave Pallone in the 9th inning of a 6–5 loss to the Mets, inciting a near riot among Cincinnati fans.

Reds pitcher Ron Robinson is one out away from a perfect game against the Astros when pinch hitter Wallace Johnson singles, and Tim Raines follows with a home run. John Franco preserves the Reds' 3–2 victory.

4th Joe Niekro, 43, is released by the Twins, joining Steve Carlton and Tippy Martinez as the 3rd veteran pitcher to be released by the club since Opening Day.

8th Pittsburgh's Doug Drabek takes a no-hitter into the 9th before allowing a pinch single to Randy Ready and a home run to Marvell Wynne, but wins a 6–2 two-hitter over the Padres.

9th Jerry Reuss picks up his 200th career victory with 7⅓ shutout innings in Chicago's 3–0 win over Baltimore.

Oakland beats Detroit 3–1 to extend its club-record winning streak to 14 consecutive games, the longest in the majors since 1977. The A's will finally lose tomorrow 8–2 to the Tigers.

10th Mark Langston strikes out a 16 batters in a 4–2 win over Toronto, equaling the 1988 ML high set yesterday by Boston's Roger Clemens in a 2–0 three-hitter over the Royals.

11th Six games go into extra innings, tying the one-day ML record. The Mets beat the Astros 9–8 in 10; the Pirates beat the Dodgers 2–1 in 11; the Phillies beat the Reds 4–3 in 11; the Cubs beat the Padres 1–0 on Vance Law's 10th-inning squeeze bunt; the Giants beat the Cardinals 5–4 on Kevin Mitchell's home run in the 16th; and the Indians beat the Angels 4–3 on Bryan Harvey's 13th-inning balk.

14th IF Jose Oquendo becomes the first nonpitcher in 20 years to get a ML decision in the Cardinals' 7–5, 19-inning loss to the Braves. St. Louis had used 7 pitchers when Oquendo was brought in to pitch the 16th inning. He shut out the Braves for 3 innings before surrendering the game-winning 2 runs.

18th In Oakland's 39th game of the season, pitcher Dave Stewart breaks the ML record with his 12th balk in a 4–1 loss to the Red Sox. Stewart will finish the season with 16 balks.

In a deal made possible by the emergence of rookie 1B Mark Grace, the Cubs deal veteran 1B Leon Durham to the Reds for reliever Pat Perry.

20th Mike Schmidt hits his 535th career home run to move past Jimmie Foxx into 8th place on the all-time list, but the Phillies lose to San Diego 4–3.

22nd Pedro Guerrero throws his bat at David Cone after being hit by a pitch in the Dodgers' 5–2 loss to the Mets and will be suspended for 4 games by NL president Bart Giamatti.

23rd Braves manager Chuck Tanner is fired and replaced by Russ Nixon. The Braves were 12-27 under Tanner, last in the NL West.

27th Boston's Dwight Evans collects his 2,000th career hit, in a 3–2 Red Sox loss to Oakland.

28th The Padres fire manager Larry Bowa and replace him with Jack McKeon, who is also the club's vice president of baseball operations.

Seattle's infield records 22 assists in a 6–1 win over the Yankees, a ML record.

In his first start since 1981, Milwaukee's Odell Jones no-hits the Indians for 8⅓ innings before allowing a pinch single to Ron Washington. Dan Plesac saves the 2–0 victory.

31st Jeff Pico throws a 4-hit shutout against the Reds to win his ML debut with the Cubs 4–0.

JUNE

3rd The Royals trade P Bud Black to Cleveland for versatile Pat Tabler.

4th Rickey Henderson steals 2 bases in New York's 7–6, 14-inning loss to the Orioles, giving him a club-record 249 as a Yankee.

6th Dick Williams is fired as manager of the Mariners and replaced on an interim basis by 1B coach Jimmy Snyder. Seattle was 23-33 under Williams, 6th in the AL West.

Tom Browning no-hits the Padres for 8⅓ innings before allowing a single to Tony Gwynn, but finishes with an easy 12–0 one-hitter.

8th In a pair of trades, the Giants send OF Jeff Leonard to the Brewers for IF Ernest Riles, and the Reds deal P Dennis Rasmussen to the Padres for reliever Candy Sierra. Jose Rijo will replace Rasmussen in the Reds' starting rotation.

10th Dodgers OF John Shelby goes 0-for-4 in a 4–3 loss to the Padres, ending his hitting streak at 24 consecutive games.

11th DH Rick Rhoden for the Yankees hits a sacrifice fly in New York's 8–6 win over Baltimore. He is the first pitcher to start a game as a DH since the rule was adopted in 1973.

12th Robin Yount hits for the cycle, leading Milwaukee to a 16–2 rout of the White Sox.

Houston's Mike Scott is one out away from his 2nd career no-hitter when Ken Oberkfell singles, and Scott settles for a 5–0 one-hitter against the Braves.

19th Bert Blyleven wins his 250th career game as Minnesota beats Seattle 3–1. Jeff Reardon picks up his 20th save of the season, giving him 7 straight 20-save seasons.

23rd George Steinbrenner fires Billy Martin for the 5th time, replacing him with Lou Piniella. In 1985, Piniella was fired and replaced by Martin. In 1985, Martin was fired and replaced by Piniella. New York's 40-28 record is the 4th best in the big leagues, but the Yankees had just completed a 2-7 road trip.

24th Cleveland's Doug Jones celebrates his 31st birthday by saving his 14th game in 14 appearances, breaking the ML record for consecutive saves set last season by Steve Bedrosian. Jones retires all 7 batters he faces to close out the Indians' 7–5 win over the Yankees.

25th Cal Ripken, Jr. plays in his 1,000th consecutive game, a 10–3 loss to Boston. Ripken's streak is the 6th longest in ML history.

Expos P Floyd Youmans, who underwent alcohol rehabilitation last fall, is suspended indefinitely by Commissioner Peter Ueberroth for failing to comply with his drug-testing program.

30th Alarmed by the White Sox' threatened move to St. Petersburg, Florida, Illinois lawmakers grant state subsidies for a new stadium to replace venerable but decaying Comiskey Park.

JULY

3rd Oakland's Gene Nelson steals a base while pinch running for Don Baylor in a 9–8, 16-inning win over Toronto, becoming the first AL pitcher to steal a base since John "Blue Moon" Odom in 1973.

Jose Canseco's 3 HRs are not quite enough, and the game is not decided until Mark McGwire connects in the 16th inning to end it. McGwire will hit another 16th-inning HR to clip the Blue Jays tomorrow.

4th Kansas City releases pitcher Dan Quisenberry, whose 238 saves are the 4th most in ML history. He will sign with St. Louis next week.

Rangers P Charlie Hough strikes out 4 batters in the first inning of a 13–2 loss to the Yankees.

Doug Jones pitches 3 shutout innings but gets no decision in Cleveland's eventual 4–2, 16-inning loss to the A's, ending his ML-record streak of 15 consecutive saves.

NL umpire Lee Weyer, 51, dies of a heart attack after working the Cubs 3–2 win over San Francisco.

8th Cleveland's Bud Black hits Jack Howell, Devon White, and Johnny Ray with pitches in the 4th inning of a 10–6 loss to the Angels, tying the ML record.

9th Chris Speier hits for the cycle and Ernest Riles hits the 10,000th home run in Giants history to lead San Francisco to a 21–2 rout of the Cardinals. The 21 runs are a San Francisco record.

Nolan Ryan wins his 100th game as an Astro 6–3 over the Mets, and becomes the 7th pitcher in ML history to win 100 for 2 different clubs. Ryan won 138 games for the Angels in the 1970s.

12th After being maligned by the press as an unworthy All-Star starter, A's catcher Terry Steinbach hits a solo home run and a sacrifice fly to lead the AL to a 2–1 victory at Riverfront Stadium and is named the game's MVP.

13th The Red Sox fire manager John McNamara and replace him with 3B coach Joe Morgan. Boston was 43-42 under McNamara.

14th Ken Griffey singles for his 2,000th career hit in Atlanta's 9–8 loss to the Mets.

Mike Schmidt hits his 537th career home run in Philadelphia's 7–5 loss to Houston, moving past Mickey Mantle into 7th place all-time.

15th Roger Clemens strikes out 16 Royals for the 2nd time this season, sparking the Red Sox to a doubleheader sweep in Joe Morgan's managerial debut.

California's Bob Boone catches his 2,000th ML game as the Angels beat Detroit 6–4.

17th Philadelphia's Ricky Jordan homers in his first ML at bat and the Phillies go on to beat Houston 10–4.

18th Seattle's Gene Walter balks 4 times in 2⅓ innings in a 12–3 loss to Detroit. He is the 3rd AL pitcher to tie the ML record this season.

21st In a pair of trades, Seattle sends DH Ken Phelps to the Yankees for OF Jay Buhner and 1B-DH Steve Balboni, and deals OF Glenn Wilson to the Pirates for IF-OF Darnell Coles.

Red Sox veteran Jim Rice is suspended for 3 games by the club for shoving manager Joe Morgan. Rice was angered when Morgan replaced him with pinch hitter Spike Owen in the 8th inning of Boston's eventual 9–7 win over Minnesota.

27th Tommy John achieves what is believed to be a ML first by committing 3 errors on one play in the Yankees' 16–3 rout of the Brewers. The feat ties the ML record for errors in one inning by a pitcher.

29th Baltimore trades veteran pitcher Mike Boddicker to the Red Sox for minor leaguers Brady Anderson and Curt Schilling.

30th John Franco saves his 13th game of July in Cincinnati's 2–0 win over San Diego, setting a ML record for saves in one month.

31st Jose Canseco belts 2 home runs in the A's 6–2 win over Seattle to become the first player to hit 30 or more home runs in each of his first 3 ML seasons.

AUGUST

6th Pirates reliever Jim Gott balks 3 times in the 8th inning to force in the winning run in a 5–3 loss to the Mets.

Rich Gossage becomes the 2nd pitcher in ML history to record 300 saves by retiring one batter in the Cubs 7–4 win over Philadelphia.

7th Darnell Coles, Alvin Davis, Jim Presley, Jay Buhner, and Rey Quinones all hit sacrifice flies in a 12–7 win over Oakland, giving the Mariners a record.

8th The Cubs and Phillies attempt to play the first night game ever at Wrigley Field, but are rained out in the 4th inning with Chicago leading 3–1.

9th The Cubs and Mets play the first official night game at Wrigley Field, a 6–4 Chicago victory. New York's Lenny Dykstra hits the first night home run, supplanting Phil Bradley, whose leadoff home run last night was washed out.

10th The Dodgers release Don Sutton, the 12th-winningest pitcher in ML history and the club's all-time victory leader.

11th After going 225 at bats, Gary Carter finally hits his 300th career home run as the Mets beat the Cubs 9–6.

12th The Red Sox beat the Tigers 9–4 for their 23rd consecutive win at home, breaking the AL record held by the 1931 A's. Boston has not lost at Fenway Park since June 24th.

14th Detroit pounds Boston 18–6 at Fenway Park to end the Red Sox' AL-record home winning streak at 24 games, 2 shy of the ML record held by the 1916 Giants. Roger Clemens gives up 8 runs in 1⅓ innings.

16th The Dodgers trade Pedro Guerrero to the Cardinals for pitcher John Tudor, whose 2.29 ERA is leading the NL.

27th Tommy Lasorda wins his 1,000th game as a manager as Los Angeles tops Philadelphia 4–2.

30th Kent Tekulve becomes the 2nd pitcher in ML history to appear in 1,000 games by pitching 2 innings in Philadelphia's 7–5 win over San Francisco.

31st Arbitrator George Nicolau rules against the ML owners in the "Collusion II" case, agreeing with the players' contention that the owners had conspired to fix the free-agent market after the 1986 season. Twelve players will be granted no-risk free agency after the season.

The first-place Tigers try for pennant insurance: Ted Power from Kansas City and Fred Lynn from Baltimore for players to be named later.

SEPTEMBER

3rd Dennis Eckersley sets an A's record with his 37th save of the season in Oakland's 5–4 win over New York. Eckersley will save 45 games this season, one shy of Dave Righetti's ML record.

4th Cincinnati's Danny Jackson becomes the NL's first 20-game winner by shutting out the Cubs on 6 hits as the Reds romp 17–0.

8th NL president Bart Giamatti is unanimously elected baseball's 7th commissioner, and will succeed Peter Ueberroth next season.

9th Bruce Sutter joins Rollie Fingers and Rich Gossage as the only pitchers to save 300 games as Atlanta beats San Diego 5–4 in 11 innings.

10th Orel Hershiser shuts out the Reds 5–0 to become a 20-game winner for the first time. It is his 2nd straight shutout.

12th Baltimore's Eddie Murray collects his 2,000th career hit in a 6–1 loss to Boston, and Atlanta's Dale Murphy drives in his 1,000th career run in a 5–4 loss to Los Angeles.

14th Mike Greenwell hits for the cycle to help Mike Boddicker earn a victory in his first game against his former club, a 4–3 Boston win over the Orioles.

16th Cincinnati's Tom Browning pitches the 14th perfect game in ML history, striking out 7 in a 1–0 win over the Dodgers. Tracy Woodson strikes out to end the only no-hitter in the major leagues this season.

17th Jeff Reardon saves his 40th game of the season in Minnesota's 3–1 win over Chicago, becoming the first pitcher ever to save 40 games in a season in each league. Reardon saved 41 for the Expos in 1985.

18th Baltimore's Bob Milacki allows one hit over 8 innings in his ML debut and Tom Niedenfuer pitches the 9th to complete a 2–0 one-hitter against the Tigers.

19th Oakland clinches the AL West title with a 5–3 win over the 2nd-place Twins.

20th Wade Boggs goes 3-for-3 in Boston's 13–2 rout of Toronto to become the first player this century to collect 200 hits in 6 consecutive seasons. Willie Keeler had 8 straight 200-hit seasons from 1894-1901.

Darrell Evans hits his 400th career home run off John Farrell in the 5th inning, and Chet Lemon hits his 200th career home run off Scott Bailes in the bottom of the 9th to lead Detroit to a 3–1 win over Cleveland.

22nd The Mets clinch their 2nd NL East title in 3 years with a 3–1 win over Philadelphia.

23rd The Angels fire manager Cookie Rojas and the Phillies fire manager Lee Elia. Moose Stubing

(California) and John Vukovich (Philadelphia) will manage the clubs for the remainder of this season.

Oakland's Jose Canseco becomes the founder of baseball's 40-HR, 40-SB club by stealing two bases in a 9–8, 14-inning win over Milwaukee. He also hits his 41st home run.

24th Toronto's Dave Stieb is one out away from a no-hitter when Julio Franco's apparent game-ending grounder takes a bad hop over 2B Manny Lee's head and Stieb is forced to settle for a 1–0 one-hitter.

Dave Stewart wins his 20th game of the season and the A's win their 100th 5–2 over Milwaukee.

26th The Dodgers beat the Padres 3–2 to clinch the NL West title and earn a playoff date with the Mets, who won 10 of their 11 meetings this season.

28th In his last start of the regular season, Orel Hershiser pitches 10 shutout innings to extend his consecutive-scoreless-inning streak to 59, breaking Dodger Don Drysdale's ML record by one. San Diego's Andy Hawkins also pitches 10 shutout innings and the Padres eventually win 2–1 on Mark Parent's home run in the bottom of the 16th.

29th The Cubs trade veteran C Jody Davis to the Braves for pitchers Kevin Coffman and Kevin Blankenship.

30th The Red Sox lose to Cleveland 3–2 but clinch the AL East title anyway when 2nd-place Milwaukee loses to Oakland 7–1.

Dave Stieb is one out away from a no-hitter for the 2nd consecutive game, but falls short again when Jim Traber bloops a single over the head of 1B Fred McGriff. Stieb finishes with his 2nd straight one-hitter 4–0 over the Orioles.

New York's David Cone beats St. Louis 4–2 to improve his record to 20-3.

OCTOBER

1st Boston's Jeff Sellers no-hits the Indians for 7⅓ innings before Luis Medina homers and Cleveland goes on to win 1–0.

2nd Minnesota's season-ending 3–2 win over the Angels is watched by 35,952 fans, making the Twins the first AL club ever to break 3 million in season attendance.

3rd After 2 disappointing seasons in Philadelphia, C Lance Parrish is traded to to California for a minor leaguer.

Astros manager Hal Lanier is fired after leading the club to an 82-80 record.

Cardinals coach Nick Leyva becomes the Phillies 3rd manager in 3 years, replacing Lee Elia, who was fired in September.

4th Dwight Gooden and Orel Hershisher start but neither get the decision. New York rallies for three 9th-inning runs to win the opening NLCS game over the Dodgers 3-2.

5th Tim Belcher strikes outs 10 Mets to give the Dodgers a 6–3 win in game 2.

Oakland wins the ALCS opener 2–1 over Boston.

6th Canseco's 2-run HR in the 3rd ties the game and Oakland goes on to win 4–3.

7th Lou Piniella is fired as manager of the Yankees for the 2nd time, and Jim Fregosi is fired as manager of the White Sox. Dallas Green replaces Piniella, while Yankee coach Jeff Torborg will eventually replace Fregosi on November 3rd.

8th Dodgers ace reliever Jay Howell is ejected in the 8th inning of game 3 of the NLCS for having pine tar on his glove, and the Mets go on to score 5 times in the inning on the way to an 8–4 win. Howell will be suspended for 3 days by the NL.

Down 5–0, Oakland cracks 4 HRs to beat Boston 10–6 for their 3rd win.

9th Oakland beats Boston 4–1 to complete a 4-game sweep of the ALCS. Dennis Eckersley saves all 4 games and is named series MVP.

Mike Scioscia's 9th-inning 2-run HR powers the Dodgers to a 5–4 win.

10th The Dodgers take a 6–0 lead and hold on to beat the Mets 7–4.

11th David Cone's 5-hitter evens the NLCS at 3 apiece. New York wins 5–1.

12th Series MVP Orel Hershiser shuts out New York on 5 hits to win game 7 of the NLCS 6–0 and put the Dodgers into the World Series for the first time since 1981.

15th In one of the most improbable finishes in World Series history, pinch hitter Kirk Gibson hits a 2-run home run off Dennis Eckersley with 2 out in the bottom of the 9th inning to give the Dodgers a 5–4 win in game one. The injured Gibson was not expected to play in the NLCS, and will not play again in the Series. It is the first World Series game to end on a home run since game 6 in 1975.

16th Orel Hershiser gives up 3 hits and hits 3 himself to beat Oakland 6–0.

18th Mark McGwire's home run off Jay Howell in the bottom of the 9th gives Oakland a 2–1 win in game 3 of the World Series.

19th The Dodgers win 4–3, taking advantage of Oakland errors to beat Dave Stewart.

20th Series MVP Orel Hershiser ends his dream season with a 5–2 four-hitter over the A's in game 5 of the World Series, which gives the Dodgers their first World Championship since 1981. Los Angeles is the only team to win more than one World Series in the 1980s.

24th Less than a year after signing him as a free agent, the Yankees trade 1B-DH Jack Clark to the Padres with P Pat Clements for pitchers Lance McCullers, Jimmy Jones, and Stan Jefferson.

The Phillies trade P Shane Rawley to Minnesota for 2B Tom Herr, OF Eric Bullock, and C Tom Nieto.

28th The Tigers trade P Walt Terrell to San Diego for versatile Keith Moreland and 3B Chris Brown.

NOVEMBER

1st Chris Sabo, who hit .271 with 11 home runs and 46 stolen bases as the Reds 3B, wins the NL Rookie of the Year award. Chicago's Mark Grace is runner-up.

2nd Oakland SS Walt Weiss becomes the 3rd consecutive A's player to win the AL Rookie of the Year award, joining sluggers Jose Canseco (1986) and Mark McGwire (1987).

3rd Veteran pitcher Bert Blyleven changes clubs for the 5th time, going from the Twins to the Angels for a package of minor leaguers.

7th Art Howe, who played for Houston from 1976-83, is named manager of the Astros, while Jim Lefebvre is named manager of the Mariners.

10th Orel Hershiser (23-8) is a unanimous choice as NL Cy Young Award winner.

14th Doug Rader, who piloted the Rangers from 1982-85, is named manager of the California Angels.

15th Dodgers OF Kirk Gibson wins the NL MVP Award, edging Mets Darryl Strawberry and Kevin McReynolds. Gibson hit .290 with 25 home runs and just 76 RBI.

16th Jose Canseco becomes the first unanimous AL MVP since Reggie Jackson in 1973.

23rd Free-agent 2B Steve Sax leaves the World Champion Dodgers and signs a 3-year contract with the Yankees.

28th Mike Moore, 9-15 last season for Seattle, signs as a free agent with the AL champion A's.

28th The Red Sox sign Rich Gedman to a one-year, $1.2 million contract that makes him the highest-paid catcher in the AL. He will hit .212 in 1989.

30th The Royals sign veteran catcher Bob Boone, who hit a career-high .295 last season.

DECEMBER

3rd Two free-agent pitchers sign 3-year contracts, Jesse Orosco with Cleveland and Dave LaPoint with the Yankees.

4th The Orioles trade veteran 1B Eddie Murray to the Dodgers for pitchers Ken Howell and Brian Holton and infield prospect Juan Bell.

5th The Cubs and Rangers complete a 9-player swap, with Chicago giving up OF Rafael Palmeiro, P Jamie Moyer, and P Drew Hall in exchange for IF Curtis Wilkerson and pitchers Mitch Williams, Paul Kilgus, and Steve Wilson, and a pair of minor leaguers to be named.

6th The Rangers complete their 2nd major trade in as many days, sending 1B Pete O'Brien, OF Oddibe McDowell, and 2B Jerry Browne to Cleveland for 2B Julio Franco. The Expos and Phillies also complete a trade, P Kevin Gross to Montreal for pitchers Jeff Parrett and Floyd Youmans.

7th The Rangers sign free-agent pitcher Nolan Ryan to a one-year contract.

8th Pitcher Bruce Hurst, considered the cream of this year's free-agent crop, signs a 3-year contract with the Padres. The Yankees sign free-agent pitcher Andy

Hawkins, and the Expos trade P John Dopson and SS Luis Rivera to Boston for SS Spike Owen, and OF Tracy Jones to San Francisco for OF-1B Mike Aldrete.

10th Free-agent Willie Randolph signs with the Dodgers. He will replace Steve Sax in the lineup, who earlier this month signed with Randolph's former club, the Yankees.

13th The Red Sox trade 1B-OF Todd Benzinger, P Jeff Sellers, and a player to be named later to the Reds for 1B Nick Esasky and P Rob Murphy.

1989

JANUARY

5th Three weeks after signing a record 4-year, $1.1 billion network television contract with CBS, major league baseball signs a $400 million contract with ESPN that will put 175 games per year on cable television beginning in 1990.

9th Johnny Bench and Carl Yastrzemski are elected to the Hall of Fame by the BBWAA in their first year of eligibility. Bench was named on 96.4 percent of the ballots, the 3rd-highest figure in history behind Ty Cobb and Hank Aaron.

17th Free-agent Claudell Washington leaves the Yankees to sign a 3-year contract with the Angels.

26th Last season's tougher balk rules are rescinded, and the rule is returned to its pre-1988 form.

29th The game-winning RBI is dropped as an official statistic after 9 years of use. The Mets Keith Hernandez is the all-time leader with 129.

FEBRUARY

2nd Bill White, a 6-time All-Star and longtime Yankees broadcaster, is elected president of the National League. He becomes the highest-ranking black official in American professional sports.

16th Orel Hershiser becomes the first player in ML history to sign a contract that calls for a $3 million salary by inking a 3-year, $7.9 million contract with the Dodgers that will pay him $3,166,667 in 1991.

21st Reds manager Pete Rose meets with Commissioner Peter Ueberroth and Commissioner-elect Bart Giamatti to discuss his gambling habits. "You can read anything you want into it," says Rose. "But I don't see anything bad."

26th A California court throws out a major part of Margo Adams $12 million breach-of-contract suit against Red Sox 3B Wade Boggs. Adams claimed that Boggs had promised her a salary and expenses during a 4-year affair.

28th Red Schoendienst, a former 2B and manager of the Cardinals, and Al Barlick, a ML umpire for over 29 seasons, are elected to the Hall of Fame by the Special Veterans Committee.

MARCH

9th Bob Horner, 31, announces his retirement because of a damaged left shoulder.

19th With Dave Winfield sidelined, the Yankees trade C Joel Skinner and a minor leaguer to the Indians for OF Mel Hall. Winfield will miss all of the 1989 season after undergoing back surgery.

20th The commissioner's office announces that Reds manager Pete Rose is under investigation for unnamed "serious allegations."

25th The Indians and Pirates swap shortstops, with Felix Fermin going to Cleveland in exchange for Jay Bell.

28th AL umpire Nick Bremigan, 43, dies of a heart attack.

APRIL

3rd The Mets win their 11th consecutive home opener 8–4 over St. Louis at Shea Stadium. New York has won on Opening Day in 18 of the last 20 seasons.

4th Forty-five-year-old Tommy John starts for the Yankees on Opening Day and sets a modern ML record by appearing in his 26th season. He also wins his 287th game 4–2 over the Twins.

Rangers DH Buddy Bell gets his 2,500th career hit, a single off Jack Morris in a 4–0 win over Detroit.

6th In his first start of the season, Orel Hershiser gives up a run in the first inning of a 4–3 loss to the Reds to end his ML-record consecutive-scoreless-inning streak at 59.

8th One-handed pitcher Jim Abbott makes his ML debut but lasts only 4⅔ innings in California's 7–0 loss to Seattle. Abbott, who bypassed the minors completely after starring at the University of Michigan, will finish the season 12-12 with a 3.92 ERA.

9th Rickey Henderson steals his 800th career base in New York's 4–3 loss to the Indians.

10th Dave Stieb pitches a one-hitter against the Yankees, giving him 3 one-hitters in his last 4 starts (dating back to last September). Jamie Quirk's 5th-inning single is the only hit off Stieb in the 8–0 Blue Jays' victory.

Ken Griffey, Jr. hits his first ML home run in Seattle's 6–5 win over the White Sox. He and his father, a reserve outfielder on the Reds, are the first father-and-son duo to play in the major leagues at the same time.

San Diego's Bruce Hurst pitches a one-hitter and collects his first ML hit in a 5–2 win over the Braves.

Eddie Murray hits his first NL home run, a grand slam in the top of the 9th inning that leads the Dodgers to a 7–4 win over the Giants. It is Murray's 15th career grand slam.

11th At Washington's RFK Stadium, the Soviet national baseball team loses to George Washington University 20–1. Soviet 1B Nugzar Pophadze stuns the crowd with a long HR in the left-field stands, one of 2 Russian hits. Two days earlier, the Russians were beaten 21–1 by a team from Annapolis.

12th In his 2nd start for Texas, Nolan Ryan no-hits the Brewers for 7 innings before Terry Francona singles. Ryan also sets a club record with 15 strikeouts on the way to an 8–1 win.

16th Kelly Gruber becomes the first Blue Jay to hit for the cycle as Toronto beats Kansas City 15–8.

17th Kent Tekulve pitches 2 shutout innings in the Reds 3–2, 10-inning win over the Dodgers to pass Hoyt Wilhelm as the major leagues' all-time leader in relief appearances with 1,019.

19th Mets SS Kevin Elster plays his 73rd consecutive errorless game in a 4–2 win over the Phillies, breaking Ed Brinkman's ML record for shortstops.

23rd Nolan Ryan is 2 outs from a no-hitter when Nelson Liriano triples and Ryan settles for a 4–1 one-hitter over the Blue Jays. It is Ryan's 10th career one-hitter.

28th Nelson Liriano breaks up a no-hitter in the 9th inning for the 2nd time in 6 days, ending Kirk McCaskill's bid with a pinch-hit double. McCaskill settles for a 9–0 one-hitter.

30th The Yankees trade 23-year-old lefthander Al Leiter to the Blue Jays for OF Jesse Barfield.

MAY

4th Toronto's Junior Felix hits the first pitch he sees in the big leagues for a home run off Kirk McCaskill, but the Blue Jays lose 3–2 in 10 innings. He is the 57th player ever to homer in his first ML at bat, and the 11th to do so on the first pitch.

Cleveland's John Farrell no-hits the Royals for 8 innings before Kevin Seitzer singles. Doug Jones nails down the 3–1 one-hitter.

9th For the first time since April 10th, no ML games are shutouts, ending a streak of 29 consecutive days with at least one shutout.

Mets SS Kevin Elster and Red Sox catcher Rick Cerone end their ML-record errorless game streaks for their positions. Elster had played 88 consecutive games without an error while Cerone had played 159.

10th Mark Langston no-hits Toronto for 8 innings before Tom Lawless singles and the Blue Jays rally for 3 runs to beat Seattle 3–2. It is the 3rd time this season that the Blue Jays have broken up a no-hit bid in the 9th inning.

11th Just 3 days after vetoing a proposed trade to Pittsburgh for OF Glenn Wilson, 37-year-old catcher Alan Ashby is waived by the Astros.

The Tigers, with the worst record in the ML, lose 3–1 to their Toledo farm club. The winning pitcher is 40-year-old Mud Hens manager John Wockenfuss, who never pitched during his 12-year ML career.

12th San Francisco's Rick Reuschel beats Montreal 2–1 for his 200th ML win.

13th Kirby Puckett hits 4 doubles in the Twins 10–8 win over the Blue Jays, tying the ML single-game record. He will hit 2 more doubles in a 13–1 win tomorrow to tie the 2-game record.

15th The Blue Jays fire manager Jimy Williams and replace him with hitting coach Cito Gaston. Williams led the club to a 12-24 start and had several publicized run-ins with star slugger George Bell, who refused to be the DH.

23rd Cleveland loses to Detroit 7–2 to drop its record to 21-22, but remains in first place in the AL East by percentage points. It is the latest in a season a sub-.500 team has ever been in first place.

24th Yankees reliever Lee Guetterman gives up 5 runs in the 9th inning of New York's 11–4 loss to California, ending his consecutive scoreless inning streak at 30⅔. It is the longest season-opening streak in the majors since Harry Brecheen's in 1948, and the longest season-opening streak ever by a reliever.

25th After shopping him for several months, the Mariners finally trade star pitcher Mark Langston to

Montreal for pitchers Randy Johnson, Brian Holman, and Gene Harris.

29th   Phillies 3B Mike Schmidt, 39, retires. He is 7th on the all-time home run list with 548, but was hitting just .203 this season.

31st   Cito Gaston is named manager of the Blue Jays on a permanent basis.

The Senior Professional Baseball Association announces that it will begin its inaugural season on November 1st with 8 teams of players age 35 and over.

JUNE

2nd   Eric Davis hits for the cycle in Cincinnati's 9–4 win over San Diego, becoming the first Red to do so since Frank Robinson in 1959.

3rd   Nolan Ryan pitches his 2nd one-hitter this season and 11th overall, allowing only a first-inning single to Harold Reynolds, in a 6–1 win over Seattle. Ryan also strikes out 11 to tie Don Sutton's ML record of 21 seasons with at least 100 strikeouts.

Houston beats Los Angeles 5–4 in 22 innings in a game that takes 7:14 to complete. When the Dodgers run out of players, 3B Jeff Hamilton becomes the losing pitcher and P Fernando Valenzuela finishes the game at 1B.

4th   Toronto beats Boston 13–11 in 12 innings after trailing 10–0 after 6. It is the biggest lead the Red Sox have ever blown, and is also their 12th consecutive loss to the Blue Jays at Fenway.

5th   The Toronto SkyDome opens, but the Blue Jays lose 5–3 to the Brewers. Baseball's newest and most modern stadium features a fully retractable roof, a hotel, the world's largest video display board, and a Hard Rock Cafe.

The Orioles select Louisiana State University pitcher Ben McDonald with the first pick in the annual amateur draft.

6th   San Francisco's Kevin Mitchell hits 3 home runs in a doubleheader split with Cincinnati, giving him 22 already this season.

8th   After taking a 10–0 lead in the top of the first inning (Pittsburgh's best inning since 1942), the Pirates lose to the Phillies 15–11. After the season, Pirates broadcaster Jim Rooker will conduct a charity walk from Philadelphia to Pittsburgh as a result of his on-air promise to walk home if the Pirates blew their early lead.

9th   Mets OF Darryl Strawberry hits his 200th career home run in a 4–3, 10-inning loss to Pittsburgh.

12th   Cardinals utilityman Tim Jones plays catcher during a 10–3 loss to the Cubs, becoming the first player named Jones to catch in the major leagues since Philadelphia's Bill Jones caught 4 games in the Union Association in 1884.

13th   Despite this year's relaxed balk rule, Red Sox pitcher John Dopson manages to tie the AL record with 4 balks in just 3⅔ innings in Boston's 8–7 win over Detroit.

Houston's Terry Puhl plays in his 1,403rd ML game, a 3–2 loss to the Dodgers, to break Jack Graney's record for Canadian–born players.

San Diego's Jack Clark strikes out 4 times in a 9–6 loss to the Reds, giving him a ML-record 9 strikeouts in 2 games. Clark struck out 5 times against the Giants on June 11th.

16th   Rick Wolff, 37, writing an article on minor-league baseball for *Sports Illustrated,* finishes a 3-day stint playing 2B for the South Bend White Sox (Midwest League). He replaces Cesar Bernhardt and goes 4-for-7 against the Burlington Braves. Wolff will finish the year with the highest average of any Chicago White Sox farmhand.

18th   The struggling Phillies trade. Reliever Steve Bedrosian and a player to be named later go to the Giants for pitchers Dennis Cook and Terry Mulholland and 3B Charlie Hayes, then send 2B-OF Juan Samuel to the Mets for OF Len Dykstra, P Roger McDowell, and another player to be named later.

19th   Mets pitcher Dwight Gooden wins his 100th career game, 5–3 over the Expos. His 100-37 career record is 2nd only to Whitey Ford's 100-36 start.

21st   The Yankees trade OF Rickey Henderson back to the A's for journeymen pitchers Eric Plunk and Greg Cadaret and OF Luis Polonia.

24th   Cleveland's Joe Carter hits 3 home runs in a game for the 3rd time in his career as the Indians beat Texas 7–3.

Cardinals OF Vince Coleman steals his 39th and 40th consecutive bases in a 5–2 loss to the Pirates to break the ML record set by Davey Lopes in 1975.

Coleman has not been caught stealing since last September 15th.

25th The Mets' defense does not record a single assist in a 5–1 win over Philadelphia, tying the ML record set by the Indians in 1945. New York pitchers retire the Phillies on 13 strikeouts, 12 fly outs, and 2 ground balls to 1B.

29th Boise (Northwest League) manager Mal Finchman is ejected during an 8–4 loss to Salem, but returns to the field disguised as Humphrey the Hawk, the club's mascot. He will be suspended one game for the stunt.

JULY

2nd Brewers OF Robin Yount, 33, collects his 2,500th hit in a 10–2 win over the Yankees. Ty Cobb, Rogers Hornsby, Hank Aaron, and Mel Ott are the only players to reach that milestone at a younger age.

The Braves send OF Dion James to the Indians for OF Oddibe McDowell, and P Zane Smith to Montreal for 3 minor leaguers.

4th Cincinnati's Tom Browning is 3 outs away from his 2nd career perfect game when Dickie Thon doubles, and Browning is eventually relieved by John Franco in a 2–1 win over Philadelphia.

5th Barry Bonds homers in Pittsburgh's 6–4 loss to the Giants, giving Barry and father Bobby the ML father-and-son home run record with 408. The Bells (Gus and Buddy) and the Berras (Yogi and Dale) had shared the record of 407.

6th Despite having retired on May 29th, Mike Schmidt is elected to start at 3B for the NL in the All-Star Game. A's OF Jose Canseco, who has not played all season because of a wrist injury, is picked to start for the AL, but neither will play in the game.

11th Bo Jackson and Wade Boggs lead off the bottom of the first inning with back-to-back home runs off Rick Reuschel to spark the AL to a 5–3 win in the All-Star Game at Anaheim Stadium. Jackson earns MVP honors.

14th The Mets Sid Fernandez strikes out 16 Braves, but still loses 3-2 on Lonnie Smith's leadoff home run in the bottom of the ninth.

15th Jeff Reardon saves his 250th game as the Twins beat the Red Sox 3–2.

17th White Sox C Carlton Fisk gets his 2,000th career hit in a 7–3 win over the Yankees.

Reds reliever Kent Tekulve retires, just 20 appearances shy of Hoyt Wilhelm's all-time games-pitched record of 1,070. Tekulve had posted a 5.02 ERA in 37 games this season.

18th Donnie Moore, 35, shoots himself to death at his home after shooting and critically wounding his estranged wife Tonya. Friends said Moore was haunted by the 2-run home run he surrendered to Dave Henderson in game 5 of the 1986 ALCS, costing the Angels a trip to the World Series, and that he had been even more depressed since his release last month by minor league Omaha.

The Dodgers trade P Tim Leary and SS Mariano Duncan to the Reds for OF Kal Daniels and IF Lenny Harris.

19th Cleveland's Joe Carter hits 3 home runs in a game for the 2nd time this season in a 10–1 win over Minnesota. It is his 4th career 3-HR game, tying Lou Gehrig's AL record, and also gives him a ML-record-tying 5 homers in 2 games.

22nd The Yankees trade 3B Mike Pagliarulo to San Diego for pitcher Walt Terrell.

Johnny Bench, Carl Yastrzemski, Red Schoendienst, and Al Barlick are inducted into the Hall of Fame at ceremonies in Cooperstown, New York.

27th Atlanta's Dale Murphy hits 2 home runs in the 6th inning of a 10–1 rout of San Francisco, becoming the first Brave to accomplish the feat since Robert Lowe in 1894. Murphy also drives in 6 runs in the inning to tie another ML record.

28th Cardinal Vince Coleman is caught stealing by Nelson Santovenia in a 2–0 win over Montreal, ending his ML-record streak of 50 consecutive stolen bases.

29th The White Sox trade their all-time home run leader, Harold Baines, and IF Fred Manrique to the Rangers for IF Scott Fletcher, OF Sammy Sosa, and P Wilson Alvarez.

31st The Twins trade AL Cy Young Award winner Frank Viola to the Mets for 5 players, including pitchers Rick Aguilera, David West and minor leaguer Kevin Tapani. Viola is the first Cy Young winner to be traded during the following season.

AUGUST

1st The Mets trade OF Mookie Wilson to the Blue Jays for P Jeff Musselman and minor leaguer Mike Brady.

3rd The Reds score 14 runs in the first inning of an 18–2 demolition of the Astros. ML records set during the onslaught include most hits in an inning (16), most players with 2 hits in an inning (7), and most singles in an inning (12). Mariano Duncan and Luis Quinones each tie the ML record by batting 3 times.

4th Hard-luck pitcher Dave Stieb loses a perfect game when New York's Roberto Kelly doubles with 2 out in the 9th inning, and Stieb finishes with a 2–1 two-hitter. It is the 3rd time that Stieb has lost a no-hitter with 2 out in the 9th.

8th Mauro Gozzo pitches 8 shutout innings in his ML debut as Toronto beats Texas 7–0 to go over .500 for the first time since Opening Day. The Blue Jays will eventually overtake the surprising Orioles and win the AL East.

10th Nolan Ryan falls short in yet another no-hit bid, giving up a one-out single to Dave Bergman in the 9th inning and eventually needing relief in a 4–1 win over the Tigers.

15th In his 2nd start since returning to the major leagues after cancer treatment, the Giants Dave Dravecky breaks his pitching arm while throwing to Tim Raines in the 6th inning of a 3–2 San Francisco win. Dravecky will not pitch again in the major leagues.

Rangers Charlie Hough pitches his 2nd career one-hitter and gets his 2nd career one-hit loss 2–0 to Seattle. Hough walks 5, balks, and throws a wild pitch, while the Rangers collect 13 hits but no runs, one hit shy of the ML record while being shut out.

16th Yankees OF Luis Polonia is arrested in his hotel room for having sex with a 15-year-old girl. He will be sentenced to 60 days in jail after the season.

Lefty Tom Drees, 26, pitches his 3rd no-hitter of the season for Vancouver (Triple A), beating Las Vegas 5–0 in the 7-inning opener of doubleheader. He beat Calgary 1–0 in 9 innings (May 23rd) and Edmonton in 7 (May 28th).

17th Orioles SS Cal Ripken plays in his 1,208th consecutive game to move past Steve Garvey into 3rd place on the all–time list. He goes 3-for-5 with a home run to help Baltimore to an 11–6 win over Toronto.

18th Andre Dawson gets his 2,000th career hit in the Cubs' 6–5 loss to Houston.

Dallas Green is fired as manager of the Yankees and replaced by former SS Bucky Dent. It is the 17th time the Yankees have changed managers since George Steinbrenner took over the club in 1973.

The Astros trade Billy Hatcher to the Pirates for Glenn Wilson.

20th Howard Johnson hits his 30th home run of the season in the Mets 5–4 loss to the Dodgers and joins Barry Bonds and Willie Mays as the only players to achieve 30 HRs and 30 SBs in 2 different seasons.

21st Cubs rookie OF Jerome Walton goes 0-for-4 in a 6–5, 10-inning loss to the Reds, ending his hitting streak at 30 consecutive games.

22nd Nolan Ryan strikes out Rickey Henderson in the 5th inning of a 2–0 loss to Oakland to become the only pitcher in ML history to strike out 5,000 batters.

Cleveland's Felix Fermin ties the ML record with 4 sacrifice bunts in a 3–2, 10-inning win over Seattle. He is the first player to accomplish the feat since Ray Chapman in 1919.

In his only inning of work, Braves reliever Paul Assenmacher strikes out 4 batters in the 5th inning of a 10–5 loss to St. Louis.

23rd Rick Dempsey homers off Dennis Martinez in the top of the 22nd inning to break up a scoreless tie and give the Dodgers a 1–0 win over the Expos. Expos pitchers issue no walks during the 6:14 marathon.

24th After weeks of legal wrangling, Commissioner Bart Giamatti permanently bans Pete Rose from baseball for his alleged gambling on ML games. Although the 5-page document signed by both parties includes no formal findings, Giamatti says that he considers Rose's acceptance of the ban to be a no-contest plea to the charges. Coach Tommy Helms is named Rose's interim replacement as Cincinnati manager.

25th Pittsburgh's Gary Redus hits for the cycle in a 12–3 win over the Reds.

26th Toronto's Dave Stieb pitches his 5th career one-hitter, 7–0 over Milwaukee. The spoiler is Robin Yount's 6th-inning single.

28th Frank Viola and the Mets outduel Orel Hershiser and the Dodgers 1–0 in the first-ever regular-season matchup of defending Cy Young Award winners.

29th Trailing 9–0 after 5 innings, the Cubs rally to beat Houston 10–9 in 10 innings. Rafael Ramirez drives in 7 runs for the Astros.

30th St. Louis leaves 16 runners on base in a 2–0, 13-inning loss to the Reds, setting a ML record for runners left on base in a shutout.

31st Arbitrator Thomas Roberts orders the ML owners to pay $10.5 million in damages as a result of their collusion against free agents after the 1985 season.

SEPTEMBER

1st Eight days after banning Pete Rose from baseball for life, Commissioner Bart Giamatti dies suddenly of a heart attack at the age of 51.

4th Fred Lynn hits his 300th career home run to help the Tigers to a 5–1 win over Kansas City.

8th Kansas City's George Brett singles for his 2,500th career hit in a 6–0 win over the Twins.

10th Five days after hitting a home run for the Yankees in a 12–2 win over the Mariners, Deion Sanders returns a punt 68 yards for a touchdown in his NFL debut with the Atlanta Falcons. Sanders hit .234 in 14 games for New York this year in his first attempt at playing 2 sports professionally.

12th The Indians fire manager Doc Edwards and replace him for the remainder of the season with scout John Hart.

13th Fay Vincent is elected baseball's 8th commissioner, succeeding the late Bart Giamatti, whom he served as deputy commissioner.

14th The ML owners approve the sale of the Mariners to Jeff Smulyan and Michael Browning for $77 million, the highest price ever paid for an AL club.

Jeff Reardon saves Minnesota's 2–0 win over Toronto to become the first pitcher ever to record at least 30 saves in 5 consecutive seasons.

Houston's Mike Scott (20-8) becomes a 20-game winner for the first time by beating the Dodgers 11–3. He is the first ML pitcher to reach that plateau this season.

19th San Diego's Mark Davis becomes the 7th pitcher ever to save 40 games in a season by nailing down the Padres' 5–1 win over the Reds. He will finish the season with 44 saves, one shy of Bruce Sutter's NL record.

22nd Dave Stewart becomes the first pitcher since Jim Palmer (1975-78) to win 20 games in 3 straight seasons by beating the Twins 5–2. It is also Stewart's 100th ML win.

25th Wade Boggs goes 4-for-5 in a 7–4 win over the Yankees to become the first player in ML history to achieve both 200 hits and 100 walks in 4 consecutive seasons. It is Boggs's 7th straight 200-hit season overall, extending his own modern ML record.

The Red Sox say that they will not exercise their option on Jim Rice's contract next season, while Bob Stanley, the team's all-time save leader with 132, announces his retirement.

26th The Cubs become the first team to clinch a division title this season, wrapping up the NL East with a 3–2 win over the Expos.

27th The 2 San Francisco Bay teams clinch their divisions. Oakland wins the AL West by beating Texas 5–0, while San Francisco loses 1–0 to the Dodgers but is assured of the NL West crown when the 2nd-place Padres lose to the Reds 2–1 in 13 innings.

30th The Blue Jays earn the final spot in the playoffs by scoring 3 runs in the bottom of the 8th to beat Baltimore 4–3 and clinch the AL East. The surprising Orioles led the division most of the season and will finish 2nd just one season after losing 107 games.

Nolan Ryan strikes out 13 Angels in a 2–0 three-hitter to raise his season total to 301. It is his 6th 300-strikeout season, but first since 1977.

OCTOBER

1st Minnesota's Kirby Puckett and San Diego's Tony Gwynn each win batting titles on the final day of the regular season. Puckett goes 2-for-5 to edge Carney Lansford .339 to .336, while Gwynn goes 3-for-4 to beat Will Clark .336 to .333.

3rd Oakland's Dave Stewart wins the ALCS opener 7–3 over Toronto.

4th Will Clark goes 4-for-4 with 2 home runs, including the first NLCS grand slam since 1977, to lead the Giants to a 11–3 win over the Cubs in game one of the NL playoffs. Clark's 6 RBI tie Bobby Richardson's single-game post season record set in the 1960 World Series.

Rickey Henderson swipes 4 bases as Oakland beats Toronto again 6–3.

5th The Cubs even the NLCS with 6 runs in the first inning. Jerome Walton has 2 hits in the outburst. Chicago wins 9–5.

6th Back at home Toronto wins its first ALCS game 7–3.

7th Robby Thompson's 2-run HR gives the Giants the 5–4 victory in game 3.

Two Rickey Henderson HRs and a Jose Canseco upper deck HR give Oakland a 6–5 win.

8th Oakland beats Toronto 4–3 to win the ALCS 4-1 and advance to the World Series for the 2nd straight year. Rickey Henderson, who hit .400 with 8 stolen bases, is named series MVP.

Matt Williams snaps a 4–4 tie with a 5th-inning HR, and the Giants hold on to win 5–4.

9th The Giants win their first NL pennant since 1962 by defeating the Cubs 3–2 in game 5 of the NLCS. Will Clark bats .650 in the series with 8 RBI to win MVP honors.

13th Bob Quinn resigns as GM of the Yankees to accept the same position with the Cincinnati Reds.

14th Dave Stewart shuts out the Giants 5–0 on 5 hits in game 1 of the World Series. He is the first pitcher to start consecutive WS openers since the Reds Don Gullett in 1975 and '76.

15th Terry Steinbach's 3-run HR is the big blow as Oakland wins 5–1.

17th Game 3 of the World Series is postponed when an earthquake strikes the San Francisco Bay area a half hour before game time, causing minor damage to Candlestick Park and major damage to the surrounding area.

27th After a 10-day earthquake delay, the rumbling continues as Oakland hits 5 HRs in a 13–7 win.

28th The A's take an 8–0 and beat the Giants 9–6 to complete a 4-game sweep of the World Series, the first WS sweep since 1976. Oakland's Dave Stewart, who won 2 games, is named MVP.

NOVEMBER

3rd Lou Piniella is named manager of the Reds, replacing the banned Pete Rose, and John McNamara will manage the Indians.

7th Baltimore's Gregg Olson becomes the first relief pitcher to win the AL Rookie of the Year Award.

8th Cubs OF Jerome Walton wins the NL Rookie of the Year Award, collecting 22 of 24 first-place votes to defeat teammate Dwight Smith. They are the first NL teammates to finish 1-2 in the voting since the Phillies Jack Sanford and Ed Bouchee in 1957.

14th Padres reliever Mark Davis wins the NL Cy Young Award. He saved 44 games with a 1.85 ERA.

15th Twenty-five-year-old Bret Saberhagen becomes the 4th pitcher ever to win the AL Cy Young Award twice, getting 27 of a possible 28 first-place votes for his 23-6, 2.16 ERA season. He also won the award in 1985.

16th The NL champion Giants sign free-agent OF Kevin Bass, who hit .300 for Houston last season.

17th Nick Esasky, who became one of the major leagues' most coveted free agents after hitting .277 with 30 HRs and 108 RBI for the Red Sox last season, signs a 3-year contract with his hometown Atlanta Braves.

20th Brewers centerfielder Robin Yount edges the Rangers Ruben Sierra to win his 2nd AL MVP Award. Yount, who won as a SS in 1982, hit .318 last season with 21 HRs and 103 RBI.

21st Giants Kevin Mitchell, who led the big leagues with 47 HRs and 125 RBI, wins the NL MVP Award.

22nd Twins OF Kirby Puckett re-signs with the club for $9 million over 3 years, making him the first ML player ever to sign a contract that calls for an average salary of $3 million per year. More will follow.

27th Five-time NL All-Star Tony Pena signs as a free agent with the Red Sox.

DECEMBER

1st Free-agent pitcher Mark Langston signs a 5-year contract with the Angels.

3rd Thirty-eight-year-old DH Dave Parker, who had 22 HRs and 97 RBI for the World Champion A's, signs with the Brewers as a free agent.

6th The Mets trade reliever Randy Myers to the Reds for fellow closer John Franco; free-agent outfielders Joe Carter and Fred Lynn sign with the Padres; and free-agent relief specialist Jeff Reardon signs with the Red Sox.

7th Storm Davis, 19-7 for the A's last season, signs as a free agent with the Royals. Other free-agent signees include Craig Lefferts (San Diego), Pete O'Brien (Seattle), Oil Can Boyd (Montreal), and Keith Hernandez (Cleveland).

11th The Royals sign free agent Mark Davis to a 4-year contract. Davis and Bret Saberhagen will make the 1990 Royals the first team ever to have both defending Cy Young Award winners.

12th The Yankees trade minor leaguers Hal Morris and Rodney Imes to the Reds for P Tim Leary and OF Van Snider.

20th Six months after obtaining him from the Phillies, the Mets trade 2B-OF Juan Samuel to the Dodgers for 1B Mike Marshall and P Alejandro Pena.

21st The Dodgers sign free agent Hubie Brooks.

25th Billy Martin, former infielder and 5-time manager of the Yankees, dies in a car accident at the age of 61.

1990

JANUARY

9th Jim Palmer, a 3-time AL Cy Young Award winner, and Joe Morgan, a 2-time NL MVP, are elected to the Hall of Fame in their first years of eligibility.

15th Former Blue Jay Cecil Fielder signs with Detroit as a free agent after spending last season with Japan's Hanshin Tigers, where he hit 38 HRs.

26th Boston hires Elaine Weddington as assistant GM, making her the highest-ranking black female in the major leagues.

FEBRUARY

4th The St. Petersburg Pelicans get home runs from Lamar Johnson and Steve Kemp and rout the West Palm Beach tropics 12–4 to win the first-ever championship of the Senior Professional Baseball Association.

15th ML owners refuse to open the spring training camps without a new Basic Agreement with the Players' Association, beginning a lockout that will last 32 days and postpone the start of the regular season by one week.

24th Former Red Sox slugger Tony Conigliaro dies of pneumonia and kidney failure at the age of 45. Conigliaro was the youngest ML player ever to reach 100 career home runs and was nearly blinded by a 1967 beaning.

27th For the 2nd time in 3 years, the Special Veterans Committee fails to elect a single player to the Hall of Fame in its annual balloting.

MARCH

18th The players and owners reach a new collective-bargaining agreement that will end the 32-day lockout of spring training camps. Highlights of the deal include increasing the clubs' contributions to the players' pension fund, raising the minimum ML salary to $100,000, and a compromise on salary arbitration that leaves 17 percent of players with between 2 and 3 years of ML experience eligible.

22nd The ML umpires announce that they will boycott exhibition games to protest not having been consulted in the revision of the regular season schedule after the lockout. They will return to work on April 1st.

28th A plan to allow starting pitchers to earn victories with only 3 innings pitched (because of the abbreviated spring training period) is scrapped, but teams will be allowed to open the regular season with 27-man rosters instead of the allowed maximum of 25.

APRIL

9th Houston's Glenn Davis ties a ML record when he is hit by pitches 3 times in an 8–4, 11-inning loss to the Reds. For the Reds, it is just their 3rd road opener since 1876.

10th Wade Boggs is intentionally walked 3 times in Boston's 4–2 win over Detroit, tying the ML record for a 9-inning game.

11th California's Mark Langston and Mike Witt combine to no-hit the Mariners 1–0 for the first combined no-hitter in the major leagues since 1976. It is Langston's first start for the Angels since signing as a free agent in the off-season.

12th San Francisco's Brett Butler ties the ML record by drawing 5 walks in a 13–4 win over Atlanta.

14th Bret Saberhagen gets the win and Mark Davis earns the save as Kansas City beats Toronto 3–1. It is the first time ever that 2 reigning Cy Young Award winners have figured in the same victory.

16th The Brewers have 20 hits, but no HRs, in pounding Boston 18–0. It is Milwaukee's largest shutout margin ever.

20th Less than a year after being banished from baseball for his illegal gambling activities, all-time hit king Pete Rose pleads guilty to 2 felony counts of filing false income tax returns. On July 19th, he will be sentenced to 5 months in prison and fined $50,000.

Seattle's Brian Holman has a perfect no-hitter for 8⅔ innings but loses it on his first pitch to the A's Ken Phelps. Phelps's hits a HR, but then Holman fans Rickey Henderson for a 6–1 win.

21st The Reds beat the Braves 8–1 to run their record to 9-0, the best start in club history. They will lose tomorrow to Atlanta, the team with the best (13–0 in 1982) start ever.

23rd In a White Sox-Cubs exhibition game, Steve Lyons plays all 9 positions for the South Siders.

26th Nolan Ryan pitches a one-hitter and sets a Ranger record with 16 strikeouts in a 1–0 win over the White Sox. It is Ryan's 12th career one-hitter (which ties him with ML leader Bob Feller,) and 200th career game with at least 10 strikeouts.

27th Dodgers ace Orel Hershiser will miss the rest of the season after undergoing surgery on his pitching shoulder. He hadn't missed a start since joining the club's rotation in 1984.

Wally Backman goes 6-for-6 in Pittsburgh's 9–4 win over San Diego to become the first NL player in 15 years to get 6 hits in a game.

28th Frank Tanana wins his 200th career game, as Detroit tops Milwaukee 13–5.

29th The Cubs Greg Maddux sets a ML record for pitchers when he records 7 putouts in a 4–0 win over the Dodgers.

Rather than go on the disabled list for the first time in his career, Dan Quisenberry announces his retirement. The Q man is the all-time AL save king with 238.

MAY

1st The Braves Derek Lilliquist homers twice in a 5–2 win over the Mets, becoming the first pitcher to do so since Jim Gott in 1985.

3rd New York rookie Mike Blowers, handed the starting 3B job, ties an AL record by committing 4 errors at 3B in the Yankees' 10–5 loss to the Indians.

4th The Red Sox trade reliever Lee Smith to the Cardinals for OF Tom Brunansky.

6th Cecil Fielder clubs 3 home runs, but the Tigers still lose to the Blue Jays 11–7. Toronto's Kelly Gruber hits 2 HRs to give him 9 for the year, one behind Fielder. Ten home runs are hit in the game, one shy of the ML record.

Mariners 3B Edgar Martinez makes 4 errors in a 5–4 win over the Orioles, tying the AL record last equaled by Mike Blowers just 3 days ago.

11th Citing a no-trade clause in his contract, Yankee OF Dave Winfield refuses to report to the Angels after being traded for Mike Witt. Winfield will eventually accept the trade on May 16th, ending his often stormy relationship with Yankee owner George Steinbrenner.

13th The Dodgers trade veteran 2B Willie Randolph to the A's for OF Stan Javier.

18th In a 7–0 loss to the Astros, Cubs 2B Ryne Sandberg finally commits an error. This ends his ML-record errorless streaks at 123 games and 584 chances. Joe Morgan held the previous record of 91 games.

22nd Andre Dawson sets an ML record when he is intentionally walked 5 times during a 2–1 Cubs' win over the Reds. Cincinnati issues 7 intentional passes altogether to tie a record set by Houston in 1984.

27th John Smoltz is 2 outs away from a no-hitter when the Phillies Len Dykstra doubles. Smoltz finishes with a 6–1 two-hit win for the Braves.

29th Rickey Henderson steals his 893rd career base in Oakland's 2–1 loss to the Blue Jays, surpassing Ty Cobb as the AL's all-time leader. Lou Brock's mark of 938 is next.

With the team struggling (20-22), the Mets fire manager Davey Johnson, whose 6-year winning percentage was .593. Coach Buddy Harrelson replaces him and the Mets will win 20 of their next 23 games before cooling down.

JUNE

2nd Seattle's Randy Johnson, at 6 feet 10 inches the tallest pitcher in ML history, pitches the first Mariners' no-hitter, a 2–0 win over the Tigers. He walks 6 and strikes out 8.

4th The Dodgers Ramon Martinez, 22, strikes out 18 Braves in a 2–0 win. He ties Sandy Koufax's club record and is one short of the NL mark. Martinez whiffed none in the 9th inning.

The Braves select Florida high school SS Chipper Jones with the first pick in the annual free-agent draft. The A's use their 17th choice to take the much sought after Todd Van Poppel, passed over because of his stated intention to pitch at the University of Texas. The A's change his mind and he signs on July 16th.

6th A week after the Mets fire their manager, the Yankees follow suit. Bucky Dent, the Yank's skipper for just 89 games, is replaced by Stump Merrill, who managed the Columbus farm team.

For the 2nd time this season, Cecil Fielder belts 3 HRs in a game, as Detroit beats the Indians 6–4. Fielder is only the 4th AL player to have two 3-HR games in a season.

9th Dodger Eddie Murray homers from each side of the plate for the 10th time in his career (the 2nd time in 1990) to tie Mickey Mantle's ML record. The Dodgers beat the Padres 5–4 in 11 innings.

11th Ageless Nolan Ryan pitches his unprecedented 6th career no-hitter, striking out 14 batters in a 5–0 win over the A's. He is the first to pitch a no-hitter for 3 different teams, and the first to throw a perfecto in 3 different decades.

The Phils Lenny Dykstra's hitting streaks stops at 23 games, as he goes 0-for-8 in a doubleheader with Montreal. Dykstra's average drops from .407 to .392.

12th Orioles SS Cal Ripken plays in his 1,308th consecutive game to move past Everett Scott into 2nd place on the all-time list. Ripken will need to maintain his streak into 1995 to pass Lou Gehrig's mark of 2,130.

13th Kansas City's Willie Wilson steals his 600th career base in an 11–4 win over California.

Highly touted prospect Steve Avery makes his ML debut for the Braves and gives up 8 runs in 2⅓ innings. The Reds scalp the Braves 13–4.

The Giants Trevor Wilson no-hits the Padres for 8 innings before Mike Pagliarulo singles. Wilson settles for a 6–0 one hitter, the Giants' 14th win in their last 15 games.

14th The NL announces plans to expand from 12 to 14 teams for the 1993 season. The price of admission is 95 million dollars.

19th Gary Carter catches his 1,862nd career game to break Al Lopez's NL mark. He goes 0-for-3 in the Giants' 4–3 loss to San Diego.

22nd The last-place Braves fire manager Russ Nixon and replace him with GM Bobby Cox, who last managed Toronto in 1985.

27th Brewers DH Dave Parker gets his 2,500th career hit in a 5–4 win over the Yankees.

29th Oakland's Dave Stewart and the Dodgers Fernando Valenzuela both throw no-hitters today, the first time this has happened since Hippo Vaughan and Fred Toney's double no-hitter in 1917. Stewart blanks the Blue Jays 5–0, and a few hours later Valenzuela beats the Cardinals 6–0.

JULY

1st Yankees Andy Hawkins throws the season's 6th no-hitter, but still loses 4–0 to the White Sox. With 2 out in the bottom of the 8th, New York's Mike Blowers misplays a grounder for an error, and Hawkins walks 2 to load the bases. Outfielders Jim Leyritz and Jesse Barfield drop back-to-back fly balls to allow all 4 runs to score. Ken Johnson in 1967 was the last pitcher to lose a no-hitter.

2nd Nolan Ryan strikes out 7 batters in a 3–2 loss to the Red Sox. This gives him a record 22 seasons with at least 100 strikeouts. He had shared the record of 21 with Don Sutton.

6th In his first start since losing a no-hitter, Hawkins pitches 11⅔ innings of shutout ball only to lose in the 12th 2–0 to the Twins. Hawkins is now 1-6.

Disgusted with the team's performance, Whitey Herzog resigns as manager of the Cardinals after 10 years. Red Schoendienst will replace him temporarily and Joe Torre will be named permanent manager on August 1st.

8th Losing 7–0 to California in the 3rd, the Brewers score 20 unanswered runs, including 13 in the 5th, to win.

10th Six AL pitchers combine for a 2-hitter and a 2–0 victory over the NL in a rain-delayed All Star game at Wrigley Field. Rangers 2B Julio Franco drives in both runs in the 7th inning and is named MVP.

At the half-way mark in the season, the Reds are leading the NL West by 8 games, while Pittsburgh is ½ game ahead in the East. In the AL, Boston leads by ½ game and Oakland by one game.

11th At Comiskey Park, the White Sox honor their 1917 World Championship team by donning old-fashioned uniforms and scaling concessions back to W W I prices. Chicago then loses 12–9 to Milwaukee in 13 innings.

Jack McKeon resigns as manager of the Padres but keeps his position as San Diego's vice president of baseball operations. He is replaced in the dugout by Greg Riddoch. Later in the season, McKeon will lose his front-office job as well.

12th   The White Sox Melido Perez pitches a rain-shortened 6-inning no-hitter over the Yankees, as Chicago wins 8–0. This is the 7th no-hitter this season, the most since 1917.

14th   Dante Bichette, Dave Winfield, and Brian Downing each homer twice in California's 8–7 win over Toronto. This is the 8th time 3 teammates have done this in the ML.

15th   Bo Jackson slugs 3 straight HRs, the 3rd his career 100th, then separates his shoulder in the 6th inning diving for a line drive off the bat of Yankee Deion Sanders. Sanders ends up with an inside-the-park HR but Kansas City takes home a 10–7 win. Jackson will be out for 6 weeks.

17th   The Twins pull an ML first—2 triple plays in the same game. Both are started on grounders to Gary Gaetti, who has started 5 of the Twins' last 6 triple killings. The Red Sox win anyway 1–0.

18th   The Red Sox hit into 6 double plays, while the Twins ground into 4 for an ML record, as the Red Sox win again 5–4.

21st   In his first ML start, Baltimore's Big Ben McDonald shuts out Chicago 2–0. McDonald was the first pick in the 1989 June draft.

25th   For the 2nd time in his career, George Brett hits for the cycle, as Kansas City beats Toronto 6–1.

Twenty-five-year veteran umpire Bob Engel resigns after pleading no contest to charges of shoplifting baseball cards in California.

28th   Cal Ripken's errorless streak ends at 95 consecutive games, as Baltimore loses to Kansas City 10–9. The streak is a new ML record for a SS, eclipsing Ken Elster's 89-game mark.

Cubs SS Shawon Dunston ties a ML record with 3 triples in a 10–7 win over the Expos.

The Red Sox bang out 12 doubles, an AL record, in a 13–3 win over Detroit.

With one out to go, the Giants Scott Garrelts loses a no-hitter when the Reds Paul O'Neill singles. Garrelts finishes with a 4–0 one-hit win.

30th   In a surprisingly harsh ruling, Commissioner Fay Vincent orders Yankees owner George Steinbrenner to resign as the club's general partner by August 20th and bans him from day-to-day operation of the team for life. The ruling is a result of Steinbrenner's $40,000 payment to confessed gambler Howie Spira for damaging information about since-traded Yankee star Dave Winfield.

Jack Clark hits his 300th career HR in San Diego's 4–3 eleven-inning loss to the Braves.

Nolan Ryan becomes the 20th 300 game winner in history, in a 11–3 Texas win over Milwaukee. Ryan is not around to finish, joining Steve Carlton and Early Wynn as the only pitchers not to hurl a complete game for their 300th win.

AUGUST

2nd   Yankees rookie Kevin Maas hits his 10th HR in just 77 at bats, the fastest any player has ever reached that mark. But the Yanks lose to Detroit 6–5 in 11 innings.

3rd   In just his 2nd week in the majors, Cleveland's Alex Cole ties a ML record by stealing 7 bases in 2 games, as the Indians lose to New York 6–4. He set the club record by swiping 5 bases against the Royals on August 1st.

The Braves trade 2-time MVP OF Dale Murphy to the Phillies for reliever Jeff Parrett and a pair of players to be named later.

Pittsburgh's Doug Drabek is one out away from a no-hitter when he gives up a single to the Phillies Sil Campusano, who is hitting .188. Drabek finishes with an 11–0 one-hitter.

5th   Hall of Fame induction ceremonies for Jim Palmer and Joe Morgan are rained out in Cooperstown, NY. The ceremony will be conducted the following day at a local high school.

7th   Dave Winfield collects his 2,500th career hit, a single off Tom Bolton, as California loses to Boston 6–3.

8th   Pete Rose begins serving his 5-month prison sentence at Marion (IL) Federal prison camp.

9th   San Diego SS Garry Templeton collects his 2,000 ML hit, exactly 14 years after getting his first. The Padres beat the Braves 7–0.

12th   After a 7½ hour rain delay, the White Sox-Rangers game is finally postponed.

15th   The Phillies Terry Mulholland spins the major leagues' 8th no-hitter of the season. Mulholland faces the minimum 27 batters in blanking the Giants 6–0, as just one runner reaches base on a throwing error by

Charlie Hayes. Hayes makes the last putout by grabbing a line drive

Mark McGwire hits a game-winning grand slam in the bottom of the 10th to give Oakland a 6–2 win over Boston. He becomes the first player to hit 30 HRs in each of his first 4 seasons.

17th In Chicago's 4–2 win over Texas, Carlton Fisk homers off Charlie Hough to become the White Sox' all-time HR leader (with 187) and the all-time leader in HRs by a catcher (328).

Oakland's Bob Welch wins his 20th game of the season, 8–3 over the Orioles.

19th Dodger SS Jose Offerman leads off the bottom of the first with a HR in his first ML at bat, but that is all the LA scoring as Montreal wins 2–1. Offerman had not homered all season in the minors.

21st Trailing 11–1 after 7 innings, the Phillies score 2 in the 8th and 9 more in the 9th inning to beat the Dodgers 12–11.

26th In his first game after 6 weeks on the disabled list, Bo Jackson homers in his first at bat to tie a ML record with 4 consecutive homers. The Royals top Seattle 8–2 at home.

The Red Sox shut out the Blue Jays for the 3rd consecutive day to extend their lead in the AL East to 4 games. Toronto, leading the ML in runs scored, loses 2–0, 1–0, and 1–0.

27th Boston's Ellis Burks homers twice in the 4th inning of a 12–4 pasting of Cleveland.

The Brewers-Blue Jays game is delayed 35 minutes when a huge swarm of gnats descends onto the field through the open SkyDome roof. Milwaukee scratches out a 4–2 win.

28th Ryne Sandberg homers in the Cubs' 5–2 win over theAstros to become the first 2B ever to post back-to-back 30-HR seasons. He will finish the year with 40 HRs to become the first 2B since Rogers Hornsby in 1925 to lead the league in that category.

29th The Defending World Champion A's seemingly lock up another pennant by acquiring slugger Harold Baines from the Rangers for a pair of minor leaguers, and OF Willie McGee from the Cardinals for Felix Jose and 2 more minor leaguers. McGee, a free agent at the end of the year, is leading the NL in hitting (.335).

30th Boston's Roger Clemens reaches 20 wins for the 3rd time in 5 years by beating Cleveland 9–2.

31st Ken Griffeys, Jr. and Sr., become the first father-and-son combination in ML history to play as teammates, and they each go 1-for-4 in Seattle's 5–2 win over the Royals, The Mariners had signed the elder Griffey after he was waived by the Reds last week.

Dennis Eckersley saves his 40th game of the season in Oakland's 4–2 win over Texas to join Dan Quisenberry and Jeff Reardon as the only pitchers to save 40 games twice.

SEPTEMBER

1st The 3rd inside-the-park grand slam of the season (Luis Polonia on August 14th, and Ron Karkovice on August 30th) is hit by Boston's Mike Greenwell off Greg Caderet, as the Red Sox beat New York 15–1. Greenwell's only other inside-the-park slam was also off Caderet. Boston jumped on Yankee starter Andy Hawkins who lasted ⅓ of an inning. Hawkins has now pitched a total of one inning in 3 starts at Fenway Park and given up 18 runs (ERA 162.).

2nd In the year of no-hitters, Dave Stieb pitches the 9th and final one of the season, blanking Cleveland 3–0. It is the first no-hitter in Blue Jays' history, and the first for Stieb after numerous close-calls.

3rd The White Sox Bobby Thigpen tops Dave Righetti's ML record with his 47th save of the season in Chicago's 4–2 win over the Royals. Thigpen will finish the season with a superlative 57 saves.

5th The Pirates beat the Mets 1–0 and 3–1 to open a 2½ game lead over New York in the NL East. Zane Smith pitches a one-hitter in the opener for the Bucs, which has swept all 5 of its doubleheaders this season.

9th Oakland beats New York 7–3 to complete a 12-game sweep of the Yankees this year. The season sweep is a first for the Yankees.

Seattle's Matt Young strikes out 4 batters in the first inning of a 3–1 win over the Red Sox.

10th In the first head-to-head matchup of pitchers named Abbott, Jim's Angels beat Paul's Twins 3–1. Minnesota's Carmen Castillo pinch hits late in the game to complete the successful "Abbott and Castillo" revival.

11th New York beats Texas 5–4 to snap pitcher Bobby Witt's personal 12-game winning streak.

12th Yankees starter Steve Adkins doesn't allow a hit in his ML debut, but he walks 8 batters in just 1⅓ innings, as Texas wins 5–4.

14th Ken Griffey, Sr. and Jr., hit back-to-back home runs in the first inning of a Seattle 7–5 loss to California.

Oakland's Dave Stewart wins his 20th game of the season 9–1 over the Twins to become the first pitcher since Jim Palmer (1975-78) to post 4 straight 20-game seasons.

17th The Blue Jays' 6–4 win over the Yankees is watched by 49,902 at the SkyDome, giving Toronto a ML-season attendance record. The Jays will finish the season with 58 consecutive sellouts and a total attendance of 3,885,284.

19th Doug Drabek wins his 20th game and Bobby Bonds hits his 30th and 31st HRs, as Pittsburgh beats Chicago 8–7. Two days later Bonds will steal his 50th base of the season.

21st The Padres fire Jack McKeon, who has been the San Diego GM for 10 years.

23rd Gary Gaetti hits a grand slam off the Rangers Charlie Hough for his 200th career HR, as the Twins win 6–4. It comes 9 years and 4 days after his first ML homer, also off of Hough.

25th The Oakland A's clinch their 3rd consecutive AL West title by beating Kansas City 5–0.

The Yankees tie a ML record when their first 8 batters all hit safely in a 15–3 rout of the Orioles.

29th The Reds clinch the NL West title during a rain delay of their 3–1 loss to the Padres when the 2nd-place Dodgers lose 4–3 to San Francisco. The Reds, never out of first place, are the first NL team ever to lead from wire to wire in a 162-game schedule.

30th Pittsburgh beats St. Louis 2–0 behind Doug Drabek's 3-hitter to clinch its first NL West title since 1979. The loss assures the Cards of finishing last for the first time since 1918.

The White Sox beat Seattle 2–1 in the last game played at historic Comiskey Park, which is to be torn down after 80 seasons of major-league ball. Chicago will play next season at the new Comiskey Park located across the street.

OCTOBER

1st The Dodgers young ace Ramon Martinez wins his 20th game of the season 2–1 over the Padres.

3rd Boston beats Chicago 3–1 on the final day of the season to wrap up its 3rd AL East title in 5 seasons. Tom Brunansky ends the game with a spectacular sliding catch in the RF corner with the tying runs on base.

Cecil Fielder becomes the 11th player ever to hit 50 HRs when he belts his 50th and 51st in the Tigers' season finale, a 10–3 win over New York. He is the first AL player since 1961 to reach the 50 mark.

George Brett pinch hits a single in Kansas City's finale to end the season at .329 and win the AL batting crown, his 3rd in 3 decades. Willie McGee's .335 wins the NL batting title despite having been traded out of the league in August.

Frank Viola wins his 20th when the Mets beat the Pirates 6–3. Viola also won 24 for the Twins in 1988.

4th Trailing 3–0 after one inning, the Pirates come from behind to beat the Reds 4–3 in game 1 of the NLCS.

5th Rightfielder Paul O'Neill drives in both Cincinnati runs and throws out a runner at 3rd base to spark the Reds to a 2–1 win in game 2 of the NLCS, tying the series at one game apiece.

6th Boston's Roger Clemens pitches 6 shutout innings, but Oakland rallies for one run in the 7th, one in the 8th, and 7 in the 9th to win game 1 of the ALCS 9–1. The A's 7-run 9th ties the ALCS record for runs in an inning.

7th Late-season acquisition Harold Baines drives in 3 runs to lead the A's to a 4–1 win over the Red Sox and a 2-0 lead in the ALCS.

8th Mariano Duncan belts a 3-run home run and Reds relievers Rob Dibble, Norm Charlton, and Randy Myers combine to strike out 7 batters in 3⅔ innings as Cincinnati beats Pittsburgh 6–3 in game 3 of the NLCS.

9th The Red Sox fail to hold a 1–0 lead for the 3rd consecutive game as Oakland opens up a commanding 3-0 lead in the ALCS with a 4–1 victory. In Pittsburgh, Paul O'Neill and Chris Sabo each homer to lead the Reds to a 5–3 win and a 3-1 lead in the NLCS.

10th After Red Sox starter Roger Clemens is ejected in the 2nd inning for cursing at home plate umpire

Terry Cooney, Oakland beats Boston 3–1 to complete a 4-game sweep of the ALCS and earn its 3rd-straight trip to the World Series.

Bob Patterson gets Jeff Reed to hit into a game-ending double play with the bases loaded to save the Pirates' 3–2 win over the Reds and send the NLCS back to Cincinnati for game 6.

12th Danny Jackson, Norm Charlton, and Randy Myers combine on a one-hitter, as Cincinnati beats the Pirates 2–1 to win the NLCS in 6 games.

16th In game 1 of the World Series, Eric Davis becomes the 22nd player ever to homer in his first WS at bat and the Reds go on to rout the A's 7–0, ending Oakland's 10-game post-season winning streak.

17th In the first extra-inning WS game since 1966, the underdog Reds beat the A's 5–4 in 10 innings to take a surprising 2-0 lead in in the Series. Reds OF Billy Hatcher goes 4-for-4 to run his consecutive hit streak to 7, tying Thurman Munson's WS record.

19th Cincinnati moves within one game of a shocking World Series sweep by beating Oakland 8–3 in game 3. 3B Chris Sabo slugs a pair of home runs for the Reds.

20th The talk of an Oakland dynasty is proven premature, as Cincinnati beats Oakland 2–1 to complete one of the most stunning sweeps in WS history. Series MVP Jose Rijo (2-0, 0.59 ERA) retires the last 20 batters he faces to give the Reds their first World Championship since 1976.

24th The Red Sox announce that they will not renew the contract of veteran Dwight Evans, who had been with the club since 1972. Evans will eventually sign a one-year contract with Baltimore.

NOVEMBER

6th Braves OF Dave Justice wins the NL Rookie of the Year award. He hit .282 with 28 HRs, 20 coming after he replaced Dale Murphy in RF in early August.

7th Cleveland's Sandy Alomar, Jr. wins the AL Rookie of the Year Award unanimously, joining Carlton Fisk and Mark McGwire as the only players to do so.

8th Free-agent slugger Darryl Strawberry signs a 5-year contract with his hometown Dodgers, formally ending his 8-year stay with the Mets. He is the Met's all-time HR leader with 252.

11th California's Chuck Finley and Seattle's Randy Johnson combine to pitch a no-hitter in the finale of an 8-game exhibition series between American and Japanese all-star teams. But Japan still wins the series 4-3 with one tie, the first time since 1970 that a touring US team has left Japan with a losing record.

13th Oakland's Bob Welch wins the AL Cy Young Award. His 27 wins were the most in the majors since Steve Carlton in 1972.

14th Doug Drabek (22-6) wins the NL Cy Young Award, collecting 23 of a possible 24 first-place votes.

19th Pittsburgh's Barry Bonds wins the NL MVP Award, easily outdistancing teammate and runner-up Bobby Bonilla. Bonds hit .301 with 23 home runs, 114 RBI, and 52 stolen bases.

20th Oakland's Rickey Henderson edges Detroit's Cecil Fielder for the AL MVP Award. Henderson hit .325 with 28 HRs and a ML-best 65 stolen bases.

Red Sox ace Roger Clemens is suspended for the first 5 games of the 1991 season and fined $10,000 for his outburst in game 4 of the ALCS.

21st Veteran P Mike Boddicker (17-8 with Boston) signs as a free agent with the Royals, while Danny Jackson signs with the Cubs. Tom Browning re-signs with the Reds.

23rd Former catcher Bo Diaz, 37, is crushed to death when a rooftop satellite dish topples over at his home in Venezuela. Diaz last played for the Reds in 1989.

29th A consortium of Canadian investors led by Expos president Claud Brochu agrees to buy the club from Charles Bronfman for a reported $85 million, assuring that the team will remain in Montreal.

DECEMBER

3rd NL batting champion Willie McGee signs as a free agent with the Giants, ending his 3-month stint across the bay with Oakland.

4th Reliever Dave Righetti signs as a free agent with the Giants. San Francisco now has spent $33 million for free agents Righetti, Willie McGee, and Bud Black since the end of the season.

5th   In a major trade, the Blue Jays send 1B Fred McGriff and veteran SS Tony Fernandez to San Diego for 2B Roberto Alomar and slugging OF Joe Carter.

Free-agent OF Vince Coleman signs a 4-year contract with the Mets. He has led the NL in stolen bases each of the last 6 seasons, and this year (June 3rd) copped his 500th theft in his 804th game, the quickest player to reach that plateau.

6th   Free agent George Bell signs with the Cubs.

Fifteen more players become "free look" free agents as part of the settlement of the most recent collusion case against the owners. It will also cost the clubs a whopping $280 million in damages.

At Leland's auction house in New York City, Shoeless Joe Jackson's signature is sold for $23,100, the most money ever paid for a 19th or 20th century signature. Jackson, who could not read or write, copied the signature from one written out by his wife. The signature, which was resold within hours, was cut from an unknown document.

15th   AL Cy Young winner and free agent Bob Welch re-signs with Oakland, while "free look" free agents Jack Clark and Brett Butler sign with the Red Sox and Dodgers, respectively.

The Mets send veteran lefty Bob Ojeda and minor leaguer Greg Hansell to the Dodgers for OF Hubie Brooks.

18th   The NL announces the 6 finalist cities for the 2 expansion clubs that will join the league in 1993: Buffalo, Denver, Miami, Orlando, Tampa-St. Petersburg, and Washington, DC.

24th   The Expos trade Tim Raines and a pair of minor leaguers to the White Sox for OF Ivan Calderon and reliever Barry Jones.

26th   The Senior Professional Baseball Association folds in the middle of its 2nd season when the Fort Myers Sun Sox franchise collapses due to a financial dispute among club owners.

31st   A's 3B Carney Lansford is severely injured in a New Year's Eve snowmobile accident.

INDEX